DATE DUE

DEMCO 38-296

ANTARCTICA

ANTARCTICA

An Encyclopedia

JOHN STEWART

Foreword by
Sir Edmund Hillary

VOLUME II
M–Z, Chronology, Expeditions, Bibliography

McFarland & Company, Inc., Publishers
Jefferson, North Carolina, and London

British Library Cataloguing-in-Publication data are available

Library of Congress Cataloguing-in-Publication Data

Stewart, John, 1952–
Antarctica : an encyclopedia / by John Stewart.
p.   cm.
Includes bibliographical references.
(lib. bdg. : 50# alk. paper)∞
1. Antarctic regions—Dictionaries.   I. Title.
G855.S74   1990
919.8′9—dc20   89-43631
CIP

ISBN 0-89950-470-1 (2 vol. set)
ISBN 0-89950-597-X (Vol. I)
ISBN 0-89950-598-8 (Vol. II)

Printed in the United States of America

McFarland & Company, Inc., Publishers
Box 611, Jefferson, North Carolina 28640

TABLE OF CONTENTS

VOLUME I

VOLUME II

Maagoe Peak. 79°33'S, 85°W. 1,850 m. At the north end of the Gifford Peaks. Named for Steffen Maagoe, ionosphere scientist at Eights Station in 1964.

Maaske Dome. 85°58'S, 144°W. An ice-capped, domelike elevation. 2 miles long. On the northern part of California Plateau. Named for Lt. Gary L. Maaske, USN, helicopter pilot at McMurdo Station, 1962–63 and 1963–64.

Mabee, Henry. Seaman on the Wilkes Expedition 1838–42. Joined in the USA. Run at Sydney.

Cape Mabel. 60°41'S, 44°40'W. Forms the northern tip of Pirie Peninsula on the north coast of Laurie Island. Charted by Bruce in 1903. Named by him for the wife of J.H. Harvey Pirie.

Mabel Island. 60°40'S, 44°42'W. 1½ miles NW of Cape Mabel, off the north coast of Laurie Island, South Orkneys. Charted by the *Discovery II* in 1933, and named by them for nearby Cape Mabel.

Mabel One. A small, remote US field camp of a temporary nature in Marie Byrd Land, about 800 miles from McMurdo Station, in the late 1970s. There were about 15 scientists and 20 military, and 3 helicopters, in 5 Jamesway huts which had been airlifted there.

Mount Mabelle Sidley *see* **Mount Sidley**

Mabus Point. 66°33'S, 93°01'E. A coastal point just south of the Haswell Islands. Marks the eastern limit of McDonald Bay. Charted by the AAE 1911–14. Named for Lt. Cdr. Howard W. Mabus, USN, executive officer on the *Edisto* during Operation Windmill, 1947–48. Later became the site of Mirnyy Station.

Mount McAllister. 68°42'S, 65°54'W. On the east coast of Graham Land, overlooking the Larsen Ice Shelf.

MacAlpine Hills. 84°13'S, 160°30'E. Mainly ice-free. Extend from Mount Achernar SW along the south side of Law Glacier, to Sylwester Glacier. Named for Ensign Kenneth D. MacAlpine, USNR, a member of VX-6 injured in a plane crash at McMurdo Sound in Oct. 1956.

Macaroni penguins. *Eudyptes chrysolophus.* Orange-plumed. Found in the South Shetlands and South Orkneys, and similar to rockhoppers (which are not found in Antarctica). They are 28 inches high and weigh 8 pounds. They smell like goats. Four of them live on Signy Island, and these four come back each year, amid all the chinstraps and gentoos, and live quite amicably in this foreign company. One was said to have been seen on Humble Island, near Palmer Station, on Jan. 6, 1956 (but this may have been a hoax). The macaroni penguin was discovered by Brandt.

Macaroni Point. 62°54'S, 60°32'W. Also called Punta Noreste. The NE extremity of Deception Island. Surveyed and named by the FIDS in Jan. 1954 for the colony of macaroni penguins here.

McArthur Glacier. 71°20'S, 67°29'W. Between the Christie Peaks and Swine Hill, flowing west from Palmer Land into George VI Sound. Named by the UK for Alistair H. McArthur, BAS geophysicist at Base E, 1967–68.

MacArty, Timothy. Able seaman on the *Endurance* during Shackleton's 1914–17 expedition. He was one of the *James Caird* party. Killed in action in the English Channel in 1917.

Mount Macbain. 83°06'S, 162°18'E. 2,205 m. Between the mouths of the Cornwall and Helm Glaciers. Named for Cdr. Merle Macbain, USN, public information officer, US Naval Support Force, Antarctica, 1957–58 and 1958–59.

MacBride, Hugh. Ordinary seaman on the Wilkes Expedition 1838–42. Joined at Upolu. Served the cruise.

McCain Bluff. 70°19'S, 160°05'E. On the north side of the mouth of Svendsen Glacier in the Usarp Mountains. Named for John C. McCain, biologist at McMurdo Station, 1967–68.

McCall Point. 67°02'S, 66°38'W. On the east side of Lallemand Fjord. 4 miles NW of Salmon Cove in Graham Land. Named by the UK for John G. McCall, US engineer who first measured the internal movement of a cirque glacier, in 1951–52.

McCallum Lake. In the Mule Peninsula of the Vestfold Hills.

McCallum Pass. 67°23′S, 68°18′W. Between the NE ridge of Mount Mangin and the ridge on the south side of Stonehouse Bay, in the southern part of Adelaide Island. Named by the UK in 1963 for Hugh C.G. McCallum of the BAS who traversed it in 1961 with Alan Crouch.

McCalman Peak. 63°37′S, 57°47′W. 550 m. 3 miles north of Crystal Hill, Trinity Peninsula. Named by the UK for Donald McCalman, FIDS surveyor at Base D, 1958–59.

McCance Glacier. 66°43′S, 65°55′W. Flows into Darbel Bay, just west of Widdowson Glacier on the west coast of Graham Land. Named by the UK for Robert A. McCance of the Dept. of Experimental Medicine at Cambridge who advised British polar expeditions on sledging rations between 1938 and 1958.

Mount McCann. 73°34′S, 77°37′W. Between Espenschied Nunatak and Mount Thornton in the west-central part of the Snow Nunataks of Ellsworth Land. Discovered by the USAS. Named for Capt. Kenneth McCann, captain of the *Eltanin* from Sept. 1965 to Sept. 1966.

McCann Glacier. 71°33′S, 164°33′E. Flows from the eastern slopes of Mount Stirling, then between Mount Radspinner and Markinsenis Peak, into Lillie Glacier. Named for J.M. McCann, USN, chief utilitiesman at McMurdo Station, 1962, 1963–64, and 1964–65.

McCann Point. 83°22′S, 169°38′E. The east side of the mouth of Beaver Glacier, where it enters the Ross Ice Shelf. Named for K.A. McCann, captain of the *Private Joseph F. Merrell* in 1965.

Cape McCarroll *see* **McCarroll Peak**

McCarroll Peak. 66°03′S, 62°46′W. 1,105 m. At the south side of Richthofen Pass on the east coast of Graham Land. In 1902 Nordenskjöld named the pass as Richthofen Valley, thinking that was what it was. On Dec. 20, 1928, Wilkins flew over it and named the south side of the "valley" Cape McCarroll, for H.G. McCarroll of Detroit. The name has since been given instead to this peak.

¹Mount McCarthy. 70°24′S, 66°31′E. 1,860 m. The most easterly peak in the Porthos Range of the Prince Charles Mountains. First visited in Dec. 1956 by W.G. Bewsher's ANARE party. Named by the Australians for James W. McCarthy, senior meteorologist and second-in-command at Mawson Station in 1956.

²Mount McCarthy. 72°35′S, 166°14′E. 2,865 m. 1 mile NW of Schofield Peak at the north side of the Webb Névé, in Oates Land. Named by the New Zealanders in 1962–63 for Mortimer McCarthy.

McCarthy, Mortimer. Crew member on the *Terra Nova*, 1910–13. In 1962–63 he visited Antarctica again with two other veterans of that expedition, as guests of the US Navy.

McCarthy, Robert J. Lt. US Marines, pilot on Operation Highjump, 1946–47.

McCarthy Glacier. 86°04′S, 127°24′W. At the south side of Wisconsin Plateau, it flows into the lower part of Olentangy Glacier before they both enter Reedy Glacier just SW of Mount McNaughton. Named for Lt. Robert J. McCarthy.

McCarthy Inlet. 78°50′S, 45°W. Also called Fierle Bay, McCarty Inlet. Ice-filled. The largest and most northerly of three inlets indenting the eastern side of Berkner Island. Discovered by personnel from Ellsworth Station in 1957–58. Named for Lt. Cdr. Charles J. McCarthy, USNR, VX-6 commander at Ellsworth Station during the IGY.

McCarthy Island. 67°16′S, 59°25′E. 2 miles long. Just NE of Fold Island, off the coast of Enderby Land. Photographed by the LCE 1936–37 and mapped by the Norwegians as part of Fold Island. Identified as a separate island in 1961 by an ANARE geological party. Named by the Australians for W.R. McCarthy, Australian petrologist, who described several hundred specimens from Antarctica.

McCarthy Nunatak. 69°07′S, 64°45′E. It just pokes above the surface, 5 miles SE of Depot Peak, Mac. Robertson Land. Discovered in 1970 from an ANARE airplane. Named by the Australians for I. McCarthy, senior weather observer at Mawson Station in 1970, and a member of the ANARE Prince Charles Mountains survey party of 1971.

McCarthy Point. 74°25′S, 130°59′W. Ice-covered. Marks the NE extremity of Grant Island on the seaward edge of the Getz Ice Shelf. Discovered from the *Glacier* on Feb. 4, 1962. Named for Lt. (jg) J.F. McCarthy, USN, disbursing officer on the *Glacier* at the time.

McCarthy Ridge. 74°37′S, 163°03′E. Mostly ice-covered. Forms the east wall of Carnein Glacier, in the foothills of the SE part of the Eisenhower Range. Named for Peter C. McCarthy, biolab manager at McMurdo Station, 1966.

McCarthy Valley. 85°18′S, 119°20′W. Ice-filled. 3 miles long. Between Peters Butte and Todd Ridge in the NW part of the Long Hills. Named for James E. McCarthy, meteorological electronics technician at Byrd Station, 1960.

McCarty, Owen. Petty officer, USN. Photographer on the Martin Mariner which crashed on Thurston Island on Dec. 30, 1946. He survived.

McCaslin Nunatak. 85°38′S, 140°57′W. Isolated. 5 miles south of the west end of the Bender Mountains. Named for James C. McCaslin, with the US Army Aviation Unit here in 1962–63.

Mount McCauley. 73°12′S, 63°15′E. Between Mounts Scherger and Dummett on the north side of Fisher Glacier. Discovered from an ANARE airplane in 1956 and visited by ANARE in 1960. Named for Air Marshal Sir John McCauley, chief of the Australian Air Staff, 1954–57.

McCauley Rock. 83°02′S, 48°53′W. 1,020 m. Just off the east edge of Lex-

ington Table. 6 miles north of Mount Zirzow, in the Forrestal Range of the Pensacola Mountains. Named for Clyde J. McCauley, USN, seaman at Ellsworth Station, 1957.

McCaw, Homer W. Lt., USNR. Led the helicopter division of the US Navy Antarctic Expedition, 1954–55.

McCaw Ridge. 75°21′S, 65°W. Isolated. 4 miles south of the central part of Ueda Glacier, near the base of the Antarctic Peninsula. Named for D. McCaw, construction electrician at Amundsen-Scott South Pole Station in 1963.

McClary, Nelson. Ship's mate on the RARE 1947–48.

McClary Glacier. 68°04′S, 67°W. 10 miles long. 2 miles wide. On the west coast of Graham Land. It flows along the north side of Buttress Ridge into Marguerite Bay between Cape Calmette and the Debenham Islands. Surveyed by the BGLE in 1936–37, and by the FIDS in 1946–50. Named by the UK for George B. McClary, the father of Nelson McClary (*see also* **McClary Ridge**).

McClary Ridge. 66°55′S, 64°09′W. Crescent-shaped. 5 miles SSE of Mount Hayes on the south side of Cole Peninsula in Graham Land. In Dec. 1947 it was charted by the FIDS. Named during that same period by Finn Ronne during the RARE, for George B. McClary of Winnetka, Ill., a contributor to Ronne's expedition.

McCleary Glacier. 79°33′S, 156°50′E. 10 miles long. Flows into the Darwin Glacier just west of Tentacle Ridge. Named for George McCleary, public information officer on the staff of the US Antarctic Projects Officer (1959–61), who helped create the Bulletin put out by that office. That bulletin eventually became the *Antarctic Journal*.

Mount McClintock. 80°13′S, 157°26′E. 3,490 m. The highest mountain in the Britannia Range. Surmounts the south end of the Forbes Ridge. 6 miles east of Mount Olympus. Discovered during

Scott's 1901–4 expedition and named by them for Adm. Sir Leopold McClintock, RN, a member of the Ship Committee for the expedition.

M'Clintock Bastion. 80°28′S, 22°28′W. In the Shackleton Range.

McClinton Glacier. 74°40′S, 114°W. Flows to the coast of Marie Byrd Land.

Mount McClung. 77°11′S, 144°26′W. Between Asman Ridge and Mount Crow in the Ford Ranges of Marie Byrd Land. Discovered by the USAS 1939–41. Named for Lt. Herbert C. McClung, USN, officer-in-charge of Byrd Station, 1963.

McCollum Peak. 65°32′S, 64°02′W. 735 m. South of Beascochea Bay. 2 miles SE of Mount Waugh on the west coast of Graham Land. Charted by Charcot in 1908–10. Named by the UK in 1959 for Elmer V. McCollum, US pioneer in vitamins.

McConnel Islands. 66°29′S, 65°51′W. Also called Islote Trumao. In Darbel Bay. SE of the Kidd Islands. Off the west coast of Graham Land. Named by the UK in 1960 for James C. McConnel (1860–1890), British physicist specializing in the plastic deformation of ice.

Cape McCormick. 71°50′S, 170°58′E. Marks the eastern extremity of Adare Peninsula in Victoria Land. Discovered by Ross in 1841, and named by him for Robert McCormick. Originally thought to be an island, and called McCormick Island, or McCormick's Island.

Mount McCormick. 77°S, 144°26′W. 2 miles SE of Mount Ralph in the Ford Ranges of Marie Byrd Land. Discovered by the USAS 1939–41. Named for W.S. McCormick.

McCormick, James. Seaman on the Wilkes Expedition 1838–42. Joined in the USA. Served the cruise.

McCormick, Robert. Surgeon on the *Erebus* during Ross' expedition of 1839–43.

McCormick, W.S. Airplane pilot on the shore party of Byrd's 1933–35 expedition.

McCormick Island *see* **Cape McCormick**

McCormick's Skuas *see* **Skuas**

Mount McCoy. 75°52′S, 141°10′W. Also called Mount Alma McCoy. A high, table-topped massif with dark, snow-free vertical walls. At the east side of the Land Glacier in Marie Byrd Land. Discovered by personnel from West Base during the USAS 1939–41, and named for James C. McCoy's wife, Alma.

McCoy, James C. Lt. cdr., USN. Chief pilot at West Base during the USAS 1939–41. Was back again during Operation Highjump, and was the pilot who carried Byrd to the Pole on Feb. 16, 1947.

McCrillis Nunatak. 85°27′S, 128°55′W. Marks the north end of the Gierloff Nunataks on the northern side of the Wisconsin Range in the Horlick Mountains. Named for Harold G. McCrillis, construction electrician at Byrd Station in 1959 and at Amundsen-Scott South Pole Station in 1964.

McCristel, William. Crewman on the *Bear of Oakland*, 1934–35.

Mount McCrory. 75°29′S, 139°26′W. 2 miles ESE of Mount Vance in the eastern part of the Ickes Mountains of Marie Byrd Land. Named for Capt. Eugene E. McCrory, captain of the *Glacier* in 1969 and 1970.

McCuddin Mountains. 75°47′S, 128°42′W. 40 miles east of the Ames Range in Marie Byrd Land. Mounts Flint and Petras are the main peaks. Discovered during a flight from West Base on Dec. 14, 1940, during the USAS. Named for Rear Adm. Leo B. McCuddin, USN, commander of the US Naval Support Force, Antarctica, 1972.

Mount McCue. 84°45′S, 174°41′W. 1,710 m. 5½ miles NW of Mount Wade in the Prince Olav Mountains. Discovered by the USAS 1939–41. Surveyed by Albert P. Crary in 1957–58 and named by him for James A. McCue, USN, radio mechanic who was in charge of the first Beardmore Glacier Camp, 1957–58.

McCuistion Glacier. 84°49'S, 175°30' W. 4 miles long. Flows along the north side of Lubbock Ridge into Shackleton Glacier, in the Queen Maud Mountains. Named for Joshua P. McCuistion, construction driver 1st class, USN, who was injured in an Otter airplane crash on Dec. 22, 1955, following take-off from the Cape Bird area.

MacCurrach, Peter, Jr. 3rd assistant engineer on the *Jacob Ruppert*, 1933–34, and 2nd assistant engineer, 1934–35.

McDaniel Nunatak. 75°48'S, 161°48' E. A ridgelike projection at the north side of the head of Davis Glacier. 5 miles north of Mount George Murray in the Prince Albert Mountains of Victoria Land. Named for James R. McDaniel, satellite geodesist at McMurdo Station, 1966.

Cape MacDonald. 71°32'S, 61°11'W. Headland. 435 meters high. Forms the south side of the entrance to Odom Inlet, on the east coast of Palmer Land. Discovered in 1940 by the USAS, and named for J.E. MacDonald, field representative and secretary of the USAS 1939–41.

Mount Macdonald. 84°31'S, 173°10'E. 3,630 m. Between Ludeman Glacier and Pain Névé in the Commonwealth Range. Named by the New Zealanders in 1961–62 for T.L. Macdonald, minister of external affairs and of defence when the BCTAE 1955–58 was being planned, and who was a major factor in getting NZ involved in the Antarctic.

Mount McDonald. 72°30'S, 166°36'E. 2,470 m. On the north side of Trafalgar Glacier. 4 miles NW of Mount Burton, in the Victory Mountains, in Victoria Land. Named by the New Zealanders in 1962–63 for William McDonald.

McDonald, Alexander. Landsman on the Wilkes Expedition 1838–42. Joined in the USA. Served the cruise.

McDonald, Edwin A. b. Nov. 23, 1907, California. d. March 19, 1988, Williamsburg, Va. USN career officer. Commander of the *Burton Island* during Operation Windmill, 1947–48. He was on the *Glacier,* 1957–58 and in 1958–59 was deputy commander, US Naval Support Force, Antarctica, in charge of ships, a post he held until he retired in 1962. Later that year he was back, as a consultant on the *Edisto.* He was director of Polar Operations for Lindblad Travel from 1968 to 1972, and was 4 seasons as the commander of the *Lindblad Explorer.* Wrote *Polar Operations* in 1969.

[1]McDonald, William. Seaman on the Wilkes Expedition 1838–42. Joined in the USA. Served the cruise.

[2]McDonald, William. Crew member of the *Terra Nova* during Scott's 1910–13 expedition. With two others from that expedition, he was a guest of the US Navy in Antarctica in 1962–63. He was alive in NZ in the 1980s.

McDonald Bay. 66°36'S, 92°44'E. 10 miles wide at its entrance between Adams Island and the Haswell Islands. Just west of Mabus Point on the coast of East Antarctica, near Mirnyy Station. Drygalski Island is in it. Charted by the AAE 1911–14. Named by the USA for Edwin A. McDonald.

McDonald Beach. 77°15'S, 166°21'E. West of Inclusion Hill. 6 miles SW of Cape Bird on Ross Island. Named by the NZGSAE 1958–59 for Capt. Edwin A. McDonald (q.v.), deputy commander, US Naval Support Force, Antarctica that year. He supported the expedition in its exploration of the Cape Bird area.

Macdonald Bluffs. 83°15'S, 157°50'E. Also called Macdonald Cliffs. Between Argosy and Argo Glaciers in the Miller Range. East-facing, they descend to Marsh Glacier. Named by the NZ Southern Party of the BCTAE in 1957–58 for W.J.P. Macdonald, scientist at Scott Base in 1957.

Macdonald Cliffs *see* **Macdonald Bluffs**

McDonald Glacier *see* **McDonald Ice Rumples**

McDonald Heights. 74°55'S, 136°W. Mainly snow-covered. 35 miles long. Over 1,000 meters high. Between Cape Burks and Morris Head on the Marie Byrd Land coast. To the south are the Hull, Kirkpatrick, and Johnson Glaciers. Named for Capt. Edwin A. McDonald.

McDonald Ice Rumples. 75°28'S, 26°18'W. Also called McDonald Glacier. A very broken up area on the Brunt Ice Shelf. It covers an area of 3 by 2 miles. In Jan. 1915 Shackleton discovered it and called it the Allan McDonald Glacier, for Allan McDonald of the British Association of Magallanes at Punta Arenas, Chile, who was the person most responsible for raising the funds for sending the *Emma* out to rescue (unsuccessfully, as it happened) the 22 men left on Elephant Island. The ice rumples undoubtedly looked more like a glacier then than they do today.

MacDonald Nunataks. 85°27'S, 157°38'W. Two nunataks overlooking the head of the Ross Ice Shelf, just east of the terminus of Amundsen Glacier. 5 miles west of O'Brien Peak. Named for John A. MacDonald, biologist at McMurdo Station, 1964.

MacDonald Peak. 77°40'S, 86°40'W. 1,940 m. Between Shockey Peak and Mount Crawford near the northern end of the main ridge of the Sentinel Range. Discovered aerially by Ellsworth on Nov. 23, 1935. Named in 1961 for William R. MacDonald, US Geological Survey cartographer who helped prepare the 1962 map of this range. He later went down to Antarctica many times to supervise the aerial photography used in making maps of the continent. He died in 1977, aged 52, having seen more of Antarctica than probably anyone.

MacDonald Point. 79°52'S, 160°20'E. On the south side of the mouth of the Darwin Glacier, where that glacier flows into the Ross Ice Shelf. Named for James H. (Scot) MacDonald, VX-6 journalist at McMurdo Station in 1958-59, 1959-60, 1960-61.

McDonald Point. 67°21'S, 59°40'E. Marks the western end of Islay in the William Scoresby Archipelago. Named by the personnel on the *William Scoresby* in Feb. 1936.

McDonald Ridge. 66°20'S, 52°15'E. Mostly ice-covered. Between Johnston and Douglas Peaks. 22 miles SE of Mount Biscoe in Enderby Land. Named by the Australians for K.R. McDonald, radio officer at Mawson Station in 1961.

MacDonald Spur. 76°47'S, 159°33'E. A long, low ridge extending eastward from Ballance Peak in the Allan Hills of Victoria Land. Named by the New Zealand Antarctic Research Program Allan Hills Expedition of 1964 for Ivan MacDonald, field assistant with the expedition.

McDonough Nunataks. 85°08'S, 179°59'E. Isolated. At the south edge of the Queen Maud Mountains. A small group rising above the ice plateau 5 miles west of Mount Rosenwald. Named for John W. McDonough, ionosphere physicist at the Amundsen-Scott South Pole Station in 1962.

Macdougal, J. 3rd mate on the *Scotia* during Bruce's expedition of 1902-4.

Macdougal Bay. 60°42'S, 44°33'W. Between Ferguslie and Watson Peninsulas on the north coast of Laurie Island in the South Orkneys. Charted in 1903 by Bruce, who named it for J. Macdougal.

McEacharn-Summerlees, Herbert Oliver Peter. b. 1903, Tasmania. Nicknamed "Bullet." Australian whaling laborer on the *Sir James Clark Ross* on its Antarctic expedition of 1923-24. Formerly a navvy's mate.

Mount McElroy. 74°09'S, 63°12'W. At the west end of the Hutton Mountains, in the SE part of Palmer Land. Discovered by the RARE 1947-48 and named by Finn Ronne for T.P. McElroy of Boston, who contributed the radio and communication instruments for the expedition.

McElroy Glacier. 70°58'S, 166°58'E. Just west of Matthews Ridge on Tapsell

Foreland in Victoria Land. It flows south to join Barnett Glacier. Named for Clifford T. McElroy, geologist at McMurdo Station, 1964–65 and 1966–67.

McElroy Ridge. 72°37′S, 168°03′E. 16 miles long. In the Victory Mountains of Victoria Land. Bounded by the Gruendler, Trainer, Trafalgar, and Rudolph Glaciers. Named for William D. McElroy, director of the NSF, 1969–72.

Mount Macelwane. 81°54′S, 89°30′W. The highest peak in the eastern part of the Nash Hills. Named in 1958 for the Rev. James B. Macelwane (1883–1956), a Jesuit priest and first chairman of the Technical Panel for Seismology and Gravity of the US National Committee for the IGY.

Mount Macey. 69°52′S, 65°18′E. Also called The Castle. 1,960 m. Isolated. 15 miles SE of Stinear Nunataks in Mac. Robertson Land. Discovered in 1954 by an ANARE party led by Robert G. Dovers, and named for L.E. Macey, technical superintendent at Mawson Station, 1954. Macey had been with the ANARE since 1948.

Estrecho Mac Farlane *see* **McFarlane Strait**

McFarlane, Capt. British sealer, captain of the brig *Dragon*. He arrived in the South Shetlands in the early part of Nov. 1820, and stayed through the austral summer. He may have made a landing on the Antarctic Peninsula prior to John Davis, but this is far from certain.

McFarlane Strait. 62°32′S, 59°55′W. Also called Estrecho Mac Farlane, Détroit de MacFerlane. Between Greenwich and Livingston Islands in the South Shetlands. It is 5 miles at its widest point, 4 at its narrowest. First explored by Palmer on Nov. 20, 1820. In the early sealing days it was called Yankee Sound, and Weddell called it Duff's Straits. The current name, which appeared on an 1822 chart made by Powell, is almost certainly for Capt. McFarlane.

MacFee, Peter. Ordinary seaman on the Wilkes Expedition 1838–42. Joined at Callao. Served the cruise.

Macfie Sound. 67°22′S, 59°43′E. Also called Homresund. A marine passage 1 mile wide at its narrowest point. Between Islay and Bertha Island in the William Scoresby Archipelago. Discovered in Feb. 1936 by personnel on the *William Scoresby* and named by them for Lt. A.F. Macfie, RNR, who prepared the charts of the expedition.

McGaw Peak. 75°52′S, 140°59′W. Over 800 m. Between Land Glacier and Paschal Glacier in Marie Byrd Land. Between Mount McCoy and Pearson Peak. Named for Maj. Hugh R.L. McGaw, US Army, logistics research officer on the staff of the commander, US Naval Support Force, Antarctica, 1971 and 1972.

Mount McGee. 74°03′S, 164°33′E. 1,410 m. At the north side of Clausnitzer Glacier in the Random Hills of Victoria Land. Named for Lawrence E. McGee, geologist at McMurdo Station, 1965–66.

McGee Rock. 75°54′S, 142°59′W. Isolated. At the south side of Parker Pass. 5 miles south of Zunich Hill in Marie Byrd Land. Named for Wayne R. McGee, USN, equipment operator at Byrd Station, 1966.

McGeever, Paddy. Irish/Australian whaling laborer on the *Sir James Clark Ross* expeditions of 1923–24 and 1924–25. In between expeditions he went to Norway on the ship.

Mount McGhee. 66°56′S, 52°39′E. 4 miles south of Mount Smethurst in Enderby Land. Named by the Australians for J. McGhee, mechanic and driver at Wilkes Station in 1961.

McGill, Arthur. Seaman on the Wilkes Expedition 1838–42. Joined at Upolu. Discharged at Oahu, Nov. 20, 1841.

McGill, Laurence. Ordinary seaman on the Wilkes Expedition 1838–42. Joined in the USA. Run at Manila.

McGillan, Thomas. Otherwise spelled McGillon. Seaman on the *Nimrod*,

1907–9, and fireman on the *Terra Nova*, 1910–13.

McGinnis Peak. 84° 32′ S, 177° 52′ W. 1,270 m. Has a large, bare cirque in the northern slope. Just east of the lower part of the Kosco Glacier. 3 ½ miles SW of Oppegaard Spur, near the edge of the Ross Ice Shelf. Discovered by the USAS 1939–41. Surveyed by Albert P. Crary in 1957–58, and named by him for Lyle McGinnis, seismologist in the US Victoria Land Traverse Party of 1958–59, and a leading authority on Antarctica.

MacGogger, Gregory Archibald. Tasmanian whaling laborer on the *Sir James Clark Ross* expedition of 1923–24.

McGomey, Joseph. Ordinary seaman on the Wilkes Expedition 1838–42. Joined at Callao. Discharged at Oahu, Oct. 31, 1840.

McGrady Cove. 66° 16′ S, 110° 34′ E. At the head of Newcomb Bay in the Windmill Islands. Named for Chief Photographer's Mate E.D. McGrady, USN, who took part in Operation Windmill here in 1947–48.

Mount McGrath. 70° 53′ S, 65° 28′ E. 1 mile NE of Mount Bewsher in the Aramis Range of the Prince Charles Mountains. Named by the Australians for A.E. McGrath, assistant diesel mechanic at Mawson Station in 1963.

McGrath Nunatak. 68° 03′ S, 63° 01′ E. Ridgelike. At the west end of the Blånabbane Nunataks. 7 miles SE of Van Hulssen Nunatak in Mac. Robertson Land. Photographed by the LCE 1936–37. Named by the Australians for P.J. McGrath, radio officer at Mawson Station in 1965.

Mount McGregor. 70° 37′ S, 66° 39′ E. Surmounts the SW end of Thomson Massif in the Aramis Range of the Prince Charles Mountains. Discovered in Dec. 1956 by an ANARE party led by W.G. Bewsher, and named for Peter McGregor, geophysicist at Mawson Station, 1956.

MacGregor, Capt. Commander of the *Minstrel*, in the South Shetlands, 1820–21.

McGregor Glacier. 85° 08′ S, 174° 50′ W. 14 miles long. 3 miles wide. Flows from the SW slopes of the Prince Olav Mountains into Shackleton Glacier just north of the Cumulus Hills. Named by the Southern Party of the NZGSAE 1961–62 for V.R. McGregor, geologist with that party.

McGregor Range. 71° 58′ S, 167° 51′ E. 13 miles long. In the south-central part of the Admiralty Mountains. Named for Cdr. Ronald K. McGregor, USN, leader of Antarctic Support Activities at McMurdo Station, 1962.

McGuinness, Charles J. First mate on the *Eleanor Bolling* during Byrd's 1928–30 expedition. One of the true characters of Antarctic exploration, he had fought on both sides during World War I, had been a gun runner, and a general in Ireland during the troubles.

McGuire Island. 64° 46′ S, 64° 24′ W. In the NE part of The Joubin Islands. Named for Thomas J. McGuire, oiler on the *Hero* during that vessel's first trip to Palmer Station in 1968.

Mount Machatschek. 66° 52′ S, 68° 04′ W. Mostly snow-covered. In northern Adelaide Island. 14 miles SW of Mount Vélain. Named by the UK for Fritz Machatschek (1876–1957), Austrian geomorphologist who wrote *Gletscherkunde* in 1942 with Erich von Drygalski (*see* the Bibliography).

Machin Nunatak. 72° 48′ S, 64° 53′ E. Small, domed nunatak. 7 miles east of Mount Cresswell in the southern part of the Prince Charles Mountains. Named by the Australians for D.K. Machin, radio officer at Mawson Station, 1960.

McHugh Peak. 69° 51′ S, 68° 06′ W. On the west side of the Antarctic Peninsula.

McIlroy, Dr. J.A. Surgeon on Shackleton's 1914–17 expedition. He was one of the 22 men left on Elephant Island. Back again with Shackleton on the *Quest* in

1920–21, this time he was surgeon and meteorologist.

McIntosh Cove *see* **Mackintosh Cove**

Mount McIntyre. 87°17′S, 153°W. Forms the NE extremity of D'Angelo Bluff. At the west side of the Robert Scott Glacier, near the head of that glacier, just opposite Mount Howe. This is one of the most southerly mountains in the world. Discovered in Dec. 1934 by Quin Blackburn's party during Byrd's 1933–35 expedition, and named by Byrd for Marvin H. McIntyre, President Roosevelt's secretary.

McIntyre, Eugene C. Lt. cdr., USN. Co-pilot of Flight 8A, the second R4D aircraft during Byrd's flight to the Pole on Feb. 16, 1947, during Operation Highjump.

¹McIntyre Island. 66°14′S, 110°34′E. Just west of Blakeney Point, Clark Peninsula, in the Windmill Islands. Named by Carl Eklund in 1957 for Robert McIntyre, USN, construction mechanic at Wilkes Station that year.

²McIntyre Island. 67°22′S, 49°05′E. The most easterly of the Hydrographer Islands, just south of Sakellari Peninsula in Enderby Land. Named by the Australians for Sgt. H. McIntyre, RAAF, engine fitter at Mawson Station in 1959.

McIntyre Promontory. 84°57′S, 179°40′W. At the head of the Ramsey Glacier in the Bush Mountains of the Queen Maud Mountains. Discovered aerially on Feb. 16, 1947, by Flight 8A during its flight to the Pole. Named for Eugene C. McIntyre.

McKaskle Hills. 70°01′S, 73°E. Between Rogers Glacier and the Mistichelli Hills, on the eastern edge of the Ross Ice Shelf. Photographed by Operation Highjump flights and mapped from these photos in 1952 by US cartographer John H. Roscoe, who named these hills for H.A. McKaskle, air crewman on the flights over this area.

Cape MacKay. 77°42′S, 168°31′E. Ice-covered. Forms the SE extremity of Ross Island. Discovered by the Royal Society Expedition, 1901–4, and named by Scott for Capt. Harry MacKay.

Mackay, A.F. b. 1878. Alistair Forbes Mackay. Lost in the Arctic in Feb. 1914. Physician and biologist on Shackleton's 1907–9 expedition. He was, with Mawson and David, one of the first men to reach the South Magnetic Pole.

McKay, Donald. New York seaman, probably a captain, he took part in the New York Sealing Expedition of 1820–22, and for a time commanded the *Sarah* during the 1820–21 period in the South Shetlands. He was pilot of the *Cecilia* during its 2-day exploratory cruise from Feb. 22 to 24, 1821. He sent minerals and some kelp to New York via B. Astor on the *Jane Maria*.

MacKay, Harry. Captain of the *Terra Nova* during the 1903–4 relief of Scott's Royal Society Expedition.

McKay Cliffs. 82°19′S, 156°E. Also called Alexander McKay Cliffs. 20 miles long. They form the north wall of the Geologists Range. Named by the New Zealanders in 1961–62 for Alexander McKay, pioneer NZ geologist.

Mackay Glacier. 76°58′S, 162°E. One of the major glaciers in Victoria Land, it flows from the Polar Plateau, between the Convoy and Clare Ranges, into the southern part of Granite Harbor, between Evans Piedmont Glacier and Wilson Piedmont Glacier. It flows into the Ross Sea as the Mackay Glacier Tongue. Discovered in 1908–9 by the South Magnetic Pole party of Shackleton's 1907–9 expedition, and named for A.F. Mackay.

Mackay Glacier Tongue. 76°58′S, 162°20′E. The seaward extension of the Mackay Glacier. It juts out into the Ross Sea at Granite Harbor in Victoria Land. Named by Scott's 1910–13 expedition in association with the glacier.

Mackay Mountains. 77°30′S, 143°20′W. 10 miles south of the Allegheny Mountains in the Ford Ranges of Marie

Byrd Land. Discovered in 1934 by Byrd's 1933–35 expedition. One of the peaks was named Mount Clarence Mackay, for the head of the Postal Telegraph and Mackay Radio Companies, who was a patron of the expedition. The name was later extended to the whole range, and shortened to Mackay Mountains.

MacKay Peak. 62°43′S, 60°18′W. Between Brunow Bay and False Bay on Livingston island in the South Shetlands.

Mackay Tongue *see* **Mackay Glacier Tongue**

M'Kean, Capt. Commander of the *Princess Charlotte* in the South Shetlands, between 1821 and 1825.

M'Kean Point. 62°42′S, 60°01′W. 3½ miles east of Brunow Bay on the SE coast of Livingston Island in the South Shetlands. Named by the UK in 1961 for Capt. M'Kean.

M'Keen, John. Ship's cook on the Wilkes Expedition 1838–42. Joined in the USA. Served the cruise.

Fiord Mac Kellar *see* **Mackellar Inlet**

Mount Mackellar. 83°59′S, 166°39′E. 4,295 m. At the head of Mackellar Glacier. 3 miles south of Pagoda Peak in the Queen Alexandra Range. Discovered by Shackleton during his push toward the Pole in 1908–9, and named by him for Campbell Mackellar, a patron of the expedition.

Mackellar Glacier. 83°47′S, 167°15′E. Also called Bell Glacier. Flows along the east side of the Hampton Ridge, from Mount Mackellar into the Lennox-King Glacier in the Queen Alexandra Range. Named by the New Zealanders in 1961–62 in association with the nearby mountain.

McKellar Glacier. 72°12′S, 167°07′E. Flows along the east side of Evans Ridge into Pearl Harbor Glacier in the Victory Mountains of Victoria Land. Named by the New Zealanders in 1962–63 for I.C. McKellar, geologist and glaciologist with the NZGSAE 1957–58, who worked in the area of nearby Tucker Glacier that season.

Mackellar Inlet. 62°05′S, 58°28′W. Also called Fiord Mac Kellar, Mackeller Inlet. Forms the NW head of Admiralty Bay, just to the west of Keller Peninsula, on the coast of King George Island in the South Shetlands.

Mackellar Islands. 66°58′S, 142°40′E. A group of about 30 small islands and rocks 1½ miles north of Cape Denison, in the middle of Commonwealth Bay, on the coast of East Antarctica. Discovered by the AAE 1911–14, and named by Mawson for C.D. Mackellar of London, a patron of the expedition.

Mackeller Inlet *see* **Mackellar Inlet**

Mount McKelvey. 85°21′S, 87°18′W. 2,090 m. Mostly ice-free. Less than 1 mile east of Mount Walcott in the eastern part of the Thiel Mountains. Named for Vincent E. McKelvey, ninth director of the US Geological Survey, 1971–78.

McKelvey Valley. 77°26′S, 161°33′E. A dry valley. Between the western part of the Olympus Range and the Insel Range in Victoria Land. Named by the New Zealanders in 1958–59 for Barry C. McKelvey, a NZ geologist who, with P.N. Webb (*see* **Webb Glacier**), did the first geological exploration of this area, in 1957–58. He was back again, in the Wright Valley, in 1958–59.

Mackemer Point. 66°27′S, 110°29′E. The NW point of Peterson Island in the Windmill Islands. Named for Frederick W. Mackemer, aerographer's mate at Wilkes Station, 1958.

Mount McKenny. 71°40′S, 160°22′E. 1,890 m. At the south end of the Daniels Range. 4 miles SE of Mount Toogood, in the Usarp Mountains. Named for Clarence D. McKenny, meteorologist at South Pole Station in 1959 and 1961, and at Eights Station in 1963.

Mount McKenzie. 70°40′S, 67°01′E. 2,255 m. Pyramidal. 3½ miles SE of Saxton Ridge in the Amery Peaks of the Aramis Range in the Prince Charles Mountains. Named by the Australians for John A. McKenzie, cook at Mawson Station in 1956.

Mackenzie, James. Private of marines on the Wilkes Expedition 1838–42. Joined in the USA. Served the cruise.

MacKenzie, K.N. Took over from John King Davis as captain of the *Discovery* for the second half of the BANZARE (i.e., from 1930–31).

MacKenzie Bay. 68°38′S, 70°35′E. At the western extremity of the Amery Ice Shelf. 20 miles NE of Foley Promontory. On Feb. 10, 1931, the BANZARE discovered a huge embayment here, and called it the MacKenzie Sea, for Capt. K.N. MacKenzie. Subsequent to this the Amery Ice Shelf changed its shape by parts breaking away into the sea, and this feature was greatly reduced in size. In 1968 it was only 15 miles wide.

Mackenzie Glacier. 64°17′S, 62°16′W. 4 miles long. Flows from Mount Parry into Malpighi Glacier on the east coast of Brabant Island. Charted by de Gerlache, 1897–99. Named by the UK for Sir James Mackenzie (1853–1925), British heart specialist.

McKenzie Nunatak. 71°14′S, 163°25′E. 1,620 m. Between McLin and Graveson Glaciers in the Bowers Mountains. Named for Garry D. McKenzie, glaciologist studying Meserve Glacier in 1966–67.

McKenzie Peak. 70°18′S, 65°38′E. Just south of Mount Albion in the Athos Range of the Prince Charles Mountains. Named by the Australians for J.F. McKenzie, radio technician at Wilkes Station, 1963.

Mackenzie Peninsula. 60°45′S, 44°48′W. Forms the west end of Laurie Island in the South Orkneys. Discovered and charted by Powell and Palmer in Dec. 1821. Surveyed in 1903 by Bruce, who named it for his wife (her maiden name).

MacKenzie Sea *see* **MacKenzie Bay**

Mount McKeown. 77°56′S, 85°31′W. 1,880 m. On the north side of Embree Glacier. 3 miles NE of Mount Schmid, in the northern part of the Sentinel Range. Named for 1st Lt. Donald F. McKeown,

USAF, who helped build South Pole Station in 1956–57.

Mount McKercher. 86°09′S, 150°02′W. 2,230 m. On the east side of the Robert Scott Glacier, just north of the mouth of Griffith Glacier, in the Queen Maud Mountains. Discovered in Dec. 1934 by Quin Blackburn's party during Byrd's 1933–35 expedition, and named by Byrd for Hazel McKercher, his secretary during the period of this expedition.

Mackerel Island. 66°01′S, 65°26′W. Just west of Flounder Island in the Fish Islands off the west coast of Graham Land. Charted by the BGLE 1934–37. Named by the UK in 1959 in keeping with the fish motif.

Mount McKerrow. 81°45′S, 159°48′E. On the east side of Starshot Glacier. 5 miles north of Thompson Mountain in the Surveyors Range. Discovered by the New Zealanders in 1960–61 and named by them for James McKerrow, a former surveyor-general of NZ.

Mackey, Frank. Seaman on the Wilkes Expedition 1838–42. Joined at Rio. Served the cruise.

Mackey Rock. 76°36′S, 146°22′W. Isolated. On the east side of the Sulzberger Ice Shelf. 8 miles SW of Mount Iphigene, on the coast of Marie Byrd Land. Named for Steven Mackey, field assistant with the USARP Marie Byrd Land Survey, 1967–68.

Mount McKibben. 75°23′S, 64°42′W. 5 miles SW of Hansen Inlet. 3 miles SE of McCaw Ridge, near the base of the Antarctic Peninsula. Named for L.D. McKibben, USN, shipfitter at Amundsen-Scott South Pole Station, 1963.

Mackin Table. 84°57′W, 64°W. Ice-topped. Wedge-shaped. A plateau about 20 miles long. Just north of the Patuxent Ice Stream in the Patuxent Range of the Pensacola Mountains. Named for J. Hoover Mackin, professor of geology at the University of Washington at Seattle, by several of his former students who worked in Antarctica.

McKinley, Ashley C. Capt. American surveyor/photographer on Byrd's 1928–11 expedition. He was one of the four to make the south Polar flight in the *Floyd Bennett* in 1929.

McKinley Nunatak. 85°18′S, 170°03′ 1. The most southerly of three large nunataks in the upper part of the Liv Glacier. 5 miles NNE of Barnum Peak. Named by the Southern Party of the NZGSAE 1961–62 for Ashley C. McKinley.

McKinley Peak. 77°54′S, 148°18′W. 15 miles west of Hershey Ridge at the south end of the Ford Ranges in Marie Byrd Land. Discovered during the Dec. 5, 1929 flight by Byrd, and named Mount Grace McKinley by Byrd for Grace McKinley, wife of Ashley C. McKinley. The name has since been amended.

McKinnis Peak. 69°34′S, 159°21′E. 510 m. 2 miles SE of Holladay Nunataks in the Wilson Hills. It surmounts the peninsula that is bounded by Tomilin and Noll Glaciers on the west and Gillett Ice Shelf on the east. Named for Joe D. McKinnis, VX-6 aviation electronics technician and air crewman in Antarctica five times with Operation Deep Freeze until 1969.

McKinnon Glacier. 70°38′S, 67°45′E. Flows SE from the Nemesis Glacier to Beaver Lake in the eastern part of the Aramis Range in the Prince Charles Mountains. Named by the Australians for Graeme W. McKinnon, geographical officer with the Antarctic Division, Melbourne, and officer-in-charge of the ANARE Prince Charles Mountains survey party in 1969. He was also secretary of the Antarctic Names Committee of Australia.

McKinnon Island. 67°36′S, 47°35′E. Mostly ice-covered. In the Hannan Ice Shelf along the coast of Enderby Land. Named by the Australians for Graeme W. McKinnon (*see* **McKinnon Glacier**).

Cape Mackintosh. 72°53′S, 60°03′W. Ice-covered. Forms the northern tip of Kemp Peninsula and the eastern side of the entrance to Mason Inlet, on the east coast of Palmer Land. Named by the FIDS for Neil A. Mackintosh.

Mount Mackintosh. 74°22′S, 161°49′ E. 2,300 m. On Skinner Ridge. 2 miles SW of Mount Fenton, on the western edge of the Eisenhower Range of Victoria Land. Charted by Shackleton's 1907–9 expedition, and named by them for Aeneas L.A. Mackintosh.

Mackintosh, Aeneas L.A. b. 1881. Aeneas Lionel Acton Mackintosh. Former officer on a P&O liner, he was captain of the *Aurora* during the abortive British Imperial Transantarctic Expedition. He had to have his eye removed by Dr. Marshall on Jan. 31, 1908, while second officer on the *Nimrod* during Shackleton's 1907–9 expedition. During the second expedition, 1914–17, Mackintosh brought the Aurora into McMurdo Sound, and then was responsible for laying down depots from Ross Island to the Beardmore Glacier, down which Shackleton was to traverse on his trip across the continent. Beginning in Sept. 1915 Mackintosh and his party of 5, in terrible conditions, succeeded in laying depots for the man who would never arrive. On the way back, three of the party died, including Mackintosh on May 8, 1916, when he and Hayward tried to get back on the last leg from the Discovery Hut to Cape Evans.

Mackintosh, D.R. Crewman on the *Jacob Ruppert*, 1934–35.

MacKintosh, M.P. Crewman on the *Jacob Ruppert*, 1933–34.

Mackintosh, Neil A. British marine biologist, oceanographer, and zoologist, he was one of the most important figures on the Discovery Committee. In 1925 he set up a scientific station on South Georgia (54°S). In the early 30s he was on the zoological staff of the Committee, and led the *Discovery II* expedition of 1933–35. In 1936 he became director of Research of the Discovery Investigations, and from Oct. 1937 to Jan. 1938 he led another expedition on the *Discovery II.*

Mackintosh Cove. 60°42'S, 44°30'W. Also spelled (erroneously) McIntosh Cove. Just SE of Fraser Point on the north coast of Laurie Island in the South Orkneys. Charted by Bruce in 1903. Later named for Neil A. Mackintosh.

McKinzie Islands. 74°03'S, 101°50'W. In the NE extremity of Cranton Bay, south of Canisteo Peninsula at the eastern end of the Amundsen Sea. Named for Richard H. McKinzie, USN, hospital corpsman at Byrd Station, 1967.

Mount Macklin. 69°57'S, 64°36'E. A mainly snow-covered ridge with an exposed summit. 2,005 m. Just east of Mount Shaw in the Anare Nunataks of Mac. Robertson Land. Visited in Nov. 1955 by an ANARE party led by J.M. Béchervaise. Named by the Australians for Eric L. Macklin (*see* **Macklin Island**).

Macklin, Dr. Alexander H. Surgeon on Shackleton's 1914–17 expedition. He was one of the 22 men left on Elephant Island. He was back in Antarctica in 1921 on the *Quest,* this time also in charge of stores and equipment. From 1939 to 1945 he was president of the Antarctic Club.

Macklin Island. 67°29'S, 63°39'E. In the eastern part of the Robinson Group. 3 miles NW of Cape Daly, Mac. Robertson Land. Photographed by the LCE 1936–37. Later named by the Australians for Eric L. Macklin, radio officer at Mawson Station, 1955 and 1959.

Mackworth Rock. 66°02'S, 66°34'W. A rock in water, in the Pendleton Strait. 2 miles north of Cape Leblond, Lavoisier Island. Named by the UK for Norman H. Mackworth, British experimental psychologist who, in 1953, first demonstrated beyond doubt that man acclimatizes to cold.

Maclaren Monolith. 80°20'S, 25°23'W. In the Shackleton Range.

McLaren Ridge. 70°52'S, 67°38'E. At the head of Battye Glacier. 5 miles west of Radok Lake in the Aramis Range of the Prince Charles Mountains. Named by the Australians for W.A. McLaren, glaciologist at Wilkes Station, 1965.

McLaughlin Cliffs. 71°35'S, 67°32'W. Overlook the George VI Sound between the Armstrong and Conchie Glaciers, in the western part of Palmer Land. Named for Lt. Donald J. McLaughlin, USNR, officer-in-charge of Palmer Station, 1970. A colony of snow petrels lives here.

McLaughlin Peak. 74°35'S, 64°18'W. 9 miles ESE of Mount Aaron in the northern part of the Latady Mountains in Palmer Land. Named for Robert H. McLaughlin, USN, engineman at Amundsen-Scott South Pole Station, 1964.

McLea Nunatak. 75°59'S, 159°30'E. Between Richards Nunatak and Sharks Tooth in the Prince Albert Mountains of Victoria Land. Named by the Southern Party of the NZGSAE 1962–63 for F. McLea, radio operator at Scott Base who was responsible for the field party radio communications.

McLean, Archie L. Medical officer and bacteriologist on the AAE 1911–14.

McLean, Dr. Donald. Medical officer on the RARE 1947–48.

McLean Buttress. 77°19'S, 160°58'E. A buttresslike mountain or promontory at the north side of Webb Lake and Barwick Valley in Victoria Land. Marks the southern limit of The Fortress. Named for Capt. Frank E. McLean, captain of the *Burton Island* in 1970 and 1971.

McLean Glacier. 70°59'S, 164°45'E. North of Mount Hemphill in the SW part of the Anare Mountains. It flows west into the lower part of the Ebbe Glacier, just south of Beaman Glacier. Named for Kenneth S. McLean, topographic engineer here in 1962–63.

McLean Nunataks. 67°50'S, 143°57'E. 3 nunataks in the western part of the Mertz Glacier, near the head of that glacier. Discovered by the AAE 1911–14, and named by Mawson for Dr. Archie L. McLean.

McLean Peak. 85°51'S, 141°35'W. 2,290 m. Surmounts a spur descending from the NW end of Stanford Plateau, along the Watson Escarpment. Named for Lt. William E. McLean, USN, medical officer and officer-in-charge of Amundsen-Scott South Pole Station, 1964.

McLean Ridge. 70°44'S, 66°51'E. Partly ice-covered. 3 miles SE of Mount Butterworth in the Aramis Range of the Prince Charles Mountains. Named by the Australians for C.V. McLean, senior diesel mechanic at Wilkes Station, 1963.

¹Mount McLennan. 67°12'S, 51°05'E. 4 miles south of Howard Hills in the NE part of the Scott Mountains of Enderby Land. Named by the Australians for K. McLennan.

²Mount McLennan. 77°35'S, 162°56' E. Over 1,600 m. At the north side of the Taylor Valley. It surmounts the area at the heads of the Canada, Loftus, and Commonwealth Glaciers, in Victoria Land. Named by Charles S. Wright in 1910–13 for Professor McLennan, physicist at Toronto University in Canada.

McLennan, K. Crew member on the *Discovery* during the BANZARE, 1929–31.

McLennon, T. Crewman on the *Jacob Ruppert*, 1933–34.

McLeod, Michael. Scottish sealing captain from Leith who commanded the *Beaufoy of London,* Weddell's consort ship, from 1819 to 1922. On Dec. 12, 1821, he landed on the South Orkneys.

McLeod, Thomas. Able seaman. Fireman on the *Terra Nova* during Scott's expedition of 1910–13, on the *Endurance* during Shackleton's ill-fated British Imperial Transantarctic Expedition of 1914–17 (McLeod was one of the 22 men left on Elephant Island), and on the *Quest,* Shackleton's last expedition, 1921–22.

¹McLeod Glacier. 60°44'S, 45°38'W. 1 mile long. Flows into Clowes Bay on the south side of Signy Island in the South Orkneys. Named by the UK in 1954 for Michael McLeod, following a FIDS 1947 survey.

²McLeod Glacier. 69°22'S, 158°22'E. Flows from the Wilson Hills, between Stanwix and Arthurson Ridges, into Davies Bay. Named by the Australians for Ian R. McLeod, geologist here with the ANARE in 1961 (*see also* **McLeod Massif**).

McLeod Hill. 68°05'S, 66°30'W. Also called Glacier Dome, The Dome. Ice-covered. 1,790 m. 1 mile east of the head of Northeast Glacier in Graham Land. Surveyed by the BGLE in 1936, and by the USAS in 1939–41. Resurveyed by the FIDS in 1946 and named by them for Kenneth A. McLeod, FIDS meteorological observer here during the last six months of 1947.

McLeod Massif. 70°46'S, 68°E. Just south of Manning Massif in the eastern part of the Aramis Range of the Prince Charles Mountains. Named by the Australians for Ian R. McLeod (*see also* **McLeod Glacier**), geologist-in-charge of field operations during the ANARE Prince Charles Mountains surveys of 1969 and 1970. This feature was first visited on the 1969 survey. McLeod had long been involved with the Antarctic, having been geologist at Mawson Station in 1958.

McLeod Nunataks. 67°29'S, 52°42'E. Isolated group. 35 miles SE of the Tula Mountains in Enderby Land. Visited in Dec. 1958 by an ANARE dog-sledge party from Mawson Station. The party included Ian R. McLeod (*see* **McLeod Massif**), for whom this feature is named.

Macleod Point. 64°06'S, 61°58'W. Forms the SE tip of Liège Island. Named by the UK for John J.R. Macleod (1876–1935), Scottish discoverer of insulin.

McLin Glacier. 71°12'S, 163°27'E. Flows north of McKenzie Nunatak into Graveson Glacier in the Bowers Mountains. It shares a common saddle with Carryer Glacier to the west, and is fed partly by the Edlin Névé. Named by the New Zealanders in 1967–68 for Lt. Cdr. Robert D. McLin, USN, Hercules aircraft pilot here that year.

Mount McMahon. 70°52'S, 65°09'E. 5 miles west of Mount Bewsher in the

Prince Charles Mountains. Named for R. McMahon, officer-in-charge at Mawson Station in 1963.

McMahon Glacier. 70°45'S, 165°45'E. Also called Nielsen Glacier. 18 miles long. In the Anare Mountains of Victoria Land. It flows north between Buskirk Cliffs and Gregory Bluffs into Nielsen Fjord. Named by the Australians for F.P. McMahon, logistics officer with the Australian Antarctic Division, many times in Antarctica and the sub–Antarctic islands.

McMahon Islands. 67°38'S, 45°58'E. Two islands, half a mile north of the Thala Hills of Enderby Land. 3½ miles east of Molodezhnaya Station. Named by the Australians for F.P. McMahon (*see* **McMahon Glacier**).

McManus, Thomas. Ordinary seaman on the Wilkes Expedition 1838–42. Joined in the USA. Served the cruise.

McMorrin Glacier. 67°59'S, 67°10'W. Flows from Mount Metcalfe to Marguerite Bay in Graham Land. Named by the UK for Ian McMorrin, BAS general assistant at Base E, 1961–63. He helped survey this area in 1962.

McMullin Island. 66°17'S, 110°31'E. Just over ¼ mile long. Between Shirley and Kilby Islands in the southern part of the entrance to Newcomb Bay, in the Windmill Islands. Named for John P. McMullin, air crewman on Operation Windmill.

McMurdo, Archibald. A lieutenant on the *Terror* during Ross' 1839–43 expedition to the Antarctic. Ross named McMurdo Bay (later called McMurdo Sound) for him.

McMurdo Base. This was the more common name by which NAF McMurdo (Naval Air Facility McMurdo) went from 1957 to 1961. Before 1957 it was an Air Operating Facility (an AirOpFac) of the US Navy, and called simply the AirOpFac at McMurdo Sound. It was established by the Americans in Jan. 1956, at Cape Evans, on Ross Island. The original Hut Point site had been considered too icy by Adm. Ketchum. Following the death of Richard Williams immediately after this site selection was made, Ketchum then relocated the site back to Hut Point, near the original one. This new site was at 77°50'S, 166°36'E, and 102 feet above sea level. A semi-permanent base of about 30 buildings in the shade of Mount Erebus, its first base leader was Lt. Cdr. David Canham, who led the first wintering party (1956) of 93 men. John C. Condit was first chaplain. The chaplain at the end of 1956 was Lt. Leon Darkowski, who suggested to Admiral Dufek, head of Operation Deep Freeze, that the name of the facility become Williams Air Operating Facility (q.v.). In 1957–58 the station was upgraded to a Naval Air Facility, and renamed NAF McMurdo, in preparation for the IGY (1957–58), although McMurdo would not be an IGY station as such (i.e., it would be a depot rather than a scientific station). Scott Marshall led the 1957 wintering-over party, and was relieved on Nov. 28, 1957, by Lt. Cdr. E.E. Ludeman, who in turn was relieved by Lt. Cdr. William A. Lewiston. From 1956 to 1961 it spread out and got metal-frame buildings, etc., and in 1961 it became a permanent station (*see* **McMurdo Station**).

McMurdo Bay *see* **McMurdo Sound**

McMurdo Ice Shelf. 78°S, 166°30'E. Strictly speaking, this is part of the Ross Ice Shelf, the much-traveled part between McMurdo Sound and Ross Island to the north, and Minna Bluff to the south. The characteristics of this part of the Ross Ice Shelf differ from the main shelf itself, and in 1962–63, after careful study, scientist A.J. Heine suggested the new ice shelf have as its borders Ross Island, Brown Peninsula, Black Island, and White Island. The US has since enlarged the area southward to Minna Bluff. Named for McMurdo Sound.

The *McMurdo News*. Newspaper produced at McMurdo Base during IGY. Replaced by the *McMurdo Sometimer*.

The *McMurdo Sometimer*. Originally a weekly, this was a newspaper produced at McMurdo Base as a successor to the *McMurdo News* of the IGY period. It carried American, international (radio-carried), and local news (i.e., station scuttlebutt).

McMurdo Sound. 77°30′S, 165°E. Also called McMurdo Strait. 35 miles long and wide. In the SW corner of the Ross Sea, at the junction of that sea and the Ross Ice Shelf. Between Ross Island and Victoria Land. Discovered by Ross in Jan. 1841 and named McMurdo Bay by him for Archibald McMurdo. The next person to visit was Scott in 1902. He redefined it as a sound. It is one of the main access routes to the interior of the continent, and thus has been the base for many expeditions. The sound is kept free of ice by icebreakers, so that supplies can get into McMurdo Station.

McMurdo Station. 77°50′52″S, 166°40′26″E. Its official name is NAF McMurdo (*see* **McMurdo Base** for a history of the station prior to 1961). The largest of the US stations, and indeed of all the stations in Antarctica, this has been the name of the base since 1961 when it became a permanent station. The oldest part of the base is now called Downtown McMurdo. The main street is called Burke Avenue (after Adm. Arleigh Burke), and (for a sampler) one of the living quarters buildings is called the Mammoth Mountain Inn. McMurdo is now the "largest city in Antarctica," an epithet it took over from Little America V in 1958–59. About 80 people winter-over every year, and in the summer this number swells to about 800. It has an ice runway (*see* **Williams Field**), the world's most southerly radio station (*see* **AFAN McMurdo**), many of the conveniences of home, and it even had a nuclear power plant. In 1974 it had a woman as leader — Mary Alice McWhinnie.

McMurdo Strait *see* **McMurdo Sound**

McMurdo Volcanics. A line of dormant and extinct volcanoes running along the coast of Victoria Land. They include Mount Melbourne.

Cape McNab. 66°56′S, 163°14′E. 350 meters high. Forms the south end of Buckle Island in the Balleny Islands. Named for John McNab.

McNab, John. 2nd mate on the *Eliza Scott* during Balleny's expedition of 1838–39. Made a sketch of the Balleny Islands when they were discovered in 1839.

McNair Nunatak. 67°52′S, 63°23′E. 12 miles east of the central part of the Masson Range. 5 miles SSE of Russell Nunatak. Discovered by Robert Dovers and his ANARE southern party of 1954. Named by the Australians for Richard McNair, cook at Mawson Station in 1955.

McNally Peak. 86°35′S, 153°24′W. 2,570 m. 3½ miles west of Mount Farley, near the SE side of Holdsworth Glacier in the Queen Maud Mountains. Named for Cdr. Joseph J. McNally, USN, supply officer at McMurdo Base in 1959. Later, 1967, he was on the staff of the commander, US Naval Support Force, Antarctica.

McNamara, John. Bosun on the *Jacob Ruppert*, 1933–35.

MacNamara Glacier. 84°20′S, 63°40′W. In the Patuxent Range of the Pensacola Mountains. It flows between the Thomas Hills and the Anderson Hills into the Foundation Ice Stream. Named for Edlen E. MacNamara, US exchange scientist at Molodezhnaya Station, 1967.

McNamara Island. 72°34′S, 93°12′W. 6 miles long. Mostly ice-covered. Partly within the northern edge of the Abbott Ice Shelf. 20 miles east of Dustin Island. Discovered on Feb. 27, 1940, on flights from the *Bear*, during the USAS 1939–41. Named by Byrd for John McNamara.

Mount McNaughton. 85°58′S, 128°12′W. Over 3,000 m. 2 miles south of Haworth Mesa in the western part of the Wisconsin Range. Named for John T. McNaughton, assistant secretary of defense for international security affairs, a member of the Antarctic Policy Group from 1965 until he died in 1967.

McNaughton Ridges. 67°32'S, 50°27' E. A group of ridges 12 miles NE of Simpson Peak in the Scott Mountains of Enderby Land. Named by the Australians for I.L.K. McNaughton, physicist at Mawson Station, 1961.

McNeile Glacier. 63°54'S, 59°26'W. Flows to the SE side of Almond Point to enter Charcot Bay, on the west side of Graham Land. Charted in 1948 by the FIDS, and named by them for S. St. C. McNeile, surveyor at Base D, 1948–49.

McNeish, Harry "Chips." 1886–1930. Name also spelled McNish. Carpenter on Shackleton's 1914–17 expedition. He was one of the men to go with Shackleton on the *James Caird* to South Georgia.

Mount Macnowski. 74°59'S, 64°57'W. In the northern part of the Scaife Mountains. 5 miles WSW of Schmitt Mesa, near the base of the Antarctic Peninsula. Discovered aerially by the RARE, 1947–48. Later named for Francis B. Macnowski, construction mechanic at Amundsen-Scott South Pole Station, 1967.

Mount Macpherson. 82°29'S, 155°50' E. 2,360 m. 1½ miles north of Mount Csejtey on the south edge of Boucot Plateau in the Geologists Range. Named by the New Zealanders in 1961–62 for E.O. Macpherson, formerly chief geologist of the NZ Geological Survey.

McPherson, Frank. Chief engineer on the *Eleanor Bolling* during Byrd's 1928–30 expedition.

MacPherson Peak. 70°33'S, 159°43'E. 2,290 m. On the NW end of the Pomerantz Tableland in the Usarp Mountains. Named for Frank L. MacPherson, US Army helicopter mechanic here in 1961–62 and 1962–63.

McPherson Peak. 78°32'S, 84°42'W. 2,200 m. On the west side of the head of Remington Glacier in the Sentinel Range. Named for William C. McPherson, Jr., USN, radio man at South Pole Station in 1957.

Macquarie Edge. 80°32'S, 30°03'W. At the eastern edge of the Filchner Ice Shelf, dominated by the western part of the Shackleton Range.

Mac. Robertson Land. 70°S, 65°E. Also called the Mac. Robertson Coast. The name has variously been seen as Mac Robertson Land, Mac-Robertson Land, MacRobertson Land and Mac. Robertson Land. Finally the definitive form was accepted as Mac. Robertson Land. It is the stretch of coastal East Antarctica between Enderby Land and the American Highland, or more specifically between William Scoresby Bay and Cape Darnley. In the east it includes the Prince Charles Mountains. Discovered by the BANZARE on Dec. 29, 1929, on a flight from the *Discovery,* and named by Mawson for MacPherson Robertson, an Australian patron.

McSaveney, Eileen R. American geologist, one of Lois Jones' all-women team of 1969–70, and one of the first 6 women to stand at the Pole (*see* **Women in Antarctica**). With her husband, Maurice J. McSaveney (*see* **McSaveney Spur**), she was back in the Antarctic in the early 1970s, investigating glaciers.

McSaveney Spur. 77°17'S, 160°35'E. 2 miles NE of Mount Bastion in the Willett Range of Victoria Land. It descends NE from the plateau level toward the NW flank of Webb Glacier. Named for Maurice J. McSaveney, US geologist in the Antarctic 1968–69, 1972–73, and 1973–74, and his wife Eileen R. McSaveney (q.v.).

McSweeney Point. 82°49'S, 166°40'E. 3 miles east of the terminus of Davidson Glacier. It overlooks the Ross Ice Shelf. Named for Lt. R.H. McSweeney, USN, commander of the *Tombigbee,* 1963.

Cape McVitie *see* **Cape Hartree**

McWhinnie, Dr. Mary Alice. Elmshurst, Illinois, biologist, the first American woman to do Antarctic field work. She made 11 research trips to Antarctica between 1962 and 1979. Between 1962 and 1972 she worked the Antarctic continent from the *Eltanin* during 5 summers, mostly studying krill, without setting foot on land, because the US government forbade women to do so. Finally, in 1972, she did. In 1974 she wintered-over as chief scientist at McMurdo Station, the first woman ever to head a scientific station in Antarctica. In 1975–76 she was at Palmer Station with her pupil Charlene Denys, and again every summer from 1976–79. She wrote *Polar Research* in 1979, and died on March 17, 1980. The Mary Alice McWhinnie Biology Center at Palmer Station was renamed for her in 1980–81.

McWhinnie Peak. 77°16′S, 162°14′E. 2 miles NE of Mount Harker in the Saint Johns Range of Victoria Land. Named for Mary Alice McWhinnie.

Macy, Richard. Nantucket captain of an unknown vessel who, in 1825, claimed to have discovered an island at 59°S, 91°W. He reported many seals here. It is therefore possible that he journeyed south of 60°S.

Macy, Robert R. Captain of the *Aurora*, 1820–21. He joined the *Huron* in 1821–22.

Macy Glacier. 62°43′S, 60°09′W. Flows into Brunow Bay, Livingston Island, in the South Shetlands. Named by the UK in 1958 for Robert R. Macy.

Islote Madariaga *see* **Diamonen Island**

Madden Island. 77°27′S, 149°03′W. 4 miles long. Ice-covered. In the Marshall Archipelago. Between Moody Island and Grinder Island in the Sulzberger Ice Shelf. Named for Michael C. Madden, USN, electrician's mate at Byrd Station, 1966.

Madder Cliffs. 63°18′S, 56°29′W. Reddish rock cliffs rising steeply from the sea to about 305 meters. They form the north side of the entrance to Suspiros Bay, at the west end of Joinville Island. Surveyed by the FIDS in 1953–54.

Named by the UK in 1956. Madder is a red vegetable dye, and seems to describe the color of the cliffs.

Maddox Peak. 65°09′S, 62°50′W. At the south side of the mouth of Carbutt Glacier, east of Flandres Bay, on the west coast of Graham Land. Named by the UK in 1960 for Richard L. Maddox (1816–1902), British photography pioneer.

Madell Point. 66°35′S, 66°22′W. 2 miles NE of Cape Rey on the coast of Graham Land. Named by the UK for James S. Madell, FIDS surveyor at Base W in 1957. He was responsible for the triangulation of this area.

Madey Ridge. 83°28′S, 55°50′W. Trends NW from Mount Moffatt along the north side of Berquist Ridge in the Neptune Range of the Pensacola Mountains. Named for Jules Madey of Clark, N.J., ham radio operator who, between 1957 and 1967, acted as a major link between Antarctica and the USA.

Madigan, Cecil T. Meteorologist on the AAE 1911–14. He led the Eastern Coastal Party in late 1912 to Horn Bluff and back to Main Base.

Madigan Nunatak. 67°09′S, 143°21′E. Isolated. 18 miles south of Cape Gray. Discovered by the AAE 1911–14. Named by Mawson for Cecil T. Madigan.

Mount Madison. 80°26′S, 160°10′E. 1,385 m. Mostly ice-covered. 7 miles west of Cape Selborne, on the south side of the Byrd Glacier. Named for Lt. Cdr. Douglas W. Madison, aide to the commander, US Naval Support Force, Antarctica, 1961–62, and public information officer, 1963–64.

Mae-hyoga Rock. 70°04′S, 38°54′E. 3 miles NW of Oku-hyoga Rock on the east side of Shirase Glacier, in Queen Maud Land. Named Mae-hyoga-iwa (outer glacier rock) by the Japanese in association with nearby Oku-hyoga Rock.

Mount Maere. 72°32′S, 31°17′E. 2,300 m. On the west side of Norsk Polarinstitutt Glacier, just SW of Mount Bastin, in the Belgica Mountains. Discovered by the Belgian Antarctic Expedition 1957–58 under Gaston de Gerlache, who named it for Xavier de Maere d'Aertrijcke, second-in-command and chief meteorologist of the expedition.

Magee Rock. 66°13′S, 110°37′E. A rock in water, 350 yards NE of Cameron Island, in the Swain Islands. Named by Carl Eklund in 1957 for George E. Magee, USN, carpenter at Wilkes Station, 1957.

Magellan Whaling Company. Norwegian whaling outfit, which had a base on Deception Island. In 1908–9 Andresen was manager.

The *Magga Dan*. Danish ship owned by the J. Lauritzen Lines of Copenhagen. It was the second ship used by Fuchs during the BCTAE 1955–57. The captain during 1956–57 was Hans C. Petersen, and from 1958–59 it was Harald Møller Pederson. Much used as an ANARE ship, it also took south the Belgian Antarctic expeditions of 1964, 1965, and 1966. It was later used as a tour ship.

Magga Peak. 69°10′S, 157°11′E. A triangular, flatiron-shaped wall of sheer rock. Forms the end of the most northerly of the Burnside Ridges. The summit is a sharp point. Named by the Australians for the *Magga Dan*.

Mount Maglione. 77°18′S, 141°47′W. 1 mile NE of Mount Ekblaw in the Clark Mountains of Marie Byrd Land. Named for Lt. (jg) Charles R. Maglione, USNR, navigator on Hercules aircraft, 1968.

The *Magnet*. Peter Kemp's 148-ton ship of 1833–34, probably an Enderby Brothers vessel out of London.

Magnet Bay. 66°22′S, 56°20′E. 7 miles wide. It recedes 2 miles into the East Antarctica coast, 9 miles west of Cape Davis at the NW side of the Edward VIII Plateau. Charted by the BANZARE 1929–31 as lying between Cape Borley and Cape Davis. Mawson named it for the *Magnet*. When the LCE 1936–37 photographed it aerially they found it to be much smaller than had been charted. Either the BAN-ZARE had been inaccurate or the coast had reformed in the intervening 5 years.

Magnet Hill. 63°22′S, 57°22′W. Snow-covered. On Mott Snowfield, 4 miles NE of Camel Nunataks, Trinity Peninsula. There were magnetometer and topographical survey stations here set up by the British in the 1950s. Named by the British geophysical and survey party which worked here in 1959.

Magnetic Island. 68°33′S, 77°54′E. ¼ mile NE of Turner Island, off Breidnes Peninsula, Vestfold Hills. Photographed by the LCE 1936–37. Visited on March 3, 1954, by an ANARE party led by Phillip Law. Law named it for the magnetic observations taken here by J. Brooks.

Magnetic South Pole *see* **South Magnetic Pole**

Magnetite Bluff. 83°22′S, 51°15′W. At the western edge of the Pensacola Mountains.

Magnier Peak *see* **Magnier Peaks**

Magnier Peaks. 65°40′S, 64°18′W. Two peaks, the higher being 1,345 m. They surmount the peninsula between Leroux and Bigo Bays on the west coast of Graham Land. Charcot, in 1908–10, discovered them, and thinking them to be one peak, named it Magnier Peak. The name was later amended to include both.

Magoke Point. 69°40′S, 39°29′E. On the SE part of Skallen Hills in Queen Maud Land. It juts out into the inlet between Skallen Hills and Skallen Glacier. Named by the Japanese in 1972.

Mount Maguire. 74°01′S, 66°55′E. Flat-topped. It has a distinctive pointed nunatak on its eastern side. 22 miles south of Cumpston Massif near the head of the Lambert Glacier. Named by the Australians for Sgt. O. Maguire, RAAF, radio technician at Mawson Station, 1958.

Mahalak Bluffs. 68°17′S, 65°23′W. On the east coast of the Antarctic Peninsula, overlooking the Larsen Ice Shelf.

Mount Mahan. 85° 32'S, 140° 04'W. 1,260 m. 3 miles east of Mount Fiedler in the Bender Mountains. Named for Shirley F. Mahan, radioman at Byrd Station, 1960.

Maher, Eugene H. Captain of the *Glacier,* 1955–56. On Nov. 28, 1957, he took over from Mills Dickey as commander of Naval Support Units, Antarctica.

Maher Island. 72° 58'S, 126° 22'W. Horseshoe-shaped. 7 miles north of the NW end of Siple Island, off the Marie Byrd Land coast. Discovered aerially during Operation Highjump, 1946–47. Named for Eugene H. Maher.

Mahler Spur. 69° 48'S, 70° 52'W. 6 miles long. It extends west into the Mozart Ice Piedmont 7 miles east of the south end of Debussy Heights, in the northern part of Alexander Island. Discovered aerially by the BGLE in 1937. Named by the UK for the composer.

Mahogany Bluff. 63° 53'S, 57° 14'W. 5 miles SW of Cape Gordon. Forms the east side of Pastorizo Bay, Vega Island. Named for its color by the UK.

Mount Mahony. 77° 12'S, 161° 35'E. 1,870 m. Just east of the head of Victoria Upper Glacier, in Victoria Land. Mapped by Grif Taylor's Western Geological Party, during the British Antarctic Expedition, 1910–13. Named for D. Mahony, a Melbourne geologist.

Maiden Castle. 76° 39'S, 159° 50'E. A prominent rock feature east of Halle Flat in the Allan Hills of Victoria Land. Named by the NZ Antarctic Research Program Allan Hills Expedition of 1964 for its resemblance to the ancient British earthwork of the same name.

Maigetter Peak. 76° 27'S, 146° 29'W. The most northerly of the Birchall Peaks, on the south shore of Block Bay in Marie Byrd Land. Discovered aerially on Dec. 5, 1929, during Byrd's 1928–30 expedition. Named for Robert C. Maigetter, biologist with the USARP Marie Byrd Land Survey II, 1967–68.

Cape Maignan *see* **Maignan Point**

Maignan Point. 65° 03'S, 64° 02'W. Also called Cape Maignan. Marks the NE end of Cholet Island, and the west side of the entrance to Port Charcot, just off the NW part of Booth Island in the Wilhelm Archipelago. Charted by Charcot in 1903–5, and named by him for F. Maignan, a seaman on the *Français* who was killed two minutes after the ship left Le Havre on Aug. 15, 1903.

Maigo Peak. 68° 08'S, 42° 42'E. A rocky hill. 1½ miles ESE of Cape Hinode and just west of Bohyo Heights on the Queen Maud Land coast. Named Maigoyama (stray child mountain) by the Japanese in 1973.

Cape Main. 73° 33'S, 169° 54'E. 5 miles north of Cape Anne, on the east side of Coulman Island, Victoria Land. Named by New Zealand in 1966 for Brian Main, scientific technician at Hallett Station, 1962–63.

Main Base. A term often used for an expedition's principal base when other, outlying, bases are also set up. Mawson seems to have been the first to use the term, for his base at Cape Denison during the AAE 1911–14. The Main Base of the RARE 1947–48 was on Stonington Island.

Main South Range *see* **Prince Charles Mountains**

Mount Maines. 66° 39'S, 53° 54'E. 2,190 m. 8 miles SE of Stor Hånakken Mountain in the Napier Mountains of Enderby Land. Photographed by the LCE 1936–37, and named Stornuten (the big peak) by the Norwegians. Renamed by the Australians for R.L. Maines, cook at Wilkes Station in 1961.

Mainland *see* **Coronation Island**

Mainsail Rock. 60° 37'S, 46° 03'W. Just over ½ mile SW of Spine Island in Sandefjord Bay in the South Orkneys. It is the largest and most easterly of a chain of three rocks trending in a NW-SE direction off the SE side of Monroe Island. Surveyed by the Discovery Committee in 1933, and named by them.

The *Maipo*. Chilean oil tanker which took part in several Antarctic expeditions undertaken by that country: 1948–49 (Capt. Carlos Bonafós), 1949–50 (Capt. Mario Espinoza Gacitúa), 1952–53 (Capt. Ramón Barros), 1954–55 (Capt. Ramón Pinochet).

Maipo Island. 64°25′S, 62°17′W. Also called Buls Island. Snow-covered. At the entrance to Buls Bay, in eastern Brabant Island. Charted by de Gerlache, 1897–99. Named by the Chileans before 1947 for the *Maipo.*

Maipu Refugio. Argentine refuge hut built in Bills Gulch in 1956.

Maish Nunatak. 74°36′S, 99°28′W. 5 miles WSW of Mount Moses in the central part of the Hudson Mountains. Named for F. Michael Maish, ionosphere physicist at Byrd Station, 1967, and US exchange scientist at Vostok Station in 1969.

Maitland Glacier. 68°43′S, 65°W. Flows along the west flank of Hitchcock Heights into Mobiloil Inlet, on the east coast of the Antarctic Peninsula. Named in 1952 for O. Maitland Miller of the American Geographical Society, who constructed the first reconnaissance map of this area.

Bahía Maldita *see* **Brialmont Cove**

Maling Peak. 60°39′S, 45°40′W. 430 m. The more southerly of two peaks ½ mile NW of Cape Vik on the south coast of Coronation Island in the South Orkneys. Surveyed by the Discovery Committee in 1933. Named by the UK for Derek H. Maling, FIDS meteorologist at Signy Island Station in 1948 and 1949.

Grupo Malleco *see* **Pauling Islands**

Mount Mallis. 75°40′S, 160°48′E. 1,360 m. Between Mount Joyce and Mount Billing in the Prince Albert Mountains of Victoria Land. Named for Robert R. Mallis, seismologist at Amundsen-Scott South Pole Station, 1966.

Mallory Bluff. 84°02′S, 165°50′E. On the NW slope of the Grindley Plateau, just NE of the head of Wahl Glacier.

Named for Roger P. Mallory, Jr., meteorologist at Amundsen-Scott South Pole Station, 1962, and at Wilkes Station, 1963.

Mallory Point. 66°49′S, 108°39′E. Just north of Blunt Cove. Juts out from the ice cliffs along the west side of Vincennes Bay. Named for Ensign Charles W. Mallory, USN, construction officer on Operation Windmill, 1947–48.

Mallows, Capt. An Enderby Brothers man, commander of the *Rose,* 1833–34.

Malmgren Bay. 65°45′S, 66°07′W. Also called Bahía Sobenes. Indentation into the west side of Renaud Island, just north of Speerschneider Point, in the Biscoe Islands. Named by the UK in 1959 for Finn A.E.J. Malmgren (1895–1928), Swedish specialist in sea ice.

Mount Malone. 77°52′S, 85°36′W. 2,460 m. 8 miles east of Mount Barden in the northern part of the Sentinel Range. Named for Capt. Wallace R. Malone, USAF, who helped build the South Pole Station in 1956–57.

Mount Maloney. 85°41′S, 163°35′W. 1,990 m. 4 miles north of Mount Alice Gade at the SE side of the Bowman Glacier, in the Queen Maud Mountains. Discovered during Byrd's 1928–30 expedition. Named for John H. Maloney, Jr., meteorologist at South Pole Station, 1960.

Malpighi Glacier. 64°16′S, 62°15′W. 5 miles long. 1 mile wide. Flows from Harvey Heights into Mackenzie Glacier at the east coast of Brabant Island. Charted by de Gerlache in 1897–99. Named by the UK for Marcello Malpighi (1628–1694), Italian founder of microscopic anatomy.

Malta Plateau. 72°58′S, 167°18′E. Ice-covered. 25 miles in extent. In the Victory Mountains of Victoria Land. It is bounded on the south and west by the Mariner Glacier, on the north by tributaries to Trafalgar Glacier, and on the east by tributaries to Borchgrevink Glacier. Named by New Zealand for the Mediterranean island of Malta, in a wartime reference following the Victory motif.

Malus Island. 66°14'S, 65°45'W. 4½ miles south of Cape Evensen, in Auvert Bay, off the west coast of Graham Land. Charted by the BGLE 1934–37. Named by the UK in 1960 for Étienne L. Malus (1775–1812), French physicist whose studies in reflective light played a part in the design of snow goggles.

Malva Bluff. 71°55'S, 62°21'W. At the base of Condor Peninsula, it looks south over the NW extremity of Hilton Inlet on the east side of Palmer Land. Named for Antonio I. Malva-Gomes, topographic engineer with the US Geological Survey Lassiter Coast geologic and mapping party in 1970–71. He was also a member of the Pine Island Bay Reconnaissance on the *Burton Island* in 1974–75.

Mount Malville. 82°44'S, 48°10'W. 1,030 m. 5 miles SW of Ackerman Nunatak in the northern part of the Forrestal Range of the Pensacola Mountains. Named for J. McKim Malville, aurora scientist at Ellsworth Station, 1957.

Malysh Mountain. 72°09'S, 11°24'E. 2,640 m. Just SW of Skeidshovden Mountain in the Wohlthat Mountains of Queen Maud Land. Discovered during Ritscher's 1938–39 expedition. Named Gora Malysh (small child mountain) by the USSR in 1966.

Malyutki Nunataks. 72°04'S, 10°46'E. A group that trends north-south for 4 miles, at the SE end of the Orvin Mountains. 13 miles WNW of Skeidsberget Hill, in Queen Maud Land. Named Skaly Malyutki (baby nunataks) by the USSR in 1961.

Mame Island. 69°01'S, 39°29'E. Also called Mame-zima Island. 175 yards west of Ongul Island in the eastern part of Lützow-Holm Bay. Named Mame-jima (bean island) by the Japanese.

Mame-zima Island *see* **Mame Island**

Mamelon Island *see* **Mamelon Point**

Mamelon Point. 67°19'S, 64°49'W. 11 miles ENE of Cape Northrop on the east coast of Graham Land. Charted as an island, Mamelon Island, in 1947 by the FIDS. A mamelon is a small, rounded hillock. It was later redefined.

Mammals *see* **Fauna**

Man-o-War Glacier. 72°04'S, 168°03'E. Flows from the area south of Mount Black Prince and Mount Royalist into Tucker Glacier between the McGregor Range and Novasio Ridge, in the Admiralty Mountains. Named by the New Zealanders in 1957–58 in association with the Admiralty Mountains.

Mana Mountain. 72°51'S, 3°22'W. Ice-free. Borders the south side of Frostlendet Valley, 5 miles SW of Møteplassen Peak, on the Borg Massif of Queen Maud Land. Named by the Norwegians.

Manchot Island. 66°49'S, 141°24'E. In the entrance to Port-Martin, 350 yards west of Bizeux Rock, and 350 yards north of Cape Margerie. Charted by the French in 1949–51, and named by them for the large Adélie penguin rookery on the island. Manchot is a French word meaning penguin.

Manchurian ponies. Used by Scott on his last expedition, 1910–13, largely because Shackleton had used Siberian ponies (q.v.) in 1907–9, and had gotten to within 97 miles of the Pole. What Scott overlooked was that the ponies had been a hindrance, and had had to be killed off (that is, the ones that had not died already of the cold, or by falling into crevasses, etc.), and eaten. They were expensive to provision. Cecil Meares bought 19 old and worn out Manchurians in Harbin, and out of these Scott used 10 on his trek south in 1911. He thought they would be better than dogs, but their hoofs were not equipped for ice travel, and they kept getting bogged down. None of the ponies made it back alive. But then, none of the men did either.

Manciple Island. 64°56'S, 63°56'W. Between Reeve Island and Host Island in the Wauwermans Islands, in the Wilhelm Archipelago. Named by the UK in 1958 for one of the *Canterbury Tales* characters.

Mandible Bay *see* **Mandible Cirque**

Mandible Cirque. 73°07'S, 169°15'E. Also called Mandible Bay. A spectacular cirque indenting the coast of Daniell Peninsula 5 miles WSW of Cape Phillips, in Victoria Land. Named in 1966 by New Zealand for its shape.

Mandolin Hills. 69°55'S, 67°20'W. On the west coast of the Antarctic Peninsula.

Mandon, Justin. Captain's cook on the Wilkes Expedition 1838–42. Joined at Rio. Served the cruise.

Mane Skerry. 67°50'S, 67°18'W. Also called Islote Norte. A little island in the central part of Lystad Bay, off Horseshoe Island. Named in association with nearby Mite Skerry. This latter skerry had been originally misspelled at Base Y, as Might Skerry, and the FIDS deliberately and humorously perpetuated the error by naming this second skerry as Mane Skerry.

Manfull Ridge. 75°05'S, 114°39'W. Snow-covered. Descends from the north side of the Kohler Range, 5 miles west of Morrison Bluff, in Marie Byrd Land. Named for Byron P. Manfull, US Department of State, chairman of the Interagency Committee on Antarctica, 1967–69.

Mount Manger. 77°29'S, 153°15'W. Snow-covered. 3 miles NW of Mount Josephine in the Alexandra Mountains, on Edward VII Peninsula. Named by Byrd for William Manger, of Manger Hotels, who gave free room for office space and for expedition personnel in the early stages of Byrd's 1928–30 expedition.

Mount Mangin. 67°25'S, 68°26'W. 2,040 m. 5 miles NE of Mount Barré on Adelaide Island. Discovered by Charcot in 1908–10 and named by him for Louis A. Mangin, the French botanist.

Manhaul Glacier. 72°24'S, 169°45'E. Flows from the eastern slopes of Mount Humphrey Lloyd into Edisto Inlet just south of Luther Peak, in Victoria Land. Named by the New Zealanders in 1957–58 because they manhauled their equipment across the floating tongue of this glacier.

Manhauling *see* **Sledges**

Cape Manhue. A high promontory of the Ross Ice Shelf, the western point of an inlet in the Bay of Whales, 2½ miles south of Little America I. It was discovered by Amundsen on Jan. 15, 1911, and called Kap Manhue (Cape Man's Head) by him for its shape. Due to the changing shape of the Bay of Whales, it disappeared in later years, as did the Bay of Whales itself.

Manju Rock. 68°45'S, 40°25'E. Also spelled Manzyu Rock. Between Tama Glacier and Tama Point on the Queen Maud Land coast. Named Manju-iwa (bun-shaped rock) by the Japanese.

Mount Manke. 85°28'S, 144°42'W. 900 m. Marks the eastern limit of the Harold Byrd Mountains. Named for Robert M. Manke, utilitiesman at Byrd Station in 1960.

Mount Mankinen. 73°54'S, 163°06'E. 2,910 m. 2 miles NE of Mount Adamson in the Deep Freeze Range of Victoria Land. Named for Edward A. Mankinen, geologist at McMurdo Station, 1965–66.

Mount Mann. 83°12'S, 49°20'W. 1,680 m. On the SE edge of Lexington Table. 4 miles south of Mount Zirzow, in the Forrestal Range of the Pensacola Mountains. Named for Capt. Edward K. Mann, USAF, an assistant in the Research Division of the US Naval Support Force, Antarctica, 1966–68.

Manna Glacier. 69°45'S, 159°40'E. North of Stevenson Bluff and Mount Steele in the Wilson Hills. It flows into the eastern part of the Gillett Ice Shelf. Named by the Northern Party of the NZGSAE 1963–64 for the airdrop of goodies from an aircraft which carried the governor-general of NZ over this area.

Mount Mannering. 71°48'S, 164°57'E. 4 miles SSE of Toilers Mountain in the

King Range of the Concord Mountains. Named by the Northern Party of the NZGSAE of 1963–64 for Guy Mannering, a NZ photographer who could not have picked a more appropriately named base to be at, Scott Base, in 1962–63.

Manning Automatic Weather Station. 78°48′S, 166°54′E. Elevation approximately 210 feet. Just south of Minna Bluff on the Ross Ice Shelf. This American AWS began operating on Dec. 1, 1980, and ceased on Jan. 15, 1986.

Manning Massif. 70°42′S, 67°50′E. Between Loewe Massif and McLeod Massif in the eastern part of the Aramis Range of the Prince Charles Mountains. Named by the Australians for J. Manning, surveyor at Mawson Station in 1967, surveyor in charge of field survey operations during the ANARE Prince Charles Mountains surveys of 1969, 1971, and 1972.

Manning Nunataks. 71°S, 71°12′E. In the eastern side of the southern part of the Amery Ice Shelf. 20 miles NNE of Pickering Nunatak. Named by the Australians for Sgt. A.S. Manning, RAAF, airframe fitter at Mawson Station in 1958.

Manoury Island. 64°27′S, 62°50′W. 1½ miles south of Gand Island at the north end of the Schollaert Channel in the Palmer Archipelago. Discovered by Charcot in 1903–5 and named by him for G. Manoury, secretary of the expedition.

Mansergh Snowfield. 82°01′S, 159°50′E. Feeds the central portion of the Starshot Glacier, separating the Surveyors Range from the Holyoake Range. Discovered by the Holyoake, Cobham, and Queen Elizabeth Ranges party of the NZGSAE 1964–65, and named by them for G. Mansergh, geologist with the party.

Mansfield Point. 60°39′S, 45°44′W. Marks the eastern side of the entrance to Norway Bight on the south coast of Coronation Island in the South Orkneys. Surveyed by the Discovery Committee in 1933 and again by the FIDS in 1948–49. Named by the UK for Arthur W. Mansfield, FIDS meteorologist and biologist, leader of the Signy Island Station in 1952.

Mantell Screes. 80°38′S, 24°26′W. In the Shackleton Range.

Mount Manthe. 74°47′S, 99°21′W. 575 m. 5 miles NNE of Shepherd Dome, in the southern part of the Hudson Mountains. Named for Lawrence L. Manthe, meteorologist at Byrd Station, 1967.

Manuela Automatic Weather Station. 74°55′S, 163°36′E. Elevation 260 feet. American. Began operating on Feb. 6, 1984. Ceased operating on June 27, 1987.

Manzyu Rock *see* **Manju Rock**

Mapping of Antarctica. The Ancient Greeks featured Antarctica on their maps without ever having seen it. They just figured that it was there, to balance out the Arctic. They guessed at its shape. The Piri Re′is map (*see* **Mysteries**) which came to light in 1929, and which was said to have been compiled in 1513, not only showed Antarctica, but also the islands and indentations in the coast of what is today Queen Maud Land. More, that map showed Antarctica as it had been in the ancient days, before the ice covered it. Other, later maps show Tierra del Fuego as the northern tip of a huge continent centering on the South Pole. Drake′s discovery in 1578 of the Drake Passage disproved the Tierra del Fuego part at least, and Cook′s epic voyage of 1772–75 certainly narrowed the boundaries of the proposed continent when he circumnavigated Antarctica at high latitudes — without ever seeing land. This discovery negated the many inventive theories about Terra Australis Incognita, but even at this stage the existence of a solid continent was debated. Some thought that the South Pole was located in water, but Cook rightly supposed that the mass of icebergs that he saw must have come from land, or at least a frozen mass of considerable size. The first maps of Antarctica proper (i.e., south of 60°S) were prepared by the early sealers in the South Shetlands, and some of them published charts. The first chart of the South Shetlands was prepared in 1820–21 by John Miers, based on the voyages of William Smith. The first manuscript maps of these islands were compiled by Hampton Stewart in 1820–21. Richard Sherratt made an inaccurate map of the islands in the early part of 1821, and on Nov. 1, 1822, R.H. Laurie, chartseller to the British Admiralty, published a map of the South Shetlands, South Orkneys, and the SE tip of the Antarctic Peninsula, based on the explorations of Powell. Inaccuracies abounded, of course, but gradually the maps got better. As more and more of the continent was sighted, by navigators such as von Bellingshausen, Palmer, Bransfield, Biscoe, Kemp, Balleny, Dumont d'Urville, Wilkes, and Ross, there appeared in the 19th century the probability of a roughly circular body of land of enormous size. Chartings were done of the coast, especially by the Wilkes Expedition of 1838–42. Wilkes was fooled by a lot of looming, or mirages, and, although it has now been proved that he reported honestly that which he saw, his reputation suffered considerably for decades as a result of his unwitting inaccuracies. Ross did his best to damage Wilkes in the early days. In 1886 John Murray drew a map of Antarctica which turned out to be surprisingly accurate, even though on the *Challenger* the previous decade, he had not even sighted land. In 1895 Ludwig Friederichsen, the German cartographer, made the then definitive map of Antarctica, and in 1905 J.G. Bartholomew of London brought it up to date, at a scale of 1:14 million. The vast expanse of the continent was still a white circle with nothing in it, except the Pole marked at 90°S. But the coasts and islands were now well charted. In fact, doubt still existed as to the actual continental properties of Antarctica. Speculation now arose as to the possibility of the Ross-Weddell Graben (q.v.), which would split the

continent in two. (This was partly disproved by Byrd in 1928–30, and totally by Ronne in 1947–48.) Scott and Amundsen, Shackleton, and Mawson opened up long, narrow chunks of the interior as they made the first traverses of the continent, but it was the airplane which really opened up Antarctica, in the late 1920s. In 1929 the American Geographical Survey published its 1:12.5 million map of Antarctica, and after that, with aerial photography, ground control checks, and more and more land traverses, the Antarctic was gradually filled in. As late as the 1960s some maps were still showing ice shelves as part of the land mass, but since then the shelves have been clearly defined as such. Many details remain uncertain, many parts of Antarctica have yet to be explored and mapped (*see* **Unexplored areas**), and whole regions and mountain ranges can disappear. Moreover, the coastline is constantly changing its appearance as ice calves off from the continental shelf (*see* **Bay of Whales** under W for a good example of this). Since the 1940s ever-increasingly sophisticated sounding techniques have been producing better and better maps of the bedrock, in other words what the continent looks like without the ice. Name changes play havoc with the interested reader. Several features have more than one name, or spelling. Different countries use different names sometimes, for the same feature. The names used in this encyclopedia are generally the ones accepted by the US ACAN (Advisory Committee on Antarctic Place Names). Great Britain, NZ, and Australia all have their own place names committees, and usually these all work with the Americans to produce an order of things in the naming of Antarctic geographic features. Chile, Argentina, Norway, USSR, France, Belgium, and Japan all have a tendency to go their own way, but it is the purpose of this encyclopedia to clarify this confusion as much as possible, aware even then that names are being added and amended all the time.

Sometimes hundreds of new names are given each year. The USSR has produced a 4-volume atlas of Antarctica. The US Geological Survey has produced a batch of maps which may be ordered from Map Distribution, US Geological Survey, Box 25286, Federal Center, Denver, Colorado, 80225. Prepayment is required, but an index can be mailed to you free of charge on request. These maps sell well and are often out of stock. A comprehensive catalog of maps and charts issued by the USA and other countries has been published by SCAR: *Catalog of Antarctic Maps and Charts,* 4th Edition, 1974 (revised 1976). It is available from the Division of National Mapping, Department of Minerals and Energy, Canberra, Australia. For up-to-date information contact the Division of Polar Programs, National Science Foundation, Washington, D.C. 20550, or in Britain the Scott Polar Research Institute (q.v.) in Cambridge. In Australia contact the Canberra department listed above. In any other countries contact your local polar institute or related government department.

Mapple Glacier. 65°25'S, 62°15'W. 15 miles long. Flows into the southern arm of Exasperation Inlet on the east side of Graham Land. 2 miles north of Melville Glacier and separated from it by a line of small peaks. Surveyed by the FIDS in 1961. Named by the UK for the *Moby Dick* character.

Marambio Station *see* **Vicecomodoro Marambio Station**

Maranga Island. 65°12'S, 64°22'W. The most westerly of the Anagram Islands. On the south side of French Passage in the Wilhelm Archipelago. Named anagramatically by the UK in 1961 for the Anagram Islands.

Marble. Covers the ground all around the Marble Point–Arnold Cove area of Victoria Land.

Marble Cape *see* **Marble Point**

Marble Hills. 80°17'S, 82°05'W. Mostly ice-free. On the west side of Horseshoe Valley, between the Liberty Hills and the Independence Hills in the southern part of the Heritage Range. Named by the University of Minnesota Ellsworth Mountains Party of 1962–63 because the rocks in these hills are composed of marble.

Marble Knolls. 60°42'S, 45°37'W. Near the shore of Borge Bay, just SW of Waterpipe Beach, in the eastern part of Signy Island in the South Orkneys. Named descriptively by the UK in 1974.

Marble Peak. 85°29'S, 156°28'W. 2 miles NW of its twin, O'Brien Peak, and almost the same height. It overlooks the head of the Ross Ice Shelf between Amundsen Glacier and Robert Scott Glacier. Named by the New Zealanders in 1969–70 for the bands of marble crossing its summit.

Marble Point. 77°26'S, 163°50'E. Also called Marble Cape. Due east of Cape Royds (Ross Island) it is a rocky promontory of red marble on soil. It juts out from the coast of Victoria Land near the Wilson Piedmont Glacier. 3 miles north of Cape Bernacchi and 5 miles north of New Harbor. On March 12, 1957, a 2-year feasibility study was begun to see if it could be a permanent land runway. Apparently it could not.

Marble Point Automatic Weather Station. 77°24'S, 163°48'E. Elevation approximately 380 feet. An American AWS which began operating on Feb. 5, 1980, at Marble Point, Victoria Land.

Marble Rock. 67°36'S, 62°50'E. At the edge of the ice cliff almost a mile WSW of West Arm and Mawson Station, on the coast of Mac. Robertson Land. Photographed by the LCE 1936–37. Named by the Australians for the marble beds described there by D.S. Trail (*see* **Mount Trail**).

March, John C. Private on the Wilkes Expedition 1838–42. Joined in the USA. Served the cruise.

Marchesi, V.A.J.B. Captain of the *William Scoresby*, 1943–46.

Bahía Marcial Mora *see* **Zubov Bay**

Marcoux Nunatak. 69°55′S, 159°04′E. 1,530 m. Between Schmidt Nunataks and Poorman Peak in the Wilson Hills, near the head of Manna Glacier. Named for John S. Marcoux, USN, VX-6 aviation structural mechanic at McMurdo Station, 1967.

Marégraphe Island. 66°40′S, 140°E. Not quite a hundred yards west of the north end of Carrel Island in the Géologie Archipelago. Charted in 1951 by the French and named by them for the marigraph, or tide recording gauge placed here that year, and which obtained data through 1952.

Cap Marescot *see* **Marescot Point**

Marescot-Duthilleul, Jacques-Marie-Eugène. Name also spelled du Thilleul. b. 1808. Ensign on the *Astrolabe* during Dumont d'Urville's expedition of 1837–40. Died on board, Nov. 23, 1839.

Marescot Point. 63°29′S, 58°35′W. Also called Cabo Negrita. Juts out from the Trinity Peninsula 2½ miles east of Thanaron Point. This is the Cap Marescot discovered by Dumont d'Urville in 1837–40 and named by him for J.-M.-E. Marescot-Duthilleul.

Marescot Ridge. 63°32′S, 58°32′W. A ridge consisting of several ice-covered hills, the highest being Crown Peak (1,185 m.) at the south end of the ridge. 2 miles inland from Marescot Point on the NW coast of Trinity Peninsula. Surveyed by the FIDS in 1946, and named by them because they thought this was the Cap Marescot discovered by Dumont d'Urville in 1837–40. It was not, as it turned out—that was Marescot Point.

Margaret Bay *see* **Marguerite Bay**

Margaret Goodenough Glacier *see* **Goodenough Glacier**

Mount Margaret Wade *see* **Mount Fitzsimmons**

Cape Margerie. 66°49′S, 141°23′E. Ice-covered. Between Cape Mousse and La-croix Nunatak. It is bounded on the north by several rocky islands. Charted by the AAE 1911–14, and named by Mawson for Emmanuel de Margerie, French geographer and geologist. The French were based here in the 1950s.

Marguerite Bay. 68°30′S, 68°30′W. Also called Margaret Bay. A great bay on the west side of the Antarctic Peninsula. It is bounded on the north by Adelaide Island and on the south by the Wordie Ice Shelf, George VI Sound, and Alexander Island. Discovered by Charcot in late Jan. 1909, and named by him for his second wife.

Marguerite Island. 66°47′S, 141°23′E. Almost ¾ mile NW of Empereur Island and 1¾ miles NNW of Cape Margerie on the coast of East Antarctica. Charted in 1951 by the French and named by them for a character in Goethe's *Faust*.

Marian Cove. 62°13′S, 58°48′W. Also called Caleta Mariana, Marion Cove. Indents the SW part of King George Island in the South Shetlands, between Collins Harbor and Potter Cove. Certainly named before 1913.

Caleta Mariana *see* **Marian Cove**

Pointe Marie *see* **Marie Island**

Marie Byrd Land. 80°S, 120°W. A huge tract of land, unclaimed by any country but usually regarded as an American domain, which borders the southernmost part of the Pacific Ocean. It lies to the east of the Ross Ice Shelf and the Ross Sea. It also overlooks the Amundsen Sea, and large glaciers run from here into the Ross Ice Shelf. Geologically it is an island, covered with ice to connect it to the main bedrock continent. Discovered on Dec. 5, 1929, by Byrd in a flight over it, and named by him for his wife, Marie Ames Byrd. Later the extent of Marie Byrd Land was enlarged. It was first mapped and surveyed by Paul Siple in 1935. It has resisted the obvious abbreviation so common in Antarctic place naming—Byrd Land.

Marie Byrd Land Survey. USARP's largest scientific field undertaking in the period 1966–68. It was done in two phases, in successive summers, 1966–67 and 1967–68, and these phases were known as Phase I and Phase II. There were various reasons for it: 1. to provide a ground control network for mapping; 2. to produce a general geological map; 3. to select areas for future geological study; 4. to do whatever geological study it could; 5. to collect biological specimens; 6. to produce a species-distribution map; 7. to find and study geological anomalies. There were 4 topographic engineers, 5 geologists, 3 biologists, and a paleomagnetician. There were also 13 officers and men of the US Army Aviation Detachment, a navy aerographer, 2 navy cooks, and a USARP field assistant. Available were 3 UH-1D turbine-powered helicopters. It was led by Alton Wade.

Marie Island. 66°07′S, 65°45′W. 2 miles long. Just north of Cape Evensen in Graham Land. In 1903–5 Charcot named a point on the coast just to the north of Cape Evensen as Pointe Marie, for his elder sister. During his 1908–10 expedition Charcot reapplied the name to the southern tip of what he thought was an island, Île Waldeck-Rousseau, a few miles to the SE. In 1934–37 the BGLE found that this island was in fact a peak on the mainland, and called it Waldeck-Rousseau Peak. The island near the peak had been unnamed, yet was the most prominent feature in the vicinity of the peak. So it was named Marie Island.

Mariholm. 60°45′S, 45°42′W. Also seen (erroneously) as Hariholm. The highest and most easterly island in a small group a third of a mile south of Moe Island in the South Orkneys. Named before 1912.

Marilyn Automatic Weather Station. 80°S, 165°E. Elevation approximately 230 feet. An American AWS on the Byrd Glacier. Began operating on Jan. 16, 1984.

Marin Bluff. 69°25′S, 68°36′W. On the west side of the Antarctic Peninsula.

Marin Darbel Bay *see* **Darbel Bay**

Marin-Darbel Fjord *see* **Darbel Bay**

Marin Darbel Islands *see* **Darbel Islands**

Marin Glacier. 76°04′S, 162°22′E. Just west of Cape Hickey, flowing into Charcot Cove on the Victoria Land coast. Named by the USA in 1964 for Bonifacio Marin, engineman at McMurdo Station, 1962.

Marina Point. 65°15′S, 64°16′W. Forms the NW tip of Galíndez Island in the Argentine Islands of the Wilhelm Archipelago. Surveyed in 1935–36 by the BGLE and named by them for Princess Marina, later Duchess of Kent, who was married in Nov. 1934 while the *Penola* was on its way to the Argentine Islands.

Marine Plain. 68°38′S, 78°08′E. On the southern side of Mule Peninsula, between Crooked Fjord and Ellis Fjord in the Vestfold Hills. It is SSSI #25, and includes Burton Island. It is 9.14 square miles in area, and is of interest because of the vertebrate fossil finds, and because of the limnological research at nearby Burton Lake.

Marine Worms *see* **Worms**

Mariner Glacier. 73°15′S, 167°30′E. Over 60 miles long. Flows from the plateau of Victoria Land, between Malta Plateau and the Mountaineer Range, into Lady Newnes Bay in the Ross Sea, where it forms the Mariner Glacier Tongue. Named by the New Zealanders in 1958–59 for all mariners in Antarctic waters.

Mariner Glacier Tongue. 73°27′S, 168°20′E. The floating seaward extension of the Mariner Glacier in Victoria Land. It is just west of, and abuts, the Borchgrevink Glacier Tongue where that glacier flows into Lady Newnes Bay. Named in association with the glacier.

Mariner Islands. 66°01′S, 101°09′E. They form the north-central part of the Highjump Archipelago. Edisto Channel bounds them on the west, Glossard Channel on the south and Remenchus

Glacier on the east. Include Miles Island. Named for Bunger's Martin Mariner which flew over this area during Operation Highjump, 1946–47.

Puerto Marinero Lagarrigue *see* **Lagarrigue Cove**

Mount Marion *see* **Marion Nunataks**

Marion Cove *see* **Marian Cove**

Marion Mountain *see* **Marion Nunataks**

Marion Nunataks. 69°33′S, 75°06′W. Also called Marion Mountain, Mount Marion, Marion Peak. On the north shore of Charcot Island, between Mount Monique and Mount Martine. Discovered on Jan. 11, 1910, by Charcot, and named by him for one of his daughters.

Marion Peak *see* **Marion Nunataks**

Maris Nunatak. 69°59′S, 73°09′E. 2 miles ENE of Whisnant Nunatak, at the junction of Rogers Glacier and the east side of the Amery Ice Shelf on the coast of East Antarctica. Named by US cartographer John H. Roscoe in 1952 for R.L. Maris, air crewman on Operation Highjump flights which provided the aerial photos from which Roscoe worked.

Maritime Polar Air Mass. Fairly mild and wet air mass which forms over the sea around Antarctica.

Mount Mark *see* **Mount Hawthorne**

Mount Markab. 70°56′S, 67°02′W. On the north side of the Pegasus Mountains. 10 miles NE of Gurney Point on the west coast of Palmer Land. Named by the UK for the star of that name in the constellation of Pegasus.

Marker Rock. 66°05′S, 65°47′W. 1½ miles NNW of Turnabout Island in the Saffery Islands off the west coast of Graham Land. Charted by the BGLE 1934–37. Named by the UK in 1959 because it marks the passage of vessels through the Saffery Islands.

Mount Markham. 82°51′S, 161°21′E. Also called Markham Mountains. One of the major mountains in Antarctica, it has a twin summit, one peak being 4,350 m., and the other 4,280 m. It surmounts the northern end of the Markham Plateau in the Queen Elizabeth Range. Discovered by Scott, Wilson, and Shackleton on Dec. 27, 1902, and named by Scott for Sir Clements Markham, president of the Royal Geographical Society and patron of the Royal Society Expedition. Markham, a seminal figure in Antarctic exploration, even though he never went there, was the person who picked Scott from obscurity to lead the 1901–4 expedition.

Markham Bay. 64°17′S, 57°18′W. Also called Clements Markham Bay. 8 miles wide. Between Ekelöf Point and Hamilton Point on the east side of James Ross Island. Charted by Nordenskjöld in 1901–4, and named by him for Sir Clements Markham (*see* **Mount Markham**).

¹Markham Island *see* **Clements Island**

²Markham Island. 74°36′S, 164°55′E. Just off Oscar Point in the northern part of Terra Nova Bay in Victoria Land. Discovered by Borchgrevink in Feb. 1900, and named by him for Sir Clements Markham (*see* **Mount Markham**).

Markham Mountains *see* **Mount Markham**

Markham Plateau. 82°56′S, 161°10′E. Extends south from Mount Markham for 10 miles and forms the divide between east and west flowing glaciers in the northern part of the Queen Elizabeth Range. Named by the US in association with the mountain.

Markinsenis Peak. 71°35′S, 164°29′E. 1,790 m. On the south side of McCann Glacier at the junction of that glacier with Lillie Glacier in the Bowers Mountains. Named for Ronald Markinsenis, USN, radioman at Amundsen-Scott South Pole Station in 1965.

Cape Markov. 66°46′S, 50°16′E. An ice cape on the east side of Amundsen

Bay. 7 miles west of Mount Riiser-Larsen in Enderby Land. Named by the USSR in 1961–62 for K.K. Markov, professor of geography at Moscow University and author of several reports on Antarctica.

Marks Peak. 76°30'S, 125°45'W. 3,325 m. On the south side of the crater rim of Mount Hampton in the Executive Committee Range of Marie Byrd Land. Named for Keith E. Marks, electronics engineer from the National Bureau of Standards, a member of the Marie Byrd Land Traverse Party of 1959–60.

Marks Point. 85°29'S, 155°40'W. Extends east from the north end of Medina Peaks at the south edge of the Ross Ice Shelf. Discovered during Byrd's 1928–30 expedition. Named for George R. Marks, logistics worker at McMurdo Station in 1962.

Marø, Harald. From Nova Scotia, he was captain of the *Theron*, 1955–58.

Marø Cliffs. 79°04'S, 28°30'W. SW of Jeffries Glacier in the Theron Mountains. Named by the BCTAE in 1956–57 for Harald Marø.

Mount Marr. 66°24'S, 52°07'E. 8 miles south of Johnston Peak and 8 miles west of Douglas Peak in Enderby Land. Discovered in Jan. 1930 by the BANZARE, and named by Mawson for J.W.S. Marr.

Marr, J.W.S. b. 1902. James William Slesser Marr. British Boy Scout picked by Shackleton to go on his last voyage, 1921–22, on the *Quest*. An important member of the Discovery Committee, he was zoologist on the *William Scoresby* 1927–29, and chief scientist on that ship from April to June 1929. From 1929 to 1930 he was on the *Discovery* as part of the ship's party during the BANZARE under Mawson. In 1931–33 he was on the *Discovery II*, and again in 1935–37, and was whaling inspector in the Antarctic from 1939 to 1940. He was marine biologist on the Discovery Investigations in Graham Land on the *William Scoresby* from 1943–45, and leader of the first phase of Operation Tabarin, 1943–44. He commanded Port Lockroy Station in 1944. He has been called the first FIDS leader. In a way he was, even though the Falkland Islands Dependencies Surveys were not known by that name until after the war. He later became an authority on krill (*see* the Bibliography).

Marr Bay. 60°42'S, 44°31'W. Between Cape Valavielle and Fraser Point on the north coast of Laurie Island in the South Orkneys. Mapped by Bruce in 1903. Named by personnel on the *Discovery II* in 1933 for J.W.S. Marr.

Marr Bluff. 69°47'S, 69°20'W. 1,065 m. Just north of Wager Glacier on the east coast of Alexander Island. Surveyed by the FIDS in 1948 and named by them for John E. Marr, British geologist and professor of geology at Cambridge from 1917 to 1930.

Marr Glacier. 77°43'S, 162°44'E. 2 miles west of Goldman Glacier, flowing north from the Kukri Hills into Taylor Valley in Victoria Land. Charted and named by Scott in 1911–12.

Marr Ice Piedmont. 64°33'S, 63°40'W. Covers the NW half of Anvers Island. Surveyed by Charcot in 1903–5 and again in 1908–10. Named by the UK for J.W.S. Marr.

Marra, John. Gunner's mate on the *Resolution*, 1772–75, during Cook's second voyage. In Sept. 1775 he published a book called *Journal of the Resolution's Voyage in 1772, 1773, 1774, and 1775*, which preempted Cook's official narrative of the voyage.

Marret, Mario. French photographer, leader of the Pointe Géologie winter camp in 1952–53. He wrote *Antarctic Adventure* (*see* the Bibliography).

Marret Glacier. 66°26'S, 137°44'E. A channel glacier 4 miles wide and 4 miles long. It flows NE from the continental ice to the coast just east of Cape Robert. Named by the USA for Mario Marret.

Mount Marriner. 68°10'S, 49°03'E. 2 miles WSW of Mount Flett in the central part of the Nye Mountains. Named by the Australians for A. Marriner, radio officer at Wilkes Station in 1959.

Mars Glacier. 71°54'S, 68°23'W. In the SE corner of Alexander Island. 6 miles long. 2 miles wide. Flows south into the ice shelf of George VI Sound between Two Step Cliffs and Phobos Ridge. Discovered aerially by Ellsworth on Nov. 23, 1935. Surveyed in 1949 by the FIDS and named by the UK for the planet.

Mount Marsden. 67°52'S, 66°03'E. 600 m. 3 miles SW of Mount Rivett in the Gustav Bull Mountains of Mac. Robertson Land. Named by the BANZARE in Feb. 1931 for Ernest Marsden, director of the Department of Scientific and Industrial Research in NZ.

Cape Marsh. 65°15'S, 59°28'W. A rock cliff cape over 235 m. Marks the SE extremity of Robertson Island on the edge of the Larsen Ice Shelf. Surveyed by the FIDS in July 1953. Named by the UK for George W. Marsh.

Marsh, George W. British medical officer and leader at the FIDS Base D at Hope Bay in 1952 and 1953. During the IGY (1957–58) he was surgeon at Scott Base, and took part in the BCTAE (*see* Marsh Glacier).

Marsh Glacier. 82°52'S, 158°30'E. 70 miles long. Flows from the Polar Plateau between the Miller Range and the Queen Elizabeth Range into the Nimrod Glacier. Discovered by one of the NZ parties of the BCTAE 1956–58 and named by them for George W. Marsh, a member of the party (*see* **Marsh, George W.**).

Marsh Ridge. 85°46'S, 146°10'W. 3 miles long. Halfway along the south side of Leverett Glacier. 11 miles ENE of Mount Gould. Named for Robert D. Marsh, cook at Byrd Station, 1957.

Marsh Spur. 65°53'S, 62°38'W. 4½ miles south of Bildad Peak and 4½ miles west of Scar Inlet on the east side of Graham Land. Important geologically for the contact between Basement Complex gneisses and volcanics of probably Upper Jurassic age. Named by the UK for

Anthony F. Marsh, BAS geologist at Fossil Bluff Station, 1963–64, and at Base D, 1964–65.

Mount Marshall. 84°41'S, 164°39'E. 3,160 m. 4 miles SE of Blizzard Peak in the Marshall Mountains of the Queen Alexandra Range. Named in association with the Marshall Mountains.

Marshall, E.H. Surgeon and member of the Marine Executive Staff of the Discovery Committee. He accompanied the 1928–29 Norwegian whaling expedition on the *C.A. Larsen* and made observations on whales.

Marshall, Dr. Eric. b. May 23, 1879. Eric Stewart Marshall. British surgeon, one of the four men to reach within 97 miles of the South Pole in 1909 (*see* **British Antarctic Expedition 1907–9**). He was also the cartographer on this expedition.

Marshall, James. Seaman on the Wilkes Expedition 1838–42. Joined in the USA. Served the cruise.

Marshall, Scott W. Lt. cdr., USN. Military leader of McMurdo Base for the winter-over of 1957. On Nov. 28, 1957, he handed over to E.E. Ludeman.

Marshall Archipelago. 77°S, 148°30' W. An extensive group of large, ice-covered islands within the Sulzberger Ice Shelf. Several of these islands were discovered during Byrd's first three expeditions. The group includes Beaton Island, Cronenwett Island, Gould Island, Grinder Island, Nolan Island, Przybyszewski Island, Radford Island, Steventon Island, Vollmer Island, Hannah Island, Hutchinson Island, Kramer Island, Madden Island, Orr Island, Spencer Island, Thode Island. The archipelago was named by Byrd for General George Marshall, advisor to and patron of Byrd's 1933–35 expedition.

Marshall Bay. 60°39'S, 45°38'W. 2 miles wide. Between Cape Vik and Cape Hansen on the south side of Coronation Island in the South Orkneys. Charted in 1912–13 by Petter Sørlle and in 1933 by the personnel on the *Discovery II*. The latter named it for E.H. Marshall.

Marshall Mountains. 84°37′S, 164°30′E. Overlook the Beardmore Glacier in the Queen Alexandra Range. Bounded on the north by Berwick Glacier and on the south by Swinford Glacier. Discovered by Shackleton in 1908 and named by him for Dr. Eric Marshall, one of his companions.

Marshall Nunatak. 74°10′S, 75°41′W. Isolated. 23 miles ESE of FitzGerald Bluffs in Ellsworth Land. 9 miles east of Schwartz Peak. It is the most easterly in a chain of small summits SE of FitzGerald Bluffs. Named for William F. Marshall, US Geological Survey topographical engineer in Antarctica, 1967–68.

Marshall Peak. 71°09′S, 61°32′W. 1,205 m. Mostly ice-covered. 6 miles NW of the head of Palmer Inlet on the east coast of Palmer Land. Explored by the USAS in 1940, and charted by the FIDS and RARE in 1947. Named by the FIDS for Norman B. Marshall, zoologist at Base D in 1945–46.

Marshall Stream. 78°04′S, 164°18′E. Also called Rivard Creek. A meltwater stream 6 miles long. Flows through the Marshall Valley from the Rivard Glacier to the Koettlitz Glacier in Victoria Land. Named by NZ and the USA in association with the valley.

Marshall Valley. 78°04′S, 164°10′E. Ice-free except for Rivard Glacier at its head. Between the Garwood and Miers Valleys on the coast of Victoria Land. Named by the NZ Blue Glacier Party of the BCTAE in 1956–57 for Dr. Eric Marshall.

Mount Marsland. 67°11′S, 51°14′E. 6 miles south of the eastern part of Beaver Glacier in Enderby Land. Named by the Australians in 1962 for F.L. Marsland.

Marsland, F.L. A crew member on the *Discovery* during the BANZARE 1929–31.

Marsteinen Nunatak. 71°26′S, 1°42′W. 6 miles NE of Valken Hill, at the north end of the Ahlmann Ridge in Queen Maud Land. Name means "the sea stone" in Norwegian.

Mount Marston. 76°54′S, 162°12′E. Also called Whaleback. 1,245 m. Whaleback-shaped. At the north side of the Kar Plateau. 3 miles north of the terminus of the Mackay Glacier in Victoria Land. Named by Shackleton in 1907–9 for George Marston.

Marston, George E. b. March 20, 1882. George Edward Marston. d. 1940. British art teacher who was artist and general handyman on Shackleton's 1907–9 and 1914–17 expeditions. Known as "Putty," he was later director of the Rural Industries Bureau.

Marston Glacier. 76°54′S, 162°30′E. Flows from Mount Marston and Doublefinger Peak and enters Granite Harbor between Dreikanter Head and the Kar Plateau. The NZ Northern Survey Party of the BCTAE traveled up this glacier on their way to Mount Marston in Oct. 1957. They named the glacier in association with the mountain.

Fjord Martel *see* **Martel Inlet**

Martel Inlet. 62°05′S, 58°22′W. Also called Fjord Martel. Forms the NE head of Admiralty Bay, King George Island, in the South Shetlands. It is almost certain that Charcot named it in Dec. 1909.

Martello Rock *see* **Martello Tower**

Martello Tower. 62°06′S, 58°08′W. Also called Martello Rock. 10 meters high. A rock in King George Bay, 2 miles NNW of Lions Rump in the South Shetlands. Charted in 1937 by personnel on the *Discovery II*, who named it for European coastal defense towers of that name.

Martens Peak. 85°34′S, 131°02′W. In the NE part of the Ford Nunataks in the Wisconsin Range of the Horlick Mountains. Named for Edward A. Martens, radioman at Byrd Station in 1960 and at McMurdo Station in 1965.

The *Martha*. British sealer out of London, in the South Shetlands in 1821–23, under the command of Capt. Bond (this is almost certainly Ralph Bond).

Martha Automatic Weather Station.
78°18'S, 172°30'W. Elevation approximately 148 feet. American AWS on the Ross Ice Shelf. Began operating Feb. 1, 1984.

Martha II Automatic Weather Station.
73°23'S, 173°25'W. American AWS at an elevation of approximately 59 feet. Began operating on Feb. 11, 1987.

Cabo Martillo *see* **Cape Wollaston**

Cap Martin *see* **Martins Head**

Mount Martin. 69°40'S, 62°59'W. Also called Mount Briesemeister. 1,360 m. Just north of the head of Anthony Glacier, on the east coast of Palmer Land. Named by Finn Ronne in 1948 for Orville Martin, who helped obtain radio equipment in the USA for the RARE.

Point Martin. 60°47'S, 44°41'W. On the east side of Mossman Peninsula, almost a mile NW of Cape Murdoch, on the south coast of Laurie Island in the South Orkneys. Charted in 1903 by Bruce, who named it for J. Martin.

Port Martin. 66°49'S, 141°24'E. Anchorage just off Cape Margerie. Discovered in 1950 by the French, and named by Liotard for André-Paul Martin, second-in-command of the expedition who had died on his way to the Antarctic. Port-Martin Station was here.

Martin, J. Able seaman on the *Scotia* during Bruce's expedition in 1902–4.

Martin, James H. Bosun on the *Discovery* during the BANZARE 1929–31, and first mate on the *Penola* during the BGLE 1934–37.

Martin, William K. Lt. (jg), USN. Pilot on Operation Highjump, 1946–47.

Martin Dome. 83°18'S, 157°21'E. Also called Martins Dome. An elevated snow-covered prominence between Argosy Glacier and Argo Glacier in the Miller Range. Discovered in Dec. 1957 by the NZ Southern Party of the BCTAE. Named by them for L. Martin, leader at Scott Base in 1958.

¹Martin Glacier *see* **Balch Glacier**

²Martin Glacier. 68°29'S, 66°53'W. 3 miles wide and 9 miles long. Flows from the south side of Mount Lupa to the SE corner of Rymill Bay where it joins the Bertram Ice Piedmont, on the west coast of Graham Land. Surveyed in 1936 by the BGLE, and again in 1948–49 by the FIDS. Named by the FIDS for James H. Martin.

Martin Hill. 72°48'S, 169°14'E. Ice-free. At the west side of Whitehall Glacier in the Victory Mountains of Victoria Land. Named by the USA for P.J. Martin, senior NZ scientist at Hallett Station in 1961.

Martin Hills. 82°04'S, 88°01'W. Isolated range. 4 miles long. 50 miles south of the Pirrit Hills. Named for Larry R. Martin, scientific leader at Byrd Station in 1962.

Martin Island. 66°44'S, 57°E. In the northern part of Edward VIII Bay, just off the southern shore of Edward VIII Plateau. Photographed by the LCE 1936–37 and called Utvikgalten (the outer bay boar) by the Norwegians. Renamed by the Australians in 1958 for A.R. Martin, officer-in-charge of the ANARE party at Macquarie Island (not in the Antarctic) in 1948.

Martin Islands. 65°37'S, 65°22'W. Also called Islas Mataquito. 5 miles in extent. East of the north part of Renaud Island and 1 mile west of Vieugué Island in the Grandidier Channel. In 1903–5 Charcot discovered a group of small islands to the north of Pitt Island (Pitt Island is now known to be a group of small islands, and is called Pitt Islands). He named them Martin Islands, for Capt. Martin of the Argentine navy. After aerial surveys had made clearer the arrangement of the mass of islands in the area, the islands north of Renaud Island were considered to be one group, and called the Pitt Islands. Charcot's group, the Martin Islands, fell into that. His naming was then transferred to the group with the above coordinates.

Martin Massif. 70°28'S, 65°40'E. In the Porthos Range of the Prince Charles

Mountains. Just east of Mount Lied to which it is connected by a low col. Named for P.J. Martin, officer-in-charge at Mawson Station in 1964.

Martin Mountain *see* **Mount Martine**

Martin Nunataks. 74°57'S, 158°46'E. Two isolated nunataks. On the northern edge of David Glacier. 9 miles SE of Mount Wood in Victoria Land. Named for Robert D. Martin, US Geological Survey topographical engineer at McMurdo Station in 1961–62.

Martin Peak. 84°22'S, 65°21'W. 1,045 m. 2 miles NE of Nance Ridge in the Thomas Hills in the northern part of the Patuxent Range of the Pensacola Mountains. Named for Christopher Martin, biologist at Palmer Station, 1966–67.

Martin Peninsula. 74°25'S, 114°10'W. 60 miles long. 20 miles wide. Mostly ice-covered. Between the Getz Ice Shelf and the Dotson Ice Shelf on the Marie Byrd Land coast. Forms the eastern edge of the Bakutis Coast. Named for Col. Lawrence Martin, US Army (retired), authority on the history of Antarctic exploration.

Martin Reef. 67°34'S, 65°31'E. Also called Martinskjeret. 7 miles north of the coast and slightly west of Cape Fletcher. Named by Mawson in Feb. 1931 for James H. Martin.

Martin Ridge. 84°25'S, 165°30'E. Ice-covered. Borders the west side of the upper part of the Moody Glacier in the Queen Alexandra Range. Named for Maj. Wilbur E. Martin, US Army, in charge of trail operations during Operation Deep Freeze 1963.

Mount Martine. 69°33'S, 74°58'W. Also called Martine Mountain, Martin Mountain. 750 m. Overlooks the north shore of Charcot Island, just south of Cheesman Island. Discovered on Jan. 11, 1910, by Charcot and named by him for one of his daughters.

Martine Mountain *see* **Mount Martine**

Martínez Díaz, Alfredo. Chilean leader of his country's 1955–56 expedi-

tion to the Antarctic. His ships were *Baquedano, Rancagua, Lientur, Leucotón.*

Punta Martins *see* **Martins Head**

Martins Dome *see* **Martin Dome**

Martins Head. 62°11'S, 58°14'W. Also called Punta Martins, Cap Martin. A headland forming the southern side of the entrance to Legru Bay on the south coast of King George Island in the South Shetlands. Named before 1820.

Martinskjeret *see* **Martin Reef**

Mount Martyn. 69°24'S, 157°10'E. 3 miles south of Eld Peak in the Lazarev Mountains, on the west side of the Matusevich Glacier. Named by the Australians for D.F. Martyn, a member of the ANARE Executive Planning Committee.

Maruff Peaks *see* **Billingane Peaks**

Mount Marujupu *see* **Marujupu Peak**

Marujupu Peak. 76°31'S, 145°37'W. Also called Mount Marujupu. A nunatak above the main flow of Ochs Glacier, between Mount Iphigene and Mount Ferranto in the Ford Ranges of Marie Byrd Land. Discovered on a flyover by Byrd on Dec. 5, 1929, and named by him for Marian, Ruth, Judy, and Punch, the four children of Arthur Sulzberger, a patron of the expedition.

Mount Marvel. 78°45'S, 159°22'E. 1,540 m. 7 miles south of Escalade Peak, near the head of the Mulock Glacier. Named in 1964 for Cdr. R. Marvel, USN, at McMurdo Station, 1963.

Mount Mary Louise Ulmer *see* **Mount Ulmer**

Mount Mary Ulmer *see* **Mount Ulmer**

Marze Peak. 78°52'S, 84°30'W. Has twin summits. Near the south end of the ridge between Wessbecher and Hudman Glaciers, at the south end of the Sentinel Range. Named for Marion O. Marze, USN, aviation machinist's mate (*see* Deaths, 1956).

Mount Marzolf. 70°28'S, 159°41'E. Partly ice-free. At the head of Svendsen Glacier. 2 miles west of Mount Gillmor, in the Usarp Mountains. Named for John E. Marzolf, biologist at McMurdo Station, 1967–68.

Cape Mascart. 66°38'S, 67°41'W. Also called Punta Longavi. Forms the northern extremity of Adelaide Island. Discovered by Charcot in 1903–5 and named by him for Eleuthère Mascart, French physicist and director of the Bureau Central Météorologique.

Mascías Cove. 64°54'S, 63°01'W. Also called Sturm Cove. Indents the west coast of Graham Land just east of Mount Banck. Charted by de Gerlache in 1897–99 and by David Ferguson in 1913–14. Named by the Argentines for Lt. Eladio Mascías of the *Chiriguano,* here in 1949–50.

Maskelyne Passage. 65°50'S, 65°24'W. Between Larrouy and Tadpole Islands to the east and Cat Island, Runnelstone Rock, and Hummock Island to the west, off the west coast of Graham Land. Named by the UK in 1959 for Nevil Maskelyne (1732–1811), British Astronomer Royal from 1757 until he died. He started the *Nautical Almanac* in 1767.

Mount Maslen. 67°42'S, 49°07'E. 1,200 m. 1 mile west of Mount Currie in the Raggatt Mountains of Enderby Land. Named by the Australians for A.W.G. Maslen, officer-in-charge at Mawson Station in 1961.

Mount Masley. 72°59'S, 162°54'E. Flat-topped. 2,605 m. In the northern part of the Pain Mesa, 11 miles east of Silva Ridge in the Mesa Range. Named for Andrew J. Masley, ionosphere physicist at McMurdo Station in 1962–63.

Mount Mason. 84°43'S, 169°48'W. 815 m. At the edge of the Ross Ice Shelf. Surmounts the northern extremity of the Lillie Range. Discovered by Byrd's 1928–30 expedition and named by Byrd for Howard F. Mason.

Mason, Douglas P. Surveyor with the FIDS in 1947. Part of the Weddell Coast Sledging Party.

Mason, Howard F. Radio engineer on the shore party during Byrd's 1928–30 expedition. He had been with Byrd in the Arctic.

Mason Glacier. 78°53'S, 161°41'E. Flows from the eastern slopes of the Worcester Range, just south of Bareface Bluff. It flows east into the Skelton Glacier. Named in 1964 for David T. Mason, biologist at McMurdo Station, 1961–62 and 1962–63.

Mason Inlet. 72°57'S, 60°25'W. Ice-filled. Recedes 15 miles SW between Cape Mackintosh and the coastline south of Cape Herdman, on the east coast of Palmer Land. Discovered aerially in Dec. 1940 by the USAS. Named by the FIDS for Douglas P. Mason.

Mason Peaks. 72°46'S, 74°44'E. A prominent serrated ridge with several peaks. 8 miles NW of Mount Harding in the Grove Mountains. Named by the Australians for A.C. Mason, topographic draftsman with the Division of National Mapping at the Australian Department of National Development. He contributed greatly to Antarctic mapping.

Mason Spur. 78°33'S, 164°25'E. Over 1,300 m. Partly ice-covered. Projects eastward from Mount Morning in Victoria Land. Named in 1963 for Robert Mason, USARP representative at McMurdo Station, 1962–63.

Masquerade Ridge. 83°04'S, 164°40'E. 5 miles long. 16 miles north of Clark Peak on the east side of Robb Glacier. Named in 1970 by US geologist John Gunner, who, with John Splettstoesser, collected rocks here in Dec. 1969. The ridge was shown on the cover of the Feb. 7, 1970, issue of *Saturday Review,* in which there was an article about the 1969–70 Ohio State University Geological Expedition here. The ridge on the photo was confused with Coalsack Bluff, and the man in the foreground is not David H. Elliot (*see* **Elliot Peak**) as the caption says. Hence the name.

Mount Massam. 81°44'S, 158°12'E. Ice-covered. 8 miles west of Mount

Lindley in the Churchill Mountains. Named by the Holyoake, Cobham, and Queen Elizabeth Ranges Party of the NZGSAE 1964–65 for D. Massam, a member of the party. The season before, Massam had been a member of the Southern Party of the NZGSAE 1963–64.

Massam Glacier. 84°33′S, 175°12′W. 11 miles long. Flows between Waldron Spurs and Longhorn Spurs into the Ross Ice Shelf just east of the mouth of Shackleton Glacier. Named for D. Massam (see **Mount Massam**) by the 1963–64 party that he was a member of.

Mount Massell. 72°29′S, 163°21′E. 1,880 m. 6 miles SE of Mount Jackman in the Freyberg Mountains. Named for Wulf Massell, biolab manager at McMurdo Station in 1967.

Massey Glacier. 71°53′S, 168°24′E. 6 miles long. Flows from the western slopes of Meier Peak in the Admiralty Mountains. It flows along the south side of the Wylie Ridge into Man-o-War Glacier. Named for C. Stanton Massey, meteorologist at Amundsen-Scott South Pole Station, 1968.

Massey Heights. 63°58′S, 57°58′W. Flat-topped. 6 miles SW of Andreassen Point on James Ross Island. Surveyed by the FIDS in 1945 and 1955. Named by the UK for Paul M.O. Massey, FIDS medical officer at Base D in 1955.

Masson Island. 66°08′S, 96°35′E. Also called Mission Island. Ice-covered. 17 miles long. 465 meters high. 9 miles NW of Henderson Island, within the Shackleton Ice Shelf. Discovered in Feb. 1912 by the AAE 1911–14, and named by Mawson for Professor Sir David Orme Masson of Melbourne, a member of the AAE Advisory Committee (see also **Masson Range**).

Masson Range. 67°51′S, 62°50′E. Part of the Framnes Mountains, this range extends 15 miles in a north-south direction and comprises the North Masson Range, the Central Masson Range, and the South Masson Range. Discovered by the BANZARE 1929–31 and named by Mawson for

Professor Sir David Orme Masson, a member of the BANZARE Advisory Committee (see also **Masson Island**).

Mast Hill. 68°11′S, 67°W. 14 m. At the west end of Stonington Island on the west side of the Antarctic Peninsula. Surveyed by members of the USAS from East Base 1939–41. They built a flagstaff on this hill.

Mast Point. 66°22′S, 110°26′E. The most westerly point on Ardery Island in the Windmill Islands. Named for Clarence W. Mast, USN, constructionman at Wilkes Station in 1958.

Matador Mountain. 85°10′S, 176°50′W. 1,950 m. Ice-free. At the south side of the mouth of Gallup Glacier, where that glacier enters Shackleton Glacier. Matador is the general name for the student body at Texas Tech. Alton Wade, leader of the Texas Tech Shackleton Glacier Expedition of 1962–63 named it because all three members of the expedition were affiliated with Texas Tech.

Islas Mataquito see **Martin Islands**

Mount Mateer. 66°59′S, 51°08′E. 1 mile east of Mount Degerfeldt in the Tula Mountains of Enderby Land. Named by the Australians for N.C. Mateer.

Mateer, N.C. Crew member of the *Discovery* during the BANZARE 1929–31.

Matha, A. Lt. French hydrographer, second-in-command of the *Français* expedition of 1903–5 under Charcot.

Matha Bay see **Matha Strait**

Matha Strait. 66°34′S, 67°30′W. Between Adelaide Island and the south end of the Biscoe Islands. In 1908–10 Charcot charted it as a bay, Matha Bay, naming it for Lt. A. Matha. The BGLE 1934–37 redefined it.

Mount Mather. 73°34′S, 61°E. 3½ miles west of Mount Menzies in the Prince Charles Mountains. Discovered aerially by Flying Officer John Seaton during an ANARE flyover in 1956. Named by the Australians for Keith B. Mather, who led the ANARE seismic party which mapped this feature in 1957–58. Mather was also leader of Mawson Station in 1957.

¹**Mount Matheson.** 66°57'S, 50°56'E. Between Mount Harvey and Mount Degerfeldt in the western part of the Tula Mountains of Enderby Land. Named by the Australians for J. Matheson.

²**Mount Matheson.** 75°05'S, 72°10'W. 2 miles NW of Mount Boyer in the Merrick Mountains of Ellsworth Land. Named for Lorne D. Matheson, ionosphere physicist at Eights Station in 1963.

Matheson, J. A crew member of the *Discovery* during the BANZARE 1929–31.

Matheson Glacier. 70°47'S, 62°05'W. 11 miles long. 2 miles south of Ashton Glacier which it parallels. It flows in an easterly direction to the west side of Lehrke Inlet on the east coast of Palmer Land. Discovered in 1940 by members of the USAS. Charted by the Weddell Coast Sledge Party in 1947. Named by the FIDS for J. Matheson, a member of the FIDS at Port Lockroy Station in 1944 and at Base D in 1945.

Mount Mathew. 81°41'S, 159°57'E. Also called (erroneously) Mount Mathews. 2,030 m. At the east side of Starshot Glacier. 2 miles north of Mount Hotine in the Surveyors Range. Named by the New Zealanders in 1960–61 for Felton Mathew, the first surveyor-general of New Zealand in 1840.

Mount Mathews *see* **Mount Mathew**

Mathewson Point. 74°23'S, 132°33'W. At the north tip of Shepard Island, off the coast of Marie Byrd Land. It is the site of an Adélie penguin rookery. Algae, lichens, mosses, and petrels are also found here. Charted on Feb. 4, 1962, by personnel from the *Glacier*. Named for Lt. (jg) David S. Mathewson, USN, supply officer on the *Glacier* at that time.

Mathias, J.V. Crewman on the *Bear of Oakland* in 1934–35.

Mathieu Rock. 66°20'S, 136°49'E. Ice-free. Between Cape Bickerton and Rock X, at the east side of the entrance to Victor Bay. Charted by the French under Marret in 1952–53, and named by them for Claude-Louis Mathieu (1783–1875), French astronomer.

Mathis Nunataks. 77°08'S, 143°27'W. Isolated. Near the head of Arthur Glacier, 8 miles ESE of Mount Warner, in the Ford Ranges of Marie Byrd Land. Named for Terry R. Mathis, engineer at Byrd Station, 1967–68 and 1968.

Mathis Spur. 83°20'S, 51°17'W. Along the west side of the Saratoga Table, 3 miles north of Mount Stephens in the Forrestal Range of the Pensacola Mountains. Named for Melvin Mathis, hospital corpsman at Ellsworth Station, 1957.

Mathys Bank. 80°19'S, 28°30'W. In the Shackleton Range.

Matikonis Peak. 75°21'S, 138°14'W. Isolated. In the central Coulter Heights, near the Marie Byrd Land coast. Named for William P. Matikonis, USN, damage controlman on the *Glacier*, 1961–62.

Mount Matin. 65°08'S, 63°40'W. Mostly snow-covered. North of Hotine Glacier on the west side of Graham Land. Charted by Charcot in 1903–5 and named by him for *Le Matin,* the French newspaper which was a contributor to the expedition.

Matkah Point. 63°58'S, 58°19'W. The northern entrance point to Holluschickie Bay, on the west coast of James Ross Island. Named by the UK for the *Jungle Book* character.

Matney Peak. 79°10'S, 86°14'W. Mostly ice-free. 1,810 m. Near the middle of the line of peaks at the east side of Webster Glacier in the Heritage Range. Named for William R. Matney, USN, chief aviation bosun's mate and fuel officer in Antarctica, 1966.

Matsuyama Rocks. 66°40'S, 66°35'W. Just off the west side of Stefan Ice Piedmont in Graham Land. Named by the UK for Motonori Matsuyama (1884–1958), Japanese geophysicist specializing in the geomagnetic poles.

Matterhorn. 77°40'S, 162°27'E. 1,600 m. Surmounts the north wall of the

Taylor Valley between Lacroix and Matterhorn Glaciers. Named for the Swiss mountain of that name by Grif Taylor in 1910–13.

Matterhorn Glacier. 77°41′S, 167°27′E. Alpine glacier. On the edge of the north wall of the Taylor Valley, just west of the Matterhorn in Victoria Land. Named in Dec. 1957 by visitor Troy L. Péwé (*see* **Lake Péwé**), for the Matterhorn.

Matterhorn Valley. A dry valley in the Asgard Range of Victoria Land.

Matterson Inlet. 80°50′S, 160°30′E. Ice-filled. Between Penny Point and Cape Douglas, on the west side of the Ross Ice Shelf. Named by the NZGSAE 1960–61 for Garth John Matterson, leader of the party which surveyed this area.

Matthes Glacier. 67°30′S, 65°40′W. 9 miles long. Flows into Whirlwind Inlet between Demorest and Chamberlin Glaciers, on the east side of Graham Land. Discovered aerially by Wilkins on Dec. 20, 1928. Charted by the FIDS in 1947, and named for François E. Matthes, chief geologist with the US Geological Survey.

Matthews Glacier. 75°45′S, 65°30′W. On the east side of the Wilkins Mountains. It flows into the Ronne Ice Shelf just west of the Dodson Peninsula. Named for J.D. Matthews, engineman at Amundsen-Scott South Pole Station, 1963.

Matthews Island. 60°45′S, 45°09′W. The largest of the Robertson Islands in the South Orkneys. Just SE of Coronation Island, from which it is narrowly separated by The Divide. Mapped as part of Coronation Island until Jan. 1957 when the FIDS determined that it was an island unto itself. Named by the UK in 1959 for Drummond H. Matthews, FIDS geologist at Signy Island Station in 1956.

Matthews Peak. 67°40′S, 67°47′W. On the west coast of the Antarctic Peninsula.

Matthews Ridge. 70°57′S, 167°03′E. 6 miles long. Mostly snow-covered. On the south side of Tapsell Foreland in Victoria Land. It forms the east wall of McElroy Glacier and terminates to the south at Barnett Glacier. Named for Jerry L. Matthews, geologist who worked in the Horlick Mountains, 1965–66, and the McMurdo Sound area in 1966–67.

Mount Matthias. 71°13′S, 164°41′E. 1,610 m. 2 miles ENE of Mount Dockery in the Everett Range of the Concord Mountains. Named for Lt. Cdr. Jack M. Matthias, USN, maintenance officer and aircraft commander with VX-6, 1968 and 1969.

Mattox, John. Seaman on the Wilkes Expedition 1838–42. Joined at Rio. Served the cruise.

Mattox Bastion. 77°38′S, 160°56′E. One of the peaks of the Inland Forts, surmounting the NE part of Flory Cirque in the Asgard Range of Victoria Land. Named for Cdr. Benjamin G. Mattox, USN, officer-in-charge of the Naval Support Force winter-over detachment at McMurdo Station in 1971.

Matusevich Glacier. 69°20′S, 157°27′E. Also called Pennell Glacier. 50 miles long. Flows to the coast of Oates Land between the Lazarev Mountains and the NW end of the Wilson Hills. It terminates in the Matusevich Glacier Tongue. Named by the USSR in 1957–58 for N.N. Matusevich, hydrographer and geodesist.

Matusevich Glacier Tongue. 69°50′S, 157°15′E. 18 miles long. The massive seaward extension of the Matusevich Glacier. On Feb. 21, 1959, when Phillip Law's ANARE party sailed around it in the *Magga Dan*, it was floating in 300 fathoms of water.

Mount Matz. 74°42′S, 162°17′E. 1,300 m. At the west side of the terminus of Anderton Glacier. Forms the end of a ridge descending south from the Eisenhower Range to Reeves Glacier in Victoria Land. Named for David B. Matz, geologist at McMurdo Station, 1965–66.

Maud Bank *see* **Maud Seamount**

Maud Seamount. 63°30'S, 2°E. Also called Maud Bank. Subsurface feature off the coast of New Schwabenland, north of the Antarctic Circle.

Maud Subglacial Basin. 81°S, 15°E. A large subglacial basin southward of the Wohlthat Mountains in the southern part of Queen Maud Land. Named for its position in Queen Maud Land.

Cape Maude. 83°09'S, 168°25'E. Ice-covered. Forms the east end of Vaughan Promontory in the Holland Range. Overlooks the Ross Ice Shelf. Discovered by Shackleton's 1907–9 expedition and named for Col. I.A. Maude, who donated the "Maudgee" pony ration for the expedition.

Maudheim Base. 71°03'S, 10°56'W. On the Quar Ice Shelf, one mile south of Norsel Iceport, on the coast of Queen Maud Land. This was the base for the Norwegian-British-Swedish Antarctic Expedition 1949–52 (seen listed in this book as the NBSAE 1949–52).

Mauger, C.C. Carpenter on the *Aurora*, 1914–16.

Mauger Nunatak. 85°44'S, 176°44'E. 2,780 m. 3 miles NE of Mount Block in the Grosvenor Mountains. Named by the New Zealanders in 1961–62 for C.C. Mauger.

The *Maumee*. US Naval T-5 tanker, 620 feet long. Sister ship to the *Yukon*. Many times in at McMurdo Station delivering fuel. In 1969 it supplied 7 million gallons of petroleum to McMurdo — in one trip. L.O. Hess was its captain in 1970 and 1971.

Maumee Ice Piedmont. 74°44'S, 113°22'W. On the Marie Byrd Land coast.

Maurice Faure Islands *see* **Faure Islands**

Maurstad Point. 65°39'S, 66°05'W. Also called Punta Micalvi. 6½ miles NNE of Speerschneider Point, on the west side of Renaud Island in the Biscoe Islands. Named by the UK in 1959 for Alf Maurstad, author of *Atlas of Sea Ice* in 1935.

Maury, William L. US naval lieutenant on the *Porpoise* during the Wilkes Expedition 1838–42.

Maury Bay. 66°33'S, 124°42'E. Ice-filled. Indentation in the Banzare Coast just east of Cape Lewis. Named for William L. Maury.

Maury Glacier. 72°42'S, 61°40'W. 4 miles wide. Flows to the SW corner of Violante Inlet, on the east coast of Palmer Land. Discovered aerially in Dec. 1940 by the USAS. Named by the FIDS in 1947 for Matthew F. Maury (1806–1873), a US Navy commander who, in 1860 tried to get several nations to study Antarctica together. The Civil War put an end to that.

Mautino Peak. 77°21'S, 162°03'E. At the west side of Packard Glacier in the Saint Johns Range of Victoria Land. Named for Cdr. Robert L. Mautino, officer-in-charge of the Naval Support Force winter-over detachment at McMurdo Station in 1972.

Cape Mawson. 69°59'S, 74°40'W. Ice-covered. Forms the SE extremity of Charcot Island. Discovered aerially and charted by Wilkins on Dec. 29, 1929, and named by him for Sir Douglas Mawson.

Mawson, Sir Douglas. b. 1882, Yorkshire, England. d. 1958. In Australia since childhood, he studied geology under Edgeworth David, and with David went on Shackleton's 1907–9 expedition, and the two of them were among the first group to reach the South Magnetic Pole. Mawson was also one of the first six men to climb Mount Erebus, in 1908. He turned down a place on Scott's 1910–13 expedition in order to lead his own Australasian Antarctic Expedition (see listed in this book as AAE 1911–14). He barely survived an epic traverse after the death of Mertz and Ninnis. This expedition, and his BANZARE of 1929–31, proved a continuous 2,500 mile coastline between Cape Freshfield in George V Land, and Enderby Land. Knighted by the British. Mawson's discoveries formed the basis of the Australian Antarctic territorial claim.

Mawson Bank. 73°30′S, 173°30′E. Submarine feature of the Ross Sea. Named for Sir Douglas Mawson.

Mawson Canyon. 65°S, 140°E. Submarine feature off Adélie Land. Named for Sir Douglas Mawson.

Mawson Coast. 67°40′S, 63°30′E. Between William Scoresby Bay (59°34′E) and Murray Monolith (66°54′E) in Mac. Robertson Land. Discovered by the BANZARE 1929–31 under Mawson. Later named by the Australians for Mawson.

Mawson Corridor. 67°S, 63°E. A sea passage between grounded icebergs on the way into Mawson Station at Holme Bay. 22 miles long and between 4 and 5 miles wide. It opens out at the southern end to give the feature a funnel shape. The northern end at 66°45′S, 63°20′E is sharply defined and coincides with the edge of the continental shelf. Discovered by the ANARE in 1954 and used regularly by ANARE relief ships in their approach to Mawson Station. Named by the Australians for Sir Douglas Mawson.

Mawson Escarpment. 73°05′S, 68°10′ E. Flat-topped. Faces west. Extends in a north-south direction for 70 miles along the east side of the Lambert Glacier. Discovered by Flying Officer John Seaton of the RAAF during an ANARE reconnaissance flight in Nov. 1956. Named by the Australians for Sir Douglas Mawson.

Mawson Glacier. 76°13′S, 162°05′E. On the east coast of Victoria Land. It flows from the Polar Plateau, to the north of Trinity Nunatak and the Kirkwood Range, and enters the Ross Sea, at the northern end of the Scott Coast, where it forms the Nordenskjöld Ice Tongue. Named by Shackleton's 1907–9 expedition for Douglas Mawson.

Mawson Peninsula. 68°35′S, 154°11′E. 455 meters high. Ice-covered. Narrow. On the west side of the Slava Ice Shelf, and the east side of the Cook Ice Shelf. It extends in a NW direction for more than 30 miles, terminating in Cape Hudson. Discovered by Phillip Law on a flight from the *Magga Dan* on Feb. 21, 1959, and named by him for Sir Douglas Mawson.

Mawson Station. 67°36′S, 62°52′E. Australian year-round scientific station finished on Feb. 13, 1954, by Phillip Law's ANARE party on the *Kista Dan*. A natural harbor, snow-free in summer, it is at the head of Horseshoe Harbor, near the Murray Monolith, on the coast of Mac. Robertson Land. Named for Sir Douglas Mawson, it was Australia's first station in the Antarctic, and the world's first permanent station there, as well as being the first station ever established south of the Antarctic Peninsula. It was built in order to consolidate Australia's vast claim in Antarctica. Robert Dovers was the first leader, in 1954, and he was succeeded by John M. Béchervaise in 1955, W.G. Bewsher in 1956, Keith B. Mather in 1957, Ian L. Adams in 1958, and Béchervaise again in 1959. It is still active.

Maxwell Bay. 62°15′S, 58°51′W. Also called Bahía Fildes, Bahía Guardia Nacional. 10 miles long. Between King George Island and Nelson Island in the South Shetlands. At the foot of the Fildes Peninsula. Fildes Strait is on the NW side. The name Maxwells Straits was given to this bay and also to Fildes Strait by Weddell in 1822–24, for Lt. Francis Maxwell, who had served with Weddell a decade before (not in the Antarctic). In 1960 the UK altered and limited the name to the bay in question. A commemorative historic site plaque is now mounted on the shore cliffs which says, "In memory of the landing of members of the first Polish Antarctic Marine Research Expedition on the vessels *Professor Siedlecki* and *Tazar* in Feb. 1976." The plaque bears the Polish eagle and the dates 1975 and 1976.

Maxwells Straits *see* **Maxwell Bay**

Cape May. 81°50′S, 162°50′E. Also called May Point, Cape William Henry May. On the west side of the Ross Ice Shelf. 8 miles SE of Cape Laird. Discovered by Scott's 1901–4 expedition and named by Scott for Admiral of the Fleet Sir William Henry May, lord of the admiralty and controller of the navy, 1901–5.

May, William. Passed midshipman on the Wilkes Expedition 1838–42. He served variously on the *Vincennes* and on the *Flying Fish*. He was later court-martialed for insubordination.

May Glacier. 66°13′S, 130°30′E. A channel glacier. 5 miles wide. 6 miles long. Flows to the coast between Cape Morse and Cape Carr. Named for William May.

May Glacier Tongue. 66°08′S, 130°35′ E. A term no longer used, it was the seaward extension of May Glacier in East Antarctica.

May Peak. 85°57′S, 132°23′W. 2,200 m. Pyramidal. At the west side of the Reedy Glacier, 1 mile west of Stich Peak in the Quartz Hills. Named for Lt. Cdr. Robert L. May, USN, helicopter pilot at McMurdo Station in 1962–63.

May Point *see* **Cape May**

May Valley. 83°18′S, 51°10′W. Nearly flat. Snow-covered. On the west flank of the Forrestal Range of the Pensacola Mountains, at the junction of the Lexington and Saratoga Tables. Named for Walter H. May, aerographer at Ellsworth Station in 1957.

Maya Mountain. 77°47′S, 160°33′E. Pyramidal. 2,000 m. Between Aztec Mountain and Pyramid Mountain. Just south of Taylor Glacier in Victoria Land. Named by the New Zealanders in 1958–59 because it resembles the ceremonial platforms used by the Mayas of Mexico and Central America.

Mayakovskogo Mountain *see* **Skavlhø Mountain**

Mount Maybelle Horlick Sidley *see* **Mount Sidley**

Mount Maybelle Sidley *see* **Mount Sidley**

Mayeda Peak. 84°36′S, 164°41′E. 2,890 m. In the Marshall Mountains of the Queen Alexandra Range. 4½ miles north of Mount Marshall. Named for Fred H. Mayeda, meteorologist at South Pole Station, 1959.

Mayer Crags. 84°53′S, 168°45′W. V-shaped massif. 10 miles long. Surmounted by several sharp peaks. At the west side of the mouth of Liv Glacier, where that glacier enters the Ross Ice Shelf. Named for Lt. Robert V. Mayer, USN, Hercules aircraft pilot for four Antarctic summers. He was plane commander for a mid-winter evacuation flight on June 26, 1964.

Mayer Hills. 69°33′S, 67°12′W. Mainly ice-covered. About 900 m. South of the Forster Ice Piedmont on the Antarctic Peninsula, between Prospect Glacier and Mount Leo. Surveyed by the BGLE in 1936–37, and again by the FIDS in 1958. Named by the UK for Johann Tobias Mayer (1723–1762), German mathematician who worked out a series of lunar tables for determining longitude, published by the British Admiralty in 1775.

Mayewski Lobe. Also called Mayewski Ice Lobe. In the Dominion Range, in the area of the Beardmore Glacier. It is a lobe of ice projecting from the main part of the range. Named for Paul A. Mayewski (*see* **Mayewski Peak**).

Mayewski Peak. 77°18′S, 162°14′E. In the Saint Johns Range of Victoria Land. Midway down the ridge which bounds the north side of Baldwin Valley. Named for Paul A. Mayewski, glaciologist at McMurdo Station in 1968–69, at the McGregor Glacier in 1970–71, at the Willett and Convoy Ranges in 1971–72 and at the Rennick Glacier in 1974–75.

Mount Mayhew. 65°35′S, 62°26′W. 1,200 m. Between Pequod and Starbuck Glaciers on the east side of Graham Land. Named by the UK for the *Moby Dick* character.

Mayman Nunatak. 71°05′S, 66°56′E. Has a domed appearance from the NE. 6 miles SW of Taylor Platform in the Prince Charles Mountains. Named by the Australians for Dr. K.J. Mayman, medical officer at Davis Station in 1964.

Cape Mayo. 68°54′S, 63°23′W. A bare rock cliff. Forms the east end of a flat, ice-covered platform which rises to 500 m. Between Cape Keeler and Miller Point on the east coast of Palmer Land. Discovered aerially by Wilkins on Dec. 20, 1928, and named by him for William B. Mayo of the Ford Motor Company.

Mayo Peak. 74°49′S, 110°36′W. On the coast of Marie Byrd Land.

Mayr, Rudolf. Pilot of the flying boat *Passat* during the German New Schwabenland Expedition of 1938–39 led by Ritscher.

Mayr Range *see* **Mayr Ridge**

Mayr Ridge. 72°11′S, 2°22′E. Also called Armlenet. Formerly called Mayr Range. A mountainous ridge which includes the Nupskammen Ridge and Von Essen Mountain. It forms the SW extremity of the Gjelsvik Mountains in Queen Maud Land. Ritscher's 1938–39 expedition flew over here and named a feature in this general area as Mayr-Kette (Mayr Range) for Rudolf Mayr. This may or may not be the same feature, but the name has been preserved.

Mazzeo Island. 65°09′S, 65°W. ½ mile WNW of Quintana Island in the Wilhelm Archipelago. Named by the UK for Lt. Peter Mazzeo, second survey officer on the *Endurance,* which was in the area in Feb. 1969.

Meade Islands. 62°27′S, 60°05′W. In the northern entrance to McFarlane Strait in the South Shetlands. They include Cave Island. Charted and named in 1935 by personnel on the *Discovery II.*

Meade Nunàtak. 80°23′S, 21°58′W. In the Shackleton Range.

Meads Peak. 83°45′S, 57°08′W. 1,165 m. ½ mile off the NW end of Hudson Ridge in the Neptune Range of the Pensacola Mountains. Named for Edward C. Meads, construction driver at Ellsworth Station in 1958.

Meander Glacier. 73°16′S, 166°55′E. Flows from the area around Mount Supernal and Hobbie Ridge, eastward in a meandering manner for 30 miles through the Mountaineer Range, and enters Mariner Glacier just east of Engberg Bluff, Victoria Land. Named descriptively by the New Zealanders in 1962–63.

Mear, Roger. One of Britain's leading mountain climbers, he was with the BAS in Antarctica when he met Robert Swan. He joined Swan's In the Footsteps of Scott Expedition, 1985–86. In his 30s at the time, he was one of the three men who skied to the Pole during this expedition.

Meares, Cecil H. 1878–1937. Cecil Henry Meares. Buyer (and manager) of the dogs and Manchurian ponies for Scott's 1910–13 expedition.

Meares Cliff. 71°12′S, 168°25′E. 600 m. 5½ miles WNW of Nelson Cliff on the north coast of Victoria Land. Charted by Campbell's Northern Party during Scott's 1910–13 expedition. Named by Campbell for Cecil H. Meares.

Mechnikov Peak. 71°37′S, 11°28′E. 2,365 m. At the base of the spur separating Schüssel Cirque and Grautskåla Cirque in the northern part of the Humboldt Mountains in Queen Maud Land. Discovered aerially by Ritscher's 1938–39 expedition, and named by the USSR in 1966 for geographer L.I. Mechnickov (1838–1888).

Medals. The US government has presented 4 different medals for Antarctic service, but now presents only one—the Antarctica Service Medal. On its obverse is a man standing in a determined manner, dressed in polar clothing, and to his left and right are the words, "Antarctica" and "Service." The reverse shows the words, "Courage," "Sacrifice," and "Devotion," one on top of the other in that order, on an outline polar projection of the continent, all encircled by a border of penguins and marine life. This medal was awarded to all US forces personnel who served in Antarctica from Jan. 1, 1946, onward. It is only in bronze, but clasps attachable to the suspension ribbon distinguish people who have wintered-over in Antarctica. A bronze clasp means one winter, a silver clasp two winters, and a gold clasp three or more winters. The ribbon has outer bands of dark blue which represent five-twelfths of the Antarctic year, i.e., night. The center portion graduates inward until there is a very light band, representing increasing lightness leading to aurora australis. The first medal for Antarctica was the Byrd Antarctic Expedition Medal, designed in 1930 by Francis H. Packer, which was approved by Congress on May 23, 1930. The obverse shows Byrd in a parka, holding a ski pole, with ice formations to left and right. The reverse bears a sailing ship on top of the inscription, "presented to the officers and men of the Byrd Antarctic expedition to express the high admiration in which the Congress and the American people hold their heroic and undaunted services in connection with the scientific investigations and extraordinary aerial explorations of the Antarctic continent." Below that is a tri-motored airplane. The ribbon has a saxe blue center vertical band on an eggshell field. 66 gold, 7 silver, and 9 bronze were issued by the secretary of the navy. Gold was for full-time expedition members, silver for those who were not in at the start but were at the finish, and bronze for those who were in at the start but not at the finish. The Second Byrd Antarctic Expedition Medal was approved by Congress on June 2, 1936, was silver, and was presented to winterers-over, and commanders of the *Bear of Oakland* and the *Jacob Ruppert*. Byrd recommended 57 recipients. The obverse portrays Byrd, and the reverse has an inscription similar to the 1930 medal, and is surrounded by an airplane on top, a sailing ship to the right, a dog team at bottom with a sledge, and radio towers on left. It was designed by Heinz Warneke. The ribbon is all-white grosgrain. The US Antarctic Expedition Medal 1939–1941 was authorized by Congress on Sept. 24, 1945. 60 gold medals were awarded to men who wintered-over. 50 silver medals to men who had spent the summers 1939–40 and 1940–41, and 50 bronze medals to those who had only one summer. The obverse shows Antarctica on a partial globe, with the words, "Science, Pioneering, Exploration," with the name of the expedition around the circumference of the medal. The reverse has an inscription similar to the two previous medals. The ribbon has wide bands of sistine blue at each edge, and a white center band, on which are thin stripes of Old Glory red. In 1970 the USSR Academy of Sciences struck a medal commemorating the 150th anniversary of von Bellingshausen's voyage. The obverse shows von Bellingshausen and Lazarev, and their two ships. On the reverse is a map of Antarctica with the cruise tracks of the 1819–21 expedition. For religious medals *see* **Churches.**

Medea Dome. 66°11′S, 62°03′W. A snow dome, 350 m. Marks the eastern end of Philippi Rise on the east coast of Graham Land. Surveyed by the FIDS in 1953. Named by the UK in 1956 for the Greek mythological female involved with Jason (this feature is near Jason Peninsula).

Medhalsen Saddle. 72°09′S, 3°10′E. An ice saddle just south of Risemedet Mountain in the Gjelsvik Mountains of Queen Maud Land. Name means "the landmark neck" in Norwegian.

Medhovden Bluff. 72°01′S, 3°18′E. Ice-covered. Forms the NE end of Risemedet Mountain in the Gjelsvik Mountains of Queen Maud Land. Name means "the landmark bluff" in Norwegian.

Median Snowfield. 83°30′S, 52°30′W. In the Pensacola Mountains. Between Torbert Escarpment in the Neptune Range, and the southern part of the Forrestal Range. Named for its position between the Neptune and Forrestal Ranges.

Mount Medina. 68°27′S, 66°15′W. 1,845 m. Ice-covered. In the NE part of the Hadley Upland. It overlooks the head of Gibbs Glacier in southern Graham Land.

Surveyed by the FIDS in 1958. Named by the UK for Pedro de Medina (1493–1567), Spanish cosmographer royal, who wrote *Arte de Navigar* in 1545, an important manual of navigation.

Medina Peaks. 85°36'S, 155°54'W. Mostly ice-free. They surmount a ridge 15 miles long, and extend north along the east side of Goodale Glacier to the edge of the Ross Ice Shelf. Parts of them were discovered during Byrd's 1928–30 expedition. Named for Guillermo Medina, technical director of the US Navy Hydrographic Office, 1954–60, and of the Naval Oceanographic Office, 1960–64.

Medley Rocks. 62°58'S, 56°01'W. Also called Islotes Mom. Just off the NE side of D'Urville Island. Surveyed by the FIDS in 1953–54, and named by the UK in 1956 for the medley of reefs and rocks in this group.

Medmulen Spurs. 72°01'S, 3°08'E. A group of rock spurs extending from the north side of Risemedet Mountain in the Gjelsvik Mountains of Queen Maud Land. Name means "the landmark snout" in Norwegian.

Medvecky Peaks. 70°34'S, 67°38'E. In the NW part of the Loewe Massif in the eastern part of the Aramis Range, in the Prince Charles Mountains. Named by the Australians for A. Medvecky, geologist with the ANARE Prince Charles Mountains survey in 1969.

Meek Channel. 65°15'S, 64°15'W. A narrow channel separating Galíndez Island from Grotto and Corner Islands in the Argentine Islands of the Wilhelm Archipelago. Charted by the BGLE in 1935, and named by them for William McC. Meek, marine architect and surveyor, who helped ready the *Penola* for the expedition.

Mount Meeks. 86°13'S, 148°51'W. 2,470 m. Surmounts the rocky divide between Griffith Glacier and Howe Glacier in the Queen Maud Mountains. Named for Lt. Harman T. Meeks of VX-6, aircraft navigator in the Antarctic, 1966 and 1967.

Meeley Automatic Weather Station. 78°30'S, 170°12'E. On the Ross Ice Shelf, due east of Minna Bluff, at an elevation of approximately 150 feet. An American AWS, it operated from Dec. 4, 1980, until Dec. 31, 1985.

Mefford Knoll. 76°01'S, 136°16'W. A rocky knoll or ledge on the lower west slopes of the Mount Berlin massif, in the Flood Range of Marie Byrd Land. Named for Michael Mefford, a member of the USARP team which studied ice sheet dynamics in the area to the NE of Byrd Station in the summer season of 1971–72.

Mefjell *see* **Mount Griffiths**

Mefjell Glacier. 71°58'S, 25°E. 5 miles long. Flows into Gjel Glacier between Menipa Peak and Mefjell Mountain in the Sør Rondane Mountains. Named Mefjellbreen (the middle mountain glacier) by the Norwegians.

Mefjell Mountain. 72°05'S, 25°03'E. Also called Middle Mountain. 3,080 m. 5 miles west of Mount Bergersen in the Sør Rondane Mountains. Photographed by the LCE 1936–37 and mapped 10 years later by Norwegian cartographers, and mapped again in 1957 by the same country's cartographers, but this time from photos taken during Operation Highjump, 1946–47. Named Mefjell (middle mountain) by the Norwegians, because of its central location in the Sør Rondanes.

Megalestris Hill. 65°11'S, 64°10'W. 35 m. In the southern part of Petermann Island in the Wilhelm Archipelago. Charted by Charcot in 1908–10 and named by him for the megalestris (an archaic name for the South Polar skua).

Megaptera Island *see* **Huemul Island**

Megaw Island. 66°55'S, 67°36'W. The most easterly of the Bennett Islands in Hanusse Bay. Named by the UK for Helen Dick Megaw, British physicist who, in 1934, made accurate measurements of the cell dimensions of ice.

Mehaugen Hill. 71°44'S, 25°33'E. The central hill in the group at the east side of Kamp Glacier in the Sør Rondane Mountains. Photographed by the LCE 1936–37 and mapped 10 years later by Norwegian cartographers using these photos. Norwegians also mapped it again in 1957, using photos taken during Operation Highjump, 1946–47. Name means "the middle hill" in Norwegian.

Meholmane *see* **Jocelyn Islands**

Meholmen Island. 68°58'S, 39°32'E. Between Ongul Island and Utholmen Island in Lützow-Holm Bay. Photographed by the LCE 1936–37. Name means "the middle island" in Norwegian.

Cape Meier *see* **Meier Point**

Meier Peak. 71°51'S, 168°40'E. 3,450 m. At the south side of the head of Ironside Glacier, 4 miles SSW of Mount Minto in the Admiralty Mountains. Named for Lt. Cdr. Miron D. Meier, USNR, VX-6 helicopter pilot in Antarctica, 1967 and 1968.

Meier Point. 60°38'S, 45°54'W. Also called Cape Meier. Forms the west side of the entrance to Norway Bight on the south side of Coronation Island in the South Orkneys. Named before 1912–13, when Petter Sørlle listed it as such on his chart.

Meier Valley. 67°08'S, 67°24'W. Just east of Mount St. Louis on Arrowsmith Peninsula in Graham Land. Named by the UK for Mark F. Meier, US geologist who made the first detailed study of strain all over the surface of a glacier, in 1952.

Meiklejohn, Ian F. Radio operator on the BGLE 1934–37.

Meiklejohn Glacier. 70°33'S, 67°44'W. 12 miles long. 4 miles wide. Flows from the Dyer Plateau of Palmer Land into George VI Sound, just south of Moore Point. In its lower reaches the south side of this glacier merges with Millett Glacier. Surveyed in 1936 by the BGLE. Named by the UK in 1954 for Ian F. Meiklejohn.

Meinardus Glacier. 73°22'S, 61°55'W. Flows in an ENE direction to a point just

east of Mount Barkow, where it is joined from the NW by the Haines Glacier, and then east to enter New Bedford Inlet just west of Court Nunatak, on the east coast of Palmer Land. Discovered aerially in Dec. 1940 by the USAS. Named by the FIDS in 1947 for Wilhelm Meinardus, German meteorologist and climatologist who drew up the meteorological results of von Drygalski's expedition of 1901–3.

Meiney, John. Master-at-arms on the Wilkes Expedition 1838–42. Joined in the USA. Served the cruise.

Mount Meister. 74°14'S, 162°47'E. 2,520 m. On the west side of Priestley Glacier. It surmounts the north end of Nash Ridge in the Eisenhower Range of Victoria Land. Named for Laurent J. Meister, geologist at McMurdo Station in 1965–66.

Mekammen *see* **Central Masson Range**

Mekammen Crest *see* **Central Masson Range**

Meknattane Nunataks. 69°48'S, 75°12'E. On the east side of Polarforschung Glacier where that glacier flows into Publications Ice Shelf. Photographed by the LCE 1936–37 and named Meknattane (the middle crags) by the Norwegians.

Mel Moraine. 71°53'S, 9°18'E. At the north end of the Gagarin Mountains, in the Orvin Mountains of Queen Maud Land. Name means "meal" in Norwegian.

Melaerts, Jules. Belgian second officer on the *Belgica* expedition, 1897–99.

Mount Melania. 78°07'S, 166°08'E. 330 m. At the north end of Black Island in the Ross Archipelago. It was first climbed by Bernacchi and Ferrar during the Royal Society Expedition of 1901–4. Named by the New Zealanders in 1958–59. Melania is a Greek word meaning an ink blob, an apt name for such a rounded hill on an island called Black Island.

Melba Peninsula. 66°31'S, 98°18'E. Ice-covered. Between Reid Glacier and the Bay of Winds, fronting on the Shackleton Ice Shelf. Discovered by the AAE 1911–14, and named by Mawson for Dame Nellie Melba, the Australian opera star, and a patron of the expedition.

Melbert Rocks. 78°02′S, 155°07′W. Just NW of Mount Paterson in the Rockefeller Mountains, on Edward VII Peninsula. Discovered during Byrd's 1928–30 expedition. Named for George W. Melbert, USN, utilitiesman at Byrd Station, 1966.

Mount Melbourne. 74°21′S, 164°42′E. 2,730 m. A dormant volcano between Wood Bay and Terra Nova Bay in Victoria Land. Part of the McMurdo Volcanics, it last exploded probably in 1837. The crater is ⅛ mile across, and Cryptogram Ridge is on top of it. The summit is SSSI #24, and is special for its microflora and microfauna. First sighted in 1841 by Ross, who named it for Lord Melbourne, British prime minister when the expedition was being planned. It was first climbed in Jan. 1967 by a NZ party, and subsequently by NZ parties in Dec. 1972 and Nov. 1984. Several other parties have since gone up.

Melbourne Glacier *see* **Campbell Glacier**

Île Melchior *see* **Melchior Islands**

Puerto Melchior *see* **Melchior Harbor**

Melchior Archipelago *see* **Melchior Islands**

Melchior Harbor. 64°19′S, 62°59′W. Small harbor in the Melchior Islands of the Palmer Archipelago. It is formed by the semicircular arrangement of Delta Island, Alpha Island, Beta Island, Kappa Island, and Gamma Island. Surveyed by Discovery Investigations personnel in 1927. They may have named it. It is certainly named for the island group. It was resurveyed by the Argentines in 1942, 1943, and 1948. They call it Puerto Melchior.

Melchior Island *see* **Melchior Islands**

Melchior Islands. 64°19′S, 62°57′W. Ice-covered. Near the center of Dallmann Bay in the Palmer Archipelago. Discovered by Dallmann in 1873–74. Charted by Charcot in 1903–5. He named what he thought was the large easternmost island in the group as Île Melchior, for Vice Adm. Melchior of the French Navy, but later surveys proved Charcot's Île Melchior to be two islands, now called Eta Island and Omega Island. The term Melchior Archipelago was subsequently used for the group, and divided into two parts, the East Melchior Islands and the West Melchior Islands. But, even later, the feature was redefined as Melchior Islands — pure and simple, a group within the Palmer Archipelago. Eta Island and Omega Island form the eastern part. Other islands include Alpha Island, Beta Island, Gamma Island, Delta Island, Epsilon Island, Theta Islands, Kappa Island, Lambda Island, Omicron Islands, Rho Islands, Sigma Islands, Tau Islands, Psi Islands, Omega Island.

Melchior Station. 64°20′S, 62°59′W. The second Argentine scientific station to be built in Antarctica (*see* **Orcadas**), this was established on Jan. 31, 1947, on Gamma Island in the Melchior Islands (or Melchior Archipelago as it was called then). A meteorological station primarily, its first leader was Nadau, in 1947. He was succeeded by Leonardo Roque de Costillas in 1948. Daniel Canova led the 1952 party, and A.A. Giuntini was leader during the IGY (1957–58) when the station studied meteorology, glaciology, and oceanography.

Melchoir Archipelago *see* **Melchior Islands**

Melfjellet. 68°21′S, 59°12′E. Also called Whiting Nunatak. In the eastern part of the Hansen Mountains. A prominent rock outcrop about 2 miles SE of See Nunatak. Photographed by the LCE 1936–37 and named later by the Norwegians.

Mount Mellanby *see* **Mount Rouge**

Melleby, Peter. In charge of sledge dogs on the NBSAE 1949–52.

Melleby Peak. 73°16'W, 1°15'W. Marks the eastern end of the Neumayer Cliffs in Queen Maud Land. Named by the Norwegians for Peter Melleby.

Pináculos Mellizos *see* **Twin Pinnacles**

Mello Nunatak. 72°21'S, 165°03'E. Isolated. 7 miles east of Mount Staley of the Freyberg Mountains, in the NE part of the Evans Névé. Named for Gerald L. Mello, chief engineman, USN, petty officer in charge of Hallett Station for the summer of 1966–67, and a member of the wintering-over party at McMurdo Station in 1967.

The *Mellona.* British sealer out of Newcastle, in the South Shetlands for the 1821–22 season under Capt. Johnson. Anchored at Clothier Harbor for most of the season with the *Liberty,* in whose company it sailed. The *Mellona* also anchored in Shirreff Cove for a while and just escaped being wrecked on Desolation Island on March 25, 1822.

Mellona Rocks. 62°18'S, 59°30'W. 2 miles NE of Newell Point, Robert Island, in the South Shetlands. Named by the UK in 1961 for the *Mellona.*

Mellor Glacier. 73°30'S, 66°30'E. Flows between Mounts Newton and Maguire, and coalesces with Collins Glacier just prior to its junction with the Lambert Glacier at Patrick Point in the Prince Charles Mountains. Named by the Australians for Malcolm Mellor, glaciologist at Mawson Station, 1957.

Melrose, Cecil. Crewman on the *Jacob Ruppert,* 1934–35.

Melrose Peak. 82°19'S, 160°14'E. 4 miles south of Peters Peak in the Holyoake Range. Named for Robert L. Melrose, meteorologist at Hallett Station, 1963–64.

Melsom Rocks. 60°31'S, 46°10'W. Isolated. 2 miles north of Despair Rocks and 7 miles west of Penguin Point, the NW end of Coronation Island, in the South Orkneys. Discovered and charted by Powell and Palmer in Dec. 1821. Named by Petter Sørlle in 1912–13 for Capt. H.G. Melsom, manager of the Thule Whaling Company.

¹The *Melville.* Norwegian whaler in the South Shetlands 1929–30. Owned by the Hecktor Whaling Company. It transported Wilkins' expedition part of the way.

²The *Melville.* US research ship of the 1970s and 1980s. Built by the US Navy in 1970, and operated by the Scripps Institution of Oceanography, it is 2,000 tons and 245 feet long. It has wet and dry labs and can accommodate up to 30 scientists and 20 crew.

Cape Melville. 62°02'S, 57°37'W. Also called South Foreland. Forms the eastern extremity of King George Island in the South Shetlands. Some early charts show this name for the NE cape of the island, but for the last hundred years the eastern cape has been the one with the name. Named before 1820, probably by Bransfield.

Mont Melville *see* **Melville Peak**

Melville, Frederick C. Captain of the *City of New York,* during Byrd's 1928–30 expedition.

Melville Glacier. 65°28'S, 62°10'W. 12 miles long. Between Mapple and Pequod Glaciers on the east coast of Graham Land. It flows into Exasperation Inlet southward of Mount Ahab. Surveyed by the FIDS in 1947 and 1955. Named by the UK for Herman Melville (1819–1891), the author of *Moby Dick.*

Melville Peak. 62°01'S, 57°41'W. Also called Mont Melville. Surmounts Cape Melville (hence its name), the eastern cape of King George Island in the South Shetlands. Charted by Charcot in 1908–10.

Melville Point. 74°35'S, 135°31'W. Marks the eastern side of the entrance to Siniff Bay on the coast of Marie Byrd Land. Named for Capt. Frederick C. Melville.

Melvilles' Island *see* **Laurie Island**

Melvold Nunataks. 72°51'S, 74°09'E. 14 miles west of Mount Harding in the Grove Mountains. Named by the Australians for C.D. Melvold, radio officer at Mawson Station, 1962.

Mendeleyev Glacier. 71°55'S, 14°33'E. 10 miles long. Flows through the northern portion of the Payer Mountains in Queen Maud Land. Named by the USSR for chemist Dmitri I. Mendeleyev (1834–1907).

Mendelssohn Inlet. 71°15'S, 73°W. 25 miles long. 9 miles wide. Ice-filled. The most northeasterly of the three inlets indenting the north side of Beethoven Peninsula on Alexander Island. Discovered aerially by the USAS 1939–41. Named by the UK for the composer.

Mendenhall Peak. 85°24'S, 87°19'W. 2,130 m. ½ mile west of Mount Wrather in the eastern part of the Thiel Mountains. Named by Bermel and Ford, leaders of the US Geological Survey Thiel Mountains party here in 1960–61, for Walter C. Mendenhall, fifth director of the US Geological Survey, 1931–43.

Mendori Island. 69°S, 39°32'E. The most northerly in a group of three small islands ½ mile NW of the strait separating Ongul Island and East Ongul Island. Named Mendori-jima (hen island) by the Japanese in 1972 in association with Ondori Island, which is 350 yards to the north.

The *Mendoza*. Destroyer on Argentine naval maneuvers in the South Shetlands in 1948, under the overall command of Contra-Almirante Harald Cappus.

Menelaus Ridge. 64°35'S, 63°40'W. Snow-covered. Has four small summits. 1,370 m. Between Mount Agamemnon and Mount Helen in the Achaean Range of central Anvers Island. Surveyed in 1955 by the FIDS and named by the UK for the Homeric character.

The Menhir. 60°39'S, 45°12'W. 395 m. An isolated pinnacle rock. Overlooks the west side of Gibbon Bay in eastern Coronation Island in the South Orkneys. Surveyed by the FIDS in 1956–58 and named by the UK in 1959. A menhir is a single standing monumental stone built in ancient Europe.

Islotes Menier *see* **Screen Islands**

Ménier Island. 64°59'S, 63°37'W. Also called Guyou Island. Largest of a small island group in the mouth of Flandres Bay, 4 miles NE of Cape Renard, off the west coast of Graham Land. Charcot discovered the group in 1903–5 and named them Îles Ménier. Later the name was reduced in its scope to this one island.

Menipa *see* **Menipa Peak**

Menipa Mountain *see* **Menipa Peak**

Menipa Peak. 71°56'S, 25°10'E. 2,590 m. 5 miles north of Mefjell Mountain in the central part of the Sør Rondane Mountains. Photographed by the LCE 1936–37. Named Menipa (the middle peak) by the Norwegians, and in English this became first Menipa Mountain and then Menipa Peak.

Mensa Bay *see* **Table Bay**

Mount Mentzel. 71°22'S, 13°40'E. 2,330 m. 6 miles east of Mount Zimmermann in the Gruber Mountains of Queen Maud Land. Discovered during Ritscher's 1938–39 expedition, and named by Ritscher for the president of the German Research Society.

Cape Menzel. 72°S, 95°43'W. Also called Craddock Nunatak. Ice-free. Marks the northern extremity of the ice-covered Lofgren Peninsula in the NE part of Thurston Island. Discovered on helicopter flights from the *Glacier* and the *Burton Island* during the USN Bellingshausen Sea Expedition of Feb. 1960. Named for Reinhard W. Menzel, seismologist at Eights Station, 1965.

Mount Menzies. 73°30'S, 61°50'E. 3,355 m. On the massif between Mounts Mather and Bayliss, on the south side of the Fisher Glacier in the Prince Charles Mountains. Discovered by Flying Officer John Seaton, RAAF, from an ANARE aircraft in 1956. Named by the Australians for Robert Menzies, Australia's greatest prime minister.

Meoto Rocks. 68°07'S, 42°36'E. Also called Myoto Islands. Two large rocks, just west of Cape Hinode, off the coast of Queen Maud Land. Named Meoto-iwa (husband and wife rocks) by the Japanese.

Meöya *see* **Alphard Island**

Mercanton Heights. 67°30'S, 67°26' W. Between Bigourdan Fjord and Nye Glacier in the SW part of Arrowsmith Peninsula in Graham Land. Named by the UK for Paul-Louis Mercanton, Swiss glaciologist who was, for many years, secretary of the International Commission on Snow and Ice.

Mercator Ice Piedmont. 68°37'S, 65° 30'W. At the head of Mobiloil Inlet in eastern Graham Land. It is formed by the confluence of the Gibbs, Lammers, Cole, and Weyerhaeuser Glaciers. Surveyed by the FIDS in Dec. 1958. Named by the UK for Gerardus Mercator (1512–1594), creator of the famous map of 1568.

Mount Mercer. 70°13'S, 65°39'E. 2 miles west of Farley Massif in the Athos Range of the Prince Charles Mountains. Named by the Australians for B. Mercer, weather observer at Davis Station in 1961.

Mercer Lobe. Also called Mercer Ice Lobe. A lobe of ice projecting from the main body of the Dominion Range, in the area of the Beardmore Glacier. Named for John H. Mercer (*see* **Mercer Ridge**).

Mercer Ridge. 84°50'S, 113°45'W. Partly ice-free. Forms the SW end of Mount Schopf in the Ohio Range of the Horlick Mountains. Named for John H. Mercer (1922–1987), British geologist, a member of the Ohio State University expedition to the Horlicks in 1960–61. He was back in the same area in 1964–65. It was Mercer who named the Sirius Formation (q.v.).

Mercik Peak. 85°05'S, 169°06'W. 1,425 m. 7 miles NE of Mount Wells, on the ridge descending from that mountain, in the Prince Olav Mountains. Named for James E. Mercik, aurora scientist at Amundsen-Scott South Pole Station in 1965.

The *Mercury*. British sealer from Liverpool, in the South Shetlands in 1820–21. Capt. Wetherell commanding.

Mercury Bluff. 62°29'S, 60°49'W. SW of Cape Shirreff and Scarborough Castle on the north coast of Livingston Island in the South Shetlands. Named in 1958 by the UK for the *Mercury*.

Mercury Glacier. 71°34'S, 68°14'W. On the east coast of Alexander Island. 5 miles long. 2 miles wide. It flows east into George VI Sound between Waitabit Cliffs and Keystone Cliffs. Surveyed by the FIDS in 1948 and 1949. Named by the UK for the planet.

Mount Meredith. 71°12'S, 67°45'E. Flat-topped. 10 miles north of Mount Fisher in the Prince Charles Mountains. Named by the Australians for Sgt. N. Meredith, RAAF, engine fitter at Mawson Station, 1957.

Merger Island. 70°06'S, 71°13'W. Ice-covered. 3 miles long. At the entrance to Haydn Inlet, off the west coast of Alexander Island. Named descriptively by the UK for the way in which it merges with the surrounding ice shelf.

Mericle Rock. 73°39'S, 163°15'E. A nunatak in the middle of Campbell Glacier, 9 miles from the head of that glacier, in Victoria Land. Named for David L. Mericle, USN, electronics technician at McMurdo Station, 1967.

Meridian Glacier. 68°45'S, 66°37'W. 9 miles long. Flows along the west side of Godfrey Upland and joins the Clarke Glacier between Behaim Peak and Elton Hill, in southern Graham Land. Finn Ronne and Carl Eklund traversed this glacier in Jan. 1941 as part of the USAS. Surveyed by the FIDS in Dec. 1958. Named by the UK because the glacier flows from north to south along the meridian.

Merle, René. French deputy-leader of the expedition led by Alfred Faure which, in Jan. 1959, relieved Rouillon and Garcia at Charcot Station.

Merrell Valley. 76°50′S, 160°50′E. Ice-free. In the Convoy Range. It runs north from the head of the range just east of Mount Gunn, into the Greenville Valley. Named by the NZ Northern Survey Party of the BCTAE in 1957 for the *Private Joseph F. Merrell.*

Merrem Peak. 76°03′S, 136°03′W. 3,000 m. The secondary summit on the Mount Berlin massif in Marie Byrd Land. It is 2 miles west of Berlin Crater. Discovered and charted by the Pacific Coast Survey Party, led by Leonard Berlin, during the USAS, in Dec. 1940. Named for Frank H. Merrem, ionosphere physicist and scientific leader at Amundsen-Scott South Pole Station in 1970.

The *Merrick.* US supply ship which formed part of the Central Group during Operation Highjump, 1946–47. Captain John J. Hourihan.

Mount Merrick. 67°42′S, 49°18′E. 1,120 m. 3 miles west of Mount Humble in the Raggatt Mountains. Named by the Australians for W.R. Merrick, geophysicist at Mawson Station in 1960.

Merrick Glacier. 80°13′S, 158°52′E. Just east of Sennett Glacier in the Britannia Range. It flows into Byrd Glacier at the west end of Horney Bluff. Named for the *Merrick.*

Merrick Mountains. 75°06′S, 72°04′W. 8 miles in extent. 7 miles NE of the Behrendt Mountains in eastern Ellsworth Land. Discovered aerially by the RARE 1947–48. Named for Conrad G. Merrick, US Geological Survey topographic engineer with the Antarctic Peninsula Traverse Party, 1961–62, who took part in the survey of these mountains.

Merrick Point. 74°28′S, 110°09′W. On the coast of Marie Byrd Land.

Merritt, Everett L. Photogrammetrist with the Navy Hydrographic Office, who was a surveyor on Operation Windmill, 1947–48. He landed in the Bunger Hills on Jan. 12, 1948.

Merritt Island. 66°28′S, 107°12′E. 13 miles WNW of Cape Nutt, just off the coast of East Antarctica. Named for Everett L. Merritt.

Mersey Spit. 62°05′S, 57°55′W. On the south coast of King George Island, just north of Penguin Island, in the South Shetlands. Charted and named in 1937 by personnel on the *Discovery II.*

Mertz, Xavier. b. 1884, Basle, Switzerland. A Swiss law graduate, he was his nation's ski-running champion. He was the skiing expert on the AAE 1911–14, and died of Vitamin A poisoning on Jan. 7, 1913, while on his way back to base, as part of the Far Eastern Party under Mawson. His death on the trail left Mawson alone to face one of the most harrowing adventures in Antarctic annals.

Mertz Basin. 66°45′S, 147°E. A submarine feature 100 miles out to sea from George V Land.

Mertz Canyon. 65°S, 148°E. Submarine feature in the southern Indian Ocean, out beyond the coast of Wilkes Land.

Mertz Glacier. 67°30′S, 144°45′E. Heavily crevassed. 45 miles long. 20 miles wide on average. It flows into the sea at the East Antarctica coast, between Adélie Land and George V Land, or more specifically between Cape de la Motte and Cape Hurley, where it forms the Mertz Glacier Tongue. Discovered by the AAE 1911–14 and named by Mawson for Xavier Mertz.

Mertz Glacier Tongue. 67°10′S, 145°30′E. 45 miles long. 25 miles wide. The seaward extension of the Mertz Glacier, on the coast of East Antarctica. Discovered by the AAE 1911–14 and named by Mawson in association with the glacier.

Mertz-Ninnis Trough *see* **Mertz-Ninnis Valley**

Mertz-Ninnis Valley. 67°30′S, 146°E. Also called Mertz-Ninnis Trough, Adélie Depression. A submarine feature off the coast of George V Land.

Mount Mervyn. 70°31'S, 65°13'E. Also called Mount Christensen. South of the main part of the Porthos Range in the Prince Charles Mountains. 6 miles south of Mount Kirkby. Discovered in Dec. 1956 by an ANARE party led by W.G. Bewsher, and named for Mervyn Christensen, weather observer at Mawson Station in 1956.

Merz Peninsula. 72°15'S, 61°05'W. Ice-covered. 15 miles long in an east-west direction. 25 miles wide on average. Between Hilton Inlet and Violante Inlet on the east coast of Palmer Land. Discovered aerially in Dec. 1940 by the USAS. Named by the FIDS in 1947 for Alfred Merz (1880–1925), German oceanographer and original leader of the *Meteor* expedition of 1925–26. He died before he reached the Antarctic.

Bahía Mesa *see* **Table Bay**

Isla Mesa *see* **Table Island**

Mesa Range. 73°11'S, 162°55'E. A range of flat-topped mesas, the Pain Mesa, the Sheehan Mesa, the Tobin Mesa, and the Gair Mesa. At the head of the Rennick Glacier in Victoria Land. Named descriptively by the New Zealanders in 1962–63.

Meserve Glacier. 77°31'S, 162°17'E. A hanging glacier on the south wall of the Wright Valley in Victoria Land. Between the Bartley and Hart Glaciers. Named by Robert Nichols (*see* **Nichols Snowfield**), for William Meserve, geological assistant to Nichols at nearby Marble Point in 1959–60.

Messent Peak. 69°24'S, 66°13'W. On the west side of the Antarctic Peninsula.

Mesteinene *see* **Wigg Islands**

Mesyatseva Mountain *see* **Gårenevkalven Nunatak**

Metavolcanic Mountain. 86°13'S, 126°15'W. Flat-topped. 2,480 m. 5 miles north of Hatcher Bluffs on the east side of the Reedy Glacier. Made up of dark, metavolcanic rock, it contrasts sharply with the lighter-colored granites everywhere else along the glacier. Named by John H. Mercer (*see* **Mercer Ridge**).

Mount Metcalfe. 67°59'S, 66°57'W. At the south side of the head of McMorrin Glacier. 1½ miles south of Mount Wilcox in Graham Land. Named by the UK for Robert J. Metcalfe, BAS surveyor at Base E, 1960–62. He surveyed the area in 1962.

Metchnikoff Point. 64°03'S, 62°34'W. Forms the western extremity of Pasteur Peninsula in northern Brabant Island. Charted by Charcot in 1903–5 and named by him for Élie Metchnikoff (1845–1916), Russian-born French microbiologist who succeeded Pasteur as director of the Pasteur Institute in Paris. De Gerlache, Amundsen, Cook, Arctowski, and Danco camped here from Jan. 30, 1898–Feb. 6, 1898.

¹The *Meteor*. German ship at the South Shetlands on an oceanographic cruise in 1925–27. Capt. Alfred Merz died at sea on Aug. 25, 1925, before reaching the South Shetlands, and Capt. Fritz A. Spiess took over.

²The *Meteor*. West German research ship of the 1980s.

Meteorite Hills. 79°40'S, 155°36'E. In the Darwin Mountains of Victoria Land.

Meteorites. There are 4 kinds of meteorites. 1. Chondrites. These are stony meteorites containing chondrules (rounded aggregates of silicate minerals). These are by far the most common. 2. Achondrites. These are stony meteorites without chondrules. 3. Stony irons. These are meteorites consisting of subequal amounts of silicate minerals and nickel-iron. 4. Irons. These are meteorites consisting of a nickel-iron alloy. A rare achondrite, called a shergottite, was found in 1979 at Elephant Moraine. Polymict eucrites are also rare finds in Antarctica. Some of these come from the moon. Frank Bickerton discovered the first meteorite in Antarctica, in 1912, during the AAE 1911–14. Between then and 1969 only 4 meteorite fragments were found in Antarctica. In 1969 Japanese scientists discovered 9 fragments in the Queen Fabiola Mountains. Since then over

4,000 fragments have been discovered in that area. In the Allan Hills, another profitable area for Antarctic meteorite hunters, scientists discovered 364 (one was 4–6 billion years old). Meteorites come from the moon, Mars or the asteroid belt, and the trick is to find out if they are single meteorites, or fragments of the same one.

Meteorology. A major scientific study in Antarctica, meteorology consists of temperatures, atmospheric pressures, precipitation, wind velocity and direction, and forecasting of the weather, the last being very difficult until recently due to the few reporting stations. Photography is aiding it tremendously.

Methuen Cove. 60°46'S, 44°33'W. Between Capes Anderson and Whitson on the south coast of Laurie Island in the South Orkneys. Charted in 1903 by Bruce, and named by him for H. Methuen, the expedition's accountant.

Metoppen *see* **Gap Nunatak**

Mount Metschel. 78°18'S, 159°E. 1,845 m. Ice-free. 4 miles SE of Angino Buttress and the Skelton Icefalls. Named for Cdr. John J. Metschel, USN, commander of the *Staten Island* in 1962 and 1963. He was killed in the Arctic, Oct. 15, 1963, while in a helicopter, doing ice reconnaissance from his ship.

Mount Meunier. 74°58'S, 113°19'W. On the coast of Marie Byrd Land.

Meusnier Point. 64°33'S, 61°38'W. 4 miles SE of Portal Point, within Charlotte Bay, on the west coast of Graham Land. Charted by de Gerlache in 1897–99. Named by the UK in 1960 for Jean-Baptiste-Marie Meusnier (1754–1793), French military engineer and aeronautics pioneer.

Meyer Desert. 85°08'S, 166°45'E. A triangular ice-free area of about 50 square miles at the north end of the Dominion Range, near the confluence of the Beardmore and Mill Glaciers. Named by the New Zealanders in 1961–62 for George Meyer, scientific leader at McMurdo Station in 1961. He led a field party into this area in 1961–62.

Meyer Hills. 79°47'S, 81°06'W. Between the Enterprise Hills and the head of Constellation Inlet, in the Heritage Range. Named by the University of Minnesota Ellsworth Mountains Party of 1962–63 for Harvey J. Meyer, geologist with that party.

Meyers Nunatak. 74°54'S, 98°46'W. 10 miles ESE of Mount Manthe, at the SE end of the Hudson Mountains. Named for Herbert Meyers, geomagnetist at Byrd Station, 1960–61.

Mezzo Buttress. 66°03'S, 64°31'W. At the head of Barilari Bay just east of Lawrie Glacier, on the west coast of Graham Land. Charted by the BGLE 1934–37. Named by the UK in 1959 because the face of this buttress is conspicuously divided diagonally, half of it being of black rock, the other half of red rock.

Mhire Spur. 79°33'S, 83°50'W. Descends from the heights around Mount Sporli to form the southern limit of the Larson Valley in the Heritage Range. Named for chief equipment operator Clifford J. Mhire, USN, responsible for supervising the movement of jet fuel from McMurdo Station to Williams Field in 1966.

Mica Islands. 69°20'S, 68°36'W. Four mainly ice-covered islands. 7 miles west of Mount Guernsey and 6 miles NE of Cape Jeremy, off the west coast of the Antarctic Peninsula. Discovered aerially in 1936 by the BGLE. Visited and surveyed in 1948 by the FIDS, who named them for the mica in the schists which form them.

Punta Micalvi *see* **Maurstad Point**

Michailoff's Island *see* **Cornwallis Island**

Michell, Dr. W.A.R. Canadian surgeon on the *Nimrod* during Shackleton's 1907–9 expedition.

Michelsen Island. 60°44'S, 45°02'W. Small island in the South Orkneys, joined to the southern end of Powell Island by a narrow isthmus of occasionally submerged boulders. Discovered by Powell and Palmer in Dec. 1821. Named before 1912–13 when Petter Sørlle listed it as such on his chart. It is part of Specially Protected Area #15.

Camp Michigan. 78°34'S, 163°57'18" W. A base at the edge of the Ross Ice Shelf for the Ross Ice Shelf Deformation Project during IGY. Established in Nov. 1957, it comprised a sledge-mounted wanigan and a prefabricated hut about 8 feet high. A couple of Weasels were part of the equipment. It was vacated in Feb. 1958. It was again occupied in the summer of 1958–59, and then revacated. It was visited and photographed in Dec. 1959. Heavy snow then buried it and it was visited again by the Ross Ice Shelf Survey Party in Jan. 1963. In Feb. 1972 the crew of the *Eltanin* saw something from their ship which they listed as X-72 (X the unknown). This is almost certainly the remains of Camp Michigan.

Michigan Plateau. 86°08'S, 133°30'W. Ice-covered. 30 miles long. 3,000 m. At the western side of the Reedy Glacier. The northern and eastern sides of the plateau are marked by the steep Watson Escarpment. The western and southern sides grade gently to the level of the interior ice. Named for the University of Michigan, at Ann Arbor, which has sent several parties to the Antarctic.

Michotte, Louis. Belgian sailor on the *Belgica* during de Gerlache's expedition of 1897–99.

Mickle Island. 77°34'S, 166°13'E. 1 mile SE of Flagstaff Point, just off the west side of Ross Island. Charted and named by Shackleton's 1907–9 expedition. Mickle means "great," and a joke is intended in the naming because the island is very small.

Mickler Spur. 85°49'S, 130°45'W. 4 miles long, and narrow. Forms the south wall of Hueneme Glacier in the western part of the Wisconsin Range. It terminates at Reedy Glacier. Named for Raymond R. Mickler, equipment operator at Byrd Station in 1961 and at McMurdo Station in 1964.

Mid Barrier Depot. Scott's depot at 81° 30'S, 170°04'E, during his last expedition.

Midas Island. 64°10'S, 61°07'W. Also called Isla José Hernández. NW of Apéndice Island in Hughes Bay, off the west coast of Graham Land. Discovered by de Gerlache in 1898 and described as an island with two summits like the ears of an ass. Named by the UK in 1960 for Midas, the mythical Phrygian king portrayed in Greek satyrical drama as having the ears of an ass.

Midbresrabben Hill. 72°44'S, 2°06' W. Isolated. Between the Penck Trough and Jutulstraumen Glacier, east of the Borg Massif in Queen Maud Land. Name means "the mid glacier ridge" in Norwegian.

Middle Crater. Between Ski Slope and Crater Hill at Hut Point, Ross Island.

Middle Crest *see* **Central Masson Range**

Middle Glacier *see* **Wiggins Glacier**

¹Middle Island. 61°58'S, 57°38'W. 1½ miles south of Foreland Island, and midway along the east coast of King George Island in the South Shetlands. Charted in 1937 by personnel on the *Discovery II*. They named it for its position.

²Middle Island *see* **Day Island**

³Middle Island. Legendary island in the Bransfield Strait, reported by sealers in the 19th century. Refuted by Dr. Gunnar Andersson in the *Antarctic* in 1902–3, during Nordenskjöld's expedition. It was probably an iceberg. Named for its position between the South Shetlands and the mainland.

Middle Mountain *see* **Mefjell Mountain**

Midge Lake. 62°38'S, 61°06'W. Tiny lake on Byers Peninsula, Livingston Island, in the South Shetlands. Named for its size.

Midges. Order: Diptera. There are two species in Antarctica (*see* **Fauna**). They are parasitic on seals and birds.

Midgley Island. 66°20′S, 110°24′E. Almost 1 mile long. Just south of Hollin Island in the Windmill Islands. Named for Lt. E.W. Midgley, Army Medical Corps observer on Operation Windmill.

Midgley Reefs. 66°20′S, 110°22′E. Several tidal and submerged rocks among the islands off the west side of Midgley Island in the Windmill Islands. Discovered from small craft from Wilkes Station in 1961. Named by the Australians in association with Midgley Island.

Midkiff Rock. 77°28′S, 145°06′W. Between Hammond and Swope Glaciers. On an ice-covered ridge 6 miles ESE of Mount West in the Ford Ranges of Marie Byrd Land. Named for Frank T. Midkiff, Jr., aviation machinist's mate, USN, helicopter flight crewman in Antarctica in 1968.

Mount Midnight. 71°56′S, 167°28′E. 2,000 m. On the north side of Tucker Glacier. 3½ miles west of Shadow Bluff in the Admiralty Mountains. Climbed by a geological team of the NZGSAE 1957–58, in Jan. 1958. Named by them in association with Mount Shadow, just to the east, and Shadow Bluff.

Midnight Plateau. 79°53′S, 156°15′E. Ice-covered, 2,200 m. The central feature of the Darwin Mountains. It is the only area of snow accumulation in these mountains. Discovered by the VUWAE 1962–63 and named by them because this plateau was visited by members of the expedition at midnight on Dec. 27, 1962.

Lake Midori. 69°01′S, 39°36′E. A small lake just NE of Lake Kamome, and just under ⅓ mile SE of Hachinosu Peak on East Ongul Island. Named Midori-ike (green pond) by the Japanese.

Midway Glacier. 72°10′S, 166°50′E. Also called Midway Island Glacier. Flows along the west side of Evans Ridge into Pearl Harbor Glacier in the Victory Mountains of Victoria Land. At the head it shares a common snow saddle with Jutland Glacier which flows north, while Midway Glacier flows south. Named by

the New Zealanders in 1962–63 following the motif in this area of famous naval battles.

Midway Island Glacier *see* **Midway Glacier**

Midwinters Day Message. Sent by the president of the USA to winterers in the Antarctic. This has been going on since Eisenhower did it in 1959, and the message, normally sent on June 21 or June 22, is now received by all stations operated by all countries. It is designed to boost morale, and demonstrate the interest of the American people in the Antarctic.

Lake Miers. 78°06′S, 163°51′E. A small lake in Miers Valley, 1 mile east of the snouts of Miers and Adams Glaciers. It is filled by meltwater from these glaciers. A stream from the lake flows down the valley during hot summers to reach the coast of Victoria Land. Named in 1957 by the NZ Blue Glacier Party of the BCTAE, in association with the glacier.

Miers Bluff. 62°43′S, 60°27′W. Also called Miers Point. Marks the south end of Hurd Peninsula which separates False Bay from South Bay on the south coast of Livingston Island in the South Shetlands. This feature was for many years erroneously called Elephant Point. Robert Fildes had named another feature in the area as Elephant Point, and somehow the name was given to this bluff. Things are now sorted out. The original Elephant Point is now called that again, and this feature was renamed for John Miers (1789–1879), British engineer and botanist who was responsible for the first published chart of the South Shetlands, based on the work of William Smith.

Miers Glacier. 78°05′S, 163°40′E. North of Terminus Mountain in Victoria Land. It occupies the upper (western) portion of Miers Valley, between Hobbs Glacier and Koettlitz Glacier. Mapped and named by members of Scott's 1910–13 expedition.

Miers Point *see* **Miers Bluff**

Miers Valley. 78°06′S, 164°E. Just south of Marshall Valley and west of

Koettlitz Glacier, on the coast of Victoria Land. It is ice-free except for Miers Glacier in its upper (western) part and Lake Miers near its center. Mapped and named by members of Scott's 1910–13 expedition.

Miethe Glacier. 64°56'S, 63°06'W. 3 miles long. Flows NW into Gerlache Strait to the south of Mount Banck on the west coast of Graham Land. Named by the UK in 1960 for Adolf Miethe (1862–1927), German photography pioneer.

Migley, William. Quarter-gunner on the Wilkes Expedition 1838–42. Joined in the USA. Served the cruise.

Migmatitovaya Rock. 71°47'S, 10°38' E. At the east end of a spur, 3 miles NE of Terletskiy Peak in the Shcherbakov Range of the Orvin Mountains in Queen Maud Land. Named Skala Migmatitovaya (migmatite rock) by the USSR in 1966.

Miharashi Peak. 69°S, 39°37'E. Also spelled Miharasi Peak. A hill 40 meters high. The highest point in the NE extremity of East Ongul Island. Named Miharashi-iwa (extensive view peak) by the Japanese.

Miharasi Peak *see* **Miharashi Peak**

Cape Miho *see* **Cape Akarui**

The *Mikhail Somov.* USSR supply ship of 7,400 tons, 450 feet long, sister ship of the *Kapitan Bondarenko.* Named for the leader of the USSR effort during the IGY (1956–58). Used on WEPOLEX 81 (the Weddell Polynya Expedition). In March 1985 it got trapped in the pack-ice while conducting the annual resupplying of Russkaya Station. By Aug. 3, 1985, it had been freed by the *Vladivostok.* In 1986–87 it freed the *Nella Dan* from the ice.

Cape Mikhaylov. 66°54'S, 118°32'E. An ice-covered point 42 miles east of Totten Glacier in Wilkes Land. Named by the USSR for Pavel Mikhaylov.

Mikhaylov, Pavel N. Artist on von Bellingshausen's expedition of 1819–21.

Mikhaylov Island. 66°48'S, 85°30'E. Ice-covered. In the West Ice Shelf. 240

m. 6 miles SE of Leskov Island. Discovered by the USSR in 1956, and named by them for Pavel Mikhaylov.

Mikheyeva Mountain *see* **Skeidshovden Mountain**

Mikkelsen, Caroline. Wife of Klarius Mikkelsen, she became the first woman on record to have set foot on the Antarctic continent when, on Feb. 20, 1935, she stepped ashore at the Vestfold Hills, spent a short time ashore, then went back to the *Thorshavn.*

Mikkelsen, Klarius. Norwegian whaling captain. In 1930–31 he commanded the *Torlyn* in Antarctic waters, and in 1933–34 was in command of the *Thorshavn.* In 1934–35 he took a fleet directed by Lars Christensen (the owner) to the Antarctic, he himself commanding the *Thorshavn* again. That year he discovered the Ingrid Christensen Coast, and named it for his boss' wife. He and his wife Caroline stepped ashore on Feb. 20, 1935, near today's Davis Station.

Mikkelsen, Otto. Norwegian diver who inspected the hull of the damaged *Pourquoi Pas?* belonging to Charcot when it pulled into the Norwegian whaling depot on Deception Island during the French expedition of 1908–10.

Mikkelsen Bay. 68°43'S, 67°10'W. 15 miles wide at the mouth. It indents 10 miles. Entered between Bertrand Ice Piedmont and Cape Berteaux on the west coast of Graham Land. Surveyed by the BGLE in 1936 and again by the FIDS in 1948–49. Named by the BGLE for Ejnar Mikkelsen, Danish Arctic explorer.

Mikkelsen Harbor. 63°54'S, 60°47'W. Also called Hoseason Harbor. A small bay indenting the south side of Trinity Island in the Palmer Archipelago, between Skottsberg and Borge Points. Discovered during Nordenskjöld's 1901–4 expedition. Named before 1913, possibly for Ejnar Mikkelsen (1880–1971), (*see* **Mikkelsen Bay**), or for Otto Mikkelsen.

Mikkelsen Island *see* **Watkins Island**

Mikkelsen Islands. 67°38'S, 68°11'W. Off the SE coast of Adelaide Island, 2 miles SE of the Léonie Islands. Discovered by Charcot in 1908–10, and named by him for Otto Mikkelsen.

Mikkelsen Peak. 67°47′S, 66°43′E. Also called Klarius Mikkelsen Fjell. 420 m. The highest peak of the Scullin Monolith in Mac. Robertson Land. Named by Norwegian whalers here in Jan. and Feb. 1931, for Klarius Mikkelsen.

Mikus Hill. 70°27′S, 63°50′W. Surmounts the SW wall of Richardson Glacier in Palmer Land. Named for Edward J. Mikus, USN, photographer of the cartographic aerial mapping crew in VX-6 Hercules aircraft in 1968–69.

Milan Ridge. 83°15′S, 156°08′E. Mostly ice-free. 5 miles long. Borders the west side of Ascent Glacier in the Miller Range. Named for Frederick M. Milan, physiologist at Little America, 1957.

Milan Rock. 76°01′S, 140°41′W. On the eastern edge of the Land Glacier, 2 miles SE of Mount Hartkopf, in Marie Byrd Land. It is the most southerly outcrop near the head of the glacier. Named for Frederick T. Milan, USN, aviation structural mechanic on VX-6 Hercules aircraft for several seasons in Antarctica. He was a crew member on the first midwinter flight to Antarctica, on June 25, 1964.

Milburn Bay. 63°44′S, 60°44′W. Indents the NW side of Trinity Island in the Palmer Archipelago. Named by the UK in 1960 for M.R. Milburn, air traffic control officer of the FIDASE, which photographed this area in 1955–57.

Mile High Plateau. Between Stonington Island and Cape Keeler, on the Antarctic Peninsula.

Miles Island. 66°04′S, 101°15′E. 3 miles long. Just north of Booth Peninsula in the Mariner Islands. Named for R.A. Miles, air crewman on Operation Highjump, 1946–47.

Milestone Bluff. 67°38′S, 68°45′W. 830 m. Just WSW of Mount Liotard, in the southern part of Adelaide Island. Named by the UK in 1964 because it is an important landmark on the inland route north of Base T.

Glacier du Milieu *see* **Wiggins Glacier**

Milky Way. 71°11′S, 68°55′W. A col between the southern part of the LeMay Range and Planet Heights. It is the highest point on a possible sledging route between Uranus and Jupiter Glaciers in the eastern part of Alexander Island. Named by the UK in association with the plethora of names astronomical in the area.

¹Mount Mill *see* **Mill Mountain**

²Mount Mill. 65°15′S, 64°03′W. Also called Mill Peak. 735 m. 2 miles west of Mount Balch on the NE shore of Waddington Bay, on the west coast of Graham Land. Charted by de Gerlache in 1897–99. Named by Charcot in 1908–10 for Hugh Robert Mill (*see* **Mill Cove**).

Mill Cove. 60°46′S, 44°35′W. Between Cape Anderson and Valette Island on the south coast of Laurie Island in the South Orkneys. Charted by Bruce in 1903, and named by him for Hugh Robert Mill (1861–1950), Scottish geographer and Antarctic historian, the eminence grise of his time in that subject, and possibly the most respected of all the Antarctic historians (*see* the Bibliography).

Mill Glacier. 85°10′S, 168°30′E. 10 miles wide. Flows NW between the Dominion Range and the Supporters Range into the Beardmore Glacier. Discovered during Shackleton's 1907–9 expedition and named by them for Hugh Robert Mill (*see* **Mill Cove**).

Mill Inlet. 67°S, 64°20′W. Also called Sullivan Inlet. Ice-filled. Recedes 8 miles in a NW direction. 20 miles wide at its entrance between Cape Robinson and Monnier Point, on the east coast of Graham Land. Charted by the FIDS in 1947 and named by them for Hugh Robert Mill (*see* **Mill Cove**).

Mill Island. 65°30′S, 100°40′E. Ice-domed. 25 miles long. 16 miles wide. 25 miles north of the Bunger Hills, and partly on the Shackleton Ice Shelf. Discovered in Feb. 1936 by personnel on the *William Scoresby,* and named by them for Hugh Robert Mill (*see* **Mill Cove**).

Mill Mountain. 79°26′S, 157°52′E. 2,730 m. Flat-topped. Forms the eastern end of Festive Plateau in the Cook Mountains. In 1901–4 Scott named a peak in nearby Reeves Bluffs as Mount Mill, for Hugh Robert Mill (*see* **Mill Cove**). Later surveys show no feature which could possibly be this Mount Mill. In 1965 the USA renamed and reapplied the Mill term to this nearby mountain.

¹**Mill Peak**   *see*   **Mount Mill**

²**Mill Peak.** 67°58′S, 61°08′E. 1,760 m. 10 miles south of Pearce Peak and 30 miles south of Cape Simpson. Discovered in Feb. 1931 by the BANZARE 1929–31, and named by Mawson for Hugh Robert Mill (*see* **Mill Cove**).

Mill Stream Glacier. 85°20′S, 171°E. 10 miles wide. Flows between the Supporters Range and the Otway Massif into Mill Glacier. Named by the New Zealanders in 1961–62 in association with Mill Glacier.

Millen Range. 72°20′S, 166°15′E. West of the Cartographers Range in the Victory Mountains of Victoria Land. Named by the NZ Federated Mountain Clubs Antarctic Expedition of 1962–63, for John M. Millen, leader of the expedition.

¹**Mount Miller.** 66°57′S, 51°16′E. 1 mile NW of Pythagoras Peak in the Tula Mountains of Enderby Land. Named by the Australians for J.J. Miller.

²**Mount Miller.** 83°20′S, 165°48′E. 4,160 m. In the Holland Range, 7 miles south of Mount Lloyd. Discovered and named by Shackleton's 1907–9 expedition.

Miller, David. Ordinary seaman on the Wilkes Expedition 1838–42. Joined in the USA. Returned in the *Relief* in 1839.

Miller, J.H. "Bob." NZ surveyor (b. 1919), now known as Sir Holmes Miller. Right name: Joseph Holmes Miller. Second-in-command, under Hillary, of the NZ team during the BCTAE 1955–58. He was leader/surveyor of the Northern Party of the NZGSAE 1963–64, and traveled over 3,000 miles by sledge throughout Oates Land. He was chair-

man of the Ross Dependency Research Committee from 1970–83, and president of the NZ Antarctic Society from 1960–63.

Miller, J.J. Crew member on the *Discovery* during the BANZARE 1929–31.

Miller, Jack. Seaman on the Wilkes Expedition 1838–42. Joined at the Sandwich Islands. Served the cruise.

Miller, Linwood T. Sailmaker in the shore party on Byrd's 1933–35 expedition.

Miller, Michael. Ordinary seaman on the Wilkes Expedition 1838–42. Joined in the USA. Died at sea, Aug. 15, 1839.

Miller, Walfred. Crewman on the *Bear of Oakland*, 1933–35.

Miller, William. Ordinary seaman on the Wilkes Expedition 1838–42. Joined in the USA. Lost in the *Sea Gull* on April 29, 1839.

Miller Bluffs. 77°35′S, 85°45′W. 15 miles long. Extend WNW from the mouth of Newcomer Glacier in the Sentinel Range. Named for George P. Miller, former chairman of the House Science and Astronautics Committee, who was a great friend of US involvement in the Antarctic from 1958–72.

Miller Butte. 72°42′S, 160°15′E. 2 miles SE of Roberts Butte in the Outback Nunataks. Named for Carl D. Miller, geophysicist at McMurdo Station, 1967–68.

Miller Crag. 73°40′S, 94°42′W. 1,450 m. 3 miles WSW of Sutley Peak in the western extremity of the Jones Mountains. Named by the University of Minnesota–Jones Mountains Party of 1960–61 for Thomas P. Miller, geologist with the party.

Miller Glacier. 77°12′S, 162°E. 1 mile wide. Grif Taylor described it as a transection glacier lying in a transverse trough and connecting the Cotton and Debenham Glaciers in Victoria Land. Discovered by Taylor's Western Geological Party of 1910–13, and named by Taylor for M.J. Miller, mayor of Lyttelton, NZ, and the shipwright who repaired the *Terra Nova* before it left NZ.

Miller Heights. 66°01'S, 65°14'W. They extend eastward from Sharp Peak, on the west coast of Graham Land. Charted by the BGLE in 1934-37. Named by the UK for Ronald Miller, FIDS general assistant at Base W in 1956 and at Base J in 1957.

Miller Ice Rise. 69°05'S, 67°38'W. On the west side of the Antarctic Peninsula.

Miller Island. 64°54'S, 63°59'W. 1 mile NE of Knight Island in the Wauwermans Islands in the Wilhelm Archipelago. Named by the UK in 1958 for the *Canterbury Tales* character.

Miller Nunatak. 74°26'S, 164°15'E. At the lower end of Campbell Glacier. 5 miles ESE of Mount Dickason, in Victoria Land. Named for Herman T. Miller, biologist at McMurdo Station, 1965-66.

Miller Nunataks. 67°02'S, 55°11'E. 11 miles SW of Mount Storegutt in Enderby Land. Named by the Australians for K.R. Miller, weather observer at Mawson Station in 1962.

¹Miller Peak. 70°59'S, 162°53'E. 2,420 m. 2 miles south of Mount Ford in the Explorers Range of the Bowers Mountains. Explored by the Northern Party of the NZGSAE 1963-64, and named by them for J.H. "Bob" Miller.

²Miller Peak. 78°49'S, 84°14'W. Has twin summits. On the central part of the ridge between Hudman and Carey Glaciers, at the south end of the Sentinel Range. Named for Charles S. Miller, USN, aviation electronics technician (*see* **Deaths, 1956**).

Miller Point. 68°56'S, 63°23'W. A black, rock cape. 250 m. Forms the north side of the entrance to Casey Inlet, on the east coast of Palmer Land. Discovered aerially by Wilkins on Dec. 20, 1928, and named by him for George E. Miller of Detroit.

Miller Range. 83°15'S, 157°E. Extends south from Nimrod Glacier for 50 miles

along the western edge of the Marsh Glacier. Named for J.H. "Bob" Miller by the New Zealanders.

Miller Ridge. 70°08'S, 65°30'E. 1 mile east of Mount Seedsman on the north side of the Athos Range in the Prince Charles Mountains. Named by the Australians for L.D. Miller, radio operator at Mawson Station, 1964.

Miller Spur. 75°07'S, 137°29'W. Ice-covered. Descends NE from Mount Giles, near the coast of Marie Byrd Land. It terminates in a small rock bluff 1 mile west of the lower part of the Hull Glacier. Discovered aerially on Dec. 18, 1940, by the USAS. Later named for Linwood T. Miller.

Miller Valley. 83°39'S, 55°14'W. Dry valley between Drury Ridge and Brown Ridge in the Neptune Range of the Pensacola Mountains. Named for Lt. Donald R. Miller, VX-6 pilot, 1963-64.

Cap Millerand *see* **Millerand Island**

Millerand Island. 68°09'S, 67°13'W. Also called Cap Millerand. 3 miles across. 4 miles south of Cape Calmette, off the west coast of Graham Land. Discovered by Charcot in 1908-10, and named by him for the French statesman, Alexandre Millerand (1859-1943).

Milles Nunatak. 70°55'S, 160°06'E. 3 miles NE of Howell Peak at the north end of the Daniels Range in the Usarp Mountains. Named for David B. Milles, biolab technician at McMurdo Station, 1967-68.

Millett, Hugh M. Chief engineer on the *Penola* during the BGLE 1934-37.

Millett Glacier. 70°37'S, 67°40'W. Heavily crevassed. 13 miles long. 7 miles wide. Flows from the Dyer Plateau of Palmer Land into the George VI Sound, just north of Wade Point. In its lower reaches it merges with Meiklejohn Glacier. Surveyed in 1936 by the BGLE. Named in 1954 by the UK for Hugh M. Millett.

Millington Glacier. 84°32'S, 178°E. 10 miles long. Flows from the eastern slopes of the Hughes Range into Ramsey Glacier, northward of Mount Valinski. Named for Lt. Cdr. Richard E. Millington, USN, medical officer during Operation Deep Freeze 63 and 64.

The *Mills*. US ship DER-383, weather reporting on ocean station duty at 60°S, for several seasons in the 1960s. Cdr. Henry C. Morris, Jr., was captain 1964–66, and Lt. Cdr. Joseph A. Felt 1966–68. H. King Triplett was ensign on the 1966–67 cruise, and combat information center officer on the 1967–68 cruise.

Mount Mills. 85°12′S, 165°17′E. 2,955 m. Forms part of the northern escarpment of the Dominion Range, overlooking the Beardmore Glacier. 8 miles north of Mount Saunders. Discovered during Shackleton's 1907–9 expedition and named by them for Sir James Mills who, with the NZ Government, paid for the towing of the *Nimrod* to the Antarctic by the *Koonya*.

Mills Peak. 74°14′S, 163°54′E. 1,420 m. In the Deep Freeze Range. On the west side of Campbell Glacier between Mount Queensland and the terminus of Bates Glacier in Victoria Land. Named for Peter J. Mills, geologist at McMurdo Station, 1965–66.

Mills Valley. 73°06′S, 163°12′E. Ice-filled. Indents the east side of Pain Mesa, between Biretta Peak and the Diversion Hills, in the Mesa Range of Victoria Land. Named for Cdr. Norman J. Mills, USNR, officer-in-charge of the Detachment A winter party at McMurdo Station, 1967.

Milnes Island. 65°35′S, 65°02′W. 2 miles north of Woolpack Island, in the Biscoe Islands. Charted by the BGLE 1934–37. Named by the UK in 1959 for Leading Seaman Arthur R. Milnes, RN, member of the British Naval Hydrographic Survey Units here in 1956–57 and 1957–58.

Mount Milton. 78°48′S, 84°48′W. 3,000 m. 11 miles SSE of Mount Craddock and 1½ miles SE of Mount Southwick, in the southern part of the Sentinel Range.

Named for Patrick G. Milton, USN, aviation machinist's mate, and plane captain on a reconnaissance flight to these mountains on Jan. 28, 1958.

Milward, C.A. Chief officer on the *William Scoresby*, 1930–32.

Mimas Peak. 71°56′S, 69°36′W. 1,000 m. West of the head of Saturn Glacier and 9 miles west of Dione Nunataks in the SE part of Alexander Island. Discovered aerially by Ellsworth on Nov. 23, 1935. Named by the UK for the satellite of the planet Saturn.

Mime Glacier. 77°37′S, 161°45′E. At the southern (upper) end of Tiw Valley in the Asgard Range of Victoria Land. Named by the New Zealanders for the smith in Norse mythology.

Mims Spur. 86°02′S, 125°35′W. Juts out from the southern extremity of the Wisconsin Plateau, just SE of Polygon Spur on the north side of McCarthy Glacier. Named for Julius E. Mims, Jr., radioman at Byrd Station, 1962.

Caleta Mina de Cobre *see* **Coppermine Cove**

Lake Minami. 69°01′S, 39°35′E. Just south of Lake Tarachine in the southern part of East Ongul Island. Named Minami-ike (south pond) for its small size, by the Japanese.

Mount Minami-heito. 69°17′S, 39°48′E. 480 m. Surmounts the SE extremity of the Langhovde Hills on the Queen Maud Land coast. Named Minami-heito-zan (south flat-top mountain) by the Japanese in association with Mount Heito just to the north.

Minami-karamete Rock. 69°13′S, 35°26′E. 9 miles south of Kita-karamete Rock in the eastern part of the Riiser-Larsen Peninsula of Queen Maud Land. Named Minami-karamete-iwa (south back gate rock) by the Japanese in 1972.

Minamino-seto Strait. 69°02′S, 39°33′E. Between Ongul Island and the Te Islands in the Flatvaer Islands. Photographed by the LCE 1936–37. Named Minamino-seto (southern strait) by the Japanese.

Minamo Island. 69°39'S, 39°37'E. The largest of several small islands in the narrow inlet between Skallen Glacier and the Skallen Hills, on the Queen Maud Land coast. Named by the Japanese in 1972.

The Minaret. 64°46'S, 63°39'W. 1,065 m. A steep rock pinnacle on the ridge extending NE from Mount William in the southern part of Anvers Island. Surveyed by the UK in 1944 and 1955, and named by them for its shape.

Minaret Nunatak. 72°42'S, 162°10'E. 2,115 m. 1 mile west of Burkett Nunatak, in the Monument Nunataks. Named for its shape by the New Zealanders in 1962–63.

Minaret Peak. 80°15'S, 82°22'W. At the NW end of the Marble Hills in the Heritage Range. Named by the University of Minnesota Ellsworth Mountains Party of 1962–63 for its shape.

Mincey, A.V. US marine master sergeant, radio operator on Flight 8A during Byrd's Feb. 16, 1947, flight to the Pole during Operation Highjump (*see* **South Pole**).

Mincey Glacier. 84°57'S, 177°30'W. 10 miles long. Flows from the southern slopes of Anderson Heights in the Bush Mountains, then SE into the Shackleton Glacier at Thanksgiving Point. Discovered aerially during Byrd's flights to the Pole on Feb. 16, 1947. Named for A.V. Mincey.

Mineral exploitation. The search for minerals was an incentive of the early explorers, the first samples being brought back to the USA by B. Astor. These were quartz, amethysts, porphyry, Rouen onyx, flint, zealite, pumice stone, and pyrites. Over the years other minerals have been found—coal, chromium, copper, zinc, lead, tin, molybdenum, gold, titanium, antimony, but none of these have yet been found in economically feasible quantities. There are indications of high concentrations of ferro-manganese nodules on the floor of the South Eastern Pacific, and the Scotia Sea, particularly beneath the Antarctic Convergence, and it looks as if sedimentary phosphate exists in Antarctica. If the minerals discovered in the future warrant mining, and it becomes economically viable, and it could prove disastrous for Antarctica ecologically. Because of this frightening prospect, an international regime for the exploration and exploitation of mineral resources became a pressing demand in the 1980s.

Mineral Hill. 63°29'S, 57°03'W. 445 m. Round-topped. It has ice-free, talus-covered slopes. 1½ miles west of Trepassey Bay on Tabarin Peninsula. Charted by the FIDS in 1946, and named by them for the small quantities of reddish-colored mineral in the rock.

Minerals *see* **Mineral exploitation**

¹The *Minerva*. British sealer from London, in the South Shetlands for the 1820–21 season. Capt. Binn commanding.

²The *Minerva*. One of the whale catchers from the British whaling factory ship the *Pythia*. It went aground on the Minerva Rocks, off Chionis Island in the Palmer Archipelago in March 1922. It was abandoned, and because of the heavy swell, became a total wreck.

Minerva Rocks. 63°53'S, 60°37'W. Off Chionis Island near Trinity Island in the Palmer Archipelago. Named by British whalers for the *Minerva*, the whale catcher of the 1920s.

The *Ministro Ezcurra*. Argentine ship on the first two postwar expeditions which that country sent to the Antarctic. In 1946–47 the captain was Vinquales, and in 1947–48 it was Luís E. Reynaud.

Rocas Ministro Ezcurra *see* **Sewing-Machine Needles**

Mink Peak. 86°14'S, 129°56'W. 2 miles north of Cleveland Mesa at the east end of the Watson Escarpment. Named for Harold D. Mink, utilitiesman at Byrd Station in 1962 and 1966.

Minke. *Balaenoptera acutorostrata*, or *Balaenoptera bonaerensis*. Another name for the lesser rorqual, a whale that frequents Antarctic waters. The smallest of the rorquals (or whalebone whales), it is just over 30 feet long, and was named for the Norwegian whaler, *Miencke*. In 1964–65 only 6 were taken in the Antarctic. In 1972–73, 5,745 were taken.

Minna Bluff. 78°31′S, 166°25′E. A 3,000 foot-high peninsula, 25 miles long and 3 miles wide, jutting out into the western Ross Ice Shelf from the SE foot of Mount Discovery. 46 miles south of McMurdo Station. Discovered during Scott's 1901–4 expedition, and named by Scott for Minna, wife of Sir Clements Markham (*see* **Mount Markham**).

Minna Saddle. 78°26′S, 165°33′E. A sweeping snow saddle, several miles long and wide, at the junction of Minna Bluff and the eastern slopes of Mount Discovery. Named by the NZ party of the BCTAE in 1957 in association with Minna Bluff.

Minnehaha Icefalls. 77°02′S, 162°24′ E. Heavily crevassed icefall. Flows from the steep western slopes of Mount England and forms a southern tributary to the New Glacier, just west of its terminus at Granite Harbor in Victoria Land. Charted and named by Frank Debenham while a part of Grif Taylor's Western Geological Party during Scott's 1910–13 expedition.

Camp Minnesota. 73°30′S, 94°30′W. At Basecamp Valley in the Jones Mountains. This was a Jamesway hut installed in Nov. 1961 for USARP use by the University of Minnesota–Jones Mountains Party of 1961–62.

Minnesota Glacier. 79°S, 83°W. 40 miles long. 5 miles wide. Flows east through the Ellsworth Mountains and separates the Sentinel and Heritage Ranges. It is fed by ice from the plateau west of the mountains and by the Nimitz and Splettstoesser Glaciers. It merges into the Rutford Ice Stream at the eastern edge of the Ellsworth Mountains. Named for the University of Minnesota, at Minneapolis, which sent major research parties to the Ellsworth Mountains in 1961–62, 1962–63, and 1963–64.

The Minnows. 66°01′S, 65°23′W. East of Flounder Island in the Fish Islands, off the west coast of Graham Land. Charted by the BGLE 1934–37. Named by the UK in 1959 because of its location in the Fish Islands.

Minot Point. 64°16′S, 62°31′W. Also called Cabo Pirámide. On the west coast of Brabant Island, in the Palmer Archipelago. 3 miles west of the summit of Mount Parry. Named by the UK for George R. Minot (1885–1950), US physician and Nobel Prize winner for his work on liver therapy in pernicious anemia.

Mount Minshew. 85°43′S, 129°22′W. Mostly ice-covered. 3,895 m. 3½ miles west of Faure Peak at the NW end of the elevated plateau part of the Wisconsin Range in the Horlick Mountains. Named for Velon H. Minshew, geologist with the Ohio State University geological party here in 1964–65.

The *Minstrel*. British sealer from London, in the South Shetlands in the 1820–21 season. Capt. MacGregor commanding.

Minstrel Point. 61°04′S, 55°25′W. Between Capes Lindsey and Yelcho on the west coast of Elephant Island in the South Shetlands. Named by the Joint Services Expedition of 1970–71 for the *Minstrel*.

Mount Minto. 71°47′S, 168°45′E. 4,165 m. Mostly ice-free. 2½ miles east of Mount Adam in the central part of the Admiralty Mountains. Discovered in Jan. 1841 by Ross, who named it for the Earl of Minto, first lord of the admiralty.

Mintz Peak. 76°53′S, 126°03′W. In the SE corner of Mount Hartigan in the Executive Committee Range of Marie Byrd Land. Named for Jerome Mintz, meteorological electronics technician at Byrd Station in 1959.

Mirabilite Pond. 78°11′S, 163°56′E. An alkali pond at a high elevation in the southern part of Hidden Valley, west of Koettlitz Glacier. It is on the north side of the ridge which bounds the SE part of the valley. Troy L. Péwé, the geologist, found mirabilite here in 1957–58.

Mirabito Range. 71°40′S, 165°27′E. 40 miles long. 4 miles wide. Trends NW. Between the upper part of Lillie Glacier and the Greenwell Glacier in northern Victoria Land. Named for Lt. Cdr. John A. Mirabito, USN, staff meteorological officer in Antarctica, 1955–56, 1956–57, 1957–58, and 1958–59.

Mirage Island. 66°48′S, 141°27′E. ¼ mile long. Almost a third of a mile west of Cape Mousse. Charted in 1950 by the French and named Île des Mirages for the mirages often seen here.

Mirages. Phenomena produced by rays of light refracted on superimposed layers of hot and cold air. They are images of things, those things being in a place different from the place of the images. They can be well defined and very clear, or they can be blurred and elongated (this is called looming). They have led to many errors in navigation and exploration (notably by Wilkes, Scott and Amundsen). (*See also* **Phenomena**).

Île des Mirages *see* **Mirage Island**

Miranda Nunataks *see* **Miranda Peaks**

Miranda Peaks. 71°28′S, 68°36′W. Also called Miranda Nunataks. A line of half a dozen peaks trending north-south on the south side of Uranus Glacier, in the eastern part of Alexander Island. Named by the UK for the moon of the planet Uranus.

Mirazh Mountain. 71°18′S, 13°25′E. 1,485 m. On the north-central part of Steinmulen Shoulder in the Gruber Mountains of Queen Maud Land. Discovered aerially during Ritscher's 1938–39 expedition. Named Gora Mirazh (Mirage Mountain) by the USSR in 1966.

The *Mirfak*. US Navy supply ship in at McMurdo Station in 1963, and again during the 1970s.

Mirfak Nunatak. 81°58′S, 156°05′E. Near the Polar Plateau, 10 miles SW of Vance Bluff. Named for the *Mirfak*.

The Mirnyy. Russian corvette of 528 tons, designed by Kolodkin, built of pinewood and commanded by Lazarev during the von Bellingshausen expedition of 1819–21. Older and slower than the flagship, the *Vostok*, it somewhat hindered the progress of the expedition (the name means "peaceful"). It had 72 people on board. On Jan. 20, 1820, 7 days before the expedition sighted the Antarctic continent (or the shelf ice, at least), the *Mirnyy* collided with a berg, and only on its return to Sydney was there found a three-foot hole in the hull. The interior canvas lining was the only thing holding the water out.

Mirnyy Peak. 69°20′S, 72°34′W. 750 m. 4 miles NE of Enigma Peak in the northern part of Rothschild Island. Named by the UK for the *Mirnyy*.

Mirnyy Station. 66°33′S, 93°01′E. The USSR's first station in Antarctica, it was opened on Feb. 13, 1956, on the Queen Mary Land coast. Designed by A.M. Afnasyev, its main street was in 1989 called Lenin Street, and is 200 yards long. Mikhail Somov was the first leader, in 1956, and A.F. Treshnikov succeeded him for the 1957 winter. It was USSR's main station until 1972 when Molodezhnaya took over. G.I. Greku was the station's first elected mayor.

Mount Mirotvortsev. 71°50′S, 12°17′E. 2,830 m. 1½ miles NE of Mount Neustruyev in the Südliche Petermann Range of the Wohlthat Mountains. Discovered aerially by the Ritscher expedition of 1938–39. Named in 1966 by the USSR for geographer and explorer K.N. Mirotvortsev (1880–1950).

Mirounga Flats. 60°42′S, 45°36′W. A small, partly enclosed tidal area in the inner, NW corner of Borge Bay, Signy Island, in the South Orkneys. Its eastern limit is formed by the Thule Islands, and its northern and western limits by Signy Island itself. The tidal area dries at low water. Surveyed in 1933 by Discovery Investigations personnel, and again in 1947 by the FIDS, who named it for the elephant seals *(Mirounga leonina)* found here in large numbers during the molting period.

Mirsky Ledge. 84°37'S, 111°40'W. Snow-covered. A shelflike feature about 10 miles NE of Mount Schopf in the Ohio Range. Urbanak Peak and Iversen Peak rise above the ledge which seems to be the NE extremity of the Horlick Mountains. Named for Arthur Mirsky, assistant director of the Institute of Polar Studies at Ohio State University, which sent researchers to the Horlicks in the period between 1958–62.

The *Mirzak.* US cargo vessel supplying McMurdo Station in 1963. Captain that year was B. Senia.

The *Mischief.* 45-foot pilot cutter skippered by Bill Tilman, which reached the South Shetlands in 1966 (*see also* **Tilman Ridge**).

Misery Peak. 85°31'S, 178°16'W. 2,725 m. At the extreme west side of Roberts Massif. It is occupied as a survey station. Named by the Southern Party of the NZGSAE 1961–62 for the many miserable hours spent here while waiting for the clouds to pass.

Misery Trail. Nickname for the trail forged by Finn Ronne from the Ross Ice Shelf in 1933 during Byrd's 1933–35 expedition.

The *Misiones.* Destroyer on Argentine naval maneuvers, in the South Shetlands in 1948 under the overall command of Contra-Almirante Harald Cappus.

Misnomer Point. 62°22'S, 59°42'W. Just north of Carlota Cove on the west coast of Robert Island in the South Shetlands. Named by the UK in 1971. For years this was erroneously called Cornwall Point (*see* **Cornwall Island**).

The *Miss American Airways.* The Pilgrim single-engine monoplane — NC74N — taken by Byrd on his expedition of 1933–35. It returned home to the USA at the end of the expedition.

Missen Ridge. 70°41'S, 166°24'E. Ice-covered. South of the Davis Ice Piedmont. It extends along the peninsula of which Cape Hooker is the NE point, on the northern coast of Victoria Land. Named by the ANARE for R. Missen, weather technician on the ANARE cruise on the *Thala Dan* along this coast in 1962.

Mission Island *see* **Masson Island**

Mission Rock. 67°49'S, 68°25'W. SW of the Guébriant Islands, off the SW end of Adelaide Island. Named by the UK in 1963 in association with the Guébriant Islands, themselves named for the missionary Père Guébriant.

Mist Rocks. 66°48'S, 66°37'W. Rocks in water NW of Holdfast Point at the entrance to Lallemand Fjord in Graham Land. Discovered on Aug. 21, 1956, by the first FIDS party sledging north from Base W. The FIDS group was searching in the mist for a secure camp site.

Mistake Peak. 77°26'S, 160°13'E. 2,600 m. 3 miles WSW of Shapeless Mountain, at the south end of the Willett Range in Victoria Land. Named by the NZ Northern Survey Party of the BCTAE in 1957 because they climbed it in the mistaken belief that they were climbing Shapeless Mountain.

Misthound Cirque. 79°46'S, 156°12'E. A large embayment in the east side of Haskell Ridge in the Darwin Mountains. Named by the New Zealanders in 1962–63 for the hound-shaped boulders lying on the mist-filled floor of this dramatic place.

Mistichelli Hills. 70°02'S, 72°52'E. 1 mile SW of McKaskle Hills on the eastern edge of the Amery Ice Shelf. Named by US cartographer John H. Roscoe in 1952 for G. Mistichelli, air crewman on Operation Highjump, 1946–47, during which time the photos were taken from which Roscoe prepared his maps 5 years later.

Mistral Ridge. 69°33'S, 68°04'W. On the west side of the Antarctic Peninsula.

Misty Mountain *see* **Mount Elder**

Misty Pass. 63°29'S, 57°59'W. 700 m. Between the head of Broad Valley and a valley descending north to Bransfield Strait, 8 miles SE of Cape Ducorps on

Trinity Peninsula. Mapped by the FIDS in 1946 and named by them for the misty clouds rolling east through the pass to signal bad weather ahead.

Mount Mitchell. 82°43'S, 165°36'E. 1,820 m. 5 miles SW of Cape Goldie in the northern part of the Holland Range. Named for Cdr. G.W. Mitchell, captain of the *Burton Island* in 1964.

Mitchell, G.M. Crewman on the *Jacob Ruppert*, 1933–35.

Mitchell, George. Quartermaster on the Wilkes Expedition 1838–42. Joined at Valparaiso. Served the cruise.

Mitchell, John. Ordinary seaman on the Wilkes Expedition 1838–42. Joined at Rio. Served the cruise.

Mitchell Island *see* **Mitchell Peninsula**

Mitchell Nunatak. 70°58'S, 71°30'E. The central of three nunataks in the northern part of the Manning Nunataks. Named by the Australians for R. Mitchell, senior diesel mechanic at Mawson Station in 1969.

Mitchell Peak. 76°25'S, 147°22'W. 13 miles west of Birchall Peaks on the south side of Guest Peninsula in Marie Byrd Land. Discovered aerially by Byrd on Dec. 5, 1929, and named by Byrd for Hugh C. Mitchell, mathematician who ascertained that Byrd had actually flown over the North and South Poles.

Mitchell Peninsula. 66°20'S, 110°32'E. 2½ miles long. 2 miles wide. Between O'Brien Bay and Sparkes Bay at the east side of the Windmill Islands. At first thought to be an island, and called Mitchell Island for Ray A. Mitchell, captain of the *Cacapon* during Operation Highjump, 1946–47. In 1957 personnel from Wilkes Station redefined it.

Mitchell Point. 64°13'S, 62°03'W. At the south side of the entrance to Hill Bay on the east coast of Brabant Island. Named by the UK for S. Weir Mitchell (1829–1914), US novelist.

Mitchells Island *see* **Robert Island**

Mite Skerry. 67°52'S, 67°19'W. Also called Islote Sur. A small island in the southern part of the entrance to Lystad Bay, off Horseshoe Island. Named for its size by the UK in 1958.

Mites. Order: Acarina. There are 67 nonparasitic species in Antarctica, living under stones, and associated with spore-reproducing plants (*see* **Fauna**).

Isla Mitre *see* **Lavoisier Island**

Mitsudomoe Islands. 69°57'S, 38°45'E. Also spelled Mitudomoe Islands. Three small islands close together, 1 mile west of Strandnebba in the SE extremity of Lützow-Holm Bay. Named Mitsudomoe-shima (commas-which-have-been-joined-together-to-form-a-circle island).

Mitsui. A member of the Dash Patrol during Shirase's expedition of 1910–12.

The Mitten. 75°59'S, 160°30'E. Bare, flat-topped mountain. Looks like a mitten when seen from above. 3 miles NW of Mount Armytage in Victoria Land. Named for its shape by the New Zealanders in 1962–63.

Mittens *see* **Gloves**

Mitterling Glacier. 66°50'S, 64°18'W. On the east coast of Graham Land, it flows between Mount Vartdal and Mount Hayes into the northern part of Mill Inlet. Named by the UK for Philip I. Mitterling, US historian (*see* the Bibliography).

Mittlere Petermann Range. 71°30'S, 12°28'E. One of the Petermann Ranges. It extends north-south for 17 miles from Johnson Peaks to Store Svarthorn Peak, in the Wohlthat Mountains of Queen Maud Land. Discovered aerially by Ritscher's 1938–39 expedition, and named by them for its middle (mittlere) position in the northern part of the Petermann Ranges.

Mitudomoe Islands *see* **Mitsudomoe Islands**

Mixon Rocks. 76°43'S, 159°23'E. 2½ miles west of Gadarene Ridge in the Allan Hills of Victoria Land. Named by the NZ Antarctic Research Project Allan

Hills Expedition for Lt. William A. Mixon, US Navy medical officer at McMurdo Station who treated an injured member of the expedition.

Miyoda Cliff. 68°22'S, 65°05'W. On the east coast of Graham Land.

The *Mizar.* US cargo vessel which helped supply McMurdo Station in 1962. Captain B. Senia.

Mizar Nunataks. 81°52'S, 154°35'E. 12 miles south of Wilhoite Nunataks, near the Polar Plateau. Named for the *Mizar.*

Mizir, Thomas. 1st class boy on the Wilkes Expedition 1838–42. Joined at Tahiti. Served the cruise.

Mizuho Plateau. 71°30'S, 39°E. Ice-plateau east of the Queen Fabiola Mountains and south of the Shirase Glacier in Queen Maud Land. Named by the Japanese in 1961, first as Japan Highland, and then renamed for one of the old names for Japan.

Mizuho Station. 70°42'S, 44°19'E. The second Japanese year-round station in Antarctica. It is further inside Enderby Land than is Showa Station. It studies glaciology and meteorology.

Mizukuguri Cove. 69°11'S, 39°38'E. In the east side of Lützow-Holm Bay, Queen Maud Land. It indents the western shore of the Langhovde Hills ½ mile west of Mount Choto. In Feb. 1968 members of the Japanese Antarctic Research Expedition (JARE) scuba-dived here. Named Mizukuguri-ura (diving-cove) by the Japanese in 1972.

Mizukumi Stream. 69°S, 39°35'E. A small meltwater stream 175 yards north of Hachinosu Peak on East Ongul Island. Named Mizukumi-zawa (water-drawing stream) by the Japanese.

Mjell Glacier. 72°07'S, 26°06'E. 9 miles long. Flows between Mount Bergersen and Isachsen Mountain in the Sør Rondane Mountains. Named Mjellbreen (the dry snow glacier) by the Norwegians.

Mjøllføykje Bluff. 73°32'S, 3°45'W. At the east side of Belgen Valley, in the Kirwan Escarpment of Queen Maud Land. Named by the Norwegians.

Mjøllkvaevane Cirques. 71°53'S, 14°27'E. A series of small snow-filled cirques which indent the eastern side of the Kvaevefjellet Mountain in the Payer Mountains of Queen Maud Land. Named by the Norwegians.

Moawhango Névé. 72°15'S, 163°34'E. Between Mount Camelot and Monte Cassino in the Freyberg Mountains. Named by the New Zealanders in 1967–68 for a locality of the same name in NZ.

Mount Moberly. 64°44'S, 63°41'W. 1,535 m. Snow-covered. At the end of the ridge extending SW from Mount Français in the southern part of Anvers Island. It is separated from Mount William to the south by the col at the head of Hooper Glacier. In 1832 John Biscoe discovered a mountain in this area and named it for Capt. John Moberly, RN. Subsequent expeditions could not find this mountain, but later, the FIDS identified it.

Mobiloil Bay *see* **Mobiloil Inlet**

Mobiloil Inlet. 68°35'S, 64°45'W. Formerly called Mobiloil Bay. Ice-filled indentation into the Larsen Ice Shelf on the east coast of the Antarctic Peninsula. Between Rock Pile Peaks and Hollick-Kenyon Peninsula, just west of Cape Agassiz. Discovered aerially by Wilkins on Dec. 20, 1928, and named by him for the product of the Vacuum Oil Co. of Australia.

Mock Suns *see* **Phenomena**

Moe, M. Thoralf. A whaling captain from Sandefjord, Norway, in the South Orkneys 1912–13 as captain of the *Tioga.* He surveyed the west coast of Signy Island.

Moe Island. 60°45'S, 45°42'W. About ⅝ mile by ⅝ mile. Separated from the SW end of Signy Island by the Fyr Channel in the South Orkneys. It is Specially Protected Area (SPA) #13. Named probably for M. Thoralf Moe.

Moe Point. 70°19'S, 62°23'W. Just south of Croom Glacier on the NW side of Smith Inlet in Palmer Land. Named for Richard Moe, biologist at Palmer Station in 1974.

Moewik. Norwegian captain of the whale catcher *Star V*, during the 1923–24 *Sir James Clark Ross* expedition.

Mount Moffat. 83°32'S, 55°17'W. 1,250 m. 4 miles NE of Mount Ege in the Neptune Range of the Pensacola Mountains. Named for Robert J. Moffat, construction electrician at Ellsworth Station, 1958.

Moffet Glacier. 85°52'S, 161°W. 13 miles long. Flows from the Rawson Plateau into Amundsen Glacier just south of Mount Benjamin in the Queen Maud Mountains. Discovered aerially by Byrd during his South Polar flight of Nov. 28–29, 1929, and named by him for Rear Adm. William A. Moffet, USN, first chief of the Bureau of Aeronautics, Department of the Navy.

Mount Mogensen. 77°34'S, 85°50'W. 2,790 m. Snow-covered. 5 miles NE of Mount Ulmer in the northern part of the Sentinel Range. Discovered aerially by Ellsworth on Nov. 23, 1935. Named for Palle Mogensen.

Mogensen, Palle. Took over from Paul Siple as scientific leader at South Pole Station on Nov. 30, 1957. He remained the rest of the summer.

Isla Mogote *see* **Hummock Island**

Islotes Mohai *see* **Sewing-Machine Needles**

Mohaupt Point. 66°04'S, 100°47'E. The eastern point of Currituck Island in the Highjump Archipelago. The name Mohaupt Island was given by the USA in 1956 to the northern part of Currituck Island, and the two were thought to be two islands. The USSR in 1956–57 found that the so-called Mohaupt Island was in fact part of Currituck Island, and the USA did some redefining here. H.E. Mohaupt was an air crewman on Operation Highjump, 1946–47.

Mount Mohl. 78°33'S, 85°05'W. At the east side of the Vinson Massif. It surmounts the ridge between the heads of Dater and Thomas Glaciers, in the Sentinel Range. Named for Cdr. Edgar A. Mohl, USN, hydrographic officer on the staff of the Commander of Task Force 43, during Operation Deep Freeze I and II.

Mohn Basin. 86°30'S, 168°W. A major depression in the surface near the edge of the Polar Plateau. It extends southward from the western limit of the Quarles Range for about 100 miles and includes the névé area adjacent to the heads of the Bowman, Devils, Amundsen, and Robert Scott Glaciers, in the Queen Maud Mountains. Discovered in Dec. 1911 by Amundsen on his way to the Pole. Later named by the USA for Henrik Mohn, Norwegian meteorologist and author of the meteorological report of Amundsen's 1910–12 expedition.

Mohn Peaks. 73°07'S, 61°15'W. Two ice-covered peaks. The northern one is 1,275 m. and the southern one is 1,230 m. 9 miles WSW of the head of Mason Inlet, on the east coast of Palmer Land. Discovered aerially in Dec. 1940 by the USAS. Named by the FIDS for Henrik Mohn (*see* **Mohn Basin**).

Moider Glacier. 67°43'S, 67°38'W. On the west side of the Antarctic Peninsula.

Moider Peak. 65°55'S, 63°09'W. 1,165 m. Between Fleece Glacier and the upper reaches of Leppard Glacier. 12 miles west of Mount Alibi, on the east side of Graham Land. Surveyed by the FIDS in 1955, and named by them for the confusion (moider means to confuse) experienced here due to the low cloud while trying to determine its position.

Molar Massif. 71°38'S, 163°45'E. Just east of the Lanterman Range in the Bowers Mountains. Named because when viewed in plan it looks like a molar.

Molar Peak. 64°41'S, 63°19'W. Also called Pico Elevado. 1,065 m. Between Mount Camber and Copper Peak in the Osterrieth Range of Anvers Island. Surveyed by the FIDS in 1955 and named by the UK for its shape.

Molchaniya Rock. 72°09'S, 14°08'E. Isolated. 6 miles WNW of Rokhlin Nunataks in the Payer Mountains of Queen Maud Land. Discovered aerially by Ritscher's 1938–39 expedition. Named Skala Molchaniya (silent rock) by the USSR in 1966.

Molds. There are many species in Antarctica (see **Flora**).

Molecule Island. 66°28'S, 66°24'W. The most easterly of the Bragg Islands, in Crystal Sound, 7½ miles north of Cape Rey, Graham Land. Surveyed by the FIDS in 1958–59. Named by the UK in association with nearby Atom Rock.

Molholm, John R.L. US glaciologist at Wilkes Station, 1957.

Molholm Island. 66°16'S, 110°33'E. At the entrance to McGrady Cove in the eastern part of Newcomb Bay in the Windmill Islands. Named by Carl Eklund in 1957 for John R.L. Molholm.

Molholm Shoal. 66°16'S, 110°33'E. A shoal area 175 yards west of Molholm Island in the Windmill Islands. Discovered and charted in Feb. 1957 by personnel from the *Glacier*. Named by the Australians for nearby Molholm Island.

Molina Point. 64°48'S, 62°51'W. On the west side of Graham Land.

Molina Rocks. 63°22'S, 58°27'W. 4 miles west of Tupinier Islands, Trinity Peninsula. Named by the Chileans before 1951.

Möll Spur. 76°23'S, 112°09'W. Juts out southward from Jaron Cliffs on the southern slope of Mount Takahe in Marie Byrd Land. Named for Markus Möll from the University of Bern in Switzerland, glaciologist at Byrd Station in 1969–70.

Molle Glacier. 67°31'S, 47°10'E. Also called Hannan Glacier. 4 miles wide. Flows NNE into the northern part of the Hannan Ice Shelf of Enderby Land. Named by the Australians for J.D. Molle, radio officer at Davis Station, 1960.

Møller Bank. 67°34'S, 62°52'E. A marine bank with a least depth of 32 meters. At the north end of the Kista Strait, 1 mile west of Welch Island in Holme Bay, Mac. Robertson Land. Charted by d'A. Gale during an ANARE hydrographic survey in Feb. 1961. Named by the Australians for J. Wennerberg Møller, third mate on the *Thala Dan* that year. Møller assisted with the survey.

Molloy, William. Midshipman on the *Terror*, 1839–43.

Mollusks. There is a variety of these living on the sea beds near the shores (see **Fauna**).

Molnar Rocks. 66°11'S, 66°58'W. Rocks in water 4 miles west of the middle of Lavoisier Island in the Biscoe Islands. Named by the UK for George W. Molnar, US physiologist who specialized in the reactions of the human body to the cold.

Molodezhnaya Station. 67°40'S, 45°51'E. On the Prince Olav Coast of Enderby Land. Official name: Antarctic Meteorological Center Molodezhnaya. Opened on Jan. 14, 1963. It is the USSR's biggest Antarctic station, succeeding Mirnyy Station as headquarters in 1972. Meteorology is the main study. Rocketry and geophysics are also studied. About 128 people winter-over every year, and there are over 200 in the summer. It has a synoptic meteorology bureau and a landing strip. Named for the "molodezh" or "young people" who constructed the station.

Moltke Group *see* **Moltke Nunataks**

Moltke Nunatak *see* **Moltke Nunataks**

Moltke Nunataks. 78°58'S, 35°30'W. Also called Moltke Group. Just to the NE end of the Filchner Ice Shelf. They trend north-south in a chain. In 1911–12 Filchner mapped and named one of them as Moltke Nunatak for Gen. Helmuth von Moltke (1848–1916), chief of the German General Staff and secretary of state for home affairs. Later surveys indicate that there are four or five nunataks in the chain, and the feature was redefined slightly.

Molybdenum. Mawson was the first to find it in Antarctica. It has since been found several times.

Islotes Mom *see* **Medley Rocks**

Mom Peak. 85°27'S, 173°E. 3,260 m. In the eastern part of the Otway Massif. 5 miles SE of Mount Petlock. Named for "Antarctica Mom," i.e., Mrs. Shirley Anderson of San Diego, Calif., who, in the years following 1961 wrote to thousands of American winterers in Antarctica, thus boosting morale.

Cape Monaco. 64°43'S, 64°18'W. Also called Cape Albert de Monaco. Forms the SW tip of Anvers Island. Discovered by Dallmann in 1873–74, but he did not realize what it was. Charcot charted it in 1903–5, and named it for Prince Albert of Monaco, a patron.

Cape Monakov. 67°09'S, 48°41'E. On the west coast of Sakellari Peninsula in Enderby Land. Named by the USSR for S.Y. Monakov, polar aviator who died in the Arctic.

Monastery Nunatak. 77°58'S, 160°35' E. Isolated. At the head of Ferrar Glacier, between Mount Feather and Pivot Peak, in Victoria Land. Named for its likeness to a Tibetan monastery by the NZ Northern Survey Party of the BCTAE 1956–58. It is composed of a cap of pale sandstone, with vertical walls, standing above a horizontal base of black dolerite.

Mondai Rock *see* **Kasumi Rock**

Mondor Glacier. 63°28'S, 57°08'W. 3½ miles long. Flows SW from the head of Depot Glacier into Duse Bay on Trinity Peninsula. These two glaciers fill the depression between Hope Bay and Duse Base which marks the northern limit of the Tabarin Peninsula. Named by the FIDS in association with the French "Bal Tabarin" from literature. Tabarin and Mondor were both characters from the same book.

Cape Monflier *see* **Monflier Point**

Monflier Point. 65°55'S, 66°04'W. Also called Cape Monflier, Cape Mont-flier. Marks the SW end of Rabot Island in the Biscoe Islands. Charted and named by Charcot in 1903–5.

Monge Island. 66°47'S, 141°29'E. Just south of La Conchée and ½ mile NE of Cape Mousse. Charted in 1951 by the French and named by them for Gaspard Monge (1746–1818), French mathematician.

Monica Rock. 62°20'S, 59°44'W. Almost ¾ mile west of Cornwall Island in the English Strait in the South Shetlands. It has two humps on it and for most of the time it looks like two islands. Charted by the Chilean Antarctic Expedition of 1949–50, and named by them for the eldest daughter of one of the officers on the expedition, Lt. Venturini.

Roca Monigote *see* **Lay-Brother Rock**

Mount Monique. 69°32'S, 75°14'W. Also called Monique Mountain, Monique Peak. 750 m. 3 miles west of Marion Nunataks, on the north coast of Charcot Island. Discovered and charted by Charcot on Jan. 11, 1910, and named by him for his daughter, Monique.

Monique Mountain *see* **Mount Monique**

Monique Peak *see* **Mount Monique**

Monk Islands. 60°40'S, 45°55'W. Also called Monk Islet. A group of very small islands and rocks 1½ miles south of Meier Point, off the south coast of Coronation Island in the South Orkneys. Charted and named Munken (the monk) by Petter Sørlle in 1912–13. The name was later translated into English by the UK.

Monnier Point. 67°06'S, 64°45'W. Mainly ice-covered. Forms the south side of the entrance to Mill Inlet, on the east coast of Graham Land. Named by the FIDS in 1947 for Franz R. von Le Monnier, Austrian polar bibliographer.

The Monolith. 66°57'S, 163°17'E. 80 m. A pinnacle rock, broad at the base and tapering to a point to produce a remarkable effect. Just off the north end of the islet south of Sabrina Island in the Balleny Islands. Named for its shape.

El Monolito *see* Petes Pillar

¹Monroe Island. 60°36'S, 46°03'W. Largest of the Larsen Islands in the South Orkneys. Off the west end of Coronation Island. Named Larsen Island in 1933 by personnel on the *Discovery II.* Renamed in 1954 by the UK for the *James Monroe.*

²Monroe Island *see* Snow Island

Monroe Point. 62°49'S, 61°30'W. 3 miles NW of Cape Conway on the SW side of Snow Island in the South Shetlands. In 1935 it was named Low Point by personnel on the *Discovery II,* but this name seems never to have been used. In 1961 the UK changed it officially to commemorate the old name for Snow Island — i.e., Monroe Island.

Monsimet. A member of the 1908–10 French expedition under Charcot in the *Pourquoi Pas?*

Monsimet Cove. 62°11'S, 58°34'W. ½ mile west of Hervé Cove, on the south side of Ezcurra Inlet in Admiralty Bay, King George Island, in the South Shetlands. Charted by Charcot in 1908–10 and named by him for Monsimet (q.v.).

Mount Monson. 77°31'S, 143°31'W. 1,155 m. The highest summit in the Mackay Mountains. 1½ miles NE of Vivian Nunatak in the SW part of the group, in the Ford Ranges of Marie Byrd Land. Named for Lt. Laurence C. Monson, III, USNR, Hercules aircraft co-pilot, 1968.

Montague. Cook on the *Nimrod* during Shackleton's 1907–9 expedition.

Monte Cassino. 72°19'S, 163°40'E. 2,270 m. A peak at the SE side of Moawhango Névé in the Freyberg Mountains. Named for the battle by the Northern Party of the NZGSAE 1963–64 in association with Lord Freyberg.

Mount Monteagle. 73°43'S, 165°28'E. 2,780 m. 10 miles north of Cape Sibbald in the Mountaineer Range of Victoria Land. It surmounts Aviator Glacier to the west and the large cirque of Parker Glacier to the east. Discovered in Jan. 1841 by Ross, who named it for Lord

Monteagle, chancellor of the exchequer from 1835 to 1839.

Montecchi Glacier. 72°04'S, 167°35'E. Flows from Bertalan Peak into Tucker Glacier just north of Mount Hazlett, in the Victory Mountains of Victoria Land. Named for Pietrantonio Montecchi, geophysicist at McMurdo Station, 1966–67.

Monteverdi Peninsula. 72°30'S, 72° W. Ice-covered. Between the Bach Ice Shelf and the George VI Sound. Forms the most southerly part of Alexander Island. The southern side of the peninsula was discovered and charted by Finn Ronne and Carl Eklund who traversed the entire length of the George VI Sound during the USAS 1939–41. Surveyed by the FIDS in 1948–50. Named by the UK for the composer.

Cape Montflier *see* Monflier Point

Montgolfier Glacier. 64°47'S, 62°15' W. Flows to Piccard Cove between Rozier Glacier and Woodbury Glacier on the west coast of Graham Land. Named by the UK in 1960 for Joseph M. Montgolfier (1740–1810) and his brother Étienne J. Montgolfier (1745–1799), the pioneer balloonists.

Montgomerie Glacier. 83°47'S, 166° 55'E. Also spelled (erroneously) Montgomery Glacier. 10 miles long. Flows along the west side of the Hampton Ridge in the Queen Alexandra Range to enter the Lennox-King Glacier. Named by the Northern Party of the NZGSAE 1961–62 for John Montgomerie, assistant surveyor with the party.

Montgomery Glacier *see* Montgomerie Glacier

Montigny Glacier. 71°05'S, 163°24'E. Flows east in the Bowers Mountains and at its terminus coalesces with Irwin Glacier (from the south), with which it enters Graveson Glacier. Named for Raymond J. Montigny, glaciologist who studied the Meserve Glacier in 1966–67.

Montravel Rock. 63°09'S, 58°02'W. 11 miles NW of Cape Legoupil off the NW coast of Trinity Peninsula. Discovered in Feb. 1838 by Dumont d'Urville, and

named by him for Louis Tardy de Montravel.

Mount Montreuil. 73°04′S, 166°11′E.
2,680 m. On the north side of Gair Glacier. 8½ miles east of Mount Supernal in
the Mountaineer Range of Victoria Land.
Named for Paul L. Montreuil, biologist
at McMurdo Station, 1964–65.

Rocas Montrol *see* **Northtrap Rocks**

Montrol Rock. 62°58′S, 56°21′W. Also
called Rocas Pico. The largest of a group
of rocks east of Cape Juncal on D'Urville
Island. Discovered and named by Dumont d'Urville during his expedition of
1837–40.

Montserat, Francis. Officer's steward
on the Wilkes Expedition 1838–42.
Joined in the USA. Served the cruise.

Île Montura *see* **Saddle Island**

The Monument. 63°44′S, 57°53′W.
An isolated rock pillar on the NW side of
Red Island. It is 495 meters high and
level with the main summit of Red Island. It looks like a monument. In the
Prince Gustav Channel, 2 miles south of
Trinity Peninsula. Discovered by Nordenskjöld's 1901–4 expedition and
charted and named by the FIDS in 1945.

Monument Nunataks. 72°35′S, 162°
15′E. North of Sculpture Mountain in the
upper part of the Rennick Glacier.
Named by the Northern Party of the
NZGSAE 1962–63 for the many monu-
ment-shaped pinnacles here.

Monument Rocks. 64°01′S, 60°57′W.
4 miles NE of Cape Sterneck in the entrance to Curtiss Bay in northern Graham
Land. Charted and named descriptively
by James Hoseason in 1824.

Cape Moody *see* **Moody Point**

Mount Moody. 71°31′S, 162°52′E.
2,040 m. 5 miles SE of Carnes Crag in the
NW part of the Lanterman Range of the
Bowers Mountains. Named by the Northern Party of the NZGSAE 1963–64 for Lt.
Daniel M. Moody, USN, of VX-6, who
flew support flights for the expedition
(*see also* **Moody Nunatak**).

Moody, E.L. Dog driver on the shore
party of Byrd's 1933–35 expedition.

Moody, William. Quartermaster on
the Wilkes Expedition 1838–42. Joined
in the USA. Served the cruise.

Moody Glacier. 84°30′S, 165°48′E.
Between Martin Ridge and Adams
Mountains in the Queen Alexandra
Range. It flows south into Berwick Glacier. Named for P.R. Moody, construction electrician at McMurdo Station,
1963.

Moody Island. 77°20′S, 149°12′W. 10
miles long. Ice-covered. Between Kizer
and Steventon Islands in the Sulzberger
Ice Shelf. Named for E.L. Moody.

Moody Nunatak. 83°07′S, 159°30′E.
Isolated. At the east side of Marsh Glacier. 4 miles west of Bartrum Plateau in
the Queen Elizabeth Range. Named by
the NZGSAE 1964–65 for Lt. Daniel M.
Moody (*see also* **Mount Moody**) who flew
the southern party of this expedition in
and out of the field.

Moody Peak. 78°22′S, 158°35′E. Over
1,800 m. Marks the northern limit of the
Boomerang Range. Named in 1964 for
Junior L. Moody, USN, aviation bosun's
mate in charge of loading and offloading
aircraft at McMurdo Station in 1959–60.

Moody Point. 63°18′S, 55°01′W. Also
called Cape Moody, Punta Rara. Forms
the east end of Joinville Island, off the NE
end of the Antarctic Peninsula. Discovered by Ross in 1839–43 and named by
him for Lieutenant Governor Moody of
the Falkland Islands.

Moon Bay. 62°35′S, 60°W. 7 miles
wide. Recedes 4 miles between Edinburgh Hill and Renier Point on the east
side of Livingston Island in the South
Shetlands. Discovered before 1821.
Named in 1935 by personnel on the *Discovery II* for nearby Half Moon Island.

Mount Mooney. 86°34′S, 145°48′W.
2,850 m. Also called Mount English.
Ridge-shaped. Between the Albanus
Glacier and the Robert Scott Glacier, just
north of the La Gorce Mountains, where
it rises above the middle of Robison
Glacier, in the Queen Maud Mountains.

Discovered in Dec. 1934 by Quin Blackburn during Byrd's 1933–35 expedition. Named by Byrd for James E. Mooney, who assisted this and later Byrd expeditions. From 1959–65 Mooney was deputy US Antarctic Projects Officer.

Mount Moonie. 70°13′S, 65°07′E. Just south of Mount Dart and 1 mile west of Mount Cardell in the Athos Range of the Prince Charles Mountains. Named by the Australians for P.J. Moonie, radio operator at Mawson Station in 1967 and 1969. He was also a member of the Prince Charles Mountains survey party of 1969.

Moonlight Range *see* **Athos Range**

Cape Moore. 70°56′S, 167°54′E. At the east end of the Tapsell Foreland which forms the north side of the entrance to Smith Inlet, on the north coast of Victoria Land. Discovered by Ross in 1841, and named by him for Lt. Thomas E.L. Moore.

Mount Moore. 80°25′S, 97°45′W. Isolated. 305 m. above the snow surface. 8 miles north of Mount Woollard, and 150 miles west of the Heritage Range. Discovered on Feb. 4, 1958, by the Marie Byrd Land Traverse Party, and named by them for Lt. John P. Moore.

Moore, James I. Second engineer on the *Penola* during the BGLE 1934–37.

Moore, John P. Lt. (jg), USN. Flew his helicopter into the ice during a whiteout while part of the US Navy Antarctic Expedition 1954–55, at Kainan Bay on Jan. 22, 1955. He died the same day, aged 27.

Moore, Thomas E.L. Lt. Midshipman on the *Terror*, during Ross' 1839–43 expedition.

Moore, William. Chief mate on the *Eliza Scott*, 1838–39.

Moore Bay *see* **Moore Embayment**

Moore Dome. 74°20′S, 111°20′W. On the coast of Marie Byrd Land.

Moore Embayment. 78°45′S, 165°E. Also called Moore Bay. Ice-filled. Between Shults Peninsula and Minna Bluff, on the NW side of the Ross Ice Shelf. Discovered by Scott's 1901–4 expedition,

and named by Scott for Admiral Sir Arthur Moore, naval commander-in-chief at Cape Town who was of enormous help in getting the *Discovery* fixed up before it went on to NZ and then Antarctica.

Moore Island. 69°40′S, 68°39′W. Off the west coast of the Antarctic Peninsula.

Moore Mountains. 83°21′S, 160°45′E. Just north of New Year Pass in the Queen Elizabeth Range. Named by the NZ Southern Party of the BCTAE in 1957–58 for R.D. Moore, treasurer of the Ross Sea Committee for that expedition.

Moore Point. 70°30′S, 67°53′W. Surmounted by a small peak. Fronts the George VI Sound and marks the north side of the mouth of Meiklejohn Glacier on the west coast of Palmer Land. Surveyed in 1936 by the BGLE and named by the UK in 1954 for James I. Moore.

Moore Pyramid. 70°18′S, 65°08′E. Snow-covered. Looks like a pyramid. 1 mile NW of Mount Wishart on the north side of Scylla Glacier in the Prince Charles Mountains. Named by the Australians for A.L. Moore, radio operator at Mawson Station in 1963.

Moore Ridge. 73°07′S, 161°45′E. The most northerly ridge of the Caudal Hills in Victoria Land. Named for Bruce F. Moore, VX-6 photographer at McMurdo Station in 1966.

Moores, Prince B. Captain of the *George Porter,* in the South Shetlands, 1821–22.

Moorey, George. Midshipman on the *Adventure* during Cook's second voyage of 1772–75.

Mooring Point. 60°43′S, 45°37′W. On the south side of Borge Bay between Drying Point and Knife Point, on the east side of Signy Island in the South Orkneys. Named before 1927.

Moos Inseln *see* **Moss Islands**

Moot Point *see* **Redondo Point**

Moraine Bluff. 78°46′S, 162°12′E. 930 m. On the east side of the Skelton Glacier, north of Red Dike Bluff. Surveyed and named in 1957 by the NZ party of the BCTAE for the long morainic strip which extends from the foot of the bluff to the Skelton Glacier.

Moraine Canyon. 86°09′S, 157°30′W. Has very steep rock walls. 8 miles long. Indents the northern part of the Nilsen Plateau just west of Fram Mesa in the Queen Maud Mountains. Named for the glacial moraine which completely covers the floor of the canyon.

Moraine Cove. 68°35′S, 67°08′W. At the north end of Mikkelsen Bay on the west coast of Graham Land. A moraine descends to this cove from the SW end of Pavie Ridge. In 1947 Robert L. Nichols, part of the RARE 1947–48, examined the geology in this area and called this feature Moraine Point. Later redefined.

Moraine Point *see* **Moraine Cove**

Moraine Ridge. 72°18′S, 168°03′E. In the NE part of the Cartographers Range in Victoria Land. It descends to the SW flank of the Tucker Glacier just south of the junction of that glacier with the Pearl Harbor Glacier. Named by the New Zealanders in 1957–58.

Moraine Valley. 60°43′S, 45°37′W. A valley filled with morainic debris. ¾ mile long. It drains north into Elephant Flats on the east side of Signy Island in the South Orkneys. In summer, a stream, fed by the ice slopes at its southern end, runs in this valley. Surveyed and named by the FIDS in 1947.

Moraines. These are piles of rocky rubble deposited glacially. There are three types: 1. lateral moraines—this is material derived from the sides of valleys. 2. median moraines—this is rubble carried on top of a glacier. 3. terminal moraines—this is rubble from the bed of a glacier pushed along in front of it.

Islotes Morales *see* **Wideopen Islands**

Morales Peak. 86°15′S, 126°22′W. In the southern part of Metavolcanic Mountain, just east of Reedy Glacier. Named for Tommy S. Morales, radioman at Byrd Station, 1962.

Moran, James. 1st class boy on the Wilkes Expedition 1838–42. Joined in the USA. Returned home on the *Relief,* 1839.

Moran Bluff. 74°23′S, 132°37′W. Just west of Mathewson Point on the north side of Shepard Island, on the edge of the Getz Ice Shelf. Named for Gerald F. Moran, USN, construction mechanic at McMurdo Station, 1965; at Plateau Station, 1968; and at Byrd Station, 1969–70.

Moran Buttress. 85°31′S, 125°38′W. A steep bluff 2 miles south of Koopman Peak. Over 2,600 m. Forms a major projection between Davisville Glacier and Quonset Glacier along the north wall of the Wisconsin Range. Named for Lt. Cdr. Clifford D. Moran, USN, aircraft pilot in Antarctica, 1966 and 1967.

Mordrins Island *see* **Elephant Island**

More, John. Seaman on the Wilkes Expedition 1838–42. Joined in the USA. Discharged at Oahu, Oct. 31, 1840.

More, Samuel. Captain of the topsail on the Wilkes Expedition 1838–42. Joined in the USA. Discharged at Oahu, Nov. 20, 1841.

Moreland Nunatak. 81°15′S, 87°05′W. Isolated. 15 miles west of the Pirrit Hills. Named for William B. Moreland, meteorologist at Little America, 1957.

Morelli Glacier. 72°59′S, 102°33′W. In the western part of the King Peninsula, 18 miles SE of Cape Waite. It flows NE to the Abbott Ice Shelf in Peacock Sound. Named for Panfilo S. Morelli, glaciologist at Byrd Station, 1961–62.

Morency, Anthony J.L. American gravity physicist who served as tractor driver/communications man at East Base during the USAS 1939–41. He also took part in Operation Highjump, 1946–47, and in 1957 served at Byrd Station.

Morency Island. 71°02′S, 61°09′W. 1 mile long. Just west of Steele Island and 10 miles NW of Cape Bryant, off the east coast of Palmer Land. Discovered in 1940 by members of East Base during the USAS. Named for Anthony J.L. Morency.

Morennaya Hill. 66°34'S, 93°E. 40 m. 1 mile SW of Mabus Point on the coast of East Antarctica. Discovered by the AAE 1911–14. Named Morennaya (morainic) by the USSR in 1956.

Islote Moreno *see* **Diamonen Island**

Point Moreno. 60°45'S, 44°42'W. At the east side of the entrance to the small cove at the head of Scotia Bay, on the south coast of Laurie Island in the South Orkneys. Charted by Bruce in 1903, and named by him for Francisco P. Moreno, Argentine scientist.

Moreno Island *see* **Moreno Rock**

Moreno Rock. 64°05'S, 61°18'W. Also called Moreno Island. A rock in the Gerlache Strait, 7 miles WSW of Cape Sterneck, on the west side of the Antarctic Peninsula. Named by de Gerlache in 1897–99 for Francisco P. Moreno (*see* **Point Moreno**).

Moreton Point. 60°37'S, 46°02'W. 1 mile north of Return Point at the west end of Coronation Island in the South Orkneys. Charted by Powell and Palmer in 1821. Charted again by personnel on the *Discovery II* in 1933, and named by them.

Mount Morgagni *see* **Mount Cabeza**

Mount Morgan. 76°53'S, 143°34'W. 5 miles NE of Mount Swan in the Ford Ranges of Marie Byrd Land. Discovered by the USAS 1939–41. Named for C.G. Morgan.

Morgan, C.G. Geologist on the shore party of Byrd's 1933–35 expedition.

Morgan Inlet. 72°12'S, 96°W. 18 miles long. Ice-filled. Has two branches. Indents the eastern end of Thurston Island between Lofgren and Tierney Peninsulas. Discovered in helicopter flights from the *Glacier* and *Burton Island* during the USN Bellingshausen Sea Expedition of Feb. 1960. Named for Lt. Cdr. Joseph R. Morgan, USN, hydrographic and oceanographic officer of Task Force 43 during this expedition.

Morgan Nunataks. 75°22'S, 70°35'W. At the SW end of the Sweeney Moun-

tains, in Ellsworth Land. Discovered aerially by the RARE 1947–48. Named for William R. Morgan, cook at Eights Station, 1965.

Morgan Ridge. 70°29'S, 64°41'E. Between Mounts Pollard and Small in the Porthos Range of the Prince Charles Mountains. Named by the Australians for P.J. Morgan, glaciologist at Wilkes Station, 1964.

Morgan Upland. 69°S, 66°W. An undulating snow plateau in the central part of the Antarctic Peninsula. Bounded by Cole Glacier and Clarke Glacier on the north and west, by Weyerhaeuser Glacier on the east, by Airy Glacier on the south, and by Hariot Glacier on the SW. Mapped by BAS Surveyor Ivor P. Morgan, for whom this featureless plateau is named.

Mount Moriarty. 73°40'S, 165°58'E. 1,700 m. 4 miles NE of Mount Casey in the Mountaineer Range of Victoria Land. Named for Lt. Cdr. Jack O. Moriarty, USN, air operations officer at McMurdo Station, 1966.

Mørkenatten Peak. 71°52'S, 10°34'E. 2,515 m. 1 mile south of Chervov Peak in the Shcherbakov Range of the Orvin Mountains in Queen Maud Land. Name means "the dark night" in Norwegian.

Mount Morley. 69°33'S, 71°37'W. 1,750 m. Surmounts the southern part of the Lassus Mountains in the northern part of Alexander Island. Named by the UK for the composer.

Morley Glacier. 71°12'S, 162°45'E. Flows south between Hicks Ridge and Mount Tokoroa in the Explorers Range of the Bowers Mountains, to enter Carryer Glacier. Named for Keith T. Morley, Australian IGY observer, Weather Central meteorologist at Little America, 1958.

The *Morning*. Norwegian whaler built by Svend Foyn, the inventor of the harpoon gun. It was 140 feet long, 452 tons, and was originally called the *Morgen*. Bought by Sir Clements Markham (father of the Royal Society Expedition) with monies publicly subscibed in Britain. It was renamed into English. It was the relief ship commanded by Colbeck which went south to relieve Scott's 1901–4 Royal Society Expedition in 1902–3. It left McMurdo Sound for home on March 2, 1903, with Shackleton aboard. Colbeck returned with the *Morning* again in 1904, again to relieve Scott's expedition (this time successfully), and this time accompanied by the *Terra Nova*.

Lake Morning. 78°21′S, 163°53′E. An ice lake, almost 2 miles long. 9 miles north of Mount Morning on the east side of the Koettlitz Glacier in Victoria Land. Named in 1963 in association with the mountain.

Mount Morning. 78°31′S, 163°35′E. 2,725 m. Dome-shaped. WSW of Mount Discovery and east of the Koettlitz Glacier in Victoria Land. Discovered during Scott's 1901–4 expedition and named by Scott for the *Morning*.

Morozumi Range. 71°39′S, 161°55′E. Extends for 25 miles in a NW-SE direction. Its northern heights overlook the convergence of the Gressitt and Rennick Glaciers. For spectacular beauty this is one of the ranges to see. Named for Henry M. Morozumi, aurora scientist at South Pole Station, 1960, and scientific leader at Byrd Station, 1963.

Morrell, Benjamin, Jr. b. 1795, Rye, NY. d. 1839, of fever in Mozambique. Son of a Stonington, Conn. shipbuilder. Went to sea in 1811, and was first mate on the *Wasp* in 1821–22 in the Antarctic. He got his first captaincy in 1822–23, as captain of the aforementioned vessel, in which, that austral summer, he made a controversial survey of East Antarctica waters.

Morrell's Land *see* **New South Greenland**

Morrill Peak. 69°39′S, 72°18′W. In the extreme north of Alexander Island.

Cape Morris *see* **Fort William**

Mount Morris. 78°19′S, 86°10′W. 1 mile south of Mount Ostenso, in the main ridge of the Sentinel Range. Named for Wesley R. Morris, meteorologist at Byrd Station, 1957.

Morris Basin. 75°39′S, 159°09′E. 9 square miles in area. In the northern part of the Ricker Hills, in the Prince Albert Mountains of Victoria Land. The southern part of the basin is ice-free but the northern part is occupied by a large lobe of ice. Named for Robert W. Morris, biologist at McMurdo Station, 1965–66, 1966–67.

Morris Cliff. 80°20′S, 81°49′W. Between the Marble Hills and the Independence Hills in the Heritage Range. Named for Lt. Harold M. Morris, USN, pilot of the plane which crashed in 1966 (*see* **Deaths, 1966**).

Morris Glacier. 84°46′S, 169°30′W. 10 miles long. Flows north from Mount Daniel to the Ross Ice Shelf between the Lillie Range and Clark Spur. Named by the Southern Party of the NZGSAE 1963–64 for Cdr. Marion E. Morris, USN, executive officer (later commanding officer) of VX-6, who piloted the aircraft which flew that party's reconnaissance.

Morris Head. 74°54′S, 134°50′W. An ice-covered headland. Marks the seaward end of Hagey Ridge and the NE extremity of McDonald Heights, on the coast of Marie Byrd Land. Named for Lloyd Morris, USN, chief quartermaster and senior member of the bathythermograph team on the *Glacier* off this coast in 1961–62.

Morris Heights. 83°28′S, 169°42′E. Ice-covered. They form a peninsula-like divide between Beaver Glacier and King Glacier at the north end of the Queen Alexandra Range. Named for Lt. Clarence T. Morris, USN, aerology officer on the staff of the commander, US Naval Support Force, Antarctica, 1962 and 1963.

Morris Hills. 80°23′S, 27°27′W. Also called Morris Nunataks. A scattered group of hills. 6 miles NE of Petersen Peak, in the La Grange Nunataks of the north-central part of the Shackleton

Range. Named by the UK for Leslie F. Morris, a member of the Royal Society IGY Expedition. In 1957 he helped ready the BCTAE.

Morris Island. 76°37′S, 147°48′W. 7 miles long. Ice-covered. 5 miles west of Farmer Island in the Sulzberger Ice Shelf. Named for Lt. (jg) J.E. Morris, USNR, who was on the *Glacier* in this area in 1961–62.

Morris Nunataks *see* **Morris Hills**

Morris Peak. 84°56′S, 167°22′W. 910 m. Marks the NW end of the Duncan Mountains at the east side of the mouth of Liv Glacier where that glacier enters the Ross Ice Shelf. Named for Lt. Cdr. H.C. Morris, USN, captain of the *Mills* in 1963.

Morris Rock. 62°23′S, 59°48′W. 2 miles west of Fort William in the Aitcho Islands of the South Shetlands. Named by the UK in 1961 in association with Cape Morris, a name given by personnel on the *Discovery II* in 1935 to the western extremity of Robert Island. This cape was later found to be the original location of Fort William, so that term was reinstated. The name of this rock is meant to preserve the naming of Morris in the area.

¹Mount Morrison. 66°48′S, 51°27′E. 1½ miles NE of Mount Best in the Tula Mountains of Enderby Land. Named by the Australians for H.C. Morrison.

²Mount Morrison. 76°54′S, 161°32′E. 1,895 m. Between the head of the Cleveland Glacier and the Benson Glacier in Victoria Land. Discovered during Scott's 1901–4 expedition and named by them for J.D. Morrison.

Morrison, H.C. Crew member on the *Discovery* during the BANZARE 1929–31.

Morrison, J.D. Chief engineer on the *Morning*, 1902–4.

Morrison, John H. Crewman on the *Jacob Ruppert*, 1934–35.

Morrison Bluff. 75°05′S, 114°20′W. On the west side of the Kohler Glacier. 12 miles SW of Mount Isherwood in the

Kohler Range of Marie Byrd Land. Lichens are found here. Named for Charles E. Morrison, US Geological Survey topographic engineer who took part in surveys of Marie Byrd Land in 1966–67 and Ellsworth Land in 1967–68.

Morrison Glacier. 66°10′S, 63°30′W. 3 miles long. Between Attlee and Eden Glaciers. Flows to the head of Cabinet Inlet, on the east coast of Graham Land. Charted in 1947 by the FIDS, and named by them for Herbert Morrison (1888–1965), British member of the War Cabinet which created Operation Tabarin.

Morrison Hills. 84°12′S, 168°40′E. They trend east-west in the Queen Alexandra Range, between Garrard Glacier and Hewson Glacier. Named for Lt. I. James Morrison, who did preliminary work leading to the induction of C-130 aircraft into Antarctica, and who was in Antarctica many times after 1958–59.

Morrison Rocks. 76°51′S, 117°39′W. On the southern slope of Mount Frakes in the Crary Mountains of Marie Byrd Land. Named for Paul W. Morrison, USN, hospital corpsman at Amundsen-Scott South Pole Station, 1974.

Morriss Peak. 76°50′S, 144°29′W. 950 m. At the SW end of the Wiener Peaks in the Ford Ranges of Marie Byrd Land. Named by Byrd for P.G.B. Morriss, manager of the Hotel Clark in Los Angeles, who provided office space and living quarters for Byrd's first two expeditions before they set out.

Punta Morro *see* **The Naze**

Península Morro Chato *see* **Flat Top Peninsula**

Cape Morse. 66°15′S, 130°10′E. Ice-covered. Marks the east side of the entrance to Porpoise Bay and forms the division between the Wilkes Coast and the Banzare Coast of Wilkes Land. Named for William H. Morse (*see also* **Morse Glacier**).

Morse, William H. Purser's steward on the *Porpoise* during the Wilkes Expedition 1838–42.

Morse Glacier. 66°21'S, 130°05'E. A channel glacier flowing to the east side of Porpoise Bay, 3 miles SW of Cape Morse. Due to a spelling mistake this feature was spelled Mose Glacier for many years, as Cape Morse was similarly misspelled. Named for William H. Morse.

Morse Nunataks. 84°16'S, 160°50'E. Isolated. 4½ miles south of Mount Achernar, between Lewis Cliff and Mac-Alpine Hills in the Queen Maud Mountains. Named for Oliver C. Morse, III, ionosphere scientist at South Pole Station, 1960.

Mount Morton. 64°24'S, 61°01'W. Between Blériot and Cayley Glaciers on the west coast of Graham Land. Named by the UK in 1960 for Grant Morton, US aviator who was the first man to bail out of a plane carrying a loose parachute.

Morton Glacier. 83°12'S, 168°E. 15 miles long. Flows east from the Holland Range between Vaughan Promontory and Lewis Ridge into the Ross Ice Shelf. Named for Lt. Cdr. John A. Morton, officer-in-charge of VX-6 Detachment ALFA at McMurdo Station, 1964.

Morton Strait. 62°42'S, 61°14'W. 5 miles across at its narrowest point. Between Snow Island on the SW and Rugged and Livingston Islands on the NE in the South Shetlands. Discovered in 1819 and called Strait Despair or Strait of Despair. Renamed by Weddell in 1823 as Morton's Strait, which became shortened soon thereafter.

Morton's Strait *see* **Morton Strait**

Mosby, Haakon. Norwegian oceanographer and meteorologist. Scientific leader of the *Norvegia*'s first trip to the Antarctic, in 1927–28.

Mosby Glacier. 73°09'S, 61°40'W. 5 miles wide at its mouth. Flows SE to the NW corner of New Bedford Inlet, on the east coast of Palmer Land. Discovered aerially by the USAS in Dec. 1940. Named by the FIDS in 1947 for Haakon Mosby.

Moscow University Ice Shelf. 66°30'S, 118°30'E. Off the Sabrina Coast.

Cape Mose *see* **Cape Morse**

Mose Glacier *see* **Morse Glacier**

Moseley, H.N. Naturalist on the *Challenger,* 1872–76.

Moser Glacier. 64°51'S, 62°22'W. Also spelled (erroneously) Mozer Glacier. Flows into Andvord Bay just SE of Arago Glacier on the west coast of Graham Land. Charted by de Gerlache in 1897–99. Named by the UK in 1960 for Ludwig F. Moser (1805–1880), German inventor of stereoscopic photography in 1844.

Mount Moses. 74°33'S, 99°11'W. 750 m. The highest and most prominent of the Hudson Mountains, near the center of the group, 14 miles NNE of Mount Manthe. Named for Robert L. Moses, seismologist at Byrd Station, 1967.

Moss Islands. 64°09'S, 61°03'W. East of Midas Island and north of Apéndice Island in Hughes Bay off the west coast of Graham Land. Charted by Nordenskjöld's expedition in 1902, and named descriptively as Moos Inseln (Moss Islands) by them.

Moss Lake. 60°42'S, 45°37'W. The most southerly lake in Paternoster Valley on Signy Island. Named by the UK for the luxuriant growth of moss which covers the deeper part of the lake.

Mosses. Found in Antarctica. Along with liverworts they make up the Bryophytes. They predominate in maritime areas, but can grow anywhere that lichens can (*see* **Flora**).

Mossman, Robert C. 1870–1940. British meteorologist and climatologist. A member of Bruce's expedition of 1902–4.

Mossman Inlet. 73°17'S, 60°32'W. Ice-filled. Recedes north 10 miles. Between Cape Kidson and the SW end of the Kemp Peninsula, on the east coast of Palmer Land. Discovered aerially by the USAS in Dec. 1940. Named by the FIDS in 1947 for Robert C. Mossman.

Mossman Peninsula. 60°46'S, 44°43'W. 3 miles long and narrow. It extends south from the western part of Laurie

Island, and separates Scotia and Wilton Bays, in the South Orkneys. Discovered by Powell and Palmer in Dec. 1821, and charted on Powell's map of 1822. Surveyed in 1903 by Bruce, and named by him for Robert C. Mossman in 1904.

Cape Mossyface *see* **Cape Canwe**

Møteplassen Peak. 72°47'S, 3°09'W. The most northerly peak of the group bordering the southern side of Frostlendet Valley in the Borg Massif of Queen Maud Land. Name means "the meeting place" in Norwegian.

Mötesudden *see* **Cape Well-Met**

Motherway Island. 66°26'S, 110°31'E. Also called Motherway Rock. A small rocky island about 350 yards north of Peterson Island, near the south end of the Windmill Islands. Named for Paul T. Motherway, who took part in Operation Windmill, 1947–48, as a photographer.

Motherway Rock *see* **Motherway Island**

Mothes Point. 67°14'S, 67°52'W. 7 miles SW of The Gullet on the east side of Adelaide Island. Named by the UK for Hans Mothes, German glaciologist who, in 1926, with B. Brockhamp, made the first seismic soundings of a glacier, in Austria.

Motor sledges *see* **Sledges**

Motor vehicles *see* **Aircraft, Amphibious vehicles, Automobiles, Cletracs, Ships, Sledges, Snowmobiles, Weasels,** and other direct entries.

Mott Snowfield. 63°20'S, 57°20'W. In the NE part of the Trinity Peninsula between Laclavère Plateau and Antarctic Sound. Named by the UK for Peter G. Mott, leader of the FIDASE 1955–57.

Moubray, George H. Clerk in charge of the *Terror* during Ross' expedition of 1839–43.

Moubray Bay. 72°11'S, 170°15'E. Indents the coast of Victoria Land between Capes Roget and Hallett. Discovered in 1841 by Ross, and named by him for George H. Moubray.

Moubray Glacier. 71°52'S, 170°18'E. Flows south to Moubray Bay from the Adare Saddle on Adare Peninsula. It is one of the main glaciers feeding the Moubray Piedmont Glacier. Named by the New Zealanders in 1957–58 in association with the nearby bay.

Moubray Piedmont Glacier. 71°55'S, 170°20'E. Fills the northern part of Moubray Bay. It is formed by the confluence of Moubray Glacier and ice streams falling from the west side of the south end of Adare Peninsula. The greater part of it is probably afloat. Named by the New Zealanders in 1957–58 for the nearby bay.

Mouillard Glacier. 64°18'S, 60°53'W. Flows into the SE corner of Brialmont Cove, on the west coast of Graham Land. Named by the UK in 1960 for Louis P. Mouillard (1834–1897), French gliding pioneer.

Moulder Peak. 80°05'S, 83°02'W. 3 miles SE of Mount Rosenthal in the Liberty Hills of the Heritage Range. Named for Andrew B. Moulder (*see* **Deaths, 1966**).

Mount Moulton. 76°03'S, 135°08'W. 3,070 m. Ice-covered. 10 miles east of Mount Berlin in the Flood Range of Marie Byrd Land. Lichens are to be found here. Discovered aerially by the USAS in 1940 and named for Richard S. Moulton.

Moulton, Richard S. Photographer/ chief dog driver at West Base during the USAS 1939–41. He was a member of the survey party which sledged to the west end of the Flood Range in Dec. 1940.

Moulton Escarpment. 85°10'S, 94°45'W. 8 miles long. 10 miles west of the Ford Massif where it forms a western shoulder of the Thiel Mountains. Surveyed by the US Geological Survey Thiel Mountains party in 1960–61. Named for Kendall N. Moulton of the NSF, who was in Antarctica more than 12 times between the years 1958 and 1977.

Moulton Icefalls. 76°S, 134°35'W. Steep icefalls flowing from the northern slopes of Mount Moulton (hence the name), in the Flood Range of Marie Byrd Land.

Mount Bird Ice Cap. On top of Mount Bird, Ross Island.

The *Mount Olympus.* Specially designed command ship/communications ship, and flagship of the Central Group during Operation Highjump, 1946–47. It had positions for 50 radio operators, and carried the Noorduyn Norseman airplane. Captain R.R. Moore commanded.

Mountain Ranges *see* **Ranges**

Mountain Travel. 6420 Fairmount Ave., El Cerrito, Calif., 94530. They were formerly at 1398 Solano Ave., Albany, Calif., 94706. Tel: 1-415-527-8100 or (toll-free) 1-800-227-2384. Tour operator extraordinaire. Founded by Leo Le Bon in 1968. It specializes in "handcrafted travel adventures for small groups." They now do over 50 trips to 7 continents. They do trips similar to those of Society Expeditions and Lindblad Travel, i.e., 15-day cruises to the South Shetlands and the northern tip of the Antarctic Peninsula for $3,975–$6,975 (depending on cabin), including the air fare (all Mountain Travel Antarctica expeditions include Lan Chile economy class air fare out of Miami, Fla.). The difference is that they use (from 1989–90) the *Nordbrise,* and before that the *Bahía Paraíso* of painful memory. These are not tourist ships, and more time is spent on land. Skiing and Sno-trac rides are available. The tours typically call at Primavera Bay, Esperanza Bay, Pyramid Peak, Mount Flora, the Danco Coast, Gerlache Strait, Paradise Harbor, Almirante Brown Station, Neumayer Channel, Palmer Station, Anvers Island, Melchior Islands, Deception Island, Jubany Station and King George Island—if all goes well with the weather and politics. A more exciting trip is the assault on the Vinson Massif, the highest point in Antarctica. For 4 years Mountain Travel has led a successful climb up this mountain massif. A ski-equipped Twin Otter flies 7 members out to the peaks and they climb

under the supervision of a professional. It is a 30-day expedition, generally leaving Nov. 15 and Jan. 15, and costs in excess of $15,900 per person. But the most exciting of all, and one which has the whole world talking, is the Polar Trek, an idea conceived by Leo Le Bon, who organized it and advertised for 10 paying travelers minimum and maximum. It was claimed that it was not economically feasible, at only $69,950 per person, to take fewer than 10, yet in the end only 6 went: Col. J.K. Bajaj, from the Nehru Institute of Mountaineering in Uttarkashi, India; Ron Milnarik, a USAF colonel and dentist (b. 1942) from Belleville, Ill.; Shirley Metz, a woman from Capistrano Beach, Calif.; Jerry Corr, from East Lansing, Mich.; Victoria E. Murden, from Somerville, Mass.; and Joe Murphy, from Minneapolis, Minn. These 6 civilians had trained for a year. There were 3 guides: Stuart Hamilton, from Canada; Mike Sharp, from Britain; and Alejo Contreras, from Chile. Canadian Martyn Williams, co-owner of Adventure Network International (see that entry for the relationship between the two companies) led the group and American Jim Williams was co-leader. These were the 11 people who took part in one of the most dangerous and astonishing treks available to mankind. The plan was to cross the continent of Antarctica on skis from the Weddell Sea, via the Ellsworth Mountains, to the South Pole, and then fly back—that is, if they made it to the Pole alive! What actually happened is not only astoundingly true to the plan, but worthy of some examination. Under the coordination of Nadia Le Bon in California, the party set out on Nov. 15, 1988. Mountain Travel and Adventure Network had put this historic first together, with Mountain Travel very much the senior partner. Adventure Network provided logistical back-up. Sponsored by Lan Chile, this was intended to be a one-shot deal, not a regularly offered expedition, partly because the National Science Foundation was against

it, considering it too much of a risk for ordinary civilians to undertake a 60-day expedition of this nature, with 50 days or so
on the actual continental traverse. On
Nov. 26, 1988, the band of intrepids flew
from Punta Arenas, Chile, to the Patriot
Hills area at 80°S, and then flew again, in
a ski-equipped Twin Otter, to Hercules
Inlet, not far away on "the edge of the
Ronne Ice Shelf, where the journey
started." They left there on Nov. 28,
1988, arriving at the Patriot Hills camp
on Dec. 1, 1988. They had snowmobiles
(for pulling supplies only), air back-up
(Giles Kershaw was the expedition pilot)
and medical assistance available from
Amundsen-Scott South Pole Station
should they need it. Fuel for the snowmobiles was at depots created by airdrops
every 120 miles at 82°S, 84°S, 86°S, and
88°S. The 11-person party left the Patriot
Hills on Dec. 3, 1988, and skied 770
miles in 49 days, or, in the words of
Mountain Travel, "they covered the
750-mile distance to the Pole by skiing
across the high Polar Plateau at an
average distance of 15 miles per day," arriving at noon (Pacific time) on Jan. 17,
1989. They were then airlifted back to
the Patriot Hills, and then by DC4 to the
USA. Mountain Travel produced a news-
letter in the spring of 1989 in which they
claim that this trip was the first time that
an American had reached the Pole by an
overland route. This is an innocent error,
made in the enthusiasm of the moment.
Many Americans had traversed to the
Pole. But Mountain Travel is right in that
the first Indian and the first women did
so on this trip. They are incorrect in that
only 10 men had ever crossed to the Pole
on foot (Amundsen's party of 5, and
Scott's party of 5), the rest having used
mechanized transport. They forgot the
In the Footsteps of Scott Expedition.
Although Mountain Travel enjoyed the
luxury of snowmobiles, they were not for
the travelers, only for the supplies. The
astonishing thing is that 6 ordinary people (including 2 women) did in 49 days
what it took the very fast Amundsen 55
days to do. Granted, it was a different

route, and when the Norwegian did it no
one else had ever done it before—but
then Shackleton had come within 97
miles of the Pole a couple of years before,
so there was no real 4-minute mile type
mental barrier to face. Also, Amundsen
had no back-up, not even radio. Perhaps
more to the point, Fuchs, during the
BCTAE 1955–58, took 57 days with
mechanized transport, along a route
close to that taken by Mountain Travel.
And the Mountain Travel expedition had
the remarkable luck/coincidence/plan-
ning to arrive at the Pole on the 77th anniversary of Scott's arrival there during
his last expedition.

Mountaineer Range. 73°28′S, 166°15′
E. Between the Mariner and Aviator
Glaciers in Victoria Land. First seen in
part by Ross in 1841. Named by the New
Zealanders in 1958–59 for the moun-
taineers who had explored this area.

Mountains. *See also* **Highest points in
Antarctica, Ranges, Nunataks,** and the
names of the individual mountains and
ranges. It would seem that a range is
smaller than a group of mountains, so
the Transantarctic Mountains, for example, the largest group in Antarctica, will
contain ranges. Since IGY, mountains
have been visited mostly only by reconnaissance parties, but in the early days of
exploration peaks were climbed with
regularity (and necessity sometimes) by
the parties.

Mountainview Ridge. 78°55′S, 83°42′
W. Ice-covered. Forms the SE extremity
of the Sentinel Range. Named by the
University of Minnesota Geological Party
here in 1963–64 for the excellent view of
the high peaks of the range as seen from
here.

Cap Moureaux *see* **Moureaux Point**

Moureaux Islands. 65°05′S, 63°08′W.
Two islands and off-lying rocks 2½ miles
WNW of Pelletan Point in Flandres Bay,
off the west coast of Graham Land. De
Gerlache landed on one of the islands in
Feb. 1898, and he charted and named
the group.

Moureaux Point. 63°57′S, 61°49′W. Forms the northern extremity of Liège Island. Charted by Charcot in 1903–5 and named Cap Moureaux by him for T. Moureaux, director of the Parc Saint-Maur Observatory, near Paris.

Mousinho Island. 70°38′S, 71°58′E. 235 m. Partly ice-covered. 2 miles from the south end of Gillock Island in the Amery Ice Shelf. Named by the Australians for A. Mousinho, pilot of the Beaver aircraft with the 1969 ANARE Prince Charles Mountains party.

Cape Mousse. 66°48′S, 141°28′E. Fringed by many small islands. It is backed by moraine just to the south. A small rocky cape, it juts out through the coastal ice-cap 2½ miles SW of Cape Découverte. Charted by the French in 1949–51 and named by them for the several patches of lichens found here. Mousse is the French for "moss."

Moutonnée Lake. 70°52′S, 68°20′W. A meltwater lake 4 miles south of Ablation Point on the east side of Alexander Island. Named by the UK for the roches moutonnées (sheep back rocks) here.

Moutonnée Valley. 70°51′S, 68°25′W. On the east side of Alexander Island, in the vicinity of Moutonnée Lake, for which this valley was named by the UK.

Movies set in Antarctica. There have not been many movies set in Antarctica. The most famous is *Scott of the Antarctic* (see that entry) made in 1948. The most spectacular has been the Japanese feature, *Antarctica*, released in 1984 (see that entry, too). Aside from *The Thing* (1982), that seems to be about all, although Antarctica has been mentioned many times in movies (the funniest moment perhaps being in *Mr. Belvedere Goes to College* when Clifton Webb claims to have been part of Admiral Byrd's expedition), and Sean Connery did play Amundsen in *The Red Tent*, but that was an Arctic story. There have been stacks of documentaries, the most well-received being, perhaps, *The Secret Land* (see that entry), a 1948 film about Byrd; Frank Hurley's magnificent documentaries (*see* Hurley for a list of his films); and Herbert Ponting's silent film, *90 Degrees South*, which he remade in 1933 with sound. Shackleton, during the British Antarctic Expedition of 1907–9, was the first to take moving pictures in the Antarctic. A company called Image Associates has produced many 1970s documentaries on the Antarctic for the NSF: *Antarctica* was 57 minutes long, and produced in 1975, and narrated by Burgess Meredith; *Antarctica: Laboratory for Science* was 27 minutes long, produced in 1978, and showed research being done by the USA. There are many, many others, constantly seen on TV.

Mount Moxley. 78°25′S, 162°21′E. Surmounts the divide between Potter and Wirdnam Glaciers in the Royal Society Range. Named in 1963 for Lt. (jg) Donald F. Moxley, USN, VX-6 Otter and helicopter pilot at McMurdo Station in 1960.

Islas Moyano *see* **Pitt Islands**

Cape Moyes. 66°35′S, 96°25′E. Ice-covered. Fronts the Shackleton Ice Shelf, 18 miles west of Cape Dovers. Discovered by the AAE 1911–14, and named by Mawson for Morton H. Moyes.

Moyes, Morton H. Australian naval man who was meteorologist with the Western Base Party during the AAE 1911–14. Later, during the BANZARE 1929–31, when he was a commander, he was cartographer to that expedition.

Moyes, William. British government representative on Signy Island in 1912–13.

Moyes Islands. 67°01′S, 143°51′E. In the western part of Watt Bay, 2½ miles SE of Cape-Pigeon Rocks, on the coast of East Antarctica. Discovered by the AAE 1911–14, and named by Mawson for Morton H. Moyes.

Moyes Peak. 67°45′S, 61°13′E. 2 miles north of Pearce Peak. 12 miles SW of Falla Bluff, on the coast of East Antarctica. Discovered in Feb. 1931 by the BANZARE, and named by Mawson for Morton H. Moyes.

Moyes Point. 60°45'S, 45°40'W. In the SW part of Signy Island, it forms the east side of the SE entrance to the Fyr Channel. Charted by personnel on the *Discovery II* in 1933. Surveyed by the FIDS in 1956–58 and named by the UK in 1959 for William Moyes.

Mozart Ice Piedmont. 70°S, 71°W. 60 miles long in a NW-SE direction. 15 miles at its widest. On the west coast of Alexander Island. Named by the UK for the composer.

Mozer Glacier *see* **Moser Glacier**

Nunataki Mramornyye *see* **Sigurd Knolls**

Mt. Ginnis Peak *see* **McGinnis Peak**

Muchmore, Donna. One of the first women ever to work at the South Pole (*see also* **Nan Scott**). She was a former hospital nurse married to Oklahoma professor, Dr. Harold Muchmore, who had also worked in the Antarctic on infectious diseases.

Muck Glacier. 84°39'S, 177°30'E. Between Campbell Cliffs and Sullivan Ridge in the Queen Maud Mountains. It flows north from Husky Heights, and then east around the north end of Sullivan Ridge to enter Ramsey Glacier. Named for Major James B. Muck, of the US Army Aviation Detachment which supported the Texas Tech Shackleton Glacier Expedition to this area in 1964–65.

Muckle Bluff. 61°09'S, 54°52'W. 5 miles west of Walker Point on the south coast of Elephant Island in the South Shetlands. Named by the UK in 1971. Muckle means large.

Mudrey Cirque. 77°39'S, 160°44'E. Between Northwest Mountain and West Groin in the southern part of the Asgard Range of Victoria Land. Named for Michael G. Mudrey, Jr., geologist with the Dry Valley Drilling Project in Victoria Land in 1972–73, 1973–74, and 1974–75.

Mount Mueller. 66°55'S, 55°32'E. Ice-covered. Just east of Mount Storegutt. 22 miles west of Edward VIII Bay. Named by the Australians for F. von Mueller, a member of the Australian Antarctic Exploration Committee of 1886.

Mügge Island. 66°55'S, 67°45'W. Also called Isla Fresia. One of the Bennett Islands. 1½ miles north of the west end of Weertman Island in Hanusse Bay. Named by the UK for Johannes O.C. Mügge (1858–1932), German mineralogist who made pioneer studies of the plasticity of ice, in 1895.

Mugridge, W. Fireman on the *Aurora*, during Shackleton's 1914–17 expedition.

Mühlig-Hofmann Mountains. 72°S, 5°20'E. 65 miles long in an east-west direction between the Gjelsvik Mountains and the Orvin Mountains in Queen Maud Land. Discovered by Ritscher in 1938–39 and named by him for the division director of the German Air Ministry.

Muir, J.J. 3rd officer on the *Jacob Ruppert*, 1933–34, and 1st officer, 1934–35.

Muir Peak. 79°09'S, 86°25'W. Near the middle of Frazier Ridge in the Founders Peaks of the Heritage Range. Named for Hugh M. Muir, aurora scientist at Plateau Station, 1966.

Mukai Rocks. 69°03'S, 39°42'E. On the Queen Maud Land coast, on the eastern margin of Ongul Sound, opposite East Ongul Island, in the region of Showa Station. Named Mukai-iwa (rocks which face) by the Japanese in 1972.

Mukluks. High, canvas, felt-lined, very warm boots with thick rubber soles.

Mount Mulach. 71°07'S, 164°04'E. 1,080 m. 4 miles NE of Mount Draeger on the east side of the Posey Range in the Bowers Mountains, where it overlooks the Lillie Glacier. Named for William J. Mulach, chief electrician's mate at McMurdo Station, 1967.

Muldoon, Robert. Prime minister of NZ who visited Antarctica in 1982 with Sir Edmund Hillary to mark New Zealand's 25 years of continuous research on the continent.

Mule Island. 68°39'S, 77°50'E. Just SW of Hawker Island, off the west tip of

Mule Peninsula in the Vestfold Hills, in Prydz Bay. Photographed by the LCE 1936–37 and named Mulöy (snout island) by the Norwegians.

Mule Peninsula. 68°39′S, 77°58′E. The southernmost of the three major peninsulas which comprise the Vestfold Hills in Princess Elizabeth Land. It lies between Ellis Fjord and Krok Fjord. Photographed by the LCE 1936–37 and named Breidnesmulen (the broad point snout) by the Norwegians. The Australians adapted the name.

Mule Point. 67°05′S, 58°12′E. Just south of East Stack, at the east side of the Hoseason Glacier in East Antarctica. Photographed by the LCE 1936–37 and named Mule (snout) by the Norwegians.

Mulebreen. 67°28′S, 59°21′E. Also called Dovers Glacier. A glacier, 6 miles wide and flowing WNW into the SE side of Stefansson Bay on the coast of East Antarctica. Photographed by the LCE 1936–37. Name means "the snout glacier" in Norwegian.

Pico Muleta *see* **Crutch Peaks**

Mulga Island. 67°14′S, 46°43′E. 3 miles off the coast of Enderby Land. 5 miles NE of Kirkby Head. Named for the Australian shrub of that name.

Mulgrew, P.D. Chief radio operator at Scott Base in 1957–58 who went with Hillary to the Pole as part of the BCTAE.

Mulgrew Nunatak. 79°38′S, 157°56′E. 1,600 m. 4 miles east of Tentacle Ridge in the Cook Mountains. Named by the Darwin Glacier Party of the BCTAE in 1957 for P.D. Mulgrew.

Mount Mull. 74°33′S, 63°08′W. On the east flank of Irvine Glacier. 11 miles SW of Mount Owen in the Guettard Range of Palmer Land. Named for William B. Mull, cook at Amundsen-Scott South Pole Station, 1964.

Müller, Johannes. Navigation officer on the *Deutschland* during Filchner's expedition of 1911–12. He was also second officer.

Müller, Leonhard. Stoker on the *Gauss* during von Drygalski's 1901–3 expedition.

Müller Crest. 72°11′S, 8°08′E. Also called Johannes Müller Crests. A short, ridgelike nunatak. 2,620 m. Marks the SE extremity of the Filchner Mountains, in the Orvin Mountains of Queen Maud Land. Discovered during Ritscher's 1938–39 expedition and named Müllerkammen by Ritscher for Johannes Müller. Later translated.

Müller Glacier. 72°16′S, 166°24′E. Flows from the Millen Range into Pearl Harbor Glacier just NW of Mount Pearson. Named for Dietland Müller-Schwarze.

Müller-Schwarze, Dietland and Christine. A husband and wife team working in Antarctica in the 1960s and 1970s. Dietland was an ethologist (a zoologist specializing in animal behavior), a Ph.D. from the Max Planck Institute of Behavioral Psychology in Seewiesen, Bavaria. In 1964 he became the first German scientist to be invited to work on USARP, and was the biologist at Hallett Station during the 1964–65 summer season. In 1965, back in Germany, he met Christine at Freiburg University. She was a German psychologist, also a Ph.D. They married and came to the USA. Dietland became associate professor of wildlife resources at Utah State University. He received a grant from the NSF to continue his penguin studies in Antarctica, and his wife went with him in Oct. 1969. This set a few records. They became the first husband and wife team to work in Antarctica, Christine became the first woman to come out of the USA to work on the Antarctic continent, and she was the only woman to work with USARP. They studied penguin behavior at Cape Crozier, Ross Island, during the 1969–70 and 1970–71 summer seasons. In 1971–72 they were in the Antarctic Peninsula, studying chinstraps and gentoos. Dietland then transferred to Syracuse, N.Y., and continued alone in Antarctica until 1976 (Christine was a mother by now). From

1977 they were in the Arctic studying reindeer.

Müllerkammen *see* **Müller Crest**

Mulligan Peak. 77°11'S, 160°15'E. Ice-free. 1 mile north of Robison Peak, at the north end of the Willett Range in Victoria Land. Named for John J. Mulligan of the US Bureau of Mines, who climbed this peak and the peak to the south of it during Dec. 1960, and found coal beds and fossil wood.

Mulock, George F.A. 1882–1963. 3rd lieutenant and surveyor, RN. Came to Antarctica on the *Morning* and replaced Shackleton (who was invalided home) in 1903 on the Royal Society Expedition. He compiled the survey on that expedition.

Mulock Glacier. 79°S, 160°E. Flows from the southern part of the Worcester Range, through the Hillary Coast, into the NW corner of the Ross Ice Shelf. Named by NZ in association with Mulock Inlet.

Mulock Inlet. 79°08'S, 160°40'E. A re-entrant (a bay, not of water, but of shelf ice, indenting the main part of the continent) 10 miles wide between Capes Teall and Lankester. It is occupied by the lower Mulock Glacier which flows through it to the Ross Ice Shelf. Discovered during Scott's 1901–4 expedition and named by them for Lt. George Mulock.

Muløy *see* **Mule Island**

Mulroy, Thomas B. Chief engineer on the shore party of Byrd's 1928–30 expedition. He had been in the Arctic with Byrd.

Mulroy Island. 71°45'S, 98°06'W. Just off Black Crag, the eastern extremity of the Noville Peninsula on Thurston Island. Discovered by the USN Bellingshausen Sea Expedition of Feb. 1960. Named for Thomas B. Mulroy.

Mulvik *see* **Ellis Fjord**

Mount Mumford. 71°33'S, 65°09'W. The central summit in the line of low rock peaks 4 miles north of the west end of Rathbone Hills in the Gutenko Mountains of central Palmer Land. Named for

Lt. Joel H. Mumford, USN, medical officer at Palmer Station, 1972.

Mumm Islands. 65°01'S, 63°59'W. 1½ miles NW of Turquet Point, Booth Island, off the west coast of Graham Land. Discovered and named by Charcot in 1903–5.

Mummery Cliff. 80°27'S, 21°23'W. In the Shackleton Range.

Mummification. The dryness and cold in Antarctica can mummify and preserve anything. Some seals, dying many miles inland in a vain search for food, were found years later, their leathery carcasses preserved. Explorers who visit huts left by the old pioneers are constantly amazed at the fresh state of things, including the food, some of which can still be eaten, decades later.

Mummy Pond. 77°40'S, 162°39'E. Between Suess and Lacroix Glaciers in the Taylor Valley of Victoria Land. Named by US geologist Troy L. Péwé, in Dec. 1957, for the mummified seals found here.

Mundlauga Crags. 71°57'S, 8°24'E. A group of rock crags. 2,455 m. They form the southern end of Fenriskjeften Mountain in the Drygalski Mountains of Queen Maud Land. Named by the Norwegians.

Península Munita *see* **Waterboat Point**

Munizaga Peak. 85°32'S, 177°37'W. 2,590 m. Ice-free. 3 miles ESE of Misery Peak in the Roberts Massif of the Queen Maud Mountains. Named by the USA for Fernando S. Munizaga, Chilean geologist who took part in the USARP Ellsworth Land Survey of 1968–69, and the same season accompanied a Texas Tech geological party in a survey of the Roberts Massif.

Munken *see* **Monk Islands**

Muñoz Point. 64°50'S, 62°54'W. On the west coast of Graham Land.

Munro Kerr Mountains. 70°50'S, 73°30'E. Form the NE flange of the Amery Ice Shelf on the Ingrid Christensen Coast.

Mount Munson. 84°48′S, 174°26′W. 2,800 m. On the NW flank of Mount Wade, 3 miles from its summit, in the Prince Olav Mountains. Discovered aerially by Byrd in Nov. 1929. Named for Capt. William H. Munson, USN, commander of VX-6, 1959–61.

Mural Nunatak. 64°59′S, 61°32′W. On the east side of Hektoria Glacier. 5 miles NW of Shiver Point in Graham Land. Surveyed by the FIDS in 1947 and again in 1955. Named by the UK for its wall-like appearance when seen from the SW.

The *Murature*. Argentine ship on the 1946–47 and 1947–48 expeditions undertaken by that country in the Antarctic.

Mount Murch. 84°38′S, 65°25′W. 1,100 m. 5 miles south of Mount Suydam in the Anderson Hills of the central Patuxent Range of the Pensacola Mountains. Named for Paul L. Murch, cook at Palmer Station, 1966.

¹**Mount Murchison.** 67°19′S, 144°15′E. 565 m. Dome-shaped. Snow-covered. On the west side of the Mertz Glacier. 11 miles SW of the head of Buchanan Bay. Discovered by the AAE 1911–14 and named by Mawson for Roderick Murchison of Melbourne, a patron.

²**Mount Murchison.** 73°25′S, 166°18′E. 3,500 m. Between Fitzgerald and Wylde Glaciers in the Mountaineer Range of Victoria Land. Discovered in Jan. 1841 by Ross, and named by him for Sir Roderick Murchison (1792–1871), general secretary of the British Association.

Murchison Cirque. 80°42′S, 24°33′W. In the Shackleton Range.

Cape Murdoch. 60°48′S, 44°41′W. Also called Cape Burn Murdoch. Forms the SE tip of Mossman Peninsula on the south coast of Laurie Island in the South Orkneys. Charted by Bruce in 1903, and named by him for W.G. Burn Murdoch.

Murdoch, W.G. Burn. Scottish artist on the *Balaena* during the Dundee Whaling Expedition of 1892–93. Later he was a supporter of Bruce's Scottish National Antarctic Expedition of 1902–4.

Murdoch Nunatak. 65°01′S, 60°02′W. Also called Burn Murdoch Nunatak. 3 miles NE of Donald Nunatak in the Seal Nunataks, off the east coast of the Antarctic Peninsula. Charted by the FIDS in 1947 and named by them for W.G. Burn Murdoch.

Cape Murmanskiy. 69°40′S, 13°20′E. Juts out from the west side of the Lazarev Ice Shelf, 25 miles NNE of Leningradskiy Island, in Queen Maud Land. Named by the USSR in 1959 for their city back home, Murmansk.

Mount Murphy. 75°20′S, 110°44′W. A massive, snow-covered volcano. 2,705 m. Just south of the Bear Peninsula, overlooking the Walgreen Coast of Marie Byrd Land. It is bounded by the Smith, Pope, and Haynes Glaciers. Algae and petrels are found here. Named for Robert Cushman Murphy of the American Museum of Natural History, an authority on Antarctic and sub–Antarctic bird life. He was the naturalist on the *Daisy* during the 1912–13 summer at South Georgia (he never got south of 60°S).

Murphy, Charles J.V. Assistant to Byrd after the latter's 1928–30 expedition. He was one of the shore party during Byrd's 1933–35 expedition.

Murphy, Herbert D. A member of the AAE 1911–14.

Murphy, John. Crewman on the *Bear of Oakland*, 1933–35.

Murphy Bay. 67°42′S, 146°19′E. 7 miles wide. Between Penguin Point and Cape Bage on the coast of East Antarctica. Discovered by the AAE 1911–14 and named by Mawson for Herbert D. Murphy.

Murphy Glacier. 66°54′S, 66°20′W. Flows west to Orford Cliff and merges with Wilkinson Glacier before terminating in Lallemand Fjord in Graham Land. Named for Thomas L. Murphy, FIDS leader and assistant surveyor at Base W in 1956.

Murphy Inlet. 71°56′S, 98°03′W. Ice-filled. 18 miles long. Has two parallel branches at the head. Between Noville and Edwards Peninsulas on the north side of Thurston Island. Named for Charles J.V. Murphy.

Murphy Rocks. 77°35'S, 144°55'W. 12 miles SE of Mount West on the ice-covered ridge between the Hammond and Boyd Glaciers, in the Ford Ranges of Marie Byrd Land. Named for Dion M. Murphy, USN, aviation machinist's mate and helicopter flight crewman in Antarctica with Operation Deep Freeze 68.

¹Cape Murray. 64°21'S, 61°38'W. Forms the west end of Murray Island, off the west coast of Graham Land. Charted by de Gerlache in 1897–99. He thought it was part of the mainland, and named it for Sir John Murray.

²Cape Murray. 79°35'S, 160°11'E. Mostly ice-covered. At the north side of the mouth of Carlyon Glacier on the west side of the Ross Ice Shelf. Discovered during Scott's 1901–4 expedition, and named by Scott for George R.M. Murray, temporary director of the scientific staff of the expedition, who had accompanied the *Discovery* as far as Cape Town in 1901.

Mount Murray. 76°09'S, 161°50'E. 1,005 m. Granitic. 8 miles west of Bruce Point on the north side of Mawson Glacier in Victoria Land. Charted by Shackleton's 1907–9 expedition and named by them for James Murray.

Murray, James. b. 1895, Glasgow. Biologist on Shackleton's 1907–9 expedition. He was in charge of Cape Royds when Shackles was away. He was lost in the Arctic in Feb. 1914, with A.F. Mackay.

Murray, John. b. March 3, 1841, Cobourg, Ontario, Canada. d. March 16, 1914, in a car accident near Kirkliston, West Lothian, Scotland. Oceanographer, naturalist in charge of bird specimens on the *Challenger,* 1872–76. He did much to organize the expedition. He believed strongly in Antarctic research, and was knighted in 1898.

Murray Dome. 70°42'S, 67°12'E. A dome-shaped rock 3 miles SE of Mount McKenzie in the Aramis Range of the Prince Charles Mountains. Named by the Australians for D.L. Murray, medical officer at Wilkes Station in 1964.

Murray Foreland. 74°S, 114°30'W. Ice-covered. 20 miles long. 10 miles wide. A peninsula which forms the NW arm of the larger Martin Peninsula on the coast of Marie Byrd Land. Named for Grover E. Murray, NSF geologist and president of Texas Tech from 1966–76 (Texas Tech in Lubbock, Texas, has sent down several expeditions to Antarctica).

Murray Glacier. 71°39'S, 170°E. A valley glacier, 20 miles long. It flows along the eastern side of the Geikie Ridge in the Admiralty Mountains. Its terminus coalesces with that of Dugdale Glacier, where both glaciers discharge into Robertson Bay in Oates Land. Charted by Borchgrevink, and named by him for Sir John Murray.

Murray Harbor. 64°21'S, 61°35'W. East of Cape Murray on the north side of Murray Island, off the west coast of Graham Land. Named by local whalers in 1922.

Murray Island. 64°22'S, 61°34'W. Also called Bluff Island, Isla Teniente Kopaitic. 6 miles long. At the SW side of Hughes Bay, off the west coast of Graham Land. Originally thought to be part of the mainland, its actual status was proved in 1922 by the whale catcher *Graham* passing through the channel separating it from the mainland. Named in association with Cape Murray, the seaward extremity of the island.

Murray Islands. 60°47'S, 44°31'W. Almost 1¼ miles SE of Cape Whitson, off the south coast of Laurie Island in the South Orkneys. Discovered in 1823 by Matthew Brisbane, and named by Weddell as Murry's Islands, which really should have read Murray's Islands, for James Murray of London, maker of the chronometers used on Weddell's voyage.

Murray Monolith. 67°47'S, 66°54'E. 370 m. The detached front of Torlyn Mountain. 4 miles east of Scullin Monolith in Mac. Robertson Land. Named in Feb. 1931 by Mawson for Sir George Murray, chief justice of South Australia and chancellor of the University of Adelaide, and a patron of the BANZARE 1929–31.

Murrish Glacier. 71°02'S, 61°45'W. 15 miles long. On the east side of Palmer Land. It flows ENE to the north of Stockton Peak and Abendroth Peak, and merges with the north side of Gain Glacier before the latter enters the Weddell Sea opposite Morency Island. Named for David E. Murrish, biologist and leader of the Antarctic Peninsula bird study program from 1972–75.

Murry Peak *see* **Mount Nemesis**

Murrys Islands *see* **Murray Islands**

Murtaugh Peak. 85°41'S, 130°15'W. 3,085 m. Surmounts a ridge 4 miles WNW of Mount Minshew in the Wisconsin Range of the Horlick Mountains. Named for John E. Murtaugh, geologist here in 1964–65 with the Ohio State University geological party.

Museum Ledge. 84°45'S, 113°48'W. A flat sandstone bed about 25 yards long and 10 yards wide, exposed by erosion. Fossils are found here. On the SW shoulder of Mount Glossopteris in the Ohio Range of the Horlick Mountains. Named by William E. Long (*see* **Long Hills**) for the display of fossil wood found here.

Mushketov Glacier. 71°20'S, 14°55'E. Flows from the area between the Wohlthat Mountains on the west and the Weyprecht Mountains, Payer Mountains, and Lomonosov Mountains on the east, in Queen Maud Land. Discovered aerially by Ritscher's 1938–39 expedition. Named by the USSR in 1958–59 for geologist and geographer Ivan V. Mushketov (1850–1902).

Mushroom Island. 68°53'S, 67°53'W. Ice-covered. 10 miles WSW of Cape Berteaux, off the west coast of Graham Land. Charted by the BGLE 1934–37 and named by them because it looks like a mushroom cap.

Muskeg Gap. 64°23'S, 59°39'W. A low isthmus at the north end of Sobral Peninsula in Graham Land. It provides a coastal route which avoids a long detour around the peninsula. Surveyed by the FIDS in 1960–61. Named by the UK for the Muskeg tractor.

Muskegs. Canadian tractors in use in the Antarctic. Fuchs took one on the BCTAE 1957–58.

Cape Musselman. 71°17'S, 61°W. Forms the south side of the entrance to Palmer Inlet, on the east coast of Palmer Land. Discovered in 1940 by members of East Base during the USAS 1939–41. Named for Lytton C. Musselman.

Musselman, Lytton C. Communications man at East Base during the USAS 1939–41.

Musson Nunatak. 71°31'S, 63°27'W. Pyramidal. 10 miles south of Mount Jackson at the eastern edge of the Dyer Plateau in Palmer Land. Named for John M. Musson, USN, photographer and member of the cartographic aerial mapping crew in LC-130 aircraft with VX-6 in Antarctica, 1968–69.

Mussorgsky Peaks. 71°30'S, 73°19'W. Two rocky peaks of 500 m. They overlook the northern shore of Brahms Inlet, 6 miles NW of Mount Grieg in the SW part of Alexander Island. Named by the UK for the composer.

Gora Musy Dzhalilya *see* **Mount Dzhalil'**

Mutel Peak. 76°31'S, 146°03'W. 860 m. 2 miles SW of Mount Iphigene in the Ford Ranges of Marie Byrd Land. Named for Robert L. Mutel, ionosphere physicist at Byrd Station, 1969.

Islas Mutilla *see* **Palosuo Islands**

Mutton Cove. 66°S, 65°39'W. An anchorage ½ mile NE of the south end of Beer Island in the Biscoe Islands. It is formed by four small islands, Harp

Island, Upper Island, Cliff Island, and Girdler Island. Beer Island shelters the cove from the west. Charted in 1936 by the BGLE. Named that year by Robert E.D. Ryder.

Mutton Cove Island *see* **Beer Island**

Muus Glacier. 71°26'S, 61°36'W. Enters the north side of Odom Inlet between Snyder Peninsula and Strømme Ridge, on the east coast of Palmer Land. Named for David Muus, oceanographer on the *Northwind* in the Ross Sea area, 1971–72, and on the *Glacier* in the Weddell Sea area, 1974–75.

Myall Islands. 67°40'S, 45°43'E. 6 small islands a mile offshore from Gaudis Point, in Alasheyev Bight, in the area of Molodezhnaya Station, just west of the Thala Hills off the coast of Enderby Land. By far the biggest of the group is about 600 yards long and a quarter mile wide.

Myers Glacier. 72°14'S, 100°18'W. A valley glacier 7 miles long. Flows from Mount Noxon on Thurston Island to the Abbott Ice Shelf in Peacock Sound. Named for Lt. (jg) Dale P. Myers, USN, helicopter pilot on the *Burton Island* in the area during the USN Bellingshausen Sea Expedition of Feb. 1960.

Myoto Islands *see* **Meoto Rocks**

Myres, John. Seaman on the Wilkes Expedition 1838–42. Joined in the USA. Served the cruise.

Myres, John H. 2nd class boy on the Wilkes Expedition 1838–42. Joined at Callao. Served the cruise.

Myriad Islands. 65°05'S, 64°25'W. A scattered group of small islands, including Flank Island and Final Island, and also rocks, extending for 5 miles. West of the Dannebrog and Vedel Islands in the Wilhelm Archipelago. Charted by the BGLE 1934–37. Named by the UK in 1959 because of the large number of islands in the group.

Mysteries. These are some of the more famous: Was Edwards Island the same as Deception Island? What was the mysteri-

ous New South Greenland discovered by Capt. Robert Johnson in 1821–22? The ancient Piri Re'is map (*see* **Mapping of Antarctica**) depicts Antarctica as an ice-free continent. How? And why? Why are there oases in Antarctica? When was the Français Glacier formed? On Jan. 17, 1823, the writer of the log of the *Jenny* signed off. This sealer had been in Antarctic waters looking for seals. It was discovered in Dec. 1840, floating aimlessly in the Drake Passage, its crew all long dead. What had happened? In 1893 Carl Larsen discovered on Seymour Island 50 clay balls neatly arranged on small clay pillars, which seemed to have been fashioned by human hands. If they were, who left them? When the FIDS were surveying Whistling Bay in 1948 they heard curious and still unidentified whistling sounds in the area. The FIDS would have recognized the sounds of whales, so what were they?

N.A.F. McMurdo *see* **McMurdo Station**

Mount N.D. Lorette *see* **Mount Lorette**

N. Persson Island *see* **Persson Island**

Mount Naab. 76°36'S, 160°57'E. 1,710 m. Surmounts the eastern part of Eastwind Ridge in the Convoy Range. Named in 1964 for Capt. Joseph Naab, commander of the *Eastwind*, 1961 and 1962.

Nabbodden *see* **Tilley Nunatak**

Nabbøya. 69°16'S, 39°35'E. An ice-free island 1 mile west of Hamnenabben Head, in the eastern part of Lützow-Holm Bay. Photographed by the LCE 1936–37. Name means "the peg island" in Norwegian.

Nabbvika *see* **Tilley Bay**

Nadeau Bluff. 84°04'S, 175°09'E. Mainly ice-covered. Just SW of Giovinco Ice Piedmont. Juts out into Canyon Glacier from the east side of that glacier. Named for F.A. Nadeau, Jr., at McMurdo Station in 1963.

The *Nadezhda Krupskaya*. A small passenger liner chartered by the Arctic and Antarctic Research Institute, Leningrad, for use during the 17th Soviet Antarctic Expedition, 1971–72. Left Leningrad in Jan. 1972, and 4 weeks later was in Antarctica. Sailed back to the USSR in early March 1972.

Nadezhdy Island. 70°44′S, 11°40′E. Ice-free. Nearly 1 mile long. Just off the north-central side of the Schirmacher Hills of Queen Maud Land. Named Ostrov Nadezhdy (hope island) by the USSR in 1961.

Naess Glacier. 70°22′S, 67°55′W. Separated from Chapman Glacier to the north by a rocky ridge. Flows from the west coast of Palmer Land into George VI Sound. Named by the UK in 1954 for Erling D. Naess, manager of the Vestfold Whaling Company, who gave a lot of help to the BGLE, who surveyed this glacier in 1936.

Naga-iwa Rock. 68°27′S, 41°31′E. A rock on land which juts out into the sea 2 miles east of Cape Akarui in Queen Maud Land. Named Naga-iwa (long rock) by the Japanese.

Nagagutsu Point. 69°41′S, 38°21′E. Also spelled (erroneously) as Nagagutu Point. Ice-covered. Forms the SE end of Padda Island in Lützow-Holm Bay. Photographed by the LCE 1936–37. Named later by the Japanese as Nagagutsu-misaki (boot point).

Nagagutu Point *see* **Nagagutsu Point**

Nagata, Takeshi. Japanese professor who led JARE I and JARE II (i.e., the first two Japanese Antarctic Expeditions, in 1956–57 and 1957–58 respectively—the second one having to be aborted due to thick ice). He masterminded the establishment of Showa Station in 1956–57. He was back in Antarctica again, later, in the *Fuji*, and in 1968 he was director of the University of Tokyo's Geophysical Institute. He was also, in his career, director of the Japanese National Institute of Polar Research. He took part in JARE 25 in 1983–84.

Naisbitt, Christopher. Ship's clerk on the *Quest*, 1921–22. He joined the expedition at Rio. Later lived in London.

Nakano-seto Strait. 69°01′S, 39°33′E. Very narrow. Between Ongul Island and East Ongul Island, in the eastern part of Lützow-Holm Bay. The Japanese discovered it in 1957 and called it Nakano-seto (central strait).

Nakaya Islands. 66°27′S, 66°14′W. Small group in Crystal Sound. 10 miles NE of Cape Rey, Graham Land. Named by the UK for Japanese physicist Ukichiro Nakaya, specialist in ice-crystals and snow-crystals.

Cape Nakayubi. 69°14′S, 39°39′E. Marks the southern extremity of a U-shaped peninsula which juts out into the sea like a finger from the west side of the Langhovde Hills in Queen Maud Land. Named Nakayubi-misaki (middle finger point) by the Japanese in 1972, in association with Cape Koyubi, ½ mile to the north.

Nålegga Ridge. 72°39′S, 4°03′W. Marks the north end of the Seilkopf Peaks in the Borg Massif of Queen Maud Land. Name means "the needle ridge" in Norwegian.

Nameless Glacier. 71°37′S, 170°18′E. Flows from the Adare Peninsula into Protection Cove, Robertson Bay, Victoria Land. 2 miles east of Newnes Glacier. Charted and named by Campbell's Northern Party during Scott's 1910–13 expedition. It was the only Robertson Bay glacier left unnamed by Borchgrevink in 1898–1900.

Cape Nan Anderson *see* **Cape Anderson**

The *Nana*. A Noorduyn C-64 Norseman single-engine cargo plane developed in Canada for cold-weather operations, it was named by Ronne during the RARE for the North American Newspaper Alliance for which his wife was a reporter. One of the three planes on the expedition, it was test-flown in the Antarctic on Sept. 14, 1947.

Nance Ridge. 84°23'S, 65°36'W. 2 miles NE of Mount Yarbrough in the Thomas Hills, in the northern part of the Patuxent Range of the Pensacola Mountains. Named for Vernon L. Nance, radioman at Palmer Station in 1966.

The *Nancy*. US sealing brig, registered in Salem, Mass., on Aug. 11, 1820. It was part of the Salem Expedition which spent the 1820–21 and the 1821–22 seasons in the South Shetlands, anchored for a lot of the time in Clothier Harbor. Captain Benjamin Upton.

Nancy Automatic Weather Station. 77°55'S, 168°10'E. American AWS at an elevation of approximately 83 feet. It operated from Jan. 17, 1983, to Nov. 25, 1983.

Nancy Rock. 62°13'S, 59°06'W. A rock in water 2 miles west of Flat Top Peninsula, King George Island, in the South Shetlands. Named by the UK in 1961, for the *Nancy*.

The *Nanok S.* Australian ship which supplied that country's bases in the 1970s.

¹Mount Nansen *see* **Mount Fridtjof Nansen**

²Mount Nansen. 74°34'S, 162°36'E. 2,740 m. In Victoria Land, just north of the Reeves Glacier. In the Eisenhower Range, 11 miles south of Mount Baxter. Discovered by Scott's 1901–4 expedition and named by them for Fridtjof Nansen, the Arctic explorer, who gave advice to Scott.

Nansen Ice Sheet. 74°58'S, 163°10'E. An ice shelf 30 miles long and 10 miles wide. Behind Terra Nova Bay in Victoria Land. It is fed by the Priestley and Reeves Glaciers. It adjoins the northern side of the Drygalski Ice Tongue. Explored by David's party of 1908–9 during Shackleton's 1907–9 expedition, and by Campbell's Northern Party during Scott's 1910–13 expedition. Debenham, on the latter, called it the Nansen Sheet, for the nearby

mountain. The name was changed slightly, later.

¹Nansen Island *see* **Lavoisier Island**

²Nansen Island. 64°35'S, 62°06'W. Also called Isla Nansen Sur. The largest of the islands in Wilhelmina Bay, off the west coast of Graham Land. Discovered and named by de Gerlache in 1897–99 for Fridtjof Nansen, the Arctic explorer.

Isla Nansen Norte *see* **Enterprise Island**

Nansen Sheet *see* **Nansen Ice Sheet**

Isla Nansen Sur *see* **Nansen Island**

Nantucket Inlet. 74°35'S, 61°45'W. Also called Innes-Taylor Inlet, Fran Inlet. 6 miles wide, it recedes 13 miles between the Smith and Bowman Peninsulas. In effect it is a Weddell Sea indentation into the southern coast of Palmer Land, just north of where the Ronne Ice Shelf meets the Antarctic Peninsula. Discovered on Dec. 30, 1940, on a flight from East Base during the USAS 1939–41. Named for Nantucket Island, Mass., home port for many of the early sealers to the South Shetlands.

Napier, William. Captain of the *Venus* in the South Shetlands in 1820–21. He brought back several specimens of a lichen he found there.

Mount Napier Birks. Wilkins flew over the Antarctic Peninsula in 1928 and discovered what he called Crane Channel. Just north of Crane Channel he saw two conspicuous black peaks which he named Mount Napier Birks for Napier Birks of Adelaide, Australia. The FIDS charted this coast in 1947 and proved the Crane Channel to be a glacier, the Crane Glacier (as it was renamed). They could not find Mount Napier Birks. To the north of the mouth of the glacier, however, at 65°18'S, 62°10'W, lies a conspicuous, pyramid-shaped mountain, which in 1950 the UK called Mount Birks (*see also* **Mount Alibi**).

Napier Ice Rise. 69°14'S, 67°47'W. In the SW part of the Wordie Ice Shelf, on the western part of the Antarctic Peninsula, 12 miles NW of Mount Balfour. Surveyed by the FIDS in Nov. 1958. Named by the UK for John Napier (1550–1617), the Scottish inventor of logarithms.

Napier Mountains. 66°30'S, 53°40'E. Also called the Napier Range. 40 miles long in a NW-SE direction. 40 miles south of Cape Batterbee on the coast of Enderby Land. Discovered in Jan. 1930 by the BANZARE and named by Mawson for John Mellis Napier, South Australian Supreme Court judge.

Napier Range *see* **Napier Mountains**

Napier Rock. 62°10'S, 58°26'W. A rock in water 1¾ miles ESE of Point Thomas in Admiralty Bay, King George Island, in the South Shetlands. Charted by Charcot in 1908–10. Named by the UK in 1960 for Ronald G. Napier (1925–56), FIDS general assistant and handyman at Signy Island Station in 1955, and leader at Base G until he was drowned on March 24, 1956 (*see* **Deaths, 1956**).

Narabi Rocks. 68°24'S, 41°47'E. Three rocks in a line, extending almost 3 miles along the coast (on land) between Temmondai Rock and Kozo Rock in Queen Maud Land. Named Narabi-iwa (row rocks) by the Japanese.

Mount Nares. 81°27'S, 158°10'E. Over 3,000 m. Just south of Mount Albert Markham. It overlooks the head of the Flynn Glacier in the Churchill Mountains. Scott discovered and named it in 1901–4 for Sir George S. Nares.

Nares, George S. b. 1831, Aberdeen, Scotland. d. 1915. Sir George Strong Nares. British Naval captain who joined the RN in 1845 and in 1852 went looking for Sir John Franklin in the Arctic. He was captain of the *Challenger* for the first half of the 1872–76 expedition, crossing the Antarctic Circle in 1874. Later that year he left the ship to go to the Arctic again.

Narrow Isle *see* **Gibbs Island**

Narrow Neck. 73°07'S, 169°02'E. An isthmus between Langevad Glacier and Mandible Cirque in the south part of the Daniell Peninsula of Victoria Land. Joins Tousled Peak and the Mount Lubbock area to the main part of the Daniell Peninsula. Descriptively named by NZ in 1966.

The Narrows. 67°36'S, 67°12'W. A marine channel between Pourquoi Pas Island and Blaiklock Island. Connects Bigourdan and Bourgeois Fjords off the west coast of Graham Land. Discovered and named descriptively by the BGLE 1934–37.

Nascent Glacier. 73°22'S, 167°37'E. In the eastern extremity of the Mountaineer Range, it flows to the coast of Victoria Land between Gauntlet Ridge and Index Point. Named by NZ in 1966.

Mount Nash. 74°14'S, 62°20'W. 1,295 m. 13 miles WNW of the head of Keller Inlet and 12 miles NNE of Mount Owen, on the east coast of Palmer Land. Discovered by the RARE 1947–48. Named by Ronne for H.R. Nash, of Pittsburgh, Pa., a contributor.

Nash Canyon. 64°S, 126°E. Submarine feature off the East Antarctica coast.

Nash Glacier. 71°15'S, 168°10'E. 20 miles long. Flows from the northern slopes of Dunedin Range in the Admiralty Mountains. Merges with Wallis and Dennistoun Glaciers before reaching the sea east of Cape Scott. Named for Lt. Arthur R. Nash, USN, VX-6 helicopter pilot in 1967 and 1968.

Nash Hills. 81°53'S, 89°23'W. Ice-covered. 25 miles NW of Martin Hills. Named for Lt. Archie R. Nash, USN, officer-in-charge at Byrd Station in 1962.

Nash Range. 81°55'S, 162°E. 40 miles long. Ice-covered. Between the Dickey and Nimrod Glaciers, behind the Shackleton Coast. It overlooks the Ross Ice Shelf, and is in turn overlooked by the Churchill Mountains. Named by the Ross Sea Committee during the BCTAE 1955–58 for Walter Nash, NZ politician who supported the NZ participation in the BCTAE.

Nash Ridge. 74°17′S, 163°E. 10 miles long. 5 miles wide. Juts out between the flow of the O'Kane and Priestley Glaciers in the eastern part of the Eisenhower Range of Victoria Land. Named for Harold A. Nash, biologist at McMurdo Station in 1965–66 and 1966–67.

Nashornet Mountain. 72°22′S, 2°W. 6 miles NE of Viddalskollen Hill, on the south side of Viddalen Valley in Queen Maud Land. Name means "the rhinoceros" in Norwegian.

Nashornkalvane Rocks. 72°19′S, 1°56′ W. A group of rocks on land, 2 miles north of Nashornet Mountain, at the south side of the mouth of Viddalen Valley in Queen Maud Land. Name means "the calves of the rhinoceros" in Norwegian.

Nåsudden see **The Naze**

Natani Nunatak. 84°46′S, 66°30′W. 1½ miles NNE of the extremity of Snake Ridge in the Patuxent Range of the Pensacola Mountains. Named by the US for Kirmach Natani, biologist at Amundsen-Scott South Pole Station in 1967.

Nathan Hills. 73°25′S, 164°24′E. In the east part of the Arrowhead Range of the Southern Cross Mountains in Victoria Land. Named by the Southern Party of the NZGSAE 1966–67 for Simon Nathan, senior geologist with the party.

Punta Natho see **Aguda Point**

National Antarctic Expedition see **Royal Society Expedition**

National Science Foundation. Also seen as the NSF. An independent US Federal agency founded in 1950 and headed by a presidentially-appointed director. After IGY (1957–58) it assumed the responsibility for all US Antarctic research, and in 1970 was designated the leading agency for American activities in Antarctica. At that stage all USARP was consolidated under the NSF. Logistical backup is provided by the US Naval Support Force, Antarctica. The NSF also hires a contractor (see **Antarctic Services Associates**). About 1,100 scientists and other staff are employed by the NSF. Its research ship in the Antarctic from 1968 to 1984 was the *Hero*, this being replaced in 1984 by the *Polar Duke*.

Natural resources. Science, freedom, ice, water, storage, space, and the land itself are all natural resources of Antarctica, but nothing of economic value has yet been found. The minerals and biological resources are not, as yet, exploitable to any great degree.

Nausea Knob. Part of Mount Erebus, on Ross Island.

Nautilus Head. 67°38′S, 67°07′W. A headland. 975 m. Near the NE end of Pourquoi Pas Island, off the west coast of Graham Land. Surveyed by the BGLE in 1936–37, and again by the FIDS in 1948. The FIDS named it for Jules Verne's fictional submarine.

Navarette Peak. 75°55′S, 128°45′W. 4 miles SW of Mount Petras in the McCuddin Mountains of Marie Byrd Land. Named for Capt. Claude Navarette, USN, deputy commander of the US Naval Support Force, Antarctica, in 1972. He had also served on the staff in 1969 and 1970.

The *Navarin*. USSR reinforced dry cargo vessel with an icebreaker hull. Sometimes in the Antarctic.

The *Navarino*. Argentine motor vessel, not an ice-worthy ship, leased to Linblad Travel in Feb. 1968, for a tour of the Antarctic Peninsula and the islands. A Jan. 1968 trip had been cut short by an accident at Cape Horn.

Navarrete Torres, Alejandro. Leader of the Chilean Antarctic Expedition of 1956–57. His ships were the *Baquedano*, the *Rancagua*, the *Angamos*, the *Lientur* and the *Lautaro*.

Islote Navegante Vidal see **Vidal Rock**

Navigator Nunatak. 73°15′S, 164°13′ E. In the middle of the head of Aviator Glacier, in Victoria Land. Named by the New Zealanders in 1962–63 because it is a good landmark, and also in association with nearby Aviator, Pilot, and Co-Pilot Glaciers.

Navigator Peak. 79°23'S, 85°48'W. 1,910 m. 4 miles east of Zavis Peak, in the northern part of the White Escarpment in the Heritage Range. Named by the University of Minnesota Geological Party here in 1963–64 because it was a landmark for pilots.

Mount Navy *see* **Mount Butler**

Navy Range *see* **Colbert Mountains**

The Naze. 63°57'S, 57°32'W. Also called Punta Morro. A peninsula which marks the SE entrance to Herbert Sound in the northern part of James Ross Island. Extends about 5 miles NE from Terrapin Hill toward the south-central shore of Vega Island. Discovered and named Nåsudden by Nordenskjöld's expedition of 1901–4. Later translated into English.

Neall Massif. 72°04'S, 164°28'E. Between the Salamander and West Quartzite Ranges. Named by NZ for V.E. Neall, geologist and leader of the NZGSAE 1967–68.

Neb Bluff. 67°S, 66°35'W. 6 miles south of Orford Bluff in Graham Land. Overlooks the east side of Lallemand Fjord. Surveyed by the FIDS in 1956, and named by them for its neblike appearance.

Bukhta Nebesnaya *see* **Sparkes Bay**

Nebhut, John. Private on the Wilkes Expedition 1838–42. Joined in the USA. Served the cruise.

Nebles Harbor *see* **Nebles Point**

Nebles Point. 62°12'S, 58°52'W. Forms the west side of the entrance to Collins Harbor, in the SW part of King George Island in the South Shetlands. In 1825 Weddell named a harbor near here, possibly what is now Collins Harbor, as Nebles Harbour. In 1960, unable to be sure of Weddell's location, the UK named this point in order to preserve the spirit of Weddell's naming in the area.

Neck or Nothing Passage. 62°29'S, 60°21'W. Leads from Blythe Bay between the south end of Desolation Island and a small group of islands 350 yards to the south. Named by whalers before 1930 as they used to race their vessels to this neck in order to get out in time to miss the bad weather.

Mount Neder. 71°02'S, 167°40'E. 1,010 m. Surmounts the NW part of Quam Heights in the Anare Mountains of Victoria Land. Named for Irving R. Neder, geologist in the Ohio Range and Wisconsin Range areas in 1965–66, and at McMurdo Station in 1966–67.

Nedresjöen *see* **Lake Unter-See**

The Needle *see* **The Spire**

Needle Peak. 62°44'S, 60°11'W. Also called Pico Aguja. 370 m. At the west side of Brunow Bay on the south coast of Livingston Island. Named Barnard's Peak by Weddell in 1825. Renamed in 1935 by the personnel on the *Discovery II.*

The Needles *see* **Les Dents**

Mesa Negra *see* **Birdsend Bluff**

Cabo Negrito *see* **Marescot Point**

Cabo Negro *see* **Siffrey Point**

Islote Negro *see* **Stark Rock**

Nunatak Negro *see* **Spigot Peak**

Negro Hill. 62°39'S, 61°W. Also called Cerro Negro. On the southern side of Byers Peninsula, Livingston Island, in the South Shetlands. Not to be confused with False Negro Hill.

Neil Peak *see* **Neill Peak**

Neill, William. Quartermaster on the Wilkes Expedition 1838–42. Joined in the USA. Served the cruise.

Neill Peak. 67°50'S, 66°37'E. Also called Neil Peak, Heil Peak. 460 m. 3 miles SW of Scullin Monolith in Mac. Robertson Land. Discovered on Feb. 13, 1931, by the BANZARE, and named by Mawson.

Neilson Peak. 70°57'S, 62°13'W. In the central part of the Parmelee Massif at the head of Lehrke Inlet on the east coast of Palmer Land. Named for David R.

Neilson, biologist at Palmer Station, 1975.

Neith Nunatak. 83°17'S, 55°55'W. 3 miles north of Baker Ridge in the northern Neptune Range of the Pensacola Mountains. Named for Willard Neith, photographer on the US Air Force Electronics Test Unit 1957–58.

The *Neko*. Floating factory whaler owned by Christian Salvesen. It operated in the South Shetlands and Antarctic Peninsula waters for many seasons between 1911–12 and 1923–24.

Neko Harbor. 64°50'S, 62°33'W. A bay which indents the east shore of Andvord Bay, 6 miles SE of Beneden Head, on the west coast of Graham Land. Discovered by de Gerlache and named by him for the *Neko*.

The *Nella Dan*. 2,206-ton ship under charter to Australia. It was used by the ANARE in 1962–63 and 1968–69, for example, as their transport vessel. The captain in 1968–70, and in 1972, was B.T. Hansen. In 1985, 45 days of krill research were done from it in Prydz Bay, and in late October of that year it got trapped in 13-foot-thick ice off Enderby Land. The *Icebird* tried to help, but almost got trapped itself, and after 52 days it was released by the *Shirase*. It was trapped again in the 1986–87 season, and was freed by the *Mikhail Somov*. The ship ran aground off Macquarie Island (not in the Antarctic) in Dec. 1987, and it was sunk a little while later.

Nella Island. 70°39'S, 166°04'E. The northern of 2 small islands just off the NW edge of the Davis Ice Piedmont, off the northern coast of Victoria Land. Named by the ANARE for the *Nella Dan*.

Nella Rock. 67°31'S, 62°51'E. In the entrance to Holme Bay. 500 yards from the eastern extremity of the largest of the Sawert Rocks. Named by the Australians for the *Nella Dan*, which struck this rock on March 4, 1969.

Nelly Island. 66°14'S, 110°11'E. The largest and most easterly of the Frazier Islands, in Vincennes Bay. Visited on Jan. 21, 1956, by an ANARE party which established an astronomical control station here. Named by the ANARE for the "nelly" (a nickname for the giant petrel) rookeries here.

The *Nelson*. A London sealer which left England in Dec. 1818 under Capt. Burney. It was in the South Shetlands for the 1820–21 season, and returned to England in July 1821. It was back again in the South Shetlands during the period 1821–23.

[1]Mount Nelson. Discovered near the Bay of Whales by Amundsen in 1910–11, along with Mount Ronniken. These two mountains were not very tall, and by 1928, when Byrd arrived, they were covered with snow.

[2]Mount Nelson. 85°47'S, 153°48'W. 1,930 m. 3 miles NE of Mount Pulitzer, near the west side of the Robert Scott Glacier in the Queen Maud Mountains. Named for Randy L. Nelson, geodesist at McMurdo Station in 1965.

Nelson, A.L. Lt., RNR. Chief officer and navigator on the *Discovery II* in 1930, and its captain on the 1933–35 expedition.

Nelson, Edward W. Invertebrate biologist on the British Antarctic Expedition of 1910–13. He was part of Campbell's Northern Party.

Nelson, Horatio. Seaman on the Wilkes Expedition 1838–42. Joined in the USA. Discharged at Oahu, Oct. 31, 1840.

Nelson, O. Bosun on the *Porpoise* during the Wilkes Expedition 1838–42. Was detached at Rio.

Nelson Cliff. 71°14'S, 168°42'E. At the west side of Simpson Glacier on the northern coast of Victoria Land. Charted by Campbell's Northern Party during Scott's 1910–13 expedition, and named by them as Nelson Cliffs, for Edward W. Nelson. The name was amended slightly a little later.

Nelson Cliffs *see* **Nelson Cliff**

Nelson Island. 62°19'S, 59°03'W. Also called Nelson's Island, Nelson's Isles, Leipzig Island, Strachan's Island. 12 miles long. 7 miles wide. SW of King George Island, it is one of the main islands in the South Shetlands. It is also one of the main homes of the chinstrap penguin. Briefly called O'Cain's Island (by the sealers in the 1820–21 season) it was renamed before the end of that season.

Nelson Nunatak. 72°56'S, 167°54'E. Mainly ice-covered. In the middle of Hand Glacier in the Victory Mountains of Victoria Land. Named for Thomas R. Nelson, USN, construction mechanic at McMurdo Station in 1967.

Nelson Peak. 83°40'S, 55°03'W. 1,605 m. At the east end of Drury Ridge and Brown Ridge where these two ridges abut the Washington Escarpment in the Neptune Range. Named for Willis H. Nelson, geologist here in 1963–64.

Nelson Rock. 67°23'S, 62°46'E. A solitary, partially ice-covered rock in water, 3 miles north of the Williamson Rocks, off the coast of Mac. Robertson Land. Named by the Australians for R. Nelson, weather observer at Mawson Station in 1962.

Nelson Strait. 62°19'S, 59°20'W. Separates Robert Island from Nelson Island in the South Shetlands. Palmer named it Harmony Strait in 1821. Powell renamed it King George's Strait in 1822, and this name has variously appeared as King George Straits. In 1825 Weddell renamed it again as Parry's Straits. It later became known by its present name, probably in association with the island.

Nematodes. Round worms, microfauna of Antarctica (*see also* **Fauna**).

Mount Nemesis. 68°12'S, 66°54'W. Also called Nemesis Peak, Nemesis Mountain, Murry Peak. 790 m. 2 miles NE of the seaward extremity of Roman Four Promontory, and just north of Neny Fjord, on the west coast of Graham Land. Named by the USAS 1939–41.

Nemesis Glacier. 70°35'S, 67°30'E. Flows through the Aramis Range of the Prince Charles Mountains into the Amery Ice Shelf. Discovered by W.G. Bewsher's ANARE party in Jan. 1957, and named after the Homeric character for the difficulties it caused while traversing here.

Nemesis Mountain *see* **Mount Nemesis**

Nemesis Peak *see* **Mount Nemesis**

Nemeth, Joseph. Commander of Little Rockford Station from Oct. 11, 1960, through that summer.

Nemo Cove. 67°43'S, 67°18'W. On the east side of Pourquoi Pas Island, off the west coast of Graham Land. The FIDS surveyed it and named it in 1948 for the Jules Verne character.

Nemo Glacier. 67°43'S, 67°22'W. On Pourquoi Pas Island, off the west coast of Graham Land. Named in association with nearby Nemo Cove.

Nemo Peak. 64°46'S, 63°16'W. 865 m. 1 mile NE of Nipple Peak in the north part of Wiencke Island. Discovered by de Gerlache in 1897–99. Named before 1927 for the Jules Verne character.

Neny Bay. 68°12'S, 66°58'W. Also called Bahía Isla Neny (a Spanish translation of Neny Island Bay—see a little further on in this entry). A Marguerite Bay indentation into the Fallières Coast of the Antarctic Peninsula's west side. Stonington Island forms its northern flange and Neny Island (hence the name) is on its west. Named Neny Island Bay by members from East Base during the USAS 1939–41. The name was later shortened.

Neny Fjord. 68°16'S, 66°50'W. 10 miles long. 5 miles wide. An indentation into the Fallières Coast, between Rymill Bay and Stonington Island. It is actually 4 miles from Stonington Island, in Marguerite Bay. Strictly speaking it is a bay, and lies between Red Rock Ridge and Roman Four Promontory on the west coast of Graham Land. It is not to be confused with nearby Neny Bay. Charcot, in 1909, discovered and thus named a bay further to the north, but over the years this one had gradually been accorded the name Neny Fjord.

Neny Fjord Thumb *see* **Little Thumb**

Neny Glacier. 68°15′S, 66°25′W. Also called Neny Trough. Flows into the north part of Neny Fjord, on the west side of the Antarctic Peninsula. Named by the USAS 1939–41, in association with the fjord.

Neny Glacier Island *see* **Pyrox Island**

Neny Island. 68°12′S, 67°03′W. Also called Neny Islands. 675 m. 1½ miles long. 1 mile NW of Roman Four Promontory, at the entrance to Neny Bay, just south of Stonington Island in Marguerite Bay, off the west coast of Graham Land. Discovered by the BGLE 1934–37, and named by them for the fjord.

Neny Island Bay *see* **Neny Bay**

Neny Islands *see* **Neny Island**

Neny Matterhorn. 68°20′S, 66°51′W. Over 1,125 m. Pyramidal. In the NW part of the Blackwall Mountains on the south side of Neny Fjord, Graham Land. Named by the RARE 1947–48, and by the FIDS in the same year, for the nearby fjord, and for its resemblance to the Swiss mountain.

Neptune Glacier. 71°44′S, 68°17′W. On the east coast of Alexander Island. 12 miles long. 4 miles wide. Flows into George VI Sound, to the south of Triton Point. Discovered aerially by Ellsworth on Nov. 23, 1935, and surveyed in 1949 by the FIDS. Named by the UK for the planet.

Neptune Nunataks. 76°37′S, 145°18′W. A small group between the Chester Mountains and the Fosdick Mountains in the Ford Ranges of Marie Byrd Land. Named for Gary D. Neptune, geologist on the Marie Byrd Land Survey II, 1967–68.

Neptune Range. 83°30′S, 56°W. 70 miles long. WSW of the Forrestal Range in the Pensacola Mountains. It comprises the Washington Escarpment, the Iroquois Plateau, the Schmidt Hills, and the Williams Hills. Discovered aerially on Jan. 13, 1956 (*see* the Chronology for that date). Named for the P2V-2N Neptune aircraft from which the observation was made.

Neptune's Bellows. 63°S, 60°34′W. Also called Passe du Challenger. The narrow gap which leads through the horseshoe shape of Deception Island into Port Foster. A marine channel, it was named by US sealers here before 1822, because of the strong winds in the area.

Neptune's Window. 62°59′S, 60°33′W. Also called Ventana del Chileno. A narrow gap between two pillars, just east of Whalers Bay on the SE side of Deception Island. Named by Lt. Cdr. D.N. Penfold, following his survey of the island in 1948–49, because he could observe conveniently the weather conditions at Neptune's Bellows from here.

The *Nereide.* British ship under the command of P.R.H. Harrison. It visited FIDS stations and foreign stations in the South Orkneys and South Shetlands in the 1953–54 season.

Nereide Patch. 61°57′S, 56°44′W. A reef named for the *Nereide.* Just off King George Island in the South Shetlands. It is a term no longer used.

Nergaard Peak. 72°S, 9°27′E. 2,475 m. 3 miles south of Niels Peak, in the Gagarin Mountains of Queen Maud Land. Named by the Norwegians for Niels Nergaard, scientific assistant with the Norwegian Antarctic Expedition of 1956–58.

Mount Nero. 71°12′S, 159°50′E. 2,520 m. Surmounts the west wall of the Daniels Range. 3 miles north of Forsythe Bluff in the Usarp Mountains. Named for Leonard L. Nero, biologist at McMurdo Station in 1967–68.

Mount Nervo. 83°14′S, 58°W. 1,070 m. 3 miles north of Mount Coulter in the Schmidt Hills of the Neptune Range. Named for George W. Nervo, radioman at Ellsworth Station in 1958.

Nesholmen Island. 69°44'S, 38°13'E. A small island ½ mile off Djupvikneset Peninsula in the southern part of Lützow-Holm Bay. Photographed by the LCE 1936–37 and named Nesholmen (the ness island) by the Norwegians for its proximity to the peninsula (ness).

Neshyba Peak. 71°14'S, 62°45'W. Mostly snow-covered. 16 miles ENE of Mount Jackson in the eastern part of Palmer Land. Named for Stephen Neshyba, US oceanographer near here in 1972–73.

Mount Nesos. 78°12'S, 167°05'E. Over 400 m. A hill, the remains of a volcanic cone. Near the SW end of White Island, in the Ross Archipelago, it is isolated from the main part of the island by the ice sheet, but nonetheless it is still part of the island. Named by the New Zealanders in 1958–59 (Greek "nisos" means "island").

Nesøya. 69°'S, 39°35'E. An island, ½ mile long, just off the north point of East Ongul Island on the east side of the entrance to Lützow-Holm Bay. Photographed by the LCE 1936–37. Name means "the point island" in Norwegian.

The *Nespelen*. US tanker which took part in Operation Deep Freeze I and II during IGY.

Mount Nespelen. 76°48'S, 161°48'E. Between Mackay Glacier and Fry Glacier on the north side of Benson Glacier, 4 miles south of Mount Davidson. Named by the NZ Northern Survey Party of the BCTAE 1957–58 for the *Nespelen*.

Mount Ness. 71°20'S, 66°52'W. 1,890 m. The most northerly of the Batterbee Mountains. 9 miles NE of the summit of Mount Bagshawe. 14 miles inland from George VI Sound, on the west coast of Palmer Land. Discovered aerially by Ellsworth on Nov. 23, 1935. Surveyed in 1936 by the BGLE, and named by the UK in 1954 for Mrs. Patrick Ness, a patron of the BGLE.

Nestling Rock. 71°23'S, 170°24'E. A rock in water just east of the northern

portion of Adare Peninsula, on the coast of Victoria Land, in the shade of the huge Downshire Cliffs. Named descriptively by NZ.

Mount Nestor. 64°25'S, 63°28'W. 1,250 m. The most northerly of the Achaean Range on Anvers Island. Surveyed by the FIDS in 1955 and named by the UK for the Homeric character.

Netherlands. Ratified as the 16th signatory to the Antarctic Treaty on March 30, 1967. Dutch scientists have not worked in Antarctica since the 1964–66 period.

Neu Schwabenland *see* **New Schwabenland**

Neuburg Peak. 82°38'S, 52°54'W. 1,840 m. 2½ miles east of Walker Peak in the SW part of the Dufek Massif. Named for Hugo C. Neuburg, US glaciologist at Ellsworth Station, and one of the first party to visit the Dufek Massif in Dec. 1957.

Neumann Peak. 67°04'S, 67°35'W. On the north end of Hansen Island, in Hanusse Bay, Graham Land. Named by the UK for Franz E. Neumann (1798–1895), German physicist specializing in ice.

Cape Neumayer. 63°42'S, 60°34'W. Forms the NE end of Trinity Island. Charted and named by Nordenskjöld's 1901–4 expedition, for Georg von Neumayer (*see* **Neumayer Channel**). Not to be confused with Cape Wollaston, which is the NW cape of Trinity Island (Foster named that one in 1829).

Mount Neumayer. 75°16'S, 162°17'E. 720 m. Surmounts D'Urville Wall on the north side of the terminus of the David Glacier in Victoria Land. Discovered by Scott's 1901–4 expedition, and named by them for Georg von Neumayer (*see* **Neumayer Channel**).

Neumayer Channel. 64°46'S, 63°30' W. A marine channel, 16 miles long, running in a NE-SW direction. 1½ miles wide, it separates Anvers Island from Wiencke Island, off the west coast of the

Antarctic Peninsula. Discovered in 1874 by Dallmann, who named it Roosen Channel. De Gerlache sailed through it in 1897–99 and renamed it for Georg von Neumayer (1826–1909), German physicist.

Neumayer Cliffs. 73°07′S, 1°45′W. Form the NE end of the Kirwan Escarpment in Queen Maud Land. Discovered by Ritscher in 1938–39, and named for Georg von Neumayer (*see* **Neumayer Channel**).

Neumayer Escarpment *see* **Neumayer Cliffs**

Mount Neuner. 75°18′S, 72°41′W. 3½ miles SW of Mount Chandler in the Behrendt Mountains of Ellsworth Land. Named for Charles S. Neuner, station engineer at Sky-Hi Station (*see* **Eights Station**), 1961–62.

Neupokoyev Bight. 70°05′S, 4°45′E. 30 miles wide. Indents the Queen Maud Land ice shelf, 20 miles NE of Tsiolkovskiy Island. Named by the USSR in 1961 for K.K. Neupokoyev, Arctic hydrographer in the 1920s.

Mount Neustruyev. 71°51′S, 12°14′E. 2,900 m. 5 miles NNE of Gneiskopf Peak in the Südliche Petermann Range of the Wohlthat Mountains of Queen Maud Land. Discovered by Ritscher in 1938–39. Named by the USSR in 1966 for geographer S.S. Neustruyev (1874–1928).

Isla Nevada *see* **Snow Island**

¹Névé *see* **Firn snow**

²Névé. A snowfield at the head of a glacier that has become transformed into ice.

Névé Nunatak. 78°18′S, 160°54′E. Isolated. Just north of Halfway Nunatak, between the Upper Staircase and the east side of Skelton Névé. Surveyed by the NZ Northern Survey Party of the BCTAE in 1957, and named by them in association with Skelton Névé.

Nevlingen Peak. 67°59′S, 55°05′E. Also called Mount Channon. Isolated. 2,100 m. 13 miles SE of Doggers Nunataks in Enderby Land. Photographed by the LCE 1936–37. Named by the Norwegians.

Nevskiye Nunataks. 71°40′S, 8°05′E. In the Drygalski Mountains of Queen Maud Land. They comprise the Sørensen Nunataks and the Hemmestad Nunataks. Named by the USSR in 1961 for the Neva River in their home country.

New Bedford Inlet. 73°22′S, 61°15′W. Also called Douglas Inlet. A Weddell Sea inlet into the northern part of the Lassiter Coast, on the east coast of the Antarctic Peninsula, between Cape Kidson and Cape Brooks. It is ice-filled. Discovered aerially by the USAS in Dec. 1940, and named for New Bedford, the New England whaling center of the 19th century.

New Byrd Station *see* **Byrd Station**

New College Valley. 77°14′S, 166°23′E. Name given to SPA #20, the area of ice-free land between the cliff top above Caughley Beach, and about 330 feet east of the Mount Bird Ice Cap, on Ross Island, and between a line south of the main stream bed of Keble Valley, and the south ridge of New College Valley. Surrounded on three sides by Caughley Beach. There are algae, mosses, and lichens here in abundance.

New Glacier. 77°02′S, 162°24′E. A tiny glacier which flows from the low, ice-covered plateau at the south side of the Mackay Glacier to the SW extremity of Granite Harbor, just north of Mount England, and immediately to the south of the Mackay Glacier Tongue, in Victoria Land. Charted by Grif Taylor during the British Antarctic Expedition of 1910–13, and named by him. He walked around a bluff one day, and there it was, unexpected, a new glacier.

New Harbor. 77°35′S, 163°50′E. 10 miles wide. Between Cape Bernacchi and Butter Point, it is a McMurdo Sound indentation into the southern coast of Victoria Land. Behind it are the Taylor Valley, the Kukri Hills, and the Ferrar Glacier. Discovered in 1901–2 by Scott's expedition of 1901–4, and named New Harbour by them because at that stage it was the harbor furthest south that they had ever found. The current name can be and is spelled New Harbor or New Harbour, depending on which country's spelling you uphold.

New Harbor Dry Valley *see* **Taylor Valley**

New Harbor Glacier *see* **Ferrar Glacier**

New Harbour Heights *see* **Mount Barnes**

New Mountain. 77°52'S, 161°06'E. 2,260 m. At the axis of the Ferrar and Taylor Glaciers in southern Victoria Land, between Arena Valley and Windy Gully. Charted and named by Scott's 1901–4 expedition.

New Plymouth. 62°37'S, 61°12'W. A bay, south of Start Point, on the extreme west coast of Livingston Island, in the South Shetlands. It is bordered by an extensive line of beaches. Named in various ways by the early sealers: the British called it New Plymouth Harbour, the Americans called it President Harbor and a mixture of the two called it Rugged Harbor (it looks out toward Rugged Island). The name as we know it today was given before 1822. The Argentines call it Puerto Echeverría.

New Rock. 63°01'S, 60°44'W. 105 m. A rock in water ¾ mile off the SW coast of Deception Island in the South Shetlands. Charted and named in 1929, a relatively new charting.

New Schwabenland. 72°30'S, 1°E. Also called New Swabia, Neu Schwabenland. More than 500 miles in extent, this is the mountainous upland of Queen Maud Land, extending from the Kraul Mountains to Vorposten Peak. Ritscher was the first to explore it, aerially, on his German New Schwabenland Expedition of 1938–39. They named the area for their ship, the *Schwabenland.*

New snow. Recent snow in the form of crystals or flakes.

New South Greenland. Mysterious land discovered to the SE of the Seal Islands in the South Shetlands by Capt. Robert Johnson in the *Wasp* in 1821–22. It was probably a part of the South Shetlands he saw, or maybe even the Antarctic Peninsula. Hence it is also another (arcane) name for Antarctica. Morrell (q.v.) assumed it to be the whole continent, or at least part of it, and hence another name for New South Greenland is Morrell's Land. Filchner spent over a week looking for it in June 1912. It is reckoned to be somewhere before 62°S and 69°S, and around 48°W.

New South Shetland *see* **South Shetland Islands**

New Year Nunatak. 71°02'S, 71°12'E. In the central part of the Manning Nunataks, in the SE part of the Amery Ice Shelf. Named by the Australians. It was visited by a USSR party on Jan. 1, 1966.

New Year Pass. 83°28'S, 160°40'E. Between the Moore Mountains and Mount Weeks in the Queen Elizabeth Range. Used on Jan. 1, 1958, by a NZ party of the BCTAE to get from Marsh Glacier to January Col on the Prince Andrew Plateau, overlooking Bowden Névé.

New York Sealing Expedition. 1820–22. A two-part expedition, 1820–21 and 1821–22, to the South Shetlands. Organized by New York sealing magnate James Byers after he had heard of William Smith's discovery of the South Shetlands the year before (i.e., 1819). The *Henry* left first, on June 24, 1820, commanded by Capt. Brunow. The *Aurora* was the next to leave, on July 1, 1820, under Capt. Robert R. Macy. The *Venus* sailed under Capt. Napier on Oct. 9, 1820. Later that year, in the Falklands, they met up with Capt. Robert Johnson, another Byers man, who was to lead the expedition. He was captain of the *Jane Maria,* and Donald McKay was captain of its tender, the *Sarah.* Tagging along, but not part of the expedition, was the *Charity,* under Charles Barnard. They all arrived in the South Shetlands in Dec. 1820, late in the season, and the expedition was a financial loss. The *Venus* was wrecked on March 7, 1821. The *Sarah* was lost in a storm, and the *Aurora* was so badly damaged it was sold off for salvage in the Falklands, where the remaining vessels wintered-over. What was left of the fleet was back in the South Shetlands on Oct. 31, 1821, for the 1821–22 season, still accompanied by the *Charity*. The *Henry* was still commanded by Brunow, and this time Johnson captained the *Wasp*, the *Jane Maria* being under the command of Blauvelt. The *Lynx*, an Australian vessel, accompanied them. They all left Antarctica in early 1822.

New Zealand. The country of New Zealand was at first thought to be part of the great southern continent (whatever that was in people's minds). Cook disproved this notion when he sailed around New Zealand in 1768. On July 30, 1923, Britain awarded to New Zealand the Ross Dependency, a huge chunk of Antarctica. In 1959 New Zealand was one of the 12 original signatories to the Antarctic Treaty. Well represented in IGY (1957–58), New Zealand has been researching in Antarctica continuously since 1957. The NZARP (New Zealand Antarctic Research Program) is centered at Scott Base, on Ross Island. Other stations in Antarctica are Hallett (formerly a US/NZ station), Vanda, Cape Bird Station. On Nov. 11, 1969, Pam Young (a New Zealander) became one of the first women to stand at the South Pole (*see* **Women in Antarctica**). In 1982 New Zealand's prime minister, Robert Muldoon, visited the continent with Sir Edmund Hillary, another great New Zealander. The country has an organization called the New Zealand Antarctic Society (founded in Wellington on Nov. 15, 1933).

Mount New Zealand. 74°11′S, 162°30′E. 2,890 m. Just NW of the Nash Ridge, on the south side of Priestley Glacier in the Eisenhower Range of Victoria Land. Discovered by Scott's expedition of 1901–4, and named by them for the country of New Zealand.

Mount Newall. 77°30′S, 162°42′E. Also spelled (erroneously) as Mount

Newell. 1,920 m. The NE extremity of the Asgard Range, 12 miles west of New Harbor in southern Victoria Land. Discovered by Scott's 1901–4 expedition, and named by them for one of the men who helped raise funds to send the *Morning* to the relief of the expedition.

Newall Glacier. 77°30′S, 162°50′E. In the east part of the Asgard Range of Victoria Land. Flows between Mount Newall and Mount Weyant into the Wilson Piedmont Glacier. Named by the NZ Northern Survey Party of the BCTAE in 1957 in association with the mountain.

Newbold, Neville. Seaman on the *Eleanor Bolling*, 1929–30, i.e., during the second half of Byrd's 1928–30 expedition. He was back in the Antarctic on the *Bear of Oakland* during the second half of Byrd's 1933–35 expedition, i.e., 1934–35.

Newburg Point. 66°06′S, 66°46′W. On the NW coast of Lavoisier Island in the Biscoe Islands. Named by the UK for Louis H. Newburg, US physiologist specializing in cold areas.

Newcomb Bay. 66°16′S, 110°32′E. 1 mile in extent. Between the Clark and Bailey Peninsulas in the Windmill Islands. Named by Willis L. Tressler in Feb. 1957 (he charted it) for Lt. Robert C. Newcomb, USN, navigator of the *Glacier* from which the survey was done. Newcomb also took part in the survey party.

Newcomer Glacier. 77°47′S, 85°27′W. 20 miles long. Runs through the northern portion of the Sentinel Range from Allen Peak to Bracken Peak. Named for Cdr. Loyd E. Newcomer, VX-6 pilot, 1959–60.

Mount Newell   *see*   **Mount Newall**

Newell Point. 62°20′S, 59°32′W. On the north side of Robert Island, 2½ miles east of the north end of the island, in the South Shetlands. Charted and named in 1935 by personnel on the *Discovery II*.

Newman Island. 75°40′S, 145°30′W. The largest of the three grounded islands in the Nickerson Ice Shelf on the Marie Byrd Land coast. 15 miles long. Named for Cdr. J.F. Newman, USN, ship's officer on the staff of the commander, Task Force 43 in 1966.

Newman Nunataks. 66°40′S, 54°45′E. Between the Napier Mountains and the Aker Peaks. Photographed by the LCE 1936–37. Named by the Australians for A.J. Newman (*see* **Newman Shoal**).

Newman Shoal. 68°35′S, 77°54′E. At the SW side of the Davis Anchorage, just off the Vestfold Hills. 175 yards SE of Hobby Rocks. It has depths of one fathom or less. Named by the Australians for A.J. Newman, senior diesel mechanic at Mawson Station in 1961.

Newnes Glacier. 71°41′S, 170°10′E. Flows from the Adare Saddle into Protection Cove at the head of Robertson Bay, Victoria Land. Charted by Borchgrevink in 1898–1900, and named Sir George Newnes Glacier by him for Sir George Newnes, his major sponsor. The name was later shortened.

Newspapers *see* *McMurdo News, McMurdo Sometimer, Showa Station, South Polar Times,* and the Bibliography

Mount Newton. 74°01′S, 65°30′E. Has a conical peak. Between the Collins and Mellor Glaciers in the Prince Charles Mountains. Named by the Australians for Dr. G. Newton, medical officer at Mawson Station in 1960.

Newton Island. 66°46′S, 141°27′E. ½ mile NW of Laplace Island. Just under 1¼ miles NNW of Cape Mousse. Charted by the French in 1951, and named by them for Sir Isaac Newton.

Nextdoor Glacier. Unofficial name given by the Americans in the area in the 1960s to a glacier in the Wright Valley region.

Cape Neyt *see* **Neyt Point**

Neyt Point. 63°58′S, 61°48′W. 1 mile SE of Moureaux Point, the northern extremity of Liège Island. Discovered and named by de Gerlache in 1897–99 for General Neyt, a supporter of the *Belgica* expedition.

Niban Rock. 68°14′S, 42°28′E. A rock on land, protruding into the sea, 8 miles SW of Cape Hinode, on the Queen Maud Land coast. Named Niban-iwa (number two rock) by the Japanese.

Nibelungen Valley. 77°37′S, 161°20′E. Ice-free. Just west of Plane Table and Panorama Peak in the Asgard Range of Victoria Land. Named by the New Zealanders for the Teutonic gods.

The Niblets. 66°S, 65°40′W. Small, niblet-type rocks in water between Harp Island and Beer Island, 8 miles west of Prospect Point, off the west coast of Graham Land. Charted and named descriptively by the BGLE 1934–37.

Cape Nicholas *see* **Mount Nicholas, Nicolas Rocks**

Mount Nicholas. 69°22′S, 69°50′W. 1,465 m. 5½ miles SSW of Cape Brown. Forms the northern limit of the Douglas Range on the east side of Alexander Island. Charcot discovered it from a distance in 1909, and named it Île Nicolas II, for the Russian tsar. He thought it was an island, or perhaps a headland. The BGLE charted it in error 13 miles to the NNW in 1934–37, and renamed it Cape Nicholas. What they saw was the seaward bulge of Mount Calais. During the FIDS survey of 1948, Charcot's island was identified as this mountain.

Nicholas Mountains *see* **Nicholas Range**

Nicholas Range. 66°40′S, 55°28′E. Just east of the Aker Peaks, 23 miles SW of Magnet Bay. Discovered in Jan. 1930 by the BANZARE and named by Mawson for Mr. G.R. Nicholas of Melbourne, a patron of the expedition. The individual peaks were plotted by Norwegian cartographers working off photos taken by the LCE 1936–37.

Nicholl Head. 67°47′S, 67°06′W. Western extremity of the ridge separating Dogs Leg Fjord and Square Bay, on the west coast of Graham Land. Surveyed in 1936 by the BGLE and again in 1948 by the FIDS. The FIDS named it for Timothy M. Nicholl, their base leader at Faraday Station in 1948 and 1949.

Mount Nichols. 85° 27′ S, 146° 05′ W. 670 m. In the central part of the Harold Byrd Mountains. Named for William L. Nichols, construction mechanic at Byrd Station in 1957.

Nichols, Dr. Robert L. Geologist, head of the Department of Geology at Tufts University, he was geologist, senior scientist, and trailman on the RARE 1947–48. In 1958 he was working in the dry valleys in southern Victoria Land, and was back in the same area in the 1959–60 season.

Nichols Glacier *see* **Nichols Snowfield**

Nichols Rock. 75° 23′ S, 139° 13′ W. On the west side of Kinsey Ridge in the middle of Strauss Glacier in Marie Byrd Land. Named for Clayton W. Nichols, geophysicist at Byrd Station in 1969–70.

Nichols Snowfield. 69° 25′ S, 71° 05′ W. Also called Nichols Glacier. 22 miles long. 8 miles wide. Bounded by the Rouen Mountains and Elgar Uplands to the east, and the Lassus Mountains to the west. In the north part of Alexander Island. Discovered aerially in 1937 by the BGLE. Named by the RARE 1947–48 for Robert L. Nichols.

Nicholson, Charles H. Seaman on the Wilkes Expedition 1838–42. Joined in the USA. Discharged at Oahu, Nov. 25, 1841.

Nicholson Island. 66° 17′ S, 110° 32′ E. The most westerly of the Bailey Rocks. 175 yards NE of Budnick Hill, in Newcomb Bay, Windmill Islands. Named by the Australians for R.T. Nicholson, senior carpenter who helped construct Casey Station in 1966.

Nicholson Peninsula. 80° 43′ S, 160° 30′ E. Ice-covered. 15 miles long. Between Couzens Bay and Matterson Inlet on the west side of the Ross Ice Shelf. Named for

Capt. W.M. Nicholson, USN, chief of staff to the US Antarctic Projects Officer, 1964.

Nicholson Rock. 75° 50′ S, 114° 56′ W. 2½ miles east of Cox Bluff, on the Spitz Ridge, in the eastern part of the Toney Mountain massif in Marie Byrd Land. Named for Charles E. Nicholson, USN, construction electrician at Amundsen-Scott South Pole Station in 1974.

Nickell Peak. 77° 19′ S, 161° 28′ E. Ice-free. At the west side of Victoria Upper Lake. 1 mile SE of Sponsors Peak in Victoria Land. Named for Gregory W. Nickell, manager of the Eklund Biological Center, and the Thiel Earth Sciences Laboratory at McMurdo Station in 1974 (*see* **Deaths, 1974**).

Mount Nickens. 73° 56′ S, 100° 20′ W. A snow-covered, mesa-type mountain which marks the NW extremity of the Hudson Mountains. Just east of the base of Canisteo Peninsula. Overlooks the Cosgrove Ice Shelf. Named for Herbert P. Nickens, US cartographer.

Mount Nickerson. 83° 28′ S, 168° 48′ E. Between Lennox-King Glacier and Beaver Glacier. 1,480 m. 4 miles SW of Yeates Bluff in the Queen Alexandra Range. Named for Cdr. N.E. Nickerson, USN, captain of the *Edisto* in 1965.

Nickerson Ice Shelf. 75° 44′ S, 145° W. 35 miles wide. Off the Ruppert Coast, north of Siemiatkowski Glacier. It contains 3 grounded islands—Groves Island, Newman Island, Stephen Island. Discovered during Byrd's 1928–30 expedition. Named for Cdr. H.J. Nickerson, USN, administrative officer on the staff of the commander, Task Force 43, in 1966.

Nicknames of Antarctica. The early Russian nickname was "The Ice Continent." Mawson called it "The Home of the Blizzard." Other names have been, "The White Desert," "The Pulsating Continent," "The Last Continent," "The Sixth Continent," "Down South," "Down Under," "The Ice." The Antarctic Peninsula, because of its comparatively warm climate, is often called "The Banana Belt."

Nicol Crags. 80°44'S, 24°05'W. In the Shackleton Range.

Cape Nicolas *see* **Nicolas Rocks**

Nicolas Rocks. 60°34'S, 46°06'W. Rocks in water at the NW side of the Larsen Islands. 2½ miles off the west end of Coronation Island. Discovered in Dec. 1821 by Palmer and Powell, and named by Powell as Cape Nicolas, for the feast day of Saint Nicholas, Dec. 6, the day of discovery. The name was later redefined.

Île Nicolas II *see* **Mount Nicholas**

Niels Peak. 71°57'S, 9°23'E. 2,525 m. 3 miles north of Nergaard Peak in the Gagarin Mountains of the Orvin Mountains of Queen Maud Land. Named by the Norwegians as Nielsnapen for Niels Nergaard (*see* **Nergaard Peak**).

Nielsen. Captain of the whale catcher *Star IV* during the *Sir James Clark Ross* expedition of 1923–24. This may be Oscar Nilsen.

Nielsen Bay *see* **Nilsen Bay**

Nielsen Fjord. 70°42'S, 165°50'E. 2 miles wide. Between Cape North and Gregory Bluffs on the north coast of Victoria Land. Named by the ANARE for Capt. Hans Nielsen, captain of the *Thala Dan,* 1961–62.

¹Nielsen Glacier *see* **McMahon Glacier**

²Nielsen Glacier. 71°32'S, 169°43'E. 4 miles long. Flows into the west side of Robertson Bay, just west of Calf Point, in northern Victoria Land. Charted by Borchgrevink in 1898–1900, and named Yngvar Nielsen Glacier by him for Prof. Yngvar Nielsen of Christiania University, Norway. The name was later shortened.

Nielsnapen *see* **Niels Peak**

Nielson Bay *see* **Nilsen Bay**

Niepcé Glacier. 65°07'S, 63°22'W. Joins with Daguerre Glacier into Lauzanne Cove, Flandres Bay, on the west coast of Graham Land. Named by the UK in 1960 for Joseph N. Niepcé (1765–1833), French photography pioneer.

Niewoehner, Victor. Crewman on the *Bear of Oakland,* 1933–34, and 2nd assistant engineer, 1934–35.

The *Nigeria.* British cruiser in the Antarctic in the late austral summer of 1948. Capt. B.L. Moore commanding. It visited FIDS stations with the governor of the Falkland Islands aboard. Sometimes in company with the *Snipe.*

Nigg Rock. 60°43'S, 44°51'W. Also misspelled as Eigg Rock. 155 m. A rock in water, ½ mile NW of Route Point, the NW tip of Laurie Island, in the South Orkneys. Discovered and charted by Powell and Palmer in Dec. 1821. Recharted and named by Bruce in 1903 for the birthplace of his wife in Scotland.

Niggli Nunataks. 80°38'S, 23°20'W. In the Shackleton Range.

Night. There are 3 months of continual night in Antarctica, and another 3 of twilight. These 6 months are the so called "night" months of Antarctica. At the Pole itself, there are more dark days (*see* **Seasons**).

Mount Nikolayev. 71°44'S, 12°26'E. 2,850 m. The central peak in the Aurdalsegga Ridge in the Südliche Petermann Range of the Wohlthat Mountains of Queen Maud Land. Discovered by Ritscher in 1938–39 and named by the USSR in 1963 for photographer V.A. Nikolayev.

Nikolayev Range. 71°54'S, 6°02'E. Between Austreskorve Glacier and Lunde Glacier in the Mühlig-Hofmann Mountains of Queen Maud Land. Named by the USSR in 1961 for astronaut Andriyan G. Nikolayev.

Nila. Gray, sludge ice which can be up to 4 inches thick.

Niles Island. 66°26'S, 110°24'E. Also called Niles Rock. 350 yards long. Just off the south end of Holl Island in the Windmill Islands. Named for G.W. Niles, aerial photographer on Operation Highjump, 1946–47, and Operation Windmill, 1947–48.

Niles Rock *see* **Niles Island**

Mount Nils. 68°04'S, 48°01'E. Ice-covered. Just west of Rayner Glacier. 3 miles south of Mount Christensen in Enderby Land. Named by the Australians for Nils Larsen.

Nils Jørgen Peaks. 71°53'S, 2°36'W. 6 miles NE of Mount Schumacher on the Ahlmann Ridge of Queen Maud Land. Named by the Norwegians for Nils Jørgen Schumacher.

Mount Nils Larsen. 72°13'S, 23°06'E. 2,190 m. 3 miles SW of Mount Widerøe in the Sør Rondane Mountains. Named by the Norwegians for Nils Larsen.

Nils Larsen Glacier. 68°44'S, 90°39'W. Flows to the west coast of Peter I Island, just north of Norvegia Bay. Named by the Norwegians for Nils Larsen, who made a survey of the island in 1929.

Nils Plain. 72°07'S, 0°27'E. Also called Nilsevidda. An ice plain 25 miles in extent. North of Mount Roer in the Sverdrup Mountains of Queen Maud Land. Named by the Norwegians for Nils Roer.

Mount Nilsen. 78°02'S, 155°W. 4 miles WSW of Mount Paterson in the Rockefeller Mountains, on the Edward VII Pensinsula, in Marie Byrd Land. Discovered in 1929 during Byrd's 1928-30 expedition, and named by Byrd for Oscar Nilsen.

Nilsen, Oscar. Norwegian Antarctic whaler. Took over as captain of the *Sir James Clark Ross* when Larsen died on board during the early stages of the 1924-25 expedition. He then led the expedition to a reasonably successful conclusion. He was skipper of the *C.A. Larsen* in the 1928-29 season, and towed the *City of New York* in through the Antarctic pack-ice during Byrd's 1928-30 expedition. In 1930-31 he was captain of the new *Sir James Clark Ross*. It was this ship which transported coal to the *Discovery* during the BANZARE 1929-31.

Nilsen, Thorvald. Norwegian naval lieutenant. Captain of the *Fram*, on the

Norwegian Antarctic Expedition of 1910-12, led by Amundsen. Nilsen was second-in-command of the expedition.

The *Nilsen-Alonzo.* Norwegian whaler, formerly a tramp steamer, in Antarctic waters 1928-29, under the command of Capt. H. Andresen. It was formerly commanded by Gjertsen.

Nilsen Bay. 67°36'S, 64°34'E. Just west of Strahan Glacier. 18 miles ESE of Cape Daly. Discovered by the BANZARE in Feb. 1931, and named by Mawson for Oscar Nilsen. Mawson misspelled it as Nielsen Bay, and mapped it incorrectly. The name has also been misspelled as Nielson Bay.

Nilsen Mountains *see* **Nilsen Plateau**

Nilsen Peak. 84°32'S, 175°25'W. On the north end of Waldron Spurs. Marks the east side of the mouth of Shackleton Glacier. Named for W.B. Nilsen, captain of the *Chattahoochee*, 1965.

Nilsen Plateau. 86°20'S, 158°W. Ice-covered. 30 miles long. Between 1 and 12 miles wide. 3,040 meters at its highest. Between the upper reaches of the Amundsen and Robert Scott Glaciers, between the Prince Olav Mountains and the Horlick Mountains, in the Queen Maud Mountains. When Amundsen was rushing toward the Pole, he discovered this plateau on Nov. 28, 1911. He named it the Thorvald Nilsen Plateau, for Thorvald Nilsen, captain of the *Fram*. Over the years this feature has been seen named and spelled in a variety of ways, including: Thorvald Nilsen Mountains, Mount Thorvald Nilsen, as well as several variants of the names Thorvald and Nilsen, such as Thorold, Nielsen, Nielson, etc.

Nilsevidda *see* **Nils Plain**

Nilsson Rocks. 71°45'S, 67°42'E. Rocks on land which enclose a meltwater lake 9 miles south of the Fisher Massif in the Prince Charles Mountains. Named by the Australians for C.S. Nilsson, physicist at Mawson Station in 1957.

Nimbus Hills. 79°35'S, 82°50'W. 14 miles long. They form the SE part of the

Pioneer Heights in the Heritage Range. Named for the NASA weather satellite Nimbus, which, on Sept. 13, 1964, took photos of Antarctica from 500 miles up.

Nimitz Glacier. 78°55'S, 85°10'W. 40 miles long. 5 miles wide. Flows from the area 10 miles west of the Vinson Massif, then between the Sentinel Range and the Bastien Range, into Minnesota Glacier, in the central Ellsworth Mountains. Discovered aerially by VX-6 flights on Dec. 14–15, 1959. Named for Fleet Adm. Chester W. Nimitz, USN (*see* **Nimitz Hall**).

Nimitz Hall. A building at McMurdo Station. Named for Fleet Adm. Chester W. Nimitz, USN, chief of naval operations at the time of Operation Highjump in 1946–47.

The *Nimrod*. Shackleton's ship during his British Antarctic Expedition of 1907–9. Built in 1866 by Alexander Stephen and Sons, of Dundee, it was a 200-ton sealer which was altered and repaired by R&H Green of Blackwall, and given a brand new engine which gave a 6-knot speed. Shackleton first saw it in the Thames on June 15, 1906. Rupert England was captain during the first part of the expedition, from 1907–8, with John King Davis as chief officer. When the ship left Cape Royds, on Feb. 22, 1908, England carried sealed instructions to his superiors from Shackleton, instructing them to send down Capt. F.P. Evans as captain for the next (relief) season. There is definitely truth in that Shackleton and England disagreed. Evans was, indeed, captain for the second season. He was replaced later in 1909 by John King Davis.

Mount Nimrod. 85°25'S, 165°45'E. 2,835 m. 4 miles SSE of Mount Saunders in the Dominion Range. Discovered and named by Shackleton in 1907–9 for the *Nimrod*.

Nimrod Glacier. 82°22'S, 163°E. 85 miles long. One of the major glaciers feeding the Ross Ice Shelf from the Transantarctic Mountains. It flows from the Polar Plateau between the Geologists Range and the Miller Range, then between the Churchill Mountains and the Queen Elizabeth Range. It flows into the Ross Ice Shelf between Capes Wilson and Lyttelton, at the Shackleton Inlet. Named for the *Nimrod*.

Nimrod Passage. 64°59'S, 63°58'W. Marine passage leading to the northern end of the Lemaire Channel between the Wauwermans Islands and the Dannebrog Islands, in the Wilhelm Archipelago. Named by the UK for the motor survey boat, the *Nimrod*, which was used to take most of the soundings when the RN Hydrographic Survey Unit navigated this passage in the *John Biscoe* in March and April, 1964.

Nims Peak. 72°34'S, 160°58'E. 3 miles NW of Mount Weihaupt in the Outback Nunataks. Named for David J. Nims, ionosphere physicist at McMurdo Station in 1968.

The *Nina Sagaydak*. USSR ship, sometime in the Antarctic, in the 1970s.

Ninnis, A.H. Motor engineer on the Ross Sea Party during the British Imperial Transantarctic Expedition of 1914–17. He was on the *Aurora* when it drifted away from Ross Island.

Ninnis, B.E.S. Lt. British Army lieutenant. Nicknamed "Cherub." He looked after the dogs on the AAE 1911–14. While on the Far Eastern sledge journey with Mawson and Mertz, he fell down a crevasse and disappeared on Dec. 14, 1912.

Ninnis Glacier. 68°12'S, 147°12'E. Heavily crevassed. Flows from the interior of East Antarctica, between Mertz Glacier and the Cook Ice Shelf, to the sea at the George V Land coast. Discovered by the AAE 1911–14, and named by Mawson for B.E.S. Ninnis.

Ninnis Glacier Tongue. 68°07'S, 147°51'E. The seaward extension of the Ninnis Glacier, projecting out to sea for 30 miles from the coast of George V Land. Discovered by the AAE 1911–14, and named by Mawson in association with the glacier.

Nipe Glacier. 71°52'S, 25°15'E. Between the Austkampane Hills and Menipa Peak in the Sør Rondane Mountains. Name means "the mountain peak glacier" in Norwegian.

Mount Nipha. 78°10'S, 167°25'E. 760 m. A hill in the middle of White Island in the Ross Archipelago. Named by the New Zealanders in 1958–59 because it is surrounded by ice and snow ("nipha" means "snow," in Greek).

Nipple Peak. 64°47'S, 63°17'W. 675 m. 1 mile NE of Channel Glacier in the northern part of Wiencke Island, in the Palmer Archipelago. Discovered by de Gerlache in 1897–99. Named descriptively by the personnel on Operation Tabarin in 1944.

Nishi-naga-iwa Glacier. 68°31'S, 41°18'E. Flows to the sea between Daruma Rock and Cape Akarui in Queen Maud Land. Named by the Japanese as Nishi-naga-iwa-hyoga (western long rock glacier) in association with Higashi-naga-iwa Glacier.

Nishino-seto Strait. 69°01'S, 39°29'E. Between Ongulkalven Island and Ongul Island, in Lützow-Holm Bay. Photographed by the LCE 1936–37. Named Nishino-seto (western strait) by the Japanese for its location in the Flatvaer Islands.

Nishino-ura Cove. 69°01'S, 39°34'E. Indents the western side of East Ongul Island. Photographed by the LCE 1936–37. Named in 1957 by the Japanese as Nishino-ura (western cove).

Mount Nivea. 60°35'S, 45°29'W. 1,265 m. Snow-topped. At the head of Sunshine Glacier, in the north central part of Coronation Island, in the South Orkneys. Surveyed by the FIDS in 1948–49, and named by them for *Pagodroma nivea* (the snow petrel) which breeds here.

Niznik Island. 69°47'S, 68°30'W. In the north part of George VI Sound, opposite the mouth of Eureka Glacier, near the coast of Palmer Land. Discovered by the RARE 1947–48 and named by Ronne

for Theodore T. Niznik, a contributor from Baltimore.

No Name Valley. Unofficial name given by the Americans here to a dry valley in southern Victoria Land.

Nob Island. 65°12'S, 64°19'W. The largest of the Anagram Islands, on the south side of French Passage, in the Wilhelm Archipelago. Named by the UK in 1961. There is a black knob of rock, snow-free, on the north side of the island.

Nobble Head *see* **Knobble Head**

Nobby Nunatak. 63°25'S, 56°59'W. 270 m. 1 mile south of Lake Boeckella. 1 mile east of Mount Flora, at the NE end of the Antarctic Peninsula. Charted and named descriptively by the personnel of Operation Tabarin in 1945.

Nobile Glacier. 64°32'S, 61°28'W. Flows into the SE part of Recess Cove, Charlotte Bay, on the west coast of Graham Land. Charted by de Gerlache in 1897–99. Named by the UK in 1960 for Umberto Nobile, the Arctic explorer.

Mount Noble. 60°39'S, 45°16'W. 1,165 m. On the north side of Roald Glacier. 2 miles west of Gibbon Bay in the eastern part of Coronation Island, in the South Orkneys. Named Noble's Peak by Weddell in 1823 for James Noble of Edinburgh, the orientalist. The name was later amended slightly.

Noble, Thomas. Seaman on the Wilkes Expedition 1838–42. Joined at Rio. Sent home on the *Relief* in 1839.

Noble, William. Seaman on the Wilkes Expedition 1838–42. Joined in the USA. Run at Valparaiso.

Noble Glacier. 62°04'S, 58°26'W. Just north of Flagstaff Glacier on the east side of Keller Peninsula, King George Island, in the South Shetlands. Named by the UK in 1960 for Hugh M. Noble, FIDS glaciologist at Base G in 1957.

Noble Nunatak. 85°12'S, 121°29'W. Isolated. In the northern part of the Horlick Mountains, 8 miles north of Widich Nunatak, on the north side of the Shimizu Ice Stream. Named for

William C. Noble, meteorologist at Byrd Station in 1958.

Noble Peak. 64°48′S, 63°25′W. 560 m. 1 mile SW of Lockley Point, on the NW side of Wiencke Island. Discovered by de Gerlache in 1897–99. Named before 1927.

Noble Rocks. 67°52′S, 68°41′W. 19 small rocks in Marguerite Bay, east of Jester Rock in the Dion Islands. Surveyed by the FIDS in 1949 and named by the UK in association with Emperor Island.

Noble's Peak *see* **Mount Noble**

Nødtvedt, J. Second engineer on the *Fram* during the Norwegian Antarctic Expedition of 1910–12. He was not part of the shore party led by fellow Norwegian Roald Amundsen.

Nødtvedt Nunataks. 86°32′S, 162°18′W. Isolated. In the flow of the Amundsen Glacier, 7 miles ENE of Mount Bjaaland. Named for J. Nødtvedt.

Nodule Nunatak. 63°19′S, 56°05′W. 440 m. Isolated. 3 miles south of Mount Tholus, in the southern part of Joinville Island. Surveyed by the FIDS in 1953–54. Named descriptively by the UK in 1956.

Nodwell Peaks. 64°18′S, 59°47′W. Two peaks, less than a mile apart, on the east side of Edgeworth Glacier, in Graham Land. Named by the UK for nodwells (q.v.).

Nodwells. The RN 50 Nodwells are tracked vehicles built by Robin-Nodwell Mgf. Ltd. of Calgary, Canada. Used in Antarctica since 1960.

Mount Noel. 69°55′S, 67°55′W. In the western part of the Antarctic Peninsula.

Noel Hill. 62°14′S, 58°46′W. 255 m. A slate knob on Barton Peninsula, King George Island, in the South Shetlands. Named by David Ferguson in 1913–14.

Mount Noice. 73°17′S, 164°39′E. 2,780 m. Surmounts the SW edge of Deception Plateau, 8 miles south of Mount Overlord, in Victoria Land. Named for Lt. Gary E. Noice, USN, VX-6 navigator at McMurdo Station, 1966.

Rocher Noir *see* **Tristan Island**

Noire Rock. 64°40′S, 62°35′W. Also called Mount Doble, Sable Pinnacles. A dark pinnacle rock, 1½ miles SW of Mount Dedo on the west coast of Graham Land. Charted by de Gerlache in 1898 and named descriptively by him.

Nøkkel Island. 69°28′S, 39°28′E. The most southerly of the Nøkkelholmane Islands, in the eastern part of Lützow-Holm Bay. Name means "the key" in Norwegian.

Nøkkelholmane Islands. 69°24′S, 39°29′E. 24 islands and rocks (including Nøkkel Island) scattered about just off the west side of Skarvsnes Foreland, in the east part of Lützow-Holm Bay. Photographed by the LCE 1936–37. Name means "the key islands" in Norwegian.

Nolan Island. 77°12′S, 147°24′W. Ice-covered. 6 miles long. 2 miles north of Court Ridge, in the Sulzberger Ice Shelf, on the coast of Marie Byrd Land. Discovered by the USAS 1939–41. Named for William G. Nolan, USN, radarman on the *Glacier*, 1957–58 and 1961–62.

Nolan Pillar. 85°27′S, 86°52′W. 1,940 m. A mountain, or pinnacle, 3 miles SE of Smith Knob. Marks the eastern extremity of the Thiel Mountains. Named by Peter Bermel and Arthur Ford, leaders of the Thiel Mountains party, 1960–61, for Thomas B. Nolan, 7th director of the US Geological Survey, 1956–65.

Noll Glacier. 69°33′S, 159°10′E. 20 miles long. Flows from Jones Nunatak in the central part of the Wilson Hills, into the Tomilin Glacier. Named for Major Edmund P. Noll, US Marines, VX-6 cargo officer and aircraft commander, 1968.

Nomad Rock. 63°13′S, 57°42′W. An isolated rock in water in the Bransfield Strait. 5 miles off the northern coast of Trinity Peninsula. 9 miles NE of Cape Legoupil. Named by the UK because of the confusion about geographic features in this area. Names seem to wander.

Nomenclature *see* **Mapping of Antarctica, Nicknames of Antarctica**

Nomura, Captain. Commander of the *Kainan Maru*, 1910–12. He led a party back to Japan, mid-expedition, in the summer of 1911–12, to get more funds for the Shirase expedition.

Nonplus Crag. 70°58′S, 69°10′S. 1,250 m. A rock cliff in the LeMay Range, near the head of Jupiter Glacier, in the east central part of Alexander Island. Named by the UK for the perplexity facing them over identification of this crag.

Noonan, Paul F. US Navy photographer based at Wilkes Station during the winter of 1957.

Noonan Cove. 66°16′S, 110°31′E. On the west side of Clark Peninsula, to the south of Stonehocker Point and Wilkes Station. Named by Carl Eklund (who surveyed it in 1957), for Paul F. Noonan.

Nora Island *see* **Stedet Island**

Nord Island. 66°45′S, 141°33′E. A small island, the most northerly of the Curzon Islands. Charted and named descriptively by the French.

The *Nordbrise*. Ice-strengthened Norwegian ship of 485 tons. 145 feet long, it has a cruising speed of 11 knots and can carry 39 passengers. In 1989–90 it became Mountain Travel's new chartered vessel for tours in the Antarctic. It had been 8 years in Greenland, and now had 19 newly-decorated cabins, 4 zodiacs, 5 decks—observation, sun, main, salon, and sauna.

Nordbukta. 69°38′S, 38°21′E. A bay on the north side of Padda Island in Lützow-Holm Bay. Photographed by the LCE 1936–37. Name means "the north bay" in Norwegian.

Nordenskjöld, Otto. b. Dec. 6, 1869, Småland, Sweden. d. June 2, 1928, Göteborg, Sweden. Nils Otto Gustaf Nordenskjöld. Swedish explorer and geographer, the only explorer to do any interior investigations of the Antarctic Peninsula during the Heroic Era (q.v.). Nephew of the Arctic explorer Adolf Erik Nordenskjöld. He was leader of the 1901–4 Swedish Antarctic Expedition, which

left Göteborg on Oct. 16, 1901, in the *Antarctic*. Captain of the ship was Carl Anton Larsen. Under his command were 16 officers and men. 8 scientists (including Dr. Nordenskjöld) were also on board. *See* these individual names: **Grunden, Skottsberg, Haslum, Åkerlundh, Karl Andreas Andersson, F.L. Andreassen, Ekelöf, Bodman, Ula, Ohlin, Wennersgaard, Duse, Jonassen.** The ship arrived at Buenos Aires on Dec. 15, 1901, and there they picked up F.W. Stokes, the American artist, and Lt. José M. Sobral, an Argentine Naval officer, whose presence as observer was desired by the Argentines in exchange for free food, fuel, and help for the expedition. On Dec. 21, 1901, the *Antarctic* left for the South Shetlands, arriving there on Jan. 11, 1902. Nordenskjöld landed on one of the islands, then went off to explore Orléans Strait and the west coast of the Antarctic Peninsula. Then up the coast again to the tip of the peninsula, through Antarctic Sound, and then landed on Paulet Island. They then crossed the Erebus and Terror Gulf and established a depot on Seymour Island. After an exploratory cruise Nordenskjöld chose Snow Hill Island as his winter campsite because of the fossils he found there. Nordenskjöld, Jonassen, Bodman, Åkerlundh, and Sobral set up camp with several sledge dogs, the stores, and equipment. The *Antarctic* then returned to the Falkland Islands for the winter of 1902. The wintering group built a hut and spent the winter on Snow Hill Island. In October Nordenskjöld, Jonassen, and Sobral set out on a 380-mile sledging journey on foot, covering the NE part of the Antarctic Peninsula coast from Snow Hill Island, through Robertson Island and the Larsen Ice Shelf, to Borchgrevink Nunatak, and then back. They arrived back at Snow Hill Island on Oct. 31, 1902, after 33 days. Meanwhile, in the Falklands, the *Antarctic* had picked up Dr. J. Gunnar Andersson, who was to be in command of the expedition when Nordenskjöld was not there. On Nov. 5, 1902, the *Antarctic* again left for the south to pick up the Snow Hill party. On Nov. 9, 1902, the ship encountered pack-ice at 59°30'S. Within 2 days it was stuck in the ice. Finally it got free and sailed to the South Shetlands. It stopped at Deception Island, then went along the Bransfield Strait, refuting the existence of Middle Island (q.v.). They next explored the Orléans Strait and the Gerlache Strait. Their charting of the area was completed by Dec. 5, 1902. They then headed toward Nordenskjöld's winter campsite on Snow Hill Island. At Antarctic Sound, however, they found their way blocked by pack ice in the sound. Larsen tried to ram it, but to no avail. At this point, in early December 1902, Nordenskjöld sledged to Seymour Island and found some important fossils. But it began to look as if the *Antarctic* was not coming for them. On Dec. 29, 1902, the *Antarctic* landed Andersson, Duse, and Grunden at Hope Bay. The 3 men set up a depot, then set off on foot for Snow Hill Island, 200 miles away, in order to let Nordenskjöld know what was happening with the ship. The *Antarctic* continued to hit the ice in an effort to get through the sound to Nordenskjöld. It reached Paulet Island, but then got trapped in the pack-ice. On Jan. 9, 1903, the ice began squeezing the ship. On Jan. 10, 1903, it began to sink to starboard. On Jan. 16, 1903, the ship became upright again, and on Feb. 3, 1903, it was afloat again. But the leaks in the vessel were too great for it to continue. On Feb. 12, 1903, the *Antarctic* sank, crushed by the ice, 25 miles from Paulet Island, to which the crew and scientists now had to make their way over shifting sea ice. They had to carry stores, equipment, and themselves. After 14 days and a 6-hour row in a boat, they got ashore on Paulet Island on Feb. 28, 1903. Nordenskjöld saw the pack-ice around Snow Hill Island freeze on Feb. 19, 1903, and knew he would have to winter-over again, that the ship was definitely not going to make it. Meanwhile the Hope Bay party of Andersson, Duse, and Grunden had

set out toward Snow Hill Island. They crossed the Crown Prince Gustav Channel to Vega Island, and thought they had reached James Ross Island. They saw open water ahead and "knew" that the *Antarctic* would be able to get through to Snow Hill Island. So they headed back to their base at Hope Bay, arriving there on Jan. 13, 1903. They then waited for the *Antarctic* to pick them up, with Nordenskjöld's party aboard too. On Feb. 11, 1903, they began to build a more substantial hut, and started killing penguins for food. They wintered there, then left again, on foot, for Snow Hill Island, on Sept. 29, 1903. On Oct. 6, 1903, they began the long trip over the pack ice from the mainland to Vega Island, which they reached on Oct. 9, 1903. On Oct. 12, 1903, they reached a point which was later called Cape Well-Met. It was here that they saw 2 figures coming toward them in the distance. Nordenskjöld, in the spring (Aug.-Sept.) of 1903 had set off with Jonassen on a sledging journey to the Crown Prince Gustav Channel. He then headed toward Paulet Island to continue exploration, and at Cape Well-Met he and Jonassen saw 3 figures coming toward them in the distance. The Hope Bay party and the Snow Hill Island party had finally met up. Meanwhile, on Paulet Island, where the men of the *Antarctic* had been forced to land, they set about killing 1,100 penguins for food, and building a stone hut. On June 7, 1903, Ole Wennersgaard died. On Oct. 31, 1903, Capt. Larsen and 5 of the crew set out in a boat to rescue the Hope Bay party. They reached Hope Bay on Nov. 4, 1903. They found that the 3 men had gone toward Snow Hill Island, so they started rowing there too. Also meanwhile, Sweden was concerned about the safety of the expedition, and sent down the *Frithiof* to rescue them. The French explorer, Charcot, who was also leading his own expedition, went looking for Nordenskjöld, as did the Argentines in the *Uruguay* under Irízar. While this was happening, Nordenskjöld, Jonassen, Andersson, Duse, and Grunden got back to Snow Hill Island. On Oct. 26, 1903, Nordenskjöld, Andersson, and Sobral sledged to Seymour Island. On Nov. 7, 1903, Bodman and Åkerlundh left Snow Hill Island for Seymour Island, and were rescued by the *Uruguay* later that day. The Argentines then rescued Nordenskjöld and his party, and at that moment Larsen rowed into sight from Hope Bay. The *Frithiof* arrived to find the expedition already rescued. Nordenskjöld published a book about his scientific results (*see* the Bibliography).

Nordenskjöld Barrier *see* **Nordenskjöld Ice Tongue**

Nordenskjöld Basin. 76°S, 164°30′E. A submarine feature of the Ross Sea.

Nordenskjöld Coast. 64°30′S, 60°30′W. Between Cape Longing and Cape Fairweather, on the NE coast of the Antarctic Peninsula. Named in 1909 by Edwin Swift Balch (*see* the Bibliography) for Otto Nordenskjöld, who explored here in 1902.

Nordenskjöld Glacier Tongue *see* **Nordenskjöld Ice Tongue**

Nordenskjöld Ice Barrier *see* **Nordenskjöld Ice Tongue**

Nordenskjöld Ice Tongue. 76°12′S, 163°E. Also called Nordenskjöld Barrier, Nordenskjöld Glacier Tongue, Nordenskjöld Ice Barrier, Nordenskjöld Tongue. A glacier tongue, the Ross Sea end of the Mawson Glacier in southern Victoria Land. Discovered by Scott in 1902 and named by him for Otto Nordenskjöld.

Nordenskjöld Tongue *see* **Nordenskjöld Ice Tongue**

Nordhaugen Hill. 71°43′S, 25°27′E. The northernmost of three hills bordering the east side of Kamp Glacier in the Sør Rondane Mountains. Photographed by the LCE 1936–37. Name means "the north hill" in Norwegian.

Mount Nordhill. 70°55′S, 63°27′W. Between Steel Peak and Kosky Peak in the east ridge of the Welch Mountains in Palmer Land. Named for Cdr. Claude H.

Nordhill, USN, VX-6 operations officer, 1970, and commanding officer, 1972.

Nordkammen *see* **North Masson Range**

Nordkammen Crest *see* **North Masson Range**

Nordøyane *see* **Sirius Islands**

Nordston, Andrew. Ordinary seaman on the Wilkes Expedition 1838–42. Joined in the USA. Served the cruise.

Nordtoppen Nunatak. 71°29′S, 25°14′E. 1,100 m. 16 miles north of the Austkampane Hills in the Sør Rondane Mountains. Photographed by the LCE 1936–37. Name means "the north peak" in Norwegian.

Nordwestliche Insel Mountains. 71°27′S, 11°33′E. Islandlike mountains which form the northern extremity of the Humboldt Mountains, and at the same time the NW extremity of the overall group the Wohlthat Mountains, in Queen Maud Land. Discovered and named Nordwestliche Insel (northwest island) by Ritscher in 1938–39.

Punta Noreste *see* **Macaroni Point**

Norfolk Glacier. 85°53′S, 130°18′W. 12 miles long. Flows from the Wisconsin Range into Reedy Glacier between Mounts Soyat and Bolton. Named for Norfolk, Virginia, location of Detachment Three, the Meteorological Support Unit of the US Naval Support Force, Antarctica.

Norman Glacier. 71°25′S, 67°30′W. 5 miles long. Flows from Palmer Land into the George VI Sound, just north of Bushell Bluff. Named by the UK for Shaun M. Norman, BAS leader at Base E, 1966–68.

Norman Peak. 69°09′S, 66°08′W. In the Antarctic Peninsula.

The *Normanna*. Norwegian whaling factory ship plying the waters of the South Orkneys, South Shetlands, and Antarctic Peninsula in the 1912–13 season. Owned by the Normanna Whaling Co., of Sandefjord, Norway. The captain was K.O. Stene.

Normanna Reef. 64°21'S, 62°59'W. Near the center of the south entrance to The Sound in the Melchior Islands. Named before 1927 for the Normanna Whaling Co., of Sandefjord, Norway, which worked ships in this area, including the *Normanna*.

Normanna Strait. 60°40'S, 45°38'W. 1 mile wide. Between Signy Island and Coronation Island in the South Orkneys. Discovered by Matthew Brisbane in 1823. Named in 1912–13 by Petter Sørlle for the Normanna Whaling Co. (*see* **Normanna Reef**).

Norris Island *see* **Teksla Island**

The Norsel. Norwegian sealing vessel used as the expedition ship of the NBSAE 1949–52. Captain was Guttorm Jakobsen. Each winter during this long expedition, the ship returned to Norway. The FIDS chartered it for the 1954–55 season, and in Feb. 1955 it was in Arthur Harbor. Olav Johannessen was captain that season, and Torstein Torgersen was first mate. It was also the vessel which brought the French to Antarctica in 1955–56.

Norsel Bay *see* **Norsel Iceport**

Norsel Iceport. 71°01'S, 11°W. A small iceport in front of the Quar Ice Shelf, on the icy coast of Queen Maud Land. Used by the NBSAE 1949–52 to moor and unload the *Norsel*. Maudheim was established 1 mile south of the iceport. Named Norselbukta (Norsel Bay) for the expedition ship. The name was later redefined slightly.

Norsel Point. 64°46'S, 64°06'W. About 1½ miles north of Palmer Station, on Anvers Island, it forms the southern flange of Wylie Bay and Loudwater Cove. Surveyed by the FIDS in 1955. Named by the UK for the *Norsel*.

Norseman Point. 68°12'S, 67°W. The easternmost point on Neny Island, off the west coast of Graham Land. Named by the FIDS for the Norseman airplane which landed near here to relieve the FIDS party at Base E, on Stonington Island, in Feb. 1950.

Norsk Polarinstitutt Glacier. 72°34'S, 31°16'E. Flows SW between Mount Perov and Mount Limburg Stirum in the Belgica Mountains. Discovered by the Belgian Antarctic Expedition of 1957–58 under Gaston de Gerlache, and named by him for the Norwegian Polar Institute in Oslo.

Nørsteholmen *see* **Wyatt Earp Islands**

Brazo Norte *see* **Lientur Channel**

Islote Norte *see* **D'Hainaut Island, Mane Skerry**

Cape North. 70°41'S, 165°48'E. A large, snow-covered bluff of 500 meters in height. At the foot of the Anare Mountains in Oates Land, on the west side of the Nielsen Fjord. Discovered by Ross in 1841, and named by him because it was the most northerly cape observed westward of Cape Hooker.

North, James H. Acting ship's master on the Wilkes Expedition 1838–42. He joined the *Porpoise* at Callao, and later transferred to the *Vincennes*.

North Anchorage *see* **Visca Anchorage**

North Bay. 77°38'S, 166°23'E. Between Cape Evans and Cape Barne, off the west coast of Ross Island. Named by Scott's 1910–13 expedition because it is on the north side of Cape Evans.

North Crest *see* **North Masson Range**

North Forel Glacier *see* **Sharp Glacier**

[1]**North Foreland** *see* **Brimstone Peak**

[2]**North Foreland.** 61°54'S, 57°44'W. Also called Cabo Promontorio Norte. A cape, the most northeasterly point on King George Island, in the South Shetlands. Named on Oct. 16, 1819, by William Smith, for England's most easterly point. It has also been known as Cape North Foreland.

North Foreland Head *see* **Caroline Bluff**

[1]**North Fork** *see* **Taylor Glacier**

²**North Fork.** 77°32'S, 161°15'E. The northern arm of the Wright Valley in Victoria Land. Separated from the South Fork by The Dais. Named descriptively by the New Zealanders in 1958–59.

North Fork Basin. 77°32'S, 161°24'E. An area in the Wright Valley in southern Victoria Land.

North Heim Glacier *see* **Antevs Glacier**

North Island *see* **Hansen Island**

North Korea. Ratified as the 35th signatory of the Antarctic Treaty on Jan. 21, 1987.

North Masson Range. 67°47'S, 62°49' E. Also called Nordkammen, Nordkammen Crest, North Crest. 1,030 m. Extends 3 miles. The most northerly of the segments of the Masson Range. Photographed by the LCE 1936–37. Named Nordkammen (the north crest) by the Norwegians. The Australians renamed it in 1960.

North Nansen Island *see* **Enterprise Island**

¹**North Point.** 60°41'S, 45°38'W. Marks the northern extremity of Signy Island in the South Orkneys. Named by the personnel on the *Discovery II* in 1933.

²**North Point.** 66°46'S, 64°05'W. On Anvers Island. The British Base N was here, as was its American successor Palmer Station (now called Old Palmer—*see* **Palmer Station** for details).

North Spit. 62°13'S, 58°49'W. Forms the northern entrance to Marian Cove on King George Island, in the South Shetlands. Named by the personnel on the *Discovery II* in 1935.

The North Star. A US Bureau of Indian Affairs diesel-powered ship of 1,434 tons. A wooden ice-ship, built in 1932, it was used as the vessel for West Base (Little America III) during the USAS 1939–41. Lt. Cdr. Isak Lystad commanded.

North Star Island *see* **Eta Island**

North Thor Island. 64°32'S, 61°59'W. A little island just NE of South Thor Island (now called simply Thor Island), in Foyn Harbor, Wilhelmina Bay, off the west coast of Graham Land. Named by whalers in 1921–22 for the *Thor I* which operated here that season. Later, the UK renamed both these islands, or rather they renamed South Thor Island as Thor Island, and the little island NE of it lost its name altogether (it is now unnamed).

North Victoria Land *see* **Victoria Land**

Mount Northampton. 72°40'S, 169° 06'E. 2,465 m. Just east of Bowers Glacier, behind the Borchgrevink Coast, in the Victory Mountains in northern Victoria Land. Discovered in Jan. 1841 by Ross, who named it for the Marquis of Northampton, president of the Royal Society.

Northcliffe Glacier. 66°40'S, 98°52'E. Flows from Queen Mary Land into the Shackleton Ice Shelf just east of Davis Peninsula. Discovered by the AAE 1911–14, and named by Mawson for Lord Northcliffe, a patron.

Northcliffe Peak. 78°44'S, 161°08'E. 2,255 m. 4 miles SE of Mount Harmsworth in the Worcester Range. Surveyed in 1957 by the NZ party of the BCTAE, and named by them in association with Mount Harmsworth. Sir Alfred Harmsworth, a sponsor of the Royal Society Expedition of 1901–4, later became Lord Northcliffe.

Northeast Glacier. 68°09'S, 66°58'W. Flows from McLeod Hill (between Stonington Island and Cape Keeler on the Antarctic Peninsula) on the Mile High Plateau, into Marguerite Bay between the Debenham Islands and Roman Four Promontory on the west coast of Graham Land. 13 miles long, and 5 miles wide at its mouth, it is heavily crevassed. Named by the personnel at East Base on Stonington Island during the USAS 1939–41, because the glacier lies at the northeast side of their base.

Northern Foothills. 74°45'S, 163°55' E. A line of coastal hills, south of Browning Pass. They form a peninsular continuation of the Deep Freeze Range, and overlook Terra Nova Bay in Victoria Land, between Gerlache Inlet and Inexpressible Island. Named by Campbell's Northern Party during Scott's 1910–13 expedition because Inexpressible Island was originally called the Southern Foothills.

Northern Islands *see* **Wyatt Earp Islands**

Northern Victoria Land Expedition. 1981–82. On Oct. 24, 1981, Allan Priddy and his Antarctic Services Inc. employees flew into northern Victoria Land in an LC-130 airplane to build the camp for this expedition. At the end of 2 weeks they had erected a field camp called NVL at 72°12'S, 163°50'E, at the north end of Evans Névé, near the head of the Canham Glacier. The camp consisted of 5 Jamesway huts and a plywood generator hut. On Nov. 6, 1981, the first scientists arrived, and science flights began on Nov. 9, 1981. Between this time and the end of the expedition on Jan. 13, 1982, 22 geology and geophysics projects were carried out in a 100-mile radius area by USA, NZ, West Germany, and Australia. The American Edmund Stump was chief scientist, and camp manager was Philip V. Colbert of ITT/Antarctic Services. Three UH-1N helicopters were used for local transportation, as well as motor toboggans. Information gained helped perfect 12 Antarctic Geological Reconnaissance series maps. Other studies included glaciation, gravity, airborne radiometric surveys, a search for meteorites, and lichen studies.

Cape Northrop. 67°24'S, 65°16'W. 1,160 m. Forms the north side of the entrance to Whirlwind Inlet, on the east coast of Graham Land, where it juts out into the Larsen Ice Shelf north of Francis Island. Discovered by Wilkins on Dec. 20, 1928, from his plane, a Lockheed Vega, made by John K. Northrop, who had founded Lockheed in 1927.

Northrup Head. 69°52'S, 160°09'E. Ice-covered headland, a coastal extension

of the Wilson Hills, on the north side of Suvorov Glacier, 3½ miles WSW of Belousov Point. Named for David A. Northrup, USN, VX-6 aviation electronics technician at McMurdo Station in 1967.

North's Coast. 67°S, 127°45'E. Part of what is now the Banzare Coast. This was a term given to a stretch of coast in East Antarctica which Wilkes had inadequately described as North's High Land. Because Wilkes' definition was unspecific, as was his terminology, in both geographical and topographical terms, latter day geographers gave the coastal area the name North's Coast. After 1930 the term became defunct because Mawson included it in the Banzare Coast. In 1955 the USA verified the existence of a highland section here, which had been Wilkes's original 1840 discovery (but he had not been believed). They now called it Norths Highland.

Norths Highland. 66°40'S, 126°E. Ice-covered upland behind the Voyeykov Ice Shelf in Wilkes Land. Just south of Cape Goodenough, it surmounts the Banzare Coast between Maury and Porpoise Bays. Discovered by Wilkes in 1840, and named North's High Land by him for James H. North.

North's Land *see* **North's Coast, Norths Highland**

Northstar Island. 68°11'S, 67°07'W. A tiny island, no more than ¼ mile long by a few hundred yards wide. 1 mile NW of the western tip of Neny Island, and 1½ miles east of Stonington Island, in Marguerite Bay. Surveyed by the FIDS in 1947, and named by them for the *North Star*.

Northtrap Rocks. 62°54'S, 56°34'W. Also called Rocas Montrol. Isolated rocks in water NW of Cape Juncal, D'Urville Island. Named by the UK in 1963 because they are the more northern of two groups of features to be avoided by vessels coming into Antarctic Sound from the north (*see also* **Southtrap Rocks**).

Northwest Mountain. 77°39'S, 160°38'E. Just NE of Beehive Mountain, on the north side of the upper Taylor Glacier in Victoria Land. Named by Scott's 1910–13 expedition.

¹The *Northwind* *see* **The *Staten Island***

²The *Northwind*. 6,515-ton US Coast Guard icebreaker/research ship of 10,000 hp. Launched in 1945. Part of Task Force 68 during Operation Highjump, 1946–47, during which it was the icebreaker for the Central Group. Its captain was Charles W. Thomas. It also took part in Operation Deep Freeze II and IV, and was decommissioned on Jan. 20, 1989, after which it resided at Wilmington, N.C.

Northwind Glacier. 76°40'S, 161°18'E. Flows from a high névé SW of Flagship Mountain on the east side of the Convoy Range, into the Fry Glacier. A lobe flows west a little way into Greenville Valley. Named by the NZ Northern Survey Party of the BCTAE 1957–58 for the *Northwind*.

Norton, Benjamin. Ordinary seaman on the Wilkes Expedition 1838–42. Joined in the USA. Served the cruise.

Norton, Nelson. Captain of the topsail on the Wilkes Expedition 1838–42. Joined in the USA. Discharged at Oahu, Nov. 2, 1840.

The *Norton Sound*. US ship which, on Aug. 22, 1958, fired an atom bomb-armed missile from Antarctic waters, 300 miles into the atmosphere where it was exploded.

The *Norvegia*. Norwegian ship owned by whaling magnate Lars Christensen. It first went to Antarctica in 1927–28 on a scientific expedition led by Haakon Mosby. Harald Horntvedt was ship's captain. In 1928–29 it was back again on an expedition led by Ola Olstad. Ship's captain this time was Nils Larsen. The first landing on Peter I Island was effected from this ship, on Feb. 2, 1929. It was one of the ships which carried Riiser-Larsen to the Antarctic in 1929–31. Once

again, Nils Larsen was ship's captain. The ship was crushed in the ice in the Arctic in 1933, and was replaced by the *J.H. Bull*.

Cape Norvegia. 71°25'S, 12°18'W. Marks the NE limit of the Riiser-Larsen Ice Shelf on the coast of Queen Maud Land. Discovered in Feb. 1930 by Riiser-Larsen while on a flight from the *Norvegia*. He named it for his ship.

Mount Norvegia. 67°51'S, 48°08'E. 1,340 m. Ice-covered. 6 miles north of Mount Christensen in Enderby Land. Named by the Australians for the *Norvegia*.

Norvegia Bay. 68°45'S, 90°42'W. A cove at the north side of Cape Ingrid on the west side of Peter I Island. Named by the Norwegians for the *Norvegia*.

Norway. In 1897–99 Norway's Roald Amundsen was part of the *Belgica* expedition. In 1910–12 he led the Norwegian Antarctic Expedition and was the first man to get to the South Pole. Even before that time Norway was establishing a major whaling presence in the Antarctic, and in 1929 Riiser-Larsen discovered, named, and explored Queen Maud Land. In 1939 Norway claimed Queen Maud Land (*see* **Norwegian Dependency**). One of the 12 original signatories of the Antarctic Treaty in 1959, Norway had a scientific station there, the Princess Martha Coast Station, but it no longer has bases there, having transferred them to South Africa. It still sends summer research parties, however, with the cooperation of other countries. Norway took part in the Filchner Ice Shelf Program (FISP) and in 1986–87 it fielded a small expedition to Peter I Island for mapping and aerial photography. The Norsk Polarinstitutt looks after all national interests in the Antarctic. Its address is Rolsstangveien 12, 1330 Oslo Lusthaven, Norway.

Camp Norway. There have been several camps established by the Norwegians in Queen Maud Land, and using this name. They have been field camps only, expendable after the season. They have been designated Camp Norway I,

Camp Norway II, etc. Camp Norway III was at 72°30'S, 15°W. Camp Norway IV was at 73°45'S, 14°30'W. Camp Norway V was in the area of Svarthamaren Mountain, in the Mühlig-Hofmann Mountains of Queen Maud Land, and was established in early 1985 by the Norwegian Antarctic Research Expedition of 1984–85.

Norway Bight. 60°37'S, 45°49'W. Also called Norway Fjord. A bay, 4 miles wide, which indents the south coast of Coronation Island, between Meier Point and Mansfield Point. Named by Petter Sørlle in 1912–13.

Norway Fjord *see* **Norway Bight**

Norway Glacier. 86°34'S, 164°02'W. 10 miles long. Flows from the Polar Plateau just west of Mount Prestrud and enters Amundsen Glacier between Mount Bjaaland and Mount Hassel, in the Queen Maud Mountains. Discovered by Amundsen on Nov. 29, 1911, and named by him for his country.

Norway Rocks. 76°10'S, 168°20'E. A reef of rocks which extend 4 miles southward of Bernacchi Head, Franklin Island, in the Ross Sea. Discovered in 1841 by Ross. Named by Borchgrevink in 1898–1900 for his country.

Norway Station *see* **Princess Martha Coast Station**

Norwegian Antarctic Expedition. 1910–12. Led by Roald Amundsen. On Sept. 9, 1910, at Madeira, Amundsen announced to his crew that they were not going to the North Pole at all, but to the South Pole instead. He asked them if that was all right. They said it was. So the *Fram* sailed south, instead of north. The reason was that the North Pole had recently been reached, by Peary (at least, so he claimed), so Amundsen considered his own assault on that point to be redundant. He had decided this some time before but had kept it a secret, fearing that his funding would be taken away. Only when he was at sea did he consider it safe to make his announcement. He then sportingly sent a telegram to Scott ("Beg leave to inform you, *Fram* pro-

ceeding Antarctica. Amundsen") who was in Melbourne preparing to set out for the same destination. This telegram started the so-called Race for the Pole of 1911. The Norwegians versus the British. On Jan. 2, 1911, the *Fram* crossed the Antarctic Circle, and on Jan. 3, 1911, they entered the pack-ice. On Jan. 7, 1911, after an unbelievably short time in the pack-ice, they broke through into the calm of the Ross Sea. The *Fram* having a diesel engine, this was the first motor passage of the Antarctic pack ice. On Jan. 14, 1911, they arrived at the Bay of Whales. On Jan. 15, 1911, they began unloading the *Fram*, and building their base, which, on Feb. 4, 1911, they named Framheim. There was a shore party of 9 men — Amundsen, Hassel, Hanssen, Wisting, Bjaaland, Johansen, Prestrud, Lindstrøm, and Stubberud. The others on the ship's party included Thorvald Nilsen (captain of the *Fram* and second-in-command of the expedition), Martin Rønne, Beck, Gjertsen, Sundbeck, Kutchin, Ludvig Hansen, Nødtvedt, H. Kristensen, Karinius Olsen. On Feb. 10, 1911, Amundsen, Prestrud, Johansen, and Hanssen went on a depot-laying expedition in preparation for their push to the Pole later that year. They took 3 sledges and 18 dogs, and other men went as far as the Barrier to help them up the slope onto the ice shelf. On Feb. 14, 1911, they reached 80°S, returning to Framheim on Feb. 16, 1911, after having marked the trail. The *Fram* had left earlier that day to winter-over at Buenos Aires. In the Ross Sea it met the *Terra Nova* (Scott's ship, sans Scott, who was already at Ross Island). On Feb. 22, 1911, the entire Norwegian shore party, with the exception of Lindstrøm, set out, reaching 80°S on Feb. 27, 1911. On March 3, 1911, they reached 81°S. It was from here that Hassel, Bjaaland, and Stubberud returned to Framheim. On March 8, 1911, the main party reached 82°S, setting up depots at each degree south as they went, laying massive amounts of fuel and food for themselves and the dogs. 8 dogs died on this assault, for the return journey was one of great hardship, arriving back at Framheim on March 23, 1911. They then wintered-over in preparation for the summer push on the South Pole. On Sept. 8, 1911, they all (except Lindstrøm again) left on a premature dash south, but the temperature was 68 below, and they got as far as 80°S before returning. On Oct. 20, 1911, they set out again with 45 dogs, four light sledges, and five men — Amundsen, Bjaaland, Wisting, Hassel, and Hanssen. By Oct. 26, 1911, they were on their way from the 80°S depot to the one at 81°S, which they reached on Oct. 31, 1911. They got to the southernmost depot, at 82°S, on Nov. 5, 1911, leaving here on Nov. 7, 1911. Each dog was now pulling just under 80 pounds, and on Nov. 10, 1911, they lost three of their best dogs. On Nov. 17, 1911, they reached the Transantarctic Mountains, and on Nov. 18, 1911, they came to the Axel Heiberg Glacier. This glacier was steep, but led directly to the Polar Plateau above them. Scott, on the other hand was taking the route pioneered by Shackleton five years before, the Beardmore Glacier, which was longer, less direct, but also less dangerous. Axel Heiberg had never been climbed before, and on Nov. 20, 1911, Amundsen and his men began the ascent, reaching the Polar Plateau with 18 dogs, the first animals on the Polar Plateau. On Dec. 7, 1911, they reached 88°S and on Dec. 14, 1911, they became the first men ever to reach the South Pole. They left a dark colored silk tent, the Norwegian flag and a wooden plaque bearing the name *"Fram."* Also a letter to the King of Norway, a sextant, a spirit level, several pieces of clothing, a plate bearing the name of the crew, and a letter "For Robert F. Scott." The actual Pole point was reached first probably by Olav Bjaaland, at 11 a.m., on Dec. 17, 1911, and that day they left for the return journey, with 16 dogs and the desire to get back to civilization with the news. On Dec. 25, 1911, they reached their first return depot at 88°25'S, and on Jan. 2, 1912, they were at the Devil's Glacier, at

the top of the Axel Heiberg Glacier. By Jan. 7, 1912, they were back down the Axel Heiberg Glacier and back onto the Ross Ice Shelf, and headed for home. On Jan. 17, 1912, they reached their 82°S depot, and arrived back at Framheim at 4 a.m. on Jan. 26, 1912. "Good morning, my dear Lindstrøm, have you any coffee for us?," were Amundsen's first words to the cook at Framheim, the first of the base members to welcome the Polarfarers back. They had done the whole trip in 99 days. "The whole thing went like a dream," Amundsen said. Meanwhile Prestrud, Johansen, and Stubberud had gone off on a separate expedition, on Nov. 29, 1911 becoming the first men to set foot on Edward VII Peninsula (as it was to become known — then it was called Edward VII Land), and sledging as far as Scott's Nunataks. Also the *Fram* had returned on Jan. 9, 1912, gone off again on local trips, then come back on Jan. 27, 1912. Amundsen left the Antarctic on Jan. 30, 1912, with 39 dogs altogether, crossing the Antarctic Circle on Feb. 9, 1912. At that triumphant moment for Amundsen, Scott and his party were returning from the Pole and heading toward oblivion.

Norwegian Antarctic Expedition. 1968–69. 6-man expedition organized by the Norsk Polarinstitutt in Oslo. Its aim — to carry out mapping, geological, and glaciological investigations of the Kraul Mountains (or Vestfjella as the Norwegians call them) in western Queen Maud Land. Thore S. Wisnes was geologist and leader; Audun Hjelle, geologist; Torbjørn Lunde, glaciologist; Dag Norberg, topographer; Ola Steine, geodesist; Kåre M. Bratlien, radio operator. They were taken from McMurdo Station to the Kraul Mountains on Nov. 22, 1968, by US transport, and returned on Jan. 20, 1969, a successful expedition.

Norwegian-British-Swedish Antarctic Expedition. 1949–52. Seen in this book as the NBSAE 1949–52. Led by John Giaever. The first truly international Antarctic expedition. The *Norsel* took down the expedition to the Quar Ice Shelf on the coast of Queen Maud Land. The ship was unloaded at Norsel Bay (now called Norsel Iceport). Their base, Maudheim, was built on the ice shelf. Other members of the expedition were Stig Valter Schytt, glaciologist and second-in-command; Gordon de Q. Robin, physicist and third-in-command; Ove Wilson, medical officer; John P. Jelbart, Australian observer; C.W.M. Swithinbank; Stig Hallgren; Nils Roer; Bjarne Lorentzen; Peter Melleby; Nils Jørgen Schumacher; John Snarby; Ernest F. Roots; Kåre Friis-Baastad; Leslie Quar; Sigvard Kjellberg; R.G.D.J. von Essen; Bertil Ekström; Egil Rogstad; Gösta H. Liljequist. 3 men died (see **Deaths**) out of the 20 Norwegians, British, Swedes, Australians, and Finns. US military surplus M-29 Weasel tracked vehicles were used. Much exploration of Queen Maud Land was carried out from Maudheim and from a subsidiary base set up 185 miles inland. Land traverses and aerial photography covered an area of 38,000 square miles of Queen Maud Land, the territory claimed by Norway in 1939. This expedition began a series of annual expeditions in Queen Maud Land sponsored by the 3 governments and national societies.

Norwegian Dependency. About a quarter of a million square miles of land, mostly Queen Maud Land, between 20° W and 45° E, claimed by Norway on Jan. 14, 1939. The claim was inspired by Ritscher's Nazi expedition of 1938–39 to the Queen Maud Land area, an area that Riiser-Larsen had really discovered in 1929–31 — for Norway. Nazi Germany refused to accept the Norwegian claim, but Britain, France, New Zealand, and Australia did recognize it. The USA and the USSR do not make or recognize claims. The northern and southern limits of this claim are undefined, and rather ragged, but the wedge-shaped part of the pie that the Norsemen claim does not extend to the South Pole, which is significantly strange considering Amundsen (a Norwegian) was the first human being

to get to the Pole, in 1911. In addition to this continental claim, the Norwegian Dependency also includes Peter I Island (or Peter I Øy, as the Norwegians themselves refer to it), which was claimed even earlier, on May 1, 1931.

Norwood Scarp. 68°50′S, 65°23′W. 1,525 meters at its highest. An escarpment 11 miles long. Forms part of the east flank of the Weyerhaeuser Glacier, in the eastern part of the Antarctic Peninsula. Named by the UK for Richard Norwood (1590–1675), navigation pioneer.

Nøst Island. 67°37′S, 62°41′E. Less than ¼ mile long. 2 miles WSW of Evans Island in the southern part of Holme Bay. Photographed by the LCE 1936–37 and named Nøstet (the boatshed) by the Norwegians.

Nostoc Lake. 80°24′S, 30°05′W. 1 mile SW of Mount Provender in the west part of the Shackleton Range. Named by the BCTAE in 1957 for the freshwater algae found here.

Mount Notre Dame de Lorette   see **Mount Lorette**

Nottarp Glacier. 82°37′S, 162°54′E. Flows into Lowery Glacier just south of Mount Damm in the Queen Elizabeth Range. Named for Klemmens J. Nottarp, glaciologist on the Ross Ice Shelf, 1962–63 and 1965–66.

Notter Point. 63°40′S, 59°11′W. 6 miles NE of Mount Kjellman. Marks the western limit of Bone Bay, Trinity Peninsula. Named by the Argentines in 1953 for hero Tomás Notter (d. 1814).

Novasio Ridge. 72°03′S, 168°22′E. Ice-covered. Separates the lower portions of the Freimanis and Man-o-War Glaciers in the Admiralty Mountains. Named for Richard A. Novasio, USN, radioman at Hallett Station in 1957.

Novel Rock   see   **Nueva Rock**

Mount Noville. 86°27′S, 146°10′W. 2,410 m. Between the Van Reeth and Robison Glaciers, 4 miles east of Mount Bowlin, in the Queen Maud Mountains. Discovered by Quin Blackburn's party in Dec. 1934, during Byrd's 1933–35 expedition. Named by Byrd for G.O. Noville.

Noville, George O. Executive officer of Byrd's 1933–35 expedition and one of the shore party. Known as G.O. Noville.

Noville Mountains *see* **Hudson Mountains**

Noville Peninsula. 71°50′S, 98°46′W. 30 miles long. Ice-covered. Forms the eastern flange of Peale Inlet, on the northern side of Thurston Island. Murphy Inlet is on the west. Named for G.O. Noville.

Novocin Peak. 76°01′S, 69°33′W. In the Bean Peaks, near the SE end of the group, in the Hauberg Mountains of Ellsworth Land. Named for Norbert W. Novocin, meteorologist at Byrd Station in 1965–66.

Novolazarevskaya Station. 70°46′S, 11°50′E. USSR scientific station opened on Feb. 18, 1961, on the edge of the Lazarev Ice Shelf, on the Princess Astrid Coast, and named for Mikhail Lazarev. It was moved further inland, on a lake at the eastern end of the Schirmacher Oasis. It has 8 buildings and several smaller storage buildings. The chief's house is known as "The White House." About 16 men winter-over.

Novosad Island. 70°42′S, 167°29′E. Small and ice-covered, it is one of the Lyall Islands. 4 miles NNE of Cape Dayman, off the north coast of Victoria Land. Named for Lt. Charles L. Novosad, Jr., USN, medical officer at McMurdo Station in 1957.

Cape Novosil'skiy. 68°38′S, 154°46′E. On the Oates Land coast. Named for Pavel M. Novosil'skiy.

Novosil'skiy, Pavel M. Naval lieutenant on the *Mirnyy* during von Bellingshausen's expedition of 1819–21.

Novyy Island. 70°50′S, 2°50′W. Also called Eskimo Ysbult. 250 m. The larger and southern of two similar ice-covered islands which mark the border of the Jelbart and Fimbul Ice Shelves, on the Queen Maud Land coast. Named Kupol Novyy (new dome) by the USSR in 1961.

Nowland, James. Captain of the topsail on the Wilkes Expedition 1838–42. Joined in the USA. Run at Sydney.

Mount Noxon. 72°08′S, 100°06′W. In the Walker Mountains, at the head of the Myers Glacier on Thurston Island. Named for Sgt. W.C. Noxon, US Marines, VX-6 navigator in the Antarctic, 1959–60.

Noyes, William. First mate on the *Seraph*, 1829–31.

Nozal, M. Seaman, and later lieutenant, on the *Pourquoi Pas?* in 1908–10, under Charcot.

Nozal Hill. 65°11′S, 63°57′W. Also called Nozal Peak. 620 m. Ice-covered. 1 mile north of Mount Shackleton. Between Régnard Peaks and Blanchard Ridge on the west coast of Graham Land. Discovered and named by Charcot in 1908–10 for M. Nozal.

Nozal Peak *see* **Nozal Hill**

The Nozzle. 79°55′S, 159°05′E. A defile near Diamond Hill. The lower Darwin Glacier flows through it. Named descriptively by the Darwin Glacier Party of the BCTAE 1956–58.

Mount Nubian. 78°15′S, 166°25′E. At the head of a ridge formed by a lava flow. 1 mile SE of Mount Aurora on Black Island, in the Ross Archipelago. Consists of black basalt, and was named descriptively by the New Zealanders in 1958–59.

Nuclear Power. Antarctica's first and only nuclear power plant, PM-3A, arrived at McMurdo Station on Dec. 12, 1961. Authorization to construct had come from Congress in 1960. Capt. Herbert Whitney had supervised the site preparation for the plant in 1961 halfway up Observation Hill, on Hut Point Peninsula, Ross Island, in the immediate vicinity of McMurdo. Julian P. Gudmondson, USN, had blasted the foundation that year. PM-3A was a Portable Medium Power Range plant, and was the third in an AEC series (hence the name PM-3A) prefabricated at the Martin Marietta Corporation's plant in Baltimore. A pressurized-water reactor, it came in a series of 30-foot modules, and its function was to produce power and heat for the USA's largest Antarctic base. It was duly set up on Observation Hill, and went critical on March 3, 1962. On July 10, 1962, it started producing power for the station, generating an electrical output of 1,800 kilowatts gross. Originally it was operated by Navy men under the direction of the Martin Marietta Corporation, but on May 27, 1964, the Naval Nuclear Power Unit took it over. All nuclear wastes were returned to the USA for dumping, as per the rules of the Antarctic Treaty. Although for 10 years it operated perfectly safely and produced 78 million kilowatt hours of electricity and ran at 78 percent availability, it was not really reliable until 1966. The plant had fires, leakages, and shutdowns, and in Sept. 1972 big problems started happening. It was deactivated that month, mainly because it was no longer economical. Decommissioning of PM-3A began in Oct. 1973, and the dismantling of the plant took 3 years. Over 390,000 cubic feet of contaminated rock had to be shipped back to the USA for dumping, and it was not until May 25, 1979, that the US Department of Energy released the site as safe. A plant at Byrd Station was cancelled on Oct. 1, 1962, due to the cost and predicted inefficiency.

Nueva Rock. 67°44′S, 69°10′W. Also called Novel Rock. A submerged rock south of Cono Island, and west of Cox Reef, off the south end of Adelaide Island. Named by the Argentines in 1957 (nueva means new).

Numbat Island. 67°34′S, 47°58′E. A small island, just east of Pinn Island, off the coast of Enderby Land. Named by the Australians for their native animal.

Nunakols. A nunakol is a nunatak rounded by glacial erosion, or, put another way, a rounded island of rock in a glacier.

Nunataks. Isolated mountain peaks rising from the bedrock and poking through the surface of the ice. They usually occur near the edge of an ice sheet.

Nuñez Point. 65°33′S, 64°15′W. Forms the western extremity of Takaki Promontory, between Beascochea Bay and Leroux Bay, on the west coast of Graham Land. Discovered by Charcot, and named by him for Capt. Nuñez of the Argentine Navy.

Nunn Island. 74°17′S, 117°W. 9 miles long. Ice-covered. Within the Getz Ice Shelf, just south of Wright Island, along the coast of Marie Byrd Land. Named for Rear-Adm. Ira Nunn, USN, legal adviser to the Navy during IGY (1957–58).

Nupkins Island. 65°26′S, 65°41′W. Also called Isla Comodor de Quito. 3 miles west of Sawyer Island in the Pitt Islands, in the Biscoe Islands. Named by the UK for the Dickens character.

Nupshamrane Peaks. 71°57′S, 3°20′W. Just east of the Klumpane Peaks, on the west side of the Ahlmann Ridge in Queen Maud Land. Name means "the high peaks" in Norwegian.

Nupskammen Ridge. 72°09′S, 2°19′E. 8 miles long. Has several jagged peaks on it. North of Von Essen Mountain in the Gjelsvik Mountains of Queen Maud Land. Name means "the peak crest" in Norwegian.

Nupskåpa Peak. 72°44′S, 0°16′E. 2,450 m. Ice-capped. Just south of Reece Valley in the Sverdrup Mountains of Queen Maud Land. Name means "the peak cloak" in Norwegian.

Nupsskåka Valley. 71°58′S, 8°48′E. Ice-filled. On the SW side of Nupsskarvet Mountain in the Kurze Mountains of Queen Maud Land. Name means "the peak shaft" in Norwegian.

Nupsskarvet Mountain. 71°56′S, 8°52′E. At the north side of Hålisrimen Peak in the Kurze Mountains of Queen Maud Land. Named by the Norwegians.

Nurket Rock. 73°25′S, 3°06′W. A rock on land just east of Mount Hallgren in the Kirwan Escarpment of Queen Maud Land. Name means "the pygmy" in Norwegian.

Nursery Glacier. 81°16′S, 160°30′E. 20 miles long. Flows along the west side of the Darley Hills into the Ross Ice Shelf just south of Cape Parr. Named by the NZGSAE 1959–60 for the litter of husky pups born here.

Mount Nussbaum *see* **Nussbaum Riegel**

Nussbaum Bar *see* **Nussbaum Riegel**

Nussbaum Riegel. 77°40'S, 162°46'E. Also called Mount Nussbaum, Nussbaum Bar. It is a riegel, or rock bar, across Taylor Valley in Victoria Land. It extends from the area of the Sollas Glacier toward Lake Chad. Charted and named during Scott's 1910–13 expedition.

Nusser Island. 65°43'S, 65°43'W. 1½ miles north of Laktionov Island, off the east side of Renaud Island, in the Biscoe Islands. Named by the UK in 1959 for Franz Nusser, Austrian meteorologist specializing in sea ice studies.

Cape Nutt. 66°37'S, 108°09'E. Mostly ice-covered. Has several rock outcrops at the extremity. Forms the west side of the entrance to Vincennes Bay. Named for Cdr. David C. Nutt, USNR, marine biologist on Operation Windmill, 1947–48.

Nutt Bluff. 82°34'S, 51°45'W. At the very north of the Pensacola Mountains.

Nye Glacier. 67°28'S, 67°31'W. On Arrowsmith Peninsula, it flows into Whistling Bay, in Graham Land. Named by the UK for John F. Nye, British glaciologist.

Nye Islands. 66°10'S, 110°25'E. 2 small islands between Midgely Island and Pidgeon Island in the Windmill Islands. Named for Harvey M. Nye, meteorological electronics technician at Wilkes Station in 1959.

Nye Mountains. 68°10'S, 49°E. 30 miles long. Between 10 and 15 miles wide. They trend east from the head of Rayner Glacier and overlook Casey Bay, in Enderby Land. Discovered aerially by Douglas W. Leckie (*see* **Leckie Range**) during an ANARE flight in Oct. 1956. Named by the Australians for P.B. Nye, director of the Bureau of Mineral Resources in Australia.

Cape Nygren *see* **Nygren Point**

Mount Nygren. 65°09'S, 63°48'W. In the middle of Hotine Glacier, in the western part of the Antarctic Peninsula. Named for Rear-Adm. Harley D. Nygren, director of the National Oceanic and Atmospheric Administration Corps in the 1970s and 1980s. He had been the US observer on the BAS 1961–62, when he conducted oceanographic research in the *Shackleton,* the *John Biscoe,* and the *Kista Dan.*

Nygren Point. 64°23'S, 58°13'W. 4 miles SE of Cape Broms, on the SW side of James Ross Island. Discovered and surveyed in 1903 by Nordenskjöld's 1901–4 expedition. He named it Cape Nygren, for G. Nygren, Swedish chemist who contributed to the expedition. The name was later redefined.

Mount O. Wisting *see* **Mount Wisting**

Cape Oakeley. 71°01'S, 167°54'E. Also spelled Cape Oakley. On the NE side of the Quam Heights. Forms the south side of the entrance to Smith Inlet, on the west side of Robertson Bay in Oates Land. Discovered by Ross in 1841, and named by him for Henry Oakeley.

Oakeley, Henry. Midshipman on the *Erebus* during Ross's expedition of 1839–43.

Cape Oakley *see* **Cape Oakeley**

Oakley Glacier. 73°42'S, 166°08'E. In the Mountaineer Range of Victoria Land. Flows from Mount Casey, to merge with the floating tongue from the Icebreaker Glacier at Lady Newnes Bay. Named for Lt. Cdr. Donald C. Oakley, USN, Protestant chaplain at McMurdo Station in 1967.

Oases. Russian name for deglaciated, ice-free coastal areas, unfrozen lakes, and sometimes huge areas of snow-free ground. Antarctica once had a mild climate, with forests and flowers, and the oases remain as a legacy. No one knows why.

Oasis Station   *see*   **Oazis Station**

Oates, Laurence. b. March 17, 1880, London. d. March 17, 1912, at 79°50'S in the Antarctic. Laurence Edward Grace Oates, commonly known in history as L.E.G. Oates, or Captain Oates, and to his friends as "Titus," or "The Soldier." A captain of the 6th Inniskillin Dragoons, he paid £1,000 to join Scott's 1910–13 expedition. His job was to take care of the ponies. Scott picked him for the fateful Polar party of 1911–12. One of the first ten men to reach the Pole, he suffered from severe frostbite and scurvy on the return trip, and left the tent on his 32nd birthday, to perish in the blizzard. His remaining in the tent would have been a real liability to the others, and would have threatened their existence. This act of self sacrifice and his witty remarks would have been typical of Oates. He wrote to his mother in 1910 prior to setting out for Antarctica, "The climate is very healthy, although inclined to be cold," or his final quote as he left the tent, "I am just going outside and may be some time."

Oates Coast   *see*   **Oates Land**

Oates Land. 70°S, 160°E. Also called Oates Coast. This is not yet a recognized US term, as that country prefers Oates Coast as part of northern Victoria Land. Between Cape Hudson and Cape Williams, or between the Rennick Glacier and the Cook Ice Shelf. Discovered by Pennell in the *Terra Nova* on Feb. 22, 1911, and named for Laurence Oates.

Oates Piedmont Glacier. 76°25'S, 162°35'E. East of the Kirkwood Range, it occupies the whole of the coastal platform between the Fry and Mawson Glaciers in Victoria Land. Named by the NZ Northern Survey Party of the BCTAE 1957–58, for Laurence Oates.

Oazis Station. 66°16'S, 100°45'E. USSR IGY station opened in the Bunger Hills. Established entirely by air in Oct. 1956. Its first leader, from Oct. 1956, was A. Tselishchev. Leader of the 1957 winter

party was G. Paschenko. In 1958 the USSR transferred it to Poland, and it became Dobrowolski Station.

The *Ob'*. 12,500-ton USSR icebreaker/research ship/transport ship, named for the river. It was in Antarctica every year between 1955 and 1961. I.A. Man commanded it during its first two trips, 1955–56 and 1956–57.

Ob' Bay. 70°35'S, 163°22'E. Between Lunik Point and Cape Williams, or between Yule Bay and Rennick Bay, in northern Victoria Land. The Lillie Glacier Tongue occupies the east part of the bay. Charted by the USSR in 1958, and named by them for the *Ob'*.

Ob' Passage. 66°32'S, 93°E. Almost ½ mile wide, between Khmara Island and Mabus Point, on the coast of East Antarctica. Discovered by the AAE 1911–14. The USSR named it in 1956 for the *Ob'*.

The Obelisk. 71°50'S, 70°33'W. 750 m. A pillar in the Staccato Peaks. 18 miles WNW of Mimas Peak, in the southern part of Alexander Island. Discovered aerially by Ellsworth on Nov. 23, 1935. Named descriptively by the UK.

Cape Obelisk. 64°08'S, 58°27'W. Also called Pointe Obélisque. At the north side of the entrance to Röhss Bay, on the west side of James Ross Island. Discovered and named by Nordenskjöld's 1901–4 expedition. There is an obelisk-type pillar 2 miles inland from the headland.

Obelisk Mountain. 77°38'S, 161°36'E. 2,200 m. Between Catspaw Glacier and Mount Odin, near the Wright Valley, in the Asgard Range of Victoria Land. Named descriptively by Grif Taylor's Western Journey Party during Scott's 1910–13 expedition.

Pointe Obélisque   *see*   **Cape Obelisk**

Lake Ober-See. 71°17'S, 13°39'E. The Norwegians call it Övresjöen. A meltwater lake between Sjøneset Spur and Mount Seekopf in the Gruber Mountains of Queen Maud Land. Discovered by Ritscher in 1938–39. He named it Ober-See (Upper Lake).

Oberon Peak. 71°24′S, 69°32′W. 1,250 m. An isolated nunatak. At the head of Uranus Glacier. 8 miles NNW of Titania Peak, in the central part of Alexander Island. Named by the UK in association with Uranus Glacier (Oberon is a satellite of the planet Uranus).

Oberst Glacier. 72°03′S, 27°04′E. Flows from the west side of Balchen Mountain in the Sør Rondane Mountains. Named by the Norwegians for Bernt Balchen, who reached the rank of colonel (oberst) in the US Army Air Force in World War II (Oberstbreen means "colonel glacier" in Norwegian).

Mount Obiglio. 74°27′S, 131°50′W. 510 m. A volcano on Grant Island, along the edge of the Getz Ice Shelf, in Marie Byrd Land. Discovered by the *Glacier* on Feb. 4, 1962. Named for Lt. G.M. Obiglio, Argentine naval officer on the *Glacier*. Named at the suggestion of Capt. Edwin A. McDonald.

Oblachnaya Nunatak. 67°41′S, 51°16′E. 6 miles SE of the Perov Nunataks at the east edge of the Scott Mountains in Enderby Land. The USSR called it Gora Oblachnaya (cloudy mountain) in 1962.

Obrecht Pyramid. 68°09′S, 65°32′W. On the east side of Graham Land.

O'Brien, B.P. Crewman on the *Jacob Ruppert*, 1933–34.

O'Brien, Esmonde M. Chief engineer on the *City of New York* during Byrd's 1928–30 expedition.

O'Brien, John S. Surveyor on the Geological Party led by Gould in Dec. 1929 during Byrd's 1928–30 expedition.

O'Brien Bay. 66°18′S, 110°32′E. Also called Bukhta Lagernaya. Between Bailey Peninsula and Mitchell Peninsula, in the area of the Windmill Islands. Named for Lt. Clement E. O'Brien, USN, communications officer on Operation Windmill, 1947–48.

O'Brien Island. 61°30′S, 55°58′W. 540 m. 2 miles SW of Aspland Island, it is one of the easterly group of the South Shetlands, south of Elephant Island. Named before 1822.

O'Brien Islet *see* **Pidgeon Island**

O'Brien Peak. 85°28′S, 156°42′W. 670 m. 3 miles west of the northern extremity of the Medina Peaks, between the Robert Scott Glacier and the Amundsen Glacier, overlooking the Ross Ice Shelf. Discovered by Gould's party of Dec. 1929 during Byrd's 1928–30 expedition, and named by Byrd for John S. O'Brien.

Mount Obruchev. 68°54′S, 154°12′E. A massif 15 miles ESE of Scar Bluffs, near the base of Mawson Peninsula. Named by the USSR in 1958 for geologist Vladimir A. Obruchev (1863–1956).

Obruchev Hills. 66°35′S, 99°46′E. Between Denman Glacier and Scott Glacier on the coast of East Antarctica. Plotted as a rock face by the Western Base Party of the AAE 1911–14. Later redefined, and named in 1956 by the USSR, for Vladimir Obruchev (*see* **Mount Obruchev**).

Observation Bluff. 60°43′S, 45°36′W. 110 m. The eastern summit of the ice-free ridge which forms the northern side of Paal Harbor on Signy Island, in the South Orkneys. Surveyed by the FIDS in 1947, and named by them because it was from here that they made daily observations of the sea ice.

Observation Hill. 77°51′S, 166°41′E. 230 m. (750 feet). A half mile east of, and above, McMurdo Station, and a half mile north of Cape Armitage, it stands in the shadow of Mount Erebus, on Ross Island. Discovered and named by Scott in 1902, it was used to observe the comings and goings of sledge parties during the Royal Society Expedition of 1901–4. Called Ob Hill for short, halfway up it was the nuclear plant, and at the top is the Polar Party Cross.

Observation Island. 67°01′S, 50°24′E. A small island just to the west of the mouth of Beaver Glacier, in the eastern part of Amundsen Bay. Visited in 1956 by P.W. Crohn's ANARE party and named by the Australians because the island was used as a magnetic and astronomical observation station.

Isla Observatorio *see* **Gamma Island**

Observatory Island *see* **Gamma Island**

The *O'Cain*. 280-ton Boston sealer built at Scituate, Mass., in 1802. Registered May 12, 1818, and owned by Abel Winship. 93 feet long. Part of the Boston Expedition to the South Shetlands, in 1820–21, under the command of Capt. Jonathan Winship. It took home some of the crew of the wrecked *Clothier*.

O'Cain Point. 62°16′S, 58°33′W. 3 miles NW of Duthoit Point on the east side of Nelson Island, in the South Shetlands. Named by the UK in 1961 in order to preserve the name in this area. Nelson Island was called O'Cain's Island in the 1820–21 period.

O'Cain's Island *see* **Nelson Island**

Ocean Camp. Built on the sea ice 1½ miles from the trapped *Endurance* by Shackleton's crew during the British Imperial Transantarctic Expedition of 1914–17. Established on Nov. 1, 1915, it served the 28 men until the ice floe broke up and they left the island in long boats on April 10, 1916.

Ocean currents *see* **Currents**

Oceana Insel *see* **Oceana Nunatak**

Oceana Nunatak. 65°08′S, 59°48′W. Also called Oceana Insel. One of the Seal Nunataks, at the NW corner of the Robertson Islands, off the east coast of the Antarctic Peninsula. Discovered by Larsen in 1893 and named by him for the Oceana Co., of Hamburg, a sponsor.

Oceanography. Established as a science by John Murray on the *Challenger* expedition of 1872–76.

Mount Ochre. 78°15′S, 166°32′E. A partly-eroded volcanic crater, 3 miles east of Mount Aurora, on Black Island, in the Ross Archipelago. Named by the New Zealanders in 1958–59 for the color of its upper slopes.

Ochs Glacier. 76°30′S, 145°35′W. Also called Adolph Ochs Glacier. Flows to the head of Block Bay between Mount Iphigene and Mount Avers, in the Ford Ranges of Marie Byrd Land. Discovered in 1929 during Byrd's 1928–30 expedition, and named by Byrd for Adolph S. Ochs, publisher of the *New York Times*, a patron.

Ocoa Point. 62°37′S, 61°08′W. On the west coast of Byers Peninsula, Livingston Island, in the South Shetlands.

O'Connell Nunatak. 84°43′S, 65°08′W. 1,210 m. 6 miles SSE of Mount Murch in the southern part of the Anderson Hills, in the Patuxent Range of the Pensacola Mountains. Named for Richard V. O'Connell, seismologist at Amundsen-Scott South Pole Station in 1967.

O'Connor, Raymond. Member of West Base during the USAS 1939–41.

O'Connor, W.P. RNR. Midshipman on the *Discovery* in 1927.

O'Connor Island. 66°25′S, 110°28′E. 1 mile long. Between Holl and Ford Islands, in the south part of the Windmill Islands. Named for Joseph J. O'Connor, air crewman on Operation Highjump, 1946–47, and on Operation Windmill, 1947–48.

O'Connor Nunataks. 76°26′S, 143°25′W. Near the head of Balchen Glacier. 5 miles NE of the Griffith Nunataks, in the Ford Ranges of Marie Byrd Land. Discovered in 1940, aerially from West Base, by the USAS, and named by Byrd for Raymond O'Connor.

O'Connors Rock. 62°05′S, 58°24′W. A rock in water 175 yards SW of Stenhouse Bluff, on King George Island, in the South Shetlands. It is located in Visca Anchorage in the north part of Admiralty Bay. Charted by Charcot in 1908–10. Named by the personnel on the *Discovery* in 1927 for W.P. O'Connor.

Odbert Island. 62°22′S, 110°33′E. 1½ miles long. Between Ardery Island and Robinson Ridge, in the Windmill Islands. 7 miles south of Wilkes Station. With Ardery Island, it forms an SPA because of the petrel life abundant here. Named for Lt. Jack A. Odbert, USN, assistant aerological officer on Operation Windmill, 1947–48.

The *Odd 1*. Norwegian whaler owned by Lars Christensen, which did whale reconnaissance in the Bellingshausen Sea in the summer of 1926–27, on an expedition led by Eyvind Tofte. Under the command of Capt. A.S. Anderson, it visited and charted Peter I Island that summer, but could not land. It also visited the South Shetlands and the Palmer Archipelago.

Odde Nunatak. 72°02'S, 10°43'E. The most northerly of a small chain of nunataks at the east side of Glopeflya Plain, just south of the eastern part of the Orvin Mountains, in Queen Maud Land. Named by the Norwegians for Odde Gjeruldsen, scientific assistant on the Norwegian Antarctic Expedition of 1956–58.

Oddera, Alberto J. Captain of the *Primero de Mayo* in 1942.

Oddesteinen Nunatak *see* **Odde Nunatak**

Odell Glacier. 76°46'S, 159°47'E. Flows between the Allan Hills and the Coombs Hills, into the upper part of the Mawson Glacier, in Victoria Land. Named by NZ for Prof. N.E. Odell, formerly of Otago University, NZ.

Oden Rock *see* **Ko-iwa Rock**

Odiddy. Native from Bora Bora, Tahiti, on the *Resolution* from Sept. 1773 to May 1774, including a trip to 71° 11'S on Jan. 30, 1774, during Cook's second voyage.

¹Mount Odin. 66°26'S, 64°03'W. A saddle-top mountain. Has 2 ice-covered peaks of 1,465 m. Just SW of Frigga Peak between the Anderson and Sleipnir Glaciers, on the east coast of Graham Land. Named by the FIDS for the Norse god.

²Mount Odin. 77°35'S, 161°38'E. Over 2,000 m. The most prominent, but not the highest, peak in the Asgard Range of Victoria Land. Just south of Lake Vanda. Named by the New Zealanders in 1958–59 for the Norse god.

Odin Glacier. 77°35'S, 161°36'E. Flows from the west slopes of Mount Odin in the Asgard Range of Victoria Land. Named by NZ in association with the mountain.

Odin Valley. 77°36'S, 161°43'E. Ice-free. Just east of Mount Odin, in the Asgard Range of southern Victoria Land. Named by NZ in association with the mountain.

Odinokaya Nunatak. 71°32'S, 6°10'E. Isolated. 15 miles NW of the Jaren Crags in the Mühlig-Hofmann Mountains of Queen Maud Land. Named Gora Odinokaya (solitary hill) by the USSR in 1961.

Mount Odishaw. 84°42'S, 174°54'E. 3,695 m. 9 miles SSW of Mount Kaplan, in the Hughes Range. Discovered by Byrd on the baselaying flight of Nov. 18, 1929. Surveyed and named by Albert Crary in 1957–58, for Hugh Odishaw.

Odishaw, Hugh. b. 1916, Saskatchewan, Canada. d. March 4, 1984. In the USA since 1922. Executive director of the US-IGY Committee, of the National Academy of Sciences. Known as "Mr. IGY."

Odom, Howard T. Communications man at East Base during the USAS 1939–41.

Odom Bay *see* **Odom Inlet**

Odom Inlet. 71°30'S, 61°20'W. Also called Odom Bay. An ice-filled indentation into the east coast of the Antarctic Peninsula, between Cape Howard and Cape MacDonald, or between Hilton Inlet and Steele Island. Discovered by the USAS from East Base in 1940, and named by them for Howard T. Odom.

O'Donnell Peak. 72°24'S, 166°01'E. On the Polar Plateau. 5 miles west of Joice Icefall in the Millen Range. Named for Frank B. O'Donnell, meteorologist at Hallett Station in 1962.

Oehlenschlager Bluff. 75°03'S, 136°42'W. Overlooks Hull Glacier from the north. Marks the SW extremity of the Erickson Bluffs and McDonald Heights, in Marie Byrd Land. Named for Richard J. Oehlenschlager, biologist here in 1971–72.

Oeschger Bluff. 76°24′S, 111°48′W. Flat-topped. Juts out from the SE part of Mount Takahe, in Marie Byrd Land. Named for Hans Oeschger, Swiss glaciologist on the US team at Byrd Station, 1968–69 and 1969–70.

The Office Girls. 72°20′S, 160°01′E. Also called Bray Nunatak. 2 prominent nunataks on an ice cliff, 7 miles SW of Welcome Mountain, in the Outback Nunataks. Named for the women office workers in the USA who provided support for the USARP.

Offset Ridge. 71°41′S, 68°32′W. Extends west from Triton Point, between Venus Glacier and Neptune Glacier, in eastern Alexander Island. It is formed of two ridges offset from one another by a kink in the middle. Named by the UK.

Ogara, Alicio E. Leader of the Argentine Antarctic Expeditions of 1953–54 and 1954–55. His ships on the first one were the *Bahía Buen Suceso*, the *Bahía Aguirre*, the *Punta Loyola*, the *Chiriguano*, the *Yamana*, the *Sanavirón*, and the *Les Éclaireurs*. His ships on the second were the *General San Martín*, the *Bahía Buen Suceso*, the *Bahía Aguirre*, the *Punta Loyola*, the *Sanavirón*, the *Chiriguano*, and the *Yamana*.

Ogden Heights. 73°58′S, 161°40′E. Flat. Ice-covered. 7 miles long. They form part of the south wall of the upper Priestley Glacier, to the SE of Tantalus Peak, in Victoria Land. Named by the southern party of the NZGSAE 1962–63 for Lt. John H. Ogden, USN, pilot who airlifted the party to this point, flew in their resupply, and later flew the party out again.

Ogi Beach. 69°08′S, 39°26′E. Also called Oogi-hama. At the head of the cove in the southern part of Rumpa Island, in the eastern part of Lützow-Holm Bay. Named Ogi-hama (fan beach) by the Japanese in 1973.

Ogives. Bands, or "waves" across the surface of a valley glacier, arched in the direction of the flow.

Ogle, Alexander. Marine corporal on the Wilkes Expedition of 1838–42. Joined in the USA. On Aug. 12, 1839, he died at sea (not in Antarctic waters) of an inflammation of the brain. Buried at sea, with honors.

O'Gorman Rocks. 68°34′S, 77°57′E. Two small rocks in water off the Vestfold Hills. ½ mile south of Trigwell Island. Named by the Australians for M. O'Gorman, weather observer at Davis Station in 1959.

O'Hara Glacier. 70°49′S, 166°40′E. Just west of Ackroyd Point, it flows into the south side of Yule Bay, Victoria Land. Named for Norbert W. O'Hara, who was on the Ross Ice Shelf in 1965–66.

O'Higgins Land. Named for the Chilean liberator, Bernardo O'Higgins. More properly Tierra de O'Higgins, it is the Chilean name for the area of Antarctica claimed by that country. This is the same area claimed by Argentina (they called it Tierra San Martín) and Great Britain (they called it Graham Land). The Americans (who did not claim it) called it Palmer Land. It is now called the Antarctic Peninsula.

The Ohio. 126-ton, 2-masted schooner built in Baltimore, Md., in 1840, and owned by Gilbert Chase of Newport, R.I. On July 14, 1841, it left Newport with 16 men, all from Newport, under the command of William Smyley. In Feb. 1842 it picked up the two thermometers left by Foster on Deception Island 13 years before. As the *Ohio* left Deception Island, the place was erupting. The ship arrived back in New York on July 28, 1842. Smyley then bought into the vessel, and captained it again, wrecking it (accidentally) off the South American coast on March 27, 1843.

Ohio Range. 84°45′S, 114°W. 30 miles long. 10 miles wide. Extends from Eldridge Peak to Mirsky Ledge, just to the east of the Wisconsin Range. It forms the NE end of the Horlick Mountains, and consists primarily of a large, snow-topped plateau with steep northern cliffs, and several flat-topped ridges and mountains. Mount Schopf, at 2,990 m., is the highest. Named for the Institute of Polar Studies at Ohio State University.

Ohlin, Axel. Zoologist on Nordenskjöld's 1901–4 expedition.

Ohlin Island. 63°30'S, 60°06'W. Also called Bailys Island. A tiny island, 6 miles NW of Tower Island, to the north of Charcot Bay, off the coast of the Antarctic Peninsula. First seen by Palmer on Nov. 17, 1820. Named by Nordenskjöld during his 1901–4 expedition, for Axel Ohlin.

Lake O-ike. 69°01'S, 39°34'E. Just south of Showa Flat in the eastern extremity of Ongul Island. Named O-ike (big pond) by the Japanese because it is the largest lake on the island.

Oil exploration. Not a big deal at the moment, but it could be. Offshore drilling would pose major problems with icebergs, etc. Oil looks most promising near Coats Land, the Adélie Land coast and the George V Land coast. There is no petroleum.

O'Kane Canyon. 74°19'S, 162°30'E. At the head of O'Kane Glacier. It indents the eastern side of the Eisenhower Range between Mount Baxter and Eskimo Point, in Victoria Land. Named by the New Zealanders in 1962–63 for H.D. O'Kane, photographer at Scott Base in 1961–62.

O'Kane Glacier. 74°26'S, 163°06'E. 15 miles long. Flows from the east wall of the Eisenhower Range between Mount Baxter and Eskimo Point. It ends at the north end of the Nansen Ice Sheet in Victoria Land, opposite the mouths of the Priestley and Corner Glaciers. Named in assocation with O'Kane Canyon, at the head of the glacier.

Okanogan Nunatak. Nickname given to a nunatak in the Patuxent Range of the Pensacola Mountains. It is not yet an accepted name.

O'Keefe Hill. 70°20'S, 64°24'E. Isolated. Ice-covered. 1½ miles south of Baldwin Nunatak. 8 miles SSW of Mount Starlight, in the Prince Charles Mountains. Named by the Australians for J. O'Keefe, cook at Mawson Station in 1964.

Okskaya Nunatak. 71°58'S, 13°47'E. 2,295 m. At the north end of the Rimekalvane Nunataks in the Weyprecht Mountains of Queen Maud Land. Discovered by Ritscher in 1938–39. Named by the USSR in 1966.

Oku-hyoga Rock. 70°06'S, 39°01'E. The farthest south bare rock exposed along the east side of the Shirase Glacier in Queen Maud Land. Named Okuhyoga-iwa (inner glacier rock) by the Japanese because of its position.

Oku-iwa Glacier. 68°42'S, 40°46'E. Flows to the sea just west of Oku-iwa Rock on the Queen Maud Land coast. Named by the Japanese for nearby Oku-iwa Rock.

Oku-iwa Rock. 68°42'S, 40°50'E. Also called Pinboko Rock. A rock on land just east of the Oku-iwa Glacier, on the coast of Queen Maud Land. Named Oku-iwa (interior rock) by the Japanese.

Okuma Bay. 77°48'S, 158°20'W. Also called Hal Flood Bay. An iceport on the coast of Edward VII Peninsula. Discovered by Scott in 1902. Named by Shirase in 1911–12 for his patron, Count Okuma (1838–1922), the great Japanese politician.

Olander Nunatak. 74°25'S, 72°07'W. 5 miles east of Tollefson Nunatak, and 27 miles NNW of Sky-Hi Nunataks, in eastern Ellsworth Land. It is usually grouped together with Tollefson Nunatak, Horner Nunatak, and the Sky-Hi Nunataks, for cartographic purposes. Named for R.E. Olander, electronics technician at Eights Station in 1963.

Mount Olav Bjaaland *see* **Mount Bjaaland**

Olav Prydz Bukt *see* **Prydz Bay**

Old Mans Head. 72°22'S, 60°45'W. A headland which marks the south side of the entrance to Wüst Inlet, on the east coast of Palmer Land. Discovered in Dec. 1940 by the USAS from East Base. Named descriptively by the FIDS.

Mount Oldenburg. 82°04'S, 87°55' W. Partly snow-covered. ½ mile east of Mount Helms in the eastern part of the Martin Hills. Named for Margaret Oldenburg, supporter of polar exploration.

Mount Oldfield. 66°50'S, 50°38'E. On the east side of Amundsen Bay, just west of Mount Hardy in the Tula Mountains. Named by the Australians for R.E.T. Oldfield, radio officer at Mawson Station in 1958.

Oldham Island. 67°32'S, 61°43'E. In the east part of the Stanton Group, off the coast of Mac. Robertson Land. Photographed by the LCE 1936–37. Named Andøya (Duck Island) by the Norwegians. Renamed by the Australians for Hugh Oldham, biologist at Mawson Station in 1955.

Oldroyd Island. 68°32'S, 77°54'E. A small island, 350 yards NW of Magnetic Island, off the Vestfold Hills, in the eastern part of Prydz Bay. Photographed by the LCE 1936–37. Named by the Australians for K.C. Oldroyd, weather observer at Davis Station in 1960.

Olds Peak. 84°40'S, 174°40'W. 1,480 m. 6 miles NE of Mount Kenney in the south part of Longhorn Spurs in the Queen Maud Mountains. Named for Cdr. Corwin A. Olds, USN, in Antarctica, 1964.

Mount Ole Engelstad *see* **Mount Engelstad**

The *Ole Wegger.* One of Lars Christensen's huge factory whaling ships, in Antarctic waters in the summer of 1940–41, under the command of Capt. Normann Andersen. On Jan. 13, 1941, it was seized by Germans (*see* **Lt. Bach**), just north of Queen Maud Land.

O'Leary Peak. 84°27'S, 179°14'W. 1,040 m. Partly snow-covered. The most northerly summit along the east wall of Erickson Glacier where that glacier enters the Ross Ice Shelf. Discovered by the USAS 1939–41. Named for Paul V. O'Leary, USNR, builder, a member of the US Naval Support Force, Antarctica, 1959–60 (*see* **Deaths, 1959**).

O'Leary Ridges. 70°58'S, 67°19'E. Three partly snow-covered ridges. They extend for 5 miles. 20 miles SE of Mount Bunt, in the Prince Charles Mountains. Named by the Australians for R.A. O'Leary, officer-in-charge at Wilkes Station in 1964.

The *Olenek.* USSR ship of the 1970s, sometime seen in Antarctic waters.

Olentangy Glacier. 86°S, 127°20'W. Flows from the sector of the Wisconsin Plateau ENE of Sisco Mesa. Flows into McCarthy Glacier, in the Horlick Mountains. Named by the Ohio State University explorers in 1964–65 for the river which flows through their campus back home.

Oliphant Islands. 60°45'S, 45°36'W. A group of small, ice-free islands and rocks. South of Gourlay Peninsula, the SE extremity of Signy Island in the South Orkneys. Dove Channel runs through this group from east to west. Charted by Petter Sørlle in 1912–13, and again in 1933 by the Discovery Committee. Surveyed by the FIDS in 1947, and named by them for Prof. Marcus L.E. Oliphant, who helped the FIDS get equipment.

Olivar, Ambrose W. Ordinary seaman on the Wilkes Expedition of 1838–42. Joined in the USA. Served the cruise.

Mount Oliver. 84°56'S, 173°44'W. Over 3,800 m. 2 miles SE of Mount Campbell, in the Prince Olav Mountains. Discovered by the USAS 1939–41. Surveyed by Crary in 1957–58, and named by him for Norman Oliver, of the Air Force Cambridge Research Center, who was Antarctic project leader for aurora operations, 1957–60.

Oliver Bluffs. In the Dominion Range. A term no longer used.

Oliver Glacier. 82°34'S, 163°45'E. Flows from the area west and south of Mount Christchurch, into Lowery Glacier just north of the Taylor Hills. Named for Edward J. Oliver, glaciologist at Amundsen-Scott South Pole Station, 1961–62.

Oliver Island. 69°19'S, 68°37'W. Off the west coast of Graham Land.

Oliver Nunatak. 84°06'S, 66°08'W. In the Rambo Nunataks. 2 miles south of

Sowle Nunatak on the west side of the Foundation Ice Stream in the Pensacola Mountains. Named for Thomas H. Oliver, electronics technician at Plateau Station in 1967.

Oliver Peak. 77°37'S, 161°03'E. 2,410 m. 4 miles NNW of Round Mountain, in the Asgard Range of Victoria Land. Named for Leon Oliver, of New Zealand, chief driller on the Dry Valley Drilling Project, 1973–74, and drilling superintendent on it in 1974–75.

Oliver Platform. A geologic structure in the Dominion Range, composed of the Upper Oliver Platform and the Lower Oliver Platform.

Olivine Point. 60°40'S, 45°29'W. The southern end of the peninsula which forms the eastern limit of Iceberg Bay on the south coast of Coronation Island, in the South Orkneys. Surveyed by the FIDS in 1948–49, and named by them for the mineral olivine found here.

Olliver Peak. 84°34'S, 173°33'W. 630 m. On the edge of the Ross Ice Shelf. On the east side of the mouth of Barrett Glacier, it is the most northwesterly summit in the Gabbro Hills. Named for Cdr. George R. Olliver, USN, who was injured in the crash of an Otter aircraft on Dec. 22, 1955, following take-off from Cape Bird.

Olsen, Hartveg. Norwegian whaler who was first mate on the *Wyatt Earp* during Ellsworth's expeditions of 1933–34 and 1934–35. He had been on whaling expeditions to the Antarctic before that as well. In 1935–36 he was captain of the *Wyatt Earp* during Ellsworth's most successful expedition.

Olsen, John. Seaman on the *Eleanor Bolling* during the first half of Byrd's 1928–30 expedition.

Olsen, Karinius. Cook on the *Fram,* during Amundsen's 1910–12 expedition. He was not one of the shore party.

Olsen, Magnus. Norwegian whaler, younger brother of Hartveg Olsen. He was a crewman on the 1933–34 and 1934– 35 expeditions that Ellsworth made to Antarctica on the *Wyatt Earp,* and second mate on the same ship during Ellsworth's more successful 1935–36 expedition.

Olsen Crags. 86°12'S, 160°48'W. Just north of Epler Glacier, on the east side of Amundsen Glacier, in the Queen Maud Mountains. Amundsen had called a mountain in this general area Mount K. Olsen, for Karinius Olsen. Modern geographers can not be quite sure which mountain Amundsen meant, so they arbitrarily selected this one, in order to preserve Olsen's name in this area.

Olsen Névé *see* **Olson Névé**

Olsen Peak. 77°32'S, 86°30'W. 2,140 m. 2 miles NW of Mount Wyatt Earp, in the northern part of the Sentinel Range. Discovered aerially by Ellsworth on Nov. 23, 1935. Named for Hartveg Olsen.

Olson Glacier. 72°49'S, 166°41'E. Flows from Malta Plateau into Seafarer Glacier, in the Victory Mountains of Victoria Land. Named for Richard D. Olson, National Science Foundation official who was at McMurdo Station in 1967–68, in research administration activities.

Olson Island. 77°14'S, 153°17'W. The largest, and most northerly, of the White Islands, in Sulzberger Bay. In 1928–30 Byrd described it as "low ice cliffs" that rise above the ice shelf, but the USA redefined the feature in the early 1960s. Named for Michael L. Olson, ionosphere physicist at Byrd Station in 1968, and at Plateau Station in 1968–69.

Olson Névé. 82°07'S, 158°E. Also seen spelled (erroneously) as Olsen Névé. On the NW side of the Cobham Range, it feeds Lucy Glacier and Prince Philip Glacier, in the Churchill Mountains. Named by the Holyoake, Cobham, and Queen Elizabeth Ranges Party of the NZGSAE 1964–65, for Lt. Dennis A. Olson, USN, who flew the party in, and supported them during the summer.

Olson Nunatak. 74°55'S, 162°28'E. Ice-free. At the south side of the terminus of the Reeves Glacier. 4 miles north of the summit of Mount Gerlache, in Victoria Land. Named for James J. Olson, geophysicist on the Ross Ice Shelf, in 1961–62.

Olson Peaks. 79°16′S, 160°05′E. Two peaks close together. The higher one is 1,335 m. 4 miles west of Cape Lankester, on the north side of the Bertoglio Glacier. Named for Gary D. Olson, US Army Aviation Support Unit in Antarctica, 1961–62.

Olstad, Ola. Norwegian zoologist who conducted zoological and geological research in the South Shetlands and the Palmer Archipelago in the summer season of 1927–28. He used various whaling ships to get around (cf. Olaf Holtedahl), most notably being part of Horntvedt's 1927–28 expedition on the *Norvegia.* The next season, 1928–29, he was chief scientist on the *Norvegia* under Nils Larsen.

Olstad Glacier. 68°50′S, 90°41′W. Heavily crevassed. Flows to the west coast of Peter I Island, 2 miles south of Tofte Glacier. Named for Ola Olstad.

Oluf Rocks. 63°41′S, 60°10′W. A small group of rocks in water. 3½ miles east of Cape Neumayer, Trinity Island. Named by the UK in 1960 for the *Oluf Sven.*

The *Oluf Sven.* Danish freighter under the command of Capt. J.C. Ryge. Chartered by the FIDASE 1955–57. It transported the expedition to Deception Island in 1955 and 1956, and was used throughout the expedition as a mobile base for operations by ground survey parties.

Mount Olympus. 80°13′S, 156°46′E. Over 2,400 m. Flat-topped. Ice-covered. 5 miles east of Mount Henderson, in the Britannia Range. Named for the *Mount Olympus.*

Olympus Range. 77°29′S, 161°30′E. Ice-free. Between the Victoria and McKelvey Valleys on the north, and the Wright Valley on the south, in Victoria Land. Named by the New Zealanders in 1958–59 for the home of the Greek gods.

Cape Omega. 68°34′S, 40°59′E. Between Omega Glacier and Daruma Rock on the coast of Queen Maud Land. Named by the Japanese.

Omega Glacier. 68°37′S, 41°01′E. Flows to the coast just south of Cape Omega, in Queen Maud Land. Named by the Japanese.

Omega Island. 64°20′S, 62°56′W. Also called Lystad Island, Isla Sobral. 2 miles long. Just south of Eta Island, in the Melchior Islands. Surveyed by the Discovery Investigations personnel on the *Discovery* in 1927, and again in 1942 and 1943 by the Argentines, who named it in 1946 for the Greek letter.

Omega Nunatak. 81°55′S, 29°12′W. Isolated. Flat-topped. 21 miles SSW of Whichaway Nunataks. Named by the BCTAE 1955–58 because it was the last rock outcrop seen on the way to the Pole in 1957–58.

Omega Peak. 72°09′S, 166°03′E. 1 mile NE of Le Couteur Peak, in the Millen Range. Named by the Southern Party of the New Zealand Federated Mountain Clubs Antarctic Expedition of 1962–63 because this was the last major peak climbed by them, on Jan. 2, 1963.

Omel'chenko, Anton. A Russian jockey picked up by Cecil Meares in Manchuria while looking for ponies for the British Antarctic Expedition of 1910–13. Taken on as a pony groom and dog driver. With Cherry-Garrard he tried to relieve Scott's doomed Polar party in 1912.

Omicron Islands. 64°21′S, 62°55′W. Also called Islas Silveyra. A group of small islands and rocks just SE of Omega Island, in the Melchior Islands. Surveyed in 1942 and 1943 by the Argentines who, in 1946, named them for the Greek letter.

Ommanney Bay. 60°33′S, 45°32′W. 2 miles wide. Between Prong Point and Foul Point, on Coronation Island, in the South Orkneys. Discovered by Powell and Palmer in Dec. 1821. Named by personnel on the *Discovery II* in 1933 for Francis D. Ommanney, zoologist on the staff of the Discovery Committee.

Ommanney Glacier. 71°32′S, 169°29′E. 20 miles long. A valley glacier which flows through the Admiralty Mountains into Relay Bay, on the west side of Robertson Bay, in northern Victoria Land. Charted by Borchgrevink in 1898–1900, and named by him for Adm. Sir Erasmus Ommanney, Arctic explorer.

Ommundsen Island. 66°20′S, 110°22′E. Just west of Midgley Island, in the Windmill Islands. Named for Audon Ommundsen, transport specialist at Wilkes Station in 1958.

Omond House. Bruce's stone hut on Jessie Bay, Laurie Island, in the South Orkneys, during his expedition of 1902–4. The first scientific station in Antarctica, it was taken over by the Oficina Meteorologica Argentina in Feb. 1904, and in Jan. 1905 it was renamed Orcadas Station.

Ondori Island. 69°S, 39°32′E. A small island 1 mile north of Ongul Island, and almost 1 mile west of Nesøya in the NE part of Lützow-Holm Bay. Named Ondori-jima (rooster island) by the Japanese in 1972, in association with nearby Mendori Island.

One Day Islet *see* **Hedgehog Island**

150-mile Depot. A depot set up in 1929 by Byrd's 1928–30 expedition. It was 20 miles SE of Prestrud Inlet in Marie Byrd Land, i.e., 150 miles from Little America.

105-mile Depot. 78°16′45″S, 155°32′08″W. Established 105 miles east of West Base by the depot-laying team headed by Warner in late Sept. and early Oct. 1940, during the USAS. It was to be used by the mountains sledging parties from West Base that year.

One Ton Depot. 79°28′30″S. It was laid by Scott on Feb. 17, 1911, and contained a ton of food. It was 150 miles from Hut Point, and was the depot which Scott was less than 11 miles away from when he died in 1912.

O'Neal Ridge. 72°48′S, 168°45′E. In the Victory Mountains of Victoria Land. Bounded by the Ingham and Humphries Glaciers. Named for Russell D. O'Neal, member of the National Science Board, 1972–77. He was in Antarctica in 1975.

Mount O'Neil. 85°40′S, 136°20′W. 2,090 m. Just NE of Mount Ratliff, at the north side of the Kansas Glacier. Named for Robert J. O'Neil, utilitiesman at Byrd Station in 1961.

O'Neill, Boris Kopaitic. Lt. Argentine soldier, leader of the first wintering party at Capitán Arturo Prat Station in 1947.

O'Neill Nunataks. 79°01′S, 84°59′W. A line of nunataks which mark the southern end of the Bastien Range, in the Ellsworth Mountains. Named by the University of Minnesota geological parties to the Ellsworths, for Jerry O'Neill, aerographer with these parties in 1963–64 and 1964–65.

O'Neill Point. 64°49′S, 63°06′W. On Anvers Island.

Onezhskiye Nunataks. 71°35′S, 7°03′E. A small group, 9 miles NNE of Slettefjellet, in the Mühlig-Hofmann Mountains of Queen Maud Land. The largest is Storkvarvsteinen Peak. Named by the USSR in 1961 for the Onega River in the USSR.

Ong Valley. 83°14′S, 157°38′E. 5 miles long. Mainly ice-free. In the Miller Range, just west of Kreiling Mesa. Named for John S. Ong, American traverse engineer on the South Pole Traverse of 1962–63.

Ongley Island. 62°26′S, 59°54′W. A small island 2½ miles west of Dee Island, just off the north side of Greenwich Island, in the South Shetlands. Charted by the personnel on the *Discovery II* in 1935, and named in 1948 by the UK.

Ongul Island. 69°01′S, 39°32′E. 1½ miles long. The largest of the Flatvaer Islands, just within the east side of the entrance to Lützow-Holm Bay. Photographed by the LCE 1936–37. Norwegian cartographers, working off these aerial photos, determined it to be connected to what is now East Ongul Island, and gave the name Ongul (fishhook), which is descriptive of the two islands together. In 1957 the Japanese, landing here for the first time, found that a passage separates the two islands, and redefined the area accordingly.

Ongul Islands *see* **Flatvaer Islands**

Ongul Sound. 69°02′S, 39°38′E. Also called Ongul Strait. 2 miles wide. Between the east shore of Lützow-Holm Bay and the Flatvaer Islands. Photographed by the LCE 1936–37, and named by the Norwegians for nearby Ongul Island.

Ongul Strait *see* **Ongul Sound**

Ongulgalten Island. 69°04′S, 39°36′E. The most northerly of 3 aligned islands 1 mile SE of the Te Islands, at the south end of the Flatvaer Islands. Photographed by the LCE 1936–37. In association with Ongul Island, the name means "the fishhook boar" in Norwegian.

Ongulkalven Island. 69°01′S, 39°27′E. 1 mile west of Ongul Island in the Flatvaer Islands, in Lützow-Holm Bay. Photographed by the LCE 1936–37. Name means "the fishhook calf" in Norwegian.

Onguløy *see* **Partizan Island**

Onley Hill. 67°43′S, 63°03′E. Ice-free. 1 mile south of Mount Henderson, in the NE part of the Framnes Mountains, in Mac. Robertson Land. Photographed by the LCE 1936–37, and named Sörkollen (the south knoll) by the Norwegians. Renamed by the Australians for L. Onley, weather observer at Mawson Station in 1959.

Onlooker Nunatak. 71°54′S, 162°22′E. Isolated. In the Rennick Glacier. Just SE of the Morozumi Range. Named descriptively by the New Zealanders in 1963–64.

The Ontos. A 145 hp anti-tank vehicle tried as transport by the Americans during the IGY. It was too heavy.

Onville Escarpment *see* **Orville Coast**

Onyx River. 77°32′S, 161°45′E. An evanescent meltwater stream (rather than a real river), which flows from the terminus of the Wright Lower Glacier westward for 19 miles to empty into Lake Vanda, as that lake's major source of water. It flows intermittently and only during the warmest part of the summer. It consists mainly of meltwater from the Wright Lower Glacier and the alpine glaciers that are present along the valley walls. Named by the New Zealanders in 1958–59.

Oogi-hama *see* **Ogi Beach**

Oom, K.E. Lt. Royal Australian Navy cartographer on the BANZARE 1929–31. In 1948, by now a captain, he commanded the *Wyatt Earp*.

Oom Bay. 67°26′S, 60°44′E. Also called Uksvika. 2 miles wide. Indents the coast of East Antarctica between Mount Bruce and Campbell Head. Discovered in Feb. 1931 by the BANZARE, and named by Mawson for Lt. K.E. Oom.

Oom Island. 67°24′S, 60°39′E. A small island 2½ miles NE of Campbell Head, off the coast of Mac. Robertson Land. Photographed by the LCE 1936–37, and named Uksöy by the Norwegians. Renamed by the Australians for Lt. K.E. Oom.

Mount Oona. 83°09′S, 162°36′E. 2,170 m. Between Helm Glacier and Lowery Glacier, in the Queen Elizabeth Range. Named for Henn Oona, US aurora scientist at Amundsen-Scott South Pole Station in 1964, and ionosphere physicist at the same station in 1968.

Oona Cliff. 72°27′S, 160°09′E. 4 miles long. Just NW of Mount Walton in the Outback Nunataks. Named for Henn (Hain) Oona (*see* **Mount Oona**).

Operation Baby Face. A ham radio station in Syracuse, NY, faxed down to Little America and McMurdo Base pictures of children newly born to fathers wintering-over in Antarctica. The first fax was received on May 5, 1957, at Little

America. Calvin Larsen had a baby girl, Sonya. McMurdo received their first fax on May 30, 1957.

Operation Deep Freeze. The greatest peace-time operation ever launched by the US Navy. It is the code name for the Navy's participation in Antarctica from 1955 to date, the ongoing yearly operation headed by the Commander, US Naval Support Force, Antarctica (q.v.), who leads military units from the Navy, Army, and Coast Guard to Antarctica between late Sept. and Feb. every austral summer, to provide the technical backup services necessary to USAP (formerly USARP). Originally called Project Longhaul, the name was changed to Operation Deepfreeze. However, the Amana Corporation informed the Navy of a copyright infringement, so the name was changed to Operation Deep Freeze (two words) about Oct. 1956. The *Atka's* pre-IGY expedition of 1954–55 to scout out sites for US bases for the upcoming International Geophysical Year, was a prelude to the Naval invasion which began in late 1955, as Operation Deep Freeze I (1955–56), under Adm. George Dufek (Adm. Byrd was technical director). Task Force 43 (the Navy group itself which comprised Operation Deep Freeze) had 4 objectives: to construct Little America V and AirOpFac McMurdo (later to become known as McMurdo Base, and then McMurdo Station, the Operation's headquarters), to set up an airfield at McMurdo Sound (Williams Field as it became known), and to establish a base in Marie Byrd Land (this was Byrd Station, and this objective was not achieved until the following year). 1,800 men supported the US scientific involvement in Antarctica during Operation Deep Freeze I, and 7 ships took part, the *Eastwind*, the *Edisto*, the *Glacier*, the *Arneb*, the *Greenville Victory*, the *Wyandot*, and the *Nespelen*. Operation Deep Freeze II (1956–57) began in Oct. 1956, again led by Dufek, this time with 3,400 men, and 11 ships, the *Glacier*, the *Atka*, the *Arneb*, the *Staten Island*, the *North-*

wind, the *Wyandot*, the *Curtiss*, the *Towle*, the *Nespelen*, the *Greenville Victory*, and the *Private Joseph F. Merrell*. In Nov. 1956, Dufek flew to the South Pole to scout out a site for the South Pole Station (*see* **South Pole**, and **Amundsen-Scott South Pole Station**). This was built that season, as were Wilkes, Ellsworth, Hallett, and Byrd Stations. Operation Deep Freeze III (1957–58) began in Nov. 1957, once again led by Dufek, and at the end of it he handed over as commander to Adm. Tyree, who led Operation Deep Freeze IV (1958–59). It was then decided to enumerate the Operations from 1959 onwards as Operation Deep Freeze 60 (1959–60), Operation Deep Freeze 61 (1960–61), Operation Deep Freeze 62 (1961–62), etc., and it has been that way ever since. On Nov. 26, 1962, Tyree handed over to Adm. James R. Reedy, and in April 1965 Reedy handed over to Adm. Fred Bakutis. Subsequent commanders were J. Lloyd Abbott, Jr. (1967–June 19, 1969), Rear Adm. David Fife Welch (June 19, 1969–Aug. 16, 1971), Adm. Leo B. McCuddin (Aug. 16, 1971–1972), Capt. Alfred N. Fowler (1972–June 25, 1974), Capt. Eugene W. Van Reeth (June 25, 1974). On July 1, 1974, Task Force 43 became Task Force 199 (see this entry for further COs of Operation Deep Freeze).

Operation Gangotri. Indian oceanographic, glaciologic, meteorologic, seismologic, and magnetism research expedition sent to the Enderby Land coast, on the hired ship *Polarsirkel* in 1982. The 20-man team put ashore at 70°45'S, 11°38'E, on the Princess Astrid Coast, and this site is now a historic site (q.v.). They set up a temporary camp at 70°03'S, 41°02'E, and began operations in Jan. 1982. Data were transmitted back to India via satellite, and they left behind weather stations.

Operation Highjump. 1946–47. Correct name — US Navy Antarctic Developments Project. The largest assault on Antarctica to that date. It consisted of 13 sea vessels, 33 aircraft, 8 Weasels, 10 Caterpillar tractors, Cletracs, jeeps, and tracked landing vehicles (LVTs). Over 4,700 men took part, and there were 11 journalists, 24 civilian scientists and observers, and 16 military observers. Icebreakers and helicopters were used in Antarctica for the first time. Bigger than all previous Antarctic expeditions put together, it was basically an aerial expedition. Its mission was to train personnel and test equipment under Antarctic conditions, to consolidate and extend the basis for US claims in Antarctica, should claims ever be made, plan for bases, carry out air operations, and conduct scientific studies. The Operation was established on Aug. 26, 1946, and only 7 weeks later it was under way, and Task Force 68 (q.v.) was ready to sail—a phenomenally fast piece of organization. On Dec. 2, 1946, the first ships left the USA heading south. The *Mount Olympus,* the *Pine Island,* the *Northwind,* and the *Brownson* sailed out of Norfolk, Va., and went through the Panama Canal, meeting up with the *Canisteo* and the submarine *Sennett.* Also on Dec. 2, 1946, the *Currituck* and the *Henderson* sailed from San Diego, as did the *Cacapon* from San Pedro, and the *Yancey* from Port Hueneme, Calif. The *Merrick* sailed on Dec. 5, 1946 (*see* the Chronology appendix for dates while the expedition was south of 60° S). Admiral Byrd was technical leader of Operation Highjump, and Admiral Cruzen was tactical leader, and commanding officer of Task Force 68. The Operation was split into 3 groups, each group organized around a ship with aircraft-carrying facilities. The Central Group (Task Group 68.1), led by Cruzen, had 2 icebreakers (the *Burton Island* and the *Northwind*), 2 supply ships (the *Yancey* and the *Merrick*), a communications ship (the *Mount Olympus*), and a submarine (the *Sennett*). The *Burton Island* and the *Northwind* each had a single-engine amphibian plane and a helicopter. The *Mount Olympus* carried a Norseman ski plane, a helicopter, and

two OY Grasshoppers. The Western Group (Task Group 68.2), led by George Dufek, had the *Currituck,* the *Henderson,* and the *Cacapon.* The *Currituck* carried 3 Martin Mariner seaplanes—*Baker 1, Baker 2,* and *Baker 3.* It also carried a 2-engine seaplane and 2 helicopters. The Eastern Group (Task Group 68.3), led by Charles Bond, had the *Pine Island,* the *Brownson,* and the *Canisteo.* The *Pine Island* carried 3 Martin Mariner seaplanes—*George 1, George 2,* and *George 3.* It also carried a 2-engine seaplane and 2 helicopters. Admiral Byrd himself arrived in Antarctica on the aircraft carrier *Philippine Sea* in late Jan. 1947. This ship carried 6 R4D Dakota airplanes. The Central Group entered the astonishingly thick Ross Sea pack-ice on Dec. 31, 1946, and on Jan. 14, 1947, broke through it into the Ross Sea itself, arriving at the Bay of Whales on Jan. 15, 1947. For the next 3 days the *Northwind* smashed up about 15 million tons of pack-ice in the Bay of Whales. In only 7 weeks the Central Group established Little America IV at the Bay of Whales. An airfield was also built at this base. The Western Group was to go around the continent until it met the Eastern Group at the Ross Sea. The Eastern Group set out from 90° E and went around the continent the other way until it met the Western Group. The Eastern Group was the first party to set foot on Ross Island since 1917, and quit operations on March 4, 1947. The Western Group discovered the Bunger Hills on Feb. 11, 1947. This "Shangri-la" caused a sensation in the press at the time. The Western Group quit operations on March 1, 1947. On Jan. 29, 1947, Byrd took off from the recently arrived *Philippine Sea,* in a plane for Little America IV. Subsequently R4D Dakotas landed at the base. Admiral Byrd made his second flight to the South Pole, leaving Little America at 11 a.m., on Feb. 15, 1947, and flew for 12 hours at an average speed of 144 mph (Byrd never actually set foot at the Pole, although he flew over it 3 times in his life, the last time being during Operation Deep Freeze I). For the crews and further details of this flight, see **South Pole**. On Feb. 22, 1947, the *Burton Island* arrived at the Bay of Whales to take the Central Group back to New Zealand. The main names of Operation Highjump were Byrd, Cruzen, Bond, Dufek; the following ships captains: R.R. Moore (the *Mount Olympus*), J.E. Cohn (the *Yancey*), John J. Hourihan (the *Merrick*), Charles W. Thomas (the *Northwind*), Gerald L. Ketchum (the *Burton Island*), Joseph B. Icenhower (the *Sennett*), C.F. Bailey (the *Henderson*), R.A. Mitchell (the *Cacapon*), John E. Clark (the *Currituck*), Henry Howard Caldwell (the *Pine Island*), Edward K. Walker (the *Canisteo*), H.M.S. Gimber (the *Brownson*), and Delbert S. Cornwell (the *Philippine Sea*); the most prominent pilots were Lt. Cdr. James C. McCoy, Major Robert R. Weir, Lt. George H. Anderson, Capt. Eugene C. McIntyre, Lt. Robert J. McCarthy, 1st Lt. Pitman, Lt. George W. Warden, Lt. Conrad S. Shinn, Lt. (jg) William K. Martin, Lt. (jg) Erwin Spencer, Lt. (jg) Harry W. Summers, Lt. W.R. Kreitzer, Lt. Fred L. Reinbolt, Lt. Robert H. Gillock, Lt. James C. Jennings, Lt. James C. Stevenson, Lt. Cdr. John D. Howell, Lt. (jg) Ralph P. LeBlanc, Lt. (jg) William H. Kearns, Jr., Lt. (jg) James L. Ball, Lt. (jg) Robert G. Goff, Lt. Cdr. David E. Bunger (the most well-known of all of them, thanks to his discovery of the Bunger Hills), Lt. Cdr. William J. Rogers, Jr.; aide and chief of staff was Capt. Robert S. Quackenbush, Jr., USN, and chief of staff Antarctic Developments Project was Capt. H.R. Horney, USN. Capt. George F. Kosco was in charge of aerology and special projects. Capt. M.A. Norcross was in charge of logistics. Other names were Fred Dustin, William M. Hawkes, Cdr. Clifford M. Campbell, Lt. Cdr. J.C. Heide (hydrographic officer), Lt. Charles C. Shirley (photographic officer), Capt. Vernon D. Boyd (transportation officer), John H. Roscoe (photogrammetric officer), Paul Siple (senior representative, War Department), Amory H. Waite,

A.J.L. Morency (boat maintenance), Murray Wiener (air sea rescue), Capt. C.H. Harrison (meteorologist), Lt. C.A. Schoene (Coast and Geodetic survey), B.C. Haynes (Weather Bureau), J.R. Balsley (US Geological Survey), Dr. A.D. Howard (US Geological Survey), J.E. Perkins (Fish and Wildlife Service), R.M. Gilmore (Fish and Wildlife Service). All in all 49,000 aerial photos were taken, 60 percent of the Antarctic coastline was photographed by aircraft on over 100 flight missions, and 350,000 square miles of previously unknown territory was discovered. Byrd was to have led a sequel, Operation Highjump II, but it was canceled. Operation Windmill followed it, in 1947–48.

Operation Ice Cube. A yearly New Zealand operation begun in 1965, and enumerated as Operation Ice Cube I, Operation Ice Cube II, etc. The RNZAF flies into Williams Field, McMurdo Sound, with mail, passengers, and high priority cargo for Scott Base.

Operation Tabarin. 1943–45. A British Admiralty secret military plan to establish a base on Deception Island in the South Shetlands, to maintain a watch there during the rest of World War II, and to thwart the persistent Argentine claims in the area. Two ships were used, the *William Scoresby* and the *Fitzroy*. There were two phases to Operation Tabarin. The first was 1943–44, and was led by J.W.S. Marr. It established Port Lockroy Station on Wiencke Island, and Base B on Deception Island. They removed the Argentine emblems here and at the Melchior Islands, and tried unsuccessfully to land a party at Hope Bay. They visited the South Orkneys and the South Shetlands, and the *William Scoresby* hoisted the British flag at Cape Renard, and left a record of the vessel's visit. Scientific programs were also carried out. Phase 2 was 1944–45, and was led by A. Taylor. Both stations were relieved, and Base D was established at Hope Bay. In 1945, after the War, responsibility for the British sector of

Antarctica was transferred from the War Office to the Colonial Office, and the area became administered by the newly-formed FIDS (Falkland Islands Dependencies Survey).

Operation Windmill. 1947–48. Officially called the US Navy Second Antarctic Developments Project. After the expedition was over it was nicknamed "Windmill" due to the large amount of helicopter exploration conducted during it. Its missions were to train personnel and to test equipment in Antarctica, as a follow-up to the objectives and achievements of Operation Highjump the season before, to check on Little America IV, to carry out scientific and exploratory work, to survey from the ground 30 major features (most notably the Bunger Hills) which had been photographed aerially by Operation Highjump. The 69-day expedition was carried out by Task Force 39, led by Cdr. Gerald L. Ketchum, USN. There were two icebreakers, the *Edisto* (commanded by Cdr. Edward C. Folger), and the *Burton Island* (commanded by Cdr. Edwin A. McDonald). Lt. Cdr. C.L. Browning was chief staff officer, and Capt. Vernon D. Boyd was among the 14 staff officers. There were 3 military officers and 10 civilians as observers. One of these was cartographer John H. Roscoe. The *Burton Island* carried 2 helicopters — a Sikorsky HO3S-1 and a Bell HTL-1. The *Edisto* carried an HO3S-1 helicopter and a Grumman J2F-6 amphibian airplane. 500 men took part in the operation, and 4 Weasels were used as land transport. The *Edisto* left Boston on Nov. 1, 1947, for Norfolk, Va., where the observers and scientists boarded. On Nov. 6, 1947, the ship left Norfolk, and, via the Panama Canal, went to American Samoa, arriving there on Dec. 2, 1947. The *Burton Island* left San Pedro, Calif., on Nov. 20, 1947, rendezvousing with the *Edisto* at American Samoa on Dec. 3, 1947. On Dec. 5, 1947, the two icebreakers which made up Task Force 39 left American Samoa for the Antarctic, traveling 20 miles apart. Their first objective was to get to Scott Island, but this had to be abandoned 40 miles north of the island due to bad pack-ice, which they reached on Dec. 25, 1947. Then they sailed around the Wilkes Land coast to the Davis Sea, did their work there (*see* the Chronology appendix for dates while the expedition was south of 60° S), including surveying 9 points along a 600-mile stretch of coastline in 23 days, as well as landing a team by helicopter at the Bunger Hills and other places. They fell short of the 30 points to be surveyed because of weather conditions. From the Davis Sea they went around the coast to the Ross Sea, then to Little America, and Peter I Island, and on to Marguerite Bay, Graham Land, where they helped out the RARE (q.v.). The operation was generally a success, and established 17 geodetic positions, and conducted a considerable amount of oceanography. The *Edisto* arrived back at Norfolk on March 28, 1948, and the *Burton Island* arrived at San Pedro on April 1, 1948.

Opornyy Point. 69°48′S, 13°E. An ice point along the west side of the Lazarev Ice Shelf. 15 miles north of Leningradskiy Island in Queen Maud Land. Named Mys Opornyy (support point) by the USSR in 1959 because the ice shelf here rests on the ocean floor.

Oppegaard Spur. 84°29′S, 177°22′W. 2 miles long. Extends NW from the SW portion of Mount Speed, just east of the Kosco Glacier, where that glacier enters the Ross Ice Shelf. Discovered by the USAS 1939–41. Named for Richard D. Oppegaard, seaman apprentice, USN (*see* **Deaths, 1957**).

Oppkuven Peak. 72°37′S, 0°24′E. 2 miles north of Gavlen Ridge, in the Roots Heights of the Sverdrup Mountains of Queen Maud Land. Name means "the ascent peak" in Norwegian.

Orbell, J.R. Radio operator on the *City of New York* during Byrd's 1928–30 expedition.

Orcadas Station. 60°45′S, 44°43′W. Year-round Argentine scientific base on

Jessie Bay, Laurie Island, in the South Orkneys (Orcadas means "Orkneys" in Spanish). In Feb. 1904 the Argentines took over Bruce's Omond House station there, and in Jan. 1905 renamed it. Leader of the 1950 wintering party was J. Smiter Estrada, and of the 1957 party, Miguel J. Guruceaga.

Orde-Lees, T.H. Storekeeper on the *Endurance* during the British Imperial Transantarctic Expedition of 1914–17, during which he was formally the motor expert. He later lived in NZ.

Oread Spur. 72°35′S, 168°53′E. On the south side of the Tucker Glacier, 10 miles west of Crater Cirque. The NZGSAE 1957–58 established a survey station here at a height of 1,185 m. They named it for the Greek mountain nymph.

Orejas Blancas *see* **Shewry Peak**

Islas Orejas de Burro *see* **Asses Ears, Potmess Rocks**

Orejas Negras *see* **Gateway Ridge**

Orel Ice Fringe. 64°46′S, 62°36′W. A strip of coastal ice piedmont which borders the south side of Errera Channel between Beneden Head and Porro Bluff, on the west coast of Graham Land. Named by the UK in 1960 for Eduard von Orel (1877–1941), Austrian surveyor.

Islas Orella *see* **Vize Islands**

Mount Orestes. 77°29′S, 161°55′E. Over 1,600 m. Just east of Bull Pass in the Olympus Range of Victoria Land. Named by the New Zealanders in 1958–59 for the Greek mythological character.

Orestes Valley. 77°28′S, 161°55′E. A small, ice-free valley on the north side of Mount Orestes, in the Olympus Range of Victoria Land. Named by Parker Calkin, a US geologist here in 1964, in association with the mountain.

Orford Cliff. 66°55′S, 66°29′W. Overlooks the east side of Lallemand Fjord, just east of Andresen Island, on the coast of Graham Land. Surveyed by the FIDS in 1956, and named by them for Michael J.H. Orford, FIDS assistant surveyor at Base W that year.

Organ Peak. 66°56′S, 67°W. The most northerly peak on Arrowsmith Peninsula in Graham Land. Named descriptively by the FIDS in 1956. The fluted appearance resembles the pipes of an organ.

Organ Pipe Cliffs. 68°25′S, 149°04′E. A line of coastal cliffs in the form of palisades, of columnar dolerite (hence the descriptive name given by Mawson when the AAE 1911–14 discovered them). They overlook the sea to the west of Cape Wild.

Organ Pipe Peaks. 86°03′S, 150°W. 7 miles long. Just north of Mount Harkness, at the east flank of the Robert Scott Glacier, in the Queen Maud Mountains, in the shade of the Gothic Mountains. Named descriptively by Byrd's 1928–30 expedition.

The Organ Pipes. 82°37′S, 52°42′W. A mountainous ridge in the Shackleton Range. Named descriptively.

Orheim Point. 79°24′S, 84°19′W. At the end of Inferno Ridge in the Heritage Range. Named for Olav Orheim, Norwegian glaciologist on the USARP South Pole – Queen Maud Land Traverse II (1965–66).

Oriana Ridge *see* **Igloo Spur**

Origin of Name Antarctica. The Arctic was associated with the northern Bear constellation (Arktos in Greek). The Ancient Greeks reasoned that because there was land in the extreme north, there had to be also in the extreme south, in order to balance the earth. This they called Antarktos, and so listed it on their maps, even though they had no way of proving that it actually existed.

Orion Massif. 70°23′S, 66°47′W. 14 miles long. 4 miles ENE of Scorpio Peaks, between the upper parts of Meiklejohn Glacier and Millett Glacier in Palmer Land. Named by the UK for the constellation.

Orléans Channel *see* **Orléans Strait**

Orléans Inlet *see* **Orléans Strait**

Orléans Strait. 63°50′S, 60°20′W. Also called Canal d'Orléans, Orléans

Channel, Orléans Inlet. 10 miles wide. 20 miles long. Separates Trinity Island from the Antarctic Peninsula. Discovered by Palmer on Nov. 16, 1820, or possibly by Bransfield around the same time. Mapped by Dumont d'Urville in Feb. 1838, as a bay, and named by him for the French House of Orléans. It was later redefined.

Mount Ormay. 70°44'S, 66°42'E. 1 mile south of Mount Butterworth, in the Aramis Range of the Prince Charles Mountains. Named by the Australians for P.I. Ormay, plumber at Wilkes Station in 1963.

Ormehausen Peak. 72°01'S, 14°38'E. The USSR calls it Mount Bagritskogo. At the north end of the Linnormen Hills, in the Payer Mountains of Queen Maud Land. Name means "the serpent's head" in Norwegian.

Ormeryggen. 72°04'S, 14°33'E. The 3 major hills forming the central portion of the Linnormen Hills, in the Payer Mountains of Queen Maud Land. SE of Skavlhø Mountain. Name means "the serpent's back" in Norwegian.

Ormesporden Hill. 72°05'S, 14°19'E. At the SW end of the Linnormen Hills, in the Payer Mountains of Queen Maud Land. Name means "the serpent's tail" in Norwegian.

Mount Orndorff. 84°37'S, 175°26'W. 1,520 m. 5 miles south of Nilsen Peak, at the west side of the Massam Glacier, in the Queen Maud Mountains, overlooking the Shackleton Glacier. Named for Howard J. Orndorff.

Orndorff, Howard J. Lt. cdr., USNR. Military leader of Little America during the winter of 1957, until Nov. 28, 1957. In 1963 he wintered-over at McMurdo Station.

Orne, William B. Captain of the *General Knox,* 1820–21.

Orne Harbor. 64°37'S, 62°32'W. A cove, 1 mile wide, which indents the west coast of Graham Land, 2 miles SW of Cape Anna. Discovered by de Gerlache

in 1897–99, and named presumably for William Orne.

Orne Islands. 64°40'S, 62°40'W. A group of small islands just north of Rongé Island, off the west coast of Graham Land. Surveyed by de Gerlache in 1897–99. Named presumably for William Orne.

The *Ørnen.* Whale catcher with the *Admiralen* in the South Shetlands in 1905–06. With the *Hauken* it was one of the first two modern whale catchers. Went aground at Ørnen Rocks in 1908–9.

Ørnen Rocks. 62°01'S, 57°35'W. A group of rocks in water, some submerged, some above the water level. 1 mile NE of Cape Melville, King George Island, in the South Shetlands. Named for the *Ørnen.*

Orr, John. Ordinary seaman on the Wilkes Expedition 1838–42. Joined in the USA. Served the cruise.

Orr, William. Ordinary seaman on the Wilkes Expedition 1838–42. Joined in the USA. Served the cruise.

Orr Glacier. 71°36'S, 162°52'E. Flows from the large cirque between Mounts Moody and Bernstein, in the Lanterman Range of the Bowers Mountains. Flows into Rennick Glacier. Named for Major Thomas L. Orr, US Army assistant logistics officer on the staff of the Commander, US Naval Support Force, Antarctica, 1968 and 1969.

Orr Island. 77°38'S, 149°36'W. 5 miles long. Ice-covered. 3 miles SW of Grinder Island, in the Marshall Archipelago, off the coast of Marie Byrd Land. Named for Lt. Cdr. Thomas E. Orr, VX-6 pararescue team leader in 1968.

Orr Peak. 83°29'S, 157°48'E. Overlooks Marsh Glacier, in the Miller Range, just south of Argo Glacier. Discovered in Dec. 1957 by the NZ Southern Party of the BCTAE. Named by them for H. Orr, IGY scientist at Scott Base in 1957.

Ortiz, Irving Spencer. Crewman on the *Jacob Ruppert,* 1934–35.

Ortiz Island. 63°18'S, 57°52'W. In the Duroch Islands, 350 yards south of the eastern end of Largo Island. 350 yards from the northern coast of Trinity Peninsula. Named by Martin Halpern (*see* **Halpern Point**) for Marcos Ortiz (*see* **The Lientur**).

Orton Cave. 66°22'S, 110°27'E. In the western wall of Cape Ravine, Ardery Island, in the Windmill Islands. Discovered in 1961 by Dr. M.N. Orton, medical officer at Wilkes Station that year. The Australians named it for him.

Orton Reef. 66°16'S, 110°33'E. In the north part of Newcomb Bay. ½ mile north of Molholm Island, in the Windmill Islands. Discovered and charted in Feb. 1957 by a party from the *Glacier*. Named for Dr. M.N. Orton (*see* **Orton Cave**).

Orville Coast. 75°45'S, 65°30'W. Between Cape Adams and Cape Zumberge, it is the northern coast of the Ronne Ice Shelf, at the foot of the Hauberg Mountains, in Ellsworth Land. Discovered by the RARE 1947–48, and named Orville Escarpment by Ronne for Capt. Howard T. Orville, who formulated the meteorological program for the expedition. The feature was later redefined.

Orville Escarpment *see* **Orville Coast**

Orvin Mountains. 72°S, 9°E. 65 miles long. Between the Wohlthat Mountains and the Mühlig-Hofmann Mountains in Queen Maud Land. Named by the Norwegians for Anders K. Orvin, director of the Norsk Polarinstitutt, 1945–48, and under-director after 1948.

The Orwell. Norwegian transport ship belonging to the Tønsberg Hvalfangeri Company. It was the second ship of that name to belong to that company. Under the command of Capt. Søren Berntsen, it anchored at Signy Bay in 1925–26, 1926–27, 1927–28, 1928–29, and 1929–30.

Orwell Bight. 60°43'S, 45°23'W. Also called Fondeadero Ventisquero. South of the eastern half of Coronation Island, in the South Orkneys. Bounded on the west by Signy Island, and on the east by the Robertson Islands. Named by the UK for the *Orwell*.

Orwell Glacier. 60°43'S, 45°38'W. Less than ½ mile long. Flows from the Snow Hills and terminates in 20 meter-high ice cliffs on the south edge of Elephant Flats, in the eastern part of Signy Island, in the South Orkneys. Surveyed by personnel on the *Discovery* in 1927, and named by them for the *Orwell*.

Mount Osborne. 78°37'S, 84°47'W. 2,600 m. On the SW side of Thomas Glacier. 5 miles east of Mount Craddock, in the Sentinel Range. Named for Thomas M. Osborne, Navy builder, one of the men who helped construct South Pole Station in 1956–57, and who wintered-over there in 1957.

Oscar Cove. 64°55'S, 62°55'W. On the east coast of Graham Land.

Oscar Island *see* **Inexpressible Island, Oscar Point**

Oscar Point. 74°35'S, 164°53'E. On the north shore of Terra Nova Bay, 1 mile NW of Markham Island, in Victoria Land. Discovered by Borchgrevink in 1898–1900 and named by him as Oscar Island, for the King of Norway. It was also called Inexpressible Island for a while, and was later redefined as a point.

Oscar II Coast. 65°45'S, 62°30'W. Between Cape Fairweather and Cape Alexander, on the NE coast of the Antarctic Peninsula. Discovered by Larsen in 1893, and named King Oscar Land by him for the King of Norway. Later redefined and slightly renamed.

Mount Oscar Wisting *see* **Mount Wisting**

Osechka Peak. 71°31'S, 15°26'E. 1,740 m. 6 miles south of Vorposten Peak in the Lomonosov Mountains of Queen Maud Land. The USSR named it Gora Osechka (misfire mountain) in 1966.

Osen Cove. 69°27'S, 39°40'E. A lake-like cove. Indents the north part of Skarvsnes Foreland. Opens in Byvågen

Bay at the east side of Lützow-Holm Bay. Photographed by the LCE 1936–37. Name means "the outlet" in Norwegian.

Mount O'Shea. 70°15′S, 65°35′E. 2 miles NNW of Mount Albion in the Athos Range of the Prince Charles Mountains. Named by the Australians for A.J. O'Shea, assistant diesel mechanic at Mawson Station in 1964.

O'Shea Peak. 70°26′S, 66°30′E. Just south of Mount McCarthy in the eastern part of the Porthos Range in the Prince Charles Mountains. Named by the Australians for J.H. O'Shea, radio officer at Wilkes Station in 1962 and 1964.

Oshiage Beach. 69°38′S, 39°27′E. On the NE side of the Skallen Hills, on the Queen Maud Land coast. It is actually between the Skallen Hills and the terminus of Skallen Glacier. Named Oshiage-hama (raised beach) by the Japanese in 1972.

Osicki Glacier. 84°41′S, 170°45′E. Just south of Mount Deakin in the Commonwealth Range. It flows into the Beardmore Glacier. Named for Kenneth J. Osicki, American biologist at McMurdo Station in 1963.

Oskeladden Rock. 71°18′S, 11°27′E. Almost a mile south of Pål Rock, in the Arkticheskiy Institut Rocks, at the NW extremity of the Wohlthat Mountains of Queen Maud Land. Discovered by Ritscher in 1938–39. Named by the Norwegians.

Osmand, Daniel. Seaman on the Wilkes Expedition 1838–42. Joined in the USA. Run at Valparaiso.

Bajo Osorno *see* **Pesky Rocks**

Osøya. 69°27′S, 39°37′E. In the middle of Osen Cove. An island. On the north coast of Skarvsnes Foreland, on the east side of Lützow-Holm Bay. Photographed by the LCE 1936–37. In association with the cove, the name means "the outlet island" in Norwegian.

Mount Ostenso. 78°19′S, 86°12′W. 4,180 m. 2 miles south of Mount Giovinetto in the main ridge of the Sentinel Range. Named by Charles Bentley in 1957–58 for Ned A. Ostenso, traverse seismologist at Byrd Station in 1957, and a member of the Marie Byrd Land Traverse Party of 1957–58. First climbed on Jan. 12, 1967.

Osterrieth Mountains *see* **Osterrieth Range**

Osterrieth Range. 64°40′S, 63°15′W. Runs NE-SW along the SE coast of Anvers Island. Discovered by de Gerlache in 1897–99, and named by him as Osterrieth Mountains, for Mme. Ernest Osterrieth, a patron. The feature was later more correctly defined as a range.

Östliche Petermann Range. 71°26′S, 12°44′E. One of the Petermann Ranges, it runs north-south for 15 miles from Per Spur to Gornyy Inzhenery Rocks in the Wohlthat Mountains of Queen Maud Land. Discovered by Ritscher in 1938–39, and named by him for its eastern location.

Östre Shelf-Is *see* **Ekström Ice Shelf**

Ostryy Point. 69°55′S, 12°E. Juts out from the Queen Maud Land ice shelf, forming the west side of the entrance to Leningradskiy Bay. Mapped by the USSR in 1959 and named Mys Ostryy (angular point) by them.

Osuga Glacier. 72°34′S, 166°55′E. Flows into Trafalgar Glacier just east of Mount Burton, in the Victory Mountains of Victoria Land. Named for David T. Osuga, biologist at McMurdo Station in 1966–67.

O'Sullivan Peak. 71°26′S, 62°06′W. 1,765 m. Ice-covered. 11 miles west of the north arm of Odom Inlet, on the east coast of Palmer Land. Named by the FIDS for T.P. O'Sullivan, FIDS worker at Base D, 1946–47.

Otago Glacier. 82°32′S, 161°10′E. 20 miles long. Feeds the Nimrod Glacier from the area around Mount Markham. Named by the New Zealanders in 1961–62, for Otago University, NZ.

Mount Otis. 75°05′S, 136°13′W. On the north side of the Kirkpatrick Glacier.

1½ miles SE of Mount Sinha at the SE edge of the Erickson Bluffs in the Mc-Donald Heights of Marie Byrd Land. Named for Jack Otis, biologist here in 1971–72.

Otlet Glacier. 65°48'S, 64°38'W. 9 miles long. Flows along the south side of the Fontaine Heights to the west coast of Graham Land. Named by the UK for Paul Otlet (1868–1944), Belgian who pioneered the classification of polar information.

Otome Point. 68°08'S, 42°36'E. 2 miles SW of Cape Hinode on the Queen Maud Land coast. Named Otome-no-hana (girl's nose) by the Japanese in 1973.

Ottehallet Slope. 72°12'S, 0°13'W. An ice slope between Straumsvola Mountain and Brekkerista Ridge, in the Sverdrup Mountains of Queen Maud Land. Name means "the early morning slope" in Norwegian.

Otter Highlands. 80°38'S, 30°W. In the western part of the Shackleton Range.

Otter Pass. 80°37'S, 23°W. In the Shackleton Range. Not yet an accepted name.

Otter Plain. 71°30'S, 7°30'E. An ice plain between Sigurd Knolls on the north and the Mühlig-Hofmann Mountains on the south, in Queen Maud Land. Named by the Norwegians for the Otter aircraft used on the Norwegian Antarctic Expeditions between 1956 and 1960.

Otter Rock. 63°38'S, 59°12'W. A rock in water 3 miles north of Notter Point, Trinity Peninsula. Named by the UK for the Otter aircraft.

Ottoborchgrevinkfjella *see* **Mount Borchgrevink**

Otway Massif. 85°27'S, 172°E. 10 miles long. 7 miles wide. Mainly ice-free. At the NW end of the Grosvenor Mountains, at the confluence of the Mill and Mill Stream Glaciers. Named by the Southern Party of the NZGSAE 1961–62 for P.M. Otway, a member of this party.

He was also a member of the Northern Party of the NZGSAE 1960–61. He had wintered-over at Scott Base in 1961.

Ouellette Island. 64°47'S, 64°25'W. ½ mile west of Howard Island, in the southern part of the Joubin Islands. Named for Gerald L. Ouellette, chief engineer on the *Hero* on its first voyage to Palmer Station in 1968.

Outback Nunataks. 72°30'S, 160°30'E. 40 miles long. 20 miles wide. South of Emlen Peaks, in the Usarp Mountains, and west of Monument Nunataks and the upper part of the Rennick Glacier. Named for their remote position.

Outcast Islands. 64°48'S, 64°08'W. Two small islands and about 14 rocks, 3 miles SW of Palmer Station, off Anvers Island. The 2 main islands (themselves little more than rocks) are ½ mile apart. Surveyed by the FIDS in 1955, and named by the UK for their position in relation to Arthur Harbor.

Outer Island. 60°43'S, 45°35'W. Fringed by submerged rocks. ⅓ mile east of Berntsen Point on the east side of Signy Island, in the South Orkneys. Charted by personnel on the *Discovery II* in 1933, and named by them for its position just outside the entrance to Borge Bay.

Outlaw Rock. 67°53'S, 68°53'W. An isolated rock in water, west of the Dion Islands, off the south end of Adelaide Island. Named by the UK for its isolated position.

Outlet glaciers. An outlet glacier is one which drains an inland ice-cap or which flows through a gap between mountains.

Outlook Peak. 85°59'S, 150°50'W. 2 miles SE of Mount Zanuck in the Queen Maud Mountains. Named by the NZGSAE 1969–70, who got a good outlook of the next stage of their trip from here.

The Outpost *see* **Vorposten Peak**

Outpost Nunataks. 75°50'S, 158°12'E. 3 aligned nunataks. 4 miles SW of Brimstone Peak, in the Prince Albert Mountains of Victoria Land. Named by the New Zealanders in 1962–63 because of their position near the edge of the Polar Plateau.

Outrider Nunatak. 69°28′S, 156°23′E. 1,250 m. In the north-central part of the Arkhangel'skiy Nunataks. Named by the New Zealanders in 1963–64 because of its forward position in the group.

Ovbratten Peak. 72°47′S, 3°44′W. Pyramidal. 2 miles SW of Høgfonna Mountain in the Borg Massif of Queen Maud Land. Named by the Norwegians.

Ove Peak. 72°11′S, 3°27′W. The most northerly of the group at the west side of the Wilson Saddle, near the SW end of the Ahlmann Ridge, in Queen Maud Land. Named Ovenuten by the Norwegians for Ove Wilson.

Ovenuten *see* **Ove Peak**

Overflow Glacier. 77°46′S, 163°11′E. Flows into Ferrar Glacier, just east of Briggs Hill, in southern Victoria Land. Named descriptively (it overflows, rather than flows, into Ferrar Glacier) by Grif Taylor's Western Journey Party during Scott's 1910–13 expedition.

Mount Overlord. 73°10′S, 164°36′E. 3,395 m. An extinct stratovolcano, at the NW limit of Deception Plateau, just east of the head of Aviator Glacier, in northern Victoria Land. Named by the New Zealanders in 1962–63 because of its dominance in the area.

Overton Peak. 69°41′S, 72°05′W. In the NW extremity of Alexander Island.

Overwintering *see* **Wintering-over**

Övresjöen *see* **Lake Ober-See**

Øvrevollen Bluff. 72°11′S, 3°45′E. Just south of Festninga Mountain in the Mühlig-Hofmann Mountains of Queen Maud Land. Name means "the upper wall" in Norwegian.

Isla Owen *see* **Tartar Island**

Mount Owen. 74°25′S, 62°30′W. Also called Mount Arthur Owen. 1,105 m. 2 miles NW of Kelsey Cliff at the south side

of Johnston Glacier, on the east coast of Palmer Land. Named by Finn Ronne in 1948 for Arthur Owen.

Owen, Arthur. Boy scout, he was the trail man on the RARE 1947–48.

Owen, Russell. *New York Times* correspondent, one of the shore party on Byrd's 1928–30 expedition.

Owen Hills. 83°44′S, 169°50′E. Ice-covered. On the west side of the Beardmore Glacier, between Socks Glacier and Evans Glacier, in the Queen Alexandra Range. Named for George Owen, special assistant for Antarctica in the Department of State, 1959–62.

Owen Island. 61°56′S, 58°26′W. Also called Isla Redonda. Between Round Point and Pottinger Point, just off the north coast of King George Island, in the South Shetlands. Charted and named in 1935 by the personnel on the *Discovery II*.

Owen Peak. 71°52′S, 63°08′W. Inland from Hilton Inlet, in eastern Palmer Land. On the south side of the Gruening Glacier. Discovered aerially on Nov. 21, 1940, by members of East Base during the USAS 1939–41. Named Mount Russell Owen, for Russell Owen. Name later amended by the USA.

Owen Ridge. 79°50′S, 84°50′W. 22 miles long. Forms the most southwesterly part of the Sentinel Range. Extends SSE from Mount Strybing, and includes Mount Southwick and Lishness Peak. Named in 1974 for Thomas B. Owen, National Science Foundation official.

Owlshead Peak. 66°19′S, 65°49′W. 1½ miles east of Cape Bellue, on the west coast of Graham Land. Named descriptively by the UK.

Owston Islands. 66°23′S, 66°06′W. Also spelled (erroneously) as Owlston Islands. A group of small islands 1 mile west of the Darbel Islands, in Crystal Sound. Named by the UK for P.G. Owston, British crystallographer.

Oyako Islands. 68°28′S, 41°24′E. Two small islands just north of Cape Akarui on the coast of Queen Maud Land. Named Oyako-shima (parent and child islands) by the Japanese because one of the islands is tiny.

Oyayubi Island. 69°14′S, 39°40′E. 1½ miles long. Just off the Langhovde Hills, 2 miles south of Mount Choto, in eastern Lützow-Holm Bay. Named Oyayubi-jima (thumb island) by the Japanese in 1972 in association with Oyayubi Point.

Oyayubi Point. 69°15′S, 39°39′E. Marks the southern end of Oyayubi Island off the Langhovde Hills of Queen Maud Land. Named Oyayubi-misaki (thumb point) by the Japanese in 1972 in association with Cape Nakayubi, just to the north.

Mount Øydeholmen. 67°24′S, 55°42′E. Also called Mount Kernot. Mostly ice-covered. 4 miles west of Rayner Peak, south of Edward VIII Bay, in Enderby Land. Photographed by the LCE 1936–37. Name means "the desolate island" in Norwegian.

Øygarden Group. 66°58′S, 57°25′E. Also called Øygarden Islands, Guardian Islands. 11 miles in extent. In the south part of the entrance to Edward VIII Bay. They include Ackerman Island, Alphard Island, Borg Island, Depot Island, Håkollen Island, Shaula Island, Karm Island, the Sirius Islands, and the Rigel Skerries. They were discovered in Feb. 1936 by the Discovery Committee personnel on the *William Scoresby,* and considered by them to be part of the mainland. Photographed by the LCE 1936–37 in Jan. and Feb. 1937, and charted as islands by Norwegian cartographers working off these aerial photos. Named Øygarden (Guardian Islands) by the Norwegians.

Øygarden Islands *see* **Øygarden Group**

Ozhidaniya Cove. 70°44′S, 11°39′E. ½ mile east of Tyuleniy Point on the north side of the Schirmacher Hills in Queen Maud Land. Nadezhdy Island lies across the mouth of the cove. Named Zaliv Ozhidaniya (anticipation cove) by the USSR in 1961.

Ozone. The Earth's ozone layer, located in the stratosphere, screens out biologically harmful ultraviolet rays from the sun. Whether one believes in creation or evolution, it is a very pleasant thing to have above us. If this ozone layer were to thin out, or if a hole were to appear, we could be in trouble. A true "hole," as such, could melt the Antarctic ice, and that could mean that people now living inland could find themselves coastal dwellers. In 1975 the ozone layer over Antarctica started to thin. This was discovered in 1977 by the BAS (British Antarctic Survey) who kept it quiet for fear of panicking the world. They did not release the information until 1985. Since 1983 the ozone layer above the Antarctic has thinned by half. A "hole" about the size of the USA appears in late August and patches up again in November. However, the "hole" is gradually lasting longer and longer, but this is not a constant. Some years are better than others, but there is a gradual worsening of the situation. Actually it is a springtime decrease in the ozone layer, and thus allows more potentially harmful ultraviolet radiation into Antarctica. The "hole" seems to be caused by chlorofluorocarbons in the atmosphere, merging with the intense cold in the lower stratosphere, a strong polar vortex centered over the South Pole, and the presence of polar stratospheric clouds. Since 1986–87 there have been National Ozone Expeditions (NOZE I, NOZE II, etc.) from the USA each summer. In addition, a smaller "hole" has appeared over Spitsbergen in the Arctic.

Pointe P. Curie *see* **Curie Point**

Mount P.L. Smith *see* **Mount F.L. Smith**

The *Paal.* Norwegian whaler in the South Orkneys in the 1911–12 and 1912–13 seasons. Petter Sørlle made his investigations of these islands from this vessel in those years. Sometimes, erroneously, recorded as the *Palmer* (see also **The** *Powell*).

Paal Harbor. 60°43′S, 45°36′W. ½ mile south of Borge Bay on the east side of Signy Island in the South Orkneys. Named before 1912, probably by Petter Sørlle, and definitely for the *Paal*.

Paape, Frank. Seaman on the *Eleanor Bolling* during the second half of Byrd's 1928-30 expedition.

Pabellón Island. 64°19′S, 62°57′W. The more southerly of two islands just off the northern tip of Omega Island. It marks the southern side of the western entrance to Andersen Harbor in the Melchior Islands. Surveyed by Discovery Investigations personnel in 1927. Named by the Argentine Antarctic Expedition of 1946-47 for their flag which they flew from a mast they erected on the island (pabellón is the Spanish for "national flag").

The *Pacific*. US sealer from New London, in the South Shetlands during the 1829-31 season, commanded by Capt. James Brown.

Pacific-Antarctic Basin *see* **Southeast Pacific Basin**

Pacific-Antarctic Ridge. Also called Antarctic Pacific Ridge, South Pacific Rise, South Pacific Ridge. A submarine feature centering on 62°S, 157°W.

Pacific South Polar Basin *see* **Southeast Pacific Basin**

Pack-ice. Ice forming a pack in the sea around Antarctica. The cold air masses coming off the continent freeze the ice in this manner: when the temperature of the water reaches −1.86°C frazil ice is formed. As long as the temperature remains below −2°C this forms into grease ice, and then into pancake ice, which eventually forms into floes, then pack-ice. The pack-ice around Antarctica is in constant motion, retreating in the summer, advancing in the winter, pushed by the winds and currents. It reaches north to about 56°S in the Atlantic, and to about 64°S in the Pacific, and because of

its variation in area, it may play a great role in world weather. As long as humans have been going down to the Antarctic, their ships have been getting caught in the pack-ice. Some have been merely pinched by it, some have been freed by other ships—if they were lucky. Sometimes vessels would be beset for a year or more, traveling with the pack-ice until the thaw came. Even icebreakers get caught occasionally. However, only 4 recorded ships have ever been crushed and sunk by the pack: the *Antarctic* in 1903; the *Endurance* in 1915; the *Gotland II* in 1981; and the *Southern Quest* in 1986. If you are going down to the ice in a vessel it's best to make sure an ice pilot is on board. If not, the easiest passage through the pack is at 178°E.

Packard Glacier. 77°21′S, 162°10′E. Just west of Purgatory Peak in the Saint Johns Range of Victoria Land, flowing south into Victoria Valley. Named by the New Zealanders in 1958-59 for Andrew Packard, biologist who worked here with the NZ party of the BCTAE the season before.

Padack, A. Capt. Commander of the *Geneva*, 1836-37.

Padda Island. 69°39′S, 38°20′E. Near the west side of the entrance to Havsbotn in Lützow-Holm Bay. Photographed by the LCE 1936-37. Name means "the toad" in Norwegian (because of its shape).

Pagano Nunatak. 83°41′S, 87°40′W. Also called Semper Shaftus. 1,830 m. Isolated. 8 miles east of the Hart Hills and 80 miles NNE of the Ford Massif in the Thiel Mountains. Examined and sketched by Edward Thiel during an airlifted seismic traverse along the 88°W meridian in 1959-60. Named for CWO Gerald Pagano (1913-1981), US Army, assistant for plans and operations on the staff of the Commander, US Naval Support Force, Antarctica, 1960-65.

Cape Page. 63°55′S, 60°18′W. Also called Cabo Byers, Cabo Comandante Byers. 13 miles SW of Cape Kater on the west coast of Graham Land. Named by the UK in 1960 for Sir Frederick Handley Page (1885–1962), British pioneer aircraft designer.

Page Bluff. 69°38′S, 66°11′W. On the Antarctic Peninsula.

Page Rock *see* **Jester Rock**

Pageant Point. 60°44′S, 45°36′W. The central and highest of three ice-free points at the east end of the Gourlay Peninsula on Signy Island in the South Orkneys. Surveyed in 1933 by personnel from the Discovery Committee, and again in 1947 by the FIDS. Named by the FIDS for the pageantry seen in the penguin rookery there.

Pagoda Peak. 83°56′S, 166°45′E. 3,040 m. Between the heads of the Tillite and Montgomerie Glaciers. 3 miles north of Mount Mackellar in the Queen Alexandra Range. Named by the New Zealanders in 1961–62 for its shape.

Pagoda Ridge. 71°53′S, 68°33′W. It has a small peak looking like a pagoda at its summit. Between Phobos Ridge and Deimos Ridge on the north side of Saturn Glacier in the SE part of Alexander Island. Named descriptively by the UK.

Pagodroma Gorge. 70°50′S, 68°08′E. 3 miles long and steep-sided. It joins Radok Lake with Beaver Lake in the Prince Charles Mountains. Traversed by A. Medvecky, ANARE geologist, in Jan.–Feb. 1969. Named by the Australians for the snow petrels *(Pagodroma nivea)* which nest in the weathered sandstone walls of the gorge.

Mount Paige. 76°20′S, 144°42′W. 3 miles west of Mount Carbone in the Phillips Mountains of Marie Byrd Land. Discovered aerially during Byrd's 1928–30 expedition. Named for David Paige.

Paige, David. Artist on the shore party of Byrd's 1933–35 expedition.

Pain Mesa. 73°08′S, 163°E. Also called Pain Tableland. Just north of Tobin Mesa, in the Mesa Range of Victoria Land. Named by the northern party of

the NZGSAE 1962–63 for Kevin Pain, deputy leader of this party *(see also* **Pain Névé**).

Pain Névé. 84°36′S, 174°20′E. Between the Commonwealth Range and the Hughes Range. The Keltie Glacier flows from here into the Beardmore Glacier. Named by the southern party of the NZGSAE 1961–62 for Kevin Pain, field assistant with the party *(see also* **Pain Mesa**).

Pain Tableland *see* **Pain Mesa**

Mount Paine. 86°46′S, 147°32′W. 3,330 m. Flat-topped. Forms a buttress-type projection of the western part of the La Gorce Mountains in the Queen Maud Mountains. Discovered in Dec. 1934 by Quin Blackburn's party during Byrd's 1933–35 expedition, and named by Byrd initially as Mount Katherine Paine, for the wife of Stuart D.L. Paine. The name was later shortened.

Paine, Stuart D.L. From Durham, N.H. The navigator and radio operator on Quin Blackburn's party to the Queen Maud Mountains during Nov. and Dec. of 1934, on Byrd's 1933–35 expedition.

Paine Ridge. 71°50′S, 162°E. Saber-shaped. Bare rock. Extends southward from DeGoes Cliff at the SW end of the Morozumi Range. Named for Roland D. Paine, public information officer of the NSF, who was at McMurdo Station, 1960–61 and 1968–69.

Painted Cliffs. 83°50′S, 162°20′E. They extend SW from Mount Picciotto and mark the SE edge of the Prince Andrew Plateau. Named by the New Zealanders in 1961–62 for the colored sedimentary and igneous rock layers exposed on the face of this irregular line of cliffs.

Painted Hill *see* **Painted Peak**

Painted Peak. 67°45′S, 62°51′E. Also called Painted Hill. 710 m. A peak on the northern spur of the North Masson Range in the Framnes Mountains of Mac. Robertson Land. Photographed by the LCE 1936–37. Visited by an ANARE party in 1955, and named by the Australians for its notable red-brown coloring.

Mount Paish. 66°51'S, 52°48'E. 1½ miles east of Mount Torckler and 27 miles SW of Stor Hånakken Mountain in Enderby Land. Named by the Australians for P.G. Paish, weather observer at Wilkes Station in 1961.

Pål Rock. 71°18'S, 11°26'E. Between Per Rock and Oskeladden Rock in the Arkticheskiy Institut Rocks at the NW extremity of the Wohlthat Mountains of Queen Maud Land. Discovered by Ritscher's 1938–39 expedition. Name means "Paul" in Norwegian (*see also* **Per Rock**).

Palaver Point. 64°09'S, 61°45'W. On the west side of Two Hummock Island in the Palmer Archipelago. Named by the British for the palaver created here in the penguin rookery.

Paleosols. Buried soils, usually those which developed during an interglacial period, and were buried by later ice deposits.

Palestrina Glacier. 69°21'S, 71°35'W. In the northern part of Alexander Island. 11 miles long. 8 miles wide. Flows west from the Nichols Snowfield into Lazarev Bay. Named by the UK for the composer.

Palets Rock. 70°46'S, 11°36'E. Isolated. Between Aerodromnaya Hill and the Schirmacher Hills of Queen Maud Land. Named Skala Palets (toe rock) by the USSR in 1961.

Palindrome Buttress. 70°59'S, 71°17'W. 500 m. Marks the south end of the north group of the Walton Mountains in the western central part of Alexander Island. Discovered aerially on Nov. 23, 1935, by Ellsworth. Named by the UK because its shape is recognizable from quite a distance from all angles.

Palisade Nunatak. 64°04'S, 58°15'W. Just north of Röhss Bay and 2 miles SE of Hidden Lake on James Ross Island. Surveyed by the FIDS in 1960–61. This distinctive ridge-backed nunatak with a vertical columnar structure is the largest outcrop of hard obtrusive rock on the island. Named by the UK for its resemblance to a palisade.

Palisade Valley. 79°47'S, 158°26'E. 2 miles long. 1,000 meters high. It is dominated for its entire length by a large dolerite sill. At the SW side of Pleasant Plateau, and 3 miles NE of Bastion Hill in the Brown Hills. Named by the New Zealanders in 1962–63 for its resemblance to the Palisades bordering the Hudson River in New York.

The Palisades. 82°50'S, 159°10'E. A steep escarpment at the west side of Cotton Plateau in the Queen Elizabeth Range. Overlooks Marsh and Nimrod Glaciers. Discovered by the northern party of the NZGSAE 1961–62 and named by them for its resemblance to a protective wall at the junction of 2 rivers.

Pallas Peak. 72°06'S, 69°43'W. Between Ceres Nunataks and Stephenson Nunatak, in the southern part of Alexander Island. The western face of this steep triangular peak is lined with several gullies, but the eastern side has a gentle slope of snow and rock. Named by the UK for the minor planet.

Pallid Peak. 84°37'S, 178°49'W. 1,500 m. On the west side of the Kosco Glacier. 7 miles SW of McGinnis Peak, in the Queen Maud Mountains. It is composed entirely of white crystalline marble. Named descriptively by Edmund Stump of the Ohio State University party which geologically mapped this peak on Dec. 3, 1970.

Palma, Emilio Marcos. The first human being to be born in Antarctica (*see* **Births**). This Argentine was born at Esperanza Station on Jan. 7, 1978.

Cape Palmer *see* **Mount Palmer**

Mount Palmer. 71°40'S, 98°52'W. Ice-covered. Visible from the sea. Surmounts the northern end of Noville Peninsula on Thurston Island. Named for James Troxall Palmer. Originally thought to be a cape and called Cape Palmer. Later redefined.

Palmer, Alexander S. Brother of Nat Palmer. Commander of the *Penguin*, 1829–31. He was back again in the South Shetlands in the *Charles Adams*, 1831–33.

Palmer, James T. James Troxall Palmer. Acting surgeon on the *Relief*, 1838–39, and on the *Peacock*, 1839–40, during the Wilkes Expedition 1838–42. Wrote *Thulia: A Tale of the Antarctic* in 1843, and *Antarctic Mariner's Song* in 1868 (*see* the Bibliography). He was later surgeon-general of the US Navy.

Palmer, Nathaniel B. b. Aug. 8, 1799, Stonington, Conn. d. 1877, San Francisco. Nathaniel Brown Palmer. Son of a shipyard owner, and brother of Alex Palmer. Nat went to sea at 14. He was 2nd mate on the *Hersilia* during its 1819–20 voyage to the South Shetlands. The following season, 1820–21, he was a major part of the Fanning-Pendleton Sealing Expedition, in which he was captain and part-owner of the *Hero,* and co-owner of the *Express*—at the age of 20! On Nov. 17, 1820, he sighted the Antarctic Peninsula, and on Feb. 6, 1821, he met von Bellingshausen (see that entry for details). Yet again, the following season, he was back in the South Shetlands, as commander of the *James Monroe,* and on Dec. 6, 1821, with British sealer George Powell, discovered the South Orkneys. Powell, unlike Palmer, was not part of the Fanning-Pendleton Sealing Expedition of that season. In 1829–31 he and Ben Pendleton led the Palmer-Pendleton Expedition to the same area, with Palmer commanding the *Annawan,* which he co-owned. At the end of the expedition Palmer's vessel was boarded by pirates. Later Palmer became a clipper ship master and designer.

Palmer, Robert. Supply officer/assistant to the meteorologist at East Base during the USAS 1939–41.

Palmer Archipelago. 64°15′S, 62°50′W. Also called Antarctic Archipelago,

Palmer Islands. A group of islands NW of the Antarctic Peninsula, and separated from it by the Gerlache Strait. It extends from Tower Island in the north to Anvers Island in the south. Discovered in 1898 by de Gerlache and named by him for Nat Palmer. Aside from the two mentioned above, some of the main features of this group are Liège Island, Brabant Island, Two Hummock Island, Wiencke Island, Hoseason Island, Christiania Islands, Paul Islands, Lecointe Island, Lajarte Islands, Guesalaga Island, Cobalescou Island, Bernard Rocks, Harry Island, Hydrurga Rocks, Abbot Island, Davis Island, Haller Rocks, Lobodon Island, Chance Rock, Yoke Island, Grinder Rock, D'Hainaut Island, Tetrad Islands, Klo Rock, Chionis Island, Farewell Rock, Minerva Rocks, Babel Rock, Judas Rock, Spert Island, Trinity Island, Cetacea Rocks, Hydrodist Rocks, Ryge Rocks, Oluf Rocks, Chanticleer Island, Pearl Rocks, Zigzag Island, Catodon Rocks, Ohlin Island, Physeter Rocks, Jurien Island, Dumoulin Rocks, Kendall Rocks, Beaumont Skerries, Beauprés Rocks, Bills Island, Bob Island, Breaker Island, Breakwater Island, Buff Island, Capstan Rocks, Casabianca Island, Christine Island, Cormorant Island, Dobrowolski Island, Doumer Island, Dream Island, False Island, Fournier Island, Fridtjof Island, Gand Island, Goetschy Island, Gossler Islands, Green Reef, Guépratte Island, Joubin Islands, Lion Island, Vázquez Island, Halfway Island, Hermit Island, Huemul Island, Humble Island, Janus Island, Litchfield Island, etc.

¹**Palmer Bay.** 60°37′S, 45°20′W. 1 mile wide. Just west of Crown Head on the north coast of Coronation Island in the South Orkneys. Discovered in Dec. 1821 by Palmer and Powell and named by Powell for Nat Palmer.

²**Palmer Bay**   *see*   **False Bay**

Palmer Coast   *see*   **Davis Coast**

Palmer Inlet. 71°15′S, 61°10′W. Also called Robert Palmer Bay. Ice-filled. 7 miles long. Between Capes Bryant and

Musselman on the east coast of Palmer Land. It is rectangular in shape and bordered by almost vertical cliffs. Discovered in 1940 by members of East Base during the USAS 1939–41, and named for Robert Palmer.

Palmer Inseln *see* **Palmer Archipelago**

Palmer Islands *see* **Palmer Archipelago**

Palmer Land. 71°30′S, 65°W. The half of the Antarctic Peninsula south of a line joining Cape Jeremy and Cape Agassiz. Until 1964 the USA officially used the name for the entire Antarctic Peninsula (see that entry for an explanation of this). Supposedly discovered by Nat Palmer, for whom it was supposedly named in 1820 by von Bellingshausen (*see also* Graham Land, and **Antarctic Peninsula**).

Palmer-Pendleton Expedition. 1829– 31. Also called the American Sealing and Exploring Expedition. A private expedition organized by Edmund Fanning, it was a forerunner of the Wilkes Expedition of 1838–42, in that it was government-sanctioned, being organized after a proposed US Naval Expedition was canceled. Jeremiah N. Reynolds was a major fund raiser for it, public subscriptions making it possible. The organization of the expedition was undertaken by the South Sea Company, which comprised Ben Pendleton, Edmund Fanning, Capt. Leslie, James E. Bleecker, Benjamin Rodman, and Nat Palmer, and the scientific program was sponsored by the Lyceum for Natural History of the City of New York. Sealing was done to bring in some revenue. Technically there were only 2 vessels—the *Seraph*, commanded by Pendleton, the field commander, which left New York on Aug. 31, 1829, and the *Annawan*, commanded by Palmer, which left the same port on Oct. 17, 1829. However, a third vessel, the *Penguin*, commanded by Alexander S. Palmer, Nat's brother, left Stonington, Conn., on Oct. 2, 1829, on its own expedition. The *Penguin* and the

Annawan arrived at Elephant Island in the South Shetlands together on Jan. 20, 1830, and did sealing, exploring, and scientific studies. The scientists, Eights, Watson, Reynolds, and 2 others unidentified, were on the *Annawan*, although Eights was the only real scientist, and they managed to collect 15 chests of specimens, and left Antarctica on Feb. 22, 1830. The *Seraph* sealed in the South Shetlands from Jan.–Feb. 1830, and then the 3 vessels went sealing in South American waters. The *Penguin* arrived back in Stonington on June 22, 1831, and the *Annawan* arrived in New York on Aug. 6, 1831. The *Seraph* arrived back in New York on Aug. 8, 1831, minus 6 deserted crew members.

Palmer Peninsula *see* **Antarctic Peninsula**

Palmer Point. 69°43′S, 74°02′E. 2 miles west of Strover Peak and 8 miles WNW of Mount Caroline Mikkelsen on the coast of East Antarctica. Named by the Australians for J. Palmer, helicopter pilot off the *Nella Dan* during the ANARE of 1968.

Palmer Station. 64°46′27.771″S, 64° 03′15.753″W. US scientific station on Gamage Point, at Arthur Harbor, Anvers Island. This is the new site, anyway, the old one (now called Old Palmer) being located at 64°46′S, 64°05′W, on North Point, in the same general area. The site for the original was selected by the *Staten Island* in early 1963. Work began on Jan. 12, 1965, and it was opened on Feb. 25, 1965, being named for Nat Palmer. It was on the site of the burned-down Base N, which the British had closed in 1958. It is 2,360 miles from McMurdo Station, and is 25 feet above sea level. New Palmer Station (still called Palmer Station) was commissioned on March 20, 1968. For most of its history, New Palmer was resupplied by the *Hero*. About 40 people in the summer and a maximum of 10 in the winter study marine life and birds. There is no permanent runway, and the station no longer welcomes visitors—the tourists' fault, not Palmer's!

Palmers Bay *see* **Palmer Bay, False Bay**

Palmer's Harbor. 61°41'S, 45°27'W. About a mile within the entrance to Washington Strait in the South Orkneys. It was discovered in Dec. 1821 by Palmer and Powell and named by Powell for Palmer.

Mount Palombo. 77°29'S, 143°12'W. 1,030 m. Marks the NE end of the Mackay Mountains in the Ford Ranges of Marie Byrd Land. Named for Lt. Robert A. Palombo, USN, aircraft commander during Operation Deep Freeze 68.

Palosuo Islands. 65°37'S, 66°05'W. Also called Islas Mutilla. 1½ miles north of Maurstad Point off the west side of Renaud Island in the Biscoe Islands. Named by the UK in 1959 for Erkki Palosuo, Finnish oceanographer specializing in sea ice studies.

Mount Pálsson. 67°20'S, 65°32'W. 1,190 m. At the north end of Whirlwind Inlet between Flint Glacier and Demorest Glacier on the east coast of Graham Land. Named by the UK for Sveinn Pálsson (1762–1840), Icelandic naturalist and pioneer glaciologist.

The *Pampa*. Argentine transport vessel used in the 1947–48 expedition undertaken by that country to the Antarctic (Captain Oscar H. Rousseau). It also took part in the 1948–49 expedition.

Bahía Pampa *see* **Pampa Passage**

Pampa Island. 64°20'S, 62°10'W. Also called Hunt Island, Isla Jenie. 1½ miles long. 475 meters high. Off the east coast of Brabant Island. 1 mile NE of Pinel Point, it is separated from Brabant Island by the southern part of the Pampa Passage. Charted by de Gerlache in 1897–99. Named by the Argentine Antarctic Expedition of 1947–48 in association with the passage.

Pampa Passage. 64°18'S, 62°10'W. Also called Freud Passage, Boca Pampa. A ship passage along the east side of

Brabant Island. It trends SW between Brabant Island and Lecointe and Pampa Islands. It was named Bahía Pampa by the Argentine Expedition of 1947–48, for the *Pampa*. It was later redefined.

Pampero Pass. 69°31'S, 66°11'W. On the west side of the Antarctic Peninsula.

Islote Pan de Azúcar *see* **Sugarloaf Island**

Pico Pan de Azúcar *see* **Mount Zuckerhut**

Pan Glacier. 68°48'S, 64°24'W. 7 miles long. Flows north and terminates at the east coast of the Antarctic Peninsula 2 miles SW of Victory Nunatak. Surveyed by the FIDS in Dec. 1958. Named by the UK for the Greek god.

Pancake ice. Small, circular pieces of ice, with raised edges, looking like pancakes. They are an accumulation of frazil ice, congealed in the calm sea. In turn the pancakes form ice floes.

Pandemonium Point. 60°45'S, 45°40'W. Marks the south end of a sharp ice-free ridge which forms the southern extremity of Signy Island in the South Orkneys. Surveyed in 1947 by the FIDS, and named by them for the pandemonium caused by the penguins in their rookeries on the west side of the ridge just north of the point.

Pandora Spire. 77°47'S, 161°13'E. 1,670 m. The highest point in the Solitary Rocks, on the north side of Taylor Glacier in Victoria Land. Named by the New Zealanders in 1957–58 for its sharply pointed shape.

Panhard Nunatak. 63°42'S, 58°17'W. The nearest nunatak to the coast on the north side of Russell East Glacier in Trinity Peninsula. Named by the UK for René Panhard (1841–1908), the French automobile designer.

Isla Panimavida *see* **Roux Island**

Pankratz Bay. 73°27'S, 126°38'W. In the western end of Siple Island, off the coast of Marie Byrd Land. Just south of Lovill Bluff, it opens on Wrigley Gulf. Named for Leroy M. Pankratz, seismologist at Byrd Station in 1965.

Panorama Peak. 77°37'S, 161°24'W. ½ mile north of Mount Thundergut on the ridge extending to Plane Table, in the Asgard Range of Victoria Land. Named for the wide scenery seen from here by the New Zealanders.

Panorama Point. 82°49'S, 159°10'E. Has a small hill on it. On the NW side of Cotton Plateau. Overlooks the junction of Marsh and Nimrod Glaciers. Named for the panoramic view from here as seen by the New Zealanders in 1964-65.

Panther Cliff. 66°23'S, 65°36'W. At the NE corner of Darbel Bay, just north of the mouth of Cardell Glacier, on the west coast of Graham Land. Named for its shape.

Pantomime Point. 60°44'S, 45°36'W. The most northerly of three ice-free points at the east end of the Gourlay Peninsula on Signy Island, in the South Orkneys. Surveyed in 1933 by personnel from the Discovery Committee, and again in 1947 by the FIDS. Named by the FIDS for the funny behavior of the penguins in their rookeries on Gourlay Peninsula.

Panzarini, Rodolfo N. Argentine Naval officer who led the 1950-51 expedition which his country put together for the Antarctic. He led the 1952-53 expedition too, with the ships *Bahía Buen Suceso, Bahía Aguirre, Punta Ninfas, Chiriguano, Sanavirón, Yamana.* Later in the decade, as an admiral, he was director of the Instituto Antártico Argentino.

Panzarini Hills. 82°10'S, 41°30'W. North of San Martín Glacier. They form the northern half of the Argentina Range in the Pensacola Mountains. Named by the USA for Rodolfo Panzarini.

Papanin Nunataks. 68°13'S, 50°15'E. 11 miles east of Alderdice Peak in the Nye Mountains of Enderby Land. Named by the USSR in 1961-62 for Adm. Ivan D. Papanin, the polar expert.

Pape Rock. 75°32'S, 159°04'E. A single rock, somewhat isolated, at the south side of the David Glacier, 3 miles NW of Shomo Rock, in the Prince Albert Mountains of Victoria Land. Named for Bernard C. Pape, builder at Amundsen-Scott South Pole Station, 1966.

Papua Island. 63°07'S, 55°57'W. Circular. 4 miles west of Boreal Point, off the northern coast of Joinville Island. Named by the Argentine Antarctic Expedition of 1954-55 for the large numbers of gentoo penguins (*Pygoscelis papua*) seen here.

Papua New Guinea. When it became independent of Australia, it automatically carried with it membership of the Antarctic Treaty, and was ratified as the 23rd signatory on March 16, 1981.

Parachutes. The first parachute jump at either the North or the South Pole took place at 90°S on Nov. 22, 1956, by the 1710th Aerial Port Squadron, when Sgt. Richard J. Patton, USAF, parachuted to the South Pole. On Jan. 19, 1969, R. Spaulding set a McMurdo Station parachute altitude record of 12,500 feet. On Jan. 12, 1972, Parachute Rigger 1st Class H.V. Gorick, set an Antarctic record of 20,500—freefalling for 90 seconds. The previous record had been 16,500 feet.

Paradise Bay *see* **Paradise Harbor**

Paradise Harbor. 64°51'S, 62°54'W. A wide embayment behind Lemaire and Bryde Islands. Indents the west coast of Graham Land between Duthiers and Leniz Points on the Danco Coast. It is surrounded by huge ice-cliffs and is famous for its spectacular scenery. Originally called Paradise Bay before 1920 by the whalers in the area, the feature was slightly redefined in the 1970s.

Paradise Ridge. 85°27'S, 157°10'W. Parallels the coast at the head of the Ross Ice Shelf. East of the Amundsen Glacier and between the MacDonald Nunataks and O'Brien Peak. Named by the New Zealanders in 1969-70 for its flat top which provides astoundingly easy traverses.

Paragon Point. 65°38'S, 64°17'W. On the SW side of Leroux Bay. 3 miles WSW of Eijkman Point on the west coast of Graham Land. Charted by the BGLE 1934–37. Named by the UK in 1959.

Parallactic Island. 67°32′S, 62°46′E. The most northwesterly of the Parallactic Islands in Holme Bay, Mac. Robertson Land. Photographed by the LCE 1936–37. Named by the Australians for the photo-theodolite erected on the island for parallactic measurement of the aurora by the ANARE in 1961.

Parallactic Islands. 67°32′S, 62°46′E. Group of 6 small islands between the Azimuth Islands and the Kellas Islands, in Holme Bay, Mac. Robertson Land. Photographed by the LCE 1936–37. Named by the Australians for Parallactic Island.

Paraselenae   *see*   **Phenomena**

Parasite Bay. 66°46′S, 141°33′E. Also called Baie des Parasites. Between Péage Island and the coastal angle formed by the west side of Découverte Island. Charted by the French in 1951 and named by them for the study of atmospheric parasites made here, and by analogy with Ionosphere Bay at the east side of Cape Découverte on the coast of East Antarctica.

Parasite Cone. 73°06′S, 164°18′E. A small parasite cone (a small cone on the side of a mountain) on the NW flank of Mount Overlord. It is 6½ miles from that mountain's summit, in the Mountaineer Range of Victoria Land. Named descriptively by the New Zealanders in 1962–63.

Baie des Parasites   *see*   **Parasite Bay**

Luís Pardo   *see*   **Luís Pardo Villalón**

Pardo Ridge. 61°07′S, 54°51′W. Extends from The White Company in the west to Cape Valentine in the east. On Elephant Island in the South Shetlands. Named by the UK for Luís Pardo Villalón.

Mount Pardoe. 67°08′S, 50°11′E. 790 m. Between the Wyers Ice Shelf and Priestley Peak on the shore of Amundsen Bay in Enderby Land. Named by the

Australians for Dr. R. Pardoe, medical officer at Mawson Station in 1961.

Pardoe Peak. 73°29′S, 61°38′E. The summit at the SW end of the Mount Menzies massif, it is 3½ miles SW of the summit of Mount Menzies itself, in the Prince Charles Mountains. Named by the Australians for Dr. R. Pardoe (*see* **Mount Pardoe**).

Pardoner Island   *see*   **Guido Island**

Pardue Peak. 79°06′S, 86°30′W. 1,840 m. The most northerly peak on the Smith Ridge in the Founders Peaks of the Heritage Range. Named for Lt. A. Michael Pardue, USN, VX-6 flight surgeon, 1960–61.

Paré Glacier. 64°08′S, 62°13′W. 7 miles long. 1 mile wide. Flows east and then NE into the head of Bouquet Bay on the NE side of Brabant Island. Named by the UK for Ambroise Paré (1510–1590), French surgeon.

Parhelia   *see*   **Phenomena**

Massif Paris   *see*   **Mount Paris**

Mount Paris. 68°58′S, 70°50′W. Also spelled (erroneously) as Mount Parks. 2,750 m. 4 miles SE of Mount Bayonne in the northern part of Alexander Island. Named by Charcot in 1908–10 for the capital of his country. He called it Massif Paris. In 1936 the BGLE charted it as mountains, calling them the Paris Mountains. However, studies of photos taken by the RARE 1947–48 show that this is a single mountain.

Paris Mountains   *see*   **Mount Paris**

Paris Peak. 64°30′S, 63°22′W. 1,645 m. 4 miles NE of Mount Priam in the Trojan Range on Anvers Island. Surveyed by the FIDS in 1955. Named by the UK for the Homeric character.

Parizhskaya Kommuna Glacier. 71°38′S, 12°04′E. 8 miles long. Flows between Zwiesel Mountain and Gråkammen Ridge to Humboldt Graben in the Petermann Ranges of the Wohlthat Mountains. Discovered by Ritscher's 1938–39 expedition. Named Lednik Parizhskoy Kommuny (Paris Commune Glacier) by the USSR in 1966.

Lednik Parizhskoy Kommuny *see* **Parizhskaya Kommuna Glacier**

Mount Park. 67°14'S, 51°E. 3 miles west of Mount Tomlinson in the NE part of the Scott Mountains of Enderby Land. Named by the Australians for J.A. Park.

Park, David B. Sailmaker's mate on the Wilkes Expedition 1838–42. Joined in the USA. Served the cruise.

Park, J.A. Crew member on the *Discovery* during the BANZARE 1929–31.

Park Glacier. 74°20'S, 110°38'W. On the northern part of the Bear Peninsula. It flows to the sea along the west side of the Gurnon Peninsula, in Marie Byrd Land. Named for Chung G. Park, ionosphere physics researcher at Byrd Station in 1966.

The *Parker*. Ship on the Argentine Antarctic Expedition of 1947–48. Captain Guillermo José Zarrabeitia.

Mount Parker. 71°15'S, 168°05'E. 1,260 m. A bluff-type mountain. On the west side of the Nash Glacier in the Admiralty Mountains of Victoria Land. This may or may not be the Mount Parker seen by Ross from his ship in 1840, but it is in the general area. Vice Adm. Sir William Parker was a senior lord of the admiralty from 1834–41.

Parker, Alton N. From Mississippi. Aviation pilot on the shore party of Byrd's 1928–30 expedition. He was the first ashore.

Parker, George. Captain of the topsail on the Wilkes Expedition 1838–42. Joined in the USA. Run at Sydney.

Parker, Thomas. Seaman on the Wilkes Expedition 1838–42. Joined at Rio. Run at Sydney.

Parker Bluff. 86°17'S, 145°38'W. At the south end of the California Plateau. Overlooks the Van Reeth Glacier, about 5 miles east of Mount Blackburn in the Queen Maud Mountains. Named for John J. Parker, VX-6 photographer, 1966 and 1967.

Parker Glacier. 73°47'S, 165°33'E. A valley glacier in the Mountaineer Range

of Victoria Land. It flows from the area just east and NE of Mount Monteagle, and flows south to Lady Newnes Bay where it terminates in a floating glacier tongue adjacent to Andrus Point. Named for Anthony G.H. Parker, biologist at Hallett Station in 1963–64, and at McMurdo Station in 1964–65 and in 1966–67.

Parker Hill. 68°31'S, 78°26'E. Over 135 m. Just east of Lake Cowan in the eastern part of the Vestfold Hills. A wind-run pole was erected here by an ANARE party from Davis Station in 1969. Named by the Australians for Dr. D. Parker, officer-in-charge and medical officer at Davis Station in 1969.

Parker Mesa. 77°15'S, 160°55'E. Snow-covered. 4 miles SE of Skew Peak, in the southern part of the Clare Range of Victoria Land. Named for Bruce C. Parker, biologist on the Antarctic Peninsula in the 1969–70 summer season and in Victoria Land during the 1973–74 and 1974–75 seasons.

Parker Pass. 75°53'S, 142°48'W. Ice-covered. On the south side of Zuncich Hill in Marie Byrd Land. It leads from the head of Siemiatkowski Glacier to the névé area to the SW of El-Sayed Glacier. Named for Dana C. Parker, geophysicist at McMurdo Station, 1967–68.

Parker Peak. 72°14'S, 97°30'W. At the base of Evans Peninsula, in the Walker Mountains of Thurston Island. Named for Alton N. Parker.

Parkinson Peak. 69°33'S, 159°E. 690 m. Pyramidal. Near the coast in the north-central part of the Wilson Hills, between Tomilin and Noll Glaciers. Visited in March 1961 by an ANARE airborne field party led by Phillip Law from the *Magga Dan*. Named by the Australians for W.D. Parkinson, geophysicist with the expedition.

Mount Parks *see* **Mount Paris**

Parks Glacier. 77°07'S, 125°55'W. Flows from the Weiss Amphitheater, in the southern part of Mount Sidley, in the

Executive Committee Range of Marie Byrd Land. Named for Perry E. Parks, Jr., exploration geophysicist and assistant seismologist on the Marie Byrd Land Traverse of 1959–60.

Parmelee Massif. 70°58′S, 62°10′W. West of the base of Imshaug Peninsula at the head of Lehrke Inlet, on the east coast of Palmer Land. Named for David F. Parmelee, biologist who studied birds of the Antarctic Peninsula from aboard icebreakers in the seasons 1972–73, 1973–74, and 1974–75.

Parpen Crags. 60°35′S, 45°49′W. Isolated rock face near the head of Norway Bight on the south side of Coronation Island in the South Orkneys. Surveyed by the FIDS in 1948–50 and named by the UK. Parpen is a masonry term meaning a stone extending through the thickness of a wall.

Cape Parr. 81°14′S, 161°04′E. Snow-covered. On the west side of the Ross Ice Shelf. 8 miles south of Gentile Point. Discovered by Scott's 1901–4 expedition, and named by Scott for Adm. Alfred Arthur Chase Parr, Arctic explorer and one of Scott's advisors.

Parrish Peak. 79°55′S, 82°01′W. 1,775 m. Partly snow-topped. Surmounts the ridge just to the south of Seal Glacier in the Enterprise Hills of the Heritage Range. Named for Edward N. Parrish, glaciologist on the first two South Pole–Queen Maud Land traverses, 1964–65 and 1965–66.

Mount Parry. 64°16′S, 62°25′W. Also called Parry Berg. 2,520 m. East of Minot Point. It dominates the central part of Brabant Island. Named by Henry Foster in 1829.

Parry Berg *see* **Mount Parry**

Parry Patch. 62°17′S, 59°22′W. A shoal in the Nelson Strait, 3 miles NW of Harmony Point, Nelson Island, in the South Shetlands. Named by the UK in 1961 in order to preserve the name Parry in the area. What Richard Sherratt had called Parry's Straits in 1820–21 had long ago become Nelson Strait.

Parry Point. 79°30′S, 30°20′W. North of the mouth of Slessor Glacier. 25 miles SW of Mount Faraway in the Theron Mountains, on the east side of the Filchner Ice Shelf. Named by the BCTAE in 1957–58 for Adm. Cecil R.L. Parry, secretary to the BCTAE 1955–58.

Parry's Straits *see* **Nelson Strait**

Mount Parsons. 67°47′S, 62°35′E. 1,120 m. 1 mile SSW of the northern extremity of the David Range. Photographed by the LCE 1936–37. Visited in Jan. 1956 by an ANARE party led by J.M. Béchervaise. Named by the Australians for Neville Parsons, cosmic ray physicist at Mawson Station in 1955.

Punta Partida *see* **Start Point**

Partizan Island. 68°31′S, 78°10′E. Hook-shaped. 3 miles long. In the middle of the entrance to Langnes Fjord in the Vestfold Hills. Photographed by the LCE 1936–37. Named Ongulöy (fishhook island) by the Norwegians, but subsequently renamed by the USSR in 1956 as Ostrov Partizan (partisan island) in order to avoid confusion with Ongul Island.

Partridge Nunatak. 75°42′S, 140°20′W. The most westerly of three aligned nunataks south of the Ickes Mountains in Marie Byrd Land. It is 730 meters high and is on the north side of White Glacier, 5 miles west of Bailey Nunatak. Named for Billy W. Partridge, USN, chief equipment operator at Byrd Station in 1966.

Gora Parus *see* **Småsponen Nunatak**

Parvenu Point. 67°34′S, 67°17′W. Forms the northern extremity of Pourquoi Pas Island, off the west coast of Graham Land. Surveyed in 1936 by the BGLE, and again in 1948 by the FIDS, who found it to be more conspicuous from the west than had been supposed, hence the name.

Mount Parviainen. 66°45′S, 51°07′E. Just NE of Mount Henksen, in the northern part of the Tula Mountains of Enderby Land. Named by the Australians for L. Parviainen.

Parviainen, L. Crew member on the *Discovery* during the BANZARE 1929–31.

Pascal Island. 66°47′S, 141°29′E. 350 yards ESE of Descartes Island and 1 mile NE of Cape Mousse off the coast of East Antarctica. Charted by the French in 1951 and named by them for Blaise Pascal (1623–1662), French physician and philosopher.

Paschal Glacier. 75°54′S, 140°40′W. 20 miles long. 4 miles wide. Flows NW between 2 ridges, the terminal points of which are Mount McCoy and Lewis Bluff. The lower end of this glacier merges with the flow of White Glacier and Land Glacier near Mount McCoy before Land Glacier ends up in Land Bay on the coast of Marie Byrd Land. Named for Evans W. Paschal, scientific leader at Byrd Station, 1970.

Mount Pasco. 66°59′S, 54°44′E. West of Edward VIII Bay. 18 miles WSW of Mount Storegutt. Named by the Australians for Cdr. C. Pasco, RN, member of the Australian Antarctic Exploration Committee of 1886.

Passage Rock. 62°23′S, 59°45′W. In the Aitcho Islands in the South Shetlands. At the northern entrance to English Strait. ½ mile west of Fort William on Robert Island. Charted in 1935 by personnel on the *Discovery II,* and named by them because it is a guide to shipping passing through the strait.

The *Passat.* One of the Dornier flying boats on the German New Schwabenland Expedition of 1938–39 led by Ritscher. (*See* **The *Boreas*** for description. Both planes were the same type.)

Passat Nunatak. 71°18′S, 3°55′W. 145 m. Almost a mile NE of Boreas Nunatak at the mouth of the Schytt Glacier in Queen Maud Land. Discovered by the Ritscher expedition of 1938–39, and named by Ritscher for the *Passat.*

Mount Passel. 76°53′S, 144°56′W. Ridgelike. 4 miles north of the Swanson Mountains, in the Ford Ranges of Marie Byrd Land. Discovered in Dec. 1940 by a party from West Base during the USAS 1939–41. Named for Charles F. Passel (q.v.), radio operator with that party.

Passel, Charles F. Geologist and radio operator at West Base during the USAS 1939–41.

Passel Pond. 76°53′S, 145°05′W. A meltwater pond at the SW foot of Mount Passel in the Denfeld Mountains of the Ford Ranges of Marie Byrd Land. Mapped by the USAS 1939–41. Named in association with the nearby mountain.

Passes Peak. 63°27′S, 57°03′W. 535 m. Pyramidal. Just south of Mount Carrel, and 2 miles south of the head of Hope Bay, at the NE end of the Antarctic Peninsula. Charted in 1945 by the FIDS, and named by them because it lies between two passes used by Base D sledging parties while traveling to Duse Bay and to the head of Depot Glacier.

Pasteur Island. 66°37′S, 140°06′E. At the SE end of the Dumoulin Islands just north of the Astrolabe Glacier Tongue. Charted by the French in 1949–51 and named by them in 1951–52 for Louis Pasteur (1822–1895), the French chemist.

Pasteur Peninsula. 64°04′S, 62°24′W. 5 miles long in a north-south direction, and between 5 and 8 miles broad. Between Guyou Bay and Bouquet Bay, it forms the northern end of Brabant Island. Named by Charcot in 1903–5 for Louis Pasteur (*see* **Pasteur Island**).

Pastor Peak. 85°54′S, 134°42′W. 2,000 m. On the north wall of Colorado Glacier, between Teller Peak and the Eblen Hills, on the ridge descending from the Michigan Plateau. Named for Stephen E. Pastor, equipment operator at the AirOpFac (the early McMurdo Base) in 1956, at Byrd Station in 1960, and at McMurdo Station in 1964.

Pastorizo Bay. 63°54′S, 57°17′W. 2 miles wide. Indents the south side of Vega Island, just west of Mahogany Bluff. Named by the Argentines before 1959.

The *Patagonia.* Transport ship on the 1946–47 Argentine Antarctic Expedition

(Capt. L.M. Maloberti). It was also on the 1948 Argentine Naval maneuvers led by Admiral Cappus.

Patcha Point. 64°37'S, 62°08'W. The southern end of Nansen Island in Wilhelmina Bay off the west coast of Graham Land. Charted by de Gerlache in 1897–99. Named by the UK in 1960 for Jan Patcha, helicopter pilot with the FIDASE 1955–57, which photographed this area.

Patella Island. 63°08'S, 55°29'W. Also called Isla Ruiz. Over 75 m. 2 miles NW of Ambush Bay off the north coast of Joinville Island. Surveyed by the FIDS in 1953. Named by the UK for its limpet shape (patella is Latin for limpet).

Paternoster Valley. 60°41'S, 45°37'W. Extends southwestward from Stygian Cove in northern Signy Island in the South Orkneys. Named by the UK for the three small paternoster lakes (small lakes in rock basins in a glacial valley) at different levels in the valley.

Paternostro Glacier. 69°24'S, 158°37' E. 11 miles long. In the Wilson Hills. It flows between Cook Ridge and the Goodman Hills to enter the eastern part of Davies Bay. Named for Lt. (jg) Joseph L.A. Paternostro, USNR, Hercules aircraft navigator, 1967 and 1968.

Mount Paterson. 78°02'S, 154°36'W. Also spelled (erroneously) Mount Patterson. Pyramidal. 2 miles NE of Mount Schlossbach, at the NE end of the southern group of the Rockefeller Mountains, on the Edward VII Peninsula. Discovered by Byrd's 1928–30 expedition and later named by Byrd for Seward M. Paterson, manufacturer who furnished shoes and ski boots for Byrd's 1933–35 expedition.

Paterson Islands. 67°32'S, 63°10'E. 4 miles NE of the Klung Islands, close to the coast of Mac. Robertson Land. Photographed by the LCE 1936–37. Named by the Australians for A.J.F. Paterson, supervisory technician (radio) at Mawson Station in 1963.

Patience Rocks. 67°45'S, 68°56'W. 1½ miles NW of Avian Island, just off the south end of Adelaide Island. Named by the UK for Leading Engineer Mechanic Donald Patience, a member of the RN Hydrographic Survey Unit which charted this area in 1963.

Paton, James. British seaman who has the distinction of being the first man on Beaufort Island in the Ross Sea. As a crew member on the *Morning* in 1903, he left the ship against orders, crossed the ice, and walked onto the island. Presumably he was castigated on his return to the ship. This did not stop him returning in the *Morning* the following year, 1904, part of Scott's relief party. He was back again on the *Nimrod*, during the second half of Shackleton's expedition, i.e., 1908–9, and again on the *Terra Nova*, first when that ship took Scott down to the Antarctic, and again in 1912 when it came to pick him up (Scott was, of course, dying on the trail at that time, and never made it back). Paton was back in Antarctica on the *Aurora* in 1914–16, as part of the Ross Sea expedition, itself a part of Shackleton's ill-fated British Imperial Transantarctic Expedition of 1914–17.

Paton Peak. 76°57'S, 166°57'E. 740 m. The highest point on Beaufort Island in the Ross Archipelago. Named by the New Zealanders in 1958–59 for James Paton.

Patricia Islands. 66°51'S, 56°47'E. Also called Georges Islands. Three small islands 15 miles SW of Austnes Point in the western part of Edward VIII Bay. Discovered and named in Feb. 1936 by personnel on the *William Scoresby*.

Mount Patrick. 84°13'S, 172°E. Mostly ice-covered. In the Commonwealth Range. 2,380 m. Just east of Wedge Face on the eastern side of the Beardmore Glacier. Discovered and named by Shackleton's expedition of 1907–9.

Patrick Automatic Weather Station. 89°53'S, 45°E. An American AWS at the South Pole (or close to it). It began operating on Jan. 28, 1986.

Patrick Nunatak. 84°04'S, 55°35'W. 3½ miles SE of Gambacorta Peak in the southern part of the Neptune Range in the Pensacola Mountains. Named for Frank M. Patrick, aerographer at Ellsworth Station, 1958.

Patrick Point. 73°28'S, 66°51'E. The northern point of Cumpston Massif at the junction of the Mellor and Lambert Glaciers in the Prince Charles Mountains. Named by the Australians for Patrick Albion, radio operator at Mawson Station in 1956.

Patriot Hills. 80°20'S, 81°25'W. A line of rock hills 5 miles long, 3 miles east of the north end of the Independence Hills in Horseshoe Valley, in the Heritage Range of the Ellsworth Mountains, just south of the Ronne Ice Shelf. There is an ice runway here, and a base camp, both built by Adventure Network International. Named in association with the Heritage theme.

Patroclus Hill. 64°28'S, 63°37'W. Rounded. Snow-covered. 760 m. Separated by a low col from the NW side of Mount Achilles in the Achaean Range of Anvers Island. Surveyed by the FIDS in 1955 and named by the UK for the Homeric character.

Mount Patterson *see* **Mount Paterson**

Patterson, James. Landsman on the Wilkes Expedition 1838–42. Joined in the USA. Returned home in the *Relief,* 1839.

Patterson Peak. 85°44'S, 155°59'W. 1,610 m. At the south end of Medina Peaks. 4 miles NW of Anderson Ridge, in the Queen Maud Mountains. Named for Clair C. Patterson, glaciologist at Byrd Station, 1965–66.

Patterson Rock. 66°13'S, 110°35'E. A rock in water ½ mile west of Cameron Island in the Swain Islands. Surveyed in 1957 by a party led by Carl Eklund from Wilkes Station, and named by Eklund for Acy H. Patterson, USN, electrician at that station in 1957.

Patton, James. Surgeon on the *Resolution* during Cook's voyage of 1772–75.

Patton Bluff. 75°13'S, 133°40'W. Between Shibuya Peak and Coleman Nunatak on the east side of Berry Glacier in Marie Byrd Land. Named for Delbert E. Patton, ionosphere physicist at Byrd Station in 1962.

Patton Glacier. 78°16'S, 85°25'W. It flows from the eastern slope of the main ridge of the Sentinel Range, between Mounts Ostenso and Tyree, to enter Ellen Glacier. Named for Sgt. Richard J. Patton (*see* **Parachutes**).

Patuxent Ice Stream. 85°15'S, 67°45' W. Between the Patuxent Range and the Pecora Escarpment in the Pensacola Mountains. It flows northwestward to the upper part of the Foundation Ice Stream. Named in association with the nearby range.

Patuxent Mountains *see* **Patuxent Range**

Patuxent Range. 84°43'S, 64°30'W. One of the major ranges of the Pensacola Mountains. It comprises the Thomas Hills, the Anderson Hills, Mackin Table, and several nunataks and ridges bounded by the Foundation Ice Stream, the Academy Glacier, and the Patuxent Ice Stream. Discovered aerially on Jan. 13, 1956 (*see* the Chronology). Named originally as the Patuxent Mountains, for the US Naval Air Station at Cedar Point, Md., on the south side of the mouth of the Patuxent River. This was VX-6's first base in the USA. The range was redefined as such later.

Paul, B.W. 1st assistant engineer on the *Jacob Ruppert,* 1933–35.

Mount Paul Block *see* **Mount Block**

Paul Block Bay *see* **Block Bay**

Paul Islands. 64°16'S, 63°44'W. 3 miles in extent. NW of Quinton Point off the NW coast of Anvers Island. Discovered and named by Dallmann in 1873–74.

Mount Paul Lee *see* **Mount Lee**

Mount Paulcke. 65°59'S, 64°53'W. 915 m. West of Huitfeldt Point, at Barilari Bay, on the west coast of Graham Land. Named by the UK in 1959 for Wilhelm Paulcke (1873–1949), pioneer in long-distance ski-mountaineering.

Paulding Bay. 66°35'S, 123°15'E. On the coast of East Antarctica, just west of Clark Point. The outer portions of the bay are bounded by the Moscow University Ice Shelf and the Voyeykov Ice Shelf. Named for James K. Paulding (1778–1860), dramatist who also happened to be secretary of the Navy under President Van Buren. Prior to that he had been instrumental in outfitting the Wilkes Expedition 1838–42.

Paulet Island. 63°35'S, 55°47'W. Circular. 1 mile in diameter. 3 miles SE of Dundee Island, off the coast of the Antarctic Peninsula. Discovered by Ross during his expedition of 1839–43, and named by him for Lord George Paulet, Capt. RN. One of the Nordenskjöld expedition huts is on this island.

Pauling Islands. 66°32'S, 66°58'W. Also called Islotes Condell, Grupo Malleco. 3 miles SE of the Barcroft Islands in Crystal Sound, off the west coast of Graham Land. Surveyed by the FIDS in 1958–59. Named by the UK for Linus C. Pauling (b. 1901), US chemist who, in the mid-1930s, originated a theory of the structure of ice.

Pauls Hole. 64°41'S, 62°38'W. A small harbor on the east side of Rongé Island, just south of Cuverville Island, off the west coast of Graham Land. Named by whalers in the area before 1921.

Paulsen, Karl-Heinz. Oceanographer on the German New Schwabenland Expedition of 1938–39, led by Ritscher.

Paulsen Mountains. 72°10'S, 1°21'E. In the northern part of the Sverdrup Mountains in Queen Maud Land. Discovered on the German New Schwabenland Expedition of 1938–39, and named by Ritscher for Karl-Heinz Paulsen.

Mount Paulus. 72°37'S, 31°E. 2,420 m. Just south of Mount Rossel in the SW

part of the Belgica Mountains. Discovered by the Belgian Antarctic Expedition of 1957–58, led by Gaston de Gerlache, who named it for Jean-Pierre Paulus, a patron of the expedition.

Paulus Glacier. 69°24'S, 70°31'W. In the northern part of Alexander Island.

Paumelle, R. Steward of the *Français* during Charcot's first Antarctic expedition of 1903–5.

Paumelle Point. 65°04'S, 64°03'W. Marks the south side of the entrance to Libois Bay and the NW end of the peninsula which forms the western extremity of Booth Island in the Wilhelm Archipelago. Charted by Charcot in 1903–5, and named by him for R. Paumelle.

The *Pavel Korchagin*. USSR ice-reinforced cargo ship supplying Molodezhnaya Station in the 1980s.

Cap Pavie *see* **Pavie Ridge**

Île Pavie *see* **Pavie Ridge**

Pavie Ridge. 68°34'S, 66°59'W. An isolated rocky ridge over 500 m. It extends south and west from Martin Glacier to Moraine Cove, and forms the SE limit of the Bertrand Ice Piedmont, on the west coast of Graham Land. Charcot, in 1909 named a feature in this area as Île Pavie, for Auguste J.M. Pavie (1847–1925), French diplomat and explorer. As Charcot was not sure whether this was an island or a cape, he also called it Cap Pavie, just to be sure. He put the feature at 68°27'S, 66°40'W. Maurice Bongrain, during the expedition, made sketches of this feature from a position 15 miles SE of Jenny Island. In 1936 the BGLE, who were surveying this area, could not find this island/cape, but in 1948 the FIDS, using Bongrain's sketches, identified it as a feature which the BGLE in 1936 had called Red Rock Ridge. Red Rock Ridge stuck, and the name Pavie Ridge was given to this other feature, not far away.

Pavlak Glacier. 82°58'S, 163°12'E. Flows from the Queen Elizabeth Range into Lowery Glacier just south of Mount Predoehl. Named for Thomas L. Pavlak, glaciologist at Amundsen-Scott South Pole Station, 1962–63.

Pavlov Peak. 64°03'S, 61°58'W. Also called Monte Centro. North of Mount Vesalius on Liège Island. Named by the UK in 1960 for Ivan P. Pavlov (1849–1936), Russian experimental physiologist who worked on conditioned reflexes.

Pawley Nunataks. 69°59'S, 67°36'W. On the west side of the Antarctic Peninsula.

Mount Pawson. 73°10'S, 61°01'W. 7 miles SE of Mohn Peaks, on the east coast of Palmer Land. Named for David L. Pawson, biologist working in the area of the Antarctic Peninsula, off the *Eastwind* and out of Palmer Station, during the summer season of 1965–66.

Pawson Peak. 62°11'S, 58°28'W. Between Sphinx Hill and Hervé Cove on King George Island in the South Shetlands.

Payer Group *see* **Payer Mountains**

Payer Mountains. 72°02'S, 14°35'E. Also called the Payer Group. A group of scattered mountains extending north-south for 23 miles. 10 miles east of the Weyprecht Mountains. They form the eastern half of the Hoel Mountains in central Queen Maud Land. Discovered during Ritscher's 1938–39 expedition and named by Ritscher for Julius von Payer (1842–1915), Austrian Arctic explorer who, with Karl Weyprecht, in 1873 discovered Franz Josef Land, now the most northerly territory of the USSR.

Paz Cove. 66°14'S, 100°47'E. 1 mile wide and 4 miles long. Indents the northern side of the Bunger Hills, 2½ miles SE of Cape Henderson. Named for H.J. Paz, air crewman on Operation Highjump, 1946–47.

Peace Island. 64°18'S, 62°57'W. Also called Isla Iota. The most northerly of several islands which extend northward about a mile from the western extremity of Eta Island in the Melchior Islands. Surveyed by personnel of the Discovery Committee in 1927, and probably named by them.

Peachey, A.T.G.C. Captain of the *Queen of Bermuda* in 1941.

The *Peacock.* 559-ton American sloop of war, 118 feet long, 31½ feet in the beam, 15½ feet depth in hold, 10 guns, 11 knot speed, with a crew of 130. In 1828 it was selected for the US Government Expedition which never took place. 10 years later, and in disastrous condition, it took part in the Wilkes Expedition 1838–42, and, under the command of Capt. William L. Hudson, acted as consort to Wilkes's flagship, the *Vincennes.* In March 1839, during the first foray of the expedition into Antarctic waters, the *Peacock* and the *Flying Fish* sailed along the edge of the pack-ice off the west coast of the Antarctic Peninsula, as far as the north of Thurston Island. Later, the *Peacock* got hit badly by icebergs, and had to return to Sydney in 1840. It was wrecked in the USA in 1841.

Mount Peacock. 72°13'S, 169°27'E. 3,210 m. Directly at the head of Kelly Glacier, just over 1½ miles SW of Mount Herschel in the Admiralty Mountains of Victoria Land. Discovered by Ross in Jan. 1841, and named by him for Dr. George Peacock, dean of Ely.

Peacock, Capt. Commander of the *Liberty,* in the South Shetlands, 1821–22.

Peacock, D. Crew member on the *Discovery* during the BANZARE 1929–31.

¹Peacock Bay *see* **Peacock Sound**

²Peacock Bay. This is probably what is now called Deakin Bay. It was discovered by Wilkes and named Peacock's Bay, for the *Peacock.*

Peacock Peak. 75°11'S, 134°30'W. 1 mile south of Bennett Bluff on the western side of the upper part of the Berry Glacier, in Marie Byrd Land. Named for Dennis S. Peacock, ionosphere physicist at Byrd Station in 1970–71.

Peacock Ridge. 66°48'S, 51°E. Between Mount Soucek and Mount Porteus in the northern part of the Tula Mountains in Enderby Land. Named by the Australians for D. Peacock.

Peacock Sound. 72°45′S, 99°W. Also called Peacock Bay. 135 miles long. 40 miles wide. It is ice-filled and is occupied by the western part of the Abbott Ice Shelf. It separates Thurston Island from the Eights Coast. Discovered in Feb. 1940 on flights from the *Bear* during the USAS 1939–41. Named for the *Peacock*.

Peacock's Bay *see* **Deakin Bay**

Péage Island. 66°46′S, 141°32′E. ½ mile SW of Cape Découverte, off the coast of East Antarctica. Charted by the French in 1951 and named by them for its position, which looks as if it commands access to the Curzon Islands for parties arriving from Port Martin. Péage is French for "toll."

Peak 1600. 78°50′S, 83°45′W. In the Sentinel Range.

Peake-Jones Rock. 67°38′S, 62°48′E. Bean-shaped. Just off the coast. 2 miles NE of Ring Rock in Holme Bay, Mac. Robertson Land. Photographed by the LCE 1936–37. Named by the Australians for K. Peake-Jones, weather observer at Mawson Station, 1959.

Peale, Titian Ramsay. b. Oct. 10, 1799, Philadelphia. d. March 13, 1885, Philadelphia. He was the naturalist on the *Peacock* during the Wilkes Expedition 1838–42, the only 1 of the 6 scientists on that expedition to go as far south as 60°S. His life and diary were published by Jessie Poesch (*see* the Bibliography).

Peale Inlet. 71°55′S, 99°12′W. 16 miles long. Ice-filled. Just west of Noville Peninsula. It indents the northern side of Thurston Island. Named for Titian Ramsay Peale.

Pear Island. 64°31′S, 62°54′W. Just SW of False Island, off the NE coast of Anvers Island. Discovered before 1929, and named by the British before 1952 for its shape.

Pearce Peak. 67°48′S, 61°12′E. 1,200 m. Partly snow-covered. It is actually a

ridge, which when seen from the north, looks like a peak. 2 miles south of Moyes Peak and 15 miles SSW of Falla Bluff. Discovered in Feb. 1931 by the BAN-ZARE, and named by Mawson for Sir George Pearce, chairman of the Australian Antarctic Committee in 1929.

Mount Pearigen. 72°01′S, 168°50′E. 3,020 m. 6 miles NW of Mount Hart in the Admiralty Mountains. Named for Lt. Cdr. Jare M. Pearigen, USN, helicopter pilot in Antarctica, 1967–68, 1968–69, and 1969–70.

Pearl Harbor Glacier. 72°15′S, 167°40′ E. Flows east from the Victory Mountains into the SW side of the Tucker Glacier 17 miles NW of Bypass Hill. Named by the New Zealanders in 1957–58 for the Americans at Pearl Harbor 16 years before.

Pearl Rocks. 63°35′S, 59°56′W. They cover an area 3 miles by 2, just off the west coast of Tower Island in the Palmer Archipelago. Named by the FIDASE 1955–57, and is descriptive of the several snow-covered rocks in the group.

Pearse Valley. 77°43′S, 161°32′E. Dry valley, 3 miles long, just west of Catspaw Glacier, at the south side of the Asgard Range in Victoria Land. Named for John S. Pearse, biologist at McMurdo Station in 1961 and in 1961–62.

¹Mount Pearson. 72°17′S, 166°43′E. 2,440 m. Snow-covered. At the west side of the mouth of Lensen Glacier where that glacier joins Pearl Harbor Glacier, in the Victory Mountains of Victoria Land. Named by the northern party of the NZ Federated Mountain Clubs Antarctic Expedition of 1962–63, for F.H. Pearson, surveyor with the party.

²Mount Pearson *see* **Pearson Peak**

Pearson, Jean. Science writer for the *Detroit News*, the first woman journalist in Antarctica since Edith Ronne. She went to the South Pole while covering Lois Jones's all-women expedition of 1969–70 (*see* **Women in Antarctica**).

Pearson Peak. 75°54′S, 140°57′W. Also called Mount Pearson. 1 mile south of McGaw Peak on the ridge that trends south from Mount McCoy on the coast of Marie Byrd Land. Named for Herbert E. Pearson, seismologist at Byrd Station, 1963.

Massif Peary *see* **Mount Peary**

Mount Peary. 65°15'S, 63°52'W. Also called Mount Matin, Massif Peary. 1,900 m. A massif. It has a flat, snow-covered summit several miles in extent, surmounted by a marginal peak on the west. 7 miles ENE of Cape Tuxen. It dominates the area between the Wiggins and Bussey Glaciers on the west coast of Graham Land. Discovered by Charcot in 1908–10, and named by him for Robert E. Peary (1856–1920), the man who is generally supposed to have been the first to reach the North Pole, in 1909.

Pebbly Mudstone Island. 63°18'S, 57°51'W. In the SE part of the Duroch Islands. About ⅓ mile SW of Halpern Point on Trinity Peninsula. Named by Martin Halpern (*see* **Halpern Point**) for the outcrop of pebbly mudstone found on this island.

Mount Pechell. 71°05'S, 167°16'E. 1,360 m. Surmounts the western end of Hedgpeth Heights in the Anare Mountains. Discovered and mapped in Jan. 1841 by Ross, who named it for Capt. Sir Samuel J. Brooke Pechell, a junior lord of the admiralty.

Peck, Capt. Commander of the *Richard Henry,* in the South Shetlands, 1843–45.

Peckham Glacier. 80°21'S, 157°25'E. Flows from Mount McClintock into the Byrd Glacier in the Britannia Range. Named for Verne E. Peckham, biologist at McMurdo Station in 1962. He made several dives into the water, under the sea ice, using scuba gear.

Pecora Escarpment. 85°38'S, 68°42'W. 7 miles long. 35 miles SW of the Patuxent Range. It marks the southernmost exposed rocks of the Pensacola Mountains. Named by Dwight Schmidt (*see* **Schmidt Hills**) for William T.

Pecora, eighth director of the US Geological Survey, 1965–71.

Mound Peddie. 76°01'S, 145°01'W. Isolated. 5 miles north of Webster Bluff, at the north end of the Ford Ranges in Marie Byrd Land. Named for Norman W. Peddie, seismologist at Byrd Station, 1964.

Peden Cliffs. 74°57'S, 136°28'W. 6 miles long. Breached near the center by the Rhodes Icefall. They border the north side of Garfield Glacier in the western part of the McDonald Heights in Marie Byrd Land. Named for Irene C. Peden, ionosphere physicist at Byrd Station, 1970–71.

Mount Pedersen. 72°05'S, 164°02'E. 2,070 m. 9 miles SE of Galatos Peak in the Salamander Range of the Freyberg Mountains. Named for John M. Pedersen, biologist at McMurdo Station, 1965–66 and 1966–67.

Pedersen, Morten. Norwegian whaler, captain of the *Castor* in the South Shetlands from 1893–94.

Pedersen Nunatak. 64°56'S, 60°44'W. The most westerly of the Seal Nunataks, 8 miles NE of Cape Fairweather, off the east coast of the Antarctic Peninsula. Charted in 1947 by the FIDS, and named by them for Morten Pedersen.

Monte Pedro *see* **Mount Pierre**

Punta Pedro *see* **Azufre Point**

Pedro Aguirre Station *see* **Presidente Pedro Aguirre Cerda Station**

Isla Pedro Nelson *see* **Jinks Island**

Peeler Bluff. 72°35'S, 93°20'W. Also called Peeler Point. Along the middle of the west coast of McNamara Island. It is a useful navigation mark from the seaward. Named for Lt. Cdr. James C. Peeler, USN, who camped here from Feb. 7–9, 1961, and obtained position data for the bluff and other points in the area, which was explored by personnel from the *Glacier* and *Staten Island.*

Peeler Point *see* **Peeler Bluff**

Pegasus Mountains. 71°S, 67°12'W. 16 miles long. They consist of a system of ridges and peaks broken by two passes. Between the Bertram and Ryder Glaciers, and just east of Gurney Point, on the west coast of Palmer Land. Named by the UK for the constellation.

Pegmatite Peak. 85°39'S, 154°39'W. 790 m. On the west side of the Koerwitz Glacier, between the main summits of Medina Peaks and Mount Salisbury in the Queen Maud Mountains. Named by the New Zealanders in 1969–70 for the large, whitish pegmatite dikes in a rock wall at the SE spur of the peak.

Pegmatite Point. 85°01'S, 165°20'W. Juts out into the head of the Ross Ice Shelf from the Duncan Mountains. 7 miles ENE of Mount Fairweather. Named by the New Zealanders in 1963–64 for the pegmatite found in this distinctively banded point.

Pegtop Mountain. 77°04'S, 161°15'E. Also called Pegtop Nunatak. An elongated mountain marked by several conspicuous knobs, the highest and most westerly rising to 1,395 m. At the south side of the Mackay Glacier, 3 miles west of Sperm Bluff, in Victoria Land. Mapped and named descriptively by Scott's 1910–13 expedition.

Pegtop Nunatak *see* **Pegtop Mountain**

The *Pelagos*. Norwegian factory whaling ship owned by Lars Christensen, which, on Jan. 14, 1941, was taken by Nazi raiders from the *Pinguin*.

Pelecypods. Also known as Bivalvia. All bivalves, e.g., oysters and clams, belong to this class of mollusks. Found in the Antarctic.

Peleg Peak. 65°51'S, 62°33'W. 920 m. On the massif between Flask Glacier and Leppard Glacier on the east coast of Graham Land. 4 miles north of Ishmael Peak. Surveyed by the FIDS in 1955. Named by the UK for the *Moby Dick* character.

Peletier Plateau. 83°55'S, 159°40'E. Ice-covered. 20 miles long. 5 miles wide. Forms the southern part of the Queen Elizabeth Range. Named for Rear Adm. Eugene Peletier, USN, of the Bureau of Yards and Docks, who assisted Adm. Dufek in the preparation of Operation Deep Freeze II, 1956–57.

Mount Peleus. 77°29'S, 162°05'E. 1,790 m. 3 miles west of Mount Theseus in the Olympus Range of Victoria Land. Named by the New Zealanders in 1958–59 for the Thessalian king of Greek mythology.

Peleus Glacier. Unofficial American name in the 1960s for a glacier in the area of the Wright Valley, close to Mount Peleus, in association with which it was named.

Pelias Bluff. 66°04'S, 61°23'W. Over 150 m. At the head of the inlet just west of Standring Inlet, on the northern coast of Jason Peninsula in Graham Land. Surveyed by the FIDS in 1953. Named by the UK in 1956 in association with Jason. In Greek mythology Pelias was his uncle.

Islotes Peligro *see* **Danger Islands**

Punta Peligrosa *see* **Foul Point**

Cabo Peligroso *see* **Cape Danger**

Pelletan Point. 65°06'S, 63°02'W. Also called Bayet Point. Long narrow point jutting out into the head of Flandres Bay 3 miles south of Briand Fjord, on the west coast of Graham Land. Charted by Charcot in 1903–5, and he named the indentations to the north and south of this point as one bay, Baie Pelletan. In 1960 the UK decided that these two indentations did not form one feature, and transferred the name to the point between them, and left the two indentations nameless. Charles-Camille Pelletan (1846–1915) was minister of the French Navy, 1902–5.

Pelseneer Island. 64°39'S, 62°13'W. 2 miles long. 1 mile wide. Has three prominent rocky peaks projecting through its ice-cap. 2 miles west of Brooklyn Island in the south-central part of Wilhelmina Bay, off the west coast of Graham Land. Discovered by de Gerlache in 1897–99 and named by him for P. Pelseneer, member of the *Belgica* commission and writer of some of the zoological reports of the expedition.

Pelter, J.A. Aerial photographer on the shore party of Byrd's 1933–35 expedition.

Pelter Glacier. 71°52′S, 98°20′W. 5 miles long. Flows from the east side of the Noville Peninsula into the west side of Murphy Inlet on Thurston Island. Named for J.A. Pelter.

Peltier Channel. 64°52′S, 63°32′W. 6 miles long, in a NE-SW direction. Separates Doumer and Wiencke Islands to the south of Port Lockroy, in the Palmer Archipelago. Discovered by Charcot in 1903–5 and named by him for Jean Peltier (1785–1845), French physicist.

Peltier Island. Off the coast of the Antarctic Peninsula.

Pemmican *see* **Food**

Pemmican Bluff. 73°31′S, 94°22′W. It overlooks the west side of the upper section of Basecamp Valley just west of Pillsbury Tower, in the Jones Mountains. Named by the University of Minnesota–Jones Mountains Party of 1960–61 because the bluff is composed of complex volcanic rocks giving the steep rock northern face a very mottled appearance similar to pemmican.

Pemmican Step. 72°S, 167°33′E. A steplike rise in the level of the Tucker Glacier above its junction with Leander Glacier, in Victoria Land. It is very crevassed in its southern half, but toward the northern end traveling is easier going. It is the second of the steps on this glacier. Named by the New Zealanders in 1957–58.

Penance Pass. 78°04′S, 163°51′E. The lowest and most easterly of the passes from Shangri-la to the Miers Valley. Named by the New Zealanders in 1960–61.

Penca Hill. 62°37′S, 61°07′W. At the extreme west of Livingston Island in the South Shetlands.

Cape Penck. 66°43′S, 87°43′E. Ice-covered point fronting on the West Ice Shelf. 35 miles WNW of Gaussberg. It separates the Leopold and Astrid Coast from the Wilhelm II Coast. Charted by the Western Base Party of the AAE 1911–14, and named by Mawson for Albrecht Penck (1858–1945), noted German geographer and authority on the ice ages.

¹Penck Glacier *see* **Albrecht Penck Glacier**

²Penck Glacier. 77°57′S, 34°42′W. Flows along the west side of Bertrab Glacier to Vahsel Bay. Discovered by Filchner in 1911–12, and named by him for Albrecht Penck (*see* **Cape Penck**).

Penck Ledge. 73°03′S, 4°18′W. Also called Pencksökkrabbane. Ice-covered. At the west side of the head of Penck Trough in Queen Maud Land. Named by the Norwegians in association with the trough.

Penck-Mulde *see* **Penck Trough**

Penck Trough. 73°S, 2°45′W. Also called Penck-Mulde (German), Pencksökket (Norwegian). A broad ice-filled valley trending SW-NE for 60 miles or so between the Borg Massif and the NE part of the Kirwan Escarpment, in Queen Maud Land. Discovered by Ritscher's 1938–39 expedition and named by him for Albrecht Penck (*see* **Cape Penck**).

Pencksökket *see* **Penck Trough**

Pencksökkrabbane *see* **Penck Ledge**

Pendant Ridge. 85°04′S, 174°45′W. 3 miles long. Extends SW to the north side of the mouth of McGregor Glacier. 1½ miles NW of Simplicity Hill, in the Queen Maud Mountains. Named by the Texas Tech Shackleton Glacier Expedition of 1964–65 because a pyramidal peak at its southern extremity looks as if it is dangling from the ridge like a pendant.

Baie Pendleton *see* **Pendleton Strait**

Pendleton, Capt. Commander of the *Sarah E. Spear,* in the South Shetlands, 1852–53.

Pendleton, Benjamin. Connecticut sealer who commanded three major expeditions to the South Shetlands: the Fanning-Pendleton Sealing Expeditions of 1820–21 and 1821–22, and the Palmer-Pendleton Expedition of 1829–31.

Pendleton, Harris. Commanded the *Hero* during the Fanning-Pendleton Sealing Expedition of 1821–22.

Pendleton Island *see* **Tower Island**

Pendleton Strait. 66°S, 66°30'W. Between Rabot and Lavoisier Islands in the Biscoe Islands. Charcot named it Baie Pendleton in Jan. 1909, thinking it was a bay, and naming it for Ben Pendleton. It was redefined by the BGLE in 1934–37.

Mount Pendragon. 61°15'S, 55°14'W. Also called The Fortress. 975 m. 1½ miles NW of Cape Lookout, Elephant Island in the South Shetlands. It is the highest mountain on Elephant Island. Mapped by the UK Joint Services Expedition of 1970–71, and named by the UK in 1971 for Prince Charles, the royal patron of the expedition (Pendragon is the ancient title for a British or Welsh prince).

Péndulo Refugio. Argentine refuge hut built in Telefon Bay, Deception Island, in 1949.

Pendulum Cove. 62°56'S, 60°36'W. On the NE side of Port Foster, Deception Island, in the South Shetlands. Discovered and named in 1828–29 by Henry Foster, who was here to do pendulum studies in an effort to measure gravity forces. One can swim here in the natural sulfur hot springs.

Penelope Point. 71°30'S, 169°47'E. A bold rock headland between Nielsen Glacier and Scott Keltie Glacier on the north coast of Victoria Land. Charted by Campbell's Northern Party during Scott's 1910–13 expedition, and named by them for Harry Pennell (his nickname was "Penelope").

Peneplain Peak. 83°51'S, 167°02'E. 2,650 m. Midway along Hampton Ridge, between Montgomerie Glacier and Mackellar Glacier in the Queen Alexandra Range. Named by the Ohio State University Geological Party of 1967–68 for the

excellent exposure of the Kukri Peneplain, an ancient erosion surface, present on this peak.

Penfold, D.N. RN Lt. Cdr. from Yorkshire, England. He surveyed Deception Island in 1948–49.

Penfold Point. 62°59'S, 60°35'W. Forms the NW side of the entrance to Whalers Bay, Deception Island, in the South Shetlands. Named by the UK for Lt. Cdr. D.N. Penfold, RN.

Pengin Dai *see* **Penguin Heights**

The *Penguin*. Stonington, Conn., sealing schooner of 84 tons, owned by Ephraim Williams. It went to the South Shetlands on its own expedition in 1829–31, but teamed up with the *Annawan*, and became an unofficial part of the Palmer-Pendleton Expedition of 1829–31. It had a crew of 16. Alex Palmer was captain, and Phineas Wilcox was first mate.

Penguin Heights. 68°08'S, 42°38'E. 1 mile SW of Cape Hinode on the coast of Queen Maud Land. Named Pengin Dai (Penguin Heights) by the Japanese in 1973.

¹Penguin Island. 62°06'S, 57°54'W. Also called Georges Island, Île Pingouin, Penguin Isle, Isla Pengüino. 1 mile long. Just off the south coast of King George Island. Marks the east side of the entrance to King George Bay, in the South Shetlands. Discovered by Bransfield in Jan. 1820, and named by him for the penguins seen on the shores of the island.

²Penguin Island *see* **Afuera Islands, Pingvin Island**

Penguin Isle *see* **Penguin Island**

¹Penguin Point. 60°31'S, 45°56'W. Also called Pointe Foca. Forms the NW extremity of Coronation Island in the South Orkneys. Discovered on Dec. 7, 1821, by Powell and Palmer. Named by Powell for the penguins here.

²Penguin Point. 64°19'S, 56°43'W. Also called Pinguinenkap. On the south-central shore of Seymour Island, SE of

James Ross Island, at the southern edge of the Erebus and Terror Gulf. Carl A. Larsen landed on the island in 1892 and 1893 and charted it. Nordenskjöld's expedition recharted it in 1901–4 and named it for the large penguin colony found here.

³Penguin Point. 67°39′S, 146°12′E. At the west side of the entrance to Murphy Bay on the coast of East Antarctica. 95 meters high. Marks the termination of a granite wall about 3 miles long. Discovered and named in 1912 by Cecil T. Madigan's Eastern Coastal Party during the AAE 1911–14.

Penguin rookeries. Places where penguins breed. The world's most southerly is the Adélie penguin rookery at Cape Royds, Ross Island. That island also sports other penguin rookeries. The world's largest is probably the Adélie rookery at Hope Bay, on the tip of the Antarctic Peninsula. Low flights by aircraft over rookeries are prohibited because frightened penguins leave nests and chicks unattended and undefended against predators such as skuas and petrels.

Isla Pengüino *see* **Penguin Island**

Penguins. Birds which evolved about 40 million years ago into the family *Spheniscidae.* Imagine a 6 foot tall penguin! Well, the primordial penguin was this high, or close to it. In 1930, on Seymour Island, the giant fossilized penguin *Anthropornis nordenskjöldi* was discovered. This fellow stood probably about 5½ feet tall, and weighed 200–300 pounds. There are between 16 and 25 species worldwide (no one agrees as to the exact number), ranging from the Antarctic to the Equator. You will read sources saying that there are 2 or 3 species only which inhabit Antarctica, but in fact those to be seen south of 60°S number 7, if you include the King Penguin, which used to live in the South Shetlands and South Orkneys, but not any more. The others are the gentoo penguin (or jackass penguin), the chinstrap penguin, the

macaroni penguin, the Robert Island penguin, the Adélie penguin, and the emperor penguin. These birds are perfectly adapted for swimming, diving, and the cold, and feed mostly on small fish, plankton, squids, and crustaceans, but they in turn are prey to leopard seals, skuas and petrels, killer whales, and humans, although they like people. To be fair to humans, they do not massacre penguins like they used to, and even in the old days they never killed them in the quantities in which they killed the seals. Occasionally young penguins are food for skuas and giant petrels, which is why penguins travel in flocks. They have strong homing instincts and can navigate by the sun. They have found their way home 2,000 miles away within a year. The sexes are generally alike in size and plumage (although, see each individual penguin listed above), and the eggs, usually 1 or 2, are brooded by both parents, who take no food during incubation. The young penguins are fed by regurgitated food. First studied by the Bruce expedition of 1902–4, penguins in Antarctica (except the emperor, the largest and the most magnificent) migrate north for the winter, following the new ice boundaries. They form pebble nests in the summer (the Emperor is the only one who does not). All species but the emperor are found elsewhere in the world, and the Adélie is the funniest and the most common.

Penitent Peak. 67°52′S, 67°14′W. Between Mount Breaker and Ryan Peak on Horseshoe Island. Surveyed by the FIDS in 1955–57, and named by them for the snow penitents which are a characteristic feature in the vicinity of this peak.

Pennell, Harry L.L. Lt., RN. Commander of the *Terra Nova* during the 1910–13 expedition which was Scott's last trip south (or anywhere, for that matter). After leaving Scott at Ross Island, Pennell (nicknamed "Penelope" by his men) did oceanography studies in the Ross Sea, and explored large sections of Oates Land and Victoria Land.

Pennell Bank. 74°S, 177°E. A submarine feature of the Ross Sea. Thought to be a vast terminal moraine (*see* **Moraines**), or ridge of glacier-deposited material, it was possibly the extent of the Ross Sea during the ice age. Named for Harry Pennell.

Pennell Coast. 71°S, 167°E. The northern part of Victoria Land, between Cape Williams and Cape Adare. Named by New Zealand in 1961 for its discoverer, Harry Pennell.

Pennell Glacier *see* **Matusevich Glacier**

Pennell Glacier Tongue *see* **Matusevich Glacier Tongue**

Penney Bay. 66°26′S, 110°36′E. Extends from Robinson Ridge to Browning Peninsula at the east side of the Windmill Islands. Named for Richard L. Penney, Australian ornithologist and biologist at Wilkes Station in 1959 and 1960.

Penney Landing. 66°22′S, 110°28′E. The only practical landing place toward the eastern end of Ardery Island in the Windmill Islands. Discovered in 1959 by Richard L. Penney (*see* **Penney Bay**), for whom it was named by the Australians.

Penney Ravine. 66°22′S, 110°27′E. A small ravine on Ardery Island in the Windmill Islands. It is on the northern side of the island, just west of the center. Discovered in Feb. 1960 by a biological field party from Wilkes Station. Named by the Australians for Richard L. Penney (*see* **Penney Bay**).

Lake Pennilea *see* **Kroner Lake**

Penny, Thomas. Ordinary seaman on the Wilkes Expedition 1838–42. Joined in the USA. Run at Oahu.

Penny Lake. 78°16′S, 163°12′E. A coin-shaped lake (hence the name) perched in moraine near the mouth of Roaring Valley, just south of the Walcott Glacier in Victoria Land. It was the site of a base camp of the VUWAE 1960–61, and was named by them.

Penny Point. 80°48′S, 160°41′E. Ice-covered. On the south side of Nicholson Peninsula. Marks the northern side of the entrance to Matterson Inlet, along the Ross Ice Shelf. Named for Lt. Cdr. H.C. Penny, USN, commander of the *Vance*, ocean station ship in support of aircraft flights between NZ and Antarctica in 1961–62.

The *Penola.* The BGLE ship, 1934–37. A 130-ton Brittany fishing schooner with twin auxiliary screws, it was built in 1905, and bought by Rymill for £3,000. He renamed it the *Penola*, for his home town in Australia. Its rig was altered in the Falklands to one more suited to the ice, but its engine mounting was misaligned. It sailed to the Antarctic from the Falklands (*see* **British Graham Land Expedition**).

Glacier Penola *see* **Zélée Glacier**

Penola Island. 62°03′S, 57°51′W. In Sherratt Bay, just off the south coast of King George Island in the South Shetlands. Charted in 1937 by personnel on the *Discovery II*, and named for the *Penola*, the BGLE ship which helped the *Discovery II* look for a survey party stranded on King George Island in Jan. 1937.

Penola Strait. 65°10′S, 64°07′W. 11 miles long. An average of 2 miles wide. Separates the Argentine Islands, Petermann Island, and Hovgaard Island from the west coast of Graham Land. Traversed by de Gerlache on Feb. 12, 1898. Named by the BGLE 1934–37 for their ship, the *Penola.*

Roca Peñón *see* **Fort Point**

Penrod Nunatak. 85°35′S, 134°53′W. 2 miles NW of Abbey Nunatak, at the west side of the Reedy Glacier, just north of the mouth of the Kansas Glacier. Named for Jack R. Penrod, builder at Byrd Station, 1957.

Pensacola Mountains. 83°45′S, 55°W. Extend 280 miles in a NE-SW direction. Comprise the Argentina Range, Forrestal Range, Dufek Massif, Cordiner Peaks,

Neptune Range, Patuxent Range, Rambo Nunataks, and Pecora Escarpment. Discovered aerially on Jan. 13, 1956 (see the Chronology). Named for the US Naval Air Station in Pensacola, Florida, in honor of that establishment's role in training so many US Navy aviators.

Penseroso Bluff. 71°04'S, 160°06'E. 1,945 m. Surmounts the narrow northern neck of the Daniels Range, 10 miles NE of Mount Nero, in the Usarp Mountains. The Northern Party of the NZGSAE 1963–64 reached it on a gloomy day, and the bluff appeared dark and sombre, hence the name, from Milton's *Il Penseroso* (a title meaning "the brooding one"), in antithesis to Allegro Valley, 14 miles to the south.

Pensyl, Samuel. Private of Marines on the Wilkes Expedition 1838–42. Joined in the USA and served the cruise.

The *Penzhina*. A 1970s USSR diesel-electric cargo ship of the icebreaker class, sometimes in the Antarctic.

The *Pep Boy's Snowman?* The Kellett autogiro, NR 2615, taken by Byrd on his 1933–35 expedition. It was the first rotary-winged aircraft to be used in Antarctica, or any polar region, and crashed on Sept. 28, 1934, at Little America.

Cape Pépin. 66°32'S, 138°34'E. Ice-covered. Between Ravin Bay and Barré Glacier on the coast of East Antarctica. Discovered by Dumont d'Urville in 1840, and named by him for his wife, Adèle Pépin. Charted by the AAE in 1912–13, and again by the BANZARE in 1931.

Pepper Peak. 83°12'S, 57°55'W. 940 m. 2 miles north of Mount Nervo in the Schmidt Hills of the Neptune Range. Named for Clifford G. Pepper, hospital corpsman at Ellsworth Station, 1958.

Isla Pequeña *see* **Small Island**

Pequod Glacier. 65°30'S, 62°03'W. Over 15 miles long. Flows east into Exasperation Inlet on the east coast of Graham Land. It is parallel to and just south of Melville Glacier. The lower reaches were surveyed by the FIDS in 1947 and the upper reaches in 1955. Named by the UK for the ship in *Moby Dick*.

Per Nunatak. 71°52'S, 7°04'E. 4 miles NE of Larsen Cliffs in the Mühlig-Hofmann Mountains of Queen Maud Land. Named by the Norwegians for Per Larsen, steward with the Norwegian Antarctic Expedition of 1956–57.

Per Rock. 71°17'S, 11°26'E. Almost a mile north of Pål Rock in the Arkticheskiy Institut Rocks, at the NW extremity of the Wohlthat Mountains of Queen Maud Land. Discovered aerially by the Ritscher expedition of 1938–39. Name means "Peter" in Norwegian (*see also* **Pål Rock**—Peter and Paul).

Per Spur. 71°19'S, 12°36'E. Also called Persaksla. Marks the northern extremity of the Östliche Petermann Range in the Wohlthat Mountains of Queen Maud Land. Discovered by Ritscher's expedition of 1938–39. Named by the Norwegians for J. Per Madsen, meteorologist with the Norwegian Antarctic Expedition of 1958–59.

Peralta Rocks. 63°16'S, 58°08'W. 8 small rocks. They cover an area of 4 miles by 2 miles. 7 miles north of Cape Ducorps, Trinity Peninsula. Named by the Chilean Antarctic Expedition of 1949–50 for Lt. Roberto Peralta Bell, second-in-command of the *Lientur*.

Cape Perce *see* **Perce Point**

Perce, Earl B. Co-pilot and radio operator at East Base during the USAS 1939–41. Later, 1946–47, he was on Operation Highjump.

Perce Point. 72°08'S, 74°38'W. Ice-covered. 12 miles WNW of Berlioz Point on the southern coast of Beethoven Peninsula, Alexander Island. Discovered by Snow, Perce, and Carroll on a flight from East Base on Dec. 22, 1940, during the USAS 1939–41. Named Cape Perce, for Earl B. Perce. Later redefined.

Perch Island. 66°S, 65°22'W. Just off Prospect Point in the Fish Islands, off the west coast of Graham Land. Charted by the BGLE 1934–37. Named by the UK in 1959 in continuation of the fish theme.

Mount Perchot. 65°44'S, 64°10'W. 2,040 m. It is surmounted by a prominent ridge which extends in a general north-south direction. 4 miles SE of Magnier Peaks on the west coast of Graham Land. Discovered by Charcot in 1908–10 and named by him for Monsieur Perchot, an acquaintance who donated 70 pairs of boots to the expedition.

Percival, Isaac. Pilot on the Wilkes Expedition 1838–42. Joined the *Relief* at Callao, and was later transferred to the *Sea Gull.*

Mount Percy. 63°15'S, 55°49'W. Also called Percy Berg. 765 m. The highest point on Joinville Island, just north of Mount Alexander, near the center of the island. Discovered on Dec. 30, 1842, by Ross, who named it for Rear Adm. Josceline Percy, RN (1784–1856). Ross said that it is surmounted by twin peaks. It is not. So this may, or may not be, the Mount Percy described by him, but there are several other mountains of similar height in the area, and he may have seen two mountains as one.

Percy Berg *see* **Mount Percy**

Peregrinus Peak. 69°09'S, 65°50'W. Also spelled Perigrinus Peak. 1,915 m. On the north side of the Airy Glacier. 3 miles SE of Mount Timosthenes, in the central part of the Antarctic Peninsula. Surveyed by the FIDS in Dec. 1958. Named by the UK for Petrus Peregrinus de Maricourt, French crusader and the greatest experimental scientist of his time (the 13th century), who wrote the first detailed description of the compass as an instrument of navigation, in his *Epistola de Magnete* (1269).

Cape Peremennyy. 66°12'S, 105°24'E. An ice point on the coast of East Antarctica, 45 miles WNW of Merritt Island. Named by the USSR in 1956. The name means "variable," and refers to the nature of the ice coastline along the Knox Coast.

Cape Pérez. 65°24'S, 64°06'W. Between Collins Bay and Beascochea Bay on the west coast of Graham Land. Discovered by de Gerlache in 1897–99. The Belgians did not name it until 1904, when they called it Cap de Trooz in their scientific reports of de Gerlache's expedition. Meanwhile, in Nov. 1904, Charcot rediscovered it and named it Cap Trois Pérez, for the three Pérez brothers, Fernando, Leopoldo, and Manuel, of Buenos Aires. The Americans, later, shortened Charcot's name to Cape Pérez, and gave the name Trooz to a glacier 5 miles NE of the cape.

Mount Perez. 70°S, 159°32'E. 1,610 m. At the south side of the upper reaches of the Suvorov Glacier, 6 miles SW of Hornblende Bluffs, in the Wilson Hills. Named for Manuel J. Perez, USN, photographer's mate in the area in 1962–63.

Perez Glacier. 84°06'S, 177°E. 10 miles long. Flows from Mount Brennan in the Hughes Range to the Ross Ice Shelf east of the Giovinco Ice Piedmont. Named for Ensign Richard Perez, USN, VX-6 member at McMurdo Station in 1961. He was back in the Antarctic in 1963–64.

Pérez Peak. 65°25'S, 64°05'W. 1 mile SE of Cape Pérez on the peninsula between Collins Bay and Beascochea Bay in western Graham Land. Named Sommet du Grand Pérez by Charcot in 1908–10, in association with Cap Trois Pérez (now called Cape Pérez) nearby. The present name has been in general use since 1957.

Roca Perforada *see* **Hole Rock**

Périgot, Germain Hector. Crew member on the *Zélée* during Dumont d'Urville's expedition of 1837–40. He left sick at Valparaiso on May 29, 1838.

Perigrinus Peak *see* **Peregrinus Peak**

Periphery Point *see* **Rock Pile Point**

Mount Perkins. 76°32'S, 144°08'W. At the east end of the Fosdick Mountains in the Ford Ranges of Marie Byrd Land. Discovered by Byrd's 1933–35 expedition during the Northeastern Flight of Dec.

15–16, 1934, and named by Byrd for Jack E. Perkins.

Perkins, A. Walker. Seaman on the *Eleanor Bolling* during Byrd's 1928–30 expedition.

Perkins, Earle B. Biologist on the shore party of Byrd's 1933–35 expedition.

Perkins, Jack E. Biologist at West Base during the USAS 1939–41. Later, 1946–47, he was part of Operation Highjump.

Perkins Canyon. 85°27′S, 124°20′W. At the head of Quonset Glacier, between Ruseski Buttress and Mount LeSchack, on the north side of the Wisconsin Range. Named for David M. Perkins, geomagnetist at Byrd Station, 1961.

Perkins Glacier. 74°54′S, 136°37′W. 8 miles SSE of Cape Burks on the coast of Marie Byrd Land. It flows from the McDonald Heights into the east side of Hull Bay. Named for Earle B. Perkins.

Perks, R. Seaman on the *Eleanor Bolling* during Byrd's 1928–30 expedition.

The Perla Dan. Ship belonging to the J. Lauritzen Lines of Copenhagen. Has been to the Antarctic.

Perlebandet Nunataks. 71°56′S, 23°03′E. 5 miles NW of Tanngarden Peaks in the Sør Rondane Mountains. Name means "the string of pearls" in Norwegian.

Permanent ice. This is the ice of the ice shelves, the glaciers and the Polar Plateau, and is relatively permanent when compared to the sea-ice, or annual ice as it is also called.

Mount Perov. 72°34′S, 31°12′E. 2,380 m. Just west of the terminus of Norsk Polarinstitutt Glacier in the Belgica Mountains. Discovered by the Belgian Antarctic Expedition of 1957–59 under Gaston de Gerlache, who named it for Cdr. Viktor Perov, USSR pilot who rescued 4 members of this Belgian expedition after their plane crashed.

Perov Nunataks. 67°35′S, 51°06′E. On the eastern edge of the Scott Mountains. 19 miles SE of Debenham Peak. Surveyed in Nov. 1958 by an ANARE airborne field party. Named by the Australians for Viktor Perov (*see* **Mount Perov**).

Perplex Ridge. 67°39′S, 67°43′W. Over 915 m. It is composed of four rocky masses separated by small glaciers. Extends 6 miles northeastward from Lainez Point on the NW side of Pourquoi Pas Island, off the west coast of Graham Land. Discovered and charted in 1909 by Charcot. Surveyed in 1936 by the BGLE and again in 1948 by the FIDS, who named it for the confusion in trying to identify this ridge from earlier maps.

Perrier Bay. 64°23′S, 63°45′W. Also called East Perrier Bay. 6 miles wide. Indents the NW coast of Anvers Island between Giard Point and Quinton Point. Discovered by Charcot in 1903–5 and named by him for Edmond Perrier, French naturalist.

Perry, O.H. US Naval lieutenant on the Wilkes Expedition 1838–42. He was first on the *Peacock* and then on the *Vincennes.*

Perry Bay. 66°08′S, 132°49′E. 12 miles wide. Ice-filled. Indents the coast of East Antarctica between Freeman Point and Cape Keltie. Named for O.H. Perry.

Perry Range. 75°S, 134°12′W. 6 miles long, and narrow. Separates the lower ends of Venzke Glacier and Berry Glacier, where they enter the Getz Ice Shelf on the Marie Byrd Land coast. Discovered aerially in Dec. 1940 by members of West Base during the USAS 1939–41. Named for Lt. John E. Perry, USN, public works officer at McMurdo Station, 1968. He commanded the Antarctic Construction Battalion Unit from Jan. 1969 until it was decommissioned in May 1971, when he became project manager for Amundsen-Scott South Pole Station.

Perry Sound   *see*   **Nelson Strait**

Perry's Straits   *see*   **Nelson Strait**

Persaksla   *see*   **Per Spur**

Perseus Crags. 70°36′S, 66°11′W. 12 small nunataks dominated by a high whale-backed hill, on the west edge of the Dyer Plateau in Palmer Land. 30 miles ENE of Wade Point. Named by the UK for the constellation.

Mount Perseverance. 76°48′S, 162°12′ E. The high peak near the south end of the ridge from Mount Whitcombe, overlooking the lower part of the Benson Glacier in Victoria Land. So named because it was the final station occupied by the NZ Northern Survey Party of the BCTAE during a particularly long day's field work on Oct. 22, 1957.

Perskjeret *see* **Per Nunatak**

Persson Island. 64°13′S, 58°24′W. 1½ miles long. In the entrance to Röhss Bay on the SW side of James Ross Island. Discovered by Nordenskjöld's expedition of 1901–4, and named by him as N. Persson Island, for Nils Persson, a patron of the expedition. The name was later shortened.

Peru. Ratified as the 25th signatory of the Antarctic Treaty on April 10, 1981. Peru sent observers to Antarctica in 1982–83, one working with the Australians and two with the Chileans. The first Peruvian Antarctic expedition was in Jan.–March 1988, in the *Humboldt*. They studied the ecosystem in the Bransfield Strait. A Peruvian base on King George Island in the South Shetlands is a distinct possibility.

The *Peru*. US sealer from New London, in the South Shetlands in 1871–72 under the command of Capt. George Gilderdale, and in company with the *Franklin*.

Perutz Glacier. 67°36′S, 66°33′W. 10 miles long. 2 miles wide. Flows WNW into Bourgeois Fjord, just east of Thomson Head, on the west coast of Graham Land. The mouth of this glacier was surveyed in 1936 by the BGLE. The entire glacier was surveyed in 1946–47 and 1947–48 by the FIDS, who named it for Max F. Perutz of the Cavendish Laboratory, Cambridge, who was an authority on glacier flow.

Pervomayskaya Peak. 71°47′S, 11°40′ E. 2,795 m. 1 mile NE of Mount Skars-

hovden in the central portion of the Humboldt Mountains in Queen Maud Land. Discovered by the Ritscher expedition of 1938–39. Named Gora Pervomayskaya (May 1st Mountain) by the USSR in 1966.

Pesky Rocks. 66°09′S, 65°54′W. Also called Bajo Osorno. A small group of rocks, 3½ miles west of Cape Evensen, off the west coast of Graham Land. Named by the UK in 1959 because they obstruct an otherwise clear shipping route.

Mount Peter. 70°11′S, 64°56′E. Dome-shaped. 2 miles east of Mount Béchervaise in the Athos Range of the Prince Charles Mountains. Visited in Nov. 1955 by an ANARE party led by J.M. Béchervaise. Named by the Australians for Peter Crohn, geologist at Mawson Station in 1955–56.

Peter Glacier. 73°20′S, 1°09′W. Flows NE into Jutulstraumen Glacier just east of the Neumayer Cliffs and Melleby Peak in Queen Maud Land. Named by the Norwegians for Peter Melleby.

Peter Nunatak. 75°55′S, 128°33′W. 2,440 m. Conical. 3½ miles SE of Mount Petras at the southern extremity of the McCuddin Mountains in Marie Byrd Land. Named for Capt. Peter J. Anderson, USAF, technical editor, History and Research Division, US Naval Support Force, Antarctica, 1971 and 1972.

Peter Snow-Millers. Trench-cutting machines which create snow-tunnels. They are made in Switzerland by the Konrad Peter Company.

Peter I Island. 68°47′S, 90°35′W. Said as Peter the First Island. A glaciated volcanic island. 9½ miles long and 4 miles wide. In the Bellingshausen Sea, about 240 miles off the Eights Coast. It rises from the continental rise, and is one of the true oceanic islands in Antarctic waters. It was discovered at 3 p.m. on Jan. 21, 1821, by von Bellingshausen, the first land to be discovered within the Antarctic Circle. He named it for the old ruler of Russia. Charcot was the next to see it, in 1910. In 1927 the *Norvegia* dredged some rocks off its west coast, and it was first landed on on Feb. 2, 1929, by the crew of the *Norvegia*. The Norwegians call it Peter I Øy, and they claimed it on May 1, 1931. A crew from the *Burton Island* went ashore at Norvegia Bay in 1960.

Petermann Island. 65°10′S, 64°10′W. 1 mile long. Just over ½ mile wide at its broadest. 1 mile SW of Hovgaard Island in the Wilhelm Archipelago, off the west coast of the Antarctic Peninsula. Discovered by Dallmann, and named Petermann Islands (as a group) for August Petermann, the German geographer. In 1897–99 de Gerlache named the largest island in the area as Lund Island. Later, the USA renamed it yet again as Petermann Island.

Petermann Islands *see* **Petermann Island**

Petermann Range *see* **Petermann Ranges**

Petermann Ranges. 71°40′S, 12°20′E. A group of associated mountain ranges just east of the Humboldt Mountains in Queen Maud Land. They include the Östliche Petermann Range, the Westliche Petermann Range, the Mittlere Petermann Range, the Südliche Petermann Range, and the Pieck Range. Discovered by Ritscher in 1938–39 and named Petermann Range by him for August Petermann (*see* **Petermann Island**). The feature was nicely pluralized, presumably by the Australians, after the Petermann Ranges of Australia (these ranges were also named for August Petermann).

Peters Bastion. 70°27′S, 62°54′W. Mostly ice-free. The northernmost summit of the Eland Mountains in Palmer Land. Named for Cdr. Vernon W. Peters, USN, commander of VXE-6 in 1974.

Peters Butte. 85°19′S, 119°32′W. Flat-topped. On the south side of McCarthy Valley in the Long Hills of the Horlick

Mountains. Named for Norman L. Peters, meteorologist at Byrd Station, 1958.

Peters Peak. 82°14′S, 160°04′E. 2,220 m. Snow-covered. 4 miles north of Melrose Peak in the central part of the Holyoake Range. Named for Merrill J. Peters, USARP field assistant, 1962–63.

Cape Petersen. 71°56′S, 101°46′W. Ice-covered. On the north side of Thurston Island. 18 miles ENE of Cape Flying Fish. Named for Carl O. Petersen.

Mount Petersen *see* **Mount Peterson**

Petersen, Carl O. Norwegian radio engineer on the shore party of Byrd's first two expeditions.

Petersen, Hans C. Norwegian captain of the *Kista Dan*, 1954–55 and 1955–56, then of the *Magga Dan*, 1956–57, then of the *Kista Dan* again, 1957–58 and 1958–59, and then of the *Thala Dan*, 1959–61.

Petersen, Harris-Clichy. Physicist on the RARE 1947–48. In charge of meteorological, solar radiation, atmospheric refraction, and cosmic ray investigations. For his adventure *see* **Plateau Weather Station**. (*See also* his name in the Bibliography.)

Petersen Bank. Submarine feature centering on 65°45′S, 110°10′E. It is a bank extending NNW from the coast of East Antarctica, just west of the Balaena Islands. Named by the ANARE in 1957 for Hans C. Petersen.

Petersen Island. 67°35′S, 62°54′E. The largest and most northerly of the Jocelyn Islands in Holme Bay, Mac. Robertson Land. Photographed by the LCE 1936–37. Named by the Australians for Hans C. Petersen.

Petersen Peak. 80°27′S, 27°57′W. 1,215 m. 6 miles SW of the Morris Hills in the north-central part of the Shackleton Range. Named in 1957 by the BCTAE for Hans C. Petersen.

The *Peterson*. US ship DE-152 in Antarctica 1959–60.

Mount Peterson. 74°40′S, 76°59′W. Also spelled Mount Petersen. 22 miles

NW of Mount Rex in Ellsworth Land. Named by Finn Ronne in 1948 for Harris-Clichy Petersen (sic).

Peterson, Harries-Clichy *see* **Harris-Clichy Petersen**

Peterson Bluff. 71°09′S, 165°53′E. 1,480 m. On the north side of Ebbe Glacier. Forms the SE end of the broad ridge descending from Mount Bolt in the Anare Mountains. Named for Donald C. Peterson, USN, photographer's mate with VX-6 at McMurdo Station in 1967–68 and 1968–69.

Peterson Glacier. 66°25′S, 110°44′E. Flows west into Penney Bay opposite Herring Island in the Windmill Islands. Named for Louie N. Peterson, radio operator and recorder on Operation Windmill, 1947–48.

Peterson Hills. 75°50′S, 67°55′W. Just east of Spear Glacier, between the Hauberg Mountains and the Wilkins Mountains, in Ellsworth Land. Named for D.G. Peterson, electronics technician at Amundsen-Scott South Pole Station in 1963.

Peterson Icefalls. 70°05′S, 72°44′E. A line of icefalls at the terminus of Stevenson Glacier, where that glacier enters the east part of the Amery Ice Shelf. Named by US cartographer John H. Roscoe in 1952 for J.C. Peterson, Jr., air crewman on Operation Highjump, 1946–47, on flights which provided the photos from which Roscoe was to work 5 years later.

Peterson Island. 66°28′S, 110°30′E. 2 miles long. Has two inlets indenting the northern side. Just west of Browning Peninsula in the southern part of the Windmill Islands. Named for Lt. Mendel L. Peterson, USN, supply officer on Operation Windmill, 1947–48.

Peterson Ridge. 84°34′S, 163°56′E. Extends north from the western part of Storm Peak massif in the Queen Alexandra Range. Named by the Ohio State University Geological Expedition of 1969–70 for Donald N. Peterson, party member who collected basalt lavas from

the ridge for petrologic and paleomagnetic studies.

Petes Pillar. 63°S, 60°33′W. Also called Kats Pillar, El Monolito. A pillar rock or stack just east of Fildes Point at the north side of the entrance to Port Foster in Deception Island in the South Shetlands. It was a well-known landmark to the early sealers. Named in 1950 by the UK for Pilot Officer Pete St. Louis, Royal Canadian Air Force, pilot with the FIDS in 1949–50.

Mount Petinos. 74°25′S, 132°43′W. 500 m. 1 mile ESE of Worley Point in the NW part of Shepard Island. Named for Lt. (jg) Frank Petinos, USN, first lieutenant on the *Glacier* when it mapped this mountain on Feb. 4, 1962.

Petite Rocks. 82°40′S, 51°30′W. Two small isolated rocks in the western part of the Sallee Snowfield, about 5 miles east of the central Dufek Massif in the Pensacola Mountains. Named for their size.

Mount Petlock. 85°25′S, 172°16′E. 3,195 m. The most prominent mountain in the NE part of the Otway Massif. It surmounts the north end of the ridge which borders the east side of the Burgess Glacier. Named for James D. Petlock, ionosphere physicist at Amundsen-Scott South Pole Station, 1963.

Mount Petras. 75°52′S, 128°39′W. 2,865 m. Ridge-shaped. 10 miles SE of Mount Flint in the McCuddin Mountains behind the Hobbs Coast of Marie Byrd Land. Discovered by the USAS on a flight from West Base on Dec. 14–15, 1940, and named Mount Josephine Petras, for the wife of Theodore Petras. The name was later shortened. Lichens are to be found here.

Petras, Theodore A. US Marine master technical sergeant and aircraft pilot on the USAS 1939–41. At West Base, he was initially one of the four men looking after the Snowcruiser.

Mount Petrel *see* **Petrellfjellet**

Petrel Cove. 63°28'S, 56°13'W. At the west end of Dundee Island, between Welchness and Diana Reef. It is next to Petrel Station, and was named Rada Petrel in the 1950s by the Argentines. The name has since been translated into English.

Petrel Island *see* **Dynamite Island**

Pétrel Island. 66°40'S, 140°01'E. ½ mile long. 45 meters high. NW of Rostand Island. It is the largest feature in the cluster of islands at the SE end of the Géologie Archipelago. Charted by the French in 1949–51, and named by them for the several snow petrel nests here. In Jan. 1952 this became the basis for Dumont d'Urville Station. The French call it Île des Pétrelles.

Petrel Station. 63°28'S, 56°17'W. Argentine station built initially as a refugio (refuge hut) on Dundee Island in 1952, and subsequently expanded into a scientific station.

Île des Pétrelles *see* **Pétrel Island**

Petrellfjellet. 71°59'S, 4°50'E. A mountain. Also called Mount Petrel. Mostly ice-free. Between Slokstallen Mountain and Mount Grytøyr in the Mühlig-Hofmann Mountains of Queen Maud Land. Name means "the petrel mountain" in Norwegian.

Petrels. Also called tubenoses because of their tubular nostrils. They are the most numerous birds in the Antarctic. Of the order Procelariiformes, they are related to the fulmars (q.v.), prions (q.v.), albatrosses (q.v.), and shearwaters (q.v.), and sometimes the differences are vague. Superbly equipped for the Antarctic, with their webbed feet and dense plumage, they lay a single egg. The name means "little Peter" and comes from the birds' habit of walking on water. Wilson's Petrel *(Oceanites oceanicus)* is a storm petrel, and breeds on the Antarctic continent. It is one of the most abundant seabirds in the world. Others seen south of 60°S include black-bellied storm petrel *(Fregetta tropica)*; mottled petrel *(Pterodroma inexpectata)*; white-

headed petrel *(Pterodroma lessoni)*; blue petrel *(Halobaena caerulea)*; Kerguélen petrel *(Pterodroma brevirostris)*; white-faced storm petrel *(Pelagodroma marina)*. There are various fulmars called petrels; *see* that entry also.

Mount Petrides. 75°04'S, 136°30'W. Between Oehlenschlager Bluff and Mount Sinha, in the southern part of the Erickson Bluffs of Marie Byrd Land. It overlooks the confluence of the Kirkpatrick and Hull Glaciers from the north. Named for George A. Petrides, biologist working off the *Southwind* in the Bellingshausen and Amundsen Seas in 1971–72.

Petrie Ice Rises. 70°33'S, 72°12'W. On Wilkins Sound, off the west coast of Alexander Island.

Havre Petter *see* **Potter Cove**

Petter Bay. 60°43'S, 45°10'W. A bight ½ mile south of Spence Harbor on the east coast of Coronation Island in the South Orkneys. Named as Petters Bay before 1912. It may well have been named by Capt. Hans Borge for Capt. Petter Sørlle.

Petters Bay *see* **Petter Bay**

Pettersen. Captain of the whale catcher *Star I* during the *Sir James Clark Ross* expedition of 1923–24.

Pettersen Ridge. 71°47'S, 9°42'E. Extends north for 6 miles from Sandhø Heights in the Conrad Mountains of the Orvin Mountains in Queen Maud Land. Discovered by Ritscher's expedition of 1938–39. Named Pettersenegga by the Norwegians for Sverre Pettersen, steward with the Norwegian Antarctic Expedition of 1957–58.

Pettersenegga *see* **Pettersen Ridge**

Pettus Glacier. 63°48'S, 59°04'W. 9 miles long. Flows north from Ebony Wall into the Gavin Ice Piedmont between Poynter Hill and Tinsel Dome on Trinity Peninsula. Named by the UK for Robert N. Pettus, aircraft pilot with the FIDASE, 1956–57.

Petty Rock *see* **Petty Rocks**

Petty Rocks. 67°34′S, 67°29′W. 3 miles SE of Cape Sáenz in the center of the western part of Bigourdan Fjord, off the west coast of Graham Land. Surveyed in 1936 by the BGLE, and again in 1948 by the FIDS. They named it Petty Rock for its size. Later air photos have shown that there are several rocks, so the feature was redefined slightly.

Petzval Glacier *see* **Suárez Glacier**

Mount Pew. 72°19′S, 169°11′E. 2,950 m. Surmounts the central part of the ridge separating Kelly Glacier and Towles Glacier in the Admiralty Mountains. Named for James A. Pew, geophysicist at McMurdo Station, 1966–67.

Lake Péwé. 77°56′S, 164°18′E. A small lake at a height of 580 m. On the uppermost bench of the Koettlitz Glacier, 1 mile SE of Blackwelder Glacier in Victoria Land. Named by the New Zealanders in 1960–61 for Troy L. Péwé, glacial geologist from the University of Alaska. In 1957–58 he explored parts of Victoria Land, including this lake.

Péwé Peak. 78°02′S, 163°40′E. 860 m. A bedrock peak. Composed of granite and topped with a dolerite sill. Just south of Joyce Glacier. It is surrounded by glacial ice except on the south side. Named for Troy L. Péwé (*see* **Lake Péwé**).

Pfaff Island. 66°54′S, 67°44′W. One of the Bennett Islands, just south of Gränicher Island, in Hanusse Bay. Named by the UK for Alexius B.I.F. Pfaff (1825–1886), German physicist specializing in the plasticity of ice.

Pfrogner Point. 72°37′S, 89°35′W. Ice-covered. On the NW extension of Fletcher Peninsula; it is partly within the Abbott Ice Shelf. It marks the division of the Eights Coast and the Bryan Coast. Named for Ray L. Pfrogner, seismologist at Byrd Station, 1961–62.

Phalaropes. Red phalaropes—*Phalaropus fulicarius*—are rare birds in the Antarctic.

Phantom Point. 66°25′S, 65°41′W. Also called Cabo Bellue. A point within Darbel Bay. 1½ miles west of Shanty Point on the west coast of Graham Land. In 1957 a FIDS sledge party visited it and it suddenly loomed up at them out of the thick fog, looking like a phantom.

Mount Phelan. 71°59′S, 160°37′E. 2,000 m. Mostly ice-free. 5 miles SE of Killer Nunatak in the southern portion of the Emlen Peaks in the Usarp Mountains. Named for Michael J. Phelan, seismologist at Amundsen-Scott South Pole Station in 1962, and a member of the Byrd Traverse, 1963–64.

Phelps Island. 66°17′S, 110°30′E. Just west of the north end of Shirley Island in the Windmill Islands. Named for Robert F. Phelps, air crewman on Operation Windmill, 1947–48.

Phenomena. The nature of the Antarctic lends itself to phenomena, the flatness and vastness of the continent optimizing their viewing, aided by the cold dry climate. Haloes are the most common. Haloes are called parhelia when the source of light is the sun, and paraselenae when the source of light is the moon. They are produced by the refraction and reflection of sun or moon rays on the ice crystals of cirrus clouds and of fog, and are spectacular displays. When a halo occurs, 3 suns or 3 moons are seen on a given line parallel to the horizon. The sun or moon in the center is the true one. Haloes are often confused with coronas, which are colored areas of light, usually extending over no great distance, and are arranged concentrically in alternating bands of blue or green and red around the sun or moon. They are not caused by refraction in ice crystals (as a halo is) but by diffraction of light around the small water droplets which form the cloud. The more uniform the size of the droplets the purer the colors of the corona. Glories are common. They are caused by the diffraction of light from the edge of water drops (which must be present to form a glory), that light being reflected back to the sun, and mixing with the incoming light causes circular zones of darkness and brightness. Note: in order to see a glory, look away from the sun. Mock suns, or sun dogs, are caused by the sun's light being reflected and refracted by ice crystals in the atmosphere. This seems to expand and whiten the sun. A sun-pillar is a long, thin dagger of orange light which sometimes rises from the horizon high into the sky above the setting sun at the Pole. This is due to the refraction of ice crystals in the air. Also due to the refraction of ice crystals in the air are rainbow circles, which often form around the sun. A false sun is a mirage at the Pole, where the sun rises and sets for several days instead of following the horizon in a circle as the proper Antarctic sun should. Another phenomenon is wind clouds, which can form after severe storms. (*See also* **Looming, Mirages, Whiteout, Ice-blink, Airglow, Aurora, Fog bows, Rainbows, Barrier wind phenomenon.**)

Philately *see* **Stamps**

Philbin Inlet. 74°04′S, 113°58′W. 15 miles long. Ice-filled. Indents the northern end of Martin Peninsula in Marie Byrd Land. Named for Brig. Gen. Tony Philbin, US Army, who served the secretary of defense in liaison with the US Navy during the IGY (1957–58).

Philip, Prince. b. 1921. The Duke of Edinburgh. Led the *Britannia* expedition to the Antarctic in 1956–57.

Philip Wrigley Gulf *see* **Wrigley Gulf**

Cape Philippi. 75°14′S, 162°33′E. A rock cape rising abruptly to 490 m. Marks the northern side of the terminus of the David Glacier in Victoria Land. Discovered during Shackleton's 1907–9 expedition, and named by Shackleton for Emil Philippi.

Philippi, Emil. German professor of geology at Jena University. He was glaciologist and geologist on von Drygalski's 1901–3 expedition.

Philippi Glacier. 66°45′S, 88°20′E. 15 miles long. Flows north to the east end of the West Ice Shelf, 15 miles west of Gaussberg. Named by the Australians for Emil Philippi.

Philippi Ice Plateau *see* **Philippi Rise**

Philippi Rise. 66°06′S, 62°18′W. Also called Philippieis, Philippi Ice Plateau. A low, snow-covered promontory. 7 miles wide. Extends about 10 miles SE from the east coast of Graham Land. The ice surface is highest in the west where it rises to 395 m., and is broken by Borchgrevink and Gemini Nunataks. Nordenskjöld, in 1901–4, reported an ice wall or glacial terrace in the area of Borchgrevink Nunatak. Although he was unable to determine its true nature he called it Philippigletscher (Philippi Glacier) for Emil Philippi. In 1947 the FIDS determined that it is a snow-covered promontory.

Philippieis *see* **Philippi Rise**

Philippigletscher *see* **Philippi Rise**

The *Philippine Sea*. Aircraft carrier during Operation Highjump, 1946–47. It carried 6 R4D transport planes and a helicopter. Captain Delbert S. Cornwell.

Philips, Charles. Second mate on the *Huron*, 1820–21.

Cape Phillips. 73°04′S, 169°36′E. On the east side of the Daniell Peninsula, 8 miles SE of Mount Brewster, in Victoria Land. Discovered in Jan. 1841 by Ross, who named it for Lt. Charles G. Phillips.

Mount Phillips. 73°01′S, 167°15′E. 3,035 m. In the southern part of the Malta Plateau in Victoria Land. Discovered in Jan. 1841 by Ross, who named it for Prof. John Phillips, assistant secretary of the British Association.

Phillips, Charles G. Lieutenant on the *Terror*, 1839–43.

Phillips Glacier *see* **Albanus Glacier**

Phillips Mountains. 76°16′S, 145°W. On the north side of Balchen Glacier and Block Bay in the Ford Ranges of Marie Byrd Land. Discovered by Byrd's 1928–30 expedition and named by Byrd for Albanus Phillips, Sr., a Maryland manufacturer and patron of the expedition. Originally called the Albanus Phillips Mountains, the name was later shortened. Mount June is the highest peak in this range.

Phillips Nunatak. 84°45′S, 62°35′W. A small nunatak along the edge of a small ice escarpment 7 miles north of Mount Wanous in the Patuxent Range of the Pensacola Mountains. Named for Harry G. Phillips, cook at Palmer Station, 1967.

Phillips Ridge. 67°50′S, 62°49′E. ½ mile long. ½ mile west of the main massif of the Central Masson Range in the Framnes Mountains of Mac. Robertson Land. Photographed by the LCE 1936–37. Named by the Australians for J. Phillips, physicist at Mawson Station, 1962.

Phils Island. 64°30′S, 63°W. The southern of two small islands just south of Guépratte Island in the Discovery Sound in the Palmer Archipelago. Charted and named in 1927 by personnel on the *Discovery.*

Phleger Dome. 85°52′S, 138°24′W. Dome-shaped mountain. 3,315 m. At the NE end of Stanford Plateau on the Watson Escarpment. Named for Herman Phleger, one of the US representatives in the discussions on the Antarctic Treaty in 1959.

Phobos Ridge. 71°52′S, 68°30′W. A rocky ridge of sandstone and shale. Forms the west side of Mars Glacier in the SE corner of Alexander Island. Surveyed in 1949 by the FIDS. Named by the UK for the satellite of the planet Mars.

Mount Phoebe. 71°47′S, 68°47′W. Between the head of Neptune Glacier and Saturn Glacier in eastern Alexander Island. It is situated at the junction of four radial ridges. The summit is a small mesa of conglomerate rising 300 meters above the surrounding ice. Named by the UK for one of the satellites of the planet Saturn.

Phoenix Peak. 64°24′S, 59°39′W. Just south of Muskeg Gap at the north end of

Sobral Peninsula, Graham Land. Surveyed by the FIDS in 1960–61. Named by the UK for the Phoenix Manufacturing Co., of Eau Claire, Wisconsin, pioneers of locomotive sleds.

Phoque Island. 66°49′S, 141°24′E. 175 yards long. The most southerly island in a small group 175 yards north of Cape Margerie. Charted in 1951 by the French and named by them for the large number of seals here (phoque is French for seal).

Île aux Phoques *see* **Phoque Island**

Îles des Phoques *see* **Seal Islands**

Phosphate. It looks as if sedimentary phosphate exists in Antarctica.

Photography. Shackleton and Marshall took pocket cameras with them on their trek to the Pole in 1908–9, and Mawson had a box-camera with him when he went to the South Magnetic Pole during the same expedition. Herbert Ponting was the first professional photographer in the Antarctic, when he went down on Scott's last expedition, 1910–13. Byrd was the first to use a fixed aerial survey camera (*see also* **Aerial photography, Movies set in Antarctica**).

Physeter Rocks. 63°31′S, 60°09′W. Just NW of Ohlin Island in the Palmer Archipelago. Named by the UK in 1960 for the sperm whale *(Physeter catodon).*

Pi Islands. 64°20′S, 62°53′W. Also called Islotes Sidders, Islotes Subofi Rubianes. Two islands and several rocks 1 mile east of the NE end of Omega Island, in the Melchior Islands. Named by the Argentines in 1946 for the Greek letter.

Piccard Cove. 64°45′S, 62°19′W. Forms the southernmost part of Wilhelmina Bay, on the west coast of Graham Land. Charted by de Gerlache in 1897–99. Named by the UK in 1960 for Auguste Piccard (1884–1962), Swiss balloonist.

Mount Picciotto. 83°46′S, 163°E. Mostly ice-free. 2,560 m. Surmounts the NE end of Painted Cliffs on the Prince Andrew Plateau of the Queen Elizabeth Range. Named for Edgard E. Picciotto, glaciologist at Amundsen-Scott South Pole Station in 1962–63, and a member of the South Pole–Queen Maud Land Traverses of 1964–65 and 1965–66.

Pickering Nunatak. 71°24'S, 70°47'E. At the eastern side of the mouth of Lambert Glacier. 20 miles SSW of the Manning Nunataks. Discovered aerially on Nov. 2, 1957, on a flight by an ANARE Beaver aircraft over the Amery Ice Shelf. Named by the Australians for Flight Sgt. R. Pickering of the RAAF Antarctic Flight at Mawson Station, 1957.

Pickering Nunataks. 71°49'S, 68°57'W. 2 miles SW of Mount Phoebe. On the NE side of Saturn Glacier in the eastern part of Alexander Island. Named by the UK for William Pickering (1858–1938), US astronomer who discovered Phoebe, the satellite of the planet Saturn.

Pickersgill, Richard. b. 1749, West Tanfield, Yorkshire, England. Drowned in the Thames, 1779, a drunkard. Lieutenant on the *Resolution* during Cook's voyage of 1772–75.

Pickwick Island. 65°29'S, 65°38'W. Also called Isla Alferez Maveroff. The largest of the Pitt Islands in the Biscoe Islands. Charted by the BGLE in 1934–37. Named by the UK in 1959 in continuation of the *Pickwick Papers* theme (the islands in the group were named for characters in the Dickens book).

Picnic Passage. 64°20'S, 56°55'W. Also called Estrecho Arguindeguy. A marine channel, 1½ miles long and ½ mile wide. Between Snow Hill Island and Seymour Island. Surveyed in 1902 by Nordenskjöld's expedition. Named by the UK for the easy sledging conditions experienced here by the FIDS resurveying party in 1952.

Picnics. To relieve the boredom aboard the frozen-in *Français* during the winter of 1904 at Port Charcot on Booth Island, Charcot took a party of men on a picnic to nearby Hovgaard Island. They left their ship at 10:30 a.m. on May 30, 1904, and walked across the ice. They

had to break up the meat and butter with axes, and then eat very quickly, dancing as they did so to keep warm.

Isla Pico *see* **Beak Island**

Mount Pico. 64°10'S, 62°27'W. Also called Mount Rokitansky. Over 1,700 m. In the northern part of Brabant Island. 3½ miles NE of Driencourt Point. Named as such before 1957 by the Argentines. The name means "peak."

Rocas Pico *see* **Montrol Rock**

Pidgeon Island. 66°19'S, 110°27'E. 1 mile long. Between Midgley Island and Mitchell Peninsula in the Windmill Islands. Named for E.C. Pidgeon, USN, photographer's mate on Operation Highjump, 1946–47. The eastern part of this feature was once thought to be a separate island, and called O'Brien Islet. The name O'Brien is now applied to the bay north of Mitchell Peninsula.

Pieck Range. 71°45'S, 12°06'E. A short mountain range surmounted by Zwiesel Mountain. At the east side of the Humboldt Graben, in the Petermann Ranges of the Wohlthat Mountains of Queen Maud Land. Discovered by Ritscher's expedition of 1938–39. Named by the USSR in 1966 for Wilhelm Pieck, president of East Germany from 1949–60.

Piedmont glacier. The lobe-shaped expanded terminal part of a valley glacier spread out over broad lowlands at the base of a mountain. Differs from an ice-sheet (q.v.) in its origin.

Piedmont Tongue. 77°01'S, 163°07'E. A tiny glacier tongue at the very north of the Wilson Piedmont Glacier. Juts out into the southern part of Granite Harbor, in Victoria Land.

Isla Piedrabuena *see* **Eta Island**

Pierce-Butler, K.S. British major who, on Feb. 5, 1947, relieved E.W. Bingham as commander of the 11-man FIDS Base E on Stonington Island. For a while he teamed up with Finn Ronne of the RARE.

Pierce Peak. 84°52'S, 63°09'W. 1,790 m. 2 miles south of Sullivan Peaks at the NE edge of the Mackin Table in the

Patuxent Range of the Pensacola Mountains. Named for Chester M. Pierce who, with Jay T. Shurley, studied the psychophysiology of men while asleep and awake, before, during, and after stays at Amundsen-Scott South Pole station in 1966–67.

¹Mount Pierre. 63°58′S, 61°50′W. Also called Monte Pedro. 210 m. Conical. Just south of Moureaux Point on Liège Island. Discovered and named by de Gerlache in 1897–99.

²Mount Pierre. 71°18′S, 35°45′E. 2,220 m. A massif. Just north of Mount Goossens in the Queen Fabiola Mountains. Discovered by the Belgian Antarctic Expedition of 1960–61 led by Guido Derom, on Oct. 7, 1960. Derom named it for Michel Pierre, aircraft mechanic, a member of the Belgian flight reconnoitering party in this area.

Cap Pierre Baudin *see* **Baudin Peaks**

Cap Pierre Willems *see* **Cape Willems**

Pig Rock. 62°19′S, 58°48′W. 65 m. Also called Rocas Chanchito. The largest of a group of rocks 1 mile east of the east end of Nelson Island in the South Shetlands. Discovered by sealers before 1821. Charted and named by personnel on the *Discovery II* in 1935.

Pigmy Rock. 68°43′S, 67°33′W. Also spelled Pygmy Rock. Just off the SW side of Alamode Island at the southern extremity of the Terra Firma Islands, off the west coast of Graham Land. Surveyed in 1948 by the FIDS. They named it for its size.

Pigs. Charcot took a cochon called Toby with him on the *Français* during his first expedition. He was very upset when the animal died in Dec. 1904 after eating fish with hooks still in them. Charcot had operated, but Toby had died anyway.

Pila Island. 67°35′S, 62°43′E. Also called Arrow Island. 1½ miles west of the

Flat Islands in Holme Bay, Mac. Robertson Land. Photographed by the LCE 1936–37. Named means "arrow" in Norwegian.

Pilarryggen. 72°42′S, 3°56′W. A rock ridge at the west side of Portalen Pass in the Borg Massif of Queen Maud Land. Name means "the pillar ridge" in Norwegian.

Pilbeam, Arthur. Leading seaman, RN. Part of the Royal Society Expedition of 1901–4.

Pilcher Peak. 64°19′S, 60°49′W. Between Mouillard and Lilienthal Glaciers on the west coast of Graham Land. Named by the UK in 1960 for Percy S. Pilcher (1866–1899), British gliding pioneer.

Pillar Peak *see* **Waldeck-Rousseau Peak**

Pillow Knob. 83°39′S, 58°41′W. 810 m. At the NE end of the Williams Hills in the Neptune Range of the Pensacola Mountains. Named descriptively by Dwight L. Schmidt (*see* **Schmidt Hills**).

Pillsbury Tower. 73°31′S, 94°20′W. 1,295 m. A remnant volcanic cone. It has a sheer north-facing rock cliff and a gradual slope at the south side. Directly at the base of Avalanche Ridge in the Jones Mountains. Its dark rock rises over 100 meters above the surrounding area, thus making it an excellent landmark. Named by the University of Minnesota–Jones Mountains Party of 1960–61 for Pillsbury Hall, which houses the Department of Geology at the University of Minnesota.

Pilon Peak. 71°14′S, 164°57′E. 1,880 m. 2 miles NE of Mount Works. On the west side of Horne Glacier in the Everett Range of the Concord Mountains. Named for Cdr. Jerome R. Pilon, USN, commander of VXE-6, 1969–70. He had been operations officer of VX-6 (as it was known then) from 1967–68 and executive officer from 1968–69. Later, 1976–78 he served on the Advisory Committee on Antarctic Names of the US Board on Geographic Names.

Pilot Glacier. 73°23'S, 165°03'E. Descends along the SE side of Deception Plateau, through the Mountaineer Range, to enter Aviator Glacier, in Victoria Land. Named by the New Zealanders in 1962–63 for the members of VX-6, and also in association with Aviator Glacier.

Pilot Peak. 65°51'S, 65°16'W. 745 m. The highest peak on Larrouy Island, off the west coast of Graham Land. Charted by Charcot in 1908–10. Named by the UK in 1959 because of its usefulness as a navigation mark for the passage of Grandidier Channel. This peak is conspicuous from a long way away.

Pilot Whales. *Globicephala melaena.* Formerly rarely seen in Antarctic waters, they are actually the third most visible whales south of 60°S. They feed on squid and fish, and are probably seasonal visitors.

The *Piloto Pardo.* Chilean ship of the 1980s. Seen in Antarctic waters. Named for Capt. Luís Pardo Villalón.

Pilseneer Island *see* **Pelseneer Island**

Pilten Nunatak. 71°53'S, 24°48'E. In the northern part of the Gjel Glacier in the Sør Rondane Mountains. Name means "the nipper" in Norwegian.

The Pimple. 77°59'S, 162°40'E. 3,215 m. A cone-shaped peak between Mount Lister and Camels Hump in the Royal Society Range of Victoria Land. Discovered and named by Scott's 1901–4 expedition.

Pin Point *see* **Renier Point**

Pinafore Moraine. 76°53'S, 159°26'E. A sheet of moraine which extends northeastward from Carapace Nunatak in Victoria Land. Named descriptively by the New Zealanders in 1964.

Pinball Machines. American automatic weather stations in Antarctica. Ac-

tually ice stations, they are more reliable than grasshoppers.

Pinboko Rock *see* **Oku-iwa Rock**

Pincer Point. 85°34'S, 150°30'W. 4 miles ESE of Durham Point, near the NW end of the Tapley Mountains. Discovered by Byrd's 1928–30 expedition. It looks like part of a pincers.

Pinckard Table. 74°S, 164°03'E. An ice-covered tableland. 8 miles long by 3 miles wide. Between the Styx and Burns Glaciers in Victoria Land. Named for William Pinckard, biologist at McMurdo Station, 1965–66.

Pinckney, Robert F. First lieutenant, USN, on the Wilkes Expedition 1838–42. Also spelled Pinkney. He joined the *Peacock* at Orange Bay, and took over command of the *Flying Fish* from Lt. Walker at Callao. He was detached at Honolulu in 1840.

Pinder Gully. 60°43'S, 45°35'W. A small gully in the eastern part of Signy Island in the South Orkneys. It runs north from Observation Bluff down to the sea. Named by the UK for Ronald Pinder, radio operator and meteorologist at Signy Island Station in 1959–61.

The *Pine Island.* Seaplane tender, and flagship of the Eastern Task Group during Operation Highjump, 1946–47. Captain Henry Howard Caldwell.

Pine Island Bay. 74°50'S, 102°40'W. 40 miles long. 30 miles wide. It is fed by the Pine Island Glacier. An indentation of the Amundsen Sea into the Walgreen Coast. Named for the *Pine Island.*

Pine Island Glacier. 75°10'S, 100°W. Flows along the south side of the Hudson Mountains into Pine Island Bay, on the Walgreen Coast, at the SE extremity of the Amundsen Sea. Named in association with the bay.

Pinegin Peak. 71°44'S, 12°33'E. 2,595 m. A central peak on Isdalsegga Ridge in the Südliche Petermann Range of the Wohlthat Mountains. Discovered by the Ritscher expedition of 1938–39. Named by the USSR in 1966 for polar explorer N.V. Pinegin (1883–1940).

Pinel Point. 64°21'S, 62°12'W. 5 miles NE of D'Ursel Point on the east side of Brabant Island. Charted by de Gerlache in 1897–99. Named by the UK for Philippe Pinel (1745–1826), French pioneer of humane psychiatry.

Piner, Thomas. Signal quartermaster on the *Vincennes* during the Wilkes Expedition of 1838–42. He served the cruise.

Piner Bay. 66°43'S, 140°17'E. 8 miles long. 2 miles wide. An indentation in the coast of Adélie Land between Cape Bienvenue and the east side of the Astrolabe Glacier Tongue. Discovered on Jan. 30, 1840, by Wilkes, who named it Piner's Bay, for Thomas Piner.

Piñero Island. 67°34'S, 67°49'W. Also called Isla Carrera, Île Piniero. 2 miles long. ½ mile wide. 4½ miles NW of Pourquoi Pas Island, off the west coast of Graham Land. Discovered by Charcot in 1908–10, and named by him for Dr. Antonio F. Piñero, member of the Chamber of Deputies of Argentina, on whose motion the government voted unlimited credit to meet the needs of Charcot's expedition.

Piñero Peak. 67°34'S, 67°49'W. In Graham Land.

Piners Bay *see* **Piner Bay**

Pinet Butte. 73°10'S, 161°41'E. Forms the westernmost portion of the Caudal Hills in Victoria Land. Named for Paul R. Pinet, geologist at McMurdo Station, 1966–67.

Île Pingouin *see* **Penguin Island**

The *Pinguin.* A Nazi raider, Hilfskreuzer 33 of the German Navy. Capt. Ernst-Felix Krugge. In the early morning of Jan. 13–14, 1941, this vessel succeeded in capturing 40,000 tons of Norwegian whaling vessels, in the form of three of Lars Christensen's factory ships, the *Pelagos,* the *Solglimt,* and the *Ole Wegger,* as well as 11 whale catchers. This act was committed off the Queen Maud Land coast, probably at around 59°S, 2°30'W. All the ships concerned had been in the

Antarctic. The *Pinguin* was sunk by the British Navy in May 1941 (*see also* Lt. Bach).

Pinguinenkap *see* **Penguin Point**

Punta Pingüinera *see* **Stranger Point**

Pingvin Island. 65°45'S, 81°50'E. Also called Penguin Island. Off the NW side of the West Ice Shelf. Named by the USSR in 1956–57 as Pingvin (penguin).

Pingvinane Nunataks. 72°S, 23°17'E. Just north of Tanngarden Peaks in the Sør Rondane Mountains. Name means "the penguins" in Norwegian.

Île Piniero *see* **Piñero Island**

Pinkham, S.A. 1st assistant engineer on the *Bear of Oakland,* 1933–34, and chief engineer, 1934–35.

Pinkney, Robert F. *see* **Pinckney, Robert F.**

Pinn Island. 67°34'S, 47°55'E. Just off the NE end of McKinnon Island, off the coast of Enderby Land. Named by the Australians for John Pinn, geophysicist at Mawson Station in 1957.

Pinnacle *see* **The Spire**

Pinnacle Gap. 73°15'S, 163°E. Between Pain and Tobin Mesas in the Mesa Range of Victoria Land. Traversed and named by the northern party of the NZGSAE 1962–63. It is easily identified by the high rock pinnacle of Mount Ballou on the northern ridge overlooking the gap.

Pinnacle Island *see* **Pinnacle Rock**

Pinnacle Rock. 61°06'S, 54°47'W. Also called Pinnacle Island. 120 m. 2½ miles east of Point Wild and just off the north coast of Elephant Island in the South Shetlands. Named by Shackleton's men in 1916 after the failed British Imperial Transantarctic Expedition of 1914–17.

Pintails. The yellow-billed pintail—*Anas georgica*—is a rare bird in the Antarctic, but seen nonetheless.

Pinther Ridge. 70°22'S, 64°20'W. Arc-shaped. 6 miles long. Isolated.

Mostly snow-covered. At the eastern edge of the Dyer Plateau in Palmer Land. 22 miles south of the Eternity Range. Named for Miklos Pinther, chief cartographer of the American Geographical Society in the 1970s, who was responsible for many excellent maps of Antarctica.

Pioneer Crossing. 68°29′S, 78°22′E. A low pass across Langnes Peninsula in the Vestfold Hills. It leads from the SE arm of Tryne Fjord to Langnes Fjord. Photographed by the LCE 1936–37. Visited by an ANARE sledging party led by Bruce H. Stinear in 1957, and named by the Australians to commemorate this first known traverse.

Pioneer Heights. 79°30′S, 83°30′W. Also called Pioneer Hills. The large area of hills, ridges, and peaks east of Schneider and Schanz Glaciers and between Splettstoesser and Union Glaciers in the Heritage Range. Included in these heights are Inferno Ridge, the Nimbus Hills, the Buchanan Hills, the Collier Hills, and the Gross Hills. Named in association with the Heritage theme.

Pioneer Hills *see* **Pioneer Heights**

Pioneers Escarpment. 80°28′S, 21°10′ W. In the Shackleton Range.

Pionerskaya Station. 69°44′S, 95°31′E. USSR operational support station used during the IGY. 250 miles inland from Mirnyy Station, it was established in May 1956 by sledge parties from Mirnyy, with assistance from aircraft. The first leader, in the winter of 1956, was A.M. Gusev. Leader for the 1956–57 summer season was N. Rusin (Nov. 1956–Feb. 1957). The leader briefly in Feb. 1957 was G. Paschenko before he was transferred to Oazis Station for the winter. Pionerskaya closed in 1958, at the end of the IGY.

Pionerskiy Dome. 73°59′S, 73°08′E. An ice-covered summit about 60 miles SSW of the Grove Mountains. Discovered by the USSR in 1958 and named Kupol Pionerskiy (Pioners Dome).

Piore Ridge. 72°40′S, 168°55′E. 11 miles long. Between Elder Glacier and

Bowers Glacier in the Victory Mountains of Victoria Land. Named for Emanuel Ruben Piore, US physicist with the NSF, 1961–72.

Pipe Peak. 79°09′S, 86°15′W. 1,720 m. 1½ miles north of Matney Peak in the Founders Peaks of the Heritage Range. Named by the University of Minnesota Geological Party in 1963–64 for a pipe that was left here after a visit.

Pipecleaner Glacier. 78°14′S, 162°51′ E. Formed by the coalescence of several small alpine glaciers on the east side of Mount Huggins. With Glimpse Glacier it joins the Radian Glacier where that glacier meets the northern arm of Dismal Ridge. Its surface is marked by innumerable bands of moraine which look like pipecleaners. Named by the New Zealanders in 1960–61.

Pipkin Rock. 68°05′S, 68°50′W. 260 yards long. Ice-free. Just NE of Dismal Island in the Faure Islands, off the west coast of Graham Land. Named by the FIDS in 1949 for its insignificant nature.

Pippin Peaks. 65°39′S, 62°28′W. They range in height from 880 meters to 1,160 meters. They are formed of white or pink granite. They form a line running east-west. At the west end of Stubb Glacier where they form a part of that glacier's north wall. Named by the UK for the *Moby Dick* character.

Cabo Pirámide *see* **Minot Point**

Pirie, J.H. Harvey. Doctor/bacteriologist/geologist on Bruce's Scottish National Antarctic Expedition of 1902–4.

Pirie Peninsula. 60°42′S, 44°39′W. Extends northward for 3 miles from the center of Laurie Island in the South Orkneys. Surveyed in 1903 by Bruce who named it for J.H. Harvey Pirie in 1904.

Mount Pirrit *see* **Mount Tidd**

Pirrit, John. US glaciologist with the US Ellsworth-Byrd Traverse Party of 1958, based at Ellsworth Station that winter. He took over from S. Barnes as scientific leader of Byrd Station for the 1959 winter.

Pirrit Hills. 81°17′S, 85°21′W. Isolated. 7 miles in extent. South of the Ellsworth Mountains, between the Heritage Range and the Nash Hills. Named for John Pirrit.

Mount Pisco *see* **Mount Pisgah**

Mount Pisgah. 62°57′S, 62°29′W. There are two peaks next to each other in the north-central part of Smith Island in the South Shetlands. American sealers who saw them in the 1819–20 season thought that there was a twin-peaked mountain on the island, similar to the mountain in Durham, Connecticut, called Mount Pisgah. They duly named it Mount Pisgah. However, there are two separate peaks. This one was later called Mount Pisgah, and the one 4 miles to the SW was called Mount Foster (q.v.). There is another mountain, 3 miles to the NE, called Mount Christi. Mount Pisgah is 1,860 m. It is also seen spelled as Mount Pisco, and Mount Piso.

Mount Piso *see* **Mount Pisgah**

Pitkevitch Glacier. 71°23′S, 168°52′E. 20 miles long. Flows north from the Admiralty Mountains along the west side of the DuBridge Range. It reaches the sea just east of Atkinson Cliffs, where it forms the Anderson Icefalls. A portion of the terminus merges with Fendley Glacier. Named for Staff Sgt. Leonard M. Pitkevitch (*see* **Deaths, 1958**).

Mount Pitman. 70°09′S, 67°42′W. Has two mainly ice-covered, dome-shaped summits, the higher and northern rising to 1,830 m. 9 miles inland from the George VI Sound, between Riley and Chapman Glaciers on the west coast of Palmer Land. Surveyed in 1936 by the BGLE. Named by the UK in 1954 for E.L. Pitman, a British airplane carpenter who made the sledges used by the BGLE (*see* **Sledges**).

Piton Island. 66°47′S, 141°36′E. 175 yards SW of Guano Island in the Curzon Islands. Charted in 1951 by the French and named by them for its very pointed shape.

Pitt, K.A.J. Captain of the *Fitzroy,* 1943–46.

Pitt Island *see* **Pitt Islands**

Pitt Islands. 65°26′S, 65°30′W. Also called Islas Moyano. Just off the northern extremity of Renaud Island in the Biscoe Islands. Charted by the BGLE in 1935–36. Named for Pitt's Island (q.v.). The islands within the group have generally been given names of characters in Charles Dickens's book, *The Pickwick Papers*: Fizkin, Snubbin, Pickwick, Buzfuz, Nupkins, Sawyer, Tupman, Winkle, Trundle, Jingle, Slumkey, Weller, Smiggers, and Snodgrass Islands, as well as Bardell Rock and Dickens Rocks.

Pitt Point. 63°51′S, 58°22′W. A promontory. 90 m. At the south side of the mouth of Victory Glacier on the south coast of the Trinity Peninsula. Charted by the FIDS in 1945, and named for K.A.J. Pitt.

Pittar, Jack. Electronics man on the *Solo* in 1978.

Mount Pittard. 71°31′S, 166°54′E. 2410 m. 12 miles east of the northern part, of the Homerun Range in the Admiralty Mountains. Named for Donald A. Pittard, biologist at McMurdo Station, 1966–67 and 1967–68.

Pitt's Island. About 65°10′S, 65°50′W. In the area of Alexander Island, this was an island discovered by Biscoe on Feb. 19, 1832. He landed on it and named it for William Pitt, the former British prime minister. The island now can not be found in this area, and modern geographers think Biscoe charted it in error. This may be so, but the name has been transferred to the Pitt Islands, 25 miles to the ESE.

Pitzman Glacier. 70°41′S, 160°10′E. 6 miles long. Flows from the SE slopes of the Pomerantz Tableland in the Usarp Mountains, between Mount Lowman and Williams Bluff to an ice piedmont just eastward. Named for Frederick J. Pitzman, biologist at McMurdo Station, 1967–68.

Mount Pivot. 80°41'S, 30°10'W. 1,095 m. Between Mount Haslop and Turnpike Bluff, in the western part of the Shackleton Range. Named in 1957 by the BCTAE because this prominent landmark was the turning point for aircraft and sledging parties of the expedition rounding the SW end of the Shackleton Range.

Pivot Peak. 78°02'S, 161°01'E. 2,450 m. Conical. 6 miles SE of Monastery Nunatak at the NE edge of the Skelton Névé. The NZ Northern Survey Party of the BCTAE established a survey station on its summit on Jan. 21, 1958. Named by them for its prominent position and appearance.

Plaice Island. 66°01'S, 65°27'W. West of Mackerel Island in the Fish Islands, off the west coast of Graham Land. Charted by the BGLE 1934–37. Named by the UK in 1959 in continuation of the fish theme.

Planck Point. 79°18'S, 85°11'W. Snow-covered. Spurlike. On the north side of Splettstoesser Glacier. 10 miles SE of Landmark Peak in the Heritage Range. Named by the University of Minnesota Geological Party here in 1963–64, for Russell E. Planck, helicopter crew chief with the 62nd Transportation Detachment, who assisted the party.

Plane Table. 77°36'S, 161°27'E. An ice-free mesa in the northern part of the Asgard Range of Victoria Land. Surmounts the area between the Nibelungen Valley and the Sykes Glacier and commands an extensive view of the Wright Valley. Named descriptively by New Zealand.

Planet Heights. 71°13'S, 68°47'W. A series of summits along a ridge, extending 24 miles in a north-south direction between the southern part of the LeMay Range and George VI Sound in the eastern part of Alexander Island. Named by the UK in association with the many features nearby named for planets.

Plankington Bluff. 84°58'S, 64°37'W. On the SW edge of the Mackin Table. 5 miles SE of Shurley Ridge in the Patuxent Range of the Pensacola Mountains. Named for John C. Plankington, Jr., meteorologist at Amundsen-Scott South Pole Station in 1967.

Plankton. Minute aquatic organisms which abound in the seas, especially near the coasts, and float near the surface of the water. Part of the marine chain of life, the phytoplankton are eaten by the zooplankton, which in turn are gobbled up as the basic diet by whales, seals, fish, squid, and seabirds. They are the marine equivalent to pasture land for cattle (*see also* **Flora, Fauna**).

Morro Plano *see* **Flat Top Peninsula**

Plants *see* **Flora**

Plasmon. A milk-protein health food carried in powder form by Scott and Shackleton during their expeditions. Also used as a food supplement (*see also* **Sledging biscuits**).

Plata Passage. 64°40'S, 62°01'W. Also called La Plata Channel. Separates Brooklyn Island from the west coast of Graham Land in Wilhelmina Bay. Charted by de Gerlache in 1897–99 and named for the estuary between Argentina and Uruguay to honor the people of Argentina for all their help on the *Belgica* expedition.

Plateau Station. 79°15'S, 40°30'E. The smallest, highest, coldest, and most inaccessible of all the US scientific stations in Antarctica. It was 11,890 feet above sea level and 1,350 miles from McMurdo Station. Built by Cdr. S.K. Kauffman, USN, in Dec. 1965, it comprised 5 fabricated vans assembled into a building 8 by 25 meters, plus an additional van and a Jamesway hut for emergency shelter. Meteorology, geophysics, and upper atmosphere physics were studied. Between 4 and 8 people wintered-over on average, until the station closed in Jan. 1969.

Plateau Weather Station. Meteorological station set up on the mainland of the Antarctic Peninsula, NE of Stonington Island, from July 16–24, 1947, during the RARE. Manned by Petersen and Dodson, it was abandoned by them on July 25, a day after completion. The two returned to Main Base on Stonington Island, but on the way back Petersen fell down a crevasse and was trapped upside down, 110 feet down the crevasse, for 12 hours. Dodson brought back a rescue squad and Petersen was hauled out with no damage. This was the highlight of their wild adventure.

Platt Cliffs. 62°11'S, 58°35'W. Between Monsimet Cove and Goulden Cove on King George Island in the South Shetlands.

Platt Point. 68°36'S, 64°14'W. Juts out into the Larsen Ice Shelf from the east coast of the Antarctic Peninsula.

Platypus Ridge. 70°42'S, 163°43'E. Ice-covered. Borders the west side of the mouth of Lillie Glacier. It extends NE from the Bowers Mountains to the head of Ob' Bay. Named by the ANARE for the Australian animal.

Ostrov Plau *see* **Plog Island**

Playfair Mountains. 73°55'S, 63°25'W. Between Swann Glacier and Squires Glacier in SE Palmer Land. Discovered aerially by the USAS from East Base in 1939–41. Named by the USA for John Playfair (1748–1819), Scottish mathematician and geologist.

Plaza Point. 62°06'S, 58°26'W. Also called La Plaza Point. Forms the southern tip of Keller Peninsula, which separates Mackellar and Martel Inlets in the northern part of Admiralty Bay, on King George Island, in the South Shetlands. Charted by Charcot in 1908–10, and named by him for the plazalike position of this feature at the head of Admiralty Bay.

Pleasant Plateau. 79°46'S, 158°30'E. Isolated. Ice-free. Just west of Blank Peaks and Foggydog Glacier in the Brown Hills. Named by the New Zealanders in 1962–63 for the pleasant weather conditions here.

The Pleiades. 72°42'S, 165°32'E. Several extinct volcanic peaks in a cluster,

overlooking the west side of the head of Mariner Glacier. Named by the New Zealanders in 1962–63 for the cluster of small stars in the constellation Taurus.

Mount Pleiones. 72°45'S, 165°29'E. The southernmost and highest peak of The Pleiades, at the head of Mariner Glacier. Named by New Zealand for Pleione, the Greek mythological mother of the Pleiades.

Pointe Pléneau *see* **Pléneau Island**

Pléneau, Paul. French director of an engineering company, he was a friend and supporter of Charcot, and went with the explorer on his first Antarctic expedition, 1903–5, as photographer on the *Français*. When Charcot telegrammed him an invitation to come on the expedition in 1903, Pléneau replied, "Where you like. When you like. For as long as you like."

Pléneau Island. 65°06'S, 64°04'W. Almost a mile long. Just NE of Hovgaard Island in the Wilhelm Archipelago. Charted as a peninsula of Hovgaard Island by Charcot in 1903–5, and he named its NE point as Pointe Pléneau, for Paul Pléneau. The Argentines mapped it as an island in 1957.

Plog Island. 68°32'S, 78°E. Also called Plow Island, Plough Island, Ostrov Plau. 1 mile long. In Prydz Bay. ½ mile north of Lake Island, and ½ mile west of Breidnes Peninsula, Vestfold Hills. Photographed by the LCE 1936–37. Named Plogöy (plow island) by the Norwegians for its shape.

Plogöy *see* **Plog Island**

Plogskaftet Nunataks. 71°48'S, 5°12'E. A row of nunataks about 5 miles long. Just NW of Cumulus Mountain in the Mühlig-Hofmann Mountains of Queen Maud Land. Name means "the plow handle" in Norwegian.

Plogsteinen *see* **Lucas Island**

Plough Island *see* **Plog Island**

Plow Island *see* **Plog Island**

Plumley, Frank. British blacksmith who was a stoker in the Royal Navy. Part of the crew on the *Discovery* during Scott's 1901–4 expedition.

Plummer Glacier. 79°58'S, 81°30'W. Flows east through the Enterprise Hills to the north of Lippert Peak and the Douglas Peaks, in the Heritage Range. Named for Charles C. Plummer, glaciologist at Palmer Station in 1965.

Plumstead Valley. 76°37'S, 159°49'E. At the northern end of Shipton Ridge in the Allan Hills of Victoria Land. Named by the New Zealanders in 1964 for Dr. E.P. Plumstead, for her work on glossopteris fossils.

Plunder Fish. *Pogronphryne scotti.* Coastal fish of the order *Harpagiferidae.* Found in Antarctic waters.

Plunket Point. 85°05'S, 167°06'E. Marks the northern end of the Dominion Range and the confluence of the Beardmore and Mill Glaciers. Discovered by Shackleton's 1907–9 expedition and named for Lord Plunket, governor of NZ.

Pluto Glacier. 71°07'S, 68°22'W. On the east coast of Alexander Island. 10 miles long. 4 miles wide. Flows into George VI Sound to the north of Succession Cliffs. Surveyed by the BGLE in 1936, and again by the FIDS in 1948 and 1949. Named by the UK for the planet Pluto.

Mount Plymouth. 62°28'S, 59°49'W. 635 m. 1½ miles NW of Discovery Bay in the northern part of Greenwich Island in the South Shetlands. Charted in 1935 by personnel on the *Discovery II*. Not named, it seems, until 1948, by the British.

Plymouth, Charles. Midshipman on the *Resolution* during Cook's voyage of 1772–75.

PM-3A *see* **Nuclear Power**

Pobeda Ice Island. 64°30'S, 97°E. 100 miles from the Shackleton Ice Shelf, out to sea. It is about 75 miles long by 50 wide.

Poch, Julio. Lieutenant 1st class in the Argentine Navy. He was an observer on the USAS, 1939–41.

Pod Rocks. 68°09'S, 67°30'W. 5 miles west of Millerand Island in Marguerite Bay, off the west coast of Graham Land. Surveyed in 1936 by the BGLE, and again in 1949 by the FIDS, who established a sealing camp here. The FIDS named it for the old sealers' pods (groups of seals hauled ashore).

The Podium. 78°56'S, 161°09'E. A high, flat, ice-covered bluff. 1 mile in extent. Projects at the southern end of the Worcester Range and surmounts the ice-filled embayment between Cape Teall and Cape Timberlake. Named in 1964 for its position relative to nearby features and for its resemblance to a podium.

Podprudnoye Lake. 70°45'S, 11°37'E. A small lake just SE of Prilednikovoye Lake in the Schirmacher Hills of Queen Maud Land. Named Ozero Podprudnoye (by-the-pond lake) by the USSR in 1961.

Cape Poindexter *see* **Mount Reynolds**

Poindexter Peak. 75°13'S, 134°25'W. 1,215 m. Snow-covered. 4 miles SE of Bennett Bluff, on the west side of the upper part of the Berry Glacier in Marie Byrd Land. Named for Monte F. Poindexter, meteorologist at Byrd Station, 1962.

Cape Poinsett. 65°46'S, 113°13'E. Ice-covered. The northern extremity of Budd Coast. Named for Joel R. Poinsett, secretary of war under President Van Buren, who was instrumental in the compilation and publication of the many scientific reports based on the work of the Wilkes Expedition 1838–42. This expedition may well have been the first actually to sight this cape, albeit through a mirage.

Pointe Géologie *see* **Géologie Archipelago**

Pointer Nunatak. 80°37'S, 29°W. 1,245 m. Just east of Wedge Ridge in the western part of the Shackleton Range. Named in 1957 by the BCTAE because it is an important landmark on the route from Blaiklock Glacier to Stratton Glacier, which provides access from the west to the east part of the Shackleton Range.

The Pointers. 62°36'S, 61°19'W. Two rocks NW of Rugged Island in the South Shetlands. Named by sealers in the 1820s.

Pointing Cliff   *see*   **Ponting Cliff**

Isla Poisson   *see*   **Bob Island**

Poisson Hill. 62°29'S, 59°39'W. 80 m. Ice-covered. Almost ⅓ mile NE of Iquique Cove, Greenwich Island, in the South Shetlands. Named variously as Cerro Poisson and Promontorio Poisson by the Chileans in the early 1950s for Maurice Poisson who signed the official act of inauguration of nearby Capitán Arturo Prat Station in 1947.

Poland. The thirteenth country to sign the Antarctic Treaty, and the 10th to be ratified (this last on June 8, 1961 — ahead of Australia, Argentina, and Chile, 3 of the original 12 signatories). On July 29, 1977, it became the 13th Consultative party to the treaty. The only Polish scientific station is Arctowski.

Polar Air Mass. Great body of air forming over the South Pole, or nearby, either over land or water. (*See also* **Continental Polar Air Mass**, and **Maritime Polar Air Mass**.)

The *Polar Circle* *see* **The *Polarsirkel***

The *Polar Duke*. Canadian-flag steel ship, 219 feet in length. Ice-strengthened, it was built in Norway in 1983, designed for polar work. It has a 43-foot beam, 19-foot draft, a helicopter deck and 4 labs. Modified for the Antarctic it is 615 gross tons, and has 2 diesel engines, each 2,250 bhp. It carries 12 crew and 28 scientists. It was leased by the NSF as a replacement for the *Hero* in Jan. 1985, as their ship servicing Palmer Station. In Nov. 1985 it helped rescue the crew of the trapped *John Biscoe*, and in Jan.–Feb. 1989 it was involved in the fight against the oil slick from the capsized *Bahía Paraíso* (*see* **Pollution**).

Polar Party Cross. A giant cross made of Australian jarrah wood standing 9 feet out of the very top of Observation Hill on Ross Island. It was erected on Jan. 22, 1913, to honor Scott and his 4 companions, by those members of that expedition who did not die. They took 2 days to carry it to the top of the 750 foot hill. The inscription says, "To strive, to seek, to find, and not to yield." In July-Aug. 1974 it blew down in a tremendous storm, and was reuprighted on Sept. 24, 1974, by New Zealanders from Scott Base.

Polar Plateau. Also called the South Polar Plateau, the King Haakon VII Plateau (by Amundsen), the King Edward Plateau (by Shackleton), and the polar plateau (i.e., small letters). It is a broad, relatively smooth plateau discovered by Armitage in 1902. The South Pole lies on it.

The *Polar Queen*. Norwegian ship of the 1980s. Used on GANOVEX III.

Polar Record Glacier. 69°45'S, 75°30' E. Flows from the American Highland, between the Meknattane Nunataks and Dodd Island, to the central part of the Publications Ice Shelf in East Antarctica. Named by US cartographer, John H. Roscoe, in 1952, for the *Polar Record*, the polar journal published in England by the Scott Polar Research Institute.

Polar Record Glacier Tongue. 69°40'S, 75°10'E. The seaward extension of the Polar Record Glacier in East Antarctica.

The *Polar Sea*. One of the US Coast Guard's most powerful icebreakers. Commissioned in Jan. 1977. Sister ship of the *Polar Star*.

¹**The *Polar Star*.** 216-ton whaler in the Dundee Whaling Expedition of 1892–93. Captain James Davidson.

²**The *Polar Star*.** Ellsworth's Northrop Gamma all-metal, cantilever, low-wing monoplane, NR12269. It weighed 7,800 pounds, had a 600 hp Wasp engine, and could do 5,000 miles non-stop at 230 mph. It could carry 2 passengers and could land at 42 mph. In the 1930s Lincoln Ellsworth tried three times to fly

across the continent of Antarctica. He used this plane on each occasion. On the first try, 1933–34, it was damaged in a storm at Little America II. The following season, 1934–35, Ellsworth failed to get off the Antarctic Peninsula with it. On the 3rd attempt, 1935–36, he and Hollick-Kenyon flew in it across the continent from the Weddell Sea to a point 16 miles from Little America, where they ran out of fuel, and the plane had to be abandoned. The men made their way to Little America.

³The *Polar Star*. US Coastguard icebreaker used in Antarctic waters also as a research vessel. Commissioned in Jan. 1976, it was the most powerful US icebreaker ever made (including the *Glacier*). Sister ship of the *Polar Sea*. It was the 7th ship to circumnavigate Antarctica at high latitudes when it carried an Antarctic Treaty inspection team to 12 international bases around the continent in 1982–83.

Polar Subglacial Basin. 85°S, 110°E. A subsurface feature beneath the Polar Plateau, generally between the Gamburtsev Subglacial Mountains and the Dominion Range in East Antarctica. Also called the Eastern Plain, it was roughly delineated by US, UK, and USSR seismic sounding parties in the period 1958–61. Named by the USA in 1961 for its proximity to the South Pole.

Polar Times Glacier. 69°46′S, 74°35′E. On the Ingrid Christensen Coast, it flows northward between Svarthausen Nunatak and Boyd Nunatak into the western part of the Publications Ice Shelf. Named by John H. Roscoe, the US cartographer, in 1952, for the *Polar Times*, a polar journal published by the American Polar Society of New York.

Polarårboken Glacier. 69°36′S, 76°E. 3 miles NE of the Stein Islands, flowing westward into the northern part of the Publications Ice Shelf. Named by US cartographer John H. Roscoe in 1952 for the *Polarårboken*, a polar journal published by the Norsk Polarklubb of Oslo, Norway.

The *Polarbjörn*. Norwegian ship of 486 tons. Under Capt. Bern Brandal it accompanied the *Polarsirkel* to Antarctica with the Norwegian Antarctic Expedition of 1956–57. It took the first SANAE down to Antarctica in 1959–60.

Polarforschung Glacier. 69°50′S, 75°07′E. Heavily crevassed. Flows north along the west side of the Meknattane Nunataks to the Publications Ice Shelf. Vestknatten Nunatak lies within the mouth of the glacier. Named by US cartographer John H. Roscoe in 1952 for the *Polarforschung*, a polar journal published by the Archiv für Polarforschung in Kiel, Germany.

The *Polarhav*. Tiny Norwegian sealer which in 1959 was sent to resupply the Belgian Roi Baudoin Station with a relief party, dogs, supplies, and equipment. It got trapped in the ice 200 miles from the station, and was helped out by the *Glacier*. It was not its first time in Antarctic waters. It transported the Belgian Antarctic Expedition of 1957–58, and was commanded that season by Capt. Sigmund Boë. In 1960–61 it took down the second SANAE.

Polaris Glacier. 64°14′S, 59°31′W. 4 miles long. Flows southward from the Detroit Plateau of Graham Land, between Pyke and Eliason Glaciers. Surveyed by the FIDS in 1960–61. Named by the UK for the Polaris motorsledge (*see* **Sledges**).

Polaris Peak. 84°39′S, 172°40′W. 970 m. 4 miles SW of Mount Roth in the Gabbro Hills of the Queen Maud Mountains. Named by the Southern Party of the NZGSAE 1963–64 because they drove a Polaris motor toboggan to the top.

The *Polarsirkel*. Norwegian ship which carried various Norwegian expeditions to the Antarctic. Under the command of John Jakobsen, it took down the Belgian Antarctic Expedition of 1957–58. From the 1976–77 season onwards it conducted marine geophysical surveys in Antarctic waters, and in 1981–82 was hired by the Indians to take down their Operation

Gangotri. The ship is sometimes referred to as the *Polar Circle*.

Polarstar Peak. 77°32'S, 86°09'W. 2,400 m. 3 miles north of Mount Ulmer in the northern part of the Sentinel Range. Discovered aerially by Ellsworth on Nov. 23, 1935. Named for Ellsworth's *Polar Star*.

Polarstar Ridge. 71°49'S, 70°27'W. In the NW part of Alexander Island.

The *Polarstern*. West German icebreaker (the name means "Polar Star") commissioned in Jan. 1982. 387 feet long, 82 feet wide, it has a 34½-foot draft and can carry 3,900 tons at 15½ knots. It can take 106 passengers and 36 crew and 40 scientists as well as 30 replacement crew for the scientific station Georg von Neumayer. On Nov. 20, 1985, it freed the trapped *John Biscoe*. From June 17–Dec. 14, 1986, it conducted the Winter Weddell Sea Project.

Poldervaart Ridge. 80°45'S, 26°W. In the Shackleton Range.

Pole of Inaccessibility Station *see* **Polyus Nedostupnosti Station**

Pole of Relative Inaccessibility. 82°06' S, 54°58'E. Also called the Pole of Inaccessibility, this is the point in the Antarctic which is farthest inland from all shore lines. About 550 miles from the South Pole itself, it was first reached on Dec. 14, 1958, by a USSR IGY tractor traverse.

Pole Station *see* **Amundsen-Scott South Pole Station**

Poles *see* **South Pole, South Geomagnetic Pole, South Magnetic Pole, Spin Pole, Pole of Relative Inaccessibility**

Polex South. International project proposed by the USSR and begun in 1975 as part of GARP (The Global Atmospheric Research Program). There is a Polex North too, and their mission was to understand the dynamics of the climate. The first phase was 1975–76, and this involved the USSR and the USA. Argentina studied the circumpolar current in the Drake Passage.

Polheim. Amundsen's tent base at the South Pole. Erected on Dec. 14, 1911, it was abandoned on Dec. 17, 1911.

Mount Pollard. 70°28'S, 64°37'E. Partly snow-covered. Just south of the Corry Massif and 3 miles west of the Crohn Massif in the Porthos Range of the Prince Charles Mountains. Named by the Australians for J.R. Pollard, ionosphere physicist at Wilkes Station in 1964.

Pollard Glacier. 65°49'S, 64°13'W. Flows into the south side of Comrie Glacier to the east of Bradford Glacier on the west coast of Graham Land. Named by the UK for Alan F.C. Pollard (1877–1948), first president of the British Society for International Biography. He also pioneered the use of the Universal Decimal System into public libraries.

Pollen. Pollen fell from flowers eons ago when there were flowers in Antarctica. It was then fossilized. Palynologist Rosemary Askin has pioneered Antarctic work in dating fossilized pollen spores.

Pollholmen. 69°01'S, 39°36'E. An island almost ⅓ mile long. 175 yards off the SE side of East Ongul Island in the east side of the entrance to Lützow-Holm Bay. Photographed by the LCE 1936–37, and named Pollholmen (the bay island), by the Norwegians for its position opposite the narrow inlet or bay separating East Ongul Island from Ongul Island.

Cape Pollock. 68°03'S, 146°50'E. The northern point of Dixson Island, at the west side of the mouth of the Ninnis Glacier. Discovered by the AAE 1911–14, and named by Mawson for Prof. J.A. Pollock of the Expedition Advisory Committee.

Mount Pollock. 73°45'S, 162°47'E. 2,640 m. Symmetrical. In the mid section of Recoil Glacier just south of Archambault Ridge, in the Deep Freeze Range of Victoria Land. Named for Herbert W. Pollock, USN, construction electrician at McMurdo Station in 1962 and 1967.

Pollution. Pollution was in Antarctica long before man came here. Penguin droppings, for example, can be pretty overpowering en masse, as the men at Hallett Station found out during IGY. The volume of natural human waste will never rival that of the Adélie penguin, to name but one animal in Antarctica. The big, and dangerous, problems are tourists and oil spills. Tourists are becoming a nuisance to the penguins and the scientists; the first oil spill occurred in 1989, and represented the biggest earthbound environmental threat to Antarctica yet. On Jan. 28, 1989, the *Bahía Paraíso* ran aground in the Bismarck Strait, about 1½ miles from Palmer Station. On Jan. 31, 1989, after passengers and crew had been rescued, and the ship had floated free in heavy seas, it capsized, spilling oil and several hundred propane gas containers into the sea, leaving a 2-mile slick.

Pollux Nunatak. 65°05′S, 59°53′W. One of the Seal Nunataks. 2 miles NW of Robertson Island in the Larsen Ice Shelf. Its existence was postulated by the FIDS in 1947, and proved by them during a 1953 survey. Named by the UK for the Greek mythological character, brother of Castor (Castor Nunatak is 4½ miles to the SSW).

Polnell, John. Quarter-gunner on the Wilkes Expedition 1838–42. Joined in the USA. Served the cruise.

Polo Glacier *see* **Il Polo Glacier**

Polotsk Island *see* **Robert Island**

Polychaeta *see* **Worms**

Polygon Spur. 86°S, 126°W. Ice-free. 2 miles SE of Tillite Spur at the south end of the Wisconsin Plateau in the Horlick Mountains. Named by John H. Mercer in 1964–65 for the network of unsorted polygons covering the surface of this spur.

The *Polynesia*. Norwegian floating factory ship belonging to the Rethval Whaling Co., of Oslo. Under the command of Capt. Hans Borge, it worked in the South Shetlands and South Orkneys

in 1913–14, and again in the Antarctic Peninsula area in 1914–15.

Polynesia Point. 60°43′S, 45°36′W. Ice-free. Forms the north side of the entrance to Paal Harbor, on the east side of Signy Island in the South Orkneys. Surveyed in 1933 by personnel from the Discovery Committee and again in 1947 by the FIDS. Named by the UK in 1954 for the *Polynesia*.

Polynya. A Russian word meaning an area in an ice-field which is constantly free of ice. Discovered in 1974, some are as large as France, and may be vents for gas and excess heat. (*See* **Weddell Polynya**, and **Terra Nova Polynya**.)

Polyus Nedostupnosti Station. Also called Pole of Inaccessibility Station. A USSR scientific station at 82°06′S, 54°58′E. At the Pole of Relative Inaccessibility, it was used only for the 1958–59 season.

Pomerantz, Dr. Martin A. Director of the Barthol Foundation, and innovator in Antarctic solar studies. He conducted cosmic ray studies in the McMurdo Sound area in 1959–60 and 1960–61. On Jan. 6, 1987, he was awarded the Distinguished Public Service Award by the NSF for his contributions to research at the South Pole and to USAP.

Pomerantz Tableland. 70°38′S, 159°50′E. 2,290 m. Ice-covered. 10 miles long. 15 miles NW of the Daniels Range in the Usarp Mountains. Named for Martin A. Pomerantz.

Pomona *see* **Coronation Island**

The *Pomona*. British sealer in the South Shetlands, 1821–23. From London, it was commanded by Capt. Robinson.

Pomona Plateau. 60°35′S, 45°55′W. Ice-covered. Over 300 m. Extends between Sandefjord Peaks and Deacon Hill in the western part of Coronation Island in the South Orkneys. Surveyed by the FIDS in 1948–50. Named by the UK to preserve the name Pomona in the area (*see* **Coronation Island**).

Pomornaya Hill. 70°45'S, 11°47'E. On the Princess Martha Coast.

Ponce Island. 63°18'S, 57°53'W. 175 yards east of Ortiz Island and almost ⅓ mile SE of Largo Island in the Duroch Islands. 1 mile NE of General Bernardo O'Higgins Station. Named by Martin Halpern (see **Halpern Point**) for Lautaro Ponce, chief of Antarctic Operations at the University of Chile, in appreciation of the Chilean logistical support provided to the Wisconsin field party led by Halpern.

Mount Pond. 62°57'S, 60°33'W. Also called Monte Campbell. 550 m. 1½ miles ESE of Pendulum Cove on Deception Island in the South Shetlands. Named probably by Henry Foster's expedition here in 1828–31 for John Pond (1767–1836), the 6th British astronomer royal.

Pond Peak. 77°19'S, 162°24'E. 1,430 m. Ice-free. At the south side of the mouth of Baldwin Valley in the Saint Johns Range of Victoria Land. Named in 1964 for James D. Pond, USN, in charge of electronic repair and maintenance at Hallett Station in 1962.

Pond Ridge. 73°25'S, 93°33'W. Extends north from Mount Loweth in the Jones Mountains. Named by the University of Minnesota–Jones Mountains Party here in 1960–61 for a small pond that was discovered on the ridge.

Ponies *see* **Manchurian ponies, Siberian ponies**

Ponting, Herbert G. b. 1870, Salisbury, England, d. 1935. Herbert George Ponting, FRGS. Australian camera artist, he was already famous in 1909 when he was picked to go south with Scott on that explorer's last expedition. The first professional photographer in the Antarctic, he made a movie, *90 Degrees South,* which he remade in sound in 1933. He wrote the book, *The Great White South.*

Ponting Cliff. 71°12'S, 168°21'E. Also seen spelled (erroneously) as Pointing Cliff. Similar in appearance to Meares Cliff just to the eastward. 3 miles east of the terminal confluences of the Nash, Dennistoun, and Wallis Glaciers on the northern coast of Victoria Land. Charted by Campbell's Northern Party in 1911–13, during Scott's last expedition. Campbell named it for Herbert G. Ponting.

Ponton Island. 65°06'S, 63°05'W. 1½ miles SE of the Moureaux Islands near the head of Flandres Bay, off the west coast of Graham Land. In 1954 the Argentines named it Islote Solitario. In 1957 they applied the same name to another island further to the SW (see **Solitario Island**). In 1960 the UK renamed this first one as Ponton Island, for Mungo Ponton (1802–1880), Scottish photography pioneer.

Pony Lake. 77°33'S, 166°09'E. Also called Home Lake. A little lake just north of Flagstaff Point, and ¼ mile north of Cape Royds, Ross Island. Named by Shackleton's 1907–9 expedition for the ponies they tethered near here. The expedition's winter hut was next to this lake.

Mount Pool. 86°13'S, 127°W. 2,090 m. At the NW side of Metavolcanic Mountain, at the eastern flank of the Reedy Glacier. Named for Douglas A. Pool, construction electrician at Byrd Station, 1962.

Poorman Peak. 69°57'S, 159°15'E. 1,610 m. Near the head of Suvorov Glacier. 9 miles WSW of Mount Ellery in the Wilson Hills. Named for Dean A. Poorman, USN, aviation machinist's mate with VX-6 at McMurdo Station, 1967.

Pope Glacier. 75°15'S, 111°30'W. 20 miles long. Flows north along the west side of Mount Murphy into the lower part of the Smith Glacier, in Marie Byrd Land. Named for Maj. Donald R. Pope, US Army, civil engineer on the staff of the Commander, US Naval Support Force, Antarctica, 1965–67.

Pope Mountain. 69°44'S, 158°50'E. 1,345 m. Mostly ice-free. Directly at the head of Tomilin Glacier. 3 miles SE of Governor Mountain in the Wilson Hills.

Named for Lt. Thomas J. Pope, USNR, Hercules aircraft navigator, 1968.

Populations. Before Oct. 1956 the human population was nil, really, except for whalers and government representatives in the South Shetlands. After 1956, however, the continent began to be populated on a permanent continuous basis, by relays of scientists. The population varies seasonally, and at times (in the summer) can reach 2,000 or more. The animal population is a different story. It is exceedingly difficult to count them. Some say the total number of seals, for example, is between 50 and 75 million, but others break it down like this: crabeater seals — 5 to 30 million; Weddell seals — ½ to 1 million; leopard seals — ½ million; elephant seals — 600,000 to 750,000; Ross seals — 50,000 to 200,000; fur seals — 30,000 to 200,000. The penguins are pretty uncountable, but the emperors are estimated at 1 million.

Lake Porkchop. 78°16′S, 163°08′E. Near the middle of Roaring Valley. Named for its shape by the New Zealanders in 1960–61.

Porphyry Bluff. 64°27′S, 59°11′W. Extends from the coast to two miles inland, between Larsen Inlet and Longing Gap in Graham Land. Surveyed by the FIDS in 1960–61. Named by the UK for the buff-colored quartz-plagioclase-porphyry rock characteristic of this bluff.

The *Porpoise*. 224-ton American brig, 88 feet long and 25 feet in the beam. 11 feet deep in the hold, it had 4 guns, a crew of 65 and a speed of 10 knots. Commanded by Cadwalader Ringgold during the Wilkes Expedition 1838–42, it helped chart the coastline of East Antarctica in 1840. On Jan. 29, 1840, it met Dumont d'Urville's expedition off the coast. Unsure flag signals made by each of the expeditions made each of the commanders think that there was snubbing going on by the other, and this caused a bit of international hostility until it was all cleared up.

Porpoise Basin. 66°15′S, 128°30′E. Also called Porpoise Trough. A submarine feature off the Banzare Coast of East Antarctica. Named for the *Porpoise*.

Porpoise Bay. 66°30′S, 128°30′E. 90 miles wide. Ice-filled. Indents the Banzare Coast between Cape Goodenough and Cape Morse. Discovered by Wilkes in 1840 and named by him for the *Porpoise*. The trouble is, he saw it through a mirage and logged it as being in 66°S, 130°E. This bay, to the SW, must be what he saw, and the USA applied the Wilkes naming to this one.

Porpoise Canyon. 64°S, 128°E. Submarine feature off the Banzare Coast of East Antarctica. Named for the *Porpoise*.

Porpoise Trough *see* **Porpoise Basin**

Porpoises. Cetaceous marine creatures similar to whales, they do not cross the Antarctic Convergence, and are therefore not seen in Antarctic waters.

Porro Bluff. 64°45′S, 62°33′W. South of Birdsend Bluff. Overlooks Errera Channel on the west coast of Graham Land. Named by the UK in 1960 for Ignazio Porro (1795–1875), Italian engineer and inventor in 1851 of the Porro prism, an optical device that inverts and reverses right and left an image viewed through it. This was important in the development of stereo-plotting instruments.

Port Lockroy *see* **Lockroy**

Port Lockroy Station. 64°49′S, 63°31′W. Also called Base A, it is a British scientific station at Port Lockroy, Wiencke Island. The second permanent British station in Antarctica, Base A was established in 1944 during Operation Tabarin on the site of an old whaling station. Geology and geography were the main studies, and J.W.S. Marr was the first leader, that winter. G.J. Lockley succeeded Marr, in the winter of 1945, when the FIDS took over the base. Lockley continued as FIDS leader in 1946, and in 1947 the station was vacated. It was reopened in 1948 under the leadership of

G.P.J. Barry, and vacated again in 1949. J.H. Chaplin led it in 1950, and it was vacated again in 1951. Ralph A. Lenton was leader in 1952, W.S.P. Ward in 1953, F.G. Bird in 1954, A.M. Carroll in 1955 and 1956, and C.C. Clement in 1957. During IGY ionosphere observations were made.

Port Martin *see* **Martin**

Port-Martin Station. 66°49′S, 14°24′E. Main Base for the French Polar Expedition of 1949–53, built on Pointe Géologie in Adélie Land in Jan. 1950. It had a hut with a kitchen, a washroom, storeroom, and an electric power plant fed by a diesel engine. At 3:20 a.m. on Jan. 24, 1952, the main building burned down, but all baggage and scientific results were saved. It was replaced by Dumont d'Urville Station. It is now a historic site. It was named for Martin, the photographer who had died on the *Commandant Charcot* on his way south in 1949.

The *Port of Beaumont, Texas.* 1,190-ton wooden-hulled, ocean-going tug, 183 feet long, formerly called the ATA-215. It had two 750 hp diesel-electric motors. It was Ronne's ship during the RARE 1947–48. Captained by Isaac Schlossbach, it was deliberately frozen in while the expedition wintered-over at Stonington Bay. Named by Ronne for the port of Beaumont in Texas, which had extended every courtesy to the expedition when it had docked there.

The Portal. 78°02′S, 159°45′E. The gap between the Lashly Mountains and Portal Mountain, through which the main stream of the Skelton Glacier enters the Skelton Névé from the Polar Plateau. Named descriptively in Jan. 1958 by the NZ Party of the BCTAE.

Portal Mountain. 78°06′S, 159°10′E. 2,555 m. Has a broad, ice-capped summit. South of the Lashly Mountains on the south side of the main stream of the Skelton Glacier, where it leaves the Polar Plateau. Discovered by the NZ Party of the BCTAE in 1957, who named it in association with The Portal.

Portal Point. 64°30′S, 61°46′W. In the NE part of Reclus Peninsula, on the west coast of Graham Land. In 1956 a FIDS hut was built here, from which a route to the plateau of Graham Land was established. Named by the UK in 1960 because this point is the gateway of the route.

Portal Rock. 83°50′S, 165°36′E. 1,990 m. A turretlike rock knob in the Queen Alexandra Range. 1½ miles NW of Fairchild Peak, just south of the mouth of Tillite Glacier. Named by the Ohio State University geological party here in 1966–67 because the only safe route to Tillite Glacier runs between this rock and Fairchild Peak.

Portalen Pass. 72°43′S, 3°53′W. A mountain pass between Domen Butte and Pilarryggen in the Borg Massif of Queen Maud Land. Name means "the gateway" in Norwegian.

Porten Pass. 72°12′S, 2°23′E. A mountain pass between Von Essen Mountain and Nupskammen Ridge in the Gjelsvik Mountains of Queen Maud Land. Name means "the gateway" in Norwegian.

Porteous, A.N. Second engineer on the *Discovery II*, 1933–35.

Porteous Point. 60°44′S, 45°41′W. Forms the north side of the NW entrance to Fyr Channel, at the SW end of Signy Island in the South Orkneys. Charted in 1933 by personnel on the *Discovery II*, and named for A.N. Porteous.

Porter, George. Seaman on the Wilkes Expedition 1838–42. Joined in the USA. Died at sea (not in the Antarctic) on March 3, 1842. He was buried at sea.

Porters Pinnacles. 71°33′S, 99°09′W. A group of low, ice-covered rocks forming a threat to shipping along the north coast of Thurston Island. 4 miles north of the eastern extremity of Glacier Bight. Discovered by the *Glacier* during the USN Bellingshausen Sea Expedition of Feb. 1960. Named for Cdr. Philip W. Porter, commander of the *Glacier* at the time.

Mount Porteus. 66°49'S, 51°03'E. Just east of Peacock Ridge in the Tula Mountains of Enderby Land. Named by the Australians for F.W. Porteus.

Porteus, F.W. Crew member on the *Discovery* during the BANZARE 1929–31.

Porthos Range. 70°25'S, 65°50'E. The second range south in the Prince Charles Mountains. It extends for about 30 miles in an east-west direction between the Scylla and Charybdis Glaciers. Visited in Dec. 1956 by W.G. Bewsher's ANARE southern party and named by Bewsher for one of the *Three Musketeers,* the most popular book read on the southern journey.

Portnipa Peak. 72°14'S, 2°24'E. 2,665 m. Surmounts Von Essen Mountain and Porten Pass in the Gjelsvik Mountains of Queen Maud Land. Name means "the gateway peak" in Norwegian.

Poryadin, Yaroslav. Navigator of the *Vostok* during von Bellingshausen's expedition of 1838–42.

Poryadin Island. 66°32'S, 92°59'E. ½ mile south of Haswell Island in the Haswell Islands. Discovered by the AAE 1911–14. Named by the USSR in 1956 for Yaroslav Poryadin.

Posadowsky Bay. 66°47'S, 89°27'E. An open embayment in the area of Gaussberg, just east of the West Ice Shelf. Discovered in Feb. 1902 by von Drygalski, who named it for Graf Arthur von Posadowsky-Wehner, German imperial home secretary who secured the government grant which covered the cost of von Drygalski's expedition.

Posadowsky Glacier. 66°50'S, 89°25' E. 9 miles long. Flows north to Posadowsky Bay, just east of Gaussberg in East Antarctica. It was observed from the summit of Gaussberg by members of von Drygalski's expedition in 1901–3. Named by the US in 1955 in association with the bay.

Poseidon Pass. 68°47'S, 63°40'W. 375 m. On the east side of the Antarctic Peninsula. It leads from Mobiloil Inlet to the Larsen Ice Shelf between Capes Keeler and Mayo. Surveyed by the FIDS in Nov. 1947. It was used by the east coast geological party from Base E on Stonington Island in Nov. 1960, and was found to provide an ideal sledging route. Named by the UK for the Greek god.

Posey, Julian W. US meteorologist who took over as scientific leader from Palle Mogensen at South Pole Station for the winter of 1959.

Posey Range. 71°12'S, 164°E. In the eastern part of the Bowers Mountains. It is bounded by the Smithson, Graveson, Lillie, and Champness Glaciers. Named for Julian W. Posey.

Cape Possession. 63°43'S, 61°51'W. Forms the western extremity of Chanticleer Island, just west of Hoseason Island, in the Palmer Archipelago. Named by Capt. Henry Foster's *Chanticleer* party which landed in this area on Jan. 7, 1829.

Possession Island. 71°52'S, 171°12'E. Almost 2 miles long. The most northerly and largest of the Possession Islands in the Ross Sea. Discovered by Ross on Jan. 11, 1841, and named by him in commemoration of the planting of the British flag here on that day.

Possession Islands. 71°56'S, 171°10'E. A group of small islands and rocks extending over an area of about 7 miles, in the western part of the Ross Sea. 5 miles SE of Cape McCormick, Victoria Land. They include: Possession Island, Bull Island, Foyn Island, Heftye Island, Kemp Rock, Dickson Pillar, and Favreau Pillar. Ross landed here on Jan. 11, 1841, and dedicated them to Queen Victoria. In 1895 Kristensen discovered a lichen here, the first vegetation found south of the Antarctic Circle.

Possession Nunataks *see* **Possession Rocks**

Possession Rocks. 66°45'S, 98°51'E. Also called Possession Nunataks. Two small rock outcrops just east of Northcliffe Glacier, above which they rise to 160 m. Discovered by the Eastern Sledge

Party under Frank Wild during the AAE 1911–14, and named following a ceremony in Dec. 1912 which claimed all the land around here for Britain.

Post Office Hill. 77°28'S, 169°14'E. 430 m. 4 miles NW of The Knoll. It overlooks the Adélie penguin rookery of Cape Crozier on Ross Island. Named by the New Zealanders in 1958–59 because the *Discovery,* in Jan. 1902, left messages attached to a pole in a cairn of rocks in the rookery for the relief ship *Morning.*

Post offices. *See also* **Stamps.** Before Shackleton left NZ in 1907 he was sworn in as a postmaster before Prime Minister Sir Joseph Ward, and authorized to open a post office on Edward VII Peninsula. It was actually opened at sea on Jan. 14, 1908, and closed March 4, 1909. There was a post office on Deception Island in the 1930s, and Byrd's 1933–35 expedition had PO facilities, but no actual post office, at Little America II. Finn Ronne started one on Stonington Island in 1947 during the RARE. Nowadays all the stations have one.

Post Ridge. 76°56'S, 143°38'W. A rock ridge, 3 miles long. It trends WNW-ESE. Just NE of Mount Swan in the Ford Ranges of Marie Byrd Land. Discovered by the USAS 1939–41. Named for Madison J. Post, ionosphere physicist at Byrd Station in 1970.

Poste, L. Stoker on the *Français,* during Charcot's 1903–5 expedition.

Poste Point. 65°05'S, 64°01'W. On the west side of Booth Island. Marks the southern limit of Salpêtrière Bay, in the Wilhelm Archipelago. Charted by Charcot in 1903–5 and named by him for L. Poste.

Postel Nunatak. 84°53'S, 67°46'W. 1,450 m. 8 miles SW of Snake Ridge along the ice escarpment that trends SW from the ridge, in the Patuxent Range of the Pensacola Mountains. Named for Philip A. Postel, meteorologist at Amundsen-Scott South Pole Station, 1967.

Mount Poster. 74°41'S, 65°39'W. West of the Latady Mountains and 9

miles NW of Mount Tenney in Palmer Land. Named for Carl K. Poster, geophysicist with the USARP South Pole–Queen Maud Land Traverse, 1967–68.

Postern Gap. 63°15'S, 55°59'W. A pass in the central ridge of Joinville Island, just east of Mount Tholus. Surveyed by the FIDS in 1954. This is the only pass through the ridge giving access to the central part of the south coast of the island, hence the name given by the UK.

Postillion Rock. 68°14'S, 66°53'W. Ice-free. In the northern part of Neny Fjord, just south of Roman Four Promontory on the west coast of Graham Land. Surveyed in 1936 by the BGLE, and again in 1949 by the FIDS, and named by them for its outlying position.

Potaka, Dr. Louis H. Medical officer on the shore party of Byrd's 1933–35 expedition.

Potaka Glacier *see* **Potaka Inlet**

Potaka Inlet. 71°57'S, 99°35'W. Also called Potaka Glacier. A narrow ice-filled inlet. 8 miles long. Indents the northern side of Thurston Island, just east of Starr Peninsula. Named for Dr. Louis H. Potaka.

Potmess Rocks. 62°19'S, 59°45'W. A group of large rocks. The Argentines call the group Islas Orejas de Burro (Asses Ears), but in the English language Asses Ears is only a feature within Potmess Rocks. Almost 1¼ miles west of Heywood Island in the South Shetlands. Charted by personnel on the *Nimrod* in Jan.–March 1967, during a Royal Navy Hydrographic Survey Unit expedition here. Named for the midday stew served on board the ship.

Potter, James. Ordinary seaman on the Wilkes Expedition 1838–42. Joined in the USA. Run at Rio.

Potter Cove. 62°14'S, 58°42'W. Indents the SW side of King George Island to the east of Barton Peninsula, in the South Shetlands. Bellingshausen Station is here. Also known as Havre Petter, it was discovered by the sealers before 1821, and originally called Potter's Cove.

Potter Glacier. 78°23'S, 162°12'E. 12 miles long. Between Mounts Huggins and Kempe in the Royal Society Range. It flows generally SW into the Skelton Glacier. Named in 1963 for Lt. Cdr. Edgar A. Potter, USN, helicopter pilot at McMurdo Station in 1960.

Potter Nunataks. 72°02'S, 161°10'E. Isolated. 6 miles SW of the Helliwell Hills and 20 miles NE of Welcome Mountain of the Outback Nunataks. Named for Neal Potter, economist at McMurdo Station in 1965–66, there to study the economic potentials of Antarctica.

Potter Peak. 75°07'S, 68°45'W. 6 miles east of Mount Jenkins in the Sweeney Mountains of Ellsworth Land. Discovered aerially by the RARE 1947–48. Named for Christopher J. Potter, glaciologist at Byrd Station, 1965–66.

Potter Peninsula. 62°15'S, 58°40'W. Almost a mile east of Three Brothers Hill, in the area of Potter Cove on the SW side of King George Island in the South Shetlands. It is Site of Special Scientific Interest #13.

Potters Cove *see* **Potter Cove**

Pottinger, Capt. Captain of the *Tartar* in the South Shetlands, in 1821–22.

Pottinger Point. 61°56'S, 58°24'W. Also called Punta Redonda. 2 miles east of Round Point on the northern coast of King George Island in the South Shetlands. Named by the UK in 1960 for Capt. Pottinger.

Pottle, James M. Private who joined the Wilkes Expedition 1838–42 in the USA and was later run at Rio.

Potts, Capt. Commander of the *L.P. Simmons,* in the South Shetlands, 1873–75.

Potts Glacier. 72°58'S, 166°50'E. Flows from the west slopes of Malta Plateau into the Mariner Glacier, in the Victory Mountains of Victoria Land. Named for Donald C. Potts, biologist at McMurdo Station, 1966–67.

Potts Peak. 61°58'S, 58°18'W. At the west side of Eldred Glacier on the north coast of King George Island in the South Shetlands. Named by the UK in 1960 for Capt. Potts.

Poulter, Dr. Thomas C. d. 1978. Scientific director of the Armour Research Foundation in Chicago. He was second-in-command and senior scientist on the shore party of Byrd's 1933–35 expedition. Later he designed and built the Snowcruiser (q.v.), and came down to the Antarctic again during the first part of the USAS, in 1939, to set it up.

Poulter Glacier. 86°50'S, 153°30'W. Flows east along the south flank of the Rawson Mountains of the Queen Maud Mountains, into Robert Scott Glacier. Discovered during Byrd's 1933–35 expedition and named for Thomas C. Poulter.

Poulton Peak. 68°02'S, 63°02'E. The highest point on the elongated rock ridge in the NE part of the Blånabbane Nunataks in Mac. Robertson Land. The summit looks like a rock cairn. The peak was used as an unoccupied trigonometrical station by ANARE surveyor M.A. Corry in 1965. Named by the Australians for M.A. Poulton, weather observer at Mawson Station in 1965.

The *Pourquoi Pas?* Charcot's 3-masted schooner during his second Antarctic voyage, of 1908–10. It was the most modern polar vessel until that time, taking 8 months to build at Saint-Malo, France, by Gauthier Senior, at a cost of 780,000 gold francs. It had 800 tons capacity, was 131 feet long, 30 feet wide, and had 550 hp. It had all the modern equipment — telephones, a searchlight, ship-to-shore electric cables, a motor launch, and 3 laboratories. It was launched May 18, 1908. Charcot was obviously leader of the expedition, and the scientists included Gourdon, Bongrain, Godfroy, Gain, Rouch, Liouville, and one other. Of the 22 crew, 8 had sailed with Charcot on the *Français* a few years before. The captain was Ernest Cholet, and the crew included: Boland, Thomas, Denais, Hervé, Monsimet, J. Guéguen, F. Guéguen. Charcot froze the ship in the ice deliberately at Petermann Island in 1909. He disappeared with the ship on Sept. 16, 1936, in the area of Greenland.

Pourquoi Pas Glacier. 66°15′S, 135°55′ E. 4 miles wide. 15 miles long. Flows NNW from the continental ice and terminates in the Pourquoi Pas Glacier Tongue 9 miles WNW of Pourquoi Pas Point. Named by the French in 1952 for the *Pourquoi Pas?*

Pourquoi Pas Glacier Tongue. 66°10′ S, 136°E. 4 miles wide. 6 miles long. The prominent seaward extension of the Pourquoi Pas Glacier. Named for the *Pourquoi Pas?*

Pourquoi Pas Island. 67°41′S, 67°28′ W. 17 miles long. Between 5 and 11 miles wide. Mountainous. Between Bigourdan and Bourgeois Fjords off the west coast of Graham Land. Discovered by Charcot in 1908–10. Charted by the BGLE in 1934–37 and named by them for the *Pourquoi Pas?* Features on the island are named for Jules Verne characters.

Pourquoi Pas Point. 66°12′S, 136°11′E. Ice-covered. Forms the west side of the entrance to Victor Bay on the coast of East Antarctica. Charted by the French in 1950–52 and named by them in 1954 for the *Pourquoi Pas?*

Powder Island. 69°32′S, 68°47′W. 8 miles SSE of Cape Jeremy and 2 miles off the west coast of Palmer Land, in the George VI Sound. Surveyed in 1948 by the FIDS and named by them for the crumbly type of rock on this island, a rock which when easily crushed turns to a powder.

The *Powell.* Whale catcher used by Petter Sørlle to get about while he made his running survey of the South Orkneys in 1912–13. It belonged to the factory ship, the *Paal*, a name which sounds very much like Powell and Palmer.

Mount Powell. 85°21′S, 87°56′W. 2,195 m. Shares a small massif with King

Peak 1½ miles to the WNW. In the eastern part of the Thiel Mountains. Named by Bermel and Ford, leaders of the Thiel Mountains Survey Party here in 1960–61, for John Wesley Powell (1834–1902), the second director of the US Geological Survey, from 1881–94.

Powell, Capt. Commander of the *Eliza* in the South Shetlands in 1820–21. This may be George Powell, but this is highly uncertain.

Powell, George. British sealing captain in the South Shetlands in the *Dove* in 1821–22. From Nov. 30, 1821–Dec. 22, 1821, he teamed up with the *James Monroe* under the command of Nat Palmer, and together the two captains discovered the South Orkneys on Dec. 6, 1821, Powell annexing them for Britain. He did some charting here and while cruising the South Shetlands. His charts of 1822 are seminal in the history of Antarctic cartography. He died at sea on a later, non-Antarctican, voyage. This could be Capt. Powell (*see* **Powell, Capt.**).

Powell Basin. 62°15′S, 49°30′W. A submarine feature in the South Shetlands. Named for George Powell.

Powell Channel. 68°08′S, 67°07′W. A narrow marine channel between Millerand Island and the Debenham Islands, off the west coast of Graham Land. Named by the UK for Lt. John M. Powell, RN, who surveyed the channel in 1972.

Powell Cove. 66°15′S, 110°32′E. In the western side of Clark Peninsula, between Whitney and Stonehocker Points, on the coast of East Antarctica. Named by Carl Eklund in 1957 for James T. Powell, USN, chief aerographer at Wilkes Station in 1957 (*see also* **Powell Hill**).

Powell Group *see* **South Orkney Islands**

Powell Hill. 81°56′S, 161°11′E. Rounded. Ice-covered. 6 miles WSW of Mount Christmas, overlooking the head of Algie Glacier. Named for Lt. Cdr. James T. Powell, USN, chief aerographer at Wilkes Station, 1957 (see *also* **Powell Cove**).

Powell Island. 60°41'S, 45°03'W. Also called Cruchleys Island, Dibdins Island. A narrow island, 7 miles long and 2 miles wide. Between Coronation Island and Laurie Island in the South Orkneys. Discovered by Powell and Palmer in Dec. 1821, and named by 1839, at least, for George Powell. There is a Specially Protected Area here (an SPA) which takes in the southern half of Powell Island, Fredriksen Island, Michelsen Island, Christoffersen Island, Grey Island and the unnamed islets nearby. This is SPA #15.

Powell Islands *see* **South Orkney Islands**

Powell Rock. 60°42'S, 45°36'W. A small submerged rock on the east side of Signy Island in the South Orkneys. Off the mouth of Starfish Cove, about a third of a mile NE of Balin Point. Charted by Petter Sørlle in 1912–13 and named by him as Powellboen, for his whale catcher, the *Powell*.

Powellboen *see* **Powell Rock**

Power, James S. Purser's steward on the Wilkes Expedition 1838–42. Joined the *Peacock* at Callao and later transferred to the *Flying Fish*.

Power Glacier. 66°35'S, 125°15'E. In Norths Highland, Wilkes Land, in East Antarctica.

Poynter. Master's mate on the *Williams* under Bransfield in 1819–20.

Poynter Col. 63°49'S, 59°07'W. Over 700 m. Snow-filled. Joins Poynter Hill and Ivory Pinnacles in northern Graham Land. 9 miles ESE of Cape Kjellman. Charted by the FIDS in 1948. Named by the UK in association with the hill.

Poynter Hill. 63°46'S, 59°06'W. 825 m. 8 miles ESE of Cape Kjellman on the west side of the Trinity Peninsula. Charted in 1948 by the FIDS. Named by the UK in 1950 for Poynter (q.v.).

Prahl Crags. 76°04'S, 134°43'W. 2,750 m. On the south slopes of the Mount Moulton massif, in Marie Byrd Land. Named for Sidney R. Prahl who studied ice-sheet dynamics in the area NE of Byrd Station in 1971–72.

Pram Point. 77°51'S, 166°45'E. A low rounded point on the SE side of Hut Point Peninsula, about 1½ miles NE of Cape Armitage on Ross Island. Discovered by Scott in Feb. 1902, and named by him for the pram (a Norwegian-style skiff) they had to use to travel between here and Winter Quarters Bay. Scott Base is here.

Pranke Island. 73°14'S, 124°55'W. Ice-covered. Close to Siple Island in the western extremity of Russell Bay, off the coast of Marie Byrd Land. Named for James B. Pranke, aurora researcher at Byrd Station in 1965.

Punta Prat *see* **Edwards Point**

Mount Pratt. 85°24'S, 176°41'E. Also called Stenhouse Nunatak. The most northerly nunatak in the Grosvenor Mountains. Just east of the head of Mill Stream Glacier. 17 miles north of Block Peak. Between Mount Bumstead and the Ross Ice Shelf, in the Queen Maud Mountains. Discovered by Byrd on his flight to the Pole in Nov. 1929, and named by him for Thomas B. Pratt, US financier and contributor to the expedition.

Pratt, David L. Engineer who went with Fuchs across the continent during the BCTAE 1957–58.

Pratt, Geoffrey. John Geoffrey D. Pratt. Geophysicist who went with Fuchs across the continent during the BCTAE 1957–58.

Pratt Peaks *see* **Pratts Peak**

Pratts Peak. 80°24'S, 29°21'W. Also called (erroneously) Pratt Peaks. 6 miles east of Mount Provender in the western part of the Shackleton Range. Named by the UK for David and Geoffrey Pratt.

Prebble Glacier. 84°16'S, 164°30'E. 9 miles long. Flows westward from Mount Kirkpatrick in the Queen Alexandra Range to enter the Walcott Névé north of

Fremouw Peak. Named by the Northern Party of the NZGSAE 1961–62 for Michael Prebble, of the base support party, who assisted the party with preparations and training.

Prebble Icefalls. 79°54′S, 155°55′E. On the SW side of Midnight Plateau in the Darwin Mountains. They occupy 2 large cirques SW of Mount Ellis and fall about 900 m. Discovered by the VUWAE 1962–63, and named for W.M. Prebble, geologist with the expedition.

Precious Peaks. 62°04′S, 58°20′W. A line of about 3 dark peaks at the NE side of the Martel Inlet on Admiralty Bay, King George Island, in the South Shetlands. Charted by Charcot in 1908–10. Named by the UK in 1960 for Alan Precious, FIDS meteorological observer at Base D in 1954 and 1955, and leader at Base G in 1957.

Mount Predoehl. 82°56′S, 163°11′E. 1,710 m. Partly snow-covered. Just north of the lower part of Pavlak Glacier in the Queen Elizabeth Range. Named for Martin C. Predoehl, meteorologist at McMurdo Station in 1961–62 and 1962–63.

Prehn Peninsula. 75°06′S, 63°30′W. 20 miles long. 10 miles wide. Mainly ice-covered. Between Hansen and Gardner Inlets, on the southeast coast of Palmer Land. Discovered aerially by the RARE 1947–48. Named for Lt. Cdr. Frederick A. Prehn, Jr., USN, pilot over this area in 1967 and 1968.

Preikestolen Ridge. 72°06′S, 2°51′W. In the western part of Liljequist Heights, on the Ahlmann Ridge of Queen Maud Land. Name means "the pulpit" in Norwegian.

Prensa Islands. Small group in the northern part of the Wilhelm Archipelago. They cannot be mapped properly yet, because the photos of the area are not detailed enough.

President Beaches. 62°39′S, 61°09′W. A series of beaches extending for 6 miles along the western end of the Byers Peninsula on Livingston Island in the South Shetlands. In Feb. 1969 Kaye R. Everett, US geologist on the island, named them West Beaches. He was making a reconnaissance soil survey in the area. However, the US thought that the name would not really be distinctive enough, or meaningful enough, and they were right. Instead, they called it President Beaches, to preserve the name that had once been used for Plymouth Harbor — i.e., President's Harbor, which is an anchorage just off these beaches.

President Harbor *see* **New Plymouth**

President Head. 62°44′S, 61°12′W. A headland forming the southern extremity of Snow Island in the South Shetlands. Named by the UK in 1961 to preserve the original name of the island, i.e., President Island as the Connecticut sealers called it in 1820–21. That name did not catch on.

President Island *see* **Snow Island**

Presidente Frei Station. 62°12′S, 58°54′W. Also called Presidente Eduardo Frei Station, it is a year-round Chilean scientific base on King George Island in the South Shetlands. Built in 1969 it is the center of the Chilean meteorological program in Antarctica, and is maintained by the Chilean Air Force. It collects meteorological data, and uses the airstrip of its neighbor, Teniente Rodolfo Marsh Station.

Presidente Gabriel González Videla Station. 64°49′S, 62°52′W. Permanent Chilean meteorological station built in 1951 on Waterboat Point, Paradise Harbor (or Paradise Bay as it was called then), on the Danco Coast of the Antarctic Peninsula. Leaders of the wintering parties were 1951 — Roberto Araos Tapia; 1952 — Gerardo López; 1953 — Sergio Espinoza; 1954 — Eleuterio Molina; 1955 — Orlando Pérez; 1956 — Ernesto L. Gález; 1957 — Vicente Rodrigues Bustos. The station was closed after the IGY, subsequently reopened in 1980 by the Chilean Air Force, but closed again.

Presidente Pedro Aguirre Cerda Station. 62°56′S, 60°36′W. Chilean scientific base at Pendulum Cove, Deception Island, in the South Shetlands. Nearby are warm volcanic springs. Established in 1955. Leaders of the first wintering parties were 1955 — Hernán del Rio; 1956 — Hugo Sage; 1957 — Mario Jiménez Vargas. The station was destroyed by the volcano of Dec. 5, 1967, which also wiped out the British Base B.

The *Presidente Pinto*. Chilean ship which took down the Presidential Antarctic Expedition of 1948. Also part of the 1948–49 expedition (Capt. Jorge Gándara).

Presidential Antarctic Expedition. Chilean expedition of 1948, which took to the Antarctic President General González Videla, and the minister of National Defense, Gen. Guillermo Barrios Tirado. The president inaugurated Capitán Arturo Prat Station in Feb. 1948.

President's Harbor *see* **New Plymouth**

Preslik Spur. 82°32'S, 51°20'W. In the extreme northern part of the Pensacola Mountains.

Mount Press. 78°05'S, 85°58'W. 3,830 m. Just east of the main ridge of the Sentinel Range and 3½ miles ENE of Mount Bentley, in the Ellsworth Mountains. Named by Charles R. Bentley during his Marie Byrd Land Traverse of 1957–58, for Frank Press, vice-chairman of the technical panel on glaciology of the US National Committee for the IGY. In 1965 he became chairman of the Department of Earth and Planetary Sciences at M.I.T., and in 1977 became White House science advisor.

Pressure Bay. 71°25'S, 169°20'E. An arm of Robertson Bay. 3 miles wide. Between Cape Wood and Birthday Point, on the north coast of Victoria Land. Charted in 1911 by Campbell's Northern Party. They had a great deal of trouble sledging across the pressure ice in this area caused by the nearby Shipley Glacier descending to the sea ice. Hence the name given by Campbell.

Pressure ice *see* **Pressure ridges**

Pressure ridges. Also known as pressure ice. Ridges, hummocks, or any kind of sharp mass of ice thrust up by the collision of slowly-moving ice with a land mass.

Preston Island. 67°48'S, 68°59'W. The largest of the Henkes Islands, off the south end of Adelaide Island. Named by the UK in 1963 for Frank Preston, FIDS officer-in-charge and surveyor at Base T in 1961–62. He was a member of the first party to winter there.

Preston Point. 70°17'S, 71°48'E. Ice-covered. Marks the north end of Gillock Island in the Amery Ice Shelf. Named by US cartographer John H. Roscoe in 1952 for J.C. Preston, Jr., air crewman on Operation Highjump flights over this area which provided the photos from which Roscoe was to work 5 years later.

Mount Prestrud. 86°34'S, 165°07'W. Over 2,400 m. In the SW part of the massif at the head of the Amundsen Glacier, in the Queen Maud Mountains. During his race to the Pole in Nov. 1911 Amundsen named a mountain in this general area as Mount K. Prestrud, for Lt. Kristian Prestrud. This may or may not be the same mountain, but the USA picked one and named it to preserve Prestrud's name in the area.

Prestrud, Kristian. Lt. Scientific observations chief on the Norwegian Antarctic Expedition of 1910–12, and first officer on the *Fram*. He did not go with Amundsen to the Pole, but he did lead an independent sledge journey, the Eastern Sledge Party of 1911, to Scott's Nunataks (or Scott Nunataks, as they are now also called), on the Edward VII Peninsula (or Edward VII Land, as it was then called).

Prestrud Coast *see* **Shirase Coast**

Prestrud Inlet. 78°18'S, 156°W. A re-entrant (an ice-shelf indentation into the mainland) in the south side of Edward VII Peninsula. It forms the neck of this peninsula, at the NE corner of the Ross

Ice Shelf. Named by the USAS 1939–41 for Lt. Kristian Prestrud.

Preuschoff, Franz. Engineer on the flying boat *Passat* during the German New Schwabenland Expedition of 1938–39.

Preuschoff Range. 72°04′S, 4°03′E. Comprises Mount Hochlin and associated features. Just west of Kaye Crest in the Mühlig-Hofmann Mountains of Queen Maud Land. Discovered aerially by the Ritscher expedition of 1938–39 and named Preuschoff-Rücken by Ritscher for Franz Preuschoff. Because Ritscher's photos were inaccurate, this may or may not be the feature that he intended, but it is pretty close to it if it is not.

Prévost, Jean. Biologist on the French Polar Expedition of 1952.

Prevot Island. 64°53′S, 63°58′W. Also called Tangent Island, Isla Primer Teniente Prevot. ½ mile NE of Miller Island. The northernmost of the Wauwermans Islands in the Wilhelm Archipelago. The Argentines called it first Isla Fernando, and in 1956 changed it to honor First Lieutenant (Primer Teniente) Prevot, commander of the mobile detachment in the operations of the Argentine Air Force unit for Antarctica. He died on the job.

Prezbecheski Island *see* **Przybyszewski Island**

Mount Priam. 64°34′S, 63°24′W. The central mass of the Trojan Range. 4 miles north of Mount Français on Anvers Island. Flat-topped. Snow-covered. 1,980 m. Surveyed in 1955 by the FIDS. Named by the UK for the Homeric character.

Mount Price. 84°29′S, 166°38′E. The eastern of two peaks at the north end of the Adams Mountains. 3,030 m. In the Queen Alexandra Range. Named for Rayburn Price, meteorologist at Hallett Station in 1963.

Price Bluff. 86°32′S, 144°34′W. 5 miles NE of Mount Mooney, Near the head of Robison Glacier in the Queen

Maud Mountains. Named for Lt. Robert P. Price, USN, photographic officer on many flights as an in-flight observer during the periods 1965 and 1966.

Price Nunatak. 67°57′S, 62°43′E. Marks the northern end of the Trilling Peaks. 3 miles south of Mount Burnett in the Framnes Mountains of Mac. Robertson Land. Photographed by the LCE 1936–37. Named by the Australians for H. Price, senior diesel mechanic at Mawson Station in 1959.

Price Peak. 85°43′S, 142°24′W. 1,510 m. At the north side of the Leverett Glacier. 8 miles north of the end of California Plateau. Named for Floyd W. Price, VX-6 personnel man in Antarctica every summer season between 1963 and 1967, as well as one winter-over.

Priest Island *see* **Goetschy Island**

Mount Priestley. 75°11′S, 161°53′E. 1,100 m. At the north side of the David Glacier. 5 miles SW of Mount Bellingshausen in the Prince Albert Mountains of Victoria Land. Named by Shackleton's 1907–9 expedition for Raymond Priestley.

Priestley, Raymond. b. 1886, Tewkesbury, England. d. 1974. Raymond Edward Priestley. Assistant geologist on the British Antarctic Expedition of 1907–9, led by Shackleton. He later studied geology in Sydney under Edgeworth David. He was back in Antarctica on Scott's 1910–13 expedition, and was the leader of the second ascent of Mount Erebus. He was a member of Victor Campbell's Northern Party during the same expedition, and thus a part of their wild adventure. He was later knighted, and was chancellor of Birmingham University in England. He made two more visits to Antarctica in his old age.

Priestley Glacier. 74°20′S, 163°22′E. Also spelled (erroneously) as Priestly Glacier. A major valley glacier. 60 miles long. Flows SE from the Polar Plateau of Victoria Land between the Deep Freeze Range and the Eisenhower Range and enters the northern end of the Nansen

Ice Sheet. Explored by Campbell's Northern Party of 1911–13, and named by Campbell for Raymond Priestley.

Priestley Névé. 73°35'S, 160°20'E. At the head of the Priestley Glacier (in association with which it was named by New Zealand in the 1960s), in Victoria Land.

Priestley Peak. 67°12'S, 50°23'E. Between Mount Pardoe and Mount Tod on the south side of Amundsen Bay in Enderby Land. Discovered on Jan. 14, 1930, by the BANZARE, and named by Mawson for Raymond Priestley.

Priestly Glacier see **Priestley Glacier**

Prilednikovoye Lake. 70°45'S, 11°35'E. 1¼ miles SSW of Tyuleniy Point in the Schirmacher Hills, at the edge of the continental ice-sheet in Queen Maud Land. Named Ozero Priyednikovoye (foreglacier lake) by the USSR in 1961 for its location.

Cape Primavera see **Spring Point**

Primavera Bay see **Brialmont Cove**

Primavera Station. 64°09'S, 60°57'W. Year-round Argentine scientific base on Cape Primavera (Spring Point as it is called by the US, and as it is listed in this book), near Brialmont Cove, on the Danco Coast of the Antarctic Peninsula. Started as a refugio (refuge hut) in 1954, it later became a real scientific station.

Prime Head. 63°13'S, 57°17'W. Snow-covered headland. Forms the northern extremity of the Antarctic Peninsula. During his 1837–40 expedition Dumont d'Urville discovered and named as Cap Siffrey a point in this area. For ages this was thought to be the same point, and was called Cape Siffrey in English. Later, however, the UK found Dumont d'Urville's Cap Siffrey to be another point, 2 miles to the ESE. The UK then named that one Siffrey Point, and renamed this one as Prime Head, to indicate that this is, indeed, the northernmost point on the Antarctic continent.

Monte Primer Teniente Aciar see **Mount Aciar**

Isla Primer Teniente Aciar see **Prevot Island**

The Primero de Mayo. Also written The 1° de Mayo. Argentine ship first in the South Shetlands in 1930. A. Rodríguez was surveyor. It was back in the South Shetlands in 1942, surveying and claiming Deception Island for Argentina. Alberto J. Oddera was captain that year. In 1943 it was back again, to do more surveying. In March 1943 it landed a party at Stonington Island, the first visitors since the USAS left it in 1941. They rescued much of the US equipment. Captain on this 1943 cruise was Silvano Harriague.

Isla Primero de Mayo see **Lambda Island**

Primero de Mayo Bay. 62°58'S, 60°42'W. Also called Surgidero Iquique, Fumarole Bay. The largest bay in Port Foster, Deception Island, on the SW side of that natural harbor. Named Bahía 1° de Mayo (Bahía Primero de Mayo) by the Argentines before 1953, for the Primero de Mayo.

Primero de Mayo Station. 62°59'S, 60°42'W. Argentine scientific station opened in 1948 on Primero de Mayo Bay, Deception Island. Also called Decepción Station, it was maintained by the Argentine Navy, and collected meteorological data. Its first leader was Roberto A. Cabrera. Alberto Fort led it in 1956, and Z.S. Bolino was leader in 1957, during the IGY, when the station studied meteorology, geomagnetism, glaciology, ionosphere observations, and oceanography.

The Primeroso-Mariana. Spanish vessel out of Cádiz in 1819, which went south of 60°S in an effort to save its partner ship, the San Telmo (q.v. for details).

Mount Prince. 74°58'S, 134°11'W. 640 m. A prominent butte. Marks the northern end of the Perry Range on the Marie Byrd Land coast. Algae, lichens, mosses and petrels are to be found here. Discovered aerially by the USAS in 1939–41.

Named for Joseph F. Prince, USN, VX-6 aviation machinist's mate who spent several summer seasons in Antarctica, as well as wintering-over at Little America in 1956 and at McMurdo Station in 1966.

Prince Albert Mountains. 76°S, 161°30'E. Over 200 miles long. Extend north-south between the Priestley Glacier and the Ferrar Glacier in Victoria Land. Discovered on Feb. 17, 1841, by Ross, who named them for Prince Albert, husband of Queen Victoria.

Prince Andrew Plateau. 83°38'S, 162°E. Ice-covered. 40 miles long. 15 miles wide. South of Mount Rabot in the Queen Elizabeth Range. Named by the New Zealanders in 1961–62 for the son of Queen Elizabeth II.

Prince Charles Mountains. 72°S, 67°E. Also called Main South Range. In Mac. Robertson Land. They include the Athos, Porthos, and Aramis Ranges. Form an arc of about 260 miles in length, extending from the vicinity of Mount Starlight in the north to Goodspeed Nunataks in the south. Discovered aerially and from a distance during Operation Highjump, 1946–47. They were much explored by ANARE parties over the years, and named by the Australians in 1956 for Prince Charles, son of Queen Elizabeth II.

Prince Charles Strait. 61°05'S, 54°35'W. 5 miles wide. Between Cornwallis and Elephant Islands in the South Shetlands. Known to sealers in 1820–21. The first recorded navigation of this strait was in 1839 by the *Porpoise* during the Wilkes Expedition. Named for Prince Charles (*see* **Prince Charles Mountains**).

Prince de Ligne Mountains. 72°20'S, 31°14'E. 2,285 m. 10 miles north of the Belgica Mountains. Discovered by the Belgian Antarctic Expedition of 1957–58 led by Gaston de Gerlache, who named them for Prince Antoine de Ligne, pilot and photographer with the expedition.

Prince Edward Glacier. 82°46'S, 159°32'E. Flows from the north side of Cot-

ton Plateau in the Queen Elizabeth Range, and north for about 6 miles along the west side of Hochstein Ridge. Named by New Zealand for Prince Edward, son of Queen Elizabeth II.

Prince Gustav Channel. 63°50'S, 58°15'W. 80 miles long. Between 4 and 15 miles wide. Separates James Ross Island and Vega Island from Trinity Peninsula. Discovered in Oct. 1903 by Nordenskjöld's expedition, and named by the Swedish explorer as Crown Prince Gustav Channel, for the man who later became king. The name was later shortened.

Prince Harald Coast. 69°30'S, 36°E. The coast of Queen Maud Land between Riiser-Larsen Peninsula (34°E) and the eastern entrance point to Lützow-Holm Bay, marked by the coastal angle at 40°E. Or, between the Princess Ragnhild Coast and the Prince Olav Coast. It actually encompasses the Lützow-Holm Bay area. Discovered aerially by an LCE 1936–37 flight carrying Viggo Widerøe, Nils Romnaes, and Ingrid Christensen. Named Prins Harald Kyst for the young son of the Crown Prince of Norway. It is also called Prince Harald Land.

Prince of Wales Glacier. 82°44'S, 160°10'E. In the Queen Elizabeth Range. Flows north for 10 miles between Hochstein Ridge and Kohmyr Ridge into Hamilton Glacier. Named by the New Zealanders in 1961–62 for the Prince of Wales, i.e., Prince Charles, son of Queen Elizabeth II.

Prince Olaf Mountains *see* **Prince Olav Mountains**

Prince Olav Coast. 68°30'S, 42°30'E. Also called Crown Prince Olav Land, Kronprins Olav Kyst (in Norwegian), Prince Olav Land. The section of the Queen Maud Land coast between the eastern entrance point of Lützow-Holm Bay, marked by the coastal angle at 40°E, and Shinnan Glacier at 44°38'E. Discovered by Riiser-Larsen on a flight from the *Norvegia* in Jan. 1930. Named for Crown Prince Olav of Norway.

Prince Olav Land *see* **Prince Olav Coast**

¹Prince Olav Mountains. 84°57′S, 173° W. Also spelled Prince Olaf Mountains. Extend from Shackleton Glacier to Liv Glacier in the Queen Maud Mountains, at the head of the Ross Ice Shelf. Discovered in 1911 by Amundsen, and named by him as Crown Prince Olav Mountains, for the Crown Prince of Norway. The name was later shortened.

²Prince Olav Mountains *see* **Bush Mountains**

Prince Philip Glacier. 82°21′S, 159°55′ E. Flows south for 20 miles between the Cobham and Holyoake Ranges into the Nimrod Glacier. Named by NZ for Prince Philip, the Duke of Edinburgh, husband of Queen Elizabeth II, and himself an Antarctic visitor (*see* **Philip**).

Prince-Regent Luitpold Land *see* **Luitpold Coast**

Princess Anne Glacier. 82°59′S, 159° 20′E. In the Queen Elizabeth Range. Flows from the area south of Mount Bonaparte between the Cotton and Bartrum Plateaus, into Marsh Glacier. Named by the New Zealanders in 1961–62 for the daughter of Queen Elizabeth II.

Princess Astrid Coast. 70°45′S, 12°30′ E. The section of the Queen Maud Land coast between 5°E and 20°E. The entire coast is bordered by ice shelves. Discovered in March 1931 by Capt. H. Halvorsen of the *Sevilla,* and named by him as Prinsesse Astrid Kyst, for the Norwegian princess.

The *Princess Charlotte.* British sealer out of Calcutta, India. It was in the South Shetlands in 1821–22 under the command of Capt. M'Kean. It moored in Johnson's Dock.

Princess Elizabeth Land. 70°S, 83°E. Also called Princess Elizabeth Coast. That section of the coast of East Antarctica between Gaussberg and Mac. Robertson Land. Discovered by the BANZARE during the 1930–31 season, and named by Mawson for the princess who would later become Queen Elizabeth II.

Princess Martha Coast. 72°S, 7°30′W. That section of the Queen Maud Land coast between 5°E and the terminus of the Stancomb Wills Glacier (20°W). A long coast, it connects Coats Land with New Schwabenland. The entire coast is bounded by ice shelves with ice cliffs 20 to 35 meters high. Discovered aerially by Riiser-Larsen in a flight from the *Norvegia* on Feb. 8, 1930, and called Crown Princess Martha Land, for the Norwegian princess.

Princess Martha Coast Station. 70°30′ S, 2°32′W. Also called Norway Station. On the Princess Martha Coast of Queen Maud Land, to the east of the Weddell Sea. Established in 1957, it was Norway's only IGY station. It operated until Jan. 8, 1960, when Norway handed it over to South Africa and it became Tottenbukta Sanae Station, or simply Sanae Station.

Princess Ragnhild Coast. 70°30′S, 27° E. Also called Ragnhild Coast. That section of the Queen Maud Land coast between 20°E and the Riiser-Larsen Peninsula (34°E). The entire coast, except the eastern end, is fringed by ice shelves. Discovered by Riiser-Larsen and Capt. Nils Larsen in flights from the *Norvegia* on Feb. 16, 1931. Named Prinsesse Ragnhild Kyst, or Princess Ragnhild Land, by the Norwegians for their princess.

Cabo Principal *see* **Principal Point**

Canal Principal *see* **The Sound**

Principal Point. 64°55′S, 63°27′W. Also called Pursuit Point. Ice-covered. 4 miles east of Cape Errera. Forms the SE end of Wiencke Island. Charted by Charcot in 1903–5. Named Cabo Principal by the Argentine Antarctic Expedition of 1953–54, for its prominence as a feature.

Canal Príncipe Gustavo *see* **Prince Gustav Channel**

Prins Harald Land *see* **Prince Harald Coast**

Prinsesse Astrid Kyst *see* **Princess Astrid Coast**

Prinsesse Ragnhild Kyst *see* **Princess Ragnhild Coast**

Prinzregent Luitpold Land *see* **Luitpold Coast**

Prions. The prion is a type of petrel. There are three species: dove prion, or Antarctic prion *(Pachyptila desolata)*, fulmar prion, and thin-billed prion. All are seen in the Antarctic, but only the Dove breeds south of 60°S — in the South Orkneys.

Mount Prior. 72°58'S, 168°47'E. 1,220 m. 10 miles west of Mount Brewster, at the head of Whitehall Glacier in the western part of the Daniell Peninsula of Victoria Land. Named by the New Zealanders in 1957–58 for George T. Prior *(see* **Prior Island).**

Prior Island. 75°41'S, 162°52'E. 1 mile long. Just east of Lamplugh Island, off the coast of Victoria Land. Charted by Shackleton's 1907–9 expedition. Named by Shackleton for George Thurland Prior, keeper of the Department of Minerals at the British Museum from 1909–27. He studied all the rocks brought back by British Antarctic expeditions.

Prioress Island. 64°56'S, 63°53'W. ½ mile east of Host Island in the Wauwermans Islands of the Wilhelm Archipelago. Named by the UK in 1958 for the *Canterbury Tales* character.

Prism Ridge. 73°33'S, 94°14'W. Just north of Haskell Glacier and 2 miles SSW of Bonnabeau Dome, in the Jones Mountains. Named by the University of Minnesota–Jones Mountains Party, 1960–61, for the large block of ice in the shape of a square prism which they found standing as an isolated feature at the south end of this ridge.

The *Private John R. Towle* *see* **The** *Towle*

The *Private Joseph F. Merrell.* US icebreaker/freighter with a diesel-electric engine. In at McMurdo Sound 1956–57, 1957–58, and 1964–65.

Proclamation Island. 65°51'S, 53°41'E. 2½ miles west of Cape Batterbee and just east of the Aagard Islands. The BANZARE discovered it and on Jan. 13, 1930, a proclamation was read on its summit claiming the vast area in this region for Britain.

Procyon Peaks. 70°29'S, 66°30'W. Two ridges of peaks connected by a pass which can be sledged through. Between the upper parts of the Millett and Bertram Glaciers. 25 miles east of Moore Point on the west coast of Palmer Land. Named by the UK for the star.

The *Professor Siedlecki.* Polish ship which, with the *Tazar,* carried out the 1975–76 Polish Antarctic Marine Research Expedition. The party landed at Maxwell Bay (q.v. for details), on King George Island, in Feb. 1976.

The *Professor Vize.* Also spelled the *Professor Viese.* Big USSR research ship of 6,934 tons and 384 feet long. It was built in 1967, and is sister ship to the *Professor Zubov.* Designed for polar work, it can accommodate 200 scientists and crew. It alternates every year with the *Professor Zubov.* Named for Vladimir Vize *(see* **Vize Islands).**

The *Professor Zubov.* Sister ship to the *Professor Vize,* consequently it is like it in most respects, and alternates in the Antarctic with it. It also was built in 1967.

Progress Station. 69°24'S, 76°24'E. USSR scientific station just SW of Davis Station.

Project Array. Current measurements conducted by the *Westwind* between Feb. 5 and Feb. 19, 1968.

Islote Promontorio *see* **Foreland Island**

Cabo Promontorio Bajo *see* **Low Head**

Cabo Promontorio Norte *see* **North Foreland**

Prong Point. 60°32'S, 45°34'W. Forms the west side of the entrance to Ommanney Bay on the north side of Coronation Island in the South Orkneys. Discovered by Powell and Palmer in Dec.

1821. Surveyed by the FIDS in 1956–58. Named descriptively by the UK in 1959. It is a narrow, protruding point.

Proshchaniya Bay. 70°10'S, 4°20'E. Indents the SW side of Neupokoyev Bight, along the ice shelf that fringes the coast of Queen Maud Land. Named Bukhta Proshchaniya (farewell bay) by the USSR in 1961.

Prospect Col *see* **Prospect Glacier**

Prospect Glacier. 69°32'S, 67°20'W. Between the Kinnear Mountains and the Mayer Hills. It flows north into the Forster Ice Piedmont on the west coast of the Antarctic Peninsula. Surveyed in 1936 by the BGLE. In 1954 the UK named a col here as Prospect Col. This col runs between Eureka Glacier and the glacier of this entry. In 1958, during a resurvey, the FIDS found that the col was not even worthy of a name, but that this glacier was, so they transferred the name to the glacier.

Prospect Mesa. 77°30'S, 161°52'E. Below Bull Pass on the north side of the Wright Valley in Victoria Land. Named by geologists C.G. Vucetich and W.W. Topping of the VUWAE 1969–70 to designate the type locality of the geological "Prospect Formation."

Prospect Point. 66°01'S, 65°21'W. Almost 2 miles south of Ferin Head, and just east of the Fish Islands, on the west coast of Graham Land. Charted by the BGLE 1934–37. Named in 1957 by Edwin P. Arrowsmith, governor of the Falkland Islands.

Prospect Point Station *see* **Base J**

Prospect Spur. 83°57'S, 173°25'E. At the SW base of Cleft Peak in the Separation Range. It descends westward to the edge of Hood Glacier. Named by the NZ Alpine Club Antarctic Expedition of 1959–60. They had to climb up here to get a view of Hood Glacier in order to prospect a route to the south.

Protection Cove. 71°39'S, 170°12'E. A bay, 3 miles wide. At the east side of Cape Klövstad where it forms the head of

Robertson Bay in northern Victoria Land. Named by Borchgrevink in 1898–1900 for the protection it afforded his ship, the *Southern Cross.*

The *Protector.* British naval guardship in Antarctic waters in 1955–56 and 1956–57, both seasons under the command of Capt. John V. Wilkinson. It was back again in 1957–58 and 1958–59, those two seasons under Capt. Adrian R.L. Butler. It was used by the Royal Navy Hydrographic Survey Unit in Antarctic waters from 1961–63, and in 1964 it was back yet again, under the command of Capt. Martin S. Ollivant.

Protector Heights. 66°42'S, 66°15'W. Mountainous coastal heights separated from the Graham Land plateau by a narrow col. They dominate the area between Wilkinson Glacier and the southern part of Darbel Bay. Named by the UK for the *Protector.*

Mount Provender. 80°23'S, 29°55'W. 900 m. Marks the NW extremity of the Shackleton Range. Named in 1957 by the BCTAE for the food and fuel depot, and the airplane camp established by them that year to support sledging parties working in the Shackleton Range.

Providence Cove. 68°19'S, 66°47'W. Bounded by ice cliffs. At the foot of Remus Glacier in the SE corner of Neny Fjord, on the west coast of Graham Land. Surveyed in 1936 by the BGLE. Resurveyed in 1940–41 by members of USAS and named by them because when they first arrived here it seemed providential that a site for East Base was found so quickly. It was soon found, however, that the cove was not a good place for the base.

Pryamougol'naya Bay. 70°10'S, 5°30'E. Indents the SE side of Neupokoyev Bight along the ice shelf that fringes the coast of Queen Maud Land. Named Bukhta Pryamougol'naya (rectangle bay) by the USSR in 1961.

Prydz Bay. 69°S, 75°E. Also called Olav Prydz Bukt. A deep embayment of the continent between the Lars Christensen Coast and the Ingrid Christensen Coast. Partially discovered in Jan. and Feb. 1931 by the BANZARE, and also by Norwegian whalers. It was explored in Feb. 1935 by Mikkelsen in the *Thorshavn*. It was photographed by the LCE 1936–37. Named by the Norwegians for Olav Prydz, general manager of the Hvalfangernes Assuranceforening in Sandefjord, Norway.

Pryor Cliff. 73°53′S, 100°W. Faces northward toward Cosgrove Ice Shelf. 5 miles NE of Mount Nickens at the north end of the Hudson Mountains. Named for Douglas A. Pryor, map compilation specialist who contributed greatly to the preparation of US Geological Survey sketch maps of Antarctica.

Pryor Glacier. 70°05′S, 160°10′E. Flows northeastward to the north of Mount Shields and Yermak Point, into Rennick Bay. 30 miles long. It forms a separation between the Wilson Hills and the Usarp Mountains. Named for Madison E. Pryor, scientific leader at McMurdo Station in 1959, and US exchange scientist at Mirnyy Station in 1962.

Przybyszewski Island. 76°58′S, 148°45′W. Also spelled (erroneously) as Prezbecheski Island. This is without doubt the Antarctic name that is the most difficult to pronounce and to spell. Ice-covered. 12 miles long. In the Marshall Archipelago. 3 miles east of Cronenwett Island in the western part of the Sulzberger Ice Shelf. Charted from aircraft off the *Glacier* in 1962. Named by the captain of the ship, Capt. Edwin A. McDonald, for Lt. (jg) V.A. Przybyszewski, USNR, helicopter pilot who sighted this island from the air on Jan. 26, 1962.

Mount Przywitowski. 86°36′S, 154°08′W. 2,770 m. At the SE side of Holdsworth Glacier. 2½ miles west of McNally Peak in the Queen Maud Mountains. Named for Richard F. Przywitowski, scientific leader at Amundsen-Scott South Pole Station, 1966.

Psi Islands. 64°18′S, 63°01′W. Also called Islotes Ballesteros, Islotes La Madrid. Just to the west side of Lambda Island in the Melchior Islands in the Palmer Archipelago. Named by the Argentines before 1946 for the Greek letter.

Mount Ptolemy. 68°33′S, 65°58′W. An isolated block mountain with 4 main summits, the highest being 1,370 m. Just north of the Traffic Circle on the NW side of the Mercator Ice Piedmont on the Antarctic Peninsula. Discovered by Finn Ronne and Carl Eklund as they sledged their way through the Traffic Circle during the USAS 1939–41. Surveyed by the FIDS in 1947. Named by the UK for Ptolemy, the ancient Egyptian geographer.

Publication Glacier Tongues *see* **Publications Ice Shelf**

Publications Ice Shelf. 69°38′S, 75°20′E. 35 miles long. On the south shore of Prydz Bay, on the Ingrid Christensen Coast, between Mount Caroline Mikkelsen and Stornes Peninsula. Fed by several glaciers, all named by US cartographer John H. Roscoe in 1952 for international polar journals, and these glaciers are (from SW to NE): Polar Times Glacier, Il Polo Glacier, Polarforschung Glacier, Polar Record Glacier, and Polarårboken Glacier. Photographed by the LCE 1936–37, and again by Operation Highjump, 1946–47. Roscoe worked off these last photos and first called this area Publication Glacier Tongues. Later redefined.

Puccini Spur. 69°53′S, 70°50′W. 6 miles long. Extends SW into the Mozart Ice Piedmont just south of Mahler Spur in the northern part of Alexander Island. Discovered aerially by the BGLE in 1937. Named by the UK for the composer.

Pudding Butte. 75°52′S, 159°59′E. Also called Pudding Tableland. 2 miles SW of Beta Peak in the Prince Albert Mountains of Victoria Land. Named by the Southern Party of the NZGSAE 1962–63 for the feast they had at the nearby camp.

Pudding Tableland *see* **Pudding Butte**

The *Puerto Deseado.* Argentine ice-strengthened research ship bought by that country in 1980 for Antarctic work.

Puffball Islands. 69°02′S, 68°30′W. A scattered group of small, low, mainly ice-covered islands and rocks which extend about 10 miles in a NE-SW direction, in the southern portion of Marguerite Bay off the west coast of the Antarctic Peninsula. The center of the group lies 23 miles NNE of Cape Jeremy. Visited and surveyed in 1948 by the FIDS, who named them in association with Mushroom Island, which is 14 miles NE of this group.

Cape Puget *see* **Puget Rock**

Puget Rock. 63°29′S, 55°39′W. Also called Islote Redondo. East of the Eden Rocks, off the east end of Dundee Island. On Dec. 30, 1842, Ross named a feature in this area as Cape Puget, for Capt. William D. Puget, RN, but it is not clear what exact feature Ross was naming. In 1956 the UK named this rock in order to preserve Ross's naming.

Pujals, Carmen. Argentine professor of hydrography. One of the first women scientists to work on the continent, in 1968–69 (*see* **Women in Antarctica**).

Pujato Bluff. 82°40′S, 42°57′W. 660 m. Forms the south end of the Schneider Hills in the Argentina Range of the Pensacola Mountains. Named by the USA for General Hernán Pujato, officer-in-charge of General Belgrano Station in 1955 and 1956.

The *Pukaki.* NZ frigate, under Capt. R.T. Hale, in Antarctic waters with the *Hawea* (q.v. for details) in 1956–57.

Mount Pukaki. 82°49′S, 162°06′E. Between Mount Hawea and Mount Rotoiti in the Frigate Range. Named by the New Zealanders in 1961–62 for the *Pukaki.*

Pukkelen Rocks. 72°15′S, 27°09′E. Just west of Bollene Rocks at the head of Byrdbreen, in the Sør Rondane Mountains. Name means "the hump" in Norwegian.

Pulfrich Peak. 64°41′S, 62°28′W. Near the eastern part of Wild Spur on the

Arctowski Peninsula, on the west coast of Graham Land. Named by the UK in 1960 for Carl Pulfrich (1858–1927), the "father of stereophotogrammetry."

El Pulgar. 71°29′S, 161°46′E. A granite monolithic peak of 1,660 m. 3 miles north of Berg Peak in the northern part of the Morozumi Range. Named by the four members of the NZGSAE 1967–68 who climbed it that season. Named for its steep sides (el pulgar means "the thumb" in Spanish).

Mount Pulitzer. 85°49′S, 154°16′W. 2,155 m. 7 miles NE of Mount Griffith on the elevated platform between the Koerwitz and Vaughan Glaciers, in the Queen Maud Mountains. Discovered by Quin Blackburn's party during Byrd's 1933–35 expedition and named by Byrd for Joseph Pulitzer, son of the more famous father of the same name, and a patron of the expedition.

Pullen, William A. Aviation machinist's mate at East Base during the USAS 1939–41.

Pullen Island. 72°35′S, 60°57′W. Snow-covered. 5 miles long. Rises to 495 meters at its northern end. Near the center of Violante Inlet, on the east coast of Palmer Land. Discovered aerially on Dec. 30, 1940, by USAS members from East Base. Named for William A. Pullen.

Pully, Robert. Quartermaster on the Wilkes Expedition 1838–42. Joined in the USA. Served the cruise.

Pulmar, Benjamin. Ordinary seaman on the Wilkes Expedition 1838–42. Joined in the USA. Run at Sydney.

Pulpit Mountain. 60°41′S, 45°13′W. 940 m. Red-colored. Conspicuous. 1½ miles west of Spence Harbor at the east end of Coronation Island in the South Orkneys. Surveyed by the FIDS in 1948–49 and named by them for its shape when seen from the east.

Pumphouse Lake. 60°42′S, 45°37′W. The most southerly of the three lakes in Three Lakes Valley on Signy Island in the South Orkneys. Named by the UK for the abandoned pumphouse and pipeline on the east side of the lake, which were built by whalers.

Punch Bowl *see* **Devils Punchbowl**

Punchbowl Cirque. 76°42'S, 159°47' E. In the southern part of the Shipton Ridge, about ½ mile SW of Roscolyn Tor, in the Allan Hills of Victoria Land. Named descriptively by the New Zealanders in 1964.

Punchbowl Glacier. 65°11'S, 61°57'W. Enters the north end of Exasperation Inlet, north of Jorum Glacier, on the east side of Graham Land. Surveyed by the FIDS in 1947 and 1955. The glacier, being hemmed in by mountains, was named descriptively by the UK.

Pico Puño *see* **Admiralen Peak**

The *Punta Loyola*. Argentine vessel on the following Antarctic expeditions: 1950–51; 1953–54; 1954–55 (Capt. Jorge Federico Pablo Wicht); 1956–57.

The *Punta Ninfas*. Argentine vessel on the following Antarctic expeditions: 1948–49; 1949–50 (Capt. Enrique Arizzi); 1951–52 (Capt. M. Sanguinetti); 1952–53 (Capt. Roberto L. Arenas); 1955–56; 1956–57.

Pico Puntiagudo *see* **Sharp Peak**

Pup Rock. 68°22'S, 67°03'W. 200 meters in diameter. Between the Refuge Islands and the Tiber Rocks in Rymill Bay, off the west coast of the Antarctic Peninsula. Discovered by Robert L. Nichols during the RARE 1947–48, and he named it Three Pup Island. The name has since been shortened for convenience.

Puppis Pikes. 71°16'S, 66°24'W. A loosely-defined group of pointed nunataks and smaller rock outcrops running roughly east-west. 7 miles NE of Mount Cadbury in Palmer Land. Named by the UK for the constellation.

Purcell Snowfield. 70°29'S, 69°55'W. 15 miles wide. Between the Colbert Mountains and the Douglas Range in the central part of Alexander Island. Named by the UK for the composer.

Purdy Point. 60°32'S, 45°26'W. 1½ miles ESE of Foul Point on the north coast of Coronation Island in the South Orkneys. Discovered by Powell and Palmer in Dec. 1821, and shown on Powell's 1822 chart. Surveyed by the FIDS in 1956–58 and named by the UK in 1959 for John Purdy (1773–1843), British hydrographer who compiled nautical directories and charts, including one of the South Orkneys.

Purgatory Peak. 77°21'S, 162°18'E. 2 miles SW of Pond Peak in the Saint Johns Range of Victoria Land. Named by the NZ Northern Survey Party of the BCTAE 1956–58, for the extremely bad weather and terrain conditions here.

Purka Mountain. 68°15'S, 58°35'E. Also called Mount Corry. A mountain ridge with two outliers. 5 miles SE of Mount Gjeita in the Hansen Mountains. Photographed by the LCE 1936–37. Name means "the sow" in Norwegian.

Pursuit Point *see* **Principal Point**

Cape Purvis. 63°35'S, 55°58'W. Forms the southern extremity of Dundee Island, off the northern tip of the Antarctic Peninsula. Discovered in Dec. 1842 by Ross, and named by him for Commodore John B. Purvis, RN, who had helped Ross get his expedition together.

Purvis Peak. 72°38'S, 169°09'E. 2,250 m. 2 miles NE of Mount Northampton in the Victory Mountains of Victoria Land. Overlooks the terminus of Tucker Glacier from the south. Named for Lt. Ronald S. Purvis, USN, VX-6 pilot of Otter aircraft at Ellsworth Station in 1956–57, and of R5D Skymaster aircraft at McMurdo Station in 1957–58.

Putzke Peak. 75°49'S, 128°32'W. 2,325 m. At the end of the spur which descends NE from Mount Petras, from which mountain this peak is 3½ miles to the SW, in the McCuddin Mountains of Marie Byrd Land. Named for Capt. Stanley G. Putzke, commander of the *Staten Island*, 1970–71 and 1971–72.

Puzzle Islands. 64°59'S, 63°40'W. At the mouth of Flandres Bay, 1 mile west of

Ménier Island off the west coast of Graham Land. Charted by Charcot in 1903–5. Named by the UK in 1958. This group of small islands, rocks, and reefs is often hidden by icebergs which come to rest in the shallow waters around here.

Py Point. 64°53'S, 63°37'W. Forms the southern extremity of Doumer Island in the Palmer Archipelago. Discovered by Charcot in 1903–5 and named by him for Monsieur Py, president of the French Chamber of Commerce in Buenos Aires.

Pycnogonids. Ten-legged, crablike, foraging sea-spiders which live on the sea-bed near the coasts (*see* **Fauna**). Eights discovered them in 1830, but he was not believed until they were rediscovered by Bruce in 1903. There are several species, and some have twelve legs (*Dodecalopoda mawsoni*).

Pygmy Right Whale. Endemic to Antarctica and the southern oceans.

Pygmy Rock *see* **Pigmy Rock**

Pyke Glacier. 64°15'S, 59°36'W. 5 miles long. Flows southward from Detroit Plateau in Graham Land, between the Albone and Polaris Glaciers. Surveyed by the FIDS in 1960–61. Named by the UK for Geoffrey N. Pyke (1894–1948), designer of the Weasel (q.v.).

Pylon Point. 68°06'S, 65°05'W. Also called Clarkson Point. 4 miles SW of Three Slice Nunatak. It marks the north end of the main mountainous mass of the Joerg Peninsula, on the east coast of Graham Land. Named because it was a turning point for sledge parties during the USAS 1939–41.

¹**The Pyramid** *see* **Pyramid Island**

²**The Pyramid.** 63°26'S, 57°01'W. Also called Pyramiden. 565 m. A pyramidal nunatak. 1 mile east of Mount Carrel and 1½ miles SE of the head of Hope Bay, at the NE end of the Antarctic Peninsula. Discovered and named by Dr. J. Gunnar Andersson's party of the Nordenskjöld expedition of 1901–4.

³**The Pyramid.** 78°21'S, 163°30'E. A peak. Also called Pyramid Nunatak. Just south of Pyramid Trough, at the west side of the Koettlitz Glacier. Named descriptively by members of Scott's 1910–13 expedition.

Pyramid Island. 62°26'S, 60°06'W. Also called The Pyramid. A pillar-shaped island, 205 meters high, 2 miles NNE of Williams Point, Livingston Island, in the South Shetlands. Charted and named descriptively by personnel on the *Discovery II* in 1935.

¹**Pyramid Mountain** *see* **Mount Rhamnus**

²**Pyramid Mountain.** 81°19'S, 158°15'E. 2,810 m. Pyramidal. 4 miles north of Mount Albert Markham in the Churchill Mountains. Discovered and named by the Royal Society Expedition of 1901–4.

¹**Pyramid Peak** *see* **Mount Rhamnus**

²**Pyramid Peak.** 72°16'S, 165°35'E. Pyramidal. On the Polar Plateau. 7 miles SW of Gless Peak of the Millen Range and 1 mile north of Sphinx Peak. Named descriptively by the New Zealanders in 1962–63.

Pyramid Point *see* **Tilt Rock**

Pyramid Rock. 64°23'S, 63°07'W. Close to the extremity of Gourdon Peninsula, off the NE coast of Anvers Island. Charted and named by personnel on the *Discovery* in 1927.

Pyramid Trough. 78°18'S, 163°27'E. A deep trough just west of The Bulwark, through which a part of the Koettlitz Glacier formerly flowed north to Walcott Bay. Named by the New Zealanders in 1960–61 for its nearness to The Pyramid.

Pyramiden *see* **The Pyramid**

Pyramiden Nunatak. 72°17'S, 3°48'W. 2 miles east of Knallen Peak, on the east side of the head of Schytt Glacier in Queen Maud Land. Name means "the pyramid" in Norwegian.

Pyrite Islands *see* **Pyrites Island**

Pyrites Island. 61°55'S, 57°59'W. Also called Pyrite Islands. The largest of three small islands SE of Gam Point. Forms the eastern side of Esther Harbor, off the north coast of King George Island in the South Shetlands. Named by the UK in 1960 in order to avoid confusion with the other Esther names in the area. In 1913–14 David Ferguson explored this area, and he charted several islands here, and called them Esther Islands, or Pyritis Islands, or even Pyritic Islands. In those days there were more islands here, but since then the ice cliff behind Gam Point has advanced and swallowed up these islands. There are only a few remaining now, and this is the largest of them. It is composed of pyrites and vein quartz.

Pyritic Islands *see* **Pyrites Island**

Pyritis Islands *see* **Pyrites Island**

Pyrox Island. 68° 12′ S, 66° 41′ W. Also called Neny Glacier Island. At the head of Neny Fjord, on the west coast of Graham Land. Surveyed by the USAS 1939–41. Resurveyed in 1949 by the FIDS, who named it for the pyroxenic rocks here.

Pyroxenite Promontory. 82° 37′ S, 53° W. In the northern part of the Pensacola Mountains.

Pythagoras Peak. 66° 59′ S, 51° 20′ E. 1,275 m. The highest peak in the central Tula Mountains. On the north side of Beaver Glacier. 8 miles SE of Mount Storer. It has a prominent notch, the eastern aspect being a right-angled triangle with a perpendicular northern face. Named by the Australians for that old Greek triangle man, Pythagoras.

The *Pythia*. British whaling factory ship belonging to Christen Christensen, in the Palmer Archipelago in 1921–22 (*see also* **The *Minerva***).

Pythia Island. 64° 32′ S, 61° 59′ W. About 350 yards long. The largest of a group of small islands off the east side of Enterprise Island in Wilhelmina Bay, off the west coast of Graham Land. Named by the UK in 1960 for the *Pythia*.

Pyxis Ridge. 71° 16′ S, 66° 48′ W. A narrow ridge of nunataks separated by passes. 5 miles NNW of Mount Cadbury from where it projects into the southern side of Ryder Glacier in Palmer Land. Named by the UK for the constellation.

Mount Quackenbush. 80° 21′ S, 157° E. 2,435 m. Flat-topped. Just west of Peckham Glacier and north of Byrd Glacier. Named for Capt. Robert S. Quackenbush, Jr., chief of staff to Admiral Cruzen during Operation Highjump, 1946–47.

The Quadrangle. 71° 35′ S, 68° 36′ W. Ice-covered glacial cirque between Mount Umbriel and Venus Glacier in eastern Alexander Island. Named by the UK for its shape.

Quam Heights. 71° 03′ S, 167° 48′ E. Mostly snow-covered. 15 miles long. 4 miles wide. Over 1,000 m. Forms the coastline between the Barnett and Dennistoun Glaciers in northern Victoria Land. Named for Louis O. Quam, National Science Foundation scientist from 1967–72.

Mount Quandary. 64° 52′ S, 61° 34′ W. On the east side of the head of Hektoria Glacier. 12 miles NW of Shiver Point in Graham Land. Surveyed by the FIDS in 1955. When first seen, it was not certain if it was part of the central plateau of Graham Land or a detached mountain in Hektoria Glacier.

Quar, Leslie. British radio mechanic and technician on the NBSAE 1949–52. Died on Feb. 24, 1951, when the Weasel he was in fell over the edge of the Quar Ice Shelf.

Quar Ice Shelf. 71° 20′ S, 11° W. Also called Maudheim Shelf Is (i.e., Maudheim Shelf Ice in Norwegian). Between Cape Norvegia and Soråsen Ridge in Queen Maud Land. Maudheim was on this ice shelf. Named for Leslie Quar.

Quarles Range. 85° 36′ S, 164° 30′ W. Extends from the Polar Plateau between Cooper and Bowman Glaciers to the edge of the Ross Ice Shelf, in the Queen Maud Mountains. Amundsen first saw peaks in this range in Nov. 1911. Named by the

USA for Donald A. Quarles, secretary of the Air Force, 1955–57.

Quarterdeck Ridge. 72°27'S, 170°17' E. The snow crest of Hallett Peninsula, near to the Cotter Cliffs. Named by the New Zealanders in 1957–58 for its similarity to the quarterdeck of a ship.

Quartermain Glacier. 67°01'S, 65°09' W. Heavily crevassed. On the north side of Fricker Glacier. Flows from the plateau of Graham Land into Mill Inlet on the east coast of the Antarctic Peninsula. Named by the UK for Leslie B. Quartermain, New Zealand historian (see the Bibliography), and former president of the NZ Antarctic Society.

Quartermain Point. 72°03'S, 170°08' E. In the northern part of Moubray Bay between Helm Point and Cape Roget. Named by the New Zealanders in 1957–58 for Leslie B. Quartermain (see Quartermain Glacier).

Quartermain Range. In southern Victoria Land. A term no longer used.

Quartley, Arthur L. Chief stoker, RN, on the Royal Society Expedition, 1901–4.

Quartz. Has been found in the Antarctic.

Quartz Hills. 85°56'S, 132°50'W. Mostly ice-free hills and peaks just south of Colorado Glacier on the west side of the Reedy Glacier in the Transantarctic Mountains. Named by John H. Mercer for the rose quartz found here.

Quartz Pebble Hill. 84°44'S, 113°59' W. Flat-topped. On the northern escarpment of Buckeye Table, Ohio Range, just where Discovery Ridge joins the main escarpment. The hill is composed of sandstone and quartz pebble conglomerate. Named by William E. Long (see Long Hills).

Quaternary Icefall. 77°18'S, 166°30'E. A western lobe of the Mount Bird Ice Cap, descending steeply into Wohlschlag Bay 1 mile south of Cinder Hill on Ross Island. Named by the New Zealanders in 1958–59 for the Quaternary glacial

period marine shells carried by the icefall and deposited in terminal moraines.

The *Que Sera Sera*. The American DC3 aircraft piloted by Gus Shinn, which took Admiral Dufek to the South Pole on Oct. 31, 1956, to kick off Operation Deep Freeze II. It left behind a US flag and a radar beacon. For a list of the crew of this momentous flight *see* **South Pole.**

Queen, W.K. Chief engineer on the *Jacob Ruppert*, 1933–34.

Queen Adelaide Island *see* **Adelaide Island**

Queen Alexandra Range. 84°20'S, 168°E. Also called Alexandra Range, and also seen spelled (erroneously) as Queen Alexandria Range. 100 miles long. Between the Beardmore Glacier and the Queen Elizabeth Range in the Transantarctic Mountains. It overlooks the Ross Ice Shelf and consists of some important features such as Mounts Kirkpatrick, Darwin, Hope, Bell, Buckley, Wild, Falla, Mackellar, Elizabeth, and Sirius, as well as The Cloudmaker, Coalsack Bluff, Fremouw Peak, the MacAlpine Hills, the Marshall Mountains, Blizzard Heights, Blizzard Peak, Storm Peak, Tempest Peak, Prebble Glacier and Tillite Glacier. Discovered by Shackleton in 1907–9 and named by him for the Queen of England at the time.

Queen Elizabeth Range. 83°20'S, 162° E. Parallels the east side of Marsh Glacier for 100 miles, from the Nimrod Glacier in the north to the Law Glacier in the south. To the west of the Queen Alexandra Range, it overlooks the Ross Ice Shelf. It includes some important features such as Mounts Ropar, Picciotto, Weeks, Angier, Counts, Rabot, Markham, and Christchurch, as well as Moody Nunatak, the Moore Mountains, Cranfield Peak, and Claydon Peak. Named by J.H. Miller for Queen Elizabeth II.

Queen Fabiola Mountains. 71°30'S, 35°40'E. 30 miles long. They consist mainly of 7 small massifs. 90 miles SW of the head of Lützow-Holm Bay, between the Belgica Mountains and the Shirase

Glacier. Discovered aerially by the Belgian Antarctic Expedition of 1960–61, on Oct. 8, 1960, and named by them for Queen Fabiola of Belgium. In Dec. 1960 the Japanese gave them their own name, the Yamato Mountains. The Norwegians call them Dronning Fabiolafjella.

Queen Mary Coast *see* **Queen Mary Land**

Queen Mary Land. 67°S, 96°E. Also called Queen Mary Coast, Mary Coast, Pravda Coast (this last by the USSR during the IGY). Between Cape Filchner (91°54′E) and Cape Hordern (100°30′E), on the shores of the Davis Sea, behind the Shackleton Ice Shelf, in the vicinity of Mirnyy Station. Discovered in Feb. 1912 by the *Aurora* party of the AAE 1911–14, and named by them for Queen Mary of England.

Queen Maud Land. 72°30′S, 12°E. Called Dronning Maud Land by the Norwegians. One of the major lands of East Antarctica, its current boundaries are the terminus of the Stancomb Wills Glacier in 20°W and the Shinnar Glacier in 44°38′E, between New Schwabenland and Enderby Land. The original Queen Maud Land (between 37°E and 50°E) was discovered on Jan. 15, 1930, by Riiser-Larsen. He named it Dronning Maud Land, for the Queen of Norway, and also explored it in 1930–31. Norway claimed it on Jan. 14, 1939, and it forms the bulk of the Norwegian Dependency.

Queen Maud Mountains. 86°S, 160°W. Part of the Transantarctic Horst, it is the group of mountains nearest the Pole, and bounds the Ross Ice Shelf at the south of that mass of ice. Between the Beardmore and Reedy Glaciers. Discovered by Amundsen on Nov. 11, 1911 (11/11/11), and named by him as the Queen Maud Range for the Queen of Norway. Later redefined.

Queen Maud Range *see* **Queen Maud Mountains**

Queen Mountain *see* **Queer Mountain**

The Queen of Bermuda. British ship (*see* **Wars** for details), commanded by Capt. Peachey while at Deception Island in March 1941.

Queens Bay *see* **Borge Bay**

Mount Queensland. 74°16′S, 163°56′E. 1,910 m. 7 miles north of Mount Dickason, in the Deep Freeze Range of Victoria Land. Discovered by Scott's 1901–4 expedition and named by them for the state of Queensland for its assistance to the expedition.

Mount Queequeg. 65°39′S, 62°07′W. Partly snow-covered. Has 3 conical summits, the highest being 900 m. Between the mouths of the Starbuck and Stubb Glaciers on the east coast of Graham Land. Surveyed by the FIDS in 1947. Named by the UK in 1956 for the *Moby Dick* character.

Queer Mountain. 77°08′S, 161°45′E. Also spelled (erroneously) as Queen Mountain. 1,180 m. A black mountain 1 mile west of Killer Ridge, between the Cotton and Miller Glaciers of Victoria Land. Mapped and named by Scott's 1910–13 expedition because it has all sorts of rocks in it, even though it is surrounded by glacier.

Querthal *see* **Cross Valley**

Quervain Peak. 67°23′S, 66°39′W. In the central part of the Boyle Mountains in Graham Land. Named by the UK for Alfred de Quervain, Swiss glaciologist.

Query Island. 68°48′S, 67°12′W. Between the foot of Clarke Glacier and Keyhole Island on the south side of Mikkelsen Bay, off the west coast of Graham Land. Surveyed and named by the FIDS in 1948 because of the question as to whether, from a distance, the feature was an island or part of the mainland.

[1]**The *Quest*.** The ship used by Shackleton on his 1921–22 expedition. Formerly a Norwegian sealer, it was in disastrous condition when it sailed from England in Sept. 1921. It had a 5 mph maximum speed, was wooden, and weighed 125

tons. The expedition, otherwise known as the Shackleton-Rowett Antarctic Expedition, was financed by Shackleton's old school chum John Q. Rowett. Its mission was to map 2,000 miles of Antarctic coastline, to pioneer aviation in Antarctica, to look for lost islands, and to do scientific research. Shackleton was the leader and Frank Wild was second-in-command. Also on the expedition were Macklin, McIlroy, Wilkins, McLeod, Hussey, Worsley, Marr, Argles, Young, Watts, C.E. Smith, Ross, Naisbitt, Kerr, Jeffrey, Green, Douglas, Dell, Carr. At Madeira, on the way down, Bee Mason (the cinematographer/photographer), Gerald Lysaght, and Boy Scout Norman E. Mooney all left to return home. At Rio A. Eriksen, a Norwegian harpoon expert, left for home. The *Quest* left Rio on Dec. 18, 1921, arriving at South Georgia (54°S) on Jan. 4, 1922. Shackleton died on Jan. 5, 1922, at South Georgia, and Wild took over, completing the expedition, which stayed in the Antarctic until March 21, 1922, making observations and soundings. The ship returned to South Georgia on April 5, 1922, and, via Cape Town, arrived back in Plymouth, England, on Sept. 16, 1922.

²**The *Quest*.** In 1963 this British survey motor boat was used by the RN Hydrographic Survey Unit in Antarctic waters off the Antarctic Peninsula. A.J. Jennings was coxswain.

Quest Channel. 67°48′S, 69°01′W. A marine channel which leads SW from Adelaide Anchorage between Hibbert Rock and Henkes Islands off the south end of Adelaide Island. Named by the UK for the *Quest* (the 1963 vessel).

Quest Cliffs. 82°36′S, 155°06′E. Also called Quest Nunatak. Just north of The Slot in the Geologists Range. Named by the New Zealanders in 1961–62 for the *Quest* (the 1921–22 vessel).

¹**Quest Nunatak** *see* **Quest Cliffs**

²**Quest Nunatak.** 81°31′S, 28°10′W. 1,065 m. The most northeasterly of the Whichaway Nunataks. Mapped in 1957 by the BCTAE and named by them because it was the last nunatak visited by them on the way to the Pole in Dec. 1957.

Mount Quilmes. 63°14′S, 55°37′W. 715 m. Mainly snow-covered. NE of Haddon Bay on Joinville Island. Named by the Argentine Antarctic Expedition of 1953–54 for the famous Argentine naval battle.

Quilp Rock. 67°37′S, 67°47′W. An isolated rock in water in Laubeuf Fjord. 3½ miles SSE of the southern tip of Piñero Island. 1½ miles off the NW side of Pourquoi Pas Island, off the west coast of Graham Land. Surveyed in 1948 by the FIDS, and named by them for the Dickens character.

Quilty Nunataks. 75°45′S, 71°45′W. Extend over 8 miles. 15 miles SW of the Thomas Mountains in eastern Ellsworth Land. Discovered by the RARE 1947–48. Named for Patrick Quilty, geologist here in 1965–66.

Quin, James. Ordinary seaman on the Wilkes Expedition 1838–42. Joined in the USA. Discharged at Oahu on Nov. 2, 1840.

Quintana Island. 65°09′S, 64°57′W. Isolated. 6 miles NE of the Betbeder Islands in the SW part of the Wilhelm Archipelago. Charcot charted it as a group in 1903–5 and named it Quintana Islets for Manuel Quintana (1836–1906), president of Argentina. Redefined by the UK as one island in 1957–58.

Quintana Islets *see* **Quintana Island**

Quinton Point. 64°19′S, 63°41′W. At the north side of the entrance to Perrier Bay, on the NW coast of Anvers Island. Charted by Charcot in 1903–5, and named by him for Dr. Quinton, assistant at the Collège de France.

Islas Quirihue *see* **Darbel Islands**

Quonset Glacier. 85°19′S, 127°05′W. 20 miles long. Flows from the northern slopes of the Wisconsin Range between Mount LeSchack and Ruseski Buttress, to enter the northern side of the Davisville

Glacier. Named for Quonset Point, Rhode Island, home of VX-6.

R4D Nunatak. 72°44'S, 162°21'E. 2 miles SE of Burkett Nunatak at the SE end of the Monument Nunataks. Named by the Northern Party of the NZGSAE 1962–63, for the R4D Dakota aircraft used by the US Navy to transport the party to the area, and to resupply and return the party to Scott Base.

The R.S.A. Republic of South Africa research vessel of 1,550 tons launched in Japan in 1961. Its first voyage was in early 1962, taking down the South African National Antarctic Expedition III to Antarctica from South Africa.

Mount Rabben. 66°27'S, 54°07'E. 1,540 m. 2 miles NE of Mount Griffiths in the Napier Mountains of Enderby Land. Photographed by the LCE 1936–37. Name means "the small elongated elevation" in Norwegian.

Rabben Ridge. 71°52'S, 2°49'E. Isolated. 5 miles north of Stabben Mountain in the northern part of the Gjelsvik Mountains of Queen Maud Land. Name means "the small elongated elevation" in Norwegian.

Mount Rabot. 83°11'S, 161°17'E. 3,335 m. 3 miles SE of Mount Lecointe in the Queen Elizabeth Range. Discovered by Shackleton's 1907–9 expedition, and named by them for Charles Rabot (*see* Rabot Island).

Rabot Glacier. 83°11'S, 160°10'E. Flows west from Mount Rabot between Mount Counts and the Bartram Plateau to enter Marsh Glacier, in the Queen Elizabeth Range. Named by the New Zealanders in 1961–62 in association with Mount Rabot.

Rabot Island. 65°54'S, 65°59'W. 5 miles long. 2 miles wide. 1 mile south of Renaud Island in the Biscoe Islands. Charted by Charcot in 1903–5, and named by him for Charles Rabot, French glaciologist and editor of *La Géographie*, bulletin of the Société Géographique of Paris.

Rabot Point. 64°17'S, 57°20'W. On the east side of James Ross Island, in Markham Bay. It separates the mouths of the Gourdon and Hobbs Glaciers. During his 1901–4 expedition, Otto Nordenskjöld named a small glacier just west of The Watchtower on the south side of the island as Rabot Gletscher (Rabot Glacier) for Charles Rabot (*see* **Rabot Island**). In 1953 the FIDS, while surveying the south side of the island, found that this glacier was so small it did not even warrant a name. The UK named the glacier of this entry in order to preserve the name Rabot in the area.

Rachel Glacier. 65°37'S, 62°10'W. 6 miles long. On the east coast of Graham Land. Flows east along the north side of Mount Baleen into the Larsen Ice Shelf. Named by the UK for one of the ships in *Moby Dick*.

Racine Nunatak. 85°28'S, 136°18'W. 960 m. 3 miles west of the lower part of the Reedy Glacier. 7 miles ESE of the Berry Peaks. Named for Edward J. Racine, crew member on the *Eastwind*, 1967.

Racovitza, Emile G. Rumanian zoologist let out of the Rumanian army for the *Belgica* expedition led by de Gerlache in 1897–99. On the way south he left the ship at Rio on Oct. 30, 1897, to travel overland to Punta Arenas where he picked up the ship again.

Racovitza Islands. 64°31'S, 62°05'W. Three islands just north of Nansen Island, off the west coast of Graham Land. Surveyed by the FIDS from the *Norsel* in 1955. Named by the UK for Emile G. Racovitza.

Radford Island. 76°54'S, 146°36'W. Ice-covered. Surmounted by several peaks. 6 miles west of Saunders Mountain in the eastern part of the Sulzberger Ice Shelf. Discovered by the Eastern Flight of Dec. 5, 1929, during Byrd's 1928–30 expedition. Mapped as part of the mainland by the USAS 1939–41, and named Radford Mountains by Byrd for Vice Adm. Arthur W. Radford, USN, deputy chief of Naval Operations (Air) during Operation Highjump. It was determined to be an island by the US Geological Survey from aerial photos taken by the US Navy in 1962–65.

Radford Mountains *see* **Radford Island**

Radian Glacier. 78°13′S, 163°E. On the east side of the Royal Society Range. It descends from a high cirque just SE of Mount Rücker, and flows east toward the Walcott Glacier in Victoria Land. Measured by the New Zealanders in 1960–61, and during these measurements one of the survey angles, quite by chance, was exactly one radian, and the glacier became known by this name.

Radiation. More radiation is lost than kept in Antarctica (except in midsummer) due to the white surface reflecting the sun's rays back into the atmosphere. This heat loss explains in part why it is so cold in Antarctica.

Radio. Scott rejected its use for his last expedition of 1910–13. The first time radio was used in the Antarctic was by Mawson during the AAE 1911–14. After that time the pioneers erected high radio masts, but these are now covered over by drifting snow and ice. Byrd pioneered the use of 2-way radio, and the radio set at Little America (1928–30) was so powerful that it could transmit to the North Pole. The world's most southerly radio station is AFAN McMurdo, at McMurdo Station.

Radio Hill. 66°33′S, 93°E. 50 m. Almost ½ mile SW of Mabus Point, in Mirnyy Station, on the coast of East Antarctica. Discovered and mapped by the AAE 1911–14. Remapped and named by the USSR in 1956.

Radiolaria. A type of microfauna (*see* Fauna) found in Antarctic waters.

Mount Radlinski. 82°31′S, 103°34′W. Ice-covered. 2,750 m. 4 miles SE of Mount Seelig in the NE part of the Whitmore Mountains. Surveyed on Jan. 2,

1959, by William H. Chapman, a member of the Horlick Mountains Traverse of 1958–59, and named by him for William A. Radlinski, special assistant (Antarctic) to the chief topographic engineer of the US Geological Survey.

Radok Lake. 70°52′S, 68°E. A meltwater lake. 4 miles long. Has a slender glacier tongue feeding it from the west. 3 miles SW of Beaver Lake and 15 miles SE of the Aramis Range in the Prince Charles Mountains. Named for Uwe Radok, Australian meteorologist who greatly assisted ANARE's glaciological program. In 1984 USSR scientists discovered that it is the deepest lake in Antarctica (1,135 feet).

Mount Radspinner. 71°29′S, 164°33′E. 1,785 m. Ridgelike. Just east of Mount Freed and Copperstain Ridge in the eastern part of the Bowers Mountains. Named for Capt. Frank H. Radspinner, Jr., US Army, helicopter commander in the area in 1962–63.

Point Rae. 60°46′S, 44°37′W. Marks the NE side of the entrance to Scotia Bay, on the south coast of Laurie Island, in the South Orkneys. Charted in 1903 by Bruce, who named it for John Rae (1813–1893), Arctic explorer.

Rae, Capt. *see* **Rea, Henry**

Rafted ice. One layer of ice riding over another. This is called rafting.

Rafting *see* **Rafted ice**

Raggatt Mountains. 67°42′S, 49°E. Also spelled (erroneously) Raggett Mountains. West of the Scott Mountains, east of Rayner Glacier and north of Thyer Glacier. Named by the Australians for Dr. H.G. Raggatt, secretary of the Australian Department of National Development.

Ragged Island *see* **Rugged Island**

Ragged Peaks. 66°59′S, 51°E. Also called Rugged Peaks. On the eastern side of Amundsen Bay in a line running almost north-south. They extend for 8 miles and contain several spires. The ridge connecting the peaks is greatly serrated. There are 5 peaks over 915 m. Discovered in Oct. 1956 by the ANARE Amundsen Bay party led by P.W. Crohn. Named descriptively by the Australians.

Raggett Mountains *see* **Raggatt Mountains**

Ragle Glacier. 76°28'S, 145°32'W. Flows from the west end of the Fosdick Mountains, between Mounts Ferranto and Avers, and then NW to Block Bay in Marie Byrd Land. Named by Byrd for Dr. B. Harrison Ragle, Byrd's personal physician in the late 1930s, who was a contributor and consultant to the USAS 1939–41.

Ragotzkie Glacier. 80°02'S, 157°45'E. 10 miles long. In the Britannia Range. Flows north along the west side of Mount Aldrich. It coalesces with other north-flowing glaciers which enter the Hatherton Glacier to the SW of Junction Spur. Named for Robert A. Ragotzkie, project director for USARP studies of lakes in the dry valleys. He was in Victoria Land in 1962–63.

Cape Rahir *see* **Rahir Point**

Rahir Point. 65°04'S, 63°14'W. Also called Punta Thomson. Marks the NE end of a small peninsula which juts out into Flandres Bay just north of Thomson Cove, on the west coast of Graham Land. Charted by de Gerlache in 1897–99, and named Cap Rahir by him for Maurice Rahir, Belgian geographer.

Railroads. There have never been many in Antarctica, for obvious reasons. Dumont d'Urville Station had a ground railway and an overhead railway during IGY.

Rain. Almost unknown in Antarctica. It becomes snow before we see it (*see also* **Snow, Atmosphere**).

Mount Rainbow. 80°54'S, 156°55'E. 2,050 m. On the south side of Byrd Glacier. Surmounts the ridge between Zeller and Sefton Glaciers. Named by the New Zealanders in 1960–61 for the rainbow effect given by the multi-colored beds of

sandstone with probable dolerite sitting on pink-green limestone in this mountain.

Rainbow Ridge. 78°06'S, 165°24'E. Forms a distinct western rim to the large craterlike depression high in the central part of Brown Peninsula in Victoria Land. Named descriptively by New Zealand in the 1960s. The top of the ridge has been planed off by continual glaciation and the surface now exposes two basalt "pipes" (Nubian Formation) within the trachyte. These have altered the trachyte at their edges to various shades of brown, hence the name given to the ridge.

Rainbows. Rare in Antarctica because rain is rare. (*See also* **Phenomena.**) However, fog bows (q.v.) are quite common near coasts and on ice shelves.

Rainer Glacier *see* **Rayner Glacier**

Rainey Glacier. 73°40'S, 163°06'E. On the north side of the Archambault Ridge, it flows from the Deep Freeze Range into Campbell Glacier in Victoria Land. Named by the northern party of the NZGSAE 1962–63 for Denys B. Rainey, cartographer, who assisted this and other NZ Antarctic expeditions with their mapping problems.

Rainoff's Island *see* **Gibbs Island**

Rakebosten Ridge. 71°56'S, 7°12'E. Forms the south part of Trollslottet Mountain in the Filchner Mountains of Queen Maud Land. Name means "the shave bristles" in Norwegian.

Rakekniven Peak. 71°54'S, 7°17'E. 2,365 m. At the northern end of Trollslottet Mountain in the Filchner Mountains of Queen Maud Land. Name means "the razor" in Norwegian.

Rakuda Glacier. 68°03'S, 43°54'E. Flows to the coast just east of Rakuda Rock in Queen Maud Land. Named by the Japanese.

Rakuda Rock. 68°02'S, 43°49'E. A rock which juts out of the East Antarctica coast just to the west of Rakuda Glacier in Queen Maud Land. Named by the Japanese.

The *Raleigh* see The *Adventure*

Rallier-du-Baty Channel *see* Rallier Channel

Rallier-du-Baty Islet *see* Rallier Island

Rallier Channel. 65°04′S, 64°03′W. Also called Rallier-du-Baty Channel. A narrow marine channel between Rallier Island and the west end of Booth Island in the Wilhelm Archipelago. Discovered by Charcot in 1903–5 and named by him in association with Rallier Island.

Rallier Island. 65°04′S, 64°03′W. A small island with a small islet off its northern side. ¼ mile west of the NW extremity of Booth Island in the Wilhelm Archipelago. Discovered by Charcot in 1903–5, and named by him for Raymond Rallier du Baty.

Mount Ralph. 76°58′S, 144°32′W. Between Mount Gilmour and Mount McCormick in the Ford Ranges of Marie Byrd Land. Discovered by the USAS 1939–41. Named for Ralph W. Smith.

Ram Bow Bluff. 80°48′S, 26°42′W. On the east side of the Stephenson Bastion in the south-central part of the Shackleton Range. Visited by the BCTAE in 1957, and named descriptively by them for its resemblance to the ram bow of an old battleship.

Ramage Point. 73°39′S, 120°20′W. Ice-covered. Just west of Beakley Glacier on the north side of Carney Island, on the coast of Marie Byrd Land. Named for Rear Adm. L.P. Ramage, USN, assistant chief of Naval Operations, Ships Operations and Readiness in the period following IGY.

Rambler Harbor. 66°28′S, 66°27′W. In the northern side of Rambler Island in the Bragg Islands, in Crystal Sound. Named by Cdr. Carey on the *Discovery II* in 1930–31. Its location was doubted for several years but in 1958 the FIDS reidentified and surveyed it.

Rambler Island. 66°28′S, 66°27′W. Also called Isla Bio Bio. The largest of the Bragg Islands, in Crystal Sound, about

7½ miles north of Cape Rey, in Graham Land. Surveyed by the FIDS in 1958–59. Named in association with Rambler Harbor, which lies on the northern side of the island.

Rambo Nunataks. 83°57′S, 66°20′W. A chain of nunataks NW of the Patuxent Range. They extend along the west side of the Foundation Ice Stream for 17 miles in the Pensacola Mountains. Named for William L. Rambo, geophysicist in the Pensacola Mountains in 1965–66.

Mount Ramenskiy. 71°46′S, 12°33′E. 2,560 m. Forms the south end of Isdalsegga Ridge in the Südliche Petermann Range of the Wohlthat Mountains. Discovered aerially by Ritscher's 1938–39 expedition. Named by the USSR in 1966 for botanist L.G. Ramenskiy (1884–1953).

Rameris, Theodore. Ordinary seaman on the Wilkes Expedition 1838–42. Joined in the USA. Run at Valparaiso.

Ramirez Island. 69°09′S, 68°28′W. Off the west coast of the Antarctic Peninsula.

The Ramp. A plateau between two mountain ridges about ½ mile NE of Cape Evans on Ross Island. Two waterfalls run down from it toward the cape.

Rampart Ridge. 78°10′S, 161°55′E. On the west side of the Royal Society Range. North of Rutgers Glacier. It extends from The Spire to Bishop Peak. Surveyed and named descriptively by the NZ Northern Survey Party of the BCTAE in 1957.

Mount Ramsay. 60°45′S, 44°45′W. 475 m. At the west side of Uruguay Cove on the north coast of Laurie Island in the South Orkneys. Charted by Bruce in 1903, and named by him that year for Allan Ramsay.

Ramsay, Allan. Chief engineer of the *Scotia* during the Bruce expedition of 1902–4. He died on Aug. 6, 1903, and was buried at the foot of what is now called Mount Ramsay.

Ramsay Glacier *see* **Ramsey Glacier**

Ramsay Wedge. 80°26′S, 25°43′W. In the Shackleton Range.

Ramseier Glacier. 80°30'S, 156°18'E. A steep cirque-type glacier. 5 miles long. Flows SW to enter Byrd Glacier just east of Mount Rummage. Named for René O. Ramseier, glaciologist at McMurdo Station, 1960–61, and at Amundsen-Scott South Pole Station, 1961–62.

Ramsey Cliff. 83°28'S, 54°09'W. A rock cliff along the Torbert Escarpment. 2 miles NE of Mount Torbert in the Neptune Range of the Pensacola Mountains. Named for Robert E. Ramsey, storekeeper at Ellsworth Station in 1958.

Ramsey Glacier. 84°24'S, 179°20'E. Also seen spelled (erroneously) as Ramsay Glacier. 45 miles long. Comes off the Bush Mountains near the edge of the Polar Plateau, and flows north to the Ross Ice Shelf eastward of Den Hartog Peak. Discovered by the USAS during Flight C of Feb. 29–March 1, 1940. Named by Byrd for Adm. DeWitt C. Ramsey, USN, vice chief of Naval Operations during Operation Highjump, 1946–47.

The *Rancagua*. Argentine ship which took part in the following expeditions undertaken by that country in the Antarctic: 1946–47; 1953–54 (Capt. Vicente Reyes); 1955–56 (Capt. Juan Otazo Kelly); 1956–57 (Capt. Eduardo Beeche).

Rancho Point. 62°58'S, 60°30'W. A rock headland, 170 meters high. Marks the eastern extremity of Deception Island in the South Shetlands. It rises from the sea to become a large rock, and was named for its shape in 1947 by the commander of the *Granville* (part of the Argentine Antarctic Expedition of 1947–48).

Randall Ridge. 71°44'S, 64°38'W. Arc-shaped. At the north side of the Guthridge Nunataks in the Gutenko Mountains of central Palmer Land. Named by the US Geological Survey in 1974 for Robert H. Randall (1890–1966), assistant for cartography with the US Bureau of the Budget. His responsibility was to coordinate mapping activities of the government, 1941–60. In 1954 he set up the Technical Advisory Committee on Antarctic Mapping which established a mapping program for Antarctica based on the best technical methods.

Randall Rocks. 68°11'S, 67°17'W. ½ mile off the SW corner of Millerand Island, they trend in a NW-SE direction for 1 mile, in Marguerite Bay off the west coast of Graham Land. Surveyed in 1936 by the BGLE, and again in 1948–49 by the FIDS. Named by the UK for Terence M. Randall, FIDS radio operator at Base E in 1947–49.

Random Hills. 74°07'S, 164°25'E. Bounded on the west by Campbell Glacier and on the east by Tinker Glacier and Wood Bay. The center of this group of rugged hills is about 15 miles NNW of Mount Melbourne, in Victoria Land. Named by the New Zealanders in 1966–67 because of the random orientation of the ridges which go to form these hills.

Raney, Michele. b. 1951. Dr. Michele Eileen Raney was an L.A. doctor, the first woman to winter-over at the Pole. She was chosen ahead of all applicants, male and female, to be the Amundsen-Scott South Pole Station physician for the 1978–79 season. She wintered-over in 1979, and left in Nov. 1979.

Ranfurly Point. 84°50'S, 169°36'E. Marks the convergence of the Beardmore and Keltie Glaciers, at the northern end of the Supporters Range. Named by Denys B. Rainey, Cartographic Branch of the Department of Lands and Survey, NZ, for Lord Ranfurly, governor of NZ, 1897–1904.

Ranges. Different from a "mountains" group in that the peaks of a range tend to form one continuous mass, whereas a "mountains" is broken, and usually, although not always, larger, and may contain several ranges. Most ranges have now been photographed from the air, if not mapped topographically. Sometimes ranges disappear over the course of the centuries.

Rankin Glacier. 71°41'S, 62°15'W. 12 miles long. On the east side of Palmer Land. It flows SE, then east, along the south side of the Schirmacher Massif to join the Cline Glacier just inland from the head of Odom Inlet. Named for John S. Rankin, biologist on the International Weddell Sea Oceanographic Expeditions of 1968 and 1969.

Rankine Rock. 82°24'S, 50°35'W. 1 mile north of Cox Nunatak at the northern extremity of the Dufek Massif in the Pensacola Mountains. Named for David F. Rankine, Jr., VX-6 photographer, 1964.

Ranney Nunatak. 76°53'S, 143°55'W. In the SW extremity of the Gutenko Nunataks, in the Ford Ranges of Marie Byrd Land. Mapped by the USAS 1939–41. Named for Charles R. Ranney, ionosphere physicist at Byrd Station, 1969.

Ransom, Nelson. Seaman on the Wilkes Expedition 1838–42. Joined in the Sandwich Islands. Served the cruise.

Ranvik Bay. 69°S, 77°40'E. 15 miles wide. South of the Rauer Islands in the SE part of Prydz Bay. Discovered and charted in Feb. 1935 by Mikkelsen in the *Thorshavn*. Named for Ranvik, the bay in Norway where Lars Christensen, owner of the *Thorshavn,* had his estate.

Ranvik Glacier. 69°10'S, 77°40'E. Also called Ranvik Ice Tongue. Flows into the southern part of Ranvik Bay in the SE part of Prydz Bay on the Ingrid Christensen Coast of East Antarctica. Photographed by the LCE 1936–37, and named Ranvikbreen (Ranvik Glacier) by the Norwegians in association with the bay.

Ranvik Ice Tongue *see* **Ranvik Glacier**

Ranvik Island. 68°54'S, 77°50'E. Also called Torckler Island. 1½ miles long. The largest island in the southern part of the Rauer Islands, at the northern end of Ranvik Bay, 3 miles NW of Browns Glacier. Photographed by the LCE 1936–37, and considered to be a part of the mainland by the Norwegian cartographers

working off these photos. They called it Ranviktangen (the Ranvik tongue) in association with Ranvik Bay. The Operation Highjump photos, taken in 1946–47, enabled US cartographer John H. Roscoe in 1952 to determine that this is indeed an island, and he redefined it.

Ranvika. 68°44'S, 90°30'W. A cove indenting the east coast of Peter I Island, near the NE corner of the island. Discovered in 1927 by Eyvind Tofte in the *Odd I.* Named by him, probably for the estate of his boss, Lars Christensen, who was owner of the *Odd I.* His estate was located at the head of Ranvik, a bay in Norway.

Ranviktangen *see* **Ranvik Island**

Punta Rara *see* **Moody Point**

RARE *see* **Ronne Antarctic Research Expedition**

Rare Range. 74°24'S, 64°05'W. Between the Wetmore and Irvine Glaciers in Palmer Land. Discovered aerially by the RARE in 1947–48. Named for the RARE (Ronne Antarctic Research Expedition 1947–48) for its huge contribution toward opening up the Antarctic Peninsula.

Cape Rasmussen *see* **Rasmussen Island**

Rasmussen Island. 65°15'S, 64°05'W. In the northern part of Waddington Bay, on the west coast of Graham Land. The northern entrance to Waddington Bay was named Cap Rasmussen by de Gerlache in 1897–99. Air photos have since shown that there is no such cape, so in 1959 the UK named this feature in order to preserve the name Rasmussen in the area.

Rassa Point *see* **Rossa Point**

Rastorfer Glacier. 71°50'S, 167°06'E. Flows south from the Admiralty Mountains into the upper part of the Tucker Glacier just east of the Homerun Range. Named for James R. Rastorfer, biologist at McMurdo Station in 1967–68, and at Palmer Station in 1968–69.

Rastorguev Glacier. 70°57'S, 163°30' E. Flows from the eastern slopes of the Explorers Range between Mounts Ford and Sturm and joins the Lillie Glacier via the Flensing Icefall. Named by the USA for meteorologist Vladimir I. Rastorguev, USSR IGY observer at Weather Central at Little America V in 1957.

Rat-Tailed Fishes. *Lionarus filicauda.* Deep sea fish of the order Macrouridae. They live at the sea bottom, and are the most abundant of the deep sea fishes here. Relatives of the cod, they are elongated with large heads, and have eyes that are covered with spiny scales.

Mount Rath. 74°19'S, 62°30'W. 6 miles NNE of Mount Owen in the Hutton Mountains of Palmer Land. Named for Arthur E. Rath, electronics technician at Amundsen-Scott South Pole Station in 1964.

Rathbone Hills. 71°39'S, 64°48'W. A line of low hills or nunataks, 14 miles long. Trend east-west. 4 miles north of the Guthridge Nunataks in the Gutenko Mountains of central Palmer Land. Named for Maj. David L. Rathbone, US Marine commander of Hercules aircraft with VXE-6, 1970 and 1971.

Mount Ratliff. 85°42'S, 137°W. 2,520 m. North of the Watson Escarpment. 8 miles NNE of Mount Doumani. Named for Charles E. Ratliff, aviation machinist's mate with VX-6 on several trips to the Antarctic between 1963 and 1967.

Raudberg Pass. 72°38'S, 3°22'W. Also called Raudbergpasset. Between Kulen Mountain and Raudberget in the Borg Massif of Queen Maud Land. Named for its nearness to Raudberget.

Raudberg Valley. 72°39'S, 3°26'W. Also called Raudbergdalen. 20 miles long. The main ice-filled valley extending northeastward through the Borg Massif of Queen Maud Land. Named for its nearness to Raudberget.

Raudbergdalen *see* **Raudberg Valley**

Raudberget. 72°38'S, 3°30'W. A prominent mountain just NE of Hogskavlen Mountain in the Borg Massif of Queen Maud Land. Name means "the red mountain" in Norwegian.

Raudbergpasset *see* **Raudberg Pass**

Rauer Group *see* **Rauer Islands**

Rauer Islands. 68°51'S, 77°50'E. Also called the Rauer Group. Between Sørsdal Glacier Tongue and Ranvik Bay, in the SE part of Prydz Bay. Dominated by the Vestfold Hills. They include Filla Island, Hop Island, Ranvik Island. Discovered and charted by Mikkelsen in 1935, and named by him for the island of the same name in Oslofjorden, opposite Tønsberg, Norway, the great whaling harbor.

Rautio Nunatak. 82°37'S, 53°03'W. At the northern extremity of the Pensacola Mountains, overlooking the Ronne Ice Shelf.

Ravel Peak. 69°45'S, 71°17'W. 1,250 m. Surmounts the south side of Debussy Heights in the northern part of Alexander Island. When seen from the east it is distinctly pyramidal. Named by the UK for the composer.

Ravelin Ridge. 61°11'S, 54°05'W. Extends north-south almost the length of Clarence Island in the South Shetlands. Named by the UK in 1971 for its resemblance to a ravelin-type fortification.

Ravin Bay. 66°32'S, 138°27'E. Also called Baie des Ravins. Between Cape Pépin and the point where Français Glacier flows into the sea on the coast of East Antarctica. Discovered in 1840 by Dumont d'Urville and named by him for the ravinelike quality of the coastline at this point.

Baie des Ravins *see* **Ravin Bay**

The *Ravn.* Norwegian whale catcher based at Deception Island in 1908–9.

Ravn Rock. 63°S, 60°34'W. A submerged rock in the middle of Neptune's Bellows, which is the entranceway to Port Foster, Deception Island. Charted by Charcot in 1908–10, and named by him for the *Ravn.*

Rawle Glacier. 71°50'S, 164°40'E. In the Concord Mountains, flowing NW between Leitch Massif and the King Range into the Black Glacier. Named by the New Zealanders in 1963–64 for Russell Rawle, leader at Scott Base in 1964.

Mount Rawson *see* **Rawson Plateau**

Rawson, Kennett L. Navigator on the shore party of Byrd's 1933–35 expedition.

Rawson Mountains. 86°43'S, 154°40' W. Also called the Frederick H. Rawson Mountains. Crescent-shaped. A range of tabular, ice-covered mountains SE of the Nilsen Plateau, of which they are a continuation. They extend SE for 18 miles to the west side of the Robert Scott Glacier. Discovered in Dec. 1934 by Quin Blackburn's party during Byrd's 1933–35 expedition and named by Byrd for Frederick H. Rawson, US banker and contributor to Byrd's first 2 expeditions to the Antarctic.

Rawson Plateau. 85°52'S, 164°45'W. 15 miles long. 3,400 m. Between the heads of the Bowman, Moffett, and Steagall Glaciers in the Queen Maud Mountains. Named originally as Mount Kennett Rawson, then as Mount Rawson, and finally it was determined to be a plateau.

Mount Ray. 85°07'S, 170°48'W. 3,905 m. 1½ miles SE of Mount Fisher in the Prince Olav Mountains. Named for Carleton Ray, zoologist at McMurdo Station, 1963–64, 1964–65, and 1965–66.

Ray, Charles. Ordinary seaman on the Wilkes Expedition 1838–42. Joined in the USA. Served the cruise.

Ray, Nathaniel. Commander of the *Harmony* in the South Shetlands for the 1820–21 season. On Aug. 1, 1821, he was succeeded as captain by Isaac Hodges.

Ray Nunatak. 83°28'S, 51°58'W. 1,630 m. Just north of Beiszer Nunatak and 5 miles SW of Dyrdal Peak in the southern part of the Forrestal Range of the Pensacola Mountains. Named for James A. Ray, utilitiesman at Ellsworth Station in 1957.

Ray Promontory. 62°36'S, 61°09'W. On the north coast of Livingston Island in the South Shetlands.

Rayment, Ted. Movie photographer on David Lewis' *Solo* expedition of 1977–78.

Mount Raymond. 85°53'S, 174°43'E. 2,820 m. On the southernmost ridge of the Grosvenor Mountains. 2½ miles SE of Mount Cecily. Discovered by Shackleton during his 1907–9 expedition, and named by him for his eldest son. Shackleton thought it lay in the Dominion Range. He was wrong, but he charted it correctly.

Raymond Fosdick Mountains *see* **Fosdick Mountains**

Raymond Fosdick Range *see* **Fosdick Mountains**

Rayner, George W. British zoologist with the Discovery Committee. Chief scientist on the *William Scoresby* from June 1929 to June 1930, and again in 1934–35, 1935–36, and 1937–38.

Rayner Glacier. 67°40'S, 48°25'E. Also spelled (erroneously) as Rainer Glacier. 10 miles wide. Flows from the Nye Mountains of Enderby Land into Casey Bay, just west of the Condon Hills. Discovered aerially by Douglas Leckie in Oct. 1956, while flying over in an ANARE Beaver aircraft. Named by the Australians for J.M. Rayner, director of the Bureau of Mineral Resources in the Australian Department of National Development.

Rayner Peak. 67°24'S, 55°56'E. Also called George Rayner Peak, Kjuringen. 1,270 m. 35 miles SW of the head of Edward VIII Bay and 2 miles west of Robert Glacier. Discovered in Feb. 1936 by personnel on the *William Scoresby* and named by them for George W. Rayner.

Rayner Point. 60°39'S, 45°10'W. Forms the northern side of the entrance to Gibbon Bay on the eastern coast of Coronation Island in the South Orkneys. Charted by Petter Sørlle in 1912–13, and again by personnel on the *Discovery II* in

1933. They named it for George W. Rayner.

Rays. Rajidae. Found only in the region of the Antarctic Peninsula (*see* **Fish**).

Razlom Point. 70°S, 12°52′E. At the west edge of the Lazarev Ice Shelf. 2 miles north of Leningradskiy Island, in Queen Maud Land. Named Mys Razlom (breach point) by the USSR in 1959 for the large old break in the ice shelf nearby.

Mount Razorback. 76°50′S, 161°18′E. Just east of Staten Island Heights, on the ridge dividing the NW and SW sources of the Benson Glacier in Victoria Land. Named descriptively in 1957 by the NZ Northern Survey Party of the BCTAE.

Razorback Island *see* **Little Razorback Island, Big Razorback Island**

Razorback Islands *see* **Dellbridge Islands**

Razorback Whale *see* **Fin Whale**

Mount Razumovskiy. 71°29′S, 12°43′E. 2,285 m. On the southern part of the Deildegasten Ridge in the Östliche Petermann Range of the Wohlthat Mountains. Discovered by Ritscher in 1938–39. Named by the USSR in 1966 for geologist N.K. Razumovskiy (1893–1967).

Mount Rea. 77°04′S, 145°30′W. Has an imposing monolith on its west side called The Billboard (q.v.). Between the Arthur and Boyd Glaciers in the Ford Ranges of Marie Byrd Land. Discovered during the Eastern Flight of Dec. 5, 1929, and named by Byrd for Mr. and Mrs. Rea of Pittsburgh, contributors to that 1928–30 expedition of Byrd's.

Rea, Henry. b. ca. 1804. British RN officer who left England in the *Hopefull* and the *Rose* in 1833 on a government-endorsed Enderby Brothers sealing expedition, to follow up Biscoe's discoveries. When Capt. Prior resigned in the Falklands, Rea took over the expedition. The *Rose* was later crushed between two icebergs. This fact, plus mutinous crews, forced the *Hopefull* back to England.

Rea Peak. 62°01′S, 58°09′W. 590 m. Almost 2 miles NE of Rose Peak and 1½ miles NW of Mount Hopeful in the central part of King George Island in the South Shetlands. Named by the UK in 1960 for Henry Rea.

Rea Rocks. 77°05′S, 145°10′W. In the middle of Arthur Glacier. 6 miles east of Mount Rea in the Ford Ranges of Marie Byrd Land. Named for Peter C. Rea, USN, construction electrician at Byrd Station in 1967.

Read Mountains. 80°42′S, 24°45′W. A group of rocky summits, the highest being 1,830 m. East of Glen Glacier in the south-central part of the Shackleton Range. Named in 1957 by the BCTAE for Professor Herbert H. Read, chairman of the Scientific Committee and member of the Committee of Management of the BCTAE 1955–58.

Reade Peak. 65°06′S, 63°29′W. 1,060 m. 1 mile south of Sonia Point and Flandres Bay, on the west coast of Graham Land. Named by the UK in 1960 for Joseph B. Reade (1801–1870), British photography pioneer.

Rebholz Nunatak. 74°05′S, 100°13′W. Isolated. Just north of the Hudson Mountains. 8 miles NNW of Teeters Nunatak. Named for Maj. Edward Rebholz, operations officer of the US Army Aviation Detachment, which supported the Ellsworth Land Survey of 1968–69.

Rebo, Joseph. 2nd Class Boy on the Wilkes Expedition 1838–42. Joined at Rio. Served the cruise.

Rebuff Glacier. 73°58′S, 163°12′E. Flows from the Deep Freeze Range into the Campbell Glacier 4 miles SE of the summit of Mount Mankinen in Victoria Land. Named by the northern party of the NZGSAE 1962–63 because they were prevented from getting to it.

Recely Bluff. 73°10′S, 125°46′W. On the NE slope of Mount Siple on Siple Island, off the coast of Marie Byrd Land. 7 miles NE of the summit of the mountain. Named for Frank J. Recely, Jr., ionosphere physicist at Byrd Station in 1965.

Recess Cove. 64°30′S, 61°32′W. 2½ miles wide. In the east side of Charlotte Bay, on the west coast of Graham Land. Surveyed by the FIDS from the *Norsel* in 1955. Named by the UK in 1956 because it does, indeed, form a recess in the side of Charlotte Bay.

Recess Nunatak. 76°31′S, 144°17′W. 1 mile west of Mount Perkins in the Fosdick Mountains of the Ford Ranges of Marie Byrd Land. Named because the nunatak is recessed in the ice at the base due to windscooping.

Reckling Peak. 76°16′S, 159°15′E. 2,010 m. Isolated. Surmounts the central part of a ridge located at the icefalls at the head of the Mawson Glacier in Victoria Land. Named in 1964 for Lt. Cdr. Darold L. Reckling, VX-6 pilot in Antarctica in 1961.

Cape Reclus *see* **Reclus Peninsula**

Reclus Peninsula. 64°33′S, 61°47′W. 7 miles long. Borders the west side of Charlotte Bay, on the west coast of Graham Land. Charted in 1898 by de Gerlache, who named the northern extremity as Cap Reclus, for Élisée Reclus (1830–1905), French geographer known for his mammoth 19-volume work, *Nouvelle Géographie Universelle*. In 1960 the UK extended the name to the entire peninsula.

Recluse Nunatak. 70°18′S, 70°32′W. Isolated. On the Handel Ice Piedmont, between Haydn Inlet and the Colbert Mountains, in the west-central part of Alexander Island. Named by the UK for its location.

Recoil Glacier. 73°46′S, 163°05′E. Flows from the Deep Freeze Range, south of Mount Pollock, into the Campbell Glacier, in Victoria Land. Named by the northern party of the NZGSAE 1962–63 because the geologist of the party recoiled in horror at finding little of value there.

Recovery Glacier. 81°10′S, 28°W. 60 miles long, or more. 40 miles wide at its mouth. Flows west along the south side of the Shackleton Range. Discovered by the BCTAE in 1957, and named by them for the recovery of the tractors which were continually falling into crevasses in the early stages of the transantarctic crossing.

Recreation. There are several forms of recreation enjoyed in Antarctica. There have been theatrical shows ever since the pioneer days; now there are movies as well. Books were, from the beginning, considered a staple, as were conversation and pipe-smoking. Chess, checkers (draughts), and cards have always been popular indoor games, and Frank Wild was a popular winner of the shove ha'penny tournament in the winter of 1902. As far as outdoor activities go, skiing has always been a natural, as have sledging, tobogganing, and skijoring. Rugby, soccer, volleyball, softball, baseball, and basketball have all been played outside. Track and field has often been represented (*see* **Scott's Hut Race**). The Pole Bowl Football Game on New Year's Day was begun at the South Pole in 1974–75. Jogging has developed as a popular pastime, and the Annual South Pole Golf Tournament was first held in 1979. It has one hole — 237 yards long. An unusual recreation was Charcot's picnic (*see* **Picnics**), and in the winter of 1909, Charcot founded the Antarctic Sporting Club on Petermann Island, where ski and sledge races were held. While trapped on the ice in 1915, the crew of the *Endurance* created the Antarctic Derby (q.v.). There are innumerable other activities available in Antarctica.

Red Bay. 68°18′S, 67°11′W. Just south of the western extremity of Red Rock Ridge, on the west coast of Graham Land. Surveyed in 1936 by the BGLE, and again in 1948–49 by the FIDS, who named it in association with the ridge.

Red Buttress Peak. 76°49′S, 162°21′E. 1,060 m. Between the lower parts of the Benson and Hunt Glaciers in Victoria Land. Its eastern face is a huge cliff of red granite. Named descriptively in 1957 by the NZ Northern Survey Party of the BCTAE.

Red Dike Bluff. 78°48'S, 162°19'E. Also spelled Red Dyke Bluff. Just south of Trepidation Glacier, on the east side of the Skelton Glacier. It is distinguished by a dike made up of igneous rock against a black background of the intruded sediments. Named descriptively in 1957 by the NZ party of the BCTAE.

Red Dyke Bluff *see* **Red Dike Bluff**

Red Island. 63°44'S, 57°52'W. Circular. Flat-topped. 1 mile across. 495 meters high. Has reddish cliffs of volcanic rock. 3½ miles NW of Cape Lachman, James Ross Island, in the Prince Gustav Channel. Discovered and named descriptively by Nordenskjöld's expedition of 1901–4.

Red Raider Rampart. 85°09'S, 173°12'W. A rugged ice and rock wall just east of the junction of the Gatlin and McGregor Glaciers in the Queen Maud Mountains. Named by the Texas Tech Shackleton Glacier Expedition of 1964–65 for the student body of Texas Tech, whose athletic representatives are known as the Red Raiders.

Red Ridge. 77°06'S, 162°08'E. Just west of Robson Glacier in the Gonville and Caius Range of Victoria Land. Named descriptively by Frank Debenham during his plane table survey of 1912 while part of Scott's 1910–13 expedition.

Red Rock Ridge. 68°18'S, 67°08'W. A reddish-colored promontory. 690 m. Juts out from the west coast of Graham Land between Neny Fjord and Rymill Bay. Surveyed in 1936 by the BGLE, and named by Rymill for its color. Actually, this ridge was discovered in 1909 by Charcot and named Île Pavie, or Cap Pavie (*see* **Pavie Ridge**), but the BGLE did not know this. It was not until the FIDS did a survey in 1948 that this feature was thus identified. By that time, however, the name Red Rock Ridge had become so popular that it stuck.

Red Spur. 85°57'S, 126°44'W. 2 miles long. It descends from the southern part

of the Wisconsin Plateau to Olentangy Glacier 1 mile north of Tillite Spur. Named by John H. Mercer in 1964–65 because the surface of a flat platform on this spur is weathered bright red.

Redcastle Ridge. 72°26'S, 169°57'E. A castlelike ridge of red and black volcanic rocks between the Arneb Glacier and the terminal face of the Edisto Glacier at the head of Edisto Inlet. Named by the New Zealanders in 1957–58 for its color and shape.

Redcliff Nunatak. 77°12'S, 162°03'E. Also called Redcliffs Nunakol. 630 m. A red granite nunatak. 4 miles east of Mount Suess along the southern flank of the Mackay Glacier. Charted by members of Scott's 1910–13 expedition and named by them for its color.

Redcliffs Nunakol *see* **Redcliff Nunatak**

Reddick Nunatak. 76°17'S, 144°01'W. In the eastern part of the Phillips Mountains. 8 miles ENE of Mount Carbone, in the Ford Ranges of Marie Byrd Land. Named for Warren W. Reddick, Jr., USN, construction electrician at Byrd Station in 1967.

Redfearn Island. 68°37'S, 77°53'E. A small island just west of Warriner Island and 1 mile off the west end of Breidnes Peninsula, Vestfold Hills. Photographed by the LCE 1936–37, and plotted as two even smaller islands by Norwegian cartographers working from these photos. 1957–58 ANARE air photos showed these two islands to be one. Named by the Australians for H.T. Redfearn, diesel mechanic at Davis Station, 1961.

Mount Redifer. 85°48'S, 160°52'W. 2,050 m. 3 miles south of Mount Ellsworth in the Queen Maud Mountains. Named for Howard D. Redifer, meteorology electronics technician at South Pole Station, 1959.

Redmond Bluff. 71°08'S, 167°03'E. An abrupt east-facing bluff. 1,200 m. 2½ miles east of Mount Dalmeny in the Anare Mountains. Named for James R.

Redmond, biologist at McMurdo Station, 1967–68.

Isla Redonda *see* **Owen Island**

Punta Redonda *see* **Pottinger Point**

Cabo Redondo *see* **Redondo Point**

Islote Redondo *see* **Puget Rock**

Redondo Point. 65°12'S, 64°06'W. Just west of Blanchard Ridge on the west coast of Graham Land. In 1957 the Argentines named it Cabo Redondo (Round Point), and later the British named it Moot Point. The USA adheres to Redondo Point.

Redpath Peaks. 80°28'S, 81°18'W. Snow-covered. 3 miles SE of Mount Shattuck and the Independence Hills, at the southern end of the Heritage Range. Named for Bruce B. Redpath, geophysicist on the first South Pole–Queen Maud Land Traverse, of 1964–65.

Mount Reece. 63°50'S, 58°32'W. 1,085 m. Ice-free. 4 miles west of Pitt Point. It is the highest point of a ridge forming the south wall of Victory Glacier on the south side of the Trinity Peninsula. Charted in 1945 by the FIDS, and named by them for Alan Reece.

Reece, Alan. British geologist. FIDS leader at Base B on Deception Island in 1945, and FIDS meteorologist/geologist at Base D at Hope Bay in 1946. As geologist on the NBSAE 1949–52, he had to have his eye amputated on July 21, 1951, by novice doctor Ove Wilson. The operation was a success, but Reece died in the Canadian Arctic in a plane crash in 1960.

Reece, J.A. Radio operator at West Base during the USAS 1939–41.

Reece Pass. 76°32'S, 144°32'W. Just east of Mount Colombo and Mount Richardson, in the eastern part of the Fosdick Mountains in the Ford Ranges of Marie Byrd Land. Discovered aerially by the USAS 1939–41 on flights from West Base, and visited by a biological party of the same expedition in 1940. Named for J.A. Reece.

Reece Valley. 72°41'S, 0°22'E. Ice-filled. Between Gavlen Ridge and Nupskåpa Peak, in the southern part of the Sverdrup Mountains in Queen Maud Land. Named Reecedalen (Reece Valley) by the Norwegians for Alan Reece.

Reecedalen *see* **Reece Valley**

Mount Reed. 67°02'S, 51°38'E. On the north side of Beaver Glacier, 2 miles east of Mount Sones in the Tula Mountains of Enderby Land. Named by the Australians in 1962 for J.E. Reed.

Reed, J.E. Crew member on the *Discovery* during the BANZARE 1929–31.

Reed, Raymond. Seaman on the Wilkes Expedition 1838–42. Joined at Oahu. Served the cruise.

Reed Nunataks. 74°49'S, 161°58'E. They form a divide between the upper portions of the Reeves and Larsen Glaciers. 6 miles west of Hansen Nunatak, in Victoria Land. Named for David Reed, US Geological Survey topographic engineer at McMurdo Station, 1964–65.

Reed Ridge. 85°02'S, 91°40'W. Flat-topped. Snow-covered. Extends NW for 3 miles from the west part of the Ford Massif in the Thiel Mountains. Forms the western wall of the Compton Valley. Named for Dale R. Reed, ionosphere scientist at Ellsworth Station in 1958 and Byrd Station in 1960.

Reedy Glacier. 85°30'S, 134°W. Over 100 miles long. Between 6 and 12 miles wide. Flows from the Polar Plateau to the Ross Ice Shelf between the Michigan Plateau and the Wisconsin Range. It marks the limits of the Queen Maud Mountains on the west and the Horlick Mountains on the east. Named for Rear Adm. James R. Reedy, USN, Commander, US Naval Support Force, Antarctica, from Nov. 1962 until April 1965.

Mount Rees. 76°40'S, 118°10'W. 7 miles NW of Mount Steere in the northern end of the Crary Mountains of Marie Byrd Land. Lichens are to be found here. Named in the 1960s for Manfred H. Rees, aurora scientist at Byrd Station, 1965–66.

Reeve Island. 64°55'S, 63°58'W. 1½ miles long. Between Knight and Friar Islands in the Wauwermans Islands of the Wilhelm Archipelago. Named by the UK in 1958 for the *Canterbury Tales* character.

¹Mount Reeves. 67°07'S, 67°58'W. 1,920 m. Just NE of Mount Bouvier on the east side of Adelaide Island. Discovered and surveyed in 1909 by Charcot. Resurveyed in 1948 by the FIDS and named by them for Edward A. Reeves (*see* **Reeves Bluffs**).

²Mount Reeves *see* **Reeves Bluffs**

Reeves, Joseph. Quartermaster on the Wilkes Expedition 1838–42. Joined in the USA. Run at Sydney.

Reeves Bluffs. 79°36'S, 158°40'E. 8 miles long. East-facing. 15 miles west of Cape Murray in the Cook Mountains. Discovered by Scott in 1901–4. Scott named a summit along this bluff as Mount Reeves, for Edward A. Reeves, map curator and instructor in Survey at the Royal Geographic Society from 1900–33. In 1965 the US, on finding no prominent mountain where Scott claimed, extended the name to the whole line of bluffs.

Reeves Glacier. 74°45'S, 162°15'E. Flows from the interior upland, between the Eisenhower Range and Mount Larsen, into the Nansen Ice Sheet on the coast of Victoria Land. Discovered by Shackleton's 1907–9 expedition and named by them for William Pember Reeves, agent-general for New Zealand in London from 1896–1909.

Reeves Névé. 74°25'S, 160°E. West of the Eisenhower Range in Victoria Land. Reeves Glacier flows out of this névé. Named by New Zealand in association with the glacier.

Reeves Peninsula. 77°24'S, 152°20'W. Snow-covered. Along the northern side of Edward VII Peninsula. It extends between the lower ends of the Dalton and Gerry Glaciers into the southern part of Sulzberger Bay. Named by Byrd for John

M. Reeves, of Reeves Brothers, Inc., who contributed cold-weather clothing to Byrd's first two expeditions.

Reference Island *see* **Reference Islands**

Reference Islands. 68°12'S, 67°10'W. Also called Reference Island. 2 miles WNW of the west tip of Neny Island, and 1½ miles SE of Millerand Island in Marguerite Bay off the west coast of Graham Land. Charted in 1936 by the BGLE. Surveyed by the FIDS in 1947, and named by them because they serve as a convenient reference point for survey work.

Reference Peak. 67°15'S, 50°29'E. 1,030 m. Conical. Has a steep face to the west near its crest. 3 miles south of Amundsen Bay. Between Mounts Weller and Hollingsworth. When seen from the north it is a sharp peak with smooth, clear-cut sides. Discovered in Oct. 1956 by an ANARE party and named by them for its use as a reference point for magnetic observations at Observation Island.

Referring Peak. 76°56'S, 161°51'E. Over 1,200 m. A black peak on the north side of Mackay Glacier. 1½ miles west of the mouth of Cleveland Glacier, in Victoria Land. Charted by members of Scott's 1910–13 expedition. Named by them for its easy use as a landmark.

Refuge Islands. 68°21'S, 67°10'W. 1 mile from the ice cliffs at the SW side of Red Rock Ridge, off the west coast of Graham Land. Discovered by the BGLE 1934–37. Named by Rymill for their use as a depot for sledge journeys south from the expedition's southern base in the Debenham Islands.

Regent Reef. 67°52'S, 68°38'W. An area of submerged and drying rocks forming the NE limit of the Dion Islands, off the south end of Adelaide Island. Charted by the RN Hydrographic Survey Unit in 1963. Named by the UK in association with other islands nearby which have regality as a theme.

Mount Regina. 71°27'S, 165°45'E. 2,080 m. 10 miles WNW of Mount LeResche in the southern part of the Everett Range. Named for Thomas J. Regina, USN, photographer's mate on Hercules aircraft in the 1968–69 season. He had been in Antarctica before, at McMurdo Station, in 1963.

Régnard Peaks. 65°11'S, 63°53'W. Snow-covered. Over 1,220 m. 3 miles north of Mount Peary on the west coast of Graham Land. Discovered and named by Charcot in 1908–10.

Cap Regreso *see* **Return Point**

Regula, Herbert. Chief meteorologist on the German New Schwabenland Expedition of 1938–39, led by Alfred Ritscher.

Regula Range. 72°05'S, 3°20'W. Forms the SW portion of the Ahlmann Ridge in western Queen Maud Land. Somewhere in this very area Ritscher's 1938–39 expedition flew over and photographed a vast amount of terrain, but unfortunately there were no ground control checks for this fantastic feat to be of much worth. The Germans named several features here, including one called the Regula-Kette, for Herbert Regula. This may or may not be the same feature as the subject of this entry, but modern geographers have arbitrarily assumed that it is close enough.

Reichart, Louis. Seaman on the *City of New York* during the first half of Byrd's 1928–30 expedition, and on the *Eleanor Bolling* during the second half.

Cape Reichelderfer. 69°22'S, 62°43' W. Mainly ice-covered. 4 miles east of DeBusk Scarp, at the west side of Stefansson Strait on the east coast of Palmer Land. Charted by the USAS in 1940 and called Cape Rymill by them for John Rymill. This was one of two capes that the USAS called Cape Rymill that year, the other being just to the SE. This confusion was cleared up in 1947 when Finn Ronne, during the RARE, renamed this one for Francis W. Reichelderfer, chief of the US Weather Bureau.

Reichle Mesa. 68°09'S, 65°03'W. On the east side of the Antarctic Peninsula.

Mount Reid. 83°03'S, 166°01'E. 3,315 m. Mainly ice-free. Just east of the head of Cleaves Glacier in the Holland Range, on the edge of the Ross Ice Shelf. Discovered by Shackleton's expedition of 1907–9, and named by them for Alfred Reid, manager of the expedition.

Reid, James W.E. Passed midshipman on the Wilkes Expedition 1838–42. He started off on the *Relief*, and when Lt. Johnson transferred to the *Sea Gull*, Reid became commander of the *Relief*. He later transferred to the *Sea Gull* and was on that vessel when Johnson took it to Deception Island in March 1839. Reid was commander of the *Sea Gull* when it disappeared on April 29, 1839.

¹Reid Glacier. 66°30'S, 98°40'E. Flows between the Melba and Davis Peninsulas to the Shackleton Ice Shelf on the coast of East Antarctica. Discovered in Nov. 1912 by the Western Base Party of the AAE 1911–14, and named by Mawson for Sir George Reid, Australian high commissioner in London in 1911.

²Reid Glacier. 67°29'S, 67°16'W. 1½ miles wide. 8 miles long. Flows south to enter Bigourdan Fjord opposite The Narrows, on the west coast of Graham Land. Charted by the BGLE 1934–37. The lower reaches of the glacier were surveyed in 1948–49 by the FIDS. The glacier was named by them for Harry F. Reid (1859–1944), professor of geology at Johns Hopkins University in Baltimore. He was noted for his studies of glacier flow and stratification in Alaska and the Alps.

Reid Island. 60°41'S, 45°30'W. At the east side of the entrance to Iceberg Bay, on the south coast of Coronation Island in the South Orkneys. In 1912–13 Petter Sørlle charted a small group of islands in this area, and called them Reidholmen (Reid Islets). Surveys conducted by the FIDS in 1948–49 found that only one island exists here.

Reid Islets *see* **Reid Island**

Reid Ridge. 76°57'S, 160°23'E. At the west side of the mouth of Cambridge Glacier in Victoria Land. Named in 1964 for John R. Reid, Jr., glaciologist at Little America V in 1959–60.

Reid Spur. 84°46'S, 178°30'E. 5 miles long. Flows north along the east side of Ramsey Glacier from an unnamed prominence 3 miles NW of Mount Bellows in the Queen Maud Mountains. Named for CWO James S. Reid, member of the US Army Aviation Detachment which explored this area with the Texas Tech Shackleton Glacier Expedition of 1964–65.

Reidholmen *see* **Reid Island**

Reilly Ridge. 71°32'S, 163°18'E. 7 miles long. On the NE side of the Lanterman Range of the Bowers Mountains. It descends from the heights just east of Mount Bernstein and forms a part of the SW wall of Sledgers Glacier. Named for Cdr. Joseph L. Reilly, USN, officer-in-charge of McMurdo Station, 1964.

Reilly Rocks. 75°09'S, 114°59'W. 5 miles NNW of Detling Peak in the NW part of the Kohler Range of Marie Byrd Land. Named for Gerald E. Reilly, Jr., US Coast Guard machinery technician (*see* **Deaths, 1976**).

Mount Reimer. 77°48'S, 86°12'W. 2,430 m. In the northern portion of the Sentinel Range, on the south side of the Newcomer Glacier. 5 miles SW of Mount Warren. Named for John D. Reimer, aerial photographer with VX-6 in this area in the 1959–60 season.

Reinbolt Hills. 70°29'S, 72°30'E. 5 miles long. 9 miles east of Gillock Island at the eastern edge of the Amery Ice Shelf. Named by US cartographer John H. Roscoe in 1952 for Lt. Fred L. Reinbolt, USN, co-pilot in 1946–47 on Operation Highjump flights over this area. These flights provided the photos for Roscoe to work from.

Mount Reinhardt. 84°12'S, 177°12'E. 1,020 m. Has a spur descending NE from it. At the NW portal of Good Glacier, where that glacier flows into the Ross Ice Shelf. Discovered by the USAS on Flight C of Feb. 29–March 1, 1940. Named for Cdr. Charles O. Reinhardt, USN, engineer on Operation Highjump, 1946–47, based at Little America IV.

Reist Rocks. 66°31'S, 107°25'E. 8 miles west of the Snyder Rocks on the coast of East Antarctica. Named for Wilbur H. Reist, tractor driver on Operation Windmill, 1947–48.

Relay Bay. 71°30'S, 169°32'E. An arm of Robertson Bay. 5 miles wide. Between Islands Point and Penelope Point on the north coast of Victoria Land. Visited on Oct. 14, 1911, by Campbell's Northern Party during the 1910–13 expedition led by Scott. Named by Campbell because they had to relay their sledges due to the heavy pressure ridges here. These ridges are created by the Nielsen, Ommanney, Crume, and Reusch Glaciers flowing into the bay.

Relay Hills. 69°29'S, 68°W. Ice-covered. Mainly conical. Between Mount Edgell and the Kinnear Mountains in the western part of the Antarctic Peninsula. Surveyed by the BGLE in 1936–37, and again by the FIDS in Nov. 1958. Named by the UK because both of these surveying parties had to relay their sledge loads through this area to the head of Prospect Glacier.

Relaying. Over exceptionally difficult terrain a party of sledgers may have to relay their sledges. Instead of each sledge being pulled by its normal man or group of dogs, it will have to be pulled by everybody together. The group will then have to go back for the next sledge and do the same for that one, and so on. It is a tough, time-consuming process.

Relict Lake. 62°57'S, 60°36'W. A small lake SE of Pendulum Cove on Deception Island. Named by the UK in 1957 for the fact that this lake is now cut off from the waters of Pendulum Cove. In Jan.–March 1829, when Lt. E.N. Kendall did his survey of Deception Island from the *Chanticleer*, the cove extended inland to this lake.

The *Relief*. Very slow cargo boat taken on the Wilkes Expedition 1838–42, but sent home in 1839 while en route to the Antarctic. Thus, it seems not to have gotten south of 60° S. Commanded first by Lt. Robert E. Johnson, and then by Passed Midshipman James Reid. It had a 468-ton displacement, was 109 feet long, 30 foot in the beam, 12 feet deep in the hold. It had 6 guns, and could reach 8½ knots. It had a crew of 75.

Relief Inlet. 75°13′S, 163°45′E. At the SW corner of Terra Nova Bay. Named by Edgeworth David in 1908 as he was on the South Magnetic Pole trip. Just as they were about to give up hope of being picked up, the *Nimrod* showed up here to collect the party.

Relief Lake. A small lake in the eastern part of Deception Island.

Relief Pass. 79°49′S, 158°23′E. 1,000 m. 1 mile north of Bastion Hill in the Brown Hills. Named by the VUWAE 1962–63 for the relief this pass provided after they had climbed to it.

Reluctant Island. 67°50′S, 67°05′W. Off the eastern coast of Horseshoe Island, on the west coast of Graham Land. Surveyed by the FIDS in 1955–57. This island was strangely reluctant to be mapped. It should have, but did not appear on the charts of the BGLE 1934–37. It was mapped as a peninsula by the FIDS in 1948–50.

Remenchus Glacier. 66°02′S, 101°35′E. A channel glacier. 4 miles wide. 8 miles long. Flows NW from the continental ice, and terminates in a small, but prominent tongue just east of the Mariner Islands and 12 miles NE of the Bunger Hills. Named for John F. Remenchus, chief aviation pilot during Operation Windmill, 1947–48.

Mount Remington. 71°46′S, 161°17′E. 1,775 m. 4 miles NW of Mount Bresnahan in the northern part of the Helliwell Hills. Named for Benjamin F. Remington, Jr., meteorologist at Little America V in 1957, and at South Pole Station in 1959.

Remington Glacier. 78°34′S, 84°18′W. 7 miles long. In the SE part of the Sentinel Range. It flows from the area just north of McPherson Peak and flows ESE into the area between the terminus of Hough Glacier and Johnson Spur. Discovered aerially by VX-6 on Dec. 14–15, 1959. Named for Edward W. Remington, glaciologist at South Pole Station, 1957.

Remnant Lake   *see*   **Dingle Lake**

Islote Remolino   *see*   **Vortex Island**

Remplingen Peak. 72°05′S, 4°18′E. 2,650 m. At the north end of Langfloget Cliff in the Mühlig-Hofmann Mountains of Queen Maud Land. Name means "the calf" in Norwegian.

Remus Glacier. 68°20′S, 66°43′W. 8 miles long. Flows from the northern slopes of Mount Lupa northwestward along the NE side of the Blackwall Mountains into Providence Cove, at Neny Fjord, on the west coast of Graham Land. The lower reaches of the glacier were surveyed by the BGLE in 1936, and resurveyed by the FIDS in 1948–49. The FIDS named it in association with Romulus Glacier, the head of which lies near the head of this glacier, and with Mount Lupa.

Renagar Glacier   *see*   **Renegar Glacier**

Cape Renard. 65°01′S, 63°47′W. Forms the south side of the entrance to Flandres Bay. It separates the Danco Coast from the Graham Coast on the west coast of the Antarctic Peninsula. Discovered in 1898 by de Gerlache, and named by him for Professor A. Renard, a member of the *Belgica* Commission.

Renard Glacier. 64°40′S, 61°38′W. Flows into the most southerly part of Charlotte Bay, on the west coast of Graham Land. Charted by de Gerlache in 1897–99. Named by the UK in 1960 for Charles Renard (1847–1905), dirigible airship pioneer.

Renaud Glacier. 67°43′S, 65°35′W. Heavily crevassed. Flows SE to enter

Seligman Inlet between Lewis Glacier and Choyce Point, on the east coast of Graham Land. Named by the UK for André Renaud, Swiss glaciologist.

Renaud Island. 65°40′S, 66°W. Ice-covered. 25 miles long. Between 4 and 10 miles wide. Between the Pitt Islands and Rabot Island in the Biscoe Islands. Charted and named by Charcot in 1908–10.

Rendezvous Bluff *see* **Discovery Bluff**

Rendezvous Rocks. 69°35′S, 67°38′W. On the west side of the Antarctic Peninsula.

Mount Rendu. 67°26′S, 67°04′W. Between the Reid and Heim Glaciers on Arrowsmith Peninsula in Graham Land. Named by the UK for Louis Rendu (1789–1859), French bishop and scientist specializing in glacier flow.

Renegar Glacier. 78°22′S, 163°08′E. Flows SE from Mount Dromedary into the Koettlitz Glacier. Named for Lt. Garland Renegar, USN, R4D aircraft pilot at McMurdo Station, 1960.

Cap Renier *see* **Renier Point**

Renier Point. 62°37′S, 59°48′W. Also called Punta Alfiler, Friesland Point, Cap Renier. Forms the eastern extremity of Livingston Island in the South Shetlands. Known to sealers as Point Renier as early as 1821, but also called Dread Point. In 1935 personnel on the *Discovery II* called it Pin Point, but this name did not catch on.

Renirie Rocks. 71°20′S, 161°20′E. An elliptical rock outcrop 1½ miles long, at the west side of the terminus of the Gressitt Glacier, 10 miles NW of the Morozumi Range. Named for Jack Renirie, USARP public information officer at McMurdo Station for at least 5 seasons from 1962–63 to 1970–71.

Rennell Glacier. 79°23′S, 84°12′W. 10 miles long. In the Pioneer Heights of the Heritage Range. It flows NW to the east of Inferno Ridge, into Splettstoesser Glacier. Named by the University of Min-

nesota Geological Party here in 1963–64, for K.P. Rennell, biologist on that party.

Renner Peak. 70°21′S, 67°50′W. The dominant peak on the small mountain mass between Chapman Glacier and Naess Glacier on the west coast of Palmer Land. Named by the UK for Robert G.B. Renner, BAS geophysicist at Stonington Island's Base E, 1963–65.

Rennick, Henry E. de P. Lt. Royal Navy officer on the *Terra Nova*, 1910–13.

Rennick Bay. 70°06′S, 161°20′E. An indentation into Oates Land at the terminus of Rennick Glacier. It is bounded on the west by Belousov Point and on the east by Stuhlinger Ice Piedmont. The eastern part of the bay was discovered from the *Terra Nova* in 1911, after that ship had deposited the Scott expedition at Cape Evans. Named by Harry Pennell for Lt. Henry E. de P. Rennick.

Rennick Glacier. 70°30′S, 160°45′E. Nearly 200 miles long, it is one of the largest glaciers in Antarctica, and the largest outlet glacier in northern Victoria Land. It flows from the Polar Plateau westward of the Mesa Range, and feeds Rennick Bay on the Oates Land coast. It is generally 20 to 30 miles wide, but narrows to 10 miles wide at the coast. Named in association with the bay.

Rennick Névé. 73°10′S, 160°20′E. At the head of Rennick Glacier in Victoria Land. Named by NZ in 1966 in association with the glacier.

Mount Rennie. 64°41′S, 63°35′W. 1,555 m. Snow-covered. Forms the central part of the ridge which extends southwestward from Mount Français in the southern part of Anvers Island. Surveyed by personnel of Operation Tabarin in 1944, and resurveyed by the FIDS in 1955. Named by the UK for Alexander J. Rennie, FIDS assistant surveyor at Base N in 1955.

Mount Renouard. 67°S, 52°26′E. 3 miles south of Mount Keyser, in the eastern part of the Tula Mountains of Enderby Land. Named by the Australians for H.E. von Renouard, weather observer at Mawson Station, 1961.

Gora Rëpke *see* **Iskollen Hill**

Reptile Ridge. 67°33'S, 68°11'W. On Adelaide Island.

Rescapé Islands. 66°49'S, 141°22'E. ½ mile NW of Cape Margerie off the Adélie Land coast. Surveyed by the French in 1949–51, and named by Liotard for an incident in 1950 when they landed at Port Martin and a small craft got carried away. It was rescued. Rescapé means "survivor" in French.

Rescue Nunatak. 69°37'S, 157°27'E. 14 miles SSE of Mount Martyn in the southern portion of the Lazarev Mountains. On the west side of the upper reaches of the Matusevich Glacier. Visited by the NZGSAE 1963–64, who named it for the rescue, in adverse conditions, of a sledge and its dogs that had fallen into a nearby crevasse.

The *Resolution*. Small, 462-ton British corvette, a former Whitby coalship known originally as the *Drake*. It was Cook's flagship on his second voyage of 1772–75 (*see also* **Cook**, and **The Adventure**). It was 110 feet 8 inches long, 35 feet 5½ inches wide, and carried cannon and a large ship's launch. It had a crew of 112. Cook was the captain and John Gilbert was the master (for further crew *see* **Cook**). Joseph Banks was going to go on it, but Cook ordered his scientific fittings pulled out when the ship became top-heavy. Banks, infuriated, resigned. The *Resolution* crossed the Antarctic Circle in 1773, and twice more after that, and reached a southing record of 71°10'S. Cook also sailed in the *Resolution* on his last, fatal, voyage.

Ressac Island. 66°42'S, 141°14'E. 1 mile east of Houle Island, and 4 miles NE of the Zélée Glacier Tongue. Charted by the French in 1949–51, and named by them for the surf which breaks over the island. Ressac means "surf" in French.

Rethval Point. 60°44'S, 45°36'W. Ice-free. Forms the southern side of the

entrance to Paal Harbor, on the east side of Signy Island in the South Orkneys. Surveyed in 1933 by personnel from the Discovery Committee, and again in 1947 by the FIDS. Named by the UK in 1954 for the Rethval Whaling Company of Oslo, the first company to start whaling operations in the South Orkneys, in 1911–12.

Retour Island. 66°46'S, 141°34'E. Almost ¾ mile long. The largest of the Curzon Islands. 175 yards north of Cape Découverte. Charted in 1951 by the French, and named by them to commemorate the return (le retour, in French) of French exploring parties to the area.

Cape Retreat *see* **Point Retreat**

Point Retreat. 76°55'S, 162°33'E. Also called Cape Retreat. A point at the eastern extremity of the Kar Plateau. It juts out into Granite Harbor from the coast of Victoria Land, between Cape Archer and the Mackay Glacier Tongue. Named by members of Scott's 1910–13 expedition.

Retreat Hills. 72°59'S, 165°12'E. At the south side of the head of Astronaut Glacier, along the southern edge of the Evans Névé. Named by the Northern Party of the NZGSAE 1962–63 for the hasty retreat they had to make due to blizzards, which had prevented them from getting to these hills.

Retrospect Spur. 84°09'S, 173°12'E. 7 miles long. Descends NNW from the base of the Separation Range into the east side of Hood Glacier. Named by the NZ Alpine Club Antarctic Expedition of 1959–60 for their retrospective panoramic view of Hood Glacier which they had just traversed.

Return Point. 60°38'S, 46°01'W. A rocky slope forming the SW extremity of Coronation Island in the South Orkneys. Discovered by Palmer and Powell on Dec. 7, 1821. Powell landed on this point, and then returned directly to the *Dove,* hence the name.

Mount Reu. 71°09′S, 65°35′E. Partly snow-covered. 18 miles east of Mount Hicks in the Prince Charles Mountains. Named by the Australians for R.F. Reu, radio officer at Wilkes Station in 1962.

Reusch Glacier. 71°29′S, 169°29′E. Also called Reush Glacier, Doctor Rusch Glacier (both erroneously). Flows into Relay Bay just east of Islands Point, on the north coast of Victoria Land. Charted by Borchgrevink in 1898–1900, and named by him for Professor H. Reusch, president of the Norwegian Geographical Society.

Reush Glacier see **Reusch Glacier**

Reuther Nunataks. 79°10′S, 85°57′W. A ridgelike line of nunataks, 4 miles long. 3 miles west of Landmark Peak in the Founders Peaks of the Heritage Range. Named by the University of Minnesota Geological Party here in 1963–64, for Charles J. Reuther, helicopter technical representative with the 62nd Transportation Detachment that season.

Revelle Bay see **Revelle Inlet**

Revelle Inlet. 68°40′S, 63°26′W. Also called Revelle Bay. A broad, ice-filled inlet. Recedes west 15 miles or so between Cape Agassiz and Cape Keeler, on the east coast of Palmer Land. Charted by the USAS in 1940. Named by Finn Ronne in 1947–48 for Roger Revelle, oceanographer at the Scripps Institution, who helped Ronne during the technical preparations of the RARE.

Revsnes Island. 69°17′S, 39°37′E. Forked. Has two branches. Just off Hamnenabben Head in the eastern part of Lützow-Holm Bay. Photographed by the LCE 1936–37, and named Revsnes (fox's nose) by the Norwegians for its shape.

Mount Rex. 74°54′S, 75°57′W. 1,105 m. Isolated. On the interior ice surface of Ellsworth Land. 55 miles SSE of Fitz-Gerald Bluffs. This is what Ellsworth described as "the isolated nunatak" after his flight over on Nov. 23, 1935. Finn Ronne, during the RARE 1947–48,

resighted it and called it Mount Daniel Rex, for Lt. Cdr. Daniel F. Rex, USN, of the Office of Naval Research, who helped Ronne get his scientific equipment together for the expedition. The name of the mountain was later shortened to Mount Rex.

Cabo Rey see **King Point**

Cape Rey. 66°36′S, 66°27′W. Also called Punta Lincoyan. A dark rocky cape between the SW side of Darbel Bay and the NE side of Lallemand Fjord. 22 miles east of Cape Mascart in Adelaide Island, it juts out into the sea from the west coast of Graham Land. Discovered by Charcot in 1908–10, and named by him for Lt. Joseph J. Rey.

Rey, Joseph J. Lt. French naval officer who served as meteorologist on the *Français* during Charcot's 1903–5 expedition.

Isla Rey Jorge see **King George Island**

Rey Juan Carlos I Station. 62°40′S, 62°20′W. At South Bay, Livingston Island, in the South Shetlands. This was Spain's first Antarctic base, established in Jan. 1988 as a year-round station. Dr. A. Ballester led the first party.

Punta Reyes see **Jurva Point, Reyes Spit**

Reyes Spit. 62°29′S, 59°41′W. Also called Bajo Toro. A narrow shingle spit jutting out westward into Discovery Bay from the Guesalaga Peninsula on Greenwich Island in the South Shetlands. In 1947 the Chileans named a point at the base of the spit as Punta Reyes for Second Navigation Sergeant Camilo Reyes Ulloa, who was in charge of the gyrocompass and other navigation instruments on the *Iquique* during the 1946–47 Chilean Antarctic Expedition. This name appeared on a Chilean chart of 1951. The name Reyes has since been extended to cover the whole feature listed in this entry.

[1]Cape Reynolds. 75°25′S, 162°34′E. Marks the southern side of the terminus of the David Glacier, on the coast of Victoria Land. Discovered by Shackleton's 1907–9 expedition, and named by them for Jeremiah N. Reynolds.

²Cape Reynolds see **Mount Reynolds**

Mount Reynolds. 72°42'S, 61°16'W. Also called Cape Poindexter, Cape Reynolds. 1,130 m. Snow-capped. Has steep, rocky lower slopes. At the south side of Violante Inlet, on the east coast of Palmer Land. Discovered aerially by members of East Base on Dec. 30, 1940, during USAS. Named for Jeremiah N. Reynolds.

Reynolds, George. Ordinary seaman on the Wilkes Expedition 1838–42. Joined in the USA. Died at sea (not in the Antarctic) on Aug. 22, 1839.

Reynolds, Jeremiah N. Also called John Reynolds, but he has gone down in history as listed. b. Wilmington. He was the most active proponent for a US Government expedition to Antarctica in the 1820s, predominantly between 1827 and 1829 when the expedition for which he had so strongly campaigned, failed to go. He was historiographer and commercial investigator on the Palmer-Pendleton Expedition of 1829–31, and after that he stayed in Chile. In Oct. 1832 he joined the US frigate *Potomac* as private secretary to Commodore Downes. He later did much to promote the Wilkes Expedition 1838–42, but did not himself go on it.

Reynolds, William. Passed midshipman on the Wilkes Expedition 1838–42. On Jan. 16, 1840, he saw land from the *Peacock* and later that year he transferred to the *Flying Fish* at Honolulu. Still later, at Singapore, he transferred to the *Porpoise.*

Reynolds Bench. 70°35'S, 63°40'W. A nearly flat bench, or mesalike feature. 6 miles long. 2 miles wide. Has a smooth, snow-covered surface but has rock outcroppings along its steep sides. At the north side of the Kelley Massif, to which it appears to be joined, on the south side of the upper part of the Clifford Glacier

in Palmer Land. Named for Richard L. Reynolds, geologist with the US Geological Survey Lassiter Coast geologic and mapping party of 1970–71.

Reynolds Glacier. 77°38'S, 145°55'W. 5 miles long. Flows eastward from the Haines Mountains along the south side of Keyser Nunatak into the Hammond Glacier in Marie Byrd Land. Named for Donald K. Reynolds, ionosphere physicist at Byrd Station, 1967–68.

Reynolds Nunatak. 85°33'S, 149°40'W. At the south side of the terminus of the Leverett Glacier. 12 miles north of Mount Herr. Named for Clifford E. Reynolds, electrician at Byrd Station, 1957.

Reynolds Peak. 69°16'S, 157°01'E. 785 m. 6 miles NW of Eld Peak on the west side of the Matusevich Glacier in the Wilson Hills of Wilkes Land. It was discovered from the *Peacock* on Jan. 16, 1840, by Passed Midshipmen William Reynolds and Henry Eld. They also saw another conical peak near to it. Wilkes named them respectively for the two midshipmen. He then charted them where he thought they were, and due to a mirage, he put them at 200 miles out to sea off the Mawson Peninsula. This was one of the things which discredited Wilkes on his return and in subsequent decades of discovery. In 1959, Phillip Law selected one of the peaks to the west of the Matusevich Glacier as the one Wilkes had intended.

Reynolds Ridge. 75°40'S, 129°19'W. 1½ miles long. 5 miles NW of Mount Flint in the McCuddin Mountains of Marie Byrd Land. Named by Warren Reynolds of the US Department of State who assisted in work on the Antarctic Treaty in 1959.

Reynolds Strait. 74°15'S, 132°10'W. Between Forrester Island on the north and Shepard and Grant Islands along the edge of the Getz Ice Shelf on the south. On Feb. 4, 1962, USN personnel on the *Glacier* discovered Forrester Island, and thus established the existence of this strait. Named for Lt. Cdr. Ralph R. Reynolds (1938–1973), USN, officer-in-charge of the nuclear power unit at McMurdo Station in 1970.

Reynolds Trough. 66°50′S, 121°15′E. A subsurface feature beneath the Sabrina Coast of Wilkes Land. A term no longer used.

Mount Rhamnus. 68°11′S, 66°50′W. Also called Pyramid Mountain, Pyramid Peak. 865 m. 2 miles NE of Mount Nemesis on the northern side of Neny Fjord, Graham Land. It looks like a snow-covered pyramid when seen from the west. Surveyed in 1936 by the BGLE, and again in 1947 by the FIDS, who named it for the sanctuary of Nemesis in Greek mythology.

Rhea Corner. 71°53′S, 68°48′W. A triangular area of exposed rock on the north side of Saturn Glacier in the SE part of Alexander Island. It is a promontory at the west end of the massif that includes the Deimos, Phobos, and Pagoda Ridges. A cliff on the north face is 500 meters high. Named by the UK for one of the satellites of the planet Saturn.

Rhino Horn Rock   *see*   **Rhino Rock**

Rhino Rock. 69°34′S, 62°32′W. A prominent black rock with steep sides rising to 700 meters. 5 miles SW of Cape Rymill, opposite the southern end of Hearst Island, on the east coast of Palmer Land. Named Rhino Horn Rock for its shape by the USAS from East Base in 1940. The name was later shortened.

Rho Islands. 64°17′S, 63°W. Also called Islotes Boulier, Islotes Soler. Just north of Lambda Island in the Melchior Islands. Named before 1946 by the Argentines for the Greek letter.

Rhoads, Dr. Harman F. From Everett, Wisc. He was surgeon on Ellsworth's 1938–39 expedition.

Mount Rhodes. 66°49′S, 51°09′E. Between Mounts Hampson and Bond, in the northern part of the Tula Mountains in Enderby Land. Named by the Australians for G.J. Rhodes.

Rhodes, G.J. Crew member on the *Discovery* during the BANZARE 1929–31.

Rhodes Bluff. 79°50′S, 83°20′W. 2 miles NW of Mount Dolence. It forms the NW end of the Enterprise Hills in the Heritage Range. Named for Lt. (jg) Joseph J. Rhodes, USN, in charge of the maintenance program at McMurdo Station in 1966.

Rhodes Head. 74°42′S, 163°03′E. A prominent headland forming the extremity of McCarthy Ridge on the SE side of the Eisenhower Range. Overlooks the Nansen Ice Sheet on the coast of Victoria Land. Named for Capt. James C. Rhodes, US Marine Reserve, VX-6 Hercules aircraft commander for several seasons up to 1967.

Rhodes Icefall. 74°58′S, 136°25′W. Flows west out of the McDonald Heights, through a breach in the middle of the Peden Cliffs. It feeds the Garfield Glacier near the coast of Marie Byrd Land. Named for William L. Rhodes, USN, aviation bosun's mate and crash crew leader at Williams Field, 1968, 1969, and 1970.

Rhodes Peak. 83°20′S, 167°47′E. 780 m. At the north side of the mouth of Hoffman Glacier. Marks the seaward end of the ridge descending east from Mount Tripp, in the Holland Range. Named by the USA for Lt. Cdr. A.G. Rhodes, commander of the NZ ship *Pukaki* (q.v.), which was an ocean station vessel on duty between NZ and McMurdo Sound in 1964 and 1965.

Rhone Glacier. 77°42′S, 162°14′E. West of the Matterhorn Glacier. It flows south toward the junction of Lake Bonney and Taylor Glacier in Victoria Land. Charted and named by Scott's 1910–13 expedition.

Rhyolite Head. 62°10′S, 58°36′W. Between Ezcurra Inlet and Cardozo Cove on the west side of Admiralty Bay in King George Island, South Shetlands. Named by the UK for the rhyolite it is composed of.

Rhyolite Islands. 69°40'S, 68°35'W. They extend 4 miles in an east-west direction, just off the west coast of Palmer Land, opposite the north side of the mouth of Eureka Glacier, in George VI Sound. Surveyed in 1948 by the FIDS and named by them for the rhyolite these islands and rocks are composed of.

Rice Bastion. 64°27'S, 60°19'W. A large mountain mass surmounted by a small crown of exposed rock which appears slightly higher than the plateau behind it, projecting from the edge of Detroit Plateau in Graham Land. 8 miles SW of Mount Elliott. Surveyed by the FIDS in 1960–61. Named by the UK for Lee Rice, FIDS surveyor at Base D, 1957–58.

Rice Ridge. 73°27'S, 93°50'W. 1 mile long. Extends from the north side of Anderson Dome in the Jones Mountains. Named for Lt. Cdr. Robert A. Rice, USN, supply and fiscal officer of Mobile Construction Battalion One in 1962.

Mount Rich. 79°47'S, 158°48'E. Isolated. In the Brown ᴉ ills. 5 miles NW of Diamond Hill. Named by the VUWAE 1962–63 for Charles C. Rich, geologist and deputy leader of the expedition.

Rich, William. Botanist, one of the scientific corps on the Wilkes Expedition 1838–42. Joined the *Peacock* at Callao, and transferred to the *Vincennes* at San Francisco.

Richard Black Coast *see* **Black Coast**

Baie Richard D'Abnour *see* **D'Abnour Bay**

Richard E. Byrd Memorial. Bronze bust of Admiral Byrd on a polished black Norwegian-marble pedestal donated by the National Geographic Society and erected Nov. 1965 just south of the Chapel of the Snows, at McMurdo Station.

The *Richard Henry*. US sealer/whaler from Stonington, Conn., in the South Shetlands in 1843–45 under Capt. Peck. It was wrecked here in Feb. 1845.

Mount Richard Russell *see* **Mount Russell**

Richards, Capt. Commander of the British sealer *George* in the South Shetlands in 1820–21.

Richards, R.W. Richard W. "Dick" Richards. Australian scientist. One of the three survivors of Mackintosh's depot-laying Ross Sea Party of 6, during the British Imperial Transantarctic Expedition of 1914–17.

Richards Cove. 62°35'S, 61°09'W. 1 mile east of Essex Point on the north coast of Livingston Island in the South Shetlands. Window Island, nearby, was called Richards Island (probably for Capt. Richards) by Weddell in 1822, not knowing that Powell had already named it the year before. In order to preserve the Richards name in the area, this cove was so named.

Richards Inlet. 83°20'S, 168°30'E. Ice-filled. At the mouth of the Lennox-King Glacier, opening to the Ross Ice Shelf just SE of Lewis Ridge. Named by the New Zealanders in 1959–60 for R.W. Richards.

Richards Island *see* **Richards Cove, Window Island**

Richards Nunatak. 75°56'S, 159°45'E. Between McLea Nunatak and Pudding Butte in the Prince Albert Mountains of Victoria Land. Named by the Southern Party of the NZGSAE 1962–63 for David Richards, radio operator at Scott Base that season, who shared field party work and was responsible for the training of the base dog team in the absence of the base dog handler.

Cape Richardson *see* **Cape Bickerton**

Mount Richardson. 76°34'S, 144°39'W. Just west of Reece Pass. 3 miles south of Mount Colombo in the SE part of the Fosdick Mountains, in the Ford Ranges of Marie Byrd Land. Discovered aerially by members of West Base during the USAS 1939–41, and named for Harrison H. Richardson.

Richardson, Edgar A. Private on the Wilkes Expedition 1838–42. Joined in the USA. Served the cruise.

Richardson, Harrison H. Meteorological observer at West Base during the USAS 1939–41.

Richardson, John D. Cooper on the Wilkes Expedition 1838–42. Joined in the USA. Served the cruise.

Richardson Bluff. 70°47'S, 166°20'E. On the east side of Kirkby Glacier, opposite Frecker Ridge, in the Anare Mountains of Victoria Land. Named by the ANARE for Sgt. A. Richardson, RAAF, member of the Antarctic Flight which accompanied the ANARE on the *Thala Dan* to this coast in 1962.

Richardson Glacier. 70°28'S, 63°42'W. Flows into the Clifford Glacier just SE of Mikus Hill in Palmer Land. Named for Harriet Richardson, French zoologist and author of several reports on the crustacea collected by Charcot on his two expeditions.

Richardson Hill. 79°48'S, 156°40'E. Also called Richardson Nunatak. Ice-free. On the ice of Island Arena on the north side of the Darwin Mountains. Named by the VUWAE 1962–63 for Professor L.R. Richardson of the Victoria University of Wellington, NZ, an active supporter of the university's Antarctic expeditions.

Richardson Lakes. 66°45'S, 50°38'E. A small group of meltwater lakes at the foot of Mount Riiser-Larsen on the NW side, just east of Amundsen Bay. Named by the Australians for Sgt. A.K. Richardson, RAAF, a member of the 1958 Antarctic Flight at Mawson Station.

[1]Richardson Nunatak *see* **Richardson Hill**

[2]Richardson Nunatak. 66°22'S, 64°56'W. In the southern part of the Hugi Glacier in Graham Land. Named by the UK in 1959 for E.C. Richardson (1871–1954), the "father of British skiing."

Riches. Crew member on the *Nimrod* in 1908–9.

Richmond, William. Bosun's mate on the Wilkes Expedition 1838–42. Joined in the USA. Served the cruise.

Richmond Peak. 75°48'S, 115°49'W. 3,595 m. The central and culminating peak of the Toney Mountain massif in Marie Byrd Land. Named for Addison E. Richmond, Jr., of the US Department of State, chairman of the Interagency Committee on Antarctica, 1971–72.

Richter Glacier. 77°10'S, 155°25'W. 10 miles west of the Scott Nunataks on the north side of the Edward VII Peninsula. It shares a common saddle with the Butler Glacier, and flows NW to the sea where it forms a small glacier tongue. Shirase's Japanese party traversed up this glacier in Jan. 1912. Named for Gregory S. Richter, meteorologist and scientific leader at Byrd Station in 1968.

Richter Peaks. 71°20'S, 70°21'W. On Alexander Island.

Richthofen Pass. 66°01'S, 62°42'W. Also called Richthofen Sund. 1 mile wide. Between Mount Fritsche and the rock wall north of McCarroll Peak, at the southern end of the Oscar II Coast, on the east coast of Graham Land. Discovered in 1902 by Nordenskjöld's expedition, and named Richthofen Valley by the Swedish explorer for Baron Ferdinand von Richthofen, German geographer and geologist. In 1955 the FIDS redefined it as a pass.

Richthofen Sund *see* **Richthofen Pass**

Richthofen Valley *see* **Richthofen Pass**

Ricker Canyon. 84°47'S, 115°18'W. Steep-sided. Ice-filled. Indents the northern escarpment of the Buckeye Table between Darling Ridge and Schulthess Buttress, in the Ohio Range of the Horlick Mountains. Named for John F. Ricker, geologist with the Ohio State University expedition to the Horlick Mountains in 1961–62.

Ricker Dome. 82°04'S, 162°43'E. 1,720 m. Snow-free. 3 miles east of Smith Bluff in the Nash Range. Named for Karl E. Ricker, biologist at McMurdo Station, 1961.

Ricker Hills. 75°41'S, 159°10'E. Ice-free. 9 miles in extent. Just west of Hollingsworth Glacier in the Prince Albert Mountains of Victoria Land. Named by the Southern Party of the NZGSAE 1962–63, for J.F. Ricker, a geologist with the party.

Ricker Peak see **Ricker Hills**

Rickinson, Louis L. d. 1945. Chief engineer on the *Endurance* during the British Imperial Transantarctic Expedition of 1914–17. He had a non-fatal heart attack on April 17, 1916, as the party moved onto Cape Wild on Elephant Island.

Rickmers Glacier. 66°15'S, 64°55'W. Flows into Hugi Glacier just south of Caulfeild Glacier on the west coast of Graham Land. Named by the UK in 1959 for W. Rickmer Rickmers, German ski pioneer.

Ricky Glacier see **Blackwelder Glacier**

Riddell Nunataks. 69°54'S, 64°20'E. 5 miles NW of the Anare Nunataks in Mac. Robertson Land. Discovered by an ANARE party led by Robert Dovers in 1954. Named by the Australians for Alfred Riddell, carpenter at Mawson Station, 1955.

Riddle Islands. 65°39'S, 64°33'W. Off the SW end of Chavez Island, off the west coast of Graham Land. Charted by the BGLE 1934–37. Named by the FIDS in Aug. 1957 because these islands were difficult to find among the icebergs.

Mount Riddolls. 72°48'S, 167°46'E. 3,295 m. Directly at the head of Rudolph Glacier in the Victory Mountains of Victoria Land. Named by the Mariner Glacier geology party of the NZGSAE 1966–67 for B.W. Riddolls, assistant geologist with the party.

The Ridge see **Jabet Peak**

Ridge Island. 67°42'S, 67°06'W. Also called Isla Cabellete. Ridge-shaped. 6 miles long. 1½ miles wide. 3 miles east of Pourquoi Pas Island in the center of Bourgeois Fjord, off the west coast of Graham Land. Discovered and named by the BGLE 1934–37.

Ridge Peak. 63°30'S, 57°03'W. 510 m. Pyramidal. A prominent ridge extends eastward from it. 2½ miles SW of Trepassey Bay between Cairn Hill and Lizard Hill on the Tabarin Peninsula. First explored by a party of Nordenskjöld's expedition of 1901–4. Charted and named descriptively by the FIDS in 1946.

Ridgeway Glacier. 73°24'S, 167°14'E. Also spelled (erroneously) as Ridgway Glacier. In the eastern part of the Mountaineer Range. Flows SE between Spatulate Ridge and Gauntlet Ridge into Lady Newnes Bay on the coast of Victoria Land. Named by NZ in 1966 for Norman Ridgeway, senior scientist at Hallett Station in 1963–64.

Ridgway Glacier see **Ridgeway Glacier**

Camp Ridley. On Ridley Beach, Cape Adare. This was Borchgrevink's camp for him and his 9 men during the wintering-over of 1899. Borchgrevink named it for his English mother, formerly Miss Ridley.

Ridley Beach. 71°18'S, 170°13'E. A cuspate beach feature forming a triangle about 1 mile long on each side. 1 mile south of Cape Adare, on the west side of the Adare Peninsula in northern Victoria Land. In 1898–1900 Borchgrevink camped here at Camp Ridley (he named the camp for his mother—it was her maiden name). In 1911 Campbell's Northern Party disembarked here from the *Terra Nova,* and they extended the name to the whole beach. There is an Adélie penguin rookery here.

Ridley Head see **Ridley Island**

Ridley Island. 61°51'S, 58°03'W. Also called Ridley Head. An island 2 miles north of False Round Point on King George Island in the South Shetlands. Discovered by sealers before 1822.

Mount Rifenburgh. 82°57'S, 166°20'E. 2,690 m. 2 miles east of the head of

Davidson Glacier in the Holland Range. Named for Capt. E. Rifenburgh, commander of the *Arneb*, 1962–63.

The *Riff Raft*. A 12-foot-square plywood raft attached to the land by a steel cable. It had a steel frame and was kept afloat by eight 55-gallon oil drums welded together. It had a 42-inch hole in the middle of the deck through which marine specimens could be brought up from the water in McMurdo Sound. Three research assistants in wet suits were the crew. Named by its pioneer, Dr. Mary Alice McWhinnie, in 1974.

The *Rig Mate*. Norwegian ship in the area of the Antarctic Peninsula, 1975–76.

Mount Rigby. 85°33′S, 154°35′W. 950 m. 2 miles NW of Mount Hastings. Just west of the mouth of the Robert Scott Glacier, in the Karo Hills. Discovered by Byrd's 1928–30 expedition. Named for John F. Rigby, geologist at McMurdo Station, 1965–66.

Mount Rigel. 70°24′S, 66°52′W. On the west part of the Antarctic Peninsula.

Rigel Skerries. 66°55′S, 57°18′E. A chain of islands and rocks in the NW part of the Øygarden Group, in the southern part of the entrance to Edward VIII Bay. Photographed by the LCE 1936–37, and named Utskjera (the outer skerries) by the Norwegians. Visited by an ANARE party in 1954. Renamed by the Australians for the star, Rigel, which was used for an astrofix near here.

Rightangle Peak. 73°31′S, 94°25′W. Between Snowplume Peak and Camelback Ridge in the Jones Mountains. Named by the University of Minnesota–Jones Mountains Party of 1960–61 because when seen from Camp Minnesota (q.v.) this peak presented a right-angle profile facing west.

Rigsby Islands. 66°40′S, 67°37′W. Ice-capped. Off the NE coast of Adelaide Island. 2 miles SE of the Sillard Islands. Named by the UK for George P. Rigsby, US geologist specializing in the investigation of ice crystal structure and the plasticity of ice.

Mount Riiser-Larsen. 66°47′S, 50°40′E. 870 m. At the NW end of the Tula Mountains, on the east side of Amundsen Bay. Named by Mawson during the BANZARE 1929–31, for Hjalmar Riiser-Larsen.

Riiser-Larsen, Hjalmar. Norwegian Naval captain who led the 1929–31 whaling and exploring expedition in the *Norvegia*. He carried two airplanes, making his first flight from the ship on Dec. 7, 1929. On Dec. 22, 1929, he flew to the coast of Enderby Land, and on Jan. 15, 1930, he discovered Queen Maud Land. On Feb. 18, 1930, he discovered the Princess Martha Coast, and in early 1931 the Princess Ragnhild Coast. Major Gunnar Isachsen commanded the *Thorshavn* and was co-leader during the second half of the expedition, i.e., 1930–31. Riiser-Larsen was in the Antarctic again in 1932–33, whaling and exploring with Kjelbotn and Devold, with the *Thorshavn, Thorshammer,* and *Torlyn.*

Riiser-Larsen Ice Shelf. 72°40′S, 16°W. Also called (in Norwegian) Riiser-Larsenisen. 250 miles long, on the western coast of Queen Maud Land. Extends from Cape Norvegia in the north to Lyddan Island and Stancomb Wills Glacier in the south. Parts of the ice shelf were discovered by Bruce in 1904, Shackleton in 1915, and Riiser-Larsen in 1930. Named by the Norwegians for Hjalmar Riiser-Larsen.

Riiser-Larsen Peninsula. 68°55′S, 34°E. Also called Cook Peninsula. Forms the divide between the Prince Harald Coast and the Princess Ragnhild Coast. It forms the western portal to Lützow-Holm Bay and juts out into the Haakon VII Sea. Discovered on a flight from the *Norvegia* by Hjalmar Riiser-Larsen (for whom it is named), on Feb. 21, 1931.

Riiser-Larsenisen *see* **Riiser-Larsen Ice Shelf**

Gory Rikhtgofena *see* **Gruber Mountains**

Mount Riley. 86°11′S, 147°37′W. 2,100 m. On the NE side of Long Valley, just west of the California Plateau, in the Queen Maud Mountains. Named for Lt. (jg) Stephen G. Riley, VX-6 photographic officer 1965–66 and 1966–67.

Riley, John. Private on the Wilkes Expedition 1838–42. Joined in the USA. Served the cruise.

Riley, Quintin T.P.M. Assistant meteorologist on the BGLE 1934–37. Had been with Rymill in Greenland a few years before. Was technical adviser on the 1948 movie *Scott of the Antarctic* (q.v.).

Riley Glacier. 70°03′S, 68°20′W. Heavily crevassed. 14 miles long. 17 miles wide. Flows westward from the west side of Palmer Land into the George VI Sound between the Traverse Mountains and Mount Dixey. Discovered and surveyed in 1936 by the BGLE. Resurveyed in 1949 by the FIDS, and named by them for Quintin Riley.

Rime Crests. 60°38′S, 45°25′W. Five crestlike summits surmounting the eastern side of Sunshine Glacier, on Coronation Island in the South Orkneys. Surveyed by the FIDS in 1948–49, and the highest peak was named Rime Peak by them for the heavy cover of rime, or hoarfrost. Later the name was extended to all of the summits.

Rime Peak *see* **Rime Crests**

Rimebrekka Slope. 72°08′S, 13°14′E. A crevassed ice slope 4 miles south of Rimekalvane Nunataks in the Weyprecht Mountains of Queen Maud Land. Name means "the frost slope" in Norwegian.

Rimekalvane Nunataks. 72°03′S, 13°38′E. 4 miles east of the Dekefjellrantane Hills in the Weyprecht Mountains of Queen Maud Land. Name means "the frost calves" in Norwegian.

Rindebotnen Cirque. 72°33′S, 3°20′W. Indents the NE wall of Borg Mountain in the Borg Massif of Queen Maud Land. Name means "the mountain cirque" in Norwegian.

Rindehallet Slope. 72°25′S, 1°13′E. An ice slope between Isingen Mountain

and Egil Peak in the Sverdrup Mountains of Queen Maud Land. Name means "the mountain slope" in Norwegian.

Rinehart Peak. 70°38′S, 160°01′E. 1,710 m. On a ridge on the east-central slopes of the Pomerantz Tableland, in the Usarp Mountains. At the south side of the head of Helfferich Glacier. Named for Floyd J. Rinehart, geophysicist at McMurdo Station in 1967–68.

Ring Rock. 67°39′S, 62°43′E. 2 miles SE of Nøst Island at the head of Holme Bay. Photographed by the LCE 1936–37, and named Ringøya (ring island) by the Norwegians. Visited by an ANARE sledging party in 1956, and they redefined it.

Ringed Nunatak. 85°13′S, 173°13′W. In the icefall at the head of Gatlin Glacier, in the Cumulus Hills. Named by the Texas Tech Shackleton Glacier Expedition of 1964–65 for the ring of moraine completely surrounding the nunatak.

Ringed penguin *see* **Chinstrap penguin**

Ringgold, Cadwalader. A US naval lieutenant, commander of the *Porpoise* during the Wilkes Expedition of 1838–42.

Ringgold Knoll. 69°20′S, 157°39′E. A mountain 9 miles south of Archer Point on the east side of Matusevich Glacier. Discovered by Cadwalader Ringgold on Jan. 16, 1840, from the *Porpoise,* during the Wilkes Expedition of 1838–42. Wilkes called it Ringgold's Knoll, but his charts were inaccurate. In 1959, Phillip Law of the ANARE selected this mountain as the one discovered by Ringgold 119 years before, as it seems to be in the correct relationship with Reynolds Peak and Eld Peak (qq.v.).

Ringgold's Knoll *see* **Ringgold Knoll**

Ringøya *see* **Ring Rock**

Rink Point. 63°53′S, 58°11′W. On the NW coast of James Ross Island, 2 miles east of Carlson Island. When a FIDS party visited it in Aug. 1952 it was surrounded by a large area of slippery, snow-free sea ice resembling a skating rink.

Mount Rio Branco. 65°25'S, 64°W. Also called Mount Branco, Sommet Rio Branco. 975 m. 2½ miles east of Cape Pérez on the west coast of Graham Land. Discovered by Charcot in 1908–10, and named by him for Baron Rio Branco, minister of Foreign Affairs of Brazil.

Sommet Rio Branco *see* **Mount Rio Branco**

Rip Point. 62°15'S, 58°59'W. Also called Cabo Andrada. On Nelson Island in the South Shetlands, forming the southern side of the entrance to Fildes Strait. Probably named by personnel on the *Discovery II* in 1935.

Rippon Glacier. 66°40'S, 56°29'E. Just east of Seaton Glacier, it flows southward into the Edward VIII Ice Shelf. Named by the Australians for Sgt. R. Rippon, RAAF, airframe fitter at Mawson Station in 1959.

Islotes Riquelme *see* **Symington Islands**

The *Riquita*. A yacht in the Antarctic, 1985–86.

Risemedet Mountain. 72°03'S, 3°10'E. 2,705 m. Marks the eastern end of the Gjelsvik Mountains in Queen Maud Land. Name means "the giant landmark" in Norwegian.

Risen Peak. 71°58'S, 3°18'E. 2 miles north of Medhovden Bluff in the Gjelsvik Mountains of Queen Maud Land. Name means "the giant" in Norwegian.

Risk Rock. 66°09'S, 65°48'W. Isolated. Between Cape Evensen and Pesky Rocks, off the west coast of Graham Land. Named by the UK in 1959 because the rock lies in the way of vessels that pass southward through the channel between Marie Island and the mainland.

Ristelen Spur. 71°59'S, 5°37'E. Also called Krylov Mountain (actually Gora Krylova, by the USSR). 5 miles SE of the summit of Breplogen Mountain. Between the flow of the Vestreskorve and Austreskorve Glaciers in the Mühlig-

Hofmann Mountains of Queen Maud Land. Name means "the plowshare" in Norwegian.

Ristkalvane Nunataks. 71°41'S, 10°36'E. Form the north end of the Shcherbakov Range, in the Orvin Mountains of Queen Maud Land. Discovered aerially by members of the Ritscher expedition of 1938–39. Name means "the ridge calves" in Norwegian.

Ritala Spur. 83°07'S, 48°57'W. In the Pensacola Mountains.

Ritchie Point. 70°25'S, 68°20'E. At the extremity of the large, flat rock feature extending northeastward from the Amery Peaks in the Prince Charles Mountains. Named by the Australians for F.A. Ritchie, cook at Mawson Station, 1965.

Ritscher, Alfred. 1879–1963. German Naval captain who led the German New Schwabenland Expedition of 1938–39 in a mad Nazi claim on Antarctica. He had been first in the merchant marine. In 1912–13 he had been in the Arctic, after having transferred to the Imperial Navy.

Ritscher-Land *see* **Ritscher Upland**

Ritscher Peak. 71°24'S, 13°20'E. 2,790 m. 7 miles WSW of Mount Mentzel in the Gruber Mountains of Queen Maud Land. Discovered by Ritscher's 1938–39 expedition, and named for Alfred Ritscher.

Ritscher Upland. 73°S, 9°W. A large ice-covered upland in the western part of Queen Maud Land. It is bounded by the Kraul Mountains and the Heimefront Range to the west and SW, and by the Borg Massif and the Kirwan Escarpment to the east. Discovered by members of Ritscher's 1938–39 expedition, and named by them for their leader, Alfred Ritscher, as Ritscher-Land. The Norwegians call it Ritscherflya.

Ritscherflya *see* **Ritscher Upland**

Rivard Glacier. 78°04'S, 163°55'E. Also called David Lee Glacier. 1 mile long. At the head of the Marshall Valley in Victoria Land. Discovered and mapped by Troy L. Péwé, glacial geologist here in 1957–58, and named by him for his assistant on the trip, Norman Rivard.

Rivas Peaks. 83°35′S, 54°25′W. A line of rock peaks that juts out westward for 2 miles from the southern part of the Torbert Escarpment in the Neptune Range of the Pensacola Mountains. Named for Merced G. Rivas, radioman at Ellsworth Station, 1958.

Isla Rivera *see* **Apéndice Island**

Rivera Peaks. 73°48′S, 62°50′W. A wedge-shaped range of peaks. 14 miles in extent. Between Swann Glacier and the Watson Peaks, in Palmer Land. Named for James P. Rivera, electronics technician at Amundsen-Scott South Pole Station, 1967.

Rivers. Ordinary rivers do exist in Antarctica, but they are really short-lived streams of glacial meltwater, and are seen occasionally only in the warmer months (*see* **Onyx River**). Ice rivers are called glaciers, or ice streams (qq.v.).

Rivers, John. Ordinary seaman on the Wilkes Expedition 1838–42. Joined at Rio. Lost at sea in the *Sea Gull* on April 29, 1839.

Mount Rivett. 67°50′S, 66°14′E. Bare rock. The most northerly feature in the Gustav Bull Mountains of Mac. Robertson Land. Named by Mawson on Feb. 13, 1931, when the BANZARE landed at nearby Scullin Monolith. Sir David Rivett was deputy chairman and chief executive officer of the Australian Council for Scientific and Industrial Research from 1927 to 1945.

Rivolier, Jean. The French Polar Expedition doctor at Pointe Géologie in 1952. He wrote *Emperor Penguins* in 1956 (*see* the Bibliography).

Roadend Nunatak. 79°48′S, 158°02′E. 4 miles WNW of Bastion Hill, on the north side of the Darwin Glacier, where that glacier and the Touchdown Glacier meet in the Brown Hills of the Queen Alexandra Range. Named by the New Zealanders in 1962–63 for its use as a landmark for sledging parties.

Roads. Most of the stations in Antarctica have streets around them, or what pass for streets. Sometimes there are roads leading from the base to an airfield. The most notable is the "Mac-Willy Expressway," leading from McMurdo Station to Williams Field. It is 4 miles long, 25 feet wide, and built on a 4-foot snowpack. It was completed in Nov. 1960. Around McMurdo there are several roads which take rubber-tired vehicles.

Roald Amundsen Sea *see* **Amundsen Sea**

Roald Glacier. 60°39′S, 45°13′W. Flows from the vicinity of Mount Noble and Mount Sladen eastward into Gibbon Bay, on the east coast of Coronation Island in the South Orkneys. Charted and named by Petter Sørlle in 1912–13. Surveyed in 1948–49 by the FIDS.

Roaring Cliffs. 86°23′S, 159°24′W. Just north of Kutschin Peak on the west side of the Nilsen Plateau, in the Queen Maud Mountains. Named by William Long, a US geologist here in 1963–64. Named for the sound of the roaring wind.

Roaring Ridge. 86°14′S, 146°45′W. Descends from the Watson Escarpment 3½ miles NE of Mount Blackburn. Named by the New Zealanders here in 1969–70 for the roaring of the wind here.

Roaring Valley. 78°16′S, 163°03′ı . Moraine-filled. On the north side of Mount Dromedary. It was formerly occupied by the coalescing glaciers which descend NE and north from Mount Kempe and Mount Dromedary. Named by the New Zealanders here in 1960–61 for the incredibly strong winds which hit them at the mouth of this valley that season.

Robb, William. 1st class boy on the Wilkes ıxpedition 1838–42. Joined at Rio. Served the cruise.

Robb Glacier. 82°38′S, 165°ı . 40 miles long. Flows from Clarkson ı eak north along the east side of Softbed Ridges to the Ross Ice Shelf at Cape Goldie. Named by the NZGSAE 1959–60 for Murray Robb, leader of the expedition, who traversed this glacier to get to Lowery Glacier.

Robben Nunataks see **Seal Nunataks**

Robbenspitze see **Seal Point**

Robbery Beaches. 62°37′S, 61°05′W. Extend along the north side of Byers Peninsula, on Livingston Island, in the South Shetlands. Named by Weddell in 1822 for the "occasional" robbery of sealskins which took place in the rush of 1820–22 in the area. Specifically Weddell may have had in mind a robbery committed by the British of skins collected by the US vessel, the *Charity*. The captain of the *Charity*, Charles H. Barnard, became a friend of Weddell's and told him of his loss.

Robbin, William. Quartermaster on the Wilkes Expedition 1838–42. Joined in the USA, but returned on the *Relief* in 1839.

Robbins, James. Petty officer, USN. Radio operator on Operation Highjump 1946–47. He survived the Martin Mariner crash of Dec. 30, 1946, on Thurston Island.

Robbins Island. 64°47′S, 64°27′W. One of the islands in the SW part of the Joubin Islands, off the SW coast of Anvers Island. Named for Stephen H. Robbins, Jr., able seaman on the *Hero* during that vessel's first trip to Antarctica in 1968.

Robbins Nunatak. 83°12′S, 57°05′W. 8 miles NE of Mount Gorecki in the Schmidt Hills, Neptune Range, Pensacola Mountains. Named for Edward J. Robbins, aerographer at Ellsworth Station, 1958.

The *Robert*. British sealing brig from Liverpool, in the South Shetlands during the 1821–22 season, commanded by Capt. Robert Fildes. For most of the season it was moored in Clothier Harbor.

Cape Robert. 66°23′S, 137°39′E. Ice-covered point at the west side of Marret Glacier. Discovered by Dumont d'Urville in 1840 and named by him for a member of his family. Charted by the AAE 1911–14.

The *Robert D. Conrad*. Research vessel operated by Lamont-Doherty Geological Observatory of Columbia University. It made detailed geophysical and geological measurements in and south of the Drake Passage in support of the proposed *Glomar Challenger* deep-drilling project. It spent the summer of 1971–72 there, getting as far south as 65°23′S, 71°22′W. Dr. Stephen Eittreim was chief scientist. It did not call at Palmer Station. It was back in early 1974, between Jan. 5 and April 11 of that year, going in and out of Antarctic waters, and getting as far south as 68°20′S.

Robert English Coast see **English Coast**

Robert Glacier. 67°10′S, 56°18′E. The eastern of two glaciers flowing into the southern part of Edward VIII Bay. Discovered by Robert Dovers and the French observer G. Schwartz during an ANARE sledge journey over the bay. Named by the Australians for Dovers.

Robert Island. 62°24′S, 59°30′W. Also called Roberts Island, Mitchell's Island, Polotsk Island. 11 miles long. 8 miles wide. Between Nelson and Greenwich Islands in the South Shetlands. Named by sealers before 1821.

Robert Island penguins. Found on Robert Island in the South Shetlands.

Robert Palmer Bay see **Palmer Inlet**

Robert Point. 62°28′S, 59°23′W. Also called Cape Roberts, Roberts Point. Marks the SE tip of Robert Island in the South Shetlands. Named for the island.

Mount Robert Scott. 83°49′S, 172°48′E. Small, flat, and snow-covered. Over 1,000 m. Just south of Ebony Ridge in the Commonwealth Range. Discovered by Shackleton's 1907–9 expedition, and named by him for Robert F. Scott.

Robert Scott Glacier. 85°45′S, 153°W. Also called Scott Glacier, Thorne Glacier. 120 miles long. Flows from the Polar Plateau in the vicinity of D'Angelo Bluff and Mount Howe, then between the Nilsen Plateau and the mountains of the Watson Escarpment, and hits the Ross Ice Shelf just west of the Tapley Mountains, in the southernmost portion of ocean in the world. Discovered by Gould's geological party in Dec. 1929, during Byrd's 1928–30 expedition. Named by the USA for Robert F. Scott.

¹Cape Roberts. 77°02′S, 163°12′E. At the south side of the entrance to Granite Harbor, on the coast of Victoria Land. It forms the NE tip of the Wilson Piedmont Glacier. Discovered by Edgeworth David's South Magnetic Pole party in 1908–9, and named by him for William C. Roberts.

²Cape Roberts *see* **Robert Point**

Mount Roberts. 64°S, 58°49′W. Dark. Mostly ice-free. Has a flat, sloping top. 955 m. Isolated from the Detroit Plateau to the west. 3 miles south of Aitkenhead Glacier on the south side of Trinity Peninsula. Charted by the FIDS in 1945 and named for D.W. Roberts, manager of the Falkland Islands Co. in 1945, who helped the FIDS that year.

Roberts, Brian B. Ornithologist on the BGLE 1934–37. Left halfway through the expedition, to be replaced by Bertram. He was later secretary of the UK Antarctic Place-names Committee.

Roberts, Charles L., Jr. Meteorologist and scientific leader at Hallett Station in 1959.

Roberts, J. Capt. British commander of the *King George* in the South Shetlands in 1820–21 and 1821–22.

Roberts, Owen. Private on the Wilkes Expedition 1838–42. Joined in the USA. Served the cruise.

Roberts, William. 1st class boy on the Wilkes Expedition 1838–42. Joined in the USA. Served the cruise.

Roberts, William C. b. 1872. Cook on Shackleton's 1907–9 expedition. Al-though strictly speaking he was also assistant zoologist, he cooked throughout the day, and that was his sole job (all the others shared duties).

Roberts Butte. 72°39′S, 160°08′E. 2,830 m. Flat-topped. Extremely prominent, and useful as a landmark from great distances. 2 miles NW of Miller Butte in the Outback Nunataks. Named by the US Victoria Land Traverse Party of 1959–60. Louis J. Roberts, surveyor on the party, named it Flattop Mountain, but there was already a mountain or two with that name, so the name was changed to honor Roberts, who was the first to survey it.

Roberts Cirque. 75°45′S, 115°49′W. It is marked by a sheer rock cliff. Just west of Zurn Peak along the central-north wall of Toney Mountain in Marie Byrd Land. Named for John H. Roberts III, USN, chief commissaryman at Amundsen-Scott South Pole Station, 1974.

Roberts Cliff. 72°24′S, 170°05′E. The third prominent rock bluff south of Seabee Hook on the eastern shore of Edisto Inlet on the coast of Victoria Land. Named by the New Zealanders in 1959–60 for Charles L. Roberts, Jr.

Roberts Ice Piedmont. 69°S, 70°20′W. 20 miles long in a north-south direction, and 15 miles wide. To the north and NW of Mount Calais. It occupies the NE corner of Alexander Island. Discovered and charted by Charcot in 1908–10. Photographed aerially on Aug. 15, 1936, by the BGLE and named by the UK in 1955 for Brian B. Roberts.

Roberts Inlet. 79°15′S, 44°W. Ice-filled. The central of three inlets indenting the eastern side of Berkner Island. Discovered by IGY personnel from Ellsworth Station under Finn Ronne in 1957–58. Named by Ronne for Capt. Elliott B. Roberts, formerly chief of the geophysical branch of the US Coast and Geodetic Survey.

Roberts Island *see* **Robert Island**

Roberts Knoll. 71°27′S, 3°15′W. Also called (by the Norwegians) Robertskollen. Snow-covered. At the east side i f the mouth of Schytt Glacier in Queen Maud Land. Named by the Norwegians for Brian B. Roberts.

Roberts Massif. 85°32'S, 177°05'W. Snow-free. At the head of Shackleton Glacier. Over 2,700 m. 60 square miles in area. Visited by the NZGSAE's Southern Party in 1961–62, and named by them for A.R. Roberts, leader at Scott Base in 1961–62.

Roberts Point *see* **Robert Point**

Roberts Ridge. 86°23'S, 131°30'W. 5 miles SW of Cleveland Mesa, at the SE end of Michigan Plateau. Named for Peter Roberts of the Division of International Scientific and Technical Affairs within the US Department of State.

Robertskollen *see* **Roberts Knoll**

Cape Robertson. 60°44'S, 44°48'W. Marks the west side of the entrance to Jessie Bay, in the NW part of Laurie Island in the South Orkneys. 1 mile east of Route Point at the northern end of the Mackenzie Peninsula. In 1904 Bruce named the NW end of Mackenzie Peninsula as Cape Robertson, for Thomas Robertson, not knowing that Powell and Palmer had already named it in Dec. 1821 as Route Point. Later geographers kept the 1821 naming and switched Bruce's naming to the NE extremity of the peninsula.

Mount Robertson. 74°41'S, 64°14'W. 1,565 m. 20 miles NW of Mount Austin and the head of Gardner Inlet, on the east coast of Palmer Land. Discovered by the RARE 1947–48, and named by Ronne as Mount James Robertson for James B. Robertson. The name was later shortened.

Robertson, James B. Aviation mechanic on the RARE 1947–48.

Robertson, Dr. John. Surgeon on the *Terror* during Ross' expedition of 1839–43. He was responsible for zoological and geological research.

Robertson, Thomas. An experienced Arctic navigator from Scotland. He was captain of the *Active* during the Dundee Whaling Expedition of 1892–93, and captain of the *Scotia* during Bruce's expedition of 1902–4.

Robertson, W.A. Crewman on the *Bear of Oakland*, 1933–35.

Robertson Bay. 71°25'S, 170°E. Triangular. Indents the north coast of Victoria Land between Cape Barrow and Cape Adare. Discovered in 1841 by Ross, who named it for Dr. John Robertson.

Robertson Channel. 66°19'S, 110°29' E. The Russians call it Proliv Krivoy. A marine channel separating Mitchell Peninsula from Pidgeon Island and Warrington Island in the Windmill Islands. Named for Richard A. Robertson, glaciologist at Wilkes Station, 1958.

Robertson Glacier. 71°03'S, 165°23'E. Flows south from the Anare Mountains into Ebbe Glacier east of Springtail Bluff. Named for John W. Robertson, VX-6 photographer's mate at McMurdo Station, 1967–68 and 1968–69.

Robertson Island. 65°10'S, 59°37'W. Ice-covered. 13 miles long in a NW-SE direction. 6 miles wide. At the eastern end of the Seal Nunataks off the east coast of the Antarctic Peninsula, in the Larsen Ice Shelf. Discovered by Carl A. Larsen on Dec. 9, 1893, and named by him for William Robertson, co-owner of Woltereck and Robertson, the Hamburg company which sent Larsen to the Antarctic.

Robertson Islands. 60°46'S, 45°09'W. A group of small islands extending 4 miles southward off the SE extremity of Coronation Island in the South Orkneys. The largest is Matthews Island. Others include Coffer Island, Steepholm, Atriceps Island and Skilling Island. Discovered and charted by Powell and Palmer in Dec. 1821. Named by Weddell in 1823, as Robertson's Islands.

Robertson Landing. 66°23'S, 110°26' E. A boat-landing on the north side of Ardery Island, near the west end of the island, in the Windmill Islands. A landing was first made here by the launch *MacPherson Robertson,* which was carrying Phillip Law and his ANARE party, on Jan. 9, 1961. The landing is named for N.N. Robertson of Melbourne, the donor of the launch.

Robertson Nunatak. 71°54′S, 69°37′E. 20 miles NE of Clemence Massif on the east side of the Lambert Glacier. Named by the Australians for M.J. Robertson, geophysicist at Mawson Station in 1970. He took part in the ANARE Prince Charles Mountains survey of 1971 which mapped this nunatak.

Robertson Ridge. 77°24′S, 162°12′E. Circumscribes the NW part of Clark Glacier in Victoria Land. Named for James D. Robertson, geophysicist at Byrd Station, 1971. He also took part in the geophysical survey of the Ross Ice Shelf in 1973–74 and 1974–75.

Robertson's Islands *see* **Robertson Islands**

Robillard Glacier. 68°18′S, 65°35′W. Flows ENE into the northern side of the head of Solberg Inlet, on the east coast of Graham Land. Discovered by the USAS from East Base in 1939–41. Charted by the FIDS in 1948. Named by Finn Ronne for Capt. George Robillard, USN, of the legal section of the Bureau of Ships, who helped procure the RARE ship, the *Port of Beaumont, Texas.*

Robilliard Glacier. 70°13′S, 159°56′E. A valley glacier. 17 miles long. Flows northeastward through the Usarp Mountains. It rises southward at Mount Simmonds and comes out of the mountains at Mount Shields, where it joins Kooperatsiya Ice Piedmont. Named for Gordon Robilliard, biologist at McMurdo Station, 1967–68 and 1968–69.

Robin, Gordon de Q. Gordon de Quetteville Robin. British physicist and writer (*see* the Bibliography). He was the first leader of Signy Island Station (or Base H, as it was known then) in 1947. He was third-in-command during NBSAE 1949–52.

Robin Heights. 72°27′S, 0°38′E. A cluster of high rock summits between Hei Glacier and Kvitsvodene Valley in the Sverdrup Mountains of Queen Maud Land. Named Robinheia by the Norwegians for Gordon de Q. Robin.

Robin Peak. 60°41′S, 45°38′W. 270 m. The most northerly peak on Signy Island in the South Orkneys. Named by the UK in 1954 for Gordon de Q. Robin (q.v.), who made the first detailed survey of Signy Island.

Robinheia *see* **Robin Heights**

The *Robinson.* Argentine vessel on the 1947–48 expedition sent to Antarctica by that country.

Cape Robinson. 66°52′S, 63°43′W. Also called Cape Duemler. Marks the eastern end of Cole Peninsula, between Cabinet Inlet and Mill Inlet, on the east coast of Graham Land. On his flight of Dec. 20, 1928, Wilkins spotted an island in about 67°20′S, 61°40′W, which he named Robinson Island, for W.S. Robinson of London and Australia. It later proved impossible to find this island, and in order to preserve the naming, this cape, which was charted by the FIDS in 1947, was thus named.

Mount Robinson. 71°50′S, 169°49′E. 2,430 m. At the head of DeAngelo Glacier in the Admiralty Mountains of Victoria Land. Discovered on Jan. 15, 1841, by Ross, who named it for the Rev. Dr. Robinson of Armagh, a member of the committee of the British Association which advocated sending out Ross' expedition.

Robinson, Capt. Commander of the *Pomona* in the South Shetlands, 1821–23.

Robinson, A.G.B. 3rd mate on the *City of New York* during the second half of Byrd's 1928–30 expedition. He took over that position from S.D.I. Erickson. He was back in the Antarctic again as 2nd officer on the *Bear of Oakland,* during the second half of Byrd's 1933–35 expedition.

Robinson, J. Crewman on the *Jacob Ruppert*, 1933–34.

Robinson, John. Captain of the fo'c's'le on the Wilkes Expedition 1838–42. Joined in the USA. Served the cruise.

Robinson, R.P. Purser's steward on the *Vincennes* during the Wilkes Expedition of 1838–42.

Robinson, R.S. Crewman on the *Bear of Oakland*, 1933–34.

Robinson, William. Seaman on the Wilkes Expedition 1838–42. Joined in the USA. Served the cruise.

Robinson Bay. 66°38′S, 98°57′E. An indentation into the coast of Queen Mary Land, just to the south of the east end of the Shackleton Ice Shelf.

Robinson Bluff. 85°36′S, 159°47′W. Overlooks the western side of the lower part of the Amundsen Glacier, just north of Whitney Glacier, in the Queen Maud Mountains. Discovered in Dec. 1929 by Gould's geological party during Byrd's 1928–30 expedition. Named for Richard R. Robinson, station engineer at McMurdo Station in 1966.

Robinson Glacier. 66°30′S, 107°16′E. A channel glacier flowing to the coast of East Antarctica between Merritt Island and Reist Rocks. Named for R.P. Robinson.

Robinson Group. 67°27′S, 63°27′E. A group of islands which extend 10 miles in an east-west direction. Just NW of Cape Daly off the East Antarctic coast. In 1931 they were independently discovered by the BANZARE and by Norwegian whalers on the *Thorgaut*. Mawson named them for W.S. Robinson (*see also* **Cape Robinson**), a supporter of the BANZARE, while the Norwegians called them Thorgaut-öyane (the Thorgaut Islands). The Australians stuck with Mawson's naming, but named the largest island in the group as Thorgaut Island. Others in the group include: Andersen Island, Macklin Island.

Robinson Heights. 71°22′S, 166°40′E. 2,170 m. Mostly ice-covered. They are elliptical in plan. 15 miles long. South of the Anare Pass. They form the NW end of the Admiralty Mountains. Named for Edwin S. Robinson, geophysicist at McMurdo Station in 1960. He took part in several geophysical traverses, and led the South Pole Station Traverse of 1962–63.

Robinson Island *see* **Francis Island, Cape Robinson**

Robinson Peak. 79°23′S, 83°58′W. 2,040 m. On the ridge east of Rennell Glacier. 7 miles south of Mount Virginia in the Heritage Range. Named for Willard E. Robinson, construction mechanic at Byrd Station in 1965.

Robinson Ridge. 66°22′S, 110°36′E. A rocky coastal peninsula between Sparkes Bay and Penney Bay, at the east side of the Windmill Islands. Named for Lt. Cdr. Frederick G. Robinson, USN, aerological officer on Operation Windmill, 1947–48.

Robison Glacier. 86°29′S, 148°12′W. Flows NW along the north side of the La Gorce Mountains and enters the Robert Scott Glacier in the Queen Maud Mountains. Discovered in Dec. 1934 by Quin Blackburn's party during Byrd's 1933–35 expedition. Named for Lt. Cdr. Layton E. Robison, VX-6 pilot during Operation Deep Freeze 64, 65, and 66.

Robison Peak. 77°12′S, 160°15′E. Also spelled (erroneously) as Robinson Peak. 2,230 m. Snow-covered. 3 miles NE of Mount Dearborn, near the north end of the Willett Range in Victoria Land. Named for Leslie B. Robison, US Geological Survey engineer who surveyed this peak in Dec. 1960.

Robson Glacier. 77°05′S, 162°11′E. 3 miles long. Flows north from the Gonville and Caius Range along the east side of Red Ridge. It merges with the general flow of ice toward Granite Harbor southward of Redcliff Nunatak in Victoria Land. Named by Grif Taylor during his Western Journey, while part of Scott's 1910–13 expedition.

Cape Roca. 60°45'S, 44°49'W. Also called Cape Rock. 2 miles NW of Cape Davidson at the west end of Laurie Island in the South Orkneys. Charted in 1903 by Bruce, and named the following year by him for Julio A. Roca, the president of Argentina at the time.

Islotes Roca *see* **Anagram Islands**

¹Roca Islands. 65°11'S, 64°27'W. Also spelled (erroneously) as Rocca Islands. Between the Cruls Islands and the Anagram Islands, on the south side of French Passage in the Wilhelm Archipelago. Discovered by Charcot in 1903–5, and named by him for the president of Argentina at the time. In 1934–37 the BGLE incorrectly named the Anagram Islands as the Roca Islands, and this mistake was not cleared up until 1958.

²Roca Islands *see* **Anagram Islands**

Roca Reef *see* **Rocca Islands**

Roca Rock *see* **Rocca Islands**

Punta de Las Rocas *see* **Stone Point**

¹Rocca Islands *see* **Roca Islands**

²Rocca Islands. 67°47'S, 68°46'W. Also called Roca Reef, Roca Rock. 3 miles east of Avian Island, off the south end of Adelaide Island. Discovered in 1909 by Charcot, and named by him for Monsieur Rocca, an acquaintance in Buenos Aires.

Rochray Glacier. 72°11'S, 101°21'W. 5 miles long. Just east of Hendersin Knob on Thurston Island. It flows south to the Abbott Ice Shelf in Peacock Sound. Named for Lt. (jg) Samuel Rochray, USN, helicopter pilot on the *Glacier* in Feb. 1960, during the USN Bellingshausen Sea Expedition.

Cape Rock *see* **Cape Roca**

Rock Haven. 60°44'S, 45°35'W. On the east coast of Signy Island, between Pageant Point and Gourlay Point on Gourlay Peninsula. It provides a sheltered anchorage for small boats. Named by the UK for the prominent rock at its entrance.

Rock Pile Peaks. 68°25'S, 65°09'W. 1,110 m. Surmount the east end of the peninsula projecting from the east coast of Graham Land between Mobiloil Inlet and Solberg Inlet. Named for its confused appearance.

Rock Pile Point. 68°25'S, 64°58'W. Also called Punta Carrera Pinto, Periphery Point. At the eastern point of the extremity containing Rock Pile Peaks on the east coast of Graham Land. Named descriptively by the USA before 1947.

Rock X *see* **X**

Rockefeller Mountains. 78°S, 155°W. A group of low-lying, scattered granite peaks and ridges. Almost entirely snow-covered. 30 miles SSW of the Alexandra Mountains on the Edward VII Peninsula. Discovered aerially by Byrd on Jan. 27, 1929, and named by him for John D. Rockefeller, Jr., a patron of the expedition.

Rockefeller Plateau. 80°S, 135°W. East of the Shirase and Siple Coasts, and south of the Ford, Flood, and Executive Committee Ranges in Marie Byrd Land. It is part of the interior ice plateau, and is extensive, ice-covered, and from 1,000 m. to 1,500 m. above sea level. Discovered by Byrd in 1934 and named by him for John D. Rockefeller, Jr. (*see* **Rockefeller Mountains**).

Rockefeller Range *see* **Rockefeller Mountains**

Rockets. Rocketry studies were conducted during the IGY, the *Glacier* launching "rockoons" into the ionosphere to gather data on cosmic rays, aurora, and geomagnetism. Rockets were not used by the USA between 1963 and 1970, although they were by other countries. *See also* **Arcas rockets.**

Rockfall Cliff. 73°26'S, 93°34'W. Marks the NW face of Mount Loweth, in the Jones Mountains. Named by the University of Minnesota–Jones Mountains Party of 1960–61 for the continual rockfalls here making study of the area rather dangerous.

Rockinson, Louis L. *see* **Rickinson, Louis L.**

Rockney Ridge. 75°02′S, 133°45′W. On the NE side of Mount Goorhigian in the Demas Range of Marie Byrd Land. Named for Vaughn D. Rockney, meteorologist at Byrd Station, 1968–69.

Rockoons *see* **Rockets**

Rockpepper Bay. 63°08′S, 55°44′W. 3½ miles wide at its entrance. East of Boreal Point on the north coast of Joinville Island. Surveyed by the FIDS in 1953–54. Named by the UK for the many small islands and rocks in the bay.

Rocks. The sun can heat rocks to 59°F. Snow then melts, runs down the rock as water into the shade, and freezes, thus cracking and eroding the rock (*see also* Erosion).

Rocky Point *see* **Bell Point, Cape Dunlop, Hospital Point**

Punta Rocosa *see* **Bell Point, Hospital Point**

Isla Rodeada *see* **Beta Island**

Roderick Valley. 83°30′S, 57°30′W. Ice-filled. Trends in a north-south direction. Separates the Schmidt Hills and the Williams Hills from the main mass of the Neptune Range in the Pensacola Mountains. Named for Capt. David W. Roderick, USAF, pilot and second-in-command of the US Air Force Electronics Test Unit 1957–58.

Mount Rodger. 79°42′S, 83°34′W. 1,410 m. At the NW end of the Collier Hills in the Heritage Range. Named for Rodger A. Brown, meteorologist at Little America V in 1958.

Rodgers, George. Private on the Wilkes Expedition 1838–42. Joined in the USA. Served the cruise.

Rodman Cove. 61°07′S, 55°28′W. Also called Emma Cove. South of Cape Lindsey on the west coast of Elephant Island in the South Shetlands. Named by US geographer Lawrence Martin for Benjamin Rodman of New Bedford, Mass., owner of whaling ships in the 1820s and 1830s. The name has appeared on charts and descriptions of Elephant Island since the mid-1940s.

Rodman Passage. 65°52′S, 66°W. A marine passage between the south end of Renaud Island and Rabot Island in the Biscoe Islands. Charted by Charcot in 1908–10. Named by the UK in 1959 for Hugh Rodman of the US Hydrographic Office, a pioneer in the 1890s of ice movement studies in the North Atlantic.

Rodolfo Marsh Station *see* **Teniente Rodolfo Marsh Station**

Rödon *see* **Red Island**

Isla Rodríguez *see* **Terminal Island**

Rodríguez, A. Argentine surveyor on the *Primero de Mayo* in 1930.

Rodríguez, Ezequiel. Lt. 1st class, Chilean Navy. He was an observer on the USAS 1939–41.

Mount Roe. 85°08′S, 169°36′W. Flat, ice-covered. Overlooks the west side of Liv Glacier. 1 mile NE of Mount Wells at the SE end of the Prince Olav Mountains. Named for Lt. Donald W. Roe, Jr., with VX-6 at McMurdo Station in 1961, and squadron safety officer for VX-6 at McMurdo Station in 1962–63.

Roe Glacier. 85°36′S, 151°26′W. 10 miles long. Flows NW through the Tapley Mountains to enter the Robert Scott Glacier just south of Mount Durham. Named for Derrell M. Roe, at McMurdo Station in 1963–64 and 1964–65, and station engineer at the same station in 1966.

Roe Island. 64°S, 60°50′W. In the entrance to Curtiss Bay. 2 miles west of Cape Andreas in Graham Land. Named by the UK for Sir Alliott Verdon Roe (1877–1958), aviation pioneer who founded A.V. Roe and Co., Ltd., in Britain in 1910.

Mount Roer. 72°18′S, 0°21′E. Also called Roerkulten. 2,085 m. Isolated. 7 miles west of Fuglefjellet in the Sverdrup Mountains of Queen Maud Land. Named by the Norwegians for Nils Roer.

Roer, Nils. Surveyor on the NBSAE 1949–52.

Roerkulten *see* **Mount Roer**

Rog Point. 67°38'S, 46°04'E. 6 miles east of Molodezhnaya Station on Alasheyev Bight in Enderby Land.

Mount Rogers. 80°33'S, 29°26'W. 995 m. On the east side of Blaiklock Glacier between Williams Ridge and Wedge Ridge in the western part of the Shackleton Range. Named in 1957 by the BCTAE for Allan F. Rogers.

Rogers, Dr. Allan F. Medical officer and physiologist on the BCTAE with Fuchs in 1957–58.

Rogers Glacier. 69°59'S, 73°04'E. Enters the eastern side of the Amery Ice Shelf just north of the McKaskle Hills. Named by US cartographer John H. Roscoe in 1952 for Lt. Cdr. William J. Rogers, Jr., USN, plane commander during Operation Highjump, 1946–47.

Rogers Peak. 79°21'S, 84°14'W. 1,520 m. At the east side of the terminus of Rennell Glacier in the Heritage Range. Named by the University of Minnesota Geological Party here in 1963–64, for M. Alan Rogers, geologist to the Hart Hills and Whitmore Mountains areas in that year.

Rogers Peaks. 72°15'S, 24°31'E. Also called Rogerstoppane. Just SW of Dufek Mountain in the Sør Rondane Mountains. Named for Lt. Cdr. William J. Rogers, Jr. (see **Rogers Glacier**).

Rogers Spur. 74°30'S, 111°12'W. Wedge-shaped. At the head of the Brush Glacier on the Bear Peninsula of Marie Byrd Land. Named for James C. Rogers, electrical engineer at Byrd VLF Station, 1966.

Rogerstoppane see **Rogers Peaks**

Cape Roget. 71°59'S, 170°37'E. A steep rock cape at the southern tip of the Adare Peninsula. Marks the north side of the entrance to Moubray Bay on the coast of Victoria Land. Discovered by Ross in 1841, and named by him for Peter Mark Roget (1779–1869), British philologist who, in 1852, created the famous thesaurus which bears his name. In the time of Ross' expedition Roget was secretary of the Royal Society. The cape is the site of an emperor penguin colony. (For Roget see also **Roget Rocks**).

Roget Rocks. 64°20'S, 61°10'W. 4 miles SW of Spring Point in Hughes Bay, Graham Land. Surveyed by Ken Blaiklock from the *Norsel* in 1955. Named by the UK for Peter Mark Roget (see **Cape Roget**), a member of the committee which planned the expedition of the *Chanticleer* in 1828–31.

Rogstad, Egil. Norwegian chief radio operator on the NBSAE 1949–52.

Rogstad Glacier. 72°21'S, 1°19'E. Flows NW along the north side of Isingen Mountain in the Sverdrup Mountains of Queen Maud Land. Named by the Norwegians for Egil Rogstad.

Röhss Bay. 64°12'S, 58°16'W. 11 miles wide. Between Capes Broms and Obelisk on the SW side of James Ross Island. Discovered by Nordenskjöld's 1901–4 expedition and named by him for August and Wilhelm Röhss, patrons of the expedition.

Roi Baudoin Station. 70°25'S, 24°20'E. 10 miles inland from Breidvika on the Princess Ragnhild Coast of Queen Maud Land. Belgium's only scientific station in the Antarctic. It was built as a summer-only station by the Belgian Antarctic Expedition of 1957–58 led by Gaston de Gerlache, really as an IGY station. It was named for King Baudoin of Belgium, and was closed in 1967.

Île du Roi Georges see **King George Island**

Terre du Roi Oscar see **Oscar II Coast**

Isla Roja see **Red Island**

Isla Rojas Parker see **Vázquez Island**

Rojas Peak. 64°49'S, 62°55'W. On the western coast of Graham Land.

Rokhlin Nunataks. 72°12'S, 14°28'E. Four nunataks, 6 miles south of the Linnormen Hills at the southern end of the Payer Mountains in Queen Maud Land. Discovered by Ritscher's expedition of

1938–39. Named by the USSR in 1963 for M.I. Rokhlin (*see* **Deaths, 1958**).

Mount Rokitansky   *see*   **Mount Pico**

Mount Roland. 86°29'S, 145°42'W. 2,210 m. Directly north of Mount Mooney on the north flank of the Robison Glacier in the Queen Maud Mountains. Named for Lt. (jg) Charles J. Roland, VX-6 aircraft navigator on Operation Deep Freeze 66 and 67.

Roland, F. Seaman on the *Français* during Charcot's expedition of 1903–5.

Roland Bay. 65°04'S, 64°03'W. A cove. Its southern shore is Hervéou Point. Indents the west end of the peninsula that forms the western extremity of Booth Island in the Wilhelm Archipelago. Charted by Charcot in 1903–5, and named by him for F. Roland.

Roland Bonaparte Point   *see*   **Bonaparte Point**

Île Rollet de l'Isle   *see*   **Rollet Island**

Rollet Island. 65°02'S, 64°03'W. 1 mile north of the NW part of Booth Island in the Wilhelm Archipelago. Discovered by Charcot in 1903–5, and named by him as Île Rollet de l'Isle, for Monsieur Rollet de l'Isle, French hydrographic surveyor. The name has since been shortened.

Roman Figure Four Mountain   *see* **Roman Four Promontory**

Roman Four Promontory. 68°13'S, 66°56'W. 830 m. Marks the north side of the entrance to Neny Fjord on the west coast of Graham Land. Charted by the BGLE 1934–37. Named by the USAS from East Base in 1939–41 as Roman Figure Four Promontory. The snow-filled clefts along the face of the promontory make it look like a Roman IV. Also called Roman Four Rock, the name finally approved for this feature was Roman Four Promontory.

Roman Four Rock   *see*   **Roman Four Promontory**

Roman Passage. 65°52'S, 66°W. Also called Paso Covadonga. A marine passage north of the Biscoe Islands, off the west coast of Graham Land.

Romanes Beach. 77°17'S, 166°22'E. On the north side of Wohlschlag Bay just south of Harrison Bluff, on the west side of Ross Island. Named by NZ for W. Romanes, mountaineer assistant with the NZGSAE 1958–59, which mapped this feature while on a visit here from the *Arneb*.

The *Romeo*. British sealer from London, in the South Shetlands for the 1821–22 season. It moored in Clothier Harbor in March 1822.

Romeo Island. 62°23'S, 59°55'W. 3½ miles SW of Table Island in the South Shetlands. Named by the UK in 1961 for the *Romeo*.

Islote Romero   *see*   **Romero Rock**

Romero Rock. 63°19'S, 57°57'W. 175 yards west of Saavedra Rock in the Duroch Islands off Trinity Peninsula. Named by the Chilean Antarctic Expedition of 1947–48 as Islote Astrónomo Romero for Guillermo Romero González, the astronomer of the Chilean Army, who was on this expedition and who did astronomical work in the Antarctic. In 1951 this name was shortened to Islote Romero, and in 1962 the name Romero Rock began to gain acceptance.

Rømlingane Peaks. 72°11'S, 1°08'E. A chain extending from the west side of Vendeholten Mountain in the Sverdrup Mountains of Queen Maud Land. Name means "the fugitives" in Norwegian.

Rømlingsletta Flat. 72°16'S, 1°07'E. A flat, ice-covered area of about 40 square miles. Northward of the foot of Isingen Mountain in the Sverdrup Mountains of Queen Maud Land. Name means "the fugitive's plain" in Norwegian.

Mount Romnaes. 71°31'S, 24°E. 1,500 m. Isolated. 22 miles NW of Brattnipane Peaks and the main group of the Sør Rondane Mountains. Photographed by the LCE 1936–37, and named Romnaesfjellet by the Norwegians for Nils Romnaes.

Romnaes, Nils. Aerial photographer on the LCE 1936–37.

Romnaesfjellet *see* **Mount Romnaes**

Romulus Glacier. 68°23'S, 66°55'W. 7 miles long. 2 miles wide. Flows from the northern slopes of Mount Lupa westward to Rymill Bay between the Blackwall Mountains and Black Thumb, on the west coast of Graham Land. Surveyed in 1936 by the BGLE and again in 1948–49 by the FIDS, who named it in association with nearby Remus Glacier and Mount Lupa.

The *Ronald*. Norwegian floating factory whaling ship belonging to the Hektor Whaling Company. Anchored at Deception Island in 1911–12, and for several seasons after that.

Mount Ronald *see* **Ronald Hill**

Ronald Hill. 62°59'S, 60°35'W. Also called Mount Ronald. Ice-free. 105 m. North of Kroner Lake in Deception Island, South Shetlands. Charted by Olaf Holtedahl in 1927–28, and named by him for the *Ronald*.

Ronald Ridge. 79°37'S, 83°20'W. 5 miles long. 1 mile west of Donald Ridge, which it resembles, in the Pioneer Heights of the Heritage Range. Named for Ronald C. Taylor, meteorologist at Little America V in 1957.

Ronald Rock. 83°20'S, 49°25'W. 1,145 m. Along the cliff just north of Skidmore Cliff, east of the Saratoga Table in the Forrestal Range of the Pensacola Mountains. Named for Ronald D. Brown, aviation structural mechanic at Ellsworth Station in 1957.

Mount Ronca. 82°38'S, 155°15'E. Over 2,200 m. Surmounts the southern end of Quest Cliffs in the Geologists Range. Named for Luciano B. Ronca, geologist at McMurdo Station in 1960–61.

Ronde Island. 66°47'S, 141°15'E. Just to the NE side of Zélée Glacier Tongue. Just over 2½ miles WNW of Rescapé Islands. Charted by the French in 1949–51, and named by them for its round shape.

Rongé Island. 64°43'S, 62°41'W. Also called Cuverville Island, Rouge Island. 5

miles long. High and rugged. The largest of the group which forms the west side of Errera Channel, off the west coast of Graham Land. Discovered by de Gerlache in 1897–99, and named by him for Madame de Rongé, a patron of the expedition.

Mount Ronne. 77°34'S, 146°10'W. Juts out from the middle of the east side of the Haines Mountains in the Ford Ranges of Marie Byrd Land. Named for Martin Rønne.

Ronne, Edith. Wife of Finn Ronne, and a reporter for the North American Newspaper Alliance. She and Jennie Darlington wintered-over on Stonington Island during the RARE 1947–48 (*see* **Women in Antarctica**, and the **Ronne Antarctic Research Expedition** for further details of this strange adventure). She shared a single hut with Finn Ronne.

Ronne, Finn. b. 1898, Horten, Norway. d. Jan. 12, 1980, Bethesda, Maryland. Son of Martin Rønne (Finn changed the ø into an o when he came to the USA in 1923). From 1924–39 he was a mechanical engineer at Westinghouse, during which time he was invited by Byrd to go on his 1933–35 expedition as ski expert, dog driver, and trail radio operator. This was the first of 9 Antarctic outings for Ronne, one of the greatest figures in Antarctic exploration. He was with Byrd again on the United States Antarctic Service Expedition (better known as the USAS), from 1939–41, in which he was second-in-command (chief of staff) of the party at East Base. A captain in the USNR, he organized his own private venture to Antarctica in 1947–48, the Ronne Antarctic Research Expedition (q.v.), better known as the RARE, which wintered-over on Stonington Island in 1947. His wife, Edith, went along. His disproving of the mythical Ross-Weddell Graben finally proved Antarctica to be a continent (on the surface, at least—*see* **Geology**). He was the IGY scientific and military leader at Ellsworth Station until Jan. 16, 1958, when he handed over to

Paul Tidd and Matthew Brennan. Ronne wrote several books (see the Bibliography).

Rønne, Martin. b. 1861, Norway. d. 1932, Norway, of a cerebral hemorrhage. A sailor since childhood, he was with Amundsen on several Arctic trips, and went with Amundsen on the Norwegian Antarctic Expedition of 1910–12. He was not one of the shore party, but remained on the *Fram* as sailmaker. He was sailmaker, ski instructor, dog driver, and ice-pilot on Byrd's 1928–30 expedition, the only one on that expedition who had been in the Antarctic before. He was the father of Finn Ronne.

Ronne Antarctic Research Expedition. Better known by its initials, RARE. 1947–48. The last of the major private ventures to Antarctica, this was Finn Ronne's own private expedition, privately financed but with some government aid. It was sponsored by the American Antarctic Association, which had been formed for this purpose. 23 people left Beaumont, Texas, on Jan. 25, 1947, on the *Port of Beaumont, Texas.* They were Ronne, his wife, Schlossbach, Nichols, Petersen, Thompson, Lassiter, Charles Adams, Darlington and his wife, James Robertson, Hassage, Latady, Fiske, Walter Smith, McClary, Gutenko, Kelsey, Dodson, McLean, Wood, Owen, and Valdés. They arrived at Stonington Island in Marguerite Bay off the west coast of the Antarctic Peninsula, on March 12, 1947, with 3 aircraft, 2 Weasels, dog sledges, and 43 dogs (at least, that's the number of dogs they had when they left Texas. Half of the dogs died of distemper en route to the Antarctic). They set up Main Base at Stonington Island, froze the *Port of Beaumont, Texas* in the ice for the winter, and wintered-over in 1947. They set up an advance base at Cape Keeler (*see* **Cape Keeler Advance Base**) (*see also* **Plateau Weather Station** and **Weddell Coast Sledge Party**). They greatly extended the knowledge of Palmer Land, and explored south of 73°S, and between 35°W and 80°W. A half million square

miles were covered by 14,000 trimetrogon aerial photographs, and several scientific investigations were made. They finally disproved the existence of the Ross-Weddell Graben. Two women wintering-over with 21 men led to a few problems. Jennie Darlington became pregnant and almost had her daughter in Antarctica (she just made it back to the USA in time), and the two husbands had a violent quarrel (Ronne barely mentions Darlington in his books), and the wives stopped communicating. The party left the Antarctic on Feb. 23, 1948, and arrived back in New York on April 15, 1948. The expedition led to a great interest in the Antarctic.

Ronne Bay   *see*   **Ronne Entrance**

Ronne Entrance. 72°30′S, 74°W. The broad SW entrance to the George VI Sound where it opens on the Bellingshausen Sea at the SW side of Alexander Island. Discovered by Finn Ronne and Carl Eklund when they were on a sledge journey through the sound in Dec. 1940, as part of the USAS. It was named Ronne Bay. Since then the head of the bay has receded eastward into George VI Sound, and the shape of the area thus changed. It was no longer a bay, and was redefined. Named actually for Finn Ronne and his father, Martin Rønne.

Ronne Ice Shelf. Centers on 78°30′S, 61°W. Large body of ice at the head of the Weddell Sea, immediately to the west of the Filchner Ice Shelf, from which it is partially separated by Berkner Island. It is over 500 feet thick and extends to more than 520 miles inland. After the Ross Ice Shelf it is the largest body of ice in the world. The area was claimed by Britain in 1908, by Chile in 1940, and by Argentina in 1942. It is bounded on the west by the base of the Antarctic Peninsula and Ellsworth Land. In Nov. and Dec. 1947 Finn Ronne discovered it (or rather a thin strip along the northern portion of the entire ice shelf) and called it the James Lassiter Ice Barrier, for James Lassiter. The huge stretch of land which Ronne presumed lay to the south of the ice shelf he named Edith Ronne Land, for his wife. In 1957–58 Ronne determined that the ice shelf went inland much further than he had thought, and took in most of what he had mapped as Edith Ronne Land. (*See also* **Filchner Ice Shelf** for the history of the nomenclature of this area.)

Ronne Weddell Coast Party *see* **Weddell Coast Sledge Party**

Mount Ronniken *see* **Mount Nelson**

Röntgen Peak. 64°02′S, 62°17′W. 1 mile SE of Cape Cockburn in the NE part of Pasteur Peninsula on Brabant Island. Named by the UK for Wilhelm K. von Röntgen (1845–1923), the German physicist who discovered X-rays in 1895.

Rookeries *see* **Penguin rookeries**

¹Rookery Islands *see* **Haswell Islands**

²Rookery Islands. 67°37′S, 62°31′E. In the SW part of Holme Bay, 7 miles west of Mawson Station. It is an SPA because of the 6 species of birds which breed here. Photographed by the LCE 1936–37, and called Innerskjera (the inner skerries) by the Norwegians. The islands were visited by the ANARE in 1954 and 1955 and renamed by the Australians for the Adélie Penguin rookery which occupies the largest island in the group.

Roos, S. Edward. American oceanographer who was a seaman on the *City of New York* during Byrd's 1928–30 expedition, and again on the *Bear of Oakland* during Byrd's 1933–35 expedition.

Roos Glacier. 75°17′S, 110°57′W. Flows from the NW slopes of Mount Murphy in Marie Byrd Land. Named for S. Edward Roos.

Chenal de Roosen *see* **Neumayer Channel**

Roosen Channel *see* **Neumayer Channel**

Roosevelt Ice Dome *see* **Roosevelt Island**

Roosevelt Island. 79°25′S, 162°W. Also called Roosevelt Ice Dome. An ice-covered island, but not grounded as was

once believed. 80 miles long in a NW-SE direction and 40 miles wide. In the NE section of the Ross Ice Shelf, not far south of Little America. The northern extremity of this huge island is only 3 miles south of where the Bay of Whales used to be. Discovered by Byrd in 1934 and named by him for President F. Roosevelt.

Roosevelt Sea *see* **Amundsen Sea**

Roots, Ernest F. Ernest Frederick Roots. Known as Fred. Chief geologist on the NBSAE 1949–52.

Roots Heights. 72°37′S, 0°27′E. Also called Rootshorga. Ice-free. Between Reece Valley and Skarsdalen Valley in the Sverdrup Mountains of Queen Maud Land. Named by the Norwegians for Ernest F. Roots.

Rootshorga *see* **Roots Heights**

Mount Ropar. 83°58′S, 160°29′E. 2,420 m. At the eastern extremity of Canopy Cliffs in the Queen Elizabeth Range. Named for Nicholas J. Ropar, Jr., Weather Central meteorologist at Little America V in 1958.

Ropebrake Pass. 84°45′S, 173°25′W. A steep, narrow snow pass between the south end of Gabbro Hills and Mount Llano. It allows passage between the Barrett and Gough Glaciers. Named by the Southern Party of the NZGSAE 1963–64 for the large number of rope brakes used in its crossing.

Roper Point. 76°19′S, 112°54′W. Mostly ice-covered. At the western extremity of Mount Takahe, in Marie Byrd Land. Named for Nathaniel A. Roper, aurora researcher at Byrd Station in 1963.

Cape Roquemaurel. 63°33′S, 58°56′W. A rocky headland at the east side of the entrance to Bone Bay, on the north side of Trinity Peninsula. Discovered by Dumont d'Urville in 1837–40 and named by him for Lt. Louis de Roquemaurel.

Mount Rorqual. 65°39′S, 62°20′W. Between the Starbuck and Stubb Glaciers. 5 miles west of Mount Queequeg, on the east side of Graham Land. 1,110 m. Separated from Cachalot Peak by a narrow ridge. Named by the UK in continuation of the whaling theme for the features in this area.

Rorquals. Types of baleen whales (q.v.). They sink when dead. Antarctic ones include: Sei Whale, Minke, Blue Whale, Fin Whale, Bryde's Whale.

Islote Rosa *see* **Rosa Rock**

Rosa Rock. 63°18′S, 57°54′W. 175 yards west of Agurto Rock in the Duroch Islands off Trinity Peninsula. Named by the Chilean Presidential Antarctic Expedition of 1948 for Rosa González de Claro, daughter of the president of Chile, Gabriel González Videla.

Rosamel Island. 63°34′S, 56°17′W. Also called Christmas Island. Circular. 1 mile across. Has precipitous cliffs of volcanic rock rising to a snow-covered peak of 435 m. West of Dundee Island in the southern entrance to Antarctic Sound. Discovered by Dumont d'Urville in 1837–40 and named by him for Vice-Adm. Claude de Rosamel, French minister of marine, under whose orders the expedition sailed.

Roscoe, John H. US Marine 1st Lt. Photogrammetric officer in the central task group of Operation Highjump, 1946–47. He was an observer on Operation Windmill, 1947–48. Later he was with the Navy's Photo Interpretation Center, and wrote *Antarctic Bibliography* (*see* the Bibliography). He was scientific adviser to the director of US Antarctic Programs, but is best known as being the cartographer who worked off Operation Highjump photos in 1952 to produce a new series of maps, and who named many new features.

Roscoe Glacier. 66°30′S, 95°20′E. A channel glacier. 12 miles long. Between 3 and 5 miles wide. Feeds McDonald Bay from the Queen Mary Land coast, at the western part of the Shackleton Ice Shelf, between Cape Moyes and Junction Corner. Charted as a valley depression by the AAE in March 1912, when the Western Base Party led by Frank Wild was making a southern reconnaissance. Correctly

identified during Operation Highjump, 1946–47. Named for John H. Roscoe.

Roscolyn Tor. 76°42′S, 159°50′E. A high sandstone feature. 1 mile SW of Warren Peak in the Allan Hills of Victoria Land. Named by the New Zealanders here in 1964 for a similar feature in Anglesey, Wales.

Rose *see* **Rose Rock**

The *Rose*. An Enderby Brothers yawl in the Antarctic in 1833–34 as tender to the *Hopefull*. Capt. Mallows commanding. In Dec. 1833 or Jan. 1834, with the crews of both ships mutinying, the *Rose* got crushed between 2 icebergs at 60°17′S, 53°26′W. The men and provisions were saved and taken aboard Capt. Rea's flagship, the *Hopefull*.

Mount Rose. 66°40′S, 140°01′E. 22 m. South of Mount Cervin on the east side of Pétrel Island in the Géologie Archipelago. Charted in 1951 by the French and named by them for a mountain in the Alps.

Rose, Stephen D. 1st officer on the *Bear of Oakland*, 1933–34, and master of the *Jacob Ruppert*, 1934–35.

Rose Peak. 62°02′S, 58°12′W. 655 m. Almost 2 miles SW of Rea Peak and 3 miles NE of Ternyck Needle, in the central part of King George Island in the South Shetlands. Named by the UK in 1960 for the *Rose*.

Rose Point. 74°45′S, 136°45′W. 1 mile east of Cape Burks on the coast of Marie Byrd Land. Named for Stephen D. Rose.

Rose Rock. 71°17′S, 170°13′E. This is the southern of two rocks called The Sisters, off the northern extremity of Cape Adare. The term The Sisters was given by Borchgrevink in 1898–1900, but the individual rocks were named Rose and Gertrude by Campbell, the leader of the Northern Party during Scott's 1910–13 expedition. Murray Levick suggested the name to Campbell, Rose and Gertrude being two sisters in a comic song of the time.

Rosenau Head. 70°28′S, 162°46′E. A headland. Ice-covered. On the east side of Barber Glacier in the Bowers Mountains, on the coast of Victoria Land. Named for Darrell D. Rosenau, USN, electronics technician at Amundsen-Scott South Pole Station.

Rosenberg Glacier. 75°44'S, 132°33'W. Heavily crevassed. Flows from the western slopes of the Ames Range between Mount Kosciusko and Mount Boennighausen, in Marie Byrd Land. Named for Theodore J. Rosenberg, ionosphere physicist at Siple Station, 1970–71.

Mount Rosenthal. 80°03'S, 83°15'W. 1,840 m. At the northern end of the Liberty Hills, in the Heritage Range. Named for Lt. Cdr. Ronald Rosenthal, USN, navigator (*see* **Deaths, 1966**).

Rosenthal Islands. 64°36'S, 64°18'W. Off the west coast of Anvers Island. 6 miles north of Cape Monaco. The main island in the group is Gerlache Island. Discovered by Dallmann in 1873–74 and named by him for Albert Rosenthal, director of the German Society for Polar Navigation, who, with the Society, sponsored Dallmann's expedition.

Mount Rosenwald. 85°04'S, 179°06'W. 3,450 m. Forms a major landmark between the heads of the Gallup and Baldwin Glaciers in the Queen Maud Mountains. Completely snow-covered on the SW side but has nearly vertical exposed-rock cliffs on the NE side. Discovered by Byrd on his Polar flight of Nov. 1929, and named by him for Julius Rosenwald (1862–1932), Chicago philanthropist who contributed to Byrd's 1928–30 expedition and also, posthumously, to Byrd's 1933–35 expedition.

Cape Ross. 76°44'S, 163°01'E. A granite headland. 8 miles north of Cape Archer on the coast of Victoria Land. Charted by Shackleton in 1907–9, and named by him for Sir James Clark Ross.

Mount Ross *see* **Mount Haddington**

Ross, Alastair. Taxidermist on Bruce's 1902–4 expedition.

Ross, G.H. Fireman on the *Quest*, 1921–22.

Ross, Sir James Clark. b. April 15, 1800, London. d. April 3, 1862, Aylesbury, Bucks. Scottish navigator, nephew of Arctic explorer Sir John Ross (1777–1856) who, with the younger Ross and singly searched for the Northwest Passage. James joined the RN at 12, and between 1819 and 1827 he was in the Arctic with Parry. In 1827 he made an unsuccessful assault on the North Pole. In 1831 he and his uncle located the North Magnetic Pole. By the time he left for the Antarctic, on Sept. 30, 1839, Ross was the most experienced polar captain in history. His mission was to plant a flag at the South Magnetic Pole for the British Admiralty. He left London with 2 ships, the *Erebus*, which he commanded, and the *Terror*, under Crozier. All of his sailors were volunteers on double pay. Altogether there were 128 men, plus 4 scientists. Crozier was second-in-command of the expedition, which also included R. McCormick, J. Robertson, Hooker, Lyall, J.E. Davis, Yule, J. Wood, Kay, Bird, Cotter, Tucker, Dayman, Oakeley, P.A. Scott, Sibbald, A.J. Smith, Hallett, C.G. Phillips, T.E. Moore, Molloy, Moubray. They explored the Kerguélen Islands, then went to Tasmania, departing there on Nov. 13, 1840. The bosun of the *Erebus* had drowned while between the Kerguélens and Tasmania. On Jan. 1, 1841, they crossed the Antarctic Circle, finding the pack-ice at about 66°32'S, 174°34'E. On Jan. 5, 1841, they pushed into the pack, and on Jan. 9, 1841, they found the sea free again as they became the first men ever to enter the Ross Sea. On Jan. 11, 1841, Ross sighted the Admiralty Mountains (which he named on that day), the furthest south land had ever been seen, and finding his way south blocked he went east and then south again. On Jan. 12, 1841, the expedition landed a party on Possession Island, and discovered Victoria Land. They then cruised south, further into the Ross Sea, toward McMurdo Sound. After 400 miles Ross claimed Franklin Island for the British Crown and, on the following day, Jan. 28, 1841, he discovered Mounts Erebus and Terror, and thus Ross Island (although he thought it was part of the mainland) and McMurdo Sound. Later that day he came up against the barrier which today is called the Ross Ice Shelf. This blocked his way south again. He cruised along it for 350 miles, mapping the barrier as he went to as far eastward as 167°W before giving up any hope of penetrating it. He then returned to Cape Adare, then to the Balleny Islands, and finally to Tasmania, where he arrived on April 1, 1841. He had set a new southing record of 78°09'S on Jan. 22, 1841. On Nov. 23, 1841, he left again for Antarctica, reentering the pack-ice on Dec. 17, 1841, in incredibly cold weather. He entered the Ross Sea again at the end of Feb. 1842, and once again unable to penetrate the barrier he abandoned the voyage. He wintered at the Falklands in 1842, and on Dec. 17, 1842, he left for a third Antarctic cruise, this time to the Weddell Sea, but he found it too full of pack-ice. He spent most of that summer (1842–43) exploring the Erebus and Terror Gulf and trying to penetrate the Weddell Sea pack-ice. On March 5, 1843, after having crossed the Antarctic Circle for the third time, he reached 71° 30'S, 14°51'W, then left, arriving back in England on Sept. 4, 1843. He was knighted not long afterwards, his having been the last of the great polar sailing voyages. Scott described Ross as "the discoverer of Antarctica." He had charted over 1,000 miles of coastline and had claimed for Britain all he had discovered.

Ross Archipelago. 77°30'S, 167°E. A fabricated term for the group of islands which include Beaufort Island, Ross Island, the Dellbridge Islands, Black Island, White Island, and Brown Island (now called Brown Peninsula). All these features are in the area of McMurdo Sound. Frank Debenham wrote a report, "The Physiography of the Ross Archipelago," on the feature in 1923. Named for Sir James Clark Ross.

Ross Bank. 77°S, 176°E. A submarine feature of the Ross Sea.

Ross Barrier   *see*   **Ross Ice Shelf**

Ross Dependency. New Zealand's "share" of the Antarctic continent, it lies between 150°W and 160°E. Named for Sir James Clark Ross, and for the Ross Sea, it is also called the Ross Sea Dependency. It was claimed by Britain on July 30, 1923, and put in the care of New Zealand.

Ross Desert. Unofficial name for the area of dry valleys in southern Victoria Land. Covering 5,000 square kilometers, it is the largest ice-free region in Antarctica. The Transantarctic Mountains cut off the flow of ice from the East Antarctic Ice Sheet, and this leads to the dry, cold, desert quality of the area. Named for Sir James Clark Ross.

Ross Glacial Episodes   *see*   **Ross Sea Glaciations I–IV.**

Ross Ice Barrier   *see*   **Ross Ice Shelf**

Ross Ice Shelf. Between 78°S and 86°S, and between 155°W and 160°E. It centers on 81°30'S, 175°W. The world's largest body of ice, it lies at the head of the Ross Sea, occupying the entire southern part of the Ross Sea embayment and ending seaward in a cliffed ice front about 400 miles long, stretching from Ross Island in the west to Edward VII Peninsula in the east. It reaches 600 miles inland from the coast. It is fed by numerous glaciers coming down from the Transantarctic Mountains, including the Beardmore Glacier, and is about 200,000 square miles in area, the size of Texas, and has a gently undulating surface. The whole ice shelf is continually moving, albeit slowly, its velocity averaging 2,180 feet per year. The mean ice thickness is 1,100 feet to 2,300 feet and, although the ice shelf is firmly attached to the continent, it has no bedrock beneath it, and is therefore floating. Its 200 foot high cliffs barred Ross' way south when he discovered it on Jan. 28, 1841, and he called it the Victoria Barrier, for the Queen of Great Britain. It was subsequently called the Great Ice Barrier, the Great Southern Barrier, the Icy Barrier, the Ice Barrier, the Barrier, the Ross

Ice Barrier and the Ross Barrier, the last two names for Sir James Clark Ross, its discoverer. It was called the Ross Ice Barrier even into Byrd's day in the 1920s and 1930s. The term ice shelf is fairly recent. The Germans call it Grosse Eisebeine. It served as the starting point for many explorations.

Ross Ice Shelf Geophysical and Glaciological Survey. Better known by its initials, RIGGS. A 5-year project in the 1970s.

Ross Ice Shelf Project. Otherwise known by its initials, RISP. A US project with contributions from 9 Antarctic Treaty nations and 3 non-Treaty nations. It was begun in 1973 and investigated the Ross Ice Shelf from the ground and air, making use of coring, sampling, and drilling.

¹Ross Island *see* **James Ross Island**

²Ross Island. 77°30′S, 168°E. In the SW corner of the Ross Sea, on the east side of McMurdo Sound. At the northern edge of the Ross Ice Shelf, just to the east of southern Victoria Land, it is the world's most southern land accessible to ships. It is roughly triangular, extending 43 miles from Cape Bird in the north to Cape Armitage in the south, and a similar distance from Cape Royds in the west to Cape Crozier in the east. The entire island is a volcanic formation, and is not grounded as was once believed. The main mountains (all volcanoes, active or extinct) are Erebus, Terror, Terra Nova, and Bird. McMurdo Station, Scott Base, and Scott's and Shackleton's huts are here, and a host of other famous sites are here, owing to the fact that it was the starting point of so many explorations to the interior. Ross discovered it in Jan. 1841, but thought it was part of the mainland. Scott was the next to see it, in 1902, and he determined it to be an island, and named it for Ross.

Ross Point. 62°21′S, 59°08′W. On the SW side of Nelson Island in the South Shetlands. 2 miles SE of Harmony Cove. Charted by personnel on the *Discovery II* in 1935.

Ross Sea. It centers on 75°S, 175°W. A southern extension of the Pacific Ocean, it forms a massive embayment into the continent of Antarctica between Cape Adare on the west and Cape Colbeck on the east. Its southern limit is the Ross Ice Shelf. It is one of Antarctica's least iced and most accessible seas, thus it has been the target of explorers as a starting point for their pushes into the interior. All coastal areas are now explored, and tourist ships frequent it. It is dominated by the high ranges of Victoria Land. Going north, away from the continent, it drops into the Southeast Pacific Basin. Surface currents generally move westward along the front of the Ross Ice Shelf. It is 370,000 square miles in area, and was first entered by Ross on Jan. 9, 1841. The next vessel to do so was the *Antarctic* in 1895. Scott named it for Ross in 1902.

Ross Sea Dependency *see* **Ross Dependency**

Ross Sea Glaciations I–IV. Ice ages in Antarctica. Expansions of the Ross Ice Shelf into ice sheets, which were largely grounded on the floor of the Ross Sea. Formerly called the Ross Glacial Episodes, and named for Sir James Clark Ross.

Ross seals. Family: Phocidae. Species: *Ommatophoca rossi*. Rarely seen, usually solitary seals which breed exclusively in Antarctica (*see* **Seals**). Named for Sir James Clark Ross, there are now about 50,000, and they feed on cephalopods, fish, and plankton. They have short faces, very large eyes, greenish-gray coarse fur with yellowish stripes on the sides. They grow to about 7½ feet long, and 330 to 470 pounds in weight.

Ross Shelf Ice *see* **Ross Ice Shelf**

Ross-Weddell Graben. A mythical passage in the form of a subglacial trench between the Weddell Sea and the Ross Sea which would split Antarctica in two. This idea had been proposed since the beginning of the 20th century. Bruce, Filchner, Shackleton, and Ronne made the proving or disproving of it a priority.

Byrd's 1933–35 expedition and Operation Highjump, 1946–47, seemed to disprove its existence, and the discovery of the Ellsworth Mountains by Ronne during the RARE 1947–48 finally dispelled the idea of such a graben (an elongated trough of land produced by subsidence of the earth's crust between two faults).

Rossa Point. 65°57′S, 65°14′W. Also called Rassa Point. 2 miles NE of Ferin Head on the west coast of Graham Land. Charted by the BGLE 1934–37. Named by the UK in 1959 for Anders Rossa, a Lapp ski pioneer.

Mount Rossel. 72°36′S, 31°02′E. 2,250 m. 3 miles SW of Mount Perov in the Belgica Mountains. Discovered by the Belgian Antarctic Expedition of 1957–58, led by Gaston de Gerlache, who named it for Mlle. Marie-Thérèse Rossel, a patron.

Rosser Ridge. 82°46′S, 53°35′W. 4 miles long. Marks the northern limit of the Cordiner Peaks in the Pensacola Mountains. Named for Earl W. Rosser, topographic engineer in the Pensacola Mountains in 1965–66.

Rossini Point. 72°27′S, 72°39′W. Snow-covered. On the south coast of Alexander Island. Marks the SE side of the entrance to the embayment occupied by the Bach Ice Shelf. Discovered by the USAS 1939–41. Named by the UK for the composer.

Mount Rossman. 79°47′S, 82°48′W. Wedge-shaped. Ice-free. 1,450 m. At the northern end of the Enterprise Hills between the Union and Henderson Glaciers, in the Heritage Range. Named for Rossman W. Smith, ionosphere physicist at Eights Station in 1965 (there were already too many features in Antarctica with the name Smith, but none with Rossman).

Rostand Island. 66°40′S, 140°01′E. 350 yards long. 175 yards SE of Pétrel Island in the Géologie Archipelago. Charted in 1951 by the French, who named it Île Jean Rostand, for Jean Rostand, the biologist.

Rotch Dome. 62°38′S, 60°53′W. Also called Rotch Ice Dome. 1,170 feet. An undulating snow dome just east of Byers Peninsula, on the western side of Livingston Island, in the South Shetlands. Named by the UK in 1958 for William Rotch (1734–1828) and his brother Francis Rotch, New England oil merchants, and pioneers of the southern whale fishery.

Rotch Ice Dome   *see*   **Rotch Dome**

Rote Insel   *see*   **Red Island**

Mount Roth. 84°35′S, 172°22′W. 870 m. 3 miles east of Mount Justman in the NE corner of the Gabbro Hills, near the edge of the Ross Ice Shelf. Discovered during Byrd's 1928–30 expedition and named by Byrd for Sgt. Benjamin Roth.

Roth, Sgt. Benjamin. Assigned by the US Army to go on Byrd's 1928–30 expedition as their representative, and also as a mechanic.

Rothera Point. 67°34′S, 68°08′W. At the east side of the entrance to Ryder Bay, on the SE coast of Adelaide Island. Charted by Charcot in 1908–10. It is SSSI #9. Named by the UK in 1960 for John M. Rothera, FIDS surveyor at Base Y in 1957 and at Base W in 1958.

Rothera Station. 67°34′S, 68°08′W. British scientific station on Adelaide Island, at Rothera Point.

Cape Rothschild   *see*   **Rothschild Island**

Mount Rothschild   *see*   **Rothschild Island**

Rothschild Island. 69°25′S, 72°30′W. Also called E. de Rothschild Island, Île de Rotschild. 17 miles long. Mainly ice-covered. Has several prominent peaks on it. 3 miles west of the north end of Alexander Island, in the northern entrance to Wilkins Sound. Discovered by Charcot from a distance in 1908–10, and thought by him to be a cape. He called it Cap E. de Rothschild, for Baron Édouard-Alphonse de Rothschild (1868–1949), head of the French branch of the Rothschild family, and president of the Rothschild Brothers Bank. This cape became known in English as Cape Rothschild. In 1934–37 the BGLE redefined it (wrongly) as a mountain connected to Alexander Island, and called it Mount Rothschild. The USAS proved it to be an island in 1939–41.

Rotifers. A type of microfauna in Antarctica (*see* **Fauna**).

The *Rotoiti*. NZ frigate on Ocean Station duty between Christchurch and McMurdo Sound in 1963–64. Commander was Lt. Cdr. D.J. Cheney, RNZN.

Mount Rotoiti. 82°48′S, 162°14′E. 2,900 m. 1 mile NE of Mount Pukaki in the Frigate Range. Named by the New Zealanders in 1961–62 for the *Rotoiti*.

Mount Rotolante. 83°36′S, 168°25′E. 2,460 m. 6 miles NW of Mount Fox in the Queen Alexandra Range. Named for Ralph A. Rotolante, meteorologist at McMurdo Station in 1962.

Île de Rotschild *see* **Rothschild Island**

Rotten bergs. Icebergs wasted by the winds, ablation, sublimation, and by the waves. They are usually no longer tabular.

Rotz Glacier. 69°17′S, 65°43′W. 9 miles long. 2 miles wide. Flows west from Wakefield Highland in the central part of the Antarctic Peninsula, into Airy Glacier at a point due south of Mount Timosthenes. Surveyed by the FIDS in Dec. 1958 and Nov. 1960. Named by the UK for Jean Rotz, 16th-century French chartmaker, and hydrographer to Henry VIII of England.

Rouch, Jules. French naval ensign, the third officer on board the *Pourquoi Pas?* during Charcot's 1908–10 expedition. He was also the scientist specializing in meteorology, atmospheric electricity, and physical oceanography. Later he became director of the Oceanographic Institute of Monaco.

Rouch Point. 65°10′S, 64°11′W. Forms the NW end of Petermann Island.

Charted by Charcot in 1908–10, and named by him for Jules Rouch.

Massif Rouen *see* **Rouen Mountains**

Rouen Mountains. 69°13′S, 70°50′W. Also called Massif Rouen. 2,750 m. They extend 30 miles in a NW-SE direction between Mount Bayonne and Mount Cupola in the northern part of Alexander Island. Named by Charcot in 1908–10 for the French city.

Massif Rouge *see* **Mount Rouge**

Mount Rouge. 65°37′S, 63°42′W. Also called Mount Mellanby. Between the Funk and Cadman Glaciers at the head of Beascochea Bay, on the west side of Graham Land. Discovered and named Massif Rouge (red mountain) by Charcot in 1908–10.

Rouge Island *see* **Rongé Island**

Rougier Hill. 85°10′S, 174°30′W. Ice-free. Just east of the LaPrade Valley in the northern part of the Cumulus Hills. Overlooks the south side of McGregor Glacier. Named by the Texas Tech Shackleton Glacier Expedition of 1964–65 for Michael Rougier, staff photographer with *Life* Magazine, who was badly injured while climbing this hill with the expedition.

Rouillon, Gaston. Leader of the French Polar Expedition of 1957–59. He relieved Imbert's expedition, and his expedition was in turn relieved in Jan. 1959 by that of Alfred Faure.

Roullin Point. 65°07′S, 64°01′W. Marks the southern tip of Booth Island in the Wilhelm Archipelago. Charted by Charcot in 1903–5 and named by him for Captain Roullin of the French Navy.

Round, P.E. Crewman on the *Jacob Ruppert*, 1934–35.

Round Bay *see* **Rund Bay**

¹Round Island. 65°54′S, 65°33′W. ½ mile long. 1 mile west of Hummock Island and 7 miles NW of Ferin Head, off the west coast of Graham Land. Discovered and named by the BGLE 1934–37.

²Round Island *see* Davey Point

Round Mountain. 77°41'S, 161°06'E. 2,410 m. Overlooks the north side of Taylor Glacier at the east side of the Inland Forts in Victoria Land. Named for its outline by Scott in 1901–4.

Round Point. 61°56'S, 58°28'W. 12 miles west of False Round Point on the north coast of King George Island in the South Shetlands. Named descriptively by sealers in the area before 1822.

Roundel Dome. 65°38'S, 63°15'W. Mainly snow-covered dome. Has a small circular rock exposure at the summit. 1,770 m. On the east side of the Bruce Plateau, between the heads of the Crane and Flask Glaciers. It is a useful landmark for sledging parties in this area. Named by the UK for its resemblance to a roundel (the RAF markings on a British airplane).

Cape Rouse. 67°45'S, 67°09'E. Ice-covered. 8 miles east of Murray Monolith on the coast of Mac. Robertson Land. Discovered on Feb. 12, 1931, by the BANZARE, and named by Mawson for Edgar J. Rouse of Sydney, who provided photographic equipment for the expedition.

Rouse Islands. 67°35'S, 62°57'E. Also called Rouse Rocks. In the eastern part of Holme Bay, fringing the coast of Mac. Robertson Land just south of Welch Island. Discovered on Feb. 13, 1931, by the BANZARE, and named by Mawson for Edgar J. Rouse (*see* **Cape Rouse**).

Rouse Rocks *see* **Rouse Islands**

Route Point. 60°44'S, 44°49'W. Marks the NW extremity of Laurie Island in the South Orkneys. Discovered and named by Palmer and Powell in Dec. 1821.

Cape Roux. 64°01'S, 62°28'W. Marks the NW extremity of Pasteur Peninsula in the northern part of Brabant Island. Discovered by Charcot in 1903–5 and named by him for Émile Roux (1853–1933), a bacteriologist famous for his work on diphtheria. He was then director of the Pasteur Institute in Paris (1904–33).

Roux Island. 66°54'S, 66°57'W. Also called Charles Roux Island, Isla Panimavida. 2 miles long. ½ mile north of Arrowsmith Peninsula at the west side of the entrance to Lallemand Fjord, off the west coast of Graham Land. Discovered by Charcot in 1908–10, and named by him for Jules Charles-Roux, presumably an acquaintance.

Row Island. 66°31'S, 162°38'E. Also spelled (erroneously) as Rowe Island. Less than a mile across. Just off the SE end of Young Island in the Balleny Islands. In 1839, when John Balleny discovered this group of islands, he found an island 10 miles north of Young Island, and called it Row Island, for J. Row, one of the merchants who had gotten together with the Enderby Brothers to send out the expedition. Later explorers could not find that island, so in 1936 personnel on the *Discovery II* named this little island in order to preserve the name Row.

Rowe, Capt. Commander of the *Grace,* a Plymouth sealer from England, in the South Shetlands during the 1821–22 season.

Rowe, James G. Seaman on the Wilkes Expedition 1838–42. Joined in the USA. Served the cruise.

Rowe, John. Assistant master on the *Adventure* during Cook's voyage of 1772–75. He was killed and eaten by the Maoris on Dec. 17, 1773, in NZ.

Rowe Bluff. 68°01'S, 58°36'W. On the east side of the Antarctic Peninsula.

Rowe Island *see* **Row Island**

Rowe Point. 62°35'S, 60°54'W. 8 miles SSW of Cape Shirreff on the north coast of Livingston Island, it juts out into Barclay Bay, in the South Shetlands. Named by the UK in 1961 for Capt. Rowe.

Rowett Island. 61°17'S, 55°13'W. ½ mile long. Just off Cape Lookout, Elephant Island, in the South Shetlands. Discovered before 1822. Named by Shackleton's *Quest* expedition in 1921–22 for John Q. Rowett, the major patron of the expedition.

Rowland Glacier. 82°46'S, 163°10'E. On the north side of the Frigate Range, flowing east into the Lowery Glacier. Named for Robert W. Rowland, glaciologist at Amundsen-Scott South Pole Station in 1962–63 and again from 1963–64.

Rowles Glacier. 71°17'S, 167°39'E. Over 20 miles long. Flows NW along the east side of the Dunedin Range of the Admiralty Mountains, into Dennistoun Glacier. Named for D.S. Rowles of the NZ Department of Scientific and Industrial Research, and a member of the party at Hallett Station in 1964.

Rowley Corridor. 71°25'S, 67°15'W. A pass in the Batterbee Mountains, running north-south. It extends from Ryder Glacier to Conchie Glacier and separates Mount Ness and Mount Bagshawe from the peaks along the western edge of Palmer Land and George VI Sound. Named by the UK for David N. Rowley, senior pilot with the BAS, 1969–74.

Rowley Massif. 71°35'S, 61°55'W. Between the Haley and Cline Glaciers. It surmounts the north side of the head of Odom Inlet on the east coast of Palmer Land. Named for Peter D. Rowley of the US Geological Survey, a member of the USGS geologic and mapping party to the Lassiter Coast in 1970–71, and leader of the USGS party to the area in 1972–73.

Mount Roy. 72°31'S, 166°15'E. 2,850 m. 6 miles SSW of Mount Aorangi of the Millen Range. Named for Robert R. Roy, cook at Hallett Station in 1957.

Royal Order of Winter Knights. A society of men who had wintered-over in Antarctica during Operation Deep Freeze I (1956) and Operation Deep Freeze II (1957). 484 military men and scientists received a handsome scroll (designed by the Walt Disney Studios) signed by Admiral Dufek and Cdr. Herbert W. Whitney, USN, senior members of the wintering-over party, and themselves "knights."

Royal Society Expedition. 1901–4. Also called the *Discovery* Expedition, and the British National Antarctic Expedition 1901–4. This was Scott's first expedition, and was the brainchild of Sir Clements Markham, president of the Royal Geographical Society in London. He selected Scott to lead Great Britain's big expedition in the face of several from other countries. The *Discovery* left England on Aug. 6, 1901, sponsored by the Royal Society and the Royal Geographical Society. Seaman Charles Bonner fell to his death in New Zealand before they hit the cold, and the first icebergs were encountered at 65°30'S on Jan. 2, 1902. On Jan. 3, 1902, they passed the Antarctic Circle, and at 10:30 p.m., on Jan. 8, 1902, they saw Antarctica. On Jan. 9, 1902, they landed at Cape Adare, and on Jan. 10, 1902, left Victoria Land going south. By Jan. 23, 1902, the *Discovery* was at the Ross Ice Barrier. They discovered the Edward VII Peninsula (calling it King Edward VII Land), and on Feb. 3, 1902, anchored in the Bay of Whales. On Feb. 4, 1902, Lt. Armitage and 4 men went sledging and Scott went up in his balloon. Shackleton went up next, and the sledging party returned, having set a new southing record of 79°03'S. They set up winter quarters on Hut Point Peninsula on McMurdo Sound (which Scott had redefined on first pulling in there on Jan. 21, 1902), and the only death on the expedition proper occurred on March 11, 1902 (*see* **Vince, George**). The *South Polar Times* was begun during the 1902 winter-over. On Sept. 17, 1902, Scott, Barne, and Shackleton set out to lay a depot for their attack on the South Pole. Two days later they were back. On Sept. 27, 1902, they set out again, Barne replaced by Feather, and they set up Depot A, at 10 a.m., Nov. 2, 1902. Scott, Wilson, and Shackleton, the Polar party, set out, the next day catching up with the support party which had set out earlier. On Nov. 13, 1902, half the support party turned back as arranged, and on Nov. 15, 1902, the other half turned back. The three polar trekkers pushed on alone. On Dec. 9, 1902, the first dog died. All the animals were suffering, and so were the 3 men. At

80° 30' S they laid Depot B. By Dec. 20, 1902, only 14 out of the 19 dogs were alive. On Dec. 27, 1902, they discovered Mount Markham, and on Dec. 30, 1902, they reached 82° 16' 33" S, a new southing record. They then returned under dreadful circumstances. By Jan. 13, 1903, they got back to Depot B. All of them had scurvy and Shackleton was in a very bad way. On Jan. 28, 1903, they got to Depot A, and then the last leg was a nightmare. On Feb. 3, 1903, they got back to base. Meanwhile, Armitage had led a sledge party into Victoria Land via the Ferrar Glacier. They set out on Nov. 29, 1902, and on Jan. 5, 1903, Armitage became the first man to walk on the Polar Ice Cap, or the Polar Plateau as it is better known. By Jan. 19, 1903, they were back at base. On Jan. 23, 1903, the *Morning*, the expedition's relief ship, arrived (Scott had deliberately frozen-in the *Discovery*, and it was to remain thus until 1904). On March 2, 1903, the *Morning* left. Mulock had replaced the protesting Shackleton, and all but 2 of the merchant navy men were sent home. Scott then settled in for another winter over because he could not get his ship out of the ice. On Sept. 7, 1903, Wilson, Royds, and 4 others set out to collect emperor penguin eggs from Cape Crozier. They were unsuccessful. On Oct. 26, 1903, Scott led 9 men to the Polar Plateau in the footsteps of Armitage. Scott led what was the first sledging expedition on the Polar Plateau (as opposed to the ice shelf below). Ferrar took 2 men and explored the Ferrar Glacier valley, and on the Polar Plateau Scott split up the 6 remaining men into 2 teams: Scott, Feather, and Evans and Skelton, Handsley, and Lashly. On Nov. 22, 1903, Skelton, Handsley, and Feather had to return to base. The 3 remaining men turned back on Nov. 30, 1903, in grossly uncomfortable circumstances. At one point, Scott, Evans, and the sledge fell into a crevasse. Lashly alone supported them until they managed to struggle out. They got back to base on Dec. 24, 1903. On Jan. 5, 1904, the *Morning* returned, this time with the

Terra Nova, with instructions to abandon the *Discovery* if it could not be broken free of the ice. On Feb. 16, 1904, miraculously, the *Discovery* was freed. Altogether the Royal Society Expedition discovered 900 miles of land and 150 miles of ice shelf, and explored 200 miles of land, and they ascertained that no sea passage led through the Ross Ice Barrier (later named the Ross Ice Shelf). Scott, after trudging over 300 miles directly across the Ross Ice Shelf, concluded that dogs were a bad investment and that manhauling the sledges was the best idea. They also discovered and explored a bit of the Polar Plateau, and concluded that the Pole was on the plateau, high above sea level. This was the first real land expedition in the Antarctic. Aside from those men mentioned above, these also went on the *Discovery*: Koettlitz, Hodgson, Brett, Bernacchi, Allan, Blissett, Charles Clarke, Crean, Cross, Croucher, Dell, Dailey, Dellbridge, Charles Ford, Heald, Joyce, Kennar, Hare, Pilbeam, Plumley, Gilbert Scott (no relation to the leader), Quartley, Smythe, Weller, Whitfield, Frank Wild, and Thomas S. Williamson.

Royal Society Range. 78° 10' S, 162° 40' E. 4,025 m. Along the western shore of McMurdo Sound between the Koettlitz, Skelton, and Ferrar Glaciers. Scott was the first to explore this majestic-looking range in 1903, and named it for the Royal Society, one of the major sponsors of the expedition. Scott named many of the individual peaks for members of his expedition.

Mount Royalist. 71° 47' S, 168° 30' E. 3,640 m. 2 miles west of Mount Adam in the Admiralty Mountains of Victoria Land. Named by the New Zealanders in 1957–58 for its regal appearance, and also for the NZ cruiser, the *Royalist*, in continuation of the ship theme in the area.

Cape Royds. 77° 33' S, 166° 09' E. A dark rock cape forming the western extremity of Ross Island. It faces on McMurdo Sound. Discovered by Scott in 1902 and named by him for Charles

Royds. Shackleton built his hut here in 1908, as base for his 1907–9 expedition. It is SSSI #1.

Royds, Charles. 1876–1931. Charles W. Rawson Royds. 1st lieutenant in the Royal Navy. Meteorologist on the Royal Society Expedition of 1901–4. He rose to admiral, and later became commissioner of the Metropolitan Police in London.

Røysane Rocks. 72°19′S, 23°17′E. 4 miles SE of Mount Nils Larsen in the Sør Rondane Mountains. Name means "the pile of stones" in Norwegian.

Royster, C.P. Crewman on the *Bear of Oakland*, 1933–35.

Rozier Glacier. 64°45′S, 62°13′W. Flows into Wilhelmina Bay north of Sophie Cliff, on the west coast of Graham Land. Charted by de Gerlache in 1897–99. Named by the UK in 1960 for Jean-François Pilâtre de Rozier (1756–1785), French pioneer balloonist.

Rozo, M. Argentine cook on the *Français* during Charcot's 1903–5 expedition. He joined the cruise at Buenos Aires in Dec. 1903, and wore a pair of old slippers during the winter-over of 1904.

Rozo Point. 65°03′S, 64°03′W. Marks the NW end of Cholet Island, which lies just north of the NW part of Booth Island in the Wilhelm Archipelago. Discovered by Charcot in 1903–5, and named by him for M. Rozo.

Rubeli Bluff. 70°26′S, 72°27′E. At the north end of the Reinbolt Hills, at the eastern edge of the Ross Ice Shelf. A survey station was established here during the ANARE tellurometer traverse from the Larsemann Hills in 1968. Named by the Australians for M.N. Rubeli, surveyor at Mawson Station, who was in charge of the traverse.

Rubey Glacier. 75°11′S, 137°07′W. Heavily crevassed. Flows north to coalesce with the west side of the Hull Glacier eastward of Mount Giles, near the coast of Marie Byrd Land. Named for Capt. Ervin B. Rubey, USN, commander

of Antarctic Support Activities at McMurdo Station, 1969–70.

Mount Rubin. 73°25′S, 65°40′E. A large, gently-domed mountain with a long tail of moraine trending east. 16 miles WNW of the Cumpston Massif in the Prince Charles Mountains, just to the south of the Fisher Glacier. Named by the Australians for US meteorologist Morton J. Rubin, US exchange scientist to Mirnyy Station in 1958. Later, 1973–74, he was a member of the US Advisory Committee on Antarctic Names.

Mount Rubin de la Borbolla. 75°02′S, 135°03′W. 1,090 m. Ice-covered. In the SE extremity of the McDonald Heights. It overlooks Johnson Glacier from the west. In Marie Byrd Land. Named for George S. Rubin de la Borbolla, meteorologist at Plateau Station, 1968.

Rubner Peak. 66°44′S, 65°51′W. The highest point on the sharp ridge separating the McCance and Widdowson Glaciers, just south of Darbel Bay on the west coast of Graham Land. Named by the UK in 1960 for Max Rubner (1854–1932), German physiologist specializing in calorie requirements.

Mount Rücker. 78°11′S, 162°32′E. 3,815 m. Just south of Johns Hopkins Ridge in the Royal Society Range of Victoria Land. Discovered by members of Scott's 1901–4 Royal Society Expedition, and named by Scott for Sir Arthur Rücker, honorary secretary of the Royal Society.

Rucker, Joseph T. Photographer on the shore party of Byrd's 1928–30 expedition. He had been sent by *Paramount News*.

Rücker Ridge. 78°12′S, 162°50′E. A high spur descending east from Mount Rücker in the Royal Society Range of Victoria Land. Forms the divide between the Radian and Walcott Glaciers. Named by the New Zealanders in 1960–61 in association with the mountain.

Rucker Spur. 77°31′S, 146°30′W. Between Alexander Peak and Mount

Ronne, on the east side of the Haines Mountains of Marie Byrd Land. Named for Joseph T. Rucker.

Rude Spur. 77°27'S, 160°49'E. 2 miles NW of Mount Circe. Descends from the Polar Plateau of Victoria Land toward Balham Lake and Balham Valley. Named for Jeffrey D. Rude (*see* **Deaths, 1975**).

Rudmose Brown Peak. 66°22'S, 51°04' E. 7 miles south of the coast and 8 miles SW of Mount Hurley in East Antarctica. Discovered in Jan. 1930 by the BANZARE, and named by Mawson for Rudmose Brown.

Rudmose Rocks. 60°42'S, 44°35'W. Almost ⅓ mile NNW of Cape Geddes, off the north coast of Laurie Island in the South Orkneys. Charted in 1903 by Bruce, who named them the following year for Rudmose Brown.

¹Rudolph Glacier. 64°54'S, 62°26'W. Flows into Andvord Bay south of Moser Glacier, on the west coast of Graham Land. Charted by de Gerlache in 1897–99. Named by the UK in 1960 for Paul Rudolph, German mathematical optician who developed the first anastigmatic camera lens in 1889.

²Rudolph Glacier. 72°32'S, 167°53'E. Flows into Trafalgar Glacier opposite the mouth of Hearfield Glacier in the Victory Mountains of Victoria Land. Named for Emanuel D. Rudolph, project leader for the study of lichens in the area of Hallett Station, 1961–62, 1962–63, and 1963–64.

Rudolphy Point. 64°53'S, 63°07'W. On the west coast of Graham Land.

Mount Ruegg. 71°51'S, 170°11'E. 1,870 m. The culminating peak on the divide between DeAngelo Glacier and Moubray Glacier in the Admiralty Mountains of Victoria Land. Named by NZ for Capt. H. Ruegg, nautical adviser to the Marine Department of New Zealand. He visited the Ross Sea area in 1956.

Rugate Ridge. 65°01'S, 61°56'W. Between the Green and Evans Glaciers, on the east side of Graham Land. Named by the UK for its rugate quality (the word means "ridgy").

Rugg Peak. 66°19'S, 65°23'W. At the east side of the Widmark Ice Piedmont, south of Crookes Peak, on the west coast of Graham Land. Named by the UK in 1959 for Andrew Rugg-Gunn, pioneer in the design of snow-goggles.

Rugged Harbor *see* **New Plymouth**

Rugged Island. 62°38'S, 61°15'W. Also called Lloyds Island. 3 miles long and 1 mile wide. West of Livingston Island, it is the smallest of the major islands in the South Shetlands. It has an elevation of 650 feet. It was discovered on Jan. 22, 1820, by the crew of the *Hersilia*, and named by them as Ragged Island, for its shape. The name later became corrupted.

Rugged Peaks *see* **Ragged Peaks**

Rugged Rocks. 62°37'S, 59°48'W. Also called Rocas Escarpadas, Rocas Rugosas. At the west side of the southern entrance to McFarlane Strait, just north of Renier Point, Livingston Island, in the South Shetlands. Mapped by Powell in 1822. Recharted in 1935 by personnel on the *Discovery II,* and named descriptively by them.

Rocas Rugosas *see* **Rugged Rocks**

Mount Ruhnke. 72°05'S, 3°38'E. 2,535 m. In the NW part of Festninga Mountain, in the Mühlig-Hofmann Mountains of Queen Maud Land. A feature in this area was named Ruhnke-Berg by Ritscher in 1938–39 for Herbert Ruhnke. If this mountain is not Ruhnke-Berg, it is pretty close to that feature.

Ruhnke, Herbert. Radio operator on the *Passat*, one of the flying boats used by Ritscher during the German New Schwabenland Expedition of 1938–39.

Ruhnke-Berg *see* **Mount Ruhnke**

Isla Ruiz *see* **Patella Island**

Mount Ruker. 73°40'S, 64°30'E. A large, dark mountain just SW of Mount Rubin in the southern part of the Prince Charles Mountains. Named by the Australians for R.A. Ruker, geologist at Mawson Station, 1960.

Mount Rukhin. 71°35'S, 15°07'E. 1,740 m. 9 miles SW of Ekho Mountain in the Lomonosov Mountains of Queen Maud Land. Named by the USSR in 1963 for L.B. Rukhin (d. 1959), professor at Leningrad State University.

Rullman Peak. 79°13'S, 84°32'W. 1,910 m. Just south of Grimes Glacier in the Anderson Massif of the Heritage Range. Named for Chief Equipment Operator Gerald D. Rullman, USN, direct supervisor of the crew which first pierced the Ross Ice Shelf at 160 feet in 1965–66, near the Dailey Islands.

Rumania. Ratified as the 17th signatory of the Antarctic Treaty on Sept. 15, 1971.

Rumbler Rock. 64°47'S, 64°13'W. 3½ miles west of Bonaparte Point, off the SW coast of Anvers Island. Named by the UK for the rumble of the heavy seas breaking over this rock. The noise can be heard for a long way, and warns vessels of the danger it poses.

Rumdoodle Air Strip. Mawson Station's air strip. It is dominated by Rumdoodle Peak, which took its name from the air strip. The name came about in 1960 from the book *The Ascent of Rumdoodle* by W.E. Bowman. This novel was favorite reading at Mawson Station and the Rumdoodle of the title was a mountain.

Rumdoodle Peak. 67°46'S, 62°50'E. 1 mile SW of Painted Peak in the North Masson Range of Mac. Robertson Land. Photographed by the LCE 1936–37. Named by the Australians in association with Rumdoodle Air Strip.

Mount Rummage. 80°29'S, 156°12'E. 1,510 m. Conical. Bare rock. At the west side of Ramseier Glacier. It is the most westerly mountain along the north wall of Byrd Glacier. Named for Chief Quartermaster Laurence A. Rummage, USN, who took part in Christchurch transport and schedule operations for Operation Deep Freeze 65.

Rumpa Island. 69°08'S, 39°26'E. In the eastern part of Lützow-Holm Bay. 5

miles NW of Langhovde-kita Point. Photographed by the LCE 1936–37. Name means "the rump" in Norwegian.

Run. A polite term used in the 19th century meaning "desert from a ship."

Runaway Hills. 73°19'S, 163°33'E. Form the NW extremity of Arrowhead Range in the Southern Cross Mountains of Victoria Land. Named by the Southern Party of the NZGSAE 1966–67, because both of their motor toboggans went out of control going downhill here.

Runaway Island. 68°12'S, 67°07'W. Almost ¾ mile west of the western tip of Neny Island and almost ¼ mile NW of Surf Rock, in Marguerite Bay off the west coast of Graham Land. Charted in 1936 by the BGLE. In 1947 the FIDS surveyed it, and named it because a runaway dog team left this island and returned to base.

Runciman Rock. 65°15'S, 64°17'W. Marked by breakers. 175 yards east of Black Island, at the SE approach to Black Island Channel in the Argentine Islands. Charted in 1935 by the BGLE, and named by Rymill for Philip Runciman, chairman of the Board of Directors of Whites Southampton Yachtbuilding and Engineering Co., Ltd., where the *Penola* was refitted before sailing to the Antarctic in 1934.

Runcorn Glacier. 72°06'S, 62°34'W. On the east side of Palmer Land.

Isla Runcumilla *see* **Weertman Island**

Rund Bay. 67°02'S, 57°15'E. Indentation into the southern shore of Edward VIII Bay, immediately east of Kvarsnes Foreland. Photographed by the LCE 1936–37. Named Rundvika (round bay) by the Norwegians.

Rundle Peaks. 80°44'S, 157°12'E. Mainly ice-covered. At the south side of Byrd Glacier, just east of Sefton Glacier. Named for Arthur S. Rundle, who studied the Ross Ice Shelf in 1961–62 and 1962–63.

Rundneset *see* **Green Point**

Rundöy *see* **Trevillian Island**

Rundvåg Bay. 69°50'S, 39°04'E. The southern part is occupied by a glacier tongue. This rounded embayment indents the SE shore of Lützow-Holm Bay just west of the Rundvågs Hills. Photographed by the LCE 1936–37. Named Rundvåg (round bay) by the Norwegians.

Rundvågs Head. 69°53'S, 39°E. A rock headland. 160 m. At the SW edge of Rundvåg Bay, on the SE coast of Lützow-Holm Bay. Photographed by the LCE 1936–37 and named Rundvågshetta (the round bay cape) by the Norwegians for its nearness to Rundvåg Bay.

Rundvågs Hills. 69°50'S, 39°09'E. Bare rock hills. Just east of Rundvåg Bay on the SE shore of Lützow-Holm Bay. Photographed by the LCE 1936–37 and named Rundvågskollane (the round bay hills) by the Norwegians for their nearness to Rundvåg Bay.

Rundvågshetta *see* **Rundvågs Head**

Rundvågskollane *see* **Rundvågs Hills**

Rundvika *see* **Rund Bay**

Runnelstone Rock. 65°47'S, 65°20'W. At the SW end of the Grandidier Channel. 3 miles NW of Larrouy Island. 16 miles WSW of Cape García, Graham Land. Discovered by the BGLE 1934–37, and named by Rymill.

Runyon Rock. 76°56'S, 116°33'W. On the north side of Boyd Ridge, in the Crary Mountains of Marie Byrd Land. Named for William E. Runyon, USN, construction electrician at Amundsen-Scott South Pole Station, 1969 and 1974.

Ruotolo Peak. 86°04'S, 148°06'W. 2,490 m. Surmounts the north side of Griffith Glacier, just west of the California Plateau and the Watson Escarpment. Named for Lt. Cdr. Anthony P. Ruotolo, VX-6 aircraft pilot in 1965–66 and 1966–67.

Ruppert Coast. 75°45'S, 141°W. Also called Jacob Ruppert Coast. That portion of the coast of Marie Byrd Land behind the Nickerson Ice Shelf, between Brennan Point and Cape Burks. Named by Byrd for Col. Jacob Ruppert of New York, a supporter of Byrd's 1933–35 expedition, which made the first aerial reconnaissance along this coast. (*See also* **The Jacob Ruppert.**)

Mount Rusanov. 71°32'S, 19°38'E. Isolated. North of the Russkiye Mountains. 35 miles NE of Zhelannaya Mountain, in Queen Maud Land. Named by the USSR in 1959 for geologist and polar explorer V.A. Rusanov.

Ruser, Hans. Captain of the *Gauss*, 1901–3.

Ruseski, Peter P. Lt., USN. Medical officer and military leader of Byrd Station in 1958. He took over from Brian Dalton on Dec. 8, 1957.

Ruseski Buttress. 85°29'S, 124°23'W. A projecting buttress rock or spur. Forms the southern portal to Perkins Canyon on the north side of the Wisconsin Range of the Horlick Mountains. Named for Lt. Peter P. Ruseski.

Rush Glacier. 64°23'S, 62°37'W. 4 miles long. In the southern part of Brabant Island. Flows west from the Solvay Mountains into Dallmann Bay between Fleming and Humann Points. Named by the UK for Benjamin Rush (1745–1813), one of the signatories of the Declaration of Independence in 1776.

Russel, Elias. Ship's cook on the *Flying Fish* during the Wilkes Expedition 1838–42. Joined in the USA. Run at Callao.

Russel, Morris. Landsman on the Wilkes Expedition 1838–42. Joined in the USA. Run at Rio.

Cape Russell. 74°54'S, 163°54'E. A rock cape in Terra Nova Bay, on the coast of Victoria Land. Forms the southern extremity of the Northern Foothills. Named for Lt. Cdr. R.E. Russell, USN, officer-in-charge of the helicopter unit on the *Glacier* in 1958–59.

Mount Russell. 86°17'S, 149°08'W. Also called Mount Richard Russell. 2,280 m. On the east flank of the Robert Scott

Glacier, just south of the mouth of Howe Glacier, in the Queen Maud Mountains. Discovered in Dec. 1934 by Quin Blackburn's party during Byrd's 1933–35 expedition, and named by Byrd for Richard S. Russell, one of the expedition's supporters, and his son, Richard S. Russell, Jr., one of the shore party on the expedition.

Russell, Richard S., Jr. One of the shore party of Byrd's 1933–35 expedition. A socialite, he was the son of one of the expedition's patrons (*see* **Mount Russell**).

Russell Bay. 73°27′S, 123°54′W. In the SW part of the Amundsen Sea, extending along the northern sides of Siple Island, the Getz Ice Shelf, and Carney Island, from Pranke Island to Cape Gates. Named for Adm. James S. Russell, USN, vice chief of Naval Operations during the period after the IGY (1957–58).

Russell Bluff. 82°21′S, 161°06′E. Ice-free. At the east side of the mouth of Errant Glacier, at the junction of that glacier with the Nimrod Glacier. Named for John Russell, USARP traverse specialist at McMurdo Base in 1959.

Russell East Glacier. 63°44′S, 58°20′ W. 6 miles long. 3 miles wide. At the north end of the Detroit Plateau. It flows from Mount Canicula eastward into the Prince Gustav Channel on the south side of Trinity Peninsula. This glacier, which used to be called East Russell Glacier, together with Russell West Glacier, which used to be called West Russell Glacier, and which flows westward into Bone Bay on the north side of Trinity Peninsula, form a through glacier across the northern part of the Antarctic Peninsula. Surveyed in 1946 by the FIDS. Named by the UK for V.I. Russell, surveyor and FIDS leader at Base D in 1946.

Russell Nunatak. 67°47′S, 63°19′E. Solitary. Rounded. 10 miles east of the Masson Range and 7 miles SE of Mount Henderson. Discovered in Dec. 1954 by an ANARE party led by Robert Dovers. Named by the Australians for John Russell, engineer at Mawson Station, 1954.

Mount Russell Owen *see* **Owen Peak**

Russell Peak *see* **Brown Peak**

Russell West Glacier. 63°40′S, 58°50′ W. Also called West Russell Glacier. 11 miles long. 4 miles wide. Immediately north of the Detroit Plateau. Flows from Mount Canicula westward into Bone Bay on the north side of the Trinity Peninsula. For its relationship with Russell East Glacier, see that entry. Surveyed in 1946 by the FIDS. Named by the UK for V.I. Russell (*see* **Russell East Glacier**).

Russet Pikes. 67°49′S, 67°08′W. Just east of the mouth of Gaul Cove on Horseshoe Island. Surveyed by the FIDS in 1955–57. Named descriptively by the UK for the russet color of the slopes of these peaks, which are too steep to keep a snow cover for very long.

Russia *see* **USSR**

Russian Gap. 69°11′S, 71°13′W. Extends in a north-south direction between the Havre Mountains and the Rouen Mountains in the northern part of Alexander Island. This gap was probably sketched by the von Bellingshausen expedition of 1819–21. At least, what looks as if it could be this gap appears on a Russian sketch done at the time. Named by the UK for the Russians who discovered the general area in 1821.

Russkaya Station. 74°43′S, 137°09′W. USSR station on Cape Burks, Marie Byrd Land.

Russkiye Mountains. 72°10′S, 18°E. A widely scattered group of mountains and nunataks between the Hoel Mountains and the Sør Rondane Mountains in Queen Maud Land. Named by the USSR in 1959 as Gory Russkiye (Russian Mountains).

Rust Bluff. 82°56′S, 157°42′E. On the east side of the Miller Range. Overlooks Marsh Glacier 5 miles south of Corner Nunatak. Named for Izak C. Rust, professor of geology at the University of Port Elizabeth in South Africa. He was an international exchange scientist with the Ohio State University Geological Expedition of 1969–70, and with John Gunner, collected geological samples at this bluff.

Rustad, Ditlef. Biologist on the *Norvegia* in 1927–28.

Cape Rusty *see* **Cape Howard**

Rusty Bluff. 60°44′S, 45°37′W. Prominent cliffs rising to a rounded summit of 225 m. On the west side of Paal Harbor, on Signy Island in the South Orkneys. Surveyed in 1947 by the FIDS, who named it for the color of the bluff, and for a rusty iron post found on the summit.

Rutford Glacier *see* **Rutford Ice Stream**

Rutford Ice Stream. 79°S, 81°W. 180 miles long. Over 15 miles wide. Flows southeastward between the Ellsworth Mountains and the Fletcher Ice Rise into the SW part of the Ronne Ice Shelf. Formerly called the Rutford Glacier, for Bob H. Rutford, leader of the University of Minnesota Ellsworth Mountains Party of 1963–64. He has been on several other expeditions to Antarctica, and from 1975–77 was director of the Division of Polar Programs at the NSF. The glacier was redefined as an ice stream.

Rutgers Glacier. 78°14′S, 161°55′E. Flows SW from Johns Hopkins Ridge and Mount Rücker to enter the Skelton Glacier in the Royal Society Range. Named for Rutgers University in New Jersey, which has sent researchers to Antarctica. This is in continuation of the academic theme given to place names in this area.

Cape Ruth *see* **Ruth Ridge**

Mount Ruth. 86°18′S, 151°45′W. 2,170 m. Ridge-shaped. 3 miles west of Mount Gardiner, at the SE side of the lower reaches of the Bartlett Glacier in the Queen Maud Mountains. Discovered by Quin Blackburn's party in Dec. 1934 during Byrd's 1933–35 expedition, and named by Byrd as Mount Ruth Black for the late wife of Richard B. Black (q.v.).

Later, the name was abbreviated to Mount Black, and then to Mount Ruth.

Mount Ruth Black *see* **Mount Ruth**

Ruth Bugge Islands *see* **Bugge Islands**

Mount Ruth Gade. 85°37′S, 164°40′ W. 3,515 m. 3 miles NE of Mount Wedel-Jarlsberg in the Quarles Range of the Queen Maud Mountains. Between Cooper Glacier and Isaiah Bowman Glacier, next to Mount Alice Gade. Amundsen called it The Beehive when he discovered it on Nov. 17, 1911, and he later renamed it for one of the daughters of F. Herman Gade (*see also* **Mount Alice Gade**).

Ruth Ridge. 64°39′S, 60°48′W. A black, rocky ridge, 1½ miles long, in a north-south direction. It terminates at its southern end in a small peak. Forms the southern end of the Detroit Plateau and marks a change in the direction of the plateau escarpment along the east coast of Graham Land where it turns west to form the northern wall of Drygalski Glacier. In 1901–4 Nordenskjöld named a feature at the north side of Drygalski Glacier as Cape Ruth, for his sister. In 1947 the FIDS determined it to be a ridge, and redefined it.

Mount Ruth Siple *see* **Mount Siple**

Ruthven Bluff. 82°34′S, 42°54′W. 1 mile south of Sosa Bluff in the Schneider Hills portion of the Argentina Range of the Pensacola Mountains. Named for Richard W. Ruthven, US Geological Survey surveyor who visited this bluff in 1965–66.

Rutkowski Glacier. 85°11′S, 166°21′E. Flows from the northern part of the Dominion Range ice-cap eastward of Mount Mills. It flows northeastward into the Meyer Desert where it terminates without reaching Beardmore Glacier. Named for Richard L. Rutkowski, meteorologist at Amundsen-Scott South Pole Station in 1962.

Ruvungane Peaks. 72°54′S, 3°28′W. Just north of Ryvingen Peak in the southern part of the Borg Massif in Queen Maud Land. Named by the Norwegians.

Isla Ruy *see* **Guido Island**

Ryan, Capt. Commander of the *Instituto de Pesca I* in 1916.

Ryan, Michael. 1st class boy on the Wilkes Expedition 1838–42. Joined at Rio. Run at Sydney.

Ryan Peak. 67°52'S, 67°12'W. 1 mile east of Penitent Peak on Horseshoe Island. Surveyed by the FIDS in 1955–57. Named by the UK for Francis B. Ryan of the FIDS, meteorologist at Base Y in 1956, who broke a leg while climbing this mountain.

Rydberg Peninsula. 73°10'S, 79°45'W. 30 miles long. Ice-covered. Between Fladerer Bay and Carroll Inlet in Ellsworth Land. Named for Capt. Sven Rydberg, commander of the *Eltanin* from Feb. 1962 to June 1963.

Rydelek Icefalls. 74°28'S, 113°50'W. On Martin Peninsula on the coast of Marie Byrd Land.

Mount Ryder. 66°57'S, 52°15'E. Between Harvey Nunataks and Mount Keyser in the eastern part of the Tula Mountains of Enderby Land. Named by the Australians for B.P. Ryder, radio officer at Mawson Station in 1961.

Ryder, Lisle C.D. Second mate on the *Penola* during the BGLE 1934–37.

Ryder, Robert E.D. Known as Red Ryder. Captain, RN. As a lieutenant he was commander of the *Penola* during the BGLE 1934–37.

Ryder Bay. 67°34'S, 68°20'W. 6 miles wide at its mouth. Indents for 4 miles. 5 miles east of Mount Gaudry on the SE coast of Adelaide Island. The Léonie Islands lie across the mouth of this bay. Discovered and surveyed in 1909 by Charcot. Resurveyed in 1936 by the BGLE, and again in 1948 by the FIDS. Named by the UK for Lisle Ryder.

Ryder Glacier. 71°07'S, 67°20'W. Gently sloping. 13 miles long. 13 miles wide. Flows west from the Dyer Plateau of Palmer Land into the George VI Sound to the south of Gurney Point. Surveyed by the BGLE in 1936. Named by the UK in 1954 for Robert E.D. Ryder.

Rye, John. Seaman on the Wilkes Expedition 1838–42. Joined in the USA. Served the cruise.

Ryge, J.C. Danish captain of the *Oluf Sven* during the FIDASE 1955–57.

Ryge Rocks. 63°40'S, 60°W. East of the Oluf Rocks, in the Palmer Archipelago. Named by the UK in 1960 for J.C. Ryge. The FIDASE photographed these rocks.

¹Cape Rymill *see* **Cape Reichelderfer**

²Cape Rymill. 69°30'S, 62°25'W. A steep, metamorphic rock cliff opposite the central part of Hearst Island. It juts out from the ice-cap along the eastern coast of Palmer Land. Named in 1940 by members of East Base during the USAS, for John Rymill.

Mount Rymill. 73°03'S, 65°50'E. Has an undulating surface marked by an extensive formation of stone polygons. 6 miles west of Mount Stinear in the Prince Charles Mountains. Named by the Australians for John Rymill.

Rymill, John. b. 1905. d. 1968, after a road accident in South Australia, where he lived in a town called Penola. John Riddoch Rymill. Australian explorer. He planned and led the British Graham Land Expedition (perhaps better known by its initials—the BGLE) from 1934–37. He discovered that the Antarctic Peninsula (or Palmer Peninsula as it was known then) was in fact part of the mainland. A couple of years before he had been in the Arctic with Gino Watkins, on the British Arctic Air Route Expedition.

Rymill Bay. 68°24'S, 67°05'W. 9 miles wide at its mouth. Indents for 5 miles. It is entered between Red Rock Ridge and the Bertrand Ice Piedmont on the west coast of Graham Land. Surveyed in 1936 by the BGLE, and again in 1948 by the FIDS. Named by the BGLE for John Rymill.

Rymill's Col *see* **Safety Col**

Ryrie Rock. 67°03'S, 61°27'E. Also called Ryrieskjeret. Isolated. 11 miles NE of Kidson Island and 26 miles NE of Byrd Head. Discovered in Feb. 1931 by the BANZARE, and named by Mawson for the Australian high commissioner in London at the time.

Ryrieskjeret *see* **Ryrie Rock**

Ryswyck Island *see* **Fournier Island**

Ryswyck Point. 64°34'S, 62°50'W. Marks the eastern extremity of Anvers Island. Discovered by de Gerlache in 1897–99, and named by him as Cap. V. Ryswick. This became Van Ryswycke Point, and finally Ryswyck Point.

Cape Ryugu. 67°58'S, 44°02'E. 7 miles NE of Rakuda Rock on the coast of Queen Maud Land. Named by the Japanese as Ryugu-misaki (cape of the dragon's palace).

Ryvingen Base. Near Sanae Station, on the Queen Maud Land coast. It was the base of the Trans-Globe Expedition in 1980–81. It consisted of two huts made of two-layer cardboard which could fit easily into the airplane.

Ryvingen Mountain *see* **Ryvingen Peak**

Ryvingen Peak. 72°55'S, 3°29'W. Also called Ryvingen Mountain. 3 miles WSW of Bråpiggen Peak, on the south side of the Borg Massif of Queen Maud Land. Named by the Norwegians.

Mount S. Hassel *see* **Mount Hassel**

Saavedra Rock. 63°19'S, 57°56'W. At the SW corner of González Anchorage in the Duroch Islands. Named by the Chilean Antarctic Expedition of 1950–51 for Lt. Col. Eduardo Saavedra, chief Army delegate on the *Lautaro* during that expedition.

Cape Sabine *see* **Sabine Glacier**

Mount Sabine. 71°55'S, 169°33'E. 3,720 m. Mostly snow-free. Between the heads of Murray Glacier and Burnette Glacier in the Admiralty Mountains. Discovered on Jan. 5, 1841, by Ross, who

named it for Lt. Col. Edward Sabine, foreign secretary of the Royal Society and a supporter of the expedition.

Sabine Glacier. 63°55'S, 59°47'W. Flows into the sea between Wennersgaard Point and Cape Kater, on the NW coast of Graham Land. Foster, in 1829, named a cape in this area as Cape Sabine, for Sir Edward Sabine (1788–1883), British astronomer and a member of the committee which planned the *Chanticleer* expedition of 1828–31. Modern explorers could not find this cape, so they named this feature thus, in order to preserve the naming in this area.

Sable Pinnacles *see* **Noire Rock**

Saborido, Lorenzo. Captain of the *Austral*, 1905–6.

The *Sabrina*. A 47-ton Cowes cutter out of London, commanded by Capt. Freeman during Balleny's 1838–39 expedition. Lost in a gale on March 24, 1839, in 95°E, leaving Balleny alone with the *Eliza Scott* and 178 seal skins.

Sabrina Coast. 67°20'S, 119°E. Also called Sabrina Land. Between Cape Waldron in 115°33'E and Cape Southard in 122°05'E, or between the Budd Coast and the Banzare Coast on the coast of Wilkes Land. Discovered by Balleny on March 2, 1839, and named by him for the *Sabrina*. Mawson was the first to explore it, during the BANZARE 1929–31.

Sabrina Island. 66°56'S, 163°18'E. Off Sturge Island, and about 2 miles south of Buckle Island, in the Balleny Islands. Originally named Sabrina Islet, for the *Sabrina*, but later redefined slightly. It is an SPA because of its flora and fauna.

Sabrina Land *see* **Sabrina Coast**

Sac, John. Seaman on the Wilkes Expedition 1838–42. Joined in the USA. Discharged at Oahu, Oct. 31, 1840.

Sachse, Walter. German navigation officer on the *Valdivia*, 1898.

Sack Island. 66°26'S, 110°25'E. Also called Back Rock, Sack Rock. Almost ½ mile long. 350 yards east of the south end of Holl Island in the Windmill Islands.

Named for Norman F. Sack, photographer's mate on Operation Highjump, 1946–47, and Operation Windmill, 1947–48.

Sack Rock *see* **Sack Island**

Saddle Island. 60°38'S, 44°50'W. Also called Île Montura. Nearly 2 miles long. Has twin summits. 5½ miles north of the west end of Laurie Island in the South Orkneys, just to the east of Powell Island. Discovered in 1823 by Weddell, and named by him for its shape.

Saddle Peak. 70°40'S, 164°39'E. Twin peaks of 960 m. They have a saddle between them. 3 miles NW of Mount Kostka in the western part of the Anare Mountains. Named by the ANARE in 1962.

Saddleback Ridge. 62°35'S, 59°56'W. Just to the SW of Ephraim Bluff on Greenwich Island in the South Shetlands.

The Saddlestone. 63°26'S, 57°02'W. A nunatak of 380 m. Between Mount Carrel and The Pyramid, in the northern part of the Tabarin Peninsula. At the head of Kenney Glacier. Surveyed in 1955 by the FIDS, who named it descriptively. A saddlestone is the stone at the apex of a gable.

Sadler Point. 64°42'S, 62°04'W. Juts out into Wilhelmina Bay from the west coast of Graham Land, 2½ miles east of Garnerin Point. Charted by de Gerlache in 1897–99. Named by the UK in 1960 for James Sadler (1751–1828), ballooning pioneer.

Cape Saens Peña *see* **Cape Sáenz**

Mount Saens Valiente *see* **Valiente Peak**

Saens Valiente Peak *see* **Valiente Peak**

Cape Sáenz. 67°33'S, 67°39'W. Also called Cape Saens Peña. Between Laubeuf and Bigourdan Fjords. Forms the southern extremity of Arrowsmith Peninsula on the west coast of Graham Land. Discovered and named by Charcot in 1908–10 for Dr. Roque Sáenz Peña, president of Argentina.

Saetet Cirque. 72°01'S, 2°42'E. On the north side of Jutulsessen Mountain, in the Gjelsvik Mountains of Queen Maud Land. Name means "the seat" in Norwegian.

Saether Crags. 71°52'S, 8°54'E. Just south of Steinskaret Gap, in the Kurze Mountains of Queen Maud Land. Named by the Norwegians for Håkon Saether, medical officer with the Norwegian Antarctic Expedition of 1956–57.

Safety Camp. Scott's camp between the Discovery Hut and One Ton Depot.

Safety Col. 68°20'S, 66°57'W. Also called Bingham Col, Rymill's Col. Snow-covered. 185 m. Between Red Rock Ridge and the Blackwall Mountains, on the west coast of Graham Land. Surveyed by the BGLE in 1936, and again in 1948–49 by the FIDS, who named it because it affords a safe sledging route between Neny Fjord and Rymill Bay during the summer.

Safety Island. 67°31'S, 63°54'E. 3 miles east of Cape Daly on the coast of East Antarctica. Photographed by the LCE 1936–37. Visited by Robert Dovers and his 1954 ANARE party. This small island was named by the Australians because it was the nearest safe campsite to Scullin Monolith.

Safety Spur. 85°19'S, 168°E. Between Vandament Glacier and Mill Glacier in the Dominion Range. Named by the Southern Party of the NZGSAE 1961–62 because they arrived safely here after crossing Mill Glacier in Nov. 1961.

Saffery Islands. 66°04'S, 65°49'W. Also called Islotes Tortuga. They extend west from Black Head, off the west coast of Graham Land. Charted by the BGLE 1934–37. They include Turnabout Island, Turtle Island, Fringe Rocks. Named by the UK for J.H. Saffery, deputy leader and flying manager of the FIDASE, 1955–57.

Sagbladet Ridge. 71°47'S, 5°51'E. At the east side of the mouth of Austreskorve Glacier in the Mühlig-Hofmann

Mountains of Queen Maud Land. Name means "the saw blade" in Norwegian.

Sage Nunataks. 84°33′S, 173°W. Two ice-free mountains, 1 mile apart. At the edge of the Ross Ice Shelf, just north of Mount Justman and the Gabbro Hills. Named for Richard H. Sage, USN, builder at Byrd Station in 1959, and at Amundsen-Scott South Pole Station in 1964.

Sagehen Nunataks. 86°30′S, 153°30′ W. In the Queen Maud Mountains.

Sail Rock. 63°02′S, 60°57′W. Also called Sail Rocks, Steeple Rock, Rocher Voile. 100 feet high. 7 miles SW of Deception Island in the South Shetlands. Named by sealers before 1822. From a distance it looks like a ship under sail.

Sail Rocks *see* **Sail Rock**

The *Sailor's Return.* American schooner commanded by Smyley on two expeditions to the South Shetlands. The first left the USA on July 3, 1836, in company with the *Geneva.* The second expedition left Newport, Rhode Island, on Sept. 22, 1837, and 20 days out of port the ship was wrecked off the African coast.

Bay of Sails. 77°22′S, 163°36′E. A McMurdo Sound indentation into the Wilson Piedmont Glacier in southern Victoria Land, between Spike Cape and Gneiss Point. Named by the Western Geological Party during Scott's 1910–13 expedition because they erected sails on their man-hauled sledge, to increase their speed across the mouth of the bay.

The *St. Austell Bay.* In March 1954, under D.C.H. Ward, this British ship escorted the Argentine minister of Marine (himself on the *Les Éclaireurs*) on his tour of Argentine scientific stations in the Antarctic.

Saint George Peak. 69°06′S, 72°03′W. 1,500 m. 3 miles NE of Cape Vostok, in the western part of the Havre Mountains on Alexander Island. Discovered and inaccurately charted by von Bellingshausen in 1821, and named by him (in Russian)

as Mountain of Saint George the Victor. The UK renamed it slightly.

Baie Saint Georges *see* **King George Bay**

Saint Johns Range. 77°16′S, 162°E. Crescent-shaped. 20 miles long. In Victoria Land, south of the Cotton, Miller, and Debenham Glaciers and north of Victoria Valley, Victoria Upper Glacier, and Victoria Lower Glacier. Named in 1957 by the NZ Northern Survey Party of the BCTAE for St. John's College, Cambridge, an institution meaningful to many members of Scott's 1910–13 expedition.

Baie Saint Lauzanne *see* **Lauzanne Cove**

Mount St. Louis. 67°09′S, 67°30′W. 1,280 m. Mainly ice-covered. Just east of The Gullet, on the west coast of Graham Land. Discovered and charted in 1909 by Charcot. Surveyed in 1948 by the FIDS, and named later by them for Canadian pilot Peter B. St. Louis, who flew from the Argentine Islands to Stonington Island in Jan. and Feb. 1950 to relieve Base E.

St. Marie Peak. 71°56′S, 171°05′E. 100 m. At the north end of Foyn Island in the Possession Islands. Named for Lt. Cdr. John W. St. Marie, USN, VX-6 co-pilot on the flight of Jan. 18, 1958, which photographed this feature.

Saint Martha Cove. 63°56′S, 57°50′ W. On the NW side of Croft Bay, just south of Andreassen Point, James Ross Island. Named by the Argentines in 1959 for the saint.

Mount Saint Michael. 67°10′S, 58°21′ E. Also called Skagen. A headland on the west side of the entrance to Bell Bay in Enderby Land. Discovered in Feb. 1936 by the Discovery Investigations crew on the *William Scoresby,* and named by them for the French coastal landmark.

Saint Pauls Mountain. 77°40′S, 161° 14′E. 2 miles NE of Round Mountain on the north side of Taylor Glacier. It is joined to Round Mountain by a high ridge. Named by Scott's 1901–4 expedition.

Saint Rita Point. 64°15'S, 57°16'W. Just north of the mouth of Gourdon Glacier, on the east coast of James Ross Island. Named Cabo Santa Rita by the Argentines in 1959 for the saint.

Sakazuki Rock. 68°43'S, 40°30'E. Just east of Tama Point on the Queen Maud Land coast. Named Sakazuki-iwa (wine cup rock) by the Japanese in 1962.

Sakellari Peninsula. 67°10'S, 49°15'E. Ice-covered. Just west of Amundsen Bay, in Enderby Land. Named by the USSR in 1957 for N.A. Sakellari, scientist and navigator.

Sal Glacier. 72°03'S, 25°31'E. 7 miles long. Flows between Salen Mountain and Mount Bergersen in the Sør Rondane Mountains. Named Salbreen (the saddle glacier) by the Norwegians, in association with Salen Mountain.

Salamander Range. 72°06'S, 164°08' E. A line of peaks in the Freyberg Mountains, between the Canham and Black Glaciers, in the area of Rennick Glacier in Oates Land. Named by the New Zealanders in 1963–64 for Lord Freyberg's nickname.

The Salem Expedition. On Aug. 23, 1818, the *General Knox,* commanded by William S. Orne, and its tender, the *Governor Brooks,* commanded by Nicholas Withen, left together from Salem, Mass., for the South Seas, on a sealing expedition. Two years later, on Aug. 13, 1820, the brig *Nancy* left Boston, commanded by Benjamin Upton. The South Shetlands had been discovered by this time, and all three ships met up there for the 1820–21 season. The *Nancy* left the South Shetlands on March 10, 1821, in company with the *Huntress,* and wintered-over in the Falklands, as did the *Governor Brooks,* while the *General Knox* returned to the USA, arriving there on June 5, 1821, with 5,000 skins and 600 barrels of oil. The *Nancy* and the *Governor Brooks* were back in the South Shetlands for the following season of

1821–22, but did not do well, and left on March 6, 1822. On May 25, 1822, they arrived back in Salem with 1,800 skins and 100 barrels of oil.

Salen Mountain. 72°05'S, 25°27'E. 2,950 m. Between Komsa Mountain and Sal Glacier in the Sør Rondane Mountains. It is a descriptive Norwegian name meaning "the saddle."

Salient Glacier. 78°08'S, 163°07'E. On the east side of the Royal Society Range, flowing into the head of Blue Glacier from Salient Peak. Named in 1957 by the NZ Blue Glacier Party of the BCTAE, in association with the peak.

Salient Peak. 78°10'S, 162°45'E. In the Royal Society Range, between Mounts Rücker and Hooker. Named by the NZ Blue Glacier Party of the BCTAE in 1957 because it forms a salient.

Salient Rock. 62°22'S, 59°20'W. A rock in water to the NE of Robert Island in the South Shetlands, in Nelson Strait. Named descriptively by the Chileans in 1951 as Roca Saliente.

The *Salisbury.* British sealer from Liverpool in the South Shetlands in 1820–21 under Capt. Hodges.

Mount Salisbury. 85°38'S, 153°37'W. 970 m. Ice-free. At the west side of the lower part of the Robert Scott Glacier, at the south end of the Karo Hills. Discovered during Byrd's 1928–30 expedition. Named for James B. Salisbury, cosmic ray scientist at McMurdo Station, 1965.

Salknappen Peak. 72°19'S, 1°02'E. On the north side of Isingen Mountain in the Sverdrup Mountains of Queen Maud Land. Name means "the saddle button" in Norwegian.

Sallee Snowfield. 82°38'S, 50°20'W. In the northern part of the Pensacola Mountains, between the Dufek Massif and the Forrestal Range. Named for Lt. Cdr. Ralph W. Sallee, assistant meteorological officer on the staff of the Commander, US Naval Support Force, Antarctica, 1967 and 1968.

The *Sally*   *see*   **The *Sarah***

Sally Cove. 67°48'S, 67°17'W. Indents the NW shore of Horseshoe Island, off the coast of Graham Land. Named by the UK because all FIDS sledging parties leaving Base Y would sally forth from this cove.

Sally Rocks. 62°42'S, 60°26'W. Rocks in water in South Bay, just north of Miers Bluff, Livingston Island. Weddell, in 1820–23, named a feature in this area as Sally's Cove. Modern geographers can not find this cove, but, in order to preserve Weddell's naming, named these rocks thus.

Sally's Cove *see* **Sally Rocks**

Salmon, Kenneth J. NZ physicist who took over as scientific leader of Hallett Station from James Shear on Jan. 16, 1958.

Salmon Bay. 77°56'S, 164°34'E. Just north of Cape Chocolate on the coast of Victoria Land. Named Davis Bay by Scott's 1910–13 expedition, in association with Davis Glacier. In 1958 the NZ Northern Survey Party of the BCTAE renamed the glacier to avoid confusion with another Davis Glacier. The bay was also renamed.

Salmon Cliff. 72°22'S, 170°06'E. South of Seabee Hook on the west side of Hallett Peninsula. Named by the New Zealanders in 1957–58 for Ken Salmon.

Salmon Cove. 67°06'S, 66°28'W. 4 miles SE of McCall Point on the east side of Lallemand Fjord, Graham Land. Named by the UK for Eric M.P. Salmon, assistant FIDS meteorologist who spent several seasons in the Antarctic from 1950–56, and who visited this cove in 1956.

Salmon Creek *see* **Salmon Stream**

Salmon Glacier. 77°58'S, 164°05'E. 5 miles WSW of Cape Chocolate. Just to the north of the Garwood Valley, and just to the south of Salmon Hill, in Victoria Land. Named Davis Glacier by Scott's 1910–13 expedition. Renamed in 1958 by the NZ Northern Survey Party of the BCTAE to avoid confusion with another glacier of that name.

Salmon Hill. 77°57'S, 164°09'E. Between Salmon and Blackwelder Glaciers in Victoria Land. Named by Frank Debenham during Scott's 1910–13 expedition for the pink limestone here.

Salmon Island. 66°01'S, 65°28'W. The most westerly of the Fish Islands, off the west coast of Graham Land. Charted by the BGLE 1934–37. Named by the UK in 1959 in continuation of the fish motif.

Salmon Stream. 77°56'S, 164°32'E. A meltwater stream. 6 miles long. Flows from the Salmon Glacier into Salmon Bay in Victoria Land. Scott's 1910–13 expedition called it Davis Creek, in association with Davis Glacier (now called Salmon Glacier). In 1960 New Zealand changed the name to Salmon Creek, in accordance with the change of name of all the features in this area which had once been called Davis. Shortly thereafter, they changed it to Salmon Stream.

Salpêtrière Bay. 65°04'S, 64°02'W. 1 mile wide. Between Hervéou Point and Poste Point on the west side of Booth Island in the Wilhelm Archipelago. Charted and named by Charcot in 1903–5 for l'Hôpital de la Salpêtrière in Paris, where Charcot's father founded a clinic to treat nervous diseases.

Salsbury, Francis. Captain of the maintop on the Wilkes Expedition 1838–42. Joined in the USA. Served the cruise.

Mount Saltonstall. 86°53'S, 154°18'W. 2,975 m. 1 mile south of Mount Innes-Taylor at the south side of Poulter Glacier in the Queen Maud Mountains. Discovered in Dec. 1934 by Quin Blackburn during Byrd's 1933–35 expedition. Named by Byrd for John Saltonstall, contributor to the expedition.

Salvador Nunatak. 72°34'S, 163°20'E. 2 miles north of Schumann Nunatak, in the SW part of the Freyberg Mountains. Named for Anthony Salvador, ionosphere physicist at McMurdo Station, 1967.

Salvesen Bay *see* **Salvesen Cove**

Salvesen Cove. 64°24′S, 61°20′W. Also called Salvesen Bay. Forms the southern extremity of Hughes Bay, on the west coast of Graham Land. Charted by de Gerlache in 1897–99. Named by whalers in the area for the Scottish whaling firm of Salvesen & Co.

Samoylovich Nunatak. 71°48′S, 4°55′ E. Near the northern end of Hamarskaftet Nunataks, in the Mühlig-Hofmann Mountains of Queen Maud Land. Named by the USSR in 1961 for R.L. Samoylovich, polar explorer.

Sample Nunataks. 70°53′S, 159°52′E. At the convergence of Lovejoy Glacier and Harlin Glacier in the Usarp Mountains. Named for Gerald M. Sample, USN, radio operator in R4D aircraft, 1961–62 and 1962–63.

Mount Samsel. 70°24′S, 63°15′W. Along the north side of Clifford Glacier, just west of the junction of Kubitza Glacier, in Palmer Land. Named for Gene L. Samsel, biologist at Palmer Station in 1969–70 and 1970–71.

The *Samson* *see* **The *City of New York***

Samson, G. Radio operator on the *Eleanor Bolling*, 1929–30. Replaced H.N. Shrimpton.

The *Samuel*. Nantucket whaler of 287 tons. 92 feet long. Built at Scituate, Mass., in 1804. Registered on March 30, 1815, in New Bedford. It sailed to the South Shetlands for seals for the 1820–21 season, leaving the USA on Nov. 19, 1820, under Capt. Robert Inott. Due to its late arrival, the expedition was unsuccessful, and the vessel was condemned at Rio in 1822.

Samuel Nunataks. 79°38′S, 82°30′W. 7 nunataks at the SE end of the Nimbus Hills in the Heritage Range. Named for Samuel L. Wilson, meteorological electronics technician at Little America in 1957.

Samuel Peak. 62°33′S, 60°07′W. West of Edinburgh Hill in the NE part of Livingston Island in the South Shetlands.

Named by the UK in 1958 for the *Samuel*.

San Eladio Point. 64°50′S, 63°07′W. In Graham Land.

The *San Giuseppe Due*. Italian 2-masted lateen-rigged ketch out of the Rome area. It arrived at Deception Island on Jan. 1, 1971, under Capt. Giovanni Ajmone-Cat and his amateur crew of 3, who were making a round-the-world trip flying the Italian flag.

The *San Juan Nepomuceno*. Argentine sealing brig, probably the first in Antarctica. It was leased by a party of British sealers under Adam Guy, and went to the South Shetlands for the 1819–20 season, under the command of Capt. Carlos Timblón. It took 14,600 seal skins and returned to Buenos Aires on Feb. 22, 1820.

The *San Luís*. Destroyer on the 1948 Argentine naval maneuvers led by Admiral Cappus.

San Martín Glacier. 82°24′S, 42°14′ W. Bisects the Argentina Range in the Pensacola Mountains. Named for the *General San Martín*.

San Martín Land. 68°08′S, 67°07′W. This was Argentina's name (actually Tierra de San Martín) for the Antarctic Peninsula, which they claim. It was named for the Argentine liberator, José de San Martín.

San Martín Station. 68°07′S, 67°08′ W. Argentine base on Barry Island, in the Debenham Islands, off the west coast of Graham Land. It was also called General San Martín Station. A year-round base built in 1951, it was maintained continuously until 1960. Leaders of the first wintering parties were 1951—Julio Mottel; 1952—Juan Carlos Bassini; 1953—Bassini again; 1954—Jorge Leal; 1956—Elisagaray.

San Rafael Nunatak *see* **Mount Ferrara**

San Roque Refugio. Argentine refuge hut built on Robertson Island in 1956.

The *San Telmo*. Spanish ship which left Cádiz bound for Peru in May 1819, along with the *Alexandro*, the *Prueba*, and the *Primeroso-Mariana*. In the Drake Passage bad weather forced the ship south, and at 61°S, 60°W the *Primeroso-Mariana* took the *San Telmo* in tow, but could not hold her because the hawsers were not strong enough. The *San Telmo* was left to its fate on Sept. 4, 1819, in about 62°S, with no mast or rudder. Parts of the vessel were found by sealers on Half Moon Beach on Livingston Island in the South Shetlands in 1820–21.

San Telmo Island. 62°28'S, 60°49'W. Also called Telmo Island. Forms the west side of Shirreff Cove on the north coast of Livingston Island in the South Shetlands. Named by the UK in 1958 for the *San Telmo*.

SANAE *see* **South African National Antarctic Expeditions**

Sanae Station. 70°30'S, 2°32'W. Also called Tottenbukta Sanae. South Africa's first scientific station in Antarctica. On Totten Bay, in the Polar Circle Bight, on the Princess Martha Coast of New Schwabenland in Queen Maud Land. On Jan. 8, 1960, the South Africans took over the Princess Martha Coast station from the Norwegians and made it their base for their national expeditions (called SANAE. The expeditions acronym has all capital letters. The name of the station, which is the same, and which was named for the expeditions, has only a capital S). It lasted until 1962, when it was replaced by a newer, bigger, better station, called Sanae II. This station was built early in 1962 by the third SANAE. The later Sanae III Station was on the Fimbul Ice Shelf, and there was an even later one, called Sanae IV Station.

The *Sanavirón*. Argentine ship used on the following expeditions fielded to the Antarctic by that country: 1947–48 (Capt. Luís Ambrosini); 1948–49 (Capt. Gabino Santoro); 1950–51 (Capt. Laerte Santucci); 1951–52 (Capt. Aldo Molinari); 1952–53 (Capt. Ricardo S. Fitz-Simon); 1953–54 (Capt. Pernice); 1954–55 (Capt. Hector A. Suffern); 1956–57 (Capt. Eduardo H. Fraga).

Península Sanavirón *see* **Coughtrey Peninsula**

Sanctuary Cliffs. 64°27'S, 57°12'W. At the northern edge of the ice-cap in the central part of Snow Hill Island. Discovered and charted by Nordenskjöld's expedition of 1901–4, and named by them as Mittelnuten (middle nunatak). Redefined by the FIDS in 1952, and renamed by the UK for the shelter these cliffs provide from the sou'westerlies here.

Sanctuary Glacier. 86°01'S, 150°50'W. In the Queen Maud Mountains.

Sanctuary Islands. 65°37'S, 64°35'W. Group of small islands. Just off the west side of Chavez Island. ½ mile SW of Link Stack, off the west coast of Graham Land. Charted by the BGLE 1934–37. Named by the UK in 1959 because they provided sheltered camping sites for the FIDS sledging parties in 1957.

Sanctuary Pinnacle *see* **The Spire**

Sandau Nunatak. 71°42'S, 67°12'W. On the west side of Palmer Land.

Sandbakken Moraine. 71°34'S, 12°08'E. 2 miles NW of Gråhorna Peaks, on the west side of the Westliche Petermann Range in the Wohlthat Mountains. Name means "the sand slope" in Norwegian.

Sandbotnen Cirque. 71°44'S, 12°01'E. Indentation into the west side of Zwiesel Mountain, in the Pieck Range of the Wohlthat Mountains. Name means "the sand cirque" in Norwegian. Its floor is covered in moraine.

Sandefjord *see* **Sandefjord Bay**

¹Sandefjord Bay. 60°37'S, 46°03'W. Also called Sandefjord. 2 miles long. Between the west end of Coronation Island and Monroe Island. Spine Island is in it. Discovered and charted by Powell and Palmer in Dec. 1821. Named by Petter Sørlle in 1912–13 for the Norwegian town.

²Sandefjord Bay *see* **Sandefjord Ice Bay, Sandefjord Cove**

Sandefjord Cove. 68°47'S, 90°42'W. Also called Sandefjord Bay. Between

Cape Ingrid and the terminus of Tofte Glacier on the west side of Peter I Island. Named by the Norwegians for the town of Sandefjord, one of the main centers of the Norwegian whaling industry.

Sandefjord Ice Bay. 69°40'S, 74°25'E. 25 miles wide. On the west side of Publications Ice Shelf, on the east side of the Amery Ice Shelf. It forms the head of Prydz Bay. Discovered in Feb. 1935 by Klarius Mikkelsen in the *Thorshavn*. He named it Sandefjord Bay, for Lars Chrisensen's home town in Norway. Lars Christensen was the owner of the ship Mikkelsen was captain of. The feature was redefined slightly in later years.

Sandefjord Peak *see* **Sandefjord Peaks**

Sandefjord Peaks. 60°37'S, 45°59'W. Three conical peaks. The highest is 635 m. They mark the SW end of Pomona Plateau at the west end of Coronation Island. The most southerly was named Sandefjord Peak by personnel on the *Discovery II* in 1933 for the Norwegian whaling town. The FIDS surveyed them in 1950, and the UK extended the name to cover all the peaks.

Sandegga Ridge. 71°54'S, 9°43'E. Extends 5 miles south from the Sandhø Heights in the Conrad Mountains, in the Orvin Mountains of Queen Maud Land. Discovered by Ritscher in 1938–39. Name means "the sand ridge" in Norwegian.

Sandeggtind Peak. 71°52'S, 9°45'E. 3,055 m. 1 mile south of Sandhø Heights on Sandegga Ridge in the Conrad Mountains of Queen Maud Land. Discovered aerially by Ritscher's expedition of 1938–39. The name means "sand ridge peak" in Norwegian.

Sandeidet Moraine. 71°39'S, 12°15'E. Covers the surface between Gråkammen Ridge and a small rock spur just to its NW, in the Westliche Petermann Range of the Wohlthat Mountains in Queen Maud Land. Name means "the sand isthmus" in Norwegian.

Mount Sandell *see* **Mount Wood**

Sandercock Nunataks. 68°32'S, 52°04'E. Isolated. 45 miles ESE of the Nye

Mountains in Enderby Land. Discovered and visited in Dec. 1959 by an ANARE airborne party. Named by the Australians for Squadron Leader J.C. Sandercock, RAAF, officer commanding the Antarctic flight at Mawson Station in 1959.

Mount Sanders *see* **Mount Saunders**

Sanderson, T. Crewman on the *Jacob Ruppert*, 1933–34.

Sandford, Joseph P. Passed midshipman on the Wilkes Expedition 1838–42. He served on the *Vincennes* during the cruise of 1840, and at other times served on other ships of the fleet. He joined the *Porpoise* at Tahiti, the *Flying Fish* at San Francisco, and the *Porpoise* again at Singapore.

Sandford, Thomas. Quartermaster on the Wilkes Expedition 1838–42. Joined in the USA. Served the cruise.

Sandford Cliffs. 83°52'S, 159°20'E. Mainly ice-free. Forms the western extremity of Peletier Plateau, in the Queen Elizabeth Range. Named by the NZ Southern Party of the BCTAE in 1957–58, for N. Sandford, scientist at Scott Base in 1957.

Sandford Glacier. 66°38'S, 129°50'E. A channel glacier flowing to the east side of Porpoise Bay in East Antarctica. 25 miles SSW of Cape Morse. Named for Joseph P. Sandford.

Sandhø Heights. 71°50'S, 9°47'E. In the center of the Conrad Mountains of Queen Maud Land. Discovered aerially by the Ritscher expedition of 1938–39. Name means "sand heights" in Norwegian.

Sandhøhallet Glacier. 71°52'S, 9°50' E. Flows SE from the Sandhø Heights in the Conrad Mountains of Queen Maud Land. Name means "the sand heights slope" in Norwegian.

Sandhøkalvane Nunataks. 71°46'S, 9° 55'E. 4 miles NE of Sandhø Heights, between the Conrad Mountains and Mount Dallmann, in Queen Maud Land. Discovered by Ritscher in 1938–39. Name means "the sand heights calves" in Norwegian.

Sandilands Nunatak. 70°32'S, 67°27' E. 3 miles north of Mount Seaton. In the middle of, and near the northern end of, Nemesis Glacier, in the Prince Charles Mountains. Discovered in Dec. 1956 by an ANARE sledging party led by P.W. Crohn. Named by the Australians for A.H. Sandilands, radio operator at Mawson Station in 1957.

Sandneset Point. 71° 39′ S, 9° 33′ E. The northern point of Furdesanden Moraine in the Conrad Mountains in the Orvin Mountains of Queen Maud Land. Discovered by Ritscher in 1938–39. Name means "the sand point" in Norwegian.

Sandneskalven Nunatak. 71° 40′ S, 9° 53′ E. Isolated. 6 miles east of Sandneset Point in the Conrad Mountains of Queen Maud Land. Name means "the sand point calf" in Norwegian.

Sandnesstaven Peak. 71° 41′ S, 9° 39′ E. 2,030 m. At the northern end of the Conrad Mountains, in the Orvin Mountains of Queen Maud Land. Name means "the sand point staff" in Norwegian.

Mount Sandow. 67° 22′ S, 100° 24′ E. A nunatak overlooking the Denman Glacier, 11 miles SW of Mount Amundsen. Discovered by the Western Base Party of the AAE 1911–14, and named by Mawson for Eugene Sandow of London, a patron of the expedition.

Sandra Automatic Weather Station. 74° 30′ S, 160° 30′ E. American AWS at an elevation of approximately 4,971 feet. Operated from Jan. 19, 1988–Feb. 23, 1988.

Sandseten Mountain. 71° 33′ S, 12° 09′ E. 1 mile south of Krakken Mountain. Just SW of Gneysovaya Peak in the Westliche Petermann Range of the Wohlthat Mountains of Queen Maud Land. Discovered aerially during the Ritscher expedition of 1938–39. Name means "the sand seat" in Norwegian.

Mount Sandved. 82° 41′ S, 161° 06′ E. 2,440 m. 2 miles north of Mount Dougherty in the northern part of the Queen Elizabeth Range. Named for Kurt G. Sandved, information officer at the National Science Foundation.

Sandwich Bluff. 63° 50′ S, 57° 30′ W. 610 m. Flat-topped. In the central part of Vega Island. Discovered by Nordenskjöld's 1901–4 expedition. Charted by the FIDS in 1945, and named by them. It looks like a sandwich when seen from the north because a band of rock holds snow in it.

Sandy Beach   *see*   **Blacksand Beach**

Sandy Glacier. 77° 29′ S, 161° 57′ E. Just over 600 yards long and 80 yards wide. Just over ½ mile east of Mount Orestes in the Olympus Range, near the Wright Valley, in Victoria Land. Named by Wakefield Dort (*see* **Mount Dort**) in 1965–66. He analyzed it as being of ice and sand.

Sanitation. Sanitation in Antarctica has been woefully inadequate until recent times. Although today showers, flush toilets, and washer/dryers are the order of the day in most Antarctic bases, it is not difficult to imagine how tough it must have been in the old days. On board ship, a couple of years at a stretch, things would get pretty bad, and men rotted—literally. The relevant facilities on board the inevitably tiny vessel were astonishingly small and crude, and waste matter was dumped overboard into the icy seas. There were no showers or bathtubs, no deodorants, no toothpaste, hand cream, or toilet tissue. The situation improved only a little in the 19th century, the better diet contributing only slightly to the overall improved conditions. This is one of the unsung reasons why women were forbidden entry to high southern latitudes until recently—the impracticality of the facilities. By the time of Scott and Amundsen, things had improved still further. Amundsen had a w.c. at Framheim (his base), but out on the trail he suffered grievously from piles. He was frank about it. Most of the other pioneers suffered similarly, but they did not refer to it. Many of them were British and it would definitely have been infra dig to have alluded to such a problem. The dogs and ponies had an easier time of it, of course, and most of the dogs would eat their own excrement, and that of the humans too. The British, especially, did not look on this at all favorably, but it's a zoological fact of life, and it alleviated the problem of waste disposal somewhat, especially around the bases. Toilet paper seems to have been first taken to the Antarctic by Scott's 1910–13 expedition, and in 1934 Byrd took a 5-gallon can stuffed with it for his "Alone" stay at Bolling Advance Weather Station. One of the big problems of the Polar pioneers was functioning naturally in the extreme cold, out there on the trail at 86°S. If the weather was clement outside the small tent, it was comparatively easy. One just turned against the wind and acted smartly. If it was – 60°F, it was definitely an inside job, in a small corner of the tent especially allotted for this purpose. This little entry merely scratches the surface of a fascinating subject, one that is definitely worth further study and possibly the writing of a thesis, a monograph, or even a short book.

The *Santa Cruz*. Argentine ship in the South Shetlands in 1948.

Santa Cruz Point. 62°31′S, 59°33′W. Also called Spencer Bluff. Forms the east end of Greenwich Island in the South Shetlands. Named in 1949 by the Argentines for the *Santa Cruz*.

Santa Fe Hill *see* **Mount Spann**

Bahía Santa Marta *see* **Duperré Bay**

The *Santa Micaela*. Argentine vessel on the 1950–51 expedition sent to the Antarctic by that country.

Santa Teresita Range *see* **Dufek Massif**

Santos Peak. 64°25′S, 61°32′W. South of Murray Island, on the west coast of Graham Land. Charted by de Gerlache in 1897–99. Named by the UK in 1960 for Alberto Santos-Dumont (1873–1932), Brazilian aeronautics pioneer.

Sapin-Jaloustre, Jean. French biologist on the 1950 French Polar Expedition. Discovered the emperor penguin colony on Pointe Géologie.

Sapp Rocks. 82°30′S, 51°48′W. Two rocks on land, 2 miles north of Alley Spur on the north side of the Dufek Massif. Named for Clifton E. Sapp, hospital corpsman at Amundsen-Scott South Pole Station.

Sapper Hill. 81°24′S, 160°38′E. Ice-covered. 2 miles NE of Hermitage Peak in the northern part of the Surveyors Range. Named by the New Zealanders in 1960–61 for the Royal Engineers (they are nicknamed "the Sappers").

The *Sarah*. 40-ton shallop (or tender) to the *Jane Maria* during the New York Sealing Expedition of 1820–21 in the South Shetlands. It was assembled at the Falklands from a kit brought down on the *Jane Maria* in 1819. Nicknamed the *Sally,* it was commanded by Donald McKay, and was lost at sea on April 8, 1821, with 9 men aboard.

The *Sarah E. Spear*. American sealer in the South Shetlands in 1852–53 under Capt. Pendleton, and again in 1853–54 under Capt. Kane.

The *Sarah W. Hunt*. American sealer from New London, in the South Shetlands for the 1888–89 season, under Capt. James W. Buddington. It took only 39 skins, and was probably back the following season, 1889–90. But there were no seals left.

Saratoga Table. 83°20′S, 50°30′W. A snow-covered plateau in the Forrestal Range of the Pensacola Mountains. 8 miles long and 6 miles wide. Just south of Kent Gap and Lexington Table. Discovered on Jan. 13, 1956, during a fly over. Named for the *Saratoga,* the American aircraft carrier of the 1920s (not in the Antarctic).

Sares, Henry. Captain of the maintop on the Wilkes Expedition 1838–42. Joined at Callao. Served the cruise.

Sargent Glacier. 85°23′S, 163°50′W. Flows from the Herbert Range into the Axel Heiberg Glacier, just SE of Bell Peak, in the Queen Maud Mountains. Named for Howard H. Sargent III, ionosphere physicist at Amundsen-Scott South Pole Station in 1964.

Sarie Marais Base. Formerly an emergency base in Queen Maud Land, it was operated as a South African summer station in 1986–87.

Sarkofagen Mountain. 72°10'S, 16°45' E. Isolated. 11 miles south of Mount Yakovlev in the Russkiye Mountains of Queen Maud Land. Name means "the sarcophagus" in Norwegian.

Sarnoff Mountains. 77°10'S, 145°W. 25 miles long. 4–8 miles wide. They separate the Boyd and Arthur Glaciers in the Ford Ranges of Marie Byrd Land. Discovered aerially on Dec. 5, 1929, during Byrd's 1928–30 expedition. Named by Byrd for David Sarnoff, president of RCA, provider of radio equipment for Byrd's 1933–35 expedition.

Sartorius Island *see* **Greenwich Island**

Sartorius Point. 62°34'S, 59°39'W. Almost 2 miles east of Ephraim Bluff on the south side of Greenwich Island in the South Shetlands. In 1820 sealers called it Point Hardy. This name later became attached erroneously to Fort Point, so, in 1961, the UK, in order to avoid confusion, gave it a new name. Weddell had called Greenwich Island Sartorius Island for his old admiral, Sir George Sartorius (1790–1885). The new name was designed to preserve Weddell's naming.

Sastrugi. (Pronounced with a soft "g." The singular is Sastrugus, with a hard "g.") Wavelike irregularities which look like miniature snow dunes. They rise from a few inches in height to more than three feet from the ground. They have long tails descending downwind, sometimes to a length of 50 feet. They move continually as the wind reshapes them. At places they played hell with the early sledging expeditions.

Cape Sastrugi. 74°37'S, 163°41'E. 1½ miles NW of Snowy Point, on the west side of the Deep Freeze Range. It overlooks the northern portion of the Nansen

Ice Sheet in Victoria Land. Named by Victor Campbell during Scott's 1910–13 expedition for the sastrugi here.

Såta Nunatak. 69°46'S, 37°17'E. ½ mile north of Kista Nunatak, on the east side of Fletta Bay, on the SW shore of Lützow-Holm Bay. Photographed by the LCE 1936–37 and named Såta (the haystack) by the Norwegians.

The Satellite. 67°51'S, 61°07'E. 1,100 m. A peak 3 miles SW of Pearce Peak, and 8 miles east of Baillieu Peak. Discovered and named in Feb. 1931 by the BANZARE.

Satellite Snowfield. 71°28'S, 69°45'W. At the SE side of the Walton Mountains in the south-central part of Alexander Island. Named by the UK for the satellites (moons) in the Solar System (several individual satellite names are used in features around here).

Saturn Glacier. 72°S, 68°35'W. 15 miles long and 6 miles wide. Feeds the George VI Sound from the southern part of Alexander Island. Surveyed in 1949 by the FIDS, and named by the UK for the planet.

[1]**Mount Saunders** *see* **Saunders Mountain**

[2]**Mount Saunders.** 85°21'S, 165°26'E. Also called (erroneously) Mount Sanders. 2,895 m. 4½ miles NNW of Mount Nimrod in the Dominion Range. Discovered by Shackleton's 1907–9 expedition and named by him for Edward Saunders, Shackleton's secretary in England.

Saunders, A. Photographer on the *Discovery II* in 1933. He "captured" the South Orkneys.

Saunders, Harold E. USN cartographer for the first two Byrd expeditions. He actually went to Antarctica on the first only, the 1928–30 expedition. A friend of Byrd's, he was chairman of the US Advisory Committee on Antarctic Names, 1948–61.

Saunders Bluff. 72°45'S, 160°44'E. Isolated. 9 miles ESE of Miller Butte in the Outback Nunataks. Named for

Jeffrey J. Saunders, biolab technician at McMurdo Station in 1965–66.

Saunders Coast. 77°45′S, 150°W. Between Cape Colbeck and Brennan Point on the coast of Marie Byrd Land. Explored aerially on Dec. 5, 1929, during Byrd's 1928–30 expedition, and mapped by Harold E. Saunders from photos taken on that flight. It is named for Saunders.

Saunders Hill. 66°19′S, 110°32′E. Juts out into the SE part of O'Brien Bay, just east of the Windmill Islands. Named for William Y. Saunders, biologist at Wilkes Station, 1961.

Saunders Mountain. 76°53′S, 145°40′W. Also called Mount Saunders (not to be confused with the other Mount Saunders). A mass of peaks in the Ford Ranges of Marie Byrd Land. Between the mouths of Crevasse Valley Glacier and Arthur Glacier. Discovered aerially on Dec. 5, 1929, during Byrd's 1928–30 expedition, and named by Byrd for Harold E. Saunders.

Saunders Point. 60°42′S, 45°19′W. The southern extremity of South Coronation Island, between Amphibolite Point and Tophet Bastion, off the south coast of Coronation Island in the South Orkneys. Charted by personnel on the *Discovery II* in 1933, and named by them for A. Saunders.

Saunders Rock. 85°25′S, 127°02′W. A rock on land, 3 miles NW of Feeley Peak. Between the Davisville and Quonset Glaciers on the north side of the Wisconsin Range. Named for John T. Saunders, electronics technician at Byrd Station in 1960.

Saunders Valley. 62°12′S, 58°59′W. Just north of Clement Hill, on Fildes Peninsula, on King George Island in the South Shetlands.

Sauria Buttress. 80°32′S, 20°24′W. In the Shackleton Range.

Mount Sauter *see* **Terningskarvet Mountain**

Sauter Range *see* **Terningskarvet Mountain**

Savage Glacier. 72°25′S, 96°05′W. Also called Savage Inlet. Flows into Seraph Bay, south of Tierney Peninsula, at the east end of Thurston Island. Discovered by helicopter during the USN Bellingshausen Sea Expedition of that month. Named for Lt. John Savage, USN, dental officer on the *Glacier* during the expedition.

Savage Inlet *see* **Savage Glacier**

Savage Nunatak. 86°27′S, 124°58′W. 7 miles SE of Hatcher Bluffs, on the eastern edge of the upper Reedy Glacier. Named for Henry C. Savage, builder at Byrd Station in 1962.

Savin Nunatak. 73°52′S, 68°02′W. Isolated. 30 miles SW of Mount Vang at the base of Palmer Land. Named for Samuel M. Savin, glaciologist at Byrd Station in 1965–66.

Savoia Peak. 64°51′S, 63°26′W. Also called Pic Luigi de Savoie, Luigi Peak. 1,415 m. At the NE end of the Sierra DuFief, on Wiencke Island. Discovered by de Gerlache in 1898, and climbed by members of Charcot's 1903–5 expedition. Named by Charcot for Luigi di Savoia, duke of the Abruzzi.

Mount Saw. 68°11′S, 56°44′E. Isolated. 17 miles SSE of Mount Cook of the Leckie Range. Named by the Australians for B. Saw, ANARE helicopter pilot in 1965.

Sawert Rocks. 67°31′S, 62°50′E. Rocks in water, 2½ miles ENE of Azimuth Island in the NE part of Holme Bay, Mac. Robertson Land. Named by the Australians for A. Sawert, radio officer at Mawson Station in 1959.

Sawtooth *see* **Armadillo Hill**

Sawyer Island. 65°26′S, 65°32′W. Also called Isla Contramaestre Rivera. 2 miles long. North of Pickwick Island in the Pitt Islands, Biscoe Islands. Named in 1959 by the UK for the Dickens character.

Sawyer Nunatak. 75°44′S, 161°49′E. 3 miles SE of Mount Stephens in the Prince Albert Mountains of Victoria Land.

Named for Joseph O. Sawyer, satellite geodesist at McMurdo Station in 1966.

Saxton Ridge. 70°37′S, 66°52′E. Just south of Thomson Massif in the Aramis Range of the Prince Charles Mountains. Named by the Australians for R.A. Saxton, officer-in-charge of Wilkes Station in 1963.

Saxum Nunatak. 63°10′S, 56°02′W. 430 m. Isolated. 6 miles north of Mount Tholus on the north side of Joinville Island. Surveyed by the FIDS in 1954, and named by them because when seen from the north it looks like a wall (saxum means wall in Latin).

Sayce Glacier. 65°05′S, 62°59′W. Flows into Flandres Bay, just north of Pelletan Point on the west coast of Graham Land. Charted by de Gerlache in 1897–99 and named by the UK in 1960 for B.J. Sayce (1839–1895), photography pioneer.

Sayen Rocks. 73°41′S, 94°37′W. Two rocks on land, visible from the north. Between Miller Crag and Sutley Peak in the Jones Mountains. Named for L.D. Sayen, VX-6 photographer who photographed the Jones Mountains in Jan. 1961.

Sayer, Capt. Captain of the *General Scott,* in the South Shetlands for the 1821–22 season.

Sayer Nunatak. 62°28′S, 60°08′W. On the shore of Dragon Cove, on the NE side of Livingston Island in the South Shetlands. Named by the UK for Capt. Sayer.

Sbrosovoye Lake. 70°45′S, 11°35′E. 1 mile SW of Tyuleniy Point in the Schirmacher Hills of Queen Maud Land. Named by the USSR in 1961. The name means "fault lake."

Scaife Mountains. 75°06′S, 65°08′W. West of Prehn Glacier, between the Ketchum and Ueda Glaciers at the very south of Palmer Land. Discovered by the RARE 1947–48 and named by Ronne for Alan M. Scaife of Pittsburgh, a contributor to the expedition.

Scallop Hill. 78°12′S, 166°44′E. 225 m. A volcanic dome behind Cape Spirit on the eastern edge of Black Island in the Ross Ice Shelf. Named by the New Zealanders in 1958–59 for a fossiliferous conglomerate on top of the hill which contains a chlamid lamellibranch commonly called scallops.

Scallop Ridge. 85°26′S, 139°W. 3 miles long. Forms the SW portion of the Berry Peaks. Named descriptively for the curving outline.

Scanlan Peak. 71°05′S, 65°23′E. The most southerly of a group of 3 peaks 5 miles SE of Husky Massif in the Prince Charles Mountains. Named by the Australians for A.M. Scanlan, cook at Davis Station in 1961.

The *Scapa.* Whale catcher which capsized off Laurie Island, South Orkneys, on Jan. 23, 1928. 15 out of the 17 crew were killed.

SCAR *see* **Scientific Committee on Antarctic Research**

Scar Bluffs. 68°48′S, 153°32′E. Three black, rectangular, steep-sided rock outcrops. 27 miles south of Cape Hudson on the Mawson Peninsula. Named by the Australians for SCAR.

Scar Hills. 63°25′S, 57°01′W. A small ridge of hills extending from the head of Hope Bay 1 mile NE along the SE shore of the bay, at the NE end of the Antarctic Peninsula. Discovered by Dr. J. Gunnar Andersson of Nordenskjöld's expedition of 1901–4, and named by him as Schrammenhügel. Translated later into English.

Scar Inlet. 66°S, 62°W. Just NW of Jason Peninsula in the Larsen Ice Shelf. Discovered by Nordenskjöld in 1902, and named Scott Bay by him for Robert F. Scott. The UK renamed it in 1963 for SCAR.

Scarab Peak. 73°21′S, 163°02′E. 3,160 m. 2 miles NE of Mount Frustum on the SE end of Tobin Mesa in the Mesa Range, in Victoria Land. Named by the New Zealanders in 1962–63 for its shape.

Scarborough Castle. 62°28'S, 60°48'W. A flat-topped rock on land, with perpendicular sides. South of Cape Shirreff, on the north coast of Livingston Island in the South Shetlands. Named by Robert Fildes in 1820.

Roca Scarborough Castle *see* **Fortín Rock**

Scarlatti Peak. 71°16'S, 70°26'W. 750 m. Pyramidal. 8 miles NW of Holst Peak. 12 miles east of the Walton Mountains, in the central part of Alexander Island. Named by the UK for the composer.

Scend Rocks. 64°48'S, 64°15'W. A small group of rocks in water 1½ miles SW of Rumbler Rock. 2½ miles WNW of the Outcast Islands, off the SW coast of Anvers Island. Named by the UK in 1958. Scend is a tidal flow over a rock.

Mount Schaefer. 71°22'S, 166°23'E. 1,825 m. Marks the western extremity of Robinson Heights in the Admiralty Mountains. Named for Paul W. Schaefer, biologist at McMurdo Station, 1966–67.

Schaefer Islands. 73°40'S, 103°24'W. Small group near the NW end of Canisteo Peninsula. 2 miles SW of Lindsey Islands. Named for William A. Schaefer, geologist on the Ellsworth Land Survey of 1968–69.

Schanz Glacier. 79°45'S, 83°40'W. 8 miles long. In the Heritage Range. Flows between the Soholt Peaks and the Collier Hills to enter Union Glacier. Named for Lt. Cdr. Thomas L. Schanz, VX-6 supply officer in 1965.

Scharon Bluff. 70°58'S, 167°24'E. 1,000 m. On the south side of Tapsell Foreland in Victoria Land. It surmounts the north side of Barnett Glacier, 9 miles west of Cape Moore. Named for LeRoy H. Scharon, geophysicist, US exchange scientist at Molodezhnaya Station in 1968.

Schaumberg, Fritz. One of the mountaineers on David Lewis' 1977–78 *Solo* expedition.

Scheimpflug Nunatak. 64°48'S, 62°36'W. In the mouth of the Deville Glacier, on the Arctowski Peninsula, on the west coast of Graham Land. Named by the UK in 1960 for Theodore Scheimpflug (1865–1911), Austrian aerophotogrammetry pioneer.

Schenck, William. Carpenter's mate on the Wilkes Expedition 1838–42. Joined in the USA. Served the cruise.

Schenck Peak. 69°40'S, 72°25'W. On the NW coast of Alexander Island.

The *Schepelsturm.* West German research vessel of the early 1980s. It was the ship used on GANOVEX 79.

Mount Scherger. 73°13'S, 62°55'E. Just west of Mount McCauley in the Prince Charles Mountains. In the area of the Lambert Glacier. Named by the Australians for Air Marshal Sir Frederick Scherger (d. 1984).

Scheuren Stream. 77°24'S, 163°39'E. A meltwater stream 1 mile west of Gneiss Point in southern Victoria Land. It comes out of the Wilson Piedmont Glacier and flows into the Bay of Sails. Named by Robert L. Nichols, a geologist here, for John J. Scheuren, Jr., chief of the Metcalf and Eddy Engineering Field Party here in 1957–58.

Mount Schevill. 85°07'S, 167°12'W. 1,995 m. Overlooks the head of Somero Glacier. 5 miles SE of Mount Johnstone in the Queen Maud Mountains. Named for William E. Schevill, biologist at McMurdo Station in 1964–65.

Mount Schicht. 71°26'S, 13°08'E. Has several summits. 4 miles WSW of Ritscher Peak in the Gruber Mountains of Queen Maud Land. Discovered aerially during Ritscher's expedition of 1938–39, and named by him as Schicht-Berge (stratum mountains) because of its appearance.

Mount Schimansky. 70°50'S, 63°49'W. 6 miles NW of Heintz Peak of the Welch Mountains in Palmer Land. Named for Lt. Cdr. John A. Schimansky, USN, VX-6 Hercules aircraft commander, 1970 and 1971.

Schimper Glacier. 80°18'S, 20°05'W. In the Shackleton Range.

Schirmacher, Richardheinrich. Lufthansa airplane captain who took part in the German New Schwabenland Expedition of 1938–39, under Ritscher.

Schirmacher Hills. 70°45′S, 11°40′E. A thin strip of exposed hilly coastline about 10 miles long. Has several meltwater ponds. 40 miles north of the Humboldt Mountains, on the coast of Queen Maud Land. Discovered aerially in 1938–39 by Ritscher's expedition, and named Schirmacher Oasis by Ritscher for Richardheinrich Schirmacher. Later redefined.

Schirmacher Massif. 71°37′S, 62°20′W. Islandlike. In the east part of Palmer Land. 3 miles west of the Rowley Massif, between the Rankin and Cline Glaciers. Named by the US for Eberhard G. Schirmacher, topographic engineer on the Lassiter Coast, 1969–70 and 1970–71, and at Pine Island Bay, 1974–75, all times as expedition leader.

Schirmacher Oasis *see* **Schirmacher Hills**

Schirmacher Ponds. 70°45′S, 11°40′E. A group of meltwater ponds in the Schirmacher Hills, 40 miles north of the Humboldt Mountains on the coast of Queen Maud Land. Discovered by Ritscher's expedition of 1938–39, and named by him for Richardheinrich Schirmacher.

Schist Peak. 77°19′S, 162°01′E. 1,650 m. Between Willis Glacier and Packard Glacier in the Saint Johns Range of Victoria Land. Named by the New Zealanders in 1959–60 for the rock here.

Schist Point. 60°43′S, 45°14′W. At the west side of the Divide Peaks on the south coast of Coronation Island in the South Orkneys. Surveyed by personnel on the *Discovery II* in 1933 and again in 1948–49 by the FIDS, who named it for the rocks here.

Schlatter Glacier. 77°41′S, 161°27′E. Flows from the Asgard Range toward Lake House in the Pearse Valley of Victoria Land. Named by the US for Roberto P. Schlatter, Chilean biologist at Cape Crozier, 1969–70 and 1970–71.

Schloredt Nunatak. 75°03′S, 134°15′W. 1 mile south of Bleclic Peaks at the southern extremity of the Perry Range in Marie Byrd Land. Named for Jerry L. Schloredt, chief construction electrician, USN, who was nuclear power plant operator at McMurdo Station in 1966, 1967, and 1969.

Cape Schlossbach. 75°08′S, 63°06′W. Forms the eastern end of Prehn Peninsula, between Gardner and Hansen Inlets on the east side of the base of Palmer Land. Discovered by the RARE 1947–48 and named by Ronne for Isaac Schlossbach.

Mount Schlossbach. 78°03′S, 154°48′W. Just SE of Mount Nilsen in the southern group of the Rockefeller Mountains on Edward VII Peninsula. Discovered aerially on Jan. 27, 1929, by Byrd's 1928–30 expedition. Later named for Isaac Schlossbach.

Schlossbach, Isaac. b. Aug. 20, 1891, Neptune, N.J. d. Aug. 23, 1984, Neptune, N.J. Nicknamed "Ike." One of the major figures in Antarctic history, this one-eyed sailor/pilot first went to Antarctica as one of the shore party of Byrd's 1933–35 expedition. During the USAS 1939–41 he was at West Base, and was one of the crew who occupied the Rockefeller Mountains Seismic Station in Nov.–Dec. 1940. In 1947–48 he was captain of the *Port of Beaumont, Texas,* and second-in-command of the RARE. By this time he was a commander, USN, (retired). In 1955–56 he was at Mawson Station with the ANARE, in 1956–57 and 1957–58 he was in the Weddell Sea area, and in 1960–61 he was back in Antarctica as a consultant and observer. *See* the Bibliography (Goodrich).

Schlossbach, Theodore. Medical officer on Ellsworth's 1935–36 expedition.

Schmehl Peak. 69°34′S, 158°45′E. 750 m. At the north end of the ridge overlooking the junction of the Walsh Glacier with the Tomilin Glacier in the Wilson Hills. Named for Lt. (jg) Peter W. Schmehl, USNR, Hercules aircraft navigator, 1968.

Mount Schmid. 77°58'S, 85°40'W. 2,430 m. On the south side of Embree Glacier. 5 miles east of Mount Goldthwait in the Sentinel Range. Named for Capt. Ernest A. Schmid, USAF, who helped build the South Pole Station in 1956–57.

Schmidt Glacier. 79°15'S, 83°42'W. 20 miles long. In the Pioneer Heights of the Heritage Range. Flows from near Hall Peak, along the west side of Thomson Escarpment and the Gross Hills into the lower part of Splettstoesser Glacier north of Mount Virginia. Named by the University of Minnesota Ellsworth Mountains party of 1961–62 for Paul G. Schmidt, geologist with the party.

Schmidt Hills. 83°14'S, 57°48'W. 15 miles long. North of Childs Glacier and west of Roderick Valley in the Neptune Range. Named for Dwight L. Schmidt, geologist and important student of Antarctic rocks at Carleton College, Minnesota.

Schmidt Nunataks. 69°53'S, 158°56' E. 11 miles SE of Governor Mountain in the Wilson Hills. Named for James L. Schmidt, USN, aviation electronics mate with VX-6 at McMurdo Station in 1967.

Schmidt Peak. 86°15'S, 144°50'W. On the south side of California Plateau. 3 miles NE of Parker Bluff at the end of a narrow ridge. In the Queen Maud Mountains. Named for Dennis C. Schmidt, VX-6 photographer, 1963, 1964, and 1967.

Schmidt Peninsula. 63°19'S, 57°54' W. Connected by a low isthmus to Cape Legoupil, Trinity Peninsula. Named by the Chilean Antarctic Expedition of 1947–48 for Capt. Hugo Schmidt Prado of the Chilean Army, the first commander of General Bernardo O'Higgins Station in 1948.

Schmitt, Waldo L. Marine biologist on the *Fleurus* at Deception Island in 1927, and on the *Staten Island* in 1962–63 (sic) at Marguerite Bay and in the Weddell Sea.

Schmitt Mesa. 74°56'S, 64°05'W. 15 miles long. 5 miles wide. Mostly ice-covered. Forms the southern rampart of the Latady Mountains. Named for Waldo L. Schmitt.

Schmitter Peak. 71°16'S, 66°21'E. 3 miles SW of Mount Woinarski in the Prince Charles Mountains. Named by the Australians for U. Schmitter, cook at Davis Station in 1964.

Schneider Glacier. 79°29'S, 84°17'W. 15 miles long. Flows between the Dunbar and Inferno Ridges and merges with the Balish Glacier before joining the Splettstoesser Glacier in the Heritage Range. Named for Cdr. Arthur F. Schneider, VX-6 maintenance officer, 1965, and commander of VX-6 in 1968.

Schneider Hills. 82°36'S, 42°45'W. South of San Martín Glacier. Forms the southern half of the Argentina Range in the Pensacola Mountains. Named for Otto Schneider, chief scientist of the Instituto Antártico Argentino in the 1950s and 1960s.

Schneider Rock. 74°07'S, 114°51'W. A rock on land, 3 miles north of the Siglin Rocks. It protrudes through the ice on the west side of Martin Peninsula in Marie Byrd Land. Lichens and petrels are to be found here. The name was given by the Americans in 1966 for Lt. R.P. Schneider, USN, maintenance coordinator at Williams Field that year.

Schobert Nunatak. 85°31'S, 162°14' W. Overlooks the terminus of Bowman Glacier, 4 miles east of Mount Dean, at the NE end of the Quarles Range in the Queen Maud Mountains. Named for William J. Schobert, VX-6 aviation electrician and maintenance shop supervisor for several seasons between 1964 and 1967.

Schoeck Peak. 79°54'S, 82°51'W. 1,810 m. At the head of the Henderson Glacier in the Enterprise Hills of the Heritage Range. Named for Peter A. Schoeck, auroral scientist at Little America, 1957.

Schofield Peak. 72°36'S, 166°18'E. 1 mile SE of Mount McCarthy, at the head of Webb Névé. Named for Edmund A.

Schofield, biologist at Hallett Station in 1963–64, and at McMurdo Station in 1967–68.

Schokalsky Bay. 69°15′S, 69°55′W. Also seen spelled as Shokalsky Bay, and formerly known as Shockalski Strait (see below). 9 miles wide at its entrance. It indents 6 miles between Mount Calais and Cape Brown on the east coast of Alexander Island. Fed by the Hampton Glacier. First seen from a distance by Charcot, and defined by him as a strait. He called it Détroit Schokalsky, for Russian geographer Yuliy M. Schokal'skiy. Redefined by the FIDS in 1948.

Scholander Island. 66°22′S, 66°58′W. 1½ miles east of Watkins Island in the Biscoe Islands. Named by the UK for Per F. Scholander, US physiologist specializing in the Poles.

Schollaert Channel. 64°30′S, 62°50′ W. A strait between Brabant Island and Anvers Island. Discovered in 1898 by de Gerlache, who named it for François Schollaert (1851–1917), Belgian statesman.

Schonyan, F.H.P. Crewman on the *Jacob Ruppert*, 1934–35.

Schoofs Nunatak. 73°18′S, 64°04′W. Isolated. 20 miles WNW of Mount Barkow. West of Meinardus and Haines Glaciers in Palmer Land. Named for Gerald J. Schoofs, radioscience researcher at Byrd Station, 1965–66.

Mount Schopf. 84°48′S, 113°25′W. 2,990 m. Mostly ice-covered. Mesalike mountain just east of the Buckeye Table, between the Wisconsin Range and the Ohio Range. Named for paleobotanist James M. Schopf, a member of the Horlick Mountains Party of 1961–62.

Schott Inlet. 72°10′S, 60°52′W. Small, ice-filled inlet. Indents the east side of Merz Peninsula, just south of Cape Darlington, on the east coast of Palmer Land. Discovered aerially by the USAS 1939–41 in Dec. 1940. Charted in 1947 by a joint FIDS/RARE party. Named by the FIDS for Gerhard Schott, German oceanographer.

Schrammenhügel *see* **Scar Hills**

Schroeder Hill. 85°23′S, 175°12′W. 2,680 m. 3½ miles SE of Ellis Bluff in the Cumulus Hills. Named for Henry B. Schroeder, meteorologist at Amundsen-Scott South Pole Station in 1964, and field assistant at Byrd Station in 1964–65.

Schroeder Peak. 82°15′S, 158°37′E. 2,230 m. 3 miles NW of Mount Kopere in the Cobham Range. Named for James E. Schroeder, glaciologist at Little America, 1959–60.

Schroeder Spur. 71°38′S, 160°30′E. South of Edwards Glacier and Thomson Spur (which lies parallel), at the south end of the Daniels Range in the Usarp Mountains. Named for Lauren A. Schroeder, biologist at McMurdo Station, 1967–68.

Schubert Inlet. 70°52′S, 70°55′W. Ice-filled. 14 miles long. 5 miles wide. Indents the west coast of Alexander Island between the Colbert and Walton Mountains. Named by the UK for the composer.

Schule Island. 65°46′S, 65°33′W. Small. 4 miles east of Laktionov Island, off the east side of Renaud Island, in the Biscoe Islands. Named by the UK in 1959 for John J. Schule, Jr., US oceanographer who organized the sea-ice service of the US Hydrographic Office in 1950.

Schulte Hills. 73°35′S, 163°53′E. 5 miles SSW of Stewart Heights in the Southern Cross Mountains of Victoria Land. Named by the Southern Party of the NZGSAE 1966–67 for Frank Schulte, geologist with the party.

Schulthess Buttress. 84°47′S, 115°W. An ice-capped bluff between the Ricker and Higgins Canyons on the north side of Buckeye Table in the Ohio Range. Named for Emil Schulthess, Swiss photographer on the USARP Horlick Mountains Traverse of 1958–59, which surveyed this feature in Dec. 1958.

Schultz Glacier. 77°19′S, 162°20′E. Flows between Pond Peak and Purgatory Peak into Victoria Lower Glacier. Named for Lt. Robert L. Schultz, USN, officer-in-charge of the Naval Support Force at McMurdo Station in 1975.

Schulz Point. 66°17′S, 110°29′E. The western point of Shirley Island in the Windmill Islands. Named for Richard L. Schulz, USN, construction mechanic at Wilkes Station in 1958.

Schulze Cove *see* **Bolsón Cove**

Mount Schumacher. 71°55′S, 2°58′W. 1,230 m. 6 miles SW of Nils Jørgen Peaks on the west side of the Ahlmann Ridge in Queen Maud Land. Named by the Norwegians for Nils Jørgen Schumacher.

Schumacher, Nils Jørgen. Norwegian. Senior meteorologist on the NBSAE 1949–52.

Mount Schumann. 71°35′S, 73°38′W. 500 m. Snow-covered. Just south of the head of Brahms Inlet on Beethoven Peninsula in the SW part of Alexander Island. Named by the UK for the composer.

Schumann Nunatak. 72°35′S, 163°18′E. 2 miles south of Salvador Nunatak, at the SW end of the Freyberg Mountains. Named for Edward A. Schumann, cosmic ray scientist at McMurdo Station in 1967.

Schüssel Cirque. 71°34′S, 11°33′E. Also called Grautfatet. Contains Schüssel Moraine (q.v.). In the north-central part of the Humboldt Mountains of Queen Maud Land. Discovered by Ritscher in 1938–39. He called it In der Schüssel (in the bowl), and a little later Grosse Brei-Schüssel (great mash bowl). Renamed by the USA.

Schüssel Moraine. 71°34′S, 11°32′E. A large morainal deposit in Schüssel Cirque in the Humboldt Mountains of Queen Maud Land. Discovered by Ritscher in 1938–39. Named by the USSR in 1961 in association with the cirque.

Mount Schutz. 69°46′S, 159°16′E. 1,260 m. At the east side of the head of Noll Glacier in the Wilson Hills. Named for Lt. Cdr. Albert C. Schutz, Jr., USN, aircraft commander, 1967 and 1968.

The *Schuyler Otis Bland*. USN supply ship in Antarctic waters.

The *Schwabenland*. A Lufthansa aircraft carrier, the ship of the German New Schwabenland Expedition of 1938–39. 8,488 tons. 468 feet long. 59 feet wide at its broadest. Top speed of 11 knots. Had a powerful catapult on board for the planes. It carried two hydroplanes, the *Passat* and the *Boreas*.

Schwartz, Georges. French observer with the ANARE at Mawson Station in 1954.

Schwartz Peak. 74°10′S, 76°15′W. 15 miles ESE of FitzGerald Bluffs in Ellsworth Land. Discovered aerially by Ellsworth on Nov. 23, 1935. Named for Bruce L. Schwartz, topographic engineer in Antarctica in 1967–68.

Schwartz Range. 67°08′S, 55°38′E. 17 miles SW of Edward VIII Bay, East Antarctica. Discovered in Nov. 1954 by Robert Dovers and Georges Schwartz during an ANARE sledging journey to Edward VIII Bay. Named by the Australians for Schwartz.

Schweitzer Glacier. 77°50′S, 34°40′W. Flows along the north side of the Littlewood Nunataks into Vahsel Bay. The Lerchenfeld Glacier merges with the lower portion of it. Discovered by Filchner in 1911–12. He named it for Major Schweitzer, first president of the German Antarctic Expedition Society.

Schwerdtfeger Automatic Weather Station. 79°35′S, 169°27′E. An American AWS at an elevation of approximately 200 feet. Began operating on Jan. 24, 1985.

Schwob Peak. 75°53′S, 128°39′W. 2,715 m. 1½ miles south of Mount Petras in Marie Byrd Land. Named for Capt. William S. Schwob, US Coast Guard, commander of the *Southwind* in 1972.

Schytt, Stig Valter. Glaciologist. Second-in-command of the NBSAE 1949–52.

Schytt Glacier. 71°35′S, 3°40′W. 60 miles long. Flows between the Giaever and Ahlmann Ridges of Queen Maud Land to the Jelbart Ice Shelf. Named by the NBSAE 1949–52 for Stig Valter Schytt.

Science. Scientific studies in Antarctica, especially during the IGY, have increased incalculably the knowledge of the entire earth. The first scientific efforts were the maps drawn by the early sealers of 1820–21, and the rocks, minerals, and plants brought back by them (*see* **Donald McKay, B. Astor,** and **William Napier**).

Scientific Committee on Antarctic Research. Known as SCAR. Until 1961 this organization was known as the Special Committee on Antarctic Research, but still called SCAR. The aims are identical. It had its 19th meeting at San Diego in June 1986. Presidents: 1961–63—G.R. Laclavère of France; 1963–70—Laurence Gould of the USA; 1970–74—Gordon de Q. Robin of Great Britain; 1974–78—T. Gjelsvik of Norway; 1978–82—G.A. Knox of NZ; 1982—James H. Zumberge of the USA. For more information about the organization before 1957 *see* **Special Committee on Antarctic Research.**

Scientific stations. The first scientific base in Antarctica was Scottish, Bruce's Omond House on Laurie Island in the South Orkneys. Built in 1903 it was turned over to the Argentines in 1904 (it became Orcadas Station) because the British government did not want it. The concept of a permanently manned station with annually rotated personnel was dreamed up for the USAS 1939–41, but the first was established in Feb. 1944 by the British on Deception Island in the South Shetlands during Operation Tabarin. The second was at Port Lockroy, and the third was Base D. In the late 1940s and early 1950s other nations started to build their own bases (for lists see the individual countries concerned, then the individual stations concerned). It was during IGY (1957–58) that the bulk of today's stations were established. Some stations are permanent, some are summer only, and today most welcome

tourists. Indeed, some are tourist traps to the extent that the trend will shift toward hostility to tourists if that station has only science on its mind. If it is out to take the Yankee dollar, then it will welcome tourists with increasingly open arms, and put them up at its hotels, and welcome them to its gift shops, etc. For a description of an IGY station *see* **Amundsen-Scott South Pole Station.** In Dec. 1988, there were 40 year-round stations in Antarctica, one summer one (Italy), and one abandoned one (Norway). The year-round ones were USSR (8), Argentina (6), Great Britain (4), USA (3), Chile (3), Australia (3), Japan (2), and the following with one only: Brazil, China, the two Germanys, Korea, NZ, Poland, Uruguay, France, India, and South Africa. (*See also* **Norway, Belgium, Spain, Sweden,** and **Greenpeace.**)

Scientists. The first scientist to work in Antarctica was W.H.B. Webster, in 1829, who arrived on Deception Island in the South Shetlands that year on board the *Chanticleer* to study plants and animals, and to conduct ice experiments. He left a couple of self-recording thermometers behind him. James Eights was the first American scientist to go to Antarctica, on the Palmer-Pendleton Expedition of 1829–31. Over the next 120 years every major expedition took down its share of scientists, and since the IGY (1956–57) most of the people who go are scientists.

Scoble Glacier. 67°23′S, 60°27′E. 4 miles west of Campbell Head, Mac. Robertson Land. Photographed by the LCE 1936–37 and named Breoddane (the glacier points) by the Norwegians. Renamed by the Australians for Charles H. Scoble, diesel engineer who drowned at Macquarie Island (not in the Antarctic) in July 1948.

Cape Scoresby. 66°34′S, 162°45′E. Marks the northern end of Borrodaile Island in the Balleny Islands. Charted by the personnel on the *Discovery II* in 1936–38. Named by them for the *William Scoresby,* their sister ship.

Scoresby Bay *see* **William Scoresby Bay**

Scorpio Peaks. 70°31'S, 67°26'W. A massif with 2 high conical peaks on its western end and with a ridge of lower peaks extending eastward. Separates the Meiklejohn and Millett Glaciers on the western edge of Palmer Land. Named by the UK for the constellation Scorpio.

The *Scotia*. Norwegian whaler bought in 1901 and refitted in Scotland to be used for the Scottish National Antarctic Expedition of 1902–4, led by Bruce. Bruce renamed it, and it had a crew of 25, under Capt. Thomas Robertson. Bruce froze it in the ice at Laurie Island in the winter of 1903.

Scotia Arc *see* **Scotia Ridge**

Scotia Bay. 60°46'S, 44°40'W. 2½ miles wide. Just east of the Mossman Peninsula on the south side of Laurie Island in the South Orkneys. Discovered and charted in Dec. 1821 by Powell and Palmer. Surveyed by Bruce in 1903, and named by him in 1904 for his ship, the *Scotia*.

Scotia Ridge. Also called Scotia Arc, South Andillean Arc, South Atlantic Arc, South Sandwich Arc. An undersea ridge which runs between the Weddell Sea and South Georgia (54°S). Although it centers on 57°S, 27°W, part of it does go south of 60°S.

Scotia Sea. Although this sea centers on 57°30'S, 40°W, part of it does go further south than 60°S. It is bounded by the Shag Rocks, South Georgia, and the South Sandwich Islands. Named about 1932 for the *Scotia*.

Cape Scott. 71°08'S, 168°05'E. At the west side of the terminus of Dennistoun Glacier on the north coast of Victoria Land. Discovered and named by Ross in 1841 for Peter A. Scott.

¹Mount Scott. 65°09'S, 64°03'W. Also called Scott Massif. It is indeed a massif. 880 m. Horseshoe-shaped. Its convex side fronts on Girard Bay and its NW side fronts on the Lemaire Channel on the

west coast of Graham Land. Discovered by de Gerlache in 1897–99 and named by Charcot in 1908–10 for Robert F. Scott.

²Mount Scott *see* **Mount Robert Scott**

Scott, Gilbert. A private in the RMLI (Royal Marine Light Infantry). He took part in the Royal Society Expedition of 1901–4. Apparently no relation to the leader of the expedition, Robert F. Scott.

Scott, John G. Captain of the *Emerald*, 1820–21.

Scott, Nan. Microbiologist from Oklahoma. In 1973 she and Donna Muchmore became the first women ever to work at the South Pole (at Amundsen-Scott South Pole Station). She goes every summer to the Pole (except 1977–78) to collect blood samples from wintering-over personnel.

Scott, Peter. b. Sept. 14, 1909, London. d. Aug. 30, 1989. Peter Markham Scott. Son of Robert F. Scott. Went to the Antarctic several times, notably in 1966, and again in Feb. 1968 when he was tour leader on the *Navarino*. First person to be knighted for services to conservation.

Scott, Peter A. Midshipman on the *Terror* during Ross' 1839–43 expedition.

Scott, Robert Falcon. b. June 6, 1868, Devonport, England. d. ca. March 29, 1912, in the Antarctic. Son of a brewer, Scott was a career Navy man. He was picked out of the blue by Sir Clements Markham, president of the Royal Geographical Society, to head the Royal Society Expedition of 1901–4. The most legendary (if not the greatest, perhaps) of all the Antarctic explorers, he was the first real explorer there, as opposed to navigator/discoverer, and pioneered the use of sledges and dogs on the continent. On June 30, 1901, he was promoted to commander, and transferred to the *Discovery* as its commander, leaving England on Aug. 5, 1901. The epitome of heroism, he and two companions trekked to 82°16'S, a new southing

record, in late 1902, and barely made it
back to base alive. He preferred manhauling sledges to having dogs pull
them, and exhibited the most astonishing endurance and will power, as he did
on his second expedition of 1910–13. He
was the second leader to stand at the
South Pole, on Jan. 17, 1912, a month
after Amundsen. An excellent writer and
diary-keeper, he kept it up to the end,
dying with his four companions on the
return from the Pole. His, Wilson's, and
Bowers' bodies were discovered 8 months
later along with Scott's diary. The last
entry reads, "Every day we have been
ready to start for our depot 11 *miles* away,
but outside the door of the tent it remains a scene of whirling drift . . . we
shall stick it out to the end, but we are
getting weaker, of course, and the end
cannot be far. It seems a pity, but I do
not think I can write more." Scott was
never knighted, not even posthumously,
but his wife was later made Lady Scott in
her own right. Those are the facts surrounding Scott, but what about the
theories? Was he a bungling fool, or was
he a hero? Was he an immature martinet
who led his men to certain death, or was
he a man who knew what he wanted and
expected others to keep up with him?
Did he really run out of steam in the blizzard (and if so, did all three men run out
of steam together?), or did he decide he
could not face life, and talk the others
into dying with him in the tent? Was he
a weak, vacillating, glory seeker, or was
he an old fashioned hero who faced problems when he came to them? These ques-
tions and more are being asked with
greater and greater frequency, it seems,
as time goes by. This author believes this
of Scott: Whatever his faults he was the
greatest of the Antarctic explorers, and a
true hero who should be remembered
that way in an age now when heroes are
hard to find. He had the qualities which
we all wish we had, and some of us do,
and those who knock him probably know
they do not have—guts, determination,
physical and mental strength, romanti-
cism, theatricalism, an overriding sense

of competition and fear of failure, a
devil-may-care attitude about hardship,
a sense of glory, and a great awareness of
the Grand Gesture.

Scott, Thomas. Quartermaster on the
Wilkes Expedition 1838–42. Joined in
the USA. Served the cruise.

Scott Base. 77°51′S, 166°45′E. At
Pram Point at the end of Hut Point
Peninsula on Ross Island. About 2 miles
east of McMurdo Station. It is New Zealand's only active year-round scientific
station, and was built in 1957 by Sir Edmund Hillary as the Ross Island base for
the BCTAE, and it also served NZ during
the IGY. Hillary was its first commander
and Trevor Hatherton was scientific
leader in 1957. L. Martin was leader of
the base in 1958. It became a permanent
base in 1959–60. It tripled in size in the
early 1980s.

Scott Bay *see* **Scar Inlet**

Scott Canyon. 72°S, 179°E. Submarine feature of the Ross Sea.

Scott Coast. 76°30′S, 162°30′E. Between Cape Washington and Minna
Bluff, on the Ross Sea coast, in the
southern Victoria Land area. Named by
New Zealand in 1961 for Robert F. Scott,
who explored much of this coastline.

Scott Cone. 66°55′S, 163°15′E. A conical hill 2 miles NNE of Cape McNab on
the south end of Buckle Island in the
Balleny Islands. Next to Eliza Cone. Both
features were named for the *Eliza Scott,*
Balleny's ship.

¹Scott Glacier. 66°15′S, 100°05′E. 7
miles wide. 20 miles long. Flows to the
coast between Cape Hoadley and Grace
Rocks, behind the Shackleton Ice Shelf in
Wilkes Land. Discovered by the *Aurora*
party during the Australasian Antarctic
Expedition of 1911–14, and named by
Mawson for Robert F. Scott.

²Scott Glacier *see* **Robert Scott Glacier**

Scott Icefalls. 85°34′S, 170°E. Near the
head of Mill Glacier, between the Otway
Massif and the southern part of the

Dominion Range. Named by the New Zealanders in 1961–62 for Robert F. Scott.

Scott Island. 67°24'S, 179°55'W. ¼ mile long. ⅛ mile wide. Looks like an elephant's head when viewed from the west. 315 miles NE of Cape Adare. It was discovered on Dec. 25, 1902, by William Colbeck in the *Morning,* and named by him for Robert F. Scott, whose expedition Colbeck was on his way to relieve. It was not seen again, and its existence was doubted, until Dec. 10, 1928, when Byrd resighted it from the *City of New York.* It had always been obscured by the fog.

Scott Island Automatic Weather Station. 67°22'S, 179°58'W. American AWS at an elevation of approximately 100 feet. Began operating on Dec. 25, 1987.

Scott Island Bank. A submarine ridge centering on 67°45'S, 179°55'W. Named for Scott Island, the nearest land in the area.

Cape Scott Keltie *see* **Keltie Head**

Scott Keltie Glacier. 71°33'S, 169°49'E. Flows into Robertson Bay between Penelope Point and Egeberg Glacier on the north coast of Victoria Land. Charted by Borchgrevink in 1898–1900, and named by him for Sir John Scott Keltie, secretary of the Royal Geographical Society.

Scott Massif *see* **Mount Scott**

Scott Mountains. 67°30'S, 50°30'E. South of Amundsen Bay, which they overlook, in Enderby Land. Discovered on Jan. 13, 1930, by the BANZARE and named Scott Range by Mawson, for Robert F. Scott. Because of the isolation of the individual peaks within this group, the term "mountains" is preferred to "range," and it was redefined.

Scott Nunataks *see* **Scott's Nunataks**

Scott of the Antarctic. British movie of 1948, directed by Charles Frend, produced by Michael Balcon, from a screenplay by Ivor Montagu, Walter Meade, and Mary Hayley Bell. The players were John

Mills (as Scott), Harold Warrender (as Wilson), Kenneth More (as Teddie Evans), Derek Bond (as Oates), Reginald Beckwith (as Bowers), James Robertson Justice (as Taff Evans), James McKechnie (as Atkinson), Norman Williamson (as Lashly), Barry Letts (as Cherry-Garrard), Clive Morton (as Ponting), Bruce Seton (as Pennell), Christopher Lee (as Day), Dennis Vance (as Wright), John Gregson (as Crean), Diana Churchill (as Kathleen Scott), and Anne Firth (as Oriana Wilson). Technical advisor was Quintin Riley (q.v.).

Scott Peninsula. 74°22'S, 117°58'W. Ice-covered. 17 miles long. Extends from the coast of Marie Byrd Land into the Getz Ice Shelf toward the west end of Wright Island. Named for Lt. Col. Thomas Scott, US Army finance and liaison officer for Antarctica in 1956–57.

Scott Polar Research Institute. Seen abbreviated as the SPRI. Founded in 1926 principally by Frank Debenham (the first director, from 1926–48), with monies left over from the Scott Memorial Fund. It is at Lensfield Road, Cambridge, England, CB2 1ER.

Scott Range *see* **Scott Mountains**

Scott Shoal. 73°15'S, 177°E. A submarine feature of the Ross Sea.

Scott Uplands. 72°40'S, 66°W. On the west side of Palmer Land.

Scott's Hut Race. First held at McMurdo Station on Dec. 3, 1978, and annually since. It is a 5-mile course from the Eklund Biological Center to the tip of Hut Point, up the hill to the Cosmic Ray Lab, and back to Eklund. It came about because there were a lot of joggers at McMurdo Station. The Navy graded the roads for the first race, in which 89 runners took part, 85 finishing. Audrey Haschemeyer was the first woman to finish the race, in 48 minutes 43 seconds.

Scott's Huts. There are two still standing on Ross Island, one at Hut Point, and the other at Cape Evans. Both are protected as historic sites. The Discovery

Hut (so named by Scott on his return to the area in 1911) at Hut Point was constructed during February and early March 1902, during the Royal Society Expedition. However, it was used only for storage and other similar purposes. It is 36 feet square, and is the most historic site on the continent. Shackleton visited it again on Aug. 14, 1908, and Scott did so again on Jan. 15, 1911. Scott left the hut for the last time on Nov. 3, 1911. It had been used by Scott as a depot on his last expedition, and at that time the two smaller huts nearby, which Scott had built in 1902 of lighter wood and covered with asbestos sheets, were still standing, but they are gone now. The Discovery Hut was restored in 1963 by the New Zealand Antarctic Society, and today it is a tourist landmark. The other Scott hut is ¼ mile north of Cape Evans and was used as the base for his last expedition. It measures 50 by 20 feet.

Scott's Nunataks. 77°14′S, 154°12′W. Also called Scott Nunataks. Twin nunataks which form the north end of the Alexandra Mountains on Edward VII Peninsula. Discovered by Scott's 1901–4 expedition. Named in 1911 by Prestrud for Robert F. Scott.

Scouts. Shackleton was the first to take a Boy Scout to the Antarctic. In fact he took two on the *Quest* in 1921–22, J.W.S. Marr and Norman E. Mooney. Mooney got off at Madeira on the way south, and never made it to the ice. Marr did, and this began a lifetime of Antarctic exploration for him. Byrd advertised a competition for a Boy Scout, the winner to go with him to Antarctica in 1928. He had to be between 17½ and 19½. Paul Siple, aged 19, won from the six finalists, in New York. He wrote *A Boy Scout with Byrd*, and thus began another successful Antarctic career. The second US Scout to go down was Dick Chappell, who went with the US team in 1956 for the IGY. Mark Leinmiller, an Eagle Scout, went in 1978, and Douglas Barnhard of McMurray, Pa., was selected to go south in 1984–85. In 1985–86 two Girl Scouts,

Karen Prentice and Robin Moyle, went to McMurdo Station. In 1988–89 Julie Hagelin spent 8 weeks at McMurdo Station. Robert Scot Duncan, 19, was the 6th Boy Scout selected by the Boy Scouts of America to go to Antarctica since 1928. That was in 1989–90.

Scree Cove. 67°34′S, 67°08′W. On the SW side of Blaiklock Island, in Graham Land. Named by the FIDS for the prominent scree slopes along the southern shore of the cove.

Scree Peak. 63°38′S, 57°27′W. 560 m. Flat-topped. Has scree-covered slopes. At the NE end of Eagle Island in the Prince Gustav Channel, off the south coast of Trinity Peninsula. Discovered by the FIDS in 1945, and surveyed and named by them for the scree slopes.

Screen Islands. 65°01′S, 63°43′W. Also called Islotes Menier. They extend 1½ miles NW from Aguda Point across the entrance to Hidden Bay, off the west coast of Graham Land. Charted by de Gerlache in 1897–99. Named by the UK in 1958 because they form a screen across the entrance to Hidden Bay.

Scripps Heights. 69°08′S, 63°40′W. Also called Scripps Ridge. Largely ice-covered. Overlooks Cape Walcott at the northern edge of the Eternity Range, between the Casey and Lurabee Glaciers. Discovered aerially by Wilkins on Dec. 20, 1928, and named by him as Scripps Island for William Scripps of Detroit. In the 1930s it was redefined by the BGLE as a peninsula, and renamed Scripps Peninsula. It was later redefined again as Scripps Heights.

Scripps Island *see* **Scripps Heights**

Scripps Peninsula *see* **Scripps Heights**

Scripps Ridge *see* **Scripps Heights**

Scrivener Glacier. 76°57′S, 161°37′E. Flows into the northern side of Mackay Glacier just west of Mount Allan Thomson in Victoria Land. Charted and named by Scott's 1910–13 expedition.

Cape Scrymgeour. 63°35′S, 56°26′W. Composed of high, red-colored, volcanic rock cliffs. Forms the east end of Andersson Island in Antarctic Sound, off the NE tip of the Antarctic Peninsula. Named by Thomas Robertson of the *Active* in 1893. Reidentified and charted by the FIDS in 1947.

Scud Rock. 63°23'S, 55°01'W. An isolated rock in water, 4 miles south of Moody Point, the eastern extremity of Joinville Island. Surveyed by the FIDS in 1953. The UK named it for the scud (low, fast-moving cloud) prevalent here.

Scudder Mountain. 86°07'S, 149°36' W. 2,280 m. Between Organ Pipe Peaks and Mount McKercher on the east side of the Robert Scott Glacier in the Queen Maud Mountains. The name first appears on Paul Siple's 1938 botany report on Byrd's 1933–35 expedition, based on Quin Blackburn's visit here in 1934.

Scudder Peak. 75°53'S, 115°12'W. Just SW of Spitz Ridge, on the south side of Toney Mountain, in Marie Byrd Land. Named for Brent E. Scudder, meteorologist at Byrd Station in 1966.

Scullin Monolith. 67°48'S, 66°42'E. A crescent-shaped rock 4 miles west of Torlyn Mountain on the Mawson Coast in Mac. Robertson Land. It is next to the Murray Monolith. Mawson landed on it in a plane on Feb. 13, 1931, during the BANZARE, and named it for J.H. Scullin, the prime minister of Australia. In Jan.-Feb. 1931 Norwegian whalers charted it, and named it Mount Klarius Mikkelsen, for Klarius Mikkelsen. The Mawson naming has become accepted, and Mikkelsen Peak is now the highest feature on the monolith.

Sculpture Mountain. 72°51'S, 162°03' E. Also called Sculpture Tableland. Between the Monument Nunataks and Sheehan Mesa. The mountain is dissected. Named by the New Zealanders in 1962–63 for the cuspate embayment which has been sculpted into the feature.

Sculpture Tableland *see* **Sculpture Mountain**

Scurvy. Acute lack of vitamin C. It is always fatal if untreated. Symptoms are swollen limbs, bleeding gums, loosening teeth, depression, mental derangement. It was the scourge of sailors throughout history, but became really noticeable to the world during the long ocean voyages of the 17th and 18th centuries, when it was a long time between ports. Cook devised a cure for it—fresh fruit and vegetables, even though vitamins were not discovered until the 20th century. Cook had great success in keeping his crews alive, but some other captains did not enforce the diet so strictly. Later the lime juice, which had been so efficacious when fresh, was bottled and stored, and thus lost its value. Of course, it was lime juice that was held up to ridicule, and so more scurvy appeared in the 19th century. Davis' 1821–22 crew got it, and had to recuperate in the Falklands. Some of the crew of the *Seraph* got it in 1830, and a couple of Biscoe's crew died from it in 1831. The *Zélée* had 38 cases of it in 1838. Armitage's Sept. 1902 Western Party all returned to base with scurvy during the Royal Society Expedition of 1901–4, and Shackleton got it in 1903 during the same expedition. He got it so badly that he had to be invalided home on the *Morning*. In 1912 Oates was riddled with it, and if he had not walked out of the tent into the blizzard he would surely have died of scurvy instead. Dr. Raney (q.v.) reported a case of it at the South Pole as late as 1979.

Scylla Glacier. 70°20'S, 67°E. Flows between the Athos and Porthos Ranges of the Prince Charles Mountains, and feeds the Amery Ice Shelf from above the Lars Christensen Coast. Discovered in Dec. 1956 by Bewsher's ANARE Southern Party. Named by the Australians for the Greek mythological sea monster, due to the difficulty in crossing the glacier.

Scythian Nunatak. 76°44'S, 159°46'E. Isolated. 1 mile SE of Trudge Valley in the Allan Hills of Victoria Land. The Romans found Scythia to be shrouded in snow. So did the NZ Allan Hills Expedition of 1964 of this nunatak.

Sea elephant *see* **Elephant seals**

The *Sea Gull*. An old 110-ton pilot boat from New York. 73½ feet long. 20½ feet in the beam. 9 feet 9 inches in depth in hold. 2 guns. A crew of 15. It was part of the Wilkes Expedition of 1838–42. Lt. Johnson took over command of it at Tierra del Fuego, and after an unsuccessful venture to Deception Island (*see* **Wilkes**), Midshipman Reid took over command. It disappeared off the Chile coast in late April 1839.

Sea ice   *see*   **Annual ice**

Sea leopard   *see*   **Leopard seal**

Sea Leopard Patch. 62°05′S, 58°24′W. A shoal near the center of Visca Anchorage, Admiralty Bay, King George Island in the South Shetlands. Charted and named by the personnel on the *Discovery* in 1927.

Sea lions. Order: Otariids. Plentiful in the Falklands, but rarely, if ever seen in the Antarctic.

Sea snails. Order: Liparidae. Fish living at the sea bottom.

Sea spiders   *see*   **Pycnogonids**

Sea stars. The Antarctic sea star is *Perknaster fuscus antarcticus*. Notable for its high level of protein (38% of the dry weight).

Seabee Heights. 85°13′S, 171°15′W. 3,400 m. Snow-covered. 15 miles long. 5 miles wide. Bounded by the DeGanahl, LaVergne and Liv Glaciers in the Queen Maud Mountains. Named for the Seabees (q.v.).

Seabee Hook. 72°19′S, 170°13′E. Composed of coarse, volcanic ash. Forms the tip of Cape Hallett, in Victoria Land. Hallett Station was here. Named for the Seabees who surveyed it in Jan. 1956, from the *Edisto*.

Seabees. Construction Battalion (CB) units of the US Navy. They built Little America IV in 1947, and since then have played a great part in the building of American scientific stations in Antarctica.

Seabold, George. Seaman on the Wilkes Expedition 1838–42. Joined at Rio. Run at Aurora Island.

Seafarer Glacier. 72°54′S, 166°34′E. Flows from the Webb Névé between the Lawrence Peaks and Malta Plateau, into Mariner Glacier in Victoria Land. Named by the Mariner Glacier Party of the NZGSAE 1966–67, in association with the name Mariner.

Seal Bay. 71°45′S, 12°45′W. Indents the NE end of the Riiser-Larsen Peninsula, just south of Cape Norvegia on the coast of Queen Maud Land. Discovered in 1930 by Riiser-Larsen who named it for the many seals here.

Seal Glacier. 79°53′S, 81°50′W. Just north of Parrish Peak in the Enterprise Hills of the Heritage Range. Named for G.L. Seal, USN, radioman in Antarctica for 4 austral summers up to 1966.

¹Seal Islands. 60°58′S, 55°24′W. A group of small, rocky islets, 3–6 miles north of Elephant Island. They are the northernmost of the South Shetland Islands. Discovered by Bransfield in 1820. The largest one was named Seal Island by William Smith that year for the number of seals caught here. The group was called Seal Rocks, and later Seal Islands.

²Seal Islands   *see*   **Seal Nunataks**

Seal Nunataks. 65°03′S, 60°18′W. Also named Robben Nunataks. To the NW of Robertson Island in the north of the Larsen Ice Shelf. Discovered and named Seal Islands in Dec. 1893 by Carl A. Larsen. Surveyed and redefined in 1902 by the Nordenskjöld expedition. They include Åkerlundh, Arctowski, Bull, Bruce, Castor, Christensen, Dallmann, Donald, Evensen, Gray, Murdoch, Hertha and Oceana Nunataks.

¹Seal Point. 63°24′S, 56°59′W. Extends north from the SE shore of Hope Bay between Eagle Cove and Hut Cove, at the NE end of the Antarctic Peninsula. Discovered by J. Gunnar Andersson's party during the Nordenskjöld expedition of 1901–4. They killed a seal here to save their shortage of food and fuel.

²Seal Point. 71°22'S, 170°14'E. Also called Robbenspitze. 3½ miles south of Ridley Beach on the west side of Adare Peninsula in northern Victoria Land. Charted and named by Campbell's Northern Party during Scott's 1910–13 expedition.

¹Seal Rocks *see* **Seal Islands**

²Seal Rocks. 66°15'S, 162°16'E. Rocks in water. 15 meters high. They extend 3 miles NNW of Cape Ellsworth, the northern extremity of Young Island in the Balleny Islands.

Sealer Hill. 62°40'S, 61°06'W. On the southern coast of Byers Peninsula, on Livingston Island in the South Shetlands. Named for the old sealers who used to frequent this area.

Sealers Passage. 61°02'S, 55°23'W. A marine channel between Elephant Island and Seal Islands in the South Shetlands. It was used by sealers in the 1820s as a shortcut around the north coast of Elephant Island. Named by the UK in 1971.

Sealing. Commercial fur sealing began in the Falklands in 1766, and when Cook discovered South Georgia at 54°S, and published the fact that he had seen a lot of seals in Southern waters, this led to the first wave of exploration in search of new sealing grounds. If any sealers discovered the South Shetlands and South Orkneys before 1819, they kept it a secret. The *Hersilia*, the *San Juan Nepomuceno,* and the *Espírito Santo* confirmed the presence of the islands, and this led to the rush of 1820–21, when 30 American ships went south (the best known of the season being the Fanning-Pendleton Sealing Expedition) and at least 24 British ships, and some others of other nationalities. As an example of the toll taken on the seal population in the South Shetlands just that first season, the *Hersilia* alone took 18,000 superior sealskins (who knows how many were rejected — after the killing), while the *San Juan Nepomuceno* took 14,600. In 1820–22 alone 320,000 fur seals were killed in the South Shetlands. They were easy prey.

They had no reason to be afraid of humans. They would come up to them in a friendly manner and be clubbed to death. Sealers would be exhausted at the end of a day's work on a crowded beach, laying to left and right as they pushed their way along the beach. 1820–22 was the peak period of sealing activity in the South Shetlands, and then fur sealing died out — after well over 100 vessels had pulled in here. After 1822 the catches fell off dramatically, and expeditions were mounted to find new lands, and vessels now combined fur sealing with elephant seal oil. In the late 1860s the seal population began to grow slightly, but in 1871 James W. Buddington and others revived the US Antarctic fur sealing program in the South Shetlands. No thought was given to the extinction of species, or to what would happen to the industry in the future, until 1881 when the first controlling regulations came into effect by the British in the Falklands and the Antarctic Peninsula. In 1972 a Convention was signed to prohibit sealing in Antarctica. The Antarctic Treaty signatories were at this convention, which was fully ratified on March 11, 1978, and went into force as the Convention for the Conservation of Antarctic Seals. It restricts the number of crabeater seals taken yearly to 175,000; leopard seals to 12,000; Weddell seals to 5,000. Ross seals, southern elephant seals, and fur seals are totally protected.

Seals. Seals are pinnipeds, and true seals belong to the Phocid order. They are generally unafraid of man, and this has cost them dearly. Sometimes seals go as far as 30 miles inland, and as high up as 3,000 feet. Fur seals were slaughtered so extensively that by 1822 they had virtually disappeared (after only 2 years contact with man). (*See* **Fur seals, Weddell seals, Ross seals, Crabeater seals, Elephant seals, Leopard seals.**)

Seamounts. Submarine mountains. *See* **Barth Seamount, Maud Seamount, Vaughan Bank, Umitaka Bank.**

Seaplane Point. 64°03′S, 60°46′W. At the south side of Curtiss Bay on the west coast of Graham Land. Named by the UK for Glenn Curtiss (1878–1930), seaplane pioneer.

Seaquist Peak. 79°45′S, 81°20′W. 800 m. Surmounts the NW end of the Meyer Hills in the Heritage Range. Named for Larry R. Seaquist, meteorologist at Ellsworth Station in 1961.

Mount Searle. 67°49′S, 67°15′W. Between Sally and Gaul Coves on Horseshoe Island. Named by the UK for Derek J.H. Searle of the FIDS, surveyor at Base Y in 1955 and 1956. He surveyed this mountain.

Seas. The main Antarctic seas are Ross, Weddell, Bellingshausen, Amundsen, Davis.

Seasons. Summer is November, December, and January, and the sun never falls below the horizon. Therefore it is always light, one long day really. In late March a long dusk occurs and on April 24 the sun disappears and winter begins. This is one long night, where the sun does not shine. On Midwinters Day, June 21, the sun reaches only to the Antarctic Circle, which is a long way from the Pole (1,410 miles). In late September a gray-pink dawn heralds the spring (as it were, although there is no real spring, and no real fall), and then in November comes summer again. Needless to say, perhaps, but summer is cold, and winter is colder.

Mount Seaton. 70°36′S, 67°27′E. Domed. One of the Amery Peaks. 3 miles south of Sandilands Nunatak in the Prince Charles Mountains. Named by the Australians for Pilot Officer John Seaton, RAAF pilot with the Antarctic Flight at Mawson Station in 1956. That season he was promoted to flight lieutenant.

Seaton Glacier. 66°43′S, 56°26′E. 17 miles long. Flows into Edward VIII Ice Shelf at the NW part of Edward VIII Bay. Photographed by the LCE 1936–37.

Named by the Australians in 1958 for John Seaton (see **Mount Seaton**).

The Seaver. Ship on the Argentine Antarctic Expedition of 1947–48. Captain Alberto Patrón.

Canal Seaver see **George VI Sound**

Seavers Nunataks. 73°16′S, 61°58′E. 2 nunataks. 16 miles west of Mount Scherger, near the head of Fisher Glacier in the Prince Charles Mountains. Named by the Australians for J.A. Seavers, assistant cook at Mawson Station in 1961.

Seavers Ridge. 67°03′S, 52°51′E. 14 miles ESE of Mount Renouard in Enderby Land. Named by the Australians for J.A. Seavers (see **Seavers Nunataks**).

Seawater distillation plants. One was installed at McMurdo Station in 1965, and a new one in 1987. The new one can supply up to 80,000 gallons of fresh water every day from McMurdo Sound. The old one became a secondary machine, used only for emergencies.

Seay Nunatak. 84°03′S, 54°38′W. 3 miles south of Hill Nunatak, at the SE end of the Neptune Range in the Pensacola Mountains. Named for William K. Seay, utilitiesman at Ellsworth Station in 1958.

Seay Peak. 79°05′S, 157°30′E. 1,805 m. Ice-free. The NE summit in the Finger Ridges of the Cook Mountains. Named for Benny F. Seay, US Army Aviation Support, 1961–62.

Sechrist Peak. 75°23′S, 111°02′W. 1,350 m. On the SW spur of the Mount Murphy massif. Named for Frank S. Sechrist, US exchange scientist at Molodezhnaya Station in 1975.

Secluded Rocks. 67°32′S, 59°20′E. Between Mulebreen and Cosgrove Glacier. 6 miles SSW of Kemp Peak in Enderby Land. Named by the Australians because the rocks are in a hollow.

Second Crater. 77°49′S, 166°40′E. Just over ½ mile NE of First Crater, on Arrival Heights, Hut Point Peninsula, Ross Island. Named by Frank Debenham in

1912 while surveying the peninsula as part of Scott's 1910–13 expedition.

Second Facet. 77°11′S, 162°18′E. An ice-free escarpment just west of First Facet. The two features form the north wall of Debenham Glacier in Victoria Land. Charted and named descriptively by members of Scott's 1910–13 expedition.

Secret Lake. 71°50′S, 68°21′W. A meltwater lake. 2 miles west of Ares Cliff, in eastern Alexander Island. It is in a cirque and is fed from an area of stagnant ice. It is 100 meters above the eastern edge of Mars Glacier and can be seen only from the cirque or aerially. Named descriptively by the UK.

The Secret Land. 1948 movie produced by Orville O. Dull. It is a documentary studying Byrd's expeditions to Antarctica. Van Heflin, Robert Montgomery, and Robert Taylor narrated.

Section Peak. 73°14′S, 161°56′E. A sandstone knob at the north end of the Lichen Hills in Victoria Land. It provides for the geologists one of the few sections seen in sedimentary beds. Named by the New Zealanders in 1962–63.

Security. As it is highly unlikely that anyone is going to rob, vandalize, or otherwise threaten an Antarctic station, security as we know it in "civilized" countries is not necessary, except perhaps to keep the tourists from trampling over scientifically special ground. Besides, at most of the bases there is a military presence of one sort or another. Also, there is no need for spies—Antarctic research is open to all visitors. On a personal level of security, no one should leave the confines of an Antarctic station without at least one other person.

Security Bay. 64°51′S, 63°37′W. Also called Bahía Sin Nombre. Between Homeward and Gauthier Points on the north side of Doumer Island in the Palmer Archipelago. Charted by Charcot in 1903–5. Named by the UK in 1958 because it gives shelter to small craft.

Mount Seddon. 73°06′S, 65°E. Has 2 peaks separated by an ice-filled saddle. 20 miles west of Mount Stinear on the north side of Fisher Glacier in the Prince Charles Mountains. Discovered aerially by the ANARE in 1957. Named by the Australians for Norman R. Seddon, managing director of B.P. Australia, a continuing sponsor of the ANARE.

Sedgwick Glacier. 69°51′S, 69°22′W. 7 miles long. 2 miles wide. Flows from the foot of Mount Stephenson on the east coast of Alexander Island into George VI Sound just north of Mount King. Surveyed in 1936 by the BGLE and again in 1948 by the FIDS, who named it for Adam Sedgwick (1785–1873), British geologist who named the Cambrian period.

Cape Sedov. 69°22′S, 14°05′E. An ice cape. Forms the NW extremity of the Lazarev Ice Shelf on the Queen Maud Land coast. Named by the USSR in 1959 for G.Y. Sedov, polar explorer.

See Nunatak. 68°19′S, 59°09′E. The most northerly of the group of peaks forming the eastern part of the Hansen Mountains. Named by the Australians for R. See, chief helicopter mechanic with the ANARE in 1965.

Mount Seebeck. 85°44′S, 150°46′W. At the head of Roe Glacier in the Tapley Mountains in the Queen Maud Mountains. Named for Richard L. Seebeck, station engineer at McMurdo Station in 1962.

Mount Seedsman. 70°09′S, 65°26′E. 8 miles east of Mount Dovers in the Athos Range of the Prince Charles Mountains. Named by the Australians for D.L. Seedsman, electronics engineer at Mawson Station in 1964.

Mount Seekopf. 71°17′S, 13°42′E. Also called Sjöhausen. 1,300 m. Surmounts the eastern side of Lake Ober-See in the Gruber Mountains of Queen Maud Land. Discovered and named Seekopf (lake peak) by Ritscher in 1938–39.

Mount Seelig. 82°28′S, 103°54′W. 3,020 m. The highest of the Whitmore

Mountains, at the NE end of the group. Surveyed on Jan. 2, 1959, by William H. Chapman of the Horlick Mountains Traverse of 1958–59, and named by him for Walter R. Seelig, National Science Foundation official who has been several times to the Antarctic.

Sefton Glacier. 80°45′S, 156°52′E. 10 miles long. Flows into the south side of Byrd Glacier, just west of Rundle Peaks. Named for Ronald Sefton, ionosphere physicist at Byrd Station in 1962 and 1964.

Mount Segers. 78°25′S, 85°22′W. 2,460 m. To the east of the head of Crosswell Glacier. 7 miles east of Mount Tyree in the central part of the Sentinel Range. Discovered aerially by VX-6 on Dec. 14–15, 1959. Named for Chester W. Segers, Navy cook at the South Pole Station in 1957.

Sei whale. *Balaenoptera borealis.* A rorqual which frequents the waters of Antarctica.

Seid, Frederick. Radio operator from New York City. He was on Ellsworth's 1938–39 expedition.

Seilkopf Peaks. 72°41′S, 4°W. Mainly ice-free peaks and ridges between Portalen Pass and Nålegga Ridge in the Borg Massif of Queen Maud Land. Named by Ritscher in 1939 for Heinrich Seilkopf, head of the Marine Aerology section of the German Hydrographic Office.

Seismology. In 1985 US and French scientists conducted a major seismology expedition at the South Pole (*see also* Earthquakes).

Mount Seitz. 71°43′S, 166°05′E. 2,130 m. Between Mirabito Range and Homerun Range in northern Victoria Land. 4 miles SE of Mount Armagost. 9 miles NW of Boss Peak. Named for Thomas E. Seitz, USN, chief construction mechanic at McMurdo Station in 1967.

The *Seksern*. Norwegian whaler in Antarctic waters off the coast of East Antarctica in Jan. 1931, commanded by the Brunvoll Brothers.

Cape Selborne. 80°23′S, 160°47′E. Snow-covered. At the south side of Barne Inlet, at the end of the Byrd Glacier. It juts out from the Shackleton Coast into the western side of the Ross Ice Shelf. Discovered by Scott in 1902, and named by him for the Earl of Selborne, lord of the Admiralty.

Seligman Inlet. 67°50′S, 65°30′W. A large Larsen Ice Shelf indentation into the east side of the Antarctic Peninsula between Cape Freeman and Choyce Point. It recedes inland for 6 miles. Charted by the FIDS in 1947, and named by them for Gerald Seligman, founder and president of the British Glaciological Society.

Seller Glacier. 69°21′S, 66°24′W. 20 miles long. 4 miles wide. Flows into the Forster Ice Piedmont in the west part of the Antarctic Peninsula, just north of Flinders Peak. Surveyed by the BGLE in 1936–37, and again by the FIDS in Dec. 1958. Named by the UK for John Seller (ca. 1658–1698), navigation pioneer.

Mount Sellery. 84°58′S, 172°45′W. 3,895 m. Between Mounts Oliver and Smithson in the Prince Olav Mountains. Discovered aerially by Byrd on Nov. 18, 1929. Surveyed by Crary in 1957–58, and named by him for Harry Sellery of the US National Bureau of Standards, who was Antarctic project leader for ionosphere studies in 1957–60.

Selvick Cove *see* **Lagarrigue Cove**

Mount Selwood. 66°53′S, 51°30′E. 5 miles NE of Pythagoras Peak in the Tula Mountains of Enderby Land. Named by the Australians for C.H.V. Selwood.

Selwood, C.H.V. Crew member on the *Discovery* during the BANZARE 1929–31.

Bukhta Semerka *see* **Adams Fjord**

Semper Shaftus *see* **Pagano Nunatak**

Mount Semprebon. 82°04′S, 88°01′W. Partly snow-free. 1 mile NE of Mount Barsoum in the Martin Hills. Named in 1958 by the US Ellsworth-Byrd Traverse

Party for Louis C. Semprebon, ionosphere physicist and assistant scientific leader at Ellsworth Station in 1958.

Mount Send. 70°02′S, 159°49′E. 1,180 m. On the north flank of Pryor Glacier. 10 miles east of Basilica Peak in the southern part of the Wilson Hills. Named for Raymond F. Send, geophysicist at McMurdo Station, 1967–68.

Sengekoven Cirque. 71°53′S, 5°26′E. Indents the north side of Breplogen Mountain, just east of Høgsenga Crags in the Mühlig-Hofmann Mountains of Queen Maud Land. Name means "the bed closet" in Norwegian.

Senia Point. 80°31′S, 160°59′E. Ice-covered. 9 miles south of Cape Selborne. Marks the north side of the entrance to Couzens Bay on the west side of the Ross Ice Shelf. Named for B. Senia, captain of the *Mizar* in 1962 and of the *Mirzak* in 1963.

The *Sennett*. Submarine used by the central group of Task Force 68 during Operation Highjump, 1946–47. Commanded by Joseph B. Icenhower, USN. It failed in the Antarctic because it was unable to handle the pack-ice. It was withdrawn by the *Northwind,* Jan. 2–5, 1947, and set up in open water near Scott Island as a weather station.

Sennett Glacier. 80°13′S, 158°40′E. Flows from Mount Aldrich into the Byrd Glacier, between the Yancey and Merrick Glaciers in the Britannia Range. Named for the *Sennett.*

Sentinel Islands. 66°47′S, 141°42′E. A small group of rocky islands, the easternmost rock outcrops along the Adélie Land coast. Just off the coastal ice cliffs 2 miles east of the Curzon Islands. Charted and named descriptively by the French under Liotard in 1949–51.

Sentinel Mountains *see* **Sentinel Range**

Sentinel Nunatak. 64°46′S, 60°44′W. Black, pyramidal nunatak at the mouth of the Drygalski Glacier, on the east side of Graham Land. Charted and named by

the FIDS in 1947 for its commanding position at the mouth of the glacier.

Sentinel Peak. 77°47′S, 162°23′E. A conspicuous, pointed peak over 2,000 m. At the north side of Ferrar Glacier. It forms the highest point in the south-central part of the Kukri Hills in Victoria Land. Discovered and named descriptively by Scott's 1901–4 expedition.

Sentinel Range. 78°10′S, 85°30′W. Also called Sentinel Mountains. 115 miles long. Between 15 and 30 miles wide. The northern portion of the Ellsworth Mountains. It contains Vinson Massif, the highest point in Antarctica. Discovered aerially on Nov. 23, 1935, by Ellsworth and Hollick-Kenyon, and named by Ellsworth for its prominence. First visited in Jan. 1958 by the Marie Byrd Land Traverse Party led by Charles R. Bentley.

Sentry Cove. 62°13′S, 58°26′W. Indentation into the west side of Admiralty Bay, on the south side of King George Island in the South Shetlands. In the immediate area of Demay Point.

Sentry Rocks. 70°45′S, 167°24′E. Two high rocks in water, just off Cape Dayman on the north coast of Victoria Land. Named descriptively.

Separation Range. 84°05′S, 174°E. Also called the East Commonwealth Range. 30 miles long. Separates the Hughes Range from the Commonwealth Range. Just east of the Hood Glacier, it ends at the Ross Ice Shelf. Named by the New Zealanders in 1959–60.

Sepúlveda Point. 64°31′S, 61°35′W. On the east coast of Graham Land.

Sequence Hills. 73°03′S, 161°15′E. On the western edge of the upper part of the Rennick Glacier. 7 miles NW of the Caudal Hills in Victoria Land. There is a good geological sequence here, hence the name given by the New Zealanders in 1962–63.

Sérac. A pointed ice-ridge in a crevassed area.

The *Seraph*. Stonington, Conn. brig owned by Ben Pendleton. It was one of the two vessels scheduled to go to the Antarctic on the 1829 US Government expedition which never took place (*see* **United States**). In 1829–31 Ben Pendleton took it to the South Shetlands as part of the Palmer-Pendleton Expedition, with a crew of 22, including first mate William Noyes.

Seraph Bay. 72°28′S, 95°12′W. 15 miles wide. Indentation into the SE side of Thurston Island. The Abbott Ice Shelf is on the SW, Cape Annawan is on the NW, and Dustin Island is on the SE. Discovered aerially in Feb. 1940 on flights from the *Bear* during the USAS 1939–41. Named for the *Seraph*.

Serba Peak. 69°37′S, 159°03′E. 830 m. Along the north side of Fergusson Glacier in the Wilson Hills. Named for Lt. Edward W. Serba, USN, navigator on Hercules aircraft, 1967 and 1968.

Serlin Spur. 75°04′S, 134°42′W. Mostly snow-covered. 4 miles south of Bowyer Butte in Marie Byrd Land. Extends eastward from the divide between Johnson and Venzke Glaciers. Named for Ronald C. Serlin, ionosphere physicist at Siple Station in 1969–70.

Serpan Peak. 83°34′S, 54°50′W. 1,445 m. Surmounts Washington Escarpment, just west of the Rivas Peaks in the Neptune Range of the Pensacola Mountains. Named for Robert D. Serpan, aerologist here in 1963–64.

Isla Serrano *see* **Lavoisier Island**

Serrat Glacier. 70°24′S, 161°04′E. 10 miles long. Flows through the middle of Kavrayskiy Hills into the west side of the Rennick Glacier. Named for Javier Serrat from the University of Chile, who worked at electrical engineering at McMurdo Station in 1967–68.

Services Glacier *see* **Sultan Glacier**

Sessile hydrozoans. They live on the sea bed near the coasts (*see* **Fauna**).

Setenuten Peak. 72°03′S, 4°45′E. 2,745 m. 1 mile south of Petrellfjellet in the Mühlig-Hofmann Mountains of Queen Maud Land. Name means "the

seat peak" in Norwegian, due to its shape.

Seue Peaks. 67°19′S, 66°55′W. Between Bentley Crag and Mount Rendu on the Arrowsmith Peninsula of Graham Land. Named by the UK for Christian Martini de Seue, 19th-century Norwegian pioneer glaciologist.

Peak Seven. 69°41′S, 64°42′E. Also known as West Nunatak. 5 miles WNW of Summers Peak in the Stinear Nunataks of Mac. Robertson Land. Discovered by Dovers and his 1954 Southern ANARE party. This was their furthest south (their code for that achievement was "seven").

Seven Bay *see* **Adams Fjord**

Seven Buttresses. 63°36′S, 57°10′W. A series of 7 rock buttresses, or cliffs, 150 meters high, and separated by narrow icefalls. They extend for 4 miles along the west side of the Tabarin Peninsula, the eastern extremity of the Trinity Peninsula. Surveyed and named by the FIDS in 1946.

70 Islets. 62°14′S, 59°01′W. In the west entrance to Fildes Strait in the South Shetlands. Surveyed and named collectively by personnel on the *Discovery II* in 1934–35. At least 2 of the islets were over 70 feet high. There were 3 of these islets, what is now Dart Island and the 2 islands to the south and east of it. In other words, there were not 70 islets in the group—the name referred to the height. In 1961 the UK redefined the feature (*see* **Dart Island**) in order to remove this wrong presumption.

76th Parallel Escarpment *see* **USAS Escarpment**

Mount Severtsev. 71°43′S, 12°37′E. 2,540 m. 2 miles NE of Pinegin Peak in the Südliche Petermann Range of the Wohlthat Mountains. Discovered aerially during Ritscher's 1938–39 expedition and named by the USSR in 1966 for geographer N.A. Severtsev (1827–1885).

Sevier Nunatak. 71°22′S, 70°15′W. In the western part of Alexander Island, overlooking the Wilkins Sound.

The *Sevilla*. Norwegian whaler in Antarctic waters in 1930–31 under the command of Capt. H. Halvorsen.

Seward Mountains. 72°26′S, 66°15′W. Isolated. 10 miles ESE of Buttress Nunataks, and 10 miles east of George VI Sound, which they overlook in Palmer Land. Discovered in 1936 by the BGLE, and named by Rymill for Sir Albert Charles Seward, professor of botany at Cambridge from 1906 to 1936.

Sewing-Machine Needles. 62°58′S, 60°30′W. Also called Rocas Ministro Ezcurra, Islotes Mohai. 3 rock needles in water. The highest is 45 m. Just SE of Rancho Point, Deception Island. Originally it was a conspicuous arch, and was named Sewing-Machine Rock by whalers in the area. An earthquake in 1924 caused the arch to collapse, and the feature was later redefined.

Seymore, Frederick. Ordinary seaman on the Wilkes Expedition 1838–42. Joined at Rio. Run at Sydney.

Cape Seymour *see* **Seymour Island**

Seymour Island. 64°17′S, 56°45′W. The Argentines call it Isla Vicecomodoro Marambio. 13 miles long. Between 2 and 5 miles wide. It is sheltered and consequently receives little snow and is free of permanent ice. Although there is no vegetation here, it is the site of rich fossil deposits (*see* **Fossils**). 1 mile NE of Snow Hill Island at the southern edge of the Erebus and Terror Gulf, and east of James Ross Island, off the coast of the NE tip of the Antarctic Peninsula. Ross discovered the NE end of it on Jan. 6, 1843, and named it Cape Seymour, for Rear Adm. George Francis Seymour of the Royal Navy. Carl A. Larsen defined it as an island in 1893 and discovered fossils here that year. Nordenskjöld discovered a large number of fossils here in 1901–4. The FIDS studied the island in 1953–54 and the Argentines mapped most of the island. After that came a further rash of fossil finds.

Seymour Island Expedition. 1982. The first major US–supported field program along the NE flank of the Antarctic Peninsula. It was to the James Ross Island area, including Cockburn Island, Seymour Island, Vega Island, James Ross Island, and, to some extent, King George Island in the South Shetlands. It was also the first time a US Coast Guard icebreaker was used to support a geological field program. On Feb. 14, 1982, the *Glacier* left Punta Arenas in Chile, and made a stop later at Cape Melville on King George Island to visit a geological sequence discovered during the 1980–81 season by a Polish party. They obtained samples here for future study. On the morning of Feb. 19, 1982, the *Glacier* arrived at Seymour Island. Helicopters took personnel and equipment to the main campsite on the south side of Cross Valley. A second, smaller camp was established on the south side of the island to study cretaceous deposits there. It was a 19-day field season, and only 3 of these days were lost due to storms. The *Glacier* returned on March 7, 1982, after having carried out an on-board marine geology program in the Bransfield Strait, directed by John B. Anderson of Rice University. Equipment and samples were brought back to the ship from Seymour Island by helicopter, and a reconnaissance party was flown to the north end of Snow Hill Island that same day. A storm soon brought them all back to the ship, but on March 9, 1982, several short helicopter visits were made to Cockburn, Vega, and James Ross Islands. The expedition was a success. These are some of the achievements: 1. The first discovery of Tertiary reptiles (lizards) in Antarctica; 2. The first discovery of bony fishes (holosteans) from the Cretaceous of Antarctica; 3. The first discovery of a Tertiary coal seam in Antarctica; 4. The discovery of several large skeletons of pleiosaurs; 5. The discovery of skeletal remains (partial skull) of a mosasaur. The expedition, supported by the National Science Foundation, comprised William J. Zinsmeister, Thomas Devries, Carlos Macellari, Brian Huber, Michael O. Woodburne, William Daily, Rosemary Askin, Farley

Fleming, Sankar Chatterjee, and Gary White. There were follow-up expeditions in 1984, 1985, and 1986–87.

Sfinksen *see* **Sphinx Mountain**

Sfinksen Nunatak. 72°18′S, 3°47′W. 1 mile south of Pyramiden Nunatak, at the SW end of the Ahlmann Ridge in Queen Maud Land. Name means "the sphinx" in Norwegian.

Sfinksskolten *see* **Sphinxkopf Peak**

Shabica Glacier. 70°21′S, 62°45′W. Flows into the Clifford Glacier, joining it near its terminus just east of Mount Tenniel in Palmer Land. Named for Stephen V. Shabica, biologist and scientific leader at Palmer Station in 1970.

The *Shackleton*. FIDS relief ship commanded in 1955–56 by Capt. William Johnston. Captain in 1956–57 was N.R. Brown, and 2nd officer that year was Adam J. Kerr.

Mount Shackleton. 65°13′S, 63°56′W. Also called Shackleton Peak. 1,465 m. 2½ miles east of Chaigneau Peak, between the Leay and Wiggins Glaciers on the west side of Graham Land. Discovered in 1908–10 by Charcot, and named by him for Ernest H. Shackleton.

Shackleton, Ernest H. b. Feb. 15, 1874, Kilkee, Co. Clare, Ireland. d. Jan. 5, 1922, Grytviken, South Georgia, of heart failure brought on by angina pectoris, which is hardly surprising, considering what he had gone through on his expeditions. He was buried at South Georgia at his widow's insistence, on March 5, 1922. Ernest Henry Shackleton was the son of an Irish doctor who went to London in 1884. At 17 Shackleton was in the merchant navy. He was a sublieutenant, RNR, on the Royal Society Expedition of 1901–4, and one of the leaders under Scott. Shackles (as he was known, or Shackle) was 27 then, and was in charge of seawater analysis. He also edited the *South Polar Times*, and went up in a balloon. On Dec. 30, 1902, he, Scott, and Wilson set a new southing record of 82°16′33″S, and Shackles got

scurvy. He was in terrible condition when he made it back to base, was sent home on the relief ship *Morning* on March 2, 1903, and was replaced by George Mulock. This "failure" so irked him that he got his own expedition together, the British Antarctic Expedition, 1907–9, in which he pioneered the Beardmore Glacier route to the Pole. He got to within 97 miles of the South Pole. It took a special kind of leader to turn back at this point, rather than to press on, but he knew that he and his men would never make it back if they did get to the Pole. He told his wife that he would rather be a live donkey than a dead hero. He and his 3 companions barely made it back to Ross Island as it was. He was knighted on Dec. 14, 1909, on his return to England, for pushing the Antarctic frontier much farther than anyone had pushed it before. He set out again in 1914 on the British Imperial Transantarctic Expedition, in order to cross the continent on foot. His ship, the *Endurance,* got caught in the ice before he set foot on land. There followed the most amazing sequence of events (see the notes on the expedition) which make one revise one's concepts about the limits of human endurance and determination, the physical and mental barriers imposed by the human species upon themselves. "The Boss" (as he was known to his men) died while on his fourth expedition, on the *Quest.* His last words, to his doctor, were, "What do you want me to give up now?" He wrote 2 books (*see* the Bibliography).

Shackleton Base. 77°59′S, 37°10′W. On Vahsel Bay in the Weddell Sea. Construction began on Jan. 30, 1956, by Ken Blaiklock and his advance party of the BCTAE 1955–58. It was that expedition's base on the Weddell Sea.

Shackleton Canyon. 75°S, 162°W. A submarine feature of the Ross Sea.

Shackleton Coast. 82°S, 162°E. Between Cape Selborne and Airdrop Peak at the east side of the Beardmore Glacier, it forms the western edge of the Ross Ice

Shelf at this point. Named by New Zealand in 1961 for Ernest Shackleton.

Shackleton Glacier. 84°35′S, 176°20′W. Also called Wade Glacier. 60 miles long. Between 5 and 10 miles wide. It flows from the Polar Plateau, in the vicinity of Roberts Massif, between the Bush Mountains and the Prince Olav Mountains, to enter the Ross Ice Shelf between Mount Speed and Waldron Spurs. Discovered by the USAS 1939–41. Named for Ernest H. Shackleton.

Shackleton Harbor *see* **Duperré Bay**

Shackleton Ice Shelf. 66°S, 100°E. It stretches from 95°E, 105°E. 240 miles long. It extends about 80 miles out to sea from the Indian Ocean coast of East Antarctica. The western part of it was discovered by Wilkes on Feb. 21, 1840, and called Termination Land. That name was later changed to Termination Barrier and then to Termination Ice Tongue. The entire ice shelf was discovered and renamed for Ernest H. Shackleton by the *Aurora* party of the AAE 1911–14.

Shackleton Icefalls. 85°08′S, 164°E. Extensive icefalls. Part of the Beardmore Glacier. South of Mount Darwin and Mount Mills. Named by Scott's 1910–13 expedition for Ernest H. Shackleton, the first to pioneer this area.

Shackleton Inlet. 82°20′S, 163°55′E. 10 miles wide. Between Capes Wilson and Lyttelton, this is a Ross Ice Shelf indentation into the Transantarctic Mountains (a re-entrant), and receives the ice of the Nimrod Glacier. This is as far south as Scott got in Dec. 1902, and he named it for one of his companions on this trek, Ernest H. Shackleton.

Shackleton Mountains *see* **Shackleton Range**

Shackleton Peak *see* **Mount Shackleton**

Shackleton Range. 80°40′S, 26°W. Also called Shackleton Mountains. 85 miles long. Between the Slessor and Recovery Glaciers, behind Coats Land. The highest peak is 6,000 feet. Discovered aerially in Feb. 1956 by the BCTAE and named by them for Ernest H. Shackleton.

Shackleton's Hut. Hard by Home Lake, Cape Royds, on Ross Island, this was the 33 by 19 by 8 foot home of the British Antarctic Expedition of 1907–9, led by Shackleton. The shell went up between Feb. 3 and Feb. 13, 1908, and by March 5, 1908, it was completely finished. 15 men holed up there. Shackleton had his own room, and 7 other rooms had 2 men each. It still stands.

Mount Shadow. 71°56′S, 167°30′E. Just west of Shadow Bluff, at the junction of the Tucker and Leander Glaciers, in the Admiralty Mountains. Climbed by the NZGSAE 1957–58 in Jan. 1958, and named by them in association with Shadow Bluff and nearby Mount Midnight.

Shadow Bluff. 71°57′S, 167°38′E. Just west of the McGregor Range, at the junction of the Tucker and Leander Glaciers. Nearly always in shadow, it was named by the New Zealanders in 1957–58.

Shafer Peak. 74°01′S, 162°36′E. 3,600 m. 3 miles south of Mount Hewson in the Deep Freeze Range of Victoria Land. Named for Lt. Cdr. Willard G. Shafer, USN, officer-in-charge of the nuclear power plant at McMurdo Station in 1965.

Shag Rock. 66°S, 65°38′W. A rock in water, 175 yards east of Cliff Island. 8 miles west of Prospect Point off the west coast of Graham Land. Charted and named by the BGLE 1934–37.

Shagnasty Island. 60°44′S, 45°38′W. Small and ice-free. ⅓ mile west of Lenton Point in the northern part of Clowes Bay, just off the south coast of Signy Island. Charted in 1933 by the personnel on the *Discovery II,* and surveyed and named in 1947 by the FIDS because of the state of the island due to the blue-eyed shags living here.

Shags. Imperial shags and blue-eyed shags are found in Antarctica.

Shaler Cliffs. 80°17′S, 25°29′W. In the Shackleton Range.

Shallow Bay. 67°48′S, 67°28′E. 5 miles wide. Just west of Point Williams on the coast of Mac. Robertson Land. Discovered on Feb. 12, 1931, by the BAN-ZARE, and named by Mawson for its unusual depth (shallow waters are rare along this coast).

Shambles Camp. Scott's camp at the base of the Transantarctic Mountains.

Shambles Glacier. 67°20'S, 68°13'W. 4 miles long. 6 miles wide. Flows between Mounts Bouvier and Mangin into Stonehouse Bay, on the east side of Adelaide Island. Discovered and surveyed in part by Charcot in 1909, and resurveyed by the FIDS in 1948. The FIDS named it for its broken surface.

Shangri-la. 78°03'S, 163°42'E. A small, secluded valley (hence the name given by the New Zealanders in 1960–61, for the lost valley of Shangri-la in James Hilton's novel, *Los Horizon*) completely isolated by mountains. Just south of Joyce Glacier and Péwé Peak.

Shanklin Glacier. 84°37'S, 176°40'E. Flows from Mount Waterman, into Much Glacier, 5 miles west of Ramsey Glacier in the Hughes Range. Named for CWO David M. Shanklin, US Army Aviation Detachment which supported the Texas Tech Shackleton Glacier Expedition of 1964–65.

Shannon, R.L.V. Lt. cdr., RN. Captain of the *William Scoresby*, 1929–30.

Shanty Point. 66°25'S, 65°38'W. Within Darbel Bay. Just west of the mouth of Cardell Glacier on the west coast of Graham Land. Named by the UK for its appearance.

Shapeless Mountain. 77°26'S, 160°24' E. West of the head of Balham Valley and just to the west of Victoria Valley, in southern Victoria Land. It is 2,740 m. and shapeless from every direction. Named in 1957 by the NZ Northern Survey Party of the BCTAE.

Shapley Ridge. 86°19'S, 129°10'W. Overlooks Reedy Glacier. Extends east from Cleveland Mesa, and marks the eastern extremity of the Watson Escarpment. Named for Alan H. Shapley, vice-

chairman of the US National Committee for the IGY.

Cape Sharbonneau. 70°50'S, 61°27' W. A snow-covered headland that juts out into the very southern portion of the Larsen Ice Shelf, on the east side of Antarctic Peninsula. It forms the southern fringe of Lehrke Inlet. In was considered an island by the USAS in 1940, and called Sharbonneau Island by them for Charles W. Sharbonneau. Redefined in 1947 by the Weddell Coast Sledge Party.

Sharbonneau, Charles W. Carpenter at East Base during the USAS 1939–41.

Sharbonneau Island *see* Cape Sharbonneau

Shark Island   *see*   Håkollen Island

Shark Peak. 68°03'S, 62°41'E. Isolated nunatak. 3 ½ miles SSW of Van Hulssen Nunatak in the Framnes Mountains of Mac. Robertson Land. Photographed by the LCE 1936–37 and named Hånuten (the shark peak) by the Norwegians. The Australians translated this.

Sharks Tooth. 76°02'S, 159°38'E. A toothlike nunatak west of Beckett Nunatak, at the north side of the upper Mawson Glacier in Victoria Land. Named by the New Zealanders in 1962–63.

Sharman Rock. 62°06'S, 58°28'W. A rock in water between Plaza Point and Crépin Point, King George Island, in the South Shetlands. This term is no longer used.

Mount Sharp. 77°53'S, 86°10'W. Over 3,000 m. 2 miles SE of Mount Barden in the northern part of the Sentinel Range. Named by the Marie Byrd Land Traverse Party of 1957–58 for Professor Robert P. Sharp, member of the Technical Panel on Glaciology, US National Committee for the IGY.

Sharp Glacier. 67°20'S, 66°27'W. Also called North Forel Glacier. Flows to the head of Lallemand Fjord, just east of the Boyle Mountains in Graham Land. Named by the UK for Robert P. Sharp, US glaciologist (*see* **Mount Sharp**).

¹Sharp Peak. 62°32'S, 60°04'W. Also called Pico Agudo, Pico Puntiagudo. 425 m. 2 miles NW of Edinburgh Hill, in the NE part of Livingston Island, in the South Shetlands. Charted and named descriptively by the personnel on the *Discovery II* in 1935.

²Sharp Peak. 66°02'S, 65°18'W. 475 m. 2 miles SE of Prospect Point on the west coast of Graham Land. Discovered and named descriptively by the BGLE 1934–37.

Sharrock, George. Carpenter's mate on the Wilkes Expedition 1838–42. Joined at Valparaiso. Served the cruise.

Shatskiy Hill. 72°02'S, 13°21'E. 2,705 m. In the Dekefjellrantane Hills of the Weyprecht Mountains of Queen Maud Land. Discovered aerially by Ritscher's 1938–39 expedition. Named by the USSR in 1966 for geologist N.S. Shatskiy.

Mount Shattuck. 80°26'S, 81°28'W. 1,430 m. At the south end of the Independence Hills. 3 miles NW of Redpath Peaks in the Heritage Range. Named for Wayne M. Shattuck, USN, aviation machinist and air crewman (*see* **Deaths, 1966**).

Shaula Island. 66°58'S, 57°21'E. 3 miles long. 150 meters high at its highest point. 1 mile east of Achernar Island in the Øygarden Group. Photographed by the LCE 1936–37 and called Söröya (the south island) by the Norwegians. Visited by an ANARE party in 1954, and they renamed it for the star which they used for an astrofix.

Mount Shaw. 69°57'S, 64°33'E. 2,035 m. The highest peak of the Anare Nunataks in Mac. Robertson Land. Visited in Nov. 1955 by an ANARE party led by J.M. Béchervaise. Named by the Australians for P.J.R. Shaw, meteorologist at Mawson Station in 1955.

Shaw, H. Fireman on the *Aurora*, 1914–16.

Shaw, Peter. Seaman on the Wilkes Expedition 1838–42. Joined at Valparaiso. Served the cruise.

Shaw Glacier *see* **Kichenside Glacier**

Shaw Islands. 67°33'S, 47°44'E. 4 islands. 2 miles north of the central part of McKinnon Island, off the coast of Enderby Land. Named by the Australians for John E. Shaw, physicist at Mawson Station in 1957.

Shaw Massif. 72°S, 66°55'E. 1,355 m. Flat-topped. On the west edge of the Lambert Glacier. 12 miles south of Mount Willing in the Prince Charles Mountains. Discovered aerially by the ANARE in Nov. 1956. Named by the Australians for Bernard Shaw, radio supervisor at Mawson Station in 1957.

Shcherbakov Range. 71°51'S, 10°32'E. 20 miles long. Just east of Mount Dallmann in Queen Maud Land. Discovered aerially by the Ritscher expedition of 1938–39. Named by the USSR in 1963 for scientist D.I. Shcherbakov.

Shea Sisters Lake. 71°48'S, 162°E. An internally drained water body, or closed-basin pond, in an ice-free portion of the southeastern end of the Morozumi Range in northern Victoria Land. It has an area of 50,000 square meters, is ice-covered, and is several feet deep. It was created over 1,000 years ago. It is an unofficial name given by Americans in the field in the mid-1960s.

Sheaf, James. Ordinary seaman on the Wilkes Expedition 1838–42. Joined in the USA. Served the cruise.

Mount Shear. 78°21'S, 86°08'W. 13,100 feet. 4 miles NW of Mount Tyree in the Sentinel Range. Discovered by the Marie Byrd Land Traverse Party of 1957–58 under Charles Bentley, who named it for James A. Shear.

Shear, James A. Kentucky doctor who was scientific leader at Hallett Station until Jan. 16, 1958, when he handed over to Ken Salmon.

Shearer Stack. 61°55'S, 58°05'W. A rock stack 1½ miles SW of False Round Point off the north coast of King George Island. Named in 1960 by the UK for the *Charles Shearer.*

Shearwaters. Types of petrel. There are 4 seen in the Antarctic, although none breed south of 54°S. The grey petrel, the white-chinned petrel, the sooty shearwater *(Puffinus griseus),* and the slender-billed shearwater *(Puffinus tenuirostris).*

Sheathbills. Small, white, pigeonlike scavenging land birds which eat anything, nest in rocks, and lay 2–4 eggs. They are the only seabirds in the Antarctic which do not have webbed feet. There are three sorts, all seen in the Antarctic. The wattled sheathbill is the largest, and breeds in the Antarctic Peninsula, the South Shetlands, and the South Orkneys. The lesser sheathbill does not breed south of 60°S. The American sheathbill *(Chionis alba),* also known as the greater or snowy sheathbill, is also seen here.

Sheehan Glacier. 70°56′S, 162°24′E. Flows from the vicinity of Miller Peak in the Explorers Range of the Bowers Mountains, into Rennick Glacier just south of Alvarez Glacier. Named by the Northern Party of the NZGSAE 1963–64 for Maurice Sheehan, field assistant with the Northern Party of the NZGSAE 1962–63, mountaineer at Scott Base in 1963, and field party assistant with the Northern Party of the NZGSAE 1963–64.

Sheehan Islands. 67°22′S, 59°46′E. Also called Hamarøygalten (by the Norwegians). A group of small islands at the SE side of Islay in the William Scoresby Archipelago. Discovered on Feb. 18, 1931, by the BANZARE. Mawson named one of the group as Sheehan Nunatak for H.H. Sheehan, secretary of the Australian Antarctic Committee of the BANZARE. Mawson thought this island was part of the mainland. This feature was redefined by personnel on the *William Scoresby* on Feb. 27, 1936.

Sheehan Mesa. 73°01′S, 162°18′E. Also called Sheehan Tableland. 10 miles WNW of Pain Mesa in the NW part of the Mesa Range of Victoria Land. Named by the Northern Party of the NZGSAE 1962–

63 for Maurice Sheehan *(see* **Sheehan Glacier).**

Sheehan Nunatak *see* **Sheehan Islands**

Sheehan Tableland *see* **Sheehan Mesa**

Sheelagh Islands. 66°32′S, 50°12′E. Group of small islands 3 miles south of Cape Kolosov, near the mouth of Amundsen Bay in Enderby Land. An ANARE party landed here on Feb. 14, 1958. Named by the Australians for the wife of R.H.J. Thompson *(see* **Thompson Peak).**

Sheep. Scott took 45 live sheep on board the *Discovery* in 1901, presumably for food. They were slaughtered and hung in the rigging when the ship hit the ice. The expedition had roast mutton throughout their first winter. The *Koonya* carried down sheep for the *Nimrod* expedition, killing them on Jan. 14, 1908, as they approached the ice.

Sheets Peak. 85°28′S, 125°52′W. Over 1,800 m. 1 mile NW of Koopman Peak on the northern side of the Wisconsin Range. Named for Joseph D. Sheets, journalist in Antarctica, 1965, 1966, and 1967.

Cape Sheffield. 62°37′S, 61°19′W. Forms the NW extremity of Rugged Island in the South Shetlands. Named for James P. Sheffield.

Mount Sheffield. 80°10′S, 25°42′W. 915 m. The most northerly of the Shackleton Range. At the junction of the Gordon and Slessor Glaciers. Named in 1957 by the BCTAE for Alfred H. Sheffield, chairman of the radio communications working group for the IGY, who was of great help to the BCTAE.

Port Sheffield. On Rugged Island in the South Shetlands. Named for James P. Sheffield. A term no longer used.

Sheffield, James P. American sailor, the first American sealer known to have visited the South Shetlands. He was second mate on the *Volunteer* during Edmund Fanning's trip around the world in

1815–17. From 1817–18 he was first mate on the *Jane Maria,* and in 1818–19 was its captain. He entered the Antarctic picture in a major way in 1819–20 when he captained the *Hersilia* to the South Shetlands for the season. This was the first American vessel to visit the islands, as far as we know, and it is possible that he sighted the Antarctic Peninsula from Livingston Island in Jan. 1820. The following season he captained the *Hersilia* again as part of the Fanning-Pendleton Sealing Expedition of 1820–21 in the South Shetlands, and on May 13, 1821, he was captured by the Spaniards off the coast of Chile. He escaped on Sept. 2, 1821, minus the *Hersilia,* and in 1822–23 was captain of a new ship, also called the *Hersilia.*

Sheila Cove. 60°45′S, 44°46′W. In the SW part of Jessie Bay, on the north coast of Laurie Island in the South Orkneys. Surveyed in 1903 by Bruce and named by him for his daughter.

Mount Shelby. 68°09′S, 65°50′W. 1,520 m. Between Daspit Glacier and Bills Gulch at the head of Trail Inlet, on the east coast of Graham Land. Discovered by the USAS 1939–41 from East Base. Charted in 1948 by the FIDS. Named in 1948 by Finn Ronne for Marjorie Shelby, typist and editor for the RARE report.

Shelby Glacier *see* **Gould Glacier**

Sheldon Glacier. 67°30′S, 68°23′W. On Adelaide Island.

Shelf ice. Easily deformable crystalline rock. It is the ice found on ice shelves.

Shell Glacier. 77°16′S, 166°25′E. A western lobe of the Mount Bird Ice Cap on Ross Island. It flows through the valley north of Trachyte Hill and Harrison Bluff. Named by the New Zealanders in 1958–59 for the marine shells in the moraines.

Shelter Cove. 63°41′S, 57°57′W. Indents the north shore of the Prince Gustav Channel, between Chapel Hill and Church Point on Trinity Peninsula. Named descriptively by the UK.

Shelter Islands. 65°15′S, 64°17′W. Group of small islands just over ¼ mile west of Winter Island in the Argentine Islands in the Wilhelm Archipelago, off the west coast of the Antarctic Peninsula. Charted and named by the BGLE 1934–37.

Mount Shelton. 71°41′S, 166°48′E. 2,485 m. Just west of the upper part of Rastorfer Glacier in the Homerun Range of the Admiralty Mountains. Named for John E. Shelton, meteorologist at Hallett Station in 1964–65.

Shelton Head. 72°28′S, 97°25′W. A headland 12 miles west of Long Glacier on the south coast of Thurston Island. Named for John A. Shelton, meteorologist at Byrd Station in 1963–64.

Shelton Nunataks. 75°43′S, 70°35′W. 2 isolated nunataks. 10 miles SE of the Thomas Mountains in eastern Ellsworth Land. Named for Willard S. Shelton, electrician at Eights Station in 1964.

Shelvocke, George. b. 1675, Shropshire, England. Entered the Royal Navy in 1690. Harried Spanish shipping as a privateer. In late 1719 he went south of 60°S (so he says). He wrote *A Voyage Round the World* (*see* the Bibliography). Hatley, his 2nd captain, shot an albatross, and the voyage became the inspiration for Coleridge's *The Ancient Mariner.* On Oct. 1, 1719, William Camell, a seaman on the ship, fell from the mainsail and drowned at about 60°37′S, 5°W. Shelvocke reports having sailed as far south as 61°30′S.

Shenk Peak. 85°11′S, 174°45′W. 2,540 m. Just SE of Mount Kenyon, between Gillespie Glacier and the LaPrade Valley in the Cumulus Hills, just to the east of the Shackleton Glacier. Named by the Texas Tech Shackleton Glacier Expedition of 1964–65 for John C. Shenk, a member of the expedition.

Mount Shennan. 70°14′S, 65°34′E. 4 miles west of Farley Massif in the Athos Range of the Prince Charles Mountains. Named by the Australians for K.J. Shennan, assistant diesel mechanic at Mawson Station in 1963.

Shepard, Oliver. Member of the Trans-Globe Expedition of 1980–82, who crossed the Antarctic via the Pole.

Shepard Cliff. 74°08′S, 161°09′E. Isolated. 4 miles long. At the NE edge of the Reeves Névé in Victoria Land. Named for Danny L. Shepard, USN, construction electrician at Amundsen-Scott South Pole Station in 1966.

Shepard Island. 74°25′S, 132°30′W. 11 miles long. 6 miles west of Grant Island on the west side of the Getz Ice Shelf, off the coast of Marie Byrd Land. It is volcanic, and ice-capped except at its seaward side. Discovered by the USAS 1939–41, and named John Shepard Island by Byrd for John Shepard, Jr., a contributor to the expedition. The name was later shortened.

Shepherd, Simon. Ordinary seaman on the Wilkes Expedition 1838–42. Joined in the USA. Served the cruise.

Shepherd Dome. 74°52′S, 99°33′W. Dome-shaped mountain at the north side of Pirie Island Glacier. 4 miles SW of Mount Manthe, in the southern part of the Hudson Mountains. Named for Donald C. Shepherd, ionosphere physicist at Byrd Station, 1967.

Sheppard, R.C. Captain of the *Eagle,* 1944–45, the season when the ship landed the party which established Base D at Hope Bay. He was captain of the *Trepassey,* 1945–46.

Sheppard Nunatak. 63°22′S, 56°59′W. Conical. 60 m. Just north of Sheppard Point, the north side of the entrance to Hope Bay, at the NE end of the Antarctic Peninsula. First explored by Nordenskjöld's 1901–4 expedition. Charted by the FIDS in 1945, and named by them in association with the point.

Sheppard Point. 63°22′S, 56°58′W. Marks the north side of the entrance to Hope Bay, at the NE end of the Antarctic Peninsula. Discovered by J. Gunnar Andersson during Nordenskjöld's expedi-

tion of 1901–4. Surveyed and named by the FIDS in 1945 for R.C. Sheppard.

Sheppard Rocks. 75°37′S, 158°38′E. Rocks on land. 4 miles NW of the Ricker Hills in the Prince Albert Mountains of Victoria Land. Named for Paul D. Sheppard, storekeeper at Amundsen-Scott South Pole Station in 1966.

Sheridan Bluff. 86°53′S, 153°30′W. At the head of the Robert Scott Glacier in the Queen Maud Mountains.

Cape Sheriff *see* **Cape Shirreff**

Sheriff Cliffs. 83°24′S, 50°37′W. In the northern part of the Pensacola Mountains.

Sherlac Point. 64°44′S, 62°40′W. At the SE end of Rongé Island, off the west coast of Graham Land. Charted by de Gerlache in 1897–99, and named Cap Charles by him. To avoid confusion with Charles Point in Hughes Bay, the UK anagrammized it in 1960.

Sherman Island. 72°38′S, 100°W. Ice-covered. 32 miles long. 10 miles wide. South of Thurston Island in the middle of Peacock Sound. Named for Admiral Forrest Sherman, USN, chief of Naval Operations, 1949–51.

Sherratt, Richard. Name also seen spelled as Sherrat. British captain of the *Lady Trowbridge* in 1820–21. While waiting to be rescued after his vessel went down on Dec. 25, 1820, he made an interesting, if inaccurate, map of the South Shetlands.

Sherratt Bay. 62°02′S, 57°50′W. Between Cape Melville and Penguin Island on the south side of King George Island in the South Shetlands. Named by the UK in 1960 for Richard Sherratt.

Sherrell Point. 63°18′S, 58°42′W. At the south side of Astrolabe Island, off Trinity Peninsula. Named by the UK for Frederick W. Sherrell, surveyor and geologist here with the FIDASE in 1955–56.

Cape Sherriff *see* **Cape Shirreff**

Sherwin Peak. 82°37′S, 161°48′E. 2,290 m. Surmounts the east side of

Otago Glacier. 5 miles SE of Mount Chivers in the north part of the Queen Elizabeth Range. Named for James S. Sherwin, ionosphere physicist at Little America, 1958.

Sherwood, Charles C. Seaman on the Wilkes Expedition 1838–42. Joined at Rio. Served the cruise.

Shetland Island *see* **South Shetland Islands**

Shewry Peak. 64°45′S, 63°38′W. Also called Orejas Blancas. 1,065 m. North of Mount William in the southern part of Anvers Island. Surveyed by the personnel of Operation Tabarin in 1944 and by their successors, the FIDS, in 1955. Named by the UK for Arthur L. Shewry of the FIDS, general assistant at Base N in 1955.

Shibuya Peak. 75°09′S, 133°35′W. 840 m. An isolated nunatak. On the east side of Berry Glacier, on the Hobbs Coast of Marie Byrd Land. 4 miles SE of the Demas Range. Named for Franklin T. Shibuya, American meteorologist at Byrd Station in 1962.

Mount Shideler. 77°55′S, 154°51′W. 1 mile SE of Mount Fitzsimmons in the northern group of the Rockefeller Mountains on Edward VII Peninsula. Discovered aerially on Jan. 27, 1929, by Byrd's 1928–30 expedition. Named by the USAS 1939–41.

Shield Island *see* **Shield Nunatak**

Shield Nunatak. 74°33′S, 164°30′E. Also called Shield Island. At the east side of the terminus of Campbell Glacier on the north shore of Terra Nova Bay in Victoria Land. It is a multiple volcanic cone. Named for its shape by the New Zealanders in 1965–66.

Mount Shields. 70°11′S, 159°56′E. 1,170 m. At the junction of the Pryor and Robilliard Glaciers, at the north end of the Usarp Mountains. Named for Staff Sgt. James K. Shields, US Marine with VX-6, 1962–63 and 1963–64.

Shimizu Ice Stream. 85°11′S, 124°W. In the Horlick Mountains. Flows from the area between the Wisconsin Range and Long Hills to enter the southern flank of the Horlick Ice Stream. Named for Hiromu Shimizu, glaciologist at Byrd Station in 1961.

Shimizu Nunatak *see* **Anderson Nunataks**

Shimmering Icefield. 76°40′S, 159°44′E. Between the Shipton and Tilman Ridges in the Allan Hills of Victoria Land. Named by the New Zealanders in 1964 for its shimmering appearance when seen against the sun.

Shingle Cove. 60°39′S, 45°34′W. In the NW corner of Iceberg Bay, on the south coast of Coronation Island. Charted by the personnel on the *Discovery II* in 1933. Surveyed and named by the FIDS in 1948–49 for the shingle on the landing beach on the south shore of the cove.

Mount Shinn. 78°27′S, 85°46′W. 15,750 feet. 4 miles SE of Mount Tyree in the Sentinel Range. Discovered in Jan. 1958 on a flight piloted by Gus Shinn, for whom it was named. First climbed on Dec. 21, 1966.

Shinn, Conrad S. "Gus." Pilot in the US Navy. As a lieutenant he was a pilot during Operation Highjump, 1946–47. He was back in the Antarctic for the 1956–57 season, this time as a lt. cdr. He was the first man to land a plane at the South Pole, at 8:34 a.m., on Oct. 31, 1956. He flew the DC3 *Que Sera Sera* to the Pole to spy out the land there, to see if it was suitable for an IGY base. His passengers included Adm. Dufek and Trigger Hawkes. Shinn kept the engine running in − 58°F temperature during the 45 minutes the others stayed at the Pole outside, and a Globemaster circled overhead to make sure they got off again in the low temparature. The markers that Scott and Amundsen had left had long since been buried, as had the flag Byrd dropped when he flew over in 1929. Shinn was back in Antarctica in 1957–58, flying reconnaissance flights over the Ellsworth Mountains.

Shinnan Glacier. 67°55'S, 44°38'E. Flows to the coast of East Antarctica just east of Shinnan Rocks. Marks the division between Queen Maud Land and Enderby Land. Named Shinnan-hyoga (new south glacier) by the Japanese.

Shinnan Rocks. 67°57'S, 44°33'E. Also seen spelled as Sinnan Rocks. Rocks on land at the west side of Shinnan Glacier in Queen Maud Land. Named Shinnan-iwa (new south rocks) by the Japanese.

Shinobi Rock. 68°03'S, 43°44'E. Also spelled Sinobi Rock. A rock on land on the coast between Kabuto Rock and Rakuda Rock in Queen Maud Land. Named Shinobi-iwa (hidden rock) by the Japanese.

Ship Cone. 76°40'S, 159°35'E. A peak 1 mile south of Townrow Peak on the Tilman Ridge in the Allan Hills of Victoria Land. Named by the New Zealanders in 1964 for a similarly-shaped peak in New Zealand.

Ship Nunatak. 71°04'S, 159°50'E. Near the center of the upper portion of Harlin Glacier in the Usarp Mountains. It looks like a ship, hence the name given by the USA.

Shipley Glacier. 71°26'S, 169°12'E. 25 miles long. Flows from Mount Adam, along the east wall of the DuBridge Range in the Admiralty Mountains, to Pressure Bay on the north coast of Victoria Land. Some of it reaches the sea west of Flat Island. Named by Raymond Priestley in 1910–13 for Sir Arthur Shipley of Cambridge University.

Ships. This seems a logical place to provide a glossary of some of the types of vessel encountered in the pages of this book. It is a far from comprehensive listing, of course—this is not the place for a work of that sort—but hopefully it will be useful to the reader who is not an expert on ships and shipping. **Aircraft carrier.** A warship built with an extensive flat deck space for the launch and recovery of an aircraft. **Baltimore clipper.** A slim, fast schooner. **Barge.** Has sev-

eral nautical definitions. The only one applicable to Antarctica is that of a boat allocated to a flag officer, used especially for ceremonial occasions, and often carried on board his flagship. **Barkentine.** Also spelled barquentine, and shortened to bark, or barque. A sailing ship of 3 or more masts having the foremasts rigged square and the aftermast rigged fore and aft. **Battle cruiser.** A heavily armed warship of battleship size but with light armor, and capable of high speed. **Battleship.** A heavily armored warship of the largest size. **Boat.** A smaller vessel that can usually be carried on board a larger one. A ship can not be carried. That is the difference between a ship and a boat. **Bomb.** A small warship carrying mortars. **Brigantine.** Brig for short. A two-masted sailing ship, rigged square on the foremast and on the fore-and-aft with square topsails on the mainmast. **Caravel, or carvel.** A two- or three-masted sailing ship, especially one with a broad beam, a high poop-deck and lateen rig. **Cargo ship.** Carries cargo, but is usually bigger than a humble freighter. **Clipper.** A fast sailing ship, usually used for trade. **Coaler, or collier, or coal ship.** Used to carry coal, often locally. **Coaster.** A vessel engaged in coastal commerce. **Corvette.** A lightly-armed escort warship. **Craft.** A single vessel, of any type. **Cruiser.** A high-speed, long-range warship of medium displacement, armed with medium-caliber weapons or missiles. **Cutter.** Has 3 definitions: 1. a sailing boat with its mast stepped further aft so as to have a larger foretriangle than that of a sloop; 2. a ship's boat for carrying light cargo, or passengers; 3. a small, lightly armed boat, as used by Customs, etc. **Destroyer.** A small, fast, lightly armored but heavily armed warship. **Factory ship.** A vessel which processes whale carcasses supplied by a whale catcher. Factory ships are usually big. **Flagship.** There are 2 meanings: 1. a ship, especially in a fleet, aboard which the commander of the fleet is quartered; 2. the most important ship belonging to a shipping company. **Flat-top.** Slang for an aircraft carrier. **Freighter.** A cargo ship. **Frigate.** A medium-sized, square-rigged warship. Later, the term was applied in Britain to a warship larger than a corvette but smaller than a destroyer, and in the US to a warship larger than a destroyer but smaller than a cruiser. **Gig.** A light tender for a vessel, often for the personal use of a captain. **Hermaphrodite brig.** A sailing vessel with two masts rigged square on the foremast and fore-and-aft on the aftermast. **Hulk.** A large unwieldy vessel, or the body of an abandoned ship. **Icebreaker, or ice boat.** Has a reinforced bow for the breaking of ice. **Jollyboat.** A small boat used as a utility tender for a vessel. **Ketch.** A two-masted sailing vessel, fore and aft rigged, with a tall mainmast and a mizzen stepped forward of the rudderpost. **Landing craft.** Any small vessel designed for the landing of troops or equipment on beaches. **Launch.** A motor driven boat, used chiefly for transport. In the old days it was the largest of the boats of a man o' war. **Lifeboat.** A small craft, variously propelled, carried on board a larger vessel as a means of escape or rescue. **Lighter.** A flat-bottomed barge, used for transporting cargo, especially in loading or unloading a ship. **Liner.** A passenger ship, part of a commercial fleet. **Longboat.** The largest boat carried aboard a commercial vessel. **Lugger.** A small working boat rigged with a lugsail. **Man o' War.** A warship. **Merchantman.** A merchant ship working for the Merchant Navy (or Merchant Marine). **Oiler.** Another name for a tanker. **Packet, or packet boat.** A boat that transports mail, passengers, cargo, etc., usually on a fixed, short route. **Pilot, or pilot boat, or pilot ship.** It leads the way in a convoy. **Pinnace.** A ship's tender. **Pram.** A light tender with a flat bottom and a bow formed from the ends of the side and bottom planks meeting in a small, raised transom. **Privateer.** A small, privately owned vessel commis-

sioned for war service by a government. **Refrigeration ship.** One used to hold cold-store products. **Research ship.** One on which research is done. **Sailing ship.** A large sailing vessel. **Schooner.** A vessel with at least two masts, with all lower sails rigged fore-and-aft. **Scow.** An unpowered barge used for freight, etc. **Sealer.** A vessel engaged in sealing. **Shallop.** Has 2 definitions: 1. two-masted gaff-rigged vessel, also called a tender; 2. a light boat used for rowing in shallow water. **Ship.** A large sailing vessel with (formerly) three or more square-rigged masts. Now it is defined as a larger vessel which will not fit on to another (*see also* **Boat**). **Ship of the line.** A warship large enough to fight in the first line of battle. **Slaver, or slave ship.** Used to transport slaves from Africa to America. **Sloop.** A vessel, single-masted, rigged fore-and-aft, with the mast stepped about one-third of the overall length aft of the bow. **Sloop of war.** A small, fast-sailing warship mounting some 10 to 30 small-caliber guns on the deck. **Square-rigger.** Any vessel with square sails. **Steamboat.** A boat powered by a steam engine. **Steamer.** A vessel driven by steam engines. **Steamship.** One powered by one or more steam engines. **Storeship.** One on which stores are kept. **Submarine.** A vessel designed to go and stay under water for varying periods of time. **Supertanker.** A large, fast tanker of more than 275,000 tons capacity. **Supply ship.** One used to carry supplies to Antarctic scientific stations. **Survey vessel.** One from which surveys are carried out. **Tanker.** An oil carrier. **Tender.** A small vessel towed or carried by another ship. Also called a shallop. **Transport.** A ship used to carry troops or goods. **Tug, or tugboat.** A boat with a powerful engine, used for towing other vessels. **Vessel.** The generic term for any ship or boat, and the only safe one to use when describing a sea vehicle. **Warship.** A vessel armed, armored, and otherwise equipped for naval warfare. **Whale boat.** A narrow boat, from 20 to 30 feet long, having a sharp prow and stern, formerly used in whaling. **Whale catcher.** A vessel engaged in the actual harpooning of whales, after which it returns to its mother ship, usually the factory ship. **Whaler.** Has 2 definitions: 1. a vessel engaged in whaling; 2. another name for a whale boat. **Yacht.** A vessel propelled by sail or other power, used especially for pleasure cruising. **Yawl.** Has 2 definitions: 1. a two-masted sailing vessel, rigged fore-and-aft, with a large mainmast and a small mizzenmast stepped aft of the rudderpost; 2. a ship's small boat, usually rowed by 4 or 6 oars.

Shipton Ridge. 76°40'S, 159°51'E. Forms the NE arm of the Allan Hills in Victoria Land. Named by the New Zealanders in 1964 for Eric Shipton, Himalayan mountain climber.

The *Shirase*. Japanese icebreaker/research ship named for Nobu Shirase and launched in 1982 to replace the *Fuji*. It was the third Japanese icebreaker since IGY (*see* **The *Soya*** and **The *Fuji***). 440 feet long. 92 feet wide at its broadest. Displaces 17,000 tons. It can break continuous 5-foot-thick ice at 3 knots. Maximum speed 19 knots. At 15 knots the ship has a range of 25,000 miles. It has a flight deck, and all the latest equipment. On Dec. 3, 1983, it left Fremantle, Western Australia, for its first trip south. Captain was Manoru Sato. It was to service Showa Station. In 1985 it rescued the trapped *Nella Dan* off Enderby Land.

Shirase, Nobu. 1861–1946. First name seen variously as Choku and Naoshi. Japanese Naval lieutenant who led the Japanese South Polar Expedition of 1910–12 in the *Kainan Maru*. Because Japan never really explored outside their medieval world, he had a job getting the backing, but statesman Count Okuma came to his aid. Shirase left Tokyo on Dec. 1, 1910. Also aboard were Nomura (the captain), Takeda, and Mitsui. In early March 1911 they reached the Ross Sea, arriving at Victoria Land on March 6, 1911. They were unable to land, however. They returned to Australia, receiving a monumentally bad press in Sydney, partly

because they were Japanese and partly because they were going for the Pole, as was more local hero Scott. Although Shirase publicly restated his intention to be merely an exploration of Edward VII Land, he was disbelieved. The *Kainan Maru* was back at the Ross Ice Shelf on Jan. 16, 1912 (by which time Scott was at the Pole, and Amundsen had already been there, although Shirase could not have known this), and they visited the Bay of Whales, and discovered Kainan Bay and Okuma Bay, as well as cruising the Edward VII Peninsula (as it became known later). One of their sledge parties went to the edge of the Alexandra Mountains, while the "Dash Patrol" (q.v.) went for the Pole. It was by now a gesture only, and they got as far south as 80°05'S on Jan. 28, 1912. They left the Antarctic in Feb. 1912, and returned to Yokohama on June 20, 1912.

Shirase Coast. 78°30'S, 156°W. Also called Prestrud Coast. Between the north end of the Siple Coast (83°30'S, 155°W) and Cape Colbeck, on the southern coast of Edward VII Land, bordering the eastern portion of the Ross Ice Shelf. Named by New Zealand in 1961 for Nobu Shirase.

Shirase Glacier. 70°05'S, 38°45'E. Flows from Enderby Land into Lützow-Holm Bay at the Prince Harald Coast in East Antarctica. The LCE 1936–37 called it Instefjorden (the innermost fjord). Renamed by the Japanese for Nobu Shirase.

Cap Shireff *see* **Cape Shirreff**

Shireff's Cove *see* **Emerald Cove**

Mount Shirley. 75°39'S, 142°W. Ice-covered. Surmounts the west side of the mouth of Land Glacier on the coast of Marie Byrd Land. Discovered by the USAS in 1939 and named Mount Ann Shirley for the wife of Charles C. Shirley. The name was later shortened.

Shirley, Charles C. Lt. Chief photographer at West Base during the USAS

1939–41. He was later on Operation Highjump, 1946–47.

Shirley Glacier. Does not seem to exist, despite occasional references.

Shirley Island. 66°17′S, 110°30′E. 1 mile long. 175 yards NW of the west end of Bailey Peninsula in the Windmill Islands. Named for Q. Shirley, chief photographer's mate on Operation Highjump, 1946–47.

Cape Shirreff. 62°28′S, 60°48′W. Also called Cabo General Alvarado, Cabo Giralt. The northernmost point of Livingston Island in the South Shetlands, between Hero and Barclay Bays. It is a Specially Protected Area (q.v.). Named by Bransfield in 1820 for William H. Shirreff, the senior British Naval officer on the Pacific coast of South America in the early 19th century.

Shirreff Cove. 62°28′S, 60°48′W. Just SW of Cape Shirreff, on the north side of Livingston Island in the South Shetlands. A cove around here was named as Shirreff's Cove for William H. Shirreff (*see* **Cape Shirreff**) by Bransfield in 1820. Powell located this cove in 1821. The name was later shortened to Shirreff Cove.

Shirreff's Cove   *see*   **Shirreff Cove**

Mount Shirshov. 66°51′S, 51°37′E. 3 miles NE of Mount Selwood in the Tula Mountains of Enderby Land. Named by the USSR in 1961–62 for P.P. Shirshov, polar explorer.

Shishkoff's Island   *see*   **Clarence Island**

Shiver Point. 65°03′S, 61°22′W. There is a peak on it of 670 m. 8 miles west of Cape Fairweather on the east coast of Graham Land. Charted by the FIDS in 1947. Named by the UK in 1950 for the cold here.

Cape Shmidt   *see*   **Shmidt Point**

Shmidt Point. 66°55′S, 67°02′W. Also called Cape Shmidt, Punta Allipén. Marks the northern extremity of Arrowsmith Peninsula on the west coast of Graham Land. Discovered and surveyed

in 1909 by Charcot. Named in 1954 by the UK for Prof. Otto Shmidt, USSR Arctic explorer.

Shmidt Subglacial Basin. 72°S, 106°E. South of the Knox Coast in East Antarctica. Named by the USSR in 1957 for Prof. Otto Shmidt (*see* **Shmidt Point**).

Shockley Bluff. 73°21′S, 164°55′E. Forms the south end of Deception Plateau in Victoria Land. Overlooks the point where Pilot Glacier joins Aviator Glacier. Named for Lt. Cdr. William E. Shockley, USN, VX-6 officer-in-charge at McMurdo Station in 1966.

Shockley Peak. 77°36′S, 86°47′W. 2,010 m. 2 miles SE of Allen Peak in the Sentinel Range. Discovered aerially by Ellsworth on Nov. 23, 1935. Named for Charles C. Shockley, US cartographer of the Sentinel Range in 1962.

Shoe Island. Unidentified island somewhere in the South Shetlands. Mentioned only twice, both times in Harris Pendleton's log book of the *Hero,* 1821–22. Could well be Snow Island or Low Island.

Shoemake Nunatak. 75°33′S, 140°05′W. Just west of Billey Bluff at the SW end of the Ickes Mountains on the coast of Marie Byrd Land. Named for John L. Shoemake, USN, aerographer and weather observer at Brockton Station in 1968–69 and 1969–70.

Shoemaker Glacier. 73°46′S, 164°45′E. In the Southern Cross Mountains of Victoria Land. Flows along the south side of the Daley Hills into Aviator Glacier. Named for Lt. Brian H. Shoemaker, USN, VX-6 helicopter pilot at McMurdo Station in 1967.

Shoemaker Peak. 79°51′S, 82°19′W. On the east side of Ahrnsbrak Glacier. 3 miles ESE of Sutton Peak, in the Enterprise Hills of the Heritage Range. Named for Dawaine A. Shoemaker, meteorologist at Little America in 1958.

Shoesmith Glacier. 67°51′S, 67°13′W. Also called Glaciar Este. The largest glacier on Horseshoe Island. Flows into

Lystad Bay and Gaul Cove. Named by the UK in 1958 in association with the island.

Shokalski Strait see **Schokalsky Bay**

Shomo Rock. 75°35'S, 159°09'E. A nunatak between the Ricker Hills and Pape Rock in the Prince Albert Mountains of Victoria Land. Named for Barry C. Shomo, equipment operator at Amundsen-Scott South Pole Station in 1966.

Shor, Thomas. Seaman on the Wilkes Expedition 1838–42. Joined at the Sandwich Islands. Served the cruise.

Mount Short. 72°50'S, 162°13'E. 2,110 m. 1 mile east of Sculpture Mountain, in the upper part of the Rennick Glacier. Named for Lt. Cdr. John S. Short, USN, aircraft commander, 1967 and 1968.

Short Island. 63°57'S, 60°24'W. 2½ miles SW of Cape Page, just off the west coast of Graham Land. Named by the UK in 1960 for Short Brothers, the first manufacturers of aircraft in the world.

Shortcut Col. 64°16'S, 59°13'W. Just south of Mount Hornsby on the Trinity Peninsula. Named descriptively by the UK. It is a sledging shortcut, instead of the longer Longing Gap.

Shortcut Island. 64°47'S, 64°07'W. Crescent-shaped. Almost ½ mile long. Almost ¾ mile SSE of Gamage Point (Palmer Station) along the SW coast of Anvers Island. Named by personnel at Palmer Station. They could get to Biscoe Bay quickly by using the channel separating this island from Anvers Island.

Shostakovich Peninsula. 72°11'S, 71°20'W. Ice-covered. North of Stravinsky Inlet. Juts out into the Bach Ice Shelf in southern Alexander Island. Named by the UK for the composer.

Shotton Snowfield. 80°35'S, 23°15'W. In the Shackleton Range.

Shoulder Mountain. 76°38'S, 162°07'E. Over 1,000 m. On the north side of the lower Fry Glacier. Just south of Mount Creak in Victoria Land. Named descriptively by the NZ Northern Survey Party of the BCTAE in 1957.

Showa Flat. 69°01'S, 39°34'E. A flat area along the NW shore of Lake O-ike in the eastern part of Ongul Island. Named Showa-taira (the flat of the Emperor Hirohito's era) by the Japanese, in association with Showa Station.

Showa Station. 69°S, 39°35'E. Also called Sjowa Station. Year-round Japanese scientific station on East Ongul Island, on the eastern fringe of Lützow-Holm Bay, off the Prince Olav Coast of East Antarctica. Established by JARE I (the first Japanese Antarctic Research Expedition) during the 1956–57 season, under the leadership of Prof. Takeshi Nagata, and inaugurated on Feb. 14, 1957. Dr. Eizaburo Nishibori led the first wintering-over party, of 11 men, in 1957. The 1957–58 expedition had to be abandoned because of the severity of the pack-ice that year, the *Soya* being unable to approach the station in Jan. 1958. Men and equipment were ferried by helicopter to the *Soya* and the station went to the dogs—literally, when the Japanese abandoned it on Feb. 11, 1958. When they returned for JARE III in Jan. 1959 only two huskies, Taro and Jiro (q.v.) were left manning the station. It was occupied for the winters of 1959, 1960, and 1961, and then closed between Feb. 1962 and 1965. Since then it has been occupied continuously. It can accommodate 40 people, has a mess, radio operations building, a power plant, a Japanese-style bath, living quarters, laboratories, vehicle maintenance area, and the Lakeside Hotel. The bar is called the "Maria" Bar for Maria Kazanowska (q.v.). There is also social areas, and a library. Each man has a private room. A weekly newspaper is produced. It has a temporary sea-ice runway only, and two planes—a Cessna 185 and a Pilatus Porter PC6/BZ-HZ. All equipment at Showa is made in Japan.

Mount Showers. 71°45'S, 61°28'W. On Condor Peninsula. 13 miles SW of Cape MacDonald on the east coast of Palmer Land. Named for William Showers, biologist at Palmer Station in 1975.

Shrimpton, H.N. Radio operator on the *Eleanor Bolling* during the first part of Byrd's 1928–30 expedition. Replaced by G. Samson.

Shristi Automatic Weather Station. 74°42′S, 161°40′E. American AWS at an elevation of approximately 3,912 feet. Began operating Dec. 28, 1987.

Shropshire, Ralph M. Hydrographer on the *City of New York* during Byrd's 1928–30 expedition.

Shull Rocks. 66°27′S, 66°40′W. Snow-covered rocks in water. There is actually one small island and a chain of rocks. In Crystal Sound, 10 miles NW of Cape Rey, Graham Land. Named by the UK for Clifford G. Shull, US physicist specializing in ice.

Shults Peninsula. 78°52′S, 162°38′E. Mostly ice-covered. 10 miles long. 5 miles wide. At the east side of the mouth of the Skelton Glacier in Victoria Land. Named for Capt. Roy G. Shults, USN, chief of staff to the Commander, US Naval Support Force, Antarctica, 1962 and 1963.

Shultz Peak. 76°10′S, 160°51′E. 7 miles south of Mount Armytage. Overlooks the northern flank of Mawson Glacier in Victoria Land. Named in 1964 for Willard E. Shultz, Lt. USN, supply officer at McMurdo Station in 1962.

Shumskiy Cove. 67°04′S, 67°21′W. In southern Hanusse Bay. It indents the NW side of Arrowsmith Peninsula in Graham Land. Named by the UK for Pyotr A. Shumskiy, USSR geologist in the 1950s.

Shurley Ridge. 84°54′S, 65°23′W. Partly snow-covered. Juts out from the SW side of the Mackin Table, 6 miles SE of Snake Ridge, in the Patuxent Range of the Pensacola Mountains. Named for Jay T. Shurley, biologist at Amundsen-Scott South Pole Station in 1966–67.

Mount Shute. 71°50′S, 165°47′E. 2,070 m. 14 miles SE of Austin Peak in the Mirabito Range. Named for Larry R. Shute, meteorologist at Hallett Station in 1963–64.

Cape Sibbald. 73°54′S, 165°23′E. At the SW edge of Lady Newnes Bay on the coast of Victoria Land. Marks the SW extremity of the Mountaineer Range. Discovered in Feb. 1841 by Ross, and named by him for John Sibbald.

Sibbald, John. Lieutenant, RN. On the *Erebus* with Ross, 1839–43. Later a commander.

Sibelius Glacier. 69°55′S, 70°05′W. 12 miles long. 6 miles wide. Flows into the Mozart Ice Piedmont 10 miles SW of Mount Stephenson in the northern part of Alexander Island. Discovered aerially by the BGLE in 1937. Named by the UK for the composer.

Siberian ponies. Sturdy little ponies used to the cold, but not much use in Antarctica. Shackleton took 15 on the British Antarctic Expedition of 1907–9, but provisions were a problem, and the ponies kept sinking in the ice and crevasses. He wound up killing those who did not fall to their deaths or die in some other grisly way (*see also* **Manchurian ponies**).

Mount Sibiryakov. 67°56′S, 49°35′E. Isolated. 16 miles south of Mount Humble of the Raggatt Mountains in Enderby Land. Named by the USSR in 1961–62 for the icebreaker *Sibiryakov*.

Sickle Mountain. 68°53′S, 66°47′W. 1,250 m. On the south side of Wordie Glacier. 14 miles east of Cape Berteaux, on the west coast of Graham Land. Between the Wordie Ice Shelf and the Larsen Ice Shelf. Named for its shape by Ronne during the USAS 1939–41.

Sickle Nunatak. 71°32′S, 161°56′E. At the north side of the entrance to Jupiter Valley, on the east side of the Morozumi Range. Named for its shape by the New Zealanders in 1967–68.

Sickles, J.F. Surgeon on the *Peacock* during the Wilkes Expedition 1838–42. He had joined the *Relief* at Callao as his introduction to the voyage.

Islotes Sidders *see* **Pi Islands**

Siddons, Capt. Richard. Commander of the *Lynx*, 1820–21 and 1821–22.

Siddons Point. 62°33′S, 60°26′W. Juts out into the middle of the head of Hero Bay on the north coast of Livingston Island in the South Shetlands. Named by the UK in 1958 for Richard Siddons.

Mount Sidley. 77°02′S, 126°04′W. Also called Mount Mabelle Sidley, Mount Maybelle Horlick Sidley, and various spelling combinations thereof. 13,720 feet. An extinct volcano, still steaming, in the Executive Committee Range of Marie Byrd Land, NE of Mount Waesche. Mainly snow-covered, it is the highest peak in the range, and has a spectacular caldera on the southern side. Lichens are to be found here. Discovered aerially on Nov. 18, 1934, by Byrd, who named it for Mabelle E. Sidley, daughter of sponsor William Horlick.

Sidney Herbert Sound *see* **Herbert Sound**

Siebert Rock. 64°49′S, 63°02′W. Off the west coast of Graham Land.

Siefker Ridge. 79°09′S, 85°19′W. 6 miles long. Extends NW from the western part of the Anderson Massif in the Heritage Range. Named by the University of Minnesota Geological Party here in 1963–64 for Dennis R. Siefker, USN, electronics technician in charge of the automatic weather station at the party's base at Camp Hills.

Siege Dome. 84°16′S, 172°22′E. An ice-covered summit to the south of the head of Hood Glacier, just SE of Mount Patrick in the Commonwealth Range. Named by the NZ Alpine Club Antarctic Expedition of 1959–60. While they were trying to set up a survey station here, they ran into an 8-day snow storm.

Siegfried Peak. 77°34′S, 161°46′E. Forms a saddle with its southern neighbor, Siegmund Peak, on the east side of the entrance to Odin Valley in the Asgard Range of Victoria Land. Named by New Zealand for the Teutonic hero.

Siegmund Peak. 77°35′S, 161°46′E. Forms a saddle with its northern neighbor, Siegfried Peak, on the east side of the entrance to Odin Valley in the Asgard Range of Victoria Land. Named by New Zealand for the father of Siegfried in Teutonic myth.

Siemiatkowski Glacier. 75°54′S, 144°12′W. 25 miles long. Flows into the Nickerson Ice Shelf on the Marie Byrd Land coast. Named for Edmond R. Siemiatkowski, aurora physicist at Byrd Station in 1964.

Sierra Island. 62°24′S, 59°48′W. ½ mile NW of Dee Island in the South Shetlands. Named by the Chilean Antarctic Expedition of 1950–51 for Sgt. Victor Sierra, sick bay attendant on the *Lientur*.

Cape Siffrey *see* **Prime Head**

Siffrey Point. 63°14′S, 57°11′W. Also called Cabo Negro, Punta Negra. Juts out from the north coast of Trinity Peninsula, 6 miles NW of Cape Dubouzet. A point in this area, and it may have been this one, was named Cap Siffrey by Dumont d'Urville in 1838.

Sigaren Islands. 69°10′S, 39°28′E. 2 islands in the east part of Lützow-Holm Bay. 3½ miles west of Langhovde-kita Point. Photographed by the LCE 1936–37. Named Sigaren (the cigar) by the Norwegians for their shape.

Sighing Peak. 67°24′S, 67°59′W. Isolated. 640 m. At the south side of the entrance to Stonehouse Bay on the east side of Adelaide Island. Discovered and surveyed by Charcot in 1909, and resurveyed by the FIDS in 1948. The FIDS named it for the sighing of the wind here.

Siglin Rocks. 74°09′S, 114°54′W. Isolated. Between Schneider Rock and the Binder Rocks on the west side of Martin Peninsula on the coast of Marie Byrd Land. Lichens, mosses, and petrels are to be found here. Named for CWO D.F. Siglin, USN, maintenance coordinator at Williams Field in 1967.

Sigma Islands. 64°16′S, 62°55′W. Also called Islotes Avión. Group of small islands and rocks. 3 miles north of Eta Island. They mark the northern limit of the Melchior Islands. Named in 1946 by the Argentines for the greek letter.

Signy Island. 60°43'S, 45°38'W. 4 miles long. Less than 3 miles wide. To the immediate south of Coronation Island, it is one of the major islands in the South Orkneys. Charted by Weddell in 1825. Surveyed by Petter Sørlle in 1912–13 in the *Paal*, and named by him for his wife Signy.

Signy Island Station. 60°43'S, 45°38' W. British scientific station on Signy Island in the South Orkneys. Established by the FIDS in 1947, as Base H, it is now a British Antarctic Survey research station studying vegetation and lakes of the ecosystem. Gordon de Q. Robin was the first leader, in 1947, of a party of four. R.M. Laws (*see* the Bibliography) was leader in 1948 and 1949. Subsequent leaders: 1950—W.J.L. Sladen, 1951—J.J. Cheal, 1952—A.W. Mansfield, 1953—A.G. Tritton, 1954—H. Smith, 1955—H. Dollman, 1956—W.L.N. Tickell, 1957—C.D. Scotland. During the IGY the station conducted meteorology studies.

Sigurd Knolls. 71°21'S, 7°38'E. Also called Nunataki Mramornyye. Isolated. At the north end of Otter Plain. 20 miles NW of the Drygalski Mountains in Queen Maud Land. Named by the Norwegians for Sigurd Helle, geodesist, leader of the Norwegian Antarctic Expedition of 1956–57.

Sigyn Glacier. 71°52'S, 8°36'E. Flows between the Drygalski Mountains and the Kurze Mountains of Queen Maud Land. Named by the Norwegians.

Sikorski Glacier. 71°44'S, 98°30'W. In the NE part of the Noville Peninsula on Thurston Island. Flows into the Bellingshausen Sea between Mounts Palmer and Feury. Named for Stephen Sikorski, electronics technician on the *Glacier*, 1959–60.

Sikorsky Glacier. 64°12'S, 60°53'W. Flows into Hughes Bay north of Charles

Point on the west coast of Graham Land. Named by the UK in 1960 for Igor Sikorsky, helicoter pioneer.

Silicoflagellates. Planktonic protozoa with a flagellum, yellow or greenish-brown chromatophores, and a skeleton of hollow siliceous rods. These are found both living and fossilized.

Silk Glacier. 81°09'S, 158°55'E. 10 miles long. Flows from the Churchill Mountains, between Mount Frost and Mount Zinkovich, into Nursery Glacier. Named for Cdr. P.R.H. Silk, RNZN, commander of the *Endeavour II* in Antarctic waters, 1963–64.

Sillard Islands. 66°37'S, 67°35'W. Small, ice-covered islands close to Cape Mascart, the NE end of Adelaide Island. Discovered in 1908–10 by Charcot, and named by him for Director Sillard of the French Montevideo Co., in Uruguay. This company made repairs to the *Pourquoi Pas?*

Silva Ridge. 73°S, 162°18'E. Leads to the top of Sheehan Mesa. Named by the New Zealanders in 1962–63 for the large silicified tree stumps found here.

Silver-gray fulmars *see* **Fulmars**

Silver Ridge. 82°16'S, 161°40'E. Snow-covered. West of the mouth of Algie Glacier, on the north side of the Nimrod Glacier. Named by the New Zealanders in 1960–61.

Islas Silveyra *see* **Omicron Islands**

Silvia Rock. 63°18'S, 57°54'W. Just SE of Agurto Rock in the Duroch Islands. ⅓ mile north of Cape Legoupil, Trinity Peninsula. Named by the Chilean Antarctic Expedition of 1948 for a daughter of President Gabriel González Videla.

Simensen, Erik. Photographer on the LCE 1936–37.

Simensen Peak. 71°55'S, 25°31'E. 2,215 m. On the north side of Glitrefonna Glacier in the Sør Rondane Mountains. Named by the Norwegians for Erik Simensen.

Simler Snowfield. 66°03'S, 65°05'W. NE of Holtedahl Bay on the west coast of

Graham Land. Named by the UK in 1959 for Josias Simler (1530–1576), who wrote the first advice on glacier travel, in 1574.

Simmers, R.G. Meteorologist on the BANZARE, 1929–31. He was a New Zealander.

Simmers Peaks. 66°06′S, 52°48′E. 3 peaks, the highest of which is 840 m. 13 miles SE of Cape Close and 11 miles north of Mount Codrington. Discovered by the BANZARE in 1930 and named by Mawson for R.G. Simmers.

Mount Simmonds. 70°20′S, 159°34′E. 1,885 m. Just west of Mount Theaker on the north side of Robilliard Glacier in the Usarp Mountains. Named by New Zealand for G.A.E. Simmonds, NZ cartographer of the 1960s.

Simmonds Peak. 85°58′S, 158°32′W. 1,940 m. 4 miles south of Mount Dort, on the east side of Amundsen Glacier in the Queen Maud Mountains. Named for Willard I. Simmonds, biologist at McMurdo Station in 1964.

Mount Simmons. 80°22′S, 81°46′W. 1590 m. Forms the north end of the Independence Hills of the Heritage Range. Named for Richard S. Simmons, USN, aviation electronics technician (*see* **Deaths, 1966**).

Simmons Glacier. 75°S, 113°36′W. Flows between Mount Isherwood and Mount Strange in the eastern part of the Kohler Range of Marie Byrd Land. Named for Harry S. Simmons, assistant to the USARP representative in Christchurch, NZ, for the summers between 1969–70 and 1972–73. He was in Antarctica in 1971 and 1973.

Simon Ridge. 71°03′S, 65°31′E. Arc-shaped. 8 miles SE of Husky Massif in the Prince Charles Mountains. Named by the Australians for M.J. Simon, radio officer at Wilkes Station in 1962.

Simonov, Lt. Member of the von Bellingshausen expedition of 1819–21. With Demidov he landed on an iceberg on Jan. 17, 1820, in order to capture penguins.

Simons, Allen. Ordinary seaman on the Wilkes Expedition 1838–42. Joined in the USA. Run at Valparaiso.

Simoom Hill. 69°28′S, 68°W. On the west coast of the Antarctic Peninsula.

Simplicity Hill. 85°06′S, 174°38′W. Ice-free. 1 mile west of Crilly Hill, at the north side of McGregor Glacier in the Queen Maud Mountains. Named by the Texas Tech Shackleton Glacier Expedition of 1964–65 for the ease with which they could approach the hill, and for the simplicity of its geologic nature.

Cape Simpson. 67°28′S, 61°08′E. At the north end of Ufs Island. Forms the east side of the entrance to Howard Bay in East Antarctica. Discovered in Feb. 1931 by the BANZARE, and named by Mawson for F. Simpson of Adelaide, a patron.

Île Simpson   *see*   **Simpson Rocks**

¹Mount Simpson. 72°06′S, 100°45′W. In the Walker Mountains, just west of the head of Hale Glacier on Thurston Island. Named for Lt. B.L. Simpson, Jr., VX-6 pilot, 1959–60.

²Mount Simpson *see* **Simpson Peak**

Simpson, Dr. George C. 1878–1965. George Clarke Simpson. Known as "Sunny Jim," he was the meteorologist on the British Antarctic Expedition of 1910–13. He was knighted in 1935, and became head of the Met Office in London.

Simpson Crags. 74°24′S, 162°45′E. They descend in a line from Mount Baxter of the Eisenhower Range, and form the south wall of O'Kane Glacier in Victoria Land. Named for Lt. Cdr. William A. Simpson, Jr., USN, VX-6 aircraft commander, 1967.

Simpson Glacier. 71°17′S, 168°38′E. 6 miles long. In the Admiralty Mountains. Flows to the coast between Nelson Cliff and Mount Cherry-Garrard, where it forms the Simpson Glacier Tongue. Named in association with the Simpson Glacier Tongue.

Simpson Glacier Tongue. 71°16′S, 168°50′E. Fed by the Simpson and

Fendley Glaciers. Juts out into the sea between Nelson Cliff and Atkinson Cliffs on the north coast of Victoria Land. Charted and named by Campbell's Northern Party in 1910–13 for George C. Simpson.

Simpson Head. 73°21'S, 60°59'W. 1,065 m. A promontory which juts out into the north side of New Bedford Inlet, 4 miles NW of Cape Kidson, on the east coast of Palmer Land. Discovered aerially by the USAS in Dec. 1940. Named by the FIDS in 1948 for George C. Simpson.

Simpson Nunatak. 63°58'S, 58°54'W. 1,165 m. 2½ miles NW of Mount Roberts on the southern edge of the Aitkenhead Glacier on the Trinity Peninsula. Named by the UK for Hugh W. Simpson of the FIDS, at Base D in 1957.

Simpson Peak. 67°43'S, 50°07'E. 1,720 m. Just east of Mount George in the SW end of the Scott Mountains of Enderby Land. Discovered in Jan. 1930 by the BANZARE. Mawson named it for George C. Simpson.

Simpson Ridge. 68°06'S, 62°23'E. Isolated. 1 mile south of Mount Twintop in the Framnes Mountains of Mac. Robertson Land. Named by the Australians for C.R. Simpson, electronics engineer at Mawson Station in 1967.

Simpson Rocks. 61°58'S, 57°23'W. Rocks in water, 5 miles NE of Cape Melville, King George Island in the South Shetlands. Actually they are a rock 10 meters high and sunken rocks surrounding it. Weddell called them Simpson's Islands in 1825, but they have since been redefined.

Simpson's Islands *see* **Simpson Rocks**

Sims, Lewis S. Lt. (jg), USN. Medical officer at East Base during the USAS 1939–41.

Sims Island. 73°21'S, 78°19'W. Between Rydberg Peninsula and Case Island in the southern part of Carroll Inlet, off the coast of Ellsworth Land. Discovered aerially on Dec. 22, 1940, by the USAS 1939–41 and named for Lewis S. Sims.

Mount Simsarian. 86°06'S, 132°50'W. Projects from the east side of the Michigan Plateau just south of the head of Gardiner Glacier. Named for James Simsarian, chief of the Division of International Scientific and Technical Affairs, Department of State.

Bahía Sin Nombre *see* **Security Bay**

Sinbad Rock. 62°10'S, 59°02'W. Rock in water, 1¼ miles WNW of Square End Island, off the west end of King George Island in the South Shetlands. Charted in 1935 by personnel on the *Discovery II*. Named by the UK in 1948.

Sinclair, George T. Acting ship's master on the Wilkes Expedition 1838–42. From Dec. 19, 1838, to June 15, 1839, he was on the *Relief*, then from Aug. 13, 1839, to Sept. 6, 1839, he was on the *Porpoise*, and from Sept. 15, 1839, to Sept. 25, 1840, he was on the *Flying Fish*. In Nov. 1840 he joined the *Porpoise* again at Honolulu.

Sinclair, Thomas. Seaman on the Wilkes Expedition 1838–42. Joined in the USA. Served the cruise.

Sinclair Island. 64°55'S, 63°53'W. Also called Chaucer Island. Over 1 mile long. 1½ miles NE of Reeve Island in the Wauwermans Islands of the Wilhelm Archipelago. Named by the Argentines in 1950 as Isla Alberto, but renamed by them in 1956 as Isla Sinclair, for Capt. Enrique Sinclair (1805–1904), hero in the war against Brazil. The name was subsequently translated into English.

Singer Glacier. 74°15'S, 113°52'W. On Martin Peninsula, on the coast of Marie Byrd Land.

Single Island. 69°48'S, 68°36'E. High, ice-covered island on the west side of the Amery Ice Shelf. 14 miles south of Landon Promontory. The Australians first mapped it as a promontory, Single Promontory, and named it for M. Single, senior diesel mechanic at Mawson Station in 1962. It was later redefined as an island.

Single Promontory *see* **Single Island**

Singleton Nunatak. 71°15'S, 61°36'W. Just west of the head of Kauffman Glacier on the east side of Palmer Land. Named by the UK for David G. Singleton, BAS geologist who worked here.

Mount Sinha. 75°04'S, 136°09'W. 990 m. At the SE extremity of Erickson Bluffs in the southern part of McDonald Heights in Marie Byrd Land. It overlooks the lower part of Kirkpatrick Glacier from the north. Named for A.A. Sinha, biologist here in 1971–72.

Siniff Bay. 74°40'S, 135°50'W. 13 miles wide. Between Verleger and Melville Points on the coast of Marie Byrd Land. Named for Donald B. Siniff, biologist at McMurdo Station in 1968–69, 1969–70, 1970–71, and 1971–72. He was also part of the International Weddell Sea Oceanographic Expedition of 1967–68.

Sinker Rock. 64°49'S, 63°30'W. A rock in water off the northern tip of Goudier Island, near the center of the harbor of Port Lockroy, Wiencke Island. Named by the FIDS in 1944 for a sinker laid near here for a boat mooring.

Sinnan Rocks   *see*   **Shinnan Rocks**

Sinobi Rock   *see*   **Shinobi Rock**

Mount Siple. 73°15'S, 126°06'W. Also called Mount Ruth Siple, Mount Walker. 10,200 feet. Large, snow-covered volcano on Siple Island in Pine Island Bay. Discovered aerially in 1940 by US scientists. When it was first visited, on Feb. 22, 1984, it was discovered to have been cartographically misplaced by 30 miles. Named for Paul Siple.

Siple, Paul. b. Dec. 18, 1908, Montpelier, O. d. Nov. 25, 1968, Arlington, Va. Paul Allman Siple. A Virginia Boy Scout picked by Byrd to go on his 1928–30 expedition to the Antarctic as the winner of a national competition sponsored by Byrd. He was dog handler and naturalist on that first expedition. On Byrd's 1933–35 expedition Siple was chief biologist and led a 77-day sledge journey of exploration across Marie Byrd Land.

He gained a Ph.D. in geography in 1939, and that year went south with Byrd yet again for the USAS 1939–41, during which he was chief supply officer, and leader of West Base, actually building West Base for the operation. He took part in Operation Highjump, again with Byrd, and during the IGY (Byrd's last expedition, as it were), Siple was scientific leader at South Pole Station where he and 17 other men and a dog wintered-over. He handed over to Palle Mogensen on Nov. 30, 1957. He developed a wind-chill index as a measure of cold in different wind and temperature conditions (*see also* the Bibliography).

Siple Coast. 82°S, 152°W. Between the north end of the Gould Coast (83°30'S, 153°W) and the south end of the Shirase Coast (80°10'S, 151°W) on the eastern Ross Ice Shelf. Named by NZ in 1961 for Paul Siple.

Siple Island. 73°39'S, 125°W. A large, snow-covered island, 70 miles long, mainly within the Getz Ice Shelf, to the east of Wrigley Gulf. Named in 1967 in association with Mount Siple, the dominant feature on the NW part of the island. First defined as an island in the early 1960s.

Siple Station. 75°56'23.668"S, 84°14'55.705"W. (exact location.) US scientific station (summer only) in Ellsworth Land. Opened in Nov. 1969 at 75°55'S, 83°55'W. Named for Paul Siple. It studies upper atmospheric physics, and is the best location in the Southern Hemisphere for controlled VLF wave investigations in the upper atmosphere. A new station was opened at the new location (not far away) on Jan. 14, 1979, and has 24 building modules.

Siple Station Automatic Weather Station. 75°54'S, 84°18'W. American AWS at an elevation of approximately 3,500 feet. A climate monitoring site, it began operating on Jan. 1, 1982.

Sir George Newnes Glacier   *see*   **Newnes Glacier**

The *Sir James Clark Ross*. Enormous, fast, Norwegian factory whaling ship bought by Captain Carl Anton Larsen for his boss Magnus Konow from the British in 1923. Formerly it had been the *Custodian*, a steamer, and before that, the *Mahronda*. Konow renamed it for the great British navigator, and Larsen converted it to a factory ship. In 1923 it was the largest whaling ship in the world, 12,000 tons gross. On its first expedition, in 1923–24, it had 5 whale catchers: the *Star I*, the *Star II*, the *Star III*, the *Star IV*, and the *Star V*. These small vessels were commanded by experienced Norwegian harpoon captains, respectively Pettersen, Iversen, Hartvigsen, Nielsen, and Moewik. The fleet of 6 vessels left Hobart on Nov. 30, 1923, for their first (Antarctic) voyage. On board were: Alan J. Villiers, Wilhelm van der Does, H.O.P. McEacharn-Summerlees, Harold Wells, Paddy McGeever, Thomas Spratt, Gregory A. MacGogger, Herford Simple, and Lasman Young. These were all Tasmanian whaling laborers, all aged between 18 and 24. Capt. Gjertsen was the ice-pilot, Capt. A. Kaldager was sailing master of the big ship, Dr. Kohl was the surgeon, Capt. G. Hopper was the NZ Government representative, Dr. Vallin was a Swedish scientist, Varild was the chief engineer, and Drygalski was an engine room crewman. Altogether there were over 180 men on this expedition led by Capt. Carl A. Larsen. On Dec. 12, 1923, the *Sir James Clark Ross* was in 63°S, 180°, and on Dec. 13, 1923, it broke into the pack-ice at 65°10′S, 178°16′E. On Dec. 17, 1923, they crossed the Antarctic Circle, the largest vessel to have done so until that time, and on Dec. 21, 1923, they arrived in the Ross Sea. On Dec. 25, 1923, they arrived at the Bay of Whales, and from Dec. 31, 1923, until March 7, 1924, the ship anchored in Discovery Inlet. In early 1924 the *Star I* went exploring along the coast of Victoria Land, and on March 14, 1924, they all crossed the Antarctic Circle homeward, arriving at Otago, NZ, on April 9, 1924, the big ship having left the 5 whale catchers at

Stewart Island, NZ. The expedition took a disappointing 17,500 barrels of oil, but not one man or limb was lost. This was the first whaling done in the Ross Sea. The ship went south again in 1924–25, but Larsen died in early Dec. 1924 at the edge of the Ross Sea pack-ice. Oscar Nilsen took over, and the expedition took 32,000 barrels of oil. The new *Sir James Clark Ross* was later launched at the Tyne, England, and helped Byrd's 1928–30 expedition, and under Nilsen in 1930–31 transferred coal to the BANZARE's *Discovery*.

Sir John Murray Glacier *see* **Murray Glacier**

Siren Bay. 71°22′S, 169°15′E. Formed by the configuration of the ice at the terminus of Shipley Glacier and the NW side of Flat Island on the north coast of Victoria Land. Charted by Campbell's Northern Party of 1910–13, and named by them for a noise like a ship's siren which they heard while mapping the area.

Siren Rock. 74°33′S, 98°24′W. Isolated rock on land. 12 miles east of Mount Moses in the eastern part of the Hudson Mountains. Named for Jan C. Siren, radio scientist at Byrd Station in 1967.

Mount Sirius. 84°08′S, 163°15′E. 2,300 m. Between Walcott Névé and Bowden Névé. 3½ miles north of Bauhs Nunatak, in the SW sector of the Queen Alexandra Mountains. Named by the NZGSAE 1961–62 for the star which they used to fix the baseline here.

Sirius Cliffs. 70°33′S, 66°53′W. Isolated nunatak with steep rock cliffs along its north face. Between Mount Lepus and Procyon Peaks on the south side of Millett Glacier in Palmer Land. Named by the UK for the star.

Sirius Formation. A geologic formation in the Transantarctic Mountains which took place between 3 and 4 million years ago. Discovered and named by John H. Mercer (*see* **Mercer Ridge**) for

Mount Sirius, which exhibits this in a most classic way.

Sirius Islands. 66°57′S, 57°27′E. In the northern part of the Øygarden Group. Photographed by the LCE 1936–37 and called Nordøyane (the north islands) by the Norwegians. Visited by an ANARE party in 1954. Named by the Australians for the star Sirius, used for an astrofix by the ANARE party.

Sirius Knoll. 63°43′S, 58°36′W. 1,010 m. Ice-covered. Marks the NE end of the Detroit Plateau in the central part of the Trinity Peninsula. Charted by the FIDS in 1946, and named by them for the star.

Sirocco Glacier. 69°25′S, 68°31′W. On the SW coast of Byers Peninsula, Livingston Island, in the South Shetlands.

Sirohi Point. 83°57′S, 170°06′E. On the north side of the terminus of Alice Glacier, where that glacier enters the Beardmore Glacier. Named for Girraj S. Sirohi, biologist at McMurdo Station in 1960–61.

Sisco Mesa. 85°50′S, 127°48′W. 3,350 m. Ice-capped. The summit is 2 miles long and 2 miles wide. Just north of Haworth Mesa between the heads of the Norfolk and Olentangy Glaciers in the Wisconsin Range. Named for Joseph J. Sisco, assistant secretary of State for International Organization Affairs, chairman of the Antarctic Policy Group, 1966.

Sisson, J.G. Radio operator on the *Jacob Ruppert*, 1933–35.

Sistefjell Mountain. 73°23′S, 0°44′W. 10 miles SE of Neumayer Cliffs at the NE end of the Kirwan Escarpment in Queen Maud Land. Name means "the last mountain" in Norwegian.

Sistenup Peak. 73°17′S, 0°44′W. At the NE end of the Kirwan Escarpment. 5 miles north of Sistefjell Mountain in Queen Maud Land. Name means "the last peak" in Norwegian.

Sisterabben Hill. 73°21′S, 0°44′W. 2 miles north of Sistefjell Mountain, at the NE end of the Kirwan Escarpment in Queen Maud Land. Name means "the last hill" in Norwegian.

[1]The Sisters   *see*   **Søstrene Islands**

[2]The Sisters. 71°17′S, 170°14′E. Also called Sisters Rocks. 2 pillarlike rocks, or stacks, standing together just north of Cape Adare at the NE end of Victoria Land. Charted and named by Borchgrevink in 1898–1900. In 1910–13 Campbell's Northern Party of Scott's last expedition named the northern pillar as Gertrude Rock and the southern one as Rose Rock (see both these entries).

Sisters Rock   *see*   **[2]The Sisters**

Sites of Special Scientific Interest. More commonly known as SSSIs. They are places where scientific investigations might suffer from interference unless protected by a specific management plan. It was an idea created from one of the consultative meetings of the Antarctic Treaty system. There are 28 SSSIs, with renewable expiration dates. 1. Cape Royds; 2. Arrival Heights, Ross Island; 3. Barwick Valley; 4. Cape Crozier; 5. Fildes Peninsula; 6. Byers Peninsula; 7. Haswell Island; 8. The western shore of Admiralty Bay, King George Island; 9. Rothera Point; 10. Caughley Beach; 11. Tramway Ridge, Mount Erebus; 12. Canada Glacier; 13. Potter Peninsula; 14. Harmony Point; 15. Cierra Point and nearby islands; 16. Bailey Peninsula, Budd Coast; 17. Clark Peninsula, Budd Coast; 18. White Island, McMurdo Sound; 19. Linnaeus Terrace; 20. Biscoe Point; 21. Shores of Port Foster; 22. Yukidori Valley; 23. Svarthamaren Mountain; 24. The summit of Mount Melbourne; 25. Marine Plain; 26. Chile Bay; 27. Port Foster; 28. South Bay, Doumer Island.

Sjeldche, S. Captain of the *Lancing*, 1926–27.

Sjøbotnen Cirque. 71°22′S, 13°25′E. In the north face of the main massif of the Gruber Mountains, just east of Mount Zimmerman in the Wohlthat Mountains of Queen Maud Land. Discovered aerially during Ritscher's 1938–39 expedition. Name means "the lake cirque" in Norwegian.

Sjogren, George. Seaman on the *Eleanor Bolling,* 1928–29.

Sjögren Fjord *see* **Sjögren Glacier**

Sjögren Glacier. 64°14′S, 59°W. 15 miles long. In the south part of Trinity Peninsula. Flows SE from the Detroit Plateau to the south side of Mount Wild, where it enters Prince Gustav Channel. Discovered in 1903 by Nordenskjöld, and named by him as Hjalmar Sjögren Fjord for a patron of that name (Hjalmar Sjögren). The name was, over the years, shortened to H.J. Sjögren Fjord, and then to Sjögren Fjord. The FIDS redefined this feature in 1945.

Sjögren Glacier Tongue. 64°14′S, 58°38′W. Between 5 and 7 miles wide. The seaward extension of Sjögren Glacier, it extends 15 miles across the Prince Gustav Channel from Sjögren Glacier toward Persson Island. Named for the glacier.

Sjöhausen *see* **Mount Seekopf**

Sjöneset Spur. 71°17′S, 13°35′E. Extends along the east side of Anuchin Glacier to Lake Ober-See in the Wohlthat Mountains of Queen Maud Land. Discovered aerially by Ritscher's 1938–39 expedition. Name means "the lake ness" in Norwegian.

Sjövold, Carl. Commander of the *Bouvet III* in 1930–31.

Skaar Ridge. 84°49′S, 163°15′E. On the SE side of Mount Augusta in the Queen Alexandra Range. It runs 2 miles to the Beardmore Glacier. James M. Schopf, in 1969–70, discovered a Permian peat deposit here. Named for Lt. Gerhard E. Skaar, USN, Schopf's helicopter pilot.

Skagen *see* **Mount Saint Michael**

Skålebreen. 72°06′S, 3°52′E. A glacier flowing between Festninga Mountain and Mount Hochlin in the Mühlig-Hofmann Mountains of Queen Maud Land. Named by the Norwegians.

Skålebrehalsen Terrace. 72°16′S, 4°10′E. Ice-covered. At the south side of Skålebreen in the Mühlig-Hofmann Mountains of Queen Maud Land. Named by the Norwegians.

Skallen Glacier. 69°40′S, 39°33′E. Flows into Lützow-Holm Bay to the east of the Skallen Hills. Named by the Japanese in association with the nearby hills.

Skallen Hills. 69°39′S, 39°25′E. Ice-free coastal hills which jut out into the eastern part of Lützow-Holm Bay between Skallevika and Skallen Glacier. Photographed by the LCE 1936–37. Name means "the skull" descriptively in Norwegian.

Skallevik Point. 69°41′S, 39°15′E. Marks the NW end of Skallevikhalsen Hills on the SE shore of Lützow-Holm Bay. Photographed by the LCE 1936–37. Named Skalleviksodden (the skull bay point) by the Norwegians.

Skallevika. 69°41′S, 39°23′E. A bay just west of the Skallen Hills on the SE shore of Lützow-Holm Bay. Photographed by the LCE 1936–37. Name means "the skull bay" in Norwegian.

Skallevikhalsen Hills. 69°41′S, 39°18′E. A line of ice-free hills which fringe the SE shore of Lützow-Holm Bay for 4 miles just west of Skallevika. Photographed by the LCE 1936–37. Name means "the skull bay neck" in Norwegian.

Skappelnabben Spur. 73°43′S, 4°33′W. At the east side of Urfelldokka Valley in the SW part of the Kirwan Escarpment in Queen Maud Land. Named by the Norwegians.

Skaret Pass. 72°33′S, 0°23′E. At the east side of Skarsnuten Peak in the Roots Heights of the Sverdrup Mountains in Queen Maud Land. Name means "the gap" in Norwegian.

Skarsbrotet Glacier. 71°50′S, 11°45′E. A cirque-type glacier. Flows from the Skarshaugane Peaks in the Humboldt Mountains of Queen Maud Land. Discovered by Ritscher's expedition in 1938–39. Named by the Norwegians.

Skarsdalen Valley. 72°33′S, 0°30′E. Ice-filled. Between Roots Heights and Hamrane Heights in the Sverdrup Mountains of Queen Maud Land. Name means "the gap valley" in Norwegian.

Skarshaugane Peaks. 71°49'S, 11°37'E. Extend 3 miles south from Hovdeskar Gap in the Humboldt Mountains of Queen Maud Land. Discovered by Ritscher in 1938–39. Mount Skarshovden is one of these peaks. Named by the Norwegians.

Mount Skarshovden. 71°47'S, 11°38'E. 2,830 m. Surmounts the west side of Hovdeskar Gap in the Humboldt Mountains of Queen Maud Land. It is one of the Skarshaugane Peaks. Discovered by Ritscher in 1938–39. Named by the Norwegians.

Skarskvervet Glacier. 71°45'S, 11°30'E. Cirque-type glacier. At the east side of Botnfjellet Mountain in the Humboldt Mountains of Queen Maud Land. Discovered by Ritscher in 1938–39. Named by the Norwegians.

Skarsnuten Peak. 72°32'S, 0°22'E. In the northern part of Roots Heights in the Sverdrup Mountains of Queen Maud Land. Name means "the gap peak" in Norwegian.

Skarvhalsen Saddle. 73°20'S, 1°39'W. Ice-saddle just south of Neumayer Cliffs, between Peter Glacier and Swithinbank Slope in Queen Maud Land. Name means "the barren mountain neck" in Norwegian.

Skarvsnes Foreland. 69°28'S, 39°39'E. Juts out into the eastern part of Lützow-Holm Bay. Photographed by the LCE 1936–37. Named Skarvsnes (barren mountain headland) by the Norwegians.

Skate. Non-bony fish found in the Antarctic.

Skavlhø Mountain. 72°02'S, 14°30'E. 2,610 m. North of Ormeryggen in the Payer Mountains of Queen Maud Land. Name means "the snow-drift heights" in Norwegian.

Skavlrimen Ridge. 71°58'S, 13°32'E. Largely snow-covered. 3 miles long. Surmounted in the north by Vyatskyaya Peak. 1½ miles east of Dekefjellet Mountain in the Weyprecht Mountains of Queen Maud Land. Discovered during

the Ritscher expedition of 1938–39. Named by the Norwegians.

Skavlsletta Flat. 73°26'S, 3°42'W. Small, ice-covered area between Svartbandufsa Bluff and Tverregga Spur in the Kirwan Escarpment of Queen Maud Land. Name means "the snow-drift plain" in Norwegian.

Skeen Rocks. 67°47'S, 68°54'W. Two rocks in water south of Avian Island off the south end of Adelaide Island. Named by the UK for Lt. Michael G.C. Skeen, officer-in-charge of the helicopter flight from the *Protector* while charting the area in 1961–63.

Skeidsberget Hill. 72°06'S, 11°25'E. 2 miles NW of Skeidshovden Mountain in the Wohlthat Mountains of Queen Maud Land. Named by the Norwegians. The USSR calls it Levanevskogo Mountain.

Skeidshornet Peak. 71°50'S, 12°01'E. 2,725 m. 5 miles WSW of Mount Valikhanov in the Pieck Range of the Petermann Ranges of Queen Maud Land. Discovered by Ritscher in 1938–39. Named by the Norwegians.

Skeidshovden Mountain. 72°08'S, 11°31'E. 2,730 m. At the SW end of the Wohlthat Mountains in Queen Maud Land. Named by the Norwegians.

Skeidskar Gap. 71°46'S, 11°33'E. A narrow gap in the ridge along the SE side of Skarskvervet Glacier in the Humboldt Mountains of Queen Maud Land. Discovered by Ritscher in 1938–39. Named by the Norwegians.

Mount Skeidskneet. 71°53'S, 11°57'E. 2,600 m. Surmounts the east side of the head of Humboldt Graben at the SW end of the Petermann Ranges of the Wohlthat Mountains in Queen Maud Land. Discovered by Ritscher in 1938–39. Named by the Norwegians.

Skeidsnutane Peaks. 71°53'S, 11°35'E. Extend south for 6 miles from the Skarshaugane Peaks in the Humboldt Mountains of Queen Maud Land. Discovered by Ritscher in 1938–39. Named by the Norwegians.

Skelly Peak. 79°22'S, 85°19'W. 1,450 m. Marks the NE limit of the Watlack Hills in the Heritage Range. Named for Donald J. Skelly, USN, hospital corpsman and chief petty officer in charge of Palmer Station, 1966.

Skelton, Reginald W. 1872–1952. Lt. RN. Chief engineer on the Royal Society Expedition led by Scott in 1901–4. He had assisted in the supervision of construction of the *Discovery* in Dundee, and also designed the motor sledges for Scott's later, 1910–13, expedition (which Skelton did not go on).

Skelton Glacier. 78°35'S, 161°30'E. The southernmost point of Victoria Land, it flows from the Polar Plateau to feed the Ross Ice Shelf at Skelton Inlet. Hillary pioneered it as a route to the Pole in 1957, and named it in association with the inlet.

Skelton Icefalls. 78°15'S, 158°22'E. Extend in an arc about 15 miles from Portal Mountain to the north end of the Warren Range in Victoria Land. Named by the USA in 1964 in association with the Skelton Névé and Skelton Glacier.

Skelton Inlet. 78°54'S, 162°15'E. Icefilled. At the terminus of Skelton Glacier, on the west side of the Ross Ice Shelf. 10 miles wide at its entrance between Cape Timberlake and Fishtail Point. Discovered and named by Scott's 1910–13 expedition for Reginald W. Skelton.

Skelton Névé. 78°20'S, 160°E. The huge névé of the Skelton Glacier (it feeds that glacier) on the west side of the Royal Society Range. Circular, and 40 miles in diameter, it has an area of 1,300 square miles. Named by the New Zealanders in 1957–58 for its relationship to the glacier.

Skep Point. 64°03'S, 57°18'W. Icefree. 5 miles WNW of Ula Point on the NE coast of James Ross Island. Surveyed by the FIDS in 1945 and 1953. Named descriptively by the UK. A skep is a beehive.

Skew Peak. 77°13'S, 160°43'E. 2,535 m. Just west of the head of Frazier Glacier in the Clare Range of Victoria Land. Named in 1957 by the Northern Survey Party of the BCTAE because of its asymmetrical summit.

Ski-Doos. Snowmobile motor toboggans. The Ski-Doo Alpine 640-ER, much used by the US field parties in Antarctica throughout the 1970s and 1980s, had a 640 c.c. engine. The Trans-Globe Expedition used them during their trek across Antarctica in 1980–81, to haul sledges.

Ski Slope. In the vicinity of McMurdo Station, it is a slope descriptively named.

Mount Skidmore. 80°18'S, 28°56'W. Also called Mount Lagrange. 865 m. On the east side of the mouth of Stratton Glacier in the Shackleton Range. Named by the UK for Michael J. Skidmore, BAS geologist at Halley Bay Station, 1966–69. He was in the Shackleton Range in 1968–69.

Skidmore Cliff. 83°24'S, 49°30'W. 4 miles long. East of Saratoga Table in the Forrestal Range. Named for Donald D. Skidmore, ionosphere scientist at Ellsworth Station in 1957.

Skidsmo, Capt. Captain of the *Graham*, 1921–22.

Skigarden Ridge. 71°54'S, 4°32'E. Has several peaks on it. 2 miles NE of Mount Gritøyr in the Mühlig-Hofmann Mountains of Queen Maud Land. Name means "the rail fence" in Norwegian.

Skilift Col. 86°11'S, 148°36'W. In the mountain wall between Griffith Glacier and Howe Glacier on the west side of the Watson Escarpment. 2 miles NE of Mount Meeks, it provides a shortcut for field parties. Named by the NZGSAE 1969–70 because some members of the party used a motor toboggan here in a way similar to that of a skilift.

Skilling, Charles J. 1931–1952. FIDS general assistant at Signy Island Station in 1949, and a member of the sledge party which visited the Robertson Islands that year. He died aboard the *John Biscoe* on April 17, 1952.

Skilling Island. 60°47'S, 45°09'W. A small island, just north of Atriceps

Island, in the Robertson Islands in the South Orkneys. Surveyed by personnel on the *Discovery II* in 1933. Named by the UK for Charles J. Skilling.

Skilly Peak. 64°59′S, 61°16′W. 4 miles NE of Shiver Point on the east coast of Graham Land. Surveyed by the FIDS in 1947 and 1955, and named by them in the latter year for the skilly (thin soup) they were forced to live off when their rations ran short.

Skimten Hill. 72°13′S, 0°17′E. 5 miles north of Mount Roer in the Sverdrup Mountains of Queen Maud Land. The name means "the glimpse" in Norwegian. Only a glimpse of it can be seen protruding through the ice.

Mount Skinner. 84°45′S, 171°10′W. 1,060 m. Flat. Mainly ice-free mesa. 3 miles long. 2 miles wide. Just south of the Bravo Hills. Between Gough and Le Couteur Glaciers, near the edge of the Ross Ice Shelf. Surveyed by Albert P. Crary in 1957–58 during the US Ross Ice Shelf Traverse Party of that season, and named by him for Bernard W. Skinner.

Skinner, Bernard W. Aviation and tractor mechanic on the shore party of Byrd's 1933–35 expedition.

Skinner Glacier. 70°14′S, 68°W. On the west edge of Palmer Land, between Mounts Dixey and Flower. It enters George VI Sound, just east of Carse Point. Named by the UK for Alexander C. Skinner, BAS geologist at Fossil Bluff Station, 1968–69 and at Base E, 1969–70.

Skinner Peak. 84°46′S, 112°53′W. Over 2,600 m. Mainly snow-covered. NE of Mount Schopf in the Ohio Range. Named for Courtney J. Skinner, geological assistant and camp manager with the Ohio State University Expedition to the Horlick Mountains in 1961–62. Skinner was back in the Antarctic in 1962–63, 1963–64, 1964–65, 1965–66, 1966–67.

Skinner Ridge. 74°25′S, 161°44′E. 12 miles long. Descends SW from the west side of the Eisenhower Range in Victoria Land. Mounts Fenton and Mackintosh lie astride the northern portion of the ridge. Named by the Southern Party of the NZGSAE 1962–63 for D.N.B. Skinner, geologist with the expedition. He had also been in the Northern Party of the NZGSAE 1960–61.

Skinner Saddle. 80°58′S, 159°24′E. Snow-covered. Between the northern part of the Darley Hills and that part of the Churchill Mountains east of Mount Durnford. Named by the Northern Party of the NZGSAE 1960–61 for D.N.B. Skinner (*see* **Skinner Ridge**).

Skis. Plural was "ski" in the old days. Amundsen was the first man ever to ski in Antarctica, which he did on Two Hummock Island on Jan. 26, 1898, while he was second mate on the *Belgica*.

Skjegget Peak. 69°26′S, 39°36′E. 360 m. Surmounts the NW end of Skarvsnes Foreland on the east side of Lützow-Holm Bay. Photographed by the LCE 1936–37. Name means "the barb" in Norwegian.

Skoddemedet Peak. 72°50′S, 3°51′W. 5 miles SW of Høgfonna Mountain in the Borg Massif of Queen Maud Land. Name means "the fog landmark" in Norwegian.

Cap Skollsberg *see* **Skottsberg Point**

Skontorp Cove. 64°54′S, 62°52′W. In Paradise Harbor. 2 miles SE of Bryde Island, off the west coast of Graham Land. Named for Edward Skontorp, Norwegian whaler working for Salvesen & Co., out of Scotland.

Skorefjell. 66°27′S, 53°57′E. Also called Mount Bride. 1,520 m. A mountain 9 miles NE of Stor Hånakken Mountain in the Napier Mountains of Enderby Land. Photographed by the LCE 1936–37. Named by the Norwegians.

Skorvebradden. 72°07′S, 5°33′E. A heavily crevassed ice slope. Extends 13 miles ESE from Hamarskorvene Bluff in the Mühlig-Hofmann Mountains of Queen Maud Land. Named by the Norwegians.

Skorvehallet Slope. 71°59′S, 9°12′E. Snow-covered. Just west of the Gagarin

Mountains in the Orvin Mountains of Queen Maud Land. Named by the Norwegians.

Skorvehalsen Saddle. 72°04′S, 6°11′E. Ice saddle just south of Huldreskorvene Peaks in the Mühlig-Hofmann Mountains of Queen Maud Land. Named by the Norwegians.

Skorvetangen Spur. 72°03′S, 5°20′E. 2 miles SE of Hamarskorvene Bluff in the Mühlig-Hofmann Mountains of Queen Maud Land. Named by the Norwegians.

Cape Skottsberg *see* **Skottsberg Point**

Skottsberg, Carl. A Swedish botanist who was one of the Paulet Island party off the crushed *Antarctic* during the Nordenskjöld expedition of 1901–4. In 1907–9 he led the Swedish Magellan Expedition to South Georgia (54°S).

Skottsberg Point. 63°55′S, 60°49′W. Also called Cape Skottsberg, Punta Farias, and also seen (erroneously) as Cap Skollsberg. Forms the south end of Trinity Island. Charted and named by Nordenskjöld in 1901–4 for Carl Skottsberg.

Skotvika *see* **Stack Bay**

Skredbotnen Cirque. 71°59′S, 4°27′E. Indents the west side of Mount Grytøyr in the Mühlig-Hofmann Mountains of Queen Maud Land. Name means "the avalanche cirque" in Norwegian.

Skruvestikka Nunatak. 72°12′S, 14°28′E. Just east of Filsponen Nunatak at the south end of the Payer Mountains in Queen Maud Land. Name means "the screw driver" in Norwegian.

Skua Creek. 65°15′S, 64°16′W. A marine channel between Skua Island and Winter Island in the Argentine Islands. Charted and named Skua Inlet by the BGLE in 1935. Later redefined.

Skua Glacier. 82°57′S, 157°40′E. In the northern part of the Miller Range. Flows into the Astro Glacier. Named by the New Zealanders in 1961–62 for the skuas seen here in Dec. 1961.

Skua Gull Peak. 76°50′S, 145°24′W. Has a small lake enclosed near the summit. 2 miles NE of Saunders Mountain. ½ mile south of Mount Stancliff in the Ford Ranges of Marie Byrd Land. Discovered in Nov. 1934 by a sledging party of Byrd's 1933–35 expedition and named by them for the skua gull rookery here.

Skua Inlet *see* **Skua Creek**

Skua Island. 65°15′S, 64°16′W. Almost ¾ mile long. Between Black Island on the SW and Winter Island and Galíndez Island to the north and NE. In the Argentine Islands in the Wilhelm Archipelago. Charted and named in 1935 by the BGLE.

Skua Lake. 77°38′S, 166°25′E. A little lake just NW of Island Lake, behind Home Beach on North Bay, in the area of Cape Royds, on the west coast of Ross Island. In the summer a stream flows down to Home Beach from here, and into North Bay. Named by Scott's 1910–13 expedition for its nearness to a skua rookery.

The Skuary *see* **Cape Evans**

Skuas. Large, fearless, gull-like birds of the North and South Poles. There are two types in Antarctica, both of which prey on Adélie penguins. The South Polar skua (or McCormick's skua) breeds exclusively on the continent. This is *Catharacta mcCormicki*, and flies over the South Pole and travels to Greenland. The brown skua or great skua breeds in the South Shetlands and South Orkneys. This one is *Catharacta lonnbergi*. The world's most southerly skua rookery is at Cape Evans, on Ross Island.

Skuggekammen Ridge. 71°23′S, 13°40′E. Extends SE from Mount Mentzel in the Gruber Mountains of the Wohlthat Mountains in Queen Maud Land. Discovered by Ritscher's expedition of 1938–39. Name means "the shade ridge" in Norwegian.

Skutenes. Approximately 66°53′S, 56°44′E. On the western side of Edward VIII Bay. Photographed by the LCE 1936–37 and mapped by the Norwegians from these photos, along with nearby

Skutenesmulen. Skutenes (barge point) was considered to be a point, and Skutenesmulen a nearby part of it. ANARE later mapped Skutenes as two snow-covered islands, thus the two names became redundant. Cape Dalton (q.v.) is on one of these islands.

Camp Sky-Hi *see* **Eights Station**

Sky-Hi Nunataks. 74°52'S, 71°30'W. Extend over 8 miles. 10 miles north of the Merrick Mountains in eastern Ellsworth Land. Discovered aerially by the RARE 1947–48. Named for Project Sky-Hi (*see* Eights Station).

Skytrain Ice Rise. 79°40'S, 78°30'W. Flat, peninsulalike ice rise. Extends for 50 miles from the area around the Meyer Hills in the Heritage Range, into the Ronne Ice Shelf. Named for the "Skytrain" airplanes, otherwise known as R4Ds or Dakotas, much used by the Americans in Antarctica until the late 1960s when the Hercules took over.

Slabotnen Cirque. 71°46'S, 10°27'E. Between Mount Dallmann and the Shcherbakov Range in the Orvin Mountains of Queen Maud Land. Discovered aerially during Ritscher's 1938–39 expedition. Name means "the sloping cirque" in Norwegian.

Mount Sladen. 60°41'S, 45°17'W. 890 m. Pyramidal. 1½ miles NE of Saunders Point in eastern Coronation Island. Surveyed by the FIDS in 1948–49. Named by the UK for Dr. William J.L. Sladen.

Sladen, Dr. William J.L. FIDS medical officer/biologist at Base D at Hope Bay in 1948. In 1950 he was at Signy Island Station. During the 1960s and 1970s he was chief USARP investigator concerned with the studies of penguins at Cape Crozier.

Slagle Ridge. 71°55'S, 169°50'E. Snow-covered. Between Slone Glacier and Burnette Glacier in the Admiralty Mountains. Named for Capt. Thomas D. Slagle, USN, chief medical officer at Little America in 1958.

Slalåma Slope. 72°31'S, 3°25'W. Steep ice slope on the NE side of Borg Mountain in the Borg Massif of Queen Maud Land. Name means "the slalom" in Norwegian.

Slater Rocks. 75°05'S, 113°53'W. 4 miles north of Leister Peak in the Kohler Range of Marie Byrd Land. Named for Robert T. Slater, USN, equipment operator at Amundsen-Scott South Pole Station in 1974.

Slava Bay *see* **Slava Ice Shelf**

Slava Ice Shelf. 68°49'S, 154°44'E. Formerly called Slava Bay. Between Mawson Peninsula and Cape Andreyev. Named for the USSR whaling flotilla *Slava.*

Sledgemeters. Devices used for measuring distances covered by sledges. Usually it was a bicycle wheel with a revolution counter attached to the back of the last sledge in a party. Someone was always getting off the sledge to clean the thing free of snow.

Sledgers Glacier. 71°26'S, 162°48'E. In the Bowers Mountains. Flows from Husky Pass, along the northern flank of the Lanterman Range, and enters Rennick Glacier between Carnes Crag and Mount Gow. Traveled the hard way by the Northern Party of the NZGSAE 1963–64, and they named it for all sledgers.

Sledgers Icefall. 71°28'S, 163°12'E. Heavily crevassed. Halfway up the Sledgers Glacier in the Bowers Mountains, just north of the tip of Reilly Ridge. Named by the New Zealanders in 1967–68 in association with the glacier.

Sledges. Sledges, or sleds, were used, and still are, to transport equipment and personnel across the ice and snow of Antarctica. They can be propelled in a variety of ways: dogs (q.v.), ponies (q.v.), motors, or men. The most practical over long distances are dogs, when handled correctly by an experienced dog handler and with a good team of dogs. Otherwise it can be a disaster. Ponies are not efficient, as their feet get stuck, and they require too much feeding. Motorized sledges find it hard going, while manhauling is sure, steady, but enormously draining to the men. All four methods have been used extensively in Antarctica. The first to sledge in Antarctica was the team of de Gerlache, Amundsen, Frederick Cook, Arctowski, and Danco, on Brabant Island, on Jan. 31, 1898, during the *Belgica* expedition of 1897–99. Borchgrevink was next, in 1899, then came von Drygalski, Nordenskjöld, and Scott, all in 1902. When one discusses Antarctic sledging, one thinks of Scott and Amundsen, and the different theories these men held. Amundsen had only one theory—dogs—and he practiced it exclusively, and proved its worth by being the first to reach the South Pole. He used lightweight sledges and a lot of dogs to share the load. He always gave the dogs a target to strive for. He understood dogs and how to get the best out of them. He realized that huskies need to work, they need a challenge and tough conditions to overcome. He did not anthropomorphize them, as Scott had a tendency to do. Scott was not comfortable with dogs—or with sledges for that matter—and although he pioneered the use of the sledge in Antarctica, he had no real choice in the matter. On his first expedition, Scott took nine Nansen Sledges. A Nansen Sledge was 10 feet long, 20 inches wide and weighed 31 pounds. Made of ash, it was raised at both ends, with ⅓-inch-wide runners, slightly convex, with narrow blades made of German silver. It was developed by Arctic explorer Fridtjof Nansen. Shackleton, in 1907–9, took 30 Norwegian sledges—ten 12-footers, eighteen 11-footers, and two 7-footers. He used ponies to pull, and they proved inadequate. When Scott heard that Shackleton had reached a point 97 miles from the Pole, and had used ponies, he inaccurately ascribed Shackleton's success to the ponies, and determined to take ponies with him on his next expedition, 1910–13. He also took motor sledges with him, as a safeguard, but they failed in the field (Skelton had invented these). The ponies, of course, proved as inadequate

with Scott as they had with Shackleton, and it was not long before Scott and his companions were manhauling their sledges to the Pole and almost back. It is more than suspected by most researchers that this was the way these particular British explorers wished it. There seemed to be something heroic and self-contained in pulling one's own sledge, and possibly something suspiciously weak in having animals (i.e., someone else) pull it for one. Amundsen regarded this method as criminally backward and he was very vocal about his opposition to manhauling. For this reason, perhaps, each of Scott's sledges was designed for a crew of 3. It carried their tent and full equipment and stores. The weight of a tent alone was 33 pounds. Also on each tightly-packed sledge was a Nansen cooker and a Primus stove. The total weight of each sledge was 660 pounds, or 220 pounds per man, that is if all were able to pull. They were all able in the early stages of the expedition, but usually toward the end one or more of the men was in a desperately ill state due to scurvy, frostbite, starvation, or a combination thereof, and had to be pulled by the others. Above and beyond that, it was not unknown for sick dogs to be pulled on the sledges. All of this, of course, made the job of the remaining haulers increasingly and impossibly difficult. This, then, they manhauled hundreds of miles across the ice, snow, glaciers, and crevasses, never knowing when their sledge was going to disappear down a hidden crevasse, taking dogs, tent, equipment, and food with it. Since the 1920s motor-sledges have been used more and more. E.L. Pitman of Byfleet, Surrey, made the sledges for the BGLE 1934–37, and introduced important new elements into the design of the Nansen Sledge. The Eliason Motor Sledge, invented in Sweden in 1942, and now made in Canada, has been used in Antarctica since 1960. The Polaris Motor Sledge, made by Polaris Industries, of Roseau, Minn., has also been in Antarctica since 1960.

Sledging biscuits. Biscuits taken by the old explorers on sledging traverses as a staple item of food. Plasmon was often an ingredient.

Sledging Col. 85°51'S, 154°48'W. Between Mount Griffith and a very low peak on its NE side in the Hays Mountains of the Queen Maud Mountains. It provides a sledging route from Robert Scott Glacier to the head of Koerwitz Glacier. Named in 1969–70 by the New Zealanders who used it.

Sleds *see* **Sledges**

Sleeping bags. Have always been used on land traverses in Antarctica. Scott used reindeer skin bags during his first expedition of 1901–4, and in fact had gone to Norway to buy them.

Sleipnir Glacier. 66°29'S, 63°59'W. 10 miles long. Flows into the west side of Cabinet Inlet between Balder and Spur Points on the east coast of Graham Land. Charted in 1947 by the FIDS, and named by them for the horse of the Norse god, Odin.

Slessor Glacier. 79°50'S, 28°30'W. 75 miles long or more. 50 miles wide. Flows into the Filchner Ice Shelf to the north of the Shackleton Range. Discovered aerially by the BCTAE in 1956, and named by them for Air Marshal Sir John Slessor, chairman of the Expedition Committee.

Slessor Peak. 66°31'S, 64°58'W. 2,370 m. Mainly ice-covered. At the SW end of the Bruce Plateau in Graham Land. Just NW of Gould Glacier. Surveyed in 1946–47 by a FIDS sledging party led by Robert S. Slessor, FIDS medical officer at Base E that year. Named for him by the UK.

Slettefjellet. 71°45'S, 6°55'E. A peak one mile north of Gessner Peak, at the NE end of the Mühlig-Hofmann Mountains of Queen Maud Land. Name means "the smooth peak" in Norwegian.

Mount Sletten. 85°47'S, 153°30'W. Also spelled (erroneously) as Mount Sletton. Surmounts Taylor Ridge on the west side of the Robert Scott Glacier, 4 miles NE of Mount Pulitzer. Discovered during Byrd's 1928–30 expedition. Named for Robert S. Sletten, satellite geodesist at McMurdo Station in 1965.

Slettfjell. 72°08'S, 3°19'W. A flat mountain 1 mile west of Aurhø Peak on the Ahlmann Ridge of Queen Maud Land. Name means "level mountain" in Norwegian.

Slettfjellklumpen Spur. 72°08'S, 3°18'W. Forms the north end of Slettfjell on the Ahlmann Ridge of Queen Maud Land. Name means "the level mountain lump" in Norwegian.

Slettfjellnutane Peaks. 72°05'S, 3°18'W. Two peaks, two miles north of Slettfjell on the Ahlmann Ridge of Queen Maud Land. Name means "the level mountain peaks" in Norwegian.

Slichter Foreland. 74°08'S, 113°50'W. Ice-covered peninsula. 15 miles long. 10 miles wide. Forms the NE arm of Martin Peninsula on the coast of Marie Byrd Land. Named for Louis Slichter, professor of physics at UCLA, who has trained geophysicists for the South Pole and who has planned scientific programs for the Antarctic.

Slithallet Slope. 72°03'S, 2°57'E. Ice slope between Jutulsessen Mountain and Risemedet Mountain in the Gjelsvik Mountains of Queen Maud Land. Name means "the drudgery slope" in Norwegian.

Sloket Glacier. 71°58'S, 4°54'E. Flows between Slokstallen Mountain and Petrellfjellet in the Mühlig-Hofmann Mountains of Queen Maud Land. Name means "the millrace" in Norwegian.

Sloknuten Peak. 72°02'S, 4°52'E. 2,765 m. Just SW of Slokstallen Mountain in the Mühlig-Hofmann Mountains of Queen Maud Land. Name means "the millrace peak" in Norwegian.

Slokstallen Mountain. 72°01'S, 4°54'E. 1 mile east of Petrellfjellet in the Mühlig-Hofmann Mountains of Queen Maud Land. Name means "the millrace barn" in Norwegian.

Sloman Glacier. 67°40'S, 68°33'W. Flows between Mount Liotard and

Mount Ditte to the SE coast of Adelaide Island. Named by the UK in 1963 for William O. Sloman, BAS personnel officer for many years beginning in 1956 (when BAS was still the FIDS).

Slone Glacier. 72°S, 170°E. Flows along the north side of Slagle Ridge in the Admiralty Mountains, to enter the west side of the Moubray Glacier. Named for airman Kelly Slone (*see* **Deaths, 1958**).

Sløret Rocks. 73°43'S, 4°17'W. Rocks on the Kirwan Escarpment, 5 miles south of Enden Point in Queen Maud Land. Name means "the veil" in Norwegian.

Slossarczyk, Walter. Third officer and communications officer on the *Deutschland* during the German Antarctic Expedition of 1911–12 under Filchner. He died in South Georgia on Nov. 26, 1911.

The Slot. 82°40'S, 155°05'E. A glacier which flows from the Polar Plateau between Mount Ronca and Mount Summerson in the Geologists Range. Named by the New Zealanders in 1961–62 for its narrowness and for its crevassed nature.

Slumkey Island. 65°30'S, 65°28'W. Largest island of the group east of Tupman Island in the Pitt Islands of the Biscoe Islands. Named by the UK in 1959 for the Dickens character.

Slump Mountain. 77°55'S, 160°41'E. Between Beacon Valley and Arena Valley in southern Victoria Land. A term not used any more.

Slusher Nunatak. 74°27'S, 99°06'W. 5 miles north of Mount Moses in the Hudson Mountains. Named for Harold E. Slusher, meteorologist at Byrd Station in 1967.

Småhausane Nunataks. 71°33'S, 25°18'E. 1,180 m. Between Mount Fidjeland and Nordtoppen Nunatak at the north side of the Sør Rondane Mountains. Photographed by the LCE 1936–37. Name means "the small crags" in Norwegian.

Småknoltane Peaks. 72°07'S, 8°03'E. 4 miles long. On the east side of the mouth of Snuggerud Glacier in the Filch-

ner Mountains of Queen Maud Land. Name means "the small knolls" in Norwegian.

Småkovane Cirques. 71°54'S, 5°32'E. Two cirques separated by a narrow ridge, indenting the NE side of Breplogen Mountain in the Mühlig-Hofmann Mountains of Queen Maud Land. Name means "the small closets" in Norwegian.

Smalegga Ridge. 72°01'S, 24°04'E. 4 miles long. Extends north from Mount Walnum to the west of Gillock Glacier in the Sør Rondane Mountains. Name means "the narrow ridge" in Norwegian.

Smalegga Spur. 71°55'S, 10°37'E. 3 miles SSE of Mørkenatten Peak in the Shcherbakov Range of the Orvin Mountains in Queen Maud Land. Name means "the narrow ridge" in Norwegian.

Mount Small. 70°30'S, 64°42'E. Partly snow-covered. 2 miles SW of the Crohn Massif in the Porthos Range. Named by the Australians for G.R. Small, geophysicist at Wilkes Station in 1964.

Small, John. Baker on the Wilkes Expedition 1838–42. Joined at Rio. Discharged in NZ.

Small Island. 64°S, 61°27'W. 1 mile long. 3 miles south of Intercurrence Island in the Christiania Islands in the Palmer Archipelago. Named in the 19th century, presumably because of its size.

Small Razorback Island *see* **Little Razorback Island**

Small Rock. 60°43'S, 45°36'W. A rock in water, 350 yards NE of Berntsen Point, in the entrance to Borge Bay on the east side of Signy Island in the South Orkneys. Named by personnel on the *Discovery II* in 1933.

Mount Smart. 75°16'S, 70°14'W. 4 miles SW of Mount Ballard, in the SW part of the Sweeney Mountains in Ellsworth Land. Named for Robert G. Smart, cook at Eights Station in 1965.

Småsponen Nunatak. 72°S, 3°55'E. Just NW of Storsponen Nunatak, at the north side of Mount Hochlin in the Mühlig-Hofmann Mountains of Queen

Maud Land. Name means "the little chip" in Norwegian. The USSR calls it Parus Mountain.

Småtind Peak. 72°33'S, 2°57'W. Just SE of Fasettfjellet, near the east end of the Borg Massif in Queen Maud Land. Name means "the small peak" in Norwegian.

Point Smellie. 62°39'S, 61°09'W. Forms a point at President Beaches, on the SW coast of Byers Peninsula, Livingston Island, in the South Shetlands.

Mount Smethurst. 66°50'S, 52°36'E. 3 miles NW of Mount Torckler. 29 miles SW of Stor Hånakken Mountain in Enderby Land. Named by the Australians for N.R. Smethurst, officer-in-charge of Wilkes Station in 1961.

Smiggers Island. 65°27'S, 65°21'W. 1 mile SE of Weller Island in the Pitt Islands in the Biscoe Islands. Named by the UK in 1959 for the Dickens character.

Cape Smiley *see* **Smyley Island**

Smirnov Peak. 71°43'S, 10°38'E. 2,105 m. 2½ miles south of Ristkalvane Nunataks in the northern Shcherbakov Range of the Orvin Mountains of Queen Maud Land. Named by the USSR in 1966 for Aleksandr A. Smirnov, member of the Soviet Antarctic Expedition of 1960–61.

¹Cape Smith. 62°52'S, 62°19'W. Also called Smiths Cape, Cabo Granville. The northernmost point on Smith Island, in the South Shetlands. Named for William Smith, the discoverer of the South Shetlands.

²Cape Smith *see* **Cape Irwyn**

Mount Smith. 76°03'S, 161°42'E. Over 1,400 m. North of Mawson Glacier. 7 miles NNW of Mount Murray in Victoria Land. Discovered by Scott's 1901–4 expedition and named by them as Smith Mountains for W.E. Smith, who supervised the construction of the *Discovery*. Later redefined as a single mountain.

Smith, Alexander J. Midshipman on the *Erebus*, 1839–43, under Ross.

Smith, C.E. Second engineer on the *Quest*, 1921–22.

Smith, David. Ordinary seaman on the Wilkes Expedition 1838–42. Joined in the USA. Served the cruise.

Smith, David M. Armorer on the Wilkes Expedition 1838–42. Joined in the USA. Served the cruise.

Smith, Dean C. b. 1897. Pioneer pilot in the mail service, one of the 32 who opened the mail line between New York and Cleveland. Aviation pilot on the shore party of Byrd's 1928–30 expedition.

Smith, Dorothy. b. 1918. One of the mountaineers on David Lewis' 1977–78 *Solo* expedition. She was back again with Lewis on the *Dick Smith Explorer* expedition of 1981–82.

Smith, Frank. Officer's steward on the Wilkes Expedition 1838–42. Joined in the USA. Served the cruise.

Smith, George. Private on the Wilkes Expedition 1838–42. Joined in the USA. Served the cruise.

Smith, Hendrick. Ordinary seaman on the Wilkes Expedition 1838–42. Joined in the USA. Discharged at Oahu, Nov. 2, 1840.

¹Smith, James. Seaman on the Wilkes Expedition 1838–42. Joined in the USA. Run at Sydney.

²Smith, James. Ordinary seaman on the Wilkes Expedition 1838–42. Joined in the USA. Lost in the *Sea Gull* in late April 1839.

¹Smith, John. Ordinary seaman on the Wilkes Expedition 1838–42. Joined in the USA. Lost in the *Sea Gull* in late April 1839.

²Smith, John. Ordinary seaman on the Wilkes Expedition 1838–42. Joined in the USA. Run at Rio.

³Smith, John. Private on the Wilkes Expedition 1838–42. Joined in the USA. Served the cruise.

⁴Smith, John. Seaman on the Wilkes Expedition 1838–42. Joined at Rio. Run at Sydney.

Smith, Moses J. Ordinary seaman on the Wilkes Expedition 1838–42. Joined at Rio. Run at Sydney.

Smith, Ralph W. Airplane pilot on the shore party of Byrd's 1933–35 expedition.

Smith, Walter. Ship's mate, navigator and trail man on the RARE 1947–48.

¹Smith, William. In a way, the most important man in Antarctic history. A British sealer from Blythe in England, he sighted and landed on the first Antarctic land, i.e., south of 60°S. He was on a commercial trip from Buenos Aires to Valparaiso when he sighted the South Shetland Islands on Feb. 19, 1819, in the *Williams*, of which he was captain. He made two sightings on the same day, at 62°40′S, 60°W, and named the land New South Britain. He was not believed when he arrived at Chile. He tried returning to prove it in June 1819, but got as far south as 61°12′S on June 15, 1819. He then returned to Montevideo. On Oct. 14, 1819, he returned to the South Shetlands, and on Oct. 16, 1819, he landed near North Foreland on King George Island and took possession of the islands for Britain. He explored them and partially surveyed them, and renamed them New South Shetland (a name that stuck until about 1822). These sightings were believed, and started a seal rush to the islands. The Navy placed Bransfield in charge of the *Williams,* and with Smith as pilot, the ship returned to the area for the 1819–20 season. On Jan. 30, 1820, Smith and Bransfield were perhaps the first to sight the Antarctic continent when they sighted the peaks of Trinity Land (although *see* **von Bellingshausen** and **Palmer**). Smith was in the South Shetlands again for the 1820–21 season, on another sealing expedition, as captain of the *Williams* and another vessel. He arrived back in London on Sept. 17, 1821, after a most eventful three years.

²Smith, William. Seaman on the Wilkes Expedition 1838–42. Joined at Rio. Drowned at Fiji.

³Smith, William. Bosun on the *Vincennes* during the Wilkes Expedition 1838–42.

⁴Smith, William. Yeoman on the Wilkes Expedition 1838–42. Joined in the USA. Served the cruise.

Smith, William J. Quartermaster on the Wilkes Expedition 1838–42. Joined in the USA. Discharged at Sydney, March 19, 1840.

Smith Bay   *see*   **Smith Inlet**

Smith Bluff. 82°05′S, 162°20′E. On the west side of the Nash Range, to the west of Ricker Dome. Overlooks Algie Glacier. Named for H.T.U. Smith, geologist at McMurdo Station in 1963–64.

Smith Bluffs. 72°32′S, 94°56′W. Ice-covered. Mark the north side of Dustin Island and the southern limit of Seraph Bay. Discovered aerially in Feb. 1960 by helicopters on the USN Bellingshausen Sea Expedition of that month. Named for Philip M. Smith, NSF official and USARP representative on this expedition (*see also* **Smith Glacier**).

Smith Glacier. 75°03′S, 111°12′W. Over 100 miles long. Flows from Toney Mountain to the Amundsen Sea between Bear Peninsula and Mount Murphy. A northern distributary, Kohler Glacier, flows to the Dotson Ice Shelf. Named for Philip M. Smith (*see* **Smith Bluffs**), many times in the Antarctic between 1956 and 1971.

Smith Heights. 79°52′S, 157°07′E. Between Kennett Ridge and Junction Spur in the eastern part of the Darwin Mountains. Named by the VUWAE 1962–63 for G.J. Smith, a member of the expedition.

¹Smith Inlet. 70°25′S, 62°W. A Larsen Ice Shelf indentation into the east coast of the Antarctic Peninsula, between Wilkins Coast and Black Coast, or more specifically between Cape Boggs and Cape Collier. Discovered and charted by the USAS in 1940, but later incorrectly shown on charts as Stefansson Inlet. Named Smith Bay by Ronne in 1947–48 for Rear Adm. Edward H. Smith, Arctic explorer of the 1920s. Later redefined.

²Smith Inlet. 70°59′S, 167°52′E. Also spelled (erroneously) as Smyth Inlet. A bay, 4 miles wide, and partially filled with the ice tongue of Barnett Glacier. Between Cape Moore and Cape Oakeley on the coast of northern Victoria Land. Discovered by Ross in 1841, and named by him for Alexander J. Smith.

Smith Island. 63° S, 62° 30′ W. Also called James Island, Borodino Island, Smith's Island, Smith's Isle, Île Smyth. 45 miles west of Deception Island, it is part of the South Shetland Islands, but separated from the majority of them by the Boyd Strait. It is 19 miles long and 5 miles wide at its greatest extent. Its highest peaks are Mount Pisgah and Mount Foster. First sighted Jan. 18, 1820, by the *Hersilia,* and named Mount Pisgah Island. By the time of the U.S. Civil War (1861–65) everyone was calling it Smith Island, in honor of William Smith, discoverer of the South Shetlands.

Smith Islands. 66° 18′ S, 110° 27′ E. Two islands, close to Tracy Point, the western end of Beall Island, in the Windmill Islands. Named for aerographer's mate Roger E. Smith, USN, at Wilkes Station in 1958.

Smith Knob. 85° 25′ S, 87° 15′ W. A partly snow-covered knob (or rock peak), 1 mile SSE of Mendenhall Peak in the eastern part of the Thiel Mountains. Named by Bermel and Ford, leaders of the US Geological Survey Thiel Mountains Party here in 1960–61, for George Otis Smith, 4th director of the USGS, 1907–30.

Smith Lake. 66° 07′ S, 101° 17′ E. 1 mile long. In the Bunger Hills. Between Booth and Countess Peninsulas. Named for Kenneth R. Smith, air crewman on Bunger's flight over here during Operation Highjump, 1946–47.

Smith Mountains *see* **Mount Smith**

Smith Nunatak. 70° 13′ S, 64° 35′ E. Just SE of Mount Starlight in the Athos Range of the Prince Charles Mountains. Marked by a moraine which extends 2 miles north from it. Named by the Aus-

tralians for J.C. Smith, diesel mechanic at Wilkes Station in 1960.

Smith Peak. 72° 05′ S, 99° 28′ W. In the Walker Mountains. SE of the head of Potaka Inlet. 6 miles ENE of Mount Hubbard on Thurston Island. Named for Dean C. Smith.

Smith Peaks. 67° 57′ S, 62° 29′ E. Just south of Mount Hordern in the David Range of the Framnes Mountains. Photographed by the LCE 1936–37. Named by the Australians for F.A. Smith, diesel mechanic at Mawson Station in 1957.

Smith Peninsula. 74° 25′ S, 61° 15′ W. Ice-covered. 25 miles long. 10 miles wide. Between Keller and Nantucket Inlets, at the south end of the Lassiter Coast on the east coast of Palmer Land. Named by Ronne in 1947–48 for Walter Smith.

Smith Point. 64° 49′ S, 63° 29′ W. 150 yards NE of Besnard Point on the SE side of the harbor of Port Lockroy, Wiencke Island. Discovered by Charcot in 1903–5. Named before 1927.

¹Smith Ridge. 70° 02′ S, 72° 50′ E. In the Mistichelli Hills, at the east edge of the Amery Ice Shelf. ANARE used it for a survey station in 1968. Named by the Australians for R.S. Smith, geophysicist at Mawson Station in 1968, and a member of the survey.

²Smith Ridge. 79° 07′ S, 86° 32′ W. 4 miles long. 1 mile west of Frazier Ridge in the Founders Peaks of the Heritage Range. Named by the University of Minnesota Geological Party here in 1963–64 for Carl W. Smith, helicopter engine technical representative with the 62nd Transportation Detachment here that year.

Smith Rocks. 67° 31′ S, 63° 01′ E. Rocks in water, ½ mile NE of the Canopus Islands, in the east part of Holme Bay. Mac. Robertson Land. Photographed by the LCE 1936–37 and named Spjotøyholmane by the Norwegians. Renamed by the Australians for Capt. V. Smith, dukw driver, 1958–59 and 1959–60.

Smiths Bench. 72°10'S, 163°08'E. A benchlike mountain 5 miles NW of Mount Baldwin in the Freyberg Mountains. Named for William M. Smith, psychologist on the USARP Victoria Land Traverse Party of 1959–60.

Smiths Cape see **Cape Smith**

Smiths Island see **Livingston Island**

Smith's Island see **Smith Island**

Mount Smithson. 84°59'S, 172°10'W. Over 3,000 m. Along the northern escarpment of the Prince Olav Mountains. 3 miles east of Mount Sellery between the heads of Krout and Harwell Glaciers. Named for James Smithson, British philanthropist whose will founded the Smithsonian Institution.

Smithson Glacier. 71°15'S, 163°52'E. In the Bowers Mountains. Flows from the slopes near Mount Verhage, along the west side of the Posey Range, into Graveson Glacier next to Mount Draeger. Named for Scott B. Smithson, geologist at McMurdo Station, 1967–68.

Smolensk Island see **Livingston Island**

Smolenskaya Mountain. 71°52'S, 12° 21'E. 2,890 m. 2½ miles ESE of Mount Neustruyev in the Südliche Petermann Range of the Wohlthat Mountains. Discovered by Ritscher in 1938–39. Named by the USSR in 1966 for the city of Smolensk.

Smoot Rock. 75°15'S, 135°24'W. Isolated. East of the head of Hull Glacier. 7 miles ESE of Mount Steinfeld in Marie Byrd Land. Named for Henry T. Smoot, meteorologist at Byrd Station in 1969–70.

Smooth Island. 65°13'S, 64°16'W. The most northeasterly of the Forge Islands in the Argentine Islands of the Wilhelm Archipelago. Named by the UK for its smooth, ice-free surface.

Smoothy, F.W. Crewman on the *Jacob Ruppert*, 1934–35.

Smørstabben Nunatak. 71°30'S, 10° 52'E. Isolated. 10 miles west of Eckhörner

Peaks of the Humboldt Mountains in Queen Maud Land. Discovered by Ritscher's expedition of 1938–39. Name means "the churnstaff" in Norwegian.

Cape Smyley see **Smyley Island**

Smyley, William H. d. Feb. 15, 1868, of cholera, in Montevideo, Uruguay. Sealing captain from Newport, R.I. One of the great sailors of his day, he spent much time in the South Shetlands, first as captain of the *Sailor's Return* in 1836, and on about 7 subsequent voyages until 1850, all as a sealer. His second trip was on the *Ohio*, 1841–42, during which, in Feb. 1842, he recovered Foster's thermometers from Deception Island. He wrote a short account of the harbor there. He then bought the *Ohio* (he was part owner of at least 5 ships), which was wrecked off the South American coast in 1843. He also owned the *America*, which he was captain of, and in 1846 he was wrecked in the *Catherine* (q.v.). He last went sealing in 1849–50. In 1850 he became US commercial agent in the Falkland Islands. Wilkes spelled his name incorrectly, as Smiley, and therefore all subsequent writers did so until the middle of the 20th century.

Smyley Island. 72°55'S, 78°W. Ice-covered. 38 miles long. Between 8 and 21 miles wide. Just NE of Rydberg Peninsula to the south of the Ronne Entrance. It is surrounded by an ice shelf, which makes it look as if the island is joined to Ellsworth Land. The NW end of this large mass was viewed aerially by the USAS 1939–41, and was called Cape Smyley, for William H. Smyley. In 1968 the USA redefined the area.

Cape Smyth. 67°36'S, 164°40'E. The southern extremity of Sturge Island in the Balleny Islands. In 1841 Ross, viewing Sturge Island from a distance, thought it to be three islands, and named the southernmost one Smyth Island for William Henry Smyth, first president of the Royal Astronomical Society. In 1904 Scott redefined it.

Île Smyth see **Smith Island**

Smyth Inlet *see* **Smith Inlet**

Smythe, William. Petty officer, RN, on the Royal Society Expedition of 1901–4.

Smythe Shoulder. 74°18′S, 113°53′W. On Martin Peninsula on the Marie Byrd Land coast.

Snag Rocks. 65°08′S, 64°27′W. Also called Rocas Bravo. Rocks in water in French Passage, between the Roca Islands and the Myriad Islands, in the Wilhelm Archipelago. Named by the UK for their danger to shipping.

Snails *see* **Sea snails**

Snake Ridge. 84°49′S, 66°30′W. 4 miles long. Adjoins the NW end of Mackin Table in the Patuxent Range of the Pensacola Mountains. Named by Dwight L. Schmidt, geologist here during the years 1962–66, for its serpentine shape.

Snakeskin Glacier. 84°57′S, 170°40′E. 15 miles long. Flows into Keltie Glacier at the east side of the Supporters Range. Named descriptively by the New Zealanders in 1961–62 for the ice and snow patterns on its surface which remind one of snakeskin.

Snarby, John. Cook on the NBSAE 1949–52.

Snarby Peak. 72°02′S, 1°37′E. Isolated. 6 miles NE of Brattskarvet Mountain at the NE end of the Sverdrup Mountains in Queen Maud Land. Named by the Norwegians for John Snarby.

Sneddon Nunataks. 77°17′S, 153°46′W. On the north side of Edward VII Peninsula, overlooking the Swinburne Ice Shelf and Sulzberger Bay. 11 miles ESE of Scott's Nunataks in the northern part of the Alexandra Mountains. Named for Donald L. Sneddon, USN, electronics technician at Byrd Station in 1967.

Snedeker Glacier. 66°27′S, 106°48′E. A channel glacier flowing to the coast 9 miles west of Merritt Island in East Antarctica. Named for Robert H. Snedeker, photo interpreter on Operation Windmill, 1947–48.

Mount Snell. 70°20′S, 71°38′W. On the west coast of Alexander Island, overlooking Wilkins Sound.

Snick Pass. 70°41′S, 69°25′W. Between the Douglas and LeMay Ranges, leading from Grotto Glacier to Purcell Snowfield, in central Alexander Island. Named descriptively by the UK (a snick is a small cut).

The *Snipe*. British sloop in Antarctic waters periodically from the 1947–48 season onward. Captain that season was Cdr. J.G. Forbes, RN. In Jan. 1948, during that first tour, it visited FIDS stations, carrying the governor of the Falkland Islands. It was back at FIDS stations later in that austral summer, this time in company with the *Nigeria*. In 1953 it was back under the command of D.G.D. Hall-Wright to help four FIDS members of Base G who were marooned at Point Hennequin. In Feb. 1953 it supported the British removal of Argentine and Chilean refugio huts from Deception Island (*see* **Wars**), and deported two Argentinians from Deception Island to South Georgia. It remained on patrol until mid-April 1953, having been joined in March by the *Bigbury Bay*.

Snipe Peak. 60°45′S, 45°41′W. 225 m. The main peak on Moe Island in the South Orkneys. Surveyed in 1933 by the personnel on the *Discovery II*, and again by Gordon de Q. Robin of the FIDS in 1947. He named it for the *Snipe*.

Sno-cats. Caterpillar tractors used by the French and British during IGY. Fuchs took one with him on the BCTAE 1957–58.

Snøbjørga Bluff. 72°05′S, 4°39′E. At the east side of the head of Stuttflog Glacier in the Mühlig-Hofmann Mountains of Queen Maud Land. Name means "the snow mountain" in Norwegian.

Snodgrass Island. 65°26′S, 65°29′W. Also called Isla Ingeniero Pereira. 2½ miles long. NE of Pickwick Island in the Pitt Islands of the Biscoe Islands. Named by the UK in 1959 for the Dickens character.

Snøhetta Dome. 72°11'S, 2°48'W. A mainly snow-covered, dome-shaped bluff, 3 miles east of Hornet Peak on the Ahlmann Ridge of Queen Maud Land. Name means "the snow cap" in Norwegian.

Snøkallen Hill. 71°42'S, 1°32'W. A small nunatak 3 miles SSE of Snøkjerringa Hill on the east side of the Ahlmann Ridge in western Queen Maud Land. Name means "the snow man" in Norwegian.

Snøkjerringa Hill. 71°39'S, 1°35'W. 3 miles NNW of Snøkallen Hill, on the east side of the Ahlmann Ridge in Queen Maud Land. Name means "the snow woman" in Norwegian.

Snønutane Peaks. 72°05'S, 4°48'E. Just east of Snøbjørga Bluff in the Mühlig-Hofmann Mountains of Queen Maud Land. Name means "the snow peaks" in Norwegian.

Snønutryggen. 72°14'S, 5°20'E. An ice-covered ridge SE of Snønutane Peaks in the Mühlig-Hofmann Mountains of Queen Maud Land. Name means "the snow peak ridge" in Norwegian.

Snøskalkegga Ridge. 71°59'S, 13°13'E. Mostly snow-covered. 3 miles long. Kazanskaya Mountain is at the north end of it. 2 miles west of Dekefjellet Mountain in the Weyprecht Mountains of Queen Maud Land. Discovered by Ritscher's expedition of 1938–39. Named by the Norwegians.

Snøskalkhausen Peak. 72°02'S, 13°12' E. 2,650 m. Marks the SW end of the Weyprecht Mountains in Queen Maud Land. Named by the Norwegians.

Snøtoa Terrace. 71°57'S, 4°35'E. Flat, ice-covered terrace on the NE side of Mount Grytøyr in the Mühlig-Hofmann Mountains of Queen Maud Land. Name means "the snow patch" in Norwegian.

Snout. A glacier's lower extremity.

Snow. When water vapor precipitates and crystallizes, it becomes snow. At temperatures above −5°F crystals form snowflakes. Very little snow falls in Antarctica (*see* **Snowfall, Rain, Atmos-**

phere), even at the coast, and practically all of the snow on the ground has been accumulated over the millenia.

Snow, Ashley C. Chief pilot at East Base during the USAS 1939–41. He was back in Antarctica for Operation Highjump, 1946–47.

Snow bridges. Areas of snow forming the roofs of crevasses. Caused by drifting snow, they often hide the dangers of a crevasse.

Snow cats *see* **Sno-cats**

Snow Hill *see* **Snow Hills, Snow Hill Island**

Snow Hill Island. 64°27'S, 57°12'W. More or less totally snow-capped. 20 miles long. 6 miles wide. SE of James Ross Island, and separated from it by Admiralty Sound, and immediately south of Seymour Island. Off the NE coast of the Antarctic Peninsula. Discovered on Jan. 6, 1843, by Ross, who called it Snow Hill because he thought it might be part of Seymour Island. Redefined by Nordenskjöld in 1902.

Snow Hills. 60°42'S, 45°38'W. Two snow-covered hills. One is 240 m. The other is 265 m. They are separated by ¼ mile. 350 yards west of Cemetery Bay in the east-central part of Signy Island. The lower, eastern, hill was charted as Snow Hill by personnel on the *Discovery II* in 1933. Later the name came to encompass both hills, and was pluralized.

¹Snow Island. 62°47'S, 61°20'W. Also called Basil Halls Island, Isla Nevada, Monroe Island. 12 miles long. An average of 8 miles wide. It is snow-covered and has an elevation of 975 feet. 4 miles SW of Livingston Island, between Boyd Strait and Morton Strait, in the South Shetlands. Formerly called President Island.

²Snow Island *see* **Chionis Island**

Snow melters. Large cabinets into which snow is shoveled. They are then lighted, melting the snow for drinking water, etc. It requires much snow to be shoveled to make a little water, and the whole process takes an inordinate amount of time and energy. The *Belgica* had one, a converted condenser from the engine room.

Snow Nunataks. 73°35'S, 77°06'W. Also called Ashley Snow Nunataks. Just to the west of the English Coast. Named for Ashley C. Snow.

Snow Peak. 1,416 feet. On Livingston Island in the South Shetlands.

Snow tunnels. Tunnels cut out by people under the surface of the snow in order to connect the station (or base) to the housing for scientific instruments. They are usually 6 feet deep and 1,000 feet long. Hallett Station was the only US scientific station without one during the IGY.

The Snowcruiser. Mammoth vehicle designed and built by Thomas Poulter over a 2-year period at a cost of $150,000. It was meant to travel anywhere on the Antarctic surface, under any conditions. Byrd took one with him on the USAS 1939–41. It was operated out of West Base, and was placed under the command of Alton Wade, and his 3 men Ferranto, Griffith, and Petras. It was 55 feet long, 20 feet wide and 15 feet high, and weighed 33½ tons. There were 4 individually-powered wheels, each 10 feet in diameter and weighing 3 tons apiece. An airplane was on the roof, and the vehicle carried a year's provisions. It was a failure, being too heavy for the snow, and was abandoned. It was rediscovered under the snow by members of Little America V many years later, during the IGY.

Snowfall. Rather light in Antarctica, only 4 inches falling over the Polar Plateau every year, and maybe 20 inches over the coastal regions. There is virtually no rain (*see* **Rain, Snow, Atmosphere**). In Dec. 1969 McMurdo Station had 25 inches of snow, a record since 1911.

Snowmobiles. Motorized passenger vehicles on skis. The Bombardier Alpines are much used in Antarctica by USAP. These are Canadian machines, rugged utility models.

Snowplume Peak. 73°32'S, 94°27'W. Pyramidal. On the north front of the Jones Mountains. ¾ mile WSW of Rightangle Peak and 2 miles WSW of Pillsbury Tower. Named by the University of Minnesota–Jones Mountains Party of 1960–61 for the continual plume of wind-blown snow which trails off the peak whenever the wind blows.

Snowshoe Glacier. 68°19'S, 66°34'W. 8 miles long. Flows from a col in the SW flank of Neny Glacier into Neny Fjord, western Graham Land. Surveyed by the FIDS in 1949 and named by FIDS leader K.S. Pierce-Butler, for its shape.

Snowshoe Pass. 83°03'S, 157°36'E. A snow saddle, 4 miles NE of Aurora Heights, between Argosy and Skua Glaciers, in the Miller Range. Discovered by the Northern Party of the NZGSAE 1961–62, and named by them for the best form of travel here in the deep snow.

Snowy petrels *see* **Petrels**

Snowy Point. 74°37'S, 163°45'E. Marks the north side of the western portal of Browning Pass in the Deep Freeze Range of Victoria Land. Explored and named by Campbell's Northern Party of 1910–13.

Snubbin Island. 65°29'S, 65°50'W. 2 miles west of Pickwick Island, at the western end of the Pitt Islands in the Biscoe Islands. Named by the UK in 1959 for the Dickens character.

Snug Cove. 65°30'S, 64°26'W. On the east side of the second largest of the Lippmann Islands off the west coast of Graham Land. Named by the UK in 1959 because it is a good anchorage for small boats.

Snuggerud Glacier. 72°07'S, 7°52'E. Flows between Klevekåpa Mountain and Småknoltane Peaks in the Filchner Mountains of Queen Maud Land. Named by the Norwegians for J. Snuggerud, radio mechanic with the Norwegian Antarctic Expedition of 1956–58.

Snyder Peak. 73°31'S, 93°56'W. Ice-covered. 1 mile SW of Anderson Dome in the Jones Mountains. Named for David Snyder, VX-6 aviation electronics technician in the Antarctic, 1961–62.

Snyder Peninsula. 71°25'S, 61°26'W. Ice-covered. On the south side of Lamplugh Inlet, on the east coast of Palmer Land. Cape Howard forms its tip. Named for Rear-Adm. Joseph E. Snyder, Jr., USN, Antarctic project officer for the assistant secretary of the navy for research and development, 1967–69.

Snyder Rocks. 66°34'S, 107°45'E. Small group on the coast of East Antarctica. 3 miles west of the terminus of Underwood Glacier. Named for Mark G. Snyder, a member of Operation Windmill, 1947–48.

Sobek Expeditions, Inc. Tour operator who has had some experience in Antarctica. Did tours of the Antarctic Peninsula on the *Bahía Paraíso* when it was still afloat. They also did an Antarctic Adventure, for 11 days. Address: PO Box 1089, Angels Camp, California 95222. Tel: (209) 736-4524.

Bahía Sobenes *see* **Malmgren Bay**

Cape Sobral. 64°33'S, 59°34'W. Mainly snow-covered. Surmounts the south end of Sobral Peninsula at the very north of the Larsen Ice Shelf, just south of the Prince Gustav Channel. Discovered by Nordenskjöld in 1901–4, and named by him for José M. Sobral.

Isla Sobral *see* **Omega Island**

Sobral, José M. Argentine naval sublieutenant (or ensign) who, at Buenos Aires, joined the Nordenskjöld expedition of 1901–4 as an observer/assistant physicist/meteorologist in exchange for the Argentine government giving the expedition free food, equipment, and help. He was with Nordenskjöld in the main party at Snow Hill House.

Sobral Peninsula. 64°30'S, 59°38'W. Mainly ice-covered. 11 miles long. 5 miles wide. Juts out into the northern part of the Larsen Ice Shelf, west of Larsen Inlet, in northern Graham Land. Named by the UK in 1963 in association with Cape Sobral at the south end of the peninsula.

Sobral Station. Argentine station on the Filchner Ice Shelf. Named for Ensign José M. Sobral.

Society Expeditions Cruises, Inc. Probably the best known of the tour operators serving Antarctica. Address: 3131 Elliott Ave., Suite 700, Seattle, Washington 98121. Tel: (206) 285-9400 or, toll-free (800) 426-7794. The London number is (01) 637-9961. Founded in 1974 "for the traveler who wants to be part of the adventure, versus being just an observer." A member of Cruise Lines International Association, their Antarctic expeditions began in 1976, with the *World Discoverer* as their flagship. Thus began a variety of tours with expert guides and authorities in various disciplines. In 1985 the company added the *Society Explorer*, and in July 1987 the company was sold to West German shipowner Heiko Klein, and 30-year-old Patrick Kirkpatrick became president. The company plans a third vessel in 1990. Society Expeditions also uses its ships for some scientific work. Before one goes on a cruise, one is given notebooks, books, maps, charts, a reading list, a rucksack, and a special parka. On their ships one is given an outside cabin (an ordinary cabin which one can look out of and see things), excellent food and service, a swimming pool, sundeck, library, fitness center, beauty salon, and gift shop. Included in the price are accommodations, meals, lectures, tipping, and shore excursions. The cost of the trip depends on which tour is chosen, whether one goes ordinary, or deluxe, and on which deck, and whether one is in a suite, or an "owner's suite." Range per person in 1989 figures was US $4,990–$19,490. Air fare is additional. They offer 15- to 26-day tours; only 5 to 7 days are spent in latitudes higher than 60°S. Only a taste of the continent is offered, the ships touching Anvers, Nelson, and King George Islands, and if possible, Deception Island, Paradise Bay, Iceberg Alley, Lemaire Channel, the South Orkneys, maybe some of the other South Shetland Islands, Port Lockroy and some other scientific stations (all depending on the trip). These destinations are all maybes, depending on the weather and other conditions.

A land traverse to the Pole, à la Scott, is not available—that's the province of Mountain Travel. A tip: electrical voltage on board ship is 220, recessed round 2-pronged European type outlets.

The *Society Explorer*. 2,500 ton expedition ship used by Society Expeditions Cruises, Inc. It is 250 feet long and has an ice-hardened hull, a shallow draft, a bow-thruster and the highest ice-rating of any passenger ship. It has a 13.5 knot speed, and is a luxury ship with sophisticated equipment and safety gear, including Zodiac landing boats. It has 5 decks—Explorer, Yacht, Salon, Boat, and Bridge—and carries 98 passengers. Commissioned in 1969 as the world's first passenger expedition ship, it is owned by West German shipowner Heiko Klein as part of his company Discoverer Rederei, which also owns the *World Discoverer*, Society Expeditions' first ship. Registered in Liberia, it became Society Expeditions' second ship in 1985, and in 1987 Klein bought Society Expeditions Cruises, Inc. The *Society Explorer* has circumnavigated the Antarctic.

Socks. In Antarctica it is a good idea to wear one thin pair of wool socks beneath, and then one or two heavier wool pairs on top. Rag wool knee-highs are recommended for the outer pair(s).

Socks Glacier. 83°42'S, 170°05'E. Flows from the Queen Alexandra Range just north of the Owen Hills, to enter the west side of the Beardmore Glacier. Discovered by Shackleton on his trip to the Pole in 1908, and named by him for Socks, the last pony to die on the expedition, who fell into a crevasse near here on Dec. 7, 1908.

Softbed Nunataks *see* **Softbed Ridges**

Softbed Ridges. 83°03'S, 163°45'E. Also called Softbed Nunataks. A series of parallel rock ridges interspaced by small, snow-covered valleys. They extend 15 miles between Robb and Lowery Glaciers. Named by the New Zealanders in 1959–60.

Sögen Island. 65°04'S, 64°02'W. Forms the eastern side of Français Cove, in the SW extremity of Port Charcot, Booth Island, in the Wilhelm Archipelago. Discovered and named by Charcot for one of his dogs which died and was buried here during the 1903–5 expedition.

Sohm Glacier. 66°07'S, 64°49'W. Flows into Bilgeri Glacier on the west coast of Graham Land. Charted by the BGLE in 1934–37. Named by the UK in 1959 for Victor Sohm, Austrian skiing pioneer.

Soholt Peaks. 79°43'S, 84°12'W. Ice-free. Between Gifford Peaks and Drake Icefall in the Heritage Range. Named by the University of Minnesota Ellsworth Mountains Party 1962–63 for Donald E. Soholt, geologist with the party.

Sökkhornet *see* **Graben Horn**

Solar eclipses. On Nov. 12, 1985, the eclipse was total over northern Victoria Land (at Hallett Station, for example, it was total for 56 seconds), and partial over the rest of Antarctica.

Solberg Inlet. 68°19'S, 65°15'W. Ice-filled. Between 5 and 10 miles wide. Recedes west 14 miles between Rock Pile Peaks and Joerg Peninsula on the east coast of Graham Land. Discovered by the USAS in 1940. Named in 1947 by Ronne for Rear-Adm. Thorvald A. Solberg, USN, chief of naval research, and a supporter of the RARE.

Sölch Glacier. 67°04'S, 66°23'W. Flows into Salmon Cove, on the east side of Lallemand Fjord in Graham Land. Named by the UK for Johann Sölch (1883–1951), Austrian glaciologist.

Soldat Island. 68°31'S, 78°10'E. 2½ miles long. South of Partizan Island in the south part of the entrance to Langnes Fjord in the Vestfold Hills. Photographed by the LCE 1936–37 and mapped as a peninsula. John Roscoe, the US cartographer, working off Operation Highjump photos, redefined it in 1952. The USSR named it in 1956 (the name means "soldier island").

Solem Ridge. 71°12'S, 63°15'W. Mostly snow-covered. Arc-shaped. 4 miles long. 10 miles NNE of Mount Jackson, in Palmer Land. Named for Lt. Lynn D. Solem, USN, medical officer at Amundsen-Scott South Pole Station in 1972.

Islotes Soler *see* **Rho Islands**

The Solglimt. Huge Norwegian supply ship belonging to Lars Christensen. In the Queen Maud Land coastal area in 1941. On Jan. 13, of that year, it was taken by Nazis off the *Pinguin.*

Solhøgdene Heights. 71°22'S, 13°42' E. 1 mile east of Mount Mentzel, overlooking the north side of Asimutbreen Glacier in the eastern part of the Gruber Mountains of the Wohlthat Mountains in Queen Maud Land. Discovered by Ritscher in 1938–39. Name means "the sun heights" in Norwegian.

Islote Solitario *see* **Ponton Island**

Solitario Island. 67°52'S, 68°26'W. Also called Solus Island. A small island 3 miles south of the Guébriant Islands, off the south end of Adelaide Island. Named by the Argentines in 1957 for its solitary position.

Solitary Island *see* **Uksen Island**

Solitary Nunatak. 67°28'S, 58°46'E. Isolated. 14 miles SE of Svart Peak in Enderby Land. Named descriptively by the Australians.

Solitary Peak. 83°14'S, 161°40'E. 2,810 m. 4½ miles SE of Mount Rabot in the Queen Elizabeth Range. Named by the Ohio State University Geological Party of 1967–68 because of its isolation.

Solitary Rocks. 77°47'S, 161°12'E. Rocks on land, just NW of the Cavendish Icefalls on the north side of the major bend in the Taylor Glacier in Victoria Land. Named descriptively by Scott's 1901–4 expedition.

Sollas Glacier. 77°43'S, 162°36'E. Flows between the Marr and Hughes Glaciers, from the Kukri Hills toward the east end of Lake Bonney in southern Victoria Land. Charted by Scott's 1910–13 expedition, and named by them for William J. Sollas, professor of geology at Oxford.

The Solo. David Lewis's 62-foot steel yacht which left Sydney on Dec. 15, 1977, with 8 persons on board, on an Antarctic expedition financed by Lewis' Oceanic Research Foundation. Second-in-command was Lars Larsen. Geologist was Dr. Pieter Arriens. Botanist was Dr. Peter Donaldson. Electronics man was Jack Pittar. Mountaineers were Dorothy Smith and Fritz Schaumberg. Movie photographer was Ted Rayment. All were under the command of Lewis. They crossed the Antarctic Circle on Jan 9, 1978, and sighted Buckle Island in the Ballenys, and anchored in the island group, the first boat ever to do so. They went on to land at Cape Adare, and were back in Sydney on March 3, 1978, having used only 352 gallons of diesel fuel.

Solo Harbor. Unofficial name for a small, natural harbor in Sturge Island, in the Balleny Islands. Named for the *Solo,* which put in here in 1978. As this harbor does not have an official name, this may well become accepted in time.

Solo Nunatak. 72°50'S, 163°35'E. Isolated. 6 miles NW of Intention Nunataks, at the SW side of the Evans Névé. Named by the New Zealanders in 1962–63 for its position.

Mount Solov'yev. 74°41'S, 12°19'E. 2,715 m. On the southern part of Gråkammen Ridge in the Westliche Petermann Range of the Wohlthat Mountains of Queen Maud Land. Discovered by Ritscher in 1938–39. Named by the USSR in 1966 for cartographer M.D. Solov'yev.

The Solstreif. Norwegian whaler in the waters of the Antarctic Peninsula in the 1921–22 season.

Solstreif Island. 64°33'S, 62°W. The most southerly of the small group of islands at the eastern side of Foyn Harbor, in Wilhelmina Bay, off the west coast of Graham Land. Named by the whalers in the area for the *Solstreif* which was moored here.

Mount Solus. 68°50'S, 65°33'W. 1,290 m. Isolated. Near the mouth of Weyerhaeuser Glacier in southern Graham Land. Surveyed by the FIDS in Dec. 1958. Named by the UK for its position.

Solus Island *see* **Solitario Island**

Mount Solvay. 72°34'S, 31°23'E. 2,560 m. Just north of Mount Gillet in the Belgica Mountains. Discovered by the Belgian Antarctic Expedition of 1957–58 under Gaston de Gerlache, who named it for Ernest Jay Solvay, a supporter and descendant of Ernest Solvay (*see* **Solvay Mountains**).

Solvay Mountains. 64°25'S, 62°32'W. Also called Monts Solway. In the southern part of Brabant Island. Discovered by de Gerlache in 1897–99, and named by him for Ernest Solvay, a supporter. At one time the name applied to the entire east coast of the island, but there really are not any mountains in the north which could belong to them.

Sombre Lake. 60°41'S, 45°37'W. The most northerly lake in the Paternoster Valley in northern Signy Island in the South Orkneys. Named by the UK for its setting, and in association with nearby Stygian Cove.

Somerndyke, Benjamin. Carpenter's mate on the Wilkes Expedition 1838–42. Joined in the USA. Served the cruise.

Somero Glacier. 85°02'S, 167°10'W. 7 miles long. Flows from Mount Fairweather into Liv Glacier just south of the west end of the Duncan Mountains. Named for George N. Somero, biologist at McMurdo Station in 1963–64 and 1965.

Somers, Henri. Chief engineer on the *Belgica*, 1897–99.

Somers Glacier. 65°22'S, 63°31'W. Flows NW into Trooz Glacier on the west coast of Graham Land. Charted by the BGLE in 1934–37. Named by the UK in 1959 for Henri Somers.

Somerville Island. 65°22'S, 64°19'W. Also called Sommerville Islet. 4 miles SW of the Berthelot Islands. 2½ miles NW of Darboux Island in the Wilhelm Archipelago. Discovered in 1908–10 by Charcot, and named by him for Crichton Somerville of Christiania (later Oslo) in Norway, who supervised the making of polar equipment for the expedition.

Somigliana Glacier. 67°S, 67°09'W. Flows into Langmuir Cove on the north part of Arrowsmith Peninsula in Graham Land. Named by the UK for Carlo Somigliana, Italian mathematician and physicist who studied glacier flow in the 1920s.

Sommerville Islet *see* **Somerville Island**

Somov, Mikhail M. Leader of the first Soviet Antarctic Expedition, 1955–56, and leader of the 1956 wintering party at Mirnyy Station. He arrived in Antarctica at the beginning of Jan. 1956.

Somov Canyon. 65°S, 143°E. Submarine feature off Adélie Land.

Mount Sones. 67°02'S, 51°30'E. On the north side of Beaver Glacier, 2 miles west of Mount Reed in the Tula Mountains of Enderby Land. Named by the Australians in 1962 for F. Sones.

Sones, F. A crew member on the *Discovery* during the BANZARE 1929–31.

Sonia Point. 65°04'S, 63°29'W. 6 miles west of Rahir Point on the south side of Flandres Bay, on the west coast of Graham Land. Charted by Charcot in 1903–5, and named by him for Madame Sonia Buneau-Varilla, the wife of Philippe-Jean Buneau-Varilla, one of the leading exponents and propellors of the Panama Canal and Panamanian independence.

Sonntag Nunatak. 84°52'S, 86°40'W. Solitary. 20 miles ENE of Hamilton Cliff, in the Ford Massif of the Thiel Mountains. Discovered on Dec. 13, 1959, by Edward Thiel and Campbell Craddock, who named it for Wayne Sonntag, logistics officer for the airlifted geophysical traverse along the 88th Meridian West that year.

Mount Soond. 75°S, 134°13'W. 1 mile north of Bleclic Peaks in the Perry Range of Marie Byrd Land. Named for Robert T. Soond, geomagnetist at Plateau Station in 1968.

Sooty Rock. 65°14'S, 65°09'W. Between Lumus Rock and the Betbeder Islands in the Wilhelm Archipelago. Discovered and named Black Reef by the BGLE 1934–37. Renamed in 1970 by the UK in order to avoid confusion with Black Rock.

Sophie Cliff. 64°44'S, 62°15'W. Also called Sophie Rocks. A granite cliff at the east side of the entrance to Piccard Cove, Wilhelmina Bay, on the west coast of Graham Land. Charted and named by de Gerlache in 1898.

Sophie Rocks *see* **Sophie Cliff**

Sør Rondane Mountains. 72°S, 25°E. Also called Southern Escarpments. 100 miles long. Between the Queen Fabiola Mountains and the Wohlthat Mountains in Queen Maud Land. Discovered by the LCE 1936–37 and photographed by them on Feb. 6, 1937. The name means "the Southern Rondane Mountains" in Norwegian. The Rondanes form a massif in Norway.

Søråsen Ridge. 71°25'S, 10°W. Snow-covered. Separates the Quar and Ekström Ice Shelves on the Queen Maud Land coast. Name means "the south ridge" in Norwegian. Named by the NBSAE 1949–52.

Sorensen, J.W. Crewman on the *Bear of Oakland,* 1934–35.

Sørensen Nunataks. 71°41'S, 7°57'E. 15 nunataks which extend over 6 miles, and which form the NW part of the Drygalski Mountains in Queen Maud Land. Named by the Norwegians for Stein Sørensen, radio operator on the Norwegian Antarctic Expedition of 1956–58.

Sorensen Peak. 71°43'S, 167°48'E. 2,640 m. Between the base of the Lyttelton Range and Church Ridge in the Admiralty Mountains. Between the Dennistoun and Leander Glaciers. Named for Douglas J. Sorensen, field assistant at McMurdo Station in 1965–66.

Sorge Island. 67°11'S, 67°43'W. Just south of The Gullet in Barlas Channel, just east of Adelaide Island. Named by the UK for Ernest F.W. Sorge, German glaciologist in the 1920s and 1930s.

Sørhaugen Hill. 71°48'S, 25°37'E. The most southerly of a group at the east side of Kamp Glacier in the Sør Rondane Mountains. Photographed by the LCE 1936–37. Name means "the south hill" in Norwegian.

Sørhausane Peaks. 72°47'S, 0°15'E. 2 miles south of Nupskåpa Peak, at the south end of the Sverdrup Mountains in Queen Maud Land. Name means "the south peaks" in Norwegian.

Sørhjelmen Peak. 71°48'S, 26°28'E. 2,030 m. At the head of Hette Glacier, just east of the mouth of Byrdbreen in the Sør Rondane Mountains. Photographed by the LCE 1936–37. Name means "the south helmet" in Norwegian, and was named for its position at the south end of the group of peaks here.

Sørhortane. 72°02'S, 12°35'E. A group of rock crags along the NE edge of Horteriset Dome, south of the Petermann Ranges in Queen Maud Land. Named by the Norwegians.

Sörkammen *see* **South Masson Range**

Sörkammen Crest *see* **South Masson Range**

Sörkollen *see* **Onley Hill**

Cape Sørlle. 60°46'S, 44°59'W. Marks the south end of Fredriksen Island in the South Orkneys. Discovered and charted by Powell and Palmer in Dec. 1821. Recharted by the personnel on the *Discovery II* and named by them for Petter Sørlle.

Sørlle, Petter. 1884–1922. Norwegian whaling captain, the first manager of the United Whalers station at Stromness in South Georgia (54°S). In 1911–12 he investigated anchorages in the South Orkneys in the *Paal,* for the Rethval Whaling Company of Oslo, and he was back in the South Orkneys in 1912–13, doing a running survey of the islands aboard the

Paal. He invented the whale slipway in 1922.

Sørlle Rocks. 60°37'S, 46°15'W. Rocks in water. The highest is 20 m. 7 miles west of Moreton Point, the western extremity of Coronation Island in the South Orkneys. Petter Sørlle called them Tre Sten (three stones) in 1912–13, but the personnel on the *Discovery II* in 1933 renamed them for Sørlle.

Sorna Bluff. 83°18'S, 50°40'W. Overlooks the head of May Valley, on the north side of the Saratoga Table, in the Forrestal Range of the Pensacola Mountains. Named for Lt. Cdr. Ronald E. Sorna, USN, pilot on photographic flights in the Pensacola Mountains.

Sörnuten *see* **Fischer Nunatak**

Söröya *see* **Shaula Island**

Grupo Sorpresa *see* **Sorpresa Rock**

Islote Sorpresa *see* **Brewster Island**

Roca Sorpresa *see* **Sorpresa Rock**

Sorpresa Rock. 67°51'S, 69°34'W. Also called Roca Sorpresa, Grupo Sorpresa, Surprise Island. A rock in water, SW of Cavalier Rock, off the south end of Adelaide Island. Named by the Chileans in 1947 (sorpresa means surprise).

Sorrenson Glacier. 74°28'S, 111°22'W. On the west side of the Bear Peninsula, on the coast of Marie Byrd Land.

Sørsdal, Lief. Norwegian dentist on the *Thorshavn*, 1934–35. A member of the party which landed at the northern end of the Vestfold Hills.

Sørsdal Glacier. 68°42'S, 78°10'E. Heavily crevassed. It flows along the south side of Krok Fjord and the Vestfold Hills, and forms the northern extremity of Prydz Bay. It ends in the Sørsdal Glacier Tongue. Discovered in Feb. 1935 by Mikkelsen in the *Thorshavn*, and named by him for Lief Sørsdal.

Sørsdal Glacier Tongue. 68°43'S, 78° E. Seaward extension of the Sørsdal Glacier (for which it is named), at Prydz Bay in East Antarctica. Discovered in Feb. 1935 by Mikkelsen in the *Thorshavn*.

Sørskeidet Valley. 72°03'S, 11°30'E. Ice-filled. North of Skeidshovden Mountain, near the SW end of the Wohlthat Mountains in Queen Maud Land. Named by the Norwegians.

Sørtindane Peaks. 68°08'S, 62°24'E. Just south of Mount Twintop, at the south end of the David Range of the Framnes Mountains. Photographed by the LCE 1936–37. Name means "the southern peaks" in Norwegian. Also called Brown Range.

Sosa Bluff. 82°32'S, 42°53'W. 1 mile south of Lisignoli Bluff in the Schneider Hills of the Argentina Range in the Pensacola Mountains. Named by the USA for Lt. O.R. Sosa, Argentine officer-in-charge of General Belgrano Station in 1966.

Søstrene Islands. 69°33'S, 75°30'E. Also called The Sisters. Group of small islands and rocks, including Debutante Island, in the Publications Ice Shelf at the head of Prydz Bay. Discovered and charted by Mikkelsen in Feb. 1935 while aboard the *Thorshavn*. They named them for the islands of the same name in the entrance to Oslofjorden, Norway.

Soto Glacier. 71°31'S, 61°46'W. 12 miles long. Flows along the SW side of Strømme Ridge into Odom Inlet on the east coast of Palmer Land. Named by the USA for Luís R. Soto, Argentine oceanographer on the International Weddell Sea Oceanographic Expeditions of 1968 and 1970.

Sotomayor Island. 63°20'S, 57°55'W. Just south of the entrance to Unwin Cove, Trinity Peninsula. Named by the Chilean Antarctic Expedition of 1950–51, for 2nd Lt. Victor Sotomayor, cargo officer of the *Lientur* during that expedition.

Mount Soucek. 66°49'S, 50°58'E. Between Mount Hardy and Peacock Ridge in the NW part of the Tula Mountains in Enderby Land. Named by the Australians for Dr. Z. Soucek, medical officer at Wilkes Station in 1960 and 1962.

Soucek Ravine. 66°22'S, 110°27'E. 5 yards wide. 100 yards long. West of Penney Ravine, Ardery Island, in the Windmill Islands. Discovered in 1960 by a biological field party from Wilkes Station. Named by the Australians for Dr. Z. Soucek (*see* **Mount Soucek**).

Souchez Glacier. 86°17'S, 154°W. 17 miles long. Flows from Mount Crockett, along the east side of the Faulkner Escarpment, and then it parallels the SW side of the Hays Mountains, to join Bartlett Glacier just south of Mount Dietz in the Queen Maud Mountains. Named for Roland A. Souchez, geologist at McMurdo Station, 1965–66.

Soule, William. Landsman on the Wilkes Expedition 1838–42. Joined at Rio. Served the cruise.

The Sound. 64°19'S, 62°58'W. Also called Canal Principal. A marine passage, 3 miles long and ½ mile wide. It divides the Melchior Islands into the West Melchior Islands and the East Melchior Islands. Charted by Charcot in 1903–5, and named by personnel on the *Discovery* in 1927.

Île Sourrieu *see* **Lambda Island**

South Africa. South Africa's first real exposure to Antarctica was in the 1957–58 IGY season, when J.J. La Grange, a member of the South African Weather Bureau, was invited by Fuchs to be a part of the BCTAE, and Harry Van Loon, also of the Weather Bureau, was loaned to Little America. South Africa, which does not claim any land south of 60°S, was one of the 12 original signatories of the Antarctic Treaty in 1959, and that year sent its first expedition to Antarctica (*see* **South African National Antarctic Expedition I**). The SANAE, as these expeditions are called, have been going down every year since. South Africa acquired Norway's scientific stations when that country pulled out of Antarctica that first season. Bases include Sanae, Sanae II, Sanae III, Sanae IV, Sarie Marais, Grunehogna, Borga. In 1959–60 Gordon Artz and Johan Bothma, both also from the Weather Bureau, were loaned to the FIDS at Halley Bay Station.

South African National Antarctic Expedition I. 1959–61. More commonly known as SANAE I, or the First SANAE. Organized by SANCAR (The South African National Committee for Antarctic Research), it left Table Bay on Dec. 3, 1959, on the Norwegian sealer *Polarbjörn*, led by J.J. La Grange. The radio technician was M.J. du Preez (he was also second-in-command), and other members were V. von Brunn, Dr. A. le R. Van der Merwe, D.J. Bonnema, G.F. Strauss, M.H. Van Wyk, W.T. de Swardt, N.S. Erasmus (radio operator), and C. De Weerdt (diesel mechanic). There were observers and an American, Rear-Admiral S. Mandarich. The very first night out of South Africa, the chief steward was lost overboard. At Bouvet Island, approaching Antarctica, the ship's second officer, Reidulf Kwien, was killed by dynamite. On Dec. 31, 1959, the *Polarbjörn* was beset, but in a short while freed by the *General San Martín*. On Jan. 8, 1960, the ship arrived in Polar Circle Bight, and the expedition took over the Norwegians' Princess Martha Coast Station (Tottenbukta Station), and called it Sanae Tottenbukta (Tottenbukta is Norwegian for Totten Bay). On early Jan. 15, 1960, the *Polarbjörn* left. The first sledging trip of any length was begun on Aug. 29, 1960, by La Grange and von Brunn. Several took place after that, and La Grange and von Brunn did the last major one, from Oct. 31–Dec. 7, 1960, traversing over 350 miles on dog sledge to the mountains in the south. On Dec. 26, 1960, the *Polarhav* arrived with the members of the Second SANAE. On Jan. 9, 1961, the *Polarhav* left, taking the first expedition with it back to Cape Town.

South African National Antarctic Expedition II. 1960–62. More commonly known as SANAE II, or the Second SANAE. Went down to Antarctica in the *Polarhav*, arriving at Sanae Station on Dec. 26, 1960. This expedition took over from the first one on Jan. 9, 1961, and was led by radio engineer J.P. Van der Westhuyzen. His deputy was meteorologist D.J. Bonnema, who stayed over from the First SANAE. Also on it were B. Butt, D.W. Jacobs, P. Van As, P.M.C. Voges, Dr. R. Plotkin, A. Swanevelder (surveyor), J.W. Viljoen and H.V. Liebenberg (mechanics) and R. Van der Riel (radio operator). It was relieved in early 1962 by the Third Sanae (see below).

South African National Antarctic Expedition III. Early 1962–early 1963. More commonly known as SANAE III, or the Third SANAE. This was the expedition which put up Sanae II Station, and was transported to Antarctica from South Africa by the recently commissioned *R.S.A.* The leader was M.J. du Preez (back again after a year away). S.A. Rossouw was deputy leader, and other personnel included Dr. E.E.G. Lautenbach, D. Neethling, S. Kavanagh, D. Baker, A.J. Brand, J.T.J. Van Wyk, H.S. du Preez, D.S. Oliver, H. Fulton, A.L. Smith.

South African National Antarctic Expedition IV. Early 1963–early 1964. More commonly known as SANAE IV, or the Fourth SANAE. Physicist A.M. Ventner was leader, and others in the expedition were Dr. C.F. Wagner, J. Labuschagne, C.J. Reynolds, W.J.F. du Toit, E.E. Bester, O. Langenegger, A. du Plessis, D.G. Torr, G. Vermaak, J. Randall, A.M. Van der Meulen, J. Joubert.

South African National Antarctic Expedition V. Early 1964–early 1965. More commonly known as SANAE V, or the Fifth SANAE. W.R. Van Zyl was leader. Dr. M.L. Traut was deputy leader. Others on the expedition were A. du Plessis, W.J.F. du Toit, B.P. Booyens, H.S. du Preez, A.G. Brunt, M.B. Ezekowitz, G.J. Kuhn, P. de Waal, G.W. Bentley, J.F. Pretorius, N.H. Jay, G.T. Robertson.

South African National Antarctic Expedition VI. Early 1965–early 1966. More commonly known as SANAE VI, or the

Sixth SANAE. J.T.J. Van Wyk was leader. Others on the expedition were Dr. W.H. Pollake, D.J. Joubert, D.W. Sharwood, J.A. Strydom, H.J. Joubert, G.P. Potgieter, A.J. Steyn, M.B. Ezekowitz, N.S. Smit, E.R. Statt, Dr. J. du P. de Wit, J.C. Joubert, W. Hodsdan.

South African National Antarctic Expedition VII. Early 1966–early 1967. More commonly known as SANAE VII, or the Seventh SANAE. Surveyor S. Kavanagh was leader. Other members were Dr. J.A. Schoones, C. Woolfardt, S.M. Verbeek, S. Venter, R.G. Van der Heever, H.D. Barnard, E. de Ridder, H.A. Bastin, H.O. Polle, D.P. Homann, J.S. Smith, H. Czanik, H. Fulton, W.J. Van Staden.

South America Glacier. 77°49′S, 161°48′E. Near the SW corner of the Kukri Hills in Victoria Land. Named by Grif Taylor on his Western Journey during Scott's last expedition. The ice hangs down a cliff 2,000 meters high and resembles South America in shape.

South Antillean Arc *see* **Scotia Ridge**

South Arm *see* **Ferrar Glacier**

South Atlantic Arc *see* **Scotia Ridge**

¹South Bay. 62°40′S, 60°28′W. 6 miles long. Large bay on the south side of Livingston Island, NW of False Bay, in the South Shetlands. Weddell called it Erebys Bay in 1825, but the simpler name has caught on.

²South Bay. 64°52′S, 63°35′W. On the south side of Doumer Island in the Palmer Archipelago. Part of its waters are SSSI #28, its interest being marine ecology. Scuba divers started this study in 1972, and since 1981 advanced studies have been made of the relationships of marine life here. Weddell seals and killer whales come here.

³South Bay. 77°38′S, 166°26′E. Between Cape Evans and Turks Head in western Ross Island. Named by Scott's 1910–13 expedition.

South Beaches. 62°40′S, 61°03′W. On the south side of Byers Peninsula, on the extreme west coast of Livingston Island, in the South Shetlands. Named by George Powell in 1822.

South Beacon. 77°52'S, 160°43'E. A peak between Beacon Valley and Arena Valley. A term not used any more.

South Cape. 60°48'S, 45°09'W. Also called South Point. Marks the southern extremity of the Robertson Islands in the South Orkneys. Discovered and named descriptively by Powell and Palmer in Dec. 1821.

South Coronation Island. 60°42'S, 45°19'W. Tiny island to the south of Coronation Island in the South Orkneys.

South Crest see **South Masson Range**

South Dip Pole see **South Magnetic Pole**

South East Point. 62°59'S, 60°32'W. The SE point on Deception Island in the South Shetlands. 1 mile NE of Fildes Point. Charted by Foster in 1829. Surveyed by Penfold in 1948–49 and named by the British Hydrographic Department of the Admiralty.

South Eastern Mountains see **Grove Mountains**

South Foreland see **Cape Melville**

South Fork. 77°34'S, 161°15'E. The southern arm of the Wright Valley in Victoria Land. It is separated from the North Fork by The Dais. Named by the New Zealanders in 1958–59.

South Geographic Pole see **South Pole**

South Geomagnetic Pole. The theoretical pole of the earth's magnetic field, where the lines of the earth's magnetic field converge. It is always moving. In 1956 it was located about 790 miles from the South Pole itself, at 78°S, 110°E. It was first reached on Dec. 16, 1957, by a USSR IGY tractor traverse. It was located at that time at 78°28'S, 106°48'E.

South Ice. 81°56'S, 29°30'W. British IGY depot used by Fuchs on his way to the Pole during the BCTAE 1957–58. Equipment and food were airfreighted in

in Jan. and Feb. 1957, and it was ready by Feb. 22, 1957. The hut was built in a 5-foot-deep pit to protect it with snow during the winter. In March 1957 three winterers were installed. Hal Lister led this little group. They were relieved on Oct. 8, 1957. On Dec. 21, 1957, the main Fuchs party of the BCTAE went through the depot en route to the South Pole and the other side of the continent. South Ice was abandoned in 1958.

South Indian Basin. Submarine feature centering on 60°S, 120°E. Also called Australian Antarctic Basin, Eastern-Indian Antarctic Basin, Indian-Antarctic Basin, Knox Basin, South Indian Ocean Basin.

South Indian Ocean Basin see **South Indian Basin**

South Island see **Wyatt Island**

South Korea. In 1986 this country sent an expedition to King George Island in the South Shetlands. Part of the group went on to climb the Vinson Massif on the mainland. South Korea was ratified as the 33rd signatory of the Antarctic Treaty on Nov. 28, 1986. A scientific station on King George Island, King Sejong Station, was built by Feb. 17, 1988, as part of the Korean Antarctic Research Program.

South Magnetic Pole. Also called the South Dip Pole. This is the precise spot toward which all magnetic compass needles point, or the point of vertical orientation of a magnetic dip needle, in other words the point where the compass needle points straight down. Like the North Magnetic Pole, it is constantly changing position, and moves about 8 miles to the NW each year. It was predicted by German physicist Carl Gauss to lie at 66°S, 146°E, and was unsuccessfully sought by Dumont d'Urville and Wilkes in 1840. Ross, who was the third to try, put it at 75°30'S, 154°E in 1841. It was first reached on Jan. 16, 1909, at 72°24'S, 155°18'E, by David, Mawson, and Mackay, three members of Shackleton's 1907–9 British Antarctic Expedition. They found it on the high ice plateau of Victoria Land, after a sledge journey from Cape Royds. They marked the spot with a British flag. Bage, Webb, and Hurley got to within 50 miles of it on Dec. 21, 1912, during the AAE 1911–14, and in 1952 Mayaud led a French party there, locating it at 68°07'S, 148°E. It is no longer on the mainland, however. In 1956 it was about 1,526 miles from the South Pole, being at 68°S, 144°E. In 1971 it was at 60°05'S, 139°05'E. On Jan. 6, 1986, the *Icebird* reached it, this time at 65°18'S, 140°02'E. This was only the fourth time in history that the general area of the South Magnetic Pole had been reached.

South Masson Range. 67°53'S, 62°47' E. Also called Sörkammen, Sörkammen Crest, South Crest. The southern part of the Masson Range. It extends 2 miles in an arc from NE to SW. Photographed by the LCE 1936–37, and named Sörkammen by the Norwegians. The name means "the south crest." It was renamed in 1960 by the Australians.

South Orkney Islands. They center on 60°35'S, 45°30'W. Also called the South Orkneys, the Powell Group, Powell Islands. They lie between 60°20'S and 60°50'S, and between 44°20'W and 46°45'W. A major island group in the Antarctic, they are also the most northerly. They lie between the Scotia Sea to the north and the Weddell Sea to the south, in the South Atlantic Ocean, to the east of the South Shetlands and NE of the Antarctic Peninsula. There are two larger islands, Coronation Island and Laurie Island, and several smaller ones, the main ones being Signy Island and Powell Island. There are also many rocky islets. They are all barren and uninhabited (except for scientific station personnel), the total area being about 240 square miles. They form part of the British Antarctic Territory. They were discovered on Dec. 6, 1821, by Palmer and Powell who were out from the South Shetlands looking for new fur sealing grounds. They were subsequently named

Powell's Group. Weddell came across them in Feb. 1822 and, not knowing of their previous discovery, called them the South Orkneys because they are in roughly the same degree of latitude as the Orkney Islands in Scotland are in the northern hemisphere. Weddell claimed them for Great Britain. Over the next 75 years they were hardly visited at all: Dumont d'Urville was there in 1838, Dallmann in 1874, Lynch in 1880, and Larsen in 1892, but it was Bruce who first surveyed them, in 1903, and set up his base there for the Scottish National Antarctic Expedition of 1902–4. Working south, the islands are Karlsen Rock, Governor Islands, Coronation Island, Melsom Rocks, Despair Rocks, Nicolas Rocks, Lay-Brother Rock, Inaccessible Islands, Spine Island, Larsen Islands, Mainsail Rock, The Twins, Sphinx Rock, Sørlle Rocks, Saddle Island, Powell Island, Weddell Islands, Lynch Island, Gosling Islands, Mabel Island, Gerd Island, Monk Islands, Hart Rock, Laurie Island, Bruce Islands, South Coronation Island, Reid Island, Signy Island, Herdman Rocks, Rudmose Rocks, Eillium Island, Whale Skerries, Powell Rock, Balin Rocks, Thule Islands, Spindrift Rocks, Flensing Islands, Expedition Rock, Nigg Rock, Fredriksen Island, Outer Island, Bare Rock, Small Rock, Billie Rocks, Cam Rock, Jebsen Rocks, Baldred Rock, Graptolite Island, Michelsen Island, Christoffersen Island, Confusion Island, Shagnasty Island, Moe Island, Grey Island, Robertson Islands, Oliphant Islands, Mariholm, Valette Island, Acuña Island, Murray Islands, Florence Rock, Ailsa Craig.

South Orkney Ridge. 60°S, 40°W. Submarine feature in the area of the South Orkneys.

South Orkney Trough. 60°S, 45°W. Submarine feature in the area of the South Orkneys.

South Orkneys *see* **South Orkney Islands**

South Pacific Cordillera *see* **Albatross Cordillera**

South Pacific Ridge see Pacific-Antarctic Ridge

South Pacific Rise see Pacific-Antarctic Ridge

¹South Point. 60°45'S, 45°42'W. Marks the south end of Moe Island in the South Orkneys. Named by personnel on the *Discovery II* in 1933.

²South Point. 63°02'S, 60°37'W. The southernmost point on Deception Island in the South Shetlands.

³South Point see South Cape

South Polar Plateau see Polar Plateau

South Polar skuas see Skuas

South Polar Station see Amundsen-Scott South Pole Station

South Polar Times. The first periodical produced in the Antarctic. It was a monthly magazine edited and printed by Shackleton during the winter months at base during the first year of the Royal Society Expedition of 1901–4. He put out 5 issues, in April, May, June, July, and August of 1902. Wilson illustrated, and they contained puzzles, caricatures, humor, articles, and how-to pieces. When Shackleton was invalided home in March 1903, the magazine did not continue. It was, in a way, revived by Shackleton during his own 1907–9 expedition (*see* "**Aurora Australis**"). In 1907 Smith, Elder & Co., of London, published a limited edition of 250 copies for private circulation. This was a facsimile of the original. It was definitely revived during Scott's 1910–13 expedition, with Cherry-Garrard as the editor (*see also* **The Blizzard**).

South Pole. The bottom of the world, the point where all the Earth's lines of longitude come together, the point where there is no South, East, or West — only North (*see also* **Time, Direction**). This is the Geographic South Pole. Unlike the North Pole, the South Pole is on land, or rather on ice (*see* **Depth of ice, Bedrock**). Midwinter here is June 21, and winds are light, 9–17 mph. About 300 miles from the Ross Ice Shelf, it is at 90°S, and does not coincide with the South Magnetic Pole, the South Geomagnetic Pole, or the Pole of Relative Inaccessibility. Its altitude is 9,301 feet above sea level, and the thickness of the ice at this point is 8,850 feet. Winter comes March 23, and summer September 23. There are basically 6 months of night, and 6 months of day. Nothing lives here (that is, nothing indigenous), but humans sport a growing population at the Pole. The nearest mountains are 200 miles away. Mount Howe is the nearest nunatak, 181 miles away, and this nunatak also has the nearest indigenous life form (bacteria and yeast colony). The South Pole lies on the Polar Plateau. Scott said of it, "Great God! This is an awful place," but then, he had just been beaten to it by Amundsen. In Dec. 1956 Paul Siple placed a silvered glass ball on top of an orange and black striped bamboo pole and this became the symbolic South Pole of the Americans at South Pole Station which was built in the summer months of 1956–57. Siple had bought the ball in New Zealand on the way down to Antarctica. In Nov. 1957, when leaving South Pole Station, Siple took the ball home with him as a souvenir, and replaced it with a spare, which still stands today. There is a sign in front of the Pole, saying, "Elevation 9,186 feet. Population 21." (The height above sea level at the Pole is constantly being recalculated.) Ruth Siple, Paul's widow, donated the original ball to Canterbury Museum, Christchurch, NZ, in Jan. 1975. The average temperature at the South Pole is −56°F. The old record of −113.3°F was set in July 1956, and was not broken until June 23, 1982, when −117.4°F was recorded. The aim of many explorers, of course, the South Pole's history can be summarized as a series of firsts: 1. The first navigator to try for the Pole: Cook, in 1773. He reached only 71°10'S, a southing record for its day (*see* **Southing records**). 2. The first explorer to try to get there by land: Scott, during the Royal Society Expedition of

1901–4. He reached 82°16'33"S (500 miles short). 3. The first five men to stand at the pole: Amundsen, Bjaaland, Hassel, Hanssen, and Wisting, on Friday, Dec. 14, 1911, as the culmination of the Norwegian Antarctic Expedition of 1910–12. 4. The first British explorers to reach the Pole: Scott, Wilson, Bowers, Evans, and Oates, on Jan. 17, 1912. 5. The first men to fly over the Pole: Byrd, Balchen, June, and McKinley, on Nov. 29, 1929, in the *Floyd Bennett*. 6. The first flight to the Pole since 1929: again Byrd, in 1947. There were two planes, both US Navy twin-engine R4D aircraft which did it on Feb. 15–16, 1947, during Operation Highjump. In Plane V1 were Lt. Cdr. J.C. McCoy, pilot; Lt. George H. Anderson, co-pilot; Byrd; K.C. Swain; J.E. Valinski. In Plane V6 were Major Robert R. Weir, pilot; Capt. Eugene C. McIntyre, co-pilot; Robert P. Heekin, navigator; George E. Baldwin; Raymond J. Butters; Cdr. Clifford M. Campbell; A.V. Mincey. They took off from Little America IV at 11 p.m. on Feb. 15, 1947. V1 reached the Pole at 5 a.m. the next day, and got back to base just before noon. 7. The first men to fly to the Pole and land: Dufek, Shinn, Hawkes, Strider, Cordiner, Cumbie, and Swadener, on Oct. 31, 1956, to scout the area for an IGY station, in the airplane *Que Sera Sera*. This was only the third party in history to stand at the Pole. 8. The first leader to land at the Pole by plane in order to set up a base: Lt. Bowers, on Nov. 20, 1956, in order to build the South Pole Station for the USA's involvement in IGY. This was then built by a team (*see* Paul Siple's book *90° S* in the Bibliography. An appendix lists all the men who helped construct the station). The elevation was then considered to be 9,370 feet above sea level. 9. The first wintering-over party at the Pole: 18 men and a dog, led by Paul Siple in 1957, at the South Pole Station. *See* **Amundsen-Scott South Pole Station** for details. 10. The first US Congressman to fly over the Pole: J.P. Saylor on Nov. 16,

1957 (*see* **Distinguished visitors**). 11. The first British person to reach the Pole since Scott: Noël Barber, the British journalist, who flew in on a US plane to South Pole Station to await the arrival of Fuchs. Barber was covering the story of the first ever Transantarctic land traverse. 12. The first to reach the Pole by land traverse since Scott: Hillary, on Jan. 4, 1958, during the BCTAE 1957–58. 13. The first leader to arrive at the Pole during a Transantarctic crossing: Fuchs, on Jan. 20, 1958, during the BCTAE 1957–58. 14. The first American group to land traverse to the Pole: The Byrd–South Pole Overland Trek, on Jan. 16, 1961. 15. The first helicopters to reach the Pole: on Feb. 4, 1964. 16. The first women to reach the Pole by plane: Nov. 11, 1969 (*see* **Women in Antarctica**). 17. The first woman to spend the night at the Pole: Miss Louise Hutchinson, correspondent with the *Chicago Tribune,* when weather delayed a return flight to McMurdo Station in Dec. 1971. 18. The first women to work at the Pole: Nan Scott and Donna Muchmore, in 1973. 19. The first woman to winter-over at the Pole: Michele Raney, in 1979. 20. The first group to arrive at the Pole, as part of a Transantarctic land traverse, since Fuchs: The Trans-Globe Expedition, on Dec. 15, 1980. 21. The first commercial flight to the Pole: Jan. 11, 1988, by Adventure Network. 22. The first tourists ever to reach the Pole after a land traverse from the edge of the continent: this unbelievable feat was achieved at noon, Jan. 17, 1989, by the group from Mountain Travel (q.v. for details).

South Pole–Queen Maud Land traverses. A series of 3 USARP geological expeditions more commonly referred to as SPQMLT. They were land traverses undertaken by US scientists from the South Pole to the interior of Queen Maud Land. A Navy air reconnaissance scouted the route for each expedition, and in each expedition three diesel-powered Sno-cats were used for transportation. Exploration and geology were the main aims of the SPQMLTs. SPQMLT I was in 1964–65, and went from the Pole to Plateau Station, as did SPQMLT II in 1965–66. SPQMLT III did not leave from the South Pole directly, but from Plateau Station, on Dec. 5, 1967, under the leadership of Norman W. Peddie. This 9-man party started out with 8 scientists and 2 engineers, but on Dec. 8, 1967, 50 miles and 3 days out of Plateau Station, one of the scientists became ill and had to return to base. By Jan. 29, 1968, the expedition had covered 815 miles and had reached 78°42′S, 6°52′W, or 200 miles NE of the Shackleton Range. That was the end of the expedition, and two days later, on Jan. 31, 1968, the personnel and much of the equipment were airlifted to McMurdo Station.

South Pole Station *see* **Amundsen-Scott South Pole Station**

South Sandwich Arc *see* **Scotia Ridge**

South Sandwich Trench. Extends from 55°S, 32°W to 61°S, 27°W. A submarine trench on the east side of the South Sandwich Islands in the Atlantic-Indian Basin, it reaches a maximum depth of 27,650 feet. Incidentally, the South Sandwich Islands are not included in this book, as they lie just north of 60°S, and not a single part of them encroaches into the territory of this volume.

South Shetland Islands. They center on 62°S, 58°W. Also called South Shetlands. A major group of islands at the northern tip of the Antarctic Peninsula, north of the Bransfield Strait, and actually lying in the Drake Passage. Barren, snow-covered, and uninhabited (except by scientific station personnel and some wildlife), they extend for 320 miles and cover a total area of 1,800 square miles. The principal islands in the group are King George Island, Livingston Island, Greenwich Island, Deception Island, Elephant Island, Clarence Island, Nelson Island, Robert Island, Snow Island, Smith Island, Low Island, Desolation Island, and Rugged Island. History and Antarctica come together at the South Shetland Islands. In Sept. 1599

Dirck Gerritsz may have reached a latitude of 64°S and seen them, but this is little more than a rumor started by Edmund Fanning a couple of centuries later. In March 1603 the *Blyde Bootschap* may have sighted the South Shetlands, but once again this is almost certainly an apocryphal tale. In 1712 Frazier may have sighted them, and called them South Iceland, or New South Iceland. Again, this was a rumor perpetuated by Fanning, to take away from the British achievement of their actual discovery, which took place on Feb. 19, 1819, when William Smith became the islands' undisputed discoverer (although at the immediate time he was disbelieved by his superiors). If any sealers discovered the South Shetlands before 1819, they kept it a secret. This is what Fanning was saying, but men talked, especially sealers, and especially when they were drunk and when there was so much at stake. Therefore Smith does emerge in most serious books as the real discoverer of the South Shetlands. He named them New South Britain. On Oct. 14, 1819, he returned, landed on King George Island on Oct. 16, 1819, claimed the islands for Britain, and renamed them New South Shetland because they are in the same general degree of latitude as the Scottish islands, the Shetlands, are in the northern hemisphere. They were known also as New Shetland for a while, but it was not long before everyone was calling them the South Shetlands, and that name became official (South Shetlands is a term interchangeable with, shorter than, and actually preferred to South Shetland Islands, even though the latter is the name seen on the maps). Smith explored them, and roughly surveyed them. Between 1819 and 1833 there were 105 sealing vessels there, hunting fur seals, and in the 1820–21 season alone, there were 30 American vessels in at the South Shetlands, not to mention the British ones and the others of different nationalities. Between 1906 and 1931, the islands were used mostly for sealing and whaling bases, notably on Deception Island, and Britain claimed them in 1908. In 1945 they began to be used for scientific bases by Britain, Argentina, Chile, and others. Working south, the islands are Seal Islands, Gibbous Rocks, Borceguí Island, Cornwallis Island, Gnomon Island, West Reef, Pinnacle Rock, Sugarloaf Island, Clarence Island, Elephant Island, Cruiser Rocks, Rowett Island, Gibbs Island, Aspland Island, Eadie Island, O'Brien Island, Bransfield Rocks, Ridley Island, Hole Rock, Limit Rock, Cove Rock, Jagged Island, Pyrites Island, Shearer Stack, Kellick Island, Owen Island, Tartar Island, King George Island, Foreland Island, Simpson Rocks, Middle Island, Trowbridge Island, Hauken Rock, Ørnen Rocks, Livonia Rock, Penola Island, Bridgeman Island, Stump Rock, O'Connors Rock, Sea Leopard Patch, Penguin Island, Martello Tower, Atherton Islands, Growler Rock, Caraquet Rock, Twin Pinnacles, Denais Stack, Napier Rock, Dufayel Island, Square End Island, Sinbad Rock, Syrezol Rocks, Chabrier Rock, Upton Rock, Ardley Island, Nancy Rock, Tu Rocks, Dart Island, Weeks Stack, Withen Island, Telefon Rocks, Two Summit Island, Nelson Island, Emm Rock, Folger Rock, Low Rock, Parry Patch, Mellona Rocks, The Watchkeeper, Pig Rock, Libert Rocks, Henfield Rock, Potmess Rocks, Robert Island, Heywood Island, Monica Rock, Lone Rock, Cornwall Island, Turmoil Rock, Table Island, Bowler Rocks, Grace Rock, Salient Rock, Chaos Reef, Cheshire Rock, Aitcho Islands, Holmes Rock, Romeo Island, Sierra Island, Stoker Island, Dee Island, Burro Peaks, Ongley Island, Pyramid Island, Zed Island, Eliza Rocks, Cone Rock, Corner Rock, Ibar Rocks, Cave Island, Express Island, Tenorio Rock, Greenwich Island, Channel Rock, Livingston Island, Craggy Island, Desolation Island, San Telmo Island, González Island, Dunbar Islands, Indian Rocks, Wood Island, Fortín Rock, Fuente Rock, Honores Rock, Vidal Rock, Basso Island, Chapman Rocks, Lynx Rocks, Frederick Rocks,

Window Island, Svip Rocks, Cutler Stack, The Pointers, Eddystone Rocks, Rugged Rocks, Rugged Island, Stewart Stacks, Astor Island, Hetty Rock, Stackpole Rocks, Vietor Rock, Sally Rocks, Enchantress Rocks, Long Rock, Aim Rocks, Snow Island, Conical Rock, Castle Rock, Keep Rock, Knight Rocks, Tooth Rock, Barlow Island, Deception Island, Smith Island, Meade Islands, Sewing-Machine Needles, Ravn Rock, New Rock, Låvebrua Island, Sail Rock, Van Rocks, Low Island.

South Shetland Trough. 61°S, 59°30′ W. A submarine feature in the area of the South Shetlands.

South Shetlands *see* **South Shetland Islands**

South Spit. 62°14′S, 58°49′W. Forms the south entrance to Marian Cove in King George Island, in the South Shetlands. Named by personnel on the *Discovery II* in 1935.

South Stream. 77°27′S, 163°43′E. A meltwater stream 2 miles SW of Marble Point in southern Victoria Land. It comes out of the Wilson Piedmont Glacier and flows into Bernacchi Bay. Named by Robert L. Nichols, geologist here, for its position in relation to Marble Bay.

South Thor Island *see* **Thor Island**

South Victoria Land *see* **Victoria Land**

Cape Southard. 66°33′S, 122°04′E. Ice-covered. Separates the Banzare and Sabrina Coasts in Wilkes Land. Named for Samuel Lewis Southard, secretary of the navy under President John Quincy Adams. Southard was an important figure in the initiation of the Wilkes Expedition 1838–42.

Mount Southard. 72°10′S, 159°57′E. 2,400 m. 5 miles NW of Welcome Mountain at the NW end of the Outback Nunataks in Victoria Land. Named Rupert B. Southard, chief of the Office of International Activities, US Geological Survey.

Southard Promontory. 66°56′S, 64° 48′W. On the east coast of Graham Land.

Southeast Pacific Basin. Submarine feature centering on 60°S, 115°W. Also called Amundsen Basin, Bellingshausen Basin, Pacific-Antarctic Basin, Pacific South Polar Basin.

Mount Southern. 74°12'S, 76°28'W. A nunatak. 1½ miles NE of Mount Harry. 14 miles SE of FitzGerald Bluffs in Ellsworth Land. Discovered aerially by Ellsworth on Nov. 23, 1935. Named for Merle E. Southern, topographic engineer in Antarctica in 1967–68.

Southern Barrier Depot. Scott's depot almost at the southern edge of the Ross Ice Shelf.

Southern bottlenose whales *see* **Beaked whales**

[1]**The** *Southern Cross.* 521-ton Norwegian sealer, formerly the *Pollux*. It was reregistered in London under its new name, and under the command of Capt. Jensen was Borchgrevink's ship for his 1898–1900 expedition. It put him and his shore party onto Cape Adare on Feb. 17, 1899.

[2]**The** *Southern Cross.* US supply ship many times in at McMurdo Station in the 1980s. Retired in 1984. Capt. Bjorn Werring was its last skipper.

Southern Cross Mountains. 73°40'S, 164°E. Between the Mariner and Priestley Glaciers in Victoria Land. Ross saw parts of them in 1841 from his ship. Named by the New Zealanders in 1965–66 for the *Southern Cross,* Borchgrevink's ship.

Southern elephant seals *see* **Elephant seals**

Southern Escarpments *see* **Sør Rondane Mountains**

Southern Foothills *see* **Inexpressible Island**

The *Southern Harvest.* British whaler in Antarctic seas, 1947–48.

Southern Lights *see* **Aurora**

Southern Nunataks *see* **Stinear Nunataks**

Southern Ocean *see* **Antarctic Ocean**

The *Southern Quest.* An Icelandic trawler converted into an ice-strengthened polar ship. 139 feet long. It was the supply ship for the In the Footsteps of Scott Expedition (q.v.). As the ship stood off in the Ross Sea, 19 miles from Jack Hayward Base on Ross Island, which was the expedition headquarters, an aircraft carried by the ship was assembled in three days on an ice floe near the ship. Three men had gone to the Pole, and this expedition plane was to go out and pick them up. During these three crucial days heavy ice closed in on the ship. In the early morning of Jan. 12, 1986, ice pressure split the hull and the engine room was flooded. The vessel sank, stern first, shortly afterward, between 12:04 a.m. and 12:30 a.m. The 14 crew and 7 passengers, men and women, got onto a nearby ice floe before the vessel sank, and were rescued by US Coast Guard helicopters which transported them to Beaufort Island, and then to McMurdo Station by 5 a.m.

Southern right whales. *Eubalaena glacialis australis.* Baleen whales found in Antarctic waters. Protected in 1935.

The *Southern Sky.* Norwegian whaler from South Georgia used by Shackleton on his first unsuccessful attempt to rescue his Elephant Island party in May 1916. It was forced to retreat by the pack-ice 60 miles from Elephant Island. The commander was Capt. Thom.

Southern Thule. Some people's unofficial name for the Antarctic in the 1820s. The name now applies to a group in the South Sandwich Islands in 59° 26'S.

Southing records. 54°S, Vespucci, 1502; 55°S, Magellan, 1520; 57°S, Drake, Sept. 7, 1578; 64°S, Gerritsz, Sept. 1597 (questionable); 66°30'S, Cook, Jan. 17, 1773 (1,410 miles to the Pole); 67°15'S, Cook; 71°10'S, Cook, Jan. 30, 1774 (1,130 miles to the Pole); 74° 15'S, Weddell, Feb. 20, 1823 (945 miles to the Pole); 78°09'S, Ross, Jan. 22, 1841 (710 miles to the Pole); 78°50'S, Borchgrevink, Feb. 16, 1900 (670 miles to the Pole); 79°03'S, Armitage, 1902; 80°01'S, Scott, Nov. 25, 1902; 80°20'S, Scott, Dec. 3, 1902; 80°32'S, Scott, Dec. 16, 1902; 81°33'S, Scott, Dec. 24, 1902; 82°11'S, Scott, Dec. 28, 1902; 82°16'33"S, Scott, Dec. 30, 1902 (500 miles to the Pole); 82°18'30"S, Shackleton, Nov. 26, 1908; 83°16'S, Shackleton, Dec. 1, 1908; 84°50'S, Shackleton, Dec. 16, 1908; 85°05'S, Shackleton, Dec. 19, 1908; 85°17'S, Shackleton, Dec. 20, 1908; 86°19'S, Shackleton, Dec. 27, 1908; 86°54'S, Shackleton, Dec. 31, 1908; 88°07'S, Shackleton, Jan. 6, 1909; 88°23'S, Shackleton, Jan. 9, 1909 (97 miles to the Pole); 88°24'S, Amundsen, Dec. 8, 1911 (95 miles to the Pole); 90° 00'S, Amundsen, Dec. 14, 1911 (the Pole itself).

Southtrap Rock. 62°59'S, 56°38'W. Isolated rock in water, west of Cape Juncal, D'Urville Island. Named by the UK in 1963 because it is the southern of two features to be avoided by shipping in Antarctic Sound (cf. Northtrap Rock).

Mount Southwick. 78°46'S, 84°55'W. 3,280 m. Near the south end of the Sentinel Range. 9 miles SSE of Mount Craddock. Named for Technical Sgt. Thomas E. Southwick, US Marines, navigator on a Navy R4D flight here on Jan. 28, 1958.

The *Southwind* see **The *Atka***

Southwind Passage. 65°18'S, 65°20' W. Also called Buchanan Channel. A navigable passage between the Betbeder Islands and the Dickens Rocks at the northern end of the Biscoe Islands. Named by Capt. S.R. Dolber in 1967–68 for the ship he was commanding through here, the *Southwind*.

Southworth, Edward. Quartermaster on the Wilkes Expedition 1838–42. Joined in the USA. Served the cruise.

Soviet Antarctic Expeditions see **USSR, and the Expeditions appendix**

Sovietskaya Station. 78°24'S, 87°35'E. USSR IGY station. Established Feb. 16, 1958.

Sowle Nunatak. 84°03'S, 66°05'W. One of the Rambo Nunataks. 5½ miles SE of Wagner Nunatak, on the west side of the Foundation Ice Stream in the Pensacola Mountains. Named for Melvin L. Sowle, construction mechanic at Plateau Station in 1967.

The *Soya*. A reconstructed 4,200-ton ice-strengthened patrol ship provided by the Japanese Maritime Safety Board as the first Japanese icebreaker used during IGY. It helped set up Showa Station as the ship used by the JARE I (1956–57). It went to the Antarctic on the abortive JARE II (1957–58), JARE III (1958–59), JARE IV (1959–60), JARE V (1960–61), and JARE VI (1961–62), and then was succeeded by the *Fuji*.

Soya Coast. East Antarctica. A term no longer used.

Mount Soyat. 85°52'S, 130°46'W. 2,150 m. In the western Wisconsin Range, on the east side of Reedy Glacier, just north of the junction of Norfolk Glacier. Named for Cdr. David Soyat, USN, air operations manager with VX-6 at McMurdo Station in 1962.

Søyla Peak. 72°42'S, 3°51'W. Just north of Domen Butte in the Borg Massif of Queen Maud Land. Name means "the pillar" in Norwegian.

Soyuz Station. 70°35'S, 68°47'E. USSR summer station/field camp established in 1982 on Jetty Peninsula, near Beaver Lake, in the Prince Charles Mountains. It consists of 10 prefabricated plywood huts (PDKO huts). It has a diesel electrical generating system, radio station, sauna, dining room/kitchen, and 2 landing strips.

Mount Soza. 71°10'S, 162°34'E. 2,190 m. Forms the eastern wall of the Rennick Glacier in the Bowers Mountains, between the points where the Alt and Carryer Glaciers flow into the Rennick Glacier. Named for Ezekiel R. Soza, topographic engineer here in 1961–62 and 1962–63.

Spaatz Island. 73°12'S, 75°W. Ice-covered. 50 miles long. 25 miles wide.

Close to the coast of Ellsworth Land. 30 miles east of Smyley Island. The north side of the island forms a portion of the south edge of the Ronne Ice Shelf. The rest of the island is surrounded by the ice shelves of Stange Sound and George VI Sound. First defined as an island by Ronne during the RARE 1947–48, and named by him for Gen. Carl Spaatz, chief of staff, USAAF, who gave the RARE an airplane.

Spain. In 1756 the *León,* a Spanish ship, got as far south as South Georgia (54°S), which it discovered. On March 31, 1982, Spain became the 26th ratified signatory of the Antarctic Treaty. The following summer, (1982–83), a private voyage became a Spanish Government–sponsored expedition to the waters off the Antarctic Peninsula. Rey Juan Carlos I Station was established in Jan. 1988, and in Sept. 1988 Spain became a Consultative party to the Antarctic Treaty.

Spallanzani Point. 64°08′S, 61°59′W. Also called Punta Harry. Forms the north side of the entrance to Hill Bay and the east tip of Brabant Island. Named by the UK for Lazaro Spallanzani (1729–1799), physiologist who first interpreted the process of digestion, in 1780.

Spanley Rocks. 82°58′S, 54°40′W. Six rocks on land, 10 miles SW of Cordiner Peaks. They mark the northern extremity of the Neptune Range, in the Pensacola Mountains. Named for John A. Spanley, Jr., cook at Amundsen-Scott South Pole Station in 1965.

Mount Spann. 82°03′S, 41°21′W. Also called Santa Fe Hill. 925 m. Marks the northern extremity of the Panzarini Hills and also of the Argentina Range, at the NE end of the Pensacola Mountains. Discovered aerially on Jan. 13, 1956 (*see* the Chronology). Named for Staff Sgt. Robert C. Spann, US Marines, navigator during that flight.

Spano Island. 66°24′S, 110°36′E. ½ mile north of the west end of Herring Island in the Windmill Islands. Named for Angelo F. Spano, meteorologist at Wilkes Station in 1960.

The *Spark.* A sealing schooner, tender to the *Clothier,* in Antarctic waters during the 1820–21 season.

Spark Point   *see*   **Canto Point**

Sparkes, Robert S. Lt., USN. Took over from Donald Burnett as military leader of Wilkes Station on Jan. 30, 1958.

Sparkes Bay. 66°22′S, 110°32′E. Also called Bukhta Nebesnaya. 1 mile wide. Indents the coast for 2½ miles between Mitchell Peninsula on the north and Robinson Ridge and Odbert Island on the south, in the Windmill Islands. Named for Lt. Robert S. Sparkes.

Sparrman, Anders. b. 1747, Uppland, Sweden. d. 1820. Surgeon. He was the assistant naturalist on the *Resolution* during Cook's voyage of 1772–75. He joined at Cape Town on Sept. 19, 1772, and left at Cape Town on March 23, 1775.

The *Sparrow.* British ship which in 1948–49, under Capt. John Waterhouse, visited FIDS and foreign scientific bases in the South Shetlands, South Orkneys, and the Antarctic Peninsula.

Spartan Glacier. 71°03′S, 68°20′W. A valley glacier between the Callisto Cliffs and the Tombaugh Cliffs on the east side of Alexander Island. Named by the UK for the "Spartans," a dog team used to ascend the glacier in 1969.

Spath Crest. 80°39′S, 26°12′W. In the Shackleton Range.

Spatulate Ridge. 73°28′S, 167°13′E. Ice-covered. In the Mountaineer Range. Extends from a point between Suter Glacier and Ridgeway Glacier to the coast of Victoria Land. Named descriptively by NZ in 1966.

Mount Spatz. 72°41′S, 160°33′E. 2,270 m. 10 miles WSW of Mount Weihaupt in the Outback Nunataks. Named for Richard Spatz, station engineer at McMurdo Station in 1968.

Spaulding Peninsula. 74°26′S, 116°W. In the NW part of the Martin Peninsula, on the coast of Marie Byrd Land.

Spaulding Rocks. 77°S, 143°16′W. Isolated. 11 miles NE of Mount Warner in the Ford Ranges of Marie Byrd Land. Named for Howard R. Spaulding, USN, builder at Byrd Station in 1966.

Spaull Point. 60°44′S, 45°41′W. The northern point on Moe Island in the South Orkneys. Named by the UK for Vaughan W. Spaull, BAS biologist at Signy Island Station in 1969.

Spayd Island. 70°33′S, 72°07′E. Also called Spayd Outlier. Ice-covered. 2 miles long. At the SE side of Gillock Island on the east edge of the Amery Ice Shelf. Named by US cartographer John H. Roscoe in 1952 for A.W. Spayd, air crewman on Operation Highjump flights over this area in 1946–47.

Spayd Outlier *see* **Spayd Island**

Spear Glacier. 75°55′S, 68°15′W. Between the Hauberg Mountains and the Peterson Hills in eastern Ellsworth Land. Named for Milton B. Spear, construction electrician at Eights Station in 1965, and at Byrd Station in 1962.

Spear Nunatak. 86°32′S, 124°06′W. 3 miles south of Strickland Nunatak. It is the furthest south rock outcrop along the east side of the head of Reedy Glacier. Named for Milton B. Spear (*see* **Spear Glacier**).

Spear Spur. 82°38′S, 52°22′W. 3 miles east of Clinton Spur on the south side of the Dufek Massif in the Pensacola Mountains. Named for Albert Spear, builder at Ellsworth Station in 1957.

Spears, Robert. Captain of the maintop on the Wilkes Expedition 1838–42. Joined in the USA. Discharged at Oahu, Oct. 31, 1840.

Special Committee for Antarctic Research. More commonly known as SCAR. Organized in Sept. 1957 by the International Council of Scientific Unions (ICSU). The first meeting of this nongovernmental agency was at The Hague on Feb. 3, 1958, G.R. Laclavère of France, president. Its purpose was to encourage scientific cooperation in Antarc-tica, and to coordinate all Antarctic research. It was a successor to IGY and the signing of the Antarctic Treaty, and helps keep the Treaty in force. In 1961 it changed its name slightly to the Scientific Committee for Antarctic Research (q.v.), and was still called SCAR.

Special Odysseys. Travel agent dealing with Antarctica. Phone number in 1990: (206) 445-1960.

Specially Protected Areas. These are areas of outstanding scientific interest that are accorded special protection to preserve their unique natural system. They were created out of an idea dreamed up at one of the Consultative meetings of the Antarctic Treaty. There are 20 SPAs, as they are more commonly known: 1. Taylor Rookery, Mac. Robertson Land; 2. Rookery Islands, Holme Bay; 3. Ardery Island and Odbert Island, Budd Coast; 4. Sabrina Island in the Balleny Islands; 5. Beaufort Island, Ross Sea; 6. Cape Crozier, Ross Island; 7. Cape Hallett, Victoria Land; 8. Dion Islands, Marguerite Bay; 9. Green Island in the Berthelot Islands; 10. Byers Peninsula, Livingston Island; 11. Cape Shirreff, Livingston Island; 12. Fildes Peninsula, Livingston Island; 13. Moe Island in the South Orkneys; 14. Lynch Island in the South Orkneys; 15. southern Powell Island and adjacent islands in the South Orkneys; 16. There appears not to be a #16; 17. Litchfield Island; 18. the northern part of Coronation Island, in the South Orkneys; 19. Lagotellerie Island; 20. New College Valley.

Specimen Nunatak. 67°59′S, 66°46′ W. In Swithinbank Glacier, 4 miles south of its terminus, in Graham Land. Visited on Feb. 9, 1941, by Dorsey and Healy of the USAS 1939–41. Named by them because it is a good specimen.

Spectator Nunatak. 70°37′S, 159°29′ E. Isolated. Mainly ice-covered. Consists of hornblende. 4 miles west of the Pomerantz Tableland in the Usarp Mountains. Used as a survey station by the NZGSAE 1963–64, who named it because of the view from here.

The Spectre. 86°06'S, 150°10'W. A mountain in the Queen Maud Mountains.

Mount Speed. 84°30'S, 176°50'W. Circular and mound-shaped. Has several low summits. At the edge of the Ross Ice Shelf, at the west side of the mouth of Shackleton Glacier. Discovered by the USAS 1939–41. Surveyed by the US Ross Ice Shelf Traverse Party led by Albert P. Crary in 1957–58. Crary named it for Lt. Harvey G. Speed, USN, VX-6 member at Little America in 1957.

Speerschneider Point. 65°45'S, 66°10'W. Forms the west side of the entrance to Malmgren Bay on the west side of Renaud Island in the Biscoe Islands. Named by the UK in 1959 for C.I.H. Speerschneider, Danish meteorologist specializing in the Arctic sea ice in the early part of the 20th century.

Spellers Cove *see* **Spiller Cove**

Spence Harbor. 60°41'S, 45°09'W. 1 mile south of The Turret on the east coast of Coronation Island in the South Orkneys. Discovered by Powell on Dec. 9, 1821, and named by him.

Cape Spencer. 68°24'S, 147°28'E. Ice-covered. Marks, on the east, the seaward end of the depression caused by the Ninnis Glacier. Discovered by the AAE 1911–14 and named by Mawson for Sir Baldwin Spencer (1860–1929), director of the National Museum in Melbourne in 1911, and professor of biology at Melbourne University from 1887 to 1919.

Mount Spencer. 77°17'S, 143°20'W. 1 mile south of Mount Darling in the Allegheny Mountains of the Ford Ranges of Marie Byrd Land. Discovered aerially by members of West Base during the USAS 1939–41, and named for Herbert R. Spencer, of Erie, Pa., Paul Siple's Sea Scout commander in the days of Byrd's 1928–30 expedition.

Spencer, William H. Seaman on the Wilkes Expedition 1838–42. Joined at Rio. Run at Sydney.

Spencer Bluff *see* **Santa Cruz Point**

Spencer Island. 77°09'S, 148°04'W. A small, ice-covered island in the Marshall Archipelago. 2 miles off the NE part of Steventon Island in the Sulzberger Ice Shelf. Named for Lt. Michael P. Spencer, USNR, Hercules aircraft navigator, 1968.

Spencer Nunatak. 85°21'S, 122°11'W. 9 miles ENE of Mount LeSchack, between the Wisconsin Range and the Long Hills in the Horlick Mountains. Named for Donald J. Spencer, atmospheric noise scientist at Byrd Station in 1958.

Cape Spencer-Smith. 78°02'S, 167°30'E. The most northerly cape on White Island in the Ross Archipelago. Named by the New Zealanders in 1958–59 for the Rev. Arnold P. Spencer-Smith.

Spencer-Smith, The Rev. Arnold P. Chaplain and photographer on Mackintosh's depot-laying party during the British Imperial Transantarctic Expedition of 1914–17. He died on March 8, 1916, of scurvy and exhaustion, and during particularly miserable circumstances, on the return journey from the Beardmore Glacier to Ross Island.

Spencers Straits *see* **Lewthwaite Strait, English Strait**

Sperm Bluff. 77°05'S, 161°36'E. 3 miles long. Over 1,000 meters high. Forms the NE extremity of the Clare Range, between the Mackay Glacier and the Debenham Glacier in Victoria Land. Charted and named by Scott's 1910–13 expedition because, from the east, the north face looks like the head of a sperm whale.

Sperm whale. *Physeter catodon* or *Physeter macrocephalus.* Also called a cachalot. A blunt-snouted whale with an enormous head. This was Moby Dick. Occasionally solitary males come into Antarctic waters and swim right up to the edge of the pack-ice.

Sperre. Second engineer on the *Wyatt Earp* during Ellsworth's last expedition to Antarctica in 1938–39. A Norwegian, he had been to Antarctica at least once before with Ellsworth.

Sperring Point. 67°24'S, 59°31'E. On the west side of William Scoresby Bay in East Antarctica. Discovered and named by the personnel on the *William Scoresby* in Feb. 1936.

Spert Island. 63°50'S, 60°57'W. Triangular little island off the west coast of Trinity Island. It rises to a height of 525 feet. Charted by the Nordenskjöld expedition of 1901–4. Named by the UK in 1960 for Sir Thomas Spert, controller of the king's ships for Henry VIII, first master of the mariners of England.

Mount Speyer. 78°52'S, 160°42'E. 2,430 m. At the head of Kehle Glacier in the Worcester Range. Discovered by Scott's 1901–4 expedition, and named by them for Sir Edgar Speyer, a contributor.

Sphinx *see* **Beehive Hill, Sphinx Mountain**

Mount Sphinx. 72°21'S, 31°15'E. 2,200 m. In the Prince de Ligne Mountains, 9 miles north of the Belgica Mountains. Discovered by the Belgian Antarctic Expedition of 1957–58 under Gaston de Gerlache, who named it for its resemblance to a sphinx.

Sphinx Hill. 62°11'S, 58°27'W. 145 m. Isolated, black hill 1½ miles NNW of Demay Point, on the western shore of Admiralty Bay, King George Island. Charted by Charcot in 1908–10. Surveyed by Lt. Cdr. F.W. Hunt, RN, in 1952, and named descriptively by the UK soon afterward.

Sphinx Island. 65°54'S, 64°53'W. 2 miles long. 1 mile wide. Has an ice-free summit. In the entrance to Barilari Bay on the west coast of Graham Land. Discovered and named by the BGLE 1934–37.

Sphinx Mountain. 71°27'S, 11°58'E. 1,850 m. Extends 6 miles in linear fashion. 5 miles east of Nordwestliche Insel Mountains in the Wohlthat Mountains of Queen Maud Land. Ritscher discovered it and named its northern peak Sphinx. The Norwegians and the Soviets,

in the late 1950s and early 1960s, extended the name to the entire mountain. They called it Sfinksen (the sphinx) and Gora Sfinx (sphinx mountain) respectively, and in fact they still do call it by those names. It was set in English to follow the original German spelling.

Sphinx Peak. 72°17'S, 165°36'E. 1 mile south of Pyramid Peak, west of the Millen Range, on the Polar Plateau. Named by the New Zealanders in 1962–63 in association with Pyramid Peak.

Sphinx Point. On the western shore of Admiralty Bay on King George Island, in the South Shetlands. A term no longer used.

¹Sphinx Rock. 60°37'S, 46°05'W. A rock in water, just off the SW end of Monroe Island, in the South Orkneys. Charted and named by the personnel on the *Discovery II* in 1933.

²Sphinx Rock. 71°27'S, 169°30'E. A rock in water, in front of Islands Point in the west part of Robertson Bay in Victoria Land. Charted and named for its shape by Campbell's Northern Party of 1910–13.

Sphinxkopf Peak. 71°25'S, 11°57'E. The Norwegians call it Sfinksskolten. 1,630 m. At the northern end of Sphinx Mountain in the northern part of the Wohlthat Mountains of Queen Maud Land. Discovered and named descriptively (sphinx head) by Ritscher's expedition of 1938–39.

Cape Spieden. 66°25'S, 126°44'E. On the west shore of Porpoise Bay. 17 miles SE of Cape Goodenough. Named for William Spieden.

Spieden, William. Purser on the Wilkes Expedition 1838–42.

Spiers Nunatak. 85°20'S, 125°36'W. Isolated. 8 miles WNW of Mount Brecher on the north side of Quonset Glacier in the Wisconsin Range of the Horlick Mountains. Named for Raymond R. Spiers, cook at Byrd Station, 1959.

Spiess, Fritz A. Capt. Commander of the *Meteor* 1925–27. Succeeded Capt.

Alfred Merz, who died at sea on Aug. 25, 1925, before the ship got to the Antarctic.

Spiess Glacier. 72°15'S, 61°15'W. On the east coast of Palmer Land.

Spigot Peak. 64°38'S, 62°34'W. Also called Nunatak Negro. 285 m. A black peak. Marks the south side of the entrance to Orne Harbor, on the west coast of Graham Land. Named descriptively by the UK in 1956.

Spike Cape. 77°18'S, 163°43'E. The northern flange of the Bay of Sails. 4 miles south of Dunlop Island, in the Convoy Range, on the coast of Victoria Land. Once covered by the Wilson Piedmont Glacier. Named Spike Point by Robert Forde, one of Grif Taylor's Western Journey Party, during Scott's 1910–13 expedition, for its likeness to Spike Island, in Plymouth, England. It was later redefined.

Spike Point *see* **Spike Cape**

Spiller, Capt. Commander of the *Indian*, 1820–21.

Spiller Cove. 62°30'S, 60°43'W. Also called Spellers Cove. Just west of Black Point, on the north coast of Livingston Island, in the South Shetlands. Named by Robert Fildes in 1821 for Capt. Spiller.

Spillway Icefall. 85°03'S, 166°30'W. In the Queen Maud Mountains.

Spin Pole. The imaginary point at which the earth's axis "protrudes." Its geographic position, as it were, would be the same as the South Pole.

Spincloud Heights. 67°50'S, 67°09' W. Border the north side of Shoesmith Glacier on Horseshoe Island. Surveyed by the FIDS in 1955–57 and named by them for the clouds of spindrift blowing off the heights, giving warning of approaching storms.

Spindrift Bluff. 69°35'S, 68°02'W. On the west side of the Antarctic Peninsula.

Spindrift Col. 60°41'S, 45°37'W. Between hills in the north-central part of

Signy Island in the South Orkneys. 1,000 yards SE of Spindrift Rocks, in association with which it was named by the UK.

Spindrift Rocks. 60°42'S, 45°40'W. Ice-free rocks in water, 15 meters high. ¾ mile SW of North Point and close to the west of Signy Island, in the South Orkneys. Surveyed by the FIDS in 1947, and named by them for the spindrift, or sea spray, which forms over these rocks during westerly gales.

Spine Automatic Weather Station. 67°42'S, 66°06'W. American AWS at an elevation of approximately 1,600 feet, on the Antarctic Peninsula.

Spine Island. 60°36'S, 46°02'W. Between Coronation Island and Monroe Island in the South Orkneys. Discovered by Powell and Palmer in Dec. 1821. Surveyed by the personnel on the *Discovery II* in 1933, and named by them for its appearance.

¹The Spire. 68°18'S, 66°53'W. Also called Pinnacle, The Needle, Sanctuary Pinnacle. An isolated rock pinnacle, or peak, at the NW end of the Blackwall Mountains on the south side of Neny Fjord, Graham Land. First climbed on Jan. 17, 1948, by a combined FIDS/RARE team. Named in 1949 by William Latady.

²The Spire. 78°09'S, 161°38'E. Over 2,600 m. A rock spire, or peak, at the west end of Rampart Ridge in Victoria Land. Surveyed and descriptively named in 1957 by the NZ Party of the BCTAE.

Spiret Peak. 72°31'S, 3°38'W. In the NW part of Borg Mountain, in the Borg Massif of Queen Maud Land. Name means "the spire" in Norwegian.

Cape Spirit. 78°12'S, 166°44'E. The easternmost point on Black Island in the Ross Ice Shelf. Named by the New Zealanders in 1958–59 for the spirited winds blowing between Black and White Islands.

Spiro Hill. 62°16'S, 59°W. Also called Strachan Hill. 120 m. At the head of Edgell Bay, Nelson Island, in the South

Shetlands. Originally called Sudeste (south east) by the Argentines, but renamed by them in 1956 for Spiro, the Argentine hero who fought with Almirante Brown.

Spirogyra Lake. 60°42'S, 45°39'W. One of the group of lakes just to the SW of Paternoster Valley in the northern part of Signy Island in the South Orkneys.

Spirtle Rock. 65°13'S, 64°20'W. In the navigable passage between The Barchans and the Anagram Islands in the Argentine Islands. Spirtle means "splash," and it was named descriptively by the UK in 1971.

The Spit. 61°30'S, 55°28'W. An isthmus made of shingle and boulders. 50–80 meters long. 1 meter above the level of the high tide. In the east part of Gibbs Island in the South Shetlands. It connects the narrow, eastern part of the island (this part is sometimes called Narrow Isle) with the rest of the island. Named by the personnel on the *Discovery II* in the 1930s.

Spit Point. 62°32'S, 59°48'W. Also called Punta Lengua. Gravel spit forming the south side of the entrance to Yankee Harbor, in Greenwich Island, in the South Shetlands. Named descriptively by the personnel on the *Discovery II* in 1933.

Spitz Ridge. 75°49'S, 114°52'W. Mainly ice-covered. Forms the east end of the Toney Mountain massif in Marie Byrd Land. East of Cox Bluff. Named for Armand Lawrence Spitz, ionosphere physicist at Byrd Station in 1966. He also spent summers at Byrd Station and at Hallett Station.

Mount Spivey. 69°31'S, 69°50'W. 2,135 m. Flat-topped. Mainly ice-covered. On the west side of Toynbee Glacier. 9 miles south of Mount Nicholas, in the northern part of the Douglas Range of Alexander Island. Surveyed by the FIDS in 1948, and named by them for Robert E. Spivey, general FIDS assistant at Base E (Stonington Island), who took

part in the FIDS sledge journey to George VI Sound in 1949.

Spjotöy *see* **Canopus Island**

Spjotøyholmane *see* **Smith Rocks**

Spjotöyskjera *see* **Wiltshire Rocks**

Splettstoesser Glacier. 79°12'S, 84°09' W. 35 miles long. Flows from the plateau just south of Founders Escarpment, then through the Heritage Range to the south of Founders Peaks and the Anderson Massif, to join the Minnesota Glacier. Named by the University of Minnesota Ellsworth Mountains Party 1961–62 who explored here, for John F. Splettstoesser, geologist with the party.

Splinten Peak. 72°41'S, 3°59'W. In the Seilkopf Peaks. Just north of Pilarryggen in the Borg Massif of Queen Maud Land. Name means "the splinter" in Norwegian.

Split Rock. 64°47'S, 64°04'W. A tiny oval-shaped island split to the water-line in a north-south direction. 175 yards NW of Janus Island, off the SW coast of Anvers Island, not far from Palmer Station. Named descriptively by personnel at Palmer Station in 1972.

Splitwind Island. 65°02'S, 63°56'W. ¼ mile long. Off the north end of Booth Island, in the Wilhelm Archipelago. Charted by Charcot in 1903–5, and named de Rothschild Islets by him for Alphonse de Rothschild, French banker baron and sponsor of the expedition. Renamed in 1959 by the UK to avoid confusion with Rothschild Island. The wind to the north of the island is often very different from the wind to the south of it.

Mount Spohn. 85°28'S, 171°58'E. 3,420 m. On the west side of Burgess Glacier to the west of the Otway Massif in the Queen Maud Mountains. Named for Harry R. Spohn, meteorologist at Amundsen-Scott South Pole Station in 1963.

Sponges. Fauna which live on the sea bed near the coasts.

Sponholz Peak. 80°08'S, 83°W. 1,730 m. 2½ miles south of Moulder Peak in the Liberty Hills of the Heritage Range. Named for Martin P. Sponholz, meteorologist at Plateau Station in 1966.

Sponskaftet Spur. 71°39'S, 11°12'E. Extends west from The Altar in the Humboldt Mountains of Queen Maud Land. Discovered by Ritscher in 1938–39. Name means "the wooden spoon handle" in Norwegian.

Sponsors Peak. 77°18'S, 161°24'E. Over 1,600 m. At the west side of the mouth of Victoria Upper Glacier in Victoria Land. Named by the VUWAE 1958–59 for their sponsors.

Spooner Bay. 67°36'S, 46°15'E. 6 miles wide. On the coast of Enderby Land. 12 miles east of Freeth Bay in Alasheyev Bight. Visited by the ANARE under D.F. Styles in Feb. 1961, and named by them for Senator W.H. Spooner, Australian minister of national development.

Mount Sporli. 79°33'S, 83°39'W. 2,255 m. At the east side of the head of Driscoll Glacier in the Pioneer Heights of the Heritage Range. Named by the University of Minnesota Geological Party here in 1963–64 for Bernhard N. Sporli, geologist with the party.

Spøta Spur. 72°03'S, 4°03'E. Extends from the north-central part of Mount Hochlin in the Mühlig-Hofmann Mountains of Queen Maud Land. Name means "the knitting needle" in Norwegian.

Spouter Peak. 65°49'S, 62°23'W. 615 m. 4½ miles SSW of Daggoo Peak at the south side of the mouth of Flask Glacier on the east coast of Graham Land. Surveyed by the FIDS in 1947. Named by the UK in 1956 for the inn in New Bedford which provides the opening scene for *Moby Dick*.

Spraglegga Ridge. 71°55'S, 14°45'E. Partly snow-covered. Surmounted by Stenka Mountain. 4½ miles SE of Kvaevefjellet Mountain in the Payer Mountains of Queen Maud Land. Discovered by Ritscher in 1938–39. Named by the Norwegians.

Sprekkefjellet. 71°42'S, 5°37'E. Isolated hill. Looks like two low rock summits separated by a snow col. 5 miles north of the mouth of Austreskorve Glacier in the Mühlig-Hofmann Mountains of Queen Maud Land. Name means "the split hill" in Norwegian.

The *Sprightly*. British sealing ship from London. It was in the South Shetlands in 1820–21 under Capt. Fraser, and again in 1821–22, this time under Capt. Brown when it moored at New Plymouth for the season. Its most important voyage was in 1824–25, when it explored the waters of the Antarctic Peninsula, under the command of Capt. Edward Hughes. First mate on that trip was James Hoseason. In 1825–26, under Capt. George Norris, it was at Bouvetøya (not in the Antarctic).

Sprightly Island. 64°17'S, 61°04'W. 1 mile NW of Spring Point in Hughes Bay, Graham Land. Surveyed by de Gerlache in 1897–99. Named by the UK for the *Sprightly*.

Cape Spring *see* **Spring Point**

Spring Point. 64°18'S, 61°03'W. Also called Cape Primavera, Cape Spring, Cape W. Spring. Forms the south side of the entrance to Brialmont Cove on the west coast of Graham Land. Discovered and named Cap Spring by de Gerlache in 1897–99, for Prof. W. Spring of the University of Liège, a member of the *Belgica* Commission. Later redefined.

Springer Peak. 79°24'S, 84°53'W. 1,460 m. In the northern part of Webers Peaks in the Heritage Range. Named for Michael J. Springer, aerial photographer over Marie Byrd Land and Ellsworth Land in 1965–66.

Springtail Bluff. 71°02'S, 165°12'E. Borders the eastern section of Mount Hemphill, in the Anare Mountains. It faces south. Named by the New Zealanders in 1963–64 for the springtails (q.v.).

Springtail Point. 77°10'S, 160°42'E. 3 miles north of Skew Peak in the Clare Range of Victoria Land. Named by Heinz

Janetschek, the biologist, in 1961–62, for springtails (q.v.) he found here.

Springtails. Order: Collembola. The world's most abundant insects. Small, primitive, and wingless, they measure from 1 to 10 mm long. There are 19 species living in Antarctica, non-parasitic, mostly living under rocks, and associated with spore-reproducing plants.

Spry, William. Engineering sub-lieutenant on the *Challenger*, 1872–76.

Spume Island. 64°48′S, 64°07′W. A little island 2 miles SW of Palmer Station in the Palmer Archipelago. Named by the UK for the spume here.

Spur Point. 66°36′S, 63°48′W. At the east end of a spur extending between Anderson Glacier and Sleipnir Glacier on the west side of Cabinet Inlet, on the east coast of Graham Land.

Sputnik Islands. 70°22′S, 163°22′E. Two ice-covered islands, one much bigger than the other. Between Cape Cheetham and Cape Williams in the entrance to Ob' Bay, Oates Land. Named by the USSR in 1958 for their satellite.

Square Bay. 67°50′S, 66°59′W. Also called Bahía Caudrada. 10 miles wide. Between Nicholl Head and Camp Point. It separates Horseshoe Island from the Antarctic Peninsula, in the vicinity of Adelaide Island. Named by the BGLE 1934–37 for its shape.

Square End Island. 62°10′S, 58°59′W. Also called Isla Cuadrada. A small island 3 miles NNE of the west tip of King George Island in the South Shetlands. Charted by the personnel on the *Discovery II* in 1935, and named by them descriptively.

Squire Island. 64°55′S, 63°54′W. A small island just NE of Friar Island in the Wauwermans Islands in the Wilhelm Archipelago. Named by the UK in 1958 for the *Canterbury Tales* character.

Squires Glacier. 73°58′S, 62°35′W. Between the Playfair Mountains and the Hutton Mountains, flowing into Swann Glacier in Palmer Land. Named for Peter L. Squires, glaciologist at Byrd Station in 1965–66.

Squires Peak. 73°56′S, 62°39′W. Marks the eastern extremity of the Playfair Mountains in Palmer Land. Named for Donald F. Squires, biologist here in 1965–66.

Staack Nunatak. 74°15′S, 72°49′W. 1 mile west of Horner Nunatak. 40 miles north of the Merrick Mountains in Ellsworth Land. Named for Karl J. Staack, meteorologist at Byrd Station in 1965–66.

Stabben *see* **Stump Mountain**

Stabben Mountain. 71°58′S, 2°52′E. Just north of Mayr Ridge in the northern part of the Gjelsvik Mountains of Queen Maud Land. Name means "the stump" in Norwegian.

Staccato Peaks. 71°47′S, 70°39′W. A series of rock peaks extending for 11 miles and rising sharply out of the snowfields 20 miles south of the Walton Mountains in the southern part of Alexander Island. Discovered aerially by Ellsworth on Nov. 23, 1935. Named musically by the UK to conform with the other musical terms in the area.

Stack Bay. 67°03′S, 58°04′E. Between West Stack and the mouth of Hoseason Glacier in Enderby Land. Photographed by the LCE 1936–37. Named Skotvika (stack bay) by the Norwegians. This name was later translated into English.

Stackpole Rocks. 62°41′S, 60°58′W. Rocks in water off the SE part of Byers Peninsula, Livingston Island, in the South Shetlands. Named by the UK in 1958 for Edouard A. Stackpole, curator of the Marine Historical Association in Mystic, Conn. Mr. Stackpole is also regarded as one of the major Antarctic historians (*see* the Bibliography).

Banco Stacy *see* **Stanley Patch**

The Stadium. 61°07′S, 54°42′W. A bowl-shaped cirque with mountains on 3 sides but open on the east. A glacier occupies the floor. 1 mile north of Walker

Point on Elephant Island in the South Shetlands. Named descriptively by the UK.

Mount Stadler. 66°54'S, 53°14'E. 2½ miles SE of Mount Cordwell. 23 miles SSW of Stor Hånakken Mountain in Enderby Land. Named by the Australians for S. Stadler, weather observer at Wilkes Station in 1961.

Staeffler Ridge. 77°20'S, 162°48'E. West of Hanson Ridge. Separates Victoria Lower Glacier from Greenwood Valley in Victoria Land. Named in 1964 for George R. Staeffler, topographic engineer in the McMurdo Sound area in 1960–61.

Stafford Glacier. 72°30'S, 168°15'E. 5 miles east of Rudolph Glacier, flowing into Trafalgar Glacier, in the Victory Mountains of Victoria Land. Named for Sgt. Billy D. Stafford, US Army, in charge of the enlisted detachment of the helicopter group here in 1961–62.

Mount Stagnaro. 77°10'S, 144°20'W. In the Ford Ranges of Marie Byrd Land.

Mount Stahlman. 85°41'S, 151°36'W. Over 1,000 m. On the east flank of the Robert Scott Glacier, between Mount Wallace and Mount Hamilton, at the west end of the Tapley Mountains, in the Queen Maud Mountains. Discovered in Dec. 1929 by Gould's Geological Party during Byrd's 1928–30 expedition, and first visited by Quin Blackburn's party in Dec. 1934 during Byrd's 1933–35 expedition. Named by Byrd for James G. Stahlman, a Nashville, Tenn., newspaper publisher and supporter of Byrd's second expedition.

Stair Hill. 66°10'S, 65°14'W. At the south side of the head of Holtedahl Bay, on the west coast of Graham Land. Named by the UK in 1959 for Ralph Stair of the US National Bureau of Standards, a snow-goggles pioneer.

Staircase Glacier. 72°17'S, 168°43'E. 8 miles long. Flows between Mount Francis and Mount Titus into Tucker Glacier in the Admiralty Mountains. Named by the

NZGSAE 1957–58 for its proximity to the Staircase Survey Station established by that expedition, and the station was so named because a long line of steps were cut into the ice in order to climb it.

Mount Staley. 72°20'S, 164°41'E. 2,560 m. At the south end of the Salamander Range in the Freyberg Mountains. Named for James T. Staley, biologist at Hallett Station in 1962–63.

Mount Stalker. 70°09'S, 65°37'E. In the northern part of the Athos Range, about 5 miles NW of Farley Massif. Named by the Australians for J.F. Stalker, weather observer at Mawson Station in 1964.

Stålstuten Ridge. 72°04'S, 4°10'E. Extends from the NE side of Mount Hochlin in the Mühlig-Hofmann Mountains of Queen Maud Land. Name means "the bulldozer" in Norwegian.

Stamnen Peak. 72°16'S, 3°26'W. Also called Stäven. 1 mile north of Brabordsranten Ridge near the SW end of the Ahlmann Ridge in Queen Maud Land. Name means "the prow" in Norwegian.

Stamper Peak. 71°41'S, 169°19'E. 2,180 m. 10 miles ENE of Mount Gilruth in the Admiralty Mountains. Between the Dugdale and Ommanney Glaciers. Named for Wilburn E. Stamper, USN, radioman at McMurdo Station in 1967.

Stamps. Polar stamp collecting is a major philatelic specialty. *The Polar News,* published twice yearly by the American Polar Society, always has something on philately, while *The Ice Cap News* was a journal published regularly by the American Society of Polar Philatelists. In Britain there exists the Polar Postal History Society of Great Britain. Many countries have issued Antarctic, or Antarctica-related stamps. Here is an abbreviated chronology of Antarctic philately (only those in a series which relate to Antarctica are mentioned). **1907–9.** The New Zealand government printed special stamps for Shackleton's expedition of 1907–9 — 24,000 of them, in fact. They were overprinted KING EDWARD VII

LAND in green for use by members of the expedition, and a postmark inscribed BRIT. ANTARCTIC EXPED. was used to cancel mail posted from the NZ base (*see also* Post offices). Shackleton left some at his furthest south in 1909, in a brass cylinder buried in the snow. **1920.** The Cook Islands, being named for Captain Cook, are a natural for showing his picture on their stamps. A ½d of this year showed Cook's landing on the islands, and a 1½d in the same series showed Cook's portrait. **1931–32.** A Cook Islands series showing the same scenes as on the 1920 series, except that they were on the ½d and the 1d. **1933.** The USA printed a Byrd Antarctic Expedition II 3¢ stamp to commemorate Byrd's expedition of 1933–35. In addition to the 3¢ postage charge, letters sent by the expedition ships to be canceled in Little America were subject to an extra service charge of 50¢ each. The stamp showed the world map on Van der Grinten's projection. **1933.** The Falkland Islands have put out many Antarctic stamps over the years. The first series was in this year. ½d iceberg, 1½d whale catcher, 6d blue whale. **1935, May 1.** NZ series. 2d Cook landing at Poverty Bay, NZ. **1938–39.** France issued two semi-postals, with pictures of Charcot on them. **1938–44.** NZ series. 1d Cook. **1938–46.** Falkland Islands series. 6d the *Discovery II,* 9d the *William Scoresby,* 2/6 gentoo penguins, 10/- Deception Island. **1944.** Throughout this year the 1938–41 Falkland Islands series were reissued with words overprinted in red, saying, GRAHAM LAND, DEPENDENCY OF; SOUTH GEORGIA, DEPENDENCY OF; SOUTH ORKNEYS, DEPENDENCY OF; and SOUTH SHETLANDS, DEPENDENCY OF. They were separate issues for those individual dependencies. These dependencies existed at most momentarily, and at least as a figment of the imagination of the British government in order to stake their Antarctic claim more solidly in the face of Argentine opposition. **1946.** The Falkland Islands Dependencies (a real entity, this

one) began issuing stamps. **1946.** Cook Islands series. 1d Cook's portrait, 1/- Cook's statue. **1946, June.** Norway series. 55ö Nansen and Amundsen. **1947, May 12.** Chile. Series of 2. Showed a map with Chile's claims to the Antarctic. **1947, June.** Belgian series issued to commemorate the 50th anniversary of de Gerlache's expedition in the *Belgica.* 1.35fr de Gerlache, 2.25fr the *Belgica* and explorers. **1947–49.** Argentina series. Issued to celebrate the 43rd anniversary of the first Argentine Antarctic Mail. It had a map of the Argentine Antarctic claims. **1948–49.** Argentina. Air Post stamps showing the Antarctic Peninsula as part of Argentina. **1950, May.** Argentina. 1p Antarctic claims. **1952.** Falkland Islands series. 4d Auster plane, 6d the *John Biscoe,* 1/- gentoo penguins. **1953, Oct. 8.** Argentina. 50¢ the rescue ship the *Uruguay.* Issued to commemorate the 50th anniversary of the rescue of Nordenskjöld. **1954.** Falkland Islands Dependencies series on ships. ½d the *John Biscoe,* 1d the *Trepassey,* 1½d the *Wyatt Earp,* 2½d the *Penola,* 3d the *Discovery II,* 4d the *William Scoresby,* 6d the *Discovery,* 9d the *Endurance,* 1/- the *Deutschland,* 2/- the *Pourquoi Pas?,* 2/6 the *Français,* 5/- the *Scotia,* 10/- the *Antarctic,* £1 the *Belgica.* **1954, Jan. 20.** Argentina. 1.45p planting of the Argentine flag in the Antarctic. Issued to commemorate the 50th anniversary of Argentina's first Antarctic post office and the establishment of the La Hoy radio-post office in the South Orkneys (this latter presumably not in 1904). **1954, Nov.** Australia. 3½d flora and fauna map of Antarctica. Issued to publicize Australia's interest in Antarctica. **1955.** The Terres Australes et Antarctiques Françaises began issuing stamps. The first, this year, was actually a Madagascar stamp with TERRES AUSTRALES ET ANTARCTIQUES FRANÇAISES overprinted in red. **1956.** Falkland Islands Dependencies series of 4. Issued to commemorate the BCTAE 1955–58. **1956.** The first proper series from the Terres Australes et Antarctiques Françaises. 10fr elephant seals, 15fr elephant seals (sic). **1956.** Terres Australes et Antarctiques Françaises. Air Post stamps series of 2 with emperor penguin and map of Antarctica. **1956, Oct. 22.** USSR. 40k Antarctic bases. Issued to commemorate the USSR Scientific Antarctic Expedition. **1957-58.** During the IGY the USA issued a 3¢ stamp showing two hands about to touch over the Antarctic. **1957.** Ross Dependency series. 3d the *Erebus* and Mount Erebus, 4d Shackleton and Scott, 8d map showing location of the Ross Dependency, 1/6 Queen Elizabeth II. **1957.** The Australian Antarctic Territory began producing stamps. **1957-59.** Australian Antarctic Territory series. 5d David, Mawson, and Mackay at the South Magnetic Pole in 1908-9, 8d loading a Weasel, 1/- dog team and iceberg, 2/- Australian explorers and map of Antarctica, 2/3 emperor penguins and map. **1957.** Terres Australes et Antarctiques Françaises series of 3 celebrating the IGY. **1957, July.** Norway series. 65ö a map of the South Pole with Queen Maud Land. An IGY commemorative. **1957, July 1.** Japan. 10 yen a penguin, the *Soya*, and IGY emblem. **1957, Oct. 18.** Belgium. Semi-postal 5fr + 2.50fr dogs and Antarctic camp. **1958, July.** Argentina. 40¢ a map of Antarctica. This was an IGY commemorative. **1958, Aug. 28.** Chile. 40p a modern map of Antarctica, 10p a map of Antarctica and the ship *La Araucana*. These were IGY commemoratives. **1959.** Terres Australes et Antarctiques Françaises. Air Post stamps. 200fr wandering albatross. **1959.** South Africa. 3d a globe showing Antarctica and South Africa. Issued to commemorate the First SANAE. **1959, Sept.** Terres Australes et Antarctiques Françaises series. 30¢ light-mantled sooty albatross, 40¢ skua, 12fr king shag, 20fr coat of arms of the Terres Australes et Antarctiques Françaises. **1960.** Falkland Islands series. 1d Dominican gull, 2d gentoo penguins, 6d black-browed albatross. **1960.** Argentina. 1p Argentina and the Argentine Antarctic claim. Terres Australes et Antarctiques Françaises series. 2fr sheathbills, 4fr sea

leopard, 25fr Weddell seal, 85fr king penguin. **1960, Nov.** Japan. 10 yen Shirase and a map of Antarctica. Marked the 50th anniversary of the beginning of the First Japanese Antarctic Expedition. **1961.** Terres Australes et Antarctiques Françaises. 25fr Charcot with the *Pourquoi Pas?* in the background. **1961, July.** Australian Antarctic Territory. 5d same as the 5d in the 1957-59 series. **1961, Aug. 19.** Argentina. 2p explorers, sledge and dog team. Issued to commemorate the 10th anniversary of General San Martín Station. **1961, Oct.** Australian Antarctic Territory. 5d Mawson. Issued to commemorate the 50th anniversary of the AAE 1911-14. **1961, Nov.** Norway series of 2. Both showed Amundsen in commemoration of his 50th anniversary at the Pole. **1963.** South Georgia series. 2d sperm whale, 2½d penguins, 3d fur seals, 4d finback whale and ship, 5½d elephant seals, 6d sooty albatross, 9d whaling ship, 1/- leopard seal, 2/6 wandering albatross, 5/- elephant seals and fur seals, 10/- plankton and krill, £1 blue whale. **1963.** The first British Antarctic Territory series. ½d the *Kista Dan*, 1d skiers hauling load, 1½d muskeg, 2d skiers, 2½d Beaver seaplane, 3d the *John Biscoe*, 4d camp scene, 6d the *Protector*, 9d dog sledge, 1/- Otter seaplane, 2/- huskies and the Aurora Australis, 2/6 helicopters, 5/- Sno-cat, 10/- the *Shackleton*, £1 map of Antarctica. **1963.** Terres Australes et Antarctiques Françaises. Air Post stamps. 50fr Adélie penguins. **1963-65.** Australia series. 7/6 Cook. **1963, Feb.** Terres Australes et Antarctiques Françaises. 8fr elephant seals fighting. **1963, Sept. 16.** USSR series which had "Antarctica—Continent of Peace" as its motif. 3k map of Antarctica, penguins, research ship, southern lights, 4k map, southern lights and Sno-cats, 6k globe, camp, and various planes, 12k whaler and whales. **1964.** Ross Dependency series. Same as the 1957 series. **1964, Feb. 22.** Argentina series. 2p maps of South Georgia, South Orkneys, and South Sandwich Islands, 4p map of Argentina and the Argentine

Antarctic claims. Issued to commemorate the 60th anniversary of Argentina's claim to the South Orkneys. **1964, Oct. 10.** Argentina series of Air Post stamps issued to publicize Argentina's southern colonies. 13p Teniente Matienzo Station. **1965.** Argentina series of 2. 2p General Belgrano Station, 4p the icebreaker *General San Martín.* Issued to publicize Argentina's Antarctic claims. **1965.** USSR series on scientific conquests of the Poles. 10k the *Vostok* and *Mirnyy* and icebergs, 16k Vostok Station. **1965, Jan.** Terres Australes et Antarctiques Françaises Air Post stamps. 50fr the discovery of Adélie Land. **1965, Nov. 19.** Japan. 10 yen the Aurora Australis, a map of Antarctica and the *Fuji.* Commemorated the JARE which left on the *Fuji* on Nov. 20, 1965. **1966.** British Antarctic Territory series of a common design. **1966.** Terres Australes et Antarctiques Françaises Air Post stamps. 25 fr an ionosphere research pylon in Adélie Land. **1966-68.** Australian Antarctic Territory series. 1¢ Aurora Australis and camera dome, 2¢ banding penguins, 4¢ lookout and iceberg, 5¢ banding of elephant seals, 7¢ measuring snow strata, 10¢ wind gauges, 15¢ weather balloon, 20¢ helicopter, 50¢ ice compression tests, $1 "mock sun" (parhelion) and dogs. **1966-69.** Terres Australes et Antarctiques Françaises series. 5fr great whale, 10fr cape pigeons, 15fr killer whale, 20fr black-browed albatross. **1966, Feb. 19.** Argentina series of Air Post stamps. The only one in the series was a 27.50p which showed the Argentine Antarctic map and a Centaur rocket. Issued to commemorate the launchings of sounding balloons and of a Gamma Centaur rocket in Antarctica in Feb. 1965. **1966, Aug. 27.** Belgium series of 4 semi-postals designed to publicize Belgian Antarctic expeditions. 1fr + 50¢ surveyor and dog team, 3fr + 1.50fr de Gerlache and the *Belgica,* 6fr + 3fr surveyor, weather balloon, and ship, 10fr + 5fr penguins and the *Magga Dan.* **1966, Dec. 10.** Argentina. 10p map of Argentine Antarctica and the expedition route of the 1965 Argentine Antarc-

tic Expedition which planted their flag at the Pole. Issued to commemorate that expedition. **1967.** Ross Dependency series. Same as for the 1957 and 1964 series, except that the denominations were now 2¢, 3¢, 7¢, and 15¢. **1967.** Terres Australes et Antarctiques Françaises. 20fr Aurora Australis, map of Antarctica and a rocket. Noted the launching of the first space rocket from Adélie Land in Jan. 1967. **1967-68.** Norfolk Island series of ships. 1¢ the *Resolution* in 1774. **1967, Jan.** Chile. 40¢ blue. Showed Luís Pardo Villalón and the *Yelcho.* Commemorated the 50th anniversary of Shackleton's Elephant Island party rescue. **1967, July.** Cook Islands series. 18¢ Cook is pictured. **1968, Jan.** Terres Australes et Antarctiques Françaises. 30fr Dumont d'Urville. **1968, Feb.** Argentina series issued to publicize Argentine research projects in "Antártida Argentina." 6p map showing radio postal-stations in 1966-67, 20p Almirante Brown Station, 40p planes over map of Antarctica. **1968, Sept.** Cook Islands series. ½¢ Cook, 4¢ William Hodges' painting "The Ice Islands" (i.e. Antarctica). **1969.** British Antarctic Territory. £1 the *Endurance* and a helicopter. **1969.** Terres Australes et Antarctiques Françaises. 25fr polar camp with helicopter, plane, and Sno-cat. It noted 20 years of French Polar explorations. **1969-71.** Terres Australes et Antarctiques Françaises Air Post stamps series. 200fr Pointe Géologie. **1969, Feb.** British Antarctic Territory series of 4 to commemorate 25 years of continuous scientific work in Antarctica. 3½d Lemaire Channel, iceberg, and Adélie penguins, 6d weather sonde and operator, 1/- muskeg pulling tent equipment, 2/- surveyors with theodolite. **1969, April.** Falkland Islands series. 6d Norseman seaplane, 1/- Auster plane. **1969, June.** Norfolk Island. 10¢ Cook. **1969, Oct. 9.** NZ series. 4¢ Cook. **1969, Oct.** Cook Islands. 10¢ Cook. **1970, Jan. 27.** USSR series of 2 commemorating the 150th anniversary of von Bellingshausen's expedition. 4k map of Antarctica, the *Mirnyy,* and the *Vostok,* 16k camp and map of Antarctica with USSR Antarctic bases. **1970, April.** Norfolk Island series of 2. Both showed Cook in different situations. **1970, June.** Cook Islands. 30¢ Cook. **1971.** Australian Antarctic Territory series of 2. 6¢ sastrugi snow formation, 30¢ pancake ice. Issued to celebrate the 10th anniversary of the ratification of the Antarctic Treaty. **1971.** Terres Australes et Antarctiques Françaises series of Antarctic fish. 5fr icefish, 10fr–35fr various species of Antarctic cods, 135fr *Zanchlorhynchus spinifer.* **1971, Feb.** Argentina. 20¢ the Argentine flag, a map of Argentina and Antarctica. Marked the 5th anniversary of the Argentine South Pole Expedition. **1971, Feb.** British Antarctic Territory series of common design. **1971, May 5.** Belgium. 10fr Antarctic explorer, ship, and penguins. Issued to note the 10th anniversary of the ratification of the Antarctic Treaty. **1971, June.** British Antarctic Territory series of 4 commemorating the 10th anniversary of the ratification of the Antarctic Treaty. 1½p map of Antarctica, the Aurora Australis, and explorers, 4p seagulls instead of explorers, 5p seals instead of seagulls, 10p penguins instead of seals. The map and the aurora remained constant throughout. **1971, June.** Norway. 100ö Amundsen and the Antarctic Treaty emblem. It commemorated the 10th anniversary of the ratification of the Antarctic Treaty. **1971, June 21.** USSR 6k a map of Antarctica and a station. It honored the 10th anniversary of the ratification of the Antarctic Treaty. **1971, June 23.** USA. 8¢ a map of Antarctica. Issued to commemorate the 10th anniversary of the ratification of the Antarctic Treaty. **1971, Oct.** UK. British polar explorers series. 3p Ross, 9p Scott. **1971, Dec.** Terres Australes et Antarctiques Françaises. 75fr a map of Antarctica. Marked the 10th anniversary of the ratification of the Antarctic Treaty. **1972.** Australian Antarctic Territory series. 7¢ Capt. Cook, sextant, azimuth, compass, 35¢ a chart of Cook's circumnavigation of Antarctica, and the *Resolution.* This series was issued to commemorate the bicentenary of Cook's cir-

cumnavigation. **1972.** Terres Australes et Antarctiques Françaises series of insects. 15fr *Christiansenia dreuxi,* 22fr *Phtirocoris antarcticus,* 25fr *Microzetia dreuxi,* 140fr *Pringleophaga kerguelensis.* **1972.** British Antarctic Territory silver wedding issue with a 5p and a 10p of common type showing Queen Elizabeth II, Prince Philip, seals, and emperor penguins. **1972, Jan.** South Georgia. Shackleton series. 1½p the *Endurance* in the Weddell Sea pack-ice, 5p launching of the *James Caird,* 10p route of the *James Caird* to South Georgia, 20p Ernest Shackleton and the *Quest.* This series commemorated the 50th anniversary of the death of Shackleton. **1972, March 10.** Chile series of 2. Map of Antarctica and dog sledges on both. Marked the 10th anniversary of the ratification of the Antarctic Treaty (actually in 1961). **1972, July 13.** USSR. 6k Amundsen. This stamp honored his birth. **1972, Sept.** Norway. Polar exploration ships series. 80ö the *Fram.* **1972, Sept. 2.** Argentina. 25¢ Almirante Brown Station and a map of Antarctica. Marked the 10th anniversary of the ratification of the Antarctic Treaty. **1973.** British Antarctic Treaty series of polar explorers and their crafts. ½p Cook and the *Resolution,* 1p von Bellingshausen and the *Vostok,* 1½p Weddell and the *Jane,* 2p Biscoe and the *Tula,* 2½p Dumont d'Urville and the *Astrolabe,* 3p Ross and the *Erebus,* 4p Larsen and the *Jason,* 5p de Gerlache and the *Belgica,* 6p Nordenskjöld and the *Antarctic,* 7½p Bruce and the *Scotia,* 10p Charcot and the *Pourquoi Pas?,* 15p Shackleton and the *Endurance,* 50p Ellsworth and the airplane *Polar Star,* £1 Rymill and the *Penola.* **1973.** British Antarctic Territory series which came out later in the year. A 5p and a 15p of common design showing Princess Anne's marriage to Mark Phillips. **1973.** Tristan da Cunha. Series of 4 commemorating the centenary of the *Challenger's* visit to that island during its world trip which included Antarctic waters. **1973.** Australian Antarctic Territory series of food chain and explorers' aircraft. 1¢ plankton

962   Stamps

and krill, 5¢ Mawson's D.H. Gypsy Moth 1931, 7¢ Adélie penguin feeding on krill, 8¢ Rymill's D.H. Fox Moth returning to Barry Island, 9¢ leopard seal pursuing fish, 10¢ killer whale hunting seals, 20¢ wandering albatross, 25¢ Wilkins', Lockheed Vega, 30¢ Ellsworth's Northrop Gamma, 35¢ Lars Christensen's Avro Avian and the Framnes Mountains, 50¢ Byrd's Ford Tri-Motor dropping US flag over South Pole, £1 sperm whale attacking giant squid. 1973. Australian Antarctic Territory. A later series of 2 commemorating the 44th anniversary of Byrd's flight over the Pole. 20¢ Byrd, the *Floyd Bennett,* and a map of Antarctica, 55¢ Byrd, plane, and mountains. 1973, Jan. Norfolk Island. 35¢ the *Resolution* in Antarctica. Commemorated the first crossing of the Antarctic Circle, on Jan. 17, 1773. 1973, Jan. Terres Australes et Antarctiques Françaises Air Post stamps. 145fr the *Astrolabe.* 1973, Feb. 8. Chile. 10¢ a map of Antarctica and a flag at General Bernardo O'Higgins Station. Issued to commemorate the 25th anniversary of the opening of the station. 1973, April. Argentina. 50¢ DC3 planes over Antarctica. Noted the 10th anniversary of Argentina's first flight to the South Pole. 1973, Oct. Tonga. *Resolution* series. 1974. South Georgia series. 2p Cook's picture. Commemorated the bicentenary of Cook's discovery of South Georgia (his rediscovery, perhaps). 1974. British Antarctic Territory series of 2 to commemorate Churchill's birth. 5p Churchill and a map of the Churchill Peninsula, 15p Churchill, and the *Trepassey* of Operation Tabarin in 1943. 1974–81. Australian Antarctic Territory series of ships. 1¢ the *Aurora,* 2¢ the *Penola,* 5¢ the *Thala Dan,* 10¢ the *Challenger,* 15¢ the *Nimrod* (and another 15¢ showing the stern view of the *Nimrod*), 20¢ the *Discovery II,* 22¢ the *Terra Nova,* 25¢ the *Endurance,* 30¢ the *Fram,* 35¢ the *Nella Dan,* 40¢ the *Kista Dan,* 45¢ the *Astrolabe,* 50¢ the *Norvegia,* 55¢ the *Discovery,* $1 the *Resolution.* 1974, March. Falkland Islands series. 2p fur seals. 1974, April.

Aitutaki, although part of the Cook Islands, has occasionally printed its own stamps. One of this year was the 8¢ James Cook. 1974, May. New Hebrides series. 35¢ and 1.15fr both showed Cook. 1974, July 22. Cook Islands series of 2. Both showed Cook. 1974, Oct. Norfolk Island series. Commemorated the bicentenary of the discovery of the island by Cook. 7¢ Cook's portrait by Hodges, 10¢ the *Resolution* portrayed by Roberts. 1974, Oct. Terres Australes et Antarctiques Françaises. Air Post stamps. 150fr a penguin, a map of Antarctica, and letters. Issued to commemorate the centenary of the Universal Postal Union. 1974, Nov. Tonga series of 2. 5p Cook with the *Resolution,* 25p Cook with Jamestown, St. Helena. 1974, Dec. Falkland Islands series. 6p the *Achilles,* 16p the *Ajax.* 1974. Terres Australes et Antarctiques Françaises. Air Post stamps. 100fr the *Français,* 200fr the *Pourquoi Pas?* 1975. Ross Dependency series. 3¢ skua, 4¢ Hercules plane unloading at Williams Field, 5¢ Shackleton's hut at Cape Royds, 8¢ naval supply ship the *Endeavour* unloading, 10¢ Scott Base, 18¢ tabular ice floe. 1975, June. Argentina. Series of 2p on pioneers of Antarctica. Hugo A. Acuña and Orcadas Station, Francisco P. Moreno and Lake Nahuel Huapi, Lt. Col. Luís Piedra Buena and the icebreaker *Luisito,* Ensign José M. Sobral and Snow Hill House, Capt. Carlos M. Moyano and Cerro del Toro. 1975, Aug. Cook Islands series of 1. The $2 commemorated the completion of Cook's second voyage. 1975, Oct. Falkland Islands series. 16p Falkland Islands Dependencies coat of arms. 1975, Dec. Falkland Islands series. 5½p gentoo penguins, 10p black-browed albatross. 1976. South Georgia series commemorating the 50th anniversary of the Discovery Investigations. 2p a picture of the *Discovery* and biological laboratory, 8p the *William Scoresby* and Nansen-Pettersson water sampling bottles, 11p the *Discovery II* and plankton net, 25p biological station and krill. 1976, Jan. Terres Australes et Antarctiques Françaises series. 40¢ Antarctic tern,

50¢ Antarctic petrel, 90¢ sea lioness, 1fr Weddell seal, 1.20fr Kerguélen cormorant, 1.40fr gentoo penguin. **1976, Jan.** Terres Australes et Antarctiques Françaises Air Post stamps. 1.20fr Dumont d'Urville Base 1956, 2.70fr the *Commandant Charcot*, 4fr Dumont d'Urville Base 1976. **1976, May.** Cook Islands series of 3 show Cook and the *Resolution*. **1976, Dec.** Terres Australes et Antarctiques Françaises series of 2 commemorating Ross climbing Mount Ross on Kerguélen Island. 30¢ Ross climbing the mountain, 3fr a picture of Ross himself. **1976, Dec. 16.** Terres Australes et Antarctiques Françaises. 70¢ Cook. **1977, Jan.** British Antarctic Territory whales series. 2p sperm, 8p fin, 11p humpback, 25p blue. Issued to commemorate the conservation of whales. **1977, Feb.** Terres Australes et Antarctiques Françaises. 1.10fr blue whale. **1977, Feb.** British Antarctic Territory series commemorating the silver anniversary of Queen Elizabeth II's reign. 6p Prince Philip in Antarctica in 1956–57. **1977, Sept.** Gilbert Islands series on Cook. **1977, Dec.** Tonga. Whale protection series showing sei and fin whales. **1977, Dec. 20.** Terres Australes et Antarctiques Françaises series. 40¢ *Macrocystis algae*, 90¢ albatross, 1fr underwater sampling and scientists, 1.20fr the *Magga Dan*, 1.40 the *Thala Dan* and penguins. **1977, Dec. 24.** Terres Australes et Antarctiques Françaises. 1.90fr had a cartoon noting the 30th anniversary of the French Polar Expeditions. **1978.** South Georgia series. 25p fur seal. **1978.** British Antarctic Territory coronation anniversary series of 3. 25p emperor penguin. **1978, Jan.** Cook Islands series of 3. 50¢ Cook. **1978, Jan.** Norfolk Island series of 3 commemorating the bicentenary of Cook's arrival in the Hawaiian Islands. 18¢ Cook portrayed by Nathaniel Dance, 25¢ Cook discovering the Hawaiian Islands. **1978, July.** Maldive Islands series on Cook. **1978, July 30.** USSR series of Antarctic fauna. 1k crested penguin, 3k white-winged petrel, 4k emperor penguin and chick, 6k white-blooded pikes, 10k sea

elephants. **1978, Aug.** Tonga series showed the voyages of Cook. **1978, Dec.** Aitutaki series commemorating the bicentenary of Cook's death. 50¢ Dance's portrait of Cook, 75¢ Hodges' painting of the *Resolution* and *Adventure*. **1978, Dec.** Tonga series on the conservation of endangered species. 15¢ a whale. **1979.** South Georgia series. 3p the *Resolution*, 6p map of South Georgia and the South Sandwich Islands with Capt. Cook's route, 11p king penguin drawn by Forster, 25p Capt. Cook. These 4 stamps commemorate Cook's voyages. **1979.** British Antarctic Territory series of penguins. 3p macaroni, 8p gentoo, 11p Adélie, 25p emperor. **1979. Dominica.** Captain Cook series. 10¢ Cook and the *Endeavour*, 50¢ Cook and the *Resolution*, 60¢ Cook, the *Discovery*, and a map of the 3rd voyage, $2 Cook's portrait. **1979.** Terres Australes et Antarctiques Françaises. 1fr a petrel. **1979, Jan.** Ascension series of 4 commemorating Cook's voyages. 3p the *Resolution*, 8p Cook's chronometer, 12p a green turtle, 25p a picture of Cook. **1979, Jan. 1.** Terres Australes et Antarctiques Françaises. 1.20fr R. Rallier du Baty. **1979, Jan. 1.** Terres Australes et Antarctiques Françaises Air Post stamps. 2.70fr the *Challenger*, 10fr elephant seals. **1979, April.** Cook Islands series. 20¢ portrait of Cook by John Weber, 30¢ *Resolution* by Henry Roberts, 35¢ the *Endeavour*, 50¢ death of Capt. Cook as portrayed by George Carter. **1980.** Falkland Islands Dependencies series. 50p the *John Biscoe*, £1 the *Bransfield*, £3 the *Endurance*. **1980.** British Antarctic Territory series showed past presidents of the Royal Geographical Society. 3p John Barrow Tula, 7p Sir Clement Markham, 11p Lord Curzon, 15p William Goodenough, 22p James Wordie, 30p Raymond Priestley. **1980, Feb.** Falkland Islands series. 25p killer whale. **1980, Sept.** Argentina series of 500p showed emperor penguin, bearded penguin, Adélie penguin, Papua penguins, sea elephants, South Orkneys, Argentine base, fur seals, giant petrels, blue-eyed cormorants, stormy petrel, Antarctic doves, Puerto Soledad. All issued to commemorate Argentina's 75th anniversary in the South Orkneys. **1980, Nov. 17.** Belgium. Series showed de Gerlache painted by F.J. Navez. **1980, Nov. 24.** USSR. 4k the *Mikhail Somov.* **1980, Dec.** Terres Australes et Antarctiques Françaises. Series included Adélie penguins and sea leopards. **1980, Dec. 15.** Terres Australes et Antarctiques Françaises Air Post stamps. 7.30fr the *Norsel.* **1981.** British Antarctic Territory series commemorating the 20th anniversary of the ratification of the Antarctic Treaty. 10p map of Antarctica, 13p conservation research, 25p satellite image mapping, 26p global geophysics. **1981.** Terres Australes et Antarctiques Françaises. Air Post stamps series. 1.30fr glacial landscape, the Dumont d'Urville Sea, 1.50fr *Chionis,* 2fr Adèle Dumont d'Urville (1798–1842), 3.85fr Arcad III, 5fr 25th anniversary of Charcot Station, 8.40fr the *Antarès.* **1981, Jan. 5.** USSR series issued to publicize 25 years of USSR research in Antarctica. 4k Mirnyy Station, 6k Earth station, rocket, 15k map, supply ship. **1981, June.** Terres Australes et Antarctiques Françaises. 1.80fr a map of Antarctica. Commemorated the 20th anniversary of the ratification of the Antarctic Treaty. **1981, June 6.** Argentina series. 1,000p Esperanza Station, 2,000p cargo plane, map of Vicecomodoro Marambio Station, Marambio Island, 2,000p (another one) Almirante Irízar. This series marked the 20th anniversary of the ratification of the Antarctic Treaty. **1981, June 23.** Chile. 3.50p the Capitán Arturo Prat Naval Base. Issued to commemorate the 20th anniversary of the ratification of the Antarctic Treaty. **1981, Oct. 5.** Argentina. 1,000p a map of Argentine Antarctica and South America, and a whale. Issued to protest indiscriminate whaling. **1982.** Ross Dependency series commemorating the 25th anniversary of Scott Base. 5¢ Adélie penguins, 10¢ tracked vehicles, 20¢ Scott Base, 30¢ a field party in the upper Taylor Valley, 40¢ Vanda Station, 50¢

Scott's hut at Cape Evans. **1982.** Australian Antarctic Territory series of 2 commemorating Mawson. 27¢ Mawson and landscape, 75¢ Mawson and map. **1982, Feb.** Norfolk Island series on whales. 24¢ sperm, 55¢ southern right, 80¢ humpback. **1982, March.** British Antarctic Territory series. 3p land and water, 6p shrubs, 10p dinosaur, 13p volcano, 25p trees, 26p penguins. **1982, July.** British Antarctic Territory series of 4 of Princess Diana. **1982, Sept.** Terres Australes et Antarctiques Françaises Air Post stamps. 5fr the *Commandant Charcot.* **1982, Nov.** Tonga series showed the *Resolution* on the 29s stamp. **1982, Nov.** British Antarctic Territory series on the 10th anniversary of the Convention for Conservation of Antarctic Seals. 5p leopard seal, 10p Weddell seal, 13p elephant seal, 17p fur seal, 25p Ross seal, 34p crabeater seal. **1983.** Turks and Caicos Islands series on whales. 65¢ right, 70¢ killer, 95¢ sperm, $2 blue, $2.20 humpback. **1983.** India. The 1 rupee stamp commemorated the first anniversary of that country's Antarctic expedition. **1983, Feb. 20.** Brazil. The 150cr showed the support ship *Barão de Teffe,* and related to the Antarctic expedition that country made in 1982–83. **1983, March.** British Antarctic Territory series on marine life. **1983, March.** Falkland Islands Dependencies series. 5p *Euphausia superba.* **1983, April.** Australian Antarctic Territory series of 27¢ stamps showing local wildlife: light-mantled sooty albatross, Macquarie Island shags, elephant seals, royal penguins, Antarctic prions. **1983, July 29.** Penrhyn Island series of 5 on "Save the Whales" showing various whale-hunting scenes. **1983, Sept.** Australian Antarctic Territory. 27¢ showed the Antarctic Treaty Consultative meeting at Canberra, Sept. 13–27, 1983. **1983, Nov.** Falkland Islands series. 17p Noorduyn Norseman airplane, 50p Auster plane. **1983, Dec.** British Antarctic Territory series on the manned flight bicentenary. 5p de Havilland Twin Otter, 13p de Havilland Single Otter, 17p Consolidated Canso,

50p Lockheed Vega. **1983, Dec.** Falkland Islands Dependencies series. 50p Auster plane. **1983, Dec. 10.** Argentina series on southern pioneers and fauna showed *Diomedia exulans, Diomedia melanophris, Eudyptes chrysolophus,* Luís Piedra Buena, Carlos Maria Moyano, Luis Py, Augusto Lasserre, *Phoebetria palpebrata, Hydrurga leptonyx, Lobodon carcinophagus, Leptonychotes weddelli.* **1984–87.** Australian Antarctic Territory series. 2¢ summer afternoon, 5¢ dog team at Mawson Station, 10¢ evening, 15¢ Prince Charles Mountains, 20¢ morning, 25¢ sea ice and iceberg, 30¢ Mount Coates, 33¢ Iceberg Alley, Mawson, 36¢ winter evening, 45¢ brash ice, 60¢ midwinter shadows, 75¢ coastline, 85¢ landing field, 90¢ pancake ice, $1 emperor penguins, Auster rookery. **1984, Jan.** Australian Antarctic Territory series of 2 commemorated the 75th anniversary of the South Magnetic Pole trip of David, Mawson and Mackay in 1908–9. 30¢ a prismatic compass, 85¢ an aneroid barometer. **1984, Jan. 1.** Terres Australes et Antarctiques Françaises series showed seals and penguins. **1984, Jan. 1.** Terres Australes et Antarctiques Françaises Air Post stamps. 2.60fr the *Erebus* off the Antarctic ice-cap. **1984, March.** Tonga series on navigators and explorers of the Pacific. 1.50pa James Cook and the *Resolution.* **1984, June 18.** Chile series showed Antarctic colonization. 15p women's expedition, 15p (another one) Villa las Estrellas Station, 15p (yet another one) scouts, flag, Air Force base. **1984, Sept.** Cook Islands series. 60¢ Cook's landing, $2 Weber's portrait of Cook. **1984, Nov.** Tonga. Famous mariners series. 32s Willem Schouten. **1984, Nov.** Terres Australes et Antarctiques Françaises Air Post stamps. 9fr the *Gauss.* **1985, Jan. 1.** Terres Australes et Antarctiques Françaises series showed BIOMASS. **1985, Jan. 1.** Terres Australes et Antarctiques Françaises. Another series. 1.70fr emperor penguins, 2.80fr snowy petrel. **1985, Jan. 1.** Terres Australes et Antarctiques Françaises. Yet another series. 2.20fr Port-Martin. **1985,**

Jan. 1. Terres Australes et Antarctiques Françaises. Still another series. 2fr Liotard. **1985, March.** British Antarctic Territory series commemorated the BGLE 1934–37. 7p the *Penola* in Stella Creek, 22p Northern Base, Winter Island, 27p the D.H. Fox Moth at Southern Base, Barry Island, 54p dog team near Ablation Point, George VI Sound. **1985, April.** Norway. Series of 2 showing Antarctic mountains. **1985, May.** Falkland Islands Dependencies series on albatrosses. 7p *Diomedia chrysostoma,* 22p *Diomedia melanophris,* 27p *Diomedia exulans,* 54p *Phoebetria palpebrata.* **1985, June.** Chile series commemorating the 25th anniversary of the Antarctic Treaty. 15p krill, pack-ice, map, 20p seismological station at General Bernardo O'Higgins Station, 35p georeception station, dish receiver. **1985, July 13.** Argentina series of 10¢ stamps. One of them showed the first Argentine Antarctic flight in 1952. **1985, Nov.** Falkland Islands Dependencies series on naturalists and endangered species. 7p Dumont d'Urville and kelp, 22p John Forster and king penguin, 27p George Forster and tussock grass, 54p Sir Joseph Banks and dove prion. **1985, Nov.** British Antarctic Territory series on naturalists, fauna, and flora. 22p Sir Joseph Dalton Hooker with *Deschampsea antarctica,* 27p Jean René C. Quoy with *Lagenorhyncus cruciger,* 54p James Weddell with *Leptonychotes weddelli,* 7p (sic) Robert McCormick with *Catharacta mcCormicki.* **1986.** Australian Antarctic Territory. 36¢ commemorated the 25th anniversary of the ratification of the Antarctic Treaty and showed a mountain range in the background. **1986, Jan. 1.** Terres Australes et Antarctiques Françaises series. 1fr Antarctic fulmars, 1.70fr giant petrels. **1986, Jan. 1.** Terres Australes et Antarctiques Françaises. Another series. 3fr the *Polarbjörn.* **1986, Jan. 1.** Terres Australes et Antarctiques Françaises. Air Post stamps series. 2.10fr Charcot and the *Pourquoi Pas?,* 14fr Charcot with a ship in a storm. **1986, Jan.** British Antarctic Territory series of 4 commemorating

Halley's Comet. 22p Halley Station. **1986, May.** Terres Australes et Antarctiques Françaises. Air Post stamps. 8fr SPOT satellite over the Antarctic. **1986, May 31.** Argentina series of 10¢ stamps which showed Jubany Base, *Arctocephalus gazella, Otaria bryonia,* General Belgrano Station, *Daption capensis, Diomedia melanophris, Aptenodytes patagonica, Macronectes giganteus,* Hugo Alberto Acuña (1885–1953), *Spheniscus magellanicus, Gallinago gallinage,* Capt. Agustín del Castillo (1855–89). This was the Antarctic bases, pioneers, and fauna series. **1986, July.** St. Helena series on explorers and ships. 1p Ross and the *Erebus,* £1 Cook and the *Endeavour,* £2 Dumont d'Urville and the *Astrolabe.* **1986, July 16.** Chile series. 40p block of 4 showed Antarctic fauna: *Sterna vittata, Phalacrocorax atriceps, Aptenodytes forsteri, Catharacta lonnbergi.* **1986, Oct. 10.** USSR series. 5k icebreaker, helicopters, the *Mikhail Somov* trapped in the ice, 10k the *Mikhail Somov* port side, 50k trapped in ice. **1986, Dec.** British Antarctic Territory series commemorating the 50th anniversary of the International Glaciological Society and the 4 stamps showed different snowflakes. **1986, Dec.** Tonga. A Dumont d'Urville series of 4. The 32s showed Dumont d'Urville and the *Astrolabe.* The others related to Tonga. **1987.** Falkland Islands Dependencies series on birds. 1p Dominican gull, 2p blue-eyed cormorant, 4p brown skua, 5p cape pigeon, 9p fairy prions, 10p chinstrap penguin, 25p light-mantled sooty albatross, 50p southern giant petrel, £1 wandering albatross, £3 king penguin. **1987.** British Antarctic Territory series commemorating Scott. 10p Scott, 24p the *Discovery* at Hut Point in 1902–4, 29p Cape Evans hut in 1911–13, 58p South Pole in 1912. **1987, Jan. 1.** Terres Australes et Antarctiques Françaises. 2fr Marret Base, Adélie Land. **1987, Jan. 1.** Terres Australes et Antarctiques Françaises Air Post stamps. 14.60fr Charcot. Issued to commemorate this explorer. **1987, April.** Falkland Islands series. 29p

southern elephant seal, 58p leopard seal. **1987, June 30.** Hungary. Antarctic research 75th anniversary series. 2fo Cook and ship, 2fo (another one) von Bellingshausen and seals, 2fo (yet another one) Shackleton and penguins, 4fo Amundsen at the Pole, with dog teams, 4fo (another one) Scott and ship, 6fo Byrd and the *Floyd Bennett,* 20fo helicopter landing at Mirnyy Station. **1987, Nov.** Korea. 80w stamp commemorating the first anniversary of their signing of the Antarctic Treaty. **1987, Dec. 2.** USSR series of 18th–19th-century naval commanders. 25k Lazarev. **1988.** France. A semi-postal stamp featured Dumont d'Urville. **1988, Jan. 1.** Terres Australes et Antarctiques Françaises. 6.80fr Wilson's petrel. **1988, Jan. 1.** Terres Australes et Antarctiques Françaises Air Post stamps. Commemorated the 40th anniversary of the French Polar Expedition on its 20fr stamp.

Mount Stancliff. 76°51′S, 145°23′W. 3 miles NE of Saunders Mountain, on the south side of Crevasse Valley Glacier, in the Ford Ranges of Marie Byrd Land. Discovered by a sledging party during Byrd's 1933–35 expedition, in Nov. 1934, and named by Byrd for Olin D. Stancliff.

Stancliff, Olin D. One of the shore party of Byrd's 1933–35 expedition.

The Stancomb-Wills. One of the three longboats used by Shackleton during his abortive British Imperial Transantarctic Expedition of 1914–17. He named it for Dame Janet Stancomb-Wills, one of his patrons.

Stancomb Wills Glacier. 75°18′S, 19° W. A large glacier flowing into the eastern Weddell Sea, where it forms the Stancomb Wills Glacier Tongue, south of Lyddan Island. Discovered aerially on Nov. 5, 1967, and named by the USA in 1969 in association with Stancomb Wills Promontory (now more properly called Stancomb Wills Glacier Tongue), which Shackleton had discovered in 1915.

Stancomb Wills Glacier Tongue. 75° S, 22°W. The seaward extension of the Stancomb Wills Glacier, into the eastern part of the Weddell Sea. Shackleton discovered it in 1915, and named it Stancomb Wills Promontory for Dame Janet Stancomb-Wills, a sponsor. In 1969 the USA redefined it first as Stancomb Wills Ice Tongue, then, more properly as Stancomb Wills Glacier Tongue.

Stancomb Wills Ice Tongue *see* **Stancomb Wills Glacier Tongue**

Stancomb Wills Promontory *see* **Stancomb Wills Glacier Tongue**

Standifer Bluff. 72°32'S, 94°58'W. Part of the Smith Bluffs, which form the NW coast of Dustin Island. 10 miles WSW of the northern tip of the island. Named for J.N. Standifer, photographer in Antarctica, 1967–68.

Standring Inlet. 66°S, 61°03'W. 9 miles long and filled with ice from the Larsen Ice Shelf. The most northeasterly of 3 inlets on the north coast of Jason Peninsula, on the east coast of Graham Land. Surveyed by the FIDS in 1953, and named by them in 1956 for Anthony J. Standring, geologist at Base D in 1953 and 1954. He visited Jason Peninsula with the survey party.

Stanford Nunatak. 76°51'S, 143°18'W. Isolated. 3½ miles NE of Mount Morgan in the eastern part of the Gutenko Nunataks of Marie Byrd Land. Named for Thomas H. Stanford, ionosphere physicist at Byrd Station in 1970.

Stanford Plateau. 85°57'S, 140°W. Over 3,000 m. Ice-capped. 15 miles wide. Between the heads of Leverett Glacier and Kansas Glacier. Ends in the north at the Watson Escarpment. Named for Stanford University, which has sent many researchers to the Antarctic.

Stange Sound. 73°10'S, 76°40'W. 60 miles long. 25 miles wide. On the coast of Ellsworth Land. It is occupied by an ice shelf. On the west are Smyley and Case Islands, on the east is Spaatz Island, on the north is the Ronne Entrance, and on the south is the mainland. Named by Finn Ronne in 1948 for Henry Stange of New York, a contributor to the RARE.

Mount Stanley. 84°09'S, 165°30'E. 3,220 m. NE of the head of Wycoff Glacier, near the western limits of Grindley Plateau in the Queen Alexandra Range. Named by Shackleton's 1907–9 expedition for Dr. Eric Marshall's eldest brother.

Stanley Island. 66°32'S, 63°40'W. Also called Bertrand Island. 2 miles long. 520 meters high. 4 miles NE of Spur Point in the west part of Cabinet Inlet, off the east coast of Graham Land. Charted by the FIDS in 1947, and named by them for Oliver F.G. Stanley, secretary of state for the colonies, who helped create the forerunners of the FIDS in 1943.

Stanley Kemp Peak *see* **Kemp Peak**

Stanley Patch. 62°59'S, 60°38'W. Also called Banco Stacy. A shoal in Port Foster, Deception Island, in the South Shetlands. 2 miles WNW of Fildes Point. Surveyed and named by Lt. Cdr. D.N. Penfold, RN, in 1948–49, for the capital of the Falkland Islands.

Stansbury Peninsula. 62°14'S, 59°W. Juts out from Nelson Island into the Fildes Strait in the South Shetlands.

Mount Stansfield. 66°41'S, 52°50'E. 2½ miles SE of Mount Berrigan. 20 miles WSW of Stor Hånakken Mountain in Enderby Land. Named by the Australians for P.B. Stansfield, supervising radio technician at Wilkes Station in 1961.

Stanton, A.M. First officer on the *Discovery*, 1930–31, during the first half of the BANZARE 1929–31.

Stanton Group. 67°32'S, 61°38'E. Islands close to the coast at the east side of Utstikkar Bay. 4 miles NE of Falla Bluff. They include Kamelen Island, Oldham Island, and the Hogg Islands. Discovered by the BANZARE 1929–31 in Feb. 1931, and named by Mawson for A.M. Stanton.

Stanwix Peak. 70°43'S, 162°39'E. 2,240 m. Surmounts the south side of the head of Astapenko Glacier in the Bowers Mountains. Named by the Australians for Capt. John Stanwix, helicopter pilot with the ANARE, 1960-61 and 1961-62.

Stanwix Ridge. 69°20'S, 158°20'E. Partly ice-covered. A coastal promontory in the Wilson Hills. It extends to the SW part of Davis Bay just west of McLeod Glacier. Named by the Australians for Capt. John Stanwix (*see* **Stanwix Peak**).

The *Star I*. American-built whale catcher made of steel. 130 tons, it had triple-expansion reciprocating engines giving 550 hp and a maximum speed of 12 knots. It had a radio and an 11-man crew. It had served 10 years in Alaska when it went down to Antarctica as one of the five whale catchers serving the *Sir James Clark Ross* expedition of 1923-24. Capt. Pettersen commanded. In early 1924 it went exploring along the Victoria Land coast, and left the Antarctic with the rest of the fleet. In 1924-25 it was back in the Ross Sea with the *Sir James Clark Ross* expedition of 1924-25.

The *Star II*. Whale catcher on the first two expeditions undertaken by the *Sir James Clark Ross*, in 1923-24 and 1924-25. Capt. Iversen commanded on the first one.

The *Star III*. Whale catcher on the first two expeditions undertaken by the *Sir James Clark Ross*, in 1923-24 and 1924-25. Commanded during the first one by Capt. Hartvigsen.

The *Star IV*. Whale catcher on the first two expeditions undertaken by the *Sir James Clark Ross*, in 1923-24 and 1924-25. 90 tons. Commanded during the first one by Capt. Nielsen.

The *Star V*. Whale catcher on the first two expeditions undertaken by the *Sir James Clark Ross*, in 1923-24 and 1924-25. 70 tons. 17 years old in 1923. Commanded during the first trip by Capt. Moewik.

Starbuck Crater. 76°01'S, 133°11'W. Snow-filled. At the base of the west slope of the Mount Bursey massif in Marie Byrd Land. Named for James E. Starbuck, cosmic ray scientist at Amundsen-Scott South Pole Station in 1970.

Starbuck Glacier. 65°38'S, 62°09'W. 15 miles long. Enters Scar Inlet just north of Mount Queequeg, on the east coast of Graham Land. Surveyed by the FIDS in 1947. Named by the UK for the *Moby Dick* character.

Starfish. Live on the sea bed, near the coast.

Starfish Cove. 60°42'S, 45°37'W. Just north of Balin Point on the east side of Signy Island in the South Orkneys. Surveyed in 1933 by the personnel on the *Discovery II*. Resurveyed in 1947 by the FIDS, and named by them for the starfish found here.

Stark Point. 64°02'S, 57°44'W. On the east side of Croft Bay in the northern part of James Ross Island. Formed by almost vertical cliffs rising from the sea to 285 meters. Surveyed by the FIDS in Aug. 1953. Named descriptively by the UK.

Stark Rock. 65°15'S, 64°33'W. Also called Islote Negro. A rock in water 2 miles south of Crulls Island in the Wilhelm Archipelago. Named descriptively by the UK in 1959.

Mount Starlight. 70°12'S, 64°30'E. An extensive ridge of exposed brown rock with steep sides but no sharp peaks. At the west end of the Athos Range in the Prince Charles Mountains. Discovered in Nov. 1955 by J.M. Béchervaise's ANARE party. Named by the Australians for Operation Starlight, during which depots were laid for further work, and mapping and geological investigations done.

Starr Lake. 77°50'S, 166°40'E. A small meltwater lake, ½ mile north of McMurdo Station, on Hut Point Peninsula, Ross Island, between First Crater and Crater Hill. It is a source of water for the station. Named locally in the early 1970s for James W. Starr, USN, steelworker who helped develop the lake for water supply in 1966 and 1967.

Starr Nunatak. 75°54'S, 162°35'E. Marks the north side of the mouth of

Harbord Glacier on the coast of Victoria Land. Named for James W. Starr (see **Starr Lake**).

Starr Peninsula. 71°56'S, 99°46'W. 10 miles long. Ice-covered. Between Wagoner and Potaka Inlets on the north side of Thurston Island. Named for Robert B. Starr, oceanographer on the *Glacier* during the USN Bellingshausen Sea Expedition of 1959–60.

The *Stars and Stripes*. NX 8006. The Fairchild folding wing monoplane taken by Byrd on his 1928–30 expedition. It was 32 feet 10 inches long, had a 50-foot span overall, and an area of 332 square feet. It had a 425 hp Pratt & Whitney Wasp engine. It was abandoned at the end of the expedition, but recovered during Byrd's 1933–35 expedition and brought home to the USA on board ship.

Starshot Glacier. 81°20'S, 160°20'E. 50 miles long. Flows from the Polar Plateau through the Churchill Mountains, then along the west side of the Surveyors Range, and feeds the Ross Ice Shelf just to the east of the Byrd Glacier and to the south of Cape Parr. Named by the NZGSAE 1960–61 because the area was surveyed using star observations.

The Start *see* **Start Point**

Punta Start *see* **Essex Point**

Start Hill. 62°36'S, 61°11'W. Just to the SE of Essex Point at the west end of Livingston Island in the South Shetlands.

Start Point. 62°35'S, 61°13'W. The NW end of Livingston Island in the South Shetlands. Elevation 880 feet. Discovered and named The Start by Bransfield in Jan. 1820, for the point in England which it resembles. Later renamed slightly.

The *Staten Island*. US Navy icebreaker launched in 1942. In the late 1940s it was loaned to the USSR, who operated it as *Severny Veter* (the *North Wind*). On its return to the USA in Dec. 1951 it was named *North Wind*. In April 1952 it was renamed the *Staten Island* to prevent confusion with a US Coast Guard vessel,

the *Northwind*. It took part in Operation Deep Freeze II (1956–57), during which it helped to build Ellsworth Station in January of that summer. It returned for Operation Deep Freeze IV, 61, 63, 65, 67. On Feb. 1, 1966, it had transferred to the US Coast Guard.

Staten Island Heights. 76°49'S, 160°57'E. Flat, ice-covered upland between the Greenville and Alatna Valleys in the Convoy Range of Victoria Land. Named in 1964 for the *Staten Island*.

Statham Peak. 67°41'S, 67°47'S. On the west side of Graham Land.

Station Nunatak. 64°23'S, 57°03'W. Also called Stations Nunatak. 150 m. Isolated. Ice-free. 4½ miles SW of the east end of Snow Hill Island. Surveyed and named in 1902 by Nordenskjöld's expedition, for the closeness to their station.

Station Tarn. 68°35'S, 77°58'E. A freshwater pond near the west end of Breidnes Peninsula, Vestfold Hills, just north of Heidemann Bay. Named by the first ANARE party at Davis Station (1957) because of its proximity to the station.

Stations *see* **Scientific stations, Weather stations**

Statler Hills. 69°55'S, 73°11'E. Just north of Rogers Glacier on the eastern edge of the Amery Ice Shelf. Named by US cartographer John H. Roscoe in 1952 for L.R. Statler, air crewman on Operation Highjump flights over here in 1946–47.

Stauffer Bluff. 76°10'S, 111°46'W. At the NE extremity of Mount Takahe in Marie Byrd Land. Named for Bernhard Stauffer, Swiss geologist at Byrd Station in 1968–69 and 1969–70.

Stauren Peak. 71°51'S, 6°36'E. On Staurneset Spur in the Mühlig-Hofmann Mountains of Queen Maud Land. Name means "the Pole" in Norwegian.

Staurneset Spur. 71°50'S, 6°33'E. Extends NW from Jøkulkyrkja Mountain in the Mühlig-Hofmann Mountains of Queen Maud Land. Name means "the Pole point" in Norwegian.

Stäven *see* **Stamnen Peak**

Stayaway Skerries. 64°45′S, 64°18′W. Group of rocks and low-lying reefs. 1½ miles south of Cape Monaco, off the SW coast of Anvers Island. Named by the UK as a caution to sailors.

Steagall Glacier. 85°38′S, 161°54′W. 15 miles long. Flows from the Rawson Plateau between Mount Alice Gade and Mount Deardorff into Bowman Glacier in the Queen Maud Mountains. Named for Jack Steagall, meteorologist at South Pole Station in 1961.

Stearns, Simeon. Orderly sergeant on the Wilkes Expedition 1838–42. Joined at Tahiti. Run at Sydney.

Stedet Island. 67°33′S, 61°27′E. Also called Nora Island. A small island at the head of Utstikkar Bay. Just north of Falla Bluff, Mac. Robertson Land. Photographed by the LCE 1936–37. Name means "the place" in Norwegian.

Steel Peak. 70°54′S, 63°27′W. 1½ miles north of Mount Nordhill in the eastern ridge of the Welch Mountains of Palmer Land. Named for Capt. Henry E. Steel, US Coast Guard, commander of the *Edisto*, 1969 and 1970.

Mount Steele. 69°50′S, 159°40′E. 1,050 m. 4½ miles ENE of Stevenson Bluff, on the divide between Suvorov Glacier and Manna Glacier in the Wilson Hills. Named for Carlett D. Steele, chief aviation machinist's mate with VX-6. Between 1957 and 1968 he was in Antarctica several times as helicopter crew member and maintenance supervisor.

Steele, Clarence E. Tank driver at East Base during the USAS 1939–41.

Steele Island. 71°S, 60°40′W. 12 miles long. 10 miles wide. Snow-covered. 12 miles SE of Cape Sharbonneau, off the east coast of the Antarctic Peninsula. South of Dolleman Island. Discovered in 1940 by members of East Base during the USAS 1939–41, and named for Clarence E. Steele.

Steepholm. 60°47′S, 45°09′W. The most southerly of the northern group of the Robertson Islands in the South Orkneys. Just north of Skilling Island. In 1912–13 Petter Sørlle named the northern group (except Matthews Island, which he thought to be part of Coronation Island) as Bratholm (steep island). This later became Bratholmene (steep islands) when it was found that there were more than one island. When each individual island was named, this particular one was named Bratholm, and in English this became Steepholm.

The Steeple. 63°26′S, 57°03′W. 465 m. A rocky ridge which forms the NW arm of Mount Carrel, on the east side of Depot Glacier. 1½ miles south of the head of Hope Bay, at the NE end of the Antarctic Peninsula. Discovered by Nordenskjöld's 1901–4 expedition. Named descriptively by the FIDS in 1945.

Steeple Peaks. 71°38′S, 67°03′W. 5 peaks in a line, the NE one being Mount Ward. Sandau Nunatak is also one of them. South of Conchie Glacier on the western edge of Palmer Land. Named descriptively by the UK.

Steeple Point. 71°43′S, 67°19′W. Ice-covered. 2 miles west of Sandau Nunatak of Steeple Peaks, on the west coast of Palmer Land. Named by the UK in association with Steeple Peaks.

Steeple Rock *see* **Sail Rock**

Mount Steere. 76°44′S, 117°49′W. 3,500 m. 4 miles NNW of Mount Frakes in the Crary Mountains of Marie Byrd Land. Lichens and mosses are found here. Named for William C. Steere, biologist at McMurdo Station in 1964–65.

Steershead Crevasses. 81°10′S, 164°W. Crevasses on the Ross Ice Shelf, 70 miles south of Roosevelt Island. Distorted by the glacial outflow from Marie Byrd Land, they resemble the head of a huge steer when seen in outline from the air, as US cartographers Kenneth Bertrand and Fred Alberts did in Nov. 1962 when they named it. It is an excellent landmark for fliers from McMurdo Station to Byrd Station.

Stefan Ice Piedmont. 66°40'S, 66°30' W. Between Cape Rey and Holdfast Point in Graham Land. It overlies the coast between these points. Named by the UK for Josef Stefan (1835–1893), Austrian physicist specializing in ice.

Stefansson Bay. 67°20'S, 59°10'E. The extreme western end of the Mawson Coast of Mac. Robertson Land. It lies at the foot of the Hansen Mountains between Law Promontory and Fold Island. Mawson named it in Feb. 1931 during the BANZARE, for Vilhjalmur Stefansson, Arctic explorer. The bay was defined more accurately by the personnel on the *William Scoresby* in 1936. Photographed by the LCE 1936–37.

¹Stefansson Inlet *see* **Stefansson Strait**

²Stefansson Inlet *see* **Smith Inlet**

Stefansson Sound *see* **Stefansson Strait**

Stefansson Strait. 69°26'S, 62°25'W. Also called Stefansson Inlet, Stefansson Sound, Boggs Strait. Ice-filled. 35 miles long. 3–10 miles wide. Channel between Hearst Island and the east side of the Antarctic Peninsula. When Wilkins flew over this area on Dec. 20, 1928, he saw what he thought was a channel bisecting the Antarctic Peninsula from east to west, and called it Stefansson Strait, for Vilhjalmur Stefansson (*see* **Stefansson Bay**). He thus concluded that the Antarctic Peninsula was not part of the Antarctic mainland. In 1940 the USAS found Wilkins to be in error, and applied the name to where it is now.

Stein, Willy. Bosun on the German New Schwabenland Expedition of 1938–39, under Ritscher.

Stein Islands. 69°39'S, 75°47'E. Two islands in the east part of the Publications Ice Shelf. 8 miles SE of the Søstrene Islands. Photographed by the LCE 1936–37. Named Steinane (the stones) by the Norwegians.

Stein Nunatak. 71°42'S, 7°58'E. The Norwegians call it Steinsteinen. The

largest of the Sørensen Nunataks in the Drygalski Mountains of Queen Maud Land. Named by the Norwegians for Stein Sørensen (*see* **Sørensen Nunataks**).

Stein Nunataks. 71°36'S, 1°15'W. Also called Straumsnutane, Steinane, Steinkumpen. 15 miles east of the Witte Peaks in the NE part of the Ahlmann Ridge in Queen Maud Land. Discovered by Ritscher in 1938–39, and named by him for Willy Stein.

Steinbotnen Cirque. 71°18'S, 13°21'E. In the west wall of Steinmulen Shoulder, in the Gruber Mountains of the Wohlthat Mountains of Queen Maud Land. Discovered by Ritscher in 1938–39. Name means "the stone cirque" in Norwegian.

Steinemann Island. 66°52'S, 67°55' W. 10 miles SW of Mount Vélain, off the NE coast of Adelaide Island. Named by the UK for Samuel Steinemann, Swiss physicist specializing in ice.

Steinen *see* **Bypass Nunatak**

Mount Steinfeld. 75°12'S, 135°52'W. 685 m. Overlooks the confluence of Hull and Kirkpatrick Glaciers on the coast of Marie Byrd Land. Named for Edward F. Steinfeld, Jr., meteorologist at Byrd Station in 1962.

Steinfila Nunatak. 72°12'S, 14°23'E. The most westerly of a small group of nunataks which mark the SW extremity of the Payer Mountains in Queen Maud Land. Name means "the stone file" in Norwegian.

Steinheil Point. 64°51'S, 62°41'W. 5 miles SE of Duthiers Point on the west side of Andvord Bay on the west coast of Graham Land. Charted by de Gerlache in 1897–99. Named by the UK in 1960 for Adolf Steinheil (1832–1893), German pioneer of the telephoto lens, in 1891.

Steinmulen Shoulder. 71°18'S, 13°25' E. A rock shoulder extending north from Mount Zimmermann in the Gruber Mountains of the Wohlthat Mountains in Queen Maud Land. Discovered by Ritscher in 1938–39. Name means "the stone snout" in Norwegian.

Steinnes. 69°22'S, 76°34'E. 4 miles ENE of the Larsemann Hills, on the Ingrid Christensen Coast, at Prydz Bay, in East Antarctica. Photographed by the LCE 1936–37 in 1936. Name means "stone point" in Norwegian.

Steinskaregga Ridge. 71°49'S, 8°54'E. Ice-free. Just north of Steinskaret Gap in the Kurze Mountains of Queen Maud Land. Name means "the stone gap ridge" in Norwegian.

Steinskaret Gap. 71°51'S, 8°57'E. Ice-filled. In the central Kurze Mountains, just south of Steinskaregga Ridge, in Queen Maud Land. Name means "the stone gap" in Norwegian.

Stella Creek. 65°15'S, 64°16'W. A winding, narrow marine passage that extends from Thumb Rock to the SE end of Winter Island, and lies between Winter Island and Galíndez Island in the Argentine Islands of the Wilhelm Archipelago. Charted in 1935 by the BGLE, and named Stella Inlet by Rymill, for the BGLE motorboat, the *Stella*. The feature was subsequently redefined.

Stella Inlet *see* **Stella Creek**

Stellar Crests. 71°05'S, 69°15'W. 4 snow-covered peaks. 2,000 m. They surmount the LeMay Range west of the north part of Planet Heights in the central part of Alexander Island. Named by the UK for their proximity to features named for planets and their satellites.

Stene, K.O. Captain of the *Normanna*, 1912–13.

Stene Point. 60°39'S, 45°42'W. 1½ miles west of Cape Vik on the south coast of Coronation Island in the South Orkneys. Surveyed by the personnel on the *Discovery II* in 1933, and again by the FIDS in 1948–49. Named by the UK for K.O. Stene.

Stenhouse, J.R. b. 1887. d. in action, 1941. Chief officer of the *Aurora*, 1914–15, when that ship took down the Ross Island party of the British Imperial Transantarctic Expedition of 1914–17. He was captain of the ship from 1915–16. Later a commander, he was captain of the *Discovery* from 1925–27.

Stenhouse Bluff. 62°04'S, 58°24'W. Juts out from King George Island into Martel Inlet between Keller Peninsula and Ullman Spur, in the South Shetlands. Charted by Charcot in 1908–10. Named by the UK for J.R. Stenhouse.

Stenhouse Glacier. 62°04'S, 58°25'W. Flows into the head of Visca Anchorage just west of Stenhouse Bluff, between that bluff and Keller Peninsula, on King George Island in the South Shetlands. Charted by Charcot in 1908–10. Named West Stenhouse Glacier by the UK in 1958 in association with the bluff. The name was shortened by the UK later that year.

Stenhouse Nunatak *see* **Mount Pratt**

Stenka Mountain. 71°55'S, 14°46'E. 2,350 m. Forms the central part of Spraglegga Ridge in the Payer Mountains of Queen Maud Land. Discovered by Ritscher in 1938–39. The USSR named it (stenka means little wall) in 1963.

Stepaside Spur. 78°18'S, 161°24'E. 1,750 m. At the east side of the Upper Staircase and Skelton Glacier in Victoria Land. Surveyed and named in 1957 by the NZ party of the BCTAE.

Mount Stephen. 75°42'S, 161°43'E. 810 m. 6 miles east of Mount Howard in the Prince Albert Mountains of Victoria Land. Named for Ronald R. Stephen, meteorologist at Amundsen-Scott South Pole Station in 1966.

Mount Stephen Austin *see* **Mount Austin**

Stephen Island. 75°50'S, 146°54'W. 4 miles long. Ice-covered. The smallest and westernmost of the three grounded islands in the Nickerson Ice Shelf. Actually most of it is in the Ross Sea, only the eastern portion of it touching the western portion of the ice shelf. Named for Alexander Stephen (1795–1875), Scottish shipbuilder of Alexander Stephen and Sons, whose company built the *Terra Nova* in 1884, the *Nimrod* in 1866, and the *Bear* in 1874.

Mount Stephens. 83°23'S, 51°27'W. 2,065 m. Surmounts the western extremity of Saratoga Table in the Forrestal Range of the Pensacola Mountains. Named for Lt. Cdr. H.E. Stephens, USN, Seabee chief who led the construction of Ellsworth Station in 1957.

Mount Stephenson. 69°49'S, 69°43'W. 2,985 m. Highest mountain in the Douglas Range, at the heads of the Toynbee and Sedgwick Glaciers, 8 miles west of George VI Sound, on the east side of Alexander Island. Seen in 1909 by Charcot. Surveyed in 1936 by the BGLE. Resurveyed and named by the FIDS in 1948 for Alfred Stephenson.

Stephenson, Alfred. Surveyor on the BGLE 1934–37. He led the sledge party to the George VI Sound to about 72°S.

Stephenson, H. Name also seen spelled Stevenson. Fireman on the *Endurance*, 1914–16.

Stephenson, Dr. Jon. Phillip Jonathan Stephenson. Australian geologist who crossed the continent with Fuchs during the BCTAE 1955–58. An ANARE scientist he later (1963) worked on Heard Island (53°S).

Stephenson Bastion. 80°46'S, 27°12'W. In the southern part of the Shackleton Range. 1,850 m. Named by the UK for Dr. Jon Stephenson.

Stephenson Nunatak. 72°11'S, 69°05'W. 640 m. Pyramidal. At the NW side of Kirwan Inlet in the SE part of Alexander Island. Discovered and surveyed in 1940–41 by Ronne and Eklund of East Base during the USAS 1939–41. Resurveyed in 1949 by the FIDS. Named by the UK for Alfred Stephenson.

Stepping Stones. 64°47'S, 63°59'W. 3 tiny islands ½ mile north of Limitrophe Island, off Anvers Island, in the area of Palmer Station. A series of boat refuges, they form stepping stones for coastal trips

between Palmer Station and Biscoe Bay. Named by personnel at Palmer Station in 1972.

Stepup Col. 63°34'S, 57°51'W. Snow-covered. Links Broad Valley with Cugnot Ice Piedmont at the east end of the Louis Philippe Plateau, Trinity Peninsula. Named by the UK. When one traverses the col in a northerly direction, one gains 100 feet in height.

Steregushchiy Point. 67°40'S, 45°55'E. On Alasheyev Bight in Enderby Land, about 2 miles east of Molodezhnaya Station.

Sterna Island. 65°23'S, 64°14'W. Small island, almost ¾ mile north of Darboux Island off the west coast of Graham Land. Charted by the BGLE 1934–37. Named by the UK in 1959 for the large number of Antarctic terns *(Sterna vittata)* here.

Cape Sterneck. 64°04'S, 61°02'W. Also called Cape von Sterneck, Cape Charles, Cape Herschel, Cabo Teniente Vivot. Forms the north side of the entrance to Hughes Bay on the west coast of the Antarctic Peninsula. This is probably where Davis' landing took place in 1821. Explored and named in 1898 by de Gerlache for the German geophysicist whose apparatus was used on the expedition.

Sterneck Island *see* **Apéndice Island**

Sterrett, James M. Biologist on the shore party of Byrd's 1933–35 expedition.

Sterrett Islands. 73°48'S, 103°23'W. Small group in the Amundsen Sea. 5 miles NW of Edwards Islands. 5 miles west of Canisteo Peninsula. Named for James M. Sterrett.

Steuri Glacier. 76°23'S, 112°24'W. Flows from the southern slopes of Mount Takahe in Marie Byrd Land. 3½ miles west of Möll Spur. Named for Heinrich Steuri, Swiss glaciologist at Byrd Station in 1968–69.

Stevens, A.O. Chief of scientific staff of the Ross Sea party during the abortive British Imperial Transantarctic Expedition of 1914–17.

Stevens, Benjamin. Seaman on the Wilkes Expedition 1838–42. Joined in the USA. Returned in the *Relief* in 1839.

Stevens Rock. 67°37'S, 64°42'E. Also called Stevensskjeret. An ice-free rock in water, 1½ miles east of Strahan Glacier and one mile off the coast. Discovered in Feb. 1931 by the BANZARE, and named by Mawson for Cdr. C.W. Stevens, hydrographic department of the RAN (Royal Australian Navy).

Stevenson Bluff. 69°51'S, 159°28'E. 4 miles NW of Mount Ellery in the Wilson Hills. Forms a portion of the divide between the Suvorov and Manna Glaciers. Named for William P. Stevenson, VX-6 aviation machinist's mate and helicopter crew member at McMurdo Station in 1968.

Stevenson Cove. 66°15'S, 110°37'E. On the north side of Clark Peninsula, 2 miles ENE of Wilkes Station. Named by Carl Eklund in 1957 for Andrew Stevenson, economic adviser to the US House of Representatives Committee on Interstate and Foreign Commerce, author of a report for the committee on the IGY in the Arctic and the Antarctic.

Stevenson Glacier. 70°05'S, 72°45'E. Flows into the eastern side of the Amery Ice Shelf, just north of the Branstetter Rocks. Named by US cartographer John H. Roscoe in 1952 for Lt. James C. Stevenson, co-pilot on Operation Highjump flights here in 1946–47.

Stevenson Island. 67°26'S, 61°11'E. Small island, 120 meters high. At the east side of the Colbeck Archipelago. 2 miles NE of Cape Simpson. Discovered in Feb. 1931 by the BANZARE and named by Mawson for Capt. J.B. Stevenson, RN, a member of the Australian *Aurora* Committee of 1916–17.

Stevenson Peak. 72°25'S, 168°17'E. 1,780 m. 5 miles WNW of Bypass Hill in the Cartographers Range of the Victory Mountains of Victoria Land. Named for Robert G. Stevenson, geologist at McMurdo Station in 1967–68.

Stevensskjeret *see* **Stevens Rock**

Steventon Island. 77°15'S, 148°15'W. 24 miles long. The biggest of the grounded islands in the Sulzberger Ice Shelf. West of Court Ridge. Named for Richard F. Steventon, USN, petty officer in charge of Eights Station in 1963.

Steward, John. Seaman on the Wilkes Expedition 1838–42. Joined in the USA. Served the cruise.

Steward, Robert. Ordinary seaman on the Wilkes Expedition 1838–42. Joined at Rio. Run at Aurora Island.

Steward, Samuel. Landsman on the Wilkes Expedition 1838–42. Joined in the USA. Run at Rio.

Steward, William. Captain of the maintop during the Wilkes Expedition 1838–42. Joined in the USA. Was on the *Peacock* on March 9, 1839, when he was knocked off the yard, fell into the sea, and died two days later from internal injuries.

Stewart, Hampton. Crew member on the *Jane Maria,* 1819–21, who made manuscript maps of the South Shetlands, the first of their kind of that area.

Stewart, Reginald H.A. Meteorologist in the Advance Party of the BCTAE 1955–58.

Stewart, W.C. Crewman on the *Jacob Ruppert,* 1933–34, and 3rd assistant engineer, 1934–35.

Stewart Buttress. 79°07'S, 28°30'W. 1,005 m. A bluff 2 miles south of Marø Cliffs in the Theron Mountains. Named by the BCTAE for Reginald H.A. Stewart.

Stewart Glacier. 77°29'S, 151°25'W. On the north side of Edward VII Peninsula, flowing along the east side of the Howard Heights into the Sulzberger Ice Shelf. Named for Lt. Cdr. Wayne B. Stewart, USN, Hercules aircraft co-pilot, 1968.

Stewart Heights. 73°29'S, 163°58'E. Partly snow-covered. 2,760 meters at their highest. Just south of the Arrowhead

Range. Between the upper forks of Cosmonaut Glacier and the Southern Cross Mountains of Victoria Land. Named by the southern party of the NZGSAE 1966–67, for Ian Stewart, field assistant with the party.

Stewart Hills. 84°12'S, 86°W. 50 miles NE of the Ford Massif in the Thiel Mountains. Discovered by the USARP Horlick Mountains Traverse of 1958–59, and again on Dec. 13, 1959, by Edward Thiel and Campbell Craddock, who named them for Prof. Duncan Stewart, geologist and major student of Antarctic rocks at Carleton College, Minnesota.

Stewart Monuments *see* **Stewart Stacks**

Stewart Stacks. 62°38'S, 61°12'W. Two sea stacks on the south side of New Plymouth, between Astor and Rugged Islands, in the South Shetlands. Named Stewart Monuments by Robert Fildes in 1822 for Hampton Stewart. Redefined by the UK in 1958.

Stibbs Bay *see* **Utstikkar Bay**

Stibnite *see* **Antimony**

Stich Peak. 85°57'S, 132°01'W. 2,305 m. On the west side of Reedy Glacier. Between May Peak and Chapin Peak in the Quartz Hills. Named for Lt. Cdr. John D. Stich, USN, pilot at McMurdo Station in 1962–63 and 1963–64.

Mount Stierer. 75°06'S, 162°09'E. 1,080 m. 1½ miles NNE of Mount Bellingshausen in the Prince Albert Mountains of Victoria Land. Named for Byron A. Stierer, USAF, airman first class, at McMurdo Station, 1962.

Stig Nunatak. 73°20'S, 3°14'W. Also called Stignabben. 3 miles NE of Mount Hallgren in the Kirwan Escarpment of Queen Maud Land. Named by the Norwegians for Stig Hallgren.

Stigant Point. 62°02'S, 58°45'W. 65 m. 6 miles SW of Davey Point on the north coast of King George Island in the South Shetlands. Charted by the personnel on the *Discovery II* in 1935 and named by them for G.B. Stigant, a

member of the Hydrographic Department of the British Admiralty.

Stignabben *see* **Stig Nunatak**

Stillwell, Frank L. Geologist on the AAE 1911–14. He led a party exploring the East Antarctic coastline.

Stillwell Hills. 67°26'S, 59°28'E. On the SW side of William Scoresby Bay in Enderby Land. Included are Lealand Bluff, Kemp Peak. Explored in Feb. 1936 by the personnel of the *William Scoresby*, and by the LCE 1936–37. Named by the Australians for Frank L. Stillwell.

Stillwell Island. 66°55'S, 143°48'E. ¼ mile in diameter. Largest member of the Way Archipelago. At the west side of the entrance to Watt Bay, 1½ miles NE of Garnet Point. Discovered by the AAE 1911–14, and named by Mawson for Frank L. Stillwell.

Mount Stinear. 73°05'S, 66°24'E. 1,950 m. In the Prince Charles Mountains, just east of Mount Rymill, at the junction of the Fisher and Lambert Glaciers. Named by the Australians for Bruce H. Stinear (*see* **Stinear Nunataks**), who first visited it with his ANARE party in Oct. 1957.

Stinear Island. 67°35'S, 62°49'E. One of the Flat Islands. 350 yards north of Béchervaise Island in Holme Bay, Mac. Robertson Land. Part of what was once called Flatøy (q.v.) by the Norwegians. Discovered to be a separate island by the ANARE in 1954, and named by the Australians for Bruce Stinear (*see* **Stinear Nunataks**).

Stinear Lake. 68°34'S, 78°09'E. Salt water. 1½ miles long. ¼ mile wide. Just east of Lake Dingle in the Breidnes Peninsula of the Vestfold Hills. Visited by the ANARE in 1955. Named by the Australians for Bruce Stinear (*see* **Stinear Nunataks**).

Stinear Nunataks. 69°42'S, 64°40'E. Also called Southern Nunataks. Dark brown nunataks 16 miles north of the Anare Nunataks in Mac. Robertson

Land. Visited and named by Robert Dovers in 1954, for Bruce H. Stinear, Australian geophysicist at Mawson Station in 1954, 1957, and 1959.

Stinker Point. 61°13′S, 55°23′W. 4 miles south of Table Bay on the west coast of Elephant Island in the South Shetlands. Named by the UK for the giant petrels which breed here. Stinker is the nickname of this bird.

Stipple Rocks. 68°06′S, 67°22′W. More than 20 rocks in water, 3 miles NW of Millerand Island in Marguerite Bay, off the west coast of Graham Land. Surveyed in 1936 by the BGLE, and again in 1949 by the FIDS who named this compact group for the way it looks on a map.

Mount Stirling. 71°33′S, 164°07′E. 2,260 m. Forms part of the east wall of Leap Year Glacier, 5 miles SW of Mount Freed, in the Bowers Mountains. Named by the New Zealanders here in 1967–68 for I. Stirling, zoologist at Scott Base that season.

Stocking Glacier. 77°43′S, 161°50′E. Just east of Catspaw Glacier, it flows south toward Taylor Glacier in Victoria Land. Named by Grif Taylor during Scott's 1910–13 expedition, for its appearance as seen from above.

Stockton Peak. 71°08′S, 62°10′W. Mostly ice-covered. On the south side of the upper part of Murrish Glacier. 6 miles WNW of Cat Ridge in Palmer Land. Named for William L. Stockton, biologist at Palmer Station in 1972.

Stoker Island. 62°24′S, 59°51′W. Almost 1⅓ miles WSW of Emeline Island in the South Shetlands. There is a chinstrap penguin rookery here. Named by the UK for Donald N. Tait, stoker of the survey motor boat *Nimrod* of the RN Hydrographic Survey Unit here in 1967.

Stokes, F.W. American artist who joined the Nordenskjöld expedition of 1901–4 in Buenos Aires on Dec. 15, 1901.

Stokes Hill. 64°52′S, 63°32′W. Also called Monte Teniente. 270 m. 1 mile SE

of Doumer Hill on Doumer Island in the Palmer Archipelago. Charted by Charcot in 1903–5. Named by the UK for the engineer (stokes means stoker in British naval slang) of the Naval Hydrographic Survey Unit's motor launch here in 1956–57. He was the first to climb this hill.

Stokes Peaks. 67°24′S, 68°09′W. On the west side of Graham Land.

Stoltz Island. Just off the NW tip of Alexander Island.

Stolze Peak. 64°43′S, 62°26′W. On the Arctowski Peninsula near the head of Beaupré Cove, on the west coast of Graham Land. Named by the UK in 1960 for Franz Stolze, German pioneer in aerial photography.

Stone Point. 63°24′S, 56°56′W. Also called Punta Candado. Has a small islet lying off it. Marks the south side of the entrance to Hope Bay, at the NE end of the Antarctic Peninsula. Named by the UK for H.W. Stone, first mate on the *Trepassey*, 1946–47, following a survey by Lt. Cdr. F.W. Hunt, RN, in 1952.

Stonecracker *see* **Chinstrap penguin**

Stonehocker Point. 66°15′S, 110°31′E. Forms the western extremity of Clark Peninsula on the coast of East Antarctica. Wilkes Station is on this point. Named by Carl Eklund in 1957 for Garth H. Stonehocker, ionosphere scientist at Wilkes Station in 1957.

Mount Stonehouse. 84°25′S, 164°24′E. 2,900 m. 3½ miles SW of Mount Falla in the Queen Alexandra Range. Named by the New Zealanders in 1961–62 for Bernard Stonehouse.

Stonehouse, Bernard. FIDS meteorologist at Base E in 1947 and 1948, and biologist there in 1949. One of the leading experts on penguins (*see* the Bibliography).

Stonehouse Bay. 67°21′S, 68°05′W. 5 miles wide. Indents the east coast of Adelaide Island between Hunt Peak and Sighing Peak. Discovered and surveyed in 1909 by Charcot. Named later by the FIDS for Bernard Stonehouse.

Stoneley Point. 63°52'S, 58°07'W. On the NW coast of James Ross Island, 4 miles west of Brandy Bay. Named by the UK for Robert Stoneley, FIDS geologist at Base D in 1952.

Stonethrow Ridge. 62°58'S, 60°45'W. Snow-covered. West of Primero de Mayo Bay, and behind Fumarole Bay on Deception Island in the South Shetlands. Surveyed in Jan. 1954 by the FIDS, and named by them for the stones at the base of the steep east face thrown off the ridge.

Stonington Island. 68°11'S, 67°W. 1 mile NE of Neny Island, off the west coast of Graham Land, in the east part of Marguerite Bay. It is connected by a drifted snow slope to Northeast Glacier on the mainland. 2,500 feet long. 1,000 feet wide. Named for the Connecticut town from which many of the whaling and sealing ships issued forth over the centuries. Selected on March 8, 1940, to be the site of East Base during the USAS 1939–41. It was later the site of the FIDS station Base E.

Stopes Point. 76°37'S, 159°37'E. The most northerly point on Tilman Ridge, the NW arm of the Allan Hills in Victoria Land. Named by the New Zealanders in 1964 for Marie Stopes (1880–1958) authority on carboniferous paleobotany, and later pioneer of birth control.

Cape Stopford *see* **Stopford Peak**

Stopford Peak. 63°46'S, 61°38'W. Also called Monte Sud, Monte Sur. 495 m. On the east side of Hoseason Island in the Palmer Archipelago. Foster charted it in 1829, and called it Cape Stopford for Adm. Sir Robert Stopford (1768–1847), commander-in-chief at Portsmouth, 1827–30, where Foster's ship, the *Chanticleer,* was fitted out for the expedition. Later redefined.

Stor Hånakken Mountain. 66°32'S, 53°38'E. Also called the Great Hånakken, Mount Bennett. 1,970 m. In the central part of the Napier Mountains in Enderby Land. Photographed in 1937 by the LCE 1936–37. Name means "the great shark's neck" in Norwegian.

Store Point. 68°12'S, 67°02'W. The northernmost point of Neny Island in Marguerite Bay off the west coast of Graham Land. Surveyed by the FIDS in 1947, and named by them for their food store here.

Store Svarthorn Peak. 71°35'S, 12°33' E. 2,490 m. A black peak at the SW end of the Mittlere Petermann Range in the Wohlthat Mountains of Queen Maud Land. Discovered by Ritscher in 1938–39, and named by him as Grosses Schwarz-Horn (great black peak). The Norwegians translated it as Store Svarthorn, which means the same thing.

Mount Storegutt. 66°53'S, 55°27'E. 1,465 m. 28 miles west of Edward VIII Bay, and 10 miles south of Jennings Bluff. Photographed by the LCE 1936–37. Name means "big boy" in Norwegian.

Storeidet Col. 71°41'S, 11°31'E. 3½ miles west of Eidshaugane Peaks in the central part of the Humboldt Mountains of Queen Maud Land. Discovered by Ritscher in 1938–39. Name means "the great isthmus" in Norwegian.

Mount Storer. 66°53'S, 51°E. In the Tula Mountains, 4 miles ENE of Mount Harvey. Discovered from Observation Island in Oct. 1956 by P.W. Crohn's ANARE party. Named by the Australians for William Storer, radio operator at Mawson Station in 1954.

Storjoen Peak. 72°07'S, 0°12'W. 4 miles NW of Tvora in the Sverdrup Mountains of Queen Maud Land. Name means "the skua" in Norwegian.

Stork Ridge. 67°31'S, 68°12'W. In Adelaide Island.

Storkletten Peak. 72°03'S, 3°25'W. Ice-free. 1 mile south of Flårjuven Bluff, on the Ahlmann Ridge of Queen Maud Land. Name means "the big, steep mountain" in Norwegian.

Storknolten Peak. 72°11'S, 8°03'E. 1 mile west of Müller Crest at the south end of the Filchner Mountains in Queen Maud Land. Name means "the big knoll" in Norwegian.

Storkvaeven Cirque. 72°42'S, 0°09'E. On the NW side of Nupskåpa Peak, near the south end of the Sverdrup Mountains of Queen Maud Land. Named by the Norwegians.

Storkvammen Cirque. 71°44'S, 11°44' E. Between Eidsgavlen and Kvamsgavlen Cliffs on the east side of the Humboldt Mountains in Queen Maud Land. Discovered by Ritscher in 1938–39. Named by the Norwegians.

Storkvarvet Mountain. 71°45'S, 6°54' E. It is round with several radial spurs. North of Habermehl Peak at the NE end of the Mühlig-Hofmann Mountains in Queen Maud Land. Name means "the big round of logs" in Norwegian.

Storkvarvsteinen Peak. 71°36'S, 7°04' E. Isolated. 8 miles NE of Storkvarvet Mountain in the Mühlig-Hofmann Mountains of Queen Maud Land. Name means "the big round of logs rock" in Norwegian.

Storm Peak. 84°35'S, 163°59'E. Also called Storm Peaks. 3,280 m. Flat-topped. 3½ miles north of Blizzard Peak in the Marshall Mountains in the southern sector of the Queen Alexandra Range. Named by the NZGSAE 1961–62 for the storms here.

Storm Peaks *see* **Storm Peak**

Stornes Peninsula. 69°26'S, 76°05'E. 3 miles long. On the shore of Prydz Bay, on the Ingrid Christensen Coast, just west of the Larsemann Hills. Photographed by the LCE 1936–37. Name means "the big promontory" in Norwegian.

Stornupen Peak. 72°10'S, 2°22'E. 2,275 m. In the south part of the Nupskammen Ridge in the Gjelsvik Mountains of Queen Maud Land. Name means "the big mountain peak" in Norwegian.

Stornuten *see* **Mount Maines**

Storsåtklubben Ridge. 71°25'S, 12°25' E. 3 miles long. 5 miles NE of Mount

Hansen in the Mittlere Petermann Range of the Wohlthat Mountains of Queen Maud Land. Discovered by Ritscher in 1938–39. Name means "the large haystack mallet" in Norwegian.

Storsponen Nunatak. 72°S, 3°56'E. On the west side of Hoggestabben Butte in the Mühlig-Hofmann Mountains of Queen Maud Land. Name means "the big chip" in Norwegian.

Stout Spur. 84°52'S, 63°43'W. A knifelike rock spur descending from the north edge of Mackin Table, 3 miles east of Mount Campleman in the Patuxent Range of the Pensacola Mountains. Named for Dennis K. Stout, radioman at Palmer Station in 1967.

Strachan Hill *see* **Spiro Hill**

Strachan's Island *see* **Nelson Island**

Strachey Stump. 80°41'S, 23°10'W. A peak in the Shackleton Range.

Strafford, John. Seaman on the Wilkes Expedition 1838–42. Joined at Valparaiso. Served the cruise.

Straggle Islands *see* **Llanquihue Islands**

Straham, James. Seaman on the Wilkes Expedition 1838–42. Joined in the USA. Served the cruise.

Strahan Glacier. 67°38'S, 64°37'E. Flows into the sea, 1½ miles west of Stevens Rock, between Cape Daly and Cape Fletcher, in East Antarctica. Discovered in Feb. 1931 by the BANZARE, and named by Mawson for F. Strahan, assistant secretary, Prime Minister's Department in Australia, 1921–35.

Strand Moraines. 77°44'S, 164°31'E. Also called Stranded Moraines. An ancient lateral moraine of the Koettlitz Glacier in southern Victoria Land. Scott's 1901–4 expedition discovered and named it Eskers (the name means a morainal deposit). Scott later renamed it.

Stranded Moraines *see* **Strand Moraines**

Strandnebba. 69°57'S, 38°49'E. Ice-free hills 1 mile SW of Vesleknausen

Rock. They extend along the south shore of Lützow-Holm Bay for 1½ miles. Photographed by the LCE 1936–37. Name means "the shore beak" in Norwegian.

Strandrud. One of the mechanics on the LCE 1936–37.

Strandrud Mountain. 71°52′S, 25°36′ E. 2,070 m. At the SE side of the Austkampane Hills in the Sør Rondane Mountains. Named by the Norwegians for Strandrud (q.v.).

Mount Strandtmann. 72°07′S, 163°05′ E. 3 miles north of Smiths Bench, in the Freyberg Mountains. Named for Russell W. Strandtmann, biologist at McMurdo Station in 1966–67 and 1967–68.

Mount Strange. 74°58′S, 113°29′W. Partly ice-free. 4 miles ENE of Mount Isherwood, at the east side of the Simmons Glacier, in the Kohler Range of Marie Byrd Land. Algae and lichens are found here. Named in the 1960s for Joe F. Strange, topographic engineer on the Marie Byrd Land Survey Party of 1966–67.

Strange Glacier. 74°50′S, 63°40′W. In the Latady Mountains. It flows along the south side of Crain Ridge into Gardner Inlet, between Schmitt Mesa and Mount Austin, on the east coast of southern Palmer Land. Named for Donald L. Strange, hospital corpsman at Amundsen-Scott South Pole Station in 1964.

The *Stranger*. Boston whaling brig which sailed from Fairhaven, Mass., on a sealing expedition to the South Shetlands in 1820–21, under the command of Capt. Joseph Adams. It anchored in Yankee Harbor, and got about 1,000 skins.

Stranger Point. 62°16′S, 58°37′W. Forms the southerly tip of King George Island in the South Shetlands. Named by the UK in 1960 for the *Stranger*. Also called Punta Pingüinera.

Strath Point. 64°32′S, 62°36′W. Also called Cabo Lagrange. Ice-covered. Forms the south end of Brabant Island. Charted by de Gerlache in 1897–99.

Named by the UK. A strath is a stretch of flat land by the sea.

Mount Strathcona. 67°22′S, 99°12′E. 1,380 m. 11 miles south of Mount Barr Smith, on the west side of Denman Glacier. Discovered by the AAE 1911–14, and named by Mawson for Lord Strathcona, a patron of the expedition.

Stratton, David G. FIDS surveyor at Base D in 1952 and 1953. Made the first detailed survey of the Jason Peninsula, in May–June 1953. He was second-in-command to Fuchs during the BCTAE 1955–58.

Stratton Glacier. 80°22′S, 29°W. 20 miles long. Flows from Pointer Nunatak to the north of Mount Weston in the Shackleton Range. Named in 1957 by the BCTAE for David G. Stratton.

Stratton Inlet. 66°18′S, 61°25′W. 12 miles wide. Ice-filled. It is entered east of Veier Head on the south side of the Jason Peninsula, in Graham Land. Surveyed by the FIDS in 1953. Named in 1956 by the FIDS for David G. Stratton, who led the survey party (*see* **Stratton**).

Straumsida Bluff. 71°44′S, 1°15′W. 25 miles long. Ice-covered. Part of the east slope of the Ahlmann Ridge of Queen Maud Land. Overlooks the terminus of Jutulstraumen Glacier. Name means "the stream side" in Norwegian.

Straumsnutane *see* **Stein Nunataks**

Straumsvola Mountain. 72°07′S, 0°20′ W. 6 miles north of Jutulrøra Mountain in the NW part of the Sverdrup Mountains, overlooking the east side of the Jutulstraumen Glacier in Queen Maud Land. Name means "the stream mountain" in Norwegian.

Mount Strauss. 71°32′S, 73°11′W. Snow-covered. 250 m. 4 miles east of the head of Brahms Inlet in the SW part of Alexander Island. Named by the UK for the composer.

Strauss Glacier. 77°20′S, 139°40′W. 40 miles long. Flows between the Ickes Mountains and the Coulter Heights to enter the sea at the east side of Land Bay on the coast of Marie Byrd Land. Named by Byrd for Lewis Strauss, chairman of the Atomic Energy Commission, who proposed peaceful purposes for atomic energy in Antarctica.

Stravinsky Inlet. 72°20′S, 71°30′W. Ice-covered. Between Shostakovich Peninsula and Monteverdi Peninsula in the southern part of Alexander Island. Named by the UK for the composer.

Strawberry Cirque. 83°20′S, 157°36′E. Semi-circular glacial cirque. 1 mile wide. At the south end of the Macdonald Bluffs in the Miller Range. Indents the cliffs at the north side of the terminus of Argo Glacier where that glacier enters Marsh Glacier. Named by the Ohio State University Geological Party of 1967–68 for the color seen here in certain lights.

Strawn Pass. 75°06′S, 135°16′W. On the south side of the McDonald Heights. It connects the heads of Kirkpatrick Glacier and Johnson Glacier in Marie Byrd Land. Named for Lawrence W. Strawn, glaciologist at Byrd Station in 1967–68.

Stray Islands. 65°10′S, 64°14′W. Also called Islotes Labbe. 2 miles west of Petermann Island in the Wilhelm Archipelago. Named by the UK because the group is scattered.

Streitenberger Cliff. 85°03′S, 92°07′W. 1⅓ miles west of Reed Ridge, on the NW edge of the Ford Massif in the Thiel Mountains. Named by Bermel and Ford of the Thiel Mountains party here in 1960–61 for Staff Sgt. Fred W. Streitenberger, US Marines, VX-6 navigator of the plane which took the party into the mountains.

Strengen Valley. 72°S, 3°28′W. Ice-filled. 4 miles long. Between Flårjuvnutane Peaks and Flårjuven Bluff on the west side of the Ahlmann Ridge in Queen Maud Land. Name means "the string" in Norwegian.

Stretch, Samuel. Gunner's mate on the Wilkes Expedition 1838–42. Joined in the USA. Served the cruise.

Cape Streten. 66°49′S, 49°15′E. An ice cape at the NE tip of Sakellari Peninsula.

It forms the west side of the entrance to Amundsen Bay. Named by the Australians for N.A. Streten, meteorologist at Mawson Station in 1960.

Striated Nunatak. 67°21′S, 56°13′E. 6 miles east of Rayner Peak, on the east side of Robert Glacier in Enderby Land. Named by the Australians for its striations.

Striation Valley. 70°53′S, 68°23′W. On the east side of Alexander Island.

Strickland Nunatak. 86°29′S, 124°12′W. Between Savage Nunatak and Spear Nunatak, at the head of Reedy Glacier. Named for Ernest E. Strickland, utilitiesman at Byrd Station in 1962.

Stridbukken Mountain. 72°48′S, 3°13′W. 1 mile SW of Møteplassen Peak in the Borg Massif of Queen Maud Land. Name means "the hard head" in Norwegian.

Stride Peak. 67°41′S, 67°38′W. On Adelaide Island.

Strider, John P. Aviation machinist's mate and pilot officer second class, USN. He was crew chief and plane captain on the *Que Sera Sera* in 1956–57, and was on the flight that went to the Pole on Oct. 31, 1956. This was the famous flight that carried Admiral Dufek to 90°S.

Strider Rock. 78°02′S, 155°26′W. 1 mile NW of Mount Nilsen in the Rockefeller Mountains of the Edward VII Peninsula in Marie Byrd Land. Named for John P. Strider.

Stringfellow Glacier. 64°10′S, 60°18′W. Just west of Henson Glacier. Flows from the Detroit Plateau of Graham Land into the Wright Ice Piedmont. Named by the UK for John Stringfellow (1799–1883), aeronautics pioneer.

Striped Hill. 63°40′S, 57°53′W. Ice-free. Near the south shore of Trinity Peninsula. 1 mile ENE of Church Point. Charted by the FIDS in 1946, and named by them for the stripes on a small cliff on the seaward side of the hill.

Stroiteley Islands. 66°33′S, 92°58′E. 4 small islands in the southern part of the Haswell Islands. Close to the mainland of

East Antarctica. 1 mile west of Mabus Point. Named by the USSR in 1956 as Ostrova Stroiteley (builders' islands).

Strom, Sverre. A Norwegian ice pilot. Went to the Antarctic in 1928 as first mate on the *City of New York.* He became a member of the shore party of Byrd's 1928–30 expedition and headed the snowmobile party which hauled supplies in support of field parties. He was replaced on the ship by Harry Adams.

Strom Camp. Near the foot of Strom Glacier. Occupied in Dec. 1929 by Gould's geological party of that year, during Byrd's 1928–30 expedition. Named for Sverre Strom.

Strom Glacier. 85°10'S, 164°30'W. Flows from Mount Fridtjof Nansen, between the Duncan Mountains and the Herbert Range, or between the Liv Glacier and the Axel Heiberg Glacier, into the Ross Ice Shelf. Named for Strom Camp.

Strømme Ridge. 71°27'S, 61°42'W. Ice-covered. 15 miles long. Between the Muus and Soto Glaciers. Ends at the north side of Odom Inlet on the east coast of Palmer Land. Named for Jan A. Strømme, Norwegian member of the International Weddell Sea Oceanographic Expedition of 1968 and 1969.

Mount Strong. 70°35'S, 62°45'W. 5 miles east of the Eland Mountains in Palmer Land. Named for Frank E. Strong, biologist at Palmer Station in 1971–72.

Strong Peak. 79°56'S, 82°19'W. In the Enterprise Hills, 3 miles WSW of Parrish Peak. Overlooks the head of Horseshoe Valley in the Heritage Range. Named for Jack E. Strong, biologist at Palmer Station in 1965.

Mount Stroschein. 84°25'S, 63°35'W. 1,020 m. 2 miles SW of Weber Ridge in the Anderson Hills in the northern part of the Patuxent Range of the Pensacola Mountains. Named for Leander A. Stroschein, meteorologist at Plateau Station in 1965–66 and 1966–67.

Strover Peak. 69°43'S, 74°07'E. 6 miles WNW of Mount Caroline Mikkelsen. Photographed by the LCE 1936–37. Named Svartmulen (the black snout) by the Norwegians. Renamed by the Australians for W.G.H. Strover, radio supervisor at Davis Station in 1963.

Mount Strybing. 78°42'S, 85°04'W. 3,200 m. 3 miles SE of Mount Craddock in the southern part of the Sentinel Range. Named for Master Sgt. Henry Strybing, US Marines, navigator on R4D flights here in 1957–58.

Mount Stuart. 72°33'S, 162°15'E. 1,995 m. 5 miles north of Mount VX-6, in the Monument Nunataks. Named for A.W. Stuart, glaciologist, member of the USARP Victoria Land Traverse Party here in 1959–60.

Stuart, Frederick D. Captain's clerk on the Wilkes Expedition 1838–42. Joined in the USA. Served the cruise. He was on the *Peacock* from 1838–41 and then transferred to the *Vincennes,* staying on Wilkes' ship until the end of the cruise. He assisted Wilkes with the correction of survey data obtained on the expedition.

Stuart Doyle Point   *see*   **Doyle Point**

Stuart Point. 66°28'S, 125°10'E. Ice-covered. At the east side of the entrance to Maury Bay. Named for Frederick D. Stuart.

Stubb Glacier. 65°41'S, 62°10'W. 11 miles long. Flows into Scar Inlet between Mount Queequeg and Tashtego Point, on the east coast of Graham Land. Named by the UK in 1956 for the *Moby Dick* character.

Mount Stubberud. 86°07'S, 158°45'W. Also called Mount Jörgen Stubberud. 2,970 m. 2 miles SE of Beck Peak. North of Nilsen Plateau in the Queen Maud Mountains. In 1911, on his way to the Pole, Amundsen named a peak in this general area as Mount J. Stubberud, for Jörgen Stubberud. This may or may not be the exact peak that Amundsen had in mind, but it is the one which has been arbitrarily selected in order to honor Stubberud.

Stubberud, Jörgen. Carpenter on the *Fram* during the Norwegian Antarctic Expedition of 1910–12, led by Amundsen. One of the shore party, he took part in many of the local coastal expeditions.

Stubbs Pass. 68°11'S, 65°12'W. Runs through the middle of Joerg Peninsula, on the east side of Graham Land. Named by the UK for Guy M. Stubbs, BAS geologist at Base E, 1963–65.

Stuhlinger Ice Piedmont. 70°22'S, 162°30'E. A coastal ice piedmont 10 miles long and 10 miles wide. Just north of the Bowers Mountains, between the lower ends of the Gannutz and Barber Glaciers. Named by the USA in 1968 for Ernst Stuhlinger of NASA, a member of the NSF's advisory panel for Antarctic Programs.

Mount Stump. 86°11'S, 153°02'W. In the Queen Maud Mountains.

Stump Mountain. 67°29'S, 60°56'E. Over 310 m. 2 miles SW of Byrd Head in Mac. Robertson Land. Photographed by the LCE 1936–37. Named Stabben (the stump) by the Norwegians. The Australians translated it.

Stump Rock. 62°05'S, 58°08'W. A rock in the west part of King George Bay, ½ mile NW of Martello Tower in the South Shetlands. Charted and named in 1937 by personnel on the *Discovery II.*

Sturge Island. 67°27'S, 164°38'E. 20 miles long. 4 miles wide. Largest and most southerly of the Balleny Islands. Discovered in Feb. 1839 by John Balleny, who named it for T. Sturge, one of the merchants who sent out the expedition.

Mount Sturm. 71°04'S, 162°59'E. 2,320 m. At the head of the Rastorguev Glacier in the Explorers Range of the Bowers Mountains. Named by the northern party of the NZGSAE 1963–64 for Arnold Sturm, senior geologist on the expedition.

Sturm Cove *see* **Mascías Cove**

Stuttflog Glacier. 71°56'S, 4°45'E. Flows between Mount Grytøyr and Petrellfjellet in the Mühlig-Hofmann Mountains of Queen Maud Land. Name means "the short rock wall glacier" in Norwegian.

Stuttfloget Cliff. 72°04'S, 4°32'E. Forms the SW end of Mount Grytøyr in the Mühlig-Hofmann Mountains of Queen Maud Land. Name means "the short rock wall" in Norwegian.

Styggebrekka Crevasses. 71°58'S, 5°44'E. A crevasse field near the center of Austreskorve Glacier in the Mühlig-Hofmann Mountains of Queen Maud Land. Name means "the dangerous slope" in Norwegian.

Styggebrekkufsa Bluff. 71°55'S, 5°53'E. Overlooks the east-central part of the Austreskorve Glacier in the Mühlig-Hofmann Mountains of Queen Maud Land. Name means "the dangerous-slope bluff" in Norwegian.

Stygian Cove. 60°42'S, 45°37'W. Just west of Berry Head in the northern part of Signy Island in the South Orkneys. Named in 1947 by the FIDS because it is overshadowed by Robin Peak on its west side and a sense of Stygian gloom is felt.

Styles Bluff. 66°41'S, 57°18'E. At the SE side of Edward VIII Plateau, rising out of the sea 1 mile north of Cape Gotley. Photographed by the LCE 1936–37. Visited in Feb. 1960 by an ANARE party led by D.F. Styles (*see* **Styles Strait**). The Australians named it for Styles.

Styles Strait. 66°51'S, 48°35'E. 15 miles long. 6–9 miles wide. Separates White Island from Sakellari Peninsula. Visited in Feb. 1960 and in Feb. 1961 by the ANARE led by D.F. Styles, assistant director, Antarctic Division, Melbourne.

Styrbordsknattane Peaks. 72°13'S, 3°26'W. Just north of Kjølrabbane Hills, near the SW end of the Ahlmann Ridge in Queen Maud Land. Name means "the starboard peaks" in Norwegian.

Styx Glacier. 74°02'S, 163°51'E. In the Southern Cross Mountains of Victoria Land. It enters Campbell Glacier between Wood Ridge and Pinckard Table. Named by the New Zealanders in 1965–66 for the mythical river.

Mount Suarez. 86°27'S, 145°42'W. 2,360 m. Just east of Mount Noville. Between Van Reeth and Robison Glaciers in the Queen Maud Mountains. Named for Lt. (jg) Ralph Suarez, VX-6 navigator in Antarctica in 1965, 1966, and 1967.

Suárez Glacier. 64°56'S, 62°56'W. Also called Petzval Glacier. Flows into the small cove between Skontorp Cove and Mascías Cove on the west coast of Graham Land. Named by the Chilean Antarctic Expedition of 1950–51 for Lt. Cdr. Francisco Suárez, operations officer on the *Angamos*.

Suárez Nunatak. 82°12'S, 41°47'W. 830 m. 5 miles NW of Mount Ferrara in the Panzarini Hills of the Argentina Range of the Pensacola Mountains. Named for Capt. Jorge Suárez, Argentine officer-in-charge of Ellsworth Station in 1959–61.

Subantarctic Surface Water. This forms the northern limit of the Antarctic Ocean (q.v.), between the Subtropical Convergence (40°S) and the Antarctic Convergence (50°S – 60°S), a very broad 20° range, and it is where the warmer waters of the Indian, Pacific, and Atlantic Oceans meet the Antarctic Surface Water (q.v.) and form a mass with combined characteristics.

Sublimation. In the narrower, Antarctic, sense, it means the change from ice directly to water vapor.

Submarines. The first submarine to be tried in Antarctic waters was the *Sennett*. This was the project of Dr. Waldo Lyon, the submarine specialist, who went on Operation Highjump, 1946–47, with his sub. The machine failed, becoming icebound and unable to handle the packice. It was rescued by the *Northwind*. This was a very definite lesson for the future.

Islotes Subof Rubianes *see* **Pi Islands**

Succession Cliffs. 71°11'S, 68°16'W. 1½ miles long. On the east coast of Alexander Island. Face east onto the George

VI Sound, just south of the mouth of Pluto Glacier. Surveyed by the BGLE in 1936 and again by the FIDS in 1948. The FIDS named them for the geologic succession seen here.

Suchland Islands. 74°06'S, 102°32'W. 8 small islands. Just inside the central part of the mouth of Cranton Bay. Named for Everett B. Suchland, Jr., USN, radioman at Byrd Station in 1967.

Sucia Island. 64°58'S, 63°36'W. Also called Littlespace Island. A small, snow-covered island in Flandres Bay, just north of Ménier Island, off the west coast of Graham Land. Name means "foul" in Argentine, and describes the navigational dangers around the island.

Monte Sud *see* **Stopford Peak**

Sudare Rock. 69°42'S, 39°12'E. A rock on land, on the SE shore of Lützow-Holm Bay. 1 mile west of Skallevikhalsen Hills. Photographed by the LCE 1936–37. Named Sudare-iwa (bamboo blinds rock) by the Japanese.

Südliche Petermann Range. 71°46'S, 12°20'E. 22 miles long. Between Svarthausane Crags and Gneiskopf Peak, in the Petermann Ranges of the Wohlthat Mountains in Queen Maud Land. Discovered by Ritscher in 1938–39. Name means "Southern Petermann Range" in German.

Sudor, George. Quartermaster on the Wilkes Expedition 1838–42. Joined in the USA. Sent home on the *Relief* in 1839.

Mount Suess. 77°02'S, 161°42'E. 1,190 m. Just to the south of the Mackay Glacier in Victoria Land. Surmounts the southern part of Gondola Ridge. Discovered by Shackleton in 1907–9, and named by him for Eduard Suess (*see* **Suess Glacier**).

Suess Glacier. 77°38'S, 162°40'E. Between the Canada and Lacroix Glaciers in southern Victoria Land. It feeds the Taylor Valley from the north. Charted and named by Scott's 1910–13 expedition for Prof. Eduard Suess (1838–1914), the

Austrian geologist who first proposed the idea of Gondwanaland (q.v.).

Suffield Point. 62°12'S, 58°55'W. 1½ miles SW of Collins Harbor, on the east side of Fildes Peninsula, on King George Island, in the South Shetlands. Charted and named by personnel on the *Discovery II* in 1935.

Sugarloaf Island. 61°11'S, 54°W. Small island just to the east of Clarence Island in the South Shetlands, between Cape Lloyd and Cape Bowles. Named by sealers before 1822 for its shape.

Mount Suggs. 75°16'S, 72°13'W. 2 miles south of Mount Goodman in the Behrendt Mountains of Ellsworth Land. Named for Henry E. Suggs, Seabee equipment operator who helped open up the new Byrd Station in 1961–62.

Suggs Peak. 75°05'S, 113°06'W. Ice-covered. 6 miles SSW of Mount Wilbanks in the Kohler Range of Marie Byrd Land. Named for James D. Suggs, geologist with the Marie Byrd Land Survey Party of 1966–67.

Suicides. The only known suicide ever committed in Antarctica is also one of history's more glamorous and famous suicides, that of Oates. Frostbitten and ravaged by scurvy, he is thought to have done the honorable thing during Scott's return journey from the Pole in 1912. He was slowing up the rest of the party, and just walked out into the blizzard with the classic last line, "I am just going outside and may be some time." Some historians suspect that Scott and the others threw him out, but this is grossly unfair to Scott, and the nobility of the act is typical of Oates, as were the wry one-liners.

Sukkertoppen *see* **Istind Peak, Mount Zuckerhut**

Mount Sullivan. 69°39'S, 63°49'W. 2,070 m. 12 miles east of the northern part of the Eternity Range in Palmer Land. Charted by the BGLE in 1936–37. Named by Finn Ronne in 1948 for Col. H.R. Sullivan of the Office of Research

and Development of the USAAF, which furnished equipment for the RARE.

Sullivan, S.J. Crewman on the *Jacob Ruppert*, 1933–34.

Sullivan, Walter A. *New York Times* staff writer who was in Antarctica (*see* the Bibliography).

Sullivan Glacier. 69°42'S, 70°45'W. 6 miles long. 3 miles wide. Just south of the Elgar Uplands in the northern part of Alexander Island. Seen from a distance by the BGLE in 1937. Named by the UK for the composer, Sir Arthur Sullivan.

Sullivan Inlet *see* **Mill Inlet**

Sullivan Nunatak. 82°31'S, 156°35'E. 2 miles east of the south end of the Wellman Cliffs in the Geologists Range. Named for James G. Sullivan, geologist at McMurdo Station in 1961.

Sullivan Nunataks. 70°52'S, 65°33'E. 3 nunataks. 2 miles NE of Mount Bewsher in the Aramis Range of the Prince Charles Mountains. Named by the Australians for R.M. Sullivan, radio operator at Wilkes Station in 1968 (*see* **Deaths, 1968**).

Sullivan Peaks. 84°50'S, 63°05'W. Two peaks, over 1,400 m. on a spur descending from Pierce Peak on the north side of the Mackin Table in the Patuxent Range of the Pensacola Mountains. Named for Lt. Ronald C. Sullivan, USN, officer-in-charge of Amundsen-Scott South Pole Station in 1967.

Sullivan Ridge. 84°47'S, 177°05'E. 15 miles long. Overlooks Ramsey Glacier on the east and Much Glacier on the west. The ridge extends north from Husky Heights, and terminates at the confluence of the Ramsey and Much Glaciers. Discovered during Operation Highjump, 1946–47. Named for Walter A. Sullivan.

The *Sultan*. A shore-based Royal Navy engineering school ship at Elephant Island in the South Shetlands. Used as the base of the Joint Services Expedition of 1970–71.

Sultan Glacier. 61°08'S, 55°21'W. Also called Services Glacier. Flows into

Table Bay, Elephant Island, in the South Shetlands. Named by the UK for the *Sultan.*

Sultan's Head *see* **Sultans Head Rock**

Sultan's Head Cliffs *see* **Sultans Head Rock**

Sultans Head Rock. 77°43′S, 167°12′E. Juts out from the south of Ross Island into Windless Bight, 7½ miles SW of the Vee Cliffs. Named descriptively by Scott's 1901–4 expedition as Sultan's Head. This name later became Sultan's Head Cliffs, and then the name by which it is known today (with no apostrophe).

Sulzberger Bay. 77°S, 152°W. Also called Arthur Sulzberger Bay, Sulzberger Embayment, Biscoe Bay. A Ross Sea indentation into the front of the Sulzberger Ice Shelf between Fisher Island and Vollmer Island, on the coast of Marie Byrd Land, between Edward VII Peninsula and Guest Peninsula. Discovered on Dec. 5, 1929, during Byrd's 1928–30 expedition, and named by Byrd for Arthur H. Sulzberger, publisher of the *New York Times,* and a supporter of Byrd's first two expeditions.

Sulzberger Ice Shelf. 77°S, 148°W. A large ice shelf, 85 miles long, and 55 miles wide. It stretches from the Guest Peninsula in the north to the Edward VII Peninsula in the south. It is strictly speaking part of the Ross Sea, and is full of islands: Steventon Island, Kizer Island, Cronenwett Island, Vollmer Island, Hutchinson Island, and Morris Island. It is fed by glaciers like the Boyd Glacier, the Hammond Glacier, and the Crevasse Valley Glacier. Discovered during Byrd's 1928–30 expedition. Named in association with Sulzberger Bay.

Sumgin Buttress. 80°18′S, 25°44′W. In the Shackleton Range.

Summer *see* **Seasons**

Summers Glacier. 72°13′S, 167°28′E. Flows from the area west of Latino Peak into Pearl Harbor Glacier in the Victory Mountains of Victoria Land. Named for James L. Summers, USN, chief utilitiesman at McMurdo Station in 1967.

Summers Peak. 69°42′S, 64°53′E. Also called Bruces Peak. 2,225 m. The highest peak in the Stinear Nunataks in Mac. Robertson Land. Discovered by Robert Dovers and his ANARE southern party of 1954, and named by Dovers for Dr. R.O. Summers, medical officer at Mawson Station in 1954.

Mount Summerson. 82°43′S, 155°05′E. 2,310 m. Surmounts the north end of Endurance Cliffs in the Geologists Range. Named for Charles H. Summerson, geologist in the Mount Weaver area, 1962–63.

Summit Pass. 63°27′S, 57°02′W. 345 m. A col between Passes Peak and Summit Ridge. 2½ miles south of the head of Hope Bay. 3½ miles NE of Duse Bay, at the NE end of the Antarctic Peninsula. First explored by Nordenskjöld's 1901–4 expedition. Charted and named by the FIDS in 1945. It is the highest point on the sledging route between Hope Bay and Duse Bay.

Summit Ridge. 63°27′S, 57°02′W. 380 m. Extends east for ½ mile from Passes Peak. 2 miles south of the head of Hope Bay, at the NE end of the Antarctic Peninsula. Charted by the FIDS in 1945, and named by them in association with nearby Summit Pass.

Mount Sumner. 74°30′S, 63°45′W. At the SE end of the Rare Ridge in Palmer Land. Named for Joseph W. Sumner, utilitiesman at Amundsen-Scott South Pole Station in 1964.

Sumner Glacier. 68°52′S, 65°40′W. Flows into the lower reaches of the Weyerhaeuser Glacier just west of Mount Solus in southern Graham Land. Sketched from the air by D.P. Mason of the FIDS in Aug. 1947. Named by the UK for Thomas H. Sumner (1807–1876), navigation pioneer.

Sumrall Peak. 82°48′S, 53°33′W. 1,130 m. 1 mile south of Rosser Ridge, in the Cordiner Peaks of the Pensacola Mountains. Named for Ensign William H. Sumrall, USNR, airplane pilot at Ellsworth Station in 1957.

Sun-dogs *see* **Phenomena**

Sunburn. Perhaps surprisingly the sun can be fierce. Tourists should bring suntan lotion if they would normally do so in the tropics.

Sunday Island. 66°28'S, 66°27'W. Just north of Rambler Island in the Bragg Islands. Named by Cdr. W.M. Carey of the *Discovery II* in 1930–31. Reidentified and surveyed by the FIDS in 1958.

Mount Sundbeck. 86°10'S, 158°28'W. Also called Mount Knut Sundbeck. 3,030 m. 4 miles SE of Mount Stubberud. Just north of Nilsen Plateau in the Queen Maud Mountains. When Amundsen was speeding by here on his way to the Pole in Nov. 1911, he named a mountain in this general area as Mount K. Sundbeck, for Knut Sundbeck. Later geographers arbitrarily picked this particular mountain with which to honor Sundbeck.

Sundbeck, Knut. Swedish engineer on the *Fram* during the Norwegian Antarctic Expedition of 1910–12.

Mount Sundberg. 70°35'S, 66°48'E. Pyramidal. Surmounts the central part of the Thomson Massif in the Aramis Range of the Prince Charles Mountains. Visited in Dec. 1956 by W.G. Bewsher's southern ANARE party. Named by the Australians for Sgt. G. Sundberg, engine fitter with the RAAF Antarctic Flight at Mawson Station in 1956.

Sundholmen *see* **Hum Island**

Sunfix Glacier. 69°16'S, 64°30'W. 15 miles long. 2 miles wide. Flows between the Grimley and Lurabee Glaciers into Casey Glacier in northern Palmer Land. Surveyed by the FIDS in Nov. 1960. A rarely possible sunfix was made here (cloud cover usually forbids one).

Sunglasses. Necessary because of sun glare.

Sungold Hill. 64°23'S, 57°52'W. 860 m. Has distinctive convex slopes. 2 miles inland between Cape Foster and Jefford

Point on the south coast of James Ross Island. Surveyed by the FIDS during the 1958–61 period, and named by the UK for the color of the exposed rock cliffs here.

Sunk Lake. 77°34'S, 166°13'E. Between Deep Lake and the Cape Royds coastline on Ross Island. The surface of the ice comprising the lake is 18 feet below sea level. Named descriptively by Shackleton's 1907–9 expedition.

Sunny Ridge. 87°S, 154°26'W. Partly snow-free. Extends south for a mile from the west end of Mount Weaver, near the head of Robert Scott Glacier. Climbed by the Ohio State University Geological Party in Nov. 1962, and named by party leader George Doumani for the sunny conditions experienced during the climb.

Sunny Side Inlet. On the west entrance to the Bay of Whales. Like the Bay of Whales, it is gone now.

Sunshine Glacier. 60°38'S, 45°30'W. 3 miles long. 2 miles wide. Flows into Iceberg Bay on the south coast of Coronation Island, in the South Orkneys. It is the largest glacier on the south side of the island. It terminates in ice cliffs up to 60 meters high. Surveyed in 1948–49 by the FIDS, and named by them for the sunshine falling on this glacier.

Mount Supernal. 73°04'S, 165°42'E. Has two summits. 3,655 m. Surmounts the SE corner of Hercules Névé and the heads of the Gair and Meander Glaciers in Victoria Land. Often mistaken for Mount Murchison. Named by the New Zealanders in 1962–63 for its lofty appearance.

Support Force Glacier. 82°45'S, 46° 30'W. Flows between the Forrestal Range and the Argentina Range in the Pensacola Mountains, to the Ronne Ice Shelf. Named for US Naval Support Force, Antarctica.

Supporters Range. 85°05'S, 169°30'E. 25 miles long. Borders the east side of Mill Glacier, from Keltie Glacier in the north to Mill Stream Glacier in the south. Named by the New Zealanders in 1961–62 because several peaks in the range are named for supporters of Shackleton's 1907–9 expedition.

Supporting Party Mountain. 85°27′S, 147°33′W. 560 m. 3 miles east of Mount Fridovich, in the vicinity of the Leverett Glacier, in the Harold Byrd Mountains, overlooking the Ross Ice Shelf. Discovered in Dec. 1929 by Gould, and named by him for his supporting party. It was first climbed by Gould's party, which was part of Byrd's 1928–30 expedition.

Brazo Sur *see* **Argentino Channel**

Islote Sur *see* **Mite Skerry**

Monte Sur *see* **Stopford Peak, Mount Vesalius**

Surf Rock. 68°12′S, 67°06′W. A rock in water just to the SE of Runaway Island, and just to the west of Neny Island, in Marguerite Bay, off the west coast of Graham Land. Charted in 1936 by the BGLE. Surveyed in 1947 by the FIDS, who named it for the surf which breaks on it.

Surge Rocks. 64°47′S, 64°04′W. Five rocks, two always exposed. 175 yards SW of Eichorst Island, and just over ½ mile SSE of Bonaparte Point on Anvers Island. Named by personnel at Palmer Station in 1972. The water surges here.

Surgeon Island. 70°40′S, 166°59′E. The largest of the Lyall Islands. 4 miles ESE of Cape Hooker off the northern coast of Victoria Land. The island sports names of surgeons who have worked in Antarctica.

Mount Suribachi. 69°29′S, 39°38′E. A conical hill in the south-central portion of Skarvsnes Foreland on the Queen Maud Land coast. Named Suribachi-yama (conical mountain) by the Japanese in 1973.

Surko Stream. 77°26′S, 163°44′E. A meltwater stream coming out of the Wilson Piedmont Glacier and flowing to Arnold Cove, 1 mile south of Gneiss Point, in the Marble Point area of southern Victoria Land. Named by Robert L. Nichols, a geologist here, for Lt. Alexander Surko, USN, second-in-command of the Navy party which worked on the aircraft landing strip, just north of the stream, at Marble Point.

Cape Surprise. 84°31′S, 174°25′W. Marks the northern end of the Longhorn Spurs, between the Massam and Barrett Glaciers, at the edge of the Ross Ice Shelf. Named by the Southern Party of the NZGSAE 1963–64 because, to their surprise, they found it to be made of rocks of the Beacon and Ferrar groups.

Surprise Island *see* **Sorpresa Rock**

Surprise Spur. 86°34′S, 147°50′W. The most northerly of three spurs on the SW side of Ackerman Ridge in the La Gorce Mountains. Named by the New Zealanders in 1969–70. It consists of surprisingly varied rocks.

Surveyors Range. 81°36′S, 160°15′E. 30 miles long. Extends north along the east side of Starshot Glacier from the Thompson Mountain area to the glacier's terminus at the Ross Ice Shelf. Named by the New Zealanders in 1960–61 for all surveyors, but notably the early pioneers from NZ.

Survival school. The Snowcraft/Survival School was begun in 1962 to teach American and New Zealand personnel about cold weather living and survival in emergencies. Bill Bridge designed the first course. Summer personnel are taught at Ross Island, or on sea ice nearby, or in the dry valleys of southern Victoria Land. Wintering personnel are taught at McMurdo Station, Amundsen-Scott South Pole Station, and Siple Station. 400 students took part in the 1983–84 course.

The *Susanna Ann.* British sealer from London. In the South Shetlands between 1823 and 1825, commanded by Captain Brown.

Sushila Automatic Weather Station. 74°42′S, 161°18′E. American AWS at an elevation of approximately 4,665 feet.

Operated from Jan. 20, 1988–March 16, 1988.

Suspiros Bay. 63°19'S, 56°28'W. Also called Kinnes Cove, Bahía Koegel. Indents the west end of Joinville Island, just south of Madder Cliffs. Named by Capt. Emilio L. Díaz, leader of the Argentine Antarctic Expedition of 1951–52 for the difficulties in surrounding the bay (suspiros means sighs in Spanish).

Suter Glacier. 73°31'S, 167°10'E. In the Mountaineer Range of Victoria Land. Flows into Lady Newnes Bay just south of Spatulate Ridge. Named by NZ in 1966 for Douglas Suter, senior NZ scientist at Hallett Station in 1962–63.

Suter Island. 68°36'S, 77°54'E. A small island off the Vestfold Hills. ½ mile SW of the entrance to Heidemann Bay. Photographed by the LCE 1936–37. Named by the Australians for W. Suter, cook at Davis Station in 1960.

Sutherland Peak. 77°38'S, 161°03'E. One of the peaks of the Inland Forts. 2 miles NNW of Round Mountain in the Asgard Range of Victoria Land. Named for Cdr. William P. Sutherland, USN, officer-in-charge of the Naval Support Force at McMurdo Station in 1974.

Sutley Peak. 73°39'S, 94°32'W. 1,400 m. Just north of Wright Peak, and 3 miles ENE of Miller Crag in the Jones Mountains. Named for Lt. Cdr. Robert M. Sutley, USN, Seabee officer in 1962.

Sutton, John L. 2nd assistant engineer on the *City of New York* during Byrd's 1928–30 expedition.

Sutton, Samuel. Seaman on the Wilkes Expedition 1838–42. Joined in the USA. Served the cruise.

Sutton Peak. 79°50'S, 82°34'W. 1,410 m. Between the Henderson and Ahrnsbrak Glaciers in the Enterprise Hills of the Heritage Range. Named for Walter C. Sutton, meteorologist at Little America, 1957.

Suture Bench. 73°32'S, 162°56'E. Benchlike elevation at the SE end of Gair Mesa. Overlooks the head of Campbell Glacier in Victoria Land. Named by the northern party of the NZGSAE 1962–63 for the sutures needed for a dog after a violent dog fight here.

Suvorov Glacier. 69°56'S, 160°05'E. 5 miles wide. Flows from the Wilson Hills into the sea south of Northrup Head and Belousov Point. Named by the USSR in 1958 for V.S. Suvorov, a mechanic who died in the Arctic.

Mount Suydam. 84°32'S, 65°27'W. 1,020 m. 3 miles west of Clark Ridge in the Anderson Hills of the northern Patuxent Range in the Pensacola Mountains. Named for E. Lynn Suydam, biologist at Palmer Station in 1967.

Svart Mountain *see* **Svart Peak**

Svart Peak. 67°16'S, 58°28'E. Also called Svart Mountain. 210 m. On the SW side of Law Promontory near the coast of East Antarctica. Photographed by the LCE 1936–37. Named Svartfjell (black mountain) by the Norwegians, for its appearance.

Svartbandufsa Bluff. 73°29'S, 3°48'W. At the SW side of Tverregg Glacier in the Kirwan Escarpment of Queen Maud Land. Name means "the black band bluff" in Norwegian.

Svarthamaren Mountain. 71°53'S, 5°10'E. An ice-free area at the east side of the mouth of Vestreskorve Glacier, in the Mühlig-Hofmann Mountains of Queen Maud Land, about 125 miles from the coast. Name means "the black hammer" in Norwegian. It is SSSI #23. Contains two rock amphitheatres inhabited by breeding Antarctic petrels, and is the largest colony of those birds. This colony was first closely observed in Jan.-Feb. 1985 by Norwegian ornithologists. There are 208,000 breeding pairs here, as well as between 500 and 1,000 breeding pairs of snow petrels, and 50 pairs of South Polar skuas. Svarthamaren is the largest known seabird colony situated inland in Antarctica. The colony was discovered in Jan. 1961 by the crew of a USSR AN-2 aircraft which landed here.

Svarthausane Crags. 71°40′S, 12°40′E. Surmounted by Zhil'naya Mountain. Forms the NE end of the Südliche Petermann Range in the Wohlthat Mountains of Queen Maud Land. Discovered by Ritscher in 1938–39. Name means "the black crags" in Norwegian.

Svarthausen Nunatak. 69°49′S, 74°30′E. On the west side of Polar Times Glacier. 4 miles SSE of Mount Caroline Mikkelsen. Name means "the black crag" in Norwegian.

Svarthorna Peaks. 71°35′S, 12°37′E. 5 or more peaks in a row on the curving ridge which forms the southern end of the Mittlere Petermann Range in the Wohlthat Mountains of Queen Maud Land. Discovered by Ritscher in 1938–39, and named by him descriptively as Schwarze-Hörner (black peaks). Translated into Norwegian it means the same thing.

Svarthornbotnen Cirque. 71°35′S, 12°36′E. Just NE of Store Svarthorn Peak in the Mittlere Petermann Range of the Wohlthat Mountains of Queen Maud Land. Discovered by Ritscher in 1938–39. Name means "the black peak cirque" in Norwegian.

Svarthornkammen Ridge. 71°31′S, 12°31′E. Extends north for 5 miles from Svarthorna Peaks in the Mittlere Petermann Range of the Wohlthat Mountains of Queen Maud Land. Discovered by Ritscher in 1938–39. Name means "the black peak ridge" in Norwegian.

Svarthovden *see* **Falla Bluff**

Svartmulen *see* **Strover Peak**

Svartnupen Peak. 71°55′S, 8°53′E. On the south side of Håkon Col in the Kurze Mountains of Queen Maud Land. Name means "the black peak" in Norwegian.

Svartpiggen *see* **Tschuffert Peak**

Svarttindane Peaks. 71°39′S, 12°30′E. 2 miles south of Store Svarthorn Peak in the Südliche Petermann Range of the Wohlthat Mountains of Queen Maud Land. They include Veselaya Mountain. Discovered by Ritscher in 1938–39.

Name means "the black peaks" in Norwegian.

Svaton Peaks. 82°35′S, 161°E. At the north end of the Queen Elizabeth Range, between the mouths of Heilman Glacier and Otago Glacier. Named for Ernest M. Svaton, US ionosphere physicist at McMurdo Station in 1963 and 1964.

Svea Glacier. 72°08′S, 1°53′E. Flows between the Sverdrup Mountains and the Gjelsvik Mountains of Queen Maud Land. Named Sveabreen (the glacier of the Swedes) by the Norwegians.

Svea Station. 74°35′S, 11°13′W. The first Swedish scientific station in Antarctica. Established in Jan. 1988 at Heimefrontfjella, Queen Maud Land.

Svelget. 73°55′S, 5°22′W. A cirque between Tunga Spur and Uven Spur in the Kirwan Escarpment of Queen Maud Land. Name means "the throat" in Norwegian.

Svellnuten Peak. 72°40′S, 3°09′W. At the east side of Jøkulskarvet Ridge in the Borg Massif of Queen Maud Land. Name means "the ice sheet peak" in Norwegian.

Sven Rock. 63°44′S, 60°12′W. A rock in water south of the Oluf Rocks in Gilbert Strait, in the Palmer Archipelago. Named by the UK in 1960 for the *Oluf Sven.*

The *Svend Foyn.* Norwegian factory whaling ship in Antarctic waters in 1920–21 and 1921–22. Instrumental in the British Imperial Expedition of 1920–22 (*see also* **The *Graham***). Named for the inventor of the harpoon gun.

Puerto Svend Foyn *see* **Gouvernøren Harbor**

Svend Foyn Coast *see* **Foyn Coast**

Svend Foyn Harbor *see* **Foyn Harbor**

Svend Foyn Island *see* **Foyn Island**

Svendsen Glacier. 70°21′S, 160°E. 13 miles long. In the Usarp Mountains. Flows from Mount Marzolf, between McCain Bluff and Lenfant Bluff, into an ice piedmont just west of the terminus of the Rennick Glacier. Named for Kendall L. Svendsen, US geomagnetist at McMurdo Station in 1967–68.

Svenner Islands. 69°02'S, 76°50'E. Small group of islands and rocks 14 miles SW of the Rauer Group. In Prydz Bay, 20 miles off the Ingrid Christensen Coast. Discovered in Feb. 1935 by Mikkelsen, and named by him for the Norwegian islands.

Svensson Ridge. 70°11'S, 64°29'E. 1 mile NW of Mount Starlight in the Athos Range of the Prince Charles Mountains. Named by the Australians for A. Svensson, weather observer at Davis Station in 1964.

Sverdrup Mountains. 72°20'S, 1°E. Also called H.U. Sverdrupfjella. 50 miles long. Just west of the Gjelsvik Mountains of Queen Maud Land. Named by the Norwegians for H.U. Sverdrup, chairman of the Norwegian Committee for the NBSAE 1949–52.

Sverdrup Nunataks. 72°45'S, 63°15' W. On the east side of Palmer Land.

Mount Sverre Hassel *see* **Mount Hassel**

Sverre Peak. 71°43'S, 9°39'E. ½ mile off the north end of Pettersen Ridge in the Conrad Mountains of Queen Maud Land. Discovered by Ritscher in 1938–39. Named by the Norwegians for Sverre Pettersen, steward on the Norwegian Antarctic Expedition of 1957–58.

The *Svip*. Norwegian whale catcher in the South Shetlands in 1908–9.

Svip Rock *see* **Svip Rocks**

Svip Rocks. 62°35'S, 61°38'W. Submerged rocks, 9 miles WNW of Rugged Island in the South Shetlands. Named for the *Svip*.

Mount Swadener. 77°16'S, 153°45'W. In the Snedden Nunataks, in the northern portion of the Alexandra Mountains of Edward VII Peninsula. Named for Lt. John R. Swadener, navigator on the historic Oct. 31, 1956 flight to the Pole of the *Que Sera Sera*.

Swain, James C. American captain of an unknown vessel from Nantucket. In 1800 he reported seeing an island in 59° 31'S, 100°W. He may have gone south of 60°S, and therefore into Antarctic waters as defined in this book.

Swain, K.C. Air crewman with the Central Group of Operation Highjump, 1946–47. He was on the plane which took Byrd to the Pole on Feb. 15, 1947. He was back in the Antarctic again during Operation Windmill, 1947–48.

Swain Group *see* **Swain Islands**

Swain Islands. 66°13'S, 110°37'E. Also called the Swain Group. Group of small islands and rocks. 2 miles in extent. ½ mile north of the Clark Peninsula, at the NE end of the Windmill Islands. They include Berkley Island, Burnett Island, Cameron Island, Damel Island, Hailstorm Island, Honkala Island, Bradford Rock, Green Rocks, Wyche Island. Named for K.C. Swain.

Mount Swan. 76°58'S, 143°45'W. 4 miles south of the Gutenko Nunataks in the Ford Ranges of Marie Byrd Land. Discovered by the USAS 1939–41. Named for Paul Swan.

Swan, Paul. Airplane pilot on the shore party of Byrd's 1933–35 expedition.

Swan, Robert. b. 1956. British leader of the In the Footsteps of Scott Expedition of 1985–86, during which he got to the Pole by foot on Jan. 11, 1986. He had previously been with the BAS in Antarctica, and it had been here that he had met Roger Mear (q.v.).

Swan Glacier *see* **Swann Glacier**

Swan Point. 66°22'S, 110°30'E. The most westerly point on Odbert Island in the Windmill Islands. Named for aerographer's mate John R. Swan, USN, at Wilkes Station in 1958.

Swan Rock. 64°58'S, 63°18'W. A rock in water, 1½ miles SW of Cape Willems, off the west coast of Graham Land. Named by the UK in 1960 for Sir Joseph Swan (1828–1914), photography pioneer.

Swann Glacier. 73°53'S, 61°48'W. Flows into Wright Inlet to the north of Mount Tricorn, on the east coast of Palmer Land. Discovered aerially in Dec. 1940 by members from East Base during the USAS 1939–41. Named by Ronne in 1948 for W.F.G. Swann, director of the Barthol Research Foundation of the Franklin Institute at Swarthmore, Pa., a contributor to the RARE.

Swanson Glacier. 71°30′S, 160°24′E. 9 miles long. Flows from the Daniels Range in the Usarp Mountains, northward of Thompson Spur. Named for Charles D. Swanson, biologist at McMurdo Station in 1967–68.

Swanson Mountains. 76°58′S, 145°W. Also called Claude Swanson Mountains. 8 miles long. 6 miles SE of Saunders Mountain in the Ford Ranges of Marie Byrd Land. Discovered aerially in 1934 by Byrd's 1933–35 expedition, and named by Byrd for Claude A. Swanson, secretary of the Navy, 1933–39.

Swarm Peak. 76°29′S, 146°20′W. 610 m. The most easterly of the Birchall Peaks in the Ford Ranges of Marie Byrd Land. Named for H. Myron Swarm, ionosphere physicist at Byrd Station in 1966–67.

Swarsen Nunatak. 71°25′S, 63°39′W. Mostly snow-covered. 5 miles SW of Mount Jackson in Palmer Land. Named for Lt. Cdr. Ronald J. Swarsen, USNR, medical officer at Byrd Station in 1971, and at Amundsen-Scott South Pole Station in 1973.

Mount Swartley. 77°15′S, 143°12′W. 1 mile east of Mount Darling in the Allegheny Mountains of the Ford Ranges of Marie Byrd Land. Discovered by the USAS 1939–41 during a flight from West Base, and named by Byrd for Prof. Stanley Swartley of Allegheny College, Pa.

Swartz Nunataks. 78°39′S, 160°E. 2 nunataks. 1,565 m. Between the Worcester Range and Tate Peak. Named in 1964 for Lt. Philip K. Swartz, Jr., USN, officer-in-charge of South Pole Station in 1961.

Swash Reef. 67°34′S, 67°33′W. In the entrance to Bigourdan Fjord, just north of Pourquoi Pas Island, off the west coast of Graham Land. Named by the FIDS because most of it is awash.

Sweaters. Tourists should definitely use woolen sweaters and sweatshirts, one light one underneath, and a heavy one on top. Turtlenecks are best.

Mount Sweatt. 85°47′S, 129°39′W. 2,540 m. 6½ miles NE of Mount Soyat. Between Hueneme and Norfolk Glaciers, in the Wisconsin Range. Named for Earl E. Sweatt, construction electrician at Byrd Station in 1961.

Sweden. The first Swede south of 60°S may well have been Anders Sparrman, in 1773, with Cook. Nordenskjöld led the first Swedish expedition to Antarctica in 1901–4. In 1949–52 John Giaever led the NBSAE 1949–52 (the Norwegian-British-Swedish Antarctic Expedition of 1949–52). Swedish scientists studied astronomy at Amundsen-Scott South Pole Station in the early 1980s, and on April 24, 1984, Sweden was ratified as the 30th signatory of the Antarctic Treaty. Svea Station, the first Swedish scientific station in Antarctica, went up in Jan. 1988, and in Sept. 1988 Sweden became a Consultative party to the Antarctic Treaty.

Sweeney Mountains. 75°06′S, 69°15′W. 40 miles long. 30 miles north of the Hauberg Mountains in Ellsworth Land. Discovered by the RARE in 1947–48 and named by Ronne as Catherine Sweeney Mountains, for Catherine Sweeney, a contributor.

Sweeny Inlet. 74°27′S, 115°20′W. An Amundsen Sea indentation into the coast of Marie Byrd Land.

Mount Swift Balch *see* **Mount Balch**

Swift Glacier. 64°22′S, 57°46′W. 2 miles long. Just west of Jefford Point on James Ross Island. Surveyed by the FIDS in the period between 1958 and 1961. Named descriptively by the UK.

Swift Peak. 66°19'S, 63°08'W. At the north end of the Churchill Peninsula, on the east coast of Graham Land. Named by the UK for the author of *Gullivers Travels*.

Swimming. It is possible for humans to swim in certain freak places, such as Pendulum Cove, Deception Island, in the summer. The temperature of the water can reach 100°F due to the natural sulfur hot springs.

Swinburne Ice Shelf. 77°10'S, 153°55' W. Just north of Edward VII Peninsula and the Alexandra Mountains in the south part of Sulzberger Bay. 20 miles long. 5 miles wide. Extends from Fisher Island to the White Islands. Named for Capt. H.W. Swinburne, Jr., deputy commander and chief of staff, US Naval Support Force, Antarctica, 1970 and 1971.

Swine Hill. 71°24'S, 67°33'W. The southern of two knolls. 550 m. 10 miles WNW of Mount Bagshawe on the west coast of Palmer Land. Overlooks Gadarene Lake and George VI Sound. Discovered aerially by Ellsworth on Nov. 23, 1935. Surveyed by the BGLE in 1936 and again by the FIDS in 1948. The FIDS built a cairn on the summit. They named it for Gadarene Lake (i.e., the biblical reference to the Gadarene swine).

Mount Swinford. 77°16'S, 161°54'E. 2¾ miles WNW of Mount Harker in the Saint Johns Range of Victoria Land. Named for Lt. Cdr. Harold D. Swinford, USN, who wintered-over at the Nuclear Power Unit at McMurdo Station in 1963 and 1968.

¹Swinford Glacier *see* **Berwick Glacier**

²Swinford Glacier. 84°45'S, 164°10'E. 6 miles long. Flows between Mount Holloway and the Marshall Mountains to enter the Beardmore Glacier. Discovered in 1908 by Shackleton, and named by him for his eldest son, Raymond Swinford. Often confused on maps with Berwick Glacier, which is 12 miles to the NE.

Swinnerton Ledge. 80°43'S, 22°28'W. In the Shackleton Range.

Swire, Herbert. Sub-lieutenant on the *Challenger*, 1872–76. The last survivor of that expedition.

Swithinbank, C.W.M. British glaciologist in the Antarctic on and off between 1949 and 1962. Dr. Charles Swithinbank, as he was also known, was the glaciologist on the NBSAE 1949–52, was at Little America with the USARP in 1959–60, and was with the FIDS in the early 1960s. He was on the Ross Ice Shelf in 1960–61 and 1961–62. On one of his trips he found a can of paraffin left a half century before by Amundsen at Betty's Knoll. It was still intact.

Swithinbank Glacier. 67°56'S, 66°46' W. Flows to the SE corner of Square Bay in Graham Land. Named by the UK for C.W.M. Swithinbank.

Swithinbank Moraine. 85°S, 177°05' W. A medial moraine in the Shackleton Glacier. Of considerable note, it trends north from Matador Mountain. Named by the New Zealanders in 1961–62 for C.W.M. Swithinbank.

Swithinbank Range. 81°42'S, 159°E. In the Churchill Mountains, between Donnally Glacier and Ahern Glacier. Named by the New Zealanders in 1959–60 for C.W.M. Swithinbank.

Swithinbank Slope. 73°28'S, 2°12'W. Also called Swithinbankhallet. Semicircular ice slope. 25 miles long. Between Mount Hallgren and Neumayer Cliffs in the Kirwan Escarpment of Queen Maud Land. Named by the Norwegians for C.W.M. Swithinbank.

Swithinbankhallet *see* **Swithinbank Slope**

Swope Glacier. 77°20'S, 145°50'W. Flows west from the Ford Ranges, between Mounts Woodward and West, into the Sulzberger Ice Shelf, in Marie Byrd Land. Named by Byrd for Gerard Swope, president of General Electric, contributor to Byrd's 1933–35 expedition.

Sydney Herbert Sound *see* **Herbert Sound**

Sykes Glacier. 77°35′S, 161°32′E. Just east of Plane Table in the Asgard Range of Victoria Land. Named by NZ for Jeremy Sykes (*see* **Deaths, 1969**).

Sylwester Glacier. 84°14′S, 159°48′E. 5 miles long. Flows between Jacobs Nunatak and MacAlpine Hills into Law Glacier. Named for David W. Sylwester, aurora scientist at South Pole Station in 1961 and at Byrd Station in 1961–62.

Symington Islands. 65°27′S, 64°58′W. Also called Islotes Riquelme. Group of small islands 13 miles WNW of Lahille Island in the Biscoe Islands. Charted by the BGLE 1934–37. Named by the UK in 1959 for J.D.L. Symington, senior air photographer on the FIDASE (q.v.).

Syningen Nunatak. 68°20′S, 59°09′E. Also called Lindsay Nunatak. 1 mile south of See Nunatak in the eastern part of the Hansen Mountains. Photographed by the LCE 1936–37. Named by the Norwegians.

Syowa *see* **Showa Station**

Syrezol Rocks. 62°11′S, 58°17′W. A small group of rocks in water, 1 mile west of Martins Head at the east side of the entrance to Admiralty Bay, King George Island in the South Shetlands. Charcot, in 1908–10, named a feature somewhere between Martins Head and the Chabrier Rocks, as Cap Syrezol, but since then no cape or anything like it can be found. These rocks were named thus in order to maintain Charcot's naming.

Syrstad Rock. 75°58′S, 133°02′W. 1 mile north of Koerner Bluff on the NW slopes of Mount Bursey in the Flood Range of Marie Byrd Land. Named for Erik Syrstad, ionosphere physicist at Amundsen-Scott South Pole Station in 1970.

Systerflesene Islands. 69°17′S, 39°25′E. 3 small islands, 5 miles west of Hamnenabben Head, in the eastern part of Lützow-Holm Bay. Photographed by the LCE 1936–37. Name means "the sister islets" in Norwegian.

Szabo Bluff. 86°29′S, 144°48′W. Just north of Price Bluff, between the Van Reeth and Robison Glaciers, in southern Victoria Land. Low-level radiation was found here in 1982–83. Named for Lt. Alex J. Szabo, USN, VX-6 pilot in Antarctica, 1966 and 1967.

Szanto Spur. 73°43′S, 161°18′E. In the area of the Priestley Glacier in Victoria Land, at the head of that glacier. Named for Otto R. Szanto, USN, radioman at McMurdo Station for 4 seasons in the 1960s.

Tabarin Peninsula. 63°32′S, 57°W. 15 miles long. Between 5 and 12 miles wide. South of the trough between Hope Bay and Duse Bay. It forms the eastern extremity of Trinity Peninsula. Discovered and charted by Nordenskjöld's expedition of 1901–4. Mapped in 1946 by the FIDS, and named by them for Operation Tabarin.

¹**Table Bay.** 61°09′S, 55°24′W. Also called Mensa Bay. The largest bay on the west coast of Elephant Island, in the South Shetlands. Named before 1822.

²**Table Bay.** 84°47′S, 163°30′E. A small glacier between Mount Augusta and Mount Holloway, in the southern part of the Queen Alexandra Range. It flows into the Beardmore Glacier at Lizard Point. Named rather oddly as a bay by Scott, in 1910–12, because of its appearance.

Table Island. 62°21′S, 59°49′W. A tiny, flat-topped island 3 miles to the NW of Robert Island, in the South Shetlands. Named before 1822.

¹**Table Mountain** *see* **Tabular Mountain, Two Step Cliffs**

²**Table Mountain.** 77°56′S, 161°59′E. Over 2,000 m. Just south of the junction of the Emmanuel and Ferrar Glaciers, in the extreme south of Victoria Land. Discovered and named descriptively by Scott's 1901–4 expedition.

Table Nunatak. 68°30′S, 62°57′W. In the Larsen Ice Shelf, off the east coast of the Antarctic Peninsula. Named descriptively.

Tabor Spur. 85°15′S, 90°14′W. Juts out from the Bermel Escarpment, between Taylor Outlier and Elliott Nunatak, in the Thiel Mountains. Named by Peter Bermel and Arthur Ford, co-leaders of the Thiel Mountains Party here in 1960–61, for Rowland Tabor, geologist with the 1961–62 Thiel Mountains party.

Taborovskiy Peak. 71°48′S, 11°35′E. 2,895 m. The highest peak in the Skarshaugane Peaks of the Betekhtin Range of the Humboldt Mountains, in Queen Maud Land. Discovered by Ritscher in 1938–39. Named by the USSR in 1966 for meteorologist N.L. Taborovskiy.

Tabular bergs. These are the largest of the icebergs (q.v.). The *Glacier* sighted one on Nov. 12, 1956, which was 208 miles long and 60 miles wide.

Tabular Mountain. 77°53′S, 160°18′E. Also called Table Mountain. 2,700 m. Flat-topped. 6 miles north of Mount Feather, in the Quartermain Range of southern Victoria Land, to the south of Taylor Glacier. Named descriptively by Scott's 1901–4 expedition.

Tabuteau, François. Assistant biologist on the French Polar Expedition of 1951.

Tachimachi Point. 69°S, 89°37′E. Snow-covered. Marks the NE extremity of East Ongul Island, in the NE part of Lützow-Holm Bay. Named Tachimachi-misaki (stand and wait point) by the Japanese in 1972.

Tadpole Island. 65°56′S, 65°19′W. Just north of Ferin Head, off the west coast of Graham Land. Charted by the BGLE 1934–37. Named by the UK in 1959 for the shape of the island when seen from the air.

Taggen Nunatak. 72°10′S, 21°48′E. Between Borchgrevinkisen and Kreitzerisen in the west part of the Sør Rondane Mountains. Name means "the prong" in Norwegian.

Tail Island. 63°40′S, 57°37′W. Also called Isla Cola. 130 m. A circular island, 1¼ miles in diameter, between Egg Island and Eagle Island, in the NE part of the Prince Gustav Channel. Charted and named by the FIDS in 1945 for its position relative to Eagle and Beak Islands.

Tailend Nunatak. 78°49′S, 27°25′W. 535 m. At the north end of the Theron Mountains. Named by the BCTAE 1956–57 because it was the last rock feature at the NE end of the Theron Mountains seen during their survey.

Tait Glacier. 64°22′S, 58°02′W. 4 miles long. On the SW coast of James Ross Island. Flows into Carlsson Bay. Surveyed by the FIDS in 1945. Named by the UK for Murdo F. Tait, FIDS meteorological observer at Base D in 1952 and 1953.

Taiwan. In 1977 Taiwan sent a 700-ton fishing vessel to the Enderby Land coast for 18 days, which took a catch of about 130 tons.

Mount Takahe. 76°16′S, 112°14′W. 3,460 m. A broad, circular, symmetrical-shield extinct volcano, 18½ miles in diameter, capped by a 5 mile-wide, snow-filled summit caldera. 60 miles south of its nearest neighbor, Mount Murphy, and just south of the Kohler Range and the Dotson Ice Shelf, in Marie Byrd Land. Visited by the Marie Byrd Land Traverse Party of 1957–58, and named by them for the flightless, almost extinct, New Zealand bird, the takahe. This was the nickname of the US aircraft which supplied the party.

Takaki Promontory. 65°33′S, 64°14′W. On the NE side of Leroux Bay, on the west coast of Graham Land. Discovered and charted by Charcot in 1903–5. Named by the UK in 1959 for Baron Kanshiro Takaki, pioneer in beriberi prevention.

Takeda. Japanese leader of the scientific staff on the Shirase expedition of 1910–12. A friend of Shirase's, he was a member of the Dash Patrol.

Takrouna Bluff. 71°58′S, 163°24′E. On the east side of the Alamein Range, in the Freyberg Mountains, it overlooks the Canham Glacier. 6 miles to the SW of Galatos Peak. Named by the New Zealanders in 1963–64 for Takrouna in Tunisia, which has an association with Lord Freyberg in World War II.

Talbot Glacier. 65°12′S, 63°14′W. Flows into Étienne Fjord, Flandres Bay, on the west coast of Graham Land. Charted by de Gerlache in 1897–99. Named by the UK in 1960 for William H.F. Talbot (1800–1877), photography pioneer.

Talbott Point. 66°15′S, 67°10′W. The northern point of Dubois Island, in the Biscoe Islands. Named by the UK for John H. Talbott, US physiologist specializing in climatic change.

Talutis Inlet. 77°15′S, 81°30′W. Ice-filled. In the western side of the Fowler Ice Rise. Opens into Carlson Inlet, just south of the Keeley Ice Rise. Named for Lt. William R. Talutis, USN, officer-in-charge of Amundsen-Scott South Pole Station in 1972.

Cape Tama *see* **Tama Point**

Tama Glacier. 68°47′S, 40°22′E. Flows to the sea between Tensoku Rock and Manju Rock, on the coast of Queen Maud Land. Named Tama-hyogo (ball glacier) by the Japanese.

Tama Point. 68°43′S, 40°26′E. Also called Cape Tama. 3 miles NE of Tama Glacier, on the coast of Queen Maud Land. Named Tama-misaki (ball point) by the Japanese.

Tambovskaya Peak. 71°41′S, 12°20′E. 2,750 m. The central peak of Gråkammen Ridge in the Westliche Petermann Range of the Wohlthat Mountains, in Queen Maud Land. Discovered by Ritscher in 1938–39. Named by the USSR in 1966 for the city of Tambov.

Tammann Peaks. 66°57′S, 66°21′W. 4 miles SE of Orford Cliff, and 4 miles east of Lallemand Fjord, in Graham Land. Named by the UK for Gustav H.J.A. Tammann, German ice specialist.

Tange Promontory. 67°27′S, 46°45′E. Ice-covered. Forms the western flange of

Casey Bay, in Enderby Land. Named by the Australians for Sir Arthur Tange, secretary of the Australian Department of External Affairs, 1954–65.

Tangekilen Bay. 69°58′S, 26°20′E. An indentation of the ice shelf north of the Sør Rondane Mountains, 42 miles ENE of Breid Bay, on the coast of Queen Maud Land. Photographed by the LCE 1936–37. Name means "the tongue bay" in Norwegian. Named for the large ice tongue just to the east.

Tangent Island *see* **Prevot Island**

Tanglefoot Peak. 67°21′S, 67°33′W. 670 m. 2½ miles east of Wyatt Island, on the west coast of Graham Land. Surveyed and named descriptively by the FIDS in 1948.

Tangskjera *see* **Tongue Rock**

Tankers. For a description of these vessels, *see* **Cargo ships**, and **Ships**.

Tankobu Peak. 69°24′S, 39°48′E. 155 m. Ice-free. Marks the north end of Byvågåsane Peaks, on the east shore of Lützow-Holm Bay. Photographed by the LCE 1936–37. Later named Tankobu-san (craggy peak) by the Japanese.

[1]Tanks. Or canvas tanks. Canvas hold-alls, containing food-bags, and strapped to a sledge.

[2]Tanks. Byrd brought Army MZA-2 tanks (tracked vehicles) on the USAS 1939–41. West Base and East Base both had one. In order to lighten them, they had to be stripped of their armor. They functioned well.

Tanna Peak. 72°20′S, 1°20′E. At the east side of the mouth of Rogstad Glacier, in the Sverdrup Mountains of Queen Maud Land. Name means "the tooth" in Norwegian.

Cap Tannaron *see* **Thanaron Point**

Tanngarden Peaks. 72°02′S, 23°17′E. 2,350 m. A row of peaks just north of Viking Heights and Mount Wideroe in the Sør Rondane Mountains. Name means "the row of teeth" in Norwegian.

Tantalus Bluffs. 84°55′S, 168°25′W. They form the NE shoulder of Mount

Ferguson, overlooking the west side of the terminus of the Liv Glacier, near that glacier's entry into the Ross Ice Shelf. Named by the NZGSAE 1963–64 because they looked interesting but could not be reached.

Tantalus Peak. 73°53′S, 161°21′E. 2,220 m. The highest peak along the south wall at the head of the Priestley Glacier in Victoria Land. Named by the NZGSAE 1962–63 because they failed to establish a station here due to steep ice.

Tapley Mountains. 85°45′S, 149°W. They extend for 35 miles. Between the Leverett Glacier and the Robert Scott Glacier, in the Queen Maud Mountains. They overlook the Ross Ice Shelf. Discovered in Dec. 1929 by Gould's Southern Geological Party during Byrd's 1928–30 expedition, and named by Byrd for Harold L. Tapley of Dunedin, NZ, agent for Byrd's first two Antarctic expeditions.

Tapsell, Capt. Commander of the *Brisk*, in Antarctic waters in 1849–50.

Tapsell Foreland. 70°52′S, 167°20′E. Mostly snow-covered. Juts out into the sea between Yule Bay and Smith Inlet, in northern Victoria Land. Named by NZ in 1969 for Capt. Tapsell.

Lake Tarachine. 69°01′S, 39°35′E. Also spelled as Lake Taratine. A small lake between Lake Kamome and Lake Minami, in the south part of East Ongul Island. Surveyed and named by the JARE (Japanese Antarctic Research Expedition) of 1957.

Tarakanov Ridge. 82°19′S, 159°24′E. In the Cobham Range, between Gray Glacier and Prince Philip Glacier. Named by the USA for Gennadiy Tarakanov, USSR exchange meteorologist at McMurdo Station in 1963.

Mount Tararua. 72°07′S, 166°14′E. 2,550 m. 3 miles NE of Head Peak, in the Victory Mountains, at the head of Pearl Harbor Glacier. Climbed on Jan. 3, 1963, by the Southern Party of the New Zealand Federated Mountain Clubs Antarctic Expedition of 1962–63, and named

by them for their parent mountain club, The Tararua Tramping Club of Wellington, NZ.

Lake Taratine *see* **Lake Tarachine**

Tarbuck Crag. 68°35′S, 78°12′E. 140 m. ¾ mile SW of Club Lake, in the Vestfold Hills. Named by the Australians for J. Tarbuck, cook at Wilkes Station in 1965, and at Davis Station in 1969, and expedition assistant with the ANARE at Wilkes Station in 1967.

Tardigrades. Also called water bears, these are microfauna of Antarctica (*see also* **Fauna**).

Target Hill. 66°S, 62°57′W. 1,010 meters above the level of the Larsen Ice Shelf. 6 miles west of Mount Fritsche, on the south flank of Leppard Glacier, in eastern Graham Land. It was visible for a long way to the FIDS in 1955, when they made this their most westerly target during that year's survey.

Tarn Flats. Unofficial name for a flat area in northern Victoria Land.

Tårnet Pinnacle. 72°01′S, 25°34′E. On the NW side of Mount Bergersen, in the Sør Rondane Mountains. Name means "the tower" in Norwegian.

Taro and Jiro. When Nagata led the first Japanese team to Antarctica, in 1956–57, and wintered-over at Showa Station in 1957, 20 sledge dogs did too. When the *Soya* returned in Feb. 1958 to lift them off, it could not approach land because of the ice and weather, so the small station plane was used to ferry passengers and equipment to the *Soya*. It took 10 trips, and it was decided not to land the replacement team, and JARE 2 was abandoned. The dogs had to be left behind. In Jan. 1959 the Japanese returned for JARE 3, and reoccupied Showa Station. They found to their amazement two dogs left alive, and well—Taro and Jiro, named for the only two dogs to survive Shirase's expedition of 1910–12. These two modern survivors were Karafuto sledge dogs from Sakhalin Island, in northern Japan. Apparently they had not eaten the other 18 dogs, and it is a mystery how they survived so well. They were made real heroes in Japan. A movie was made of the story in the early 1980s.

Mount Tarr. 70°25'S, 65°46'E. 1½ miles ESE of Mount Creighton, in the Porthos Range of the Prince Charles Mountains. Named by the Australians for F. Tarr, aircraft engineer with the ANARE Prince Charles Mountains survey party of 1969.

Tarr, L.W. RNZAF Sgt., who flew with Claydon on the BCTAE 1955–58.

The *Tartar*. London sealer, in the South Shetlands in 1821–22, under the command of Capt. Pottinger.

Tartar Island. 61°56'S, 58°29'W. Also called Isla Owen. Just over ¼ mile long. ½ mile NW of Round Point, off the northern coast of King George Island, in the South Shetlands. Named by the UK in 1960 for the *Tartar*.

Tasch Peak. 76°40'S, 118°03'W. In the SE portion of Mount Rees, in the Crary Mountains of Marie Byrd Land. Named for Paul Tasch, geologist in the Sentinel and Ohio Ranges in 1966–67, and at Coalsack Bluff in 1969–70.

Tashtego Point. 65°44'S, 62°09'W. On the south side of Stubb Glacier, on the east coast of Graham Land. Surveyed and photographed by the FIDS in 1947. Named by the UK for the *Moby Dick* character.

Task Force 39. The US Naval Force which put Operation Windmill into effect in 1947–48. Created on Sept. 15, 1947, as part of the US Pacific Fleet, it comprised the icebreakers *Edisto* and *Burton Island,* and was led by Gerald L. Ketchum. Dr. Earl T. Apfel was the Task Force geologist.

Task Force 43. US Navy force created on Feb. 1, 1955, within the US Atlantic Fleet, to "implement the planned program in the Antarctic by conducting operations during the period 1954–59 and subsequent thereto as directed." In short, it backed up the scientists during Operation Deep Freeze. It set up bases, and supplied and maintained them, for the benefit of the US scientific personnel. Task Force 43, under the command of Adm. George Dufek and his second-in-command Gerald Ketchum, arrived at McMurdo Sound on Dec. 17, 1955, and did the most astonishing job in opening up the hitherto practically unknown continent of Antarctica. The force comprised not only military personnel (although this formed the lion's share of the force), but also scientific. Its air arm was VX-6 (formed on Jan. 17, 1955). Admiral Tyree took over from Dufek, and for subsequent commanders of Task Force 43 *see* **Operation Deep Freeze.** On July 1, 1974, Task Force 43 became Task Force 199, under the administrative command of the Third Fleet.

Task Force 68. Established in 1946, this was the US Naval force which executed Operation Highjump in 1946–47 (*see* **Operation Highjump** for further details).

Task Force 199. On July 1, 1974, this US Naval force replaced Task Force 43 as the USA's military support of Antarctic activity. Commanders: Capt. Eugene W. Van Reeth July 1, 1974–June 4, 1976; Capt. Claude H. Nordhill June 4, 1976–?; Capt. Darrel E. Westbrook, Jr. ?–June 24, 1980; Capt. Jare M. Pearigen June 24, 1980–July 26, 1982; Capt. Brian H. Shoemaker July 26, 1982–Aug. 16, 1985; Capt. David A. Srite Aug. 16, 1985– .

Tate Glacier. 85°54'S, 160°50'W. On the south side of Thomas Spur, merging with the Moffett Glacier, in the Queen Maud Mountains. Both of these glaciers then enter the Amundsen Glacier. Named for Robert Tate, seismologist at Amundsen-Scott South Pole Station in 1964.

Tate Peak. 78°39'S, 159°31'E. 1,885 m. 2 miles east of Escalade Peak, at the south side of the Skelton Névé. Named in 1964 for Lt. T.N. Tate, USN, public works officer at McMurdo Station in 1963.

Tate Rocks. 72°40'S, 74°33'E. Three small nunataks, 7 miles NNW of the Mason Peaks, in the Grove Mountains. Named by the Australians for K.A. Tate, radio officer at Mawson Station in 1962.

Tatimati Point *see* **Tachimachi Point**

Tau Islands. 64°18′S, 62°55′W. Also called Islotes Trio. A small group of islands and rocks just off the NE end of Eta Island, in the Melchior Islands. Named by the Argentines in 1946 for the Greek letter.

Taurus Nunataks. 70°52′S, 66°23′W. A line of nunataks, 23 miles ENE of Gurney Point, in Palmer Land. Named by the UK for the constellation Taurus.

Firth of Tay. 63°22′S, 55°45′W. 12 miles long. 6 miles wide. A sound, between Dundee Island and Joinville Island. Discovered in 1892–93 by the Dundee Whaling Expedition, and named by them for the Scottish firth.

Tay Head. 63°21′S, 55°34′W. A headland 6 miles east of Mount Alexander, it juts out into the Firth of Tay (hence the name given by the UK in 1963), on the south coast of Joinville Island.

Mount Taylor. 63°26′S, 57°08′W. 1,000 m. 2½ miles WSW of the head of Hope Bay, at the NE end of the Antarctic Peninsula. Discovered by Nordenskjöld's 1901–4 expedition. Charted by the FIDS in 1946 and named by them in 1948 for Capt. A. Taylor.

Taylor, Capt. A. Leader of Operation Tabarin Phase II, 1944–45. He became the first FIDS leader, in 1945, leading Base D that winter.

Taylor, Ashton. Private on the Wilkes Expedition 1838–42. Joined in the USA. Served the cruise.

Taylor, D. Captain of the *Caroline,* 1821–22. He was still its captain when it went down at Macquarie Island, in 1825.

Taylor, Grif. 1880–1964. Thomas Griffith Taylor. Known as "Grif." Educated in Australia, he was a geologist. He was physiographer on Scott's 1910–13 expedition, during which time he led the Western Journey Party into Victoria Land. He wrote *Scott: The Silver Lining* in 1915.

Taylor, Howard C., III. Lt., USN. Medical officer at South Pole Station in 1957.

Taylor Buttresses. 70°08′S, 67°23′W. Oval-shaped, whalebacked hill which has 3 buttresses of rock at the northern end. Near the heads of Riley Glacier and Chapman Glacier, in western Palmer Land. Named by the UK for Brian J. Taylor, BAS geologist at Fossil Bluff Station in 1961–63.

¹Taylor Glacier. 67°27′S, 60°50′E. 1½ miles wide. Just east of Hayes Peak, it flows into the sea just east of Cape Bruce. Discovered in Feb. 1931, by the BANZARE, and named by Mawson for Grif Taylor.

²Taylor Glacier. 77°37′S, 162°E. 35 miles long. Flows from the plateau of Victoria Land, into the west end of Taylor Valley. There is an emperor penguin colony here. Discovered in 1903 by Albert Armitage during the Royal Society Expedition, and considered by him to be the northern arm of the Ferrar Glacier. He named it the Upper Ferrar Glacier, or North Fork. In 1911 Scott renamed it for Grif Taylor.

Taylor Glacier Dry Valley *see* **Taylor Valley**

Taylor Hills. 82°38′S, 163°50′E. A line of ice-covered hills bordering the east side of the Lowery Glacier, between Oliver Glacier and Robb Glacier. Named for Lawrence D. Taylor, glaciologist at Amundsen-Scott South Pole Station in 1963–64.

Taylor Islands. 66°09′S, 100°16′E. A group of rocky islands and rocks, at the west side of the Edisto Ice Tongue. They mark the west end of the Highjump Archipelago. Named for Richard Spence Taylor, surveyor on Operation Windmill, 1947–48.

Taylor Nunatak. 84°54′S, 176°W. On the east side of Shackleton Glacier, just south of the terminus of Dick Glacier, in the Queen Maud Mountains. Named by the New Zealanders in 1961–62 for Thomas E. Taylor, topographic surveyor who worked in the area in 1960–61 and 1962–63.

Taylor Nunataks. 63°15'S, 55°33'W. Also called Monte Percy. Two isolated nunataks, 650 m. and 660 m., joined by a narrow ridge. SE of Mount Quilmes, in the eastern part of Joinville Island. Surveyed by the FIDS in 1953. Named by the UK for Robert J.F. Taylor, dog-physiologist with the FIDS at Base D in 1954 and 1955, who was on the FIDS survey party to Joinville Island in 1953–54.

Taylor Outlier. 85°13'S, 90°19'W. An isolated rock on land, in front of the west end of the Bermel Escarpment. 1½ miles east of the lower part of Counts Icefall, in the Thiel Mountains. Named for Alfred R. Taylor, geologist, a member of the USARP Victoria Land Traverse of 1959–60.

Taylor Peak. 72°12'S, 168°38'E. 2,550 m. The main peak of the heights separating the Helman and Tyler Glaciers, in the Admiralty Mountains. Named for C.B. Taylor, aurora scientist, NZ scientific leader at Hallett Station in 1962.

Taylor Platform. 71°01'S, 67°09'E. A massif 1 mile north of Mount Brocklehurst, in the Prince Charles Mountains. Named by the Australians for F.J. Taylor, ionosphere physicist at Mawson Station in 1964.

Taylor Point. 61°56'S, 57°40'W. Forms the northern limit of Destruction Bay, on the east coast of King George Island, in the South Shetlands. Named by the UK in 1960 for D. Taylor.

Taylor Ridge. 85°48'S, 153°21'W. 10 miles long. On the west side of the Robert Scott Glacier, between the mouths of the Koerwitz and Vaughan Glaciers, in the Queen Maud Mountains. Discovered by Quin Blackburn and his party in Dec. 1934, during Byrd's 1933–35 expedition. Named for John H. Taylor, ionosphere physicist at Amundsen-Scott South Pole Station in 1966.

Taylor Rookery. 67°50'S, 60°50'E. On the eastern side of Taylor Glacier in Mac. Robertson Land. It is the largest emperor penguin colony wholly on land, and is a Specially Protected Area (SPA).

Taylor Spur. 78°31'S, 84°09'W. Wedge-shaped. Marks the north side of the terminus of Guerrero Glacier, on the east side of the Sentinel Range. Named for Lt. Howard C. Taylor, III.

Taylor Valley. 77°37'S, 163°25'E. 25 miles long. 4 miles wide. 3,000 feet deep. A dry valley—no snow, no ice. Of spectacular nature. Just behind New Harbor, in Victoria Land, near McMurdo Sound. Once occupied by the Taylor Glacier. It is the most famous of the dry valleys in Victoria Land, indeed in Antarctica. It was also the first to be discovered—in 1902, by Scott's 1901–4 expedition. They called it Dry Valley. It later became known as New Harbor Dry Valley. In Jan. 1911 Grif Taylor explored it, and that year Scott renamed it as Taylor Glacier Dry Valley. The name was later shortened.

Taynaya Bay. 68°27'S, 78°16'E. In the north part of Langnes Peninsula, in the Vestfold Hills. Photographed by the LCE 1936–37, and plotted by the Norwegians as a lake. It looks like one from the air, having a tiny entrance to the sea on the north side. Redefined by US cartographer John H. Roscoe in 1952, as he worked off photos taken by Operation Highjump in 1946–47. Named Bukhta Taynaya (secret bay) by the USSR in 1956.

The *Tazar*. Polish ship which, with the *Professor Siedlecki*, conducted the Polish Antarctic Marine Research Expedition around the South Shetlands in 1975–76.

Mount Tchaikovsky. 71°14'S, 73°31'W. 250 m. Snow-covered. Between Mendelssohn and Brahms Inlets, in the SW part of Alexander Island. Named by the UK for the composer.

Te Islands. 69°03'S, 39°34'E. Three small islands and several rocks just south of Ongul Island, in the Flatvaer Islands. Photographed by the LCE 1936–37. The Norwegian cartographers who worked off these aerial photos plotted the three major islands as one, and named it Teöya (the tea island). Redefined by the Japanese in 1962, but the name stayed the same.

¹Cape Teall. 79°03'S, 161°04'E. Also spelled (erroneously) as Cape Teale. Forms the north side of the entrance to Mulock Inlet, on the west side of the Ross Ice Shelf. Discovered by Scott's 1901–4 expedition, and named by them for Sir Jethro Teall, director of the Geological Survey and Museum of Practical Geology, London, 1901–13.

²Cape Teall *see* **Teall Island**

Teall Island. 79°03'S, 161°54'E. Also spelled (erroneously) as Teale Island. Rises above the Ross Ice Shelf at the west side of the mouth of the Skelton Inlet. Scott's 1901–4 expedition discovered and named a feature in this area (possibly this one) as Cape Teall. It was later redefined, and its location was clarified, by the NZ party of the BCTAE 1957–58, and named in association with the nearby cape.

Teall Nunatak. 74°50'S, 162°33'E. Also called Beehive Nunatak. At the mouth of the Reeves Glacier, 3 miles SE of Hansen Nunatak, in Victoria Land. Discovered by Scott's 1901–4 expedition, and named by Shackleton's 1907–9 expedition, for Sir Jethro Teall (*see* **Cape Teall**).

Teardrop Pond. 76°54'S, 145°18'W. A meltwater pond, 1 mile SW of Greegor Peak, in the Denfeld Mountains of Marie Byrd Land. Named because of its shape when seen in plain view.

Mount Tedrow. 82°53'S, 163°E. 1,490 m. At the east side of the mouth of DeBreuck Glacier, at the junction of that glacier with the Kent Glacier. Named for Jack V. Tedrow, glaciologist at McMurdo Station in 1959–60 and 1960–61.

Tedrow Glacier. 77°59'S, 161°52'E. Flows into Ferrar Glacier along the west side of Table Mountain, in Victoria Land. Named for John C.F. Tedrow, project leader for soil studies at McMurdo Station in 1961–62.

Teeny Rock. 83°38'S, 59°10'W. A small rock at the NW end of the Williams Hills, in the Neptune Range of the Pensacola Mountains. Named for its small size.

Teeters Nunatak. 74°12'S, 100°01'W. 615 m. 5 miles north of Hodgson Nunatak, in the Hudson Mountains. Named for Robert E. Teeters, USN, storekeeper at Byrd Station in 1966.

Mount Tegge. 77°57'S, 85°15'W. 1,570 m. Isolated. At the mouth of Embree Glacier, on the east side of the Sentinel Range. Named for 1st Lt. Richard C. Tegge, USAF, who helped build South Pole Station in 1956–57.

Isla Tegualda *see* **Hansen Island**

Teigan Island. 66°27'S, 110°36'E. Also called Teigan Rock. A rocky island, 350 yards long, and 175 yards NE of Bosner Island, near the south end of the Windmill Islands. Named for B. Teigan, air crewman with the Central Task Group of Operation Highjump, 1946–47, and again on Operation Windmill, 1947–48.

Teigan Rock *see* **Teigan Island**

Teil Island *see* **Deception Island**

The *Te-Ivi-O-Atea.* The war canoe, captained by Ui-Te-Rangiora, which, legend has it, sailed from Raratonga to the Antarctic about 650 A.D.

Tejas Glacier *see* **Beaumont Glacier**

Teksla Island. 67°27'S, 60°56'E. Also called Norris Island. The largest island in the Colbeck Archipelago, near the coast of Mac. Robertson Land. 1 mile north of Chapman Ridge. Photographed by the LCE 1936–37. Name means "the cooper's axe" in Norwegian.

The *Telefon.* A vessel which went aground in Port Foster, Deception Island, in 1908, and was abandoned. It was salvaged in 1909, in what is now Telefon Bay.

Telefon Bay. 62°56'S, 60°42'W. One of the bays of Port Foster, inside Deception Island, in the South Shetlands.

Probably named by Charcot in 1909 for the *Telefon*. On Dec. 7, 1967, a new island (*see* **Yelcho Island**) was formed in Telefon Bay as the result of volcanic eruptions. This new island was made up of ash and scoriae.

Telefon Point. 62°14′S, 59°54′W. The most southerly point on the west side of Admiralty Bay, King George Island, in the South Shetlands.

Telefon Ridge. 62°56′S, 60°43′W. Behind Telefon Bay, in Deception Island, in the South Shetlands. Named by the UK in 1959 in association with the nearby bay.

Telefon Rocks. 62°15′S, 58°27′W. A group, 1½ miles SSW of Demay Point, at the west side of the entrance to Admiralty Bay, King George Island, in the South Shetlands. Named for the *Telefon*.

Isla Telegrafista Rivera *see* **Apéndice Island**

Telen Glacier. 69°38′S, 39°42′E. Flows between Telen Hill and Kjuka Headland, to the east side of Lützow-Holm Bay. Named by the Japanese in association with the nearby hill.

Telen Hill. 69°39′S, 39°41′E. Ice-free. On the coast, between Skallen Glacier and Telen Glacier, on the east side of Lützow-Holm Bay. Photographed by the LCE 1936–37. Name means "the frozen crust" in Norwegian.

Telephones. In Sept. 1911 Scott laid aluminum wire on the ice for about 12 miles, connecting the main base at Cape Evans to two outlying bases. In that month he used the first telephone in Antarctica, between Cape Evans and Hut Point.

Television. Antarctica's first TV station opened at McMurdo Station on Nov. 9, 1973. American Forces Antarctic Network Television (AFAN TV) was installed, owned and operated by the US Navy, and has reruns of US shows, local programs, and daily news and weather.

Teller Peak. 85°57′S, 135°28′W. 3,550 m. Marks the NE extremity of the Michigan Plateau and the Watson Escarpment, in the Queen Maud Mountains. Named for James T. Teller, geologist here in 1964–65.

Telmo Island *see* **San Telmo Island**

Teltet Nunatak. 71°59′S, 23°43′E. 2 miles north of Vengen Spur, in the Sør Rondane Mountains. Name means "the tent" in Norwegian.

Temmondai Rock. 68°25′S, 41°41′E. Also spelled Tenmondai Rock. On the coast at the east side of the terminus of Higashi-naga-iwa Glacier, in Queen Maud Land. Named Temmondai-iwa (astronomical observatory rock) by the Japanese.

Temnikow Nunataks. 70°37′S, 64°10′W. A group scattered over an area of 6 miles, at the east margin of the Dyer Plateau, 5 miles west of the Kelley Massif, in Palmer Land. Named for Nicolas Temnikow, US biologist at Palmer Station in 1974.

Temperatures. Temperatures in this book are generally listed in Fahrenheit (°F). There are only a few places in Antarctica where the temperature goes above freezing (32°F), even in the summer. In the South Orkneys, South Shetlands, and the northern sections of the Antarctic Peninsula, temperatures can go as high as 60°F in the summer, and during that season those areas rarely go below freezing. It is the wind chill factor that makes it colder. Indeed, one can swim in the hot caldera of Deception Island, where the water temperatures can reach 100°F. Generally, though, in those northern regions of Antarctica, summer temperatures are in the upper 30s, lower 40s, dropping in the evening, and the average year-round temperature is 26°F. In the winter, temperatures can reach 52°F in these areas. The highest temperature recorded outside of the Antarctic Peninsula and environs was 48°F, at Casey Station. At the other extreme, the coldest temperature ever recorded on earth was −129.9°F, at Vostok Station, deep in the interior of Antarctica. Mean temperatures of the coldest months in the interior are −40°F to −94°F. The average year-round temperature at the South Pole is −60°F. When Dufek landed at the Pole on Oct. 31, 1956, the temperature was −58°F. Temperatures may rise and fall 100°F within a few weeks, and, on some heated rocks as far south as 85°S, surface temperatures may reach 59°F. The coldest period on the Polar Plateau is August, just before the return of the summer sun, when it has had months of its most intense cold. Mean temperatures of the coldest months on the coast are −4°F to −22°F, although it can reach −76°F on the coast. Progressive low temperature records in Antarctica have been: −5°F, set sometime between 1829 and 1842, on Deception Island; −46°F, Sept. 8, 1898, taken by the *Belgica* in the Bellingshausen Sea; −100.4°F, May 11, 1957, South Pole; −102.1°F, Sept. 17, 1957, South Pole; −109.1°F, May 2, 1957, Sovietskaya; −113.3°F, June 15, 1958, Vostok; −114.1°F, June 19, 1958, Sovietskaya; −117.4°F, June 25, 1958, Sovietskaya; −122.4°F, Aug. 8, 1958, Vostok; −124.1°F, Aug. 9, 1958, Sovietskaya; −125.3°F, Aug. 25, 1958, Vostok; −126.9°F, Aug. 24, 1960, Vostok; −128.6°F, July 21, 1983, Vostok (recorded by platinum thermometer); −129.3°F, July 21, 1983, Vostok; −129.9°F, July 21, 1983, Vostok.

Tempest Peak. 84°32'S, 164°10'E. Also called Tempest Peaks. Ice-covered. 3,410 m. Has a smaller summit to the SW, of 3,345 m. 3 miles NNE of Storm Peak, in the Marshall Mountains, in the southern sector of the Queen Alexandra Range, in the Queen Maud Mountains. Named by the New Zealanders in 1961–62 because of the storms here.

Temple Glacier. 64°02'S, 59°55'W. Flows into the south side of Lanchester Bay, on the west coast of Graham Land. Named by the UK in 1960 for Félix du Temple (1823–1890), French aeronautics pioneer.

Mount Tempyo. 69°31'S, 39°43'E. 260 m. In the south of Skarvsnes Foreland, on the coast of Queen Maud Land. Named Tempyo-zan by the Japanese in 1973.

Ten-Year International Antarctic Glaciological Project. 1971–81. Large, cooperative venture between Australia, France, USSR, USA, and Great Britain, to determine the dynamics of the East Antarctica Ice Shelf, and to measure it precisely.

Tenaza Peak. 71°05'S, 167°24'E. 1,345 m. 2½ miles east of Mount Pechell, in the west central part of Hedgpeth Heights, in the Anare Mountains. Named for Richard R. Tenaza, biologist at Hallett Station in 1967–68.

The *Tenedos.* US whaler/sealer from New London, in the South Shetlands during the 1856–60 period, under the command of Capt. King.

Teneycke, William. Seaman on the Wilkes Expedition 1838–42. Joined in the USA. Sent home on the *Relief* in 1839.

Mount Teniente *see* **Stokes Hill**

Teniente Camara Station. 62°36'S, 59°57'W. Argentine scientific base on Halfmoon Island, in the South Shetlands. Built as a hut in 1952, it was extended in 1953, and was established as a permanent meteorological station that year. González Silvano was leader of the 1957 wintering party.

Teniente Carvajal Station. In 1985 the UK handed over their Base T, on Adelaide Island, to the Chileans, and it was renamed.

Punta Teniente Ferrer *see* **Ferrer Point**

Monte Teniente Ibáñez *see* **Mount Français**

Islote Teniente Ibar *see* **Ibar Rocks**

Teniente Jubany Station *see* **Jubany Station**

Islote Teniente Kopaitic *see* **Murray Island**

Picachos Teniente López see López Nunatak

Teniente Matienzo Station. 64°58'S, 60°02'W. Argentine station between Robertson Island and the Nordenskjöld Coast, in the Larsen Ice Shelf, off the east coast of the Antarctic Peninsula. Named for aviator Lt. Benjamin Matienzo.

Teniente Rodolfo Marsh Station. 62° 12'S, 58°54'W. On Fildes Peninsula, King George Island, in the South Shetlands. This is Chile's main tourist base in Antarctica, and doubles as a year-round scientific station. It has a motel and a 4,000-foot runway which it shares with its neighbor, Presidente Frei Station. Built in 1980, the station collects meteorological data, and is maintained by the Chilean Air Force. Several families live here.

Isla Teniente Rodríguez see Terminal Island

Cabo Teniente Vivot see Cape Sterneck

Tenmondai Rock see Temmondai Rock

¹Mount Tennant. 64°41'S, 62°41'W. 690 m. At the north end of Rongé Island, off the west coast of Graham Land. Discovered by de Gerlache in 1898. Named by personnel on the *Snipe* in Jan. 1948, for Vice-Adm. Sir William Tennant, Commander-in-Chief of the America and West Indies Station.

²Mount Tennant see Tennant Peak

Tennant, George W. Cook on Byrd's 1928–30 expedition. Had been chief cook on Byrd's North Pole expedition.

Tennant Peak. 78°09'S, 155°18'W. Also called Mount Tennant. 1 mile south of Gould Peak, in the south group of the Rockefeller Mountains. Discovered by Byrd's 1928–30 expedition, and named by Byrd for George W. Tennant.

Mount Tennent. 85°22'S, 166°45'E. 2,895 m. In the Dominion Range, 2 miles south of Vandament Glacier. Named by the New Zealanders in 1961–62 for W.B. Tennent, minister in charge of Scientific and Industrial Research, New Zealand.

Mount Tenney. 74°49'S, 65°19'W. 9 miles NW of Mount Hyatt, to the west of the Latady Mountains, at the base of the Antarctic Peninsula. Named for Philip J. Tenney, traverse engineer on the South Pole–Queen Maud Land Traverse III, in the summer of 1967–68.

Mount Tenniel. 70°20'S, 62°48'W. 7 miles WNW of the mouth of the Clifford Glacier, on the east coast of Palmer Land. Discovered in 1936 by a BGLE sledge party under Rymill. Named in 1952 by Sir Miles Clifford, governor of the Falkland Islands, for his great uncle, Sir John Tenniel (1820–1914), the artist.

Cape Tennyson. 72°22'S, 168°18'E. Also called Cape Campbell. On the north shore of Ross Island, 25 miles SE of Cape Bird. Discovered in Feb. 1900, and named by him for the British poet.

Islote Tenorio see Tenorio Rock

Tenorio Rock. 62°28'S, 59°44'W. Also called Islote Aviador Tenorio, Islote Tenorio. Almost ½ mile off the west coast of Discovery Bay, in Greenwich Island, in the South Shetlands. Humbert Tenorio was the second pilot of the Sikorsky helicopter used by the Chilean Antarctic Expedition of 1947.

Tensoku Rock. 68°48'S, 40°11'E. Also called Daiichi Rock. Between Tama Glacier and Flattunga, in Queen Maud Land. Named Tensoku-iwa (observation rock) by the Japanese, because this rock served as a point of observation for the JARE survey party in the 1950s.

Tent Island. 77°41'S, 166°22'E. 135 m. 1 mile long. The largest of the four Dellbridge Islands in McMurdo Sound. Discovered by Scott in 1901–4, and named by him for its tentlike appearance.

Tent Nunatak. 67°36'S, 65°21'W. Pyramidal. Marks the southern limit of Whirlwind Inlet, on the east coast of Graham Land. Discovered aerially by the USAS in 1940, and described as a "distinctive tent-shaped rock nunatak." Charted by the FIDS in 1947.

Tent Peak. Unofficial name for a peak just to the east of Mount Terror, on Ross Island.

Tent Rock. 75°42′S, 158°34′E. A small nunatak shaped like a ridge tent (hence the name given by the New Zealanders in 1962–63). 1 mile SW of Thomas Rock, 7 miles west of the Ricker Hills, in the Prince Albert Mountains of Victoria Land.

Tentacle Ridge. 79°37′S, 157°15′E. Partly ice-free. South of Mount Longhurst, running from the mouth of McCleary Glacier along the north side of Darwin Glacier. Named descriptively by the Darwin Glacier Party of the BCTAE 1956–58.

Tenterhooks Crevasses. 71°45′S, 162°35′E. A large system of crevasses in the Rennick Glacier, between the Morozumi Range and the Lanterman Range. Named by the Northern Party of the NZGSAE 1963–64, for the dangers here.

Teöya *see* **Te Islands**

Terletskiy Peak. 71°49′S, 10°31′E. 2,505 m. Almost 1¾ miles NW of Chervov Peak, in the Shcherbakov Range of the Orvin Mountains, in Queen Maud Land. Discovered by Ritscher in 1938–39. Named by the USSR in 1966 for hydrographer N.A. Terletskiy (1910–1954).

Terminal Island. 68°45′S, 70°35′W. Also called Isla Teniente Rodríguez, Isla Rodríguez. Snow-covered. ½ mile off the north tip of Alexander Island. Named descriptively by the UK in relation to Alexander Island.

Terminal Peak. 75°53′S, 158°24′E. 1,920 m. 1 mile north of Griffin Nunatak, in the Prince Charles Mountains of Victoria Land. Named by the Southern Party of the NZGSAE 1962–63, because it was as far west as they got.

Termination Barrier *see* **Termination Land, Shackleton Ice Shelf**

Termination Ice Tongue *see* **Termination Land**

Termination Land. The westward end of the Shackleton Ice Shelf. Discovered on Feb. 17, 1840, by Wilkes, and named by him because this was as far as he got along the coast. Mawson rediscovered it in Feb. 1912, during the AAE, and renamed it Termination Ice Tongue (rather, he redefined it as such). In 1931, Mawson, during the BANZARE, found that it had gone.

Terminus Mountain. 78°09′S, 163°36′E. Over 800 m. Just south of Adams Glacier, on the east side of the Royal Society Range, in Victoria Land. Climbed on March 1, 1911, by Grif Taylor and his Western Journey Party during Scott's 1910–13 expedition. Named by Taylor, because it was the furthest point which they ascended in this area.

Terminus Nunatak. 69°52′S, 68°20′W. 670 m. Between the Eureka and Riley Glaciers, ½ mile inland from the George VI Sound, on the west coast of Palmer Land. Photographed aerially by Ellsworth on Nov. 23, 1935. Surveyed in 1936 by the BGLE, and again by the FIDS in 1948. Named by the FIDS because this nunatak marks the end of the sledge route from the Wordie Ice Shelf to the George VI Sound.

Tern Cove. 60°42′S, 45°37′W. The entrance is blocked by submerged rocks. Just SE of Berry Head, in the north part of Signy Island, in the South Orkneys. It contains 3 small islands. Named by the FIDS after a 1947 survey, for the terns on the most southerly of the islands in the cove.

Tern Nunatak. 62°06′S, 58°20′W. Just east of Lussich Cove, Admiralty Bay, King George Island, in the South Shetlands. Charted by Charcot in 1908–10. Named by the FIDS in 1949 for the terns seen here.

Terningen Peak. 72°11′S, 2°45′E. 2,680 m. Marks the summit of Terningskarvet Mountain, in the Gjelsvik Mountains of Queen Maud Land. Name means "the die" in Norwegian.

Terningskarvet *see* **Mount Sauter**

Terningskarvet Mountain. 72°11′S, 2°46′E. Also called Mount Sauter, Sauter

Range. Just east of Mayr Ridge. Forms the SE portion of the Gjelsvik Mountains of Queen Maud Land. Name means "the die mountain" in Norwegian.

Terns *see* **Arctic terns, Antarctic terns**

Ternyck Needle. 62°05'S, 58°16'W. 365 m. A nunatak, 1½ miles east of the head of Martel Inlet, at the base of the small peninsula separating Admiralty Bay and King George Bay, on King George Island, in the South Shetlands. Charted in Dec. 1909 by Charcot, who may have named it.

Terra Australis Incognita. Latin for "unknown southern continent." The idea of a great southern land had been proposed for centuries (*see* **Origin of name Antarctica**). It was fabled as a land of great treasures, weird peoples, etc., even though no one had ever been there. Magellan's sighting of Tierra del Fuego in 1519 led to a renewed interest in its discovery, and in Jan. 1772 Kerguélen discovered the islands which now bear his name, and claimed that his "La France Australe" was the center of the Antarctic continent. He was wrong. Like Kerguélen, Captain Cook was sent to find this unknown land, but unlike the Frenchman, Cook admitted to not having seen land at all south of 60°S. It remained for the early sealers to discover Antarctic lands, in the early 1820s.

Terra Cotta Mountain. 77°54'S, 161°15'E. Also called Terra Cotta Mountains. Between Windy Gully and Knobhead, on the south side of the Taylor Glacier, in Victoria Land. Named descriptively by Scott's 1901–4 expedition.

Terra Cotta Mountains *see* **Terra Cotta Mountain**

Terra Firma Islands. 68°42'S, 67°33'W. In Mikkelsen Bay, in the Marguerite Bay area. It is a small group, 8 miles north of Cape Berteaux, off the west coast of Graham Land. They include Alamode Island, Dumbbell Island, Hayrick Island, Lodge Rock, Twig Rock. Dis-

covered and named on June 18, 1936, by the BGLE.

Terra Firma II Island *see* **Twig Rock**

The *Terra Nova*. The largest of all the Scottish whaling ships, this Dundee vessel was built by Alexander Stephen and Sons of that town, in 1884. It was 187 feet long, with a 31-foot beam, and weighed 747 tons. It had 3 masts and was rigged as a bark (barque). It was sent to the Antarctic in 1903–4, under the command of Harry Mackay, in company with the *Morning,* in order to relieve Scott's 1901–4 Royal Society Expedition. In 1910–13 it was Scott's expedition ship, and Harry Pennell commanded it in Scott's absence during the expedition.

Glacier Terra Nova *see* **Astrolabe Glacier**

Mount Terra Nova. 77°30'S, 168°03'E. 2,130 m. Snow-covered. Between Mounts Erebus and Terror, pretty much in the center of Ross Island. It is the third highest mountain on the island. Named for the *Terra Nova.*

Terra Nova Bay. 74°45'S, 164°30'E. 40 miles long. Often ice-free. A Ross Sea indentation into northern Victoria Land, between Cape Washington and the Drygalski Ice Tongue. Discovered by Scott in 1901–4, and named by him for the *Terra Nova.*

Terra Nova Bay Polynya. An ice-free area of water in Terra Nova Bay, off the coast of Victoria Land, in the Ross Sea. Between 1,000 and 5,000 square kilometers. It centers on 75°S, 163°15'E. Two things keep it ice-free: the strong katabatic winds blowing down the Reeves Glacier valley, and the Drygalski Ice Tongue, which blocks the northward flow of sea ice into Terra Nova Bay.

Terra Nova Islands. 68°53'S, 157°57'E. Two small islands, 14 miles north of Williamson Head. Discovered from the *Magga Dan* on March 8, 1961, by Phillip Law's ANARE party. Named by the Australians for the *Terra Nova.*

Terrace Island *see* **Dunlop Island**

Terrace Lake. 77°34'S, 166°13'E. A small, elongate lake in a valley, ½ mile east of Cape Barne, on Ross Island. Named probably by the Shackleton expedition of 1907–9.

Terrace Ridge. 84°49'S, 113°45'W. Mostly ice-free. Descends from the summit area at the south end of Mount Schopf, in the Ohio Range. Terraces, partly ice-covered, are formed by the resistant sandstone strata which predominate in the lower half of the slope of the ridge. Named by Ohio State University workers in 1960–61 and 1961–62.

Terrapin Hill. 63°58'S, 57°32'W. 545 m. Red-colored, and round-shaped (like a terrapin—hence the name given by the FIDS in 1948). At the south end of The Naze, on James Ross Island. Charted by the FIDS in 1945.

Mount Terrazas. 74°52'S, 63°51'W. 10 miles west of Mount Austin, in Palmer Land. Named for Rudolph D. Terrazas, builder at Amundsen-Scott South Pole Station in 1967.

Terre Adélie see **Adélie Land**

Terres Australes et Antarctiques Françaises. On March 27, 1924, all French claims in Antarctica were placed under the governor of Madagascar, and in 1925 were made a National Park. On April 1, 1938, the boundaries of this territory were fixed, and on Aug. 6, 1955, all French Antarctic and sub–Antarctic lands came under a new administration, from Paris, and achieved territorial status, independent of Madagascar.

Territorial Claims. Great Britain was the first to claim a piece of Antarctica (see **British Antarctic Territory**, and **Falkland Islands Dependencies**). This was in 1908, and the claim was based on propinquity to the Falklands as well as discovery by Ross, Scott, et al. Part of the British territory went to New Zealand in 1923 (see **Ross Dependency**). The reasons that New Zealand established the claim were 1. Britain gave it to them; 2. propinquity to New Zealand. The Ar-

gentines formulated claims to the South Orkneys in 1925, and to all of the remaining British claims in 1937. In 1942 Argentina formally claimed their stake. Their reasons were 1. propinquity; 2. geological continuity from their own country; 3. the Papal Bull, issued in Columbus' day, giving all land west of a line in the Atlantic to Spain. Norway claimed Peter I Island in 1931, and the Queen Maud Land area in 1939 (see **Norwegian Dependency**). They based their claim on the island because it was a Norwegian ship which discovered it. The claim to the continental mass was based on Amundsen's being the first man to the South Pole. It was also made to preempt the Nazis (see below). In 1933 Australia claimed a huge chunk of the Antarctic continent, based on propinquity to their own country, and on Mawson's discoveries (see **Australian Antarctic Territory**). In 1938 France formally fixed the boundaries of Adélie Land (see **Terres Australes et Antarctiques Françaises**), basing their claim on Dumont d'Urville's expedition. In 1938–39 Nazi Germany claimed the New Schwabenland area of Queen Maud Land (see **German New Schwabenland Expedition**). In 1940 Chile made a formal claim to most of the area claimed by Britain and Argentina. It used the same arguments that Argentina did. These have been the claimants. All except Nazi Germany still claim their wedge-shaped areas. Although explorers have claimed land for the USA and USSR (or Russia), these two countries have not claimed it for themselves, although they have as good a right as anybody to do so, probably better, and they do not recognize the claims of other nations (when one looks at some of the bases for these claims it is hardly surprising). Interestingly, though, the two countries have reserved the right to claim later (i.e., at some future, unspecified date). One supposes that if the economy should dictate it, they would claim. Indeed, the French claim upset the Americans who, in 1924, had stated that in order to establish a claim (anywhere in the world), a valid settlement must be made. All Antarctic land between 90°W and 150°W is unclaimed. The Antarctic Treaty does not compromise claims made before 1959 (when the Treaty was signed), but it does not allow new claims while the Treaty is in force. The spirit of the Treaty does not actually recognize pre-existing claims either. Geographically then, working the sectors from east to west, the Antarctic pie is divided as follows: 20°W–80°W, Great Britain; 25°W–74°W (overlapping), Argentina; 53°W–90°W (overlapping), Chile; 90°W–150°W, unclaimed; mostly US sphere of influence; 150°W–160°E, New Zealand; 160°E–142°E, Australia; 142°E–136°E, France; 136°E–45°E, Australia; 45°E–20°W, Norway (but only as far south as *about* 85°S, and as far north as *about* 65°S. All the other claimants go from 60°S all the way to the Pole).

The *Terror*. A small bomb/signal boat of 340 tons, made entirely of wood, and reinforced for the ice. It was Ross' cadet ship during his 1839–43 expedition. It had the same crew complement as the *Erebus*. Crozier commanded, and Pownall P. Cotter was master.

Mount Terror. 77°29'S, 168°32'E. 3,230 m. 20 miles east of Mount Erebus, in the eastern half of Ross Island. It is an extinct volcano, and is the second highest mountain on the island. Discovered in 1841 by Ross, and named by him for one of his ships.

Terror Basin. 77°15'S, 169°E. A submarine feature of the Ross Sea, to the immediate north of Ross Island.

Terror Glacier. 77°37'S, 168°E. Between Mount Terra Nova and Mount Terror, this is one of the three major glaciers on Ross Island (cf. Aurora Glacier and Barne Glacier). It feeds Fog Bay (part of Windless Bight). Named by A.J. Heine of the NZGSAE 1962–63 in association with Mount Terror.

Terror Point. 77°41'S, 168°13'E. Between Cape Mackay and Sultans Head Rock, on the south side of Ross Island. It juts out into Windless Bight, and is the eastern limit of Fog Bay. It is actually 4 miles WNW of Cape Mackay. Named by Scott's 1901–4 expedition for the mountain which overlooks this point from the NE.

Terry, Richard. Seaman on the Wilkes Expedition 1838–42. Joined in the USA. Lost in the *Sea Gull* on, or around, April 29, 1839.

Tertene Nunataks. 72°16'S, 21°57'E. Several small nunataks on the west side of Kreitzerisen, near the west end of the Sør Rondane Mountains. Name means "the tarts" in Norwegian.

Mount Terwileger. 75°13'S, 64°44'W. On the north side of Ueda Glacier, at the SE end of the Scaife Mountains, near the base of the Antarctic Peninsula. Named for Stephen E. Terwileger, hospital corpsman at Amundsen-Scott South Pole Station in 1967.

Tester Nunatak. 70°58'S, 71°29'E. In the northern part of the Manning Nunataks, in the east part of the Amery Ice Shelf. Named by the Australians for J. Tester, aircraft engineer with the ANARE Prince Charles Mountains survey party in 1969.

Tethys Nunataks. 72°10'S, 68°59'W. A group of 5 rock nunataks, 2 miles NE of Stephenson Nunatak, in the SE corner of Alexander Island. Surveyed in 1949 by the FIDS, and named by the UK for Tethys, Saturn's moon (Saturn Glacier is near the Tethys Nunataks).

Tetrad Islands. 63°53'S, 60°45'W. A group of 4 small islands, SE of Borge Point, Trinity Island. Named descriptively by the UK in 1960.

Teyssier Island. 67°36'S, 62°53'E. At the south end of the Jocelyn Islands, in Holme Bay, Mac. Robertson Land. Photographed by the LCE 1936–37. Named later by the Australians for P. Teyssier, cook at Mawson Station in 1959.

The *Thala Dan*. Ice-strengthened supply/research ship of 2,000 tons belonging to the J. Lauritzen Lines of Copenhagen. Used extensively by the ANARE in the late 1950s and early 1960s. In 1982–83 Brazil bought it for an expedition in that summer, and renamed it the *Barão de Teffe*.

Thala Hills. 67°42′S, 46°E. Between Freeth Bay and Spooner Bay, in Enderby Land, behind Molodezhnaya Station. Named by the Australians for the *Thala Dan*, from which the ANARE visited these hills in Feb. 1961.

Thala Island. 70°38′S, 166°05′E. The southern of two small rocky islands, just off the NW edge of the Davis Ice Piedmont, on the north coast of Victoria Land. Named by the ANARE for the *Thala Dan*.

Thala Rock. 68°33′S, 77°52′E. A submerged, isolated rock off the Vestfold Hills, 1⅓ miles from the western point of Turner Island. The *Thala Dan* ran into it on Jan. 16, 1959. Named by the Australians for that ship.

Thälmann Mountains. 72°S, 4°45′E. Between Flogeken Glacier and Vestreskorve Glacier, in the Mühlig-Hofmann Mountains of Queen Maud Land. Named by USSR in 1961 for German Communist leader Ernst Thälmann (1886–1944).

Thanaron, Charles. Charles-Jules-Adolphe Thanaron. Lieutenant on the *Zélée* during Dumont d'Urville's 1837–40 expedition.

Thanaron Hill *see* **Hanson Hill**

Thanaron Point. 63°30′S, 58°40′W. 8 miles east of Cape Roquemaurel, Trinity Peninsula. Named Cap Thanaron by Dumont d'Urville in 1838, for Charles Thanaron. Later redefined by the UK.

Thanksgiving Point. 84°56′S, 177°W. A nunatak at the west side of Shackleton Glacier, just north of the mouth of Mincey Glacier, in the Queen Maud Mountains. Named by the Texas Tech Shackleton Glacier Party of 1962–63,

who reached here on Thanksgiving Day, 1962.

Tharp Ice Rise. 72°25′S, 59°54′W. Off the east coast of Palmer Land.

Thawley, Elbert J. 2nd assistant engineer on the *Eleanor Bolling* during the first half of Byrd's 1928–30 expedition. During the second half he replaced John Cody as 1st assistant engineer.

Mount Theaker. 70°18′S, 159°38′E. 1,685 m. On the north wall of the Robilliard Glacier, 3 miles NE of Mount Simmonds, in the Usarp Mountains. Named for Paul R. Theaker, biologist at McMurdo Station in 1967–68.

Themis Nunatak. 71°37′S, 69°06′W. Flat-topped. 6 miles WSW of Mount Umbriel, in southern Alexander Island. Named by the UK for one of Saturn's satellites (Saturn Glacier is near Themis Nunatak).

Thène, Edwin. Seaman on the Wilkes Expedition 1838–42. Joined in the USA. Served the cruise.

Theodolite Hill. 63°29′S, 57°35′W. 690 m. 5 miles west of the NW end of Duse Bay, in the NE part of Trinity Peninsula. It stands at the SE corner of a plateau-type mountain. Discovered by the FIDS in 1946. They used this hill as a theodolite station.

Mount Theodore. 64°58′S, 62°38′W. 4 miles SE of Mount Inverleith, on the south side of Bagshawe Glacier, near the west coast of Graham Land. Named by David Ferguson in 1913.

Thermometers. Foster left two self-recording thermometers on Deception Island in 1829 which, when recovered by Smyley in 1842, gave the low reading of −5°F. The high-recording one was broken. Most expeditions, especially from the time of the Heroic Era (q.v.), took thermometers.

Thern Promontory. 74°33′S, 162°06′E. 2,220 m. Ice-covered. At the south end of the Eisenhower Range, 7 miles west of Mount Nansen, in Victoria Land. Named for Michael G. Thern, station engineer at

McMurdo Station in 1965–66 and in 1967.

The *Theron*. 839-ton, 1,310 hp Canadian motor sealer, built in Glasgow in 1950 for Arctic work. It was Fuchs' ship for the BCTAE 1955–58, and left London on Nov. 14, 1955, with a sealing crew under the command of Harald Marø (captain from 1955–58). It arrived at Vahsel Bay on Jan. 28, 1956, and on Feb. 9, 1956, left Antarctica with Fuchs and all but the advance party of the BCTAE. It arrived back in London on March 23, 1956.

Theron Mountains. 79°05′S, 28°15′W. They rise to 1,175 m., and extend for 28 miles on the east side of the Filchner Ice Shelf. Discovered aerially in 1956 by the BCTAE, and named by them for the *Theron*.

Mount Theseus. 77°26′S, 162°16′E. 1,830 m. Just south of Clark Glacier, in the Olympus Range of Victoria Land. Named by the New Zealanders for the Greek mythological hero.

Theta Islands. 64°19′S, 63°01′W. Also known as Islas Alzogaray. Several small islands and rocks, just west of Kappa Island, at the west extremity of the Melchior Islands. Charted in 1927 by the personnel on the *Discovery*. Surveyed by the Argentines in 1942 and 1943, and named by them in 1946 for the Greek letter.

Thiébault Island. 65°11′S, 64°11′W. A small island, just west of Charlat Island, in the small group off the south end of Petermann Island, in the Wilhelm Archipelago. Discovered by Charcot in 1908–10, and named by him for the French minister to Argentina.

Thiel Mountains. 85°15′S, 91°W. 45 miles long. Isolated. Mainly snow-capped. Between the Horlick Mountains and the Pensacola Mountains. They extend from the Moulton Escarpment on the west to Nolan Pillar on the east, and include the Ford Massif and the Bermel Escarpment. Named for Edward C. Thiel (*see* **Deaths, 1961**).

Thil Island. 70°08′S, 72°38′E. A small island, 1 mile NE of Jennings Promontory, in the eastern part of the Amery Ice Shelf. Delineated by John H. Roscoe in 1952, using Operation Highjump photos taken in 1946–47, and named by him for R.B. Thil, air crewman on Operation Highjump flights here.

Thimble Peak. 63°27′S, 57°06′W. 485 m. A truncated cone, consisting of rock and ice. At the east side of Mondor Glacier, 2 miles NE of Duse Bay, at the NE end of the Antarctic Peninsula. Charted by the FIDS in 1946. Named descriptively by the UK in 1948.

Thirin, Antoine Auguste. Ensign on the *Zélée* during Dumont d'Urville's 1837–40 expedition.

Thode Island. 77°02′S, 148°03′W. A small, ice-covered island in the Sulzberger Ice Shelf, 1 mile NW of Benton Island, and 5 miles east of Przybyszewski Island, in the Marshall Archipelago. Named for George C. Thode, meteorologist at Byrd Station in 1968.

Mount Tholus. 63°16′S, 56°04′W. 825 m. In the central part of Joinville Island, near Postern Gap. Surveyed by the FIDS in 1953–54, and named descriptively by the UK in 1956. A tholus is a circular, domed structure.

Thom, Capt. Commander of the *Southern Sky*, in 1916.

Lake Thomas. 77°24′S, 162°15′E. A meltwater lake in Victoria Land. Robertson Ridge is on the NW, and Clark Glacier is on the NE. Named for Robert H. Thomas, glaciologist on the Ross Ice Shelf in 1973–74 and 1974–75.

Mount Thomas. 71°01′S, 64°36′E. Mainly snow-covered. 7 miles north of Mount Hicks, in the Prince Charles Mountains. It has a domed appearance, with a ridge running east to a smaller peak. Named by the Australians for I.N. Thomas, radio officer at Wilkes Station in 1963.

Point Thomas. 62°10′S, 58°30′W. On the west side as you enter Admiralty Bay,

it is the furthest point north before Ezcurra Inlet, King George Island, in the
South Shetlands. There is a mixed penguin colony here (Gentoos, Adélies, and
Chinstraps). Charted by Charcot in
1908–10, and named by him for Thomas
(q.v.).

Thomas. Member of Charcot's 1908–
10 expedition on the *Pourquoi Pas?*

Thomas, Charles. Seaman on the
Wilkes Expedition 1838–42. Joined in
the USA. Run at Sydney.

Thomas, Charles W. Rear admiral, US
Coast Guard. d. March 3, 1973, in a car
crash in Ushuaia, Argentina. He commanded the *Northwind* during Operation Highjump, 1946–47, and during
Operation Deep Freeze I (1955–56) was
chief of staff to Admiral Dufek, and was
officer in tactical command of Little
America V. He retired in 1957. He wrote
Ice Is Where You Find It. At his death
he was ice pilot on the *Lindblad Explorer.*

Thomas, David. Officer's cook on the
Wilkes Expedition 1838–42. Joined at
Fiji. Served the cruise.

Thomas Glacier. 78°40′S, 83°58′W.
Z-shaped. Flows from the SE slopes of the
Vinson Massif, for 17 miles through the
southern part of the Sentinel Range,
leaving the range south of Johnson Spur.
Discovered by VX-6 on Dec. 15, 1959.
Named for Rear-Adm. Charles W.
Thomas.

Thomas Hills. 84°21′S, 65°12′W. A
line of hills, 17 miles long, between the
Foundation Ice Stream and MacNamara
Glacier, at the north end of the Patuxent
Range of the Pensacola Mountains.
Named by Finn Ronne for Charles S.
Thomas, secretary of the US Navy, 1954–
57.

The *Thomas Hunt.* Stonington,
Conn., sealer in the South Shetlands for
most of the seasons in the 1870s. In 1873–
74 it was under the command of Capt.
Andrew J. Eldred, and lost 7 men that
season. In 1874–75 it got only one seal
skin, due to difficult ice conditions. Cap-

tain that year was probably Eldred, but
this is not confirmed. It was there in
1875–76, 1878–79, and 1879–80, each
time under Eldred, the last season
helping in the search for the lost *Charles
Shearer.*

Thomas Island. 66°07′S, 100°57′E. 6
miles long. Between 1 and 3 miles wide.
In the Highjump Archipelago, 1946–47.
Named for Lt. (jg) Randolph G.
Thomas, USN, hydrographer officer on
Operation Windmill, 1947–48.

The *Thomas J. Gary.* US ship in Antarctica in 1965–66 and 1966–67.

Thomas Mountains. 75°32′S, 70°57′
W. Also called Lowell Thomas Mountains, Mount Lowell Thomas. 5 miles
long. 15 miles NE of Mount Horne, just
south of the Sweeney Mountains, at the
base of Palmer Land. Discovered by the
RARE 1947–48, and named by Finn
Ronne for the author Lowell Thomas, a
supporter of the expedition.

Thomas Nunatak. 78°54′S, 87°25′W.
The northern of two nunataks, about 17
miles west of the Camp Hills, in the Ellsworth Mountains. Named by the University of Minnesota Geological Party here
in 1963–64, for Hollie Thomas, helicopter crew chief with the 62nd Transportation Detachment who helped the
party.

Thomas Nunataks. 70°32′S, 65°11′E.
A group of 3 nunataks, 2 miles SW of
Mount Mervyn, in the Porthos Range of
the Prince Charles Mountains. Named by
the Australians for I.L. Thomas, physicist
at Mawson Station in 1967.

Thomas Peak. 72°46′S, 166°43′E.
2,040 m. At the west side of Malta Plateau, on the ridge between the Wilhelm
and Olson Glaciers, in the Victory Mountains of Victoria Land. Named for Francis
J. Thomas, biologist at McMurdo Station
in 1962–63 and 1964–65.

Thomas Rock. 75°42′S, 158°36′E. A
small nunatak, 1 mile NE of Tent Rock.
6 miles west of the Ricker Hills, in the
Prince Albert Mountains of Victoria

Land. Named for Kenneth E. Thomas, radioman at Amundsen-Scott South Pole Station in 1966.

Thomas Spur. 85°53'S, 161°40'W. Extends east from the Rawson Plateau, between the Moffett and Tate Glaciers, in the Queen Maud Mountains. Named for Harry F. Thomas, meteorologist at South Pole Station in 1960.

The *Thomas Washington*. Research vessel operated by the Scripps Institution of Oceanography. In 1970–71 it was on a 9-month Pacific-wide expedition, and spent about 35 days south of 60°S in Jan. and Feb. 1971.

Thomas Watson Escarpment *see* **Watson Escarpment**

Thompo Icefall. 83°18'S, 50°08'W. In the Pensacola Mountains.

The *Thompson*. Its more correct name was the *Thomas G. Thompson*. US research vessel, sometime in the Antarctic in the mid-1970s.

¹Mount Thompson. 70°40'S, 62°21'W. 1,690 m. NW of Lehrke Inlet. Surmounts the central part of the base of Eielson Peninsula, on the east coast of Palmer Land. Discovered by the RARE 1947–48, and named by Ronne for Andrew A. Thompson.

²Mount Thompson *see* **Thompson Mountain**

Thompson, Andrew A. Geophysicist on the RARE 1947–48. He was in charge of seismological, magnetic, and tidal investigations.

Thompson, Egbert. Midshipman on the *Peacock* during the Wilkes Expedition 1838–42.

¹Thompson, John. Seaman on the Wilkes Expedition 1838–42. Joined in the USA. Run at Sydney.

²Thompson, John. Captain of the fo'c's'le on the Wilkes Expedition 1838–42. Joined in the USA. Served the cruise.

Thompson, Matthew. Captain of the topsail on the Wilkes Expedition 1838–42. Joined in the USA. Sent home on the *Relief* in 1839.

Thompson, Richard H.J. Australian administrative officer, Antarctic Division, Melbourne. Second-in-command for several years in the 1950s of ANARE relief expeditions to Mawson Station.

Thompson, Robert. Australian who, in Sept. 1962, left Wilkes Station and, with his team, traveled to a deserted (he did not know it was until he got there) Vostok Station with Caterpillar tractors and sledges.

Thompson, T.N. Lt. cdr., USN. Took over as military leader of Little America from Howard Orndorff, on Nov. 28, 1957.

Thompson, William. Seaman on the Wilkes Expedition 1838–42. Joined in the USA. Served the cruise.

Thompson Escarpment. 79°27'S, 83°30'W. 8 miles long. At the head of Flanagan Glacier, in the Pioneer Heights of the Heritage Range. Named for Cdr. Robert C. Thompson, VX-6 operations officer in 1965.

Thompson Glacier. 66°45'S, 123°39'E. A channel glacier which flows into the head of Paulding Bay. Named for Egbert Thompson.

Thompson Island. 66°S, 111°07'E. The largest and most NE of the Balaena Islands, ½ mile from the coast of East Antarctica. 15 miles NE of the Windmill Islands. It consists of 2 rocky knolls separated by a low snow saddle which could mean that it is two islands connected by ice. Visited by an ANARE party on Jan. 19, 1956, and named by them for Richard Thompson.

Thompson Mountain. 81°50'S, 159°48'E. Also called Mount Thompson. 2,350 m. 5 miles south of Mount McKerrow, in the SW part of the Surveyors Range. Named by the New Zealanders in 1960–61 for Edgar H. Thompson, professor of surveying and photogrammetry at the University College of London, England.

Thompson Nunataks. 79°27'S, 85°49'W. Three evenly spaced nunataks, 4 miles south of Navigator Peak. They surmount the central part of White Escarpment, in the Heritage Range of the Ellsworth Mountains. Named for Russel W. Thompson, US meteorologist at Wilkes Station in 1963.

Thompson Peak. 69°25′S, 157°39′E. 980 m. 5 miles south of Ringgold Knoll in the NW end of the Wilson Hills. Named by the Australians for Richard H.J. Thompson.

Thompson Peaks. 84°26′S, 166°30′E. Two peaks on the divide between the upper Moody Glacier and Bingley Glacier, in the Queen Alexandra Range. Named for Douglas C. Thompson, cosmic ray scientist at McMurdo Station in 1963, and at Amundsen-Scott South Pole Station in 1965.

Thompson Peninsula. 64°28′S, 63°08′W. 3 miles long. Forms the north side of the entrance to Fournier Bay, on Anvers Island. Surveyed by the FIDS in 1955–57, and named by the UK for John W. Thompson, FIDS general assistant and mountain climber at Base N in 1956 and leader there in 1957.

¹Thompson Point *see* **Thomson Point**

²Thompson Point. 70°18′S, 161°04′E. Descends from the Kavrayskiy Hills into the western part of the terminus of the Rennick Glacier. Named for Max C. Thompson, biologist at McMurdo Station in 1966–67.

Thompson Ridge. 76°27′S, 146°05′W. 2 miles long. On the south shore of Block Bay, 3½ miles NW of Mount Iphigene, in Marie Byrd Land. Named by Byrd in 1941 for Gershom J. Thompson, doctor at the Mayo Clinic, supporter and adviser on Byrd's first two Antarctic expeditions.

Thompson Spur. 71°32′S, 160°23′E. Descends from the Daniels Range, between the Swanson and Edwards Glaciers, in the Usarp Mountains. Named for David H. Thompson, biologist at Hallett Station in 1965–66 and 1967–68.

Thomsen, C.S. Captain of the *Ajax,* in Antarctic waters in 1937.

Thomsen Islands. 65°47′S, 66°16′W. A group of small islands, 2 miles SW of

Speerschneider Point, off the west side of Renaud Island, in the Biscoe Islands. Named by the UK in 1959 for Helge Thomsen, Danish Arctic ice expert in the 1940s and 1950s.

Punta Thomson *see* **Rahir Point**

Thomson, Leslie James F. Second officer on the *Aurora,* 1914–15, and first officer, 1915–16. He died in Australia.

Thomson, Sir Wyville. b. March 5, 1830, Bonsyde, West Lothian. d. March 10, 1882, Bonsyde. Charles Wyville Thomson. Scottish marine biologist and professor of natural history. He was leader of the *Challenger* expedition of 1872–76. Knighted in 1876.

Thomson Cove. 65°06′S, 63°14′W. 1 mile wide. Just north of Étienne Fjord, in Flandres Bay, on the west coast of Graham Land. Charted by Charcot in 1903–5, and named by him as Baie Thomson, for Gaston-Arnold-Marie Thomson (1848–1932), minister of the French Navy.

Thomson Head. 67°35′S, 66°46′W. 915 m. A headland at the east side of Bourgeois Fjord, between the Perutz and Bader Glaciers, on the west coast of Graham Land. Surveyed in 1936 by the BGLE. Resurveyed in 1948–49 by the FIDS, and named by them for William H. Thomson, FIDS air pilot at Base E in 1947.

Thomson Massif. 70°35′S, 66°48′E. In the Aramis Range of the Prince Charles Mountains. Mount Sundberg and Mount McGregor come out from it. Named by the Australians for Robert B. Thomson of New Zealand, scientific leader at Hallett Station in 1960, officer-in-charge of Wilkes Station in 1962, and deputy-leader at Scott Base in 1963–64.

Thomson Peak. 72°S, 166°03′E. 2,350 m. 11 miles SE of Mount Shute, in the extreme southern limit of the Mirabito Range. Named by the New Zealanders in 1963–64 for Robert B. Thomson (*see* **Thomson Massif**).

Thomson Point. 60°43′S, 44°38′W. On the east side of Pirie Peninsula, almost 1¾ miles SE of Cape Mabel, on the north coast of Laurie Island, in the South Orkneys. Charted in 1903 by Bruce, who named it for J. Arthur Thomson, Regius professor of natural history, University of Aberdeen, Scotland.

Thomson Rock. 71°27'S, 66°56'W. A nunatak on the east edge of the Batterbee Mountains, 3 miles east of Mount Bagshawe, in Palmer Land. Named by the UK for Michael R.A. Thomson, BAS geologist at Fossil Bluff Station and at Base E between 1963 and 1966.

Mount Thor. 77°35'S, 160°42'E. 2,000 m. South of The Labyrinth, in the Asgard Range of Victoria Land. Named by the New Zealanders in 1958–59 for the Norse god.

Thor Island. 64°33'S, 62°W. The largest of a group of small islands at the east side of Foyn Harbor, in Wilhelmina Bay, off the west coast of Graham Land. Named South Thor Island in 1921–22 by whalers in the area, for the *Thor I,* which was moored here that season. Renamed in 1960 by the UK. *See also* **North Thor Island** for a more detailed description of what happened here in the naming and renaming of these features.

The *Thor I.* Norwegian factory whaling ship in Antarctic Peninsula waters in 1921–22.

Mount Thorarinsson. 67°15'S, 64°59' W. At the south side of the terminus of the Hess Glacier, on the east coast of Graham Land. Named by the UK for Sigurdur Thorarinsson, Icelandic glaciologist.

The *Thorfinn.* Norwegian whale catcher, in Antarctic waters in the 1930s.

Thorfinn Islands. 67°21'S, 60°54'E. A group of small islands (including Heckmann Island), 5 miles off the coast of Mac. Robertson Land, between Campbell Head and Cape Simpson. Photographed by the LCE 1936–37, and named by the Norwegians for the *Thorfinn.*

The *Thorgaut.* Norwegian whale catching ship in Antarctic waters in 1930–31, under the command of Rolf Walter.

Thorgaut Island. 67°27'S, 63°33'E. The largest island in the NE part of the Robinson Group, 7 miles NW of Mount Daly. Discovered by the *Thorgaut* (hence the name) in 1931.

Thorgaut Islands *see* **Robinson Group**

Mount Thorne. 85°41'S, 158°40'W. 1,465 m. On the east flank of the Amundsen Glacier, 6 miles NW of Mount Goodale, in the Hays Mountains of the Queen Maud Mountains. Discovered in Jan. 1929 by Gould's Southern Geological Party, and named by Byrd for one of this 6-man party, George A. Thorne.

Thorne, George A. Member of the shore party during Byrd's 1928–30 expedition. He took part in Gould's Southern Geological Party of Dec. 1929.

Thorne Glacier *see* **Robert Scott Glacier**

Thorne Point. 66°57'S, 67°13'W. On the west side of Langmuir Cove, marking the NE end of Arrowsmith Peninsula, in Graham Land. Named by the UK for John Thorne, FIDS meteorologist at Base W in 1956 and 1957.

Thorne Refugio. Argentine refuge hut built in Telefon Bay, Deception Island, in 1949.

Mount Thornton. 73°34'S, 77°07'W. Between Mount McCann and Mount Benkert, in the east central part of the Snow Nunataks, in Ellsworth Land. Discovered by the USAS 1939–41. Named for Capt. Richard Thornton, commander of the *Eltanin* in 1967–68.

Thorp Ridges. 66°34'S, 52°51'E. Three almost parallel ridges 18 miles west of Stor Hånakken Mountain in Enderby Land. Named by the Australians for A. Thorp, electrical fitter at Wilkes Station in 1961.

The *Thorshammer.* Norwegian factory whaling ship in Antarctic waters in 1930–31 and 1932–33, both seasons commanded by Gustav B. Bull. In 1936–37 it was back, this time with Bråvold as manager (captain).

The *Thorshavn*. Norwegian tanker owned by Lars Christensen. It came down to the Antarctic every summer between 1930–31 and 1936–37, Christensen himself leading each of the expeditions except the one of 1934–35, when Klarius Mikkelsen led it. On Feb. 20, 1935, a landing party, including Caroline Mikkelsen, made it ashore from the vessel, after having discovered the Ingrid Christensen Coast. The 1936–37 expedition is the one referred to in this book as the LCE 1936–37.

The *Thorshøvdi*. Norwegian factory whaling ship in Antarctica in 1949–50.

Mount Thorvald Nilsen   *see*   Nilsen Plateau

Thorvald Nilsen Mountains   *see* Nilsen Plateau

Bay of the Thousand Icebergs   *see* Duse Bay

Three Brothers Hill. 62°15′S, 58°41′ W. 210 m. Also called Brothers Hill. Part of an extinct volcano, on the east side of Potter Cove, King George Island, in the South Shetlands. It has 3 summits. Named before 1921.

Three Brothers Islands. Discovered in Feb. 1821 by von Bellingshausen in the South Shetlands. Named by him as Ostrova Tri Brata. Later given individual names — Aspland Island, O'Brien Island, and Eadie Island.

Three Degree Depot. 87°S, 160°03′E. One of Scott's depots.

300-Mile Depot. Established by Byrd in 1928–29, 300 miles south of Little America, on the Ross Ice Shelf.

Three Lakes Valley. 60°42′S, 45°37′ W. Contains 3 freshwater lakes. Extends from Elephant Flats to Stygian Cove, on Signy Island, in the South Orkneys. Surveyed and named descriptively by the FIDS in 1947.

Three Little Pigs. 65°14′S, 64°17′W. Three small islands. ⅓ mile NW of Winter Island, in the Argentine Islands. Charted and named by the BGLE in 1935.

Three Nunataks. 80°03′S, 154°53′E. Mostly ice-covered. 2 miles SW of Haven Mountain, at the NW edge of the Britannia Range. Named by the Darwin Glacier Party of the BCTAE in 1956–58.

Three Pup Island   *see*   Pup Rock

Three Sails. 80°27′S, 80°42′W. Three small, isolated nunataks in a row, 6 miles east of the Redpath Peaks, at the south side of the Heritage Range. Named descriptively by the University of Minnesota Geological Party here in 1963–64.

Three Sisters Cones. 77°34′S, 166°58′ E. Three aligned cones at a height of about 1,800 m., on the lower parts of Mount Erebus, Ross Island. Named by Scott's 1910–13 expedition.

Three Sisters Point. 62°04′S, 57°53′ W. Marked by 3 conspicuous boulders. Forms the west side of the entrance to Sherratt Bay, on the south coast of King George Island, in the South Shetlands. Charted and named descriptively by the personnel on the *Discovery II* in 1937.

Three Slice Island   *see*   Three Slice Nunatak

Three Slice Nunatak. 68°02′S, 64°57′ W. Also called Three Slice Island. 500 m. Looks like a serrated edge. Snow-covered, except for the 3 almost vertical rock faces, which give the name. On Joerg Peninsula, just north of Mobiloil Inlet, on the east coast of the Antarctic Peninsula. Discovered by East Base personnel during the USAS in 1940.

Threshold Nunatak. 83°46′S, 166°06′ E. Isolated. At the mouth of Tillite Glacier, 5 miles NE of Portal Rock, in the Queen Alexandra Range. Named by John Gunner of the Ohio State University Geological Expedition of 1969–70. He was landed here to collect a rock sample. Named in association with Portal Rock.

Thrinaxodon Col. 85°12′S, 174°19′W. 2 miles SE of Rougier Hill, in the Cumulus Hills of the Queen Maud Mountains. Named in 1971 by David H. Elliot of the Ohio State University

Institute of Polar Studies. Many samples of the fossil Thrinaxodon (a mammal-like creature) were found here.

The *Thule*. Owned by the Thule Whaling Company of Oslo. One of the first factory whaling ships to flense whales at sea. It operated in the South Orkneys in 1912–13 and 1913–14.

Thule Islands. 60°42′S, 45°37′W. A group of small islands and rocks, ¼ mile SW of Balin Point, in the NW part of Borge Bay, Signy Island, in the South Orkneys. Named before 1916 as Thule Rock, or Thule Rocks, for the *Thule.* Redefined by the UK in 1947 following a FIDS survey.

Thule Rock   *see*   **Thule Islands**

Thule Rocks   *see*   **Thule Islands**

The *Thulla*. Norwegian steamship which, in 1911–12, was in the South Orkneys looking for suitable anchorages for factory whaling ships.

Thulla Point. 60°43′S, 45°40′W. Ice-free. 1 mile NE of Jebsen Point, on the west coast of Signy Island. Surveyed in 1933 by personnel on the *Discovery II,* and in 1947 by the FIDS. Named in 1954 by the UK for the *Thulla.*

Thuma Peak. 69°39′S, 72°10′W. In the NW part of Alexander Island.

Thumb   *see*   **Little Thumb**

Thumb Islet   *see*   **Thumb Rock**

Thumb Point. 75°58′S, 160°28′E. A rock spur extending from the NW side of The Mitten, in the Prince Albert Mountains of Victoria Land. Named by the New Zealanders in 1962–63 because it looks like the thumb on a mitten.

Thumb Rock. 65°15′S, 64°16′W. Between Winter Island and the NW end of Galíndez Island, in the Argentine Islands. Charted by the BGLE in 1935, and named descriptively by them.

Thunder Glacier. 64°50′S, 63°24′W. A through glacier, 4 miles long, flowing across Wiencke Island from east to west between Sierra DuFief and the Wall Range. Charted in 1944 by the personnel

of Operation Tabarin, and named by them for the thunderous avalanche which nearly covered them here.

Mount Thundergut. 77°39′S, 161°24′E. 3 miles NE of Saint Pauls Mountain, in the Asgard Range of Victoria Land. Named descriptively by New Zealand. When seen from the east, it presents a very steep domed face with a vertical gut subject to rockfall.

Mount Thurman. 84°41′S, 170°49′W. 780 m. The highest summit in the Bravo Hills, on the edge of the Ross Ice Shelf, between the mouths of the Gough and Le Couteur Glaciers. Named for Cdr. Robert K. Thurman, USN, assistant chief of staff for operations, US Naval Support Force, Antarctica, 1963.

Mount Thurston   *see*   **Johansen Peak**

Thurston Glacier. 73°18′S, 125°18′W. 15 miles long. Flows from the SE slopes of Mount Siple on Siple Island. Named for Thomas R. Thurston, meteorologist at Byrd Station in 1965.

Thurston Island. 72°20′S, 99°W. 135 miles long. 55 miles wide. An ice-covered, glacially dissected island between the Amundsen and Bellingshausen Seas, off the NW end of Ellsworth Land. Separated from the mainland by the Peacock Sound. Discovered aerially on Feb. 27, 1940, on a flight from the *Bear* during the USAS 1939–41. Charted as a peninsula, and named by Byrd as Thurston Peninsula, for W. Harris Thurston, New York textile manufacturer, and a supporter. The name Eights Peninsula was also given to it, before it was redefined in Feb. 1960.

Thurston Peninsula   *see*   **Thurston Island**

Thwaites Glacier. 75°30′S, 106°45′W. Feeds the Walgreen Coast from Marie Byrd Land. Its terminus is about 30 miles east of Mount Murphy. Its seaward extensions are the Thwaites Glacier Tongue (q.v.) and the Thwaites Iceberg Tongue (q.v.). Named in association with the iceberg tongue.

Thwaites Glacier Tongue. 75°S, 106° 50′W. 40 miles long. 20 miles wide. The seaward extension of the Thwaites Glacier, in the Amundsen Sea. Named for Fredrik T. Thwaites, glacial geologist at the University of Wisconsin.

Thwaites Iceberg Tongue. 74°S, 108° 30′W. 70 miles long. 20 miles wide. 20 miles NE of Bear Peninsula, in the Amundsen Sea, off the coast of Marie Byrd Land. It is aground. In Jan. 1966 its southern end was only 3 miles north of the Thwaites Glacier Tongue, from which it had broken off. Named in association with the glacier tongue and the glacier.

Thyer Glacier. 67°45′S, 49°E. Flows along the south side of the Raggatt Mountains, between the Nye Mountains and the Scott Mountains, in Enderby Land, into Casey Bay. Named by the Australians for R.F. Thyer, chief geophysicist, Bureau of Mineral Resources, Australian Department of National Development.

Tiber Rocks. 68°23′S, 67°W. A group near the head of Rymill Bay, just west of the mouth of Romulus Glacier. 3 miles NW of the highest summit of Black Thumb, off the west coast of Graham Land. Discovered and surveyed by the BGLE in 1936. Resurveyed and named by the FIDS in 1948–49, in association with the Romulus and Remus Glaciers.

Tickell Head. 60°32′S, 45°48′W. A headland forming the east side of Bridger Bay, on the north coast of Coronation Island, in the South Orkneys. Discovered in Dec. 1821 by Powell and Palmer. Surveyed by the FIDS in 1956–58. Named by the UK for William L.N. Tickell, FIDS meteorologist at Signy Island Station in 1955, and leader there in 1956.

Tickhill, Terry Lee. b. 1950. American sophomore who, in 1969–70, went to Antarctica as part of Lois Jones' all-women party. She was one of the first six women to the South Pole. A chemistry major, she later became an aquatic ecologist with the US Fish and Wildlife Service.

Tickle Channel. 67°06′S, 67°43′W. Between 1 and 3 miles wide. 5 miles long. In the south part of Hanusse Bay, this marine channel separates Hansen Island from the east end of Adelaide Island. Discovered aerially by the BGLE in Feb. 1936. Surveyed on the ground by the FIDS in 1948, and named by them. A tickle is a narrow water passage between two islands in the Arctic.

Tidblón, Carlos *see* **Timblón, Carlos**

Mount Tidd. 81°17′S, 85°13′W. Also called Mount Pirrit. Highest summit in the Pirrit Hills. Named for Lt. Paul Tidd.

Tidd, Paul. Lt., USN. Took over from Finn Ronne as officer-in-charge of Ellsworth Station on Jan. 16, 1958.

Tierney Peninsula. 72°20′S, 95°45′W. 14 miles long. Ice-covered. Between Savage Glacier and Morgan Inlet, on the east end of Thurston Island. Discovered on helicopter flights from the *Burton Island* and the *Glacier* during the USN Bellingshausen Sea Expedition of Feb. 1960. Named for J.Q. Tierney, oceanographer on the *Burton Island* that season, i.e., 1959–60.

Tierra de O'Higgins *see* **O'Higgins Land**

Tierra San Martín *see* **San Martín Land**

Tiffany Automatic Weather Station. 77°54′S, 166°12′E. American AWS on the Ross Ice Shelf, at an elevation of approximately 132 feet. Operated from Jan. 24, 1984, to Jan. 23, 1986.

Tiger Island. 76°48′S, 162°28′E. 4 miles north of Lion Island, on the north side of Granite Harbor, in Victoria Land. The NZ Northern Survey Party of the BCTAE 1956–58 established a survey station on its highest point in Oct. 1957. Named in association with nearby Lion Island.

Tiger Peak. 70°52′S, 165°58′E. 1,490 m. Above the cirque wall near the head of Ludvig Glacier, in the central Anare Mountains. Distinguished by stripes of different colored rock. Named descriptively by the ANARE party from the *Thala Dan* here in 1962.

Tigert, E.L. Crewman on the *Jacob Ruppert*, 1933–35.

Tighe Rock. 74°28'S, 100°04'W. Along the coastal slope on the west edge of the Hudson Mountains, 15 miles NW of Mount Moses. Named for Robert F. Tighe, electrical engineer at Byrd Station in 1964–65.

Tilberg Islands *see* **Tillberg Peak**

Tillberg Islands *see* **Tillberg Peak**

Tillberg Nunataks *see* **Tillberg Peak**

Tillberg Peak. 64°46'S, 60°54'W. 610 m. Ice-free. On the ridge running east from the Foster Plateau toward Sentinel Nunatak, on the east coast of Graham Land. Discovered by Nordenskjöld's expedition in 1901–4, and named by him as Tillberg Islands, for Judge Knut Tillberg, a supporter. The feature was later redefined as nunataks, and called Tillberg Nunataks. In 1963 the UK redefined it yet again, having found that the original feature was not now distinctive enough to warrant a plural form.

Tillett Islands. 67°11'S, 59°27'E. Also called Tillet Islands, Tilletöyane. A group of small islands, the largest rising to 70 meters out of the sea. 5 miles NE of Cape Wilkins. Discovered and named in Feb. 1936 by the personnel on the *William Scoresby*.

Mount Tilley. 69°45'S, 69°29'W. 1,900 m. Flat-topped. Ice-capped. 7 miles south of Mount Tyrrell, and 3 miles inland from the George VI Sound, in the east part of Alexander Island. It is actually a foothill of the Douglas Range, from which it is separated by the Toynbee Glacier. Surveyed by the FIDS in 1948, and named by them for Cecil Tilley, professor of mineralogy and petrology at Cambridge.

Tilley Bay. 67°24'S, 60°04'E. Just east of Tilley Nunatak, on the coast of Mac. Robertson Land. Photographed by the LCE 1936–37. Named Nabbvika (peg bay) by the Norwegians. Renamed by the

Australians due to its proximity to Tilley Nunatak.

Tilley Nunatak. 67°24'S, 60°03'E. Also called Nabbodden (by the Norwegians). 5 miles south of Hobbs Islands. Projects from the coastal ice cliffs east of William Scoresby Bay. Discovered in Feb. 1936 by the personnel on the *William Scoresby*, and named by them for Cecil Tilley (*see* **Mount Tilley**).

Tillite Glacier. 83°51'S, 166°E. Flows from Pagoda Peak into Lennox-King Glacier, north of Fairchild Peak, in the western part of the Queen Alexandra Range. Named by the New Zealanders in 1961–62 for the tillite found in it.

Tillite Spur. 85°59'S, 126°36'W. 3 miles long. Descends from the southern Wisconsin Plateau, between Red Spur and Polygon Spur, and ends at the east side of Olentangy Glacier, in the area of the Reedy Glacier. Named by John H. Mercer in 1964–65 for the tillite content.

Tilman Ridge. 76°40'S, 159°35'E. Forms the NW arm of the Allan Hills, in Victoria Land. Named by the New Zealanders in 1964 for mountain climber W.H. Tilman.

Tilt Rock. 70°27'S, 68°44'W. 670 m. Isolated. Also called Pyramid Point. A peak, 2 miles inland from the George VI Sound, and 2 miles NE of Block Mountain, in eastern Alexander Island. Surveyed by the FIDS in 1948–49, and named by them for its tilted appearance.

Timber Peak. 74°10'S, 162°23'E. 3,070 m. Above Priestley Glacier, on the south side of that glacier. 2 miles WNW of the summit of Mount New Zealand, in the Eisenhower Range of Victoria Land. Named by the New Zealanders in 1962–63 for the petrified wood found here.

Cape Timberlake. 78°58'S, 161°37'E. At the west side of the mouth of the Skelton Glacier. Named in 1964 for Lt. Cdr. Lewis G. Timberlake, USN, public works officer at McMurdo Station in 1962.

Cape Timblón. 62°42'S, 61°19'W. Forms the northern extremity of Snow

Island, in the South Shetlands. Named for Carlos Timblón.

Timblón, Carlos. Name also spelled as Tidblón. Argentine captain of the *San Juan Nepomuceno,* in the South Shetlands in 1819–20.

Time zones. All time zones come together at the South Pole, so that a clock is never wrong here. It is never really right either, so for convenience, South Polers use New Zealand time.

Mount Timosthenes. 69°08′S, 65°57′ W. Between the head of Hariot Glacier and the north side of Airy Glacier, 3 miles NW of Peregrinus Peak, in the central part of the Antarctic Peninsula. Surveyed in Dec. 1958 by the FIDS. Named by the UK for Aristotle Timosthenes of Rhodes, navigation pioneer under the Ptolemies.

Tin. Has been found in Antarctica.

Tindal Bluff. 67°04′S, 64°52′W. 800 m. Between the terminus of Fricker Glacier and Monnier Point, on the east coast of Graham Land. Named by the UK for Ronald Tindal, general assistant with the BAS Larsen Ice Shelf Party in 1963–64.

Tindegga Ridge. 72°31′S, 2°54′W. Just SW of Ytstenut Peak, at the NE end of the Borg Massif, in Queen Maud Land. Name means "the summit ridge" in Norwegian.

Tindeklypa. 72°05′S, 2°22′W. A double summit separated by a deep ravine (the name in Norwegian means "the summit ravine"). 1 mile north of Istind Peak, on the east side of the Ahlmann Ridge, in Queen Maud Land.

Tindley Peaks. 71°18′S, 67°26′W. On the west coast of Palmer Land.

Tingey Rocks. 69°57′S, 67°52′E. Two small rocks SW of Single Island, on the west edge of the Amery Ice Shelf. Discovered in 1971 by the ANARE Prince Charles Mountains survey party. Named by the Australians for R.J. Tingey, geologist with the party.

Tinglof, Ivor. Cabinet maker from Boston who made the hut for Byrd to winter-over alone in at Bolling Advance Weather Station, during Byrd's 1933–35 expedition. Tinglof went on that expedition, and was a tractor mechanic on the shore party. At Little America he built the first heavy cargo sledges to be used in Antarctica.

Tinglof Peninsula. 71°59′S, 100°24′ W. 10 miles long. Ice-covered. Between the Henry and Wagoner Inlets, on the north side of Thurston Island. Named for Ivor Tinglof.

Tinker Glacier. 74°S, 164°50′E. 25 miles long. Flows from the central part of the Southern Cross Mountains, into Wood Bay, on the coast of Victoria Land. Named by the New Zealanders in 1962–63 for Lt. Col. Ron Tinker, leader at Scott Base that season.

Tinker Glacier Tongue. 74°06′S, 165° 02′E. The seaward extension of the Tinker Glacier. It juts out into the NW corner of Wood Bay, on the coast of Victoria Land. Named in association with the glacier.

Tinsel Dome. 63°44′S, 58°55′W. 700 m. Ice-covered. Between the Aureole Hills and Bone Bay, on Trinity Peninsula. Charted in 1948 by the FIDS, and named by them descriptively.

The *Tioga*. Norwegian factory whaling ship, owned by the Corral Whaling Company. It was in the South Orkneys in the 1912–13 season, with its steam whalers, the *Corral* and the *Fyr*. It was one of the first factory ships to flense whales at sea (*see also* **The *Thule***). M.T. Moe led a surveying expedition of the west coast of Signy Island from this ship. It was wrecked at Port Jebsen during a gale on Feb. 4, 1913.

Tioga Hill. 60°44′S, 45°39′W. 290 m. At the west side of the head of McLeod Glacier, it is the highest point on Signy Island, in the South Orkneys. Surveyed in 1947 by the FIDS. Named by the UK in 1954 for the *Tioga*.

Tioga Lake. 60°42′S, 45°39′W. On the west side of Signy Island, in the South

Orkneys. Named in association with nearby Tioga Hill.

Tisné Point. 64°10′S, 60°58′W. Just to the SW of Cierva Cove, on the west coast of Graham Land. This is an unofficial name. Capt. Fernando Tisné was leader of the Chilean Antarctic Expedition of 1952.

Titan Nunatak. 72°09′S, 68°43′W. 460 m. Flat-topped. Between Coal Nunatak and Tethys Nunataks, on the SE end of Alexander Island, overlooking the George VI Sound. Discovered aerially by Ellsworth on Nov. 23, 1935, but its nature was undetermined (was it an island or a nunatak in George VI Sound?) until 1949, when the FIDS surveyed it. Named by the UK for one of the satellites of the planet Saturn (Saturn Glacier is near Titan Nunatak).

Titania Peak. 71°32′S, 69°25′W. 1,250 m. Near the head of Uranus Glacier, and 11 miles WNW of Mount Umbriel, in central Alexander Island. Named by the UK for one of the satellites of the planet Uranus.

Titanium. Has been found in Antarctica, probably first by Edgeworth David.

Mount Titus. 72°18′S, 168°59′E. 2,840 m. Between the Staircase and Kelly Glaciers, in the Admiralty Mountains of Victoria Land. Named for Robert W. Titus, meteorologist and scientific leader at Hallett Station in 1961.

Tiw Valley. 77°36′S, 161°47′E. Just east of Odin Valley, in the Asgard Range of Victoria Land. Named by the USA and New Zealand for the Norse god.

Tizire Glacier *see* **Chijire Glacier**

Tizire Rocks *see* **Chijire Rocks**

Tjøntveit, Thor and **Pedersen, Einar Sverre.** Two Norwegians, Thor Tjøntveit and Einar Sverre Pedersen, arrived at the Pole on Jan. 19, 1970, in a twin-engine Cessna, after a brief fuel stop at McMurdo Station. The "Flying Vikings" stayed at the Pole for 5 hours, then returned to McMurdo Station. On Jan. 22, 1970, they left for Chile.

Tjuvholene Crags. 71°57′S, 4°28′E. 2,495 m. Form the north end of Mount Grytøyr, in the Mühlig-Hofmann Mountains of Queen Maud Land. Name means "the thief's lair" in Norwegian.

Toadstool Rocks. 68°50′S, 69°25′W. In Marguerite Bay, off the west coast of Graham Land.

Tobin Mesa. 73°17′S, 162°52′E. Also called Tobin Tableland. Between Pain Mesa on the north, and Gair Mesa on the south, in the Mesa Range of Victoria Land. Named by the Northern Party of the NZGSAE 1962–63 for James Tobin, surveyor with the party.

Tobin Tableland *see* **Tobin Mesa**

Toboggan Gap. 72°15′S, 166°05′E. A pass through the Millen Range, just north of Turret Peak, offering good sledging from the Polar Plateau to the Pearl Harbor Glacier névé. Named by the New Zealanders in 1962–63.

Toboggans. Motor toboggans were much used after IGY (1957–58). (*See also* **Ski-Doos.**)

Tocci Glacier. 72°10′S, 168°18′E. Descends from Mount Lozen, and enters the north side of the Tucker Glacier, in the Admiralty Mountains. Named for Joseph J. Tocci, II, USN, aerographer's mate at McMurdo Station in 1967.

Mount Tod. 67°13′S, 50°39′E. On the SW side of Auster Glacier, at the head of Amundsen Bay, in Enderby Land. Named by the Australians for I.M. Tod, weather observer at Mawson Station in 1961.

Todd Glacier. 68°03′S, 67°03′W. 7 miles long. Flows into Calmette Bay, in western Graham Land. Named by the UK for Gertrude E. Todd, FIDS scientific officer and editor in London, 1950–63 (the British do not send women to the Antarctic. No one else did in those days).

Todd Gully. 76°43′S, 159°42′E. A valley, almost ¾ mile west of Brock Gully, in the Allan Hills of Victoria Land. Named by the New Zealanders in 1964 for its similarity to fox-hunting country (a todd is a fox).

Todd Ridge. 85°16'S, 119°19'W. Flat-topped. At the NW end of the Long Hills, in the Horlick Mountains. Named for Marion N. Todd, aurora scientist at Byrd Station in 1958.

Todt Ridge. 71°22'S, 13°57'E. 3 miles long. Partly snow-covered. 5 miles east of Mount Mentzel, at the east end of the Gruber Mountains, in Queen Maud Land. Discovered by Ritscher in 1938–39, and named by him for Herbert Todt, assistant to Ritscher and who served as home secretary (in Germany) for the expedition.

The Toe. 62°20'S, 59°11'W. Also called Punta Dedo. A point which marks the south side of the entrance to Harmony Cove, on the west side of Nelson Island. Named descriptively by the personnel on the *Discovery II* in 1935.

Tofani Glacier. 68°21'S, 65°35'W. Flows from the east coast of Graham Land into the Larsen Ice Shelf.

Tofte, Eyvind. Leader of the *Odd I* expedition of 1926–27.

Tofte Glacier. 68°48'S, 90°42'W. Just south of Sandefjord Cove, on the west side of Peter I Island. Discovered in 1927 by the *Odd I,* and named for Eyvind Tofte.

Toilers Mountain. 71°44'S, 164°51'E. 1,955 m. A peak, 4 miles NE of Halverson Peak, in the NW end of the King Range, in the Concord Mountains. Used as a gravity station by the Northern Party of the NZGSAE 1963–64, and named by them because of the long climb up to it.

Tokarev Island. 66°32'S, 92°59'E. Also called Tokaryev's Island. 175 yards west of Gorev Island, in the Haswell Islands. Discovered and mapped by the AAE 1911–14. Named by the USSR in 1957 for Aleksey T. Tokarev (1915–1957), biologist on the Soviet Antarctic Expedition of 1956–57, who died returning from Antarctica.

Mount Tokoroa. 71°12'S, 162°53'E. Snow-covered. On a spur from the Explorers Range, in the Bowers Mountains.

6 miles SE of the summit of Mount Soza, at the junction of the Morley and Carryer Glaciers. Named by the USA in 1962–63 for Tokoroa, NZ, for that town's continued support to the US teams.

Tokroningen *see* **Kroner Lake**

Mount Tolchin. 85°06'S, 65°12'W. 1,730 m. 5 miles SW of Houk Spur, at the SW end of Mackin Table, in the southern part of the Patuxent Range, in the Pensacola Mountains. Named for Lt. Sidney Tolchin.

Tolchin, Sidney. Lt., USN. Medical officer and officer-in-charge of South Pole Station during the 1959 winter-over. Took over from Vernon Houk.

Tollefsen, Adam. Norwegian seaman who went insane during the wintering-over on the *Belgica* in 1898. Amundsen took him back to Norway in a mail boat, and he recovered.

Tollefson Nunatak. 74°25'S, 72°25'W. 5 miles west of Olander Nunatak, 40 miles north of the Merrick Mountains, in Ellsworth Land. Named for T.W. Tollefson, construction electrician at Eights Station in 1963.

Mount Tolley. 77°17'S, 143°07'W. Also seen spelled as Mount Tolly. 1,030 m. 2 miles south of Mount Swartley, in the Allegheny Mountains of the Ford Ranges of Marie Byrd Land. Discovered aerially by the members of West Base during the USAS 1939–41, and named for William P. Tolley of Allegheny College, Pennsylvania.

Mount Tolly *see* **Mount Tolley**

Glaciar Tolosa *see* **William Glacier**

Toltec Butte. 76°39'S, 159°53'E. A peak, east of Harris Valley, in the Shipton Range of the Allan Hills, in Victoria Land. It is a truncated peak, and was named by the New Zealanders in 1964 for its resemblance to Toltec buildings.

Tomandl Nunatak. 76°49'S, 144°57'W. Isolated. On the south side of Crevasse Valley Glacier. 7 miles east of Mount Stancliffe, in the Ford Ranges of Marie Byrd Land. Named for Frank

Tomandl, Jr., aviation electrician's mate, USN, at McMurdo Station in 1968.

Tombaugh Cliffs. 71°05′S, 68°20′W. Ice-free. At the north side of the mouth of Pluto Glacier (Clyde W. Tombaugh discovered the planet Pluto in 1930). They face the George VI Sound, on the east side of Alexander Island. Named by the UK.

The *Tombigbee*. US ship in Antarctica in 1963, under the command of Lt. R.H. McSweeney.

¹Tombstone Hill. 64°49′S, 63°31′W. 50 m. Just ENE of Damoy Point on Wiencke Island. Discovered and mapped by Charcot in 1903–5. Named in 1944 by the personnel of Operation Tabarin. Some of the rocks atop the hill look like tombstones.

²Tombstone Hill. 72°27′S, 169°42′E. 1,050 m. On the north side of Edisto Glacier, in the Admiralty Mountains of Victoria Land. Named by the New Zealanders in 1957–58. The summit has many rocks on it which look like tombstones.

Tomilin Glacier. 69°15′S, 158°44′E. 15 miles long. Flows from Pope Mountain in the central Wilson Hills, and enters the sea east of the Goodman Hills and Cape Kinsey in Oates Land, and forms a glacier tongue. Named by the USSR for Arctic aviator Mikhail N. Tomilin (1908–1952), who died in the Arctic.

Mount Tomlinson. 67°15′S, 51°11′E. 2 miles south of Mount Marsland, in the NE part of the Scott Mountains of Enderby Land. Named by the Australians for R.C. Tomlinson.

Tomlinson, R.C. Crew member on the *Discovery* during the BANZARE 1929–31.

Tommeliten Rock. 71°47′S, 2°29′W. Isolated. 6 miles east of Lorentzen Peak, on the Ahlmann Ridge of Queen Maud Land. Name means "Tom Thumb" in Norwegian.

Tomovick Nunatak. 74°59′S, 161°51′E. On the south side of the upper part of the Larsen Glacier. 9 miles west of Mount Gerlache, in Victoria Land. Named for

Donald S. Tomovick, USN, utilitiesman at Amundsen-Scott South Pole Station in 1966.

Tonagh Island. 67°06′S, 50°18′E. 4 miles long. 2 miles wide. Flat-topped. SW of the mouth of Beaver Glacier, in the south part of Amundsen Bay. P.W. Crohn's ANARE party discovered it in Oct. 1956, and the Australians named it for Lt. Leslie Tonagh, dukw driver with the ANARE in 1956.

Toney, George R. Scientific leader at Byrd Station for the 1957 winter. He took part in several Arctic and Antarctic explorations, both as field worker and administrator.

Toney Mountain. 75°48′S, 115°48′W. 3,565 m. Snow-covered. 38 miles long. A volcanic mountain massif on the Bakutis Coast of Marie Byrd Land, 35 miles SW of the Kohler Range. Algae and lichens are found here. Mapped by Charles Bentley in 1957–58, and named by him for George Toney.

Tongue Peak. 86°34′S, 153°02′W. In the Queen Maud Mountains.

Tongue Rock. 67°33′S, 62°01′E. A rock in water, just north of Low Tongue, off the coast of Mac. Robertson Land. Photographed by the LCE 1936–37, and named Tangskjera (the tongue rock) by the Norwegians. The Australians translated it.

Tongue Rocks. 63°38′S, 57°21′W. Small, ice-free, volcanic rocks between Eagle Island and Beak Island, off Trinity Peninsula. Named by the UK in association with the two nearby islands.

Tonkin Island. 67°49′S, 65°03′W. Also called Lewis Island. 3½ miles long. Ice-capped. Has ice-free peaks at both ends. 11 miles SE of Choyce Point, off the east coast of Graham Land. Discovered aerially by the USAS in 1940. Named by the FIDS in 1947 for J.E. Tonkin, FIDS member at Base E in 1946. He was rescued from a crevasse in Northeast Glacier by fellow FIDS member, Eric Walton.

Tønnesen Glacier. 72°04′S, 3°28′E. Flows between Risemedet Mountain and

Festninga Mountain. It separates the Mühlig-Hofmann Mountains and the Gjelsvik Mountains of Queen Maud Land. Named Tönnesenbreen by the Norwegians for J. Tønnesen, meteorologist on the Norwegian Antarctic Expedition of 1956–58.

Tönnesenbreen *see* **Tønnesen Glacier**

Tønsberg Cove. 60°32'S, 45°55'W. Also called Tønsberg Fjord. 1 mile SE of Penguin Point, on the north coast of Coronation Island, in the South Orkneys. Charted by Petter Sørlle in 1912–13. Named for the Tønsberg Hvalfangeri (q.v.).

Tønsberg Fjord *see* **Tønsberg Cove**

Tønsberg Hvalfangeri. Norwegian whaling company out of Tønsberg, Norway. It operated a permanent whaling base in the South Orkneys between 1920 and 1930. It already had a well-established base at Husvik Harbor, in South Georgia (54°S).

Mount Toogood. 71°37'S, 160°14'E. 2,100 m. At the south side of the head of Edwards Glacier, in the Daniels Range of the Usarp Mountains. Named for David J. Toogood, geologist at McMurdo Station in 1967–68 and 1968–69.

Tooth Hill *see* **Tooth Peak**

Tooth Peak. 72°47'S, 162°04'E. Also called Tooth Hill. On the north end of Sculpture Mountain, in the upper Rennick Glacier. Named descriptively by the New Zealanders in 1962–63.

Tooth Rock. 62°52'S, 61°24'W. 85 m. South of Cape Conway, Snow Island, in the South Shetlands. Named descriptively by Lt. Cdr. F.W. Hunt, RN, following his survey of 1951–52.

Tophet Bastion. 60°42'S, 45°17'W. An ice-capped rock wall, 1 mile long. 1 mile east of Saunders Point, on the south coast of Coronation Island, in the South Orkneys. Surveyed by the Discovery Committee in 1933, and again in 1948–49 by the FIDS. Named by the FIDS for the biblical place.

Topografov Island. 68°30'S, 78°11'E. Just north of Partizan Island, in the north part of the entrance to Langnes Fjord, in the Vestfold Hills area of East Antarctica. Photographed by the LCE 1936–37. Later named by the USSR as Ostrov Topografov (topographers' island).

Topping Cove. 77°29'S, 169°16'E. An exposed volcanic cone near Cape Crozier. 1¾ miles NW of the summit of The Knoll, in eastern Ross Island. Named by New Zealand for W.W. Topping, geologist here in 1969–70.

Mount Torbert. 83°30'S, 54°25'W. 1,675 m. Pyramidal. The main feature of the Torbert Escarpment, in the Neptune Range of the Pensacola Mountains. Discovered aerially on Jan. 13, 1956. Named for Lt. Cdr. John H. Torbert, USN, pilot of the P2V-2N Neptune aircraft which made this non-stop flight from McMurdo Sound to the Weddell Sea and back.

Torbert Escarpment. 83°29'S, 54°08'W. 15 miles long. Marks the west margin of Median Snowfield, in the Neptune Range of the Pensacola Mountains. Named in association with Mount Torbert, its main feature.

Torbjørn Rocks. 71°53'S, 6°21'E. A group in the mouth of Lunde Glacier, in the Mühlig-Hofmann Mountains of Queen Maud Land. Named by the Norwegians for Torbjørn Lunde, glaciologist on the Norwegian Antarctic Expedition of 1956–58.

Mount Torckler. 66°52'S, 52°44'E. 3 miles SE of Mount Smethurst, and 28 miles SW of Stor Hånakken Mountain, in Enderby Land. Named by the Australians for R.M. Torckler, radio officer at Davis Station in 1959, and at Wilkes Station in 1961.

Torckler Island *see* **Ranvik Island**

Torckler Rocks. 68°35'S, 77°56'E. Three small islands at the north side of the entrance to Heidemann Bay, in the Vestfold Hills. Photographed by the LCE 1936–37, and named by the Australians for R.M. Torckler (*see* **Mount Torckler**).

Torgersen, Torstein. First mate on the *Norsel*, 1954–55. He was the first person to enter Arthur Harbor (where the present Palmer Station is), in late Feb. 1955, preceding the *Norsel* in one of the ship's boats.

Torgersen Island. 64°46′S, 64°05′W. About ½ mile west of Palmer Station, in Arthur Harbor, off Anvers Island. Surveyed by the FIDS in 1955. Named by the UK for Torstein Torgersen.

Torgny Peak. 71°51′S, 8°06′E. Icefree. 2 miles west of Fenriskjeften Mountain, in the Drygalski Mountains of Queen Maud Land. Named by the Norwegians for Torgny Vinje, meteorologist in Antarctica in the late 1950s.

Torii Glacier. 71°19′S, 35°40′E. Flows between Mount Goossens and Mount Fukushima, in the Queen Fabiola Mountains. Discovered on Oct. 7, 1960, by the Belgian Antarctic Expedition of 1960–61, and named by leader Guido Derom for Tetsuya Torii, leader of the Japanese party which visited here in Nov. 1960.

Torinosu Cove. 69°29′S, 39°34′E. An indentation into the western side of Skarvsnes Foreland, in the eastern part of Lützow-Holm Bay. 1½ miles west of Mount Suribachi, on the coast of Queen Maud Land. Named Torinosu-wan (bird's nest cove) by the Japanese in 1973.

The *Torlyn*. Norwegian whale catcher off the coast of Mac. Robertson Land in Jan. and Feb. 1931, under the command of Klarius Mikkelsen. It was back in 1932–33.

Torlyn Mountain. 67°48′S, 66°55′E. 4 miles east of Scullin Monolith, on the coast of Mac. Robertson Land. In Jan. 1930 the BANZARE flew over it, and in Feb. 1931 they returned and named it Murray Monolith. Also in Feb. 1931 the Norwegian whalers in the area named it Torlyn Mountain, for their vessel, the *Torlyn*. The term Murray Monolith is now used only for the detached front of the feature (*see* **Murray Monolith**).

Bajo Toro *see* **Reyes Spit**

Toro, Carlos. Full name Carlos Toro Mazote G. Chilean aviation lieutenant in 1947, he was one of the men who occupied the General Bernardo O'Higgins Station that year. He was later on the *Lientur* during the Chilean Antarctic Expedition of 1950–51.

Toro, Federico Guesalaga *see* **Guesalaga Toro, Federico**

Toro Point. 63°19′S, 57°54′W. Forms the southern extremity of Schmidt Peninsula, and the north side of the entrance to Unwin Cove, on Trinity Peninsula. Named by the Chilean Antarctic Expedition of 1950–51 for Carlos Toro.

Isla Torre *see* **Cecilia Island, Tower Island**

Cape Torson. 66°40′S, 90°36′E. On the east side of Posadowsky Bay. In 1956 the USSR named it for Lt. K.P. Torson.

Torson, K.P. Lt. Officer on the *Vostok* with von Bellingshausen in 1819–21.

Tortoise Hill. 64°22′S, 57°30′W. Over 500 m. 3 miles west of The Watchtower, in the SE corner of James Ross Island. Surveyed by the FIDS during the 1958–61 period, and named by the UK in 1961 in association with Terrapin Hill, which it looks like.

Islotes Tortuga *see* **Saffery Islands**

Tot Island. 65°31′S, 64°20′W. A small island, just north of the NE end of Lahille Island, off the west coast of Graham Land. Charted by the BGLE 1934–37. Named by the UK in 1959 for its size.

Mount Toth. 86°22′S, 155°15′W. 2,410 m. The most easterly peak on the small ice-covered ridge 5 miles east of Mount Kendrick, in the Queen Maud Mountains. Named for Cdr. Arpad J. Toth, USNR, operations officer-in-charge of Williams Field, 1962–64.

Toth Nunataks. 73°33′S, 64°47′W. A small group of isolated nunataks. 17 miles NNW of Mount Coman, in Palmer Land. Named for Stephen R. Toth, glaciologist at Byrd Station in 1965–66.

The *Tottan*. Norwegian sealer chartered by France, which picked up the

French Polar Expedition (q.v.) from Adélie Land on Feb. 2, 1952. The Australians also used it occasionally as their ANARE supply ship. Captains: 1951–52, J. Engebretsen; 1952–53, H.C. Andersen.

Tottan Hills. 74°48′S, 12°10′W. 20 miles in extent. They form the SW portion of the Heimefront Range, in Queen Maud Land. Named by the Norwegians for the *Tottan*.

Totten, George M. US Naval passed midshipman who served on the *Vincennes* and the *Porpoise* during the Wilkes Expedition of 1838–42.

Totten Glacier. 66°45′S, 116°10′E. 40 miles long. 20 miles wide. Flows from the continental ice, between the Budd Coast and the Sabrina Coast, and ends in the Totten Glacier Tongue just east of Cape Waldron. Named for George M. Totten.

Totten Glacier Tongue. 66°35′S, 116°05′E. The seaward extension of the Totten Glacier, in East Antarctica. Named in association with the glacier.

Tottenbukta Sanae *see* **Sanae Station**

Totten's Highland. 67°S, 119°30′E. Off the Sabrina Coast, this area is now generally incorporated into what we know as the Sabrina Coast. Discovered by Wilkes in 1840, and named by him for George M. Totten.

Tottsuki Point. 68°55′S, 39°49′E. Also spelled Tottuki Point. 3 miles SW of Flattunga, on the coast of Queen Maud Land. Photographed by the LCE 1936–37. Later named Tottsuki-misaki (first point) by the Japanese.

Tottuki Point *see* **Tottsuki Point**

Touchdown Glacier. 79°48′S, 158°10′E. Flows between Roadend Nunatak and the Brown Hills, into Darwin Glacier. Named by the VUWAE 1962–63 because the glacier was used as a landing site for aircraft supporting the expedition.

Touchdown Hills. 78°07′S, 35°W. Snow-covered. They extend south from

Vahsel Bay on the east side of the Filchner Ice Shelf. Named by the BCTAE in 1957, because one of the expedition members landed on them, thinking they were clouds, and bounced off, undamaged.

Tour de Pise. 66°40′S, 140°01′E. 27 m. An isolated rock dome, or hill, which protrudes through the ice in the NW part of Rostand Island, in the Géologie Archipelago. Charted by the French in 1951, and named by them for the Tower of Pisa.

Mount Touring Club. 65°17′S, 63°55′W. Also called Mount Club. Snow-capped. SW of Mount Peary, on the west side of Graham Land. Discovered and named Sommet du Touring Club by Charcot in 1908–10. While a party was charting the area, they hiked along here.

Tourism. Many concerned individuals believe in one simple summary of this topic: Tourism is going to foul up the Antarctic environment, so don't go. Here is how one can proceed, nevertheless: call LAN Chile Airlines Tour Department, for example (their US number is 1-800-225-5526), but they will book you on a Society Expeditions cruise. Society Expeditions are as good as anyone's, better than most, and the best known. They are also probably the easiest to deal with. Antarctic tours are not cheap. The standard package of a few days around the Antarctic Peninsula area costs several thousand US dollars, while a trip to the Pole retails at $70,000. If you want to go it alone, you have to apply for a permit from the Antarctic authorities in your own capital city. The same applies if you go on an organized tour, and then want to strike out on your own. Other tour operators who cover Antarctica include: Mountain Travel (the most adventurous), Travel Dynamics, Lindblad Travel, Sobek, Adventure Network, Alpine Tours, Special Odysseys, Antarctica Tours. A lot of travel agents (as opposed to these tour operators) pretend they have never heard of tours to Antarctica.

They are just being protective of the environment, so those still keen to go, can call one of the tour operators listed in this book under their own entries. Expeditions start in Jan./Feb. or Nov./Dec. in order to get in on the Austral summer. The season is about 60 days, that's all, and then the Antarctic night arrives. Normally it's a matter of a cruise around the South Shetlands and the northern tip of the Antarctic Peninsula, and of going ashore at certain stations to annoy scientists. Palmer Station is becoming hostile now, as 40 man-hours are lost each season showing the tourists around the station, fixing them coffee, going out to look for them when they get lost, and cleaning up after them when they have gone — coke cans, cigarette butts, garbage, etc. Although the National Science Foundation (NSF) looks askance at tourism, and its days may be numbered, the number of ships and chartered planes is on the increase at this moment, and, before it becomes outlawed, tourism is going to be a big problem in Antarctica. Not all national authorities are averse to tourists. Antarctic tourism started in 1936 when Lars Christensen took his wife, daughter, and two female friends down to see the continent. On Dec. 22, 1956, LAN Chile flew the first tourists over Antarctica, on an aerial tour of Chile's bases. The Douglas DC6-B flew from Chabunco, Chile, and back, non-stop. In Jan.-Feb. 1958 the Argentine Naval Transport Command organized the first tours to the Antarctic Peninsula — 9 and 12 days. Since Jan. 1966 tourist ships have been going to Antarctica every summer. In 1977 Qantas started the "champagne flights" over the continent, but in 1979, 257 people were killed in an Air New Zealand DC10 when it crashed into Mount Erebus (see Disasters, Deaths). This incident put a stop to the "champagne flights," but in 1981 the Argentines announced that they would be making Vicecomodoro Marambio Station into a commercial air terminal. In 1982 Chile offered tourist flights between the mainland of South America and Teniente Rodolfo Marsh Station on King George Island, in the South Shetlands. This base is being heavily promoted for tourism. A 100-guest motel has gone up here, and in Dec. 1985, 2 Chilean pilots and 8 US tourists were killed when their light aircraft crashed coming in to land at this station (see also Lakeside Hotel — the Japanese building at Showa Station; this is not actually a tourist hotel yet). In 1983–84, 8 ships visited just Palmer Station, with 822 passengers. In 1986–87 this figure had increased to 13 ships, with 1,295 tourists. That summer there were over 5,000 tourists all over Antarctica, from all over the world. In 1987–88, despite NSF limitations, there were 10 tourist ships in at Palmer Station, with 1,102 passengers. In Jan. 1988, 50 tourists arrived at the South Pole. In early Jan. 1989 the NSF exerted its influence on tour operators to keep the number of cruise ships visiting Antarctica down to no more than the 1987–88 figure. In 1989–90 Mountain Travel sent a party to the Pole, by foot. This operator, and a few others, also conduct other exotic tours, such as regular climbs up the Vinson Massif, and other land jaunts, but such organized expeditions, by true professionals, are usually exceedingly careful of their presence on the continent. But, airstrips, hotels, recreational facilities, gift shops, motor transport, are all now in Antarctica, and one can only hope that sewage disposal, search and rescue squads, and policemen keep pace. One big uncertainty is whether the penguins are safe.

Tourmaline Plateau. 74°10′S, 163°27′E. Ice-covered. In the central portion of the Deep Freeze Range, in Victoria Land. Named by the New Zealanders in 1965–66 for the tourmaline found here.

Tournachon Peak. 64°19′S, 61°05′W. 860 m. South of Spring Point, on the west coast of Graham Land. Named by the UK in 1960 for Gaspard F. Tournachon (1820–1910), pioneer balloonist and aerial photographer known as "Nadar."

Tousled Peak. 73°11′S, 169°01′E. 1,220 m. Ice-covered. 3½ miles NW of the summit of Mount Lubbock, on the south end of Daniell Peninsula, in Victoria Land. Named by New Zealand in 1966 for its exceptionally broken ice summit.

The Tower. 62°13′S, 58°30′W. Also called Pico La Torre. 345 m. A mountain, snow-covered except at the summit. Just west of Demay Point, on the west shore of Admiralty Bay, King George Island, in the South Shetlands. Charcot charted it in 1908–10, and named it La Tour (the tower).

Mount Tower *see* **Tower Hill**

Tower Hill. 63°42′S, 60°45′W. Also called Mount Tower. 1,125 m. Surmounts the NW part of Trinity Island. Origin of the name is unknown.

Tower Island. 63°33′S, 59°51′W. Also called Pendleton Island, Isla Torre. 305 m. 4½ miles long. 20 miles north of Charcot Bay, near the Antarctic Peninsula, it marks the NE extent of the Palmer Archipelago. Mapped and named descriptively by Bransfield on Jan. 30, 1820. Palmer was the next to see it, on Nov. 17, 1820.

Tower Peak. 64°23′S, 59°09′W. 855 m. 5 miles NW of Longing Gap, in northern Graham Land. Charted and named descriptively by the FIDS in 1945.

The Towle. Full name, the USNS *Private John R. Towle.* Ice-strengthened cargo vessel of 12,450 tons, in Antarctica in Dec. 1956.

Towle Glacier. 76°38′S, 161°05′E. Flows between the Eastwind and Elkhorn Ridges, into the Fry Glacier, in the Con-

voy Range. Named by the NZ Northern Survey Party of the BCTAE in 1957, for the *Towle.*

Towle Valley. 76°41′S, 160°44′E. A deep valley, formerly occupied by the head of Towle Glacier. It is just west of the present-day Towle Glacier, in the Convoy Range of Victoria Land. Named by the NZ Northern Survey Party of the BCTAE in 1957 for the *Towle.*

Towles Glacier. 72°25′S, 169°05′E. Flows from the west slopes of Mount Humphrey Lloyd into Tucker Glacier, NW of Trigon Bluff, in Victoria Land. Named for Lt. William J. Towles, USN, medical officer at Hallett Station in 1960.

Townrow Peak. 76°38′S, 159°35′E. An outlier of Tilman Ridge, in the Allan Hills of Victoria Land. Named by the NZ Allan Hills Expedition of 1964 for J.A. Townrow, Australian paleobotanist with the expedition.

Townsend, James. Seaman on the Wilkes Expedition 1838–42. Joined in the USA. Discharged at Oahu on Oct. 31, 1840.

Toynbee Glacier. 69°35′S, 69°35′W. 17 miles long. 5 miles wide. Between the Douglas Range on the west and Mount Tyrrell and Mount Tilley on the east, it flows from Mount Stephenson to the George VI Sound, in the NE part of Alexander Island. Surveyed in 1948 by the FIDS, and named by them for Patrick A. Toynbee, FIDS air pilot at Base E in 1948 and 1949.

Trabucco Cliff. 76°37′S, 118°01′W. the NE part of Mount Rees, in the Crary Mountains. Named for William J. Trabucco, ionosphere physicist at McMurdo Station in 1969 and at Siple Station in 1973.

Trachyte Hill. 77°17′S, 166°25′E. 470 m. Just south of Shell Glacier, and about 6 miles south of Cape Bird. On the lower slopes of Mount Bird, on Ross Island. Ice-free. Named by the New Zealanders in 1958–59 for the rock type here.

Tracked Vehicles *see* **Tractors, Sno-cats, Caterpillars, Nodwells, Cletracs, Logan Sprytes**

Tractors. Scott was the first to use tractors in Antarctica, during his 1910–13 expedition. He brought 3 crawler-tracked tractors, developed by Reginald Skelton (q.v.). These had then been built by the Wolseley Company. One fell through the ice off Cape Evans, and is still there, while two were used to unload the *Terra Nova*. They failed 60 miles south of base, on the Ross Ice Shelf. From 1928 tractors became an accepted part of the Antarctic landscape. The one Byrd took on his 1928–30 expedition was a very powerful Ford "Snowmobile," with skis in front and caterpillar tracks in the rear. It had an average speed of 25 mph over the ice, and did the work of 5 or 6 dog teams. It failed at 81° S, and was abandoned. During his 1933–35 expedition, Byrd had 4 tractors which covered over 12,500 miles in a year. Two of them were light Ford tractors, and King White's Cleveland Tractor Company manufactured the heavy Cletracs. Citroën also furnished 3 trucks. During the USAS 1939–41, West Base had a T-20 International Harvester tractor for base work, and East Base had an Army artillery tractor. Tractors proliferated in Antarctica during the IGY period (1957–58). McMurdo Base had two D4 tractors, and Little America had one. Altogether the USA used 12 D8 tractors and 9 D2s, as well as the D4s mentioned above. Ten of the D8s were of the "low ground pressure" type, 23 ½ feet long (the ordinary D8 was 15 ½ feet long) and weighing 35 tons, but the width of their caterpillar tracks reduced the pressure to a maximum of 14.2 pounds per square inch. During the same period the USSR used the C80, which weighed 11.4 tons with 93 hp; Kirovets KD 35s, which weighed 3.7 tons with 37 hp; while the GAZ 47s played the largest part in the creation of Pionerskaya Station. This was the era of the great tractor

traverses over the continent, probably the most famous being Fuchs' crossing of Antarctica during the BCTAE 1957– 58. During that same expedition, but working from the other end of the continent, Hillary took 3 overhauled Ferguson farm tractors with him to the Pole.

Tracy Glacier. 65° 57′ S, 102° 20′ E. A channel glacier flowing to the Shackleton Ice Shelf, 4 miles SW of Cape Elliot. Named for Lt. Lloyd W. Tracy, USN, pilot on Operation Windmill, 1947–48.

Tracy Point. 66° 18′ S, 110° 27′ E. The most westerly point on Beall Island, in the Windmill Islands. Named for Gordon F. Tracy, USN, radioman at Wilkes Station in 1958.

Trafalgar Glacier. 72° 29′ S, 168° 25′ E. 30 miles long. Flows east into the Victory Mountains to join the Tucker Glacier below Bypass Hill, in Victoria Land. Named by the New Zealanders in 1957–58 in association with the Victory Mountains and the Battle of Trafalgar, 1805.

Traffic Circle. 68° 37′ S, 66° 03′ W. 500 m. A glacier-filled expanse in the form of a depression, on the peninsular upland of the west coast of Graham Land, overlooking Marguerite Bay, south of Mount Ptolemy. Hub Nunatak rises from its center. From this point 5 glacial troughs radiate like spokes of a wheel (hence the name). Discovered and named by the USAS members from East Base in 1940.

Mount Trail. 67° 12′ S, 50° 51′ E. On the NE side of Auster Glacier, at the head of Amundsen Bay, in Enderby Land. Named by the Australians for D.S. Trail, geologist at Mawson Station in 1961 (*see also* **Trail Glacier**).

Trail Bay *see* **Trail Inlet**

Trail Glacier. 73° 34′ S, 61° 35′ E. On the south side of Mount Menzies, 2 miles from its summit. It is 5 miles long and 3 miles wide. Named by the Australians for D.S. Trail, ANARE geologist who led a party here in Dec. 1961 (*see also* **Mount Trail**).

Trail Inlet. 68°03′S, 65°20′W. Also called Trail Bay. A Larsen Ice Shelf indentation into the east coast of the Antarctic Peninsula, between Cape Freeman and Joerg Peninsula. Discovered aerially by Wilkins on Dec. 20, 1928. Named because it is a natural trail for flights and sledge parties across the Antarctic Peninsula which, between Trail Inlet and Neny Fjord on the other side, is only 20 miles across.

Trainer Glacier. 72°34′S, 167°29′E. 7 miles west of Rudolph Glacier, flowing into Trafalgar Glacier, in the Victory Mountains of Victoria Land. Named for Charles Trainer, meteorologist and senior US representative at Hallett Station in 1960.

Trajer Ridge. 68°34′S, 78°30′E. 125 m. At the south side of the base of Breidnes Peninsula, in the Vestfold Hills. Named by the Australians for F.L. Trajer, weather observer at Davis Station in 1961. He and M. Hay visited this ridge on foot on Nov. 4, 1961.

Tramway Ridge. On top of Mount Erebus, Ross Island. It is SSSI #11.

Mount Tranchant. 65°14′S, 64°06′W. Also called Edge Hill. A hill, literally on the west coast of Graham Land. It marks the south side of the terminus of Wiggins Glacier. Charted by Charcot in 1908–10, and named by him as Mont Tranchant (sharp mountain). It is a descriptive name.

Tranquil Lake. 60°42′S, 45°39′W. On Signy Island, in the South Orkneys.

Tranquillity Valley. 82°36′S, 52°55′W. In the extreme north of the Pensacola Mountains.

Trans-Globe Expedition. 1979–82. An unusual round-the-world trip in that it went from north to south, rather than from east to west. It was a 3-man expedition comprising Sir Ranulph Fiennes, Oliver Shepard, and Charles Burton. They set out in Sept. 1979 and completed their mission in Aug. 1982. In between they had to cross Antarctica. This leg of

their journey was 2,600 miles long, and only one group in history had ever made a successful Transantarctic land crossing before — Fuchs during the BCTAE 1955–58. Fiennes led the party out of Ryvingen Base in Queen Maud Land on Ski-Doos pulling sledges, on Oct. 26, 1980. They reached the South Pole at 4:35 a.m. on Dec. 15, 1980. They reached Scott Base on Ross Island on Jan. 11, 1981, after a total of 66 days of Antarctic trekking.

Transantarctic Mountains. Also called the Transantarctic Horst. This is the great, 1,900 mile-long range which separates East Antarctica from West Antarctica. It centers on 85°S, 175°W. The mountains are composed of Precambrian to early Paleozoic metamorphic, sedimentary, and granite rocks, dating from 500 million years ago. These are overlaid by flat-lying Devonian to Jurassic strata known as the Beacon Group. The range runs, with some interruptions, from Cape Adare in northern Victoria Land to Coats Land, on the Weddell Sea. Included are the Theron Mountains, the Shackleton Range, the Pensacola Mountains, the Thiel Mountains, the Horlick Mountains, and the ranges along the western and southern sides of the Ross Ice Shelf, and those along the west side of the Ross Sea. Scott saw a small part of them in 1902, and named them the Western Mountains. Renamed (in toto) by the USA in 1962. They are completely surveyed now.

Transition Glacier. 70°26′S, 68°49′W. 8 miles long. 2 miles wide. On the east coast of Alexander Island. It flows into the George VI Sound along the north side of Block Mountain and Tilt Rock. Surveyed in 1949 by the FIDS, who named it for the transition between igneous and sedimentary rocks in the glacier.

Transportation. Many experiments have been made with travel across the ice, snow, and crevasses, but, as yet, there is no perfect answer. The Canadians developed the Foremost Delta Two, a large low ground-pressure "taxi" with 4 large wheels, which shuttles personnel between Williams Field and McMurdo Station. The Logan Spryte is the most common medium-tracked vehicle used by the USAP. *See these entries:* **Aircraft, Air-cushion vehicles, Airplanes, Amphibious vehicles, Autogiros, Automobiles, Caterpillar tractors, Cargo ships, Cletracs, Dogs, Helicopters, Icebreakers, Manchurian ponies, Railroads, Refrigeration ships, Ships, Siberian ponies, Ski-Doos, Skis, Sledges, Sno-cats, Snowcruiser, Snowmobiles, Tractors, Weasels.**

Transverse Island. 67°20′S, 59°19′E. Between Fold Island and Keel Island, on the east side of Stefansson Bay, off the coast of Enderby Land. Photographed by the LCE 1936–37, and named Tverrholmen (the transverse island) by the Norwegians. Translated by the Australians.

Tranter Glacier. 82°32′S, 161°45′E. In the north part of the Queen Elizabeth Range, flowing between Mount Chivers and Mount Boman, into the Nimrod Glacier. Named for David L. Tranter, glaciologist at Roosevelt Island in 1962–63.

Travel Dynamics. New York tour operator, servicing Antarctica. It used the *Illiria* in 1988–89.

Traverse Mountains. 69°51′S, 68°02′W. 1,250 m. Almost ice-free. At the south side of Eureka Glacier, 6 miles inland from the George VI Sound, in western Palmer Land. Surveyed by the BGLE in 1936, and named by them because the mountains are an important landmark in overland sledging.

Traverses. Crossings of Antarctica, or of any part of Antarctica, by land, i.e., by sledge, ski, tractor, etc. Strictly speaking this is called a land traverse. Scott pioneered the land traverse in 1902.

Tre Sten   *see*   **Sørlle Rocks**

Mount Treadwell. 77°01′S, 144°51′W. 820 m. At the SE end of the Swanson Mountains, in the Ford Ranges of Marie Byrd Land. Named in 1969 for Capt.

T.K. Treadwell, USN, commander, US Naval Oceanographic Office.

Mount Treatt. 68°S, 56°48′E. 9 miles SE of Mount Cooke of the Leckie Range. Named by the Australians for G. Treatt, helicopter pilot with the 1965 ANARE party led by Phillip Law from the *Nella Dan.*

Treble, George. Seaman on the Wilkes Expedition 1838–42. Joined in the USA. Served the cruise.

Trees. There used to be masses of trees in Antarctica, before glaciation set in (*see* **Flora**). The first trees to be planted by humans in Antarctica were 25 six foothigh fir trees on the McMurdo Base runway, at the beginning of Nov. 1956, for identification of the runway by pilots.

Trench Glacier. 70°12′S, 69°11′W. 6 miles long. 2 miles wide. Deeply entrenched (hence the name applied by the FIDS, who surveyed it in 1948 and 1949). On the east coast of Alexander Island, it flows into the George VI Sound, just south of Mount Athelstan.

Trenholm Point. 75°26′S, 142°23′W. Ice-covered. 8 miles NW of Eldred Point, between Holcomb Glacier and El-Sayed Glacier, on the coast of Marie Byrd Land. Named for William T. Trenholm, glaciologist at Byrd Station in 1967–68, 1968–69, and 1969–70.

The *Trepassey*. British ship chartered by the FIDS in 1945–46 as a relief vessel for Base D, and again in 1946–47 in order to conduct a survey of Antarctic Sound. Captain R.C. Sheppard commanded on the first tour. The ship arrived at Stonington Island on Feb. 23, 1946, with a FIDS crew headed by E.W. Bingham. This group would build Base E on that island. On Feb. 25, 1946, the *Trepassey* left for the winter. On Feb. 5, 1947, it returned to Stonington Island, commanded by Capt. Eugene Burden. H.W. Stone was first mate. It carried a replacement FIDS crew headed by Major K.S. Pierce-Butler, and left again on Feb. 7, 1947 (*see also* **Falkland Islands Dependencies Surveys**).

Trepassey Bay. 63°28'S, 56°58'W. Almost a mile wide. On the east side of Tabarin Peninsula. 3½ miles SE of Hope Bay. First surveyed by the FIDS and by Capt. Eugene Burden of the *Trepassey* in 1947. Named by the UK for that ship.

Trepassey Island. 68°12'S, 66°59'W. Also called Trepassey Islets. A small island in Neny Bay, just over ½ mile SE of Stonington Island, off the west coast of Graham Land. Surveyed by the FIDS in 1947, and named for the *Trepassey*.

Trepassey Islets *see* **Trepassey Island**

Trepidation Glacier. 78°48'S, 162°15' E. Enters the east side of the Skelton Glacier, between Moraine Bluff and Red Dike Bluff. Named by the NZ party of the BCTAE for the 1957 effort by an aircraft to land at the foot of the glacier.

Trerice, Burton J. From St. John's, Quebec. He had been a transport pilot in that province before becoming a reserve pilot and flight engineer on Ellsworth's 1938–39 expedition.

Tressler, Dr. Willis L. b. 1904, Madison, Wisconsin. d. Sept. 9, 1973, Denver, Colorado. Former CIA man, this oceanographer was with the US Navy Antarctic Expedition, on the *Atka,* in 1954–55, and back in Antarctica during Operation Deep Freeze II (1956–57). On Jan. 30, 1958, he took over from Carl Eklund as scientific leader of Wilkes Station, and during the period 1959–61 was at McMurdo Base. He retired in 1965.

Tressler Bank. 65°S, 95°E. A submarine feature, between 94°E and 96°E, in the eastern part of the Davis Sea. It ranges from 56 fathoms deep and greater. Sounded by the *Burton Island* and *Edisto* during Operation Windmill, 1947–48. Named for Dr. Willis L. Tressler.

Trethewry Point. 67°23'S, 59°47'E. Also called Hamrehovden (by the Norwegians). 120 m. Juts out from the coast 4 miles east of William Scoresby Bay. Discovered and named in Feb. 1936 by the personnel on the *William Scoresby.*

Treves Butte. 84°43'S, 114°20'W. 2,100 m. Partly ice-covered. Just NW of Discovery Ridge, in the Ohio Range. Named for Samuel B. Treves, geologist in Antarctica during several seasons, including 1960–61 and 1961–62 in this area.

Trevillian Island. 67°38'S, 62°42'E. A small, humped, oval-shaped island, 1 mile south of Nøst Island, in Holme Bay, Mac. Robertson Land. Photographed by the LCE 1936–37, and named Rundöy (round island) by the Norwegians. Renamed by the Australians for T. Trevillian, Australian mapper in Canberra for the ANARE.

Trey Peaks. 80°36'S, 28°52'W. 3 peaks, the highest being 1,810 m. 2 miles north of Mount Homard, and west of the Blaiklock Glacier, in the west part of the Shackleton Range. Mapped and named descriptively by the BCTAE in 1957.

Tri Valuny Point. 67°38'S, 46°01'E. On Alasheyev Bight in Enderby Land, about 5 miles east of Molodezhnaya Station.

Triad Islands. 65°36'S, 64°28'W. Three small islands, 1½ miles east of Chavez Island, off the west coast of Graham Land. Charted by the BGLE 1934–37. Named descriptively by the UK in 1959.

Triangle Point. 62°32'S, 59°51'W. A headland, 1½ miles NW of Spit Point, on the SW side of Greenwich Island, in the South Shetlands. Charted and named descriptively by the personnel on the *Discovery II* in 1935.

Trice Islands. 72°25'S, 99°48'W. A group of small, ice-covered islands, just west of Evans Point, Thurston Island. In Peacock Sound, above the level of the ice. Named for Jack L. Trice, meteorologist at Byrd Station in 1964–65.

Trickster Rocks. 65°36'S, 64°36'W. Several small rocks, 1 mile NW of Chavez Island, in Grandidier Channel, off the west coast of Graham Land. Named by the UK because when the FIDS did their 1957 survey here they thought that these rocks were icebergs and failed to chart them.

1Mount Tricorn *see* **Tricorn Mountain**

2Mount Tricorn. 73°58'S, 61°45'W. A massif on the Lassiter Coast, overlooking Wright Inlet, on the east coast of the Antarctic Peninsula. Discovered on Dec. 30, 1940, on a USAS flight from East Base. Named by them because it looks like a tri-cornered hat. In 1947–48 the RARE fixed it at 55 miles north of where it had previously been fixed.

Tricorn Bluff *see* **Trigon Bluff**

Tricorn Mountain. 85°03'S, 173°27'E. Also called Mount Tricorn. 3,475 m. 4 miles east of Graphite Peak, between the heads of the Falkenhof and Leigh Hunt Glaciers. Named by the New Zealanders in 1961–62 for its resemblance to an admiral's tricorn hat.

Tricorn Peak. 82°59'S, 156°48'E. 2,320 m. Snow-covered. Between Astro Glacier and Skua Glacier, at the extreme north of the Miller Range. Named by the New Zealanders in 1961–62 because of its resemblance to a three-cornered hat.

Mount Tricouni. 78°30'S, 161°57'E. 1,630 m. 2 miles north of Hobnail Peak, on the east side of the Skelton Glacier, in Victoria Land. Surveyed by the NZ party of the BCTAE in 1957, and named by them. A tricouni is a saw-toothed nail used on the sides of alpine boots.

Mount Trident. 72°27'S, 169°13'E. 2,480 m. Has 3 summits. Above Trigon Bluff, on the north side of Tucker Glacier, in Victoria Land. Named by the New Zealanders in 1957–58 for its summits.

Trifid Peak. 67°51'S, 67°09'W. At the head of Shoesmith Glacier, in the western part of Horseshoe Island. Named by the UK in 1958 for its 3-sided Matterhorn-type appearance.

Trigon Bluff. 72°29'S, 169°09'E. Also called Tricorn Bluff. 1,245 m. 10 miles

west of Football Mountain. On the north side of Tucker Glacier, in Victoria Land. Named descriptively by the New Zealanders in 1957–58.

Trigonia Island. 66°01'S, 65°41'W. A small island, just off the southern tip of Beer Island. 8 miles west of Prospect Point, off the west coast of Graham Land.

Trigwell Island. 68°33'S, 77°57'E. Just west of Flutter Island, and 1 mile west of Breidnes Peninsula, in Prydz Bay, in the area of the Vestfold Hills. Photographed by the LCE 1936–37. Later named by the Australians for E.A. Trigwell, radio supervisor at Davis Station in 1958.

Trilling Bay. 69°31'S, 39°41'E. Just south of Skarvsnes Foreland, on the east side of Lützow-Holm Bay. Photographed by the LCE 1936–37. Named Trillingbukta (the triplet bay) by the Norwegians, in association with the nearby Trilling Islands.

Trilling Islands. 69°30'S, 39°38'E. Three islands at the south side of Skarvsnes Foreland, in Trilling Bay, in the east part of Lützow-Holm Bay. Photographed by the LCE 1936–37. Named Trillingöyane (the triplet islands) by the Norwegians.

Trilling Peaks. 67°58'S, 62°45'E. A line of nunataks, with 3 main peaks. 3 miles south of the South Masson Range, in the Framnes Mountains of Mac. Robertson Land. Photographed by the LCE 1936–37. Named Trillingnutane (the triplet peaks) by the Norwegians.

Trillingane Nunataks. 71°50'S, 27°25'E. Three nunataks. 6 miles NE of Balchen Mountain, at the east end of the Sør Rondane Mountains. Name means "the triplets" in Norwegian.

Trillingbukta *see* **Trilling Bay**

Trillingnutane *see* **Trilling Peaks**

Trillingöyane *see* **Trilling Islands**

Mount Trimpi. 75°21'S, 72°48'W. 3 miles WNW of Mount Brice, in the Behrendt Mountains of Ellsworth Land. Named for Michael L. Trimpi, radioscience researcher at Eights Station in 1963.

Trinity Island. 63°45'S, 60°45'W. Also called Isla Trinidad, Île de la Trinité. 15 miles long. 6 miles wide. Its highest peak is 3,600 feet. Separated from the Antarctic Peninsula by the Orléans Strait. First seen by Palmer on Nov. 16, 1820, although there is a good chance that Bransfield saw it before that, in the previous Austral summer. He had named a portion of land in this area as Trinity Land. It was either this island or Trinity Peninsula (as we know them today) that he saw. Nordenskjöld clearly defined it in 1901–4.

Trinity Land *see* **Trinity Island, Trinity Peninsula**

Trinity Nunatak. 76°27'S, 160°38'E. In the flow of the Mawson Glacier, 5 miles north of the Convoy Range, in Victoria Land. Named by the NZ Northern Survey Party of the BCTAE in 1957 for its 3 summits.

Trinity Peninsula. 63°30'S, 58°W. The very northernmost part of the Antarctic continent. It is 80 miles long and extends north from an imaginary east-west line across Graham Land connecting Cape Kater to Cape Longing. This may be what Bransfield called Trinity Land (but equally well it may have been Trinity Island—see that entry) in Jan. 1820. It was discovered for sure by Dumont d'Urville on Jan. 20, 1838. He called it Louis Philippe Land. This name has been variously seen as Louis Philippe Coast, Louis Philippe Peninsula and Palmer Peninsula. It was renamed in favor of Bransfield's naming.

Islotes Trio *see* **Tau Islands**

Trio Nunataks. 75°30'S, 159°42'E. Three nunataks at the south side of the David Glacier, just west of the terminus of the Hollingsworth Glacier, in Victoria Land. Named by the New Zealanders in 1962–63.

Trioen Nunataks. 72°25'S, 3°59'W. An isolated group of 3 nunataks, 8 miles west of Borg Mountain, in Queen Maud Land. Name means "the trio" in Norwegian.

Triple Islands. 66°46'S, 141°12'E. Three small islands just east of the tip of the Zélée Glacier Tongue. Almost ½ mile SSE of the Double Islands. Charted and named by Liotard in 1949–51.

The Triplets. 62°24'S, 59°41'W. A three-pointed peak at the SE side of Coppermine Cove, near the west end of Robert Island, in the South Shetlands. Charted and named in 1935 by the personnel on the *Discovery II.*

Tripod Island. 64°19'S, 62°57'W. A small island just south of the western end of Eta Island. It marks the north side of the western entrance to Andersen Harbor, in the Melchior Islands. Surveyed and named by the personnel on the *Discovery* in 1927.

Mount Tripp. 83°18'S, 166°54'E. 2,980 m. Ice-covered. Cone-shaped. Between the Hoffman and Hewitt Glaciers, 7 miles WNW of Rhodes Peak in the Holland Range, to the west of the Lennox-King Glacier, in the Transantarctic Mountains. Discovered by Shackleton in 1907–9, and named by him for Leonard O.H. Tripp of New Zealand, who assisted Shackleton on his first two expeditions.

Tripp Bay. 76°37'S, 162°44'E. Formed by a recession in the ice between the Oates Piedmont Glacier and the Evans Piedmont Glacier, on the coast of Victoria Land. Charted by Shackleton's 1907–9 expedition, and named by Scott's 1910–13 expedition in association with Tripp Island, which is in the bay.

Tripp Island. 76°38'S, 162°42'E. In the south part of Tripp Bay, on the coast of Victoria Land. Named by Shackleton's 1907–9 expedition for Leonard O.H. Tripp (*see* **Mount Tripp**).

The *Trismus.* Belgian ship in the Antarctic Peninsula area in 1975–76.

Tristan Island. 66°44'S, 140°54'E. Also called Rocher Noir. A small island, almost ¾ mile west of Yseult Island, and

350 yards north of the western point on Cape Jules. Charted by Barré in 1951-52, and named by the French in association with Yscult Island.

Triton Point. 71°42'S, 68°12'W. Forms the east end of the high ridge separating the Venus and Neptune Glaciers, on the east coast of Alexander Island. Named by the UK for one of the satellites of the planet Neptune.

Mount Tritoppen. 67°59'S, 62°29'E. Also called Tritoppen Peak. 1,350 m. Has 3 peaks. 3 miles south of Mount Hordern, in the David Range of the Framnes Mountains. Photographed by the LCE 1936-37, and named Tritoppen (the three-peaked mountain) by the Norwegians.

Tritoppen Peak *see* **Mount Tritoppen**

Triune Peaks. 69°08'S, 66°52'W. Three peaks, 12 miles NE of Mount Balfour, and overlooking the Wordie Ice Shelf, on the west coast of the Antarctic Peninsula. Named descriptively by the UK.

Trivial Islands. 65°31'S, 65°13'W. A group of small islands, 1½ miles east of Lacuna Island, and 7 miles north of Vieugué Island, in the Biscoe Islands. Named by the UK because they are small, boring, and insignificant (and therefore of interest).

Cape Trois Pérez *see* **Cape Pérez**

Trojan Range. 64°32'S, 63°23'W. 2,135 m. Extends northward from Mount Français along the east side of Iliad Glacier, on Anvers Island. Named by the UK for the Trojans of Homer's *Iliad*.

Trollkjelen Crevasse Field. 71°17'S, 0°50'W. 12 miles long. In the Fimbul Ice Shelf. Just off the NE side of Trollkjelneset Headland, in Queen Maud Land. Name means "the troll's cauldron" in Norwegian.

Trollkjell Ridge. The crest of Jutulstraumen Glacier, in western Queen Maud Land. It is a volcanic area, and was named by the Norwegians. It is, however, an unofficial name.

Trollkjelneset Headland. 71°25'S, 1° W. Snow-domed. Between Krylvika Bight and the mouth of Jutulstraumen Glacier, in Queen Maud Land. Name means "the cape of the troll's cauldron" in Norwegian.

Trollkjelpiggen Peak. 71°35'S, 1°09' W. 5 miles SW of Utkikken Hill, on the east side of the Ahlmann Ridge, in Queen Maud Land. Name means "the peak of the troll's cauldron" in Norwegian.

Trollslottet Mountain. 71°56'S, 7°14' E. The USSR calls it Gora Zabor. Forms the NW limit of the Filchner Mountains, in Queen Maud Land. Name means "the troll castle" in Norwegian.

Cap de Trooz *see* **Cape Pérez**

Trooz Glacier. 65°20'S, 63°58'W. 1½ miles wide at its mouth. 15 miles long. Flows into the northern part of Collins Bay, on the west coast of Graham Land. Discovered by Charcot in 1908-10, and named by him for J. de Trooz, Belgian minister of the Interior and Public Information, who helped produce the scientific results of de Gerlache's *Belgica* expedition of 1897-99 (*see also* **Cape Pérez**).

Trost Peak. 67°52'S, 62°48'E. 980 m. 1½ miles NE of Mount Burnett, in the Masson Range of the Framnes Mountains. Photographed by the LCE 1936-37. Named later by the Australians for P.A. Trost, physicist at Mawson Station in 1958, and electronics engineer at Mawson Station again in 1962.

Trost Rocks. 69°45'S, 68°58'E. Two rocks at the NE end of Single Island, on the west side of the Amery Ice Shelf. Named by the Australians for P.A. Trost (*see* **Trost Peak**).

Mount Trott. 70°42'S, 66°23'E. 1 mile north of Mount Bunt, in the Prince Charles Mountains. Named by the Australians for N.E. Trott, weather observer at Wilkes Station in 1962, and officer-in-charge of Davis Station in 1964.

Mount Troubridge. 71°08'S, 167°44'E. Also spelled Mount Trowbridge. Over

1,000 m. Surmounts the east end of the Hedgpeth Heights, in the Anare Mountains. Discovered and charted by Ross in Jan. 1841, and named by him for Rear-Admiral Sir Edward Thomas Troubridge, lord of the admiralty.

Trousers. Tourists should wear good quality, pull-on waterproof trousers, with other warm trousers (jeans, etc.) underneath them.

Trout Island. 66°01'S, 65°27'W. Just east of Salmon Island, in the Fish Islands, off the west coast of Graham Land. Named by the UK in 1959 in continuation of the fish motif.

Mount Trowbridge see **Mount Trowbridge**

Trowbridge Island. 62°S, 57°39'W. 2 miles NW of Cape Melville, in Destruction Bay, off the east coast of King George Island, in the South Shetlands. Named by the UK in 1960 for the *Lady Trowbridge.*

Truant Island see **Vázquez Island**

Trubyatchinskiy Nunatak. 68°20'S, 49°38'E. 7 miles south of Alderdice Peak, in the Nye Mountains of Enderby Land. Named by the USSR in 1962 for magnetician N.N. Trubyatchinskiy (1886–1942).

Trudge Valley. 76°43'S, 159°45'E. On the south side of Windwhistle Peak, in the Allan Hills of Victoria Land. Named in 1964 by the New Zealand Allan Hills Expedition, for the many trudges along it.

True Glacier. 74°38'S, 111°45'W. On Bear Peninsula, on the coast of Marie Byrd Land.

True Hills. 80°13'S, 26°51'W. In the Shackleton Range.

Truelare, Charles. Ordinary seaman on the Wilkes Expedition 1838–42. Joined in the USA. Served the cruise.

Trueman Terraces. 80°43'S, 22°41'W. In the Shackleton Range.

Truman Nunatak. 72°44'S, 75°01'E. Partly snow-covered. 7½ miles north of

Mount Harding, in the Grove Mountains. Named by the Australians for M.J. Truman, electrical fitter at Mawson Station in 1962.

Islote Trumao see **McConnel Islands**

Trump Islands. 66°02'S, 65°57'W. A small group, 4 miles south of Dodman Island, off the west coast of Graham Land. Discovered and named by the BGLE 1934–37.

Truncated Cones. 77°32'S, 167°05'E. Unofficial name for a feature on Ross Island.

Trundle Island. 65°23'S, 65°18'W. 1 mile NE of Jingle Island, in the Pitt Islands, of the Biscoe Islands. Named by the UK in 1959 for the Dickens character.

Trundy Island. 64°47'S, 64°28'W. Almost ½ mile WNW of Robbins Island, in the west part of the Joubin Islands. Named for George B. Trundy, able seaman on the *Hero* on that vessel's first voyage to Palmer Station in 1968.

Mount Tryggve Gran see **Mount Gran**

Tryggve Point. 77°39'S, 166°42'E. Juts out from Ross Island into McMurdo Sound, between Turks Head and Cape Evans. Charted by Scott's 1910–13 expedition, and named by Scott for Tryggve Gran.

Tryne Bay. 68°24'S, 78°28'E. 3 miles wide. Between the Tryne Islands and the coast, this is the easternmost part of the Vestfold Hills. Photographed by the LCE 1936–37. Named Trynevika (the snout bay) by the Norwegians.

Tryne Crossing. 68°30'S, 78°18'E. A pass across Langnes Peninsula, in the Vestfold Hills, leading from the SW arm of Tryne Fjord (hence the name) to Langnes Fjord. Photographed by the LCE 1936–37. First traversed by an ANARE party led by Bruce Stinear on May 13, 1957, and named by the Australians.

Tryne Fjord. 68°28'S, 78°22'E. Also called Tryne Inlet. Indents the northern side of Langnes Peninsula in the Vestfold

Hills. Named by the LCE 1936–37. Means "the snout fjord" in Norwegian.

Tryne Inlet *see* **Tryne Fjord**

Tryne Islands. 68°24'S, 78°23'E. A group of several small islands and rocks, 4 miles in extent, which form the western limit of Tryne Bay and of Tryne Sound, at the NE end of the Vestfold Hills. Photographed by the LCE 1936–37. Named Trynøyane (the snout islands) in Norwegian.

Tryne Point. 67°18'S, 59°03'E. Also called Trynet Point. At the east end of Law Promontory. Forms the west side of the entrance to Stefansson Bay. Photographed by the LCE 1936–37, and named Trynet (the snout) by the Norwegians. Later translated by the Australians as Tryne Point.

Tryne Sound. 68°26'S, 78°24'E. Also called Tryne Strait. A passage on the north side of Langnes Peninsula, in the Vestfold Hills, connecting Tryne Bay and Tryne Fjord. Photographed by the LCE 1936–37. Name means "the snout sound" in Norwegian.

Tryne Strait *see* **Tryne Sound**

Trynet *see* **Tryne Point**

Trynet Point *see* **Tryne Point**

Trynevika *see* **Tryne Bay**

Trynøyane *see* **Tryne Islands**

Tschuffert Peak. 67°28'S, 60°54'E. Isolated. Between Taylor Glacier and Chapman Ridge, in Mac. Robertson Land. Photographed by the LCE 1936–37, and named Svartpiggen (the black peak) by the Norwegians. Renamed by the Australians for H. Tschuffert, meteorologist at Mawson Station in 1958.

Tsentral'naya Hill. 70°45'S, 11°40'E. 205 m. Ice-free. In the center of the Schirmacher Hills of Queen Maud Land. Mapped and named by the USSR as Tsentral'naya (central hill).

Tsiolkovskiy Island. 70°30'S, 3°E. Ice-covered. In the Fimbul Ice Shelf of Queen Maud Land. Just NE of the similar but smaller Kroshka Island. Named by the USSR in 1961 for K.E. Tsiolkovskiy (1857–1935), Russian scientist and inventor.

Tu Rocks. 62°14'S, 58°53'W. Two rocks in Maxwell Bay, 2 miles east of the SW end of King George Island, in the South Shetlands. Named phonetically by the personnel on the *Discovery II* in 1935.

Tua Hill. 72°05'S, 1°12'E. Isolated. 3 miles west of Brattskarvet Mountain, in the Sverdrup Mountains of Queen Maud Land. Name means "the knoll" in Norwegian.

Mount Tuatara. 80°34'S, 158°20'E. 1,640 m. 7 miles north of Mount Hamilton, between Byrd Glacier and the Ross Ice Shelf. Mapped by the NZGSAE 1960–61, and named by them for its resemblance to a lizard found only on some small islands near New Zealand.

Tubor, Henry. Seaman on the Wilkes Expedition 1838–42. Joined in the USA. Served the cruise.

Mount Tuck. 78°30'S, 84°50'W. 3,560 m. Pyramidal. At the head of Hansen Glacier, in the Sentinel Range. Named for Lt. John Tuck, Jr.

Tuck, John, Jr. Lt. (jg), USN. From Massachusetts. Known as "Bob" or "Jack." When he became the first leader at the new South Pole Station for the winter of 1957, he already had 23 months in the Antarctic, and had wintered-over the previous year at McMurdo Base. On Nov. 19, 1957, he handed the Pole station over to Lt. V.N. Houk. He wrote the foreword to Paul Siple's book *90°S South.*

Mount Tucker. 64°20'S, 59°16'W. 9 miles NW of Longing Gap, overlooking Larsen Inlet, in Graham Land. Named by the UK for the Tucker Sno-Cat Corporation of Medford, Oregon, manufacturer of Sno-cat vehicles.

Tucker, Charles T. Master of the *Erebus* during Ross' expedition of 1839–43.

Tucker Glacier. 72°40'S, 169°E. A valley glacier, 90 miles long, which flows between the Admiralty Mountains and the Victory Mountains into the Ross Sea at the Borchgrevink Coast of northern Victoria Land. Explored by the NZGSAE 1957–58, and named by them in association with Tucker Inlet.

Tucker Inlet. 72°39′S, 170°E. An ice-filled indentation into the coast of Victoria Land, between Capes Wheatstone and Daniell. Discovered by Ross in Feb. 1841, and named by him for Charles T. Tucker.

Tucker Point. 73°57′S, 114°49′W. On Martin Peninsula, on the coast of Marie Byrd Land.

Tuff Bluff. 78°02′S, 165°27′E. Light-colored. On the northern slopes of Brown Peninsula, Victoria Land. Trachytic tuff is found here, hence the name given by New Zealand in 1966.

Tufft Nunatak. 63°55′S, 58°42′W. 3 miles SW of Mount Bradley, on Trinity Peninsula. Named by the UK for Ronald W. Tufft, a FIDS member here in 1956–57.

Tufts College Valley *see* **Tufts Pass**

Tufts Pass. 69°25′S, 70°35′W. Also called Tufts Valley, Tufts College Valley. Runs between the Rouen Mountains and the Elgar Uplands, in the north of Alexander Island. Discovered aerially by the BGLE in 1937. Named by the RARE 1947–48 for Tufts University, Medford, Mass., Dr. Robert Nichols's university.

Tufts Valley *see* **Tufts Pass**

Tukey Island. 64°46′S, 64°26′W. Near the center of the Joubin Islands. Named for Claude C. Tukey, messman on the *Hero* on that vessel's first voyage to Palmer Station in 1968.

Mount Tukotok. 72°17′S, 164°43′E. 2,540 m. A red granite peak 5 miles ESE of Mount Apolotok, in the Salamander Range of the Freyberg Mountains. Named by the New Zealanders in 1963–64. It is an Eskimo word meaning "the little red one."

The *Tula*. 150-ton, two-masted, square-sterned schooner of 74 feet in length, used as Biscoe's flagship in 1830–32.

Cape Tula *see* **Tula Point**

Tula Mountains. 66°45′S, 51°E. Between the Scott Mountains and the Napier Mountains in Enderby Land. They include Mount Riiser-Larsen. Discovered by the BANZARE on Jan. 14, 1930, and named Tula Range by Mawson for the *Tula*. The Australians redefined the feature as mountains in 1958 following an ANARE survey by G.A. Knuckey.

Tula Point. 65°31′S, 65°39′W. Also called Cape Tula. Forms the NE end of Renaud Island, in the Biscoe Islands. Named by the UK in 1954 for the *Tula*.

Tula Range *see* **Tula Mountains**

Tumble Glacier. 69°57′S, 69°20′W. 7 miles long. 3 miles wide. Flows from the cliffs of Mount Egbert, Mount Ethelwulf, and Mount Ethelred, into the west side of the George VI Sound, just south of Mount King, on the east side of Alexander Island. Surveyed in 1936 by the BGLE, and again in 1948 by the FIDS. Named by the FIDS because of the broken condition of the lower reaches of the glacier.

Tumbledown Cliffs. 64°05′S, 58°27′W. 3 miles north of Cape Obelisk, on the west coast of James Ross Island. Surveyed by the FIDS in 1945. Named by the UK for the formation of the scree slope at the foot of the cliffs.

Tunet Valley. 72°02′S, 4°02′E. Ice-filled. Semi-circular. On the north side of Mount Hochlin, in the Mühlig-Hofmann Mountains of Queen Maud Land. Name means "the courtyard" in Norwegian.

Tunga Spur. 73°54′S, 5°20′W. Extends from the Kirwan Escarpment just SW of Gommen Valley, in Queen Maud Land. Name means "the tongue" in Norwegian.

Tuning Nunatak. 84°44′S, 115°58′W. 1 mile north of Darling Ridge, in the Ohio Range. Named for Preston O. Tuning, meteorologist at Byrd Station in 1960.

Tuorda Peak. 65°59'S, 65°10'W. 870 m. East of Ferin Head, on the west coast of Graham Land. Named by the UK in 1959 for Pava L. Tuorda, Arctic skiing pioneer.

Tupinier Islands. 63°22'S, 58°16'W. A group of pyramid-shaped islands, off the north coast of Trinity Peninsula. 3 miles NW of Cape Ducorps. Discovered by Dumont d'Urville in 1837–40, and named by him for an official with the French Navy Department who helped the expedition.

Tupman Island. 65°29'S, 65°32'W. 2 miles long. East of Pickwick Island, in the Pitt Islands, of the Biscoe Islands. Named by the UK in 1959 for the Dickens character.

Tur, Juan F. Lt., USN. From San Juan, Puerto Rico. He was military leader at Hallett Station during the winter-over of 1957. On Jan. 16, 1958, he was relieved by Lt. R.C. Bornmann.

Tur Peak. 73°06'S, 167°58'E. 1,470 m. At the SE edge of Malta Plateau, on the north wall of the lower part of the Mariner Glacier. 4½ miles SSE of Mount Alberts, in Victoria Land. Named for Juan F. Tur.

Turbidite Hill. 82°01'S, 157°45'E. 4 miles east of Laird Plateau, on the north side of Olson Névé. Named by the New Zealanders in 1964–65 for the turbidite in the hill.

Turbulence Bluffs. 67°09'S, 56°29'E. Three high bluffs with vertical faces on the NW, but merging with the ice sheet on the SE. On the east side of the Robert Glacier, 16 miles NE of Rayner Peak, in Enderby Land. Named by the ANARE because of severe turbulence while landing a helicopter here in 1965.

Mount Turcotte. 81°15'S, 85°24'W. 2½ miles NW of Mount Tidd, in the Pirrit Hills. Named for F. Thomas Turcotte, seismologist here in Dec. 1958 with the Ellsworth-Byrd Traverse Party.

Turk Peak. 81°02'S, 158°23'E. 2,000 m. Hump-shaped. 6 miles north of Mount Zinkovich, in the Churchill Mountains. Named for Lt. Col. Wilbert Turk, commander of the 61st Troop Carrier Squadron which flew the first Hercules aircraft into Antarctica in Jan. 1960.

Turks Head. 77°40'S, 166°46'E. Over 200 m. A black-colored, precipitous promontory, or headland, jutting out into McMurdo Sound from the Turks Head Ridge on Ross Island, 5 miles ESE of Cape Evans on the west side of the island, just north of the Erebus Glacier Tongue. Discovered by Scott's 1901–4 expedition, and named by them as Turk's Head (Antarctic placenames generally have since become largely free of apostrophies).

Turks Head Bay. 77°40'S, 166°44'E. Between Tryggve Point and Turks Head on the west side of Ross Island. Named by Scott's 1910–13 expedition as Turk's Head Bay, in association with Turk's Head (*see* **Turks Head** for note on apostrophes in Antarctica).

Turks Head Ridge. 77°38'S, 166°48'E. Ice-covered. A ridge coming down from Mount Erebus to McMurdo Sound, in the SW part of Ross Island. It ends partly in Turks Head. Mapped by Scott's 1910–13 expedition, and named by them as Turk's Head Ridge, in association with Turk's Head (see note on dropping the apostrophe under **Turks Head**).

Turmoil Rock. 62°21'S, 59°47'W. Almost ¾ mile SE of Table Island, in the South Shetlands. Named descriptively by the UK in 1971 since the surface of the rock is only about 18 inches below the surface of the water, and there is always turmoil around it.

Turnabout Island. 66°06'S, 65°45'W. Snow-capped. In the Saffery Islands. 2 miles SW of Black Head, off the west coast of Graham Land. Discovered by the BGLE 1934–37, and named by them for the turning point in a sledge journey in Aug. 1935.

Turnabout Ridge. 83°18'S, 162°35'E. 10 miles long. Between Linehan Glacier and Lowery Glacier, in the Queen Elizabeth Range. Named by the Ohio State

University Party here in 1966–67, because the ridge was the furthest reached from base camp by the party.

Turnabout Valley. 77°46'S, 160°32'E. A partially dry valley in southern Victoria Land, between Finger Mountain and Pyramid Mountain, to the immediate north of Beacon Valley, and on the south side of the Taylor Glacier. Named by the New Zealanders in 1958–59.

Mount Turnbull. 70°21'S, 64°02'E. 1,980 m. Partly snow-covered. 12 miles SW of Mount Starlight, in the NW part of the Prince Charles Mountains of Mac. Robertson Land. Named by the Australians for W.L. Turnbull, radio supervisor at Mawson Station in 1965.

Turnbull Point. 63°03'S, 56°36'W. At the west end of D'Urville Island. Named by the UK for David H. Turnbull, captain of the *Shackleton,* the BAS ship.

Turneaux, Tobias. This is a misprint, sometimes seen (*see* **Furneaux, Tobias**).

Turner, Henry. Captain of the foc's'le on the Wilkes Expedition 1838–42. Joined in the USA. Served the cruise.

Turner, William W. Quartergunner on the Wilkes Expedition 1838–42. Joined in the USA. Discharged at Oahu, Oct. 31, 1840.

Turner Glacier. 67°37'S, 68°29'W. On Adelaide Island.

Turner Hills. 82°59'S, 156°15'E. Between the Astro and Nimrod Glaciers, at the extreme north of the Miller Range. Named for Dr. Mort D. Turner of the National Science Foundation, long-time program manager for Polar Earth Studies. He was in the dry valleys of Victoria Land in 1959–60, and in several subsequent seasons served as USARP representative in Antarctica.

Turner Island. 68°33'S, 77°53'E. ½ mile NW of Bluff Island, and 2½ miles west of Breidnes Peninsula, in Prydz Bay, in the area of the Vestfold Hills. Photographed by the LCE 1936–37. Later named by the Australians for P.B. Turner, radio officer at Davis Station in 1958.

Turnpike Bluff. 80°44'S, 30°04'W. 5 miles SW of Mount Homard, in the SW end of the Shackleton Range. Named by the BCTAE in 1957 because it is the beginning of a badly crevassed area of Recovery Glacier.

Turnstile Ridge. 79°49'S, 154°35'E. 9 miles long. 3 miles north of Westhaven Nunatak, at the NW end of the Britannia Range, just to the west of the Darwin Mountains, in southern Victoria Land. Named in 1957 by the Darwin Glacier Party of the BCTAE for the turnstile-like snow passages along it.

Turquet, J. French naturalist who joined the *Français* at Buenos Aires in Dec. 1903, for Charcot's 1903–5 expedition.

Turquet Point. 65°03'S, 63°57'W. Marks the northern end of Booth Island, in the Wilhelm Archipelago. Charted by Charcot in 1903–5, and named by him for J. Turquet.

The Turret. 60°40'S, 45°09'W. 460 m. A headland at the south side of the entrance to Gibbon Bay, on the east coast of Coronation Island, in the South Orkneys. Charted and named descriptively by the personnel on the *Discovery II* in 1933.

Turret Island. 71°22'S, 169°13'E. A small island, ice-covered except for the north face. Lies partly within the seaward terminus of the Shipley Glacier, 1 mile west of Flat Island, on the north coast of Victoria Land. The rocky north end looks like a turret. Charted and named descriptively by Campbell's Northern Party during Scott's 1910–13 expedition.

Turret Nunatak. 82°25'S, 158°E. 1,960 m. West of the Cobham Range, in the lower portion of the Lucy Glacier. Named by the New Zealanders in 1961–62 for its turreted cliffs on the southern side.

Turret Peak. 72°16'S, 166°06'E. 2,790 m. 7 miles NW of Crosscut Peak, in the Millen Range. It has a 10-meter vertical, spirelike tower on top, which is a good landmark. Named accordingly by the New Zealanders in 1962–63.

Turret Point. 62°05'S, 57°55'W. Forms the east limit of King George Bay, on the south coast of King George Island, in the South Shetlands. Named Turret Rocks by the personnel on the *Discovery II* in 1937. Redefined by the UK in 1960.

Turret Rocks *see* **Turret Point**

Turtle Back Island *see* **Turtle Rock**

Turtle Island. 66°04'S, 65°51'W. The most northwesterly island in the Saffery Islands. A small island, it is 6 miles west of Black Head, off the west coast of Graham Land. Discovered and named by the BGLE 1934–37.

Turtle Peak. 75°22'S, 111°18'W. Mostly ice-free. 2 miles south of Hedin Nunatak, on the Mount Murphy massif, in Marie Byrd Land. Algae and petrels are found here. Named for John P. Turtle, aurora researcher at Byrd Station in 1962.

Turtle Rock. 77°45'S, 166°46'E. Also called Turtle Back Island. A rock in Erebus Bay, off the western coast of Hut Point Peninsula, Ross Island. Discovered by Scott's 1901–4 expedition, and named by them descriptively.

Tusing Peak. 76°51'S, 126°W. 2,650 m. Snow-capped. In the central portion of Mount Hartigan, in the Executive Committee Range of Marie Byrd Land. Named for Allen D. Tusing, meteorologist at Byrd Station in 1959.

The Tusk. 84°52'S, 168°15'W. 460 m. A small peak, in the east part of the Mayer Crags, 1½ miles south of Mount Henson, at the west side of the terminus of the Liv Glacier. Composed of coarsely-crystalline white marble. Named descriptively by the New Zealanders in 1963–64.

Tussebrekka Slope. 72°08'S, 6°24'E. 6 miles long. Mainly ice-covered. At the SW side of the head of Lunde Glacier, in the Mühlig-Hofmann Mountains of Queen Maud Land. Name means "the goblin slope" in Norwegian.

Tussenobba Peak. 72°S, 6°15'E. 2,665 m. 6 miles NE of Halsknappane Hills, in

the east part of the Mühlig-Hofmann Mountains of Queen Maud Land. Named by the Norwegians.

Tustane Peaks. 72°08'S, 25°17'E. At the head of Koms Glacier, in the Sør Rondane Mountains. Name means "the clumps" in Norwegian.

Tutton Point. 66°53'S, 67°36'W. The SW point of Liard Island, in Hanusse Bay, Graham Land. Named by the UK for Alfred E.H. Tutton, British mineralogist, and alpine snow and ice expert.

Mount Tuve. 73°47'S, 80°08'W. 935 m. Just south of the base of Wirth Peninsula, in Ellsworth Land. Discovered by the RARE 1947–48. Named by Ronne for Merle A. Tuve, director of the Department of Terrestrial Magnetism at the Carnegie Institution, who supplied instruments for the expedition.

Cape Tuxen. 65°16'S, 64°08'W. 2,900 feet. A promontory which forms the south side of the entrance to Waddington Bay, on the west coast of Graham Land. Discovered and named by de Gerlache in 1897–99.

Tverrbrekka Pass. 72°14'S, 1°19'E. Runs east-west through the Sverdrup Mountains, between Vendeholten Mountain and Tverrveggen Ridge, in Queen Maud Land. Name means "the transverse slope" in Norwegian.

Tverregg Glacier. 73°27'S, 3°36'W. Between the Heksegryta Peaks and Tverregga Spur, in the Kirwan Escarpment of Queen Maud Land. Named Tverreggbreen (the transverse ridge glacier) by the Norwegians.

Tverregga Spur. 73°23'S, 3°36'W. 3 miles west of Mount Hallgren, in the Kirwan Escarpment of Queen Maud Land. Name means "the transverse ridge" in Norwegian.

Tverreggbreen *see* **Tverregg Glacier**

Tverreggtelen Hill. 73°24'S, 3°33'W. Just SE of Tverregga Spur, in the Kirwan Escarpment of Queen Maud Land. Named by the Norwegians in association with Tverregga Spur.

Tverrholmen *see* **Transverse Island**

Tverrnipa Peak. 72°15'S, 1°19'E. 2,195 m. Surmounts the northern end of Tverrveggen Ridge, in the Sverdrup Mountains of Queen Maud Land. Named Tverrnipa (the transverse peak) by the Norwegians.

Tverrseten Col. 72°02'S, 4°46'E. An ice col between Setenuten Peak and Petrellfjellet in the Mühlig-Hofmann Mountains of Queen Maud Land. Name means "the transverse seat" in Norwegian.

Tverrveggen Ridge. 72°17'S, 1°20'E. Extends southward for 4 miles from Tverrbrekka Pass, in the Sverdrup Mountains of Queen Maud Land. Name means "the transverse wall" in Norwegian.

Tvetaggen Peaks. 71°45'S, 25°17'E. A short line of peaks, 1½ miles north of Austkampane Hills, on the west side of Kamp Glacier, in the Sør Rondane Mountains. Named descriptively by the Norwegians (name means "the double prongs").

Tvibåsen Valley. 71°53'S, 5°15'E. Ice-filled. Between Svarthamaren Mountain and Cumulus Mountain, in the Mühlig-Hofmann Mountains of Queen Maud Land. Name means "the double stall" in Norwegian.

Tvillingfjell *see* **Holder Peak, Young Peak**

Tvireita Moraine. 71°55'S, 14°37'E. 5 miles long. In the east part of the Mendeleyev Glacier, in the Payer Mountains of Queen Maud Land. Named Tvireita (the furrows) by the Norwegians because it is comprised of two somewhat parallel segments.

Tvistein Pillars. 68°42'S, 90°42'W. Also called Tvistern. Two flat-topped pillar rocks, 1 mile SW of Cape Eva, Peter I Island. Discovered by the *Odd I* in 1927. Named by Nils Larsen in the *Norvegia* in 1929. The name means "two stones" in Norwegian.

Tvistern *see* **Tvistein Pillars**

Tvitoppen Peak *see* **Mount Twintop**

Tvora. 72°10'S, 0°05'W. A mountain with two north-trending spurs. 3 miles east of Straumsvola Mountain, in the Sverdrup Mountains of Queen Maud Land. Name means "two ridges" in Norwegian.

Twig Rock. 68°42'S, 67°32'W. Also called Terra Firma II Island. Over 90 m. A small island, between Alamode Island and Hayrick Island, in the Terra Firma Islands, off the west coast of Graham Land. Surveyed by the FIDS in 1948, and named by them for the branching nature of the dike system exposed on its north face.

Mount Twigg. 74°17'S, 67°50'E. 16 miles SE of Mount Maguire, near the head of the Lambert Glacier. Named by the Australians for D.R. Twigg, radio supervisor at Mawson Station in 1958.

Twilight Bay. 68°32'S, 69°48'E. On the west side of the Amery Ice Shelf. It is an indentation of this ice shelf into the plateau behind it. The ANARE survey party of Feb. 1968 flew in at twilight.

Twin Crater. Unofficial name for an extinct volcano on Ross Island.

Twin Nunataks. 75°38'S, 159°36'E. Two small nunataks, between the Ricker Hills and Hollingsworth Glacier, in the Prince Albert Mountains of Victoria Land. Named descriptively by the New Zealanders in 1962–63.

¹**Twin Peaks** *see* **Gemel Peaks**

²**Twin Peaks.** 63°24'S, 57°07'W. 750 m. Two peaks. 1½ miles north of Mount Taylor, 2 miles west of the head of Hope Bay, at the NE end of the Antarctic Peninsula. Discovered by Nordenskjöld's 1901–4 expedition. Named descriptively by the FIDS in 1946.

Twin Pinnacles. 62°08'S, 58°06'W. Also called Pináculos Mellizos. 20 m. A rock in water with 2 summits. Almost 200 yards NE of Lions Rump at the west side of the entrance to King George Bay, in the South Shetlands. Charted and named descriptively by the personnel on the *Discovery II* in 1937.

Twin Rocks. 78°24'S, 161°41'E. Twin rock bluffs in the Lower Staircase of the Skelton Glacier. 6 miles east of Halfway Nunatak, in Victoria Land. Named descriptively by the NZ party of the BCTAE in 1957–58.

The Twins. 60°37'S, 46°04'W. Two rocks in water, ½ mile south of Monroe Island, in the South Orkneys. Charted and named by the personnel on the *Discovery II* in 1933.

Mount Twintop. 68°05'S, 62°22'E. Also called Tvitoppen Peak. A twin-peaked mountain, 6 miles SSW of Mount Tritoppen, in the south part of the David Range of the Framnes Mountains. Photographed by the LCE 1936–37, and named Tvitoppen (the twin peak) by the Norwegians. The Australians translated it.

Mount Twiss. 79°23'S, 85°36'W. 2,000 m. At the north end of the Watlack Hills, in the Heritage Range. Named for John R. Twiss, Jr., USARP representative at McMurdo Station in 1964–65.

Twisted Lake. 60°43'S, 45°40'W. 175 yards NE of Cummings Cove, in the western part of Signy Island, in the South Orkneys. Named by the UK for its shape.

¹Two Hummock Island *see* **Two Summit Island**

²Two Hummock Island. 64°08'S, 61°40'W. 670 m. 5 miles long. Ice-covered. Has two rocky summits. 5 miles south of Liège Island, it is between that island and Hughes Bay, off the west coast of Graham Land. Named descriptively sometime in the middle of the 19th century.

Two Step Cliffs. 71°45'S, 68°13'W. 680 m. The eastern face of a flat-topped mountain just east of Mars Glacier, on the east coast of Alexander Island. They look across the George VI Sound to the Batterbee Mountains on the Antarctic Peninsula. Discovered aerially by Ellsworth on Nov. 23, 1935. Surveyed by the BGLE in 1936, and named by them as Two Step Mountains. Resurveyed in 1940–41 by the USAS, who called the

feature Table Mountain. The FIDS gave it its current name in 1949.

Two Step Mountains *see* **Two Step Cliffs**

Two Summit Island. 62°15'S, 58°57'W. A small island with 2 summits on it. At the east entrance to Fildes Strait, in the South Shetlands. Surveyed by the personnel on the *Discovery II* in 1935, and named by them as Two Hummock Island. In 1954 the UK renamed it in order to avoid confusion with another island of that name, further south.

Twombley Glacier. 80°35'S, 157°45'E. 6 miles long. Flows from the north side of Kent Plateau into the south side of Byrd Glacier. Named for C.E. Twombley of the US Weather Bureau, at Little America V in 1956.

Mount Twomey. 71°30'S, 161°41'E. Over 1,200 m. On the NW edge of Morozumi Range. 2½ miles NW of Berg Peak. Named for Arthur A. Twomey, geologist at McMurdo Station in 1967–68 and 1968–69.

Tyler Glacier. 72°15'S, 168°35'E. Flows between Taylor Peak and Mount Francis into the Tucker Glacier, in Victoria Land. Named for Lt. Paul E. Tyler, medical officer at Hallett Station in 1962.

Tyndall Mountains. 67°15'S, 67°10'W. Just south of Avsyuk Glacier, in the central part of Arrowsmith Peninsula, in Graham Land. Named by the UK for John Tyndall (1820–1893), Irish pioneer glaciologist.

Mount Tyoto *see* **Mount Choto**

Mount Tyree. 78°24'S, 85°55'W. 4,965 m. Ice-free. 8 miles NW of the Vinson Massif, in the main ridge of the Sentinel Range. Discovered by VX-6 in Jan. 1958, and named for Admiral David M. Tyree. It was first climbed on Jan. 6, 1957.

Tyree, David M. Rear-Admiral, USN. Took over from Admiral Dufek as the head of Operation Deep Freeze on April 14, 1959. On Nov. 26, 1962, he was succeeded by Adm. James Reedy. He retired in 1963 and died on Aug. 25, 1984, in Portsmouth, Virginia.

Tyrol Valley. 77°35'S, 160°39'E. Icefree. East of Mount Baldr, in the Asgard Range of Victoria Land. Named by Heinz Janetschek, Austrian biologist, for his homeland. He was in this area in 1961–62.

Mount Tyrrell. 69°38'S, 69°31'W. Has two summits. the higher being 1,310 m. 3 miles inland from the east coast of Alexander Island, on the east side of the mouth of Toynbee Glacier. Surveyed by the FIDS in 1948, and named by them for George W. Tyrrell, geologist at Glasgow University.

Tysk Pass. 72°43'S, 3°47'W. Between Høgskavlen Mountain and Domen Butte, in the Borg Massif of Queen Maud Land. Named Tyskepasset (the German Pass—it was first photographed aerially by Ritscher's Nazi expedition of 1938–39), and later translated into English.

Tyskepasset *see* **Tysk Pass**

Tyulen'i Islands. 66°33'S, 92°57'E. 3 very small islands in the south part of the Haswell Islands, 1 mile from the mainland. Almost ¼ mile west of Mabus Point, and just west of the Stroiteley Islands. Named Ostrova Tyulen'i (seal islands) by the USSR in 1956.

Tyuleniy Point. 70°44'S, 11°36'E. ½ mile west of Ozhidaniya Cove, on the north side of the Schirmacher Hills of Queen Maud Land. Named by the USSR in 1961. Name means "seal point" in Russian.

Mount Ubique. 81°30'S, 160°30'E. Just to the east of Starshot Glacier, 4 miles south of Hermitage Peak, in the Surveyors Range of the Queen Maud Mountains. It overlooks the Ross Ice Shelf, in the area of the Byrd Glacier. Named by the New Zealanders in 1960–61 for the Royal Engineers' motto, Ubique (means "everywhere").

Uchatka Point. 62°13'S, 58°26'W. On the west shore of Admiralty Bay, King George Island, in the South Shetlands.

Ueda Glacier. 75°15'S, 64°35'W. Flows along the south side of the Scaife Mountains, to enter Hansen Inlet near the base of the Antarctic Peninsula. Named for Herbert T. Ueda who, with Lyle Hansen, was in charge of the deep core drilling program at Byrd Station, 1966–67 and 1967–68.

Ufs Island. 67°28'S, 61°08'E. 2 miles wide. In the eastern part of Howard Bay. Mawson discovered the northern end of the island, Cape Simpson, in Feb. 1931, during the BANZARE, but it was not recognized to be an island until the LCE 1936–37 photographed it and Norwegian cartographers called it Ufsöy (bluff island).

Ufsebotnen Cirque. 71°24'S, 13°09'E. 1 mile north of the summit of Mount Schicht in the Gruber Mountains of the Wohlthat Mountains in Queen Maud Land. Discovered by Ritscher in 1938–39. Name means "the bluff cirque" in Norwegian.

Ufsebrotet Bluff. 71°23'S, 13°17'E. 2 miles south of Mount Zimmermann in the central Gruber Mountains of the Wohlthat Mountains of Queen Maud Land. Discovered by Ritscher in 1938–39. Named by the Norwegians.

Ufsekammen Ridge. 71°24'S, 13°14'E. Arc-shaped. 3 miles long. Between Mount Schicht and Ufsebrotet Bluff, in the Gruber Mountains of the Wohlthat Mountains in Queen Maud Land. Name means "the bluff ridge" in Norwegian.

Ufsöy *see* **Ufs Island**

Ufsöyvågen *see* **Howard Bay**

Mount Ugolini *see* **Ugolini Peak**

Ugolini Peak. 78°01'S, 161°31'E. Also called Mount Ugolini. 2,260 m. 6 miles south of Knob Head, at the south side of the upper part of the Ferrar Glacier in southern Victoria Land. Named by the USA for Fiorenzo G. Ugolini, soil student at McMurdo Sound in 1961–62 and 1962–63.

Ui-Te-Rangiora. Cook Islander who, about 650 A.D. sailed with a crew the 2,000 miles to Antarctica in his canoe, the *Te-Ivi-O-Atea*, or so legend has it.

Uksen Island. 67°21′S, 60°09′E. Also called Solitary Island. Isolated. 4 miles NE of Tilley Nunatak, off the coast of Mac. Robertson Land. Photographed by the LCE 1936–37, and named Uksen (the ox) by the Norwegians.

Uksöy *see* **Oom Island**

Uksvika *see* **Oom Bay**

Ula, Anton Olsen. Bosun on the *Antarctic* during Nordenskjöld's expedition of 1901–4.

Ula Point. 64°05′S, 57°09′W. Ice-covered. On the NE coast of James Ross Island, 5 miles NW of Cape Gage. Discovered and surveyed by Nordenskjöld's expedition of 1901–4, and resurveyed by the FIDS in 1945. Named by the UK for Anton Olsen Ula.

Ulendet Crevasses. 72°51′S, 0°59′W. A crevasse field, 7 miles long, in the Jutulstraumen Glacier, 15 miles NE of the Neumayer Cliffs in Queen Maud Land. Name means "the rough ground" in Norwegian.

Mount Ulla. 77°32′S, 162°24′E. Also called Claymore Peak. Between the Meserve and Hart Glaciers in the Asgard Range of Victoria Land. Named by the New Zealanders in 1958–59 for the Norse god.

Ullmann Massif *see* **Ullmann Spur**

Ullmann Point. 62°05′S, 58°23′W. Also seen spelled (erroneously) as Ullman Point. The southerly tip of Ullmann Spur on Martel Inlet, King George Island, in the South Shetlands. Charted by Charcot in 1908–10. Named about 1930 in association with Ullmann Spur.

Ullmann Range *see* **Ullmann Spur**

Ullmann Spur. 62°04′S, 58°22′W. Also called Ullmann Range, Ullmann Massif. The name is also seen (erroneously) as Ullman. 275 m. A mountainous ridge jutting out from King George Island into Martel Inlet, at the head of that inlet. Charted and named by Charcot in 1908–10.

Mount Ulmer. 77°35′S, 86°09′W. 2,775 m. 2 miles north of Mount Washburn in the northern part of the Sentinel Range. Discovered aerially by Ellsworth, and named for his wife, Mary Louise Ulmer, first as Mount Mary Louise Ulmer, then as Mount Mary Ulmer, then as Mount Ulmer.

Ulvetanna Peak. 71°51′S, 8°20′E. 2,930 m. 2 miles north of Kintanna Peak, in the east part of Fenriskjeften Mountain in Queen Maud Land. Name means "the wolf tooth" in Norwegian.

Umber Island. 69°13′S, 72°W. 1½ miles long. 6 miles NW of Dint Island in Lazarev Bay, off the west side of Alexander Island. Named by the UK for the shadow caused by the Havre Mountains to the north the way it showed up on the RARE photos of 1947–48.

Mount Umbriel. 71°36′S, 68°53′W. 1,500 m. Overlooks the head of Venus Glacier in the eastern part of Alexander Island. Named by the UK for the satellite belonging to the planet Uranus.

Umeboshi Rock. 68°03′S, 43°07′E. Also spelled Umebosi Rock. 4 miles ENE of Akebono Rock on the coast of Queen Maud Land. Named Umeboshi-iwa (rumpled rock) by the Japanese in 1962.

Umitaka Bank. A seamount (submarine feature) centering on 67°25′S, 167°E.

The *Umitaka Maru*. Japanese ship which accompanied the *Soya* in 1956–57.

Underwear. Tourists should wear thermal underwear, or at least something warm, depending on the tolerance level of their more southerly regions.

Mount Underwood. 68°08′S, 49°21′E. 2 miles east of Mount Flett in the central part of the Nye Mountains. Named by the Australians for R. Underwood, geophysicist at Mawson Station in 1959.

Underwood, Joseph A. Lt., USN. On the *Vincennes* with Wilkes 1838–42. Killed at Malolo on July 24, 1840.

Underwood Glacier. 66°35′S, 108°E. A channel glacier, 15 miles long. It feeds Vincennes Bay between Reist Rocks and Cape Nutt, to the east of the Knox Coast. Named for Lt. Joseph A. Underwood.

1044   Undietch, John • United States

Undietch, John. Ordinary seaman on the Wilkes Expedition 1838–42. Joined in the USA. Served the cruise.

Ungane Islands. 69°16′S, 39°29′E. Three small islands. 4 miles WNW of Hamnenabben Head in the east part of Lützow-Holm Bay. Photographed by the LCE 1936–37. Name means "the young ones" in Norwegian.

Unger Island. 70°41′S, 166°55′E. Small, ice-free island, the westernmost of the Lyall Islands. 4 miles SE of Cape Hooker in the west side of the entrance to Yule Bay, Victoria Land. Named for Lt. Pat B. Unger, USNR, medical officer at Little America in 1957.

Unger Peak. 79°21′S, 86°10′W. Mainly ice-covered. At the south end of the Founders Escarpment, 2 miles NNW of Zavis Peak in the Heritage Range. Named for Lt. Maurice H. Unger, USN, navigator on Antarctic flights, 1965 and 1966.

Mount Unicorn. 71°16′S, 67°07′W. The most northerly of the Batterbee Mountains. 6 miles NW of Mount Ness. Named by the UK for the constellation Monoceros (the Unicorn).

Union Glacier. 79°45′S, 82°30′W. Also called Bastien Glacier. Heavily crevassed. Flows from the plateau at Edson Hills on the west side of the Heritage Range, between the Pioneer Heights and the Enterprise Hills in the middle of the Heritage Range. Named in association with the heritage theme.

United Kingdom, seen herein as UK (*see* **Great Britain**).

United Nations. The first UN discussion on Antarctica came in 1984, and on Dec. 16, 1985, the UN General Assembly voted 92–0 that all mineral resources in Antarctica should be split between all nations.

United States. Although the USA has never claimed a section of Antarctica, as some other countries have, it has been one of the most instrumental in the opening up of the continent. The sealing expeditions of the early 1820s, and people like Palmer and Pendleton, did much to discover new areas. In 1828 the US government proposed an expedition, using the *Peacock* and the *Seraph*. Jeremiah N. Reynolds was to be chief organizer, and Thomas ap Catesby Jones was selected as captain of the *Peacock*. Charles Wilkes was the astronomer. The new US president, Andrew Jackson, however, vetoed the expedition for economic reasons, and it never happened. Expeditions were sporadic after that but, in 1838–42, Wilkes led the United States Exploring Expedition (*see* **Wilkes, Charles**). The next major American expedition was Byrd's 1928–30 expedition. This was the first of five Byrd expeditions, the others following in 1933–35, 1939–41 (the United States Antarctic Service Expedition), 1946–47 (Operation Highjump), and 1955–59 (Operation Deep Freeze). There were others over that period of time, and afterward. The USA, as mentioned previously, does not make claims in the Antarctic. In 1924 Secretary of State Charles Evans Hughes announced, "It is in the opinion of this department that the discovery of lands unknown to civilization, even when coupled with a formal taking of possession, does not support a valid claim of sovereignty, unless the discovery is followed by an actual settlement of the discovered country." This policy has been restated many times since. One of the 12 original signatories to the Antarctic Treaty in 1959, the US has/had the following scientific stations in Antarctica: Mc-Murdo, Hallett, Siple, Wilkes, Ellsworth, Little America, Palmer, Byrd, Little Rockford, Beardmore, Plateau, Liv, Amundsen-Scott (also called South Pole). In 1969 4 American women reached the Pole. By the 1970s only 4 stations were operating permanently— McMurdo, Amundsen-Scott, Palmer, and Siple. Now there are only 3—Palmer, McMurdo, and Amundsen-Scott. In 1982–83 more than 285 US scientists worked on 84 projects in Antarctica, and in 1986, 150 men and 13 women wintered-over on 4 bases. In 1987, 212 men and women wintered-over at the three permanent bases. US involvement in Antarctica was called USARP (United States Antarctic Research Program) and all Antarctic activity has been handled by the National Science Foundation (of which USARP was a division) since 1959. The USARP is now called USAP (i.e., the word "research" was dropped). The Committee for Polar Research of the National Academy of Sciences was founded in 1958 and, now called the Polar Research Board, advises the NSF. The US Navy, in the form of the US Naval Support Force, Antarctica, supplies logistical backup for the USAP, and the stations are largely managed now by a contractor hired by the NSF (*see* **ITT**). The total budget for US involvement in Antarctica in 1982 (for example) was 66 billion dollars. As a matter of interest, the Antarctican Society was founded in 1959, and is located at 1619 New Hampshire Ave., Washington, D.C. 20009.

The *United States*. US sealer from Stonington, Conn., which visited the South Shetlands in 1853–54 under Capt. Wilcox. This was the furthest south this ship had ever been, although two earlier, sub–Antarctic trips may well be worth recording. In 1843–44 it had been at Crozet Islands (46°S) under Capt. Barnum on a whaling and sealing expedition, and was back at the same place, on the same mission, in 1849–51, under the same skipper (Barnum).

United States Air Force Electronics Test Unit. This was an expedition of two ski-equipped C-47 aircraft sent out from Bolling Air Force Base in Washington, D.C., to Antarctica, for the 1957–58 season, during the IGY. Its purpose was to test a Raydist electronic positioning system by surveying and photographing about 100,000 square miles within a 400-mile radius of Ellsworth Station, which was to be the base of operations. They left Washington on Oct. 1, 1957, and flew to Ushuaia, Argentina, leaving there on Oct. 16, 1957. They flew to

Robert Island in the South Shetlands, in order to refuel. They were kept on the island by severe weather until Nov. 21, 1957. The first plane, commanded by the expedition leader Major James W. Lassiter, then flew to the mainland, but had to land on Dolleman Island to wait for a storm to pass. On Nov. 22, 1957, they reached their destination – Ellsworth Station. The second plane, with Capt. David W. Roderick (second-in-command of the expedition) and 3 men arrived at Ellsworth Station on Dec. 6, 1957. By mid-January 1958 the expedition was completed and the unit left for home on the *General San Martín*. The planes were later returned to the USAF. Other members of the expedition were Dalton Webb, an electronics engineer with the Raydist Corporation, who spent a lot of time in the Pensacola Mountains; Capt. Dalton E. Alley; Staff Sgt. Robert E. Bennett, radio operator; Sgt. Ray J. Cavart, flight engineer; Master Sgt. Kitt Gray, flight engineer; Willard Neith, photographer; Capt. Samuel J. Lance; John Wall; and Neil Hinckley.

United States Antarctic Program. Known as USAP. This is the successor to USARP (*see* **United States Antarctic Research Program**). Still managed by the National Science Foundation (NSF), it is still the overall word for the US involvement in Antarctica. In 1988–89 there were 75 scientific projects on hand in the Antarctic.

United States Antarctic Research Program. Known as USARP. A division of the office of the National Science Foundation. It began on Jan. 1, 1959, as a US successor to IGY, and was headquartered in McMurdo Station. To put it succinctly, USARP was the US involvement in Antarctica. A member of USARP was called a "usarp." This was replaced by USAP.

United States Antarctic Service Expedition. 1939–41. Seen listed in this book as the USAS 1939–41. This was Byrd's third expedition to Antarctica, the first US government-sponsored expedition to that continent since 1838–42 (*see*

Wilkes). It was the largest ever expedition up to that time, and its intentions were to set up two permanent bases in the sector of American interest and to explore that area systematically; to chart the coastline between 72°W and 148°W and the Weddell Sea coast; to do other aerial investigations; and to conduct other scientific studies. Byrd, Finn Ronne, and Richard B. Black were all planning separate expeditions when President Roosevelt persuaded them to join forces as the USAS, to be led by Byrd. So the US Congress established the United States Antarctic Service, which actually sent the expedition to Antarctica. They had 2 ships, the *North Star* (commanded by Capt. Isak Lystad) and the *Bear* (commanded by Richard Cruzen, the second-in-command of the expedition), the latter ship being the renamed *Bear of Oakland* from Byrd's 1933–35 expedition. The *North Star* left Boston on Nov. 15, 1939, and the *Bear* left from the same port on Nov. 22, 1939. Byrd boarded the *North Star* at Balboa on Nov. 30, 1939. When they all got to the Bay of Whales (*see* the Chronology for dates during the expedition when they were south of 60°S) they found that it had shrunk since Byrd was last there in 1935. The ships were unloaded at the Bay of Whales, and Little America III (or West Base as it was called) was set up near the Bay of Whales, under the command of Paul Siple. On Jan. 22, 1940, the first of four major flights took place from the *Bear* over Marie Byrd Land. On Jan. 24, 1940, the *North Star* left for Valparaiso, Chile, to pick up supplies and some South American observers—Rodríguez, Bonert, Poch, and Díaz. It then headed south again, meeting the *Bear* at Horseshoe Island, Marguerite Bay, on March 5, 1940. On March 8, 1940, East Base was selected on Stonington Island, and by March 20, 1940, unloading from the ships was finished at that base. The following day both ships sailed for home, with Admiral Byrd on the *Bear*. Richard B. Black was base leader at Stonington Island, with Finn Ronne second-in-

command as chief of staff. Other personnel at East Base were Carl Eklund, Bryant, Carrol, Collier, Darlington, Dolleman, Dorsey, Dyer, Healy, Hill, Hilton, Knowles, Lamplugh, Lehrke, Morency, Musselman, Odom, Palmer, Perce, Pullen, Sharbonneau, Sims, Snow, and Steele. The total number of personnel on the expedition, including the ship's personnel, amounted to 125 men. Only 59 of these were shore party, 26 at East Base and 33 at West Base (Little America III). West Base personnel were Siple, Butler, Malcolm C. Douglass, Asman, Clay Bailey, Ferranto, Frazier, Fitzsimmons, Giles, Gilmour, Gutenko, Clyde W. Griffith, O'Connor, Shirley, Hawthorne, Alton Wade, Colombo, Perkins, Petras, Court, Berlin, Warner, McCoy, Wells, Lockhart, Passel, Wiener, Vernon D. Boyd, Bursey, Harrison H. Richardson, Orville Gray, J.A. Reece, and Isaac Schlossbach. Other persons who ventured south on this expedition, but who were not members of the shore parties, included Dana K. Bailey, Eric T. Clarke, Malcolm Davis, and Milton J. Lobell. Four planes were used on the expedition: a Barkley-Grow T8P-1 two-engine seaplane (NC18470) was carried on the *Bear* for ice reconnaissance; two Curtiss-Wright Condor twin-engine biplanes, one for East Base and one for West Base; and one single-engine Beechcraft D17A biplane (NC20778) stationed at West Base. Other machines used were 2 light Army tanks and 2 tractors, as well as the Snowcruiser (q.v.), brought to the Antarctic in 1939 by its creator Dr. Thomas Poulter, and set up by him at West Base at the beginning of the expedition. 160 dogs also took part in the USAS. Various research parties went out from West Base—a biological party and a geological survey party, both of which went to the Edsel Ford Mountains; a Pacific Coast survey party which went to Mount Hal Flood; and a geological party which went to the Rockefeller Mountains. By Jan. 7, 1941, all sledging parties had returned to West Base. At East Base various forays were made, including

Ronne and Eklund's 84-day sledge journey to the SW end of the George VI Sound. The *North Star* and the *Bear* returned that summer, evacuated West Base, then proceeded to East Base. They reached it on Feb. 24, 1941, but could not get in because of the ice. So, the personnel on the *Bear* constructed a landing strip on Mikkelsen Island (now known as Watkins Island) so the members of East Base could fly out in their Condor— without their dogs and most of their equipment, the equipment being abandoned and the dogs being destroyed. Even the Condor was abandoned once they landed on Mikkelsen Island. East Base was formally evacuated on March 22, 1941. The USAS was terminated due to lack of further financial support brought on by the War. It succeeded in most of its objectives, however, having charted most of the coast between the Ross Sea and the Antarctic Peninsula. Many of the expedition's results and activities remain unreported.

United States Army Range *see* **LeMay Range**

United States Exploring Expedition 1838–42 *see* **Wilkes, Charles**

United States Naval Support Force, Antarctica. Established in 1954 by Admiral Dufek in Washington to develop the base of operations and logistics for US participation in IGY. Split into two detachments—one at McMurdo Base, and the other at Christchurch, New Zealand. Now, it still has the same basic function, to provide logistical backup for USAP. In a sense it is the physical part of US involvement in Antarctica, whereas the National Science Foundation is strictly for research. US Naval Support Force, Antarctica, is led by the Commander, USNAVSUPFORANT (*see* **Operation Deep Freeze** and **Task Force 199**). The organization is now based out of Port Hueneme, California.

United States Navy Antarctic Expedition. 1954–55. The *Atka* sailed from

Boston on Dec. 1, 1954, to scout for scientific station locations for the US involvement in the IGY, as well as other scientific missions. Cdr. Glen Jacobsen was skipper of the ship, and William E. Davies was the geologist on board. The ship carried three Bell HTL-5 helicopters under the command of Lt. Homer W. McCaw, Jr., USNR. One of these was lost on Jan. 22, 1955, at Kainan Bay, killing Lt. John P. Moore. The *Atka* returned to the USA on April 12, 1955.

United States Navy Range *see* **Colbert Mountains**

University Peak. 77°52'S, 160°44'E. At the head of University Valley, 2½ miles SSW of West Beacon, in Victoria Land. Named by the people who named the valley, and for the same reason (*see* **University Valley**).

University Valley. 77°52'S, 160°40'E. 1 mile long. Just NE of Farnell Valley in the Beacon Valley area of Victoria Land. Named in Jan. 1962 by researchers Heinz Janetschek and Fiorenzo Ugolini for their universities.

Unneruskollen Island. 70°30'S, 6°10' W. Ice-covered. North of Halvfarryggen Ridge and between the Ekström and Jelbart Ice Shelves, on the coast of Queen Maud Land. Named in 1960 for the Norwegians.

Lake Unter-See. 71°20'S, 13°27'E. Also called Nedresjöen. A meltwater lake 3 miles SW of Lake Ober-See, in central Queen Maud Land. Occupies the southern part of a large cirque indenting the northern slopes of the Gruber Mountains. Discovered by Ritscher in 1938–39. He named it Unter-See (lower lake).

Unwin Cove. 63°19'S, 57°54'W. Just SE of Toro Point on the Trinity Peninsula. Charted by the Chilean Antarctic Expedition of 1947–48, and named by them for 1st Lt. Tomás Unwin Lambie (see below).

Unwin Lambie, Tomás. 1st. lieutenant during the Presidential Antarctic Expedition of 1947–48. Subsequently he was commander of the *Lientur* during the Chilean Antarctic Expeditions of 1949–50 and 1950–51.

Upper Ferrar Glacier *see* **Taylor Glacier**

Upper Island. 66°S, 65°39'W. At the north side of Mutton Cove, between Cliff and Harp Islands. 8 miles west of Prospect Point, off the west coast of Graham Land. Charted and named by the BGLE 1934–37.

Upper Meyer Desert. Part of the Meyer Desert in the Dominion Range of the Transantarctic Mountains.

Upper Staircase. 78°15'S, 161°05'E. The upper eastern portion of the Skelton Glacier, just north of The Landing. It merges into the Skelton Névé, in Victoria Land. Named by the NZ party of the BCTAE in 1957 for the staircase effect on its way to the Polar Plateau.

Upper Victoria Glacier *see* **Victoria Upper Glacier**

Upper Wright Glacier *see* **Wright Upper Glacier**

Upton, Benjamin. Captain of the *Nancy,* 1820–22.

Upton Rock. 62°12'S, 59°08'W. 3 miles NW of Flat Top Peninsula, King George Island, in the South Shetlands. Named by the UK in 1961 for Capt. Ben Upton.

Uragannyy Point. 69°57'S, 12°50'E. Ice point on the west edge of the Lazarev Ice Shelf. 3 miles north of Leningradskiy Island, Queen Maud Land. Mapped by the USSR in 1959, and they named it Mys Uragannyy (hurricane point). While the *Ob'* was parked there a big hurricane blew up.

Uranium. Has been detected in Antarctica since the late 1970s.

Uranus Glacier. 71°24'S, 68°20'W. 20 miles long. 6 miles wide at its mouth. On Alexander Island, it feeds the George VI Sound. Named for the planet.

Uranus Glacier Automatic Weather Station. 71°25'S, 68°W. An American AWS on the Uranus Glacier on Alexander Island, at an elevation of approximately 2,400 feet. It began operating on March 6, 1986.

Urban Point. 79°48'S, 82°W. 2 miles east of the terminus of Ahrnsbrak Glacier on the north side of the Enterprise Hills in the Heritage Range. Named for Verdis D. Urban, meteorologist at Ellsworth Station in 1958.

Urbanak Peak. 84°38'S, 111°55'W. On Mirsky Ledge in the Ohio Range. Named for Richard L. Urbanak, meteorologist at Byrd Station in 1960.

Urchin Rock. 65°19'S, 64°16'W. Also called Roca Erizo. Almost 2½ miles west of the largest of the Berthelot Islands, off the west coast of Graham Land. Named by the UK in 1959 because the rock is a hazard on the edge of the Grandidier Channel.

Urfjell Cliffs. 73°53'S, 5°17'W. Form part of the Kirwan Escarpment in Queen Maud Land. They trend sw for 10 miles from Urfjelldokka Valley. Name means "mountain with rock-strewn slopes" in Norwegian.

Urfjelldokka Valley. 73°50'S, 4°45'W. Ice-filled. Between the Urfjell Cliffs and Skappelnabben Spur along the Kirwan Escarpment in Queen Maud Land. Named by the Norwegians in association with the Urfjell Cliffs.

Islas Uribe *see* **Karelin Islands**

Mount Uritorco. 62°56'S, 60°43'W. On the south side of Telefon Ridge, Deception Island, in the South Shetlands. Named before 1956.

Urnosa Spur. 73°47'S, 5°02'W. On the west side of Urfjelldokka Valley in the sw part of the Kirwan Escarpment in Queen Maud Land. Name means "the rock-strewn peak" in Norwegian.

Uruguay. Ratified as the 22nd signatory to the Antarctic Treaty, on Jan. 11, 1980. On Oct. 7, 1985, it became the 17th nation to achieve Consultative status within the Antarctic Treaty system. It established Artigas Station in 1985.

The *Uruguay*. An old Argentine corvette sent out by that government in Nov. 1903 to rescue Nordenskjöld's expedition on Snow Hill Island. It did just that, on Nov. 7, 1903. Commander of the ship was Capt. Julian Irízar. Leader of the Navy detachment on board was Felipe Fliess, and the lieutenant was Jorge Yalour. In the 1904–5 season, under the command of Capt. Ismael Galíndez, it relieved the last of Bruce's party on Laurie Island on Dec. 30, 1904. In early 1905 Galíndez led it to look for Charcot's expedition, which was feared lost. The *Uruguay* was in the South Orkneys for many seasons after that, mostly relieving Orcadas Station. It was in the South Shetlands in 1915, with I.E. Spíndola as surveyor.

Bahía Uruguay *see* **Jessie Bay**

Uruguay Cove. 60°45'S, 44°43'W. In the west part of Jessie Bay, on the SW side of Laurie Island, in the South Orkneys. Charted by Bruce in 1903, and named later by him for the *Uruguay*.

¹Uruguay Island *see* **Andersson Island**

²Uruguay Island. 65°14'S, 64°14'W. ½ mile long. Between Irízar Island and Corner Island, in the Argentine Islands. Discovered by Charcot in 1903–5, and named by him for the *Uruguay*.

Urvantsev Rocks. 72°06'S, 5°37'E. A group 5 miles SE of Skorvetangen Spur in the Mühlig-Hofmann Mountains of Queen Maud Land. Named by the USSR for geologist N.N. Urvantsev.

USA *see* **United States**

USARP *see* **United States Antarctic Research Program**

Usarp Mountains. 71°10'S, 160°E. Extend 120 miles in Oates Land, west of the Rennick Glacier. Include: the Pomerantz Tableland, the Daniels Range, the Helliwell Hills, the Morozumi Range, the Emlen Peaks. Named for the USARP.

Usas Escarpment. 76°S, 129°W. 200 miles long, along the 76th Parallel, north of the Executive Committee Range in Marie Byrd Land. Two of its features are Mount Galla and Benes Peak. First called the 76th Parallel Escarpment by the USAS 1939–41 who discovered it. The name was later changed to honor the expedition itself.

USAS 1939–41 *see* **United States Antarctic Service Expedition**

Useful Island. 64°43'S, 62°52'W. 2 miles west of Rongé Island, in the Gerlache Strait, off the west coast of Graham Land. Discovered by de Gerlache in 1897–99, and named before 1927.

Mount Usher. 84°57'S, 172°05'E. 9,500 feet. 4 miles SW of the mouth of Brandau Glacier, just to the south of Keltie Glacier, in the Queen Maud Mountains. Discovered and named by the Shackleton expedition of 1907–9.

Usher, J. Capt. Commander of the *Caraquet*, in the South Shetlands, in the 1821–22 season.

Usher Glacier. 62°02'S, 58°37'W. 4 miles long. Flows into the sea between Stigant and Davey Points, on the north coast of King George Island, in the South Shetlands. Named by the UK in 1960 for Capt. J. Usher.

The *Ushuaia*. Argentine transport ship which took part in the 1948 Argentine Naval maneuvers led by Adm. Cappus.

Usnea Plug. 62°38'S, 61°05'W. A volcanic plug, 30 meters from base to summit, less than ½ mile SW of Chester Cone on Byers Peninsula, in the west end of Livingston Island, in the South Shetlands. Named by K.R. Everett, of the Institute of Polar Studies, Ohio State University, who was here in 1969. The Usnea is a type of lichen he found here.

USSR. Known as Russia until 1917, and, at time of writing this book, may well become so again. The first Russian on the Antarctic scene was von Bellingshausen in 1819–21. He circumnavigated the continent at high latitudes and discovered several bits of land in his ships, the *Vostok* and *Mirnyy*. The next group were Bolsheviks, in 1946 –

whalers, and since then they have done much whaling here. On June 7, 1950, the Soviet Union made a statement about not recognizing other countries' claims to pieces of Antarctica (the USSR makes no such claims itself) without the USSR participating in the decision. A big participant in IGY, the first Soviet Antarctic Expedition arrived in early Jan. 1956, led by Mikhail Somov in the *Ob'* and the *Lena*. The Air Fleet was commanded by Ivan Cherevishniy. Six scientific stations were set up, including Mirnyy, Oazis (later to be transferred to Poland and renamed Dobrowolski), Pionerskaya, Vostok, and Sovietskaya. One of the 12 original signatories to the Antarctic Treaty in 1959, the USSR has sent an expedition every year since 1956. It is of interest that a 1932–33 expedition was planned but never came off. That was in the days when the USSR was desperate to keep its secrets, and felt that exposing themselves to the world would be dangerous. The 26th (1980–81) Soviet Antarctic Expedition involved 1,400 men and women with 8 ships used to resupply the 7 permanent stations (see below). About 300 scientists and technicians wintered-over in 1981. The 27th Soviet Antarctic Expedition (1981–82) involved 800 men and women. USSR support personnel are not military, as they are in the USA, for example. Each USSR station has its own political leader (presumably not freely elected until the 1990s), i.e., the local communist party secretary. Other USSR stations in Antarctica have included Druzhnaya, Druzhnaya III, Russkaya, Soyuz, Leningradskaya, Novolazarevskaya, Bellingshausen, Lazarev. A USSR air route has been established between Maputo in Mozambique, and Molodezhnaya Station, the main USSR base in Antarctica.

Utes Point. 67°44′S, 45°43′E. Juts out from Enderby Land into Alasheyev Bight, about 4 miles west of Molodezhnaya Station.

Utholmen Island. 68°56′S, 39°31′E. The most northwesterly island in the Flatvaer Islands in Lützow-Holm Bay.

Photographed by the LCE 1936–37. Name means "the outer island" in Norwegian.

Utkikken Hill. 71°32′S, 1°01′W. The most northeasterly rock summit on the Ahlmann Ridge in Queen Maud Land. 4 miles NE of Trollkjelpiggen Peak. Name means "the look-out" in Norwegian.

Utöy *see* **Achernar Island**

Utråkket Valley. 73°40′S, 4°25′W. Between Skappelnabben Spur and Enden Point in the Kirwan Escarpment of Queen Maud Land. Named by the Norwegians.

Utrinden Point. 73°50′S, 5°18′W. On the NW side of Kuven Hill, near the SW end of the Kirwan Escarpment in Queen Maud Land. Name means "the outer ridge" in Norwegian.

Utrista Rock. 71°35′S, 10°32′E. Isolated. 10 miles NE of Mount Dallmann, at the NE extremity of the Orvin Mountains in Queen Maud Land. Discovered by Ritscher in 1938–39. Name means "the outer ridge" in Norwegian.

Utskjera *see* **Rigel Skerries**

Utsteinen Nunatak. 71°58′S, 23°34′E. 4 miles north of Viking Heights and the main group of the Sør Rondane Mountains. Named Utsteinen (the outer nunatak) by the Norwegians for its position.

Utstikkar Bay. 67°33′S, 61°28′E. Also called Stibbs Bay. 4 miles wide. Just east of Utstikkar Glacier where it indents the coast. Photographed by the LCE 1936–37. Named by the Norwegians for the glacier nearby.

Utstikkar Glacier. 67°33′S, 61°20′E. Also called Jelbart Glacier. Flows from Moyes Peak into the Utstikkar Glacier Tongue, just west of Utstikkar Bay. Photographed by the LCE 1936–37. Named by the Norwegians as Utstikkarbreen (the sticking-out glacier).

Utstikkar Glacier Tongue. 67°30′S, 61°22′E. Forms the seaward extension of the Utstikkar Glacier, just west of Utstikkar Bay. Photographed by the LCE 1936–

37. Named descriptively by the Norwegians (see **Utstikkar Glacier**).

Utvikgalten *see* **Martin Island**

Uven Spur. 73°56'S, 5°20'W. A small spur, just SW of Tunga Spur. Extends from the Kirwan Escarpment in Queen Maud Land. Named by the Norwegians.

Uversnatten Rock. 72°58'S, 3°54'W. A small rock 1 mile west of Huldreslottet Mountain, at the south end of the Borg Massif, in Queen Maud Land. Named by the Norwegians.

V. Cliffs *see* **Vee Cliffs**

V. Drygalski Bay *see* **Drygalski Glacier**

Cap V. Ryswyck *see* **Ryswyck Point**

Vaca Nunatak. 82°17'S, 41°42'W. The most southerly nunatak in the Panzarini Hills, in the Argentina Range of the Pensacola Mountains. Named by the US for Capt. José M.T. Vaca, officer-in-charge of General Belgrano Station in 1961.

Vagrant Island. 66°29'S, 66°28'W. The northern of two islands just west of Rambler Island, in the Bragg Islands, in Crystal Sound. Named by the UK in association with Rambler Island.

Vahsel, Richard. German officer on the *Gauss*, during von Drygalski's expedition of 1901–3. He led the first sledging expedition from the ice-bound *Gauss*, from March 18–26, 1902, and discovered Gaussberg. He was back in the Antarctic in 1911–12, as captain of the *Deutschland* on Filchner's German Antarctic Expedition of that year. He died on Aug. 8, 1912, of an old illness, aboard the *Deutschland*.

Vahsel Bay. 77°48'S, 35°07'W. 7 miles wide. A Weddell Sea indentation into the western part of the Luitpold Coast, at the point where Coats Land meets the Filchner Ice Shelf. It is fed by the Schweitzer and Lerchenfeld Glaciers. Discovered by Filchner in 1911–12, and named by him for Richard Vahsel. Shortly thereafter (presumably after Vahsel died) he renamed it Herzog Ernst Bucht (Duke Ernst Bay) for a more eminent personage back home. Filchner's motives may well have been noble, or at least, not as mercenary as it might seem. He renamed the bay after large portions broke away, forming a larger bay. Later explorers retained the original name.

Cape Valavielle. 60°41'S, 44°32'W. Also called Cape Buchanan. Marks the north end of Watson Peninsula, on the north coast of Laurie Island. Charted and named by Dumont d'Urville, in 1837–40.

Valdés, Jorge di Giorgio. Chilean mess cook on the RARE 1947–48.

The *Valdivia*. German ship which, while on the German Navy Oceanographic Expedition, briefly penetrated Antarctic waters in 1898. Karl Chun was leader of the expedition, Capt. Krech was ship's captain, and Walter Sachse was navigation officer.

Valdivia Basin *see* **Atlantic-Indian Basin**

Valdivia Island *see* **Valdivia Point**

Valdivia Point. 64°21'S, 61°22'W. Forms the NW side of the entrance to Salvesen Cove, on the west coast of Graham Land. Charted by Nordenskjöld's expedition of 1901–4, and named by them as Valdivia Insel (Valdivia Island), for the *Valdivia*. Aerial photos taken by the FIDASE 1955–57 show it to be joined to the mainland, and the feature was redefined.

Cape Valentine. 61°06'S, 54°39'W. Forms the NE extremity of Elephant Island, in the South Shetlands. Named before 1822, this was the place where Shackleton and his 27 men landed on April 14, 1916, during the ill-fated British Imperial Transantarctic Expedition of 1914–17.

Valette, L.H. Argentine meteorologist at Bruce's Laurie Island base in 1904.

Valette Island. 60°46'S, 44°36'W. 350 yards long. In the west side of the entrance to Mill Cove, on the south side of Laurie Island, in the South Orkneys. Charted by Bruce in 1902–4, who named it for L.H. Valette.

Mount Valhalla. 77°35'S, 161°56'E. At the west flank of the Valhalla Glacier, overlooking the south side of the Wright Valley, in the Asgard Range of Victoria Land. Named by the USA and NZ for the reward of the Norse gods.

Valhalla Glacier. 77°34'S, 161°58'E. Between Mount Valhalla and the Conrow Glacier in the Asgard Range of Victoria Land. It flows toward the Wright Valley. Named by the USA and NZ in association with the nearby mountain.

Valiente Peak. 65°27'S, 63°43'W. 2,165 m. Just north of the mouth of Lever Glacier, where that glacier enters Beascochea Bay, on the west coast of Graham Land. Discovered and named Sommet Saens Valiente by Charcot in 1908–10, for Capt. J.P. Sáenz Valiente of Argentina. The UK shortened the name in 1959.

Mount Valikhanov. 71°49'S, 12°15'E. 2,800 m. 1 mile NW of Mount Mirotvortsev, in the Südliche Petermann Range of the Wohlthat Mountains of Queen Maud Land. Discovered by Ritscher in 1938–39. Named by the USSR in 1966 for geographer Chokan Valikhanov (1935–1965).

Mount Valinski. 84°32'S, 177°30'E. 1,640 m. Just south of the Millington Glacier, 4 miles west of the Ramsey Glacier, in the Queen Maud Mountains. Named for J.E. Valinski.

Valinski, J.E. Radio operator, USN, on Operation Highjump, 1946–47. He was on Flight A during Byrd's trip to the Pole on Feb. 16, 1947.

Valken Hill. 71°29'S, 1°59'W. 6 miles SW of Marsteinen Nunatak, in the northern part of the Ahlmann Ridge, in Queen Maud Land. Name means "the roll" in Norwegian.

Mount Valkyrie. 77°33'S, 162°19'E. On the south wall of the Wright Valley. It separates the Bartley and Meserve Glaciers in the Asgard Range of Victoria Land. Named by the New Zealanders in 1958–59 for the Valkyries of Norse mythology.

Cape Vallavielle *see* **Buchanan Point**

Islote Vallenar *see* **Chanticleer Island**

Valley glaciers. Glaciers that flow down valleys, as opposed to mountain glaciers.

Vallot Glacier. 67°18'S, 67°30'W. Flows into Laubeuf Fjord just south of Lewis Peaks, on Arrowsmith Peninsula, in Graham Land. Named by the UK for Joseph Vallot, French glaciologist in the late 19th century.

Valter Butte. 71°54'S, 3°14'W. Also called Valterkulten. Ice-free. On the east side of Schytt Glacier. 5 miles WNW of Mount Schumacher in Queen Maud Land. Named by the Norwegians for Stig Valter Schytt.

Cape Van Beneden *see* **Beneden Head**

Mount Van Buren. 71°18'S, 63°30'W. 3 miles NNW of Mount Jackson, on the east side of the Dyer Plateau, in Palmer Land. Named in association with Mount Jackson (both presidents of the USA).

The *Vance.* US ocean station ship, DER-387, in support of aircraft flights between NZ and McMurdo between 1960 and 1962.

Mount Vance. 75°30'S, 139°34'W. 840 m. Between Mount LeMasurier and Mount McCrory, in the Ickes Mountains, in Marie Byrd Land. Named for Dale L. Vance, ionosphere physicist at Byrd Station in 1963, and US exchange scientist to Vostok Station in 1971.

Vance Bluff. 81°49'S, 156°55'E. Ice-covered. 10 miles north of Laird Plateau. It has a flat summit. Named for the *Vance.*

Vancleck, John. Seaman on the Wilkes Expedition 1838–42. Joined in the USA. Served the cruise.

Vancouver, George. b. June 22, 1757, Kings Lynn, Norfolk, England. d. May 10, 1798, Richmond, Surrey. British navigator famous for his surveys of the Pacific coast of North America, and for whom the city of Vancouver, Canada, is named. He was a lieutenant on the

Resolution during Cook's second and third voyages.

Lake Vanda. 77°32′S, 161°32′E. 3 miles long. A highly saline lake near McMurdo Sound, it is the largest volume closed lake in Victoria Land's dry valley area. Just east of The Dais, in the Wright Valley. It is permanently covered with ice, and the only river which feeds it is the Onyx River. Named by the VUWAE 1958–59 for a dog used by Colin Bull, leader of this expedition, when he was on the British North Greenland Expedition.

Vanda Station. A New Zealand summer-only scientific camp at the east end of Lake Vanda, in southern Victoria Land.

Vandament Glacier. 85°19′S, 167°10′E. 6 miles long. Flows from the east central portion of the Dominion Range icecap. Flows parallel to its immediate northern neighbor, the Koski Glacier, and terminates 2 miles NW of Safety Spur. Named for Charles H. Vandament, ionosphere physicist at Amundsen-Scott South Pole Station in 1962.

Van der Does, Wilhelm. Dutch artist who served as a whaling laborer on the *Sir James Clark Ross* expedition of 1923–24.

Mount Van der Essen. 72°35′S, 31°23′E. 2,525 m. Just south of Mount Gillet, in the Belgica Mountains. Discovered by the Belgian Antarctic Expedition of 1957–58 led by Gaston de Gerlache, who named it for Alfred Van der Essen, director at the Belgian Ministry of Foreign Affairs, and a patron of the expedition.

Vanderford, Benjamin. Formerly captain of several ships out of Salem, Mass., he was pilot of the *Vincennes* during the Wilkes Expedition 1838–42. He died on March 23, 1842, en route to Cape Town.

Vanderford Glacier. 66°35′S, 110°26′E. 5 miles wide. Flows into the SE side of Vincennes Bay, just south of the Windmill Islands. It moves seaward at a rate of about 7 feet per day. Named for Benjamin Vanderford.

Vanderford Valley. 66°25′S, 110°10′E.

Also called Vanderford Submarine Valley, Vanderford Strath. A submarine feature. Named for Benjamin Vanderford.

Mount Vanderheyden. 72°30′S, 31°20′E. 2,120 m. 1½ miles NE of Mount Bastin, on the north side of the Belgica Mountains. Discovered during the Belgian Antarctic Expedition of 1957–58, and named by the leader of that expedition, Gaston de Gerlache, for Henri Vanderheyden, aircraft mechanic with the group.

Mount Van der Houven. 71°54′S, 161°25′E. 1,940 m. At the north side of the head of Boggs Valley, in the Helliwell Hills of Oates Land. Named for Frans G. Van der Houven, seismologist and leader of the Victoria Land Traverse, 1959–60, from Hut Point Peninsula to the Outback Nunataks where they were picked up by VX-6 aircraft.

Mount Van der Veer. 76°41′S, 145°54′W. 8 miles south of Mount Ronne, in the Haines Mountains of Marie Byrd Land. Named for Willard Van der Veer.

Van der Veer, Willard. Photographer assigned to Byrd's 1928–30 expedition by Paramount News. He had already been with Byrd on that explorer's North Pole expedition.

Vane Glacier. 75°16′S, 110°19′W. Flows from the NE slopes of Mount Murphy in Marie Byrd Land. Enters the Crosson Ice Shelf between Eisberg Head and Boyd Head. Named for Gregg A. Vane, US exchange scientist at Novolazarevskaya Station in 1972.

Vane Hill *see* **Windvane Hill**

Mount Vang. 73°26′S, 67°09′W. Isolated. 80 miles ESE of the Eklund Islands, south of George VI Sound, between the English Coast and the Lassiter Coast, in Palmer Land. Discovered by Ronne and Eklund of the USAS 1939–41, during their sledging journey through the George VI Sound. Named later by Ronne for Knut Vang, of Brooklyn, NY, who contributed photographic materials to the RARE 1947–48.

Vangemgeym Glacier. 71°17'S, 13°48' E. 6 miles long. Flows from the area east of Mount Mentzel, toward Mount Seekopf, in the Gruber Mountains of Queen Maud Land. Discovered by Ritscher in 1938–39. Named by the USSR in 1966 for one of their meteorologists, Georgiy Vangemgeym (1886–1961).

Vanguard Nunatak. 82°33'S, 47°38' W. 715 m. Cone-shaped. At the northern extremity of the Forrestal Range, in the Pensacola Mountains. Named for its northern vanguard position in the Forrestals.

Vanhöffen, Prof. Member of the von Drygalski expedition of 1901–3.

Van Hulssen Island. 67°33'S, 62°43'E. A small island 3 miles NW of the Flat Islands, in Holme Bay. Photographed by the LCE 1936–37. It is possibly part of what the Norwegians called Ytterskjera (q.v.). In 1955 an ANARE party established an automatic weather station here. Named by the Australians for F.A. Van Hulssen, radio station supervisor at Mawson Station in 1955.

Van Hulssen Islands. 67°33'S, 62°43' E. 10 small islands. 1½ miles north of Pila Island, in Holme Bay. Photographed by the LCE 1936–37, and included by the Norwegians as part of the now-exinct Ytterskjera (q.v.). Remapped by the ANARE between 1954 and 1962, and named by the Australians for the largest island in the group (*see* **Van Hulssen Island**).

Van Hulssen Nunatak. 67°59'S, 62° 45'E. At the south end of the Trilling Peaks, in the Framnes Mountains of Mac. Robertson Land. Photographed by the LCE 1936–37. Named by the Australians for F. Van Hulssen, technical officer at Mawson Station in 1959.

Van Loon Glacier. 71°01'S, 163°24'E. 7 miles long. Flows from the eastern slopes of the Bowers Mountains between Rastorguev Glacier and Montigny Glacier, into the Graveson Glacier. Named for Harry Van Loon (*see* **South Africa**).

Mount Van Mieghem. 72°36'S, 31°14' E. 2,450 m. 1 mile south of Mount Perov, in the Belgica Mountains. Discovered by the Belgian Antarctic Expedition of 1957–58, led by Gaston de Gerlache, and named by him for Prof. Jacques Van Mieghem, president of the Scientific Committee of the expedition.

Van Mirlo, Jan. Belgian sailor on the *Belgica* expedition of 1897–99.

Vann Peak. 84°50'S, 116°43'W. 2,140 m. At the west end of the Ohio Range. Named for Charlie E. Vann, cartographer.

Vanni Peak. 67°05'S, 67°06'W. 3 miles north of Mount Lagally, in the Dorsey Mountains on Arrowsmith Peninsula, in Graham Land. Named by the UK for Manfredo Vanni, Italian hydrologist and glaciologist.

Mount Van Pelt. 71°15'S, 35°43'E. 2,000 m. Just east of Mount DeBreuck, in the northern part of the Queen Fabiola Mountains. Discovered on Oct. 7, 1960, by the Belgian Antarctic Expedition under Guido Derom. Named by Derom for Guy Van Pelt, radio operator on Belgian aircraft here in 1960.

Van Reen, Rudolph. Crewman on the *Bear of Oakland*, 1933–34, and 3rd officer, 1934–35, during Byrd's 1933–35 expedition.

Van Reen, Thomas. 2nd officer on the *Jacob Ruppert*, 1934–35.

Van Reeth Glacier. 86°25'S, 148°W. 20 miles long. Flows between Mounts Blackburn and Bowlin into the Robert Scott Glacier, in the Queen Maud Mountains. Discovered by Quin Blackburn's Dec. 1934 party, during Byrd's 1933–35 expedition. Named for Cdr. Eugene W. Van Reeth, VX-6 pilot in 1966, and commanding officer of that organization in 1969.

Van Rocks. 63°06'S, 62°50'W. Pinnacle rocks just west of Cape James, Smith Island, in the South Shetlands. In 1828–31 Foster described these rocks as a small island. The FIDASE more accurately defined the feature in 1955–57. The UK named them because they mark the westernmost land in the South Shetlands.

Van Rysselbergh, Max. Engineer on the *Belgica* expedition of 1897–99.

Van Ryswycke Point *see* **Ryswyck Point**

Vanssay Point. 65°04'S, 64°01'W. In the western part of Port Charcot, Booth Island. Discovered by Charcot in 1903–5, and named by him as Pointe de Vanssay, for M. de Vanssay de Blavous.

Vantage Hill. 80°17'S, 155°22'E. Flat-topped. Over 2,000 meters above sea level. 300 meters above the surrounding plateau. 10 miles SW of Mount Henderson in the western part of the Britannia Range. Named by the Darwin Glacier party of the BCTAE 1957–58, for the great view from here. This was their southernmost point on the expedition.

Vantage Hills. 73°33'S, 162°27'E. 5 miles west of the south end of Gair Mesa, in Victoria Land. Named by the New Zealanders in 1962–63, for their position.

Mount Van Valkenburg. 77°18'S, 142°06'W. 1,165 m. 1 mile south of Mount Burnham, in the Clark Mountains, in the Ford Ranges of Marie Byrd Land. Discovered aerially by West Base personnel during the USAS 1939–41, and named for Prof. Samuel Van Valkenburg, director of the School of Geography at Clark University.

Mount Van Veen. 71°35'S, 161°54'E. 1,510 m. Ice-free. At the south of Jupiter Amphitheatre, in the Morozumi Range of Oates Land. Named for Richard C. Van Veen, geologist at McMurdo Station in 1967–68.

Van Wyck Island *see* **Wyck Island**

Vapour Col. 62°59'S, 60°44'W. South of Stonethrow Ridge, on the SW side of Deception Island. Named by the UK in 1959 for the volcanic vapor.

Morro Varela *see* **Crimson Hill**

Varney Nunatak. 75°56'S, 162°31'E. Ice-free. On the south side of the mouth of Harbord Glacier, in Victoria Land. Named for Kenneth L. Varney, USN,

equipment operator at McMurdo Station in 1965–66 and 1966–67.

Mount Vartdal. 66°51'S, 64°23'W. 1,505 m. Snow-capped. 4 miles NE of Karpf Point, on the north side of Mill Inlet. Charted by the FIDS in 1947 and named for Hroar Vartdal, Norwegian polar bibliographer.

Lake Vashka. 77°21'S, 161°11'E. A dry valley lake near the center of Barwick Valley, 4 miles east of the Webb Glacier, in southern Victoria Land. Named by the New Zealanders in 1958–59, for Vashka, a dog on Scott's 1910–13 expedition.

Vashka Crag. 77°19'S, 161°03'E. At the east end of The Fortress, on the north side of Barwick Valley, in Victoria Land. Named by the New Zealanders in 1959–60 in association with nearby Lake Vashka.

Vassfjellet *see* **Schirmacher Hills**

The *Vassiliy Fedoseyev*. USSR ship of the 1970s, sometime seen in Antarctica.

Mount Vaughan. 85°57'S, 155°50'W. Also seen spelled (erroneously) as Mount Vaughn. 3,140 m. 4 miles SSW of Mount Griffith on the ridge at the head of Vaughan Glacier, in the Hays Mountains of the Queen Maud Mountains. Named for Norman D. Vaughan. The name originally applied to the southern portion of Mount Goodale, but the USA later reapplied the name to this peak, 15 miles to the SE.

Vaughan, Norman D. Dog driver on Byrd's 1928–30 expedition. He was one of the 6-man Southern Geological Party led by Gould during that expedition.

Vaughan Bank. 67°37'S, 163°30'E. A seamount in the area of the Balleny Islands.

Vaughan Glacier. 85°55'S, 153°12'W. 10 miles long. Flows from Mount Vaughan into the Robert Scott Glacier, just south of Taylor Ridge, in the Hays Mountains of the Queen Maud Mountains. Named in association with Mount Vaughan.

Vaughan Promontory. 83°08'S, 167°35'E. Ice-covered. Between Ekblad Glacier and Morton Glacier, in the Holland

Range. It terminates in Cape Maude, overlooking the Ross Ice Shelf. Named for Cdr. V.J. Vaughan, commanding officer of the *Glacier,* 1964 and 1965.

Mount Vaughn *see* **Mount Vaughan**

Cape Vauréal *see* **Vauréal Peak**

Vauréal Peak. 62°11'S, 58°18'W. At the east side of the entrance to Admiralty Bay, King George Island, in the South Shetlands. Charcot named it Cap Vauréal in 1908–10. It was later redefined.

Vavilov Hill. 72°02'S, 13°11'E. 2,640 m. 3 miles west of Shatskiy Hill, in the Weyprecht Mountains of Queen Maud Land. Named by the USSR in 1966 for botanist Nikolay I. Vavilov.

Vázquez Island. 64°55'S, 63°25'W. Also called Isla Rojas Parker, Truant Island. Between Fridtjof Island and Bob Island, off the SE side of Wiencke Island. Charted by Charcot in 1903–5.

Mount Vechernyaya. 67°40'S, 46°06' E. In the Thala Mountains, near Molodezhnaya Station. The landing strip for that station is here.

Veddels *see* **Weddell Islands**

Vedel Island *see* **Vedel Islands**

Vedel Islands. 65°07'S, 64°15'W. Also called Wedel Islands, Île Wedel. A group 2 miles west of Hovgaard Island in the Wilhelm Archipelago. The largest island, Vedel Island, was discovered by de Gerlache in 1898. Charcot charted the other islands in the group in 1904. In 1909 he charted them again, and named the whole group.

Vedkosten Peak. 72°01'S, 3°58'E. 2,285 m. 1 mile SE of Hoggestabben Butte in the Mühlig-Hofmann Mountains of Queen Maud Land. Name means "the wooden broom" in Norwegian.

Vedskålen Ridge. 72°03'S, 3°56'E. On the NW side of Mount Hochlin in the Mühlig-Hofmann Mountains of Queen Maud Land. Name means "the wooden shed" in Norwegian.

Vee Cliffs. 77°38'S, 167°45'E. Also spelled V. Cliffs. Steep. Mainly ice-covered. 4 miles long. Two prominent, V-shaped wedges protrude from the cliff wall (hence the name). Between Sultans Head Rock and Terror Point, or between Aurora Glacier and Terror Glacier, on the south side of Ross Island, overlooking Windless Bight. Wilson and Hodgson visited here in Nov. 1903, during Scott's 1901–4 expedition, and Wilson named the feature descriptively.

Vega Island. 63°50'S, 57°25'W. 17 miles long. 6 miles wide. In the Erebus and Terror Gulf, off the NE tip of the Antarctic Peninsula. Separated from James Ross Island by the Herbert Sound, and from Trinity Peninsula by the Prince Gustav Channel. Named by Nordenskjöld in 1901–4 for his uncle's Arctic ship, the *Vega.*

Vegetation Island. 74°47'S, 163°37'E. Also called Lichen Island. 2 miles north of Inexpressible Island, behind Terra Nova Bay, and just west of the Northern Foothills, on the coast of Victoria Land. Discovered by Campbell's Northern Party during Scott's 1910–13 expedition, and named by them for the lichens here.

Veier Head. 66°29'S, 61°42'W. A snow-covered headland. The southernmost point of Jason Peninsula on the east coast of Graham Land. On Dec. 9, 1893, Søren Andersen saw this feature, and his captain, Carl Larsen, charted it as an island, and named it for his home, Veierland, in Norway. He called it Veier Island, and other people started calling it Wetter Island, and Weather Island. It was later redefined.

The *Veinticinco de Mayo.* Cruiser which took part in the 1948 Argentine Naval maneuvers under Adm. Cappus.

Veitch, R.S. Sounding machine technician on the *Discovery II* during the Discovery Investigations of 1933.

Veitch Point. 60°36'S, 46°03'W. On the NE end of Monroe Island, in the South Orkneys. Charted and named in 1933 by personnel on the *Discovery II,* for R.S. Veitch.

Vela Bluff. 71°10'S, 66°56'W. An isolated nunatak on the lower part of the Ryder Glacier, 5 miles west of Canopus Crags, and 11 miles from the west coast of Palmer Land. Named by the UK for the constellation Vela.

Mount Vélain. 66°42'S, 67°44'W. Also called Vélain Peak. 750 m. In the northern part of Adelaide Island. Charted and named by Charcot in 1903–5, for Charles Vélain, professor of physical geography at the Sorbonne.

Vélain Peak *see* **Mount Vélain**

Isla Velez Sarsfield *see* **Jagged Island**

Veli Peak. 77°39'S, 161°28'E. Just east of Idun Peak and 1 mile south of Brunhilde Peak, in the Asgard Range of Victoria Land. Named by NZ for unknown reasons.

Velie Nunatak. 74°23'S, 99°10'W. 9 miles north of Mount Moses, in the Hudson Mountains. Named for Edward C. Velie, meteorologist at Byrd Station in 1967.

Venable Ice Shelf. 73°03'S, 87°20'W. 40 miles long. 15 miles wide. Between the Fletcher and Allison Peninsulas, in Ellsworth Land. Named for Cdr. J.D. Venable, USN, ships operations officer, US Naval Support Force, Antarctica, 1967 and 1968.

Vendehø Heights. 72°19'S, 1°28'E. Ice-covered. SE of Tverrveggen Ridge in the Sverdrup Mountains of Queen Maud Land. Named by the Norwegians.

Vendeholten Mountain. 72°12'S, 1° 20'E. 2,230 m. North of Tverrbrekka Pass in the Sverdrup Mountains of Queen Maud Land. Named by the Norwegians.

Venesta cases. Strong, light, packing cases made of layers of wood and used by Scott, Amundsen, and Shackleton on their expeditions. Venesta wood was a composite material, made of 3 layers of hard wood compressed with intermediate layers of waterproof cement.

Venetz Peak. 80°23'S, 25°30'W. In the Shackleton Range.

Vengen Spur. 72°04'S, 23°40'E. Projects north from the east part of Mount Widerøe, in the Sør Rondane Mountains. Name means "the wing" in Norwegian.

Mount Vennum. 71°33'S, 61°53'W. Surmounts the NE part of the Rowley Massif on the east coast of Palmer Land. Named for Walter R. Vennum, geologist here in 1972–73.

Isla Ventana *see* **Window Island**

Roca de la Ventana *see* **Hole Rock**

Ventifact Knobs. 77°42'S, 162°35'E. Knobs, 3 to 6 meters high, composed of lake clay covered by glacial drift. This glacial drift has cobbles that are well polished by the wind and cut into ventifacts which cover the knobs, hence the name given by Troy L. Péwé (*see* **Lake Péwé**), the first to study them, in Dec. 1957. Just east of Lake Bonney, in Victoria Land.

Fondeadero Ventisquero *see* **Orwell Bight**

Venture Dome. 68°36'S, 62°13'E. A heavily crevassed ice dome 30 miles south of Mount Twintop in Mac. Robertson Land. Named by the ANARE because of the risk taken to cross it.

[1]The *Venus*. 131-ton, 2-masted New York sealing schooner, 68 feet long, built in 1811 at Woodbridge, N.J., and registered on Oct. 7, 1820. Commanded by Capt. William Napier, it was part of the New York Sealing Expedition which went to the South Shetlands in 1820–21. It ran into a reef at Esther Harbor on March 7, 1821, and sank. Its crew were picked up by the *Emerald* and *Esther*.

[2]The *Venus*. Australian sealer/whaler out of Hobart, Tasmania. Under the command of Samuel Harvey it went on a sealing and whaling voyage to Macquarie Island (not in the Antarctic) and then sailed south, getting through the pack-ice to the Ross Sea in 1831, as far south as 72°S, the furthest south attained in the Ross Sea to that date.

Venus Bay. 61°55'S, 57°54'W. 6 miles wide. Between False Round Point and

Brimstone Peak, on the north side of King George Island, in the South Shetlands. David Ferguson called it Esther Bay in 1913–14. The UK renamed it in 1960 for the NY schooner *Venus*.

Venus Glacier. 71°38'S, 68°15'W. 10 miles long. 6 miles wide at its mouth. Flows into the George VI Sound, between the Keystone Cliffs and Triton Point, on the east coast of Alexander Island. Surveyed in 1949 by the FIDS, and named by the UK for the planet.

Venzke Glacier. 75°S, 134°24'W. Flows between Bowyer Butte and the Perry Range into the Getz Ice Shelf on the coast of Marie Byrd Land. Discovered aerially in Dec. 1940 by the USAS. Named for Capt. Norman C. Venzke, US Coast Guard, commander of the *Northwind* in 1972 and 1973. He was several other times in the Antarctic, on different ships.

Ver-sur-Mer. A Bay of Whales inlet into Marie Byrd Land, a few miles from Little America I. Named by Byrd for the French village he landed near after his 1927 transatlantic flight. The Antarctic feature is no longer there (*see* **Bay of Whales**, under W).

Verblyud Island. 70°S, 15°55'E. Ice-covered. The summit rises to 200 meters above the surrounding Lazarev Ice Shelf, of which it is on the eastern ridge, in Queen Maud Land. Named Kupol Verblyud (camel dome) by the USSR in 1961.

Laguna Verde *see* **Kroner Lake**

Pico Verde *see* **Copper Peak**

Verdi Inlet. 71°30'S, 75°W. Ice-filled. 25 miles long. 6 miles wide. Indents the north side of Beethoven Peninsula 10 miles SW of Brahms Inlet, on Alexander Island. Named by the UK for the composer.

Vere Ice Rise. 70°27'S, 72°44'W. On the Wilkins Sound, off the NW coast of Alexander Island.

Lake Vereteno. 68°31'S, 78°25'E. 1½ miles long. In the NE part of Breidnes Peninsula, of the Vestfold Hills. 1½ miles south of Luncke Ridge. Named

Ozero Vereteno (spindle lake) by the USSR because of its shape.

Verge Rocks. 65°34'S, 64°34'W. Two rocks, 2 miles north of Chavez Island, off the west coast of Graham Land. Named by the UK because they lie on the edge (verge) of Grandidier Channel.

Mount Verhaegen. 72°34'S, 31°08'E. 2,300 m. Ice-free. Just west of Mount Perov, in the Belgica Mountains. Discovered by the Belgian Antarctic Expedition of 1957–58 led by Gaston de Gerlache, and named by him for Baron Pierre Verhaegen, collaborator of the expedition.

Mount Verhage. 71°23'S, 163°42'E. 2,450 m. At the head of the Smithson Glacier, in the Bowers Mountains. Named for Lt. Ronald G. Verhage, USN, supply officer at McMurdo Station in 1967.

Mount Verlautz. 86°46'S, 153°W. 2,490 m. Just north of the mouth of Poulter Glacier, in the SE end of the Rawson Mountains, in the Queen Maud Mountains. Named for Maj. Sidney J. Verlautz, US Army Transportation Corps, in Antarctica as logistics research officer.

Verleger, W.F. Lt. (jg), USNR. Commander of the *Jacob Ruppert* on the first trip to the Bay of Whales during Byrd's 1933–35 expedition.

Verleger Point. 74°42'S, 78°25'E. Marks the west side of the entrance to Siniff Bay, on the coast of Marie Byrd Land. Named for Lt. (jg) W.F. Verleger, USNR.

Mount Verne. 67°45'S, 67°34'W. 1,645 m. 6 miles east of Bongrain Point on the southern part of Pourquoi Pas Island, off the west coast of Graham Land. Discovered and surveyed by Charcot in 1909. Resurveyed in 1948 by the FIDS, who named it for Jules Verne, the French author.

Verner Island. 67°35'S, 62°53'E. In the Jocelyn Islands, just west of Petersen Island, in Holme Bay, Mac. Robertson Land. Photographed by the LCE 1936–

37. Named later by the Australians for Verner Pedersen, chief officer of the *Thala Dan* in 1961.

Mount Vernon Harcourt. 72°32'S, 169°55'E. Also called Mount Harcourt. 1,570 m. Conical. In the south central part of Hallett Peninsula, Victoria Land. Discovered in Jan. 1841 by Ross, and named by him for the Rev. W. Vernon Harcourt, one of the founders of the British Association.

Verry, Edward. Ordinary seaman on the Wilkes Expedition 1838–42. Joined in the USA. Served the cruise.

Verte Island. 66°44'S, 141°11'E. A small island, 1 mile north of the Double Islands. 1½ miles east of the tip of the Zélée Glacier Tongue. Charted by the French in 1949–51, and named by them for its green appearance.

Vertigo Bluff. 83°35'S, 167°E. 1,950 m. 4 miles south of Asquith Bluff, on the west side of the Lennox-King Glacier. Named because of its precipitous sides by John Gunner who, with Henry Brecher, collected rock samples here in 1969–70 during the Ohio State University Geological Expedition.

The *Veryan Bay*. British frigate under the command of Capt. L.R.P. Lawford which visited FIDS stations with the governor of the Falkland Islands aboard, in 1954–55.

Mount Vesalius. 64°04'S, 61°59'W. Also called Monte Sur. 765 m. NW of Macleod Point on Liège Island. Named by the UK in 1960 for the Flemish anatomist.

Vesconte Point. 68°31'S, 65°12'W. On the north side of Mobiloil Inlet, in the northern part of the Bowditch Crests. Named by the UK for Petrus Vesconte of Genova, pioneer chartmaker.

Veselaya Mountain. 71°38'S, 12°32'E. Its sharp summit rises to 2,385 m. Forms the north end of the Svarttindane Peaks in the Südliche Petermann Range of the Wohlthat Mountains, in Queen Maud Land. Discovered by Ritscher in 1938–39.

Named Gora Veselaya (cheerful mountain) by the USSR in 1966.

Veslekletten Peak. 72°05'S, 3°26'W. 1 mile south of Storkletten Peak on the Ahlmann Ridge in Queen Maud Land. Name means "the little mountain" in Norwegian.

Vesleknausen Rock. 69°56'S, 38°52'E. 110 m. 3 miles SW of Rundvågs Head, on the SE shore of Lützow-Holm Bay. Photographed by the LCE 1936–37. Name means "the tiny crag" in Norwegian.

Veslekulten *see* **Hayes Peak**

Veslenupen Peak. 72°07'S, 2°13'E. Near the north end of Nupskammen Ridge in the Gjelsvik Mountains of Queen Maud Land. Name means "the little peak" in Norwegian.

Veslenutane *see* **Fitzgerald Nunataks**

Vesleskarvet Cliff. 71°40'S, 2°51'W. 5 miles north of Lorentzen Peak, on the west side of the Ahlmann Ridge in Queen Maud Land. Name means "the little barren mountain" in Norwegian.

Veslestabben Nunatak. 69°42'S, 37°35'E. Isolated. In the central part of Botnneset Peninsula, on the south side of Lützow-Holm Bay. Photographed by the LCE 1936–37. Name means "the little stump" in Norwegian.

Vesletind Peak. 72°10'S, 3°02'W. 3 miles ESE of Aurhø Peak in the Ahlmann Ridge of Queen Maud Land. Name means "the little peak" in Norwegian.

Vespucci, Amerigo. b. 1454, Florence. d. 1512, Seville. Italian merchant/explorer who knew Columbus. He gave his name to what is now South America, and ultimately to America as a whole. His second voyage to the New World left Lisbon on May 13, 1501, and via Cape Verde reached Brazil. He sailed as far south as Rio de la Plata, which he discovered. He then probably sailed even further south, and 54°S is his official southing record. He claimed that on April 7, 1502, he experienced a day with 15 hours of night in it. This could only have been at 72° S, which would have put him in the Weddell Sea or the Bellingshausen Sea. He claimed still to be along the coast of South America. As it is highly unlikely that he was this far south, he probably either knowingly exaggerated or was in error.

Vestbanen Moraine. 71° 35' S, 11° 59' E. A medial moraine in the Humboldt Graben, beginning near Zwiesel Mountain and extending north for 13 miles along the west flank of the Petermann Ranges of the Wohlthat Mountains, in Queen Maud Land. Name means "the west path" in Norwegian (*see also* **Austbanen**).

Vestfjella *see* **Kraul Mountains**

Vestfold Hills. 68° 40' S, 78° 30' E. Also called Vestfold Mountains. 170 square miles in area. An ice-free oasis of bedrock, glacial debris, lakes and ponds overlooking the eastern side of Prydz Bay, on the west side of the Leopold and Astrid Coast of Princess Elizabeth Land. Metabasalt dykes are a common feature. The area is made up essentially of three major peninsulas. Discovered on Feb. 20, 1935, by Mikkelsen, and named for the Norwegian county of Vestfold.

Vestfold Mountains *see* **Vestfold Hills**

Vesthaugen Nunatak. 71° 42' S, 23° 40' E. 1,400 m. 15 miles NW of Brattnipane Peaks, in the Sør Rondane Mountains. Photographed by the LCE 1936–37. Named Vesthaugen (the west hill) by the Norwegians.

Vesthjelmen Peak. 71° 42' S, 26° 18' E. 1,810 m. 8 miles west of Austhamaren Peak, in the Sør Rondane Mountains. Photographed by the LCE 1936–37. Named Vesthjelmen (the west helmet) by the Norwegians.

Vesthovde Headland. 69° 45' S, 37° 23' E. Forms the western elevated portion of Botnneset Peninsula, on the south side of Lützow-Holm Bay. Photographed by the LCE 1936–37. Name means "west knoll" in Norwegian.

Cape Vestkapp. 72° 40' S, 19° W. 60 miles west of the Kraul Mountains in Queen Maud Land. It is a projection of the Riiser-Larsen Ice Shelf. Name means "west cape" in Norwegian.

Vestknatten Nunatak. 69° 48' S, 75° 03' E. In the center of Polarforschung Glacier. 13 miles ESE of Mount Caroline Mikkelsen. Photographed by the LCE 1936–37. Name means "the west crag" in Norwegian.

Vestreskorve Glacier. 71° 57' S, 5° 05' E. To the south of Breplogen Mountain, in the Mühlig-Hofmann Mountains (cf. Austreskorve Glacier).

Vestskjera *see* **Child Rocks**

Vestskotet *see* **West Stack**

Vestskotet Bluff. 73° 13' S, 2° 09' W. Just south of Armålsryggen, at the west end of the Neumayer Cliffs, in Queen Maud Land. Name means "the west bulkhead" in Norwegian.

Veststraumen Glacier. 74° 15' S, 15° W. 45 miles long. Flows along the south end of the Kraul Mountains into the Riiser-Larsen Ice Shelf. Discovered aerially by the USA on Nov. 5, 1967. Named Endurance Glacier in 1969, for Shackleton's old ship which went down near here, but the UK had already named a glacier on Elephant Island for the more modern ship of the same name. Name means "the west stream" in Norwegian.

Vestvika Bay. 69° 10' S, 33° E. On the west side of the Riiser-Larsen Peninsula, on the coast of Queen Maud Land. Photographed by the LCE 1936–37. Name means "west bay" in Norwegian.

Vestvollen Bluff. 72° 06' S, 3° 38' E. Forms the west side of Festninga Mountain, in the Mühlig-Hofmann Mountains of Queen Maud Land. Name means "the west wall" in Norwegian.

Vestvorren Ridge. 73° 06' S, 1° 53' W. The western of two rock ridges which trend northward from the Neumayer Cliffs in Queen Maud Land. Name means "the west jetty" in Norwegian.

Veten Mountain. 72° 37' S, 3° 50' W. 2 miles NW of Høgskavlen Mountain in the

Borg Massif of Queen Maud Land. Name means "the beacon" in Norwegian.

Veterok Rock. 71°54'S, 14°43'E. Just north of Spraglegga Ridge in the Payer Mountains of Queen Maud Land. Named by the USSR in 1961.

Veto Gap. 73°24'S, 162°54'E. Between the Tobin and Gair Mesas, in the Mesa Range of Victoria Land. Named in 1962–63 by the New Zealanders because other, better routes were to be found from Rennick Glacier to Aviator Glacier.

Vetrov Hill. 66°34'S, 92°58'E. 20 m. At the east side of the entrance to McDonald Bay. Named in 1956 by the USSR. The name means "windy" in Russian. It was also named to honor A.I. Vetrov, captain of the *Lena* that year.

Mount Veynberg. 67°27'S, 67°34'W. Just west of Nye Glacier, on Arrowsmith Peninsula, Graham Land. Named by the UK for Boris P. Veynberg, USSR physicist specializing in ice flow.

Vicars Island. 65°53'S, 54°22'E. A small, ice-covered island 2 miles off the coast of Enderby Land. Discovered on Jan. 12, 1930, by the BANZARE, and named by Mawson for an Australian textile company which supported the expedition.

Isla Vicecomodoro Marambio *see* **Seymour Island**

Vicecomodoro Marambio Station. 64° 17'S, 56°45'W. Also called Marambio Station. Year-round Argentine scientific base on Seymour Island.

Vickers Nunatak. 85°20'S, 176°40'W. In the upper part of the Shackleton Glacier, 11 miles SE of Mount Black. Named by the New Zealanders in 1961–62 for E. Vickers, radio operator at Scott Base that year.

Mount Victor. 72°36'S, 31°16'E. 2,590 m. Between Mount Van Mieghem and Mount Boë, in the Belgica Mountains. Discovered by the Belgian Antarctic Expedition of 1957–58 under Gaston de Gerlache, who named it for Paul-Émile Victor.

Victor, Paul-Émile. b. 1908, Geneva, of French parents. Polar explorer, scientist, adventurer, formerly in the US Army and highly decorated. Was with Charcot in Greenland in the *Pourquoi Pas?* in 1934, and from the late 1940s was the prime mover in French Antarctic exploration. He was director of Expéditions Polaires Françaises, and from 1952–58 was special polar consultant to the US Armed Forces. He wrote several books.

Victor Bay. 66°20'S, 136°30'E. 16 miles wide. 7 miles long. An indentation into the western part of Adélie Land, between Pourquoi Pas Point and Mathieu Rock. Named by the USA for Paul-Émile Victor.

Victor Cliff. 85°20'S, 119°12'W. 1½ miles long. Forms the SW shoulder of the Long Hills, in the Horlick Mountains. Named for Lawrence J. Victor, aurora scientist at Byrd Station in 1961.

Victor Hugo Island *see* **Hugo Island**

Mount Victoria *see* **Victoria Peak**

Victoria Land. 75°S, 163°E. One of the major divisions of East Antarctica, it extends from 70°30'S to 78°S, and from the Ross Sea to the edge of the Polar Plateau. Sometimes split into two sections (but not officially)—northern Victoria Land and southern Victoria Land. Discovered by Ross in Jan. 1841, and named by him for Queen Victoria. It was first landed on—at Cape Adare—by a Norwegian party from the *Antarctic* on Jan. 24, 1895.

Victoria Lower Glacier. 77°19'S, 162° 40'E. Also called Lower Victoria Glacier. Occupies the lower eastern end of the Victoria Valley, where it appears to merge with the Wilson Piedmont Glacier, in Victoria Land. Named by the VUWAE 1958-59 for their alma mater (Victoria University of Wellington, New Zealand), which sponsored the expedition.

Victoria Peak. 64°29'S, 62°34'W. Also called Mount Victoria. 485 m. Cone-shaped. 2 miles east of Mount Bulcke in southern Brabant Island. Discovered by de Gerlache in 1897–99. Named before 1921.

Victoria Upper Glacier. 77°17′S, 161° 33′E. Also called Upper Victoria Glacier. Occupies the upper NW end of the Victoria Valley, in Victoria Land. Named by the VUWAE 1958–59 (*see* **Victoria Lower Glacier**).

Victoria Upper Lake. 77°19′S, 161°35′ E. A meltwater lake at the terminus of Victoria Upper Glacier in Victoria Land. Named descriptively, and for the glacier, by Parker Calkin (*see* **Calkin Glacier**) in 1964.

Victoria Valley. 77°20′S, 162°E. A spectacular dry valley near McMurdo Sound. It had a large glacier in it at one time. Named by the VUWAE 1958–59 (*see* **Victoria Lower Glacier**).

Victory Glacier. 63°49′S, 58°25′W. 8 miles long. Flows from the north end of Detroit Plateau on the Trinity Peninsula to the Prince Gustav Channel just north of Pitt Point. Discovered by the FIDS in Aug. 1945, a week after VJ Day.

Victory Mountains. 72°37′S, 167°30′E. 100 miles long. 50 miles wide. Bounded by Tucker Glacier, Mariner Glacier, and the Ross Sea, on the Borchgrevink Coast of Victoria Land. Named by the New Zealanders in 1957–58.

Victory Nunatak. 68°45′S, 64°22′W. Islandlike. It has 3 rocky summits. The southernmost and highest is 360 m. In the SE part of Mobiloil Inlet, 8 miles SE of Kay Nunatak, on the east coast of the Antarctic Peninsula. Named by the UK in 1961. When viewed aerially it looks like 3 dots and a dash, Morse Code for V for Victory.

Lake Vida. 77°23′S, 161°57′E. North of Mount Cerberus, in Victoria Valley, Victoria Land. Named by the VUWAE 1958–59 for Vida, a dog on Scott's 1910–13 expedition.

Vidal, Osvaldo. In charge of the echo-sounding on the *Iquique* during the Chilean Antarctic Expedition of 1947.

Vidal Rock. 62°30′S, 59°43′W. Also called Islote Navegante Vidal. Almost a mile west of Ferrer Point, in the southern part of Discovery Bay, Greenwich Island, in the South Shetlands. Named by the Chilean Antarctic Expedition of 1947 for Osvaldo Vidal.

Vidaurre Rock. 63°18′S, 57°56′W. 100 yards east of Acuña Rocks, in the Duroch Islands, off the Trinity Peninsula. Named by the Chilean Antarctic Expedition of 1949–50.

Viddalen Valley. 72°20′S, 2°45′W. Ice-filled. Flows between the south end of the Ahlmann Ridge and the Borg Massif, in Queen Maud Land. Name means "the wide valley" in Norwegian.

Viddalskollen Hill. 72°25′S, 2°19′W. 6 miles SW of Nashornet Mountain on the south side of Viddalen Valley, in Queen Maud Land. Name means "the wide valley's knoll" in Norwegian.

Isla Videla   *see*   **Bates Island**

Vietor Rock. 62°41′S, 61°06′W. Connected to the south coast of Livingston Island by a spit. In the South Shetlands. Named by the UK in 1958 for Alexander O. Vietor, curator of maps at the Yale University Library, who discovered the original logbooks of the *Hersilia*, 1819–20, and the *Huron*, 1820–21.

Mount Viets. 78°14′S, 86°14′W. Over 3,600 m. Pyramidal. 2 miles north of Mount Giovinetto, in the main ridge of the Sentinel Range. Discovered by the Marie Byrd Land Traverse Party of 1957–58 under Charles Bentley, who named it for Ronald L. Viets, geophysicist at Little America V in 1957.

Vieugué Island. 65°40′S, 65°13′W. 3 miles long. At the west side of the Grandidier Channel. 1 mile NW of Duchaylard Island. 12 miles WNW of Cape García, off the west coast of Graham Land. Discovered by Charcot in 1903–5, and named by him for M. Vieugué, French chargé d'affaires at Buenos Aires.

View Point. 63°33'S, 57°22'W. Also called Punta Visión, Punta Vista. Forms the west side of the entrance to Duse Bay, on the south coast of Trinity Peninsula. Discovered by J. Gunnar Andersson during Nordenskjöld's 1901–4 expedition. Named descriptively by the FIDS in 1945.

Vigen Cliffs. 83°23'S, 50°07'W. In the Pensacola Mountains.

Cabo Vigía *see* **Cape Lookout**

Isla Vigía *see* **The Watchkeeper**

Vigil Spur. 71°07'S, 165°33'E. Borders Ebbe Glacier. Forms the SW extremity of Mount Bolt, in the Anare Mountains. Named by the Northern Party of the NZGSAE 1963–64 because the party spent a long time here due to a blizzard.

Cape Vik. 60°40'S, 45°40'W. Marks the west side of the entrance to Marshall Bay, on the south side of Coronation Island, in the South Orkneys. Named by Petter Sørlle in 1913.

Viking Heights. 72°04'S, 23°24'E. 2,960 m. Flat-topped. Between Tanngarden Peaks and Mount Widerøe in the Sør Rondane Mountains. Named Vikinghögda (the Viking height) in Norwegian.

Vikinghögda *see* **Viking Heights**

Villalón, Luís Pardo. Chilean pilot, commander of the *Yelcho* which in 1916 rescue Shackleton's Elephant Island party.

Villard Point. 62°37'S, 61°04'W. Just to the west of Lair Point, on Livingston Island, in the South Shetlands.

Monte Villarrica *see* **Mount Bain**

Villiers, Alan J. Tasmanian whaling laborer on the *Sir James Clark Ross* expedition of 1923–24. He wrote articles about the expedition for a Hobart newspaper, and then went on to write the

book, *Whaling in the Frozen South,* and others (*see* the Bibliography).

Vince, George T. A popular, happy-go-lucky seaman, a member of the Royal Society Expedition of 1901–4, who became the first man to lose his life in McMurdo Sound when, on March 11, 1902, he was one of a party of 9 who got caught in a blizzard on Ross Island, and made their way back to the *Discovery* instead of staying put. He was wearing fur-soled boots, and slid to his death off Danger Slope, into the sea. Vince's Cross was erected to his memory at Hut Point, 90 yards SW of the Discovery Hut, in 1902.

Vincendon-Dumoulin, Clément-Adrien. Hydrographer on the *Astrolabe* during Dumont d'Urville's expedition of 1837–40.

The *Vincennes*. 780-ton American cutter-rigged coasting sloop-of-war, the USS *Vincennes* was the flagship of the United States Exploring Expedition under Charles Wilkes (q.v. for details of the expedition). 127 feet long, 34 feet 9 inches in the beam, 16½ feet depth in hold, 10 guns, 10½ knots speed, crew of 190.

Vincennes Bay. 66°30'S, 109°30'E. Also called Kreitzer Bay. V-shaped. 65 miles wide at its entrance between Cape Nutt and Cape Folger, between the Budd Coast and the Knox Coast of East Antarctica. Named by Wilkes for his flagship, the *Vincennes*. Entered in Jan. 1948 by the *Burton Island* and the *Edisto*.

Vincent, J. Able seaman, bosun on the *Endurance* during the British Imperial Transantarctic Expedition of 1914–17. He was one of the 5 to go with Shackleton to South Georgia on the *James Caird* in 1916.

Mount Vincent Astor *see* **Mount Astor**

Vincent Gutenko Mountains *see* **Gutenko Mountains**

Vindegga Ridge. 72°57'S, 3°46'W. Extends north from Huldreslottet Mountain in the south part of the Borg Massif in Queen Maud Land. Name means "the wind ridge" in Norwegian.

Vindegga Spur. 71°51'S, 11°19'E. Just south of Vindegghallet Glacier in the Humboldt Mountains of Queen Maud Land. Discovered by Ritscher in 1938–39. Name means "the wind ridge" in Norwegian.

Vindegghallet Glacier. 71°49'S, 11°15' E. 4 miles long. Flows along the south side of Mount Flånuten in the Humboldt Mountains of Queen Maud Land. Named by the Norwegians in connection with nearby Vindegga Spur. Name means "the wind ridge slope."

Vinje Glacier. 71°55'S, 8°E. 20 miles long. Flows between the Filchner Mountains and Fenriskjeften Mountain in Queen Maud Land. Named Vinjebreen by the Norwegians for T. Vinje, meteorologist on the Norwegian Antarctic Expedition, 1956–58.

Vinjebreen *see* **Vinje Glacier**

Mount Vinson *see* **Vinson Massif**

Vinson Massif. 78°35'S, 85°25'W. Also called Mount Vinson. A massif. 13 miles long. 8 miles wide. The highest elevation in Antarctica, it is 5,140 m. (or 16,864 feet). In the Sentinel Range of the Ellsworth Mountains, overlooking the Ronne Ice Shelf. Discovered in Jan. 1958 by US Navy aircraft. First climbed at 11:30 a.m., on Dec. 18, 1966, by Peter Scoening, John Evans, Bill Long, and Barry Corbet. Mountain Travel and other tour operators now organize climbing expeditions of the massif. Named for Carl G. Vinson, Georgia congressman, a major force in 20th-century US Antarctic exploration.

Vinten-Johansen Ridge. 71°49'S, 8° 58'E. In the north-central part of the Kurze Mountains of Queen Maud Land. Named by the Norwegians for A. Vinten-Johansen, medical officer on the Norwegian Antarctic Expedition of 1956–58.

Violante Inlet. 72°35'S, 61°05'W. 16 miles long. 12–15 miles wide. Ice-filled. Between Cape Fanning and Cape Herdman on the east coast of Palmer Land. Discovered aerially by the USAS in Dec. 1940, and named for Maj. André L. Violante, US Army, who designed the prefabricated buildings used on the USAS.

Virchow Hill. 64°07'S, 62°17'W. Between the Lister and Paré Glaciers in the northern part of Brabant Island. Named by the UK for Rudolph Virchow (1821–1902), German pioneer of pathological research.

Mount Virdin. 73°29'S, 61°54'W. 4 miles SW of Mount Hemmingsen, in the Werner Mountains of Palmer Land. Named for Floyd Virdin, construction mechanic at Amundsen-Scott South Pole Station in 1967.

The *Virginia*. The Fokker Super Universal monoplane—NC4453—taken to Antarctica by Byrd during his 1928–30 expedition. It was 49 feet 10 inches long, and 733 square feet in area. It had a Pratt & Whitney Wasp engine giving 425 hp. It had a 74-foot span overall. It was lost in a storm in the Rockefeller Mountains in March 1929.

Mount Virginia. 79°15'S, 84°W. In the Pioneer Heights of the Heritage Range, where the Splettstoesser and Schmidt Glaciers join. Named for Virginia S. Taylor, geographer, a staff assistant to the US Advisory Committee on Antarctic Names, 1961–65.

Visca Anchorage. 62°05'S, 58°24'W. Also called Visca Cove, North Anchorage. The NW cove of Martel Inlet, Admiralty Bay, King George Island, in the South Shetlands. Charted by Charcot in 1908–10, and named by him for Dr. Visca, a friend in Montevideo.

Visca Cove *see* **Visca Anchorage**

Vishniac Peak. 77°14'S, 160°31'E. 2,280 m. Just north of the head of Webb

Glacier. 3 miles SW of Skew Peak, in southern Victoria Land. Named for Wolf V. Vishniac (1922–1973), professor of biology at the University of Rochester, NY. Was in Antarctica in 1971–72, and 1973 (*see* **Deaths, 1973**).

Cabo Visible *see* **Cape Well-Met**

Mount Vision. 78°14'S, 166°14'E. 1 mile NW of Mount Aurora, on Black Island, in the Ross Archipelago. Named by the New Zealanders in 1958–59 because of the view from here.

Punta Visión *see* **View Point**

Visser Hill. 66°45'S, 67°44'W. 2½ miles south of Mount Vélain, in northern Adelaide Island. Named by the UK for Philipp Visser (1882–1955), Dutch mountaineer and diplomat.

Punta Vista *see* **View Point**

Cabo Vitie *see* **Cape Hartree**

Vitnesteinen Rock. 71°25'S, 12°36'E. On the west side of the Östliche Petermann Range in the Wohlthat Mountains of Queen Maud Land. Discovered by Ritscher in 1938–39. Name means "the witness stone" in Norwegian.

Mount Vito. 85°44'S, 131°30'W. 1,810 m. In the western part of the Wisconsin Range. 2 miles NE of Mount Frontz, on the east side of Reedy Glacier. Named for John Vito, electronics technician at Byrd Station in 1961.

Vittoria Buttress. 69°23'S, 71°47'W. Also spelled Vittorio Buttress. 750 m. A cliff overlooking the SE side of Lazarev Bay. Forms the NW extremity of the Lassus Mountains in northern Alexander Island. Named by the UK for Tomás Luís de Vittoria, the composer.

Vittorio Buttress *see* **Vittoria Buttress**

Vivaldi Gap. 70°40'S, 70°20'W. Snow-covered. Between the Colbert Mountains and the Lully Foothills. Connects Purcell Snowfield with Schubert Inlet, on the west central coast of Alex-

ander Island. Named by the UK for the composer.

Vivallos Glacier. 64°52'S, 62°49'W. On the east side of Graham Land.

Vivian Nunatak. 77°32'S, 143°34'W. Marks the SW extremity of the Mackay Mountains in Marie Byrd Land. Named for Lt. John F. Vivian, pilot in Antarctica in 1968.

Vize Islands. 65°40'S, 65°37'W. Also called Islas Orella. A group of small islands 2½ miles south of the Karelin Islands, off the east side of Renaud Island, in the Biscoe Islands. Named by the UK in 1959 for Vladimir Vize, USSR ice forecaster.

Vkhodnoy Island. 66°32'23"S, 92°59'30"E. 1½ miles SW of Tokarev Island, in the Haswell Islands. Almost 1½ miles NW of Mabus Point. One gets to Mirnyy Station by here. Named Ostrov Vkhodnoy (entrance island) by the USSR.

The *Vladivostok*. USSR icebreaker from the Soviet Northern Sea Route Fleet. It was sent to Antarctica in 1985 to rescue the *Mikhail Somov*, which was trapped in the frozen Bellingshausen Sea. On July 26, it took the *Somov* in tow, and by Aug. 3 had gotten it out of the pack-ice.

Vogel Glacier. 65°S, 63°10'W. Flows into Flandres Bay 3 miles SE of Cape Willems, on the west coast of Graham Land. Named by the UK in 1960 for Hermann W. Vogel (1834–1898), German photographic pioneer.

Vogt Peak. 82°22'S, 156°42'E. 2,180 m. Surmounts the east part of the McKay Cliffs in the Geologists Range. Named for Peter R. Vogt, geologist at McMurdo Station in 1962–63.

Voight, F.C. Crewman on the *Jacob Ruppert*, 1934–35.

Rocher Voile *see* **Sail Rock**

Voit Peak. 66°40'S, 65°35'W. Between the Drummond and Hopkins Glaciers on the west coast of Graham Land.

Named by the UK in 1960 for Carl von Voit (1831–1908), German physiologist specializing in calories.

Vojtech, Vaclav. Seaman on the *City of New York* during Byrd's 1928–30 expedition.

The Volcano *see* **Vulcan Nunatak**

Volcanoes. The two main active volcanoes in Antarctica are Mount Erebus and Deception Island. Erebus erupted on Jan. 26, 1841, when James Ross was there. It erupted again, for 6 hours, on Sept. 4, 1974, and again, from Sept. 13 to 19 that year. It blew again in 1979 and in 1981 three seismic stations were established by NZ, USA, and Japanese scientists to study the internal activity of the mountain. These were placed in the volcano itself. Mount Terror, Erebus' neighbor on Ross Island, was also active in 1841. Deception Island erupted in 1842, 1912, and 1917. It is a caldera, or a volcano that has a collapsed summit along ring faults which form a large, interior basin. In 1967 minor shocks occurred, increasing in frequency in November of that year. On Dec. 4, 1967, Grade 4 and 5 tremors occurred, and an underwater eruption took place in Telefon Bay. The personnel at the Chilean base of Presidente Pedro Aguirre Cerda Station evacuated to the British Base B nearby, and the island was then evacuated entirely. Base B and the Argentine bases on the island were more or less undamaged, but the Chilean base was wiped out. In early 1969 a second bout of activity destroyed Base B. Deception Island blew again on Aug. 12 and 13, 1970 (*see* **Deception Island**). Another large volcano is Mount Siple, and other extinct volcanoes include Mounts Discovery and Melbourne (last exploded probably in 1837), and in Marie Byrd Land — Mounts Berlin, Kauffman, Takahe, Bursey, Andrus, Waesche, Obiglio, Hampton, Sidley, and Murphy, as well as Toney Mountain and Shepard Island (*see also* **McMurdo Volcanics**).

Vollmer Island. 76° 44′ S, 150° 30′ W. 11 miles long. 7 miles NW of Cronenwett

Island, it is one of the grounded islands in the Sulzberger Ice Shelf. Named for Lt. T.H. Vollmer, USN, engineering officer on the *Glacier,* 1961–62, in this area.

Von Bellingshausen, Fabian. b. Aug. 18, 1778, Ösel, Russia. d. Jan. 13, 1852, Kronstadt. Also known as Thaddeus von Bellingshausen, or Fabian Gottlieb von Bellingshausen, his name in Russian was Faddey Faddeyevich Bellingsgauzen. The Bellingshausen version is German, and the von part is designed to lend him more status. Russian Navy captain who circumnavigated the world at high southern latitudes between Dec. 1819 and Feb. 1821. He was chosen by Tsar Alexander I to lead an expedition to the South Pole, the first since Cook almost 50 years before. A career man, von Bellingshausen had experience of long trips — he had gone around the world with Kruzenstern in 1803–6. Another objective of the 1819–21 expedition was to find southern harbors for the Russian fleet, and von Bellingshausen left Russia in July 1819 with two ships, the *Vostok* and the *Mirnyy,* captained respectively by Zavadovskiy and Lazarev (second-in-command of the expedition). Much to the expedition leader's regret no naturalists could be found to go the frozen wastes of Antarctica. Also on the voyage were Demidov, Simonov, Kupriyanov, Annenkov, Torson, Leskov, Mikhaylov, Poryadin. 199 men went on this trip. Von Bellingshausen crossed the Antarctic Circle for the first time on Jan. 26, 1820 (the first to do this since Cook), and on Jan. 27, 1820, reached 69° 21′ S, 2° 14′ W, on which day he saw an "icefield covered with small hillocks." He did not realize that this may well have been the first ever sighting of the Antarctic continent (he was at the Princess Martha Coast, as it is called today). He then sailed north for the winter, arriving in Sydney on April 11, 1820, the *Mirnyy* arriving on April 19, 1820. They left there for the Antarctic again on Nov. 11, 1820, and on Dec. 8, 1820, they were back in Antarctic waters to confirm the existence of the South Shetlands and to use them as a way south. Von Bellingshausen also made a preliminary map of the islands. On Dec. 24, 1820 they crossed the Antarctic Circle again at 164° W, and again on Jan. 10, 1821. By Jan. 16, 1821, they had crossed it 6 times altogether, making scientific observations and discovering new lands. On Jan. 21, 1821, they reached a furthest south of 69°53′S, 92°19′W, as they explored the seas, and on that day discovered Peter I Island. On Jan. 28, 1821, they discovered Alexander Island, which von Bellingshausen called Alexander I Land, believing it to be part of the mainland. At 10 a.m., on Feb. 6, 1821, he met the *Hero*, commanded by Nat Palmer, between Deception Island and Livingston Island, in the South Shetlands. On Feb. 11, 1821, he left Antarctica, and arrived back in Russia on Aug. 4, 1821, after a trip of 55,000 miles. When he died he was an admiral, and governor of Kronstadt.

Mount Von Braun. 71°59′S, 169°34′E. 3,275 m. 4 miles south of Mount Sabine, in the Admiralty Mountains. Named for Wernher von Braun, the German rocketeer later at NASA, who visited McMurdo Station in 1966–67.

Von Der Wall, J.H. Tractor driver and mechanic on the shore party of Byrd's 1928–30 expedition.

Von der Wall Point. 72°29′S, 98°50′W. Ice-covered. On the south side of Thurston Island. It extends into Peacock Sound toward the NE extremity of Sherman Island. Named for J.H. Von Der Wall.

Von Drygalski, Erich. b. Feb. 9, 1865, Königsberg, East Prussia. d. Jan. 10, 1949, Munich. Erich Dagobert von Drygalski, German geographer, glaciologist, and explorer. Professor von Drygalski led the German National Antarctic Expedition of 1901–3. It left Germany on Aug. 11, 1901, in the *Gauss*. Captain Hans Ruser commanded the vessel, and there were 5 naval officers, 5 scientists (including von Drygalski), and 22 crew.

An internationally-flavored cruise; some of the other people on it were Richard Vahsel, Emil Philippi, Dr. Gazert, Prof. Vanhöffen, Leonhard Müller, F. Bidlingmaier, and Hans Harlin. It was an expedition sponsored by the German government. On Feb. 21, 1902, they sighted Antarctica, and named the land they saw as Kaiser Wilhelm II Land (which later became Wilhelm II Land). That same day the *Gauss* became trapped in the ice, and they were forced to winter-over. On March 18, 1902 the first sledging expedition went out with 2 sledges, 18 dogs, and 3 men, including Vahsel. They discovered Gaussberg, 50 miles away, and returned to the ship on March 26, 1902. Von Drygalski went up in a balloon to see Gaussberg, and a second sledging party visited the mountain in late March, for 13 days. Finally von Drygalski himself went on a sledging trip, arriving at Gaussberg on April 27, 1902, after 6 days of traveling. He just survived the return trip, and on March 31, 1903, the *Gauss* left Antarctica, arriving back in Germany, via Cape Town, on Nov. 24, 1903. Von Drygalski wrote a couple of books (*see* the Bibliography).

Von Essen, R.G.D.J. Commander of the Swedish Air Force Unit (1951–52) during the NBSAE 1949–52.

Von Essen Mountain. 72°14′S, 2°23′E. 2,665 m. Marks the SW end of the Gjelsvik Mountains in Queen Maud Land. Named Von Essenskarvet by the Norwegians for R.G.D.J. von Essen.

Cape Von Sterneck *see* **Cape Sterneck**

Von Tunzelman, A.H.F. New Zealander recruited in NZ in late 1894 for the *Antarctic* expedition of 1894–95 led by Henryk Bull. Claimed to be the first ashore at Cape Adare (as did a few others).

Von Willemoës-Suhm, Rudolf. Naturalist on the *Challenger* expedition of 1872–76.

Mys Voronina *see* **Cape Hudson**

Vorposten Peak. 71° 28′ S, 15° 30′ E. Also called The Outpost. 1,670 m. Isolated. 25 miles NE of the Payer Mountains in central Queen Maud Land. Discovered by Ritscher in 1938–39, and named by him because of its location at the eastern extremity of the area he explored.

Vorrkulten Mountain. 73° 04′ S, 1° 54′ W. At the north end of the Vestvorren Ridge, just north of the Neumayer Cliffs, in Queen Maud Land. Name means "the jetty knoll" in Norwegian.

Vorrnipa Peak. 73° 08′ S, 1° 51′ W. 2,320 m. Surmounts the Neumayer Cliffs, just south of Vestvorren Ridge, in Queen Maud Land. Name means "the jetty peak" in Norwegian.

Vorrtind Peak. 73° 05′ S, 1° 35′ W. At the north end of Austvorren Ridge, just north of the Neumayer Cliffs, in Queen Maud Land. Name means "the jetty peak" in Norwegian.

Vorta Nunatak. 72° 05′ S, 1° 44′ E. Isolated. 5 miles east of Brattskarvet Mountain, in the Sverdrup Mountains of Queen Maud Land. Name means "the wart" in Norwegian.

Vørterkaka Nunatak. 72° 20′ S, 27° 29′ E. 1 mile south of Bleikskoltane Rocks, at the SE end of the Sør Rondane Mountains. The name implies a round, Norwegian sweetbread.

Vortex Col. 77° 34′ S, 160° 25′ E. Leads from the Polar Plateau into the south side of the Wright Upper Glacier, in Victoria Land. A wind vortex flows down here. Named by New Zealand.

Vortex Island. 63° 44′ S, 57° 38′ W. Also called Islote Remolino. 245 m. ½ mile long. In the NE part of the Prince Gustav Channel. 2 miles WSW of Corry Island, just south of Trinity Peninsula. Charted by the FIDS in Aug. 1945. Named by them for a whirlwind snowstorm they experienced here.

Vorweg Point. 65° 57′ S, 64° 48′ W. NW of Huitfeldt Point on the SW side of Bari-lari Bay, on the west coast of Graham Land. Charted by the BGLE 1934–37. Named by the UK in 1960 for O. Vorweg, German skiing pioneer.

Vos'moy Mart Rocks. 72° 02′ S, 14° 40′ E. A group ½ mile east of Mount Dzhalil' in the Linnormen Hills, of the Payer Mountains, in Queen Maud Land. Named Skaly Vos'mogo Marta (March 8th Rocks) by the USSR in recognition of International Women's Day.

The *Vostok*. 600-ton Russian corvette designed by Kolodkin, and made of pinewood and sheathed with copper. It was a 28-gun man-o'-war not equipped for the Antarctic. It was von Bellingshausen's flagship during his 1819–21 expedition, and was commanded by Capt. Zavadovskiy, with 117 people on board. Its escort ship was the smaller *Mirnyy*, commanded by Lazarev. On Jan. 13, 1820, it was stopped by pack-ice just south of the South Sandwich Islands (not quite in the Antarctic), and on Jan. 27, 1820, sighted the continental ice shelf. The name Vostok means "east."

Cape Vostok. 69° 07′ S, 72° 10′ W. Forms the west extremity of the Havre Mountains, and the NW extremity of Alexander Island. Discovered by von Bellingshausen in 1821. Named later by the UK for the *Vostok*.

Vostok Station. USSR IGY scientific station built at the South Geomagnetic Pole, 11,200 feet above sea level, at 78° S, 110° E. USSR tractor trains ran out from Mirnyy Station to built it, and it was opened on April 12, 1957, and closed on Nov. 30, 1957. Leader that first winter was V.G. Aver'yanov. A new Vostok Station was then built at 78° 27′ 48″ S, 106° 48′ 24″ E, and opened on Dec. 16, 1957. It was closed temporarily Jan. 21, 1962–Jan. 13, 1963. It is the coldest inhabited place on earth. 15–20 people winter-over each year.

Voyeykov Ice Shelf. 66° 20′ S, 124° 38′ E. Off the Banzare Coast, between Paulding Bay and Cape Goodenough.

Named by the USSR for the climatologist Aleksandr I. Voyeykov (1842–1916).

Vrana Dome. 69°53'S, 73°28'E. An ice dome. 4 miles NE of the Statler Hills, at the east side of the Amery Ice Shelf. The ANARE set up a survey station here in 1968. Named by the Australians for A. Vrana, cosmic ray physicist at Mawson Station in 1968. He was on the survey that year.

Vrana Peak. 70°22'S, 63°59'E. Just SW of Mount Turnbull. 14 miles SW of Mount Starlight, in the Prince Charles Mountains. Named by the Australians for A. Vrana (see **Vrana Dome**).

Vukovich Peaks. 72°23'S, 74°59'E. Two peaks surmounting the northernmost rock outcrop in the Grove Mountains. Named by the Australians for J.N. Vukovich, weather observer at Mawson Station in 1963.

Vulcan Hills. 73°39'S, 163°40'E. A group of small volcanic hills 4 miles SW of Shulte Hills in the Southern Cross Mountains of Victoria Land. Named by the New Zealanders in 1966–67 for the volcanic composition of the rocks here.

Vulcan Nunatak. 76°35'S, 144°37'W. The remains of a huge volcanic cone. 2 miles SE of Mount Richardson in the Fosdick Mountains of the Ford Ranges, in Marie Byrd Land. Discovered on Nov. 28, 1934, by Siple and Corey of Byrd's 1933–35 expedition who studied it and called it The Volcano. It was later renamed.

VX-6 see **VXE-6**

Mount VX-6. 72°38'S, 162°12'E. 2,185 m. 4 miles north of Minaret Nunatak in the Monument Nunataks of Victoria Land. Named by the USARP Victoria Land Traverse Party of 1959–60 for VX-6 (see under **VXE-6**), the air arm of the US Antarctic involvement.

VXE-6. On June 27, 1968, it was announced that VX-6 would become known as VXE-6, effective Jan. 1, 1969, i.e., Air Development Squadron Six (AirDevRonSix) would become Antarctic Development Squadron Six. It is the US Navy air squadron which supports US research in Antarctica. It is the USA's only aerial support squadron to participate in Antarctica. It operates the National Science Foundation's airplanes and the Navy's helicopters, and provides airlift, aerial photography, search and rescue operations, reconnaissance support, and other transportation services. The pararescue team was organized in Oct. 1956. VX-6 was commissioned at Naval Air Station, Patuxent River, Md., on Jan. 17, 1955, to be the flying arm of Task Force 43 during the IGY. In June 1956 it was relocated to Naval Air Station, Quonset Point, R.I. In Oct. 1973 it moved again, to Point Mugu, Calif. The first commanding officer was Gordon K. Ebbe, June 1955–June 1956. Some of the subsequent COs have been Cdr. William Munson (1960–61), Cdr. Martin D. Greenwell (1961–62), Cdr. F.S. Gallup, Jr. (1964–65), Cdr. A.F. Schneider (1967–68), Cdr. Eugene W. Van Reeth (1968–69), Cdr. Jerome P. Pilon (1969–70, the 18th CO), Cdr. David B. Eldridge (1970–71), Cdr. Claude H. Nordhill (1971–72), Cdr. John B. Dana (1972–73), Cdr. Vernon W. Peters (1973–74), Cdr. Fred C. Holt (1974–75), Cdr. D.A. Desko (1975–76), Cdr. William A. Morgan (1978–79), Cdr. David A. Srite (1979–80), Cdr. Victor L. Pesce (1980–81), Cdr. Paul R. Dykeman (1981–82), Cdr. Michael J. Harris (1982–83), Cdr. Matthew J. Radigan (1983–84), Cdr. Dwight D. Fisher (1984–85), Cdr. Paul J. Derocher (1985–86), Cdr. Joseph D. Mazza (1986–87), Cdr. Jack Rector (1987–88), Cdr. John V. Smith (1988–89).

Vyatskaya Peak. 71°57'S, 13°32'E. 2,455 m. On the north part of Skavlrimen Ridge, in the Weyprecht Mountains of Queen Maud Land. Discovered by Ritscher in 1938–39. Named by the USSR in 1966 perhaps for the Vyatka, the river in their home country.

Vysotskiy Peak. 71°34'S, 11°40'E. 2,035 m. In the northern part of the Gorki Ridge, overlooking the Schüssel Moraine, in the Humboldt Mountains of Queen Maud Land. Discovered by Ritscher in 1938-39. Named by the USSR in 1966 for geographer G.N. Vysotskiy.

Vystrel Mountain. 71°37'S, 15°04'E. 1,995 m. Partly snow-covered. 1 mile south of Mount Rukhin at the south end of the Lomonosov Mountains in Queen Maud Land. Discovered by Ritscher in 1938-39. Named before 1961 by the USSR as Gora Vystrel (shot mountain).

Cape W. Spring see **Spring Point**

Waddington Bay. 65°16'S, 64°05'W. 2 miles long. 1 mile wide. An indentation into the west coast of Graham Land, immediately north of Cape Tuxen. Discovered by de Gerlache in 1897-99. Remapped by Charcot in 1908-10, and named by him for Senator Waddington, president of the Rouen Chamber of Commerce.

Mount Wade. 84°51'S, 174°19'W. Also called Mount Bush. 4,085 m. Next to Mount Fisher, in the Prince Olav Mountains, just to the east of the Shackleton Glacier. Discovered by Byrd in Nov. 1929. Named later for Alton Wade.

Wade, F. Alton. d. 1978. Geologist. One of the shore party on Byrd's 1933-35 expedition. He was senior scientist at West Base and in charge of the "Snowcruiser" during the USAS 1939-41. He led the Texas Tech Shackleton Glacier Expeditions of 1962-63 and 1964-65, and the Marie Byrd Land Survey of 1966-68.

Wade Glacier see **Shackleton Glacier**

Wade Ice Rise. 69°01'S, 67°07'W. On the west side of the Antarctic Peninsula.

Wade Point. 70°41'S, 67°41'W. 915 m. On the George VI Sound, on the west coast of Palmer Land. Surveyed by the BGLE in 1936, and named by Rymill for Mrs. Muriel Wade, secretary of the BGLE 1934-37.

Cape Wadsworth see **Cape Wadworth**

Cape Wadworth. 73°19'S, 169°47'E. Also seen spelled Cape Wadsworth. The northern extremity of Coulman Island, in the Ross Sea. Discovered on Jan. 17, 1841, by Ross, and named by him for his wife's uncle, Robert John Coulman of Wadworth Hall.

Mount Waesche. 77°10'S, 126°54'W. 3,290 m. Of volcanic origin. Immediately SW of Mount Sidley, it marks the southern end of the Executive Committee Range. Mostly snow-covered. Discovered on Dec. 15, 1940, on a flight over by a USAS plane. Named for Vice-Adm. Russell R. Waesche, US Coast Guard, who was involved with Antarctica.

Wafer, Lionel. Surgeon and buccaneer who, in late 1687 on his way from the Pacific to the West Indies, found himself south of 60°S. In fact, on Dec. 25, 1687, he was in 62°45'S. He wrote *A New Voyage & Description of the Isthmus of America* (see the Bibliography), and in 1688 was imprisoned in Jamestown, Virginia.

Wager Glacier. 69°48'S, 69°23'W. A small, heavily-crevassed glacier on the east coast of Alexander Island. It flows into the George VI Sound, immediately south of Marr Bluff. Surveyed by the FIDS in 1948 and named by them for Lawrence R. Wager, professor of geology at Oxford.

Wagner Ice Piedmont. 69°28'S, 72°38'W. 9 miles long. 4 miles wide. It overlies the SW part of Rothschild Island. Named by the UK for the composer.

Wagner Nunatak. 83°58'S, 66°30'W. 850 m. One of the Rambo Nunataks. 9 miles south of Blackburn Nunatak, in the Pensacola Mountains. Named for John K. Wagner, radioscientist at Plateau Station in 1967.

Wagner Spur. 70°09'S, 159°36'E. A pointed rock and ice spur on the north side of Pryor Glacier, 11 miles SSE of Mount Gorton, at the SE end of the Wilson Hills. Named for John E. Wagner, glaciologist at McMurdo Station in 1967–68.

Wagoner Inlet. 71°57'S, 100°02'W. Ice-filled. Between the Tinglof and Starr Peninsulas, on the north side of Thurston Island. Named for Charles Wagoner, a seaman on the *Glacier*, in the area in 1960.

Wahl Glacier. 84°03'S, 165°15'E. 10 miles long. Flows from Grindley Plateau into the upper part of the Lennox-King Glacier, just west of Mount Mackellar, and just to the west of the Beardmore Glacier. Named for Bruno W. Wahl, scientist at McMurdo Station in 1962.

Wahr, Rudolf. German airplane captain with Lufthansa. He went on the German New Schwabenland Expedition of 1938–39, under Ritscher.

The Waifs. 64°33'S, 62°42'W. Islands in the middle of the SE entrance to the Schollaert Channel, off the NW coast of the Antarctic Peninsula. Discovered by de Gerlache in 1897–99. Charted in 1927 by the personnel on the *Discovery*, and probably named by them.

Waipuke Beach. 77°14'S, 166°24'E. Between McDonald and Caughley Beaches, 6 miles SW of Cape Bird, on Ross Island. Named by the New Zealanders in 1959 because of its periodic flooding by meltwater from the Mount Bird Ice Cap (waipuke is Maori for "flood").

The Waist. 64°38'S, 61°24'W. A col between the Herbert Plateau and the Foster Plateau, in northern Graham Land. Mapped by the FIDS. Named by the UK in 1960 for its narrowness.

Waitabit Cliffs. 71°31'S, 68°14'W. A line of sedimentary cliffs on the east coast of Alexander Island. Surveyed by the BGLE in 1936, and again by the FIDS in 1949. The FIDS delayed there (i.e., waited a bit) while they conducted rock investigations.

Cape Waite. 72°44'S, 103°16'W. At the NW end of King Peninsula, it marks the SW side of the entrance to Peacock Sound. Named for Amory H. Waite.

Waite, Amory H. "Bud" Waite was one of the 3 who rescued Byrd in 1934, during Byrd's 1933–35 expedition (*see* **Bolling Advance Weather Station**). He took part in Operation Highjump, 1946–47, and during the IGY (1957–58) was leader of the US Army Signal Corps Antarctic Research Team. He was communications specialist on the *Atka* during the US Navy Antarctic Expedition of 1954–55, and on the USN Bellingshausen Sea Expedition of 1959–60.

Waite Islands. 72°44'S, 103°40'W. In the Amundsen Sea, 6 miles west of Cape Waite. Named in association with the cape.

Waitt Peaks. 71°29'S, 62°34'W. A cluster of pointed peaks, mostly snow-covered, 4 miles NW of the Schirmacher Massif, in the eastern part of Palmer Land. Named for Richard B. Waitt, a geologist/mapper here in 1972–73.

Wakadori Island. 69°S, 39°32'E. The southernmost of 3 small islands ½ mile NW of the strait which separates Ongul Island from East Ongul Island, near Showa Station. Mapped and surveyed by the Japanese, and named Wakadori-jima (young bird island) by them in 1972.

Mount Wakefield *see* **Mount Hope**

Wakefield Highland. 69°20'S, 65°10'W. Snow-covered. In the center of the Antarctic Peninsula. Aerially photographed by the RARE on Dec. 22, 1947. Surveyed by the FIDS in Nov. 1960. Named for Lord Wakefield, a sponsor of the BGLE 1934–37.

Wakeford Nunatak. 67°50'S, 63°02'E. 3 miles east of the Central Masson Range, in the Framnes Mountains of Mac. Robertson Land. Named for R. Wakeford, cook at Mawson Station in 1962.

Cape Walcott. 69°05'S, 63°19'W. 625 m. An ice-covered headland which forms the seaward extremity of the Scripps Heights, jutting out into the Larsen Ice Shelf, to the NW of Hearst Island, on the east side of the Antarctic Peninsula. Discovered by Wilkins in 1928, and named by him for Frederic C. Walcott of the Council of the American Geographical Society.

Mount Walcott. 85°21'S, 87°23'W. 2,155 m. Ice-free. In the east part of the Thiel Mountains. Named by Peter Bermel and Arthur Ford, US geologists here in 1960–61, for Charles D. Walcott, 3rd director of the US Geological Survey, 1894–1907.

Walcott Bay. 78°15'S, 163°42'E. An indentation into the coast of Victoria Land, between the Walcott Glacier and Heald Island. Named by Scott's 1910–13 expedition in association with the nearby glacier.

Walcott Glacier. 78°13'S, 163°E. Flows from the Royal Society Range, between the Radian and Howchin Glaciers, to Walcott Bay, in southern Victoria Land. Named by Grif Taylor during Scott's 1910–13 expedition, probably for Charles D. Walcott (*see* **Mount Walcott**).

Walcott Névé. 84°23'S, 162°40'E. 350 square miles in area. Between the Law and Beardmore Glaciers. Named by the New Zealanders in 1962 for scientist in the area Richard I. Walcott.

Walcott Peak. 71°49'S, 64°22'W. A large nunatak, halfway between Mount Jukkola and Lokey Peak, in the southern sector of the Guthridge Nunataks, in central Palmer Land. Named for Lt. Fred P. Walcott, USN, officer-in-charge of Amundsen-Scott South Pole Station in 1973.

Waldeck Island *see* **Waldeck-Rousseau Peak**

Waldeck Peak *see* **Waldeck-Rousseau Peak**

Waldeck Rousseau Cape *see* **Cape Evensen**

Waldeck-Rousseau Peak. 66°09'S, 65°38'W. Also called Waldeck Peak, Pillar Peak. A monolith, 3 miles ENE of Cape Evensen, on the west coast of Graham Land. In 1903–5 Charcot named it Cap Waldeck-Rousseau, for the French statesman Pierre Waldeck-Rousseau. This name became translated into English as Waldeck-Rousseau Cape. In 1908–10 Charcot redefined it as an island, Île Waldeck (Waldeck Island). It was correctly defined by the BGLE in 1935.

Cape Walden. 71°44'S, 96°55'W. Ice-covered. At the NW end of Evans Peninsula, on Thurston Island. Named for Arthur T. Walden.

Walden, Arthur T. Dog driver, and leader of the Queen Maud Mountains supporting party during Byrd's 1928–30 expedition.

Cape Waldron. 66°34'S, 115°33'E. Ice-covered. West of the Totten Glacier. Named for R.R. Waldron.

Mount Waldron. 78°27'S, 84°53'W. 3,100 m. 3 miles north of Mount Tuck. In the Sentinel Range. Discovered by VX-6 on Dec. 15, 1959, and named for Kenneth L. Waldron, USN, a member of the South Pole Station wintering party of 1957.

Waldron, James E., Jr. Lt. Cdr. USNR. Leader at Little America V during the winter-in of 1957, and a VX-6 pilot in Antarctica during Operation Deep Freeze III (1957–58).

Waldron, R.R. Purser on the *Vincennes* during the Wilkes Expedition 1838–42.

Waldron, Thomas W. Captain's clerk on the *Porpoise* during the Wilkes Expedition 1838–42.

Waldron Glacier. 66°27'S, 130°E. A channel glacier flowing to the east side of Porpoise Bay, between the Sandford and Morse Glaciers. Named for Thomas W. Waldron.

Waldron Spurs. 84°35′S, 175°40′W. A group of rocky spurs at the east side of the terminus of the Shackleton Glacier, in the foothills of the Queen Maud Mountains. Discovered by the USAS 1939–41, and named for James E. Waldron.

Wales, William. Astronomer on the *Resolution* during Cook's second voyage, 1772–75.

Wales Glacier. 77°37′S, 163°31′E. Just west of Mount Barnes, at the east end of the Kukri Hills, in Victoria Land. Runs into Taylor Valley. Named by Scott's 1910–13 expedition, presumably for the country.

Wales Stream. 77°35′S, 163°30′E. A meltwater stream which runs from the Wales Glacier into Explorers Cove in New Harbor, Victoria Land. Named by parties unknown, in association with the glacier.

Walfe, James C. Quarter-gunner on the Wilkes Expedition 1838–42. Joined in the USA. Discharged at Oahu, Oct. 31, 1840.

Walgreen Coast. 75°15′S, 105°W. Between Cape Herlacher and Cape Waite. Discovered by Byrd in 1940 during flights from the *Bear*. Named by Byrd for Charles R. Walgreen, president of the Walgreen Drug Company of Chicago, one of Byrd's sponsors for the USAS 1939–41 and also for Byrd's 1933–35 expedition.

Walgreen Peak. 77°03′S, 145°43′W. 570 m. Forms the NW extremity of the Sarnoff Mountains, in the Ford Ranges of Marie Byrd Land. Named by its discoverer, Byrd, in 1940, for Charles R. ("Buck") Walgreen, Jr., of Chicago's Walgreen Drug Co., who contributed malted milk powder to the USAS 1939–41.

Walk Glacier. 73°38′S, 94°18′W. Flows from Christoffersen Heights to the south of Forbidden Rocks, in the Jones Mountains. Named for Lt. Donald R. Walk, USN, officer-in-charge of Byrd Station in 1961.

Walkabout Rocks. 68°23′S, 78°32′E. At the NE end of the Vestfold Hills, ½ mile south of the Wyatt Earp Islands. Photographed aerially by the LCE 1936–37. First landed on by personnel from the *Wyatt Earp* in Jan. 1939. They left records wrapped in a copy of the Australian geographical magazine, *Walkabout*. An ANARE party recovered these in May 1957, and thus named the rocks.

Cape Walker   *see*   **Walker Point**

¹Mount Walker   *see*   **Mount Siple**

²Mount Walker. 64°48′S, 62°03′W. Snow-covered. In the NE section of Forbidden Plateau, in northern Graham Land. Surveyed by the FIDS in 1955. Named by the UK for Richard Walker.

Walker, John. Captain of the *John*, 1820–21, 1821–22. He provided George Powell with descriptions and sketches of the southern shores of the South Shetland Islands for use in Powell's chart of 1822. He reported 30 American vessels in the South Shetlands in the 1820–21 season.

Walker, Richard. First officer on the *Discovery II*, 1933–37.

Walker, William M. Lt. USN, on the Wilkes Expedition 1838–42. At Tierra del Fuego, on the way down to Antarctica, in 1838, he replaced the previous captain of the *Flying Fish*. He himself was replaced as commander of that vessel in late 1839, by Lt. Pinckney.

Walker Bay. 62°38′S, 60°42′W. Between John Beach and Hannah Point, on the south coast of Livingston Island, in the South Shetlands. Named by the UK in 1958 for John Walker.

Walker Mountains. 72°07′S, 99°W. Also called Demas Mountains. They form the spine of Thurston Island, and comprise scattered nunataks of quartz-diorite-gneiss, and most are steep-sloped and ice- and snow-covered. Mount Dowling is in this group. Discovered by Byrd on a flight from the *Bear* on Feb. 27, 1940, during the USAS 1939–41. Named for Lt. William A. Walker.

Walker Nunatak. 67°55'S, 63°15'E. 10 miles east of Branson Nunatak, on the east edge of the Framnes Mountains. Discovered by the ANARE in 1962–63, and named by the Australians for K.G. Walker, assistant cook at Mawson Station in 1962, a member of the Jan. 1963 sledge party which was the first to see it from the ground. Walker was in the Prince Charles Mountains in 1970.

Walker Peak. 82°38'S, 53°13'W. 1,495 m. Marks the SW extremity of the Dufek Massif, in the Pensacola Mountains. Named for Paul T. Walker, glaciologist at Ellsworth Station, a member of the first party to visit the Dufek Massif in Dec. 1957.

Walker Point. 61°08'S, 54°42'W. Also called Walker's Point, Cape Walker, Pointe Walter (sic). A point 3 miles SW of Cape Valentine, Elephant Island, in the South Shetlands. Named by 1822, probably for John Walker.

Walker Ridge. 72°34'S, 168°22'E. Between Stafford Glacier and Coral Sea Glacier, in the Victory Mountains of Victoria Land. Named for Dr. Eric A. Walker, chairman of the National Science Board (USA), 1964–66.

Walker Rocks. 76°15'S, 161°36'E. A high rock group, 3 miles in extent. 3 miles SW of Mount Murray, near the mouth of the Mawson Glacier, in Victoria Land. Named in 1964 for Carson B. Walker, utilitiesman at South Pole Station in 1961.

Walker Spur. 85°01'S, 91°12'W. A rock spur forming the east side of Compton Valley, in the north part of the Ford Massif, in the Thiel Mountains. Named by Peter Bermel and Arthur Ford, US surveyors here in 1960–61, for Capt. Joseph G. Walker, US Marines, a VX-6 pilot here that season.

Walker Valley. 70°41'S, 67°33'E. A large, wide, snow-filled valley, immediately west of Manning Massif, in the Aramis Range of the Prince Charles Mountains. Named by the Australians for K.G. Walker (*see* **Walker Nunatak**).

Walker's Point *see* **Walker Point**

Wall Peak. 71°03'S, 65°23'E. The largest and northernmost of a group of 3 mountains 5 miles SE of Husky Massif in the Prince Charles Mountains. Named for B.H. Wall, ionosphere physicist at Wilkes Station in 1960.

Wall Range. 64°49'S, 63°22'W. It is actually a ridge, 3 miles long, with a highest point of 1,095 m. It runs from Thunder Glacier to Channel Glacier, in the center of Wiencke Island. First mapped by de Gerlache in 1897–99, and surveyed in 1944 by personnel of Operation Tabarin, who gave it this name.

Wall Rock. 83°08'S, 56°57'W. 4 miles north of Robbins Nunatak, in the Schmidt Hills part of the Neptune Range, in the Pensacola Mountains. Named for John Wall, a member of the US Air Force Electronics Test Unit (q.v.), here in 1957–58.

Wallabies Nunataks. 81°12'S, 156°20'E. A large group of nunataks near the Polar Plateau. 10 miles NE of the All-Blacks Nunataks, at the east side of the Byrd Névé. Named by the New Zealanders in 1960 for their rugby team.

Cape Wallace. 63°14'S, 62°15'W. Marks the NW end of Low Island, in the South Shetlands. Named before the 1870s.

Mount Wallace. 85°39'S, 151°24'W. 1,490 m. In the Tapley Mountains. At the south side of the mouth of the Roe Glacier at the juncture with the Robert Scott Glacier. Named for J. Allen Wallace, Jr., meteorologist at South Pole Station in 1960.

Wallace, Thomas. 1st class boy on the Wilkes Expedition 1838–42. Joined in the USA. Served the cruise.

Wallace Rock. 75°55'S, 128°27'W. 5 miles NW of Mount Petras, and 1 mile east of Peter Nunatak, at the SE end of the McCuddin Mountains in Marie Byrd Land. Named for James W. Wallace, USN, at Amundsen-Scott South Pole Station in 1965 and 1969.

Cape Wallaston *see* **Cape Wollaston**

Wallend Glacier. 64°59'S, 62°13'W. Flows from Forbidden Plateau into Green Glacier, in northern Graham Land. Surveyed by the FIDS in 1955. The UK named it because it is walled in on three sides by Forbidden Plateau.

Cape Walleston *see* **Cape Wollaston**

Wallis, Percy J. Seaman on the *City of New York,* 1928–30, during Byrd's expedition of that period.

Wallis Glacier. 71°13'S, 168°12'E. 20 miles long. In the NW part of the Admiralty Mountains. It merges into the Dennistoun and Nash Glaciers just before all three reach the sea just east of Cape Scott. Named for Technical Sgt. Nathaniel Wallis (*see* **Deaths, 1958**).

Wallis Nunataks. 66°52'S, 55°39'E. Four nunataks with steep rock faces on their south and east sides. 4 miles ENE of Mount Storegutt in Enderby Land. Named for G.R. Wallis, geologist on the *Nella Dan* in 1965.

The Wallows. 60°42'S, 45°37'W. An area in the NE part of Signy Island, in the South Orkneys. It has a small freshwater pond in the middle of it. Surveyed by the Discovery Committee in 1933, and again in 1947 by the FIDS, who named it for the wallowing elephant seals here in the summer.

Walmsley, Aaron. Sergeant of marines on the Wilkes Expedition 1838–42. Joined in the USA. Served the cruise.

Mount Walnum. 72°06'S, 24°10'E. 2,870 m. 4 miles east of Mount Widerøe, in the Sør Rondane Mountains. Photo-graphed by the LCE 1936–37, and named Walnumfjellet by the Norwegians, for Ragnvald Walnum, former chairman of the Norwegian Whaling Board, who prepared an ice chart of Antarctica.

Walsh Glacier. 69°33'S, 158°45'E. In the central part of the Wilson Hills. Enters the lower part of Tomilin Glacier. Named for Gary Walsh, biologist at Hallett Station in 1968–69.

Walsh Nunatak. 73°09'S, 63°11'W. On the north side of Haines Glacier, 8 miles SW of Mount Axworthy, in the Dana Mountains of Palmer Land. Named for John J. Walsh, biologist in Antarctica in 1965–66.

Walsh Spur. 72°40'S, 169°22'E. A pointed rock spur 4 miles east of Mount Northampton in the Victory Mountains of Victoria Land. Forms the west side of the terminus of Whitehall Glacier. Named for Cdr. Don Walsh, USN, naval researcher and explorer.

Walsham Rocks. 64°50'S, 64°32'W. Also called Islote Jorge, Islote Edgardo. 1 mile east of Buff Island, at the SW end of the Palmer Archipelago. Surveyed by the RN Hydrographic Survey Unit in 1956–57, and named by the UK for one of the Unit, Able Seaman John Walsham, RN.

Mount Walshe. 86°11'S, 152°15'W. 2,050 m. A bare rock peak on the north side of the Bartlett Glacier where it joins the Robert Scott Glacier, in the southern part of the Hays Mountains, in the Queen Maud Mountains. Named for Lt. Cdr. Edward C. Walshe, Jr., USN, in Antarctica in 1957–58, 1958–59, and 1966–67.

Pointe Walter *see* **Walker Point**

Walter, Rolf. Captain of the *Thorgaut,* 1930–31.

Walter Glacier. 69°17'S, 70°26'W. In the extreme north of Alexander Island.

Walter Kohler Range *see* **Kohler Range**

Walters Peak. 85°39'S, 126°45'W. 2,430 m. Between Faure Peak and Lentz Buttress in the Wisconsin Range. Named for Lt. Cdr. Robert E. Walters, USN, at McMurdo Station in 1960.

Waltham, Henry. Ordinary seaman on the Wilkes Expedition 1838–42. Joined in the USA. Served the cruise.

The *Walther Herwig*. West German research ship which made two krill research expeditions in the Antarctic in the mid-1970s, and was again in the Antarctic in 1980.

Mount Walton. 72°29'S, 160°18'E. 2,460 m. A sharp, bare mountain between Oona Cliff and Mount Chadwick, in the Outback Nunataks. Named for Fred W. Walton, scientist at Amundsen-Scott South Pole Station in 1968.

Walton, Eric W.K. FIDS engineer at Base E in 1946 and 1947. In 1946 he rescued fellow FIDS member J.E. Tonkin from a crevasse in Northeast Glacier.

Walton Mountains. 71°10'S, 71°15'W. 1,250 m. 3 peaks, mostly snow-covered. They extend south for 35 miles from Schubert Inlet on Alexander Island. First seen aerially by Ellsworth on Nov. 23, 1935, and photographed by him. Finn Ronne named them in 1948 for Lt. Col. R.C. Walton, US Marines, who helped get a ship and naval assistance for the RARE 1947–48.

Walton Peak. 68°09'S, 66°48'W. 825 m. 2 miles north of Mount Rhamnus, between Northeast Glacier and Neny Fjord, on the west coast of Graham Land. Surveyed in 1936 by the BGLE, and again in 1946 and 1948 by the FIDS. Named for Eric W.K. Walton.

Walts Cliff. 76°01'S, 135°42'W. Can be seen for miles. Marks the NE base of Mount Berlin, in the Flood Range. Named for Dennis S. Walts, meteorologist at Amundsen-Scott South Pole Station in 1970.

Wandel Island *see* **Booth Island**

Wandel Peak. 65°05'S, 64°W. 980 m. The highest peak on Booth Island (formerly Wandel Island), it is ½ mile south of Gourdon Peak. Named in order to preserve the name Wandel in the area.

Wanigans. Modern, boxlike refuge shelters usually made of plywood, and containing survival food and clothing.

Mount Wanous. 84°52'S, 62°20'W. 1,660 m. A bare, conical mountain 4½ miles east of Pierce Peak, at the NE edge of the Mackin Table, in the Patuxent Range of the Pensacola Mountains. Named for Richard E. Wanous, geophysicist in that area in 1965–66.

Waratah Islands. 67°24'S, 47°24'E. Two small islands just off the coast of Enderby Land, about 1 mile NW of the Hannan Ice Shelf. Named by the Australians for their plant, the waratah.

[1]Mount Ward. 71°36'S, 66°57'W. At the NE end of the Steeple Peaks, south of the Batterbee Mountains, near George VI Sound, in western Palmer Land. Discovered aerially by Ronne on Dec. 23, 1947, and mislocated by him at 71°55'S, 66°W. He named it for W.W. Ward of Beaumont, Texas, a supporter of the RARE 1947–48.

[2]Mount Ward. 85°40'S, 167°10'E. 3 miles SE of the Davis Nunataks, just south of the Dominion Range. Discovered by Shackleton's expedition of 1907–9, and named by them for the prime minister of New Zealand, Sir Joseph Ward, a supporter of the expedition.

Ward, F.J. Crew member on the *Discovery* during the BANZARE 1929–31.

Ward, Herbert G.V. Chief engineer on the *John Biscoe* from 1948–55, and on the second *John Biscoe* from 1956–62.

Ward, Michael. Private on the Wilkes Expedition 1838–42. Joined in the USA. Served the cruise.

Ward Glacier. 78°10'S, 163°26'E. Between Terminus Mountain and Howchin Glacier, on the east side of the Royal Society Range, in Victoria Land. Named by Grif Taylor of Scott's 1910–13 expedition for L. Ward, a Tasmanian geologist.

Ward Islands. 67°38'S, 69°35'W. Two small islands and a group of rocks that form the southern section of the Amiot Islands, off the SW part of Adelaide Island. Named by the UK for Herbert G.V. Ward.

Ward Lake. 78°10'S, 163°35'E. At the snout of the Ward Glacier, on the east side of the Royal Society Range, in Victoria Land. Named by members of Scott's 1910–13 expedition in association with the glacier.

Ward Nunataks. 68°07'S, 49°36'E. 4 miles north of Alderdice Peak, in the eastern part of the Nye Mountains. Named for D.J. Ward, radio officer at Wilkes Station in 1960.

Ward Rock. 67°08'S, 51°21'E. Just east of the Howard Hills, in the NE part of the Scott Mountains, in Enderby Land. Named for F.J. Ward.

Mount Warden. 86°S, 146°37'W. 2,860 m. Snow-covered. Just SE of Hunt Spur, on the NW face of the Watson Escarpment. Named for Lt. George W. Warden, USN, Operation Highjump pilot, 1946–47.

Warden Pass. 80°28'S, 28°08'W. In the Shackleton Range.

Warden Rock. 67°32'S, 67°19'W. 2 miles NW of Guardian Rock, on the north side of Bigourdan Fjord, in Graham Land. Mapped by the FIDS between 1946 and 1957, and named in association with Guardian Rock.

Wardle Entrance. 65°27'S, 65°26'W. The SE entrance to Johannessen Harbor, between Snodgrass Island and Weller Island, in the Pitt Islands of the Biscoe Islands. Named by the UK for the Dickens character.

Mount Ware. 70°27'S, 65°36'E. Just south of Mount Kerr, in the Porthos Range of the Prince Charles Mountains. Named by the Australians for W.R. Ware, weather observer at Mawson Station in 1968.

Waring Bluff. 73°01'S, 161°05'E. In the northern part of the Sequence Hills,

in Victoria Land. Named for James T. Waring, USN, air controlman at McMurdo Station in 1967.

Mount Warner. 77°05'S, 144°W. An isolated mountain just south of the head of the Arthur Glacier, and 5 miles north of Mount Crow, in the Ford Ranges of Marie Byrd Land. Discovered by the USAS 1939–41, and named for Lawrence Warner.

Warner, Lawrence. Geologist at West Base during the USAS 1939–41. He led a geological party into the Ford Ranges during that expedition.

Warning Glacier. 71°32'S, 170°23'E. Flows into Robertson Bay, 4 miles north of Nameless Glacier, in Victoria Land. First charted by Borchgrevink in 1898–1900, and named by him for the warning snow clouds over this glacier which foretold a southerly gale at Cape Adare, his base.

Mount Warnke. 84°20'S, 64°55'W. 915 m. 3 miles NE of Martin Peak, in the Thomas Hills of the Patuxent Range, in the Pensacola Mountains. Named for Detlef A. Warnke, biologist at Palmer Station in 1966–67.

Warnock Islands. 67°12'S, 59°44'E. 1 mile south of Dales Island, at the northern end of the William Scoresby Archipelago. Discovered and named in Feb. 1936 by personnel on the *William Scoresby*.

Warpasgiljo Glacier *see* **Arthur Glacier**

Warr, William. Petty officer, USN. Mechanic on the Martin Mariner which crashed on Dec. 30, 1946. Warr survived.

Mount Warren. 77°43'S, 85°57'W. 2,340 m. In the northern part of the Sentinel Range, just north of the turn in Newcomer Glacier. Named for Aviation Master Sgt. Cecil O. Warren, in this area Dec. 14–15, 1959.

Warren, A. Able seaman on the *Aurora*, 1914–17.

Warren, Guy. Right name Guyon Warren. Assistant geologist with the NZ party of the BCTAE 1957–58. He later participated in the Allan Hills Expedition of 1964, but had an accident part of the way through.

Warren Ice Piedmont. 70°S, 68°15′W. At the northern end of the George VI Sound, on the west coast of Palmer Land.

Warren Island. 67°23′S, 59°36′E. In William Scoresby Bay, just to the south of the west end of Bertha Island. Discovered and named by personnel on the *William Scoresby* in Feb. 1936.

Warren Nunatak. 79°32′S, 82°50′W. 4 miles east of Mount Capley, in the Heritage Range. Named for Arthur D. Warren, scientist at Ellsworth Station in 1958.

Warren Peak. 76°41′S, 159°52′E. SE of Halle Flat, in the Allan Hills of Victoria Land. Named by the New Zealanders in 1964 for Guy Warren.

Warren Range. 78°28′S, 158°14′E. 15 miles long. Behind the Boomerang Range, in southern Victoria Land. Discovered by the New Zealanders in 1957–58 during the BCTAE. They named the highest peak in this range Mount Warren, for Guy Warren, one of their party. As there was already another Mount Warren close by, the name was expanded to take in the whole range.

Warriner Island. 68°37′S, 77°54′E. Just to the west end of Breidnes Peninsula, in the Vestfold Hills. Photographed by the LCE 1936–37. Later named by the Australians for A. Warriner, radio officer at Davis Station in 1961.

Warrington Island. 66°20′S, 110°28′E. 7/10 mile long. A rocky island immediately south of Pidgeon Island, in the Windmill Islands. Named for W.H. Warrington, who was on Operation Highjump here in 1946–47.

Wars. The only war to touch Antarctica was World War II, which in 1941 brought a halt to the USAS 1939–41 led by Admiral Byrd. Commercial whaling also ceased for the duration. On Jan. 13, 1941, Germans took over the *Ole Weg-*

ger, the *Solglimt,* and the *Pelagos,* from their raider, the *Pinguin.* Also that year, the armed British merchant cruiser *Queen of Bermuda* destroyed the fuel left in the Hektor Whaling Company tanks on Deception Island, thus denying it to the Nazi raiders who used these seas (*see also* **The Carnarvon Castle**). The British kept the northern Antarctic Peninsula under surveillance, and Deception Island became the scene of a struggle for ownership between Britain and the pro–Nazi Argentines, which resulted in Operation Tabarin (q.v.), when Britain established military bases here. In 1952 an interesting martial incident occurred when Argentines fired on a British party going ashore at Hope Bay, to reestablish Base D there. The British retreated to their ship, the *John Biscoe,* and only after a suitable apology from Buenos Aires did the FIDS men go back ashore to get on with construction. In Feb. 1953 Royal Marines landed on Deception Island from the *Snipe,* and dismantled some offending refuge huts—one Chilean and one Argentinian, and deported a couple of Argentinians to South Georgia. The *Snipe* remained on patrol until mid-April 1953, having been joined in March by the *Bigbury Bay.* The Royal Marines spent 3 months on the island, to make sure that their "territory" was not invaded again by South Americans. In early 1954 Royal Marines spent 4 months on Deception Island, more as training than anything else.

Mount Washburn. 77°37′S, 86°08′W. 2,725 m. Between Mount Ulmer and Mount Cornwell, in the northern part of the Sentinel Range. Named by Charles Bentley on his 1957–58 exploration here, for Dr. A. Lincoln Washburn, an IGY committeeman.

Cape Washington. 74°39′S, 165°25′E. 275 m. Between Wood Bay and Terra Nova Bay, in Victoria Land. Discovered by Ross in 1841, and named by him for Capt. Washington, RN, secretary of the Royal Geographical Society, 1836–40.

Washington Escarpment. 83°42'S, 55°08'W. About 50 miles long. In the Neptune Range, of the Pensacola Mountains. Named for the University of Washington, at Seattle, several members of which took part in the Neptune Range field party of 1963–64.

Washington Ridge. 78°06'S, 154°48'W. Also called Mount Helen Washington. 1½ miles SE of Mount Franklin in the Rockefeller Mountains. Three peaks stand on it. Discovered on Jan. 27, 1929, during Byrd's 1928–30 expedition. Named by Byrd for his niece Helen A. Washington.

Washington Strait. 60°43'S, 44°56'W. 3 miles wide. Separates Powell Island from Laurie Island in the South Orkneys. Discovered in Dec. 1821 by Powell and Palmer. Named, probably by Palmer, probably for George Washington, first president of the USA.

Mount Wasilewski. 75°11'S, 71°24'W. 1,615 m. 9 miles ESE of the Merrick Mountains, in Ellsworth Land. Discovered by the RARE 1947–48, and later named for Peter J. Wasilewski, an expeditionary in the area in 1961–62 and 1965–66.

Mount Wasko. 84°34'S, 176°58'W. 1,170 m. A double-peaked, saddle-shaped mountain on the west side of the Shackleton Glacier. 3 miles north of Mount Franke, in the Queen Maud Mountains. Discovered by the USAS 1939–41. Surveyed by Crary in 1957–58, and named by him for Lt. Cdr. Frank Wasko, USNR, with VX-6 in 1957–58.

The Wasp. 123-ton, 2-masted New York sealing schooner of 76½ feet long, with a single deck. Built at East Haddam, Conn., in 1821, and registered on June 16, 1821. Under the command of Robert Johnson, it left New York, arriving in the South Shetlands on Oct. 16, 1821, as part of the second phase of the New York Sealing Expedition. First mate was Ben Morrell. The following season the *Wasp* left New York again, on June 30, 1822, commanded by Morrell. It met up with the *Henry* in the Falklands on the way south. On Dec. 13, 1822, it was at 60°11'S, 10°23'E, and was hampered by the ice for two days. In Jan. 1823 it was back in Antarctic waters, in the southern Indian Ocean, going in and out of the Antarctic Circle all the time. By Feb. 1, 1823, the *Wasp* was at 64°52'S, 118°27'E, off the Sabrina Coast (as it became known later) of Wilkes Land. Morrell then cruised westward, out to sea beyond Queen Maud Land, at about 65°S most of the way, and on March 14, 1823, reached 70°14'S, 40°03'W, in the Weddell Sea. The vessel was around the South Shetlands from March 31–April 24, 1823, claiming to get as far south as 65°42'S, 110°16'W. Morrell spent the winter of 1823 along the coast of Chile, and the *Wasp* was sold in Valparaiso on Feb. 22, 1824.

Wasson Rock. 73°50'S, 161°45'E. Ice-free. Near the head of Priestley Glacier. Named for William G. Wasson, a member of VX-6 in 1966.

The Watchkeeper. 62°18'S, 59°49'W. Also called Isla Vigía. A low rock in water 2½ miles north of Table Island, in the South Shetlands. Originally known as Flat Isle. Charted by the *Discovery II* in 1935.

The Watchtower. 64°23'S, 57°22'W. 400 m. An isolated, flat-topped, steep-sided rock at the SE end of James Ross Island. Nordenskjöld discovered, surveyed, and named it in March 1902.

Watchtower Hill. 73°16'S, 163°08'E. A small pointed hill on the SE side of Pinnacle Gap, in the Mesa Range of Victoria Land. Named by the New Zealanders in 1962–63 because of its position in relation to Pinnacle Gap.

Water. Fresh water in Antarctica is scarce. Seawater, of course, is abundant, because of the surrounding oceans. Seawater above − 2°C cannot sustain ice — it melts. Water boils at 86°C, not 100°C, in Antarctica — at least that is the case at Vostok Station.

Water Bears *see* **Tardigrades**

Waterboat Point. 64°49′S, 62°52′W. Also called Península Munita. On Paradise Bay, at the north of the Antarctic Peninsula. Named on Jan. 12, 1921, by the British Imperial Expedition which fielded two men here for the winter of 1921. A ruined waterboat lay beached here, left by a Norwegian factory whaling ship 8 years before.

Waterfalls. There are two waterfalls coming off The Ramp, in the western part of Ross Island. They flow toward Cape Evans. (*See also* **Hanging waterfalls.**) When the weather is cold enough to freeze, as it is in most places on the continent, these become known as icefalls.

Waterhouse Spur. 86°37′S, 147°25′W. 6 miles NE of Johansen Peak, in the Ackerman Range of the La Gorce Mountains. Named in 1969–70 by the New Zealanders for Barry C. Waterhouse, who was there as a geologist.

Waterloo Island *see* **King George Island**

Mount Waterman. 84°27′S, 175°24′E. 3,880 m. In the Hughes Range, 3 miles NE of Mount Wexler. Discovered by Byrd on Nov. 18, 1929, and surveyed by Crary in 1957–58. Named by Crary for Alan T. Waterman, director of the National Science Foundation.

Waterpipe Beach. 60°43′S, 45°37′W. A flat shingle beach on the west side of Borge Bay, Signy Island, in the South Orkneys. Surveyed in 1933 by personnel on the *Discovery II*. Resurveyed by the FIDS in 1947, and named by them for an old whaling waterpipe nearby.

Watkins Island. 66°22′S, 67°06′W. 5 miles long. Ice-covered. 3 miles SW of Lavoisier Island, in the Biscoe Islands. Mapped by Charcot in 1903–5 and 1908–10. Next seen by the BGLE 1934–37, and named by Rymill as Mikkelsen Island, for Ejnar Mikkelsen, Danish Arctic explorer. Renamed by the UK in 1952 for Henry G. Watkins, Arctic pioneer.

Watlack Hills. 79°26′S, 85°25′W. 10 miles long. Ice-free. In the Heritage Range. Named by the University of Minnesota Geological Party here in 1963–64, for CWO Richard G. Watlack, pilot who helped the party.

Watson, Andrew D. Geologist on the AAE 1911–14.

Watson, John Frampton. One of the scientists who went on the Palmer-Pendleton Expedition of 1829–31.

Watson, R.D. Radio operator on the *Bear of Oakland*, 1933–35.

Watson Bluff. 66°25′S, 98°57′E. 225 m. At the east end of David Island. Discovered by the AAE 1911–14, and named by Mawson for Andrew D. Watson.

Watson Escarpment. 86°04′S, 145°W. Also called Thomas Watson Escarpment. 100 miles long. Rises to 3,550 meters above sea level. Between the La Gorce Mountains and the Horlick Mountains, overlooking the Leverett Glacier. Gould was the first to survey part of it, in Dec. 1929, during Byrd's 1928–30 expedition. During Byrd's 1933–35 expedition, Quin Blackburn surveyed more of it in 1934. That year Byrd named it for Thomas J. Watson (1854–1934), shipping magnate and supporter of Byrd's second Antarctic expedition.

Watson Nunatak. 67°58′S, 62°45′E. Between Price Nunatak and Van Hulssen Nunatak in the Trilling Peaks of the Framnes Mountains in Mac. Robertson Land. Photographed by the LCE 1936–37, and later named by the Australians for K.D. Watson, at Mawson Station in 1965.

Watson Peaks. 73°45′S, 62°36′W. 2 miles NE of Rivera Peaks, in Palmer Land. Named for George E. Watson, biologist on the *Eastwind* in 1965–66 (*see also* the Bibliography).

Watson Peninsula. 60°42′S, 44°32′W. 2 miles long. Between Macdougal and Marr Bays, on the north coast of Laurie Island, in the South Orkneys. Charted in 1903 by Bruce, who named it for G.L. Watson, designer of the *Scotia*.

Watson Ridge. 67°S, 55°46′E. 9 miles SE of Mount Storegutt, in Enderby Land.

Named by the Australians for R.A. Watson, weather observer at Mawson Station in 1963.

Mount Watt. 72°28′S, 166°09′E. 2,715 m. 5 miles SW of Mount Aorangi, in the Millen Range. Named by the New Zealanders in 1962–63 for B.H. Watt, secretary of the New Zealand Federated Mountain Clubs Antarctic Expedition of that season.

Watt Bay. 67°02′S, 144°E. 16 miles wide. An indentation into the coast of East Antarctica, between Garnet Point and Cape de la Motte, or between the Mertz Glacier and Commonwealth Bay. Discovered by the AAE 1911–14, and named by Mawson for W.A. Watt, premier of Victoria, Australia, in 1912.

Watt Ridge. 84°45′S, 173°47′W. 7 miles long. In the area of Mount Llano in the Prince Olav Mountains, and the Barrett Glacier. Named for Lt. Cdr. Robert C. Watt, USN, in Antarctica in 1964.

Mount Watters. 76°44′S, 159°38′E. West of Scythian Nunatak, in the Allan Hills of Victoria Land. Named by the New Zealanders in 1964 for W.A. Watters, a geologist here with the Allan Hills Expedition that year.

Wattle Island. 67°16′S, 46°46′E. 6 miles east of Kirkby Head, in Enderby Land. Named by the Australians for their tree.

Watts, Harold. Radio operator on the *Quest*, 1921–22.

Watts Needle. 80°44′S, 24°59′W. In the Shackleton Range.

Watts Nunatak. 72°38′S, 74°13′E. Isolated. 12 miles NW of the Mason Peaks, in the Grove Mountains. Named by the Australians for J.P. Watts, at Mawson Station in 1962.

Watts Summit. 83°12′S, 50°31′W. In the Pensacola Mountains.

Mount Waugh. 65°31′S, 64°07′W. 585 m. On the south side of Beascochea Bay, 3½ miles NE of Nuñez Point, on the west coast of Graham Land. Charcot

charted it in 1908–10. Named by the UK in 1959 for W.A. Waugh, Vitamin C pioneer in the 1920s.

Waugh Peak. 86°04′S, 160°36′W. 2,430 m. Just SE of Breyer Mesa, on the west side of the Amundsen Glacier, in the Queen Maud Mountains. Named for cartographer Douglas Waugh.

Cape Wauters *see* **Wauters Point**

Wauters Point. 64°06′S, 61°43′W. Also called Cape Wauters. An ice-covered point which forms the north end of Two Hummock Island. Charted by de Gerlache in 1897–99, and named by him for Alphonse Wauters, a sponsor of the expedition.

Wauwermans Islands. 64°55′S, 63°53′W. A small, low, snow-covered group forming the northernmost group in the Wilhelm Archipelago. Discovered by Dallmann in 1873–74, and named by de Gerlache in 1897–99 for Lt. Gen. Wauwermans, a supporter of the *Belgica* expedition. The group includes Brown Island, Clear Island, Friar Island, Guido Island, Manciple Island, Prioress Island, Wednesday Island, Host Island, Knight Island, Herd Rock, Reeve Island, Miller Island, Prevot Island, Sinclair Island, Squire Island.

Wave Peak. 60°37′S, 45°36′W. 960 m. Rises from the head of Laws Glacier, in the north central section of Coronation Island, in the South Orkneys. Surveyed by the FIDS in 1948–49, and named by them for its resemblance to a wave.

Waverly Glacier. 74°01′S, 61°38′W. Also called Kasco Glacier. Flows from Mount Tricorn into Wright Inlet, on the east coast of Palmer Land. Named by Ronne in 1947 for Waverly, NY, home town of Kasco Mills, which supplied dog food to the RARE 1947–48.

Way Archipelago. 66°53′S, 143°40′E. More than 120 small islands and rocks running from Commonwealth Bay to Watt Bay in East Antarctica. The largest is Stillwell Island. Mawson discovered it in 1911–14 during the AAE, and named it for Sir Samuel Way, chancellor of the University of Adelaide.

Weasel Gap. 70°12′S, 64°37′E. Between Mount Starlight and Mount Lacey, in the Athos Range of the Prince Charles Mountains. Named by the Australians in 1955 for the Weasel vehicles.

Weasel Hill. 64°15′S, 59°33′W. 5 miles north of Larsen Inlet, in Graham Land, between Pyke Glacier and Polaris Glacier. Surveyed by the FIDS. Named by the UK for the Weasel vehicles.

Weasels. Fast, but not strong, caterpillar vehicles used mostly as exploration vehicles. The Weasel is an M-29 Tracked Cargo Carrier made by Studebaker, and designed by Geoffrey N. Pyke in 1941. Eight M-29 Cs were used during Operation Highjump, 1946–47. These were ¾-ton amphibian cargo carriers. Four were used sparingly on Operation Windmill, 1947–48, and Ronne took two on his RARE 1947–48. Weasels were much used during the IGY (1957–58) by the British, French, Australians, and Americans (who used 13). They have been much used since.

Weather Central. Collection point at Little America V for all meteorological data gathered in Antarctica during the IGY (1957–58). The data were processed here and made into records.

Weather Guesser Nunataks. 75°30′S, 71°45′W. 10 miles WNW of the Thomas Mountains, in eastern Ellsworth Land. Discovered by the RARE 1947–48. Named by Russell R. White, Jr., USN, aerographer here in 1965–66.

Weather Island *see* **Veier Head**

Weather stations. There are two types—manned and automatic. The manned ones are usually an integral part of scientific stations (q.v.). The invention and use of automatic weather stations in Antarctica was accurately predicted in the 1930s by Willis R. Gregg of the US Weather Bureau. Alan Peterson of Stanford finally designed the AWS. The first one began operating at the South Pole in

Feb. 1975. It was moved to Ross Island in Dec. 1975, and in Jan. 1976 to Marble Point, operating here until May 1977. The average AWS costs about $21,000. They provide year-round data via polar-orbiting satellites to researchers in the home country. They run on solar-powered batteries buried in the snow. Each one has a 3-meter tower with a horizontal boom on the top of the tower. The boom supports the antenna. The tower is anchored with ropes and chains. They measure air temperature, air pressure, relative humidity, and wind speed and wind direction at 10 feet above the surface. The AWS is a successful Antarctic project. Until July 1980 they were maintained by the members of the Radio Science Laboratory of Stanford University, but since then the Department of Meteorology, University of Wisconsin has seen to them. The most important American Automatic Weather Stations in Antarctica have been Allison, Arrival Heights, Asgard, Bowers, Buckle Island, Butler Island, Byrd, Clean Air, D-57, D-47, D-17, D-10, Dome C, Dolleman Island, Elaine, Ferrell, Fogle, Gill, Inexpressible Island, Jimmy, Katie, Larsen, Laurie, Lettau, Lynn, Manning, Manuela, Marble Point, Marilyn, Martha, Martha II, Meeley, Nancy, Patrick, Sandra, Schwerdtfeger, Scott Island, Shristi, Siple Station, Spine, Sushila, Tiffany, Uranus Glacier, White Island, Whitlock, Windless Bight. Others are proposed.

Weathercock Hill *see* **Cathedral Crags**

Mount Weaver. 86°58′S, 153°50′W. 2,780 m. 2 miles west of Mount Wilbur, at the top of the Robert Scott Glacier. Discovered and climbed by Quin Blackburn's party in Dec. 1934, during Byrd's 1933–35 expedition. Named by them for Charles E. Weaver, professor of paleontology at the University of Washington.

Weaver, John A. Seaman on the Wilkes Expedition 1838–42. Joined at Valparaiso. Served the cruise.

Weaver Nunataks. 79°51′S, 81°11′W. Just south of the Meyer Hills, in the

Heritage Range. Named for William E. Weaver, meteorologist at Ellsworth Station in 1962.

Weaver Peninsula. 62°12'S, 58°48'W. In the area of Buddington Peak, between Collins Harbor and Marian Cove, on the SW side of King George Island, in the South Shetlands.

Weaver Point. 65°31'S, 65°46'W. 2½ miles west of Tula Point, at the north end of Renaud Island, in the Biscoe Islands. Named by the UK in 1959 for John C. Weaver, American authority on ice.

Cape Webb. 67°52'S, 146°52'E. Between the Ainsworth and Doolette Bays in East Antarctica. In the area of the Ninnis Glacier. Discovered by the AAE 1911–14, and named by Mawson for Eric Webb.

Mount Webb. 71°12'S, 162°59'E. 2,430 m. 4 miles SE of Mount Glasgow, at the west side of Edlin Névé, in the Explorers Range of the Bowers Mountains. Named in 1968 by the New Zealanders for William Webb, the leader of the Scott Base wintering-over party of 1968.

Webb, Benjamin. Ordinary seaman on the Wilkes Expedition 1838–42. Joined in the USA. Discharged at Oahu, Oct. 31, 1840.

Webb, Eric N. "Azi." New Zealand scientist, the chief magnetician at Main Base during the AAE 1911–14. In 1912 he was one of Bage's party of 3 to go to the area of the South Magnetic Pole.

Webb Glacier. 77°19'S, 160°48'E. Just north of Mount Bastion and Gibson Spur, it flows into the head of Barwick Valley, in southern Victoria Land. Named by the New Zealanders in 1958–59 for P.N. Webb, geology pioneer here in 1957–58 and 1958–59.

Webb Icefall. 77°16'S, 160°29'E. Just south of Vishniac Peak. It flows from the Willett Range, in the area of the Webb Glacier, in Victoria Land. Named by Parker Calkin, US geologist here, in association with the glacier.

Webb Island. 67°27'S, 67°56'W. 1½ miles long. In Laubeuf Fjord, about 3 miles south of the entrance to Stonehouse Bay on Adelaide Island. Discovered by Charcot in 1908–10, and named by him for Capt. Richard C. Webb, RN, captain of a British cruiser in Argentine waters at the time.

Webb Lake. 77°20'S, 160°52'E. A meltwater lake at the terminus of Webb Glacier, in the Barwick Valley of southern Victoria Land. Named by the American geologist Parker Calkin in 1964 because of its proximity to the glacier.

Webb Névé. 72°42'S, 166°20'E. At the head of the Seafarer Glacier, in Victoria Land. Named by the New Zealanders in 1966–67 for Dexter Webb, public relations officer for the New Zealand Geological Survey Antarctic Expedition of that year. He was killed before taking up his appointment.

Webb Nunataks. 83°24'S, 56°42'W. 2 miles west of Madey Ridge, in the Neptune Range of the Pensacola Mountains. Named for Dalton Webb, a member of the US Air Force Electronics Test Unit, 1957–58.

Webb Peak. 69°38'S, 66°28'W. On the west coast of Palmer Land.

Webber Island. 77°17'S, 153°05'W. The large, central island of the White Islands, in the southern part of Sulzberger Bay, on the coast of Marie Byrd Land. First described by Byrd's 1928–30 expedition as "low ice cliffs" rising above the ice shelf. Named for James Webber, ionosphere physicist at Byrd Station in 1968–69.

Webber Nunatak. 74°47'S, 99°50'W. 495 m. 6 miles west of Mount Manthe, in the Hudson Mountains. Named for George E. Webber, at Byrd Station in 1967.

Weber Inlet. 71°50'S, 72°55'W. 13 miles long. 9 miles wide. Ice-filled. An indentation into the southern part of Beethoven Peninsula. It forms the NW arm of the Bach Ice Shelf, in Alexander Island. Named by the UK for the composer Carl Maria von Weber.

Weber Ridge. 84°20′S, 63°12′W. A bare rock ridge, 8 miles long. At the northern end of the Anderson Hills, in the northern Patuxent Range, in the Pensacola Mountains. Named for Max K. Weber, topographic engineer in the Pensacola Mountains in 1965–66.

Webers Peaks. 79°28′S, 84°40′W. In the Heritage Range. Named by the University of Minnesota Ellsworth Mountains Party 1962–63, for geologist Gerald F. Webers, a member of the party.

Mount Webster. 85°40′S, 144°24′W. 1,610 m. 3 miles north of the Leverett Glacier, and 12 miles NW of Mount Beazley, in the Byrd Mountains. Named for Lt. John B. Webster, USN, at McMurdo Station in 1962.

Webster, W.H.B. British scientist and medical doctor who made plant and animal studies and collections, as well as ice experiments, on Deception Island in 1828–29, as part of the *Chanticleer* expedition of 1828–31, led by Foster. He was the first scientist to work in Antarctica.

Webster Bluff. 76°06′30″S, 144°55′W. 9 miles long. Ice-covered. Forms a northern extension of the Phillips Mountains in Marie Byrd Land. Named for David O. Webster, ionosphere physicist at Byrd Station in 1964.

Webster Glacier. 79°06′S, 86°11′W. Flows between Frazier Ridge and Pipe Peak, in the Founders Peaks of the Heritage Range, into Minnesota Glacier. Named for Charles W. Webster, meteorologist at Wilkes Station in 1963.

Webster Knob. 85°18′S, 166°30′W. At the head of Strom Glacier, in the Queen Maud Mountains, near Mount Fridtjof Nansen. Discovered by Gould in Nov. 1929 during Byrd's 1928–30 expedition, and named by Byrd for Mrs. Laurence J. Webster, a sponsor of the expedition.

Webster Pass. 74°34′S, 111°09′W. On the Bear Peninsula of Marie Byrd Land.

¹Webster Peaks. 63°55′S, 59°40′W. 1,065 m. 4 rocky peaks west of White-cloud Glacier, at the head of Charcot Bay, on the west coast of Graham Land. Charted by the FIDS in 1948, and named for W.H.B. Webster.

²Webster Peaks. 70°28′S, 65°25′E. 5 peaks 3 miles SE of Mount Kirkby, in the Porthos Range of the Prince Charles Mountains. Named by the Australians for G.K. Webster, ionosphere physicist at Mawson Station in 1965.

Weddell, James. b. Aug. 24, 1787, Ostend (then in the Austrian Netherlands). d. Sept. 9, 1834, London. Scottish navigator, explorer, seal hunter. Son of an upholsterer. Joined the RN in 1796, was in the merchant navy, then again in the RN. He commanded the brig *Jane* on three voyages into Antarctic waters, with the prime purpose of sealing and fishing. His first voyage was in 1819–21, and on it he discovered, or rather rediscovered, the South Shetlands and South Orkneys. After this trip he bought a share of the *Jane,* and was in high southern latitudes again in 1821–22, again at the South Shetlands, as well as the South Orkneys (which he named) in Feb. 1822. His third voyage was in 1822–24. By Feb. 16, 1823, he was at 70°S, and on Feb. 20, 1823, he set a new southing record of 74°15′S, 34°16′W, and concluded that the South Pole was in an ocean (he was wrong). He was in a new sea, which he called the George IV Sea (later named the Weddell Sea). On that third voyage he also surveyed the South Shetlands and South Orkneys, and brought back Leopard seal specimens to London. In late 1823 he was back at the South Shetlands but could not land. Weddell continued as a ships captain until 1832, and wrote *A Voyage Toward the South Pole* in 1825.

Weddell Abyssal Plain. 72°S, 45°W. A submarine feature running between the Weddell Sea and the Maud Seamount.

Weddell Arm. 68°32′S, 78°08′E. A cove, the southernmost and westernmost arm of Langnes Fjord, in the Vestfold Hills. Photographed by the LCE 1936–

37. Visited in 1955 and 1957 by the ANARE, and named by them for the large number of Weddell Seals here.

Weddell Barrier *see* **Filchner Ice Shelf**

Weddell Coast Sledge Party. Joint British-American effort between the RARE and the FIDS in 1947–48. Finn Ronne, leader of the RARE, met Major K.S. Pierce-Butler, leader of the FIDS, and the 2 drew up a complex agreement, actually a contract, whereby representatives from both countries would join in a sledging expedition to the Weddell Sea coast. Four men left Stonington Island (base for both parties) on Oct. 9, 1947. They were Pierce-Butler and Douglas Mason for the FIDS, and Walter Smith and Arthur Owen for the RARE. With 3 teams of dogs, 23 dogs in toto, they crossed the Antarctic Peninsula to its east side, and then down to Mount Tricorn on the Weddell Sea coast. To this point the expedition was known as the Joint British-American Weddell Coast Sledge Party, but now the 2 teams split up. The British stayed at Mount Tricorn on Wright Inlet, while the 2 Americans pressed on south as the Ronne Weddell Coast Party, and then east, getting as far as the Bowman Peninsula overlooking Mount Austin, on Dec. 13, 1947. They then turned back. The 4 men returned to Stonington Island on Jan. 22, 1948, having covered 1,180 miles in 105 days.

Weddell Ice Shelf *see* **Filchner Ice Shelf.**

Weddell Islands. 60°39'S, 44°51'W. Also known as Weddell's Island. A group of small islands and rocks, 1 mile south of Saddle Island and 4½ miles north of the west end of Laurie Island, just to the east of Powell Island, in the South Orkneys. Named by 1823, for James Weddell.

Weddell Polynya. An ice-free area in the eastern part of the Weddell Sea. It was discovered as it was forming between 1974 and 1976 at 65°S, 0°, just to the east of the Weddell Sea proper.

Weddell Polynya Expedition. Better known perhaps as WEPOLEX 81. US-USSR joint oceanographic field expedition Oct. 9, 1981—Nov. 25, 1981. Their mission was to study the Weddell Polynya. E.I. Sarukhanyan led the expedition and his 12 Russians, while deputy leader Arnold L. Gordon led his 12 Americans. They all integrated into a single scientific team. The *Mikhail Somov* left Leningrad, stopping at Helsinki on Sept. 9, 1981, to pick up equipment and 3 Americans. The rest of the US team boarded in Montevideo, from where the *Mikhail Somov* departed on Oct. 9, 1981. On Oct. 20, 1981, they reached the edge of the Weddell Sea pack-ice at 5°E. They plowed through the ice to 62°30'S. F.A. Pesyakov was captain of the ship. The two heads of physical oceanography were Bruce A. Huber and Ivan Chuguy. The other participants in this particular discipline were David Woodroffe, Walter Richter, and Jan Szelag (USA), and Nikolai Antipov, Nikolai Bagriantsev, and Vladimir Romanov (USSR). The chemists were Arthur Chen, Joe Jennings, and Gerry Metcalf (USA), and Victor Haritonov and Vladimir Feodorov (USSR). Biologists were Jeanne Stepien, David Boardman, and Diane Clark (USA), and Valeriy M. Zhuravlev (USSR). Sea-ice scientists were Stephen Ackley (USA), and Boris Sustenov and Alexandre Samoshkin (USSR). The meteorologists were Ed Andreas (USA), and Alexandre Makshtas and Ed Lysakov (USSR). Pyotr Bogarodsky (USSR) studied velocity of ice in the ocean.

Weddell Sea. Centers on 72°S, 45°W. Forms the southernmost part of the Atlantic Ocean. It is bounded on the west by the Antarctic Peninsula, on the east by Coats Land, and on the south by the Filchner and Ronne Ice Shelves. It is deep, with an area of 3 million square miles. It is usually heavily iced. The pack-ice reaches as far north as 60°S. James Weddell discovered it in Feb. 1823, and named it George IV Sea for his new king. Morrell may have gotten there in the *Wasp* in March 1823, in fact probably did, but it is certain that Bruce was here in 1903. By that time the name had been changed (in 1900 Dr. Karl Fischer had proposed the new name, to honor its discoverer).

Weddell seals. *Leptonychotes weddelli.* Gray seals first described by James Weddell in 1823. They are nonmigratory, unafraid of man, and can be solitary although they are generally gregarious creatures. They number about 500,000. They grow to 10½ feet long, and 1,000 pounds in weight. The female is the larger. They live on fish, cephalopods, and other marine animals, including penguins. Good divers, they can go to 1,000 feet down, and can stay under water for 43 minutes. They are unique in that they can survive under fast ice, even in winter, by maintaining open breathing holes in the ice with their teeth.

Weddell's Island *see* **Weddell Islands**

Wedel Islands *see* **Vedel Islands**

Mount Wedel-Jarlsberg. 85°39′S, 165°06′W. Also called Mount Alice Wedel-Jarlsburg. Ice-covered. Between Cooper Glacier and Bowman Glacier, 2 miles SW of Mount Ruth Gade, in the Quarles Range. Discovered in Dec. 1911 by Amundsen and named by him for Alice Wedel-Jarlsberg, wife of a Norwegian diplomat.

Wedemeyer Rocks. 76°06′S, 135°56′W. Near the base of the southern slope of Mount Berlin, in the Flood Range. Named for Charles H. Wedemeyer, USN, who helped establish Byrd Station in 1956–57.

Wedge Face. 84°12′S, 171°30′E. A spur which projects from Mount Patrick to the eastern part of the Beardmore Glacier. First seen by Shackleton in Dec. 1908, but named by Scott on his way to the Pole in 1911.

Wedge Ridge. 80°38′S, 29°12′W. 1,145 m. A rock ridge in the western part of the Shackleton Range, near the head of the

Blaiklock Glacier, immediately west of Pointer Nunatak. Named by the UK.

Wedgwood Point *see* **Azufre Point**

Wednesday Island. 64°56′S, 63°45′W. 1 mile long. At the east end of the Wauwermans Islands. Discovered by Dallmann in 1873–74. Charted by the BGLE 1934–37, and named by Rymill because he sighted it on a Wednesday.

Weeder Rock. 70°23′S, 162°02′E. An isolated coastal rock 6 miles NNW of Mount Belolikov, between the Rennick and Gannutz Glaciers. Named for Courtland C. Weeder, USN, at Amundsen-Scott South Pole Station in 1965.

Mount Weeks. 83°32′S, 160°50′E. 6 miles north of Cranfield Peak, in the southern sector of the Queen Elizabeth Range, on the western edge of the Prince Andrew Plateau. Named by the New Zealanders in 1961–62 for Lt. James W. Weeks, USN, pilot in the area that season.

Weeks, Capt. Captain of the *Horatio*, 1820–21.

Weeks Stack. 62°14′S, 59°03′W. A sea stack off the northern tip of Nelson Island, in the South Shetlands. Named by the UK in 1961 for Capt. Weeks.

Mount Weems. 77°27′S, 86°10′W. 2,210 m. 8 miles north of Mount Ulmer, in the northern part of the Sentinel Range. Discovered by Ellsworth during his fly-over on Nov. 23, 1935. Named for Capt. P.V.H. Weems, inventor and consultant to Ellsworth.

Weertman Island. 66°58′S, 67°44′W. Also called Isla Runcumilla. The largest and most southerly of the Bennett Islands, in Hanusse Bay. Named by the UK for Johannes Weertman, American glaciologist.

Mount Wegener. 80°44′S, 23°31′W. In the Shackleton Range.

Wegener Range. 72°42′S, 62°23′W. On the east coast of Palmer Land.

Wegert Bluff. 69°42′S, 159°20′E. Overlooks Noll Glacier in the Wilson

Hills. Named for Lt. Cdr. Sidney J. Wegert, USN, Hercules pilot in the Antarctic in 1967 and 1968.

Wegger Peak. 62°06′S, 58°31′W. Also called The Fist. 305 m. At the west side of the entrance to Mackellar Inlet, on King George Island, in the South Shetlands. There are four peaks together, like a fist, and Charcot called it Le Poing (the fist). Renamed by the UK in 1960 for Ole Wegger, Norwegian ship builder.

Mount Weihaupt. 72°37′S, 161°02′E. 2,285 m. A bare rock mountain 10 miles east of Mount Bower. It is the dominant feature in the eastern part of the Outback Nunataks. Named for John G. Weihaupt, seismologist in the area in 1959–60.

Weikman Nunataks. 76°30′S, 143°59′W. Two nunataks between Balchen Glacier and Crevasse Valley Glacier, in the Ford Ranges of Marie Byrd Land. 2 miles east of Mount Perkins. Named for Edward R. Weikman, Jr., at Byrd Station in 1967.

Mount Weininger. 84°47′S, 65°30′W. 1,970 m. Ice-free. At the north edge of Mackin Table, in the Patuxent Range of the Pensacola Mountains. Named for Richard B. Weininger, scientific leader of Amundsen-Scott South Pole Station in 1967.

Mount Weir. 84°59′S, 177°10′E. At the head of the Ramsey Glacier. Discovered on Feb. 16, 1947, during Operation Highjump, and named for the pilot who discovered it, Maj. Robert R. Weir.

Weir, Robert R. Major, US Marines. Pilot of Flight 8-B during Byrd's flight to the South Pole on Feb. 15–16, 1947, during Operation Highjump.

Weir Glacier. 66°04′S, 64°42′W. 8 miles long. Flows into Barilari Bay, on the west coast of Graham Land. Discovered in 1909 by Charcot. Surveyed by the BGLE in 1935–36, and later named for sponsors of the BGLE, Viscount Weir and his son.

Weiss Amphitheater. 77°04′S, 126°06′W. A caldera, 2 miles wide. Occupies the south central part of Mount Sidley, in the Executive Committee Range of Marie Byrd Land. Named for Bernard D. Weiss, chief meteorologist at Byrd Station in 1959.

Welch, B.F. Second engineman on the *Discovery* during the BANZARE 1929–31.

Welch Island. 67°34′S, 62°56′E. 1 mile long. Has a rock pinnacle on it of 130 m. In the east side of Holme Bay. Discovered in Feb. 1931 by the BANZARE, and named by Mawson for B.F. Welch.

Welch Mountains. 70°57′S, 63°30′W. Also called Eternity Mountains. The highest rises to 3,015 m. 25 miles north of Mount Jackson, on the east margin of the Dyer Plateau, on the Antarctic Peninsula. Named for David F. Welch, rear admiral, USN, commander of the US Naval Support Force, Antarctic (*see* **Operation Deep Freeze**).

Welch Peak. 85°39′S, 149°15′W. 1,010 m. On the north side of the Tapley Mountains, 9 miles NW of Mount Gould. Named for Walton D. Welch, at Byrd Station in 1957.

Welch Rocks. 67°33′S, 62°54′E. Two rocks ½ mile north of Welch Island (hence the name, given by the Australians), in the east part of Holme Bay.

Welchness. 63°29′S, 56°14′W. A gravel spit which forms the western end of Dundee Island, and therefore serves as a cape. Discovered by the Dundee Whaling Expedition of 1892–93.

Welcome Mountain. 72°14′S, 160°12′E. Has 3 peaks on it, the highest being 2,505 m. 5 miles SE of Mount Southard, in the Outback Nunataks. Discovered by the US Victoria Land Traverse Party of 1959–60. It was the first mountain they saw in 3 months after coming off the Polar Plateau.

Welcome Nunatak. 79°06′S, 85°54′W. Cone-shaped. To the north of the Reuther Nunataks, in the Founders Peaks. Named by the University of Minnesota Geological Party of 1963–64. It signaled nearness to their base at Camp Hills.

Welcome Pass. 82°35'S, 52°45'W. In the Pensacola Mountains.

Weldon Glacier. 76°33'S, 29°20'W. Enters the Weddell Sea 30 miles WSW of Hayes Glacier. Discovered aerially on Nov. 5, 1967, in a flight over Coats Land. Named for Don W. Weldon, USN, photographer on the flight.

Cape Well-Met. 63°47'S, 57°19'W. Also called Mötesudden, Cabo Visible. Headland on the north side of Vega Island in the area of the Trinity Peninsula. Discovered and named by Nordenskjöld's 1901–4 expedition, originally as Cape Dreyfus. It was here that the two parties of the expedition met after a year and a half apart.

¹Mount Weller. 67°17'S, 50°40'E. 1,080 m. West of Auster Glacier. 2 miles east of Reference Peak in Enderby Land. Named by the Australians for G.E. Weller, meteorologist at Mawson Station in 1961.

²Mount Weller. 77°50'S, 160°26'E. To the immediate west of Beacon Valley, in southern Victoria Land. Named for William J. Weller.

Weller, William J. Able seaman, RN, on the *Discovery* during the Royal Society Expedition led by Scott in 1901–4.

Weller Island. 65°27'S, 65°24'W. East of Snodgrass Island, in the Pitt Islands of the Biscoe Islands. Named by the UK in 1959 for the Dickens character.

Wellman Cliffs. 82°27'S, 156°10'E. 12 miles long. On the east side of the Boucot Plateau, in the Geologists Range. Named by the New Zealanders in 1961–62 for geologist H.W. Wellman, cartographer and Antarctic veteran.

Wellman Glacier. 64°29'S, 61°26'W. Flows into Recess Cove, in Charlotte Bay, on the west coast of Graham Land. Charted by de Gerlache in 1897–99. Named by the UK in 1960 for American Arctic explorer Walter Wellman.

Wellman Valley. 79°55'S, 156°40'E. Ice-free. Just east of Midnight Plateau

and north of Mount Ash, in the Darwin Mountains. Named by the New Zealanders in 1962–63 for H.W. Wellman (*see* **Wellman Cliffs**).

Mount Wells. 85°10'S, 169°48'W. Ice-covered. In the Prince Olav Mountains. At the west side of the Liv Glacier, 4 miles NW of June Nunatak. Named for Harry Wells, with the National Academy of Sciences in the 1960s.

Wells, Loran. Photographer and observer at West Base during the USAS 1939–41.

Wells, William. Yeoman on the Wilkes Expedition 1838–42. Joined at Valparaiso. Served the cruise.

Wells Glacier. 73°32'S, 61°11'W. 9 miles west of Cape Brooks, it flows into New Bedford Inlet, on the east coast of Palmer Land. Named for James T. Wells, at Amundsen-Scott South Pole Station in 1967.

Wells Ridge. 76°58'S, 144°45'W. 4 miles long. Between the Swanson Mountains and Mount Gilmour in the Ford Ranges of Marie Byrd Land. Discovered aerially from West Base during the USAS 1939–41. Named for Loran Wells.

Wells Saddle. 76°03'S, 135°35'W. A broad, snow-filled saddle between Mount Berlin and Mount Moulton, in the Flood Range. Named for James H. Wells, in the area in 1971–72.

Welsh, Peter. Seaman on the Wilkes Expedition 1838–42. Joined in the USA. Sent home on the *Relief* in 1839.

Mount Wendland. 84°42'S, 175°18'W. 1,650 m. Near the head of the Massam Glacier, 2 miles NE of Mount Kenney, in the Prince Olav Mountains. Named for Vaughn P. Wendland, geologist here in 1970–71.

Wennersgaard, Ole Christian. Swedish seaman on the Nordenskjöld expedition of 1901–4. He died on June 7, 1903, while wintering on Paulet Island.

Wennersgaard Point. 63°51'S, 59°54'W. Forms the east side of the entrance to Lanchester Bay, on the west coast of

Graham Land. Charted by Nordenskjöld's expedition in Nov.–Dec. 1902, and named by them for Ole Christian Wennersgaard.

Wensley Beacon *see* **Wensleydale Beacon**

Wensleydale Beacon. 62°57′S, 60°42′W. Also called Wensley Beacon. 110 m. A hill, just north of Primero de Mayo Bay, on the west side of Port Foster, Deception Island. Charted by Foster in 1828–31. Named by Lt. Cdr. D.N. Penfold, RN, in 1949, after he had surveyed the island. He came from Wensleydale, in England.

Werenskiold Bastion. 67°26′S, 65°32′W. A rock headland that rises steeply to over 1,000 m. It forms the coastline between Demorest Glacier and Matthes Glacier, on the east coast of Graham Land. Mapped by the FIDS in 1947–48. Named by the UK for Norwegian geographer Werner Werenskiold.

Werlein Island. 66°25′S, 110°27′E. Almost a mile long. Just SE of Holl Island, in the Windmill Islands. Named for Ensign Richard O. Werlein, USN, who took part in Operation Windmill, 1947–48.

Werner Mountains. 73°28′S, 62°08′W. Just WSW of New Bedford Inlet, on the Lassiter Coast. First seen by the USAS members from East Base in 1940, and later named for German geologist Abraham Werner.

Werner Peak. 68°43′S, 65°14′W. 1,550 m. The highest peak on the SE side of the Mercator Ice Piedmont. Surveyed by the FIDS in 1958, and named by the UK for Johannes Werner, 16th-century German astronomer.

Wessbecher Glacier. 78°55′S, 84°25′W. 7 miles long. Flows between the Wilson and Marze Peaks at the south end of the Sentinel Range. Named for Howard O. Wessbecher, at McMurdo Base in the winter of 1956, who helped in the preparation of the South Pole Station in 1956–57.

Wesson, George. Seaman on the Wilkes Expedition 1838–42. Joined in the USA. Served the cruise.

Mount West. 77°25′S, 145°30′W. Also called Mount James E. West. 9 miles SE of Mount Woodward, between the Hammond and Swope Glaciers, in the Ford Ranges of Marie Byrd Land. Paul Siple named it for James E. West, a Boy Scout leader.

West Antarctic Ice Sheet. Formed much more recently than the East Antarctic Ice Sheet, this is the ice covering West Antarctica.

West Antarctica. Centers on 79°S, 100°W. Also called Lesser Antarctica, Andean Province (because it seems to represent a geological extension of South America. *See also* **Andean Chain**). On the Pacific Ocean side of Antarctica, it consists largely of an archipelago of mountainous islands covered and joined together by ice, or, looking at it from the surface, it comprises Marie Byrd Land, Ellsworth Land, and the Antarctic Peninsula. It was covered with temperate vegetation until about 37 million years ago. It was named before 1900, and the USA approved the name in 1962.

West Arm. 67°36′S, 62°52′E. A rock mass forming the western limit of Horseshoe Harbor, in Holme Bay. Aerially surveyed by the LCE 1936–37. The ANARE were the first to visit, on Feb. 5, 1954, and they named it.

West Balch Glacier *see* **Drummond Glacier**

West Barrier *see* **West Ice Shelf**

West Base *see* **Little America III**

West Base Antarctic Service Expedition *see* **United States Antarctic Service Expedition**

West Bay. 69°21′S, 68°26′W. On the west coast of the Antarctic Peninsula.

West Beach. About 180 yards long. On the coast of North Bay, Ross Island, about 200 yards north of Cape Evans. This term is not official.

West Beacon. 77°50′S, 160°47′E. A peak in the Beacon Valley area of southern Victoria Land. 2,420 m. Between Beacon Valley and Arena Valley, in the Beacon Heights. Originally called Beacon Heights West by Scott's 1901–4 expedition. The New Zealanders shortened the name in 1958–59.

West Budd Island. 67°35′S, 62°50′E. The western of two larger islands at the north end of the Flat Islands, in Holme Bay. Photographed by the LCE 1936–37. Named by the Australians for Dr. G.M. Budd, medical officer at Mawson Station in 1959.

West Cape. The western side of the entrance to the Bay of Whales. It is now gone, as is the Bay of Whales.

West Dailey Island. 77°53′S, 164°54′E. Also called West Dailey Isle. The largest and most westerly of the Dailey Islands, 5 miles NE of Cape Chocolate, in McMurdo Sound. Scott's 1901–4 expedition visited this group, and named it, but this particular island was named by Scott's 1910–13 expedition.

West Germany. Ratified on Feb. 5, 1979, as the 21st signatory of the Antarctic Treaty, and on March 3, 1981, as the 14th nation to achieve Consultative status within the Antarctic Treaty system. West Germany sent out the GANOVEX expeditions, and had a disaster in 1981–82 when the *Gotland II* sank. West Germany also took part in the Filchner Ice Shelf Program. It has the Georg von Neumayer Station, built in New Schwabenland in 1981 when Filchner Station was aborted.

West Gould Glacier *see* **Erskine Glacier**

West Groin. 77°39′S, 160°48′E. A rock spur between Mudrey Cirque and Flory Cirque, on the south side of the Asgard Range, in Victoria Land. Named by Scott's 1910–13 expedition for its position relative to Flory Cirque.

West Ice Shelf. 67°S, 85°E. Also called West Barrier (especially in the old days, before the term Ice Shelf caught on). Runs 180 miles in an east-west direction, between Barrier Bay and Posadowsky Bay, and fronts the Leopold and Astrid Coast of East Antarctica. Discovered by von Drygalski, in 1901–3, and named by him because of the direction in which he saw it.

West Melchior Archipelago *see* **West Melchior Islands**

West Melchior Islands. 64°19′S, 63°W. Also called West Melchior Archipelago. Ice covered rocks and little islands in the western part of the Melchior Islands, in effect those islands of the group which lie west of The Sound. Surveyed and named by the Discovery Committee in 1927.

West Nunatak *see* **Peak Seven**

West Ongul Island *see* **Ongul Island**

West Prongs. 83°54′S, 57°34′W. Three rock spurs just north of Elliott Ridge, in the Neptune Range of the Pensacola Mountains. Named for Clyde E. West, at Ellsworth Station in 1958.

West Quartzite Range. 72°S, 164°45′E. On the east side of Houliston Glacier, in the Concord Mountains. Named by the New Zealanders in 1962–63 for the geology of the feature.

West Reef. 61°05′S, 55°36′W. 3 miles NW of Cape Lindsey, on Elephant Island, in the South Shetlands. Named by the sealers before 1822.

West Russell Glacier *see* **Russell West Glacier**

West Stack. 67°03′S, 58°03′E. Also called Vestskotet. 120 m. A coastal rock outcrop, 14 miles SE of Edward VIII Bay, on the west side of Hoseason Glacier. Discovered in Feb. 1936 by the personnel on the *William Scoresby,* and named by them because of its proximity to East Stack.

West Stenhouse Glacier *see* **Stenhouse Glacier**

The *West Wind*. US icebreaker launched in 1943. It took part in Operation Deep Freeze III (1957–58), and

Operation Deep Freeze 67 and 68. It was still going to Antarctica in the 1980s.

Western Indian Antarctic Basin *see* **Atlantic-Indian Basin**

Western Mountains. Scott's name, in 1902, for the section of the Transantarctic Horst which he discovered, and which was visible from McMurdo Sound.

Western Plain *see* **Maud Subglacial Basin**

Westhaven Nunatak. 79°50′S, 154°14′ E. 2,240 m. 3 miles south of Turnstile Ridge, in the NW part of the Britannia Range, just to the west of the Darwin Mountains, in southern Victoria Land. First seen aerially, by John Claydon, who suggested the name in 1956–57, because it is the westernmost rock outcrop in this part of the range.

Westliche Petermann Range. 71°35′S, 12°10′E. The western of the three Petermann Ranges, in the Wohlthat Mountains of Queen Maud Land. This range is in the northern part of the Petermanns, extending north-south for 16 miles from Mount Hansen to the Aurdalen Valley. Discovered and named by Ritscher in 1939.

Mount Westminster. 84°59′S, 169°22′ E. 3,370 m. 4 miles south of Mount Kinsey, in the Supporters Range, between the Grosvenor Mountains and Mill Glacier, just to the east of the Beardmore Glacier. Discovered by Shackleton's 1907–9 expedition, and named by them for one of their supporters, the Duke of Westminster.

Mount Weston. 80°28′S, 29°10′W. Has several peaks, the highest being 1,245 m. In the area of the Stratton Glacier, in the Shackleton Range. Named for Peter Weston.

Weston, Peter. RAF flight sgt. mechanic who was part of the air backup during the BCTAE 1955–58.

Wetherell, Capt. Captain of the *Mercury* in the South Shetlands, 1820–21.

Wetmore Glacier. 74°38′S, 63°35′W. Also called Alexander Wetmore Glacier.

40 miles long. Flows between the Rare Range and the Latady Mountains into Gardner Inlet, on the east coast of the Antarctic Peninsula. Discovered by the RARE 1947–48, and named by Ronne for Alexander Wetmore, secretary of the Smithsonian Institution, who had helped Ronne prepare his scientific program.

Wetmore Peak. 71°28′S, 167°35′E. 2,120 m. In the north sector of the Lyttelton Range, 6 miles ENE of Mount Bierle, in the Admiralty Mountains of Victoria Land. Named for Cliff Wetmore, biologist at Hallett Station in 1963–64.

Wetter Island *see* **Veier Head**

Mount Wexler. 84°30′S, 175°01′E. 4,025 m. Ice-free. 3 miles SW of Mount Waterman, in the Hughes Range. Discovered aerially by Byrd on Nov. 18, 1929. Surveyed by Crary in 1957–58. Named by Crary for Harry Wexler, chief scientist for US Antarctic IGY programs, 1957–58.

Wexler Mountains *see* **Heritage Range**

Mount Weyant. 77°33′S, 162°42′E. 1,930 m. Between the Loftus and Newall Glaciers, in Victoria Land. Named in 1964 for William S. Weyant, chief meteorologist at Little America in 1958.

Weyerhaeuser Glacier. 68°45′S, 65° 32′W. Flows into Mercator Ice Piedmont, just west of Mobiloil Inlet, on the east coast of the Antarctic Peninsula. First defined aerially in 1940 by the USAS members of East Base. Resighted by Ronne in 1947 during the RARE, and named by him for F.K. Weyerhaeuser, a sponsor.

Weyprecht Mountains. 71°58′S, 13° 25′E. 10 miles west of the Payer Mountains, they form the western half of the Hoel Mountains of Queen Maud Land. Discovered in 1939 by Ritscher, and named by him for Karl Weyprecht, Arctic explorer, who initiated the First International Polar Year, 1882–83.

Whakawhiti Saddle. 82°38'S, 163°35' E. A low, broad snow-saddle between Oliver Glacier and the lower portion of Robb Glacier, just to the east of the Taylor Hills. Named by the New Zealanders in 1959–60. Whakawhiti means "crossing over" in Maori.

Whale Bay. 60°44'S, 45°11'W. A small bay between the SE end of Coronation Island and the NW side of Matthews Island, in the South Orkneys. Sørlle may have named it Hvalbugten (whale bay) during his surveys here in 1912–13.

Whale Rock. 60°48'S, 45°39'W. A term no longer used for a rock in the South Orkneys.

Whale Skerries. 60°42'S, 45°06'W. A small group of islands and rocks in the Lewthwaite Strait, just west of Cape Disappointment on Powell Island, in the South Orkneys. Sørlle surveyed them in 1912–13, and named them singularly as Hvalskjaer. He later changed the name to the plural, Hvalskjaerene. The UK took up the English translation in 1954.

Whaleback *see* **Mount Marston**

Whaleback Islet *see* **Whaleback Rocks**

Whaleback Rocks. 63°39'S, 59°04'W. Also called Whaleback Islet. 2 miles west of Blake Island, in Bone Bay, off the northern coast of Trinity Peninsula. Charted and aptly named by the FIDS in 1948.

Whalebone Whales *see* **Baleen Whales**

Whalers Bay. 62°59'S, 60°34'W. As one goes through Neptune's Bellows into the caldera of Port Foster, Deception Island, in the South Shetlands, this bay is on the right, between Fildes Point and Penfold Point. The whalers had a station here (*see,* for example, **The Ravn**), and the British much later had Base B here. Charcot named it aptly in 1910.

Whales. *See* **Killer whales, Pilot whales, Sperm whales, Bottle-nosed whales (or Beaked whales), Baleen whales, Rorquals, Southern right whales,** Humpback whales, Blue whales, Fin whales, Sei whales, Minke, Pygmy right whale, Right whales, whaling.

Bay of Whales. 78°30'S, 164°20'W. A Ross Sea indentation into the NE part of the Ross Ice Shelf. An iceport, and natural harbor, it was created sometime between 1902 (Scott did not see it) and 1908 (Shackleton did — and named it on Jan. 24, 1908, for the whales here). Its outline was always changing, and it shrank between 1935 (when Little America II was built here) and 1939 (when Little America III was built here). A feature of major historic importance, it was the site for several bases and the launching pad to the continent for many expeditions. It disappeared in early Oct. 1987 when the massive iceberg B-9 broke away.

Whales Bay Deeps *see* **Whales Bay Furrows**

Whales Bay Furrows. 78°S, 168°W. Also called Whales Bay Deeps. A submarine feature of the Ross Sea.

Whaling. Whaling, like sealing, is an economic activity of the past in Antarctica, as it is throughout the world. In Antarctica it is meant to be illegal, prohibited by the International Whaling Commission (IWC), although a few countries, such as Japan, still indulge for "scientific purposes." It is a sad fact that there is no real way for the IWC, or anybody else, to police the illegal Antarctic whaling; another sad fact is that no matter how much the whale is proclaimed a protected and endangered animal, this creature's days are numbered because of the human species' need to prove its own superiority. The big whaling company of the early 19th century was Enderby Brothers out of London, whose ships captains included Biscoe and Balleny. This company was responsible for the opening up of significant portions of the Antarctic continent. In the 1860s Svend Foyn, a Norwegian, invented the harpoon gun, which made slaughter much easier, quicker, and less dangerous (for the killers). Norway, one of the giants of the whaling business, was really the founder of modern Antarctic whaling. In 1906 Chris Christensen introduced the first factory ship to the South Shetlands, and by 1912–13 there were 6 shore stations, 21 factory ships, and 62 whale catchers in Antarctica, most of them Norwegian. A factory ship was a huge vessel which processed the whales caught by the catchers. Whale catchers were little steamers of 70–120 tons normally, and a group of them would operate out of a factory ship, going out and bringing back the goods. Let it be known, lest history glamorize the whaling business of old, that the smell on board a factory ship was one of the strongest and most despicable ever experienced by the human nose, and it took a man a good time to acclimatize to it, let alone spend months working in it and living in it. The Rethval Whaling Co., of Oslo, was the first to start whaling operations in the South Orkneys, in 1911–12, and the two island groups—the South Orkneys and South Shetlands— were replete with names like the Magellan Whaling Co., the Thule Whaling Co., the Corral Whaling Co., the Tønsberg Hvalfangeri. Christensen operated out of Whalers Bay, Deception Island, and Charcot, the French explorer, spent a happy Christmas with these boys in 1908. That was the year that Great Britain claimed the South Shetlands. In 1912 Britain leased a base on Deception Island to the Hektor Whaling Co., for 21 years, and during the first half of the 20th century Norway and Britain were the dominant members of the southern whaling fraternity. In fact, by 1914, Britain had licensed several whaling activities (see **Deception Island**). Whaling here reached its peak after World War I, and led to much charting and exploring. The most hunted were the blue, sei, and fin whales, and these have virtually left Antarctica now. Oil and baleen were the most profitable products. Lars Christensen, in the 1920s and 1930s, had a large whaling firm in Sandefjord, Norway, and

his company, like the Enderby Brothers a century before, was instrumental in opening up a lot of Antarctica. In 1929 Argentina, an early whaler in Antarctic waters, ceased its activities, and in 1931 stopped the killing of right whales. In 1937 Japan began Antarctic whaling, and 1937–38 was the peak year for Antarctic whaling, with 33 expeditions from several nations going south that season, and 46,000 whales killed. Also in 1937 an international convention was signed in London by 9 countries. Regulatory quotas were set in order to protect the industry from over-depletion. In 1946 the IWC was formed. In 1951 the USSR became an Antarctic whaling force, and since the 1960s the USSR and Japan have been the dominant whaling nations here. In 1963, when Britain stopped whaling, "full protection" came to the blue and humpback whales in the Antarctic. In Dec. 1965 Antarctic whaling was limited to factory ships, and in 1968 Norway quit the business. Whaling dropped off by 95 percent between 1970 and 1980, and today only minke whales are killed, for "scientific purposes." In 1976 fin whales became "fully protected" in the Antarctic, and in 1978 sei whales did so too. As of Sept. 1985 the members of the IWC were Antigua & Barbuda, Argentina, Australia, Belize, Brazil, Chile, China, Costa Rica, Denmark, Egypt, Finland, France, Iceland, India, Ireland, Japan, Kenya, Mauritius, Mexico, Monaco, Netherlands, New Zealand, Norway, Oman, Peru, Philippines, Republic of Korea, Great Britain, Saint Lucia, Saint Vincent & the Grenadines, Senegal, Seychelles, Solomon Islands, South Africa, Spain, Sweden, Switzerland, USA, USSR, Uruguay, and West Germany.

Mount Wharton. 81°03′S, 157°49′E. Over 2,800 m. 5½ miles west of Turk Peak, in the Churchill Mountains. Discovered during Scott's 1901–4 expedition, and named for Sir William Wharton, hydrographer to the Royal Navy from 1884–1904.

Mount Wheat. 64°50'S, 63°23'W. On the east side of Anvers Island.

Cape Wheatstone. 72°37'S, 170°16'E. A rock cape forming the south end of Hallett Peninsula, and marking the north entrance to Tucker Inlet, in Victoria Land. Discovered in 1841 by Ross, and named by him for Sir Charles Wheatstone, physicist.

Wheatstone Glacier. 64°44'S, 62°31'W. Flows into Errera Channel, east of Danco Island, on the west coast of Graham Land. Charted by de Gerlache in 1897–99, and named by the UK in 1960 for Sir Charles Wheatstone (see Cape Wheatstone).

Cape Wheeler. 73°58'S, 61°05'W. An abrupt rock scarp rising to 460 m. It forms the north side of the entrance to Wright Inlet, on the east coast of Palmer Land. Named Cape John Wheeler in 1948 by Finn Ronne for John N. Wheeler, president of the North American Newspaper Alliance (NANA), and a sponsor of the expedition. The name was later shortened.

Wheeler Bay. 66°18'S, 56°06'E. 3 miles wide. 2 miles NW of Magnet Bay. Photographed by the LCE 1936–37. Later named Brörvika (brother bay) by the Norwegians. They named the rocks at its entrance Brödrene (the brothers). The ANARE renamed it in 1956–57 for G.T. Wheeler, weather observer at Mawson Station in 1957.

Wheeler Rocks see **Brødrene Rocks**

Wheeler Valley. 77°12'S, 161°42'E. A hanging valley on the SW side of the Miller Glacier, immediately east of Mount Mahony. Named by the New Zealanders in 1959–60 for R.H. Wheeler, deputy leader and surveyor on that year's VUWAE.

Whelan Nunatak. 70°09'S, 64°17'E. 5 miles NW of Mount Starlight, in the Athos Range of the Prince Charles Mountains. Named by the Australians for R.F.

Whelan, radio officer at Davis Station in 1964.

Whetter, Dr. Leslie H. Surgeon on the AAE 1911–14.

Whetter Nunatak. 66°58'S, 143°01'E. 8 miles ENE of Cape Denison, on the east shore of Commonwealth Bay, in East Antarctica. Discovered by the AAE 1911–14, and named by Mawson for Dr. Leslie H. Whetter.

Mount Whewell. 72°03'S, 169°35'E. 2,945 m. Between the mouths of the Ironside and Honeycomb Glaciers, in the Admiralty Mountains of Victoria Land. Named by Ross on Jan. 15, 1841, for the Rev. Dr. William Whewell, Master of Trinity College, Cambridge.

Whewell Glacier. 72°04'S, 169°47'E. A steep, narrow glacier draining the east slopes of Mount Whewell (hence the name) and merging with the lower part of Honeycomb Glacier, in the Admiralty Mountains of Victoria Land.

Whichaway Nunataks. 81°33'S, 28°30'W. A group of rocky nunataks 7 miles long. They mark the southern side of the mouth of the Recovery Glacier. First seen from the air and visited in Jan. 1957 by the BCTAE, who did not know which way to go from here on their way south.

Mount Whillans. 84°27'S, 64°15'W. 870 m. In the northern Patuxent Range. 4 miles west of Mount Stroschein, in the Anderson Hills. Named for Ian M. Whillans, glaciologist at Palmer Station in 1967.

Whiplash Glacier. 72°16'S, 167°42'E. Flows from the Cartographers Range into the lower part of Pearl Harbor Glacier, in the Victory Mountains of Victoria Land. Named by the New Zealanders in 1962–63 for its shape.

Whirlwind Glaciers. 67°24'S, 65°32'W. Four converging glaciers, Flint Glacier, Demorest Glacier, Matthes Glacier, and Chamberlin Glacier, which flow into Whirlwind Inlet on the east coast of the Antarctic Peninsula. Discovered aerially on Dec. 20, 1928, by Wilkins, and named by him (or rather this spot where the four glaciers meet was) because they looked like the radial cylinders of his Wright Whirlwind engine. Charted by the FIDS in 1948.

Whirlwind Inlet. 67°30′S, 65°25′W. Ice-filled. 12 miles wide at its entrance between Cape Northrop and Tent Nunatak. It is a Larsen Ice Shelf indentation that cuts 7 miles inland into the east coast of the Antarctic Peninsula, between the Bowman Coast and the Foyn Coast. Wilkins discovered it aerially on Dec. 20, 1928. The Whirlwind Glaciers (q.v. for origin of name) flow into it. Charted by the FIDS in 1947.

Whisnant Nunatak. 69°59′S, 73°06′E. Protrudes above the terminus of Rogers Glacier, between the McKaskle Hills and Maris Nunatak, at the east side of the Amery Ice Shelf. John H. Roscoe, US cartographer, named it in 1952 for J.R. Whisnant, who was an airman on Operation Highjump here in 1946–47.

Whistlers. Very low frequency radio waves generated by lightning in the Northern Hemisphere, and received in Antarctica by its polar opposite points. They provide much information about the earth's magnetosphere.

Whistling Bay. 67°30′S, 67°37′W. 4 miles wide. Indents for 2½ miles into the west side of the Antarctic Peninsula, between Longridge Head and Cape Sáenz. Surveyed by the BGLE in 1936, and again in 1948 by the FIDS who named it for the curious and unidentified whistling sounds heard here at the time.

Whit Rock. 66°03′S, 65°56′W. Between the Trump and Saffery Islands, off the west coast of Graham Land. Named by the UK in 1959 for its small size.

Whitcomb Ridge. 73°07′S, 166°E. Ice-covered. On the south side of the head of Gair Glacier, 6 miles SE of Mount Supernal, in the Mountaineer Range of Victoria Land. Named for Jean P. Whitcomb, radio scientist at McMurdo Station in 1965–66 and 1966–67.

Mount Whitcombe. 76°47′S, 162°11′E. 1,425 m. Just north of Mount Perseverance and west of Mount Arrowsmith, at the west side of the Evans Piedmont Glacier, in Victoria Land. Named by the New Zealanders in 1956–58 for its similarity to the mountain of that name in Canterbury, NZ.

Mount White. 85°09′S, 170°18′E. 3,470 m. 2½ miles NNW of Mount Henry Lucy. It is the highest peak in the Supporters Range. Discovered by Shackleton's 1907–9 expedition, and named by them for the secretary of the expedition.

White, James. Captain of the fo'c's'le during the Wilkes Expedition 1838–42. Joined in the USA. Served the cruise.

White, William. Ordinary seaman on the Wilkes Expedition 1838–42. Joined at Callao. Served the cruise.

White Basin. 78°S, 168°E. A subterranean feature between Ross Island and White Island, beneath the Ross Sea.

The White Company. 61°06′S, 55°09′W. A snow-covered mountain group north of Endurance Glacier and west of Pardo Ridge, on Elephant Island in the South Shetlands. Named in 1970–71 by the Joint Services Expedition, as a descriptive name inspired by Conan Doyle's novel.

White Cross Mountain *see* **Mount Guernsey**

White Escarpment. 79°29′S, 85°37′W. In the western part of the Heritage Range. It extends for 15 miles between the heads of the Splettstoesser and Dobratz Glaciers. Named by the University of Minnesota Geological Party here in 1963–64, for CWO Ronald B. White, pilot who helped the party.

White Glacier. 75°45′S, 140°50′W. Flows into Land Glacier, on the north side of Mount McCoy, in Marie Byrd Land. Named by Byrd for Gen. Thomas D. White, USAF, Operation Deep Freeze planner.

¹**White Island.** 66°44′S, 48°35′E. Also called Kvitøya. 13 miles long. 5 miles

wide. Ice-covered. 6 miles north of Sakellari Peninsula, in Enderby Land. Between Amundsen Bay and the eastern part of the entrance to Casey Bay, more in the area of the latter. Discovered by Riiser-Larsen in Jan. 1930, and named Hvit Øya (white island) by him. Subsequent to this discovery it was not seen again, and its existence doubted, until 1957 when the personnel on the *Lena* proved it.

²**White Island.** 78°10′S, 167°20′E. 15 miles long. A huge, nunatak-type landmass with a highest point of 2,520 feet. It is in the form of a grounded island in the Ross Ice Shelf, just south of Ross Island, and next to Black Island, in the Ross Archipelago. It is SSSI #18. Discovered by Scott in 1902, and named by him for its mantle of snow.

White Island Automatic Weather Station. 77°54′S, 168°12′E. An American AWS at an elevation of approximately 116 feet. Located on White Island (see above).

White Islands. 77°17′S, 153°10′W. Ice-covered group, about 10 miles in extent. At the eastern end of the Swinburne Ice Shelf, in the southern sector of Sulzberger Bay. Called "low ice cliffs" by Byrd's 1928–30 expedition, they were later named by Byrd for Dr. Paul Dudley White, heart surgeon and consultant to Byrd during Operation Highjump 1946–47. The group includes Chandler Island, Webber Island, Olson Island.

White Massif. 70°32′S, 67°13′E. 3 miles ENE of Thomson Massif, in the Aramis Range of the Prince Charles Mountains. Named by the Australians for R.F. White (*see* **Deaths, 1963**).

¹**White Nunataks** *see* **Arkhangel'skiy Nunataks**

²**White Nunataks.** 84°46′W, 66°05′W. Three nunataks, 3 miles north of the NW tip of Mackin Table, in the Patuxent Range of the Pensacola Mountains. Named for Noah D. White, radioman at Amundsen-Scott South Pole Station in 1967.

White Spur. 71°19′S, 160°16′E. Forms part of the south wall of Allegro Valley, in the Daniels Range of the Usarp Mountains of Victoria Land. Named for Russell F. White, meteorologist at Amundsen-Scott South Pole Station in 1967–68.

White Strait. 78°15′S, 166°45′E. A small, ice-filled strait between Black Island and White Island, on the Ross Ice Shelf. Mapped by Scott's 1901–4 expedition. Named by the New Zealand Geological Survey Antarctic Expedition of 1958–59, for M. White, a member of the party.

White Valley. 76°39′S, 117°57′W. Ice-covered. It indents the northern part of the Crary Mountains, between Trabucco Cliff and Lie Cliff, in Marie Byrd Land. Named for Franklin E. White, ionosphere physicist at Byrd Station in 1966–67, 1967–68, 1969–70, and 1970–71.

Whitecloud Glacier. 63°55′S, 59°36′W. Flows into Charcot Bay just west of Almond Point, in Trinity Peninsula. Named by the UK in 1960 for the cloud formations in the area in 1948 when the FIDS surveyed it.

Whited Inlet. 69°50′S, 160°08′E. Ice-filled. Between Northrup Head and Anderson Peninsula, in East Antarctica. Named for Robert J. Whited, USN, who was in Antarctica in the late 1960s.

Whitehall Glacier. 72°43′S, 169°25′E. Flows into Tucker Inlet, between the Daniell Peninsula and the SE part of the Victory Mountains, in Victoria Land. Named by the New Zealanders in 1957–58 because of its proximity to the Admiralty Mountains (the Admiralty office in London is in Whitehall).

Whitehorn, Daniel. Quarter-gunner on the Wilkes Expedition 1838–42. Joined in the USA. Served the cruise.

Whiteout. Also spelled white-out, or white out. A dangerous weather and optical phenomenon caused by low cloud cover and snow crystals, wherein the sky and surface reflect each other, so that a pilot (for example) sees only white, and is disoriented. There are no shadows or contrasts, and the air may be very clear.

Whiteout Nunatak. 77°35'S, 86°24' W. In the northern Sentinel Range.

Mount Whiteside. 67°19'S, 59°29'E. 190 m. On the east side of Fold Island. Discovered in Feb. 1936 by the personnel on the *William Scoresby.*

Whiteside Hill. 65°08'S, 61°38'W. 330 m. An ice-covered hill. At the south side of the mouth of Evans Glacier, on the east coast of Graham Land. Discovered aerially by Wilkins on Dec. 20, 1928. First charted as a point, Whiteside Point, by the FIDS in 1947, and redefined by them in 1955. It is a descriptive name.

Whiteside Point *see* **Whiteside Hill**

Whiteston, Nicholas. Ordinary seaman on the Wilkes Expedition 1838–42. Joined at Rio. Lost in the *Sea Gull* around April 29, 1839.

Whitewhale Bastion. 65°37'S, 62°30' W. An L-shaped mass which rises to nearly 1,200 m. On the Starbuck Glacier, 10 miles from its terminus, on the east side of Graham Land. Because of the white granite walls on its east side, it was named by the UK with the *Moby Dick* connotation in mind.

Whitfield, Thomas. Chief stoker on the *Discovery* during the Royal Society Expedition of 1901–4. He went slightly insane at the end of 1903, after two winters on the continent.

Mount Whiting. 71°40'S, 62°37'W. Pyramidal. Ice-free. It is steep-cliffed on the south side. On the SW side of Rankine Glacier, near the east coast of Palmer Land. Named for Ronald F. Whiting, a geologist here in 1970–71.

Whiting Nunatak *see* **Melfjellet**

Whiting Rocks. 65°15'S, 64°20'W. 3 rocks, ½ mile south of The Barchans, in the Argentine Islands, off the west coast of Graham Land. Named by the UK for Colin S. Whiting, on the *Endurance,* with the Hydrographic Survey Unit here in Feb. 1969.

Whitlock Automatic Weather Station. 76°12'S, 168°42'E. An American AWS on Franklin Island, at an elevation of approximately 825 feet. Began operating on Jan. 23, 1982.

Whitmer Peninsula. 75°50'S, 162°45' E. 7 miles long. 7 miles wide. Ice-capped. Between the Cheetham Ice Tongue and the Harbord Glacier Tongue, on the coast of Victoria Land. Named for R.D. Whitmer, Lt. (jg), USN, at Williams Field, in the winter of 1956, and who came back in 1966 and 1967.

Whitmore Mountains. 82°35'S, 104° 30'W. An isolated group that contains 3 mountains, including Mount Chapman, and a cluster of nunataks, extending over 15 miles. Visited and surveyed by William H. Chapman, cartographer with the Horlick Mountains Traverse Party of 1958–59, and named by him for George D. Whitmore, a SCAR cartographer.

Whitney, Kembal. Ordinary seaman on the Wilkes Expedition 1838–42. Joined in the USA. Served the cruise.

Whitney Glacier. 85°39'S, 160°W. 6 miles long. Flows from Mount Ellsworth into the Amundsen Glacier, just south of Robinson Bluff, in the Queen Maud Mountains. Discovered during Byrd's 1928–30 expedition, and later named for Raymond L. Whitney, meteorologist at South Pole Station in 1961.

Whitney Island. 69°40'S, 68°31'W. Off the west coast of the Antarctic Peninsula.

Whitney Peak. 76°26'S, 126°03'W. 3,005 m. 3 miles NW of Mount Hampton, in the Executive Committee Range of Marie Byrd Land. Lichens are found here. Named for Capt. Herbert Whitney, Seabee chief in the Antarctic during the IGY (1957–58).

Whitney Point. 66°15'S, 110°31'E. At the north side of the entrance to Powell Cove, on Clark Peninsula, on the east side of the Windmill Islands. At first (1946–47) it was thought to be a small island, and in 1957 was surveyed from the ground by Carl Eklund. Named for I.A. Whitney, a member of Operation Highjump, 1946–47.

Cape Whitson. 60°46'S, 44°32'W. Between Methuen and Aitken Coves on the south coast of Laurie Island, in the South Orkneys. Bruce charted it in 1903, and named it for Thomas B. Whitson, secretary of the expedition.

Whitten, R. First mate on the *Eagle,* 1944–45.

Whitten Peak. 63°25'S, 57°04'W. 445 m. Pyramidal. Forms the NE end of Blade Ridge, at the west side of the head of Hope Bay, at the top of the Antarctic Peninsula. Discovered during Nordenskjöld's expedition of 1901–4, and later named by the FIDS for R. Whitten.

Whittle, J.S. Assistant surgeon on the Wilkes Expedition 1838–42. He did a few tours on the *Vincennes,* and transferred to the *Sea Gull.* He later joined the *Peacock* at Honolulu. He took part in Johnson's voyage to Deception Island in March 1839.

Whittle Glacier. 66°22'S, 114°13'E. A short channel glacier which flows into Colvocoresses Bay, and terminates in the Whittle Glacier Tongue, 6 miles NW of Williamson Glacier. Named for J.S. Whittle.

Whittle Glacier Tongue. 66°20'S, 114°24'E. The terminus of the Whittle Glacier, extending into Colvocoresses Bay. Named in association with the glacier.

Whittle Peninsula. 63°49'S, 59°48'W. On the NW coast of Graham Land, just SE of Hoseason Island.

Whitworth Ridge. 70°24'S, 66°08'E. 2 miles NE of Mount Leckie, in the Porthos Range of the Prince Charles Mountains. Named by the Australians for R. Whitworth, geophysicist at Wilkes Station in 1963.

Whymper Spur. 80°25'S, 21°29'W. In the Shackleton Range.

Widden, Mark. Landsman on the Wilkes Expedition 1838–42. Joined in the USA. Returned in the *Relief* in 1839.

Point Widdows. 67°42'S, 45°25'E. At the west side of the entrance to Freeth Bay, on the coast of Enderby Land. Named by the Australians for E.I. Widdows, meteorologist at Mawson Station in 1959.

Widdows, Edward. Seaman on the Wilkes Expedition 1838–42. Joined in the USA. Discharged at Oahu, Oct. 31, 1840.

Widdowson Glacier. 66°43'S, 65°46'W. Flows into Darbel Bay, between the Drummond and McCance Glaciers, on the west coast of Graham Land. Named by the UK for Elsie M. Widdowson, authority on expedition food requirements.

Wideopen Islands. 63°S, 55°49'W. Also called Islotes Furque, Islotes Libertad, Islotes Morales. Exposed, isolated, wide open islands 7 miles to the north of Joinville Island's Boreal Point. They consist of 3 little islands and some rocks.

Mount Widerøe. 72°08'S, 23°30'E. 3,180 m. Between Mount Walnum and Mount Nils Larsen in the Sør Rondane Mountains. Photographed by the LCE 1936–37, and named 10 years later by Norwegian cartographers for Viggo Widerøe.

Widerøe, Viggo. Airplane pilot on the LCE 1936–37.

Widich Nunatak. 85°20'S, 121°25'W. 3½ miles east of Spencer Nunatak, between the Wisconsin Range and the Long Hills, in the Horlick Mountains. Named for George Widich, at Byrd Station in 1960.

Widmark Ice Piedmont. 66°17'S, 65°30'W. Between Holtedahl and Darbel Bays, on the west coast of Graham Land. Named by the UK in 1959 for Eric J. Widmark, Swedish authority on snowblindness.

Widowmaker Pass. 74°55'S, 162°20'E. A dangerous, heavily-crevassed pass leading from the Larson Glacier to the

Reeves Glacier, between Mounts Janet-schek and Gerlache, in Victoria Land. Aptly named by the New Zealanders in 1962–63.

Wiegand, Alberto Karl. Leader of the Chilean Antarctic Expedition of 1952–53. His ships were the *Iquique*, the *Maipo*, the *Lientur*, and the *Leucotón*.

Wiencke, Carl. More correctly Auguste-Karl Wiencke. Norwegian sailor drowned on Jan. 22, 1898, just south of the South Shetlands, during the *Belgica* expedition of 1897–99, led by de Gerlache.

Wiencke Island. 64°45′S, 63°30′W. 16 miles long. From 2 to 5 miles wide. In the Gerlache Strait, between Anvers Island and the west coast of Graham Land. It is part of the Palmer Archipelago. Discovered in 1898 by de Gerlache, and named by him for Carl Wiencke.

Wiener, Murray A. Auroral observer at West Base during the USAS 1939–41. He was a US Army captain and observer with Air Sea Rescue on the *Mount Olympus* during Operation Highjump, 1946–47.

Wiener Peaks. 76°49′S, 144°26′W. A group of nunataks 5 miles NE of Mount Passel, in the Ford Ranges of Marie Byrd Land. Discovered aerially by members of West Base during the USAS 1939–41, and named for Murray A. Wiener.

Wiens Peak. 83°59′S, 56°20′W. At the east end of Elliott Ridge, in the southern part of the Neptune Range, in the Pensacola Mountains. Named for Rudolph H. Wiens, scientist at Ellsworth Station in 1962.

Wiest Bluff. 85°22′S, 176°20′W. 2,160 m. Just north of the confluence of the Shackleton and Zaneveld Glaciers. It marks the western extremity of the Cumulus Hills. Named for William G. Wiest, scientist at Amundsen-Scott South Pole Station in 1964.

Wigg Islands. 67°32′S, 62°34′E. Six small islands 6 miles NW of the Flat Islands, in Holme Bay. Photographed by the LCE 1936–37, and later named Mesteinene (the middle stones) by the Norwegians. Renamed by the Australians for Dr. D.R. Wiggs, medical officer at Mawson Station in 1962.

Wiggans Hills. 80°11′S, 27°03′W. In the Shackleton Range.

Wiggins Glacier. 65°14′S, 64°03′W. 10 miles long. Flows from the Bruce Plateau to the west coast of Graham Land, just south of Blanchard Ridge. Charted by Charcot in 1908–10, and named Glacier du Milieu (middle glacier) by him. Renamed by the UK in 1959 for W.D.C. Wiggins, deputy director of Overseas Surveys.

Wignall Nunataks. 70°10′S, 64°23′E. Two snow-covered nunataks, 2 miles NW of Mount Starlight, in the Athos Range of the Prince Charles Mountains. Named by the Australians for R. Wignall, weather observer at Davis Station in 1964.

Wignall Peak. 70°24′S, 66°24′E. Just west of Mount McCarthy, in the eastern part of the Porthos Range of the Prince Charles Mountains. Named by the Australians for R. Wignall (*see* **Wignall Nunataks**).

Mount Wilbanks. 75°S, 112°52′W. Partly snow-covered, with a bare rock east face. It forms the eastern end of the Kohler Range, in Marie Byrd Land. Named for John R. Wilbanks, geologist here in 1966–67.

Wilber, Jedediah. Ordinary seaman on the Wilkes Expedition 1838–42. Joined at Callao. Served the cruise.

Mount Wilbur. 86°58′S, 152°37′W. 2 miles east of Mount Weaver, at the head of the Robert Scott Glacier, in the Queen Maud Mountains. Discovered in Dec. 1934 by Quin Blackburn, during Byrd's 1933–35 expedition, and named by Byrd for the Hon. Curtis D. Wilbur, secretary of the navy, 1925–29.

Mount Wilbye. 69°25′S, 71°37′W. 2,000 m. In the Lassus Mountains, in the northern part of Alexander Island.

Named by the UK in 1960 for John Wilbye, the composer.

Mount Wilcox. 67°58'S, 66°55'W. On the SE corner of Square Bay, 8 miles east of Camp Point, on the west coast of Graham Land. Discovered by Charcot in 1909, and surveyed by the BGLE in 1936. Col. Lawrence Martin named it for Phineas Wilcox.

Wilcox, Capt. Commander of the *United States* in the South Shetlands, 1853–54.

Wilcox, Phineas. First mate on the *Hero*, 1821–22, and on the *Penguin*, 1829–31.

¹**Cape Wild** *see* **Point Wild**

²**Cape Wild.** 68°20'S, 149°05'E. On the eastern end of the Organ Pipe Cliffs, in the area of Cape Freshfield. This is probably the same Point Emmons that Wilkes discovered on Jan. 19, 1840, and named for George Emmons. During the AAE 1911–14 Mawson accurately positioned it and renamed it for Frank Wild.

¹**Mount Wild.** 64°12'S, 58°53'W. A rock ridge with several summits, the highest being 945 m. At the north side of the mouth of Sjögren Glacier, on the east coast of Trinity Peninsula. Charted by the FIDS in 1945, and named by them for Frank Wild.

²**Mount Wild.** 84°48'S, 162°40'E. 2½ miles west of Mount Augusta, at the extreme south of the Queen Alexandra Range. Discovered by Shackleton in 1907–9, and thought by him to be a range. He named it Wild Range, for Frank Wild. The name Wild Mountains became attached to it too, until it was defined as a single mountain.

Point Wild. 61°06'S, 54°52'W. The point, discovered by Frank Wild, to which, on April 17, 1916, the Shackleton party relocated from Cape Valentine, 7 miles away, on the north coast of Elephant Island, in the South Shetlands, during the disastrous British Imperial Transantarctic Expedition of 1914–17. Shackleton called this feature Cape Wild originally, and it was later redefined.

Wild, Ernest. Brother of Frank Wild. He was in charge of stores and dogs on the British Imperial Transantarctic Expedition of 1914–17. On the other side of the continent from his brother, Ernest was one of the depot layers from the *Aurora* at Ross Island, one of the three to survive the big push south under Mackintosh. He was killed while minesweeping the Mediterranean in 1917.

Wild, Frank. b. 1874, Yorkshire. d. 1930, of pneumonia, in the Transvaal. Son of a preacher, and brother of Ernest Wild, he was in the Merchant Navy at 16, and in 1900 in the RN as a gunner. He became the most experienced of the early Antarctic explorers, with 5 times in the South and a total of 10 years. His first outing was as an able seaman on the Royal Society Expedition of 1901–4, under Scott. He was with Shackleton on the British Antarctic Expedition of 1907–9, and on that expedition was one of the 4 who got to within 97 miles of the Pole. In 1911–14 he was on the AAE 1911–14, under Mawson, and led the Western Base Party of the expedition. He was second-in-command of the British Imperial Transantarctic Expedition of 1914–17, sailing with Shackleton again, this time on the *Endurance*. When Shackles left for South Georgia in the longboat, Wild was in charge of the 22 men on Elephant Island. He was on the *Quest* with Shackleton again, in 1921–22, and when the "Boss" died, Wild took over the expedition, and finished it. During the 1920s he lived in Africa, failed in business, became a drunkard, and ended his life rather ignominiously. He was, of course, intensely loyal to Shackleton, but in his diary of 1908 he said, "Following Shackleton to the Pole is like following an old woman."

Wild, J.J. Official artist, and Wyville Thomson's secretary, on the *Challenger* expedition of 1872–76.

Wild Icefalls. 84°50'S, 162°20'E. At the head of the Beardmore Glacier, between Mount Wild and Mount Buckley.

Named by the New Zealanders in 1961–62 for the nearby mountain.

Wild Mountains *see* **Mount Wild**

Wild Range *see* **Mount Wild**

Wild Spur. 64°42′S, 62°32′W. Runs from Pulfrich Peak to the west side of Arctowski Peninsula, on the west coast of Graham Land. Named by the UK in 1960 for Heinrich Wild, the Swiss instrument designer.

Wilds Nunatak. 73°01′S, 160°13′E. 2 miles west of the south end of Frontier Mountain, in Victoria Land. Named for Ronald F. Wilds, member of VX-6 in 1966.

Wilhelm Archipelago. 65°08′S, 64°20′W. Scores of islands between the Bismarck Strait and Lumus Rock, off the west coast of Graham Land. Discovered by Dallmann in 1873–74, and named by him for the Kaiser, Wilhelm I. In 1897–99 de Gerlache renamed them Îles Dannebrog, but Dallmann's original naming stuck (*see also* **Dannebrog Islands**). Booth Island and Hovgaard Island are the largest in the group, and others include the Argentine Islands, the Dannebrog Islands, the Anagram Islands, the Yalour Islands, the Cruls Islands, the Myriad Islands, the Betbeder Islands, the Roca Islands, the Stray Islands, the Vedel Islands, the Wauwermans Islands, Barbière Island, Bazzano Island, Mazzeo Island, Lisboa Island, Miller Island, Pléneau Island, Splitwind Island, Somerville Island, Indicator Island, Quintana Island, Detour Island, Charlat Island, Boudet Island.

Wilhelm Barrier *see* **Filchner Ice Shelf**

Wilhelm Carlson Island *see* **Carlson Island**

Mount Wilhelm Christophersen. 85°32′S, 167°20′W. Also called Mount Christophersen. An ice-covered knob, 3 miles west of Mount Engelstad, overlooking the south side of the head of the Axel Heiberg Glacier. Discovered in 1911 by Amundsen, and named by him for Wilhelm Christophersen, a Norwegian diplomat in Buenos Aires.

Wilhelm Glacier. 72°46′S, 166°37′E. 2 miles north of Olson Glacier, draining the north part of the western slopes of Malta Plateau, and flowing into Seafarer Glacier in Victoria Land. Named for Robert C. Wilhelm, in Antarctica in 1967–68.

Wilhelm Ice Barrier *see* **Filchner Ice Shelf**

Wilhelm Shelf Ice *see* **Filchner Ice Shelf**

Wilhelm II Coast *see* **Wilhelm II Land**

Wilhelm II Land. 67°S, 90°E. Between Cape Penck (at 87°43′E) and Cape Filchner (at 91°54′E), on the coast of East Antarctica. Discovered by von Drygalski in 1901–2 and named Kaiser Wilhelm II Land. This name became translated as King Wilhelm II Land, and finally to Wilhelm II Land. It has also been seen as King Wilhelm II Coast, and Wilhelm II Coast.

Wilhelmina Bay. 64°40′S, 62°20′W. 15 miles wide. Between Reclus Peninsula and Cape Anna, of the Danco Coast of the western part of Graham Land. Discovered by de Gerlache in 1897–99, and named for the Queen of the Netherlands.

The *Wilhoite*. A US radar picket escort destroyer operating out of Dunedin, NZ, in the early 1960s. It joined Task Force 43 on Sept. 8, 1960, and maintained an ocean station in support of aircraft flights between NZ and Antarctica for Operation Deep Freeze 61. Commanded that year by Lt. Cdr. Charles H. Willis, USN.

Wilhoite Nunataks. 81°40′S, 154°58′E. 12 miles SW of the All-Blacks Nunataks. Named for the *Wilhoite*.

Wilkes, Charles. b. April 3, 1798, NY. d. Feb. 7, 1877, Washington, DC. He entered the US Navy at 18 as a midshipman. In 1828, as a lieutenant, he was picked as astronomer for the US Government Expedition to Antarctica, which never happened. Wilkes had bought expensive equipment for this expedition, and was not refunded by the new Andrew Jackson administration which canceled the expedition. Ten years later, still a lieutenant, he was given command of the United States Exploring Expedition, on March 20, 1838, but only after a series of officers had resigned or turned the position down. It was the first American government expedition to include Antarctica, and had been authorized by Congress in 1836, and had been approved by President Jackson. Wilkes and Jeremiah N. Reynolds were the main organizers of the expedition, which left the USA on Aug. 18, 1838, in search of, among other things, the South Magnetic Pole. There were 6 ships, 82 officers, 342 sailors, and 9 naturalists, scientists, and artists (only one of this group of 9, Titian Ramsay Peale, made it to Antarctic waters). The expedition arrived at Madeira on Sept. 16, 1838, and left there on Sept. 25, 1838, bound for Cape Verde, which it reached on Oct. 7, 1838. From Nov. 23, 1838, to Jan. 6, 1839, the squadron was in Rio, and from Jan. 25 to Feb. 3, 1839, in Rio Negro. On Feb. 18, 1839, it arrived at its furthest south on the South American coast, Orange Harbor at Tierra del Fuego. Here Wilkes split the expedition into three parts. The *Porpoise* (commanded by Cadwalader Ringgold) and the *Sea Gull* (commanded by Robert E. Johnson as from Tierra del Fuego, from which port the expedition left on Feb. 25, 1839) were to push as far south as possible. The *Peacock* (commanded by William L. Hudson) and the *Flying Fish* (which, until Tierra del Fuego, had been commanded by Samuel R. Knox, and from that point south by William A. Walker) to go SW to try to better Cook's old southing record of 71° 10'S. The third party, the *Vincennes* (Wilkes' flagship, under his own command) and the *Relief* (commanded on the way to Tierra del Fuego by Robert E. Johnson, and from that point by James Reid) to do survey work around Tierra del

Fuego. Wilkes himself transferred to the *Porpoise*. On March 1, 1839, the fleet arrived in the South Shetlands, and on March 5, 1839, Wilkes ordered the *Porpoise* and the *Sea Gull* out due to bad conditions. They made their way back to Tierra del Fuego for the winter of 1839. The *Flying Fish* and the *Peacock* were still in Antarctica, however. They had sailed to the north of Thurston Island. The *Flying Fish* had lost contact for a month, getting as far south as 70° 04'S before sighting the *Peacock* again on March 25, 1839. They then both headed back to their Tierra del Fuego base on March 30, 1839. The *Relief* was sent home to the USA for being too slow, and the remaining 5 vessels left Tierra del Fuego on April 17, 1839, and sailed around the Horn to Valparaiso, reaching there on May 15, 1839. On this stretch of the voyage, the *Sea Gull* was lost at sea on or around April 29, 1839, off the Chile coast. The squadron left Valparaiso on June 6, 1839, and then spent between June 30 and July 13, 1839, in Callao, Peru. The fleet of 4 ships then crossed the Pacific, being moored at Tahiti from Sept. 10 to Sept. 29, 1839, and at Upolu, Samoa, from Oct. 25 to Nov. 10, 1839. They reached Sydney on Nov. 29, 1839. They left there on Dec. 26, 1839, bound for Antarctica. They arrived in Antarctic waters again on Jan. 10, 1840, and on Jan. 11, 1840, the *Vincennes* and the *Porpoise* reached the ice barrier at 64° 11'S, 164° 30'E, and turned westward. On Jan. 16, 1840, the *Peacock* joined them, and on Jan. 21, 1840, the *Flying Fish* did too, the latter shortly after having to return to NZ. Land was sighted on Jan. 16, 1840, and confirmed on Jan. 19, 1840. That day a party landed on an offshore island. On Jan. 21, 1840, they captured an emperor penguin. On Jan. 24, 1840, the *Peacock* was damaged by icebergs and had to leave for Sydney the following day. On Jan. 30, 1840, came the interesting meeting between the *Porpoise* and the two French ships of Dumont d'Urville's expedition (*see* **International cooperation**). The only two vessels of

Wilkes' fleet now left in Antarctic waters, the *Vincennes* and the *Porpoise,* cruised westward on their own, and apart from each other. The *Porpoise* got to 100° E on Feb. 14, 1840, and then returned to NZ to meet up with the *Flying Fish* at their rendezvous there. Wilkes, on the *Vincennes,* let some of his men land on an iceberg, and on Feb. 21, 1840, he discovered the Shackleton Ice Shelf (as it became known later). He left there for Sydney, arriving on March 11, 1840, and leaving on March 19. From March 29 to April 6, 1840, the fleet was in New Zealand, and on May 16, 1840, they landed at Malolo, one of the Pacific islands. On July 24, 1840, a battle took place between Wilkes' men and the natives here. 6 sailors were killed. They left here on Aug. 11, 1840, and from Sept. 24, 1840, to Dec. 3, 1840, the fleet was in Oahu. From Dec. 3, 1840, to March 19, 1841, they explored the Hawaiian Islands, and from March 19 to April 5, 1841, were back in Oahu. They made various stops in the USA, and on Nov. 16, 1841, were back in the islands, at Maui. From Nov. 17 to Nov. 27, 1841, they were in Oahu, and from Jan. 12 to Jan. 21, 1842, were in Manila, in the Philippines. From Feb. 19 to Feb. 26, 1842, the squadron was in Singapore, where the *Flying Fish* was sold. From April 14 to April 17, 1842, they were in Cape Town, and from May 1 to May 3, 1842, in Saint Helena. The *Vincennes, Peacock,* and *Porpoise* got back to the USA in June 1842. They had accomplished a lot. They had cruised the Antarctic coast, surveying 1,600 miles of the coastline from the Balleny Islands to the Shackleton Ice Shelf, and declared Antarctica to be a continent. The inaccuracy of his maps, as checked by Ross, led to Wilkes' court martial, but as it happens the bulk of his charts were correct, only off in places because of mirages. A tyrant, Wilkes was subject to deserting crews, and on the 1838–42 expedition 62 men were discharged as unsuitable, 42 deserted, and 15 died. The squadron was in Antarctic waters for a total of no more

than 69 days. Wilkes built the first observatory in the USA, and the data and samples he brought back from Antarctica inspired the founding of the Smithsonian Institution. During the U.S. Civil War (1861–65) Wilkes commanded the James River Fleet, and was made rear-admiral before he died. There are too many participants to list here, although each man who made Antarctic waters is listed individually. Below are the officers and other main functionaries on the expedition: Wilkes, Craven, Carr, Johnson, Alden, Maury, North, Gilchrist, R.R. Waldron, J.L. Elliott, Fox, Whittle, Totten, Reynolds, May, Sandford, Clark, Samuel Elliott, William Smith, Bright, Leighton, Hawkins, Vanderford, R.P. Robinson, Williamson, William L. Hudson, Lee, Walker, Emmons, Perry, Budd, Sickles, Holmes, Lewis, Gansevoort, Eld, Harrison, Henry, John D. Anderson, Dibble, J.D. Freeman, Insley, Peale, Long, Pinckney, Case, Underwood, Sinclair, Palmer, Davis, Blair, Howison, Thomas Lewis, Ringgold, Claiborne, Hartsene, Dale, Baldwin, Guillou, Blunt, Colvocoresses, T.W. Waldron, Chick, Joines, Morse, Frost, Reid, Bacon, Percival, Knox, Hammersly, Clemson, Cesney, De Haven, Power, Allshouse, Allman, Charles Adams, Buckett, John Black, Bateman, James Brown, Bernard, Samuel Brown, Beals, Bostwick, Robert Brown, Brisco, Charles Berry, David Burns, Burke, Babb, Butter, Blodget, Bolin, Cummings, Colson, Clute, Cann, Joseph Clark, Campbell, Cavenaugh, Cole, Clifford, Levin Clark, Crosby, Carter, John Cook, Chapman, Doughty, Demock, James Dunn, Dobleman, Disbrow, Dunbar, Days, Disney, Dewees, Dinsman, Dalton, Dickenson, Evans, Eastman, Elliotte, Edward Fox, Fritz, Fosdick, French, Foreman, Gross, Gaylard, Gibson, James Green, Greenfield, Daniel Green, Thomas Green, Goodhue, Griffith Griffith, Gallagher, Gorden, Ezra Green, John Green, Glover, Grey, Harden, Harmon, Hyde, Herron, Henderson, Heyer, Hernandez,

Husted, Hobsen, Harman, Hughes, Hefferman, Head, Hanbury, Holt, Hunt, Holden, Harris, Hammond, Jarrett, Joseph A. Jacquinot, Knight, Kirby, Kellum, Linthicum, Littleyear, Lloyd, Leavett, Lowell, Montserat, McKeen, Mandon, James McKenzie, More, Migley, Meiney, Mitchell, March, Moody, Nowland, Nebhut, Neill, Ogle, Park, Piner, Parker, Pottle, Pensyl, Pully, Polnell, Reeves, Robbin, Rodgers, Owen Roberts, Russel, Riley, Richmond, John D. Richardson, Edgar A. Richardson, William J. Smith, Southworth, Small, Stearns, Steward, Sudor, Salsbury, Thomas Scott, De Sauls, Somerndyke, Sharrock, Spears, Thomas Sandford, John Steward, Stretch, David M. Smith, Schenck, Sares, Taylor, Thomas, Thompson, Turner, Samuel Williams, Wright, Walfe, Ward, Wells, George Williams, White, Walmsley, Whitehorn, Francis Williams.

Wilkes Coast. 66°30′S, 132°E. Between Cape Morse (at 130°10′E) and Pourquoi Pas Point (at 136°11′E), or between the Banzare Coast and Adélie Land, on the coast of East Antarctica, at the extreme eastern edge of Wilkes Land. Discovered by Dumont d'Urville in Jan. 1840, and named Clarie Land by him for Jacquinot's wife, Clarie. This name changed to Clarie Coast, and later (although not everywhere accepted as such) Wilkes Coast, for Charles Wilkes.

Wilkes Land. 69°S, 120°E. Extends from Cape Hordern (at 100°31′E) to Point Alden (at 142°02′E), or between Queen Mary Land and George V Land. It fronts the Indian Ocean, on the coast of East Antarctica. Named for Charles Wilkes.

Wilkes Station. 66°15′S, 110°31′E. A scientific station on Vincennes Bay. Established on Jan. 16, 1957, and opened on Feb. 16, 1957, as the most northerly of all the US IGY stations, lying outside the Antarctic Circle, on Clark Peninsula. Named for Charles Wilkes, it had the most comprehensive scientific activity

outside of Little America. Its first wintering-over party (1957) consisted of 27 men. Lt. (jg) Donald R. Burnett, USNR, was military leader until Jan. 30, 1958, when Lt. R.S. Sparks, USN, took over. Carl R. Eklund was scientific leader until Jan. 30, 1958, when he handed over to Dr. Willis L. Tressler. The other members that winter were Richard L. "Dick" Cameron—glaciologist; Rudolph A. "Rudi" Honkala—meteorologist; Olav H. Loken and John R.L. Molhom—glaciologists; Gilbert Dewart—seismologist; Dick Berkley—geophysicist; Garth A. Stonehocker—chief ionosphere physicist; Bob L. Long, Jr.—ionosphere physicist; Ralph Glasgal—auroral physicist; Lt. Sheldon W. Grinnell, USNR—medical officer; Ken J. Hailstorm, USN—radioman; Billie R. Lilienthal, USN—aerologist; J.T. Powell and P.A. Wyche—both USN aerographers; Dave Daniel, USN—the Texan cook; and the following USN personnel—Duane J. Wonsey, Ed A. "Frenchy" Bousquet, Carl T. Bailey, Sidney E. Green, Fred E. Charlton, Bob McIntyre, Acy H. Patterson, Don L. Bradford, and Paul F. Noonan, the photographer. After the IGY, Feb. 1959, the USA transferred Wilkes Station to the Australians, and John Dingle was leader for that winter (1959). The US representative there that winter was Herbert Hansen. The station was replaced by Casey Station in 1969, because Wilkes was being buried by snow.

Wilkes Subglacial Basin. 75°05′S, 130° E. A subsurface feature south of George V Land, and west of the Prince Albert Mountains, in East Antarctica. Delineated roughly by seismological parties from the USA, in 1958–60, and named for Charles Wilkes in 1961.

Cape Wilkins. 67°15′S, 59°18′E. At the northern tip of Fold Island, forming the east side of the entrance to Stefansson Bay. Discovered on Feb. 18, 1931, by the BANZARE. At first Mawson called it Cape Hearst, for newspaper magnate William Randolph Hearst, who bought the rights to the BANZARE story.

Mawson later changed it to honor Sir Hubert Wilkins.

Wilkins, Sir Hubert. b. Oct. 31, 1888, Mount Bryan East, South Australia. d. Dec. 1, 1958, Framingham, Mass., USA. George Hubert Wilkins. Australian aviator and adventurer, son of a South Australian farmer. His first foray into Antarctica was as one of the four members of the British Imperial Expedition of 1920–22, which failed to cross too-rugged Graham Land from west to east. Embarrassed, he quit that expedition, and joined Shackleton's last expedition, on the *Quest*, in 1921–22, as photographer/ornithologist. In 1928–30 he led his first Antarctic expedition, the Wilkins-Hearst expedition, a trip financed by newspaper magnate William Randolph Hearst, and sponsored by the American Geographical Society. He took two Lockheed Vega monoplanes and an Austin motor car, and the expedition left New York on Sept. 22, 1928, the same year Wilkins had been knighted for his services to science and exploration. The party, which included two pilots, Cheesman and Eielson, as well as an engineer and a radio operator, boarded their expedition ship, the *Hektoria*, at Montevideo. On Nov. 6, 1928, they landed at Deception Island, in the South Shetlands. On Nov. 16, 1928, Eielson and Wilkins made the first Antarctic flight in an airplane. On Nov. 26, 1928, both planes took off in an unsuccessful search for a better base. On Dec. 20, 1928, Eielson and Wilkins set off again on Antarctica's first air expedition, from Deception Island going SW over Graham Land and back. They flew 1,300 miles in 11 hours, and discovered the Crane Channel, the Lockheed Mountains, and the Stefansson Strait, and incorrectly charted much of Graham Land. On Jan. 10, 1929, Wilkins and Eielson flew 500 miles over Graham Land before storing the planes for the winter. Wilkins returned to New York. In Sept. 1929 he was back at Deception Island. He made a few local flights, and then took one of his planes south on the *William Scoresby*, to look

for a better landing strip. The ship sailed from Deception Island on Dec. 12, 1929, and returned as far as Port Lockroy on Dec. 18, 1929. On a local flight Wilkins spotted Beascochea Bay, and they sailed there. But the ice was melting (it was 54° F) and he could only make an abortive flight over Charcot Land on Dec. 27, 1929. On Dec. 29, 1929, he and Cheesman flew over Charcot Land again, this time proving it to be an island (Charcot Island), and claiming it for Britain. On Jan. 5, 1930, the *William Scoresby* left Port Lockroy for Deception Island, and then on to the Falkland Islands to refuel, arriving back at Deception Island on Jan. 25, 1930. All this time Wilkins was making local flights, his last one being on Feb. 1, 1930. He mapped altogether 80,000 square miles of new territory, was the first leader to discover a new territory from an airplane, and incorrectly believed the Antarctic Peninsula (as it later became known) to be cut off from the rest of the continent. In the 1930s Wilkins was technical adviser/manager of Ellsworth's flights (*see* **Ellsworth, Lincoln**) from the *Wyatt Earp*, providing ship-base support for the American flier. Sir Hubert's ashes were scattered over the North Pole.

Wilkins Coast. 69°40'S, 63°W. Between Cape Agassiz and Cape Boggs, or between the Bowman Coast and the Black Coast, on the east coast of the Antarctic Peninsula. Named for Sir Hubert Wilkins.

Wilkins Ice Shelf. 70°15'S, 73°W. 80 miles long. 60 miles wide. Rectangular. Occupies the central part of Wilkins Sound (hence the name given by the UK in 1971).

Wilkins Island *see* **Hearst Island**

Wilkins Mountains. 75°32'S, 66°30' W. 20 miles in extent. 25 miles SE of the Sweeney Mountains, on the Orville Coast of eastern Ellsworth Land, at the very south of Palmer Land. Discovered by the RARE 1947–48, and named by Ronne for Sir Hubert Wilkins.

Wilkins Nunatak. 75°40'S, 139°55'W. The northernmost of 3 nunataks, 6 miles

SW of the Ickes Mountains, on the coast of Marie Byrd Land. Named for Melvin L. Wilkins, who explored this coast in the *Glacier* in 1961–62.

Wilkins Sound. 70°15′S, 73°W. Also called Wilkins Strait. Between Alexander Island and Charcot Island, off the west coast of Graham Land. Largely occupied by the Wilkins Ice Shelf. Charcot discovered the northern part of it in 1910, and Wilkins spotted it aerially in 1929. Named in 1940 by the USAS for Sir Hubert Wilkins.

Wilkins Strait *see* **Wilkins Sound**

Wilkinson, James. Seaman on the Wilkes Expedition 1838–42. Joined in the USA. Served the cruise.

Wilkinson, John V. RN. Captain of the *Protector,* which plied the waters of the Antarctic Peninsula in the summers of 1955–56 and 1956–57.

Wilkinson Glacier. 66°50′S, 66°20′W. On the south side of Protector Heights, flowing into Lallemand Fjord in Graham Land. Named by the UK for John V. Wilkinson.

Wilkinson Peaks. 66°37′S, 54°15′E. A group in the Napier Mountains, 5 miles SE of Mount Griffiths. Photographed by the LCE 1936–37, and later named by Norwegian cartographers as Langnabbane (the long peaks). Visited in 1961 by an ANARE sledge party, and renamed by the Australians for B.G. Wilkinson, at Mawson Station in 1961.

Will Hays Mountains *see* **Hays Mountains**

Willcox, Hilton L. Medical officer on the *City of New York* during Byrd's 1928–30 expedition.

Cape Willems. 64°57′S, 63°16′W. Forms the north side of the entrance to Flandres Bay, on the west coast of Graham Land. De Gerlache charted it in 1897–99, and named it Cap Pierre Willems, for a gentleman of that name. The name of the feature was later abbreviated.

Willett Cove. 72°19′S, 170°15′E. On the south of Seabee Hook, Cape Hallett.

Surveyed in Jan. 1956 by the *Edisto.* Named for James H. Willett, of the Navy Hydrographic Office.

Willett Range. 77°18′S, 160°25′E. Runs from Mistake Peak to the Mackay Glacier, for 20 miles, in Victoria Land. Named by the New Zealanders on the BCTAE 1957–58 for R.W. Willett, director of the NZ Geological Survey.

Willey Glacier. 70°25′S, 67°50′W. Heavily crevassed. North of Creswick Peaks, in Palmer Land. It flows from Creswick Gap into George VI Sound. Named by the UK for Laurence E. Willey, geologist at Fossil Bluff Station in the 1966–69 period, and at Base E (on Stonington Island) in 1973.

Willey Point. 84°37′S, 165°45′E. On the west side of the Beardmore Glacier, marking the southern side of the mouth of the Berwick Glacier, in the Queen Maud Mountains. Named for Francis J. Willey, III, meteorologist at Hallett Station in 1963.

Monte William *see* **Mount Banck**

Mount William. 64°47′S, 63°41′W. Also called Monte Capitán Mendioroz. 1,600 m. Snow-covered. 4 miles NNE of Cape Lancaster, the southern extremity of Anvers Island. Discovered by Biscoe on Feb. 21, 1832, and named by him for the new king, William IV.

The *William and Nancy.* 100-ton sealing schooner, 64 feet long, built in Bath, Conn., in 1810 as a whaling brig, but converted to a 2-masted schooner and registered in Nantucket on March 14, 1815. Owned by Thomas V. McClure, it was reregistered on June 1, 1819. It left the USA for the South Shetlands during the 1820–21 season, in company with the *Harmony.* Under the command of Tristan Folger, it arrived late in the islands, and did not have much luck as far as seals went. The vessel was based at Harmony Cove, Nelson Island, for most of its stay in the South Shetlands. On April 1, 1821, back in the USA, Ferdinand Gardner took over as captain.

William Bay *see* **Börgen Bay**

Mount William Block *see* **Block Peak**

Cape William Bruce *see* **Bruce Point**

Cape William Henry May *see* **Cape May**

William Glacier. 64°43'S, 63°27'W. Also called Glaciar Tolosa. Flows from the inland highlands of Anvers Island, to the head of Börgen Bay, on the SE coast of the island. Discovered by de Gerlache in 1897–99, and charted by him as simply "un grand glacier." The Discovery Committee named it in 1927.

The *William Horlick*. NR12384. The Curtiss-Wright Condor twin-engine biplane equipped with skis and floats, taken by Byrd on his 1933–35 expedition. It was damaged while loading onto a ship for the return to the USA, and was scrapped in the USA.

The *William Scoresby*. Small, fast, whale-catcher type British research vessel commissioned in 1926. It made 6 cruises in Antarctic waters from 1927 to 1939 for the Discovery Committee. From 1943 to 1945 it was used on Operation Tabarin, and from 1945–46 was a FIDS ship. The expedition leaders were 1927–30, D.D. John; 1930–32, E.R. Gunther; 1934–35, G.W. Rayner; 1935–36, G.W. Rayner; 1936–37, T.J. Hart; 1937–38, G.W. Rayner; 1945–46, A. Taylor. Captains during that time were 1927–28, H. de G. Lamotte; 1928–30, R.L.V. Shannon (it was during Shannon's time as captain that the ship helped out Wilkins during the latter's expedition of 1928–30); 1930–31, J.C.C. Irving; 1931–32, T.A. Jolliffe; 1934–37, C.R.U. Boothby; 1937–38, R.C. Freaker; 1943–46, V.A.J.B. Marchesi.

William Scoresby Archipelago. 67°20'S, 59°45'E. Extends north from the coast just east of William Scoresby Bay, East Antarctica. The main islands in the archipelago are the Klakkane Islands, the Warnock Islands, Couling Island, Sheehan Island, Islay, Bertha Island, Hum Island, Farrington Island. Discovered in

Feb. 1936 by the personnel on the *William Scoresby*.

William Scoresby Bay. 67°24'S, 59°34'E. Also called Innfjorden. 5 miles long. 3½ miles wide. Discovered in Feb. 1936 (*see* **William Scoresby Archipelago** for further details).

The *Williams*. British sealer under the command of William Smith which, while on a trading voyage from Valparaiso to Buenos Aires, discovered the South Shetlands in 1819. Smith returned to Chile, informed the Royal Navy of his find, and had his ship taken over by the RN, who placed Bransfield in command to set out on another voyage to substantiate these findings. Smith acted as pilot. Also on this cruise were midshipmen Thomas Bone and Patrick J. Blake, surgeon Adam Young, and Henry Foster and Poynter. On Jan. 18, 1820, they sighted Cape Shirreff, on Livingston Island, and on Jan. 30, 1820, they sighted the actual continent of Antarctica. Smith captained the vessel again for another voyage to the South Shetlands in 1820–21.

Cape Williams. 70°29'S, 164°05'E. Also called Williams Head. Ice-covered. On the east side of the terminus of the Lillie Glacier, in Oates Land. Discovered in Feb. 1911 by the *Terra Nova* as it explored the coast after dropping Scott off at Ross Island. Named for William Williams.

Mount Williams. 66°48'S, 50°50'E. Between Mount Riiser-Larsen and Mount Soucek, in the NW part of the Tula Mountains of Enderby Land. Named by the Australians for J. Williams, at Wilkes Station in 1959.

Point Williams. 67°49'S, 67°34'E. On the coast of Mac. Robertson Land, at the side of Shallow Bay. Discovered on Feb. 12, 1931, by the BANZARE, and named for A.J. Williams.

Port Williams. Probably a synonym for Yankee Harbor, or part of it, or a larger bay of which Yankee Harbor was a part. Palmer mentions it in his log book of

Nov. 24, 1820. Most probably it was an early name for Yankee Harbor itself, and named for Ephraim Williams. Shortly thereafter it became known as Yankee Harbor.

Williams, Capt. Commander of the *Golden West,* in the South Shetlands in 1873–74, 1874–75, and at the Kerguélen Islands (not in the Antarctic) in 1875–76. This is probably the Capt. Williams who took the *Roman* to the Kerguélens and Heard Island (53°S) in 1871–72, and who, in 1870–71 had been at Heard Island in the *Roman,* and at the Kerguélens in the same ship in 1869–70. Equally it could be the John Williams who commanded the *Golden West* at Bouvetøya (also not in the Antarctic) in 1878.

Williams, A.J. Wireless officer on the *Discovery* during the BANZARE 1929–31.

Williams, Ellis "Taffy." RAF Sgt. and radio operator in the Advance Party of the BCTAE 1955–58, and part of the RAF back-up contingent during the actual crossing of the continent by Fuchs in 1957–58.

Williams, Ephraim. Co-owner of the *Hersilia,* and one of the principal organizers of the Fanning-Pendleton Sealing Expedition of 1820–21, on which he commanded the *Express.* He was one of the owners of the *Penguin,* 1829–31.

Williams, Francis. Bosun's mate on the Wilkes Expedition 1838–42. Joined in the USA. Served the cruise.

Williams, Frederick W. Petty officer, USN. Engineer who died in the Martin Mariner crash on Thurston Island, on Dec. 30, 1946, during Operation Highjump. Actually, he died 2 hours after the crash.

Williams, George. Bosun's mate on the Wilkes Expedition 1838–42. Joined in the USA. Served the cruise.

Williams, Henry C. Landsman on the Wilkes Expedition 1838–42. Joined in the USA. Served the cruise.

Williams, Jack. Ordinary seaman on the Wilkes Expedition 1838–42. Joined in the USA. Served the cruise.

Williams, James. Landsman on the Wilkes Expedition 1838–42. Joined in the USA. Returned in the *Relief* in 1839.

Williams, Martyn. b. 1948, England. Went to Canada in 1969. Led several expeditions up the Vinson Massif, and in 1988–89 led the Mountain Travel expedition to the Pole.

Williams, Michael. Seaman on the Wilkes Expedition 1838–42. Joined in the USA. Served the cruise.

Williams, Philip. Ordinary seaman on the Wilkes Expedition 1838–42. Joined in the USA. Returned in the *Relief* in 1839.

Williams, Richard T. American Seabee tractor driver who drowned off Cape Royds on Jan. 6, 1956, when his Caterpillar D-8 tractor broke through the ice while he was en route to Cape Evans across the sea ice. The tractor weighed more than 30 tons, and plunged through a crack in the ice so quickly that Williams did not stand a chance. Williams Field is named for him.

Williams, Samuel. Gunner's mate on the Wilkes Expedition 1838–42. Joined in the USA. Served the cruise.

Williams, Thomas L. Seaman on the Wilkes Expedition 1838–42. Joined at Upolu. Served the cruise.

Williams, William. Chief engine-room artificer on the *Terra Nova* during Scott's 1910–13 expedition.

Williams Air Operating Facility. In 1956, at the suggestion of Chaplain Darkowski, Admiral Dufek renamed AirOpFac McMurdo in honor of Richard T. Williams. In 1957, a matter of a year later (certainly during the next summer season of 1957–58, Operation Deep Freeze III), he changed it again, to McMurdo Base, but Williams AirOpFac remains the name of the old part of what is now McMurdo Station. It is the nucleus of the station, in the western part of the present site.

Williams Bluff. 70°43'S, 160°14'E. A rock and ice bluff 7 miles east of Keim Peak in the Usarp Mountains, between the Pitzman Glacier and the Lovejoy Glacier. Named for Harry N. Williams of VX-6, in Antarctica in 1960–61, 1961–62, 1962–63.

Williams Cliff. 77°35'S, 166°47'E. On the SW slopes of Mount Erebus, Ross Island. Scott's 1910–13 expedition mapped it as Bold Cliff. The USA renamed it in 1964 for Richard T. Williams.

Williams Field. McMurdo Station's airfield. This is the main airport for Antarctica, and is able to take heavy, wheeled aircraft actually on the sea ice off Ross Island. A large complex, it is moved every so often whenever the snow builds up, or cracks appear in the thick ice, and also because the ice shelf is constantly moving toward the sea at the rate of 6 feet per week. There have been several Williams Fields, and when the second was built they began to enumerate them, for history's sake, as Williams Field I, Williams Field II, etc. Frank Debenham selected the site of the first in 1954–55, and it was built by 100 Seabees in late 1955 about 2½ miles south of what later became known as McMurdo Station, on 30 foot-thick sea ice. The complex was called AirOpFac, which gave its name to the whole base, AirOpFac McMurdo. In 1956–57 it was named Williams Field, for Richard T. Williams, who had died here during Operation Deep Freeze I (1955–56). It soon acquired the nicknames Willy Field or Willy. In 1957–58 the US base at McMurdo was upgraded from an AirOpFac (Air Operating Facility) to an NAF (Naval Air Facility), and Williams Field was expanded. In Oct. 1962 Williams Field II was built on the sea ice directly south of Ross Island. This move was made because of cracking ice underneath the original. In 1963–64 it was decided to create a much more livable atmosphere here, rather than just the temporary Jamesway huts. After all, more than 250 people were working here each summer. The new "comforts of home"

can best be indicated by the cost of the toilet facility—$165,000. Cracking ice led to the construction of Williams Field III during the 1965–66 season, about 3 miles SW of Pram Point. During the 1966–67 season Outer Williams Field was built about 7 miles SE of McMurdo Station, in order to extend operations, but it was closed in 1970–71. Williams Field IV was built in the summers of 1976–77 and 1977–78, about a mile to the east of Willy III. In 1980 the maintenance of the field became the responsibility of ITT/ Antarctic Services, Inc. In 1983–84 Williams Field V was built 3 miles from the site of Willy IV.

Williams Head *see* **Cape Williams**

Williams Hills. 83°42'S, 58°55'W. 10 miles long. South of Childs Glacier, and west of Roderick Valley, in the Neptune Range of the Pensacola Mountains. Named for Paul L. Williams, geologist here in 1963–64.

Williams Island. 71°54'S, 101°26'W. 1 mile long. Ice-covered. Between Cape Petersen and Dyer Point. 2 miles off the north coast of Thurston Island. Named for Frederick W. Williams.

Williams Nunatak. 66°26'S, 110°43'E. Just east of the Windmill Islands, at the SW side of the terminus of the Peterson Glacier. Named for Calvin E. Williams, member of Operation Windmill, 1947–48.

Williams Peak. 77°57'S, 163°58'E. Over 1,400 m. Between the drainage of the Hobbs, Salmon, and Garwood Glaciers in Victoria Land. Named by the VUWAE 1960–61 for Dr. J. Williams, vice chancellor of the university (i.e., the Victoria University of Wellington, New Zealand).

Williams Point. 62°28'S, 60°09'W. The extreme NE point of Livingston Island, in the South Shetlands. Probably named by Smith in 1819, for his ship, the *Williams.*

Williams Ridge. 80°30'S, 29°20'W. 1,060 m. Between the Blaiklock and Stratton Glaciers, 1 mile NW of Honnywill Peak, in the western sector of the Shackleton Range. Named for Sgt. Ellis "Taffy" Williams.

Williams Rocks. 67°26'S, 62°46'E. A group of rocks 9 miles north of the Flat Islands and Holme Bay. Mapped in 1954 by Robert G. Dovers of ANARE, and named by the Australians for J. Williams, at Mawson Station in 1962.

Williamson, John G. Gunner on the *Vincennes* during the Wilkes Expedition 1838–42.

Williamson, Thomas S. Able seaman, RN, on the Royal Society Expedition of 1901–4. He was back again with Scott, on the 1910–13 expedition, this time as a petty officer.

Williamson Bluff. 68°05'S, 65°42'W. Over 1,000 m. Flat-topped. Near the head of Trail Inlet, on the east coast of Graham Land. Named by the UK for William Williamson, glacial mathematician.

Williamson Glacier. 66°40'S, 114°06' E. Flows from Law Dome into Colvocoresses Bay, terminating in the Williamson Glacier Tongue. Named for John G. Williamson.

Williamson Glacier Tongue. 66°29'S, 114°24'E. The terminus of the Williamson Glacier, in Colvocoresses Bay. Named in association with the glacier.

Williamson Head. 69°11'S, 157°57'E. Also called Williamson Point. A headland 6 miles WNW of Drake Head, at Davies Bay, in Oates Land. Discovered from the *Terra Nova* in Feb. 1911, and named for Thomas S. Williamson.

Williamson Point *see* **Williamson Head**

Williamson Ridge. 75°47'S, 116°45' W. 10 miles long. 2 to 5 miles wide. Low, and snow-covered. A western extension of Toney Mountain in Marie Byrd Land. Named for Paul R. Williamson, ionosphere physicist at Byrd Station in 1967–68 and 1969–70.

Williamson Rock. 77°27'S, 169°15'E. A little rock off the NE coast of Ross

Island, between Cape Tennyson and Cape Crozier. It is 4 miles NW of Cape Crozier. Charted by Scott's 1910–13 expedition, and named for Thomas S. Williamson.

Mount Willing. 71°50'S, 66°55'E. 17 miles SW of the Fisher Massif, in the Prince Charles Mountains. Discovered aerially by the ANARE in Nov. 1956. Named by the Australians for Dr. Richard L. Willing, medical officer at Mawson Station in 1957.

Mount Willis. 79°22'S, 159°27'E. 2 miles south of Mount Chalmers, in the southern part of the Conway Range. Named for Lt. Cdr. Charles H. Willis, USN, commander of the *Wilhoite*.

Willis, Thomas. A lieutenant on the *Resolution* with Cook, during the second voyage, 1772–75.

Willis Glacier. 77°16'S, 162°05'E. A valley glacier in the Saint Johns Range of Victoria Land. It flows from Schist Peak along the west side of Mount Harker to the Debenham Glacier. Named and charted by the VUWAE 1959–60, for a geophysicist with the expedition, I.A.G. Willis.

Williwaw Rocks. 63°20'S, 55°01'W. Two small rocks 2 miles south of Moody Point, the eastern end of Joinville Island. Surveyed by the FIDS in 1953. Named for the williwaw winds here.

Willows Nunatak. 74°29'S, 165°17'E. 1 mile inland from the south shore of Wood Bay, on the coast of Victoria Land, between Mount Washington and Mount Melbourne. Named for A.O. Dennis Willows, biologist at McMurdo Station in 1965–66.

Wilma Glacier. 67°12'S, 56°E. The western of two glaciers entering the southern part of Edward VIII Bay. Seen by an ANARE party led by Robert G. Dovers in Nov. 1954. Named by the Australians for Dovers' wife.

The *Wilmington.* US sealer/whaler from Mystic, Conn., which, in 1853–54, in the company of the *Aeronaut* and the

Lion, was in the South Shetlands under the command of Capt. Gilderdale.

Cape Wilson. 82°14'S, 163°48'E. Snow-covered. It forms the SE end of the Nash Range, and marks the northern entrance point to Shackleton Inlet, at the southern edge of the Ross Ice Shelf. Discovered by Scott in 1902, and named for Edward Wilson.

Lake Wilson. 79°49'S, 159°33'E. Ice-covered. On the western edge of the Ross Ice Shelf, 5 miles NE of the summit of Diamond Hill, just north of the terminus of the Darwin Glacier. Named by the New Zealanders in 1962–63 for Prof. A.T. Wilson of the Victoria University of Wellington, an investigator of ice-free lakes in Victoria Land.

Mount Wilson. 68°27'S, 65°34'W. 1,675 m. 7 miles west of Rock Pile Peaks, on the east coast of Graham Land. Charted by the FIDS in 1948, and named by Finn Ronne that year for Maj. Gen. R.C. Wilson, who helped get Air Force equipment for the RARE 1947–48.

Wilson, Edward A. b. July 23, 1872, Cheltenham, Glos. d. ca. March 29, 1912, in Antarctica. Edward Adrian Wilson. British doctor, invertebrate zoologist, artist, and explorer. Known in the Antarctic as "Bill." Son of a doctor, he had tuberculosis in 1898, and later became Scott's best friend. One of the Royal Society Expedition of 1901–4, he, Scott, and Shackleton sledged to a new southing record of 82°16'33"S on Dec. 30, 1902, in an unsuccessful bid for the South Pole. He also failed in his search for emperor penguins' eggs. He refused to go on Shackleton's 1907–9 expedition, but was back with Scott on the *Terra Nova* in 1910–11, as second-in-command and chief of the scientific staff on the 1910–13 expedition. He took part in what Cherry-Garrard called "the worst journey in the world" to Cape Crozier to collect emperor penguins' eggs in the winter of 1911, and barely made it back alive. This journey would have shortened his life considerably, even if he had sur-

vived his next venture, which he did not. This was Scott's trip to the Pole in 1911–12. Like Scott, Bowers, Evans, and Oates, he died on the return journey, after having been one of the first 10 men ever to stand at the South Pole.

Wilson, J. Innes. British geologist who accompanied a whaling fleet to the South Shetlands, Palmer Archipelago, and Trinity Island in 1916–17, to collect geological specimens for the Falkland Islands government.

Wilson, John. Ordinary seaman on the Wilkes Expedition 1838–42. Joined in the USA. Run at California.

Wilson, Ove. Medical officer on the NBSAE 1949–52.

Wilson, Thomas. Sailmaker's mate on the Wilkes Expedition 1838–42. Joined in the USA. Served the cruise.

Wilson, William. Quartermaster on the Wilkes Expedition 1838–42. Joined in the USA. Sent home on the *Relief* in 1839.

Wilson Bluff. 74°20'S, 66°47'E. A large, flat-topped rock outcrop in the form of a mountain. At the south end of the Lambert Glacier, 16 miles WNW of Mount Borland. 5 square miles in area, it has a tail of moraine extending NE for several miles. Visited by an ANARE party under G.A. Knuckey in Oct. 1958. Named by the Australians for H.O. Wilson, RAAF flight lieutenant, pilot at Mawson Station in 1958–59 (*see also* **Wilson Glacier**).

¹**Wilson Glacier** *see* **Breitfuss Glacier**

²**Wilson Glacier.** 66°46'S, 56°25'E. 9 miles long. Flows into the Edward VIII Ice Shelf, just south of Seaton Glacier. Photographed aerially by the ANARE in 1956, and named for Flight Lt. H.O. Wilson, RAAF, pilot at Mawson Station in 1958–59, who was killed in an aircraft accident in Australia in 1959.

Wilson Hills. 69°40'S, 158°30'E. A group of scattered hills, nunataks, and ridges about 70 miles in extent, between the Matusevich and Pryor Glaciers, in Oates Land. Discovered by Pennell in Feb. 1911, and named for Edward Wilson.

Wilson Island. 66°27′S, 110°34′E. Ice-free. Between Browning Peninsula and Bosner Island, in the Windmill Islands. Named by the Australians for W. Stanley Wilson, biologist at Wilkes Station in 1961.

Wilson Mountains. 82°36′S, 52°22′W. In the Pensacola Mountains.

Wilson Nunataks. 80°01′S, 80°38′W. A chain, 8 miles long, between the Douglas Peaks and the head of Hercules Inlet, in the Heritage Range. Named by the University of Minnesota Geological Party here in 1963–64 for CWO Kenneth Wilson, US pilot who helped them in this area.

Wilson Pass. 68°26′S, 65°15′W. A glacier pass at 400 m., between the Bowditch Crests and Rock Pile Peaks, on the east side of the Antarctic Peninsula. Leads from Solberg Inlet to Mobiloil Inlet. Named in the 1970s for Alison Wilson of the Center for Polar Archives.

Wilson Peak. 78°52′S, 84°47′W. 2,400 m. Near the south end of the Sentinel Range, at the east side of the Nimitz Glacier, 15 miles SSE of Mount Craddock. Named for J.H. Wilson, Navy radioman here in 1957–58.

Wilson Piedmont Glacier. 77°15′S, 163°15′E. Also called Great Piedmont Glacier. A large glacier on the east coast of Victoria Land, bordering McMurdo Sound. It extends from Granite Harbor to Marble Point. Discovered by members of Scott's 1901–4 expedition, and named by members of Scott's 1910–13 expedition for Edward Wilson.

Wilson Portal. 84°28′S, 178°54′W. A peak over 1,000 m. Snow-covered except for the steep northern rock face. 2½ miles SE of O'Leary Peak, it overlooks the west side of the mouth (or portal) of the Kosko Glacier. Surveyed by Crary in 1957–58, and named by him for Charles

R. Wilson, scientist in Antarctica, 1958–59.

Wilson Ridge. 72°48′S, 75°05′E. A razorback ridge 6 miles north of Mount Harding, in the Grove Mountains. Named by the Australians for R.R. Wilson, Antarctic cartographer.

Wilson Saddle. 72°13′S, 3°15′W. Between Kjølrabbane Hills and Aurhø Peak, in the SW part of the Ahlmann Ridge of Queen Maud Land. Named Wilsonflya by the Norwegians, for Ove Wilson.

Wilson Stream. 77°17′S, 166°26′E. A meltwater stream which flows from Mount Bird to the south of Alexander Hill, and over steep sea cliffs into Wohlschlag Bay, on Ross Island. Named by the New Zealanders for J. Wilson, mountaineer assistant on the NZ Geological Survey Antarctic Expedition of 1958–59.

Wilsonflya *see* **Wilson Saddle**

Wilton, David W. Scottish naturalist living in Russia. He was turned down by Scott for the Royal Society Expedition of 1901–4, and instead went as zoologist on Bruce's Scottish National Antarctic Expedition of 1902–4.

Wilton Bay. 60°46′S, 44°45′W. Between Cape Davidson and Cape Hartree, on the SW side of Laurie Island, in the South Orkneys. Bruce charted it in 1903, and named it for David W. Wilton.

Wiltshire Rocks. 67°30′S, 63°07′E. 2½ miles ENE of Smith Rocks, off the coast of Mac. Robertson Land. Photographed by the LCE 1936–37, and named Spjotøyskjera. Renamed in 1971 by the Australians for A.C.W. Wiltshire, cook at Mawson Station in 1963.

Cape Wiman. 64°13′S, 56°38′W. Also called Cabo Gorrochátegui. Marks the northern end of Seymour Island. Surveyed by Nordenskjöld's expedition in 1902–3. Named by the UK for C. Wiman who worked on the Seymour Island fossils collected by the Swedish expedition.

Wimple Dome. 63°38'S, 58°51'W. 725 m. An ice-covered hill, 2 miles south of Hanson Hill and 2 miles east of Bone Bay, on the northern side of Trinity Peninsula. Surveyed in 1948 by the FIDS, and aptly named by them for the nuns' headdress.

Wind chill. How cold it actually feels. In other words, the ordinary temperature is not the only factor which determines how cold people feel. The speed of the wind is an important factor too, and must be added to the temperature to get a true idea of what the human skin is experiencing by way of cold. Paul Siple developed a wind chill index as a measure of cold in different wind and temperature conditions.

Windless Bight. 77°42'S, 167°45'E. A Ross Ice Shelf indentation into the south side of Ross Island. Named by Wilson on his journey to Cape Crozier in 1911, because there is no wind here.

Windless Bight Automatic Weather Station. 77°48'S, 167°42'E. An American AWS at Windless Bight, Ross Island, at an elevation of approximately 144 feet.

Windmill Islands. 66°20'S, 110°30'E. A group of rocky islands, 6 miles wide and 17 miles long, running parallel to the Budd Coast, in Vincennes Bay, immediately to the north of Vanderford Glacier. They include Ardery Island, Austral Island, Allison Island, Beall Island, Bosner Island, Boffa Island, Bousquet Island, Cloyd Island, the Cronk Islands, Denison Island, Ford Island, Herring Island, Holl Island, Hollin Island, Midgely Island, O'Connor Island, Odbert Island, Ridge Island, Bailey Rocks, Birkenhamer Island, Borrello Island, Bøving Island, Peterson Island, Phelps Island, Pidgeon Island, Sack Island, the Smith Islands, Spano Island, Teigan Island, Warrington Island, Werlein Island, Wilson Island, Zimmerman Island, etc. Named for Operation Windmill.

Windmills. Scott had one on the *Discovery* during the Royal Society Expedition of 1901–4, to supply the ship with electric light. It was damaged irreparably during a storm.

Window Island. 62°34'S, 61°07'W. Also called Isla Ventana, Richards Island. On the west side of the entrance to Barclay Bay, off the north coast of Livingston Island. Charted and named by Powell in 1822.

Winds. Moist maritime air from the oceans mixing with the cold Polar air makes the Antarctic one of the stormiest continents, if not the stormiest. Great cyclonic west wind storms circle Antarctica in a clockwise fashion in an endless west to east procession, dragging westerly ocean currents along beneath them. Katabatic winds are caused by cold, dense air flowing down the steep slopes of interior highlands, and cause a great wind chill factor (*see also* **Blizzards**). Winds on the Polar Plateau are normally light, the Plateau being so high up and not subject to the katabatics, with a mean of between 9 and 17 mph. In 1912–13 the AAE 1911–14 experienced wind velocities of 40 mph for 60 percent of their time in Adélie Land, and in Commonwealth Bay, the windiest place in the world, winds can reach 200 mph. Planes as big as DC3s have been ripped from their moorings and blown away, and in some storms ships have accumulated as much as 1,000 tons of ice in layers up to 10 feet thick (*see also* **Barrier Wind Phenomenon**).

Bay of Winds. 66°30'S, 97°35'E. Between Cape Dovers and Avalanche Rocks. Discovered by the Western Base Party of the AAE 1911–14, and named by Mawson because of the constant winds.

Windvane Hill. 77°38'S, 166°25'E. Also called Vane Hill. ¼ mile north of Cape Evans, on Ross Island. Scott, on his 1910–13 expedition, established an anemometer station here (hence the name).

Windwhistle Peak. 76°43'S, 159°46'E. A square, sandstone peak, south of Punchbowl Cirque, in the Allan Hills.

Named by the New Zealanders in this area in 1964 because the wind whistles here.

Windy Crater. Unofficial name for a crater near the Wright Valley, in Victoria Land. Aptly named.

Windy Gap. 63°34'S, 58°09'W. 975 m. A pass at the NE end of the Louis Philippe Plateau. Discovered, surveyed and named by the FIDS in April 1946. They experienced very windy weather here.

Windy Gully. 77°53'S, 161°10'E. A valley where the Ferrar Glacier meets the Taylor Glacier, in southern Victoria Land. Ice-filled, it lies between New Mountain and Terra Cotta Mountain. Named by Grif Taylor while he was leading the Western Journey Party during Scott's 1910–13 expedition, for the high winds here.

Windy Nunatak *see* **Mount Bumstead**

Windy Peak. 79°13'S, 86°04'W. 1,910 m. 2 miles SW of the Reuther Nunataks in the Founders Peaks of the Heritage Range. Named by the University of Minnesota Geological Party of 1963–64 because of the high winds here.

Windy Valley. 68°37'S, 66°50'W. A glacier-filled valley opening onto the north part of Mikkelsen Bay, on the west coast of Graham Land. In the area of the Traffic Circle. Named aptly by the BGLE 1934–37.

The "Winfly." Nickname for the first spring plane in at McMurdo every year.

Mount Winifred Cumming *see* **Mount Cumming**

Winkle, Max. Crewman on the *Jacob Ruppert*, 1934–35.

Winkle Island. 65°31'S, 65°39'W. Between Tula Point and Pickwick Island in the Pitt Islands of the Biscoe Islands. Named by the UK in 1959 for the Dickens character.

Winship, Jonathan. Captain of the *O'Cain*, out of Boston, who was in the

South Shetlands in the 1820–21 summer, and may have been the first to collect fossils in the Antarctic. His base in the South Shetlands for the season was Potter Cove.

Winship Point. 62°15'S, 58°44'W. Forms the western entrance to Potter Cove, on King George Island, in the South Shetlands. It is actually on Barton Peninsula. Named by the UK in 1960 for Jonathan Winship.

Winslow Rock. 66°17'S, 66°44'W. Off the east side of Lavoisier Island, in the Biscoe Islands. Named by the UK for Charles E.A. Winslow, US physiologist specializing in the cold.

Winter *see* **Seasons**

Winter Harbor. A term no longer used, for a little harbor off Cape Royds, Ross Island. Used and named by Scott.

Winter Island. 65°15'S, 64°16'W. ½ mile long. 200 yards north of Skua Island, in the Argentine Islands of the Wilhelm Archipelago, off the west coast of Graham Land. Named by Rymill in 1935. It was here that his BGLE made its winter base for that year.

Winter Quarters Bay. 77°51'S, 166°38' E. Also spelled Winterquarters Bay. ½ mile in width. The bay that fronts McMurdo Station on Hut Point Peninsula, Ross Island. Discovered and named by Scott in 1902. It was here that he quartered the *Discovery* for the winter.

Winter Quarters Peninsula *see* **Hut Point Peninsula**

Wintering-over. This is when a party spends the winter in Antarctica, intentionally or otherwise. The following are some notable winterings: 1821, Capt. Clark and crew aboard the *Lord Melville* in the South Shetlands; 1877, the crew of the *Florence* on King George Island; 1898, de Gerlache and crew trapped in the ice aboard the *Belgica;* 1899, Borchgrevink at Cape Adare — the first to winter-over intentionally; 1902, Nordenskjöld and crew — deliberately on Snow Hill Island; 1902, Scott and party —

deliberately on Ross Island; 1902, Von Drygalski forced to winter-over in the *Gauss;* 1903, Nordenskjöld's group forced to winter-over again when their ship was crushed; 1903, Bruce and party— deliberately at Laurie Island; 1903, Scott forced to winter-over again when the *Discovery* was trapped; 1904, Charcot deliberately at Booth Island; 1908, Shackleton's party deliberately on the British Antarctic Expedition of 1907-9; 1909, Charcot deliberately at Petermann Island. After that pretty much all expeditions wintered-over, to take advantage of the complete summer. The first women to winter-over were probably whalers' wives on Deception Island in or around 1910. Edith Ronne and Jennie Darlington did so during the RARE in 1948, and Dr. Michele Raney was the first woman to winter-over at the Pole—in 1979. The first people ever to winter-over at the South Pole were 18 men and a dog at South Pole Station in 1957. There have been some pretty perilous winterings. The 22 men on Elephant Island, for example, sheltered beneath upturned boats during the winter of 1916 (*see* **British Imperial Transantarctic Expedition 1914-17**), and never knew if they were going to be rescued, until they were. In 1921 Bagshawe and Lester, two young members of the British Imperial Expedition (not to be confused with the similar sounding expedition mentioned above) wintered-over on Waterboat Point in a makeshift hut built on an old boat. The Northern Party during Scott's 1910-13 expedition wintered-over in a snow cave. Byrd wintered-over alone at Bolling Advance Weather Station (q.v. for details) in 1934. This book contains many stories of horrific winterings, usually chronicled in the expedition entries.

Wirdnam Glacier. 78°25'S, 162°02'E. Between Mount Moxley and Mount Lisicky, in the Royal Society Range. It flows into the Skelton Glacier. Named for Squadron Leader K.A.C. Wirdnam, RAF pilot, at McMurdo Base in 1960 as an observer.

Wirth Peninsula. 73°27'S, 80°40'W. 20 miles long. Broad and ice-covered. Between Eltanin Bay and Fladerer Bay in Ellsworth Land. Named for Capt. Laurence Wirth, commander of the *Eltanin* in 1966-67.

Wisconsin Islands. 63°17'S, 57°53'W. More than a dozen small, rocky islands, 1 mile NE of Largo Island, in the NE part of the Duroch Islands. Named by Martin Halperin, leader of the University of Wisconsin's geological party here in 1961-62, for the university.

Wisconsin Plateau. 85°48'S, 125°24' W. A large, ice-capped plateau in the Wisconsin Range (hence the name) of the Horlick Mountains.

Wisconsin Range. 86°S, 125°W. In the southern part of the Horlick Mountains. It comprises the Wisconsin Plateau and several glaciers, ridges, and peaks. Named for the University of Wisconsin, which has sent many researchers to Antarctica.

Mount Wise. 78°08'S, 165°23'E. 815 m. A bare rock summit, the highest point on Brown Peninsula. Named by A.J. Heine of the McMurdo Ice Shelf Project, 1962-63, for K.C. Wise, a New Zealander who explored the peninsula in 1958-59.

Wise, E. Cook on the *Aurora,* 1914-16.

Wise Bay. 83°02'S, 167°35'E. A Ross Ice Shelf indentation into the Holland Range, at the terminus of the Ekblad Glacier, just west of Driscoll Point. Named by the New Zealanders in 1959 for K.C. Wise (*see* **Mount Wise**).

Wise Peak. 78°35'S, 158°18'E. 1,580 m. Forms the south end of the Warren Range, in Victoria Land. Named for biologist Keith A.J. Wise, at McMurdo Station every summer between 1960-61 and 1964-65.

Mount Wishart. 70°19'S, 65°16'E. Snow-covered. 5 miles north of Mount Kirkby, on the north side of Scylla Glacier, in the Prince Charles Mountains. Named for E.R. Wishart, at Mawson Station in 1963.

Wishbone Ridge. 84°56′S, 166°56′W. A Y-shaped ridge in the Duncan Mountains, 2 miles east of Morris Peak. Named by Edmund Stump, who mapped the ridge on Dec. 21, 1974, with C.E. Corbató and P.V. Colbert, all on the Ohio State University field party that year.

Wister, Horace. Ordinary seaman on the Wilkes Expedition 1838–42. Joined in the USA. Discharged at Oahu, March 31, 1841.

Mount Wisting. 86°27′S, 165°26′W. Also called Mount Oscar Wisting, Mount O. Wisting. 2,580 m. At the top of the Amundsen Glacier. Discovered in 1911 by Amundsen's party (which included Oscar Wisting), and named by Amundsen for his companion.

Wisting, Oscar. b. 1871, Norway. d. 1936, aboard the *Fram,* while it was in a museum in Oslo. A Norwegian whaler who joined the Norwegian Navy as a gunner. He was Amundsen's closest friend, and one of the first 5 men to stand at the South Pole on Dec. 14, 1911. After 1913 he was mostly in the Arctic with Amundsen.

Witalis Peak. 85°33′S, 160°18′W. 760 m. In the NE part of Collins Ridge, at the confluence of the Bowman and Amundsen Glaciers, in the Queen Maud Mountains. Discovered during Byrd's 1928–30 expedition, and named later for Ronald E. Witalis, meteorologist at South Pole Station in 1961.

Witches Cauldron. 69°56′S, 69°49′W. An ice-filled basin on the west side of the Douglas Range, just west of Mount Egbert in the northern part of Alexander Island. First seen in 1937 by the BGLE, during a flight over, and later named by the UK for its shape.

Withen, Nicholas. Captain of the *Governor Brooks,* 1820–22.

Withen Island. 62°14′S, 59°09′W. Off the NW side of Nelson Island, in the South Shetlands. Named by the UK in 1961 for Nicholas Withen.

Withrow Glacier. 77°24′S, 156°25′W. On Edward VII Peninsula, flowing into Bartlett Inlet, just east of Cape Colbeck. Named for Cdr. W.H. Withrow, USN, officer-in-charge of Detachment One at Christchurch, NZ, 1965–66.

Witt Bluff. 71°16′S, 68°27′W. On the SW side of Eros Glacier, in the eastern part of Alexander Island, in the area of Planet Heights. Named by the UK for Carl G. Witt, German astronomer who discovered Eros (Minor Planet 433).

Witte, Dietrich. Motor mechanic on the German New Schwabenland Expedition of 1938–39, under Ritscher.

Witte Nunataks. 75°29′S, 69°22′W. Isolated. Between the Sweeney Mountains and the Hauberg Mountains, on the Orville Coast of Ellsworth Land, at the very south of Palmer Land. Named for Paul F. Witte, at Eights Station in 1964.

Witte Peaks. 71°32′S, 2°04′W. 4 nunataks, 15 miles west of the Stein Nunataks, on the north part of the Ahlmann Ridge of Queen Maud Land. Discovered by Ritscher in 1938–39, and named by him for Dietrich Witte.

Wittman Island. 65°44′S, 65°49′W. 2 miles WSW of Nusser Island, off the east side of Renaud Island, in the Biscoe Islands. Named by the UK in 1959 for Walter I. Wittman, American oceanographer.

Wohlschlag Bay. 77°22′S, 166°25′E. Between Harrison Bluff and Cape Royds, on the west coast of Ross Island. Mount Bird is above it. Charted by Scott during his 1901–4 expedition. Named by the USA in 1964 for Donald E. Wohlschlag, who outfitted the biology labs on the *Eltanin* and at McMurdo Station, where he worked 5 summer seasons between 1958 and 1964.

Wohlthat Massif *see* **Wohlthat Mountains**

Wohlthat Mountains. 71°35′S, 12°20′E. Also called Wohlthat Massif. A large group consisting of the Humboldt Mountains, the Petermann Ranges, and the Gruber Mountains. Just east of the Orvin Mountains, between the Princess

Astrid Coast and the Princess Ragnhild Coast, in central Queen Maud Land. Discovered by Ritscher in 1938–39, and named by him for politician Helmuth C.H. Wohlthat, who dealt with the organization of Ritscher's expedition.

Mount Woinarski. 71°14′S, 66°30′E. Triple-peaked. 18 miles SW of Taylor Platform, in the Prince Charles Mountains. Named by the Australians for B.C.Z. Woinarski, officer-in-charge of Mawson Station in 1965.

Wolak Peak. 77°39′S, 161°08′E. In the Inland Forts, 1 mile NW of Saint Pauls Mountain, in the Asgard Range of Victoria Land. Named for Richard J. Wolak, at McMurdo Station in 1972–73 and 1973–74, and station manager at Amundsen-Scott South Pole Station in 1975.

Wold Nunatak. 74°47′S, 98°38′W. 10 miles east of Mount Manthe, in the SE sector of the Hudson Mountains. Named for Richard J. Wold, geologist at Byrd Station in 1960–61.

Wollan Island. 66°25′S, 66°38′W. Dome-shaped and ice-capped. 1 mile north of Davidson Island, in Crystal Sound. Named by the UK for Ernest O. Wollan, US physicist.

Cape Wollaston. 63°40′S, 60°47′W. Also seen as Cape Wallaston, Cape Walleston, Punta Condor, Cabo Martillo. The NW extremity of Trinity Island. Named by Foster in 1829 for William H. Wollaston, commissioner of the Royal Society on the Board of Longitude, 1818–28.

Wollesen Islands. 67°31′S, 62°41′E. In the entrance to Holme Bay, 1 mile west of the Azimuth Islands. Photographed by the LCE 1936–37, and named later by the Australians for C. Wollesen Petersen, radio officer on the *Thala Dan* and the *Nella Dan* on 9 ANARE relief voyages.

Wolseley Buttress. 64°12′S, 59°47′W. A bluff on the southern edge of the Detroit Plateau in Graham Land. Forms the west side of the Albone Glacier.

Named by the UK for the Wolseley Tool and Motor Car Co., which designed the motor sledge for Scott in 1910–13.

Womack, Lyle. Seaman on the *Eleanor Bolling*, 1928–29, i.e., during the first half of Byrd's 1928–30 expedition.

Wombat Island. 67°36′S, 47°56′E. A small island just off the east end of Mackinnon Island, off the coast of Enderby Land. Named by the Australians for their animal.

Women in Antarctica. Until the 1960s, even the 1970s, it could safely be said that Antarctica was not a place for women. In fact, Harry Darlington, in 1947, had said "There are some things women don't do. They don't become Pope, or President—or go down to the Antarctic." That was said during the RARE 1947–48, an expedition he was on, as was his wife, Jennie. Indeed, Jennie Darlington said in her 1956 book, "Taking everything into consideration, I don't think women belong in Antarctica." Below are landmark dates concerning the arrival of women on the Great White Continent: **The 1840s,** Perhaps the first woman to go south of 60°S was the wife of the captain of the *Fleetwood.* **1910,** Charcot treated the wife of a Norwegian whaling captain on Deception Island. **Feb. 20, 1935,** Caroline Mikkelsen was the first woman to set foot on the mainland of Antarctica. **1936–37,** Lars Christensen took his wife, Ingrid, and his daughter, and 2 female friends to the Antarctic as tourists (the Four Ladies Bank is named for them). **1947–48,** Mrs. Edith Ronne and Mrs. Jennie Darlington were the first women to winter-over in Antarctica, at Stonington Island during the RARE 1947–48. Their husbands were part of the expedition; in fact Ronne was the leader. Edith Ronne had been expected to leave the ship at Valparaiso, Chile, on the way down, having come to report part of the trip for the North American Newspaper Alliance. At the last moment Finn Roone had decided to bring her along for the complete tour, and had taken Harry Darlington's wife too. In Nov. 1947 they set up house with the men, and became "mothers" to the crew, washing laundry, settling fights, etc. Messrs. Ronne and Darlington had a fight, and after that the two wives ceased being friends. Jennie Darlington became pregnant (it was an Antarctic honeymoon for her) and almost had her child in Antarctica. **1956,** Marie V. Klenova became the first woman scientist to work in Antarctica. **Oct. 15, 1957,** Ruth Kelley and Pat Heppinstall, two stewardesses on the first ever commercial flight to Antarctica, became the first women ever to visit an American Antarctic base. **1962–72,** Mary Alice McWhinnie carried out shipboard research, being unable to land on the continent because of the US Navy's ban on American women there until 1969. **1968–69,** Four Argentine hydrographers did research on the Antarctic Peninsula—Professors Irene Bernasconi, Maria Adela Caria, Elena Martínez Fontes, and Carmen Pujals. **Oct. 1969,** Christine Müller-Schwarze was the first US woman to work in Antarctica, studying penguins. She spent three summers there with her husband. **Nov. 11, 1969,** With the US ban on women in Antarctica lifted in 1969 (France and Great Britain still have one), an all-women team of scientists led by Dr. Lois Jones went to Antarctica for the 1969–70 summer season. The others were Terry Lee Tickhill, Eileen McSaveney, and Kay Lindsay. Jean Pearson (a reporter) and Pam Young went along with them in a plane to the South Pole and the 6 women stepped out together, the first women ever at 90°S. They spent a few hours at the Pole and then flew back to McMurdo. It was a big news story. Jack Paulus flew the plane. **Dec. 1971,** Louise Hutchinson was the first woman to sleep over at the South Pole (*see* **South Pole**). **1972,** Yuan Lin Devries became the first woman to work at McMurdo Station. **1973,** Nan Scott and Donna Muchmore were the first women to work at the South Pole. **Jan. 2, 1974,** Patricia Nicely of the National Science Foundation, and Lt. Ann Coyer, USN, were the first US women at Vostok Station. **1974,** Mary Alice McWhinnie became the first woman to head a scientific station in Antarctica, when she took over at McMurdo Station for the 1974–75 summer season. She shared the station with Sister Mary Odile Cahoon (a nun—*see* **Cahoon**) and 100 men. **1976,** The Australians first allowed women onto the continent. **1977–78,** Dorothy Smith accompanied 7 men on the *Solo* expedition. She was 59. **1979,** Dr. Michele Raney was the first woman to winter-over at the Pole. **1980,** Martha Kane, a climatologist, replaced Raney as the only female wintering-over at the Pole. **1981,** The Australians first allowed women to winter-over in Antarctica. **Feb. 1983,** Maria Kazanowska was the first woman to visit a Japanese base. **1986,** 13 women wintered-over in 4 US bases in Antarctica. **1987,** One woman and three men wintered-over in Greenpeace Base (*see* **Greenpeace**). **Jan. 17, 1989,** Victoria E. Murden and Shirley Metz were the first two women to reach the South Pole after a land traverse.

Womochel Peaks. 72°40′S, 161°04′E. 2 miles south of Mount Weihaupt, in the Outback Nunataks. Named for Daniel R. Womochel, biologist at McMurdo Station in 1967–68.

Wonsey Rock. 66°13′S, 110°36′E. North of Cameron Island, in the Swain Islands. Named in 1957 by Carl Eklund for Duane J. Wonsey, USN, at Wilkes Station in 1957.

Wood. Larsen discovered petrified wood on Seymour Island in 1892–93. Since then wood has been discovered many times, indicating beyond doubt that there were trees in Antarctica at one time.

Cape Wood. 71°24′S, 169°20′E. The eastern point of Flat Island, at the western entrance to Robertson Bay, in northern Victoria Land. Discovered by Ross in Jan. 1841, and named by him for Charles Wood, first secretary to the admiralty.

¹Mount Wood. 74°49'S, 158°24'E. An isolated nunatak north of the David Glacier, 13 miles NE of Mount Kring in Victoria Land. Named by D.B. McC. Rainey, NZ cartographer, for the foster parents of Staff Sgt. Arthur L. Kring (*see* **Mount Kring** for further details).

²Mount Wood. 74°51'S, 64°07'W. Also called Mount Sandell. 1,230 m. West of Gardner Inlet, and 15 miles west of Mount Austin, in the Latady Mountains, on the east coast of Palmer Land. Discovered by the RARE 1947–48, and named by Ronne for Ernest A. Wood.

Port Wood. Also called Wood Harbor, both names being unofficial. On Desolation Island, in the South Shetlands. Discovered by Fildes in Dec. 1820, and named Wood Harbor by him.

Wood, Ernest A. Ship's engineer on the RARE 1947–48.

Wood, Gareth. Mountain climbing instructor from Sidney, B.C., Canada. In his 30s he became one of the three men to reach the Pole on the In the Footsteps of Scott Expedition, 1985–86.

Wood, James F.L. Lieutenant on the *Erebus* with Ross, 1839–43.

Wood Bay. 74°13'S, 165°30'E. A Ross Sea indentation into Victoria Land. It is bounded on the north by Cape Johnson and the Aviator Glacier Tongue, and on the south by Cape Washington. Discovered in 1841 by Ross, and named by him for James F.L. Wood.

Wood Glacier. 72°29'S, 166°42'E. Flows into Trafalgar Glacier, just east of Mount MacDonald, in the Victory Mountains of Victoria Land. Named by the New Zealanders in 1962–63 for New Zealand geologist B.L. Wood, who worked in this area in 1957–58.

Wood Harbor *see* **Port Wood**

Wood Island. 62°29'S, 60°19'W. SE of Desolation Island in the South Shetlands. Charted in 1820–21 by Fildes. Named in 1958 by the UK in association with Port Wood, which Fildes had named Wood Harbor in Dec. 1820. This harbor is in nearby Desolation Island.

Wood Point. 77°25'S, 168°57'E. 10 miles ESE of Cape Tennyson, on the north coast of Ross Island. Named in 1964 for Robert C. Wood, biologist here in 1961–62, 1962–63, and 1963–64.

Wood Ridge. 74°S, 163°45'E. 7 miles long. Flat-topped. Ice-covered. Between the Styx Glacier and the Campbell Glacier in the Southern Cross Mountains of Victoria Land. Named for Vernon P. Wood, USN, yeoman at McMurdo Station in 1963 and 1967.

Woodall, Vance. USN. Seaman who was killed during an unloading accident while engaged in Operation Highjump, 1946–47.

Woodall Peak. 84°17'S, 178°38'E. 720 m. A small rock peak between the Good and Ramsey Glaciers, overlooking the Ross Ice Shelf to the NE of the Hughes Range. Discovered on Flight C of Feb. 29–March 1, 1940, during the USAS, and later named for Vance Woodall.

Woodberry Glacier. 75°06'S, 161°38'E. Flows between Evans Heights and Mount Fearon, on the north side of the David Glacier, in Victoria Land. Named for Barry D. Woodberry, ionosphere physicist at Amundsen-Scott South Pole Station in 1966.

Woodberry Nunataks. 67°47'S, 62°11'E. A group of small nunataks a mile north of Lucas Nunatak, in the Casey Range of the Framnes Mountains. Photographed by the LCE 1936–37. Visited by an ANARE party in 1962, and named by them for Barry D. Woodberry (*see also* **Woodberry Glacier**), who was in this region with that 1962 party from Mawson Station.

Woodbury Glacier. 64°47'S, 62°20'W. Just west of Montgolfier Glacier, flowing into Picard Cove, in Wilhelmina Bay, on the west coast of Graham Land. Named by the UK in 1960 for Walter B. Woodbury, photography pioneer.

Wooden, Frederick E. FIDS surveyor at Base O in 1956 and at Base J in 1957.

He was also attached to the British Naval Hydrographic Survey Unit, which worked in the area of the Antarctic Peninsula in 1957–58.

Wooden Peak. 66°08′S, 65°35′W. 2 miles SE of Black Head, on the west coast of Graham Land. Charted by the BGLE in 1934–37, and named by the UK in 1960 for Frederick E. Wooden.

Woodfield Channel. 67°49′S, 68°44′ W. A deep water channel between the Dion Islands and the Henkes Islands and Roca Islands off the south end of Adelaide Island. Named by the UK in 1963 for Thomas Woodfield, first officer on the *John Biscoe* from 1959 to 1963.

Woodhouse, Thomas. Midshipman on the *Adventure* during Cook's second voyage of 1772–75. He was killed and eaten by the Maoris in NZ on Dec. 17, 1773.

Mount Woods. 84°40′S, 64°30′W. 1,170 m. A bare, ridgelike mountain. 4½ miles NE of O'Connell Nunatak, in the Anderson Hills, in the central part of the Patuxent Range of the Pensacola Mountains. Named for Clifford R. Woods, Jr., at Palmer Station in 1967.

Mount Woodward. 77°18′S, 145°46′ W. Also called Mount Donald Woodward, Donald Woodward Mountains. Has broad twin summits. To the immediate east of the Boyd Glacier, in the Ford Ranges of Marie Byrd Land. Discovered during Byrd's 1928–30 expedition, and named by Byrd for a patron, Donald Woodward.

Woolam Peak. 76°41′S, 125°49′W. In the southern part of the crater rim of Mount Cumming, in the Executive Committee Range of Marie Byrd Land. Named for Alvis E. Woolam, ionosphere physicist at Byrd Station in 1959.

Woolhouse, M.C. Seaman on the *City of New York* during Byrd's 1928–30 expedition.

Mount Woollard. 80°33′S, 96°43′W. 2,675 m. Isolated. 8 miles south of Mount Moore. 150 miles west of the Heritage

Range. Discovered by the Marie Byrd Land Traverse Party of 1957–58, and named for George P. Woollard, who trained many Antarctic geophysicists.

Mount Woolnough. 76°57′S, 161°20′ E. Over 1,400 m. On the north side of Mackay Glacier, between Mount Morrison and Mount Gran, in Victoria Land. Charted by Scott's 1910–13 expedition, and named for Walter G. Woolnough, British geologist who helped write Shackleton's 1907–9 scientific reports.

Woolpack Island. 65°37′S, 65°W. 1½ miles long. A narrow island, 4 miles NE of Vieugué Island, at the west side of the Grandidier Channel, off the west coast of Graham Land. Discovered and named by the BGLE 1934–37.

Woozle Hill. 65°15′S, 64°15′W. Near the center of Galíndez Island, in the Argentine Islands. Charted by the BGLE 1934–37, and named by the UK in 1959 for the *Winnie the Pooh* animal.

Worcester Range. 78°50′S, 161°E. 30 miles long. Between the Skelton and Mulock Glaciers, it is actually south of the Skelton Glacier. Discovered by Scott's 1901–4 expedition, and named probably for HMS *Worcester,* the British Naval training ship on the Thames.

Wordie, James M. b. 1889. James Mann Wordie. British geologist and chief of the scientific staff on the British Imperial Transantarctic Expedition of 1914–17, with Shackleton. Much in the Arctic from 1919 to 1937, he was president of the Royal Geographical Society, a member of the Discovery Committee and chairman of the Scott Polar Research Institute. He was also knighted. He was on the Antarctic cruise of the FIDS in 1946–47.

Wordie Ice Shelf. 69°10′S, 67°30′W. A small ice shelf at the south of Marguerite Bay, between Cape Berteaux and Mount Edgell, on the west coast of the Antarctic Peninsula. It is fed by the Fleming Glacier. Discovered by the BGLE 1934–37, and named by Rymill for James M. Wordie.

Wordie Nunatak. 66°16'S, 51°31'E. 4 miles SE of Mount Biscoe, and 4 miles ENE of Mount Hurley. 5 miles ESE of Cape Ann, in East Antarctica. Discovered in Jan. 1930 by the BANZARE, and named by Mawson for James M. Wordie.

Workman Rocks. 66°23'S, 65°42'W. A group in the NE part of Darbel Bay, just west of Panther Cliff, off the west coast of Graham Land. Named by the UK in 1960 for Everley J. Workman, US physicist.

Mount Works. 71°14'S, 164°50'E. 1,780 m. Just west of Horne Glacier, 2 miles SW of Pilon Peak, in the Everett Range of the Concord Mountains. Named for Lt. W.W. Works, USN, pilot in Antarctica in 1961–62 and 1962–63.

The *World Discoverer*. A 3,153-ton ship commissioned in 1974, and owned by Discoverer Rederei, Heiko Klein's West German shipping company. 285 feet 4 inches long, with a 12.5 knot speed, it is a luxury ship with sophisticated equipment and safety features, including Zodiac landing boats. It carries 136 passengers, and has 5 decks—Discoverer, Voyager, Odyssey, Boat, and Bridge. It has an ice-hardened hull and a shallow draft, and a bow thruster. It has the highest ice-rating of any passenger ship. Registered in the Bahamas, it was leased out to Society Expeditions Cruises and made its first passenger cruise to Antarctica in 1976. Subsequently Heiko Klein bought Society Expeditions, and in 1985 the tour company added another ship to their fleet, the *Society Explorer*.

World wars *see* **Wars**

Worley Point. 74°24'S, 132°47'W. A rock point which has an Adélie Penguin rookery on it. It forms the NW corner of Shepard Island, in Marie Byrd Land. Charted from the *Glacier* on Feb. 4, 1962. Named for Lt. Richard J. Worley, USN, medical officer at Amundsen-Scott South Pole Station in 1969.

Wormald Ice Piedmont. 67°29'S, 68°05'W. On the NW coast of Adelaide Island.

Worms. The annelid worm Polychaeta lives on the sea bed, near the coasts of Antarctica (*see* **Fauna**).

Cape Worsley. 64°39'S, 60°24'W. Also called Cabo Ruth. 225 m. Dome-shaped. It has snow-free cliffs on the south and east sides. 10 miles east of the south end of the Detroit Plateau, on the east coast of Graham Land. Charted by the FIDS in 1947 and named by them for Frank Worsley.

Worsley, Frank A. b. 1872, Akaroa, NZ. d. 1943, England. Frank Arthur Worsley. Went to sea in 1887, and worked his way up through the business. He was skipper of the *Endurance* during the ill-fated British Imperial Transantarctic Expedition of 1914–17. On Jan. 5, 1915, while playing soccer on an ice floe, he fell through the ice, but was rescued. After the *Endurance* sank he showed his amazing navigational skills by taking the longboat *James Caird* from Elephant Island to South Georgia. After that he, Shackleton, and Crean did another "impossible," they crossed South Georgia. He won the DSO during World War I, and in 1921–22 was hydrographer and sailing master on the *Quest*, during Shackleton's last expedition. He continued to have adventures all over the world, and was president of the Antarctic Club in 1938.

Worsley Icefalls. 82°57'S, 155°E. Near the head of Nimrod Glacier. Named by the New Zealanders in 1962–63 for Frank A. Worsley.

Worswick, Robert F. FIDS meteorologist at Signy Island Station in 1950 and 1951.

Worswick Hill. 60°34'S, 45°44'W. 575 m. A rounded summit. At the west end of Brisbane Heights, on Coronation Island, in the South Orkneys. Named by the UK for Robert F. Worswick.

Worth Reef. 67°48'S, 68°56'W. An arc of rocks forming the northernmost part of the Henkes Islands, off the south end of Adelaide Island. Named by the UK for Acting Corporal David A.

Worth, Royal Marines, of the Royal Naval Hydrographic Survey Unit here in 1963.

Worthley Peak. 82°43′S, 164°46′E. 840 m. At the north end of Benson Ridge, overlooking the lower Robb Glacier. Named for Elmer G. Worthley, bryologist at McMurdo Station in 1958–59.

Wotkyns Glacier. 86°04′S, 131°25′W. Flows from the Michigan Plateau along the west side of the Caloplaca Hills, and enters Reedy Glacier. Named for Grosenvar S. Wotkyns, at Byrd Station in 1962.

Mount Wrather. 85°23′S, 87°14′W. 2,095 m. 2½ miles SSE of Mount Walcott, on the eastern edge of the Thiel Mountains. Geologists Peter Bermel and Arthur Ford, here in 1960–61, named it for William E. Wrather, 6th director of the US Geological Survey, 1943–56.

Wray, G.B. Crewman on the *Jacob Ruppert,* 1933–34.

Mount Wright. 71°33′S, 169°09′E. Over 1,800 m. In the northern part of the Admiralty Mountains, between Shipley Glacier and the Crume Glacier, 8 miles SW of Birthday Point. Named by Scott's 1910–13 expedition for Charles S. Wright.

Wright, Charles S. b. 1887, Toronto, Canada. d. 1975. Charles Seymour Wright. Nicknamed "Silas." Physicist on Scott's 1910–13 expedition. He was a member of the party of 1912 who went out to search for the missing Scott, and was the first to sight Scott's tent. He became director of Scientific Research at the British Admiralty, and was knighted in 1946.

Wright, Daniel. Cockswain on the Wilkes Expedition 1838–42. Joined in the USA. Sent home on the *Relief* in 1839.

Wright, E. New Zealand photographer who went to the Pole with Hillary in 1957–58 during the BCTAE.

Wright Bay. 66°36′S, 93°35′E. Between the west side of the Helen Glacier

Tongue and the mainland. Discovered by the AAE 1911–14, and named by Mawson for Charles S. Wright.

Wright Glacier *see* **Wright Lower Glacier**

Wright Hill. 79°42′S, 158°46′E. Large and flat-topped. On the east side of Bowling Green Plateau, in the Cook Mountains. Named by the New Zealanders on the BCTAE 1957–58 for E. Wright.

Wright Ice Piedmont. 64°S, 60°20′W. Extends from Lanchester Bay going west along the west coast of Graham Land. Named by the UK in 1960 for the Wright Brothers, airplane pioneers.

Wright Inlet. 73°57′S, 61°26′W. Also called Mount Tricorn Inlet. An ice-filled Weddell Sea indentation into the Lassiter Coast, between Cape Little and Cape Wheeler, at the foot of Mount Tricorn, on the east coast of the Antarctic Peninsula. Named by Ronne in 1948 for John K. Wright, director of the American Geographical Society which supported the RARE 1947–48.

Wright Island. 74°03′S, 116°45′W. 35 miles long. Ice-covered. Between Carney Island and Martin Peninsula, in the northern sector of the Getz Ice Shelf, off the coast of Marie Byrd Land. Named for Adm. Jerauld Wright, USN, commander-in-chief of the Atlantic Fleet during the IGY.

Wright Lake *see* **Lake Brownworth**

Wright Lower Glacier. 77°24′S, 163°E. Also called Lower Wright Glacier. A stagnant glacier which occupies the mouth of the Wright Valley, behind the Wilson Piedmont Glacier, in southern Victoria Land. The Onyx River runs from its terminus. Named by Scott's 1910–13 expedition as Wright Glacier, for Charles S. Wright. The name was changed by the New Zealanders in 1958–59 to distinguish it from Wright Upper Glacier.

Wright Pass. 74°45′S, 110°35′W. On Bear Peninsula, on the coast of Marie Byrd Land.

Wright Peak. 73°40′S, 94°32′W. 1,510 m. ½ mile south of Sutley Peak, in the

Jones Mountains. Mapped by the University of Minnesota–Jones Mountains Party of 1960–61, which named it for Herbert E. Wright, Jr., glacial geologist and adviser to the party, who was in Antarctica in 1961–62.

Wright Peninsula. 67°28′S, 68°10′W. Between Ryder Bay and Stonehouse Bay, on the east coast of Adelaide Island. Named by the UK in 1964 for Alan F. Wright, surveyor at Base T from 1960 to 1963.

Wright Point. 66°24′S, 110°30′E. The most northerly point on Ford Island, in the Windmill Islands. Named for Robert D. Wright, USN, at Wilkes Station in 1958.

Wright Spires. 69°30′S, 68°30′W. Nunataks on the NE coast of Alexander Island, overlooking the northern entrance to the George VI Sound.

Wright Upper Glacier. 77°32′S, 160°40′E. Also called Upper Wright Glacier. An ice apron at the upper west end of the Wright Valley, formed by a glacier flowing east from the inland ice plateau. Named by the New Zealanders in 1958–59 to distinguish it from Wright Lower Glacier (q.v.).

Wright Valley. 77°33′S, 161°30′E. A spectacular dry valley near McMurdo Sound, in southern Victoria Land. Wright Upper Glacier is at its head, and Wright Lower Glacier is at its mouth. First explored in 1957 by Dr. Troy L. Péwé, and named by the New Zealanders in 1958–59 for Charles S. Wright.

Wrigley Bluffs. 84°33′S, 63°45′W. 4 miles long. 3 miles north of Mount Cross, in the Anderson Hills, in the northern part of the Patuxent Range of the Pensacola Mountains. Named for Richard J. Wrigley, equipment operator at Palmer Station in 1966.

Wrigley Gulf. 74°S, 129°W. Also called Philip Wrigley Gulf. 115 miles wide. An indentation into the Getz Ice Shelf, between Shepard Island and Cape Dart, on the coast of Marie Byrd Land.

Discovered in Dec. 1940 by the USAS, and named for Chicago manufacturer Philip Wrigley, a sponsor of the expedition.

Wu Nunatak. 72°29′S, 161°08′E. 8 miles NNE of Mount Weihaupt in the Outback Nunataks. Named for Tien H-Wu, glaciologist at McMurdo Station in 1966–67.

Wubbold Glacier. 69°20′S, 71°41′W. On the NW coast of Alexander Island.

Wujek Ridge. 82°28′S, 50°55′W. In the northern part of the Pensacola Mountains.

Wunneburger Rock. 74°42′S, 113°02′W. In the lower Kohler Glacier, near the point where that glacier flows into the Dotson Ice Shelf, in Marie Byrd Land. Named for Henry E. Wunneburger, USN, cook at Byrd Station in 1966.

Wüst Inlet. 72°20′S, 60°50′W. Between 2 and 5 miles wide. Ice-filled. An indentation into the east side of Merz Peninsula, between Cape Christmas and Old Mans Head, on the east coast of Palmer Land. Named by the FIDS for Georg Wüst, German oceanographer.

The *Wyandot*. US cargo ship in Antarctic waters from the time of the IGY (1957–58) on into the 1970s. In 1956, under the command of Francis M. Gambacorta, it helped to build Ellsworth Station, and in 1957, under Capt. F.M. Smith, it took part in Operation Deep Freeze II.

Wyandot Ridge. 76°36′S, 160°30′E. On the west side of the Chattahoochee Glacier, in the NW sector of the Convoy Range. Named in 1964 for the *Wyandot*.

Mount Wyatt. 86°46′S, 154°W. 2,930 m. Flat-topped. 3 miles west of Mount Verlautz in the Rawson Mountains of the Queen Maud Mountains. At the top of the Robert Scott Glacier. Discovered in Dec. 1934 by Quin Blackburn's party during Byrd's 1933–35 expedition, and named Mount Jane Wyatt by Byrd for the actress, a friend of expeditionary Richard S. Russell, Jr.

The *Wyatt Earp*. Lincoln Ellsworth's ship (he owned it) during his 1930s expeditions to Antarctica. A 400-ton American sealer of 135 feet with a 15-foot draft, it was formerly a Norwegian wooden herring vessel, the *Fanefjord,* built in Molde, Norway, in 1919, of Norwegian pine and oak. Refitted and ice-strengthened by Sir Hubert Wilkins, and renamed by Ellsworth for the legendary marshal of the old west (who, incidentally, had been dead only a few years). The *Wyatt Earp* had a cruising range of 11,000 miles. It carried Ellsworth to Antarctica for his 1933–34, 1934–35, 1935–36, and 1938–39 expeditions, and was managed by Wilkins. It was berthed in Norway between the first set of expeditions and the last one. For crews *see* **Ellsworth.** The *Wyatt Earp* was sold to Australia in 1939 for £4,400. In 1948 the ANARE used it on their first exploratory trip to Antarctica led by Stuart Campbell. Capt. K.E. Oom commanded that season.

Mount Wyatt Earp. 77°34′S, 86°25′W. Also called Mount Earp. 2,370 m. Snow-covered. 3 miles WNW of Mount Ulmer. Discovered by Ellsworth aerially on Nov. 23, 1935, and later named for Ellsworth's ship, the *Wyatt Earp.*

Wyatt Earp Islands. 68°22′S, 78°32′E. Also called Northern Islands. A small group of islands and rocks off the northern extremity of the Vestfold Hills, about ½ mile north of the Walkabout Rocks. Photographed by the LCE 1936–37, and later named Nörsteholmen by the Norwegians. In Jan. 1939 the *Wyatt Earp* landed at the Walkabout Rocks nearby, and later the Australians renamed these islands.

Wyatt Glacier. 68°18′S, 66°10′W. 6 miles long. Steep and narrow. Flows from near Beehive Hill into the upper part of Gibbs Glacier, in southern Graham Land. Named by the UK for Henry T. Wyatt, FIDS medical officer at Base W in 1957, and at Base E in 1958.

Wyatt Hill. 74°32′S, 110°27′W. On Bear Peninsula, Marie Byrd Land.

Wyatt Island. 67°20′S, 67°40′W. 5 miles long. 2 miles wide. 2 miles south of Day Island, near the center of Laubeuf Fjord, off the west coast of Graham Land. The BGLE surveyed it in 1936 and called it South Island. The FIDS resurveyed it in 1948 and renamed it for Vice-Adm. Sir Arthur G.N. Wyatt, hydrographer to the navy, 1945–50.

Wyche Island. 66°14′S, 110°35′E. Just south of the west end of Burnett Island, in the Swain Islands. Carl Eklund named it in 1957 for Paul A. Wyche, USN, aerographer's mate at Wilkes Station in 1957.

Wyck Island. 64°39′S, 62°06′W. Also called Van Wyck Island. A small island on the west side of Brooklyn Island, in the eastern part of Wilhelmina Bay, off the west coast of Graham Land. Discovered by de Gerlache in 1897–99, and named by Dr. Frederick Cook for R.A. Van Wyck, first mayor of New York City.

Wyckoff Glacier. 84°13′S, 164°40′E. 6 miles long. Just to the west of the Beardmore Glacier, it flows from the Grindley Plateau in the Queen Alexandra Range. Named for Kent A. Wyckoff, meteorologist at Hallett Station in 1963.

Wyers Ice Shelf. 67°11′S, 49°55′E. A small ice shelf in Enderby Land, on the east side of Sakellari Peninsula. Named by the Australians for R.W.L. Wyers, glaciologist at Mawson Station in 1961.

Wyers Nunataks. 67°13′S, 49°43′E. A group at the base of Sakellari Peninsula, just west of the Wyers Ice Shelf, in Enderby Land. Named by the Australians for R.W.L. Wyers (*see* **Wyers Ice Shelf**).

Wyeth Heights. 80°45′S, 29°33′W. In the Shackleton Range.

Wylde Glacier. 73°32′S, 166°45′E. East of Mount Murchison, in the Mountaineer Range, flowing between Dessent Ridge and Cape King, into Lady Newnes Bay, in Victoria Land. Named by the New Zealanders in 1966 for Leonard Wylde, scientific officer at Hallett Station in 1962–63.

Wylie Bay. 64°44'S, 64°10'W. Also called Bahía Arthur. 4 miles wide. Between Cape Monaco and Norsel Point, on the SW coast of Anvers Island. Charcot charted it in 1903-5. Named by the UK in 1959 for John P. Wylie, FIDS surveyor at Arthur Harbor in 1956 and 1957.

Wylie Ridge. 71°51'S, 168°27'E. Extends westward from Meier Peak in the Admiralty Mountains. It parallels the north side of Massey Glacier for 6 miles, and ends at Man-o-War Glacier. Named for Lt. Cdr. Ronald P. Wylie, USN, VX-6 pilot during 1967 and 1968.

Mount Wyman. 83°54'S, 158°57'E. 2,665 m. In the Queen Elizabeth Range, to the west of the Sandford Cliffs. Named for Carl O. Wyman, ionosphere physicist at Little America in 1957.

Mount Wyss. 82°47'S, 162°42'E. 1,930 m. 3 miles east of Mount Rotoiti, in the Frigate Range. Named for Orville Wyss, biologist at McMurdo Station in 1962-63.

Rock X. 66°20'S, 136°42'E. Off the coast of East Antarctica, in the west side of the entrance to Victor Bay, 1 mile NW of Gravenoire Rock. Charted by Marret in 1952-53. The French established an astronomical control station here, identifying the place by an X marked on the photographs taken by Operation Highjump aircraft 6 years before.

Xanthus Spur. 64°33'S, 63°30'W. Ice-covered. Extends NW from Mount Priam for 3 miles in the Trojan Range of Anvers Island. Surveyed by the FIDS in 1955 and named by the UK for the Greek god.

Yaglou Point. 66°23'S, 67°12'W. The northernmost point of Belding Island, in the Biscoe Islands. Named by the UK for Constantin P. Yaglou, American polar physiologist.

Massiv Yakkova Gakkelya *see* **Jøkulkyrkja Mountain**

Mount Yakovlev. 71°59'S, 16°38'E. 11 miles north of Sarkofagen Mountain, in the Russkiye Mountains of Queen Maud Land. Named Gora Yakovleva (Mount

Yakovlev) by the USSR for paleontologist N.N. Yakovlev.

Yalour, Jorge. Lt. Argentine Naval officer, second-in-command of the *Uruguay* under Irízar, 1903-5, including the period during which the ship rescued Nordenskjöld.

Yalour Islands. 65°14'S, 64°10'W. Also called Jallour Isles, Jalour Islands. 1½ miles in extent. In the southern part of the Wilhelm Archipelago. 1 mile NW of Cape Tuxen, Graham Land. Discovered by Charcot in 1903-5, and named by him for Lt. Jorge Yalour.

Yalour Sound. 63°34'S, 56°39'W. A passage, 1 mile wide and 4 miles long, usually icebound, linking Fridtjof Sound and Antarctic Sound, between Jonassen Island and Andersson Island, at the north of the Antarctic Peninsula. Named for Lt. Jorge Yalour.

The *Yamana*. Argentine ship which took part in some of the Antarctic expeditions conducted by that country: 1949-50 (captain unknown), 1952-53 (Capt. Alfrain Ledesma), 1953-54 (captain unknown), 1954-55 (Capt. Antonio Revuelto).

Yamana Nunatak *see* **Florence Nunatak**

Yamato Glacier. 71°25'S, 35°35'E. 6 miles wide. Flows between Mount Fukushima and Mount Eyskens, in the Queen Fabiola Mountains. Discovered on Oct. 7, 1960, by the Belgian Antarctic Expedition of 1959-61, led by Guido Derom, and named by him for a geographical feature of that name in Japan.

Yamato Mountains *see* **Queen Fabiola Mountains**

The *Yancey*. American supply ship in the Central Group of Operation Highjump, 1946-47. Capt. J.E. Cohn.

Yancey Glacier. 80°14'S, 158°32'E. A precipitous glacier in the Britannia Range, flowing from Mount McClintock into the Byrd Glacier just west of the Sennett Glacier. Named for the *Yancey*.

Yankee Bay Station. 62°32'S, 59°49'W. Chilean IGY station on Greenwich

Island. It began as a refuge hut built in 1953.

¹Yankee Harbor *see* **Port Foster**

²Yankee Harbor. 62°32'S, 59°47'W. Also called Fannings Harbor, Hospital Cove. An indentation into the south side of Greenwich Island, in the South Shetlands, between Glacier Bluff and Spit Point. Discovered by Palmer on Nov. 19, 1820, and became the main sealing base and anchorage in the islands for the 1820-21 season.

Yankee Sound *see* **McFarlane Strait**

Yanovskiy Rocks. 71°56'S, 11°40'E. Two isolated rock outcrops. 5 miles south of Mount Khmyznikov, near the SE end of the Humboldt Mountains of Queen Maud Land. Named by the USSR in 1966 for hydrographer S.S. Yanovskiy.

Yapeyú Refugio. Argentine refuge hut built on Northeast Glacier in 1955 by personnel from San Martín Station.

Mount Yarbrough. 84°24'S, 66°W. 865 m. 2 miles SW of Nance Ridge in the Thomas Hills of the northern Patuxent Range, in the Pensacola Mountains. Named for Leonard S. Yarbrough, industrial engineer at Plateau Station in 1965-66.

Yates Glacier. 70°49'S, 62°12'W. 3 miles south of Matheson Glacier, it feeds the Lehrke Inlet on the east coast of Palmer Land. Named by the UK for J. Yates, BAS surveyor in this area.

Yates Spur. 68°41'S, 64°57'W. On the east side of the Antarctic Peninsula.

Yeasts. There are many species of yeasts in Antarctica (*see also* **Flora**).

Yeates Bluff. 83°23'S, 169°10'E. Steep. Ice-covered. Has an 1,190 m. peak at its northern end. Between the Lennox-King and Beaver Glaciers, 4 miles NE of Mount Nickerson, in the Queen Alexandra Range. Named by the New Zealanders in 1960 for Peter A. Yeates, radio operator at Scott Base in that year.

Yeats Glacier. 85°01'S, 175°W. 8 miles long. Flows from Mount Finley and enters Shackleton Glacier just north of Lockhart Ridge, in the Queen Maud Mountains. Named by Alton Wade for Vestal L. Yeats, a member of Wade's 1962-63 and 1964-65 expeditions (*see* **Wade**).

¹The Yelcho. A Chilean tug out of Punta Arenas. Famous for rescuing Shackleton's men from Point Wild, Elephant Island, on Aug. 30, 1916. Capt. Luís Pardo Villalón was the pilot and Clorindo Leniz Gallejo was the chief stoker (the vessel was a steamer).

²The Yelcho. 1700-ton Chilean Naval tender/research ship of the 1970s and 1980s, named for the more famous vessel of an earlier time (see above).

Cape Yelcho. 61°03'S, 55°22'W. The NW extremity of Elephant Island, in the South Shetlands. Named by the UK in 1971 for the Yelcho (i.e., the 1916 vessel).

Paso Yelcho *see* **Graham Passage**

Yelcho Island. The 1967 volcanic eruption on Deception Island, in the South Shetlands, produced a certain disfigurement of the island, and a certain rearrangement of geographical features. One of the results of the explosion was the creation in Telefon Bay of a roughly oval-shaped volcanic islet, about 3,000 feet long and 660 feet wide, and composed of 3 principal craters and a satellite crater. It was named unofficially, by the Argentinians as Islote Marinero Suárez, by the Chileans as Isla Yelcho, and in English as Yelcho Island. After the 1970 eruption, the 3-year-old island became joined to the mainland.

Yelcho Station. Chilean scientific station on Wiencke Island.

Yeliseyev Rocks. 72°05'S, 14°30'E. They form the southern part of the Linnormen Hills in the Payer Mountains of Queen Maud Land. Ritscher discovered them in 1939. Named by the USSR in 1966 for geologist N.A. Yeliseyev.

Punta Yerbas Buena *see* **Cape Alexandra**

Yermak Point. 70°07'S, 160°41'E. In the west part of Rennick Bay, 25 miles

WNW of Znamenskiy Island. Named by the USSR in 1958 for the icebreaker *Yermak*.

Mount Yesenin. 72°03'S, 14°26'E. 2,520 m. 2 miles NW of Yeliseyev Rocks, in the Payer Mountains of Queen Maud Land. Named by the USSR in 1966 as Gora Yesenina (Mount Yesenin), for the poet S.A. Yesenin.

Cape Yevgenov. 69°03'S, 156°32'E. Ice-covered. Halfway along the NE side of Krylov Peninsula, forming the west entrance to Lauritzen Bay. Named by the USSR for hydrographer Nikolay I. Yevgenov.

Yingling Nunatak. 66°30'S, 110°37'E. Just south of the Windmill Islands, just under a mile SE of Goldenberg Ridge, in the east part of the Browning Peninsula. Named for David L. Yingling, meteorologist at Wilkes Station in 1960.

Yngvar Nielsen Glacier *see* **Nielsen Glacier**

Yoder Glacier. 75°07'S, 114°24'W. 3 miles long. Just SW of Morrison Bluff in the central part of the Kohler Range of Marie Byrd Land. It flows into Kohler Glacier. Named for Robert D. Yoder, with the US Department of State, involved with Antarctica, 1970–73.

Yoke Island. 63°58'S, 61°56'W. Also called Islotes Los Provincianos. West of the north end of Liège Island. Charted by Charcot in 1903–5, and aptly named by the UK in 1960.

York, William. Ordinary seaman on the Wilkes Expedition 1838–42. Joined in the USA. Sent home on the *Relief*, in 1839.

Yotsume Rocks. 69°44'S, 38°07'E. Also spelled Yotume Rocks. Four distinct rock exposures on the ice-covered north side of Djupvikneset Peninsula on the SW shore of Lützow-Holm Bay. Photographed by the LCE 1936–37. 20 years later surveyed by the Japanese. They call it Yotsume-iwa (the rock with 4 eyes).

Yotume Rocks *see* **Yotsume Rocks**

Mount Young. 84°28'S, 179°48'E. 770 m. A small peak on the east side of

Ramsey Glacier, just south of the Ross Ice Shelf. Discovered during Operation Highjump, on Feb. 16, 1947, and named for H. Robert Young.

Young, Dr. Adam. British surgeon on the *Williams* during the expedition led by Bransfield in 1819–20.

Young, H. Robert. Known as "Bob." A New Zealand mechanic and retired British naval rating, he was one of the shore party on Byrd's first two expeditions.

Young, Henry. Ordinary seaman on the Wilkes Expedition 1838–42. Joined in the USA. Discharged at NZ.

Young, Pam. New Zealand biologist, one of the first women to reach the South Pole (*see* **Women in Antarctica**) in 1969.

Young, R. Seaman on the *City of New York* during Byrd's 1928–30 expedition.

Young, S.S. Fireman on the *Quest*, 1921–22. Joined at Rio.

Young Glacier. 78°04'S, 84°49'W. 8 miles long. Ends at the north end of Barnes Ridge, on the east side of the Sentinel Range. Named for 1st Lt. Dale L. Young, USAF, who helped build South Pole Station in 1956–57.

Young Head. 81°29'S, 161°24'E. 350 m. A rock headland marking the north side of the entrance to Beaumont Bay, on the west side of the Ross Ice Shelf. Named for CWO Victor Young, USN, member of the Mobile Construction Battalion party at Little America in 1956.

The *Young Huron* *see* **The *Cecilia***

Young Island. 66°25'S, 162°30'E. 19 miles long. 4 miles wide. Ice-covered. Rises gently to 1,340 m. The northernmost of the Balleny Islands. Discovered in Feb. 1839 by Balleny, and named by him for merchant G.F. Young, cosponsor of Balleny's expedition.

Young Nunataks. 66°44'S, 54°08'E. 2 miles south of Mount Elkins in the Napier Mountains. Photographed by the LCE 1936–37. Named for W.F. Young, electrical fitter at Mawson Station in 1961.

Young Peak. 69°45'S, 74°31'E. Just south of Holder Peak, and 2 miles east of Mount Caroline Mikkelsen. Photographed by the LCE 1936–37, and, with Holder Peak, called Tvillingfjell (twin mountain) by the Norwegians. Renamed by the Australians for W. Young, officer-in-charge at Davis Station in 1963, who led an ANARE survey party here.

Young Point. 63°36'S, 58°55'W. 3 miles south of Cape Roquemaurel, at the east side of Bone Bay, on the west coast of Trinity Peninsula. Charted by the FIDS in 1948, and named by the UK for Adam Young.

Mount Youngman. 77°15'S, 154°21' W. 620 m. Snow-covered. A coastal mountain 4 miles SE of Scott's Nunataks, in the Alexandra Mountains. At the head of the Cumbie Glacier, it overlooks the Swinburne Ice Shelf and Sulzberger Bay. Named for Capt. Samuel A. Youngman, USN, in Antarctica in 1969 and 1970.

Yseult Island. 66°44'S, 140°56'E. To the immediate east of Tristan Island, which inspired the name Île Yseult, given by the French in 1952.

Ystekleppane Rocks. 69°59'S, 38°47' E. A group of bare rocks protruding through the ice on the east shore of Havsbotn, at the SE side of Lützow-Holm Bay. Photographed by the LCE 1936–37. Name means "the outermost lumps" in Norwegian.

Ytrehovdeholmen Island. 69°13'S, 39° 28'E. The largest of a cluster of 4 islands, 4 miles west of the Langhovde Hills, in the eastern part of Lützow-Holm Bay. Photographed by the LCE 1936–37. Name means "the outer knoll island" in Norwegian.

Ytstenut Peak. 72°30'S, 2°50'W. The most northeasterly of the peaks in the Borg Massif, in Queen Maud Land. Name means "the outermost peak" in Norwegian.

Ytterskjera. A scattered group of islands, 3 miles NW of the Flat Islands in Holme Bay, defined by the Norwegians

from photos taken by the LCE 1936–37. They included what are now the Van Hulssen Islands. It is a term no longer used.

Lake Yukidori. A little lake in Yukidori Valley. The name Yukidori means "snow petrel" in Japanese.

Yukidori Valley. 69°14'30"S, 39°46'E. 2 miles long and about ½ mile wide. In the middle of the Langhovde Hills, on the east coast of Lützow-Holm Bay. It contains Lake Yukidori and Lake Higashi Yukidori. A meltwater stream runs from the ice-cap at the head of the valley, down to Lake Yukidori, and from there to the coast. Showa Station is 19 miles to the north. There is much of biological interest here, and it is SSSI #22.

The Yukon. USNS tanker, sister ship to the *Maumee*, which it replaced after the latter's accident. Many times in at McMurdo Station, delivering fuel. On one occasion it arrived at McMurdo Sound on Jan. 28, 1982, with fuel, and left on Feb. 1, 1982. It got damaged near Beaufort Island, and went to Sydney carrying 3 passengers. The ship's cook died of a heart attack on this trip.

Yule, Henry B. Second master on the *Erebus*, during Ross's 1839–43 expedition.

Yule Bay. 70°44'S, 166°40'E. Between Cape Hooker and Cape Dayman, on the coast of northern Victoria Land. Ross discovered it in 1841, and named it for Henry B. Yule.

Yule Peak. 68°31'S, 65°37'W. 750 m. A triangular rock peak on the north side of the Mercator Ice Piedmont, in eastern Graham Land. Photographed aerially by Ellsworth on Nov. 21 and 23, 1935. Surveyed by the FIDS in Dec. 1958; they celebrated Christmas (Yuletide) near here in 1958.

Punta Yungay *see* **Bongrain Point**

Punta Z *see* **Garnerin Point**

Gora Zabor *see* **Trollslottet Mountain**

Zakharoff Ridge. 72°55'S, 75°07'E. 1½ miles SE of Mount Harding in the

Grove Mountains. Named for O. Zakharoff, radio officer at Mawson Station in 1960.

Zaneveld Glacier. 85°26'S, 176°25'W. Flows from the Polar Plateau between the Roberts Massif and the Cumulus Hills, into the upper part of the Shackleton Glacier. Named for Jacques S. Zaneveld, biologist in Antarctica in the mid-1960s.

Mount Zanuck. 85°58'S, 151°10'W. Also called Darryl Zanuck Mountain. About 5 miles long, surmounted by 3 sharp peaks, the highest rising to 2,525 m. On the south side of Albanus Glacier where that glacier joins the Robert Scott Glacier, between the La Gorce Mountains and the Watson Escarpment in the Queen Maud Mountains. Discovered by Byrd on his flight to the Pole. First visited by Quin Blackburn in 1934, during Byrd's 1933–35 expedition. Named by Byrd for Darryl Zanuck, who helped Byrd with his movie records.

Zanuck East Peak. 85°57'S, 150°53'W. The easternmost of the three peaks on Mount Zanuck. Discovered by Quin Blackburn in 1934 during Byrd's 1933–35 expedition, and named by the New Zealanders who climbed it in 1969–70.

Zapadnoye Lake. 70°44'S, 11°28'E. Half a mile long. Near the western end of the Schirmacher Hills in Queen Maud Land. Mapped and named by the USSR in 1961 as Ozero Zapadnoye (western lake).

Zapato Point. 64°36'S, 61°58'W. Also called Daedalus Point. 3 miles SW of Cañon Point on the west coast of Graham Land. First seen by de Gerlache on Feb. 7, 1898, when he sailed between it and Brooklyn Island. Named by the Argentines before 1954.

The *Zapiola*. Argentine ship, in Antarctic waters in the 1970s.

Zavadovskiy, Ivan. Captain of the *Vostok* during von Bellingshausen's expedition of 1819–21.

Zavadovskiy Island. 66°43'S, 86°24'E. Ice-covered. 200 meters high. In the West Ice Shelf, 12 miles west of Mikhaylov Island. Discovered by the USSR in 1956, and named by them for Ivan Zavadovskiy.

Zavis Peak. 79°24'S, 86°07'W. 2,195 m. 4 miles west of Navigator Peak at the south end of the Founders Escarpment in the Heritage Range. Named by the University of Minnesota Geological Party of 1963–64 for Alfred Zavis, topographic engineer with the party.

Mount Zdarsky. 66°05'S, 64°58'W. On the east side of the Simler Snowfield, between Barilari Bay and Holtedahl Bay on the west coast of Graham Land. First named Mount García by Charcot, who was the first to chart it in 1908–10. Renamed in 1959 by the UK for Mathias Zdarsky, Austrian ski pioneer.

Zebra Peak. 69°41'S, 64°56'E. 1½ miles NE of Summers Peak in the Stinear Nunataks in Mac. Robertson Land. It seems zebra-shaped.

Zebra Ridge. 70°02'S, 69°14'W. 2 miles long. A rock ridge 3 miles south of the mouth of Tumble Glacier in eastern Alexander Island. First seen aerially by Ellsworth on Nov. 23, 1935. Surveyed by the FIDS in 1948, and named because of its striped rocks.

Zed Islands. 62°26'S, 60°10'W. Also called Islas Zeta. Small group of islands almost a mile north of Williams Point on Livingston Island. The westernmost one rises to 290 m. Charted by the Discovery Investigations team in 1935, and named by them.

Mount Zeigler. 77°13'S, 143°03'W. 1,120 m. 3 miles NNE of Mount Swartley in the Allegheny Mountains of Marie Byrd Land. Named for Lt. Cdr. Luther L. Zeigler, USN, Hercules aircraft pilot during 1968.

Zeiss Needle *see* **Mount Dedo**

The *Zélée*. A small, old French corvette, commanded by Jacquinot during Dumont d'Urville's expedition of 1837–40. The cadet ship to the *Astrolabe*, it had 81 officers and men. It was not equipped for the ice.

Zélée Glacier. 66°52′S, 141°16′E. Also called Glacier Penola. 3 miles wide. 6 miles long. Flows along the west side of Lacroix Nunatak and ends in the Zélée Glacier Tongue, thus feeding Commonwealth Bay from Adélie Land. Charted by Liotard in 1949–51, and named by him for the Zélée.

Zélée Glacier Tongue. 66°47′S, 141°10′E. About 2 miles wide and 7 miles long. A prominent tongue forming the end of the Zélée Glacier, at the west side of Port Martin in East Antarctica. Named for the Zélée Glacier.

Zélée Rocks. 62°57′S, 57°15′W. In the Bransfield Strait, 17 miles north of Prime Head (the northernmost part of the Antarctic Peninsula). Discovered by Dumont d'Urville and named by him for the Zélée.

Zeller Glacier. 80°55′S, 156°30′E. 10 miles long. Flows into the south side of Byrd Glacier, just north of Mount Fries. Named for Edward J. Zeller, geologist at McMurdo Station in 1959–60 and 1960–61.

Zenith Glacier. 71°50′S, 163°44′E. 1 mile west of Johnstone Glacier. It flows from the Lanterman Range in the Bowers Mountains. Named by the New Zealanders in 1968 because of the impressive view of the Bowers Mountains from here.

Zephyr Glacier. 69°28′S, 68°30′W. On the west side of the Antarctic Peninsula.

Mount Zeppelin. 64°27′S, 61°31′W. 1,265 m. 3 miles SE of Eckener Point on the west coast of Graham Land. Charted by de Gerlache in 1897–99, and named by the UK in 1960 for the creator of the Zeppelin flying machine.

Islas Zeta see **Zed Islands**

Zeus Ridge. 64°35′S, 63°34′W. Heavily crevassed. Steep-sided. Ice-covered. Rises to 1,675 m. Extends NW from Mount Français between the Achaean and Trojan Ranges on Anvers Island. Surveyed by the FIDS in 1955, and named by the UK for the Greek god.

Zhelannaya Mountain. 72°04′S, 18°28′E. 9 miles north of Mount Karpinskiy in the Russkiye Mountains of Queen Maud Land. Named by the USSR in 1959 as Gora Zhelannaya (desired mountain).

Zhil'naya Mountain. 71°40′S, 12°38′E. 2,560 m. The central mountain of the Svarthausane Crags in the Südliche Petermann Range of the Wohlthat Mountains of Queen Maud Land. Discovered aerially by Ritscher's expedition in 1939. Named by the USSR in 1966 as Gora Zhil'naya (branching mountain) for the several mountainous ridges coming out of this summit.

Ziegler Point. 79°21′S, 83°W. A spur on the SE side of the Gross Hills in the Heritage Range. Named for Ernest L. Ziegler, at McMurdo Station in 1966.

Zigzag Bluff. 85°18′S, 163°30′W. At the foot of the Herbert Range, overlooking the Ross Ice Shelf, about 5 miles west of the terminus of the Axel Heiberg Glacier. Amundsen was probably the first to see it, and Byrd's 1928–30 expedition mapped it. The New Zealanders named it in 1962 for the peculiar folding of its marble.

Zigzag Island. 63°36′S, 59°52′W. A deeply indented island with steep cliff faces (hence the name given by the UK). Off the south coast of Tower Island.

Zilch Cliffs. 74°57′S, 134°55′W. Steep cliffs which mark the eastern end of the McDonald Heights near the coast of Marie Byrd Land. Named for Lt. Cdr. C.H. Zilch, USN, in Antarctica in 1966.

Zilva Peaks. 66°45′S, 65°23′W. Two peaks between the two arms of the Drummond Glacier in Graham Land. Named by the UK for S.S. Zilva, a pioneer in Vitamin C.

Zimmerman Island. 66°26′S, 110°27′E. Ice-free. In the Windmill Islands. Named for John R. Zimmerman, meteorologist at Wilkes Station in 1958.

Mount Zimmermann. 71°20′S, 13°21′E. 2,325 m. 3½ miles north of Ritscher Peak in the Gruber Mountains of the central part of Queen Maud Land. Discovered aerially by Ritscher's expedition in 1938-39 and named by him for the vice-president of the German Research Society.

Zinc. Has been found in Antarctica.

Mount Zinkovich. 81°08'S, 158°21'E. 2,280 m. 4 miles north of Mount Frost in the Churchill Mountains. Named for Lt. Col. Michael Zinkovich, USAF, in Antarctica, 1962.

Zircons. Are found here, especially in the Reinbolt Hills of Enderby Land.

Mount Zirzow. 83°08'S, 49°06'W. 1,615 m. 4 miles north of Mount Mann at the eastern edge of the Lexington Table in the Forrestal Range of the Pensacola Mountains. Named for Cdr. Charles F. Zirzow, USN, in Antarctica, 1966-67.

Zittel Cliffs. 80°40'S, 25°39'W. In the Shackleton Range.

Znamenskiy Island. 70°14'S, 161°51'E. A high, circular, ice-covered island. 2½ miles long. In Rennick Bay just north of the terminus of the Rennick Glacier in Oates Land. Charted by the USSR in 1958 and named by them for hydrographer K.I. Znamenskiy.

Zodiac Landing Craft. Fast, sturdy, rubberized, inflatable, and highly versatile boats which take passengers from the cruise ships to the land. The Mark II was 14 feet long, and the Mark III was 16 feet, powered by 9 and 25 hp outboard motors.

Zoller Glacier. 77°53'S, 162°18'E. In the Cathedral Rocks between Emmanuel and Darkowski Glaciers. Flows into the Ferrar Glacier in southern Victoria Land. Charted by members of Scott's last expedition, and named by the USA in 1964 for John E. Zoller, USN, chaplain with Little America V in 1957.

Zonda Glacier. 69°33'S, 68°30'W. On the west coast of the Antarctic Peninsula.

Zonda Towers. 69°34'S, 68°18'W. On the west side of the Antarctic Peninsula.

Zotikov Glacier. 85°02'S, 169°15'W. 8 miles long. Flows from Mount Fisher in the Prince Olav Mountains and runs into Liv Glacier just east of Hardiman Peak. Named by the USA for USSR exchange scientist Igor A. Zotikov, at McMurdo Station, 1965.

Zub Lake. 70°45'S, 11°44'E. ½ mile long. 1 mile ESE of Tsentral'naya Hill, in the Schirmacher Hills of Queen Maud Land. Shaped like a tooth (zub in Russian), and named and mapped by the USSR in 1961.

Zubchatyy Ice Shelf. 67°13'S, 49°05'E. A small ice shelf bordering the south side of Sakellari Peninsula in Enderby Land. The ice front is serrated, and the Russian name means "toothed."

Zubov Bay. 65°42'S, 65°52'W. Also called Bahía Marcial Mora. 2½ miles wide. An indentation into the east side of Renaud Island in the Biscoe Islands. Named by the UK in 1959 for Nikolay N. Zubov, USSR oceanographer.

Mount Zuckerhut. 71°25'S, 13°27'E. Also called Sukkertoppen (by the Norwegians). 2,525 m. 2 miles SE of Ritscher Peak in the Gruber Mountains of Queen Maud Land. Ritscher discovered it in 1939 and named it (Sugarloaf).

Zuhn, Arthur A. Physicist on the shore party of Byrd's 1933-35 expedition.

Zuhn Bluff. 72°13'S, 98°08'W. Also called Zuhn Peak. 5 miles ESE of Mount Bramhall in the Walker Mountains of Thurston Island. Named for Arthur A. Zuhn.

Zuhn Peak   *see*   **Zuhn Bluff**

Zukriegel Island. 65°54'S, 65°48'W. 1 mile long. Between Rabot Island and the Hennessey Islands in the Biscoe Islands. Named by the UK in 1959 for Josef Zukriegel, Czech geographer.

Cape Zumberge. 76°14'S, 69°40'W. Juts out into the Ronne Ice Shelf from the Orville Coast, just south of the Hauberg Mountains. It marks the SW end of the Orville Coast. This may be the Zumberge Nunatak described by Neuberg, etc., who saw it from a distance. Named for James H. Zumberge, president of the Polar Research Board in the 1970s.

Zumberge Nunatak *see* **Cape Zumberge**

Zuncich Hill. 75°50'S, 142°51'E. 1,075 m. Ice-covered. Between Siemiatkowski Glacier and El-Sayed Glacier in Marie Byrd Land. Named for Lt. Joseph L. Zuncich, USNR, Hercules aircraft navigator in Antarctica, 1966.

Zúñiga Glacier. 74°34'S, 111°52'W. On the Bear Peninsula, on the coast of Marie Byrd Land.

Zurn Peak. 75°44'S, 115°40'W. 1,515 m. At the north edge of Toney Mountain, about 4 miles NE of Richmond Peak, in Marie Byrd Land. Named for Walter A. Zurn, station scientific leader at Amundsen-Scott South Pole Station in 1972.

Lake Zvezda. 68°32'S, 78°27'E. Large, irregularly-shaped lake. ½ mile SE of Lake Cowan, in the eastern sector of the Vestfold Hills. The name means "star" in Russian, and was named and photographed by the USSR in 1956.

Zwiesel Mountain. 71°43'S, 12°08'E. Also called Zwieselhogda. 2,970 m. Highly dissected mountain. Forms the northern portion of the Pieck Range in the Petermann Ranges of Queen Maud Land. Ritscher discovered it in 1938–39 and named it Zwieselberg (forked mountain).

Zykov Glacier. 70°37'S, 164°46'E. A valley glacier. 25 miles long. In the Anare Mountains. It reaches the coast between Cape Williams and Cooper Bluffs. Named by the USSR in 1958 for Yevgeniy Zykov (*see* **Deaths, 1957**).

Zykov Island. 66°32'S, 93°01'E. Between Fulmar Island and Buromskiy Island in the Haswell Islands. Discovered and mapped by Mawson during the AAE 1911–14, and remapped by the USSR in 1956. In 1958 they named it for Yevgeniy Zykov (*see* **Zykov Glacier**).

CHRONOLOGY

Dates are Gregorian (note, e.g., the case of the Russian navigator von Bellingshausen, whose original Julian calender dates have been converted). See also the Expeditions section of this book, following.

1502
April 7   Vespucci claims a day where the night lasts 15 hours (72°S)

1687
Dec. 25   Wafer at 62°45'S

1719
Oct. 1   William Camell drowns, possibly at 60°37'S, 5°W

1773
Jan. 17   Cook crosses the Antarctic Circle at 39°35'E
Dec. 20   Cook crosses the Antarctic Circle a second time

1774
Jan. 26   Cook crosses the Antarctic Circle a third time
Jan. 30   Cook reaches a new southing record of 71°10'S (1,130 miles from the Pole)

1819
Feb. 19   Smith sights the South Shetlands
June 15   Smith reaches 61°12'S, in winter
Sept. 4   The *San Telmo* abandoned, at 62°S
Oct. 14   Smith discovers the South Shetlands properly
Oct. 16   Smith takes possession of New South Britain (South Shetlands)

1820
Jan. 16   Bransfield arrives at the South Shetlands in the *Williams*
Jan. 17   The *Hersilia* reaches 60°50'S, 58°38'W
Jan. 17   Demidov and Simonov land on an iceberg
Jan. 18   The *Hersilia* sights Smith Island in the South Shetlands
Jan. 20   The *Mirnyy* collides with an iceberg; no real damage
Jan. 22   Bransfield takes possession of King George Island
Jan. 23   The *Hersilia* anchors off Rugged Island, in the South Shetlands
Jan. 26   Von Bellingshausen crosses the Antarctic Circle
Jan. 27   Bransfield heads SW from King George Island
Jan. 27   Von Bellingshausen sights the continental ice shelf, around Princess Martha Land
Jan. 30   Smith and Bransfield sight the continent itself

1133

Feb. 4   Bransfield takes possession of Clarence Island
Feb. 7   The *Hersilia* leaves the South Shetlands
Feb. 23   The *Williams* stopped by ice at 64°50′S, off the NE coast of Graham Land
Oct. 30   The *Hersilia*, back in the South Shetlands, makes its rendezvous point
            at Hersilia Cove
Nov. 10   Palmer, in command of the *Hero*, sights Smith Island
Nov. 15   Palmer explores inside Deception Island
Nov. 17   Palmer sights the Antarctic Peninsula
Nov. 19   Palmer discovers Yankee Harbor
Nov. 28   Palmer begins a cruise around Livingston Island
Nov. 30   The *Huron, Huntress,* and *Cecilia* sight the South Shetlands
Dec. 1   Alexander Clark's expedition arrives at the South Shetlands
Dec. 5   Palmer ends his cruise around Livingston Island
Dec. 7   The wreck of the *Clothier* in Blythe Bay
Dec. 8   The *Huron, Huntress,* and *Cecilia* land at Yankee Harbor
Dec. 8   Von Bellingshausen goes south of 60°S again, at 163°E
Dec. 11   Palmer begins another tour of Livingston Island
Dec. 16   The *Dragon* meets the *Cora* off Desolation Island
Dec. 16   Palmer finishes his second Livingston Island circumnavigation
Dec. 16   Palmer, in the *Hero*, meets the *Jane Maria* at 8 p.m.
Dec. 19   The New York Sealing Expedition arrives at Yankee Harbor
Dec. 24   Von Bellingshausen crosses the Antarctic Circle at 164°W
Dec. 25   The wreck of the *Lady Trowbridge*
Dec. 25   The wreck of the *Hannah*
Dec. 30   The wreck of the *Ann*

1821
Jan. 2   The *George* badly damaged in a gale
Jan. 6   The wreck of the *Cora*
Jan. 10   Von Bellingshausen crosses the Antarctic Circle again
Jan. 13   The *Vostok* stopped by the pack-ice, just south of the South Sandwich
            Islands
Jan. 21   Von Bellingshausen discovers Peter I Island, the first land within the
            Antarctic Circle
Jan. 28   Von Bellingshausen discovers Alexander I Land (Alexander Island)
Jan. 30   Davis begins his exploration in the *Cecilia,* south of the South Shet-
            lands
Jan. 31   Davis sights Low Island
Feb. 1   Salvage auction of the wrecked *Clothier* held in Clothier Harbor
Feb. 2   Davis lands on Low Island
Feb. 6   Palmer, in the *Hero*, meets von Bellingshausen, in the *Vostok*
Feb. 6   Davis leaves Low Island
Feb. 7   Davis lands at Hughes Bay, the first landing on the continent
Feb. 8   The *Aurora* reaches Yankee Harbor, after 2 months of looking for the
            South Shetlands
Feb. 10   Davis finishes his voyage of exploration
Feb. 11   Von Bellingshausen leaves Antarctic waters
Feb. 12   Burdick takes the *Cecilia* on an exploration to Low Island
Feb. 15   Burdick sights the continent
Feb. 19   Burdick returns to Yankee Harbor
March 7   The wreck of the *Venus*
March 10   The *Huntress* leaves Antarctica

March 31   The *Huron* and *Cecilia* leave Antarctica
April 8   The *Sarah* lost at sea
Nov. 30   Powell and Palmer team up at Elephant Island
Dec. 6   Powell and Palmer discover the South Orkneys
Dec. 12   Michael McLeod lands at the South Orkneys

1822
Feb. 17   Davis leaves Antarctica in the *Huron* and *Cecilia*
March 25   The *Mellona* just escapes being wrecked on Desolation Island
Dec. 13   The *Wasp* gets hampered by the ice at 60°11'S, 10°23'E
Dec. 15   The *Wasp* clears the ice and heads north

1823
Jan. 17   Presumed date of the death of the crew of the *Jenny*
Feb. 1   Morrell in the *Wasp* is at 64°52'S
Feb. 20   Weddell sets southing record of 74°15'S, in the *Jane*
March 14   The *Wasp* reaches 70°14'S, 40°03'W, in the Weddell Sea

1829
Jan. 7   Foster takes possession of Hoseason Island

1831
Jan. 22   Biscoe crosses the Antarctic Circle
Jan. 29   Biscoe reaches 69°03'S
Feb. 24   Biscoe sights the continent at 66°08'S
Feb. 28   Biscoe sights Enderby Land

1832
Feb. 15   Biscoe discovers Adelaide Island
Feb. 19   Biscoe lands on Pitt's Island
Feb. 21   Biscoe annexes Graham Land

1833
Dec. 26   Kemp sights Kemp Land

1838
Feb. 2   Dumont d'Urville leaves the South Orkneys for the south
Feb. 4   The *Astrolabe* and the *Zélée* get stuck in the ice
Feb. 9   The *Astrolabe* and the *Zélée* get free of the ice
Feb. 27   Dumont d'Urville discovers Louis Philippe Land and Joinville Island

1839
Feb. 1   Balleny reaches 69°02'S, the furthest south at that time in the Pacific
            Ocean
Feb. 9   Balleny discovers the Balleny Islands
March 1   The Wilkes Expedition reaches Antarctica
March 2   Balleny discovers the Sabrina Coast
March 5   Wilkes abandons his first voyage to Antarctica
March 6   The *Peacock* at 62°S
March 10   The *Sea Gull* lands at Deception Island
March 11   William Steward dies on the *Peacock*
March 17   The *Sea Gull* leaves Deception Island
March 22   The *Flying Fish* gets to 70°04'S
March 24   The *Sabrina* disappears in a gale

1840
Jan. 11   Wilkes hits the ice barrier at 64°11'S, 164°30'E
Jan. 16   Hudson joins Wilkes at the ice barrier

Jan. 16   Wilkes sights the Antarctic continent
Jan. 19   Wilkes confirms sighting of the continent
Jan. 19   Dumont d'Urville sights the continent in the same area
Jan. 20   Du Bouzet of the *Zélée* lands on an island off the coast of Adélie Land
Jan. 21   Dumont d'Urville takes possession of Adélie Land
Jan. 21   The *Flying Fish* joins the Wilkes Expedition at the ice barrier
Jan. 21   The *Peacock* captures an emperor penguin
Jan. 24   The *Peacock* hit by icebergs and badly damaged
Jan. 25   The *Peacock* heads for Sydney for repairs
Jan. 30   The *Porpoise* meets the *Astrolabe*
Jan. 31   Dumont d'Urville discovers the Clarie Coast (Wilkes Coast)
Feb. 6   The *Flying Fish* leaves Antarctica for New Zealand
Feb. 12   Wilkes discovers the Budd Coast
Feb. 14   Wilkes discovers the Knox Coast and Termination Land
Feb. 21   Wilkes leaves Antarctica

1841
Jan. 1   Ross crosses the Antarctic Circle for the first time
Jan. 5   Ross pushes south through the pack-ice
Jan. 9   Ross is the first ever into the Ross Sea
Jan. 11   Ross lands a party on the Possession Islands
Jan. 15   Ross discovers the Victoria Ice Barrier (Ross Ice Shelf)
Jan. 22   Ross sets a new southing record
Jan. 25   Ross sights Mount Erebus and calls it High Island
Jan. 26   Ross names Mount Erebus more correctly when he sees it in a state of
           eruption
Jan. 27   Ross lands on Franklin Island, and takes possession
Dec. 17   Ross back in the pack-ice for another season in Antarctica
Dec. 31   The crews of Ross' ships celebrate Christmas on an ice floe

1843
March 5   Ross reaches 71° 30′ S on his third trip south

1874
Feb. 16   The *Challenger* crosses the Antarctic Circle

1893
Jan. 8   Dundee Island discovered
Jan. 10   The *Active* runs into a reef in a gale for 6 hours

1894
Dec. 25   The *Antarctic* crosses the Antarctic Circle

1895
Jan. 16   The *Antarctic* sights Cape Adare
Jan. 18   The *Antarctic* lands a party on the Possession Islands
Jan. 24   Borchgrevink and Kristensen land at Cape Adare, the first confirmed
           landing on the continent
Feb. 8   The *Antarctic* leaves Antarctica

1898
Jan. 19   The *Belgica* reaches the Antarctic
Jan. 20   The *Belgica* reaches the South Shetlands
Jan. 21   The *Belgica* hits an iceberg, but no damage

Jan. 22	Carl Wiencke drowns
Jan. 23	The *Belgica* discovers the Gerlache Strait, and sights the continent; a landing is made
Jan. 31	Amundsen leads the first sledging expedition in Antarctica (*see* **Sledges**)
Feb. 15	The *Belgica* crosses the Antarctic Circle
March 3	The *Belgica* gets stuck in the ice
May 31	The *Belgica* reaches 71° 36′ S, 87° 40′ W, its furthest south
June 5	Danco dies of scurvy
Nov. 19	In disgust, Amundsen resigns his commission on the *Belgica*

1899

Jan. 11	The crew of the *Belgica* start cutting their way out of the pack-ice
Jan. 12	Borchgrevink sights one of the Balleny Islands
Jan. 23	Borchgrevink crosses the Antarctic Circle
Feb. 14	Borchgrevink breaks free of the pack-ice
Feb. 15	The *Belgica* gets free of the pack-ice
Feb. 17	Borchgrevink sights Cape Adare
Feb. 18	Borchgrevink lands at Cape Adare for the winter
March 2	The *Southern Cross* leaves Cape Adare for the winter
March 14	The *Belgica* finally escapes the pack-ice
Oct. 14	Hanson dies on Borchgrevink's wintering-over party

1900

Jan. 28	The *Southern Cross* returns to Cape Adare to pick up Borchgrevink
Feb. 2	Borchgrevink's party taken aboard the *Southern Cross*
Feb. 16	Borchgrevink sets a new southing record of 78° 50′ S
Feb. 28	The *Southern Cross* crosses the Antarctic Circle going home

1902

Jan. 2	Scott at 65° 30′ S, in the *Discovery*
Jan. 3	Scott crosses the Antarctic Circle for the first time
Jan. 5	The *Discovery* reaches the pack-ice
Jan. 8	Scott sights Antarctica for the first time (Victoria Land)
Jan. 9	Scott calls at Cape Adare
Jan. 11	The *Antarctic* reaches the South Shetlands
Jan. 18	Scott reaches Wood Bay, Victoria Land, looking for a base
Jan. 20	Scott reaches Granite Harbor and, later in the day, McMurdo Sound
Jan. 21	Scott leaves McMurdo Sound, only the second explorer known to have visited it, and goes around Ross Island to Cape Crozier
Jan. 30	Scott discovers Edward VII Peninsula (or Land, as he called it), the first significant Antarctic discovery of the 20th century
Feb. 1	The *Antarctic* reaches 63° 30′ S, 45° 07′ W
Feb. 4	Scott goes up in a balloon to 790 feet, the first aerial view of Antarctica
Feb. 8	Scott decides to winter-over at Hut Point
Feb. 9	Nordenskjöld chooses Snow Hill Island as his winter campsite
Feb. 19	Shackleton, Wilson, and Ferrar manhaul sledges to White Island
Feb. 21	The *Gauss* gets stuck in the ice
Feb. 22	Shackleton, Wilson, and Ferrar return to base
March 2	The *Gauss* now unable to escape at all
March 4	The Royds-Skelton party sets out for Cape Crozier
March 11	Shackleton leads a whale boat party of 6 to look for Vince and Hare
March 12	Wilson leads a search party overland to look for Vince and Hare
March 13	Charles Hare walks into the camp, alone

March 18	Vahsel leads the first sledging expedition from the *Gauss*
March 26	Vahsel returns from his sledging expedition
March 31	The large depot-laying party sets out from the *Discovery*
April 2	The depot-laying party returns, foiled by low temperatures
April 21	Von Drygalski sledges to Gaussberg
April 27	Von Drygalski reaches Gaussberg
June 12	Scott decides to go for the Pole later that year
Sept. 2	Spring sledging expeditions commence from the *Discovery*
Sept. 10	Royds and Koettlitz sledge to Cape Crozier with a party of 4
Sept. 11	Armitage, Ferrar, Cross, G. Scott, Walker, and Heald sledge to the west
Sept. 17	Scott, Shackleton, and Barne set out on a depot-laying expedition to Minna Bluff
Sept. 19	Scott, Shackleton, and Barne return due to adverse conditions
Sept. 24	Scott, Shackleton, and Feather set out
Sept. 28	Nordenskjöld, Sobral, and Jonassen set out to explore Oscar II Coast
Oct. 1	Scott, Shackleton, and Feather establish Bluff Depot
Oct. 30	Barne leads support party toward the Pole for Scott
Oct. 31	Nordenskjöld's party arrives back at camp after 380 miles on foot
Nov. 2	Scott begins his trip to the Pole
Nov. 3	Scott catches up with the support party
Nov. 10	The *Antarctic* back in Antarctic waters
Nov. 13	The first half of Scott's support party returns home
Nov. 15	The second half of Barne's support party for Scott returns home
Nov. 25	Scott reaches 80°01'S, a new southing record
Nov. 29	Armitage leaves for Victoria Land
Dec. 5	The *Antarctic* sets out to relieve Nordenskjöld on Snow Hill Island
Dec. 9	Snatcher dies, the first of Scott's dogs to die on the trip
Dec. 16	Scott reaches 80°32'S, a new southing record
Dec. 25	Colbeck discovers the Scott Islands
Dec. 27	Scott discovers Mount Markham
Dec. 29	Andersson, Duse, and Grunden set ashore at Hope Bay
Dec. 30	Scott, Wilson, and Shackleton, still on the Ross Ice Shelf, reach a new southing record of 82°16'30"S

1903

Jan. 1	Spud, one of Scott's dogs, is carried on the sledge, and then killed
Jan. 5	Armitage reaches the polar ice cap
Jan. 9	Ice begins to squeeze the *Antarctic*
Jan. 10	Ice pressures the *Antarctic* to list to starboard
Jan. 13	The Hope Bay party back at its base at Hope Bay (*see* **Nordenskjöld**)
Jan. 13	Scott reaches Depot B on his return trip
Jan. 15	The last of Scott's dogs are killed
Jan. 16	The *Antarctic* returns to an upright position
Jan. 19	Armitage makes it back to base
Jan. 23	The *Morning* arrives in McMurdo Sound
Jan. 28	Scott reaches Depot A on his return trip
Feb. 3	Scott, Wilson, and Shackleton reach the *Discovery*
Feb. 3	The *Antarctic* is afloat again, but leaking badly
Feb. 3	Bruce sights the South Orkneys
Feb. 4	Bruce lands on Saddle Island
Feb. 8	The *Gauss* escapes from the ice
Feb. 11	The Hope Bay party begins to build a substantial hut

Feb. 12	The *Antarctic* sinks
Feb. 22	Bruce gets to 70°25′S on his first voyage south
Feb. 28	The crew of the *Antarctic* gets ashore at Paulet Island
March 2	The *Morning* leaves McMurdo Sound for New Zealand
March 31	Von Drygalski and the *Gauss* leave Antarctica
June 7	Ole Christian Wennersgaard dies
Sept. 29	The Hope Bay party sets out again for Snow Hill Island
Oct. 6	The Hope Bay party begins its trek across the Crown Prince Gustav Channel
Oct. 9	The Hope Bay party reaches Vega Island
Oct. 12	The Hope Bay party meets Nordenskjöld and Jonassen
Oct. 26	Scott leads an expedition to the polar ice cap
Oct. 26	Nordenskjöld, Andersson, and Sobral sledge to Seymour Island
Nov. 4	Larsen reaches Hope Bay
Nov. 7	Bodman and Åkerlundh leave Snow Hill Island for Seymour Island
Nov. 7	Larsen begins his row across Erebus and Terror Gulf
Nov. 7	The *Uruguay* reaches Nordenskjöld's party
Nov. 13	Scott reaches the polar ice cap
Nov. 22	The *Scotia* freed from the ice at Laurie Island
Nov. 22	Skelton, Handsley, and Feather forced to return to base
Nov. 27	The *Scotia* sails for Buenos Aires for refitting
Nov. 30	Scott turns back on the polar ice cap
Dec. 24	Scott makes it back to base

1904

Jan. 5	The *Morning* and the *Terra Nova* arrive at Ross Island
Feb. 1	Charcot passes the South Shetlands going south
Feb. 5	The engine on the *Français* gives trouble
Feb. 7	The *Français* anchors in Flandres Bay
Feb. 16	The *Discovery* freed from the ice after 2 years
Feb. 18	The *Français* leaves Flandres Bay
Feb. 19	The *Français* discovers Port Lockroy
March 3	The *Scotia* reaches 72°18′S on its second voyage south
March 5	The *Discovery* crosses the Antarctic Circle homeward
March 6	Bruce discovers Coats Land
May 30	Charcot goes on a picnic
Nov. 24	Charcot's party sets out to survey Graham Land
Dec. 30	The *Uruguay* relieves the last of Bruce's crew on Laurie Island

1905

Jan. 13	Charcot sights Adelaide Island
Jan. 15	The *Français* strikes a rock, sustaining damage
Jan. 29	The *Français* makes Port Lockroy
Feb. 8	The *Français* leaves Port Lockroy
Feb. 15	The *Français* leaves the Antarctic

1908

Jan. 14	The *Nimrod* and the *Koonya* reach the Antarctic Circle
Jan. 15	The *Koonya* returns to New Zealand
Jan. 16	The *Nimrod* arrives at the Ross Sea
Jan. 23	Shackleton sights the Ross Ice Shelf
Jan. 24	Shackleton names the Bay of Whales
Jan. 29	The *Nimrod* arrives at McMurdo Sound

Jan. 31	Dr.Marshall removes Mackintosh's eye (*see* **Mackintosh**)
Feb. 1	Adams, Joyce, and Wild sledge to Hut Point from the *Nimrod*
Feb. 1	Shackleton unloads the first automobile in Antarctica
Feb. 3	Shackleton goes ashore from the *Nimrod* at Cape Royds
Feb. 3	Adams, Joyce, and Wild return from the Discovery Hut
Feb. 3	Shackleton selects Cape Royds as a base area
Feb. 22	The *Nimrod* returns to New Zealand
March 2	Shackleton's crew decides to climb Mount Erebus
March 5	Mawson, David, and Mackay set off for Mount Erebus, with a supporting party consisting of Adams (supporting party leader), Marshall, and Brocklehurst
March 10	Mount Erebus climbed for the first time, at 10 a.m.
March 11	The Erebus party returns to Cape Royds
April 6	Brocklehurst's toes removed by Marshall and Mackay
July 21	Great Britain makes the first territorial claim in Antarctica
Aug. 14	Shackleton revisits the Discovery Hut
Aug. 15	Shackleton, David, and Armytage push out onto the Ross Ice Shelf
Aug. 16	Shackleton's party back at the Discovery Hut in a blizzard
Aug. 22	Shackleton's party back at Cape Royds
Sept. 19	Day, Brocklehurst, and Adams go expeditioning in the automobile
Sept. 22	Shackleton, Adams, Marshall, Wild, Joyce, and Marston leave for the Discovery Hut on a depot-laying expedition
Sept. 25	Shackleton's party at White Island
Oct. 5	David, Mawson, and Mackay leave for the South Magnetic Pole
Oct. 6	Shackleton lays Depot A at 79°36'S
Oct. 17	Shackleton's party back at the Discovery Hut
Oct. 18	Shackleton's party back at Cape Royds
Oct. 29	Shackleton leaves Cape Royds for the Pole
Oct. 30	Shackleton's Polar Party reaches the Discovery Hut
Oct. 31	Shackleton walks back to Cape Royds for more equipment and salt for the ponies
Nov. 1	Shackleton back at Hut Point
Nov. 3	Shackleton's Polar Party leaves the Discovery Hut for the Pole
Nov. 7	Shackleton's supporting party turn back for base
Nov. 15	Shackleton reaches Depot A
Nov. 16	Shackleton passes 80°S
Nov. 19	Shackleton reaches 80°32'S
Nov. 21	Shackleton shoots the pony Chinaman, and establishes Depot B
Nov. 22	Shackleton sights the Queen Maud Mountains
Nov. 26	Shackleton reaches 82°18'30"S, 168°E, a new southing record
Nov. 27	Shackleton shoots the pony Grisi, and establishes Depot C
Dec. 1	Shackleton shoots the pony Quan, and reaches 83°16'S, a new southing record
Dec. 2	Shackleton decides to attack the mountains rather than circumvent them
Dec. 3	Shackleton discovers the Beardmore Glacier
Dec. 4	Shackleton begins his ascent of the Beardmore Glacier
Dec. 6	Shackleton lays Depot D, 1,700 feet up the Beardmore Glacier
Dec. 7	Shackleton loses Socks, the last pony, down a crevasse
Dec. 16	Shackleton reaches 84°50'S, a new southing record
Dec. 17	Shackleton lays Depot E
Dec. 19	Shackleton reaches 85°05'S, a new southing record
Dec. 20	Shackleton reaches 85°17'S, a new southing record (8,000 feet and rising)

Dec. 22	Charcot reaches the South Shetlands, going south
Dec. 25	Charcot leaves Deception Island after a stay of a few days
Dec. 27	Shackleton reaches 86°19'S, a new southing record
Dec. 29	Charcot reaches Booth Island in the *Pourquoi Pas?*
Dec. 31	Shackleton reaches 86°54'S, a new southing record

1909

Jan. 1	Shackleton reaches 87°06'30"S, a new Polar record (north or south)
Jan. 1	The *Pourquoi Pas?* harbors at Port Circumcision on Petermann Island
Jan. 4	Shackleton establishes Depot F
Jan. 4	Charcot sets out to scout the Cape Tuxen coast in a long boat
Jan. 5	The *Nimrod* returns to McMurdo Sound to pick up Shackleton
Jan. 6	Shackleton reaches 88°07'S, a new Polar record
Jan. 7	Charcot's party just make it back to the *Pourquoi Pas?* alive
Jan. 8	The *Pourquoi Pas?* strikes a rock
Jan. 9	Shackleton reaches 88°23'S, 162°E, a new Polar record; at this point, with only 97 miles to go for the Pole, he turns back
Jan. 16	The *Nimrod,* under Capt. Evans, finally gets to Cape Royds
Jan. 16	David, Mackay, and Mawson discover the South Magnetic Pole
Jan. 20	Shackleton reaches Depot E, on the Beardmore Glacier, on the return trip
Jan. 28	Shackleton reaches Depot D, on the lower part of the Beardmore
Feb. 2	Shackleton reaches Depot C
Feb. 4	David, Mackay, and Mawson return to the *Nimrod*
Feb. 13	Shackleton reaches Depot B
Feb. 20	Shackleton reaches Depot A
Feb. 23	Charcot's expedition celebrates Mardi Gras in costume
Feb. 23	Shackleton reaches Bluff Depot, at Minna Bluff
Feb. 27	Shackleton and Wild leave Bluff Depot for Hut Point
Feb. 28	Shackleton gets back to the Discovery Hut with Wild
March 1	Shackleton and Wild fire signals to the *Nimrod* from Hut Point
March 2	Shackleton and Wild get back to the *Nimrod*
March 4	The *Nimrod* leaves McMurdo Sound
March 9	The *Nimrod* leaves the Ross Sea
March 10	The *Nimrod* leaves Antarctic waters for home
Sept. 18	Charcot sends an expedition to Graham Land from the *Pourquoi Pas?*
Nov. 27	The *Pourquoi Pas?* arrives back at Deception Island

1910

Jan. 7	Charcot leaves Deception Island for the south again
Jan. 10	The *Pourquoi Pas?* at 69°S, and spots Charcot Land (Charcot Island)
Jan. 11	The *Pourquoi Pas?* at 70°S, but unable to land on Charcot Island
Jan. 22	Charcot turns for home at 124°W
Dec. 9	Scott reaches the pack-ice at 177°41'W
Dec. 30	Scott reaches the Ross Sea

1911

Jan. 2	Scott reaches Cape Evans
Jan. 2	Amundsen croses the Antarctic Circle
Jan. 3	Amundsen, in the *Fram* enters the pack-ice at 175°35'E
Jan. 5	Scott unloads personnel from the *Terra Nova*
Jan. 7	Amundsen gets through the pack-ice into the Ross Sea
Jan. 14	Amundsen arrives at the Bay of Whales

Jan. 15   Scott revisits the Discovery Hut after 7 years away
Jan. 24   Scott begins his depot-laying operations for his push to the Pole later in
          the year
Jan. 28   The *Terra Nova* leaves for the Edward VII Peninsula
Feb. 3   The *Terra Nova* meets the *Fram* in the Bay of Whales
Feb. 9   Campbell's Northern Party sets out from Cape Evans
Feb. 10   Amundsen's first depot-laying team sets out
Feb. 14   Amundsen's depot-laying team reaches 80°S
Feb. 16   Amundsen back at Framheim, his base
Feb. 16   The *Fram* leaves for Buenos Aires for the winter
Feb. 22   Amundsen sets out to lay his 83°S Depot
Feb. 27   Amundsen reaches his already-laid 80°S Depot (actually at 79°59'S)
March 3   Amundsen reaches 81°S, and sets up a depot at 81°01'S
March 6   Shirase reaches Victoria Land in the *Kainan Maru*
March 8   Amundsen lays a depot at 82°S
March 23 Amundsen back at Framheim
June 27   Wilson, Bowers, and Cherry-Garrard leave for Cape Crozier
July 29   Campbell, Priestley, and Abbott go on a short sledging expedition
Aug. 1   Wilson, Bowers, and Cherry-Garrard arrive back at Cape Evans
Sept. 8   Amundsen sets out for the Pole
Sept. 14 Amundsen reaches the 80°S Depot
Sept. 16 Amundsen back at Framheim because of bad weather
Oct. 20   Amundsen sets out for the Pole again
Oct. 23   Amundsen reaches the 80°S Depot again
Oct. 24   Scott leaves Cape Evans for the Discovery Hut, en route to the Pole
Oct. 26   Amundsen leaves the 80°S Depot, going south
Oct. 31   Amundsen reaches the 81°S Depot again
Nov. 3   Scott leaves the Discovery Hut for the Pole
Nov. 5   Amundsen reaches the 82°S Depot again
Nov. 5   Grif Taylor's Western Journey Party sets out for Victoria Land
Nov. 7   Amundsen leaves the 82°S Depot, going south
Nov. 18   Amundsen reaches the Axel Heiberg Glacier
Nov. 20   Amundsen starts the ascent of the Axel Heiberg Glacier
Nov. 21   Amundsen reaches the top of the Axel Heiberg Glacier
Nov. 24   Day and Hooper turn back from Scott's party at 81°15'S
Nov. 29   Amundsen stuck in the Devil's Glacier
Nov. 29   Prestrud, Johansen, and Stubberud are the first to get to the Edward
          VII Peninsula
Dec. 3   Amundsen gets out of the Devil's Glacier
Dec. 4   Amundsen in the Devil's Ballroom
Dec. 7   Amundsen reaches 88°09'S
Dec. 8   Amundsen beats Shackleton's southing record
Dec. 10   Scott's party begins the ascent of the Beardmore Glacier
Dec. 11   Filchner in Antarctic waters in the *Deutschland*
Dec. 11   Meares and Gerof turn back on Scott's party
Dec. 14   Amundsen reaches the area of the South Pole
Dec. 16   Amundsen hoists the Norwegian flag at the South Pole (or as near to it
          as his instruments allow)
Dec. 17   Bjaaland the first to stand on the actual Pole point
Dec. 18   Amundsen leaves the Pole on his return trip
Dec. 21   Four of Scott's party turn back at the Beardmore Glacier
Dec. 25   Amundsen reaches the 86°25'S Depot on the return trip

1912

Jan. 1	Scott reaches the Polar Plateau
Jan. 2	Amundsen at the Devil's Glacier again
Jan. 3	The *Terra Nova* picks up Campbell's Northern Party from Cape Adare
Jan. 4	Crean, Teddy Evans, and Lashly turn back from Scott's party at 87° 32′ S
Jan. 7	Amundsen reaches the bottom of the Axel Heiberg Glacier
Jan. 8	Cape Denison selected by Mawson as the Main Base on the AAE
Jan. 8	Campbell's party dropped at Cape Evans by the *Terra Nova*
Jan. 9	The *Fram* returns to the Bay of Whales
Jan. 9	Scott reaches 88° 23′ S, 162° E
Jan. 16	The *Kainan Maru* reaches the Ross Ice Shelf
Jan. 17	Scott reaches the area of the South Pole
Jan. 17	Amundsen reaches the 82° S Depot on his return trip
Jan. 19	Unloading completed at Cape Denison
Jan. 25	Amundsen gets back to Framheim
Jan. 28	Shirase's Dash Patrol reaches 80° 05′ S
Jan. 30	The *Fram* leaves the Bay of Whales with Amundsen aboard
Jan. 30	Filchner sights land in the *Deutschland*
Jan. 30	Main Base completed at Cape Denison
Feb. 5	The *Terra Nova* arrives back at Cape Evans
Feb. 9	The *Fram* crosses the Antarctic Circle
Feb. 9	The unloading of the *Deutschland* begins
Feb. 17	Evans dies on Scott's return trip
Feb. 18	The Filchner Ice Shelf begins to crack under Filchner's hut
Feb. 18	Evans buried at the foot of the Beardmore Glacier
Feb. 20	The men on the Filchner expedition manage to dismantle the hut
Feb. 21	A gale damages two of Campbell's tents
March 6	The *Deutschland* is frozen in for the winter in the Weddell Sea pack-ice
March 17	Campbell's party moves into an ice cave for the winter
March 17	Oates walks out of Scott's tent in the blizzard
March 21	Browning kills a seal which contains 36 still-edible fish in its stomach
March 29	Probable date of death of Scott, Wilson, and Bowers
April 4	Erection begins of the two radio masts at Cape Denison
June 23	Filchner, Kling, and König set out to find New South Greenland
June 30	Filchner, Kling, and König return to their ship
Aug. 9	Mawson sets up Aladdin's Cave, 5½ miles south of Main Base
Sept. 1	The radio masts finally erected at Cape Denison
Sept. 30	Campbell's party makes a break for Cape Evans
Oct. 13	The radio masts wrecked by the winds at Cape Denison
Oct. 28	Campbell's party crosses Granite Harbor and can see Ross Island
Oct. 29	The search party leaves Cape Evans toward the Pole to look for Scott
Nov. 7	Campbell's party reaches Hut Point after 40 days traveling and almost 2 years away
Nov. 10	Bage's Southern Party leaves Aladdin's Cave
Nov. 12	Scott's party of 3 found dead
Nov. 26	The *Deutschland* gets free of the pack-ice
Dec. 2	Mawson tests the first airplane in the Antarctic
Dec. 14	Death of Ninnis, and the furthest east point for Mawson's Far Eastern Party
Dec. 15	Mawson kills the weakest of his dogs
Dec. 18	Madigan's Eastern Coastal Party reaches Horn Bluff, its furthest east

Dec. 21   Bage's Southern Party reaches its furthest south
Dec. 25   Bickerton's Western Party reaches its furthest west from Main Base

1913

Jan. 1   Mertz in trouble on his return to Main Base with Mawson
Jan. 6   Mawson forced to haul Mertz by sledge
Jan. 7   Mertz dies, leaving Mawson alone a long way from home
Jan. 17   Mawson falls into a crevasse
Jan. 29   Mawson arrives at the food cairn 23 miles from Aladdin's Cave
Feb. 1   Mawson arrives at Aladdin's Cave
Feb. 4   The wreck of the *Tioga*
Feb. 5   The *Aurora* leaves for Australia
Feb. 23   Wild's Western Base Party, on the Shackleton Ice Shelf, picked up by
           the *Aurora* on its way to Australia
Dec. 12   The *Aurora* returns to Cape Denison

1914

Dec. 7   The *Endurance* reaches Antarctic waters
Dec. 30   The *Endurance* crosses the Antarctic Circle

1915

Jan. 5   Shackleton's crew plays soccer on an ice floe
Jan. 7   The Ross Sea Party under Mackintosh arrives at Hut Point in the
           Aurora
Jan. 10   Coats Land sighted by Shackleton
Jan. 12   Caird Coast discovered by Shackleton
Jan. 19   The *Endurance* in trouble in the pack-ice
Jan. 21   Crews leave the *Aurora* to establish depots
Feb. 22   The *Endurance* is frozen solid in the pack-ice
May 6   The *Aurora* floats away from Cape Evans in the ice
Sept. 1   The first sledging party leaves Ross Island to lay depots for Shackleton
Oct. 24   The *Endurance* starts to leak badly under the ice-pressure
Oct. 27   Shackleton abandons the *Endurance*
Nov. 1   Shackleton sets up Ocean Camp
Nov. 21   The *Endurance* crushed by the pack-ice
Dec. 29   Shackleton establishes Patience Camp
Dec. 31   Shackleton and his 27 men cross the Antarctic Circle northward-bound
           on a floe

1916

Jan. 14   Shackleton shoots 4 dog teams
Jan. 26   Mackintosh lays the Mount Hope Depot at 83°40'S
March 1   Mackintosh reaches Bluff Depot (79°S) on his return from the south
March 8   Death of the Rev. A.P. Spencer-Smith
March 11   Wild, Richards, Joyce, and Hayward get to Hut Point
March 14   Mackintosh is collected from 40 miles out and brought to Hut Point
March 23   Shackleton sights Joinville Island
April 7   Shackleton sights Clarence and Elephant Islands
April 9   Shackleton's party loads into the three whale boats
April 10   Shackleton's party leaves the ice floe in the open boats
April 14   Shackleton's party reaches Elephant Island
April 15   Wild sets out to look for a safer camp on Elephant Island
April 17   Shackleton relocates from Cape Valentine to Cape Wild

April 24	Shackleton sets off for South Georgia in the *James Caird*
May 8	Mackintosh and Hayward die in McMurdo Sound
May 10	Shackleton reaches South Georgia (54°S)
May 23	The *Southern Sky* sails from South Georgia to try to rescue the 22 men
May 26	The *Southern Sky* turns back due to pack-ice
May 28	The *Southern Sky* fails again to get through to the men on Elephant Island
June 13	The *Instituto de Pesca I* turned back by ice 20 miles from Elephant Island
July 15	The remaining members of Mackintosh's party get to safety
July 21	The *Emma* stopped by ice 100 miles from Elephant Island
Aug. 30	Shackleton's men on Elephant Island rescued by the *Yelcho*

1917

Jan. 1	The *Aurora* arrives at McMurdo Sound
Jan. 10	The *Aurora* arrives to pick up the Ross Sea Party at Cape Royds
Jan. 17	The *Aurora* leaves with the survivors

1921

Jan. 12	The British Imperial Expedition lands on Waterboat Point
Feb. 26	Bagshawe and Lester left alone for the winter at Waterboat Point

1922

Jan. 5	Shackleton dies in South Georgia (54°S), at 3:30 a.m., aged 48
Jan. 13	Bagshawe and Lester picked up by the *Svend Foyn*
March 21	The *Quest* leaves Antarctica for South Georgia

1923

July 23	New Zealand claims the Ross Dependency
Dec. 12	The *Sir James Clark Ross* at 63°S, 180°E
Dec. 13	The *Sir James Clark Ross* breaks through the pack-ice at 65°10'S, 178°16'E
Dec. 17	The *Sir James Clark Ross* crosses the Antarctic Circle, the largest vessel until then to do so
Dec. 21	The *Sir James Clark Ross* gets into the Ross Sea
Dec. 25	The *Sir James Clark Ross* arrives at the Bay of Whales
Dec. 31	The *Sir James Clark Ross* anchors in Discovery Inlet

1924

March 7	The *Sir James Clark Ross* leaves Discovery Inlet
March 14	The *Sir James Clark Ross* crosses the Antarctic Circle homeward

1928

June 23	The *Scapa* capsizes off Laurie Island
Nov. 6	The Wilkins-Hearst Expedition lands at Deception Island
Nov. 16	First airplane flight in Antarctica made by Eielson and Wilkins
Nov. 26	Wilkins' two planes search for a better landing strip
Dec. 8	Byrd at 62°10'S, 174°27'E
Dec. 9	Byrd sees his first Antarctic icebergs
Dec. 10	Byrd confirms the existence of Scott Island
Dec. 11	The *Eleanor Bolling* returns to New Zealand
Dec. 12	The *City of New York* meets the *C.A. Larsen* for the tow through the pack-ice
Dec. 13	The *Sir James Clark Ross* stuck in the pack-ice

Dec. 17   The *C.A. Larsen* and the *City of New York* at 69°07′S
Dec. 20   Eielson and Wilkins make the first aerial expedition in Antarctica
Dec. 23   The *C.A. Larsen* and the *City of New York* break through the pack-ice
           into the Ross Sea
Dec. 25   Byrd reaches the Ross Ice Barrier
Dec. 26   Byrd moors in Discovery Inlet
Dec. 28   Byrd sights the Bay of Whales

1929

Jan. 10   Eielson and Wilkins fly over Graham Land again
Jan. 15   Byrd makes his first Antarctic flight
Jan. 27   Byrd and Balchen fly across the Ross Ice Shelf, discovering the Rocke-
           feller Mountains
Feb. 2   The *Norvegia* lands a crew on Peter I Island
March 7   Balchen, June, and Gould fly to the Rockefeller Mountains
March 14   Balchen, June, and Gould get trapped in the mountains
March 22   Byrd and Smith airlift the three trapped men out of the mountains
Nov. 4   Gould sets out at the head of the Southern Geological Party
Nov. 18   Byrd discovers Charles V. Bob Range on his base-laying flight
Nov. 28   Byrd sets off for the South Pole in the *Floyd Bennett*
Nov. 29   Byrd crosses over the Pole aerially
Dec. 7   Riiser-Larsen flies over the coast of Enderby Land in a seaplane
Dec. 12   The *William Scoresby* carries Wilkins and his planes south
Dec. 18   The *William Scoresby* anchors at Port Lockroy
Dec. 19   Wilkins flies from Port Lockroy to Evans Inlet
Dec. 20   Wilkins in Beascochea Bay
Dec. 22   Riiser-Larsen flies over the interior of Enderby Land
Dec. 27   Wilkins flies to Charcot Island
Dec. 29   Mawson discovers Mac. Robertson Land
Dec. 29   Wilkins discovers that Charcot Land is an island

1930

Jan. 5   Mawson and Campbell fly over Mac. Robertson Land
Jan. 5   Wilkins flies from Port Lockroy to Deception Island while the *William
           Scoresby* heads for the Falklands to refuel
Jan. 12   The South Pole and the North Pole are joined by radio
Jan. 13   Mawson lands a party on Proclamation Island and claims Enderby Land
           for Britain (sic)
Jan. 14   The *Discovery* meets the *Norvegia*
Jan. 15   Riiser-Larsen discovers Queen Maud Land
Jan. 19   Gould's Southern Geological Party arrives back at Little America
Jan. 25   The *William Scoresby* back in Deception Island
Jan. 30   Wilkins makes a local flight over the pack-ice
Feb. 1   Wilkins' last flight of the expedition
Feb. 18   Riiser-Larsen discovers Princess Martha Coast
Feb. 19   Little America closed
Dec. 29   The *Kosmos* supplies fuel to the BANZARE

1931

Jan. 4   Mawson arrives at Cape Denison
Jan. 7   Mawson lands in Wilkes Land
May 1   Norway claims Peter I Island

1933

| June 13 | Australia claims its territory |
| Dec. 17 | Ellsworth enters the Ross Sea pack-ice |

1934

Jan. 9	Ellsworth at the Bay of Whales
Jan. 17	Byrd arrives at the Bay of Whales
March 13	The *Blue Blade* crashes at Little America
March 16	June and Demas leave overland to set up the Bolling Advance Weather Station
March 22	Byrd, Bailey, and Bowlin fly in the Pilgrim to Bolling Advance Weather Station
March 24	The first of the parties leaves Bolling Advance Weather Station
March 29	The construction crew leave Bolling Advance Weather Station to return to Little America II
July 20	Poulter, Waite, and Demas set out to rescue Byrd
July 26	Byrd learns that Poulter's team has had to turn back
Aug. 4	Poulter leaves Little America again to rescue Byrd, but has to turn back again
Aug. 8	Poulter sets out yet again from Little America to rescue Byrd
Aug. 11	Byrd rescued from Bolling Advance Weather Station after 4½ months
Sept. 1	The autogiro makes its first flight
Sept. 25	The autogiro crashes after 10 flights
Sept. 27	A 4-man party sets out from Little America to lay dumps all the way to Mount Grace McKinley
Oct. 13	Ellsworth arrives at Deception Island
Oct. 14	Byrd flies back to Little America from Bolling Advance Weather Station
Oct. 18	Four-man party returns successfully to Little America

1935

Jan. 3	Ellsworth and Balchen set out on their unsuccessful transantarctic flight
Jan. 21	Ellsworth leaves the Antarctic for Montevideo
Jan. 22	Rymill makes the first flight on the BGLE 1934–37, as the *Penola* arrives at Port Lockroy
Feb. 14	The *Penola* makes its final trip to the Winter Island base before heading north
Feb. 20	Caroline Mikkelsen is the first woman to set foot on Antarctica
Feb. 28	Rymill makes an exploratory flight
Nov. 2	Ellsworth arrives at Deception Island
Nov. 12	Ellsworth arrives at Dundee Island
Nov. 21	Ellsworth and Hollick-Kenyon fly for 10 hours, but return to Dundee Island
Nov. 23	Ellsworth and Hollick-Kenyon set out on the first aerial crossing of Antarctica
Nov. 24	At 5 p.m. Ellsworth and Hollick-Kenyon fly out of their makeshift camp, but have to put down only half an hour later, because of weather
Nov. 27	Ellsworth and Hollick-Kenyon fly for an hour before putting down again
Dec. 5	After being trapped in a blizzard, Ellsworth and Hollick-Kenyon take off again
Dec. 6	Ellsworth and Hollick-Kenyon take off on the final leg of their trans-

antarctic crossing; then they run out of fuel, and start sledging to Little America

Dec. 15   Ellsworth and Hollick-Kenyon complete their transantarctic crossing

1936

Jan. 19   A *Discovery II* aircraft drops a parcel to Ellsworth at Little America, and he and Hollick-Kenyon are soon on board that ship

Jan. 22   Ellsworth and Hollick-Kenyon picked up by the *Wyatt Earp*

Feb. 17   The *Penola* leaves Winter Island for a cruise further south

Feb. 29   The *Penola* arrives at the Debenham Islands

March 12   The *Penola* leaves the Debenham Islands to winter-over in the Falklands

March 24   The BGLE hut on Barry Island is finished and occupied

Aug. 15   The BGLE aerially photographs Alexander Island and discovers the George VI Sound

Sept. 5   In-depth BGLE sledging parties set out to study Graham Land

Nov. 22   Rymill and Bingham succeed in their crossing of Graham Land

1937

Jan. 5   Rymill and Stephenson return to their base in the Debenham Islands

Feb. 13   The *Penola* arrives to relieve the BGLE

March 12   The *Penola* leaves the Debenham Islands for home

1938

April 1   France claims Adélie Land

1939

Jan. 1   Ellsworth flies over the Amery Ice Shelf

Jan. 3   Ellsworth flies over the Ingrid Christensen Coast

Jan. 10   Ellsworth flies over the Ingrid Christensen Coast to the West Ice Shelf

Jan. 11   Ellsworth flies over the American Highland

Jan. 14   Norway claims Queen Maud Land

Jan. 15   Liavaag's accident brings an end to Ellsworth's expedition

Jan. 20   Ritscher anchors at 69°14′S, 4°30′W; the first flight takes place from the *Schwabenland*

Jan. 29   Rudolf Wahr takes a landing party to 69°55′S, 1°09′W

Jan. 30   Germans land at 70°18′S, 4°22′E; but not for long

Jan. 31   Erich Bastlen captures 5 emperor penguins

1940

Jan. 11   The *North Star* sights the Ross Ice Shelf

Jan. 12   The *North Star* enters the Bay of Whales, and moors there

Jan. 14   The *Bear* enters the Bay of Whales

Jan. 22   The first of the four major flights from the *Bear* over Marie Byrd Land

Jan. 23   The second flight from the *Bear* over the Ford Ranges

Jan. 24   The *North Star* leaves for Valparaiso, Chile, after unloading at West Base

Jan. 25   The third flight from the *Bear*

Jan. 26   The fourth flight from the *Bear*, over the Hobbs Coast

Jan. 28   A piloted balloon goes up from West Base, the first of 219 ascents

Feb. 9   James McCoy flies from West Base into the interior of Marie Byrd Land

Feb. 12–13   Petras flies over the Ross Ice Shelf

Feb. 27   Thurston Island discovered

Feb. 29   Flight from West Base over the Ross Ice Shelf by McCoy

March 4	The *Bear* anchors at Horseshoe Island
March 5	Flight from the *North Star;* the *North Star* meets the *Bear*
March 8	East Base selected on Stonington Island
March 20	The ships complete unloading at East Base
March 21	The two ships, the *North Star* and the *Bear,* sail for home, with Admiral Byrd on the *Bear*
Sept. 18	Warner leads party to establish 105-Mile Depot
Oct. 15	Jack E. Perkins leads major sledge journey east out of West Base
Nov. 6	Chile claims the Antarctic Peninsula
Nov. 11	Three sledging parties at McKinley Peak

1941

Jan. 7	Return of all sledging parties to West Base
Jan. 13	The *Ole Wegger* taken by the Nazis off the Queen Maud Land coast
Jan. 13	The *Solglimt* taken by the Nazis off the Queen Maud Land coast
Jan. 14	The *Pelagos* taken by the Nazis off the Queen Maud Land coast
March 22	East Base evacuated

1946

Feb. 23	The *Trepassey* arrives at Stonington Island
Feb. 24	FIDS move into the old USAS East Base
Feb. 25	Work begins on Base E
March 13	Work finished at Base E
Dec. 23	The Western Group ships of Operation Highjump see their first iceberg
Dec. 24	The Eastern Task Group of Operation Highjump sees their first iceberg, at 62°41′S, 99°30′W
Dec. 24	The Western Group ships of Operation Highjump reach the edge of the Ross Sea pack-ice NE of the Balleny Islands
Dec. 25	The Eastern Task Group of Operation Highjump crosses the Antarctic Circle
Dec. 26	The first Martin Mariner launched unsuccessfully from the *Pine Island*
Dec. 29	*George-1* (a plane) flies off the *Pine Island* with Dufek aboard
Dec. 30	*George-1* crashes and kills three (*see* **Deaths, 1946**)
Dec. 30	The Central Group ships of Operation Highjump meet at Scott Island
Dec. 31	The Central Group of Operation Highjump enters the Ross Sea pack-ice

1947

Jan. 1	Bunger's 4½ hour flight in *Baker-1* over the coast and the Balleny Islands
Jan. 4	Two planes photograph the Victoria Land coast
Jan. 5	Bunger's flight over Victoria Land in *Baker-3*
Jan. 5	*George-3* flies off the *Pine Island* to look for *George-1*
Jan. 6	Kreitzer's flight over Victoria Land in *Baker-1*
Jan. 11	*George-2* flies off the *Pine Island* in a new search for *George-1*
Jan. 12	Survivors of the crashed *George-1* finally rescued by the *Pine Island*
Jan. 14	The Central Group of Operation Highjump gets through the pack-ice
Jan. 15	The Central Group arrives at the Bay of Whales
Jan. 16	Cdr. Clifford M. Campbell lands a party at Little America
Jan. 17	Dr. Paul A. Siple lands a party at Little America, and work on Little America IV begins
Jan. 17	The *Brownson* joins the *Pine Island* and they head south

Jan. 18   The *Yancey* moors in the Bay of Whales and unloading at Little
            America begins
Jan. 19   The *Merrick* moors in the Bay of Whales
Jan. 19   The helicopter in which Dufek is an observer crash lands; no one is
            hurt
Jan. 22   The *Mount Olympus* moors in the Bay of Whales
Jan. 22   Bunger and Rogers fly two planes over Wilkes Land
Jan. 23   *George-2* and *George-3* photograph Marie Byrd Land
Jan. 25   The *Philippine Sea* reaches Scott Island
Jan. 26   Kreitzer flies *Baker-1* as far east as Commonwealth Bay
Jan. 26   *George-2* and *George-3* photograph Marie Byrd Land again
Jan. 27   Rogers and Bunger fly their planes over Wilkes Land again
Jan. 27   The *Pine Island* meets and refuels from the *Canisteo*
Jan. 27   An iceberg entering the Bay of Whales forces the temporary withdrawal
            of the three ships servicing Little America IV
Jan. 28   Rogers and Kreitzer fly over Wilkes Land
Jan. 29   Hawkes pilots the first plane from the *Philippine Sea* to Little America;
            Byrd is aboard
Jan. 30   Rogers and Bunger fly yet again over Wilkes Land
Jan. 30   The *Pine Island* abandons an attempt to reach Peter I Island
Jan. 30   The rest of the planes on the *Philippine Sea* fly to Little America
Jan. 30   The *Philippine Sea* heads for home
Jan. 30   Bad weather forces the temporary withdrawal from the Bay of Whales
            of the three ships servicing Little America
Jan. 31   Melchior Station finished
Feb. 1   Kreitzer flies over the Budd Coast
Feb. 2   Bunger and Kreitzer fly over Wilkes Land; Kreitzer discovers the
            Windmill Islands
Feb. 5   The *Trepassey* returns to Stonington Island with the new FIDS crew
Feb. 6   The 3 ships in the Bay of Whales sail for home
Feb. 6   The *Burton Island* arrives at the Ross Sea pack-ice from the USA
Feb. 7   The *Trepassey* leaves Stonington Island
Feb. 8   *George-2* and *George-3* attempt a flight over Charcot Island
Feb. 9   *George-2* flies over Marguerite Bay, and *George-3* over Charcot and
            Alexander Islands
Feb. 10   Dufek unsuccessfully attempts a landing on Charcot Island
Feb. 10   The *Currituck* meets the *Balaena* at the edge of the pack-ice
Feb. 11   The *Don Samuel* arrives at Stonington Island for a visit
Feb. 11   Bunger and Rogers fly over Wilkes Land. Bunger discovers the Bunger
            Hills
Feb. 12   The Rockefeller Mountains Tractor Party sets out from Little America
Feb. 12   Amphibious aircraft flight from the *Balaena*
Feb. 13   Bunger lands in the Bunger Hills; Kreitzer aerially explores Enderby
            Land
Feb. 14   The *Don Samuel* arrives back at Melchior Station
Feb. 14   The first of ten long flights takes off from Little America IV
Feb. 15   Byrd flies over the Pole again, with two aircraft (*see* **South Pole**)
Feb. 16   The *Burton Island* arrives at McMurdo Sound
Feb. 17   Aerial photography of Victoria Land begins
Feb. 18   The Rockefeller Mountains Tractor Party leaves the mountains
Feb. 19   The Rockefeller Mountains Tractor Party arrives back at Little America IV
Feb. 20   The *Burton Island* leaves McMurdo Sound

Feb. 22	The *Burton Island* arrives at the Bay of Whales to relieve the Central Task Group of Operation Highjump
Feb. 22	Kreitzer flies over the Sør Rondane Mountains; Rogers flies along the coast of Enderby Land
Feb. 23	The *Burton Island* sails out of the Bay of Whales with all aboard
Feb. 26	The *Burton Island* and the *Mount Olympus* at Scott Island for their rendezvous
Feb. 26	Rogers flies over Enderby Land
Feb. 27	The *Pine Island* crosses the Antarctic Circle
Feb. 27	Bunger and Kreitzer fly over Enderby Land
March 1	*George-1* and *George-2* launched over Queen Maud Land
March 1	The last flights made by Western Task Group; Group quits operations
March 2	*George-2* and *George-3* launched over Queen Maud Land again
March 3	All ships of Western Task Group rendezvous
March 4	Eastern Group of Operation Highjump quits operations, and under Dufek, leaves Antarctica
March 7	The *Angamos* visits Stonington Island
March 9	The *Angamos* leaves Stonington Island
March 12	The RARE arrives in the Antarctic
Dec. 13	Gregorio Portillo flies from Argentina, across the Antarctic Circle, to drop mail over Deception Island
Dec. 14	The *Edisto* and the *Burton Island* sight their first iceberg of the season at 60° 46′ S, 177° 29′ W
Dec. 15	Operation Windmill encounters light pack-ice
Dec. 16	Operation Windmill fails to reach Scott Island due to the by now much thicker pack-ice
Dec. 18	Operation Windmill back out of the pack-ice
Dec. 24	Operation Windmill ships meet the *Southern Harvest* off Wilkes Land
Dec. 25	The Operation Windmill ships (the *Edisto* and the *Burton Island*) reach the pack-ice again
Dec. 25	Operation Windmill breaks through the pack-ice toward the Davis Sea
Dec. 26	Helicopters from Operation Windmill discover open sea for their ships
Dec. 27	Operation Windmill gets into the Davis Sea, and the two ships part company
Dec. 28	The *Edisto* lands a party 25 miles west of Haswell Island
Dec. 28	The *Burton Island* lands a party on Haswell Island
Dec. 31	The Haswell Island party evacuated

1948

Jan. 1	The *Burton Island* lands a party at Gillies Islands
Jan. 2	Lloyd Tracy, USN, completes 12 helicopter flights in 36 hours
Jan. 3	All observations of Operation Windmill completed in the Davis Sea
Jan. 6	The *Edisto* and the *Burton Island* join up again in the pack-ice and head toward the Bunger Hills
Jan. 7	Operation Windmill gets through the pack-ice into the open water
Jan. 8	Operation Windmill heads back into the pack-ice at 102° E
Jan. 12	Operation Windmill lands men in the Bunger Hills
Jan. 15	Bunger Hills party evacuated
Jan. 16	The *Edisto* and the *Burton Island* meet up again
Jan. 18	The *Edisto* lands a party on the Knox Coast
Jan. 19	The Knox Coast party evacuated
Jan. 20	Operation Windmill leaves Vincennes Bay

Jan. 25	Operation Windmill meets the *Hashedate Maru*
Jan. 26	Operation Windmill turns into the Ross Sea
Jan. 29	Operation Windmill visits Ross Island
Jan. 30	Operation Windmill heads toward Little America
Jan. 31	Operation Windmill moors at the Bay of Whales and parties go ashore
Feb. 4	The *Edisto* sets out for the north to pave a way through the pack-ice
Feb. 5	Shore parties at Little America evacuated by the *Burton Island*
Feb. 6	The *Burton Island* joins the *Edisto* in the pack-ice
Feb. 14	Operation Windmill abandons plans to go to Thurston Island, and instead heads for Peter I Island
Feb. 16	Operation Windmill leaves Peter I Island for Marguerite Bay
Feb. 19	Operation Windmill arrives at Marguerite Bay
Feb. 20	The RARE ship, the *Port of Beaumont, Texas,* is freed from the ice by the two ships of Task Force 39 (Operation Windmill)
Feb. 23	RARE leaves Antarctica, together with Operation Windmill

1950

Jan. 20	The French begin to establish Port-Martin on Adélie Land
Feb. 3	The French flag hoisted at Port-Martin
Feb. 10	The *Commandant Charcot* leaves for France

1951

Jan. 9	Liotard's crew replaced by Barré's at Port-Martin
Jan. 10	Emperor penguins seen incubating by humans for the first time

1952

Jan. 24	Fire breaks out at Port-Martin
Feb. 2	The *Tottan* picks up the French Polar Expedition
Feb. 7	Edgardo S. Andrew and Guillermo J. Campbell fly from Argentina to Deception Island in two Catalina aircraft
Feb. 10	Andrew and Campbell return to Buenos Aires

1954

Feb. 13	Mawson Station established

1955

June 28	Argentina creates Argentine province, from 46°S to the Pole, and between 25°W and 74°W
Dec. 17	The first ever planes fly in from Christchurch, New Zealand, to McMurdo Sound
Dec. 18	The *Glacier* enters McMurdo Sound
Dec. 18	Work begins on McMurdo airstrip
Dec. 20	Eight planes land at McMurdo from New Zealand
Dec. 27	Task Force 43 arrives at McMurdo Sound, bringing Operation Deep Freeze I
Dec. 30	Americans land at Little America V

1956

Jan. 6	Richard T. Williams dies
Jan. 6	Lt. Cdr. John H. Torbert flies a Neptune from McMurdo Sound to Vincennes Bay and back in 14 ½ hours
Jan. 9	The first major airplane, the Lockheed Neptune *Amen,* arrives at Little America V
Jan. 13	Nonstop flight from McMurdo Sound to the Weddell Sea and return
Jan. 14	Bursey leaves Little America to pioneer a trail to Byrd Station

Jan. 28	The *Theron,* with Fuchs and Hillary aboard, arrives at Vahsel Bay
Jan. 30	The unloading of the *Theron* begins at 8 a.m.
Feb. 3	US Navy Otter 260 goes down on Edward VII Peninsula; the pilot, Lt. Paul Streich, and crew of 6 are missing
Feb. 9	All 7 members of the Otter 260 are rescued
Feb. 9	Fuchs leaves Antarctica for the winter
Feb. 12	The *Edisto* selects the site for Hallett Station
Feb. 13	Mirnyy Station opens
March 5	Max R. Kiel dies
March 5	The *Glacier* runs aground for a few hours on an uncharted shoal
March 10	The *Glacier* leaves the Bay of Whales to scout for bases for Operation Deep Freeze II
March 26	Erskine Bay and Godel Bay are discovered
Oct. 18	Four killed in plane crash at McMurdo Base (*see* **Deaths, 1956**)
Oct. 31	Dufek flies to the Pole in the *Que Sera Sera,* and steps out
Nov. 5	Merle Dawson leads a convoy out of Little America to blaze a trail to Byrd Station
Nov. 20	Construction begins on South Pole Station
Dec. 18	Merle Dawson arrives at Byrd Station
Dec. 22	LAN Chile flies the first tourists to Antarctica (*see* **Tourism**)
Dec. 29	Landings and ground work begin at Hallett Station

1957

Jan. 3	The *Endeavour* arrives at Ross Island with Hillary aboard
Jan. 7	The *Soya* arrives at the pack-ice carrying JARE I
Jan. 9	Construction begins at Hallett Station
Jan. 13	The *Magga Dan* reaches Vahsel Bay with Fuchs aboard
Jan. 15	First, successful test flight of Hillary's Beaver aircraft.
Jan. 27	Unloading begins from the *Wyandot* at Ellsworth Station
Jan. 29	Byrd Station turned over to the scientific staff
Feb. 12	Hallett Station completed
Feb. 15	The *Soya* leaves the Antarctic coast
Feb. 16	The *Soya* beset by ice
Feb. 16	Wilkes Station opened
Feb. 22	South Ice base completed
Feb. 22	The *Endeavour* leaves for New Zealand
Feb. 28	The *Ob'* helps the *Soya* out of the ice
April 12	Vostok Station opened
July 1	IGY begins
July 12	Death of Nelson Cole
Sept. 10	Hillary leaves Scott Base for a trial run to the Ferrar Glacier
Oct. 4	The Northern Party of the Ross Island Party of the BCTAE sets out from Scott Base
Oct. 14	Hillary sets out from Ross Island for the south to lay depots
Oct. 15	The first commercial flight comes into Antarctica, carrying the first women ever to visit an American scientific station there
Oct. 16	The US Air Force Electronics Test Unit arrives in the South Shetlands
Oct. 20	Hillary reaches Skelton Depot
Oct. 22	Hillary begins ascent of the Skelton Glacier
Oct. 28	Hillary's party at 5,000 feet up the Skelton Glacier
Oct. 29	An airplane drops Hillary's mail
Oct. 31	Hillary reaches the Plateau Depot

Nov. 8	Hillary leaves Plateau Depot heading south
Nov. 13	Fuchs reaches South Ice
Nov. 15	Fuchs is flown back to Shackleton Base
Nov. 16	The Hon. John P. Saylor is the first US legislator to fly over the Pole
Nov. 21	The US Air Force Electronics Test Unit leaves the South Shetlands
Nov. 22	The first plane of the US Air Force Electronics Test Unit arrives at Ellsworth Station
Nov. 24	Six US congressmen visit Antarctica (*see* **Distinguished Visitors**)
Nov. 24	Beginning of the BCTAE crossing itself
Nov. 25	Hillary begins the building of Depot 480
Nov. 30	The original Vostok Station is closed
Dec. 1	Hillary sends out reconnaissance teams to look for a site for the last depot
Dec. 4	Fuchs leads the main BCTAE party out of Shackleton Base
Dec. 6	Hillary heads south again
Dec. 6	The second plane of the US Air Force Electronics Test Unit arrives at Ellsworth Station
Dec. 15	Hillary begins work on Depot 700
Dec. 16	The South Geomagnetic Pole reached for the first time, by a USSR tractor traverse
Dec. 16	The new Vostok Station opens
Dec. 20	The *Soya* back at the ice to relieve JARE I
Dec. 20	Depot 700 completely stocked from the air
Dec. 21	Fuchs arrives at South Ice for the second time
Dec. 24	Fuchs leaves South Ice for the Pole

1958

Jan. 2	Hillary is 70 miles from the Pole
Jan. 3	Hillary camps in sight of the Pole
Jan. 4	Hillary reaches the South Pole in a tractor
Jan. 19	Fuchs, Hillary, and Dufek rendezvous 2 miles from the Pole
Jan. 20	Fuchs reaches the Pole
Jan. 24	Fuchs leaves the Pole for Ross Island
Feb. 3	First meeting of SCAR
Feb. 7	Fuchs reaches Depot 700 and is joined by Hillary
Feb. 11	The 11 men at Showa Station are flown to the *Soya*
Feb. 14	Nagata abandons JARE II
Feb. 23	Fuchs reaches Plateau Depot
Feb. 27	Fuchs reaches Skelton Depot
March 1	Fuchs covers 75 miles in one day
March 2	Completion of the BCTAE
May 2	Eisenhower proposes the Antarctic Treaty
Oct. 15	Six men killed in a Globemaster crash near Cape Roget
Dec. 14	The Pole of Relative Inaccessibility reached for the first time — by a USSR tractor traverse
Dec. 31	IGY ends

1959

Jan. 1	USARP begins
Feb. 21	Phillip G. Law discovers the Mawson Peninsula
March 10	Lazarev Scientific Station built
Dec. 1	The Antarctic Treaty signed by 12 countries, in Washington, D.C
Dec. 31	The *Polarbjörn* beset in ice

1960

Jan. 8   The first SANAE arrives
Jan. 15   The *Polarbjörn* leaves Polar Circle Bight
July 7   Eisenhower signs the Antarctic Medal Bill
Aug. 3   Fire at Mirnyy Station kills two
Aug. 29   La Grange and von Brunn begin the first major SANAE sledging expedition
Oct. 11   Little Rockford Station opened
Oct. 31   La Grange and von Brunn set out on the last major SANAE sledging expedition
Nov. 10   New site selected for Byrd Station
Nov. 14   Charles Bentley sets out from Byrd Station on his Ellsworth Highland Traverse
Dec. 7   La Grange and von Brunn return from the last major SANAE sledging expedition
Dec. 8   Havola leaves Byrd Station on his Byrd-Pole Tractor Train
Dec. 9   First airplane landing in the Jones Mountains (*see* **Farrington Ridge**)
Dec. 10   Albert Crary leads a traverse to the Pole from McMurdo
Dec. 12   Excavation begins on New Byrd Station
Dec. 26   The *Polarhav* arrives at Sanae Station

1961

Jan. 9   The *Polarhav* takes the first SANAE home
Jan. 16   The Byrd–South Pole Overland Trek completed
Feb. 11   Bentley's Ellsworth Highland Traverse completed
Feb. 12   Albert Crary arrives at the Pole by Sno-cat
Feb. 18   Novolazarevskaya Station opens
April 9   The first Antarctic nocturnal flight and landing (*see* **Kuperov**)
June 23   The Antarctic Treaty enters into full force
Oct. 31   The first landing of a Hercules plane near Hallett Station
Nov. 9   Five men killed in a Neptune crash at Wilkes Station
Dec. 12   The first Antarctic nuclear plant arrives at McMurdo Station, by ship

1962

Jan. 21   Vostok Station closed temporarily
Feb. 9   Sky-Hi Station completed (*see* **Eights Station**)
March 3   The nuclear plant goes critical

1963

Jan. 14   Molodezhnaya Station opens
Jan. 23   Vostok Station reopens

1964

Feb. 4   Three helicopters fly to the Pole from Mount Weaver

1965

Jan. 12   Work begins on Palmer Station
Jan. 24   The first building finished at Palmer Station
Feb. 25   Palmer Station opens
Dec. 13   The first flight from McMurdo Station to Plateau Station

1966

Feb. 2   Six men are killed in an LC-47J crash on the Ross Ice Shelf
Oct. 13   A Hercules aircraft lands at Plateau Station

1967

Jan. 18	The *Atka* changes its name to the *Southwind*
May 14	McMurdo Station's water-distillation unit produces its millionth gallon of water
May 16	Amundsen-Scott South Pole Station evacuated to emergency camp following an accidental release of carbon tetrachloride fumes; they return the next day
Aug. 1	RN-50 Nodwell lost through the ice off Hut Point on its fourth attempt to reach Cape Royds
Aug. 24	Fire destroys new lavatory complex (Building 18) at Williams Field
Dec. 2	The last "Gooney Bird" flight in Antarctica (*see* **Airplanes**)
Dec. 4	Severe volcanic disturbance on Deception Island
Dec. 4	BAS asks McMurdo Station to evacuate injured Halley Bay Station physician, Dr. John Brotherhood; this is Antarctica's longest mercy flight
Dec. 5	South Pole–Queen Maud Land Traverse III sets out
Dec. 7	Two more volcanic eruptions on Deception Island
Dec. 16	Japanese traverse party arrives at Plateau Station
Dec. 19	Japanese traverse party leaves Plateau Station for the Pole
Dec. 28	The first fossilized land animals found in Antarctica

1968

Jan. 29	The South Pole–Queen Maud Land Traverse III ends at 78°42′S, 6°52′W
Jan. 30	The South Pole–Queen Maud Land Traverse III party airlifted to McMurdo Station
Feb. 22	Bellingshausen Station opened
March 19	Fire at Plateau Station (*see* **Disasters**)
March 20	The new Palmer Station is commissioned
Sept. 17	A 4.9 earthquake on Deception Island (no volcanic activity recorded)
Nov. 27	Two LH-34 helicopters belonging to VX-6 make the longest nonstop flight in Antarctic annals, 395 miles from McMurdo Station to Hallett Station, to help in emperor penguin collections
Dec. 25	The *Hero* arrives at Palmer Station for the first time

1969

Jan. 1	VX-6 becomes VXE-6
Jan. 11	R. Spaulding sets new McMurdo Station parachute altitude record of 12,500 ft.
Jan. 15	F. Michael Maish, US exchange scientist, flown to Vostok Station for the winter
Feb. 19	Casey Station opened
Feb. 21	Deception Island erupts again (*see* **1967**)
Feb. 22	All Chilean and British personnel evacuated from Deception Island
Oct. 16	The arrival of Christine Müller-Schwarze, the first US woman to work in Antarctica
Oct. 19	Christine Müller-Schwarze begins work in the field
Nov. 10	Masayoshi Murayama's Japanese traverse party reaches Plateau Station
Nov. 11	The first party of women arrive at the Pole (*see* **Women in Antarctica**)
Nov. 16	Dr. Lois Jones' party flown to Lake Bonney to begin their field work
Nov. 19	Thomas Berg and Jeremy Sykes killed in a helicopter crash
Nov. 23	Dr. David H. Elliot discovers fossilized reptiles near Coalsack Bluff
Dec. 4	Lystrosaurus fossils discovered

1970

Jan. 13   Max Conrad flies into McMurdo Station
Jan. 19   Max Conrad is the first to fly solo to the Pole
Jan. 19   Thor Tjøntveit and Einar Sverre Pedersen land at the Pole (*see* **Tjønt-veit**)
Jan. 23   Max Conrad crashes on take-off from the Pole
Feb. 25   The *Fuji* stuck in the ice outside Lützow-Holm Bay
March 19   The *Fuji* out of the ice
Aug. 11   Earthquake at 60° 36′ S, 25° 24′ W, registering 6 on the Richter Scale
Aug. 12   Deception Island erupts
Sept. 12–19 Six earthquakes on Deception Island (no volcanic activity recorded)
Oct. 21   The first C-133 Cargomaster to land in Antarctica

1971

Feb. 8   A 6.3 earthquake on Deception Island (no volcanic activity recorded)
Feb. 25   Leningradskaya Station opened
Aug. 11   A 5.4 earthquake in the Balleny Islands
Dec. 4   Juliet Delta 321 crashes in East Antarctica (*see* **Disasters**)

1972

Jan. 12   H.V. Gorick sets Antarctic parachute altitude record of 20,500 ft.
Jan. 19   Byrd Station becomes a summer only station
Jan. 21   The first borehole begun on the Dry Valley Drilling Project
Jan. 21   Mount Erebus erupts
Jan. 28   An LC-130 crashes at Amundsen-Scott South Pole Station. No one hurt
Nov. 15   David Lewis turns east at the 60th Parallel
Nov. 29   David Lewis capsizes in the *Ice Bird*
Dec. 13   David Lewis again capsizes in the *Ice Bird*

1973

Jan. 29   David Lewis arrives at Palmer Station
Feb. 19   Hallett Station closes forever
Nov. 9   AFAN-TV opens at McMurdo Station
Dec. 12   David Lewis leaves Palmer Station in the *Ice Bird*, heading south

1974

Jan. 2   The first American women visit Vostok Station (*see* **Women in Antarctica**)
Jan. 8   David Lewis leaves Signy Island for home
Feb. 25   The USSR's Amery Ice Shelf Station closes forever
Sept. 4   Mount Erebus erupts again
Sept. 24   Polar Party Cross reuprighted on Observation Hill after severe storms

1975

Jan. 9   The new Amundsen-Scott South Pole Station is dedicated
Feb. 20   The *Burton Island* becomes stuck in the ice at 71° 48′ S, 103° 33′ W
Feb. 21   The *Burton Island* breaks free of the ice
Feb. 26   The *General San Martín* becomes beset by ice at 63° 54′ S, 56° 38′ W
March 3   The *Glacier* becomes beset at 63° 44′ 42″ S, 56° 25′ 48″ W, while trying to free the *General San Martín*
March 11   The *Glacier* breaks free
March 26   The *General San Martín* breaks free of the ice after a month's besetment

1977
Feb. 26   Arctowski Station opened

1978
Jan. 7   The first human birth in Antarctica—Emilio Marcos de Palma
March 11   The Convention for the Conservation of Antarctic Seals goes into effect
Dec. 1   The first Australian Hercules aircraft lands in Antarctica, at Williams
                Field

1979
Jan. 14   The new Siple Station is opened
Jan. 19   Wladzimierz Puchalski dies (*see* **Deaths, 1979; Historic sites**)
May 25   The US Department of Energy releases the site of the decommissioned
                PM-3A nuclear plant
Nov. 28   257 people die in a "champagne" plane crash into Mount Erebus (*see*
                Tourism)

1980
Jan. 11   D-17 AWS opened
Feb. 5   Byrd AWS, Marble Point AWS, and Asgard AWS opened
April 1   ITT/ANS takes over as USARP support contractor from Holmes & Narver
June 19   D-17 AWS closed
Oct. 26   Trans-Globe Expedition begins their Antarctic crossing
Dec. 1   Manning AWS opened
Dec. 4   Meeley AWS opened
Dec. 10   Ferrell AWS opened
Dec. 15   Trans-Globe Expedition reaches the Pole

1981
Jan. 11   Trans-Globe Expedition finishes the Antarctic crossing
Oct. 20   The *Mikhail Somov* brings WEPOLEX 81 to the ice
Dec. 5   Jimmy AWS opened
Dec. 15   Laurie AWS opened
Dec. 18   The *Gotland II* sinks

1982
Jan. 1   Siple Station AWS opened
Jan. 4   The *Dick Smith Explorer* expedition arrives in Antarctic waters
Jan. 8   The *Dick Smith Explorer* sights its first ice at 65°S
Jan. 9   The Indians land on Antarctica during Operation Gangotri
Jan. 9   The *Dick Smith Explorer* reaches the Antarctic Circle and the South
                Magnetic Pole
Jan. 10   The *Dick Smith Explorer* reaches Cape Denison
Jan. 23   Whitlock AWS opened
Jan. 29   The *Dick Smith Explorer* leaves Cape Denison
Feb. 1   The *Dick Smith Explorer* reaches the Mertz Glacier Tongue
Feb. 5   The *Dick Smith Explorer* leaves the Mertz Glacier Tongue
Feb. 7   The *Dick Smith Explorer* travels along the Antarctic Circle
Feb. 8   The *Dick Smith Explorer* arrives at Dumont d'Urville Station
Feb. 19   The Seymour Island Expedition begins
Feb. 22   The *Dick Smith Explorer* leaves Dumont d'Urville Station
Feb. 26   The *Dick Smith Explorer* leaves Antarctic waters
March 9   End of the Seymour Island Expedition
April 7   CCAMLR comes into effect

Dec. 28   The *Polar Star* leaves Palmer Station on its circumnavigation of
           Antarctica
Dec. 31   Asgard AWS and Jimmy AWS closed

1983
Jan. 13   Dome C AWS opened
Jan. 17   Nancy AWS opened
Feb. 9   Katie AWS opened
March 7   The *Polar Star* completes its circumnavigation of Antarctica
July 21   New record low temperature recorded of − 128.6°F (*see* **Temperatures**)
Nov. 25   Nancy AWS closed

1984
Jan. 15   D-10 AWS opened
Jan. 16   Marilyn AWS opened
Jan. 24   Tiffany AWS opened
Jan. 25   Fogle AWS opened
Jan. 26   The *Dick Smith Explorer* takes the Frozen Sea Expedition out of Filla
           Island
Feb. 1   Martha AWS opened
Feb. 6   Manuela AWS opened
April 15   The *Hero* leaves Palmer Station for the last time
Dec. 30   The Chinese arrive to build the Great Wall Station

1985
Jan. 10   Fogle AWS closed
Jan. 24   Schwerdtfeger AWS and Gill AWS opened
Feb. 20   Great Wall Station established by the Chinese
June 28   Wood, Mear, and Stroud set out for Cape Crozier
July 26   Wood, Mear, and Stroud return to Cape Evans
Oct. 26   Swan, Mear, and Wood leave Cape Evans for the Pole
Nov. 3   Swan, Mear, and Wood leave Hut Point on the In the Footsteps of
           Scott Expedition
Nov. 13   D-47 AWS opened
Nov. 15   The *John Biscoe* trapped in the ice near the Antarctic Peninsula
Nov. 17   D-57 AWS opened
Nov. 18   The *John Biscoe* is abandoned to the ice
Nov. 20   The *Polarstern* breaks the *John Biscoe* free, and the crew reclaims it
Dec. 10   Swan, Mear, and Wood reach the foot of the Beardmore Glacier
Dec. 11   D-80 AWS opened
Dec. 19   Swan, Mear, and Wood reach the Shackleton Icefalls
Dec. 31   Meeley AWS closed

1986
Jan. 1   Larsen AWS opened
Jan. 5   Katie AWS closed
Jan. 6   The *Icebird* reaches the South Magnetic Pole
Jan. 11   Bowers AWS opened
Jan. 11   Swan, Mear, and Wood arrive at the South Pole at 11:53 p.m.
Jan. 12   The *Southern Quest* sinks at 12:04 a.m.
Jan. 12   Laurie AWS closed
Jan. 15   Manning AWS closed
Jan. 23   Tiffany AWS closed

Jan. 28   Elaine AWS, Patrick AWS, and Allison AWS opened
Jan. 29   Lettau AWS and Clean Air AWS opened
Feb. 18   Dolleman Island AWS opened
March 1   Butler Island AWS opened
March 6   Uranus Glacier AWS opened

1987

Jan. 3   Ewan Fordyce discovers a whale fossil (*see* **Fossils**) on Seymour Island
Jan. 6   Martin Pomerantz awarded NSF's highest award at South Pole ceremony
Feb. 1   Jimmy AWS reactivated
Feb. 20   Buckle Island AWS opened
Nov. 3   Bradley Lanzer takes off from McMurdo Station for Sanae Station (*see* **International cooperation**)
Nov. 4   Bradley Lanzer returns to McMurdo Station with the South African patient
Dec. 9   Two killed in Hercules crash at D-59 (*see* **Disasters**)

1988

Jan. 8   The largest ever helium balloon goes up from Williams Field
Jan. 10   Juliet Delta 321 arrives back at McMurdo Station after 16 years (*see* **Disasters, 1971**)
Jan. 11   Adventure Network International is the first to fly tourists to the Pole
Jan. 11   The big balloon comes down near Vostok Station at 78°18'S, 80°53'E
Jan. 13   US pilots from McMurdo Station retrieve the balloon's data
Feb. 17   King Sejong Station built
Nov. 28   Mountain Travel Expedition leaves Hercules Inlet in the Ronne Ice Shelf
Dec. 1   Mountain Travel Expedition arrives at the Patriot Hills camp
Dec. 3   Mountain Travel Expedition leaves Patriot Hills for the Pole

1989

Jan. 17   Mountain Travel Expedition reaches the Pole at noon (Pacific Time)
Jan. 28   The *Bahía Paraíso* runs aground
Jan. 31   The *Bahía Paraíso* capsizes, spilling oil into the water (*see* **Pollution**)
July 27   Will Steger's 6-man crew leaves the northern tip of the Antarctic Peninsula, in winter, on their land traverse to the South Pole
Oct. 4   The first MAC C-58 Galaxy airplane lands at McMurdo Station from Christchurch, New Zealand; it is the largest plane operated by the US

1990

Feb. 12   Reinhold Messner and Arved Fuchs complete a 1,700-mile trek across Antarctica without the use of dogs or mechanization
March 3   Will Steger (of Ely, Minn., USA), Jean-Louis Étienne (of France), Viktor Boyarsky (USSR), Quin Dahe (China), Geoff Somers (UK), Keizo Funatsu (Japan): this 6-man international team complete the longest ever (3,800 miles) nonmechanized transantarctic traverse, using skis and dogsleds, and taking 7 months; Steger and Étienne were the leaders

EXPEDITIONS

The first expeditions were confined to ships. It was not until the 1890s that explorers walked about on the continent itself, although vigorous seal harvesting had taken place in the first and last quarters of the 19th century in the South Shetlands and South Orkneys. The 1800s also saw the beginning of government sponsorship of expeditions, complex and costly as they are. In recent decades most expeditions have been governmental, although the In the Footsteps of Scott Expedition, for example, was privately sponsored in 1985. The last private expedition of major dimensions was the RARE, led by Finn Ronne in 1947–48. See also the **Tourism** entry in the encyclopedia proper.

Following is a list of the major expeditions to Antarctica, i.e., south of 60°S, with the following information usually: dates, the *vessel(s)*, the leader (and name of expedition, if applicable). Each vessel has its own entry.

ca. AD 650   The *Te-Ivi-O-Atea*, Ui-Te-Rangiora
1502   Vespucci
1599   Dirck Gerritsz
?   Cowley
?   Sharpe
?   Edward Davis
1603   The *Blyde Bootschap*
1687–88   Lionel Wafer
1712   Frazier
1719–20   Shelvocke
1772–75   Cook in the *Resolution* and *Adventure*
1818–19   The *Williams*, William Smith
1819   The *Williams*, William Smith
1819   The *San Telmo* and the *Primeroso-Mariana*
1819–20   The *Williams*, Bransfield
1819–20   The *Espírito Santo*
1819–20   The *San Juan Nepomuceno*, Timblón
1819–20   The *Hersilia*, Sheffield
1819–20   Unknown vessel in the South Shetlands, owned by Mr. White of Salem,
             Massachusetts
1819–21   Von Bellingshausen in the *Vostok* and *Mirnyy*
1819–21   Weddell in the *Jane* and *Beaufoy of London*

1820–21 The *Ann*
1820–21 The *Essex*, Chester
1820–21 The *O'Cain*, Winship (allied itself to the Boston Expedition)
1820–21 The Boston Expedition, comprising the *Esther* and *Emerald;* joined by the *O'Cain*
1820–21 The Fanning-Pendleton Sealing Expedition, comprising the *Frederick, Free Gift, Express, Hero,* and *Hersilia*
1820–21 The *Cora*, Fildes
1820–21 The *Dragon*, McFarlane
1820–21 John Davis in the *Huron* and *Cecilia*
1820–21 The *Hetty*, Bond
1820–21 The *Lord Melville*, Clark
1820–21 The *Horatio*, Weeks
1820–21 The *King George*, Roberts
1820–21 The *Diana*, Bunker
1820–21 The *Lady Trowbridge*, Sherratt
1820–21 The *Hannah*, Johnson [probably]
1820–21 The *Huntress*, Burdick
1820–21 Alexander Clark in the *Clothier, Catharina, Emeline,* and *Spark*
1820–21 The *Samuel*, Inott
1820–21 The *William and Nancy*, under Folger and the *Harmony*, under Ray
1820–21 The *Charity*, Barnard (allied itself to the New York Sealing Expedition)
1820–21 The *Gleaner*, Leslie
1820–21 The *Salisbury*, Hodges
1820–21 The *Lady Francis*
1820–21 The *Stranger*, Adams
1820–21 The *Williams*, and another vessel, under William Smith
1820–21 The *Nelson*, Burney
1820–21 The *John*, Walker
1820–21 The *Indian*, Spiller
1820–21 The *Lynx*, Siddons
1820–21 The *Eliza*, Powell
1820–21 The *George*, Richards
1820–21 The *Mercury*, Wetherell
1820–21 The *Minerva*, Binn
1820–21 The *Minstrel*, MacGregor
1820–21 The *Sprightly*, Fraser
1820–22 The New York Sealing Expedition, comprising the *Henry, Aurora, Venus, Jane Maria, Sarah,* and *Wasp;* joined by the *Charity* and (1821–22) *Lynx*
1820–22 The Salem Expedition, comprising the *General Knox, Governor Brooks,* and *Nancy*
1821–22 The *King George*, Roberts
1821–22 The *Charity*, Barnard
1821–22 The *General Scott*, Sayer
1821–22 The *Ann*, Kitchen
1821–22 The *George Porter*, Moores
1821–22 The *Grace*, Rowe
1821–22 The *Enchantress*, Bond
1821–22 The *Harmony*, Hodges
1821–22 The *Caraquet*, Usher
1821–22 The *Essex*, Chester

1821–22   The *Robert*, Fildes
1821–22   Powell in the *Dove* and *Eliza*
1821–22   The *Lynx*, Siddons (allied itself to the New York Sealing Expedition)
1821–22   The *Livonia*
1821–22   Thomas Johnson in the *Mellona* and *Liberty*
1821–22   The *Princess Charlotte*, M'Kean
1821–22   The *Romeo*
1821–22   The *Sprightly*, Brown
1821–22   The *George*
1821–22   John Davis in the *Huron* and *Cecilia*
1821–22   The *Henry*, Kellick
1821–22   The *Tartar*, Pottinger
1821–22   The *Caroline*, Taylor
1821–22   The *George IV*, Alexander
1821–22   The *John*, Walker
1821–22   The Fanning-Pendleton Expedition, comprising the *Alabama Packet*, *Express*, *Free Gift*, *Frederick*, *Hero*, and *James Monroe*
1821–22   Weddell in the *Jane* and *Beaufoy of London*
1821–22   The *Brusso*, Greaves
1821–23   The *Martha*, Bond
1821–23   The *Nelson*, Burney
1821–23   The *Pomona*, Robinson
1822–23   The *Henry*, Johnson
1822–23   The *Wasp*, Morrell
1822–23   The *Dart*, Duell
1822–23   The *Jenny*
1822–23   The *King George*, Alexander
1822–24   Weddell in the *Jane* and *Beaufoy of London*
1823–24   The *Alliance*, Gardiner
1823–25   The *Susanna Ann*, Brown
1824–25   The *Sprightly*, Hughes
1824–26   The *Beaufoy of London*, Brisbane
the 1820s   James Johnson
1825   Richard Macy
1828–31   The *Chanticleer*, Foster
1829–31   The *Penguin*, Alex Palmer (allied itself to the Palmer-Pendleton Expedition)
1829–31   The *Pacific*, Brown
1829–31   The Palmer-Pendleton Expedition (also called the American Sealing and Exploring Expedition), comprising the *Annawan* and *Seraph;* joined by the *Penguin*
1830–32   Biscoe in the *Tula* and *Lively*
1831   The *Venus*, Harvey
1831–33   Alex Palmer in the *Charles Adams* and *Courier*
1833–34   The *Magnet*, Kemp
1833–34   Rea in the *Hopefull* and *Rose*
1836–37   The *Sailor's Return*, Smyley
1836–37   The *Geneva*, Padack
1837–40   Dumont d'Urville in the *Astrolabe* and *Zélée*
1838–39   Balleny in the *Eliza Scott* and *Sabrina*
1838–42   The United States Exploring Expedition under Wilkes, in the *Vincennes*, *Peacock*, *Porpoise*, *Flying Fish*, *Sea Gull*, and *Relief*

1839–43   Ross in the *Erebus* and *Terror*
1841–42   The *Ohio*, Smyley
the 1840s The *Fleetwood*
1843–45   The *Richard Henry*, Peck
1845–46   The *Catherine*, Smyley
1849   The *Brisk*, Tapsell
1852–53   Eldridge in the *Aeronaut* and *Lion*
1852–53   The *Sarah E. Spear*, Pendleton
1853–54   Eldridge in the *Aeronaut*, *Lion*, and *Wilmington*
1853–54   The *Flying Cloud*, Hidden
1853–54   The *Sarah E. Spear*, Kane
1853–54   The *United States*, Wilcox
1856–60   The *Tenedos*, King
1871–72   Gilderdale in the *Peru* and *Franklin*
1872–73   There were 7 unknown US sealers in the South Shetlands this season
1872–73   The *Flying Fish*, Church
1872–76   The *Challenger*, Nares, then Wyville
1873–74   The *Francis Allyn*, Glass
1873–74   The *Thomas Hunt*, Eldred
1873–74   The *Flying Fish*, Church
1873–74   The *Franklin*, Chester
1873–74   The *Golden West*, Williams
1873–74   The *L.P. Simmons*, Potts
1873–75   The *Grönland*, Dallmann
1874–75   The *Thomas Hunt*, Eldred [probably]
1874–75   The *Francis Allyn*, Glass
1874–75   The *Charles Shearer*
1874–75   The *Golden West*, Williams
1874–75   The *Franklin*, Buddington
1875–76   The *Thomas Hunt*, Eldred
1875–77   The *Francis Allyn*, Glass
1876–77   The *Florence*, Buddington
1877–78   The *Charles Shearer*, Appleton
1877–78   The *Francis Allyn*, Glass
1878–79   The *Thomas Hunt*, Eldred
1878–79   The *Francis Allyn*, Glass
1879–80   The *Thomas Hunt*, Eldred
1879–80   The *Express*
1888–89   The *Sarah W. Hunt*, Buddington
1889–90   The *Sarah W. Hunt*, Buddington
1892–93   The Dundee Whaling Expedition, comprising the *Balaena*, *Diana*, *Active*, and *Polar Star*
1892–94   The *Jason*, Larsen
1893–94   The *Hertha*, under Evensen and the *Castor*, under Pedersen
1893–95   The *Antarctic*, Bull and Kristensen
1897–99   The *Belgica*, de Gerlache (the Belgian Antarctic Expedition)
1898–99   The *Valdivia*, Chun
1898–1900 The *Southern Cross*, Borchgrevink (the British Antarctic Expedition)
1901–03   The *Gauss*, von Drygalski (the German Antarctic Expedition)
1901–04   The *Antarctic*, Nordenskjöld (the Swedish Antarctic Expedition)
1901–04   The *Discovery*, Scott (the Royal Society Expedition, also called the British National Antarctic Expedition)

1902–03 The *Uruguay*, Irízar
1902–03 The *Morning*, Colbeck
1902–03 The *Scotia*, Bruce (the Scottish National Antarctic Expedition)
1903–04 *The Frithiof*, Gyldén
1903–04 Colbeck in the *Morning* and *Terra Nova*
1903–05 The *Français*, Charcot (the French Antarctic Expedition)
1904–05 The *Uruguay*, Galíndez (the Orcadas Expedition)
1905–06 The *Austral*, Saborido
1905–06 The *Admiralen*, Lange
1907–09 The *Nimrod*, Shackleton (the British Antarctic Expedition)
1908–09 The *Ørnen*, a whale catcher
1908–09 The *Ravn*, a whale catcher
1908–09 The *Svip*, a whale catcher
1908–10 The *Pourquoi Pas?*, Charcot (the French Antarctic Expedition)
1910–12 The *Fram*, Amundsen (the Norwegian Antarctic Expedition)
1910–13 The *Terra Nova*, Scott (the British Antarctic Expedition)
1911–12 The *Paal*, Sørlle
1911–12 The *Ronald*
1911–12 The *Neko*
1911–12 The *Thulla*, Jörgensen
1911–12 The *Deutschland*, Filchner (the German Antarctic Expedition)
1911–12 The *Kainan Maru*, Shirase (the Japanese South Polar Expedition)
1911–14 The *Aurora*, Mawson (the Australasian Antarctic Expedition)
1912–13 The *Normanna*, Stene
1912–13 The *Falkland*
1912–13 The *Thule*
1912–13 The *Tioga*, Moe
1912–13 The *Paal*, Sørlle
1913–14 Ferguson on the *Hanka*
1913–14 The *Thule*
1913–15 The *Polynesia*, Borge
1914–16 The *Endurance*, Shackleton (the British Imperial Transantarctic Expedition)
1914–17 The *Aurora*, Mackintosh (the Ross Sea party of the British Imperial
           Transantarctic Expedition)
1915   The *Uruguay*
1916   The *Southern Sky*, Shackleton
1916   The *Instituto de Pesca I*, Shackleton
1916   The *Emma*, Shackleton
1916   The *Yelcho*, Shackleton
1916–17 J. Innes Wilson's geological expeditions
1920–21 The *Svend Foyn*
1920–22 The British Imperial Expedition led by Cope on various whalers
1921–22 The *Svend Foyn*
1921–22 The *Thor I*
1921–22 The *Solstreif*
1921–22 The *Quest*, Shackleton, then Wild
1923–24 The *Neko*
1923–24 The *Sir James Clark Ross*, Larsen
1924–25 The *Sir James Clark Ross*, Larsen, then Oscar Nilsen
1925–26 The *Lancing*
1925–26 The *Discovery*, Kemp
1925–27 The *Meteor*, Spiesz

1935–37   The *Discovery II*, Deacon
1936–37   The *William Scoresby*, Hart
1936–37   Christensen in the *Thorshavn* and *Firern*
1936–37   The *Ajax*, Thomsen
1936–37   The *Thorshammer*, Bråvold
1937–38   The *William Scoresby*, Rayner
1937–39   The *Discovery II*, Mackintosh, then Herdman
1938–39   The *Schwabenland*, Ritscher (the German New Schwabenland Expedition)
1938–39   The *Wyatt Earp*, Ellsworth (the American Highland Expedition)
1939–41   The United States Antarctic Service Expedition, under Byrd, in the *North Star* and *Bear*
1940–41   The *Ole Wegger*, Andersen
1940–41   The *Solglimt*
1940–41   The *Pelagos*
1940–41   The *Pinguin*, Krüder
1940–41   The *Komet*, Eyssen
1941   The *Queen of Bermuda*, Peachey
1942   The *Primero de Mayo*, Oddera
1943   The *Carnarvon Castle*, Kitson
1943   The *Primero de Mayo*, Harriague
1943–45   Marr in the *William Scoresby* and *Fitzroy* (Operation Tabarin I)
1945   Taylor in the *Trepassey*, *Fitzroy*, *William Scoresby*, and *Eagle* (Operation Tabarin II)
1946   Bingham in the *Trepassey*, *William Scoresby*, and *Fitzroy*
1946–47   Operation Highjump, under Byrd
1946–47   Guesalaga in the *Iquique* and *Angamos* (the First Chilean Antarctic Expedition)
1946–47   The *Balaena*, Trouton
1947   Argentine Antarctic Expedition, under García
1947   Pierce-Butler in the *Trepassey* and *Fitzroy*
1947–48   The *Hashedate Maru*
1947–48   The *Bråtegg*, Holgersen
1947–48   Argentine Antarctic Expedition, under Hermelo
1947–48   The *Southern Harvest*
1947–48   Ketchum in the *Edisto* and *Burton Island* (Operation Windmill)
1947–48   González in the *Covadonga* and *Rancagua*
1947–48   The *Port of Beaumont, Texas*, Ronne (the RARE)
1947–48   The *Snipe*, under Forbes and the *Nigeria*, under Moore
1948   The *Presidente Pinto* (the Chilean Presidential Antarctic Expedition)
1948   Argentine Naval maneuvers in the South Shetlands, under Cappus
1948   The *Wyatt Earp*, Campbell (ANARE)
1948   The *John Biscoe*, Fuchs
1948–49   Fontaine in the *Covadonga*, *Maipo*, and *Lautaro* (Chilean Antarctic Expedition)
1948–49   The *Sparrow*, Waterhouse
1948–49   Argentine Antarctic Expedition, in the *Pampa*, *Chaco*, *Punta Ninfas*, *Sanavirón*, and *Chiriguano*
1949–50   Natho in the *Lientur*, *Maipo*, and *Iquique* (Chilean Antarctic Expedition)
1949–50   Argentine Antarctic Expedition, in the *Chaco*, *Punta Ninfas*, *Chiriguano*, and *Yamana*
1949–50   The *Bigbury Bay*, under Goodden and the *Gold Ranger*, under Parker
1949–51   The *Commandant Charcot*, Liotard (French Polar Expedition)

1949–52   The *Norsel,* Giaever (the Norwegian-British-Swedish Antarctic Expedition)
1949–53   Fuchs in the *John Biscoe, Sparrow, Snipe,* and *Burghead Bay*
1950–51   Munita in the *Lientur, Angamos,* and *Lautaro* (Chilean Antarctic Expedition)
1950–51   Panzarini in the *Bahía Buen Suceso, Punta Loyola, Sanavirón, Chiriguano* and *Santa Micaela* (Argentine Antarctic Expedition)
1950–51   The *Discovery II,* Herdman
1951–52   Barré in the *Commandant Charcot* (French Polar Expedition)
1951–52   Díaz in the *Bahía Buen Suceso, Bahía Aguirre, Punta Ninfas, Chiriguano,* and *Sanavirón* (Argentine Antarctic Expedition)
1952   Tisné in the *Angamos, Lientur,* and *Leucotón* (Chilean Antarctic Expedition)
1952–53   The *John Biscoe,* W. Johnston
1952–53   The Chilean Antarctic Expedition, led by Wiegand
1952–53   The *Tottan,* Marret (French Polar Expedition)
1952–53   The Argentine Antarctic Expedition, led by Panzarini
1953   The *Snipe,* under Hall-Wright, and the *Bigbury Bay,* under Sutton
1953–54   The *John Biscoe,* W. Johnston
1953–54   The *Kista Dan,* Law (ANARE)
1953–54   The Chilean Antarctic Expedition, under López Costa
1953–54   The Argentine Antarctic Expedition, under Ogara
1953–54   The *Nereide,* under Harrison, and the *St. Austell Bay,* under Ward
1954–55   The Argentine Antarctic Expedition, under Ogara
1954–55   The *Atka,* Jacobsen (the US Navy Antarctic Expedition)
1954–55   The *Veryan Bay,* under Lawford, and the *Burghead Bay,* under Hoare
1954–55   The Chilean Antarctic Expedition, led by Gándara Bofil
1954–55   The *John Biscoe,* under W. Johnston, and the *Norsel,* under O. Johannessen
1955   The *Kista Dan,* Law (ANARE)
1955–56   Somov in the *Ob'* and *Lena* (First Soviet Antarctic Expedition)
1955–56   The *Protector,* Wilkinson
1955–56   The *Shackleton,* under Johnston, and the *John Biscoe,* under Brown
1955–56   The *Tottan,* David Dalgliesh (the British Royal Society IGY Expedition)
1955–56   The *Kista Dan,* Law (ANARE)
1955–56   The Argentine Antarctic Expedition, under Díaz
1955–56   Chilean Antarctic Expedition, under Martínez Díaz
1955–56   Operation Deep Freeze I, led by Byrd
1955–56   The *Norsel,* Imbert (French Polar Expedition)
1955–57   The *Oluf Sven,* Mott (FIDASE)
1955–58   The British Commonwealth Transantarctic Expedition, led by Fuchs in the *Theron, Magga Dan,* and *Endeavour*
1956   The French Polar Expedition (wintering-over), led by Guillard
1956–57   The *Protector,* Wilkinson
1956–57   The *Shackleton,* under Brown, and the *John Biscoe,* under W. Johnston
1956–57   Nagata in the *Soya* and *Umitaka Maru* (JARE I)
1956–57   Sigurd Helle in the *Polarsirkel* and *Polarbjørn* (Norwegian Antarctic Expedition)
1956–57   Operation Deep Freeze II, under Dufek
1956–57   The 2nd Soviet Antarctic Expedition, under Treshnikov
1956–57   The *Kista Dan,* Law (ANARE)
1956–57   Argentine Antarctic Expedition, under Guozdén
1956–57   The *Britannia,* Prince Philip

1956–57 Chilean Antarctic Expedition, under Navarrete Torres
1957   French Polar Expedition (wintering-over), under Imbert
1957–58 The *Soya*, Nagata (JARE II, aborted)
1957–58 The *Protector*
1957–58 The 3rd Soviet Antarctic Expedition
1957–58 Norwegian Antarctic Expedition
1957–58 The *Thala Dan* (ANARE)
1957–58 NZGSAE [New Zealand Geological Survey Antarctic Expedition]
1957–58 IGY [International Geophysical Year]
1957–58 US Air Force Electronics Test Unit, under Lassiter
1957–58 Gaston de Gerlache in the *Polarhav* and *Polarsirkel* (Belgian Antarctic
          Expedition)
1957–58 Operation Deep Freeze III
1957–59 French Polar Expedition, led by Rouillon
1958–59 The *Protector*
1958–59 The 4th Soviet Antarctic Expedition
1958–59 Norwegian Antarctic Expedition
1958–59 The *Magga Dan*, Law (ANARE)
1958–59 Operation Deep Freeze IV
1958–59 The Belgian Antarctic Expedition, under F.E. Bastin
1958–59 VUWAE [Victoria University of Wellington Antarctic Expedition], under
          Bull
1958–59 NZGSAE
1958–59 The *Soya*, Murayama (JARE III)
1959–60 USN Bellingshausen Sea Expedition, in the *Glacier* and *Burton Island*
1959–60 Norwegian Antarctic Expedition
1959–60 The *Magga Dan*, Law (ANARE)
1959–60 Operation Deep Freeze 60
1959–60 The New Zealand Alpine Club Antarctic Expedition
1959–60 The New Zealand Geological and Topographical Survey Expedition
1959–60 VUWAE
1959–60 NZGSAE, led by Murray Robb
1959–60 The 5th Soviet Antarctic Expedition
1959–60 The *Soya*, Torii (JARE IV)
1959–61 The *Erika Dan*, Derom (Belgian Antarctic Expedition)
1959–61 The *Polarbjørn*, La Grange (SANAE I)
1959–61 The French Polar Expedition, led by Alfred Faure
1960–61 The *Soya*, Murayama (JARE V)
1960–61 The *Magga Dan*, Law (ANARE)
1960–61 NZGSAE
1960–61 VUWAE
1960–61 Operation Deep Freeze 61
1960–61 The 6th Soviet Antarctic Expedition
1961–62 The *Lientur*, Marcos Ortiz
1961–62 The *Polarhav*, van der Westhuyzen (SANAE II)
1961–62 VUWAE
1961–62 NZGSAE
1961–62 The *Soya* (JARE VI)
1961–62 Operation Deep Freeze 62
1961–62 The *John Biscoe, Kista Dan*, and *Shackleton*
1961–62 The 7th Soviet Antarctic Expedition
1961–63 The *Protector*

1962–63   The Texas Tech Shackleton Glacier Expedition, under Wade
1962–63   The 8th Soviet Antarctic Expedition
1962–63   The *John Biscoe*
1962–63   The New Zealand Federated Mountain Clubs Antarctic Expedition, led by John M. Millen
1962–63   Operation Deep Freeze 63
1962–63   NZGSAE
1962–63   VUWAE
1962–63   The *R.S.A.*, Dupreez (SANAE III)
1963–64   VUWAE
1963–64   NZGSAE
1963–64   Operation Deep Freeze 64
1963–64   The *John Biscoe*
1963–64   The *Endeavour II*, P.R.H. Silk
1963–64   The 9th Soviet Antarctic Expedition
1963–64   SANAE IV under Venter
1964   New Zealand Antarctic Research Program Allan Hills Expedition
1964–65   The 10th Soviet Antarctic Expedition
1964–65   Texas Tech Shackleton Glacier Expedition
1964–65   SANAE V under Van Zyl
1964–65   Operation Deep Freeze 65
1964–65   University of New South Wales Expedition
1964–65   NZGSAE, under Malcolm G. Laird
1965–66   First Argentine Overland Polar Expedition
1965–66   The 11th Soviet Antarctic Expedition
1965–66   The *Fuji* (JARE VII)
1965–66   NZGSAE
1965–66   Operation Deep Freeze 66
1965–66   SANAE VI, under Van Wyk
1965–66   *Nella Dan* (ANARE)
1966   The *Mischief*, Tilman
1966–67   University of New South Wales Expedition
1966–67   Operation Deep Freeze 67
1966–67   NZGSAE
1966–67   SANAE VII, under Kavanagh
1966–67   The 12th Soviet Antarctic Expedition
1966–67   The *Fuji* (JARE VIII)
1967–68   NZGSAE, under V.E. Neall
1967–68   Operation Deep Freeze 68
1967–68   The 13th Soviet Antarctic Expedition
1967–68   The *Fuji* (JARE IX)
1968–69   IWSOE [International Weddell Sea Oceanographic Expedition]
1968–69   The Norwegian Antarctic Expedition, under Thor S. Witnes
1968–69   Operation Deep Freeze 69
1968–69   The *Endurance*
1968–69   The *Hero*, in Antarctic waters every year from now until 1984
1968–69   The 14th Soviet Antarctic Expedition
1968–69   The *Fuji* (JARE X)
1969   The second IWSOE
1969–70   NZGSAE, under Don Cowie
1969–70   All-women expedition under Lois Jones (actually part of Operation Deep Freeze)

1969–70   Operation Deep Freeze 70
1969–70   The 15th Soviet Antarctic Expedition
1969–70   The *Fuji* (JARE XI)
1970   Barrett's Darwin Mountains Expedition
1970–71   The *San Giuseppe Due*, Ajmone
1970–71   The *Awahnee*, Griffith
1970–71   The *Alpha Helix*
1970–71   The 16th Soviet Antarctic Expedition
1970–71   The *Fuji* (JARE XII)
1970–71   The *Endurance* (Joint Services Expedition)
1971–72   Operation Deep Freeze 72
1971–72   The 17th Soviet Antarctic Expedition
1971–72   The *Fuji* (JARE XIII)
1971–81   The Ten-Year International Antarctic Glaciological Project
1972–73   The *Ice Bird*, Lewis
1972–73   The *Calypso*, Cousteau
1972–73   Operation Deep Freeze 73
1972–73   The 18th Soviet Antarctic Expedition
1972–73   The *Fuji* (JARE XIV)
1973–74   Operation Deep Freeze 74
1973–74   The 19th Soviet Antarctic Expedition
1973–74   The *Fuji* (JARE XV)
1974–75   Operation Deep Freeze 75
1974–75   The 20th Soviet Antarctic Expedition
1974–75   The *Fuji* (JARE XVI)
1975–   POLEX South
1975–76   The Polish Antarctic Marine Research Expedition
1975–76   Operation Deep Freeze 76
1975–76   The *Fuji* (JARE XVII)
1975–76   The 21st Soviet Antarctic Expedition
1976–77   Operation Deep Freeze 77
1976–77   The 22nd Soviet Antarctic Expedition
1976–77   The *Fuji* (JARE XVIII)
1977–78   The *Solo*, Lewis
1977–78   Operation Deep Freeze 78
1977–78   The 23rd Soviet Antarctic Expedition
1977–78   The *Fuji* (JARE XIX)
1978–79   Operation Deep Freeze 79
1978–79   The 24th Soviet Antarctic Expedition
1978–79   The *Fuji* (JARE XX)
1979–80   GANOVEX 79
1979–80   Operation Deep Freeze 80
1979–80   The 25th Soviet Antarctic Expedition
1979–80   The *Fuji* (JARE XXI)
1979–82   The Trans-Globe Expedition, under Fiennes
1980–81   Operation Deep Freeze 81
1980–81   The *Endurance*
1980–81   FIBEX
1980–81   The 26th Soviet Antarctic Expedition
1980–81   The *Fuji* (JARE XXII)
1981–82   The Northern Victoria Land Expedition
1981–82   The *Dick Smith Explorer*, Lewis

1981–82   The *Hakurei Maru*
1981–82   Operation Deep Freeze 82
1981–82   The 27th Soviet Antarctic Expedition
1981–82   The *Fuji* (JARE XXIII)
1981–   The Weddell Polynya Expedition
1982   Seymour Island Expedition
1982   The *Polar Circle* (Operation Gangotri)
1982   New Zealand Antarctic Research Program
1982–83   The *Fuji* (JARE XXIV)
1982–83   The 28th Soviet Antarctic Expedition
1982–83   The *Thala Dan* (Brazilian Expedition)
1982–83   Spanish expedition
1982–83   GANOVEX III
1982–83   The *Polar Star* circumnavigated Antarctica
1982–83   Operation Deep Freeze 83
1982–84   The *Dick Smith Explorer,* Lewis (Frozen Sea Expedition)
1983–84   The 29th Soviet Antarctic Expedition
1983–84   Operation Deep Freeze 84
1983–84   The *Shirase* (JARE XXV)
1984–85   First Chinese National Antarctic Expedition
1984–85   Norwegian Antarctic Expedition
1984–85   Operation Deep Freeze 85
1984–85   The 30th Soviet Antarctic Expedition
1984–85   The *Shirase* (JARE XXVI)
1985   GANOVEX IV
1985–86   The *Riquita*
1985–86   The *Shirase* (JARE XXVII)
1985–86   The 31st Soviet Antarctic Expedition
1985–86   Operation Deep Freeze 86
1985–86   The *Southern Quest,* Swan (In the Footsteps of Scott Expedition)
1986   The *Polarstern* (the Winter Weddell Sea Project)
1986–87   Italian Antarctic Expedition
1986–87   NOZE I [National Ozone Expedition I]
1986–87   Operation Deep Freeze 87
1986–87   The 32nd Soviet Antarctic Expedition
1986–87   The *Shirase* (JARE XXVIII)
1987   Greenpeace expedition
1987–88   The 33rd Soviet Antarctic Expedition
1987–88   Operation Deep Freeze 88
1987–88   NOZE II
1987–88   The *Shirase* (JARE XXIX)
1988–89   Mountain Travel South Pole Expedition, led by Williams
1988–89   NOZE III
1988–89   Operation Deep Freeze 89
1988–89   The 34th Soviet Antarctic Expedition
1988–89   The *Shirase* (JARE XXX)
1989–90   The 35th Soviet Antarctic Expedition
1989–90   Operation Deep Freeze 90
1989–90   The *Shirase* (JARE XXXI)
1989–90   Steger's South Pole trek from the Antarctic Peninsula
1989–90   The Messner-Fuchs expedition

BIBLIOGRAPHY

Books that proved helpful in researching this encyclopedia are annotated;
some others are lightly annotated as well; the works that are not annotated
were found to be unreliable, out of date, not generally available, or simply
superseded by others more comprehensive or authoritative.

Aagard, Bjarne. *Fangst og Forskning i Sydishavet.* Oslo: Gyldendal Norsk Forlag, 1931.
Adams, Harry. *Beyond the Barrier with Byrd.* Chicago: M.A. Donahue, 1932.
Alberts, Fred G., editor and compiler. *Geographic Names of the Antarctic.*
Washington, D.C.: United States Board on Geographic Names/National Science
Foundation, 1980. 959 pp. Foreword; The Antarctic Geographic Name Problem;
Policy Covering Antarctic Names; an article on mapping; bibliography; excellent list
of abbreviations. The body of the book is an alphabetical listing of most of the Ant-
arctic place names given up to 1979, complete with cross-references. The typical entry
gives coordinates, where it is to be found, when it was discovered, charted, and
mapped, and for whom it was named. An astonishing research effort.
Amundsen, Roald. *Mitt Liv som Polarforsker.* Oslo: Gyldendal Norsk Forlag, 1927.
Published in English by Doubleday, Page, of New York, in 1927, as *My Life as an
Explorer.*
_____. *Sydpolen.* Kristiania [Oslo]: Jacob Dybwads Forlag, 1912. 2 vols. Translated
into English by A.G. Chater, and published in London in 2 vols. in 1912 by John
Murray, as *The South Pole.*
Antarctic Bibliography. Washington, D.C.: Library of Congress/National Science
Foundation. 13 vols. Lists all material published on Antarctica from 1962 until 1984.
Later references are being compiled in *Current Antarctic Literature,* also published
by the Library of Congress/NSF. For literature before 1962 there is the *Antarctic
Bibliography 1951-61,* published by the Library of Congress, and *Antarctic
Bibliography,* published by the US Navy, listing all references prior to 1951.
Antarctic Journal of the United States. Published quarterly in March, June, Sept., and
Dec., with a thick annual review issue as well. (Division of Polar Programs, National
Science Foundation, Washington DC 20550. Tel: 202-357-7817.) Established in
1966 by editor K.G. Sandved as a natural successor to the *Report of the Commander,
US Naval Support Force, Antarctica.* It reports on US activities in Antarctica, and re-
lated activities elsewhere, and on trends in the US Antarctic Program (formerly
USARP). Guy G. Guthridge replaced Sandved as editor from the March/April 1972
issue. It used to be bimonthly, and much thicker than it is now, and went quarterly
at the beginning of 1976. Guthridge was replaced in early 1977 by a series of editors,
notably Richard P. Muldoon, and from June 1980 by Winifred Ruening.
Antarctic Magazine. A New Zealand quarterly put out by the New Zealand Antarctic

1173

Society in Christchurch, N.Z. It has been called this since 1956. Before that (Aug. 1950 through the last quarter of 1955), it was the *Antarctic News Bulletin*.

Aramayo Alzérreca, Carlos. *Historia de la Antártida*. Buenos Aires: Editorial Hemisferio, 1949. 390pp.

Armitage, Albert B. *Two Years in the Antarctic*. London: Edward Arnold, 1905. 315pp. Illus.

————. *Cadet to Commodore*. London: Cassell, 1925. 307pp.

Army Observers Report of Operation Highjump, Task Force 68, US Navy. Washington, D.C.: War Department, 1947.

Arnesen, Odd. *Roald Amundsen som Han Var*. Oslo: Gyldendal Norsk Forlag, 1929. 205pp.

————. *Fram, Hele Norges Skute*. Oslo: Jacob Dybwads Forlag, 1942. 297pp.

Arnold, H.J.P. *Photographer of the World*. London: Hutchinson, 1969. 175pp. Illus. A biography of Herbert Ponting.

————. *Herbert Ponting. Another World*. London: Sidgwick & Jackson, 1975. 128pp. Illus.

Aubert de la Rüe, Edgar. *Les Terres Australes*. Paris: Presses Universitaires de France, 1953. 126pp. Illus.

Aurora Australis. 1908-9. This was the magazine of the British Antarctic Expedition of 1907-9. "Published at the Winter Quarters of the British Antarctic Expedition, 1907, during the winter months of April, May, June, July 1908. Illustrated with lithographs and etchings by George Marston. Printed at the sign of 'The Penguins' by Joyce and Wild. Latitude 77°32'S. Longitude 166°12'E. Antarctica. (All rights reserved)." It has a couple of penguins as the logo. This was Shackleton's expedition's magazine, similar to the *South Polar Times* of Scott's 1901-4 expedition, which Shackleton had edited, except that *Aurora Australis* was a book, in one volume, a memento of the expedition of 1907-9. A hundred copies were printed and published at Cape Royds (see also the entry **Books** in the main body of this book); the intention was to sell the book on return to England. But it did not sell. At first the book was to be called *Antarctic Ice Flowers*. It is an anthology more than anything. Shackleton wrote two prefaces for it. Joyce and Wild typeset it, Marston illustrated and Day created the board covers from Venesta packing cases, smoothed these down and then bound the books. The work has 120 pages, and is dedicated to the Misses Dawson-Lambton, two major patrons of the expedition. Marston was editor and Shackleton was editor-in-chief. The title page has a lithograph of the aurora, framed in a scroll, with two sailing ships on top. It contains articles like "The Ascent of Mount Erebus" by David, "Trials of a Messman" by Priestley, "A Pony Watch" by Putty (Marston), "Southward Bound" a poem by Lapsus Linguae (Marshall), "An Interview with an Emperor" by Mackay, "Life Under Difficulties" by Murray (this article being the life history of the rotifer [q.v.]), "An Ancient Manuscript" by Shellback (Wild), "Bathybia" by Mawson, and 2 poems by Nemo (Shackleton), "Erebus" and "Midwinter Night." In 1909 Heinemann, the publishers, brought out a limited edition of 300 copies of *The Antarctic Book* as a third volume to the deluxe edition of Shackleton's narrative of the expedition, *Heart of the Antarctic*. Portions of *Aurora Australis* are in this.

Austbø, Johan. *Olav Bjåland*. Oslo: Fonna Forlag, 1945. 109pp. Illus.

Austin, O.L., Jr., editor. *Antarctic Bird Studies*. Washington, D.C.: American Geophysical Union, 1968. 262pp.

Bagshawe, Thomas W. *Two Men in the Antarctic*. New York: Macmillan, 1939. 292pp. Foreword by Frank Debenham.

Bain, J. Arthur. *Life and Explorations of Fridtjof Nansen*. London: Walter Scott, 1907. 449pp. Illus. Map. Plates.

Bakaev, V.G., editor. *Atlas of Antarctica*. Moscow: Academy of Sciences, USSR, 1966. In Russian.

Baker, J.N.L. *A History of Geographical Discovery and Exploration*. London: G.G. Harrap, 1931. 543pp. Maps.

Balch, Edwin Swift. *Antarctica*. Philadelphia: Allen, Lane & Scott, 1902. 230pp. Maps.

Balchen, Bernt. *Come North with Me*. New York: E.P. Dutton, 1958. 318pp. Illus. Bernt Balchen's autobiography. Originally published in Oslo by Gyldendal Norsk Forlag in 1958, as *Kom Nord med Meg*. (258pp. Illus.)

Barber, Noël. *White Desert*. London: Hodder & Stoughton, 1958; New York: Crowell, 1958. 205pp. Illus. A British journalist's account of the BCTAE.

Barnard, Charles H. *A Narrative of the Sufferings and Adventures of Capt. Charles H. Barnard in a Voyage Round the World*. New York: J. Lindon (private printer), 1829.

Baum, Allyn. *Antarctica: The Worst Place in the World*. New York: Macmillan, 1966. 151pp. Photos. Index.

Beaglehole, J.C., editor. *The Journals of Captain Cook*. Cambridge: Hakluyt Society, 1955.

Béchervaise, John M. *Blizzard and Fire: A Year at Mawson, Antarctica*. Sydney: Angus & Robertson, 1963. 252pp. Illus. Maps.

Begbie, Harold. *Shackleton. A Memory*. London: Mills & Boon, 1922.

Bernacchi, Louis C. *Saga of the Discovery*. London & Glasgow: Blackie and Son, 1938. 240pp. Illus.

————. *To the South Polar Regions*. London: Hurst & Blackett, 1901. 348pp. Illustrated with photos taken by the author.

————. *A Very Gallant Gentleman*. London: Thornton & Butterworth, 1933. 240pp. Illus. Maps. A biography of Capt. Oates.

Bertram, Colin. *Arctic and Antarctic: The Technique of Polar Travel*. Cambridge, England: W. Heffer & Sons, 1939.

Bertrand, Kenneth J. *Americans in Antarctica 1775–1948*. New York: American Geographical Society (Special Publication #39), 1971. 554pp. Plates, terrific maps, extensive notes, bibliography, index. Fine introduction by the author, and superb chapters on the early American sealers in the South Shetlands, including Nat Palmer. There is a 38-page chapter on the Wilkes Expedition, 50 pages on Byrd's second expedition, and 75 pages on the USAS 1939–41, surely the most detailed account of this expedition ever written. A masterpiece of research and easy reading.

Bickel, Lennard. *This Accursed Land*. Melbourne: Macmillan, 1977. 210pp. Published in the USA by Stein & Day, New York, in 1977, as *Mawson's Will*.

Billing, G., & Mannering, Guy. *South: Man and Nature in Antarctica*. London: Hodder & Stoughton, 1964. 207pp. Text by Billing, illus. by Mannering.

Bixby, William. *The Impossible Journey of Sir Ernest Shackleton*. Boston: Little, Brown, 1960. Children's book. No index. No bibliography. It details the *Endurance* expedition.

Boletín del Instituto Antártico. Argentine periodical since May 1957. Published intermittently.

Bonner, W.N., & Lewis-Smith, R.I. *Conservation Areas in the Antarctic*. Cambridge, England: SCAR/Scott Polar Research Institute, 1985. 299pp.

Bonner, W.N., & Walton, D.W.H., editors. *Antarctica*. Oxford: Pergamon Press, 1985. Part of the "Key Environments" series.

Borchgrevink, Carsten E. *First on the Antarctic Continent*. London: Newnes, 1900. 333pp. Illus. Maps.

————. *Naermest Sydpolen Aaret 1900*. Copenhagen: Gyldendalske Boghandel/Kristiania [Oslo]: Nordisk Forlag, 1905. 562pp. Illus. Maps.

Bowman, Gerald. *Men of Antarctica*. New York: Fleet Pub. Corp., 1958. 191pp. Illus.

Brent, P. *Captain Scott and the Antarctic Tragedy*. New York: Saturday Review Press, 1974. 223pp.

Brewster, Barney. *Antarctica: Wilderness at Risk*. Melbourne: Sun Books, 1980.

Brosse, Jacques. *Great Voyages of Discovery – Circumnavigators and Scientists, 1764–1843*. Paris: Bordas, 1983. Translated into English by Stanley Hockman and published in the USA by Facts on File Publications, New York. 232pp. Big coffee-table book, with plenty of illustrations. Index. Bibliography (not exhaustive, by any means, and mostly French books). Two appendices, one biographical and one geographical. Not much related to Antarctica, but there are 3 good chapters on Cook, and a particularly interesting one on the second voyage, 1772–75. Also a one-page article on von Bellingshausen, and two featuring Dumont d'Urville's pre–Antarctic career. The last section deals exclusively with Antarctica, and the great voyages of Dumont d'Urville, Ross and Wilkes.

Brown, R.N. Rudmose. *A Naturalist at the Poles: The Life, Work and Voyages of Dr. W.S. Bruce, the Polar Explorer*. London: Seeley, Service, 1923. 316pp. 38 illus. & 3 maps. 5 chapters by W. Burn Murdoch.

————; Pirie, J.H. Harvey; & Mossman, Robert C. *The Voyage of the Scotia*. Edinburgh: W. Blackwood & Sons, 1906. 375pp. Maps. These three gentlemen were on the expedition.

Bruce, William S. *Polar Exploration*. London: Williams & Norgate, 1911. 286pp. Illus.

Bull, Henryk J. *The Cruise of the Antarctic in the South Polar Regions*. London: Edward Arnold, 1896. 243pp. Illus. by W. Burn Murdoch.

Burroughs, Polly. *The Great Ice Ship Bear: Eighty-nine Years in Polar Seas*. New York: Van Nostrand Reinhold, 1970. 104pp. Illus.

Bursey, Lt. Cdr. Jack. *Antarctic Night: One Man's Story of 28,224 Hours at the Bottom of the World*. New York: Rand McNally, 1957. 256pp. Illus.

Byrd, Richard E. *Alone*. New York: Putnam's, 1938. Decorations by Richard E. Harrison. Printed in blue lettering. Dedicated by Byrd to his wife, M.A.B. (Marie Ames Byrd). Preface by Byrd. 12 chapters. 296pp. An honest account (so it seems) by an honest guy (so it seems) of his time alone at Bolling Advance Weather Station in 80°08′S, in 1934. Told in a crisp, humorous, interesting way. Useful research material for little details.

————. *Discovery*. New York: Putnam's, 1935. This is *the* book on Byrd's 1933–35 expedition. 405pp.

————. *Exploring with Byrd*. New York: Putnam's, 1937. 241pp. Illus.

————. *Little America*. New York: Putnam's, 1930. 422pp. Good index. Foreword by Byrd. 4 maps, including a very useful one of Little America and the Bay of Whales as they were in 1928–30. Appendix of all personnel on the trip, including those not on the shore party. This is *the* book on Byrd's 1928–30 expedition.

Caine, Hall. *The Woman Thou Gavest Me*. London: Heinemann, 1913. Novel. 600pp. 116 chapters. A 7-part book, a narrative of the life of the fictional Mary O'Neill, written in the first person. It is very long and hackneyed, and tells of a girl who grows up with a boy called Martin Conrad, is in love with him, marries someone else, thinks Martin died, leaves her husband and becomes a desperate in London. She is rescued by the returning Conrad, but dies as a result of exposure. It would have no interest for us if it weren't for the fact that Martin Conrad becomes North Pole–obsessed as a lad, and goes off to the Antarctic as a 20-year-old doctor (sic) in Chap. 22, as part of Lieutenant ————'s expedition. Conrad is clearly based on Shackleton (although later in the novel Caine uses a lot of Scott in Conrad as well). Lieutenant ———— is obviously Scott, and this is equally obviously the Royal Society Expedition of 1901-4, of which Shackleton was a part. For some reason, though (probably delicacy. Scott had just died in real life when the novel was written), Caine omits the name of Scott altogether, as if the man did not exist, even in his list of polar explorers, which includes even Shackleton and is otherwise quite comprehensive down to that time. Why Caine doesn't use a false name for Scott is anybody's business. Perhaps he thought he was being clever to leave it at Lieutenant ———. But, Caine takes a lot of liberties. For example, he mentions Charcot's 1903–5 expedition in an anachronistic way, and refers to a ship getting stuck in Charcot Bay (now Charcot Cove) at 76°S, at the end of the second part of the book. In the 15th Chap. of the third part the hero talks of getting down to 86°S. In the first chapter of the fourth part, he is off again, again with Lieutenant ———. We are introduced to the ship, the *Scotia* (formerly a Dundee whaler called the *Mary*) and to the crew, including the commander (this time the commander, who should be based on Scott, is based on Scott *and* Shackleton). While the *Scotia* is in London ready to leave, the commander shows a picture of the group of them from their previous expedition at the foot of Mount Erebus, and at the end of Chap. 52, in Part Four, the leader, Lieutenant ———, tells how he reached the 87th Parallel (was it the 86th or the 87th?). If Lieutenant ——— is, indeed Scott, as he must be, then the author has him going off on an expedition the real Scott never went on. But then, this is a novel. In Chap. 52, Conrad refers to the leader as "The Boss," which, in real life, was Shackleton's own nickname, not Scott's. In Chap. 83 we find that the *Scotia* has gone south again, this time under the command of the 22-year-old doctor, Martin Conrad. The ship is tossed about in a storm, pieces of wreckage imply to the world the worst, and they assume the ship has sunk. It hasn't. The first chapter of the sixth part shows Martin getting to the 88th Parallel, 100 miles from the Pole (now, this *is* Shackleton, in 1908–9). He gets back to England, is knighted, then leaves yet again for the Antarctic.

Cameron, Ian. *Antarctica: The Last Continent.* Boston: Little, Brown, 1974. 256pp. Index. Bibliography (which, incidentally, does not list Bertrand's masterpiece). Illus. Maps mostly done by Tom Stalker-Miller. There is a color map at the front showing the principal expedition routes. There is no foreword, so it is difficult to find the mind-set of this anonymous author (Ian Cameron is a pseudonym). There are 11 chapters and an epilog. There is an appendix, Principal Expeditions to the Antarctic, which would have been better left undone. Although the text of the book is okay, and even a fine introduction to Antarctica, this appendix disappoints. It is incomplete and inaccurate, notwithstanding the anonymous author's disclaimer that he had to be selective in his choice of expeditions. Even using his own criteria, where are the *Hersilia*, Morrell, the *Chanticleer*, the Palmer-Pendleton Expedition of 1929–31, Kemp, Balleny, Larsen, Charcot's first expedition, Shirase, the British Imperial Expedition of 1920–22, the *Quest* (Shackleton's last expedition), Ritscher, Operation Windmill, Ronne, and others? These are all major expeditions. Moreover, why does this appendix end at 1958, when the book was published in 1974?

Campbell, L.B., & Claridge, G. *Antarctica: Soils, Weathering Processes and Environments.* Amsterdam: Elsevier, 1987. 386pp. Illus.

Campbell, Lord George. *Log Letters from the Challenger.* London: Macmillan, 1876. 448pp.

Canepa, Luís. *Historia Antártida Argentina: Nuestros Derechos.* Buenos Aires: Imprenta Linari, 1948. 100pp.

Caras, Roger A. *Antarctica, Land of Frozen Time.* Philadelphia & New York: Chilton Books, 1962. 210pp. Good map insert. Special charts by A. Peter Ianuzzi. Index. Some fascinating appendices and charts. Brief bibliography (not much good). Very detailed appendix on the Antarctic Treaty, and an interesting one on philately, as well as others. Photos and illustrations. There is a long chapter on ice, a couple on exploration history, a good one on mammals, and one on "Penguins, Plants and Plankton." There is a good table on IGY stations, but be wary of the one on expeditions. It is too rushed to be of much value, and is badly edited. By and large, though, it is a good book to start off with, and the author has a nice, committed style of writing.

Carrington, Hugh. *Life of Captain Cook.* London: Sidgwick & Jackson, 1939. 324pp. Maps.

Carter, Paul A. *Little America: Town at the End of the World.* New York: Columbia University Press, 1979.

Chapman, Walker, editor. *Antarctic Conquest: The Great Explorers in Their Own Words.* Indianapolis: Bobbs-Merrill, 1965. Selected and introduced by Walker Chapman [a pseudonym]. 365pp. Illus. Part I deals with Terra Australis Incognita, 1506–1777; Part II with the whaling and sealing era, 1821–1839; Part III is called Toward the Magnetic Pole, 1841–1874; Part IV is The Heroic Age, 1896–1920; Part V is The Age of Mechanized Exploration, 1930 to the Present. There is an index, and some interesting material, especially in Part I. Although the idea is good, this book is unsatisfying, with no real focus.

————. *The Loneliest Continent.* Greenwich, Conn.: New York Graphic Society, 1964. 279pp. Illus.

Charcot, Jean-Baptiste. *Autour du Pôle Sud.* Paris: Ernest Flammarion, 1912. Illus. 2 vols.

————. *Le Français au Pôle Sud.* Paris: Ernest Flammarion, 1906. 486pp. Illus.

————. *The Voyage of the Why Not? in the Antarctic.* London: Hodder & Stoughton, 1911. 315pp.

Cherry-Garrard, Apsley. *The Worst Journey in the World.* London: Constable, 1922. 2 vols.

Child, Jack. *Geopolitics and Conflict in South America.* New York: Praeger. 196pp.

Christensen, Lars. *Such Is the Antarctic.* London: Hodder & Stoughton, 1935. 265pp.

Christie, E.W. Hunter. *The Antarctic Problem.* London: Allen & Unwin, 1951. 336pp.

C.I.A. *Polar Regions Atlas.* Washington, D.C.: Central Intelligence Agency, 1978. 66pp. Maps, color illustrations and diagrams. Large format book with some interesting appendices. Half the book, of course, is about the Arctic.

Clark, Joseph G. *Lights and Shadows of Sailor Life, as Exemplified in 15 Years Experience, including the More Thrilling Events of the U.S. Exploring Expedition, and Reminiscences of an Eventful Life on the "Mountain Wave."* Boston: B.B. Mussey & Co., 1848. 324pp.

Clarke, Peter. *On the Ice.* Boston: Burdette, 1966. Index. 104pp. Glossary.

Coleman-Cooke, J. *Discovery II in the Antarctic.* London: Odhams, 1963. 255pp. Illus.

Colvocoresses, George. *Four Years in a Government Exploring Expedition.* New York: Cornish, Lamport, 1852. 371pp. Tells of the Wilkes Expedition 1838–42.

Cook, Frederick A. *Through the First Antarctic Night 1898–1899.* New York: Doubleday & McClure, 1900. Reprinted in 1980 by C. Hurst & Co. in Canada with 478pp., the original introduction by Frederick A. Cook, M.D., and a new introduction by Gaston de Gerlache, son of Adrien de Gerlache, leader of the *Belgica* expedition of 1897–99, which was the expedition Cook was writing about. Illus. "A Narrative of the Voyage of the *Belgica* among Newly-discovered Lands and over an Unknown Sea about the South Pole."

Craddock, Campbell, editor. *Antarctic Geoscience.* Madison: University of Wisconsin Press, 1982. 1216pp.

Darlington, Jennie, & McIlvaine, Jane. *My Antarctic Honeymoon.* New York: Doubleday, 1956. 284pp. Illus. by Peter Spier.

David, M. Edgeworth. *Professor David: The Life of Sir Edgeworth David.* London: Edward Arnold, 1937. 320pp. Illus.

Davis, John King. *Aurora Relief Expedition. Report of Voyage by Commander, 20 December 1916 to 9 February 1917.* Melbourne: Government of Australia, 1918. 183pp. Illus. Maps.

_____. *High Latitude.* Melbourne: Melbourne University Press, 1962. 292pp. Illus. Autobiography of John King Davis.

_____. *With the Aurora in the Antarctic, 1911–14.* London: Melrose, 1919.

Deacon, George. *The Antarctic Circumpolar Ocean.* Cambridge, England: Cambridge University Press, 1984. 188pp.

Debenham, Frank. *Antarctica: The Story of a Continent.* London: Herbert Jenkins, 1959. 264pp. Illus.

_____, editor. *The Voyage of Captain Bellingshausen to the Antarctic Seas, 1819–1821.* London: Hakluyt Society, 1945. 2 vols. Translated from the Russian of the great 19th-century navigator. 474pp.

De Brosses, Charles. *Histoire de Navigations aux Terres Australes.* Paris: Durand, 1756. 2 vols. Published anonymously.

De Gerlache, Adrien. *Quinze Mois dans l'Antarctique.* Brussels: Imprimerie Scientifique, 1902. 302pp.

De Gerlache, Gaston. *Retour dans l'Antarctique.* Tournai: Casterman, 1960. 281pp. Illus.

Deryugin, K.K. *Soviet Oceanographic Expeditions.* USSR: 1974. 203pp.

Dodge, Ernest S. *The Polar Rosses.* London: Faber, 1973.

Doorly, Gerald S. *In the Wake.* London: Sampson Low, Marston, 1936. 310pp.

_____. *The Voyages of the Morning.* London: Smith, Elder, 1916. 223pp.

Dovers, Robert. *Huskies.* London: Bell, 1957. 219pp. Illus.

Dow, George F. *Whale Ships and Whaling: A Pictorial History of Whaling during 3 Centuries.* Salem, Mass.: Marine Research Society. 446pp.

Drewry, D.J., editor. *Antarctica: Glaciological and Geophysical Profile.* Cambridge, England: Scott Polar Research Institute, 1983.

Dubrovnik, L.I., & Petrov, V.N. *Scientific Stations in Antarctica, 1882–1963.* USSR: 1967. In Russian.

Dufek, George J. *Operation Deep Freeze.* New York: Harcourt, Brace, 1957. 243pp. Illus.

Dukert, Joseph M. *This Is Antarctica.* New York: Coward-McCann. 191pp. Illus. Maps.

Dumont d'Urville, J. *Voyage au Pôle Sud et dans l'Océanie sur les Corvettes l'Astrolabe et la Zélée.* Paris: Gide, 1843. 23 vols & 7 Atlases.

Dunmore, John. *French Explorers in the Pacific.* Oxford: Clarendon, 1969. 2 vols. Maps.

Ellsworth, Lincoln. *Beyond Horizons.* New York: Doubleday, 1937. 403pp.

Emmanuel, Marthe. *Charcot, Navigateur Polaire.* Paris: Les Éditions des Loisirs, 1943. 202pp. Maps.

_____. *La France et l'Exploration Polaire.* Paris: Nouvelles Éditions Latines, 1959.

_____. *Tel Fut Charcot.* Paris: Beauchesne, 1967. 293pp. Illus.

Environmental Data Inventory for the Antarctic Area. 1984. 53pp. Book of charts, maps, and data, put together by NESDIS (National Environmental Satellite, Data and Information Service) of the NOAA (National Oceanic and Atmospheric Administration) and is composed of 4 sections: geophysical, meteorological, oceanographic, and glaciological. It is available from the National Oceanographic Data Center, NOAA/NESDIS, E/OC21, Washington DC 20235. The data are international, and the book tells where you can find the data that it inventories.

Evans, E.R.G.R. *British Polar Explorers.* London: Collins, 1943.

_____. *South with Scott.* London: Collins, 1924. 318pp.

Evans, Phyllis. *The Sea World Book of Seals and Sea Lions.* New York: Harcourt Brace Jovanovich, 1986. Illus.

Fanning, Edmund. *Voyages Round the World.* New York: Collins & Hannay, 1833. 499pp.

Feeney, R.E. *Professor on the Ice.* Davis, Calif.: Pacific Portals, 1974. 164pp. Illus.

Fifield, Richard. *International Research in the Antarctic.* Oxford: Oxford University Press, 1988. 152pp. Illus.

Filchner, Wilhelm. *Ein Forscherleben.* Wiesbaden: Eberhard Brockhaus, 1950. 391pp.

————. *Zum sechsten Erdteil.* Berlin: Ullstein, 1923. 410pp.

Fisher, Margery, & James Fisher. *Shackleton and the Antarctic.* London: James Barrie Books, 1957. Reprinted in the USA in 1958 by Houghton Mifflin, Boston. Illustrated with photos, and with drawings by W.E. How, who served with the *Endurance* expedition of 1914–17. Bibliography. Index. The US version has 559pp. There is a Shackleton chronology and a set of notes referring to the text. There is also an appendix about the scientific results of Shackleton's expeditions, and another on Shackleton's writings. There is also a useful appendix on Shackleton's men.

Frazier, Paul W. *Antarctic Assault.* New York: Dodd, Mead, 1958. 237pp. Illus.

Freeman, Andrew A. *The Case for Dr. Cook.* New York: Coward-McCann, 1961. 315pp. Illus.

Fricker, Dr. Karl. *The Antarctic Regions.* New York: Macmillan, 1900. 292pp. Illus. Originally published as *Antarktis,* by Schall & Grund, in Berlin, in 1898.

Friis, Herman R., & Bale, Shelby G., Jr., editors. *United States Polar Exploration.* Athens: Ohio University Press, 1970.

Fuchs, Vivian, & Hillary, Sir Edmund. *The Crossing of Antarctica.* London: Cassell, 1958. 337pp. Maps.

Gaigerov, S.S. *Aerology of the Polar Regions.* Moscow: 1964. In Russian.

Gazetteer No. 14: Antarctica. Third Edition. Official Name Decisions of the United States Board on Geographic Names. June 1969. Geographic Names Division, US Army Topographic Command, Washington DC 20315. Available from (if you can still find it; if not, the government documents section of a good library) Geographic Names Division, Department of Technical Services, Defense Mapping Agency (better known as the DMA), Topographic Center, Washington DC 20315. You might find it listed as Official Name Decisions Gazetteer No. 14-3 – United States Board on Geographic Names 212350. Anyway, it is a blue government document, Gazetteer #14 of a series of government documents listing all the geographic features of a country (or, in the case of Antarctica, continent), up to the date published, which in this case is 1969. 217 pages of information stuffed into a slim volume, double-columned, with every Antarctic feature listed alphabetically in the left part of the entry, with the type of feature it is next to that (usually described in one, or maybe two words). There are cross-references too, of unofficial and previous names, and also of foreign names. There are a couple of general Antarctic maps (very basic) and a detailed foreword. There are 13,100 entries plus. This book really supersedes *Geographic Names of Antarctica* (1956), and was in turn superseded by Fred Alberts' book.

Gazetteer of the Australian Antarctic Territory. Melbourne: Australian Government, 1965. This is #75 of the ANARE Interim Reports.

Gazetteer of the British Antarctic Territory, South Georgia and the South Sandwich Islands. London: Antarctic Place Names Committee, 1962.

Gazetteer of Undersea Features. Washington, D.C.: Defense Mapping Agency, Topographic Center, Washington DC 20315; 1982.

The Geographical Names of Antarctica. Washington, DC: U.S. Board on Geographic Names, 1947, 1956. Superseded by *Gazetteer No. 14.*

Giaever, John. *The White Desert: The Official Account of the Norwegian-British-Swedish Antarctic Expedition.* London: Chatto & Windus, 1954. 304pp. Illus. Reprinted in the USA in 1955 by E.P. Dutton. 256pp. Originally published as *Maudheim, to År i Antarktis,* by Gyldendal Norsk Forlag, in Oslo, in 1952.

Goodrich, Peggy. *Ike's Travels.* Neptune, N.J.: 1974. Biography of Isaac Schlossbach.

Gould, Laurence M. *Cold.* New York: Brewer, Warren & Putnam, 1931. 275pp.

_____. *The Polar Regions in Their Relations to Human Affairs.* New York: American Geographical Society, 1958.

Gran, Tryggve. *Fra Tjuagutt til Sydpolfarer.* Oslo: Ernst G. Mortensens Forlag, 1974. 329pp.

_____. *En Helt.* Kristiania [Oslo]: Gyldendalske Bokhandel, 1924. 167pp.

_____. *Hvor Sydlyset Flammer.* Kristiania [Oslo]: Gyldendalske Bokhandel, 1915. 211pp. Illus.

_____. *Kampen om Sydpolen.* Oslo: Ernst G. Mortensens Forlag, 1961. 203pp.

Grattan, C.H. *The Southwest Pacific Since 1900.* Ann Arbor: University of Michigan Press, 1963.

Greely, Adolphus W. *Handbook of Polar Discoveries.* Boston: Little, Brown, 1907. 325pp. (A revision of *Handbook of Arctic Discoveries.* 1896.)

_____. *The Polar Regions in the 20th Century.* Boston: Little, Brown, 1928. 270pp.

Greene, S.W., et al. *Terrestrial Life of Antarctica.* New York: American Geographical Society, 1967.

Greenler, Robert. *Rainbows, Halos and Glories.* Cambridge, England: Cambridge University Press, 1980. 304pp. Illus.

Gressitt, J.L., editor. *Entomology of Antarctica.* Washington, D.C.: American Geophysical Union, 1974.

Greve, Tim. *Fridtjof Nansen.* Oslo: Gyldendal Norsk Forlag, 1974. 2 vols.

Grierson, John. *Challenge to the Poles.* London: Foulis, 1964. 695pp. Illus.

_____. *Sir Hubert Wilkins.* London: Robert Hale, 1960. 224pp. Illus.

Grikurov, G.E. *Geology of the Antarctic Peninsula.* USSR: 1973. 140pp. In Russian.

Guy, Michael. *Whiteout.* Martinborough, NZ: Alister Taylor, 1980. 254pp. The account of the DC-10 crash on Mount Erebus.

Hadley, J.B., editor. *Geology and Paleontology of the Antarctic.* Washington, D.C.: American Geophysical Union. 281pp. Illus.

Hansen, H.E. *Atlas of Parts of the Antarctic Coastal Lands.* Oslo: Grøndahl, 1946. 12pp.

Hanssen, Helmer. *Gjennem Isbaksen.* Oslo: H. Aschehoug, 1941. 189pp. First issued in 1936 in English as *Voyages of a Modern Viking,* by G. Routledge & Sons, of London.

Hardy, Sir Alister. *Great Waters.* London: Collins, 1967. 542pp.

Harrison, Peter. *A Field Guide to Seabirds of the World.* Penguin, 1987. 288pp. Illus.

Harrowfield, David L. *Sledging into History.* Auckland: Macmillan, 1981.

Harstad, Herlof. *Erobringen av Antarktis.* Oslo: H. Aschehoug. 1968. 208pp.

Haskell, Daniel C. *The United States Exploring Expedition 1838–1842 and Its Publications, 1844–1874.* New York: New York Public Library, 1942. 188pp. Reprinted in 1968 by the Greenwood Press.

Hatherton, Trevor, editor. *Antarctica.* London: Methuen, 1965. 511pp.

Hayes, James Gordon. *Antarctica.* London: The Richards Press, 1928. 448pp.

_____. *The Conquest of the South Pole.* London: Butterworth's, 1932. 318pp. Illus. Maps.

Hayter, Adrian. *The Year of the Quiet Sun: One Year at Scott Base.* London: Hodder & Stoughton, 1968. 191pp.

Headland, Robert K., compiler. *Chronological List of Antarctic Expeditions and Related Historical Events.* Cambridge, England: Cambridge University Press, 1990.

730pp. Bibliography, maps, graphs, photos, index. This new handbook from the Scott Polar Research Institute is a major expansion of the work done by Brian Roberts (see below). There are about 3,300 entries, showing events, names and sources; also present are a brief history and summary of the Antarctic Treaty. This book appeared just after typesetting was completed on the present work and there was no opportunity to examine it prior to publication of the present work.

_____. *The Island of South Georgia*. Cambridge, England: Cambridge University Press, 1985. 250pp. Illus.

Henderson, Daniel. *The Hidden Coasts: A Biography of Admiral Charles Wilkes*. New York: W.M. Sloane. 1953. 306pp.

Henriksen, Bredo. *Polarfareren Hjalmar Johansen og Skien*. Skien: Eget Forlag, 1961. 131pp. Illus.

Herbert, Wally. *A World of Men*. London: Eyre & Spottiswoode, 1969. 232pp.

Hill, Jo, Jr., & Hill, Ola Davis. *In Little America with Byrd*. Boston: Ginn, 1937. 263pp. Foreword by Richard E. Byrd.

Hillary, Sir Edmund. *No Latitude for Error*. London: Hodder & Stoughton, 1961. 255pp. Illus. The story of the BCTAE 1955-8.

Hobbs, W.H. *Explorers of the Antarctic*. New York: Field, 1941. 334pp.

Hooker, Joseph Dalton. *The Botany of the Antarctic Voyage of H.M. Discovery Ships Erebus and Terror in 1839–1843*. London: Reeve Bros. 1844–60.

Hoyt, Edwin P. *The Last Explorer*. New York: John Day, 1968. 380pp. Illus. About Byrd.

Huntford, Roland. *Scott and Amundsen*. London: Hodder & Stoughton, 1979. Published in the USA as *The Last Place on Earth*, by G.P. Putnam's Sons, New York. 665pp. 35 chapters. Extensive notations and bibliography (many Norwegian books listed). Good index. Maps. Excellent photos. First rate research by a talented and entertaining author. The first real chapter is a sketchy account of Antarctic exploration to the end of the 19th century. The next 3 describe the early life of Amundsen. Chapter 6 describes the *Belgica* expedition. Chapter 14 describes the *Fram*. Chapters 9–13 tell of Scott and the Royal Society Expedition. The second half of the book tells of the race to the Pole between the two men in 1911. The book is brisk, tense, you can't put it down. It reads like a novel. The author is so scathingly anti-Scott one asks why.

_____. *Shackleton*. London: Macmillan, 1986. 452pp. Illus.

_____, & Fisketjon, Gary, editors. *The Amundsen Photographs*. Atlantic Monthly, 1987. Illus. 224pp.

Hurley, Frank. *Argonauts in the South*. New York & London: Putnam's, 1925. 290pp.

_____. *Shackleton's Argonauts*. Sydney, Angus & Robertson, 1948. 140pp. Illus.

Hussey, L.D.A. *South with Shackleton*. London: Sampson Low, 1949. 182pp.

Huxley, Elspeth. *Scott of the Antarctic*. London: Weidenfeld & Nicolson, 1977. 303pp.

Huxley, Leonard, editor. *Scott's Last Expedition*. London: Smith, Elder, 1913.

Jahns, Patricia. *Matthew Fontaine Maury and Joseph Henry, Scientists of the Civil War*. New York: Hastings House, 1961. 308pp.

Jeannel, R. *Au Seuil de l'Antarctique*. Paris: Éditions du Muséum, 1941. 236pp.

Joerg, W.L. *The Work of the Byrd Antarctic Expedition 1928-30*. New York: American Geographical Society, 1930.

Joyce, E.E.M. *The South Polar Trail*. London: Duckworth, 1929. 220pp.

Karaslavov, S.G. *Antarctica: White and Blue*. Sofia: 1974. 152pp. In Bulgarian.

Kearns, William H., Jr., & Britton, Beverley. *The Silent Continent*. London: Gollancz, 1955. 237pp. Illus.

Kerguélen-Trémarec, Y.J. *Rélation de Deux Voyages dans les Mers Australes et des Indes*. Paris: Chez Knapen & Fils, 1782. 244pp.

King, Harry G.R. *The Antarctic*. London: Blandford Press, 1969. 276pp.
_____, editor. *Diary of the Terra Nova Expedition, by Edward A. Wilson*. London: Blandford Press, 1972.
_____, editor. *South Pole Odyssey: Selections from the Antarctic Diaries of Edward A. Wilson*. London: Blandford Press, 1982.
_____, editor. *The Wicked Mate: The Antarctic Diary of Victor Campbell*. England: Bluntisham Books, 1988. 192pp. Illus.
Kirwan, L.P. *The White Road*. London: Hollis & Carter, 1959. Published in the USA as *A History of Polar Exploration*, by W.W. Norton, New York, in 1960. 374pp. Illus.
Kitson, Arthur. *Captain James Cook*. London: John Murray, 1907. 525pp.
Knight, Russell. *Australian Antarctic Bibliography*. Hobart: University of Tasmania, 1987. 460pp.
Kosack, Hans-Peter. *Die Antarktis, eine Länderkunde*. Heidelberg: Keyser Verlagsbuchhandlung, 1955. 310pp.
Kozlova, Olga G. *Diatoms of the Indian and Pacific Sectors of the Antarctic*. USSR: 1964. 167pp. Illus. In Russian.
Kristensen, Leonard. *Antarctic's Reise til Sydishavet*. Tønsberg: Forfatterens Forlag, 1895. 249pp.
Kruchinin, Yuriy A. *Shelf Glaciers of Queen Maud Land*. USSR: 1969. 183pp. In Russian.
Land, Barbara. *The New Explorers: Women in Antarctica*. New York: Dodd, Mead, 1981. 224pp. Index. Photos. A fun book of 16 chapters. Mostly case studies of women in Antarctica. Not exhaustive, by any means, and should really have delivered a lot more, but it is a good, chatty, reasonably informative introduction to the subject.
Langone, John. *Life at the Bottom: The People of Antarctica*. Boston: Little, Brown, 1978. 262pp.
Lansing, Alfred. *Endurance: Shackleton's Incredible Voyage*. New York: McGraw-Hill, 1959.
Lanzerotti, L.J., & Parks, C.G., editors. *Upper Atmosphere Research in Antarctica*. Washington, D.C.: American Geophysical Union, 1978.
Laseron, C.F. *South with Mawson*. London: G.G. Harrap, 1947. 223pp. Illus.
Lashly, William. *Under Scott's Command: Lashly's Antarctic Diaries*. Edited by A.R. Ellis. Introduction by Sir Vivian Fuchs. London: Gollancz, 1967. 160pp. Illus.
Law, Phillip, & Béchervaise, John M. *ANARE: Australia's Antarctic Outposts*. Melbourne: Melbourne University Press, 1957. 152pp. Illus.
Laws, Richard M., editor. *Antarctic Ecology*. London: Academic Press, 1984. 850pp. 2 vols.
_____. *Antarctica: The Last Frontier*. UK: Boxtree, 1989.
Leatherwood, Steve, & Reeves, R. *The Sierra Club Handbook of Whales and Dolphins*. San Francisco: Sierra Club, 1981. 720pp. Illus.
Lecointe, Georges. *Aux Pays des Manchots*. Brussels: O. Schepens, 1904. 368pp. Illus. Maps.
Lee, M.O., editor. *Biology of the Antarctic Seas*. Washington, D.C.: American Geophysical Union, 1964.
Legg, Frank, & Hurley, Toni. *Once More on My Adventure*. Sydney: Ure Smith, 1966. 227pp. Illus.
Le Guillou, Élie Jean-François. *Voyage autour du Monde de l'Astrolabe et de la Zélée*. Paris: Berquet & Pétion, 1842.
Leroi-Gourhan, André. *Les Explorateurs Célèbres*. Paris & Geneva: Mazenod, 1947.
Levick, G. Murray. *Antarctic Penguins*. London: Heinemann, 1914. 139pp.
Lewis, Charles Lee. *Matthew Fontaine Maury, the Pathfinder of the Seas*. Annapolis: U.S. Naval Institute, 1927. 264pp.

Lewis, David. *Ice Bird.* London: Collins, 1975. 223pp.
————. *Icebound in Antarctica.* New York: W.W. Norton, 1987. With Mimi George. Illus. 242pp. Index. 3 appendices of a scientific type. An account of the Frozen Sea Expedition of 1982–84.
————. *Voyage to the Ice.* Sydney: ABC, 1979.
Lewis, Richard S. *A Continent for Science: The Antarctic Adventure.* New York: Viking Press, 1965. 300pp. End maps, maps, photos, charts, index. 10 chapters.
Linklater, Eric. *The Voyage of the Challenger.* London: Murray, 1972. 288pp. Illus.
List of Geographical Names of the Eastern Antarctic. Soviet Antarctic Expeditions 1955–58. Leningrad: Morskoy Transport, 1959. In Russian.
Llano, George A. *Adaptations within Antarctic Ecosystems.* Washington, D.C.: Smithsonian Institution, 1977.
————, editor. *Biology of the Antarctic Seas.* Washington, D.C.: American Geophysical Union, 1964– . A series.
Lliboutry, Luís. *Traité de Glaciologie.* Paris: Masson, 1965. 1044pp. 2 vols. Illus.
Lovering, J.F., & Prescott, J.R.V. *Last of Lands: Antarctica.* Melbourne: Melbourne University Press, 1979. 212pp.
Lubimova, T.G., editor. *Biological Resources of the Antarctic Krill.* Moscow: 1980. 251pp. In Russian.
McCormick, Robert. *Voyages of Discovery in the Arctic and Antarctic Seas.* London: Sampson Low, Marston, Seals & Rivington, 1884. 2 vols. Illus.
McPherson, John G. *Footprints on a Frozen Continent.* Sydney: Hicks Smith, 1975. 151pp.
McWhinnie, Mary Alice, editor. *Polar Research to the Present and the Future.* Boulder, Colo.: Westview Press, 1978.
Malone, T.F., editor. *Compendium of Meteorology.* Boston: American Meteorological Society, 1951.
Markham, Sir Albert H. *The Life of Sir Clements Markham.* London: John Murray, 1917. 384pp.
Markham, Sir Clements. *The Lands of Silence.* Cambridge, England: Cambridge University Press, 1921. 539pp.
Markov, K.K.; Bardin, V.I.; Lebedev, V.L.; Orlov, A.I.; & Suetova, I.A. *Geography of Antarctica.* Moscow: Mysl, 1968. 439pp. In Russian.
Marr, J.W.S. *Into the Frozen South.* London: Cassell, 1923. 245pp.
Marra, John. *Journal of the Resolution's Voyage.* London: Printed for F. Newberry. 328pp.
Marret, Mario. *Antarctic Venture.* London: William Kimber, 1955. 218pp. Originally published in French as *Sept Hommes Chez les Pingouins,* by R. Julliard in 1954.
Marston, George Edward, & Murray, James. *Antarctic Days.* London: Melrose, 1913. Illus. Introduction by Shackleton.
Marvin, Ursula B., & Mason, Brian, editors. *The Catalog of Meteorites from Victoria Land, Antarctica, 1978–1979.* Washington, D.C.: Smithsonian Institution, 1980.
Mason, A.E.W. *The Turnstile.* New York: Scribner's, 1912. A novel, quite a silly one. One of the leading characters is Capt. Harry Rames who goes to the Antarctic for three years. This is quite undoubtedly based on Scott and his first expedition. The ship is called the *Perhaps,* described as "a full-rigged ship, with auxiliary steam, broad in the beam, with strong, rounded bows" (cf. the *Discovery*). "But she's so small," cried Cynthia. "She has to be small," replied the first officer. "Length's no use for her work." Capt. Rames is introduced properly in Chapter 11, A Man on the Make. Rames, capitalizing on his fame from the Antarctic, is setting about a political career in London. Walter Hemming (based on Shackleton) is introduced in Chapter 28, Wireless. "He was one of my officers on the *Perhaps.* He has got together some

money, has bought the old ship, and is off to the south," says Rames. Read this chapter, and also Chapter 32, The Call, where Rames gets the call to go back to the Antarctic, despite a pretty wife and a budding career in Parliament. Chapter 32 also gives a summarized and accurate picture of Antarctic history up to the time of Rames (i.e., Scott). Chapter 33, A Letter from Abroad, is worth reading because of the letter which reaches Rames from Hemming in Rexland (Edward VII Land) in Antarctica, and because of the discussion that follows. This is continued in Chapter 34, The Convict at the Oar ("rames" is French for "oars"). This incident happened to Scott by Shackleton in 1909. The last chapter has Rames going off to his mistress — Antarctica.

Mason, Theodore K. *The South Pole Ponies.* New York: Dodd, Mead, 1979. 202pp. Introduction by Sir Peter Scott.

_____. *Two Against the Ice — Amundsen and Ellsworth.* New York: Dodd, Mead, 1982. 192pp. Illus., maps, bibliography, index.

Mateev, A.K. *Coal Deposits Abroad: America, Antarctica.* Moscow: Nedra, 1974. 234pp. In Russian.

Mawson, Douglas. *The Home of the Blizzard: Being the Story of the Australasian Antarctic Expedition 1911-1914.* London: Heinemann, 1915. 2 vols.

Mawson, Paquita. *Mawson of the Antarctic.* London: Longman's, 1964. 240pp. Illus. Foreword by Prince Philip.

Maxwell, W.B. *Spinster of this Parish.* London: Thornton Butterworth, 1922. This is a novel with an Antarctic involvement.

May, John. *The Greenpeace Book of Antarctica.* London: Dorling Kindersley, 1988. 192pp. Illus.

Mear, Roger, & Swan, Robert. *In the Footsteps of Scott.* London: Jonathan Cape, 1987. 306pp. Illus.

Mellor, M., editor. *Antarctic Snow and Ice Studies.* Washington, D.C.: American Geophysical Union, 1964. 277pp. Illus.

Menster, William J. *Strong Men South.* Milwaukee: Bruce, 1949. 206pp. Illus.

Mercer, John H. *Glaciers of the Antarctic.* New York: American Geographical Society, 1967.

Migot, André. *The Lonely South.* London: Hart-Davis, 1956. 206pp. Illus.

_____. *Thin Edge of the World.* Boston: Little, Brown, 1956. About the Kerguélen Islands.

Mill, Hugh Robert. *The Life of Sir Ernest Shackleton.* London: Heinemann, 1923. 312pp.

_____. *The Record of the Royal Geographical Society, 1830-1930.* London: The Society, 1930.

_____. *The Siege of the South Pole.* London: Alston Rivers, 1905. For years, this was *the* book on Antarctica. 455pp. Maps, illus.

Mitterling, Philip I. *America in the Antarctic to 1840.* Urbana: University of Illinois Press, 1959. 201pp. Illus.

Montague, Richard. *Oceans, Poles and Airmen.* New York: Random House, 1971. 307pp. Illus.

Morrell, Benjamin. *A Narrative of Four Voyages.* New York: J. & J. Harper, 1832. 492pp.

Moseley, H.N. *Notes by a Naturalist on the **Challenger**.* London: Macmillan, 1879. 620pp.

Mountevans, Admiral Lord. *Adventurous Life.* London: Hutchinson, 1946. 259pp.

_____. *The Antarctic Challenged.* London: Staples Press, 1955. 191pp. Illus.

_____. *The Desolate Antarctic.* London: Butterworth, 1950. 172pp.

Mountfield, David. *A History of Polar Exploration.* London: Hamlyn, 1974. 208pp. Illus.

Murdoch, W. Burn. *From Edinburgh to the Antarctic*. London: Longmans, Green, 1894. 364pp. Has a chapter by Bruce.

Murphy, Charles J.V. *Struggle: The Life and Exploits of Commander Richard E. Byrd*. New York: Frederick A. Stokes, 1928. 368pp.

Murphy, Robert Cushman. *Logbook for Grace: Whaling Brig Daisy 1912-13*. New York: Time, Inc., 1965. 371pp. Set in South Georgia.

Murray, George, editor. *The Antarctic Manual*. London: Royal Geographical Society, 1901. Manual for the Royal Society Expedition, 1901-4.

Myrhe, Jeffrey D. *The Antarctic Treaty System: Politics, Law and Diplomacy*. Boulder, Colo.: Westview Press, 1986. 162pp.

Neider, Charles. *Edge of the World: Ross Island, Antarctica*. Garden City, N.Y.: Doubleday, 1974. 461pp. Illus.

_____. *A Historical Guide to Ross Island, Antarctica*. Washington, D.C.: National Science Foundation, 1971. 26pp. Illus.

Newby, Eric. *The World Atlas of Exploration*. London: Mitchell Beazley, 1975. 288pp. Introduction by Sir Vivian Fuchs.

Newman, William A., & Ross, Arnold, editors. *Antarctic Cirripedia*. Washington, D.C.: American Geophysical Union, 1970. 257pp. Illus.

Nordenskjöld, Otto. *Antarctic*. Stockholm: Albert Bonniers Forlag, 1904. Reprinted in English in 1905 by Hurst, Blackett of London. 608pp. 2 vols.

Nudelman, A.V. *Soviet Antarctic Expeditions 1961-63*. USSR: 1968. 220pp. In Russian.

O'Brien, J.S. *By Dog Sled for Byrd*. Chicago: Thomas S. Rockwell, 1931. 102pp.

Olsen, Magnus L. *Saga of the White Horizon*. Lymington: Nautical, 1972. About Ellsworth. 199pp. Illus.

Ommanney, F.D. *South Latitude*. London: Longmans, Green, 1938. 308pp. Illus.

Operation Deep Freeze I — Task Force 43. Paoli, Pa.: Dorville Corporation, 1956. Compliments of the Ingalls Shipbuilding Corporation. 202pp. Black and white and color. Heavily pictorial. Brief index. Stacked full of valuable information and rare photos, it is nonetheless not as well-developed as the later annuals (see below). This is the story of Task Force 43, First Phase, 1955-56. Narrative by Joseph E. Oglesby, JOC, USN. Layout and art by Catherine M. Marriott. Under the supervision of Cdr. Robin M. Hartmann, USN, Task Force public information officer. This was the official record of the first of the Operation Deep Freeze missions, and the first of many such annuals, e.g. *Operation Deep Freeze III*, printed in 1958 by the same corporation. In 1961 was published *Operation Deep Freeze 61 — Task Force 43*, printed by the Cruise Book Firm, Burdette & Co., 120-130 Tudor Street, South Boston, Mass. 226 pages were packed with color and black and white photos. Editor was Lt. Cdr. James S. Hahn; associate editor was Lt. (jg) Steve Schmidt. It had a roster of Deep Freeze 61 personnel, including Ensign Dick Page, who loaned me this book almost 30 years later. An invaluable record.

Orrego Vicuña, Francisco. *Antarctic Bibliography*. Santiago: Institute of International Studies, University of Chile, 1987. Deals mostly with legal, political, and mineral aspects.

_____. *Antarctic Mineral Exploitation: The Emerging Legal Framework*. Cambridge, England: Cambridge University Press, 1988. 450pp. Illus.

Orvig, S., editor. *Climates of the Polar Regions*. Amsterdam: Elsevier, 1970.

Oulié, Marthe. *Charcot of the Antarctic*. London: John Murray, 1938. 235pp. Illus.

Owen, Russell. *The Antarctic Ocean*. London: McGraw-Hill, 1941. 254pp. Maps.

Palmer, James T. *Antarctic Mariner's Song*. New York: Van Nostrand, 1868. 92pp. Illus.

_____. *Thulia: A Tale of the Antarctic.* New York: Samuel Colman, 1843. 72pp. Illus.

Palmer, Wendell S. *The USS Currituck; Pictorial Log of Antarctic Cruise "Operation Highjump."* Philadelphia: Dunlap, 1948. 47pp. Illus.

Parfit, Michael. *South Light: A Journey to the Last Continent.* New York: Macmillan, 1986. 320pp.

Parker, Bruce C. *Environmental Impact in Antarctica.* Blacksburg: Virginia Polytechnic, 1978. 390pp. Illus.

Parsons, Anthony, editor. *Antarctica: The Next Decade.* Cambridge, England: Cambridge University Press, 1987. 164pp. Illus.

Paterson, W.S.B. *The Physics of Glaciers.* Oxford: Pergamon Press, 1969. 250pp. Illus.

Pergameni, Charles. *Adrien de Gerlache.* Brussels: H. Wauthoz-Legrand, 1935. 203pp.

Pinochet de la Barra, Oscar. *La Antártica Chilena: Estudio de Nuestros Derechos.* Santiago: Editorial del Pacífico, 1948. 180pp.

Poesch, Jessie. *Titian Ramsay Peale 1799–1885 and His Journals of the Wilkes Expedition.* Philadelphia: American Philosophical Society, 1961. This is Vol. 52 of the memoirs of the APS. 214pp. Endpapers. Index. There is a reference section at the back of the book, but little pertains to Antarctica, and that includes the bibliography. Illustrated. The first part (120pp.) deals with Peale's life. The next 82 pages are his diaries of the expedition, presented for the first time in their entirety. Part I is certainly a detailed biography of the naturalist; only chapters 7, 8, and 9 relate to the Wilkes Expedition. In the Diaries there is not much on the Antarctic, but the book is altogether of a quaint interest, and the Antarctic sections are dynamic.

Polar Record. Published by the Scott Polar Research Institute, Cambridge, England, and the Cambridge University Press. This is the journal of the SPRI and also of Great Britain as a whole. First published in Jan. 1931, it appeared twice yearly until Jan. 1954, and then three times yearly until Sept. 1987. Since then it is published 4 times yearly, in Jan., April, July and Sept. It reports progress in all fields of research at both polar communities, North and South. Back issues may be obtained from Bluntisham Books, Oak House, East Street, Bluntisham, Huntingdon, Hunts, UK, PE 17, 3LS.

Il Polo. 1946– . Semiannual Italian periodical.

Ponting, Herbert G. *The Great White South.* London: Duckworth, 1921. 305pp.

Porter, Eliot. *Antarctica.* London: Hutchinson, 1978. 168pp. Illus.

Potter, N. *Natural Resource Potentials of the Antarctic.* New York: American Geographical Society, 1969.

Poulter, Thomas C. *Meteor Observations in the Antarctic Byrd Expedition II, 1933–1935.* Menlo Park, Calif.: Stanford Research Institute, 1955. 2 vols.

Pound, Reginald. *Evans of the Broke.* London: Oxford University Press, 1963. 323pp. Illus. Biography of E.R.G.R. Evans.

_____. *Scott of the Antarctic.* London: Cassell, 1966. 327pp.

Powell, George. *Notes on South Shetland.* London: R.H. Laurie, 1822. 15pp.

Prévost, Jean. *Écologie du Manchot Empereur.* Paris: Hermann, 1961. 204pp. Foreword by Paul-Émile Victor.

Priestley, Raymond E. *Antarctic Adventure, Scott's Northern Party.* London: Fisher, Unwin, 1914. 382pp. Illus.

_____; Adie, R.J.; & Robin, Gordon de Q., editors. *Antarctic Research.* London: Butterworth's, 1964. 360pp. Foreword by Prince Philip.

Provisional Gazetteer of the Ross Dependency. Wellington: New Zealand Geographical Board, 1958. This had 4 supplements—1960, 1963, 1963 (again) and 1965.

Pyne, Stephen J. *The Ice: A Journey to Antarctica.* Iowa City: University of Iowa Press, 1986. 428pp. Illus.

Quam, L.O., editor. *Research in the Antarctic*. Washington, D.C.: American Association for the Advancement of Science, 1971.

Quartermain, L.B. *South from New Zealand*. New Zealand Government, 1964. 78pp.

————. *South to the Pole*. London: Oxford University Press, 1967. 481pp.

————. *Two Huts in the Antarctic*. New Zealand Government, 1963. 85pp. Illus.

Quigg, Philip W. *A Pole Apart: The Emerging Issues of Antarctica*. New York: New Press, 1982. 299pp.

Rainaud, Armand. *Le Continent Australe*. Paris: Armand Colin, 1893. 490pp.

Raling, Christopher, editor. *Shackleton*. London: BBC, 1983.

Ravich, Mikhail & Solevyev, D.S. *Geology and Petrology of the Mountains of Central Queen Maud Land, East Antarctica*. USSR: 1966. 438pp. The English translation was done by the US Department of Commerce in 1969.

Reader's Digest. *Antarctica: Great Stories from the Frozen Continent*. Sydney: Reader's Digest, 1985. 319pp. Maps, bibliography, index. There are 3 sections in this large format, colorful and informative book: The Continent and Its Wildlife, The Explorers (which includes 13 special features), and The Antarctic Atlas and Chronology, a sort of appendix which includes a Who's Who of Antarctic exploration. The book is a gem. This author called Reader's Digest US headquarters and spoke to someone who handles their books who swore there was no such book: Reader's Digest had never done a book on Antarctica! The New York bookshop that specializes in old Reader's Digest books also swore to me there was no such book. I eventually found it at Wake Forest University Library in Winston-Salem. The important detail is: it was published in Sydney, Australia.

Reboux, Michel. *Demain l'Antarctique*. Paris: Maison Mame, 1959. 186pp. Illus.

Reynolds, Jeremiah N. *Address on the Subject of a Surveying and Exploring Expedition to the Pacific Ocean and the South Seas*. New York: Harper & Bros., 1836. 300pp.

Richards, R.W. *The Ross Sea Shore Party 1914–1917*. Cambridge, England: Scott Polar Research Institute, 1962. Special Publication #2. 44pp.

Richardson, Sir John, & Grey, John Edward, editors. *The Zoology of the Voyage of HMS Erebus and Terror*. London: E.W. Janson, 1844–75. 2 vols.

Richdale, L.E. *A Population Study of Penguins*. Oxford: Clarendon Press, 1957. 195pp. Illus.

————. *Sexual Behavior in Penguins*. Lawrence: University of Kansas Press, 1951. 316pp. Illus.

Richter, Søren. *Great Norwegian Expeditions*. Oslo: Dreyers Forlag, 1954. 231pp. With chapters by Thor Heyerdahl and Hjalmar Riiser-Larsen.

Riiser-Larsen, Hjalamar. *Femti År for Kongen*. Oslo: Gyldendal Norsk Forlag, 1957. 271pp. Illus.

————. *Mot Ukjent Land*. Oslo: Gyldendal Norsk Forlag, 1930. 166pp.

Ritscher, Alfred. *Deutsche Antarktische Expedition 1938–1939*. Leipzig: Koehler & Amelang, 1943. Illus.

Rivolier, Jean. *Emperor Penguins*. London: Elek, 1956. 131pp. Illus. Translated by Peter Wiles from the French original, *Les Manchots Empereurs de Terre Adélie* (1956).

Roberts, B.B. *Edward Wilson's Birds of the Antarctic*. London: Blandford Press, 1967.

Roberts, Brian. *Chronological List of Antarctic Expeditions*. Not a book, but a highly respected couple of articles in the *Polar Record*. It was first published in the second edition of a manual called *The Antarctic Pilot* in 1948, and then again in 1959, much corrected and added to, in vol. 9, nos. 59 and 60, of the *Polar Record* (q.v.). In no. 59 most expeditions from the earliest times to 1900 are covered, and the list covers sub–Antarctic expeditions as well. It contains a lot of British material difficult to find outside of that country. The typical entry is one or two lines long, perhaps with notes, and lists year, nationality, commander and vessel. Part II continues from 1900 until the IGY (1957–8).

Robertson, Robert B. *Of Whales and Men.* New York: Knopf, 1954. 299pp. Illus.

Ronne, Finn. *Antarctic Command.* Indianapolis: Bobbs-Merrill, 1961. 272pp. Illus.

_____. *Antarctic Conquest: The Story of the Ronne Expedition 1946–1948.* New York: Putnam, 1949. 299pp. Illus.

_____. *Antarctica—My Destiny; A Personal History by the Last of the Great Explorers.* New York: Hastings House, 1979. 278pp. Illus., photos, maps, index. 22 chapters. Introduction by Lowell Thomas. The foreword gives a brief history of Ronne's early life. The first 5 chapters tell of Byrd's 1933–35 expedition. The next two are a history of exploration in Antarctica. The next 3 are about Byrd's third expedition, i.e. the USAS 1939–41. There are 5 chapters on the RARE, one on polar aviation, four on IGY, one about Ronne's life in the 1960s, and an epilog. Interesting yarn from one of the greats.

Ross, James Clark. *A Voyage of Discovery and Research in the Southern and Antarctic Regions.* London: Murray, 1847. 2 vols. Illus.

Rouch, Jules. *Le Pôle Sud; Histoire des Voyages Antarctiques.* Paris: Ernest Flammarion, 1921. 249pp.

Rubin, M.J., editor. *Studies in Antarctic Meteorology.* Washington, D.C.: American Geophysical Union, 1966.

Rusin, N.P. *Meteorological and Radiational Regime of Antarctica.* Leningrad, 1961. 355pp. Illus. In Russian.

Rymill, John. *Southern Lights.* London: Chatto & Windus, 1938. 296pp. Illus.

Sanderson, Marie. *Griffith Taylor: Antarctic Scientist and Pioneer Oceanographer.* Ottawa, Canada: Carleton University Press, 1988. 147pp. Illus. No index.

Savours, Ann, editor. *Edward Wilson's Diary of the Discovery Expedition.* London: Blandford Press, 1966. 416pp.

_____, editor. *Scott's Last Voyage—Through the Antarctic Camera of Herbert Ponting.* London: Sidgwick & Jackson, 1974. 164pp. Maps.

Schatz, G.S., editor. *Science, Technology and Sovereignty in the Polar Regions.* Lexington, Ky.: D.C. Heath, 1974. 215pp.

Scholes, William A. *Seventh Continent: Saga of Australasian Exploration in Antarctica, 1895–1950.* London: Allen & Unwin, 1953. 226pp. Maps.

Schulthess, Emil. *Antarctica: A Photographic Survey.* New York: Simon & Schuster, 1960.

Schwerdtfeger, Werner. *Weather and Climate of the Antarctic.* Amsterdam: Elsevier Science Publishers, 1984.

Scott, Robert F. *The Voyage of the Discovery.* London: Smith, Elder, 1905.

Sea Ice Climatic Atlas: Vol. 1. Antarctic. Asheville, N.C.: National Climate Center, 1985.

Seaver, George. *"Birdie" Bowers of the Antarctic.* London: John Murray, 1938. 270pp.

_____. *Edward Wilson, Nature Lover.* London: John Murray, 1937. 221pp.

_____. *Edward Wilson of the Antarctic.* London: John Murray, 1933. 301pp.

_____. *Scott of the Antarctic.* London: John Murray, 1940. 187pp.

Shackleton, Ernest H. *The Heart of the Antarctic.* London: Heinemann, 1909.

_____. *South.* London: Heinemann, 1919.

Sharp, Robert P. *Glaciers.* Eugene, Ore.: State System of Higher Education, 1960. 78pp. Illus.

Shelvocke, George. *A Voyage Round the World.* London: J. Senex, 1726. 468pp. Reprinted in 1928 by Cassell & Co., London.

Siegfried, V.W.; Condy, P.R.; & Laws, R.M., editors. *Antarctic Nutrient Cycles and Food Webs.* Berlin: Springer-Verlag, 1985. 700pp.

Simpson, Frank, editor. *The Antarctic Today*. Wellington, N.Z.: A.H. & A.W. Reed, 1952. 389pp. Illus.

Simpson, George C. *British Antarctic Expedition 1910–1913, Meteorology. Vol. 1. Discussion*. Calcutta: Thacker & Spink, 1919.

————. *Scott's Polar Journey and the Weather*. Oxford: Clarendon Press, 1926. 31pp.

Simpson, George G. *Penguins, Past and Present, Here and There*. New Haven & London: Yale University Press, 1976. 150pp. Index. Color & b/w photos. Diagrams. Short, annotated bibliography. Preface. 8 chapters.

Siple, Paul A. *A Boy Scout with Byrd*. New York: Putnam's, 1931. 165pp.

————. *90° South*. New York: G.P. Putnam's Sons, 1959. Published simultaneously in Toronto by Longmans, Green. 384pp. Foreword by John Tuck. This is the story of the setting up of the South Pole Station in 1956–57. 30 chapters. Interesting appendices on moments in South Pole history. Index. 8 interesting maps of the continent, showing its exploration development over the years, a graph showing mankind's southward advance, a couple of maps of claims, a map of the aurora zone, several photos — many in full color — and other diagrams. In this book will be found, of course, the complete list of all the men who built South Pole Station.

————. *Scout to Explorer*. New York: Putnam's, 1936. 239pp.

Smith, G. Barnett. *The Romance of the South Pole*. London: Thomas Nelson, 1900. 235pp.

Society Expeditions Cruises, Inc. *Falklands, South Georgia and Antarctica*. Seattle, Wash., 1988. This is not a book, in the true sense of the word, just a professional and entertaining 202 pages of information bound together very attractively by this cruise operator to form the expedition notebook. In other words, when one goes on a Society Expeditions cruise to the Antarctic, one gets, among other things, one of these notebooks. A must for the serious student as well, it comes with a bibliography (quite extensive but, unfortunately, not an integral part of the book). The chapters are easy to read, and cover scientific, historical, flora and fauna, the Antarctic Treaty, and an article on the International Whaling Commission.

Soudry du Kerven, Mme. A. *Dumont d'Urville: Sa Vie Intime pendant Son Troisième Voyage autour du Monde*. Paris: G. Téqui, 1886.

The South Polar Times (London). 1902–1904, 1911–1913; Smith, Elder. For details on this journal, see the entry under that name *(South Polar Times)*, in the main body of this book.

Sparks, John, & Soper, Tony. *Penguins*. London: David & Charles, 1967. Published in the USA by Facts on File, New York. Reprinted in 1987. 246pp. Index, bibliography. Illustrated by Robert Gillmor. In the 1987 edition there is an appendix on penguins in captivity. Section 8 is Species Notes, a nice overview. There is an introduction and 8 chapters. It is easy to read, a great introduction to sphenisciformes. A classic reference work. Color and b/w photos, and diagrams.

Sparrman, Anders. *A Voyage Round the World with Captain James Cook in HMS Resolution*. London: Robert Hale, 1953. Published posthumously.

Spears, John R. *Captain Nathaniel Brown Palmer, An Old Time Sailor of the Sea*. New York: Macmillan, 1922. 252pp.

Spence, Bill. *Harpooned. The Story of Whaling*. Greenwich, England: Conway Maritime Press, 1980.

Spry, W.J.J. *Cruise of Her Majesty's Ship Challenger*. New York: Harper & Bros., 1877. 380pp. Illus.

Stackpole, Edouard A. *The Sea Hunters*. Philadelphia: Lippincott, 1953. Stackpole is revered in Antarctic folklore as one of the great original researchers.

————. *The Voyage of the Huron and the Huntress*. Mystic, Conn.: Marine Historical Association, 1955.

Stanton, William. *The Great United States Exploring Expedition of 1838–1842.* Berkeley: University of California Press, 1975.

Starbuck, Alexander. *History of the American Whale Fishery.* Waltham, Mass.: Privately printed by the author, 1878. 768pp.

Steinetz, Hans. *Der 7 Kontinent.* Bern: Kümmerly & Frey, 1959. 296pp.

Stonehouse, Bernard. *Animals of the Antarctic, the Ecology of the Far South.* London: Peter Lowe, 1972. 171pp.

————, editor. *The Biology of Penguins.* London: Macmillan; Baltimore: University Park, 1975. 25 contributors to *the* book on penguins (although not the most interesting, or exciting, by far), including the Müller-Schwartzes (q.v. in Encyclopedia), who wrote on the study of 24 penguin rookeries on the Antarctic Peninsula; J.W.H. Conroy, who wrote on penguin populations in the Antarctic; G.G. Simpson, who wrote on fossil penguins; D.G. Ainley on Adélies; one on chinstraps by 3 authors; another one on the Adélies by H. Oelke; and several other chapters. There is also an introduction by Stonehouse himself. There are bibliographies after each chapter. Diagrams. Author and subject indexes. 555pp. Exhaustive.

————. *Penguins.* New York: Golden Press, 1968. 96pp. Illus.

Sullivan, Walter. *Assault on the Unknown.* New York: McGraw-Hill, 1961. 460pp. About the IGY.

————. *Quest for a Continent.* New York: McGraw-Hill, 1957. 372pp. Illus. This was, for many years after its production, *the* book on Antarctica.

Swan, Robert A. *Australia in the Antarctic.* Melbourne: Melbourne University Press, 1962. 432pp. Illus.

Taylor, A.J.W. *Antarctic Psychology.* Wellington, N.Z.: Information Publishing Centre, 1987. 145pp. Illus.

Taylor, Nathaniel W. *Life on a Whaler, or Antarctic Adventure in the Isle of Desolation.* New London, Conn.: New London County Historical Society, 1929. 208pp.

Taylor, T. Griffith. *Journeyman Taylor.* London: Robert Hale, 1958. 352pp. Illus.

————. *With Scott: The Silver Lining.* London: Smith, Elder, 1916. 464pp.

Tedrow, J.C.F., editor. *Antarctic Soils and Soil-Forming Processes.* Washington, D.C.: American Geophysical Union, 1966. 177pp.

Thomas, Charles W. *Ice Is Where You Find It.* Indianapolis: Bobbs-Merrill, 1951. 378pp. Illus.

Thomson, David. *Scott's Men.* London: Allen Lane, 1977. 331pp. Illus.

Thomson, Robert. *The Coldest Place on Earth.* Wellington, N.Z.: A.H. & A.W. Reed, 1969. 192pp. Illus. An account of the Wilkes-Vostok traverse.

Todd, Frank. *The Sea World Book of Penguins.* New York: Harcourt Brace Jovanovich, 1981. 96pp. Illus.

Toponymie de la Terre Adélie. Paris: Expéditions Polaires Françaises, 1959.

Trese, Patrick. *Penguins Have Square Eyes.* New York: Holt, Rinehart & Winston, 1962. 217pp. An account of the author's filmmaking trip during Operation Deep Freeze in 1956.

Triggs, Gillian D., editor. *The Antarctic Treaty Regime: Law, Environment and Resources.* Cambridge, England: Cambridge University Press, 1987. 239pp. Illus.

Turley, Charles. *The Voyages of Captain Scott.* New York: Dodd, Mead, 1923. Retold from *The Voyage of the Discovery* and *Scott's Last Expedition,* with an introduction by J.M. Barrie. 432pp. Map, index. Scott's Message to the Public is contained in full.

Turrill, W.B. *Joseph Dalton Hooker: Botanist, Explorer and Administrator.* London & Edinburgh: Thomas Nelson & Sons, 1963. 228pp. Illus.

Tyler, David P. *The Wilkes Expedition, the First United States Exploring Expedition (1838–1842).* Philadelphia: American Philosophical Society, 1968.

Vaeth, J. Gordon. *To the Ends of the Earth*. New York: Harper & Row, 1962. 219pp. Illus. Maps. This is a children's book about the North and South Pole explorations of Roald Amundsen. It has a short bibliography of books written by Amundsen.

Veel, Haakon Anker. *Roald Amundsen; Slekt og Miljø*. Halden: E. Sem, 1962.

Victor, Paul-Émile. *Man and the Conquest of the Poles*. New York: Simon & Schuster, 1963. 320pp. Illus., endpapers, maps, index. The original French version, *L'Homme à la Conquête des Pôles*, was published in 1962 by Librairie Plon, Paris. Translated into English by Scott Sullivan. "The Story of Polar Exploration from the Exploits of the Ancient Greeks to the Voyages of Today's Nuclear Submarines, by the Famous French Explorer who has spent more than 14 Years in the Arctic and Antarctic." Most of it is about the Arctic, but the material that there is on the Antarctic is fact-packed, unpadded, and good for the layperson. There are 28 chapters altogether. One is about Cook, another tells in a couple of pages about the sealers of the 1820s, another tells of Ross, Wilkes and the other navigators of the period. There is a page or so about the *Belgica* and other expeditions of the late 19th century, and Scott and Charcot share a chapter (which is a little odd, in anyone's book). Another chapter is called "The First Man at the South Pole." There are a few pages on Byrd's first two expeditions, two-thirds of a chapter on Operation Highjump, and one on the IGY.

Villiers, Alan J. *Captain James Cook*. New York: Scribner's, 1967. 307pp. Illus.

_____. *Sea Dogs of Today*. New York: H. Holt, 1932. 325pp.

_____. *Whaling in the Frozen South*. Indianapolis: Bobbs-Merrill, 1925. 302pp. Illus. No index. The story of the 1923–24 Norwegian whaling expedition led by Carl Anton Larsen in the *Sir James Clark Ross,* as told by one of the whaling laborers from Tasmania (see Villiers, in Encyclopedia). An erudite, observant and astute account of a typical trip on a Norwegian factory ship, written by an author with a refreshing lack of "ego" (this is disappointing in a way, as one would like to know more about an obviously fascinating author). Fun descriptions of penguins.

Viola, Herman J., & Margolis, Carolyn, editors. *Magnificent Voyagers. The US Exploring Expedition 1838–1842*. Washington, D.C.: Smithsonian Institution Press, 1985. 303pp. Illus., index. 3 appendices—the landings of the expedition, a chronology, and characteristics of the vessels. It is astonishing that in a book that implies thoroughness, there is no list of personnel. This is the story of the Wilkes Expedition, of course, and only Chapter 7 is relevant to the Antarctic. Chapters 9 and 10 are about Wilkes the man.

Von Drygalski, Erich. *Zum Kontinent des eisigens Südens*. Berlin: Reimer, 1904. 668pp.

_____, & Machatschek, Fritz. *Gletscherkunde*. Vienna: F. Deuticke, 1942. 261pp.

Wafer, Lionel. *A New Voyage and Description of the Isthmus of America*. London: J. Knapton, 1699. 224pp. Reprinted in 1934 by the Hakluyt Society.

Walton, D.W.H., editor. *Antarctic Science*. London: Cambridge University Press, 1987. 280pp. Illus.

Walton, E.W. Kevin. *Two Years in the Antarctic*. New York: Philosophical Library, 1955. 194pp.

Watson, George E., & Angle, J. Phillip. *Birds of the Antarctic and Sub-Antarctic*. Washington: American Geophysical Union, 1975. 350pp. Illus.

Watson, Lyall. *Sea Guide to Whales in the World*. London: Hutchinson, 1981. 302pp. Illus.

Weddell, James. *A Voyage Towards the South Pole*. London: Longman, Hurst, Rees, Orme, Brown & Green, 1825. 276pp.

Wild, Frank. *Shackleton's Last Voyage: The Story of the Quest*. London: Cassell, 1923. 372pp. Illus.

Wilkes, Charles. *Narrative of the United States Exploring Expedition*. Philadelphia: Lea & Blanchard, 1845. 5 vols. Illus.

Williams, A.J.; Cooper, J.; Newton, I.P.; Phillips, C.M.; & Watkins, B.P. *Penguins of the World: A Bibliography*. London: British Antarctic Survey, 1985.

Williams, Frances L. *Matthew Fontaine Maury, Scientist of the Sea*. New Brunswick, N.J.: Rutgers University Press, 1963. 720pp. Illus.

Williamson, James A. *Cook and the Opening of the Pacific*. London: Hodder & Stoughton, 1946. 251pp.

Wisting, Oscar. *16 år med Roald Amundsen*. Oslo: Gyldendal Norsk Forlag, 1930. 206pp.

Worsley, Frank A. *Endurance, an Epic of Polar Adventure*. London: Philip Allan, 1931. 316pp.

————. *The Great Antarctic Rescue*. London: Times Books, 1977. 220pp. Illus. Published in the USA in 1977 as *Shackleton's Boat Journey*, by W.W. Norton, New York.

————. *Shackleton's Boat Journey*. London: Philip Allan, 1933. 192pp.

Zapffe, Fritz G. *Roald Amundsen*. Oslo: Aschehoug & Co., 1935. 198pp.